The new edition of this best seller is
vibrant, visual, and research-based!

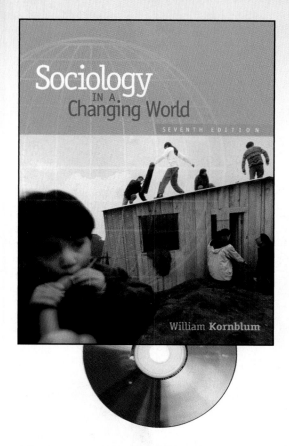

Kornblum's Seventh Edition will help your students *visualize sociology* all around them

Sociology in a Changing World, **Seventh Edition,** is unique among introductory texts!

William Kornblum's comprehensive text uses a thematic approach to emphasize the reality of social change and its impact on individuals, groups, and societies throughout the world. This fascinating theme—which is woven throughout the narrative and is evident in boxed features and chapter pedagogy—ties together the many elements of sociology while giving students a better understanding of the science and helping them see real sociology at work in the world every day.

With a careful balance of contemporary and classic theory and research, the text pays special attention to the works of female and minority social scientists and cross-cultural studies. Challenging yet accessible, interesting, and scholarly ... and now, *technologically connected* to a vast array of teaching and learning tools, the Seventh Edition could be the text that helps your students think like sociologists long after their college experience.

The chosen text for the **Exploring Society: Introduction to Sociology** *telecourse from Dallas TeleLearning!*

Kornblum's new Seventh Edition is now more *connected* to the FREE technology tools that accompany your adoption! These resources are bound into every student copy of the text:

❖ **SocCoach CD-ROM**
❖ Four months access to **InfoTrac® College Edition**
❖ An outstanding **Book Companion Web Site**

See pages 7–11 for details.

Turn the page— your sociological tour begins here!

THOMSON
✦ ™
WADSWORTH

Preview

Kornblum's emphasis on *social change* helps students understand our similarities, our differences, and society as a whole

New!

Kornblum now includes a powerful opening, Chapter 1, "Sociology: An Introduction," that emphasizes **social change** and why this emphasis is essential to studying sociology. Additionally, the book's *Preface* now addresses and thoroughly explains not only its social change philosophy but also its unique table of contents organization.

I

chapter

Sociology: An Introduction

two within society" (Mills, 1959, p. 6). Individual greed may explain why some executives manipulated company portfolios to enrich themselves beyond imagining, but in addition to these more psychological reasons, there were widespread failures of control and oversight in the accounting systems that made the excesses possible; in other words, failures at the sociological level were as important as individual motivations. In the case of the war in Iraq, the heroism of Private Jessica Lynch and her rescuers also can be explained only partially by individual characteristics. Private Lynch fully deserves to join the parade of American and British heroes who won the war, but her motivations for joining the army in the first place had a lot to do with sociological forces. She wanted to go to college and become a classroom teacher, but her family's limited resources made it desirable for her to first join the army, in the hopes of eventually going to college with support from the government based on her military service (Baker, 2003).

One of the main objectives of this book is to help you apply your sociological imagination to an understanding of the social forces that are shaping your own place in the parade—that is, the forces that are shaping your life and those of the people you care about. The sociological imagination can help us avoid blaming ourselves needlessly for the troubles we encounter in life. It can help us understand, for example, why some people are rich and powerful but many others are not; why the benefits of good health care or enriching education are available to some but not to others; or why women may find themselves resenting the men in their lives. The sociological imagination helps us sort out which facts about ourselves are explained by our place in society and which ones are a result of our own actions. Above all, the sociological imagination can suggest ways in which we can realistically effect change in our lives and in society itself.

SOCIOLOGY AND SOCIAL CHANGE

Sociology is the scientific study of human societies and human behavior in the many groups that make up a society. Sociologists must ask difficult, sometimes embarrassing questions about human life in order to explore the consequences of cataclysmic events such as those that shut down factories or enslave an entire people. To understand the possible futures of people who confront such drastic changes, sociologists are continually seeking knowledge about what holds societies together and what makes them bend under the impact of major forces such as war and migration.

We will see throughout this book that there are many ways in which sociologists can already predict the social changes that are likely to occur in coming years and

decades. For example, [...] our society increases, [...] cial change will bring [...] health care or for imp[...] finitions of the respo[...] the elderly. But there [...] of terrorism directed [...] have been predicted [...] Sociologists are tryin[...] the causes of terroris[...] hood of terrorism in [...] search to better und[...] changing or remaini[...] from social change, a[...]

The Social [...]

The knowledge socio[...] ciologists study relig[...] tary; the behavior of [...] the activities of volu[...] teacher groups and p[...] ships between men and women or between aging individuals and their elderly parents; the behavior of groups in cities and neighborhoods; the activities of gangs, criminals, and judges; differences in the behaviors of entire social classes—the rich, the middle classes, the poor, the down-and-out; the way cities grow and change; the fate of entire societies during and after revolutions; and a host of other subjects. But how to make sure the information gathered is reliable and precise, how to use it to build theories of social cohesion and social change—that is the challenge faced by the young science of sociology.

As in any science, there are many debates in sociology about the appropriate ways to study social life and about which theories or types of theories best explain social phenomena. Most sociologists, however, would agree with the following position:

> Human actions are limited or determined by "environment." Human beings become what they are at any given moment not by their own free decisions, taken rationally and in full knowledge of the conditions, but under the pressure of circumstances which delimit their range of choice and which also fix their objectives and the standards by which they make choices. (Shils, 1985, p. 805)

This statement expresses a core idea of sociology: Individual choice is never entirely free but is always determined to some extent by a person's environment. In sociology, *environment* refers to all the expectations and incentives established by other people in a person's social world. For the sociologist, therefore, the environment within which an individual's

A Focus on Social Change

The theme of *social change* is revisited and examined within the book's fascinating features

Mapping Social Change boxes—many include new maps—use clear and inviting maps, charts, and photos to illustrate how collective behaviors, social changes, and social movements are distributed throughout the United States or the world.

Global Social Change boxes explain major social changes around the world by applying sociological concepts.

Tribal Societies Within the Modern State of Nigeria

MAPPING SOCIAL CHANGE

Nigeria is the largest nation of Africa south of the Sahara desert. It is also a nation where social change is extremely rapid and unpredictable, for tribal and religious differences make it difficult to create a Nigerian identity among citizens, and the influence of Western oil companies seeking to exploit the huge oil reserves in the impoverished coastal region creates opportunities for both development and corruption.

As the detailed map shows, it is composed of many societies with their own cultures and languages. Some, like the Hausa, are spread out over vast territories in the northern savannas; others, like the Tiv and Ibo, are clustered in the more densely populated coastal plains and on the delta of the mighty Niger River. Nigeria was once considered a leader in the development of democratic political institutions. It had a lively cultural and intellectual life and produced some of Africa's best novelists and playwrights. In 1998, after many years of dictatorship, the Nigerian military began to relinquish its harsh rule over the nation, but at this writing the persistence of regional and ethnic animosities continues to hamper the emergence of national leadership. Conflict between its many societies, often over the disposal of oil revenues from the Niger delta region, and rampant political and economic corruption continually threaten the viability of its democratic institutions.

Ken Saro-Wiwa, shown in the photo, was one of the leaders of the effort to create a modern Nigerian nation even as

1995. Saro-Wiwa was the founder and leader of the movement for the survival of the Ogoni people in Nigeria's oil-rich Niger delta region. Although the government and the Dutch Shell Corporation

Source: Adapted from Kwamena-Poh, Tosh, Waller, & Tidy, 1982; Crowder, 1966.

ated a "Ken Saro-Wiwa Memorial Prize for Ethnic and Religious Tolerance." In a recent speech about this award, Nigeria's Nobel laureate, the world-famous playwright Wole Soyinka, said that "Since

have taken billions of dollars' worth of oil from their lands, the Ogoni, a small tribal society in the Cross River region, still live in mud huts and dig for yams with bamboo sticks. Acid rain and oil pollution have destroyed many productive farms. Saro-Wiwa was attempting to organize a peaceful social movement to

the death of Ken Saro-Wiwa . . . the state of ethnic consciousness has assumed a violent dimension." Worried that inequalities among Nigeria's different ethnic groups could result in civil strife, Soyinka issued an urgent call for a conference of "nationalities." Leaders around the world will be watching the

---

GLOBAL SOCIAL CHANGE

CHAPTER 18   Education   525

Poverty and Illiteracy

There is a strong correlation between illiteracy and poverty throughout the world (see the map on pages 526–527). The poor nations of the Sahel, such as Mali, Chad, Niger, Ethiopia, and the Sudan, suffer from some of the highest rates of illiteracy in the world. High rates of illiteracy are also evident in much of South Asia, especially on the Indian subcontinent. On the other hand, the correlation is not absolute: Illiteracy rates are quite low in poor nations such as Mexico and Cuba, where the ideology of social development places strong emphasis on educating the mass of citizens to the fullest extent possible.

Sociological theories of modernization stress the need for populations to become literate so that their members will be better-informed voters, more highly skilled workers, more careful parents, and generally better able to realize their human potential. Reductions in the level of ignorance yield improvements in every aspect of a nation's social and civic life.

This line of argument is clearly supported by the correlation between poverty and illiteracy in India (see the accompanying chart). Overall, the chart shows that as illiteracy decreases, the amount of money a household is able to spend each month increases. The chart also shows that illiteracy and the poverty associated with it are much more prevalent among women than among men, with rural women showing the highest rates of illiteracy and poverty (about 90 percent illiterate in the high-poverty category). That men are far more likely than women to become literate in India is a reflection of the immense gap in prestige between the sexes in that society; men are considered far more worthy of education than women.

Research on the effects of literacy on vital measures of social change such as reduced fertility clearly shows the importance of educating women. Data from research conducted in Thailand and other Southeast Asian nations suggest that until women gain access to

at least minimal educational opportunities, fertility rates in those nations will remain high. This research confirms the hypothesis that "demographic change is unlikely if the movement towards mass schooling is confined largely to males" (London, 1992, p. 306).

These relationships among gender, illiteracy, and social indicators like poverty and fertility offer a warning that investments in literacy alone are necessary but not sufficient to accelerate social change in a population. Investments in literacy must be accompanied by strategies to reach the most impoverished and discriminated against segments of the population (such as rural women in many societies). Such strategies, in turn, are difficult to develop in a society in which the powerful may fear their effects. In nations where poor rural women are offered more education, for example, the women often begin to demand greater equality. It takes farsighted leadership to actively promote such strategies.

Another consequence of increasing literacy and education in poor societies is that some of the "best and brightest" are attracted to opportunities in richer societies. This phenomenon is known as the "brain drain" and is a significant problem for developing nations (Alam, 1988; Cortes, 1980). Relatively well-educated people, often with professional training, are an important source of migration from Third World nations to the wealthier nations of North America and Western Europe. Indeed, immigration policies in North America actively

encourage immigration by well-trained individuals and establish quotas that discourage less educated persons from seeking entry.

In order to address the problems created by the brain drain phenomenon, the poorer nations have developed policies requiring that people trained at public expense (e.g., through scholarships and training programs) must serve in their own nation until it has recouped its investment in their education. Such policies are not popular with educated people in those nations, especially if they are aware of more attractive opportunities outside their own society. But if the full benefits of literacy and education are to be applied to national development, such policies are necessary.

Poverty and Illiteracy in India

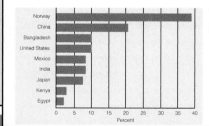

Source: Data from third quinquennial survey on employment and unemployment, Ministry of Planning, New Delhi, India.

CRITICAL SOCIOLOGY AND SOCIAL CHANGE

Empowering Women

The term *empowerment* is often used in discussions of women and development. The term refers to the process whereby relatively powerless people of any gender, race, ethnicity, or social class organize to assert their needs and

overcome obstacles to their full participation in the institutions of their societies. The term can also refer to the processes whereby people gain the ability to assert their needs in more personal contexts—in their families, work groups, schools, or communities.

Empowerment of women is a major global issue because such a large proportion of the world's females are trapped in patriarchal societies. Indeed, the extent to which different nations move toward greater parity between male and female holders of elective office (as shown in Figure 14.8) is an international measure of relative progress in dealing

Figure 14.8   Women's Share of National Legislatures in Selected Countries

Source: UNDP, 2000.

The *Research on the Cutting Edge* feature, now renamed **Critical Sociology and Social Change**, critically examines cutting-edge research and includes researchers featured in the *Exploring Society* telecourse. These sections help students understand the relevance of the field of sociology within the context of each chapter.

Popular Culture and Social Change boxes illustrate how sociological concepts are reflected in popular music, television, and other media.

POPULAR CULTURE & SOCIAL CHANGE

Jocks, Nerds, Punks, Abercrombies, and Others

The rash of high school violence, culminating perhaps in the Columbine shootings in 1998, brought to national attention the subject of high school peer groups, sometimes pejoratively called *cliques*. But educators and sociologists have been concerned for many decades about the influence of teen peer groups, an influence that can be extremely constructive and prosocial or, in some cases, can lead to destructive behavior and conflict. To understand high school peer groups, it is vital to understand the way groups of teenagers adopt particular forms of popular culture as their own.

Here is an example of how a journalist described the different peer groups of a high school he visited in Illinois:

Jocks rule and nerds still struggle for acceptance just about everywhere. But many schools have their own unique cliques. A look at Illinois' Glenbrook South High:

- *Trophy-Case Kids.* Named for their hangout under the school awards case. They're punkish in black hooded sweatshirts.
- *Wall Kids.* Mostly seniors, mostly popular.

- Lots of preppies and "Abercrombies." Their turf: a wall outside the cafeteria.
- *Bandies.* Musicians, they stick to themselves outside rehearsal room. Not especially cool or uncool, just good friends.
- *Backstage People.* Theater and arts types (both genders) lounge on couches backstage to talk, do homework, and take naps.

- *Student-Council Kids.* Clean-cut, popular. Lunch-time hangout: the council office. (Adler & McCormick, 1999, p. 56)

Surely there were more groups in the high school that the journalist did not discover. Perhaps there were technology nerds who hung out in the computer labs or the AV room, and if it was a rural school, maybe there were farm kids involved in 4-H. And what about skateboarders or cheer-

---

A Focus on Social Change

Kornblum includes dynamic *pedagogical tools* that draw students into the study of sociology

New!

More **Study Charts** have been added to the Seventh Edition to help steer students toward concept mastery. Here are just a few of the study charts in this new edition:

❖ *Types of societies* in Chapter 4, "Societies and Nations"

❖ *Primary and secondary groups* in Chapter 6, "Interaction in Groups"

❖ *Justifications for punishment* in Chapter 7, "Deviance and Social Control"

❖ *Marx's and Weber's theoretical perspectives on stratification* in Chapter 11, "Stratification and Global Inequality"

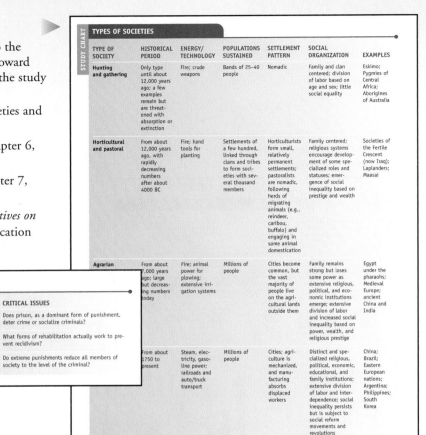

STUDY CHART

TYPES OF SOCIETIES

TYPE OF SOCIETY	HISTORICAL PERIOD	ENERGY/ TECHNOLOGY	POPULATIONS SUSTAINED	SETTLEMENT PATTERN	SOCIAL ORGANIZATION	EXAMPLES
Hunting and gathering	Only type until about 12,000 years ago; a few examples remain but are threatened with absorption or extinction	Fire; crude weapons	Bands of 25–40 people	Nomadic	Family and clan centered; division of labor based on age and sex; little social equality	Eskimo; Pygmies of Central Africa; Aborigines of Australia
Horticultural and pastoral	From about 12,000 years ago, with rapidly decreasing numbers after about 4000 BC	Fire; hand tools for planting	Settlements of a few hundred, linked through clans and tribes to form societies with several thousand members	Horticulturists form small, relatively permanent settlements; pastoralists are nomadic, following herds of migrating animals (e.g., reindeer, caribou, buffalo) and engaging in some animal domestication	Family centered; religious systems encourage development of some specialized roles and statuses; emergence of social inequality based on prestige and wealth	Societies of the Fertile Crescent (now Iraq); Laplanders; Maasai
Agrarian	From about 7,000 years ago; large but decreasing numbers today	Fire; animal power for plowing; extensive irrigation systems	Millions of people	Cities become common, but the vast majority of people live on the agricultural lands outside them	Family remains strong but loses some power as extensive religious, political, and economic institutions emerge; extensive division of labor and increased social inequality based on power, wealth, and religious prestige	Egypt under the pharaohs; Medieval Europe; ancient China and India
	From about 1750 to present	Steam, electricity, gasoline power; railroads and auto/truck transport	Millions of people	Cities; agriculture is mechanized, and manufacturing absorbs displaced workers	Distinct and specialized religious, political, economic, educational, and family institutions; extensive division of labor and interdependence; social inequality persists but is subject to social reform movements and revolutions	China; Brazil; Eastern European nations; Argentina; Philippines; South Korea

continued

STUDY CHART

JUSTIFICATIONS FOR PUNISHMENT

JUSTIFICATION	FUNCTION	CRITICAL ISSUES
Deterrence	To prevent crime and protect society from criminal predation	Does prison, as a dominant form of punishment, deter crime or socialize criminals?
Rehabilitation	To resocialize the criminal so that he or she can reenter society	What forms of rehabilitation actually work to prevent recidivism?
Retribution	To take revenge on the criminal and make punishment show society's anger about the crime	Do extreme punishments reduce all members of society to the level of the criminal?

SOCIOLOGICAL METHODS | Measures of Central Tendency

When we say that the family is a primary agent of socialization, we mean not just the child's parents but all the people who make up the "family constellation"—that is, the people who are most often in the child's home and therefore capable of influencing his or her socialization. But how can we measure such a thing across many different families? In an innovative study of whom children interact with other than their parents, Lewis and Feiring observed ten very young children from different families and counted the number of people they saw each week. Here is an example of their data and the basic methodological tools they used to analyze it.

The following table presents information from Lewis and Feiring's study of 3-year-old children's social networks:

The 3-Year-Old Child's Social Network (N = 117)*

	X	Range
Number of relatives other than parents seen at least once a week	3.20	0–15
Number of child's friends seen at least once a week	4.43	0–13
Number of adults seen at least once a week	4.38	0–24

*N refers to the number of subjects in a study.
Source: Lewis & Feiring, 1982, p. 116.

To understand this table, you must know something about the common measures of central tendency. The measure used here is the *mean*, represented by X. To arrive at this number, each child's total number of friends, relatives, and other adults seen at least once a week is added to the totals for the other children in the sample. The grand total is then divided by the number of children in the sample. The resulting number can be used to represent the entire sample.

The other common measures of central tendency are the *median* and

the *mode*. The median is the number that divides a sample into two equal halves when all the numbers in the sample are arranged from lowest to highest. The mode is simply the score that occurs most often in the sample. Sociologists make a point of specifying which of these measures they are using. They try to avoid the term *average* in statistical tables because it can refer to any one of these measures.

To illustrate all three measures of central tendency, let us use the following data from 10 of the children in Lewis and Feiring's sample:

Child	Number of Friends Seen at Least Once a Week
1	2
2	3
3	3
4	7
5	12
6	2
7	3
8	1
9	0
10	5
	38

In this example, the mode would be 3 and the median would also be 3, but the mean would be 3.8.

Sociological Methods boxes help students see and understand how sociologists go about conducting their research.

The *latest research* and coverage of *cutting-edge topics* make the Seventh Edition an outstanding teaching and learning tool

Longevity and Life Expectancy

As people live longer lives—that is, as *longevity* increases—due especially to better nutrition, more medical care, and improved economic and political stability—there are both positive and negative consequences, or risks, for societies and nations. More older people means that more people will live to be grandparents capable of helping their adult children care for their kids. Older people in good health have opportunities to travel and continue to develop their human potential. But greater longevity also means that there will be more "frail" elderly and greater incidence of illnesses such as cancer and Alzheimer's disease, which families and entire societies must learn to cope with. Despite these and other risks, increased life expectancy, as noted in earlier chapters, is a measure of social development because the overwhelming majority of people wish to live longer and more productive lives.

At age 65 and beyond, over 50 percent of North American women are widowed, whereas only 13.6 percent of men have lost their wives. This difference is due to the fact that the life expectancy of females is at least 7 years longer than that of males. (By **life expectancy** we mean the average number of years a member of a given population can expect to live beyond his or her present age.) Typically, men die before their wives do. Older men also tend to marry younger women, making widows the single largest category in the elderly population.

In the future, if male and female roles become more similar and women experience the stresses and risks that are thought to cause earlier death in men, the gap between the life expectancies of the sexes may narrow. Research on sex differences in the causes of death indicates that women may be less vulnerable to death for genetic reasons, but it is extremely difficult to prove this scientifically. The research of Lois M. Verbrugge and colleagues (Verbrugge, Gruber-Baldini, & Fozard, 1996) on health trends among males and females indicates that the lifestyles of men and women in the United States have become similar; in particular, women's lives are more like men's. This change has unfortunate implications for women's health and longevity. For example, women are now smoking almost as much as men. Smoking among men declined from 50.2 percent in 1965 to 25.9 percent in 1998, while the rate for women decreased from 31.9 percent to 22.1 percent (*Statistical Abstract*, 2001). Among older smokers, men were twice as likely to quit as women. It is no surprise that lung cancer now almost equals breast cancer as a leading cause of death for women.

AGE AND DEPENDENCY   People in the working adult cohorts—that is, those between the ages of 18 and 64 (although many continue to work well after age 64 and may start before age 18)—contribute disproportionately to the well-being of the young and the elderly. Of course, societies justify this pattern of dependency by recognizing that adults are merely doing in their turn what was done for them as children or will be done for them when they are among the frail elderly. Institutions of modern societies, such as public education and Social Security, ensure that a share of wealth passes to the dependent cohorts.

When there are very large numbers of children in a society, as is the case in the developing nations, or increasing numbers of elderly people, as is the case in the older nations of western Europe and North America, working adults may shoulder an increased burden. Figure 15.6 vividly illustrates the dependency problem. It charts the ratio of workers in the U.S. labor force to people receiving Social Security benefits. That ratio has been decreasing sharply with the aging [...] that now there [...] for every reti[...] Social Security [...] jects the ratio [...] century in ord[...] dependency situation will conti[...] aging accelerates. According to [...] of the second decade of this c[...] drawn out of the Social Security[...]

Social movements among the elderly are increasing in strength as the older population grows in numbers. Older Americans have taken an active interest in recent efforts to reform the nation's health care system.

◀ *New!*

Longevity, death and dying, and caregiving are now explored more extensively in Chapter 15, "Inequalities of Youth and Age." In this chapter, you'll also find additional coverage of aging in a global perspective.

New!

An expanded discussion of gay and lesbian relationships has been added to Chapter 16, "The Family," as well as a new section on current research on gay and lesbian families.

Gay and Lesbian Relationships

In 2003, in a stunning 6-3 decision, the U.S. Supreme Court struck down laws banning homosexual sex in Texas and 12 other states. In its ruling, the Court declared that a Texas law banning what some states have called deviate sex acts, or sodomy, was an unwarranted government violation of the right to privacy. Scholars and gay and lesbian activists said that the decision would make their efforts on behalf of gay rights easier. They also believed that it would add new credibility to their struggle to legitimate same-sex marriages, adoptions, and parental benefits. Critics, both among the minority on the Court and among opponents of gay rights, argued that the ruling would open a floodgate of efforts to legalize forms of sexuality such as prostitution and bestiality. In its ruling, however, the Court recognized that its decision follows legal precedents already established in many other democratic nations.

For sociologists who study these issues, it was clear that the Court was responding to important changes in the norms of sexuality in the American population. As noted elsewhere, attitudes toward same-sex relationships have been becoming more tolerant for the

The Sociological Observer

This photo, titled "Proud of Vermont!," appears at a Web site devoted to information about Vermont's gay and lesbian community and their efforts to convince their fellow citizens to pass the state's historic civil union bill. When you look at this photo, can you make any observations about the sexual orientations of any of the people in the photo? The crowd is celebrating the first anniversary of the civil union bill. What is the difference between civil union and marriage? Why are even civil unions among gays and lesbians still regarded as controversial? (See page 480 for further insights into the sociological content of this photo.)

New!

Entirely new sections on collective behavior now appear in Chapter 8, "Collective Behavior, Social Movements, and Mass Publics." These fascinating sections include expanded discussions of topics such as fads, fashions, rumor, gossip, panic, and mass hysteria.

New!

The social epidemiology of AIDS and the growing obesity epidemic is explored in Chapter 21, "Technology, Environment, and Health."

An outstanding art and photo program that is *beautiful*, *interesting*, and *instructive*

Chapter-opening vignettes capture students' attention and introduce them to the chapter's subject matter. Each vignette is continued in the **Visual Sociology** section at the end of the chapter.

I see them lining up for breakfast well before seven in the morning. They look exhausted and threadbare. Some have slept all night in chairs in the "day room." Others are drifting in from the street, where they have a secret hiding place to sleep—perhaps over a grate that in winter will blow warm air on them and keep them from freezing. Since the terrorist attack on New York City and the resulting loss of thousands of jobs, there is also a growing number of displaced workers, many of whom had recently struggled to get off the welfare rolls and into the labor market. But most of the homeless seeking help have been living on the streets for other reasons.

This morning, for example, I see Willie W. and his partner Samantha. They are crack addicts who roam the streets at night in search of soda and beer cans, which they will sell [for the] deposit price because [of co]caine. This morn[ing out]side the Drop-in [Center] money is around so

involved in research with the city's street population for almost three decades.

I believe that the problems of homeless adults in urban centers raise fascinating sociological issues about how a good society might deal with people who deviate from its norms and are "down and out." I find it sad that in one of the world's richest cities there are people living on the streets. Often they are mentally ill or addicted, or both. Equally often they are younger people who have been pushed out of crowded apartments after the breakup of a family. On the streets, they find many opportunities to make some money through various forms of hustling.

Race, ethnicity, and gender also play a part in the story. Two generations ago

FOCUS QUESTIONS:
• How do societies define deviant behavior?

New!

The Sociological Observer feature reinforces the book's emphasis on the analysis of actual human behavior, as presented in photos that capture aspects of social structure, social interaction, and social change. This feature presents a photo or video (from *Exploring Society, Lecture Launchers Video,* or *Core Concepts Video*) related to the images in the **Visual Sociology** feature as well as a small amount of information about what the photo or video represents. Students are encouraged to examine the photos or videos more closely and respond to critical-thinking questions in each chapter. Later, when students encounter the **Visual Sociology** photo essay at the end of each chapter, they can revisit the questions they were asked to consider earlier.

The Sociological Observer
(See photo on page 181.)

While homeless people are often considered deviant outcasts in American cities and frequently find themselves shunned into places like tunnels or public shelters, in much of the Third World, homelessness is far more common. Homeless people are often recent arrivals to urban regions who are living in makeshift shelters on the city's edges. As bad as their living situation might be, it is also likely that they have come from even more impoverished conditions in their home villages. Although the rich in their societies may see them as a nuisance, they can hardly be considered deviant since so many are in similar situations.

Coke and amphetamines started coming back to me because I had an unlimited supply [as a cook in a hospital] .... And I gave up everything, gave up everything that I had. And I moved into a place called the Amtrak Tunnel.

I have always done most of the cooking. In most cases, people will heat up stuff down there. But cooking stews, soups—I'm an excellent cook. I love to cook. People say, "That was amazing!" I've never cooked professionally. I've never had a job as a cook. They thought I was in the military or something, which I wasn't.

I got my little family [18 cats], and that's enough. I don't need any more. They are all different, and if you're feeling bad they make you feel better. They're not like people, they're not two-faced. They don't have one side and then have another the next time. So that's why I love my animals. And they know they can depend on me.

The Sociological Observer

This mother and child are standing in front of their makeshift home. Countless people in the Americas, Asia, and Africa are homeless in the sense that although they have somewhere to sleep, their shelter is grossly inadequate, cold in bad weather, boiling hot in the sun, unsanitary, unsafe, and "temporary."

Note the details of this family's "home." How is it constructed? How is the infant dressed? Where is the structure located? Do you think that this family would be considered as deviant in the region where they are living as they would were they living on the outskirts of a city in the United States? (See page 197 for further insights into the sociological content of this photo.)

art *and the sociological eye*

Graffiti—Art or Vandalism?

The teenagers who do it call it different things in different cities—writing, tagging, bombing, and even art. Most adults think of it as graffiti and consider it either a nuisance or, if it defaces their property, outright vandalism. Sociologists who study teenage behavior often explain that graffiti can send many kinds of signals. Gangs often use initials or symbols to mark their turf in an urban community. Aspiring young artists, influenced by hip-hop styles of dress and music, may become interested in graffiti as an art form. Sometimes this art is executed as a protest against the larger society, as when large graffiti murals are drawn at night on buses or trains or on public buildings. Part of the creative effort involves the daring exploit of producing art that is against the law. In some cities, youth who produce this underground or protest art are known as "bombers" because they make sudden, stealthy strikes on a building or a train. Bombers look down on mere "taggers," who scrawl their highly stylized initials ("tags") everywhere they go, even on the far more artistic bombers' work.

No matter how much we might understand and appreciate well-executed graffiti art, however, from the viewpoint of the larger society, graffiti art is a defacement of public property. Its removal

is costly; its effects can be demoralizing; and it can be read as a sign that a community's young people, or at least some of them, are alienated and angry. Realizing this, many youth workers and community leaders have found ways to reach out to graffiti artists and guide their energy and creativity into socially constructive or at least more acceptable channels. In New Orleans, for example, the Ya Ya Collective has made graffiti art into products that young people can reproduce and sell. This builds their self-esteem and provides funds for other

constructive youth activities. In New York City, where graffiti art is extremely popular, a sympathetic industrialist has hired graffiti artists to paint enormous murals on the walls of an old factory building in an industrial section of the city. In Philadelphia, Chicago, Cleveland, and many other U.S. cities, graffiti artists and their friends are applying their skills to the creation of public murals commemorating the victims of gang violence or the drug trade, and in so doing they are learning to use their art in positive ways.

Art and the Sociological Eye boxes demonstrate how fine art can be interpreted from a sociological perspective and help students improve their ability to see social relationships in action. They also help instructors to interest students in larger humanistic themes in sociology.

Art and Photo Program

Seamless integration of *multimedia and Internet resources* . . . superb teaching and learning tools linked to every chapter!

Kornblum's text works hand in hand with
SocCoach CD-ROM
0-534-62699-8

Automatically packaged with the text ... for FREE!

The exciting new *SocCoach CD-ROM* greatly improves your students' chances of success! Dynamic, interactive, and exciting, *SocCoach* helps students study and gain a better understanding of sociological concepts.

This tutorial-driven CD-ROM is firmly grounded in sociology and enables students to review chapter content, conduct online research, think critically about sociological statistics, watch well-known sociologists as they discuss important topics and concepts, and complete book-specific quizzes—all on one, easy-to-use CD-ROM! The CD's new *Study Plan* feature prompts students to take a diagnostic chapter quiz followed by a personalized *Study Plan* that illustrates exactly where they need further study. Students can then access study aids, including material from the book itself, illustrative graphs, videos, and statistics—that help them to better understand each concept.

InfoTrac® College Edition
http://www.infotrac-college.com

Give your students anytime, anywhere access to reliable resources with *InfoTrac College Edition*, the online library! This fully searchable database offers 20 years' worth of full-text articles from almost 5,000 diverse sources, such as academic journals, newsletters, and up-to-the-minute periodicals including *Time, Newsweek, Science, Forbes,* and *USA Today*. This incredible depth and breadth of material—available 24 hours a day from any computer with Internet access—makes conducting research so easy, your students will want to use it to enhance their work in every course! And, incorporating *InfoTrac College Edition* is easy—references to this virtual library are built into Kornblum's text. Both adopters and their students receive unlimited access for four months.

NEW! Students now have instant access to critical thinking and paper writing tools through *InfoWrite*.

WebTUTOR Advantage

WebTutor™ Advantage on WebCT and Blackboard
On WebCT packaged with the text: 0-534-21965-9
On Blackboard packaged with the text: 0-534-21956-X

This Web-based learning tool takes the sociology course beyond the classroom! Students gain access to a full array of study tools, including chapter outlines, chapter-specific quizzing material, interactive games and maps, and videos. With *WebTutor Advantage*, instructors can provide virtual office hours, post syllabi, track student progress with the quizzing material, and even customize the content to suit their needs. This program contains communication tools with which instructors can set up threaded discussions and conduct "real-time" chats, as well as bring the latest developments from the field into the classroom using *NewsEdge*, an authoritative news source that delivers customized news feeds daily.

Multimedia and Online Resources

Kornblum's Companion Web Site at Wadsworth's Virtual Society

http://sociology.wadsworth.com/kornblum/change7e

The Virtual Society resource center features a wealth of online book-specific study materials created especially for this text, plus a sociology timeline, a student guide to Census 2000, Sociology in the News, a career center, and much more. And for instructors, the site includes password-protected Instructor's Manuals, Microsoft® *PowerPoint*® Lectures, and important sociology links.

Click on the Companion Web Site to find useful learning resources for each chapter of Kornblum's book. Students can interact with the material as they analyze data and have their quizzes evaluated online. The site includes many password-protected resources for instructors.

Some of the site's other resources include:

- ❖ Tutorial Practice Quizzes with Feedback
- ❖ Web Links
- ❖ Internet Exercises
- ❖ Video Exercises
- ❖ InfoTrac College Edition Exercises

- ❖ Flashcards of the Text's Glossary
- ❖ Crossword Puzzles
- ❖ Learning Objectives
- ❖ MicroCase® Data-Analysis Exercises
- ❖ Virtual Explorations

Opposing Viewpoints Resource Center

http://www.gale.com/OpposingViewpoints

Newly available from Wadsworth, this online center allows you to expose your students to all sides of today's most compelling issues! The *Opposing Viewpoints Resource Center* draws on Greenhaven Press's acclaimed social issues series, as well as core reference content from other Gale and Macmillan Reference USA sources. The result is a dynamic online library of current event topics—the facts as well as the arguments of each topic's proponents and detractors. Special sections focus on critical thinking and researching and writing papers.

Additional resources for students

Study Guide

0-534-63670-5 • Packaged with the text 0-534-22225-0

by William Kornblum and Carolyn D. Smith

This student study tool contains chapter outlines, learning objectives, fill-in-the-blank review questions, key term matching exercises for each chapter of the text, *InfoTrac College Edition* and Internet exercises, and more. Also included is a set of practice tests for each chapter consisting of 15 multiple-choice, 5 true/false, and 5 short-answer questions to help students apply and master chapter concepts.

Telecourse Guide for Exploring Society: Introduction to Sociology

0-534-63677-2 • Packaged with the text 0-534-27733-0

by Jane Penney, Dallas County Community College District

This guide is keyed to Kornblum's text and provides students with valuable resources designed to direct their study in the *Exploring Society: Introduction to Sociology* telecourse. The guide includes lesson overviews, goals and objectives, specific reading assignments, practice tests, and other learning activities that connect the text and video components of each lesson of the course.

Also available . . . the perfect tool to help your students make the most of Wadsworth's online resources!

Wadsworth's Sociology Online Resources and Writing Companion

0-534-63682-9 • Packaged with the text 0-534-22207-2

New! You can package the text with this valuable guide that shows your students how they can most effectively use our exclusive online resources to help them build essential research and writing skills and integrate research findings into class assignments.

Resources

An outstanding collection of *teaching tools* designed with you in mind

Instructor's Resource Manual Notebook with Multimedia Manager CD-ROM

0-534-63678-0

With this enhanced instructor's manual, instructors can integrate their personal notes into a 3-hole-punched, tabbed notebook containing a wealth of comprehensive teaching resources. The manual contains detailed lecture outlines; instructional goals; extensive teaching suggestions; topics for discussion; strategies for how to effectively utilize the text's rich selection of tables, charts, and other visual features in class; a "Sociology versus Ideology" feature; Internet and *InfoTrac College Edition* exercises for each chapter of the text. And, there's more: a table of contents for the *CNN Today Sociology Video Series* and concise user guides for both *InfoTrac College Edition* and *WebTutor*. The Manual also includes Jerry M. Lewis's helpful booklet *Tips for Teaching Introductory Sociology* as well as *Wadsworth's Sociology Online Resources and Writing Companion* containing *InfoTrac College Edition*, **MicroCase**, and **Opposing Viewpoints Resource Center** exercises that can be assigned to students to help them build essential research and writing skills in sociology.

The **Instructor's Resource Manual Notebook** is packaged with an all-new **Multimedia Manager CD-ROM.** This new instructor resource includes book-specific *PowerPoint®* lecture slides, graphics from the book itself, the IRM Word documents, the Test Bank, CNN Video clips, and links to many of Wadsworth's important sociology resources. All of your media teaching resources in one place!

Test Bank

0-534-63672-1

The extensive *Test Bank* includes 100–125 multiple choice, 30–40 true-false, and 8–10 short-answer, and 3–5 essay questions for each chapter of the text, all with page references and question type (recall or applied) indicated. The revised test bank now includes additional questions based on the main text's rich selection of features and visuals. Further test questions specific to the *Exploring Society: Introduction to Sociology* telecourse are also provided as an appendix. The *Test Bank* is also available electronically on the *ExamView Computerized Testing CD-ROM* as well as on the *Multimedia Manager Instructor Resource CD-ROM* that comes packaged in the Instructor's Resource Manual Notebook.

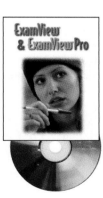

ExamView® Computerized Testing

0-534-63673-X

Create, deliver, and customize tests and study guides (both print and online) in minutes with this easy-to-use assessment and tutorial system. *ExamView* offers both a quick test wizard and an online test wizard that guide you step-by-step through the process of creating tests. The test appears on screen exactly as it will appear printed or displayed online. Using the complete word processing capabilities of *ExamView*, you can enter an unlimited number of new questions or edit existing questions.

Telecourse Faculty Guide

http://dallas.dcccd.edu/

This resource provides instructors of the *Exploring Society: Introduction To Sociology* telecourse with recommended instructional strategies, lesson summaries, suggestions for interaction with students, sample course syllabi, and other information. To order, please contact your sales representative or call Dallas TeleLearning at 972-669-6650.

Transparency Acetates

0-534-58775-5

A set of four-color acetates consisting of tables and figures from Wadsworth's introductory sociology texts is available to help prepare lecture presentations. *Free to qualified adopters.*

Dynamic *presentation tools* help you deliver interesting and interactive lectures

CNN® Today: Sociology Videos

Volume I: 0-534-52482-6 • Volume II: 0-534-55593-4 • Volume III: 0-534-55603-5
Volume IV: 0-534-58767-4 • Volume V: 0-534-58771-2 • Volume VI: 0-534-58776-3
Volume VII: 0-534-58777-1

Integrate the up-to-the-minute programming power of CNN and its affiliate networks right into your classroom! Updated yearly, *CNN Today* videos are course specific and can help you launch a lecture, spark a discussion, or demonstrate an application—using the top-notch business, science, consumer, and political reporting of the CNN networks. Produced by Turner Learning, Inc., these 45-minute videos show your students how the principles they learn in the classroom apply to the stories they see on television. Special adoption conditions apply.

Wadsworth's Lecture Launchers for Introductory Sociology

0-534-58839-5 (VHS) • 0-534-58845-X (DVD)

An exclusive offering jointly created by Thomson Wadsworth and Dallas TeleLearning, this video contains a collection of video highlights taken from the *Exploring Society: Introduction to Sociology Telecourse* (formerly *The Sociological Imagination*). Each 3 to 6 minute long video segment has been specially chosen to enhance and enliven class lectures and discussions of 20 key topics covered in the introduction to sociology course. Accompanying the video are brief written descriptions of each clip, along with suggested discussion questions to help effectively incorporate the material into the classroom.

Sociology: Core Concepts

0-534-61934-7 (VHS) • 0-534-61935-5 (DVD)

Another exclusive offering jointly created by Thomson Wadsworth and Dallas TeleLearning, this video contains a collection of video highlights taken from the *Exploring Society: Introduction to Sociology Telecourse* (formerly *The Sociological Imagination*). Each 15 to 20 minute video segment will enhance student learning of the essential concepts in the introductory course and can be used to initiate class lectures, discussion, and review. The video covers topics such as the sociological imagination, stratification, race and ethnic relations, social change, and more.

Wadsworth Sociology Video Library

This large selection of thought-provoking films is available to adopters based on adoption size. Ask your sales representative for information.

Teaching and Presentation Resources

These outstanding student resources are *FREE* when you order one packaged with Kornblum's text!

Researching Sociology on the Internet, Third Edition

0-534-62437-5 • Packaged with the text 0-534-22028-2

by D.R. Wilson

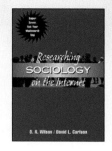

This guide is designed to assist sociology students with doing research on the Internet. Part One contains general information necessary to get started and answers questions about security, the type of sociology material available on the Internet, the information that is reliable and the sites that are not, the best ways to find research, and the best links to take students where they want to go. Part Two looks at each main topic in sociology and refers students to sites where they can obtain the most enlightening research and information.

Applied Sociology: Topics, Terms, Tools, and Tasks

0-534-52474-5 • Packaged with the text 0-534-21992-6

by Stephen Steele and Jammie Price

This concise, user-friendly book addresses a common question of many introductory sociology students: "What can I do with sociology?" The book introduces students to sociology as an active and relevant way to understand human social interaction by offering a clear, direct linkage between sociology and its practical use. It focuses on the core concepts in sociology (terms and topics), contemporary and practical skills used by sociologists to investigate these concepts (tools), and then presents concrete exercises for learning and applying these skills (tasks).

Investigating Change in American Society, Second Edition

0-534-62281-X • Packaged with the text 0-534-22180-7

by William H. Frey

This workbook and Web site combination includes exercises that allow students to analyze and manipulate huge data sets drawn from the 2000 U.S. Census.

Sociological Footprints: Introductory Readings in Sociology, Ninth Edition

0-534-58842-5 • Packaged with the text 0-534-27742-X

edited by Leonard Cargan and Jeanne Ballantine, both of Wright State University

This mainstream anthology's primary objective is to provide a link between theoretical sociology and everyday life by presenting a comprehensive balance of classical, contemporary, popular, and multicultural articles and sociological studies.

Wadsworth's Classic Readings in Sociology, Third Edition

0-534-60975-9 • Packaged with the text 0-534-22171-8

edited by Eve L. Howard

A resounding best seller in previous editions, this series of classic articles written by key sociologists will complement any introductory sociology textbook. This is a touchstone reader in which students can read original works that teach the fundamental ideas of sociology.

Wadsworth offers an array of readers for sociology.

Please visit http://www.newtexts.com **for a complete listing.**

Free Resources for Students

Instructors, welcome to your **Resource Integration Guide**! We've done some of your homework for you. This guide correlates every text chapter with the many instructor and student resources that accompany *Sociology in a Changing World,* Seventh Edition, written by William Kornblum. All of these resources have been described in detail in the preceding pages.

Chapter 1: Sociology: An Introduction

Class Preparation/ Lecture Tools	Testing Tools/ Course Management	Student Study Tools	Beyond the Book: Research, Writing, and Exploration
Instructor's Resource Manual Notebook Chapter 1 contains lecture outlines, instructional goals, teaching suggestions, discussion topics, strategies for teaching using the text's tables, charts, and visuals, "Sociology versus Ideology," Internet and *InfoTrac College Edition* exercises, and more Also consult *Tips for Teaching Introductory Sociology*, Section 1: Introduction, Section 2: Course Goals and Syllabi, Section 3: Lecture Preparation, Section 4: Core Lecture Outlines, and Section 6: Class Exercises **Telecourse Faculty Guide** Consult for instructional strategies on teaching Sociology via the "Exploring Society" telecourse **Multimedia Manager Instructor Resource CD-ROM** Text-specific graphics, customizable Microsoft® *PowerPoint*® lecture slides, lecture launcher video clips, electronic IRM and Test Bank, and more **Introductory Sociology Transparency Acetates** 2005: "Introduction" acetates **CNN® Today Videos** Sociology Vol. I–VI **Lecture Launchers Video/DVD** *The Sociological Imagination* (4.21); *The Feminist Perspective* (3.80) **Sociology: Core Concepts Video/DVD** *Introduction to Sociology* (8.92) **Wadsworth's Sociology Video Library** Select a full-length video from the collection of Films for the Humanities such as *The Development of Community*	**Test Bank** Chapter 1 contains 100–125 multiple-choice, 30–40 true/false, and 8–10 short-answer questions. Also includes "Exploring Society" telecourse test items. The Test Bank is also available electronically through **ExamView®**, which can be customized to fit your needs. *WebTUTOR Advantage* **WebTutor™ Advantage** See Chapter 1 to assign chapter quizzes, conduct online discussion, track student progress, and post course material **Instructor's Resource Manual Notebook** Consult *Tips for Teaching Introductory Sociology*, Section 5: "Examinations"	**Study Guide** Chapter 1 contains chapter outlines, learning objectives, fill-in-the-blank review questions, key term matching exercises, and practice tests containing 15 multiple-choice, 5 true/false, and 5 short-answer questions **Telecourse Guide** Chapter 1 contains lesson overviews, goals and objectives, specific reading assignments, practice tests, and other learning activities **SocCoach CD-ROM** See the Chapter 1 diagnostic quiz and personalized study plan **Web Site Highlights** http://sociology. wadsworth.com/ kornblum/change7e • Quizzes • Matching Exercises • Flashcards • Crossword Puzzles *WebTUTOR Advantage* **WebTutor™ Advantage** See Chapter 1 for chapter-specific review, quizzing, flashcards, and interactive games and exercises	**Web Site Highlights** http://sociology. wadsworth.com/kornblum/change7e • Internet links and exercises • CNN® Today videos and exercises • GSS data **InfoTrac® College Edition** http://www.infotrac-college.com *Keywords:* Karl Marx, Functionalism, Conflict Theory **Wadsworth's Sociology Online Resources and Writing Companion** "Sociological Perspectives" • InfoTrac® College Edition Exercises 1–5 • Opposing Viewpoints Resource Center Exercises 1–5 • MicroCase® Online Exercises 1–3 • InfoWrite and OVRC Research Guide **SocCoach CD-ROM** See "The Sociological Perspective" Virtual Exploration and interactive data map exercise **Researching Sociology on the Internet** Preface and Part I: "A Guide to Using the Internet" **Classic Readings in Sociology** Mills: "The Promise of Sociology" Berger: "Invitation to Sociology" Marx/Engels: "Manifesto of the Communist Party" **Applied Sociology** Chapter 1: "How Can I Use Sociology" **Six Steps to Effective Writing in Sociology** Teaches thinking and writing skills for each stage of the writing process

References

Howard, *Classic Readings in Sociology,* Third Edition
Schmidt, Hooper, and Wysocki, *Six Steps to Effective Writing in Sociology*
Steele, Price, *Applied Sociology: Terms, Topics, Tools, and Tasks*
Wadsworth, *Wadsworth's Sociology Online Resources and Writing Companion*
Wilson, *Census 2000: A Student Guide for Sociology,* Second Edition
Wilson, *Researching Sociology on the Internet,* Second Edition

Class Preparation/ Lecture Tools	Testing Tools/ Course Management	Student Study Tools	Beyond the Book: Research, Writing, and Exploration
Instructor's Resource Manual Notebook Chapter 2 emphasizes the importance of careful analysis of the data collected in research. Help students overcome the common fear of numbers and quantitative tables by walking through the tables in "Analyzing the Data." Also consult *Tips for Teaching Introductory Sociology*, Section 4 and 6 **Telecourse Faculty Guide** Consult for instructional strategies on teaching The Tools of Sociology via the "Exploring Society" telecourse **Multimedia Manager Instructor Resource CD-ROM** Text-specific graphics, customizable Microsoft® *PowerPoint*® lecture slides, lecture launcher video clips, electronic IRM and Test Bank, and more **Introductory Sociology Transparency Acetates** 2005: "Social Research" acetates **CNN® Today Videos** • Sociology Vol. I: *Science of Shopping* (5:10) • Sociology Vol. II: *Teen Suicide* (2:04) • Sociology Vol. III: *Census: Counting America* (1:45) • Sociology Vol. IV: *Census Overview* (2:07) • Sociology Vol. V: *Population Overview* (1:39) **Lecture Launchers Video/DVD** *Elian Gonzalez: A Refugee's Story* (5.13), *Mixed Research Methods & New York City's Homeless* (4.94) **Wadsworth's Sociology Video Library** Select a full-length video from the collection of Films for the Humanities such as the *Why Use Statistics?*	**Test Bank** Chapter 2 contains 100–125 multiple-choice, 30–40 true/false, and 8–10 short answer questions. Also includes "Exploring Society" telecourse test items. The Test Bank is also available electronically through **ExamView®,** which can be customized to fit your needs WebTUTOR™ Advantage **WebTutor™ Advantage** See Chapter 2 to assign chapter quizzes, conduct online discussion, track student progress, and post course material **Instructor's Resource Manual Notebook** Consult *Tips for Teaching Introductory Sociology*, Section 5: "Examinations"	**Study Guide** Chapter 2 contains chapter outlines, learning objectives, fill-in-the-blank review questions, key term matching exercises, and practice tests containing 15 multiple-choice, 5 true/false, and 5 short-answer questions **Telecourse Guide** Chapter 2 contains lesson overviews, goals and objectives, specific reading assignments, practice tests, and other learning activities **SocCoach CD-ROM** See the Chapter 2 diagnostic quiz and personalized study plan **Web Site Highlights** http://sociology. wadsworth.com/ kornblum/change7e • Practice Quizzes • Matching Exercises • Flashcards • Crossword Puzzles WebTUTOR™ Advantage **WebTutor™ Advantage** See Chapter 2 for chapter-specific review, quizzing, flashcards, and interactive games and exercises	**Web Site Highlights** http://sociology. wadsworth.com/kornblum/change7e • Internet links and exercises • CNN® Today videos and exercises • GSS data **InfoTrac® College Edition** http://www.infotrac-college.com *Keywords:* Research Methods, Data Analysis, Census, Suicide **Wadsworth's Sociology Online Resources and Writing Companion** "Research Methods" • InfoTrac® College Edition Exercises 1–5 • Opposing Viewpoints Resource Center Exercises 1–3 • MicroCase® Online Exercises 1–3 • InfoWrite and OVRC Research Guide **SocCoach CD-ROM** See the "Research Methods" interactive data map exercise **Researching Sociology on the Internet** Part II: "Research Methods" **Census 2000: A Student Guide for Sociology** Introduction and Major Trends: "The Controversy About Sampling" **Classic Readings in Sociology** Huff: "How to Lie with Statistics" **Applied Sociology** Chapter 2: "Model, Measure, and Make Sense" **Six Steps to Effective Writing in Sociology** Teaches thinking and writing skills for each stage of the writing process

Chapter 3: Culture

Class Preparation/ Lecture Tools	Testing Tools/ Course Management	Student Study Tools	Beyond the Book: Research, Writing, and Exploration
Instructor's Resource Manual Notebook Chapter 3 introduces the basic concepts and terms used in the study of culture, also introducing the broader concept of civilization. Both culture and civilization give rise to many useful discussion topics, such as whether/to what extent cultural differences have played a role in terrorism against the U.S. Also consult *Tips for Teaching Introductory Sociology*, Section 4 and 6 **Telecourse Faculty Guide** Consult for instructional strategies on teaching Culture via the "Exploring Society" telecourse **Multimedia Manager Instructor Resource CD-ROM** Text-specific graphics, customizable Microsoft® *PowerPoint®* lecture slides, lecture launcher clips, electronic IRM and Test Bank, and more **Introductory Sociology Transparency Acetates** 2005: "Culture" acetates **CNN® Today Videos** • Sociology Vol. I: *Ganges Cleanup* (4:26) • Sociology Vol. II: *Culture Watch, Hate Crimes* (2:06), *Afghanistan Taliban* (2:09), *English for Immigrants* (2:40) • Sociology Vol. III: *Cultural Change in America* (3:46) *Tattoo History* (4:03) • Sociology Vol. VI: *Selling America* (2:15) **Lecture Launchers Video/DVD** *Culture Shock* (2.93) **Sociology: Core Concepts Video/DVD** *Culture* (8.67) **Wadsworth's Sociology Video Library** Select a full-length video from the collection of Films for the Humanities such as the *Media Interrupted: The Dissection of Media in American Culture*	**Test Bank** Chapter 3 contains 100–125 multiple-choice, 30–40 true/false, and 8–10 short-answer questions. Also includes "Exploring Society" telecourse test items. The Test Bank is also available electronically through **ExamView®**, which can be customized to fit your needs. **WebTutor™ Advantage** See Chapter 3 to assign chapter quizzes, conduct online discussion, track student progress, and post course material **Instructor's Resource Manual Notebook** Consult *Tips for Teaching Introductory Sociology*, Section 5: "Examinations"	**Study Guide** Chapter 3 contains chapter outlines, learning objectives, fill-in-the-blank review questions, key term matching exercises, and practice tests containing 15 multiple-choice, 5 true/false, and 5 short-answer questions **Telecourse Guide** Chapter 3 contains lesson overviews, goals and objectives, specific reading assignments, practice tests, and other learning activities **SocCoach CD-ROM** See the Chapter 3 diagnostic quiz and personalized study plan **Web Site Highlights** http://sociology. wadsworth.com/ kornblum/change7e • Practice Quizzes • Matching Exercises • Flashcards • Crossword Puzzles **WebTutor™ Advantage** See Chapter 3 for chapter-specific review, quizzing, flashcards, and interactive games and exercises	**Web Site Highlights** http://sociology. wadsworth.com/kornblum/change7e • Internet links and exercises • CNN® Today videos and exercises • GSS data • Online Module: "Suburban Youth and School Violence" **InfoTrac® College Edition** http://www.infotrac-college.com *Keywords:* Culture, Social Darwinism, Cultural Change, Ethnocentrism, Language **Wadsworth's Sociology Online Resources and Writing Companion** "Culture" • InfoTrac® College Edition Exercises 1–5 • Opposing Viewpoints Resource Center Exercises 1–4 • MicroCase® Online Exercises 1–3 • InfoWrite and OVRC Research Guide **SocCoach CD-ROM** See the "Culture" Virtual Exploration and interactive data map exercise **Researching Sociology on the Internet** Part II: "Culture" **Classic Readings in Sociology** Merton: "Manifest and Latent Functions" Miner: "Body Ritual Among the Nacirema" **Applied Sociology** Chapter 3: "Concepts, Culture, Socialization, and Social Structure" **Six Steps to Effective Writing in Sociology** Teaches thinking and writing skills for each stage of the writing process

Chapter 4: Societies and Nations

Class Preparation/ Lecture Tools	Testing Tools/ Course Management	Student Study Tools	Beyond the Book: Research, Writing, and Exploration
Instructor's Resource Manual Notebook Besides describing the development of human societies from hunting-and-gathering to postindustrial, Chapter 4 explains the distinction between societies and nations and notes that these often do not coincide. The box on tribal societies in Nigeria illustrates this point; encourage students to think of additional examples. Also consult *Tips for Teaching Introductory Sociology,* Section 4 and 6 **Telecourse Faculty Guide** Consult for instructional strategies on teaching Societies and Nations via the "Exploring Society" telecourse **Multimedia Manager Instructor Resource CD-ROM** Text-specific graphics, customizable Microsoft® *PowerPoint®* lecture slides, lecture launcher clips, electronic IRM and Test Bank, and more **Introductory Sociology Transparency Acetates** 2005: "Social Interaction" acetates **CNN® Today Videos** • Sociology Vol. I: *Step Family Discipline* (3:05) • Sociology Vol. II: *English for Immigrants* (2:40) *Helping the Homeless* (1:45) • Sociology Vol. III: *China Internet* (1:22) **Lecture Launchers Video/DVD** *Social Interaction: The Ropes Course* (4.42) **Sociology: Core Concepts Video/DVD** *Social Interaction* (7.53) **Wadsworth's Sociology Video Library** See the *American Values* clip from the "Discovering Sociology" video	**Test Bank** Chapter 4 contains 100–125 multiple-choice, 30–40 true/false, and 8–10 short-answer questions. Also includes "Exploring Society" telecourse test items. The Test Bank is also available electronically through **ExamView®,** which can be customized to fit your needs. WebTUTOR Advantage **Advantage** See Chapter 4 to assign chapter quizzes, conduct online discussion, track student progress, and post course material **Instructor's Resource Manual Notebook** Consult *Tips for Teaching Introductory Sociology,* Section 5: "Examinations"	**Study Guide** Chapter 4 contains chapter outlines, learning objectives, fill-in-the-blank review questions, key term matching exercises, and practice tests containing 15 multiple-choice, 5 true/false, and 5 short-answer questions **Telecourse Guide** Chapter 4 contains lesson overviews, goals and objectives, specific reading assignments, practice tests, and other learning activities **SocCoach CD-ROM** See the Chapter 4 diagnostic quiz and personalized study plan **Web Site Highlights** http://sociology. wadsworth.com/ kornblum/change7e • Practice Quizzes • Matching Exercises • Flashcards • Crossword Puzzles WebTUTOR Advantage **WebTutor™ Advantage** See Chapter 4 for chapter-specific review, quizzing, flashcards, and interactive games and exercises	**Web Site Highlights** http://sociology. wadsworth.com/kornblum/change7e • Internet links and exercises • CNN® Today videos and exercises • GSS data **InfoTrac® College Edition** http://www.infotrac-college.com *Keywords:* Social Structure, Capitalism, Primary Group, Role **Wadsworth's Sociology Online Resources and Writing Companion** "Society and Social Interaction" • InfoTrac® College Edition Exercises 1–5 • Opposing Viewpoints Resource Center Exercises 1–3 • MicroCase® Online Exercises 1–3 • InfoWrite and OVRC Research Guide **SocCoach CD-ROM** See the "Social Interaction & Socialization" Virtual Exploration and the "Socialization" interactive data map exercise **Researching Sociology on the Internet** Part II: "Socialization" **Classic Readings in Sociology** Goffman: "The Presentation of Self" **Applied Sociology** Chapter 3: "Concepts, Culture, Socialization, and Social Structure" **Six Steps to Effective Writing in Sociology** Teaches thinking and writing skills for each stage of the writing process

Chapter 5: Socialization

Class Preparation/ Lecture Tools	Testing Tools/ Course Management	Student Study Tools	Beyond the Book: Research, Writing, and Exploration
Instructor's Resource Manual Notebook Chapter 5 directly addresses the possibility of confusion about the biological and social origins of behavior, contrasting the behaviorist and sociobiological views. Issues such as the extent to which intelligence is innate and whether or not sexual orientation is biologically based are sensitive ones and should be approached with care. Also consult *Tips for Teaching Introductory Sociology*, Section 6 **Telecourse Faculty Guide** Consult for instructional strategies on teaching Socialization via the "Exploring Society" telecourse **Multimedia Manager Instructor Resource CD-ROM** Text-specific graphics, customizable Microsoft® *PowerPoint*® lecture slides, lecture launcher clips, electronic IRM and Test Bank, and more **Introductory Sociology Transparency Acetates** 2005: "Socialization" acetates **CNN® Today Videos** • Sociology Vol. I: *Children and the Media* (3:58), *Self-esteem, Girls and Science* (3:46) • Sociology Vol. II: *English for Immigrants* (2:40), *Hollywood Runaways* (2:30), *Body Image* (2:23) **Lecture Launchers Video/DVD** *Nature vs. Nurture Debate* (2.77) **Sociology: Core Concepts Video/DVD** *Socialization* (12.83) **Wadsworth's Sociology Video Library** Select a full-length video from the collection of Films for the Humanities such as *Domino: Interracial People and the Search for Identity*	**Test Bank** Chapter 5 contains 100–125 multiple-choice, 30–40 true/false, and 8–10 short-answer questions. Also includes "Exploring Society" telecourse test items. The Test Bank is also available electronically through **ExamView®**, which can be customized to fit your needs. *WebTUTOR Advantage* **WebTutor™ Advantage** See Chapter 5 to assign chapter quizzes, conduct online discussion, track student progress, and post course material **Instructor's Resource Manual Notebook** Consult *Tips for Teaching Introductory Sociology*, Section 5: "Examinations"	**Study Guide** Chapter 5 contains chapter outlines, learning objectives, fill-in-the-blank review questions, key term matching exercises, and practice tests containing 15 multiple-choice, 5 true/false, and 5 short-answer questions **Telecourse Guide** Chapter 5 contains lesson overviews, goals and objectives, specific reading assignments, practice tests, and other learning activities **SocCoach CD-ROM** See the Chapter 5 diagnostic quiz and personalized study plan **Web Site Highlights** http://sociology. wadsworth.com/ kornblum/change7e • Practice Quizzes • Matching Exercises • Flashcards • Crossword Puzzles *WebTUTOR Advantage* **WebTutor™ Advantage** See Chapter 5 for chapter-specific review, quizzing, flashcards, and interactive games and exercises	**Web Site Highlights** http://sociology. wadsworth.com/kornblum/change7e • Internet links and exercises • CNN® Today videos and exercises • GSS data • Terrorism Guide: Part I, Section C **InfoTrac® College Edition** http://www.infotrac-college.com *Keywords:* Behaviorism, Socialization, Peer Group, Gender Socialization **Wadsworth's Sociology Online Resources and Writing Companion** "Socialization" • InfoTrac® College Edition Exercises 1–5 • Opposing Viewpoints Resource Center Exercises 1–3 • MicroCase® Online Exercises 1–3 • InfoWrite and OVRC Research Guide **SocCoach CD-ROM** See the "Social Interaction & Socialization" Virtual Exploration and the "Socialization" interactive data map exercise **Researching Sociology on the Internet** Part II: "Socialization" **Classic Readings in Sociology** Mead: "The Self" Rosenthal: "On Being Sane in Insane Places" **Applied Sociology** Chapter 3: "Concepts, Culture, Socialization, and Social Structure" **Six Steps to Effective Writing in Sociology** Teaches thinking and writing skills for each stage of the writing process

Chapter 6: Interaction in Groups

Class Preparation/ Lecture Tools	Testing Tools/ Course Management	Student Study Tools	Beyond the Book: Research, Writing, and Exploration
Instructor's Resource Manual Notebook Chapter 6 includes an in-depth discussion of principles of group interaction that will enable students to see groups as the basic unit of social structures of varying complexity. It explores the moral dilemmas raised by conformity to group norms—especially those of bureaucratic organizations— versus individual achievement. Also consult *Tips for Teaching Introductory Sociology*, Section 6 **Telecourse Faculty Guide** Consult for instructional strategies on teaching Interaction in Groups via the "Exploring Society" telecourse **Multimedia Manager Instructor Resource CD-ROM** Text-specific graphics, customizable Microsoft® *PowerPoint*® lecture slides, lecture launcher clips, electronic IRM and Test Bank, and more **Introductory Sociology Transparency Acetates** 2005: "Groups & Organizations" acetates **CNN® Today Videos** • Sociology Vol. III: *Tattoo History* (4:03), *KKK: A History of Hate* (1:27) • Sociology Vol.V: *Soft Pacs* (2:19) **Lecture Launchers Video/DVD** *Bystander Apathy* (2.16), *The McDonaldization of Society* (2.77) **Sociology: Core Concepts Video/DVD** *Groups* (8.58) **Wadsworth's Sociology Video Library** See the *Formal Organizations and Gangs* clips in "Discovering Sociology"	Test Bank Chapter 6 contains 100–125 multiple-choice, 30-40 true/false, and 8–10 short-answer questions. Also includes "Exploring Society" telecourse test items. The Test Bank is also available electronically through **ExamView®**, which can be customized to fit your needs. **WebTutor™ Advantage** See Chapter 6 to assign chapter quizzes, conduct online discussion, track student progress, and post course material **Instructor's Resource Manual Notebook** Consult *Tips for Teaching Introductory Sociology*, Section 5: "Examinations"	**Study Guide** Chapter 6 contains chapter outlines, learning objectives, fill-in-the-blank review questions, key term matching exercises, and practice tests containing 15 multiple-choice, 5 true/false, and 5 short-answer questions **Telecourse Guide** Chapter 6 contains lesson overviews, goals and objectives, specific reading assignments, practice tests, and other learning activities **SocCoach CD-ROM** See the Chapter 6 diagnostic quiz and personalized study plan **Web Site Highlights** http://sociology. wadsworth.com/ kornblum/change7e • Practice Quizzes • Matching Exercises • Flashcards • Crossword Puzzles **WebTutor™ Advantage** See Chapter 6 for chapter-specific review, quizzing, flashcards, and interactive games and exercises	**Web Site Highlights** http://sociology. wadsworth.com/kornblum/change7e • Internet links and exercises • CNN® Today videos and exercises • GSS data • Terrorism Guide: Part I, B **InfoTrac® College Edition** http://www.infotrac-college.com *Keywords:* Primary Group, Communities, Reciprocity, Ethnomethodology **Wadsworth's Sociology Online Resources and Writing Companion** "Groups and Organizations" • InfoTrac® College Edition Exercises 1–5 • Opposing Viewpoints Resource Center Exercises 1–4 • MicroCase® Online Exercises 1–3 • InfoWrite and OVRC Research Guide **SocCoach CD-ROM** See the "Groups and Organizations" interactive data map exercise **Researching Sociology on the Internet** Part II: "Groups and Organizations" **Classic Readings in Sociology** Goffman: "The Presentation of Self" **Applied Sociology** Chapter 4: "Groups and Organizations" **Six Steps to Effective Writing in Sociology** Teaches thinking and writing skills for each stage of the writing process

Chapter 7: Deviance and Social Control

Class Preparation/ Lecture Tools	Testing Tools/ Course Management	Student Study Tools	Beyond the Book: Research, Writing, and Exploration
Instructor's Resource Manual Notebook Chapter 7 examines deviance and social control within the context of social change, using examples such as smoking and whistleblowing to illustrate the fluidity of definitions of deviance. The controversy over capital punishment can serve as a vital topic for class discussion. Also consult *Tips for Teaching Introductory Sociology*, Section 4 and 6 **Telecourse Faculty Guide** Consult for instructional strategies on teaching Deviance and Social Control via the "Exploring Society" telecourse **Multimedia Manager Instructor Resource CD-ROM** Text-specific graphics, customizable Microsoft® PowerPoint® lecture slides, lecture launcher clips, electronic IRM and Test Bank, and more **Introductory Sociology Transparency Acetates** 2005: "Deviance and Crime" acetates **CNN® Today Videos** • Sociology Vol. II: *Hate Crimes* (2:06), *Hollywood Runaways* (2:30) • Sociology Vol. III: *Gang Violence* (1:31), *Hate Crime* (3:27), *Tattoo History* (4:03), *KKK: A History of Hate* (1:27) • Sociology Vol. V: *Execution Politics* (2:20), *Graham Execution* (1:15), *Insanity Defense* (2:41) • Sociology Vol. VI: *Support for Battered Women* (2:07); *The Reporting of Campus Crime* (6:44); *San Quentin* (4:06) **Lecture Launchers Video/DVD** *The Criminal Justice System: Plea Bargaining* (3.13) **Wadsworth's Sociology Video Library** Select a full-length video from the Films for the Humanities such as *School Shootings: America's Tragedy*. Also see the *Juveniles Locked Up* clip from the "Discovering Sociology" video	**Test Bank** Chapter 7 contains 100–125 multiple-choice, 30–40 true/false, and 8–10 short-answer questions. Also includes "Exploring Society" tele-course test items. The Test Bank is also available electronically through **ExamView®**, which can be customized to fit your needs. WebTUTOR® Advantage **WebTutor™ Advantage** See Chapter 7 to assign chapter quizzes, conduct online discussion, track student progress, and post course material **Instructor's Resource Manual Notebook** Consult *Tips for Teaching Introductory Sociology*, Section 5: "Examinations"	**Study Guide** Chapter 7 contains chapter outlines, learning objectives, fill-in-the-blank review questions, key term matching exercises, and practice tests containing 15 multiple-choice, 5 true/false, and 5 short-answer questions **Telecourse Guide** Chapter 7 contains lesson overviews, goals and objectives, specific reading assignments, practice tests, and other learning activities **SocCoach CD-ROM** See the Chapter 7 diagnostic quiz and personalized study plan **Web Site Highlights** http://sociology. wadsworth.com/ kornblum/change7e • Practice Quizzes • Matching Exercises • Flashcards • Crossword Puzzles WebTUTOR® Advantage **WebTutor™ Advantage** See Chapter 7 for chapter-specific review, quizzing, flashcards, and interactive games and exercises	**Web Site Highlights** http://sociology. wadsworth.com/kornblum/change7e • Internet links and exercises • CNN® Today videos and exercises • GSS data • Online Module: "Suburban Youth and School Violence." • Terrorism Guide: Part I **InfoTrac® College Edition** http://www.infotrac-college.com *Keywords:* Subculture, Deviance, Social Control, Stigma **Wadsworth's Sociology Online Resources and Writing Companion** "Deviance" and "Crime" • InfoTrac® College Edition Exercises (Deviance) 1–5, (Crime) 1–5 • Opposing Viewpoints Resource Center Exercises (Deviance) 1–4, (Crime) 1–5 • MicroCase® Online Exercises (Deviance) 1–3, (Crime) 1–3 • InfoWrite and OVRC Research Guide **SocCoach CD-ROM** See the "Deviance and Crime" Virtual Exploration and the "Deviance" and "Crime" interactive data map exercises **Researching Sociology on the Internet** Part II: "Deviance and Crime" **Classic Readings in Sociology** Rosenhan: "On Being Sane in Insane Places" **Applied Sociology** Chapter 5: "Deviance" **Six Steps to Effective Writing in Sociology** Teaches thinking and writing skills for each stage of the writing process

Chapter 8: Collective Behavior, Social Movements, and Mass Publics

Class Preparation/ Lecture Tools	Testing Tools/ Course Management	Student Study Tools	Beyond the Book: Research, Writing, and Exploration
Instructor's Resource Manual Notebook This chapter is placed earlier in this text than in comparable ones because collective behavior and social movements play such an important role in bringing about social change. Ask students to consider how the concept of relative deprivation and revolution can be applied to the situation of the Islamic world versus more affluent Western nations. Also consult *Tips for Teaching Introductory Sociology*, Section 4 and 6 **Telecourse Faculty Guide** Consult for instructional strategies on teaching Collective Behavior, Social Movements, and Mass Publics via the "Exploring Society" telecourse **Multimedia Manager Instructor Resource CD-ROM** Text-specific graphics, customizable Microsoft® *PowerPoint*® lecture slides, lecture launcher clips, electronic IRM and Test Bank, and more **Introductory Sociology Transparency Acetates** 2005: "Collective Behavior and Social Movements" acetates **CNN® Today Videos** • Sociology Vol. I: *Diversity in Los Angeles* (5:50), *Racism in Brazil* (7:00) • Sociology Vol. II: *Culture Watch, Subway Women* (2:25) • Sociology Vol. III: *Modernization and the American Family* (2:39) • Sociology Vol.IV: *Amazon Underwater* (3:09), *Sprawl Prescription* (1:51), *Protest Retrospective* (3:43) **Lecture Launchers Video/DVD** *AIDS Action: One Man's Personal Story* (6.31)	**Test Bank** Chapter 8 contains 100–125 multiple-choice, 30–40 true/false, and 8–10 short-answer questions. Also includes "Exploring Society" tele-course test items. The Test Bank is also available electronically through **ExamView®,** which can be customized to fit your needs. WebTUTOR Advantage **WebTutor™ Advantage** See Chapter 8 to assign chapter quizzes, conduct online discussion, track student progress, and post course material **Instructor's Resource Manual Notebook** Consult *Tips for Teaching Introductory Sociology*, Section 5: "Examinations"	**Study Guide** Chapter 8 contains chapter outlines, learning objectives, fill-in-the-blank review questions, key term matching exercises, and practice tests containing 15 multiple-choice, 5 true/false, and 5 short-answer questions **Telecourse Guide** Chapter 8 contains lesson overviews, goals and objectives, specific reading assignments, practice tests, and other learning activities **SocCoach CD-ROM** See the Chapter 8 diagnostic quiz and personalized study plan **Web Site Highlights** http://sociology. wadsworth.com/ kornblum/change7e • Practice Quizzes • Matching Exercises • Flashcards • Crossword Puzzles WebTUTOR Advantage **WebTutor™ Advantage** See Chapter 8 for chapter-specific review, quizzing, flashcards, and interactive games and exercises	**Web Site Highlights** http://sociology. wadsworth.com/kornblum/change7e • Internet links and exercises • CNN® Today videos and exercises • GSS data • Online Module: "Environmental Sociology: What's New" • Terrorism Update: Part I, D **InfoTrac® College Edition** http://www.infotrac-college.com *Keywords:* Collective Behavior, Revolution, Social Movement, Charisma **Wadsworth's Sociology Online Resources and Writing Companion** "Social Change and Social Movements" • InfoTrac® College Edition Exercises 1–5 • Opposing Viewpoints Resource Center Exercises 1–4 • MicroCase® Online Exercises 1–3 • InfoWrite and OVRC Research Guide **SocCoach CD-ROM** See the "Collective Behavior and Social Movement" interactive data map exercise **Researching Sociology on the Internet** Part II: "Collective Behavior and Social Movements" **Six Steps to Effective Writing in Sociology** Teaches thinking and writing skills for each stage of the writing process

Chapter 9: Population and Urbanization

Class Preparation/ Lecture Tools	Testing Tools/ Course Management	Student Study Tools	Beyond the Book: Research, Writing, and Exploration
Instructor's Resource Manual Notebook Chapter 9 introduces population growth and urbanization in an integrated fashion, drawing upon recent policy debates and other world convocations. Ask students why and how problems related to rapid population growth in poorer nations could be alleviated by greater education and empowerment of women. **Telecourse Faculty Guide** Consult for instructional strategies on teaching Population and Urbanization via the "Exploring Society" telecourse **Multimedia Manager Instructor Resource CD-ROM** Text-specific graphics, customizable Microsoft® *PowerPoint*® lecture slides, lecture launcher clips, electronic IRM and Test Bank, and more **Introductory Sociology Transparency Acetates** 2005: "Population and Urbanism" acetates **CNN® Today Videos** • Sociology Vol. I: *Asian Americans* (2:19) *Diversity in Los Angeles* (5:50) • Sociology Vol. II: *Subway Women* (2:25) • Sociology Vol. III: *Family Planning in Egypt* (2:39), *Changing American Immigration Policy* (2:32) • Sociology Vol. IV: *Census Overview* (2:07), *Census Undercount* (2:59), *Sprawl Brawl* (1:55), *Sprawl Prescription* (1:51), *Sprawl America* (3:10), *SUV Impact* (1:57) • Sociology Vol. V: *Population Overview* (1:39) **Lecture Launchers Video/DVD** *Urban Issues* (4.81) **Wadsworth's Sociology Video Library** Select a full-length video from the collection of Films for the Humanities such as *The Development of Community*	**Test Bank** Chapter 9 contains 100–125 multiple-choice, 30–40 true/false, and 8–10 short-answer questions. Also includes "Exploring Society" telecourse test items. The Test Bank is also available electronically through **ExamView®**, which can be customized to fit your needs. *WebTUTOR Advantage* **WebTutor™ Advantage** See Chapter 9 to assign chapter quizzes, conduct online discussion, track student progress, and post course material **Instructor's Resource Manual Notebook** Consult *Tips for Teaching Introductory Sociology*, Section 5: "Examinations"	**Study Guide** Chapter 9 contains chapter outlines, learning objectives, fill-in-the-blank review questions, key term matching exercises, and practice tests containing 15 multiple-choice, 5 true/false, and 5 short-answer questions **Telecourse Guide** Chapter 9 contains lesson overviews, goals and objectives, specific reading assignments, practice tests, and other learning activities **SocCoach CD-ROM** See the Chapter 9 diagnostic quiz and personalized study plan **Web Site Highlights** http://sociology. wadsworth.com/ kornblum/change7e • Practice Quizzes • Matching Exercises • Flashcards • Crossword Puzzles *WebTUTOR Advantage* **WebTutor™ Advantage** See Chapter 9 for chapter-specific review, quizzing, flashcards, and interactive games and exercises	**Web Site Highlights** http://sociology. wadsworth.com/kornblum/change7e • Internet links and exercises • CNN® Today videos and exercises • GSS data • Online Module: "Environmental Sociology: What's New" **InfoTrac® College Edition** http://www.infotrac-college.com *Keywords:* Urbanization, Decentralization, Subculture, Inequality **Wadsworth's Sociology Online Resources and Writing Companion** "Population, Urbanization, and the Environment" • InfoTrac® College Edition Exercises 1–5 • Opposing Viewpoints Resource Center Exercises 1–4 • MicroCase® Online Exercises 1–3 • InfoWrite and OVRC Research Guide **SocCoach CD-ROM** See the "Population and the Environment" Virtual Exploration and the "Population, Urbanism and Environment" interactive data map exercise **Researching Sociology on the Internet** Part II: "Population and Urbanism" **Census 2000: A Student Guide for Sociology** See all **Classic Readings in Sociology** Wirth: "Urbanism as a Way of Life" **Applied Sociology** Chapter 13: "Population and Human Ecology" **Six Steps to Effective Writing in Sociology** Teaches thinking and writing skills for each stage of the writing process

Chapter 10: Global Social Change

Class Preparation/ Lecture Tools	Testing Tools/ Course Management	Student Study Tools	Beyond the Book: Research, Writing, and Exploration
Instructor's Resource Manual Notebook Chapter 10 uses the major theories of social change to summarize material presented in earlier chapters, but it also emphasizes the human aspects of social change and the clash between the traditional and the new. A good topic for class discussion would be the effects of "exporting" jobs from the United States to other nations, such as Mexico. Also consult *Tips for Teaching Introductory Sociology*, Section 4 and 6 **Telecourse Faculty Guide** Consult for instructional strategies on teaching Global Social Change via the "Exploring Society" telecourse **Multimedia Manager Instructor Resource CD-ROM** Text-specific graphics, customizable Microsoft® *PowerPoint®* lecture slides, lecture launcher clips, electronic IRM and Test Bank, and more **Introductory Sociology Transparency Acetates** 2005: "Social Change" acetates **CNN® Today Videos** • Sociology Vol. I: *Diversity in Los Angeles* (5:50), *Racism in Brazil* (7:00) • Sociology Vol. II: *Culture Watch,* • Sociology Vol. III: *Modernization and the American Family* (2:39), *Migrating Peoples* (2:44) • Sociology Vol.IV: *Amazon Underwater* (3:09), *China Internet* (1:22) **Lecture Launchers Video/DVD** *Cathedrals of Consumption* (2.95) **Sociology: Core Concepts Video/DVD** *Social Change* (8.70)	**Test Bank** Chapter 10 contains 100–125 multiple-choice, 30–40 true/false, and 8–10 short-answer questions. Also includes "Exploring Society" telecourse test items. The Test Bank is also available electronically through **ExamView®**, which can be customized to fit your needs. **WebTutor™ Advantage** See Chapter 10 to assign chapter quizzes, conduct online discussion, track student progress, and post course material **Instructor's Resource Manual Notebook** Consult *Tips for Teaching Introductory Sociology*, Section 5: "Examinations"	**Study Guide** Chapter 10 contains chapter outlines, learning objectives, fill-in-the-blank review questions, key term matching exercises, and practice tests containing 15 multiple-choice, 5 true/false, and 5 short-answer questions **Telecourse Guide** Chapter 10 contains lesson overviews, goals and objectives, specific reading assignments, practice tests, and other learning activities **SocCoach CD-ROM** See the Chapter 10 diagnostic quiz and personalized study plan **Web Site Highlights** http://sociology. wadsworth.com/ kornblum/change7e • Practice Quizzes • Matching Exercises • Flashcards • Crossword Puzzles **WebTutor™ Advantage** See Chapter 10 for chapter-specific review, quizzing, flashcards, and interactive games and exercises	**Web Site Highlights** http://sociology.wadsworth. com/kornblum/change7e • Internet links and exercises • CNN® Today videos and exercises • GSS data • Online Module: "Environmental Sociology: What's New" • Terrorism Update: Part I, D **InfoTrac® College Edition** http://www.infotrac-college.com *Keywords:* Social Change, Modernization, War, Cultural Lag **Wadsworth's Sociology Online Resources and Writing Companion** "Social Change and Social Movements" • InfoTrac® College Edition Exercises 1–5 • Opposing Viewpoints Resource Center Exercises 1–4 • MicroCase® Online Exercises 1–3 • InfoWrite and OVRC Research Guide **SocCoach CD-ROM** See the "Global Social Change" Virtual Exploration and the "Social Change" interactive data map exercise **Researching Sociology on the Internet** Part II: "Globalization" and "Social Change" **Applied Sociology** Chapter 14: "Social Change and the Future" **Six Steps to Effective Writing in Sociology** Teaches thinking and writing skills for each stage of the writing process

Chapter 11: Stratification and Global Inequality

Class Preparation/ Lecture Tools	Testing Tools/ Course Management	Student Study Tools	Beyond the Book: Research, Writing, and Exploration
Instructor's Resource Manual Notebook While students will be aware of social stratification in their own society, they may be less familiar with stratification in non-Western societies. After defining stratification, caste, class, and life chances, use the photos in the vignette and "Visual Sociology" sections to dispel the myth that poverty is a result of laziness and other faults in the individual. Also consult *Tips for Teaching Introductory Sociology*, Section 6 **Telecourse Faculty Guide** Consult for instructional strategies on teaching Stratification and Global Inequality via the "Exploring Society" telecourse **Multimedia Manager Instructor Resource CD-ROM** Text-specific graphics, customizable Microsoft® *PowerPoint*® lecture slides, lecture launcher clips, electronic IRM and Test Bank, and more **Introductory Sociology Transparency Acetates** 2005: "Global Stratification" acetates **CNN® Today Videos** • Sociology Vol. I: *Racism in Brazil* (7:00) • Sociology Vol. II: *Germany Unemployed* (2:41) • Sociology Vol. III: *Challenging the Caste System in India*, (2:37), *Migrating Peoples* (2:44) • Sociology Vol.IV: *South Africa AIDS Vaccine* (2:21), *China Internet* (1:22) • Sociology Vol. V: *AIDS in Thailand* **Sociology: Core Concepts Video/DVD** *Social Stratification* (9.65) **Wadsworth's Sociology Video Library** Select a full-length video from the Films for the Humanities such as *The Media and Democracy in the Arab World*	**Test Bank** Chapter 11 contains 100–125 multiple-choice, 30–40 true/false, and 8–10 short-answer questions. Also includes "Exploring Society" telecourse test items. The Test Bank is also available electronically through **ExamView®**, which can be customized to fit your needs. WebTUTOR Advantage **WebTutor™ Advantage** See Chapter 11 to assign chapter quizzes, conduct online discussion, track student progress, and post course material **Instructor's Resource Manual Notebook** Consult *Tips for Teaching Introductory Sociology*, Section 5: "Examinations"	**Study Guide** Chapter 11 contains chapter outlines, learning objectives, fill-in-the-blank review questions, key term matching exercises, and practice tests containing 15 multiple-choice, 5 true/false, and 5 short-answer questions **Telecourse Guide** Chapter 11 contains lesson overviews, goals and objectives, specific reading assignments, practice tests, and other learning activities **SocCoach CD-ROM** See the Chapter 11 diagnostic quiz and personalized study plan **Web Site Highlights** http://sociology. wadsworth.com/ kornblum/change7e • Practice Quizzes • Matching Exercises • Flashcards • Crossword Puzzles WebTUTOR Advantage **WebTutor™ Advantage** See Chapter 11 for chapter-specific review, quizzing, flashcards, and interactive games and exercises	**Web Site Highlights** http://sociology.wadsworth. com/kornblum/change7e • Internet links and exercises • CNN® Today videos and exercises • GSS data • Terrorism Guide: Part III, A **InfoTrac® College Edition** http://www.infotrac-college.com *Keywords:* Social Stratification, Social Mobility, Class Consciousness, Refugee **Wadsworth's Sociology Online Resources and Writing Companion** "Global Stratification" • InfoTrac® College Edition Exercises 1–5 • Opposing Viewpoints Resource Center Exercises 1–4 • MicroCase® Online Exercises 1–3 • InfoWrite and OVRC Research Guide **SocCoach CD-ROM** See the "Global Stratification" interactive data map exercise **Researching Sociology on the Internet** Part II: "Social Class and Stratification" and "Globalization" **Classic Readings in Sociology** Gans: "The Uses of Poverty: The Poor Pay All" **Applied Sociology** Chapter 6: "Diversity and Inequality," Chapter 12: "Power, Politics, and Authority," and Chapter 13: "Population and Human Ecology" **Six Steps to Effective Writing in Sociology** Teaches thinking and writing skills for each stage of the writing process

Resource Integration Guide

Chapter 12: Inequalities of Social Class

Class Preparation/ Lecture Tools	Testing Tools/ Course Management	Student Study Tools	Beyond the Book: Research, Writing, and Exploration
Instructor's Resource Manual Notebook Chapter 12 describes the characteristics and life chances of social classes in the U.S. and examines the differences between equality of opportunity and equality of result. This calls for spending some time in class discussing poverty and social policy in the U.S., a topic that is sure to arouse strong opinions. Also consult *Tips for Teaching Introductory Sociology*, Section 6 **Telecourse Faculty Guide** Consult for instructional strategies on teaching Inequalities of Social Class via the "Exploring Society" telecourse **Multimedia Manager Instructor Resource CD-ROM** Text-specific graphics, customizable Microsoft® *PowerPoint*® lecture slides, lecture launcher clips, electronic IRM and Test Bank, and more **Introductory Sociology Transparency Acetates** 2005: "Social Class" acetates **CNN® Today Videos** • Sociology Vol. I: *Teen Pregnancy* (2:02) • Sociology Vol. II: *Welfare Success* (2:30), *Welfare One Year Anniversary* (2:06), *Helping the Homeless* (1:45) • Sociology Vol. IV: *African American Snapshot* (1:08), *Janitor Strike* (1:45), *Silicon Valley Lifestyles* (2:07) • Sociology Vol. VI: *Homeless in Cape Cod* (2:21) **Lecture Launchers Video/DVD** *Effects of Social Mobility: A Personal Journey* (4.24), *Life Chances: The Guerry Family* (4.06) **Sociology: Core Concepts Video/DVD** *Social Stratification* (9.65) **Wadsworth's Sociology Video Library** Select a full-length video from the Films for the Humanities such as *Educating to End Inequality*	**Test Bank** Chapter 12 contains 100–125 multiple-choice, 30–40 true/false, and 8–10 short-answer questions. Also includes "Exploring Society" telecourse test items. The Test Bank is also available electronically through **ExamView®**, which can be customized to fit your needs. WebTUTOR™ Advantage **WebTutor™ Advantage** See Chapter 12 to assign chapter quizzes, conduct online discussion, track student progress, and post course material **Instructor's Resource Manual Notebook** Consult *Tips for Teaching Introductory Sociology*, Section 5: "Examinations"	**Study Guide** Chapter 12 contains chapter outlines, learning objectives, fill-in-the-blank review questions, key term matching exercises, and practice tests containing 15 multiple-choice, 5 true/false, and 5 short-answer questions **Telecourse Guide** Chapter 12 contains lesson overviews, goals and objectives, specific reading assignments, practice tests, and other learning activities **SocCoach CD-ROM** See the Chapter 12 diagnostic quiz and personalized study plan **Web Site Highlights** http://sociology. wadsworth.com/ kornblum/change7e • Practice Quizzes • Matching Exercises • Flashcards • Crossword Puzzles WebTUTOR™ Advantage **WebTutor™ Advantage** See Chapter 12 for chapter-specific review, quizzing, flashcards, and interactive games and exercises	**Web Site Highlights** http://sociology. wadsworth.com/kornblum/change7e • Internet links and exercises • CNN® Today videos and exercises • GSS data **InfoTrac® College Edition** http://www.infotrac-college.com *Keywords:* Socioeconomic status, Middle Class, Ghetto, Educational Attainment **Wadsworth's Sociology Online Resources and Writing Companion** "Social Class and Social Stratification in the U.S." • InfoTrac® College Edition Exercises 1–5 • Opposing Viewpoints Resource Center Exercises 1–3 • MicroCase® Online Exercises 1–3 • InfoWrite and OVRC Research Guide **SocCoach CD-ROM** See "Social Stratification" Virtual Exploration and the "Social Stratification" interactive data map exercise **Researching Sociology on the Internet** Part II: "Social Class and Stratification" **Classic Readings in Sociology** Gans: "The Uses of Poverty: The Poor Pay All" **Applied Sociology** Chapter 6: "Diversity and Inequality" Chapter 12: "Power, Politics, and Authority" **Six Steps to Effective Writing in Sociology** Teaches thinking and writing skills for each stage of the writing process

Resource Integration Guide

Chapter 13: Inequalities of Race and Ethnicity

Class Preparation/ Lecture Tools	Testing Tools/ Course Management	Student Study Tools	Beyond the Book: Research, Writing, and Exploration
Instructor's Resource Manual Notebook Chapter 13 focuses on important concepts that demand close attention, including the distinction between biological and social concepts of race, the problems involved in defining ethnic groups, the difficulty of achieving true cultural pluralism, and the effects of de jure versus de facto segregation. **Telecourse Faculty Guide** Consult for instructional strategies on teaching Inequalities of Race and Ethnicity via the "Exploring Society" telecourse **Multimedia Manager Instructor Resource CD-ROM** Text-specific graphics, customizable Microsoft® *PowerPoint*® lecture slides, lecture launcher clips, electronic IRM and Test Bank, and more **Introductory Sociology Transparency Acetates** 2005: "Race and Ethnicity" acetates **CNN® Today Videos** • Sociology Vol.I: *Asian Americans* (2:19) • Sociology Vol.II: *Muslims in America* (2:04 • Sociology Vol.IV: *TV Black Culture* (2:34) • Sociology Vol. V: *Asian Growth* (2:23), *Courting Hispanics* (2:17) • Sociology Vol. VI: *Breaking Cliques* (2:03) **Lecture Launchers Video/DVD** *Genocide: Mike Jacobs' Story* (2.79), *Native American Assimilation* (2.74) **Sociology: Core Concepts Video/DVD** *Race and Ethnicity* (10.18) **Wadsworth's Sociology Video Library** Select a full-length video from the Films for the Humanities such as *How Biased Are You?, Race on Trial,* and *Kids and Sports: Racism and Athletics.* Also see the *Diversity and Culture: The Japanese-American Experience* clips from the "Discovering Sociology" video	**Test Bank** Chapter 13 contains 100–125 multiple-choice, 30–40 true/false, and 8–10 short-answer questions. Also includes "Exploring Society" telecourse test items. The Test Bank is also available electronically through **ExamView**®, which can be customized to fit your needs. WebTUTOR Advantage **WebTutor™ Advantage** See Chapter 13 to assign chapter quizzes, conduct online discussion, track student progress, and post course material **Instructor's Resource Manual Notebook** Consult *Tips for Teaching Introductory Sociology,* Section 5: "Examinations"	**Study Guide** Chapter 13 contains chapter outlines, learning objectives, fill-in-the-blank review questions, key term matching exercises, and practice tests containing 15 multiple-choice, 5 true/false, and 5 short-answer questions **Telecourse Guide** Chapter 13 contains lesson overviews, goals and objectives, specific reading assignments, practice tests, and other learning activities **SocCoach CD-ROM** See the Chapter 13 diagnostic quiz and personalized study plan **Web Site Highlights** http://sociology. wadsworth.com/ kornblum/change7e • Practice Quizzes • Matching Exercises • Flashcards • Crossword Puzzles WebTUTOR Advantage **WebTutor™ Advantage** See Chapter 13 for chapter-specific review, quizzing, flashcards, and interactive games and exercises	**Web Site Highlights** http://sociology. wadsworth.com/kornblum/change7e • Internet links and exercises • CNN® Today videos and exercises • GSS data **InfoTrac® College Edition** http://www.infotrac-college.com *Keywords:* Racism, Ethnic Nationalism, Genocide, Assimilation **Wadsworth's Sociology Online Resources and Writing Companion** "Race and Ethnicity" • InfoTrac® College Edition Exercises 1–5 • Opposing Viewpoints Resource Center Exercises 1–4 • MicroCase® Online Exercises 1–3 • InfoWrite and OVRC Research Guide **SocCoach CD-ROM** See "Race and Ethnicity" Virtual Exploration and the "Race and Ethnicity" interactive data map exercises **Researching Sociology on the Internet** Part II: "Race and Ethnicity" **Census 2000: A Student Guide for Sociology** Major Trends: "Increased Diversity," "The Hispanic Population," and "The African American Population." Also see the state demographic profiles **Classic Readings in Sociology** DuBois: "The Souls of Black Folk" **Applied Sociology** Chapter 6: "Diversity and Inequality" **Six Steps to Effective Writing in Sociology** Teaches thinking and writing skills for each stage of the writing process

Chapter 14: Inequalities of Gender

Class Preparation/ Lecture Tools	Testing Tools/ Course Management	Student Study Tools	Beyond the Book: Research, Writing, and Exploration
Instructor's Resource Manual Notebook Gender inequality is a "hot" topic. Read the lines from Tennyson's poem (in "Sociology Versus Ideology"): "Man for the field and woman for the hearth/Man for the sword and for the needle she/…All else confusion." This should give rise to an animated discussion, but be sure to end with a balanced sociological view of the issues. **Telecourse Faculty Guide** Consult for instructional strategies on teaching Inequalities of Gender via the "Exploring Society" telecourse **Multimedia Manager Instructor Resource CD-ROM** Text-specific graphics, customizable Microsoft® *PowerPoint*® lecture slides, lecture launcher clips, electronic IRM and Test Bank, and more **Introductory Sociology Transparency Acetates** 2005: "Sex and Gender" acetates **CNN® Today Videos** • Sociology Vol. I: *Divorce and Kids* (4:45), *Self-Esteem: Girls and Science* (3:46), *Teen Pregnancy* (2:02) • Sociology Vol. II: *Women's Hoop Dreams* (2:25), *Body Image* (2:23) • Sociology Vol. III: *Gay Victimization* (3:17), *Bangladesh Dowry* (2:45), *Marry for Love or Money?* (2:36) • Sociology Vol. V: *Women in Tech* (4:47), *Cyber Sperm* (1:52) • Sociology Vol. VI: *Unequal Opportunity for Women* (1:59); *Declining Number of Men on College Campuses* (2:22) **Lecture Launchers Video/DVD** *Gender Inequality* (5.28) **Wadsworth's Sociology Video Library** Select a full-length video from the Films for the Humanities such as *Lives Together, Worlds Apart: Men and Women in a Time of Change,* and *Being Gay: Coming Out in the 21st Century*	**Test Bank** Chapter 14 contains 100–125 multiple-choice, 30–40 true/false, and 8–10 short-answer questions. Also includes "Exploring Society" telecourse test items. The Test Bank is also available electronically through **ExamView®,** which can be customized to fit your needs. **WebTutor™ Advantage** See Chapter 14 to assign chapter quizzes, conduct online discussion, track student progress, and post course material **Instructor's Resource Manual Notebook** Consult *Tips for Teaching Introductory Sociology,* Section 5: "Examinations"	**Study Guide** Chapter 14 contains chapter outlines, learning objectives, fill-in-the-blank review questions, key term matching exercises, and practice tests containing 15 multiple-choice, 5 true/false, and 5 short-answer questions **Telecourse Guide** Chapter 14 contains lesson overviews, goals and objectives, specific reading assignments, practice tests, and other learning activities **SocCoach CD-ROM** See the Chapter 14 diagnostic quiz and personalized study plan **Web Site Highlights** http://sociology. wadsworth.com/ kornblum/change7e • Practice Quizzes • Matching Exercises • Flashcards • Crossword Puzzles **WebTutor™ Advantage** See Chapter 14 for chapter-specific review, quizzing, flashcards, and interactive games and exercises	**Web Site Highlights** http://sociology. wadsworth.com/kornblum/change7e • Internet links and exercises • CNN® Today videos and exercises • GSS data **InfoTrac® College Edition** http://www.infotrac-college.com *Keywords:* Gender, Sexism, Gender Roles, Patriarchy **Wadsworth's Sociology Online Resources and Writing Companion** "Gender" and "Sex" • InfoTrac® College Edition Exercises (Gender) 1–5, (Sex) 1–5 • Opposing Viewpoints Resource Center Exercises (Gender) 1–4, (Sex) 1–4 • MicroCase® Online Exercises (Gender) 1–3, (Sex) 1–3 • InfoWrite and OVRC Research Guide **SocCoach CD-ROM** See "Gender" Virtual Exploration and the "Gender" interactive data map exercise **Researching Sociology on the Internet** Part II: "Social Class and Stratification" **Census 2000: A Student Guide for Sociology** See the state demographic profiles **Classic Readings in Sociology** Bernard: "The Future of Marriage" **Applied Sociology** Chapter 6: "Diversity and Inequality" **Six Steps to Effective Writing in Sociology** Teaches thinking and writing skills for each stage of the writing process

Resource Integration Guide

Chapter 15: Inequalities of Youth and Age

Class Preparation/ Lecture Tools	Testing Tools/ Course Management	Student Study Tools	Beyond the Book: Research, Writing, and Exploration
Instructor's Resource Manual Notebook Chapter 15 emphasizes inequalities of youth as well as age. It presents data showing that poverty has increased among youth while there has been a relative improvement in the situation of the elderly. The population pyramids provide useful graphic illustrations of the effects of demographic factors—such as the baby boom—on other aspects of society. **Telecourse Faculty Guide** Consult for instructional strategies on teaching Inequalities of Youth and Age via the "Exploring Society" telecourse **Multimedia Manager Instructor Resource CD-ROM** Text-specific graphics, customizable Microsoft® *PowerPoint*® lecture slides, lecture launcher clips, electronic IRM and Test Bank, and more **Introductory Sociology Transparency Acetates** 2005: "Aging" acetates **CNN® Today Videos** • Sociology Vol. III: *Aging Baby Boomers* (2.51) • Sociology Vol. VI: *Pilots Too Old to Fly* (2:17); *Baby Boomers Moving to Retirement Communities* (2:18) **Lecture Launchers Video/DVD** *Then and Now: Aging in the Movies* (3.04)	**Test Bank** Chapter 15 contains 100–125 multiple-choice, 30–40 true/false, and 8–10 short-answer questions. Also includes "Exploring Society" tele-course test items. The Test Bank is also available electronically through **ExamView®**, which can be customized to fit your needs. WebTUTOR™ Advantage **WebTutor™ Advantage** See Chapter 15 to assign chapter quizzes, conduct online discussion, track student progress, and post course material **Instructor's Resource Manual Notebook** Consult *Tips for Teaching Introductory Sociology*, Section 5: "Examinations"	**Study Guide** Chapter 15 contains chapter outlines, learning objectives, fill-in-the-blank review questions, key term matching exercises, and practice tests containing 15 multiple-choice, 5 true/false, and 5 short-answer questions **Telecourse Guide** Chapter 15 contains lesson overviews, goals and objectives, specific reading assignments, practice tests, and other learning activities **SocCoach CD-ROM** See the Chapter 15 diagnostic quiz and personalized study plan **Web Site Highlights** http://sociology. wadsworth.com/ kornblum/change7e • Practice Quizzes • Matching Exercises • Flashcards • Crossword Puzzles WebTUTOR™ Advantage **WebTutor™ Advantage** See Chapter 15 for chapter-specific review, quizzing, flashcards, and interactive games and exercises	**Web Site Highlights** http://sociology. wadsworth.com/kornblum/change7e • Internet links and exercises • CNN® Today videos and exercises • GSS data **InfoTrac® College Edition** http://www.infotrac-college.com *Keywords:* Life Course, Baby Boom, Ageism, Life Expectancy **Wadsworth's Sociology Online Resources and Writing Companion** "Aging" • InfoTrac® College Edition Exercises 1–5 • Opposing Viewpoints Resource Center Exercises 1–4 • MicroCase® Online Exercises 1–3 • InfoWrite and OVRC Research Guide **SocCoach CD-ROM** See "Aging" Virtual Exploration and the "Age and Aging" interactive data map exercise **Researching Sociology on the Internet** Part II: "Aging and Healthcare" **Census 2000: A Student Guide for Sociology** Major Trends: "Aging Population" and "The American Household." Also see the state demographic profiles **Classic Readings in Sociology** Goffman: "The Presentation of Self" **Applied Sociology** Chapter 6: "Diversity and Inequality" **Six Steps to Effective Writing in Sociology** Teaches thinking and writing skills for each stage of the writing process

Chapter 16: The Family

Class Preparation/ Lecture Tools	Testing Tools/ Course Management	Student Study Tools	Beyond the Book: Research, Writing, and Exploration
Instructor's Resource Manual Notebook Chapter 16 stresses both family change and continuity. Emphasize the variety of family forms and norms. "Critical Sociology" on the future of the black family raises a controversial subject and offers examples of recent research. Also consult *Tips for Teaching Introductory Sociology*, Section 4 and 6 **Telecourse Faculty Guide** Consult for instructional strategies on teaching The Family via the "Exploring Society" telecourse **Multimedia Manager Instructor Resource CD-ROM** Text-specific graphics, customizable Microsoft® *PowerPoint*® lecture slides, lecture launcher clips, electronic IRM and Test Bank, and more **Introductory Sociology Transparency Acetates** 2005: "Family" acetates **CNN® Today Videos** • Sociology Vol. I: *Step Families* (2:39), *Step Family Discipline* (3:05), *Divorce and Kids* (4:45) • Sociology Vol. III: *Bangladesh Dowry* (2:45), *Marry for Love or Money?* (2:36), *Family Planning in Egypt* (2:39), *Modernization and the American Family* (2:39) • Sociology Vol. IV: *Commuter Couples* (1:31) • Sociology Vol. V: *Cyber Sperm* (1:52) • Sociology Vol. VI: *Teens and Sex* (2:54); *Divorce Study* (2:20) **Lecture Launchers Video/DVD** *Family Structures* (5.11) **Sociology: Core Concepts Video/DVD** *Family* (7.98) **Wadsworth's Sociology Video Library** Select a full-length video from the collection of Films for the Humanities such as *Love on the Rocks* and *What is Family? Defining the Tie that Binds*	**Test Bank** Chapter 16 contains 100–125 multiple-choice, 30–40 true/false, and 8–10 short-answer questions. Also includes "Exploring Society" tele-course test items. The Test Bank is also available electronically through **ExamView®**, which can be customized to fit your needs. WebTUTOR® Advantage **WebTutor™ Advantage** See Chapter 16 to assign chapter quizzes, conduct online discussion, track student progress, and post course material **Instructor's Resource Manual Notebook** Consult *Tips for Teaching Introductory Sociology*, Section 5: "Examinations"	**Study Guide** Chapter 16 contains chapter outlines, learning objectives, fill-in-the-blank review questions, key term matching exercises, and practice tests containing 15 multiple-choice, 5 true/false, and 5 short-answer questions **Telecourse Guide** Chapter 16 contains lesson overviews, goals and objectives, specific reading assignments, practice tests, and other learning activities **SocCoach CD-ROM** See the Chapter 16 diagnostic quiz and personalized study plan **Web Site Highlights** http://sociology. wadsworth.com/ kornblum/change7e • Practice Quizzes • Matching Exercises • Flashcards • Crossword Puzzles WebTUTOR® Advantage **WebTutor™ Advantage** See Chapter 16 for chapter-specific review, quizzing, flashcards, and interactive games and exercises	**Web Site Highlights** http://sociology. wadsworth.com/kornblum/change7e • Internet links and exercises • CNN® Today videos and exercises • GSS data • Online Module: "Suburban Youth and School Violence" **InfoTrac® College Edition** http://www.infotrac-college.com *Keywords:* Nuclear Family, Extended Family, Marriage, Double Standard **Wadsworth's Sociology Online Resources and Writing Companion** "Families" • InfoTrac® College Edition Exercises 1–5 • Opposing Viewpoints Resource Center Exercises 1–4 • MicroCase® Online Exercises 1–3 • InfoWrite and OVRC Research Guide **SocCoach CD-ROM** See "Family" Virtual Exploration and the "Families" interactive data map exercise **Researching Sociology on the Internet** Part II: "Marriages and Families" **Census 2000: A Student Guide for Sociology** Major Trends: "The American Household." Also see the state demographic profiles **Classic Readings in Sociology** Merton: "Manifest and Latent Functions" **Applied Sociology** Chapter 8: "Marriage and Family" **Six Steps to Effective Writing in Sociology** Teaches thinking and writing skills for each stage of the writing process

Resource Integration Guide

Chapter 17: Religion

Class Preparation/ Lecture Tools	Testing Tools/ Course Management	Student Study Tools	Beyond the Book: Research, Writing, and Exploration
Instructor's Resource Manual Notebook Secularization, fundamentalism, religiosity, and religious pluralism are important concepts that need to be highlighted in discussions of Chapter 17. Because these and related processes are accompanied by a great deal of conflict, they should be approached with care and as objectively as possible. Also consult *Tips for Teaching Introductory Sociology*, Section 4 and 6 **Telecourse Faculty Guide** Consult for instructional strategies on teaching Religion via the "Exploring Society" telecourse **Multimedia Manager Instructor Resource CD-ROM** Text-specific graphics, customizable Microsoft® *PowerPoint*® lecture slides, lecture launcher clips, electronic IRM and Test Bank, and more **Introductory Sociology Transparency Acetates** 2005: "Religion" acetates **CNN® Today Videos** • Sociology Vol. I *Ganges Cleanup* (4:26) • Sociology Vol. II: *Muslims in America* (2:04), *Afghanistan Taliban* (2:09) • Sociology Vol. IV: *Faith Based Charity* (2:41) • Sociology Vol. V: *Germany's Jews* (3:00) **Lecture Launchers Video/DVD** *The Role of Religion* (1.97) **Wadsworth's Sociology Video Library** Select a full-length video from the Films for the Humanities such as *The Sacred from the Development of Community* series. Also see the *Religion and Race in America* and *American Values* clips from the "Discovering Sociology" video	**Test Bank** Chapter 17 contains 100–125 multiple-choice, 30-40 true/false, and 8–10 short-answer questions. Also includes "Exploring Society" telecourse test items. The Test Bank is also available electronically through **ExamView®**, which can be customized to fit your needs. WebTUTOR® Advantage **WebTutor™ Advantage** See Chapter 17 to assign chapter quizzes, conduct online discussion, track student progress, and post course material **Instructor's Resource Manual Notebook** Consult Tips for Teaching Introductory Sociology, Section 5: "Examinations"	**Study Guide** Chapter 17 contains chapter outlines, learning objectives, fill-in-the-blank review questions, key term matching exercises, and practice tests containing 15 multiple choice, 5 true/false, and 5 short answer questions **Telecourse Guide** Chapter 17 contains lesson overviews, goals and objectives, specific reading assignments, practice tests, and other learning activities **SocCoach CD-ROM** See the Chapter 17 diagnostic quiz and personalized study plan **Web Site Highlights** http://sociology. wadsworth.com/ kornblum/change7e • Practice Quizzes • Matching Exercises • Flashcards • Crossword Puzzles WebTUTOR® Advantage **WebTutor™ Advantage** See Chapter 17 for chapter-specific review, quizzing, flashcards, and interactive games and exercises	**Web Site Highlights** http://sociology. wadsworth.com/kornblum/change7e • Internet links and exercises • CNN® Today videos and exercises • GSS data • Terrorism Guide: Part II **InfoTrac® College Edition** http://www.infotrac-college.com *Keywords:* Religiosity, Theism, Cult, Secularization, Islam **Wadsworth's Sociology Online Resources and Writing Companion** "Religion" • InfoTrac® College Edition Exercises 1–5 • Opposing Viewpoints Resource Center Exercises 1–4 • MicroCase® Online Exercises 1–3 • InfoWrite and OVRC Research Guide **SocCoach CD-ROM** See "Religion" interactive data maps **Researching Sociology on the Internet** Part II: "Religion" **Applied Sociology** Chapter 10: "Religion" **Six Steps to Effective Writing in Sociology** Teaches thinking and writing skills for each stage of the writing process

Chapter 18: Education

Class Preparation/ Lecture Tools	Testing Tools/ Course Management	Student Study Tools	Beyond the Book: Research, Writing, and Exploration
Instructor's Resource Manual Notebook The issue of schools and adolescent society (the development of cliques and teachers' responses to them) is an especially important one due to its possible connection with school violence. Also key is the role of education in reproducing society's stratification system, an issue that's subject to debate. Also consult *Tips for Teaching Introductory Sociology*, Section 6 **Telecourse Faculty Guide** Consult for instructional strategies on teaching Education via the "Exploring Society" telecourse **Multimedia Manager Instructor Resource CD-ROM** Text-specific graphics, customizable Microsoft® *PowerPoint*® lecture slides, lecture launcher clips, electronic IRM and Test Bank, and more **Introductory Sociology Transparency Acetates** 2005: "Education" acetates **CNN® Today Videos** • Sociology Vol. I: *Self-Esteem: Girls and Science* (3:46) • Sociology Vol. II: *English for Immigrants* (2:40), *College Costs* (3:45) • Sociology Vol. III: *Hate Crime* (3:27), *Are School Vouchers a Good Thing?* (1:53) • Sociology Vol. IV: *Census Undercount* (2:59), *Sprawl America* (3:10) • Sociology Vol. V: *School Test Trouble* (2:07) • Sociology Vol. VI: *Breaking Cliques* (2:03), *Declining Number of Men on College Campuses* (2:22) **Lecture Launchers Video/DVD** *Roles in Education* (3.17) **Wadsworth's Sociology Video Library** Select a full-length video from the Films for the Humanities such as *School Shootings: America's Tragedy* and *Educating to End Inequality*	**Test Bank** Chapter 18 contains 100–125 multiple-choice, 30–40 true/false, and 8–10 short-answer questions. Also includes "Exploring Society" tele-course test items. The Test Bank is also available electronically through **ExamView®**, which can be customized to fit your needs. **WebTutor™ Advantage** See Chapter 18 to assign chapter quizzes, conduct online discussion, track student progress, and post course material **Instructor's Resource Manual Notebook** Consult *Tips for Teaching Introductory Sociology*, Section 5: "Examinations"	**Study Guide** Chapter 18 contains chapter outlines, learning objectives, fill-in-the-blank review questions, key term matching exercises, and practice tests containing 15 multiple-choice, 5 true/false, and 5 short-answer questions **Telecourse Guide** Chapter 18 contains lesson overviews, goals and objectives, specific reading assignments, practice tests, and other learning activities **SocCoach CD-ROM** See the Chapter 18 diagnostic quiz and personalized study plan **Web Site Highlights** http://sociology. wadsworth.com/ kornblum/change7e • Practice Quizzes • Matching Exercises • Flashcards • Crossword Puzzles **WebTutor™ Advantage** See Chapter 18 for chapter-specific review, quizzing, flashcards, and interactive games and exercises	**Web Site Highlights** http://sociology. wadsworth.com/kornblum/change7e • Internet links and exercises • CNN® Today videos and exercises • GSS data • Online Module: "Suburban Youth and School Violence" **InfoTrac® College Edition** http://www.infotrac-college.com *Keywords:* Educational Attainment, Communications Media, Bureaucracy, School Choice **Wadsworth's Sociology Online Resources and Writing Companion** "Education" • InfoTrac® College Edition Exercises 1–5 • Opposing Viewpoints Resource Center Exercises 1–5 • MicroCase® Online Exercises 1–3 • InfoWrite and OVRC Research Guide **SocCoach CD-ROM** See "Education" Virtual Exploration and the "Education" interactive data map exercise **Researching Sociology on the Internet** Part II: "Education" **Classic Readings in Sociology** Kozol: "Savage Inequalities" **Applied Sociology** Chapter 9: "Education" **Six Steps to Effective Writing in Sociology** Teaches thinking and writing skills for each stage of the writing process

Chapter 19: Economic Institutions

Class Preparation/ Lecture Tools	Testing Tools/ Course Management	Student Study Tools	Beyond the Book: Research, Writing, and Exploration
Instructor's Resource Manual Notebook New to this chapter is a section on labor unions and their contributions to the well-being of workers: not only higher pay but also vacations, holidays, sick pay, family leave, and hours of employment. This material can be used to supplement your discussions of labor-management relationships and sociological perspectives on the workplace. **Telecourse Faculty Guide** Consult for instructional strategies on teaching Economic Institutions via the "Exploring Society" telecourse **Multimedia Manager Instructor Resource CD-ROM** Text-specific graphics, customizable Microsoft® *PowerPoint*® lecture slides, lecture launcher clips, electronic IRM and Test Bank, and more **Introductory Sociology Transparency Acetates** 2005: "Work and Economy" acetates **CNN® Today Videos** • Sociology Vol. I: *Divorce and Kids* (4:45) • Sociology Vol. II: *Germany Unemployment* (2:41) • Sociology Vol. IV: *Aging Baby Boomers* (2:51), *Modernization and the American Family* (2:39) • Sociology Vol. IV: *Janitor Strike* (1:45), *Unionized Doctors* (1:47) • Sociology Vol. VI: *Vacation in America* (1:46) **Lecture Launchers Video/DVD** *Globalization* (3.29) **Sociology: Core Concepts Video/DVD** *The Economy* (9.13) **Wadsworth's Sociology Video Library** See the *Downsizing in the American Workplace* and *The American Worker and the New Economy* clips from the "Discovering Sociology" video	**Test Bank** Chapter 19 contains 100–125 multiple choice, 30–40 true/false, and 8–10 short answer questions. Also includes "Exploring Society" tele-course test items. The Test Bank is also available electronically through **ExamView®,** which can be customized to fit your needs. WebTUTOR™ Advantage **WebTutor™ Advantage** See Chapter 19 to assign chapter quizzes, conduct online discus-sion, track student progress, and post course material **Instructor's Resource Manual Notebook** Consult *Tips for Teaching Introductory Sociology,* Section 5: "Examinations"	**Study Guide** Chapter 19 contains chapter outlines, learning objectives, fill-in-the-blank review questions, key term matching exercises, and practice tests containing 15 multiple-choice, 5 true/false, and 5 short-answer questions **Telecourse Guide** Chapter 19 contains lesson overviews, goals and objectives, specific reading assignments, practice tests, and other learning activities **SocCoach CD-ROM** See the Chapter 19 diagnostic quiz and personalized study plan **Web Site Highlights** http://sociology. wadsworth.com/ kornblum/change7e • Practice Quizzes • Matching Exercises • Flashcards • Crossword Puzzles WebTUTOR™ Advantage **WebTutor™ Advantage** See Chapter 19 for chapter-specific review, quizzing, flashcards, and interactive games and exercises	**Web Site Highlights** http://sociology. wadsworth.com/kornblum/change7e • Internet links and exercises • CNN® Today videos and exercises • GSS data **InfoTrac® College Edition** http://www.infotrac-college.com *Keywords:* Markets, Technology, Welfare Capitalism, Socialism **Wadsworth's Sociology Online Resources and Writing Companion** "The Economy and Work" • InfoTrac® College Edition Exercises 1–5 • Opposing Viewpoints Resource Center Exercises 1–3 • MicroCase® Online Exercises 1–3 • InfoWrite and OVRC Research Guide **SocCoach CD-ROM** See "Economy and Work" Virtual Exploration and interactive data map exercise **Researching Sociology on the Internet** Part II: "Social Class and Stratification" **Census 2000: A Student Guide for Sociology** Major Trends: "Population Growth," "The Hispanic Population," and "Aging Population" **Classic Readings in Sociology** Marx & Engels: "Manifesto of the Communist Party" **Applied Sociology** Chapter 7: "Economy and Work" **Six Steps to Effective Writing in Sociology** Teaches thinking and writing skills for each stage of the writing process

Chapter 20: Politics and Political Institutions

Class Preparation/ Lecture Tools	Testing Tools/ Course Management	Student Study Tools	Beyond the Book: Research, Writing, and Exploration
Instructor's Resource Manual Notebook The war in Iraq and subsequent efforts at nation-building will provide numerous illustrations of concepts covered in Chapter 20, such as power, authority, and legitimacy; totalitarian regimes; structural prerequisites of democracy; and civilian control of the military. Also consult *Tips for Teaching Introductory Sociology*, Section 6 **Telecourse Faculty Guide** Consult for instructional strategies on teaching Politics and Political Institutions via the "Exploring Society" telecourse **Multimedia Manager Instructor Resource CD-ROM** Text-specific graphics, customizable Microsoft® *PowerPoint®* lecture slides, lecture launcher clips, electronic IRM and Test Bank, and more **Introductory Sociology Transparency Acetates** 2005: "Politics and Government" acetates **CNN® Today Videos** • Sociology Vol. I: *Tobacco and Kids* (2:00) • Sociology Vol. II: *Minnesota Marvel* (1:42), *Hate Crimes* (2:06) • Sociology Vol. III: *Cultural Change in America* (3:46), *Are School Vouchers a Good Thing?* (1:53), *Changing American Immigration Policy* (2:32) • Sociology Vol. IV: *Faith Based Charity* (2:41), *Protest Retrospective* (3:43) • Sociology Vol. V: *Courting Hispanics* (2:17) **Lecture Launchers Video/DVD** *Integrity of the Electoral Process* (6.10) **Wadsworth's Sociology Video Library** Select a full-length video from the collection of Films for the Humanities such as *The Development of Community or In Time of War*.	**Test Bank** Chapter 20 contains 100–125 multiple-choice, 30–40 true/false, and 8–10 short-answer questions. Also includes "Exploring Society" tele-course test items. The Test Bank is also available electronically through **ExamView®**, which can be customized to fit your needs. WebTUTOR™ Advantage **WebTutor™ Advantage** See Chapter 20 to assign chapter quizzes, conduct online discussion, track student progress, and post course material **Instructor's Resource Manual Notebook** Consult *Tips for Teaching Introductory Sociology*, Section 5: "Examinations"	**Study Guide** Chapter 20 contains chapter outlines, learning objectives, fill-in-the-blank review questions, key term matching exercises, and practice tests containing 15 multiple-choice, 5 true/false, and 5 short-answer questions **Telecourse Guide** Chapter 20 contains lesson overviews, goals and objectives, specific reading assignments, practice tests, and other learning activities **SocCoach CD-ROM** See the Chapter 20 diagnostic quiz and personalized study plan **Web Site Highlights** http://sociology. wadsworth.com/ kornblum/change7e • Practice Quizzes • Matching Exercises • Flashcards • Crossword Puzzles WebTUTOR™ Advantage **WebTutor™ Advantage** See Chapter 20 for chapter-specific review, quizzing, flashcards, and interactive games and exercises	**Web Site Highlights** http://sociology. wadsworth.com/kornblum/change7e • Internet links and exercises • CNN® Today videos and exercises • GSS data • Terrorism Guide: Part I, B **InfoTrac® College Edition** http://www.infotrac-college.com *Keywords:* Legitimacy, Citizenship, Nation-State, Interest Groups **Wadsworth's Sociology Online Resources and Writing Companion** "Politics and Government" • InfoTrac® College Edition Exercises 1–5 • Opposing Viewpoints Resource Center Exercises 1–4 • MicroCase® Online Exercises 1–3 • InfoWrite and OVRC Research Guide **SocCoach CD-ROM** See "Politics" Virtual Exploration and the "Power and Politics" interactive data map exercise **Researching Sociology on the Internet** Part II: "Politics" **Census 2000: A Student Guide for Sociology** Major Trends: "Population Growth," "The Hispanic Population," and "The Controversy About Sampling" **Classic Readings in Sociology** Mills: "The Power Elite" **Applied Sociology** Chapter 12: "Power, Politics, and Authority" **Six Steps to Effective Writing in Sociology** Teaches thinking and writing skills for each stage of the writing process

Resource Integration Guide

Chapter 21: Technology, Environment, and Health

Class Preparation/ Lecture Tools	Testing Tools/ Course Management	Student Study Tools	Beyond the Book: Research, Writing, and Exploration
Instructor's Resource Manual Notebook Chapter 21 emphasizes the role of science and technology in modern societies, with special attention to environmental impacts and the quest for new sources of energy. The case of medical technology provides vivid illustrations of both the benefits and the problems associated with the rapid development of new and expensive technologies. **Telecourse Faculty Guide** Consult for instructional strategies on teaching Technology, Environment, and Health via the "Exploring Society" telecourse **Multimedia Manager Instructor Resource CD-ROM** Text-specific graphics, customizable Microsoft® *PowerPoint*® lecture slides, lecture launcher clips, electronic IRM and Test Bank, and more **Introductory Sociology Transparency Acetates** 2005: "Health Care," "Population, Urbanism, and Environment," and "Social Change" acetates **CNN® Today Videos** • Sociology Vol. I: *Tobacco and Kids* (2:00) • Sociology Vol. II: *Helping the Homeless* (1:45) • Sociology Vol. III: *What Americans Think of Their HMO* (1:33) • Sociology Vol. IV: *South Africa AIDS Vaccine* (2:21), *Unionized Doctors* (1:47), *China Internet* (1.22) • Sociology Vol. V: *Merck AIDS Drugs* (1:52), *AIDS in Thailand* (1:59), *Women in Tech* (4:47), *Cyber Sperm* (1:52) • Sociology Vol. VI: *Kids and the Internet* (3:22) **Lecture Launchers Video/DVD** *Alternative Healthcare Methods* (3.09), *Cathedrals of Consumption* (2.95) **Sociology: Core Concepts Video/DVD** *Social Change* (8.70)	**Test Bank** Chapter 21 contains 100–125 multiple-choice, 30–40 true/false, and 8–10 short-answer questions. Also includes "Exploring Society" tele-course test items. The Test Bank is also available electronically through **ExamView®**, which can be customized to fit your needs. WebTUTOR™ Advantage **WebTutor™ Advantage** See Chapter 21 to assign chapter quizzes, conduct online discussion, track student progress, and post course material **Instructor's Resource Manual Notebook** Consult *Tips for Teaching Introductory Sociology*, Section 5: "Examinations"	**Study Guide** Chapter 21 contains chapter outlines, learning objectives, fill-in-the-blank review questions, key term matching exercises, and practice tests containing 15 multiple-choice, 5 true/false, and 5 short-answer questions **Telecourse Guide** Chapter 21 contains lesson overviews, goals and objectives, specific reading assignments, practice tests, and other learning activities **SocCoach CD-ROM** See the Chapter 21 diagnostic quiz and personalized study plan **Web Site Highlights** http://sociology.wadsworth.com/kornblum/change7e • Practice Quizzes • Matching Exercises • Flashcards • Crossword Puzzles WebTUTOR™ Advantage **WebTutor™ Advantage** See Chapter 21 for chapter-specific review, quizzing, flashcards, and interactive games and exercises	**Web Site Highlights** http://sociology.wadsworth.com/kornblum/change7e • Internet links and exercises • CNN® videos and exercises • GSS data • Terrorism guide: Part I, Section D; Part III, Section A • Online Module: "Environmental Sociology: What's New?" **InfoTrac® College Edition** http://www.infotrac-college.com *Keywords:* Sustainable Development, Medicine, Energy, Cultural Lag **Wadsworth's Sociology Online Resources and Writing Companion** "Health Care" and "Technology and the Global Environment" • InfoTrac® College Edition Exercises 1–5 • Opposing Viewpoints Resource Center Exercises (Health Care) 1–4, (Technology and the Global Environment) 1–3 • MicroCase® Online Exercises 1–3 • InfoWrite and OVRC Research Guide **SocCoach CD-ROM** See the "Health and Healthcare," "Population, Urbanism, and Environment," and the "Social Change" Virtual Explorations and the "Global Social Change," and "Science and Technology," and "Healthcare" interactive data map exercises **Researching Sociology on the Internet** Part II: "Aging and Healthcare," "Globalization," and "Social Change" **Census 2000: A Student Guide for Sociology** Major Trends: "Aging Population" **Applied Sociology** Chapter 11: "Health," and Chapter 14: "Social Change and the Future" **Six Steps to Effective Writing in Sociology** Teaches thinking and writing skills for each stage of the writing process

www.wadsworth.com

www.wadsworth.com is the World Wide Web site for Wadsworth and is your direct source to dozens of online resources.

At *www.wadsworth.com* you can find out about supplements, demonstration software, and student resources. You can also send email to many of our authors and preview new publications and exciting new technologies.

www.wadsworth.com
Changing the way the world learns®

Sociology
in a
Changing World

SEVENTH EDITION

Sociology
in a
Changing
World

William Kornblum
City University of New York,
Graduate School and University Center

In collaboration with
Carolyn D. Smith

THOMSON
WADSWORTH

Australia • Canada • Mexico • Singapore • Spain
United Kingdom • United States

THOMSON
✴
WADSWORTH

Sociology Editor: Jay Whitney
Assistant Editor: Stephanie Monzon
Editorial Assistant: Melissa Walter
Technology Project Manager: Dee Dee Zobian
Marketing Manager: Matthew Wright
Marketing Assistant: Tara Pierson
Advertising Project Manager: Linda Yip
Project Manager, Editorial Production: Cheri Palmer
Print/Media Buyer: Barbara Britton

Permissions Editor: Kiely Sexton
Production Service: Beth Callaway, Graphic World
Text Designer: Lisa Buckley
Photo Researcher: Terri Wright
Illustrator: Graphic World
Cover Designer: Larry Didona
Cover Image: © Reuters/Corbis
Compositor: Graphic World
Printer: Transcontinental Printing/Interglobe

For more information about our products, contact us at:
Thomson Learning Academic Resource Center
1-800-423-0563
For permission to use material from this text or product, submit a request online at **http://www.thomsonrights.com**.
Any additional questions about permissions can be submitted by email to **thomsonrights@thomson.com**.

Library of Congress Control Number: 2004100837

Student Edition: ISBN 0-534-63666-7
Instructor's Edition: ISBN 0-534-63667-5
ISBN 0-534-63679-9

Thomson Wadsworth
10 Davis Drive
Belmont, CA 94002-3098
USA

Asia
Thomson Learning
5 Shenton Way #01-01
UIC Building
Singapore 068808

Australia/New Zealand
Thomson Learning
102 Dodds Street
Southbank, Victoria 3006
Australia

Canada
Nelson
1120 Birchmount Road
Toronto, Ontario M1K 5G4
Canada

Europe/Middle East/Africa
Thomson Learning
High Holborn House
50/51 Bedford Row
London WC1R 4LR
United Kingdom

Latin America
Thomson Learning
Seneca, 53
Colonia Polanco
11560 Mexico D.F.
Mexico

Spain/Portugal
Paraninfo
Calle Magallanes, 25
28015 Madrid, Spain

Brief Contents

Contents

Chapter 9 Population and Urbanization 228

Chapter 10 Global Social Change 260

PART 3 ▪ Social Divisions 290

Chapter 11 Stratification and Global Inequality 292

Chapter 12 Inequalities of Social Class 322

Chapter 13 Inequalities of Race and Ethnicity 355

Chapter 18 Education   518

Chapter 19 Economic Institutions   550

Features

Visual Sociology

Preface

The more I study, teach, and conduct research in sociology, the more I love the subject. My primary goal in writing this book, therefore, is to share the power and pleasures that come with sociological knowledge. No area of intellectual work overlaps with so many other fields of knowledge; none straddles the sciences and the humanities so squarely or offers such varied insights into the troubling questions of our own time. As the new century has opened on unimaginable acts of terror and bravery, sociology is now, more than ever, an essential field of study.

The sudden turn for the worse in the world situation calls our attention to the severity of social conflicts and the tasks that remain for us to accomplish if the future we leave to our children and grandchildren is to be peaceful and secure. This text demonstrates in every chapter how much sociological research has already contributed to improving our social institutions and enhancing our understandings of other societies and cultures. Throughout, it focuses on issues of social change, at every level of social organization, because an emphasis on social changes in culture, social structures, inequalities, and social institutions gives students a clear understanding of the types of theoretical and empirical questions that motivate our field.

This book introduces sociology as the preeminent field for the study of social change. Students who use this text will come to understand that whereas social change may be wrenching for some and welcomed by others, it is never without major complications. The tragic events of September 11, 2001, which as a New Yorker I witnessed firsthand, were a terrible reminder of this fact. Some of the terrorists viewed our society as threatening to their social order because of the relative freedom women enjoy here or because our movies and television programs show a society that tolerates many differing viewpoints in religion, sexual behavior, and dress.

Of course, there are groups in the United States who are also shocked by some aspects of Western culture. In our own society, we are experiencing major changes, and sociologists study them with all the concepts and methods at their command. These changes include globalization of trade and commerce, the export of industrial production and good jobs outside the developed nations, the rapid growth of metropolitan regions, the aging of our society, soaring energy consumption and the prospect of global warming, new challenges to science and technology because of infectious diseases, and many more changes discussed in this book.

Along with social change there is also continuity. Human social institutions like the family, the college, and the corporation adapt to change, but they also resist change and display many similarities over time. A challenge of sociology is to understand and predict both change and its absence. Why, for example, do poor people tend to remain poor, even as new technologies unleash new potentials for wealth and well-being? Why do people of different religions often clash, even though their faiths preach love and brotherhood? Why are women still subordinate to men in so much of the world even as women continue to press for full equality in their societies? The opportunity to address important questions like these is what makes sociology such a challenging and satisfying field.

I wanted to create a comprehensive text, one that covers all the basic methods and subjects in sociology but one that also has its own clear identity. That is why I chose to focus on the explanation and prediction of social change as a unifying theme throughout the book. After years of research as a working sociologist, and over decades of teaching sociology at the City University of New York, I also believed that I had some insights into what features of a sociology text best help students understand the concepts and their applications. As a result, I had some firm convictions about how to organize the text to assist instructors in their own approaches to the course, and I incorporated some of my own experiences in teaching the course into the book's pedagogical features.

ORGANIZATION OF THE TEXT

Some subjects in sociology, such as class, race, and gender, are so important that they cannot be segregated to a single chapter. They need to be brought up wherever they are salient, and this text tries to do that to the fullest degree possible. I also believe that students need a chance to learn more about how sociologists actually do their work than it is possible to convey in one chapter. That is why I offer methods boxes and a section on current sociological research in each chapter. I believe that instructors can judge whether their students should be required to use this material or whether it can be optional, and this provides many opportunities to use the text with students at different levels of skill and interest.

In organizing the book, I resisted the temptation to radically rearrange the standard introductory sociology course. There are traditional approaches to the subject that deserve respect, such as presenting an overview of sociology and its history, introducing the basic research methods, examining the dimensions of social inequality, and including a series of chapters on major social institutions. But I have added to this solid, time-tested framework, and in some cases I have moved a chapter from its traditional position.

In a departure from the standard ordering of chapters in most sociology texts, *Sociology in a Changing World* places chapters on collective behavior and social movements (Chapter 8), population and urbanization (Chapter 9), and global social change (Chapter 10) in Part 2 of the text ("Social Dynamics"). Normally these chapters are segregated at the very end of sociology texts and often appear to both students and instructors almost as afterthoughts. But these chapters introduce some of the most important concepts and relationships that sociologists use to predict and evaluate social change in world regions, societies, and social institutions. By giving these chapters a more central placement, the book invites their study earlier, rather than later in the semester, if at all.

The book is divided into four parts:

Part 1, Social Foundations, introduces the "human science" of sociology: Chapter 1 traces the history of sociology and introduces the major perspectives used by sociologists, and Chapter 2 describes the methods used by sociologists in conducting their research. The next two chapters focus on some of sociology's most fundamental concepts: culture (Chapter 3) and the elements of social structure (Chapter 4).

Part 2, Social Dynamics, covers many of the processes that seem to account for social stability and change: Chapter 5 discusses socialization, and Chapter 6 examines the structure of groups and how people behave in groups of different kinds. Chapters 7, 8, and 9 move from the structure and function of groups in a society to the processes that change societies. Chapter 7 deals with deviance; Chapter 8 looks at collective behavior and social movements; and Chapter 9 explores the relationships among population growth, urbanization, and community. Chapter 10 summarizes the ways in which sociologists think about and conduct research on the causes and consequences of social change.

The five chapters in **Part 3, Social Divisions,** examine social inequality, particularly in United States society. Chapter 11 introduces the concept of social stratification. Chapter 12 deals with inequalities of social class, and Chapters 13, 14, and 15 focus on social inequalities based on race, ethnicity, gender, and age.

Part 4, Social Institutions, applies the concepts and perspectives discussed earlier in the book to an analysis of several major institutions: Chapter 16 explores the changing nature of the family, Chapter 17 introduces religion, and Chapter 18 covers education. Chapter 19 deals with economic institutions, and Chapter 20 discusses political institutions. Finally, Chapter 21 analyzes the institutions of science, technology, and medicine.

DISTINCTIVE FEATURES

Early in my career, I began using photography and film in research and teaching. I also studied film-making at the New York University film school and made some professional documentary films. So, when I began working on this book, I wanted it to have a strong visual dimension. We are constantly bombarded with visual images, especially through television and other media, and I wanted students to have a chance to look at photos critically and incorporate direct observation of social phenomena into the introductory course. All textbooks use photos, of course, but I try to put a lot of thought and research into selecting all the visual elements in the book and suggesting their placement and pedagogical function.

Sociology in a Changing World also differs from its competitors in its emphasis on social change. Throughout, the book highlights the tension between attempts to modify social institutions and efforts to maintain traditional modes of behavior. The text also tries to emphasize contemporary social-scientific research. Following are the special features that incorporate this teaching philosophy:

Focus questions draw attention to key issues discussed in the chapter.

Chapter outlines serve as advance organizers, previewing the topics that will be discussed in the chapter.

Opening vignettes begin each chapter to capture students' attention and introduce them to the subject matter. The "story" presented in each vignette is continued in the Visual Sociology section at the end of the chapter.

Sociological Methods boxes show how sociologists go about conducting their research.

Global Social Change boxes apply sociological concepts to explain major social changes around the world.

Popular Culture and Social Change boxes illustrate how sociological concepts are reflected in popular music, television, and other media.

Then and Now contrasts photos of a particular social condition in the past and today.

Art and the Sociological Eye shows how fine art can be interpreted from a sociological perspective.

Mapping Social Change uses maps and photos to show the distribution of a condition or characteristic throughout the United States or the world.

The Sociological Observer, a new feature in the seventh edition, is intended to reinforce the book's emphasis on the analysis of actual human behavior as presented in photos that capture aspects of social structure, social interaction, and social change. The feature presents students with an enticing photo and a minimal amount of information about what it represents. It then motivates the student to study the photo more carefully by posing questions about details in the photo that reveal aspects of social life or interaction. These questions are left for the student to ponder until the Visual Sociology feature at the end of the chapter, where they are reprised in the context of the visual essay. The Sociological Observer photos are integrated, through both content and placement in the chapter, with the opening chapter vignette and the Visual Sociology feature.

Study Charts summarize material for ease in studying. They organize topics such as the major sociological perspectives, the basic research methods, effects of cultural contact, and elements of social structure. Several new charts have been added in this edition.

Critical Sociology and Social Change, the final section of each chapter, discusses current work by recognized sociological researchers in subject areas covered in the chapter, relating it to applied research and policy issues.

Visual Sociology, a photo essay at the end of each chapter, shows how sociologists analyze photographs or other visual material as part of their research.

Chapter summaries are found at the end of each chapter. Each summary is a thorough but concise listing of the key concepts and relationships presented in the chapter.

End-of-chapter glossaries present key terms in order of appearance so that terms that should be learned together, such as *achieved status* and *ascribed status,* occur together.

Internet Resources, also found at the end of each chapter, lists several up-to-date Internet resources, including the text-specific Web site for this book, MicroCase® Online, InfoTrac® College Edition key search terms, and chapter-related Web sites.

NEW IN THIS EDITION

The seventh edition maintains the thematic and content strengths of the previous edition but adds new content and features designed to help students better understand the momentous changes that are shaking our peace and security, as well as those that are altering our social institutions—the family, education, religion, and others—in ways that may or may not benefit future generations and invariably generate a good deal of conflict in our own.

Social Justice and Critical Research

How can we evaluate social change? If change heightens inequalities or increases animosities among groups, especially over a significant period, we can say with confidence that it is not positive social change. But what criteria do we apply to determine whether change is positive? An answer that inspires this book is that to be positive, social changes must bring about an expansion and increase in social justice throughout the world. That means more people are safe from violence and crime, fewer infants die at birth, laws are applied more equally to rich and poor, and workers who produce goods and services can afford to feed and clothe and provide health care for their families at a level considered adequate in their societies. Positive social change should improve the likelihood that in a given society, opportunities are more equal for people regardless of gender, race, religion, national origins, and much more. When sociological research points to ways in which change is moving us away from greater social justice, as is unfortunately so often the case, a critical sociological viewpoint emphasizes why this is so and what lessons we can draw. In consequence, we have selected examples of current and critical sociological research that offers constructive criticism of the status quo. The popular chapter-opening vignettes and Visual Sociology features, on the other hand, have for the most part not been substantially changed because many of the sociologists and subjects dealt with in these sections also figure in the telecourse.

Indeed, throughout, the text emphasizes research by sociologists featured in the *Exploring Society* telecourse, new from Dallas TeleLearning in 2002. *Exploring Society* replaces *The Sociological Imagination,* which for many years was the most popular telecourse offered by the Public Broadcasting System throughout the United States. The older telecourse is being replaced by an equally insightful and captivating new series of videos keyed to *Sociology in a Changing World* and featuring sociologists like Arlie Hochschild, Troy Duster, Juan Battle, Victor Ayala, Claire Renzetti, and many others who conduct original research and are experienced, charismatic classroom teachers.

Exploring Society includes twenty-two 30-minute videos, each of which features documentary footage of real social situations—including, for example, the drop-in center for the homeless in New York City that sociologist Terry Williams and I help manage. These real social situations either explore examples offered in the text (such as what parades reveal about social structure and social conflict) or develop additional examples that complement those in the text. This new version of the telecourse is organized by content modules in each video so that instructors have greater flexibility in presenting the videos during a class session if they choose, whereas students working at home will have an easier time following the presentation of concepts and examples. A telecourse study guide prepared by my colleague Jane Penney provides the essential integration of videos and text.

The new edition of *Sociology in a Changing World* continues to emphasize popular culture, both through numerous examples in the text and in a box, Popular Culture and Social Change, that appears in selected chapters.

Finally, this edition includes numerous discussions of the causes and consequences of the war on terror, the AIDS pandemic, and globalization. New material dealing with these topics appears in the discussions of how the United States is perceived abroad (Chapter 3), AIDS and social structure (Chapters 4 and 21), the war in Iraq (Chapters 10 and 20), women under the Taliban (Chapter 14), Islam in the United States (Chapter 17), and globalization and Third World poverty (Chapter 19), among others.

Major Content Revisions

Major content revisions have been made in selected chapters in response to feedback from my colleagues. Many of the chapters have been extensively revised. The introductory chapter now has an expanded discussion of the sociological imagination and increased emphasis on social change, both changes designed to help students understand the overall goals of the text. Chapter 5 ("Socialization") has been revised to reflect exciting new research on the age-old nature-nurture quandary, with more extensive material on dimensions of intelligence and a new section on role of genes in intelligence and sexual orientation. Emphasis is on the interactions between genes and social influences, as applied to intelligence in particular; in keeping with this emphasis, there is an added discussion of Howard Gardner's analysis of multiple intelligences. A new section on gender and emotional intelligence, with a table on skills of emotional competence, is designed to stimulate class discussion of a subject that arouses immediate and personal student interest.

In Part 3 of the text, which covers global social stratification and inequalities of class, race, gender, and age, each of the chapters has been updated to reflect current and worsening patterns of inequality in the United States and

on the global scene. We have expanded the discussion of welfare reform and its consequences, added material on the historical legacy of slavery, created a new section on the promotion of women to managerial positions in the United States and other industrialized nations, and worked in new material about the paradox of inequality in the United States, the world's most affluent nation. In the previous edition we had expanded the discussion of the meaning of stratification and added new sections on poverty and life chances in the context of global inequality. With the new changes added to these recent ones, the text offers a broad and lively discussion in many chapters on inequalities of class, race, gender, and age.

Each chapter of the book has been updated and revised to reflect contemporary trends in sociological research and teaching. In addition to the above-mentioned revisions, I have also added or expanded discussions of the following important topics:

Chapter 1: the sociological imagination; social change

Chapter 2: gender and research

Chapter 3: culture in nonhuman animals; how American values are perceived outside the United States

Chapter 4: AIDS and social structure in Africa

Chapter 5: the role of genes in intelligence and sexual orientation; Gardner's multiple intelligences; gender and emotional intelligence; socialization and sexual orientation

Chapter 6: performance expectations, racial groups, and poverty levels

Chapter 7: felony disenfranchisement; corporate crime

Chapter 8: fads, fashions, rumor, gossip, panic, and mass hysteria

Chapter 9: life expectancy in global context; healthy life expectancy; "environmental racism"

Chapter 10: effects of modernization; symmetrical and asymmetrical warfare; effects of war in Iraq

Chapter 11: Marx and Weber on stratification

Chapter 12: measures of inequality; the paradox of inequality in the United States; welfare reform

Chapter 13: the concept of race; legacies of slavery

Chapter 14: promotion of women to managerial positions; the beauty ideal and women's self-image

Chapter 15: aging in global perspective; longevity and life expectancy; youth and the future of civic service

Chapter 16: family poverty and food insecurity; conflict in family interactions; gay and lesbian relationships; gay and lesbian families

Chapter 17: separation of church and state; theocracy; the church and sexuality

Chapter 18: sociological perspectives on education; high-stakes testing and dropout rates; functional incompetency

Chapter 19: globalization and Third World agriculture; labor unions in global context

Chapter 20: the war in Iraq

Chapter 21: contamination of communities by toxic wastes; controversy over downloading music from the Internet; AIDS and social epidemiology; the social epidemiology of obesity

ANCILLARY PACKAGE

Sociology in a Changing World is accompanied by a wide array of supplements prepared for both the instructor and student to create the best learning environment inside as well as outside the classroom. All the continuing supplements for *Sociology in a Changing World* have been thoroughly revised and updated, and several resources are new to this edition.

For the Instructor

INSTRUCTOR'S MANUAL

Created by author William Kornblum and collaborator Carolyn D. Smith, this resource contains a lecture outline, instructional goals, extensive teaching suggestions, topics for discussion, strategies for how to effectively use the text's rich selection of tables, charts, and other visual features in class, and student exercises for each chapter of the text. Also included is a table of contents for the CNN Today Sociology Video Series and concise user guides for both InfoTrac College Edition and WebTutor.

TEST BANK

Written by Carol Chenault of Calhoun County Community College, this extensive test bank includes 100–125 multiple-choice, 30–40 true/false, and 8–10 short-answer questions for each chapter of the text, all with page references and question type (recall or applied) indicated. The revised test items now include additional questions based on the main text's rich selection of box features and visuals. Further test questions specific to the "Exploring Society: An Introduction to Sociology" telecourse are provided as an appendix.

TELECOURSE FACULTY GUIDE

This resource provides instructors of the "Exploring Society: An Introduction to Sociology" telecourse with recommended instructional strategies, lesson summaries, suggestions for interaction with students, sample course syllabi, and other information designed to assist instructors in successfully implementing the telecourse. Contact your Thomson Wadsworth Sales Representative or DALLAS TeleLearning at 972-669-6650 to order.

EXAMVIEW® COMPUTERIZED TESTING

Create, deliver, and customize printed and online tests and study guides in minutes with this easy-to-use assessment and tutorial system. ExamView includes a Quick Test Wizard and an Online Test Wizard to guide instructors step by step through the process of creating tests. The test appears on screen exactly as it will print or display online. Using ExamView's complete word processing capabilities, instructors can enter an unlimited number of new questions or edit questions included with ExamView.

INFOTRAC® COLLEGE EDITION

With InfoTrac College Edition, instructors can ignite discussions and augment lectures with the latest developments in sociology and societal change. Available as a free option with newly purchased texts, InfoTrac College Edition gives instructors and students four months of free access to an extensive online database of reliable, full-length articles (not just abstracts) from hundreds of top academic journals and popular sources. Among the journals available 24/7 are *American Journal of Sociology, Social Forces, Social Research,* and *Sociology.* (Available to North American college and university students only; journals are subject to change.)

Classroom Presentation Tools for the Instructor

WADSWORTH'S INTRODUCTION TO SOCIOLOGY TRANSPARENCY ACETATES 2003

This set of more than 150 full-color acetates—based on Wadsworth's 2003 introductory sociology texts—highlights key concepts in introductory sociology and will quickly and easily enhance lectures.

MULTIMEDIA MANAGER FOR SOCIOLOGY: A 2003 MICROSOFT® POWERPOINT® LINK TOOL

With this one-stop digital library and presentation tool, instructors can assemble, edit, and present custom lectures with ease. The MultiMedia Manager contains a selection of digital media from Wadsworth's latest titles in introductory sociology and marriage and family, including figures, tables, and photos. Also included are CNN video clips and pre-assembled Microsoft PowerPoint lecture slides based on each specific text. Instructors can use the material as is or add their own material for a truly customized lecture presentation.

LECTURE LAUNCHERS VIDEO

An exclusive offering jointly created by Thomson Wadsworth and DALLAS TeleLearning, the Lecture Launchers Video contains a collection of video highlights taken from the "Exploring Society: An Introduction to Sociology" (formerly titled "Sociological Imagination") telecourse. Each brief video segment has been especially chosen to enhance and enliven class lectures and discussion of the key topics covered in the Kornblum text.

CNN® TODAY SOCIOLOGY VIDEO SERIES, VOLUMES I–V

Illustrate the relevance of sociology to everyday life with this exclusive series of videos for the introduction to sociology course. Jointly created by Thomson Wadsworth and CNN, each video consists of approximately 45 minutes of footage originally broadcast on CNN and specifically selected to illustrate important sociological concepts. The videos are broken into short two- to seven-minute segments, perfect for use as lecture launchers or as illustrations of key sociological concepts. Each video includes an annotated table of contents, descriptions of the segments, and suggestions on their use within the course. Special adoption conditions apply.

THOMSON WADSWORTH SOCIOLOGY VIDEO LIBRARY

Bring sociological concepts to life with videos from Thomson Wadsworth's Sociology Video Library, which includes thought-provoking offerings from Films for Humanities and other excellent educational video sources. This extensive collection illustrates important sociological concepts covered in many sociology courses. Certain adoption conditions apply.

DEMONSTRATING SOCIOLOGY: SHOWCASE PRESENTATION SOFTWARE

Analyze data "live" in your classroom with this powerful yet simple-to-use software program. With ShowCase's mapping, scatterplots, cross-tabulations, or univariates, you can show your students how sociologists ask and answer questions using sociological theory. A resource book with detailed "scripts" for working with ShowCase in class accompanies the software. (For Windows users with CD-ROM compatibility.)

For the Student

STUDY GUIDE

Created by author William Kornblum and collaborator Carolyn D. Smith, this student study tool contains a chapter outline, learning objectives, fill-in-the-blank review questions, and key term matching exercises for each chapter

of the text. Also included is a practice test for each chapter consisting of 15 multiple-choice, 5 true-false, and 5 short-answer questions to help students apply and master chapter concepts. A section titled "Where to Find It" lists useful books, journals, and other sources of information relevant to the chapter.

STUDENT TELECOURSE GUIDE

Written by Jane Penney of the Dallas County Community College District, this guide is keyed to the Kornblum text and provides students with valuable resources designed to direct their study in the "Exploring Society: An Introduction to Sociology" telecourse. The guide includes lesson overviews, goals and objectives, specific reading assignments, practice tests, and other learning activities that connect the text and video components of each lesson of the course.

STUDENT GUIDE TO INFOTRAC® COLLEGE EDITION FOR SOCIOLOGY

Prepared by Michele Adams of the University of California, Riverside, this valuable guide consists of exercises based on 23 core subjects vital to the study of sociology. As students use InfoTrac College Edition's huge database of articles to complete the exercises, they learn to refine their online research skills and strengthen their understanding of important sociological concepts.

VIRTUAL EXPLORATIONS CD-ROM FOR KORNBLUM'S SOCIOLOGY IN A CHANGING WORLD, SEVENTH EDITION

This interactive CD-ROM directs students to a broad range of Web sites relevant to sociology. It then prompts them to analyze the Web material through a series of in-depth questions about the sites. Once students complete each of the exercises, it enables them to email responses to their instructors with just a few mouse clicks. Unlike the version found at Thomson Wadsworth's Virtual Society Web site, the CD-ROM's Virtual Explorations are dynamically illustrated with photos, videos, charts, and graphs that further enhance and enrich each Exploration. The CD-ROM also fully describes and directly links students to Thomson Wadsworth's Web site for Kornblum's *Sociology in a Changing World,* Seventh Edition, text. There they can take advantage of a wealth of chapter-specific online learning tools such as practice quizzes, MicroCase Online exercises, InfoTrac College Edition, and CNN videos with questions for further thought. An excellent study resource!

RESEARCHING SOCIOLOGY ON THE INTERNET, SECOND EDITION

This is a two-part guide designed to assist students in using the Internet for research. Part One provides general information necessary to get started. It discusses issues such as the type of sociology material available on the Internet, how to distinguish reliable from unreliable information, and the best ways to conduct online searches. Part Two looks at each main discipline in sociology and not only refers students to sites where the most enlightening research can be found but also notes the drawbacks and issues to be aware of in each discipline.

CLASSIC READINGS IN SOCIOLOGY, SECOND EDITION

Edited by Eve L. Howard, this excellent collection of readings teaches the fundamental ideas of sociology through classic and contemporary articles written by key sociologists. Excerpts include C. Wright Mill's "The Promise of Sociology," Erving Goffman's "Presentation of Self in Everyday Life," Max Weber's "Characteristics of Bureaucracy," and Jonathan Kozol's "Savage Inequalities." This inexpensive alternative to a full-sized reader is FREE when bundled with certain introductory sociology texts.

DOING SOCIOLOGY: A GLOBAL PERSPECTIVE USING MICROCASE® EXPLORIT®, FOURTH EDITION

This software/workbook package shows students step by step how to do real sociological research, using the same data and techniques used by professional researchers and the powerful MicroCase ExplorIt software. Written by Rodney Stark, major sociology researcher and best-selling introductory sociology author, the workbook effectively guides students through the research process and offers them a real sense of what sociologists do. A companion Instructor's Manual is also available. Ideal for classes with a methods/science emphasis.

DISCOVERING SOCIOLOGY: USING MICROCASE® EXPLORIT®, SECOND EDITION

Prepared by Steven Barkan of the University of Maine, this best-selling software-based workbook lets students explore dozens of sociological topics and issues, using the accompanying MicroCase ExplorIt software and data sets from the United States and around the world. Students won't just read about what other sociologists have done, they'll discover sociology for themselves!

Internet-Based Ancillaries

WEBTUTOR™ ADVANTAGE ON WEBCT AND BLACKBOARD

This Web-based software for students and instructors takes a course beyond the classroom to an anywhere, anytime environment. Students gain access to a full array of study tools, including chapter outlines, chapter-specific quizzing material, interactive games and maps, and videos. With WebTutor Advantage, instructors can provide virtual office hours, post syllabi, track student progress with the quizzing material, and even customize the content to suit their needs. Instructors can also use the communication tools to do such things as set up threaded discussions and conduct "real-time" chats. "Out of the box" or customized, WebTutor Advantage provides powerful tools for instructors and students alike.

VIRTUAL SOCIETY: THE WADSWORTH SOCIOLOGY RESOURCE CENTER AT HTTP://SOCIOLOGY.WADSWORTH.COM

This Web site provides instructors and students alike a wealth of FREE information and resources, such as:

- Careers in Sociology
- Virtual Explorations in Sociology (Now featuring eighteen Virtual Explorations!)
- Census 2000: A Student Guide for Sociology
- Terrorism: An Interdisciplinary Perspective
- Research Online
- MicroCase Online

And so much more!

Virtual Society also includes text-specific Web sites with chapter-specific resources for instructors and students. For instructors, the Web sites offer password-protected instructor's manuals, Microsoft PowerPoint presentation slides, and more. For students, there is a multitude of text-specific study aids. These chapter-specific features are available for students using many of Wadsworth's sociology texts:

- Tutorial practice quizzes that can be scored and emailed to the instructor
- Internet links and exercises
- InfoTrac College Edition exercises
- Flashcards
- MicroCase Online exercises
- CNN videos with discussion questions
- Crossword puzzles

And much more!

To access all these exciting text-specific Web resources, go to *Virtual Society: The Wadsworth Sociology Resource Center* at http://sociology.wadsworth.com and follow these steps:

1. Click **Course Materials**
2. Select your course
3. Click the text cover that you use
4. Click either **For Students** or **For Instructors**

ACKNOWLEDGMENTS

The new edition of *Sociology in a Changing World* is the culmination of two years of steady work—weekly writing and editing for a year, plus another year of production-related tasks. The values in a book like this are the work of many minds and hands. From the contributions of the social scientists who have reviewed the manuscript and the sociology students who have commented on previous editions, to the final touches of detail before the book is printed, there are scores of people whose contributions are essential at every step in the process. It is exciting to launch a new edition of the text, just as it is gratifying to thank those who made it possible. I have had the benefit of continuity in editors and professional friends who have advised me since the first edition. But each edition also brings in new publishing professionals whose influences help keep the book fresh and up-to-date.

First among the many people who continue to influence this project is my editor and collaborator Carolyn Smith. Carolyn first encouraged me to take on this project, and when my resolve wavered, her faith in our ability to complete it sustained me. Carolyn has untangled my prose, agonized with me over reviewers' comments, and kept track of the endless details that go into creating a scholarly text. There is not one word in this book that she has not thought about; every page bears the stamp of her expertise. Guy Smith also has my gratitude for his supportiveness during the long and demanding revision process.

The visual identity of this book, its use of photographic material for sociological example and method, has always been extremely important to me and to everyone involved in its creation. Our aim has been to create a textbook that would integrate sociological ideas with the design and layout of the book. In this edition the design, created by Lisa Buckley, and the art and photo programs continue to emphasize creative treatments of data presentation and visual sociology.

My colleagues at the City University of New York have been unstinting with their suggestions and advice. My dear friend and colleague, Vernon Boggs, was always my greatest personal ally in the making of this book. His untimely death deprives me of someone whose deep commitment to teaching and research in sociology were a sustaining example. My longtime collaborator and friend, Terry Williams, continues to influence my thinking on key issues in sociology and life. Rolf Meyersohn has been heroic in his generosity with books and articles and words of encouragement. My colleague Charles Kadushin's intimate knowledge of the publishing world has been invaluable on many occasions, as have Paul Attewell's mastery

of trends in sociological research and methods, and the profound knowledge of social movements and class theory shared by Stanley Aronowitz, William Helmreich, William DiFazio, Dean Savage, and Bogdan Denitch. If I have managed to avoid a natural predisposition toward male bias, much of the credit must go to Susan Kornblum, Cynthia Epstein, Judith Lorber, June Nash, Barbara Katz Rothman, Julia Wrigley, and many other colleagues who have shared their insights and knowledge. My colleagues Lily Hoffman, John Mollenkopf, and Mitchell Duneier are unstinting in sharing their sociological insights and knowledge of new literature. Special thanks are due to Juan Battle, Doug Meyer, Angelique Harris, and Martine Hackett for their generous help on this edition.

The thoughtful comments we receive about the book and the encouragement of many students and colleagues are immensely rewarding. Their corrections and constructive suggestions, too, are most welcome. Many colleagues throughout the United States offer me wise counsel and scholarly advice, for which I continue to be deeply grateful. But I owe a special debt to my colleague and friend, Carol Chenault of Calhoun Community College, Decatur, Alabama, for her abiding interest in the textbook and her generosity. Professor Chenault's comparative visual sociology is featured in Chapter 14.

No single author can hope to adequately represent a field as large and complex as sociology. Over several years of textbook writing, I have learned that the comments and suggestions offered by reviewers and users of the book are essential to its success. Many dedicated sales representatives have taken the time to introduce me to instructors who use the book. In addition, the comments of numerous reviewers have helped me to correct mistakes of fact, interpretation, and emphasis. I might disagree with some of them, but I always find them helpful.

Each edition of the book has benefited from the insights of reviewers. I gratefully acknowledge the following instructors who contributed to the seventh edition of *Sociology in a Changing World:*

Laura Gruntmier, Redlands Community College

Michael Miller, University of Texas, San Antonio

Juan Battle, Hunter College

J. R. Woodward, Montana State University

E. Lewis Martin, New River College

Ann Hunter, Idaho State University

Dennis Downey, University of Utah

The textbook continues to benefit from the helpful comments of the following instructors who reviewed for previous editions:

Deborah A. Abowitz, Bucknell University; Barry Adams, University of Windsor; Elizabeth Almquist, University of North Texas; Nancy Andes, University of Alaska Anchorage; Robert S. Anwyl, Miami-Dade Community College; Rita Argiros, St. Cloud State University; Ed Armstrong, University of Wisconsin—Stout; Michele Aronica, Saint Joseph's College; Augustine Aryee, Fitchburg State College; Dorothy Balancio, Mercy College; Richard Bales, Illinois Central College; Matilda Barker, Cerritos College; Roger C. Barnes, University of the Incarnate Word; Bernard Beck, Northwestern University; Scott A. Beck, East Tennessee State University; Phillip Bosserman, Salisbury State College; Kathy Brace, York College of Pennsylvania; Cliff Broman, Michigan State University; Robin Brown, Southern Union State Community College; Brent Bruton, Iowa State University; Marvin Camfield, Walters State Community College; R. E. Canjar, University of Maryland; Carole M. Carroll, Middle Tennessee State University; Chuck Carselowey, Oklahoma City Community College; Kim Catatt, SUNY Buffalo; Emilie Walter Cellucci, Francis Marion University; Carol Deming Chenault, Calhoun County Community College; Mary Beth Collins, Central Piedmont Community College; B. Keith Crew, University of Northern Iowa; Donna K. Crossman, Greenville Technical College; Glenn Currier, El Centro College; Vasilikie Demos, University of Minnesota; Mita Dhariwal, Bakersfield College; Jack Dison, Arkansas State University; Lilli Downes, Hartford Community College; Dennis R. Dubbs, Harrisburg Area Community College; Ken Elder, Southeastern Oklahoma State University; Martin Epstein, Middlesex Community College; Douglas Farley, Niagara County Community College; Charles E. Faupel, Auburn University; Frank Forwood, Northeast Louisiana University; Michael J. Fraleigh, Bryant College; Joseph Galaskiewicz, University of Minnesota; Darleen Garrett, Weatherford Community College; Eric P. Godfrey, Ripon College; James Green, St. Thomas Aquinas College; Joanna Grey, Pikes Peak Community College; Kirstin Grønbjerg, Loyola University (Chicago); Larry J. Halford, Washburn University; John Hall, University of California; Gary D. Hampe, University of Wyoming; Charles F. Hanna, Duquesne University; Scarlett Hardesty, University of Arizona; Rudy Harris, Des Moines Area Community College; Gary Heidinger, Roane State Community College; Denny Hill, Georgia Southern College; Randy Hodson, Ohio State University; Lily M. Hoffman, City College in New York; Drew Hurley, Santa Fe Community College; Mike Hurtado, Citrus College; Benton Johnson, University of Oregon; Paul Kamolnick, East Tennessee State University; Mark Kassop, Bergen Community College; Hadley G. Klug, University of Wisconsin, Whitewater; Laura Kramer, Montclair State College; Kathryn Kuhn, University of Texas; Martin L. Levin, Emory University; Ruby C. Lewis, Dekalb College—

Central Campus; Theodore Long, Merrimack College; Mits Maeda, Cypress College; Joseph Marolla, Virginia Commonwealth University; George Martin, Montclair State College; Allan McCutcheon, University of Delaware; James R. McIntosh, Lehigh University; Virginia McKeefery-Reynolds, Northern Illinois University; Anthony J. Mendonca, Community College of Allegheny County—Allegheny Campus; Jerry L. L. Miller, University of Arizona; Ephraim Mizruchi, Syracuse University; Carla Mueller, Lindenwood University; Karen Mundy, Lee College; Ann S. Oakes, Idaho State University; James D. Orcutt, Florida State University; Larry M. Perkins, Oklahoma State University; Novella Perrin, Central Missouri State University; Dick Phillips, Kalamazoo Valley Community College; Judy Porta, Las Positas College; David L. Preston, San Diego State University; Leroy Reed, Central Florida Community College; Priscilla Reinertsen, University of New Hampshire; Joseph Ribal, El Camino College; Carolyn Rivera, Florence-Darlington Technical College; Craig T. Robertson, University of North Alabama; J. D. Robson, University of Arkansas; John Roman, University of Maine; Jeffery P. Rosenfeld, Nassau Community College; Ellen Rosengarten, Sinclair Community College; Luis Salinas, University of Houston; Jon Schlenker, University of Maine at Augusta; Hasan Shapari, Villanova University; Wesley Shrum, Louisiana State University; Martin Simpson, Nicholls State University; Richard L. Simpson, University of North Carolina; Joel Charles Snell, Kirkwood Community College; Gary Spencer, Syracuse University; Larry D. Stokes, University of Tennessee—Chattanooga; Paul Stowell, Wenatchee Valley College; Lorene Taylor, Valencia Community College; Doreen Thompson, Washtenaw Community College; Marcella Thompson, University of Arkansas—Fayetteville; Kathleen Tiemann, Mercer University; Linda Tiemann, Blinn College; Jacquelyn A. Troup, Cerritos College; William Trush, Kalamazoo Valley Community College; Tim Tuinstra, Kalamazoo Valley Community College; David Van Merlo, St. Charles County Community College; Steven L. Vasser, Mankato State University; C. Edwin Vaughan, University of Missouri; Theodore C. Wagenaar, Miami University; Eric Wagner, Ohio University; Joe Walsh, Bucks County Community College; Chaim I. Waxman, Rutgers, the State University of New Jersey; Jack Weller, University of Kansas; Timothy Wickham-Crowley, Georgetown University; Kenneth Wilson, East Carolina University; Steven R. Wilson, Temple University; Leslie E. Wooten, Cleveland State Community College; Bruce T. Wyman, Delaware Community College; Thomas J. Yacovone, Los Angeles Valley College; George Yancey, University of North Texas; Stacey G. H. Yap Plymouth State College; Richard Yinger, Palm Beach Community College; Wayne Zatapek, Tarrant County Junior

College—Northeast; Herbert Zeigler, Chesapeake College; and William W. Zellner, Doane College.

In preparing this edition of *Sociology in a Changing World,* I greatly benefited from the counsel and help of a team of professional editors and publishers who recognized the strengths of the book and worked with me to make improvements. They also helped me enhance the ways in which the design and visual dimensions of the book complement the written text. In this regard I am especially grateful to Eve Howard, Jay Whitney,

Stephanie Monzon, and Melissa Walter. My thanks also go to Lisa Buckley for her text design and Larry Didona for his cover design, to Terri Wright for the development of the photo program, to Cheri Palmer and Beth Callaway for their skillful production management and editorial coordination, and to Matthew Wright for his marketing efforts.

Thanks also go to my students at the City University of New York, both graduates and undergraduates, for keeping me "turned on" to sociology.

William Kornblum

About the Author

William Kornblum is a professor of sociology at the Graduate School of the City of New York, where he helps train future instructors and researchers in the social sciences. He also teaches undergraduates at various campuses of the City University, including Queens College, Hunter College, and City College.

A specialist in urban and community studies, Kornblum began his teaching career with the Peace Corps in the early 1960s, when he taught physics and chemistry in French-speaking West Africa. He received his doctorate in sociology from the University of Chicago in 1971. He has also taught at the University of Washington at Seattle and worked as a research sociologist for the U.S. Department of the Interior. At the CUNY Graduate School, he directs research on environmental issues and urban policy. Kornblum's latest book is *At Sea in the City: New York from the Water's Edge* (Algonquin Books, 2002). With his longtime research partner, Terry Williams, he co-authored *The Uptown Kids,* a sociological portrait of teenagers and young adults growing up in high-rise public housing projects. He was also the principal investigator of Project TELL, a longitudinal study of the ways in which home computers can improve the life chances of young people at risk of dropping out of school.

The author's other publications include *Blue Collar Community,* a study of the steel-making community of South Chicago; *Growing Up Poor* (with Terry Williams), a study of teenagers growing up in different low-income communities in the United States; and *Social Problems,* a comprehensive textbook about social problems and social policies in the United States.

Sociology
in a
Changing
World

Social change is occurring around us all the time. Neighborhoods change as newcomers move in or more housing is built; factories close or open in response to changes in the economies of other continents; wars and natural disasters push people out of their homelands; new technologies alter old lifestyles and stimulate people to find new ways of living. Sociology is the science that attempts to make sense of these changes. It is devoted to studying why social change occurs and how it affects people in different societies or within a single society. But it is also the science of social order; it often asks why societies or groups do not change even when so much change is taking place around them.

The first part of this book introduces some basic sociological concepts. Chapter 1 shows

Social Foundations

how sociology developed into a science that can help us understand our world and how it changes. Chapter 2 describes the methods sociologists use in conducting their research. When we talk about culture in Chapter 3, we are referring to the making of human consciousness—how we think and communicate and how these processes make society itself possible. Chapter 4 introduces the elements of social structure and explains how various kinds of societies have developed over time.

Sociology: An Introduction

© Lee Celano/Reuters/Getty Images

Throughout the world, significant social occasions are marked by parades. The people walking or marching in the parade enjoy dressing in the appropriate uniforms or costumes and showing off before an admiring public. Spectators enjoy the pageantry, the excitement, the bands, the costumes, and much more. To sociologists and other keen observers, most parades are an occasion to observe people displaying many of the attributes of their societies that they value and enjoy.

Mardi Gras parades are among the world's most joyous and exciting public displays. In New Orleans, where Mardi Gras parades are a famous feature of the city's culture, the colorful floats and often raucous masked "krews," or clubs, dancing through different parts of the city and its suburbs are a major tourist attraction. Social scientists observe that Mardi Gras, or Carnival as it is often called, "expresses the society of New Orleans" (Trillin, 1998). An insightful and knowledgeable observer can watch how people from different social backgrounds—rich, poor, black, white, women, men, and so on—interact in the parades. And the way the parades and other Mardi Gras celebrations, especially the famous masked balls, have changed over the last few decades tells us a great deal about how New Orleans society is changing. The city's population is now more than 60 percent African American, so it is no wonder that elected officials have recently passed ordinances denying parade permits to krews like Comus and Rex, two of the oldest and most elite clubs, that exclude people of color. Nor is it surprising that as visitors and tourists from all over the United States flock to New Orleans for Mardi Gras, some of the parades include krews and floats representing other communities.

These larger forces of social change are visibly transforming the nature of the Mardi Gras parades. A sociologist can use observations of Mardi Gras to study the way the local society of New Orleans functions—for example, who presents a float and which members of the city's elite still participate in the parade. Such observations can also reveal the way conflict is affecting New Orleans society, perhaps resulting in more integrated parades in the center of the city and more segregated ones in the suburbs. The observant sociologist can also watch how interactions among parade participants and bystanders reflect issues of gender and sexuality. Some masked revelers cross-dress in order to try on different identities, and by watching them a skillful observer can learn a lot about how being a man or a woman is related to forms of communication and interaction as much as it is to biology. All of these subjects will come up in later chapters. The point here is that sociologists love parades for what they can reveal about underlying social relations.

FOCUS QUESTIONS:

• What makes sociology a "human science"?

• How does sociology differ from psychology or economics or history?

• How does developing a sociological imagination help people better understand the relationships between individual biography and history?

THE SOCIOLOGICAL IMAGINATION

It may take some thought to see why various kinds of parades tell us a great deal about our own and other societies. After all, one might argue that a parade is a special event. It is not meant to be "read" for its deeper social meanings. And no doubt most of the people who watch Mardi Gras parades are caught up in the fun of the event—by the creativity of the costumes, the flirtations that go on, the music and dance, and perhaps the drinking. They might be offended if someone asked them to look more analytically at the larger significance of their behavior. But a sophisticated understanding of social life requires some imagination. Although some participants in an event like a parade may be entirely caught up in the moment, others may also have fun while simultaneously thinking about what is going on at a deeper level.

One of the main goals of sociology courses is to help you develop the ability to both participate in social life and step back and analyze the broader meanings of what is going on. This ability is often called the **sociological imagination.** In this book, we hope to help you develop this special insight, which will equip you to use sociological knowledge in your daily life. Most of all, we hope to enable you to use your sociological imagination to gain wisdom about the society in which we all participate and for whose future we are all responsible.

Most people need some help in developing a sociological imagination. This is especially true when it comes to understanding their own place in what might be thought of as the "parade" of social life. People with a limited sociological imagination often fail to distinguish between social forces and personal troubles. If they are excluded from the "parade" because they are unemployed, they blame themselves for failing to do better; if they divorce, they blame each other. When they see crime, they blame "human nature"; when they see success, they praise individual achievement. But this tendency to think of life as a series of individual mistakes or successes blinds them to the fact that social conditions also shape their lives, often in ways for which they can hardly be held accountable. And the habit of seeing events mainly in terms of how they affect individuals blinds people to the possibility of improving the way their society is organized.

Sociologists are concerned with how **social conditions** influence our lives as individuals. Social conditions are the realities of the life we create together as social beings. Conditions such as poverty, wealth, crime, and drug use, for example, differ from biological facts (facts concerning our behavior and needs as animals) and psychological facts (facts about our patterns of behavior as individuals). Sociologists do not deny that psychological facts are impor-

tant. Differences among individuals help some people cope with stress better than others, seize opportunities that others allow to slip by, or fail where others succeed. But before saying that the success or failure of an individual or group is the result of psychological causes, the sociologist tries to look at how social conditions such as poverty or wealth, war, or changes in the availability of jobs affect the individual's chances of success.

According to sociologist C. Wright Mills, who made famous the term *sociological imagination,* people often believe that their private lives can be explained mainly in terms of their personal successes and failures. They are critical of themselves but not of their societies. They fail to see the links between their own individual biographies and the course of human history. Often they blame themselves for their troubles without grasping the effects of social change on their lives. "The facts of contemporary history," Mills points out, "are also facts about the success and the failure of individual men and women." Mills further states:

> When a society is industrialized, a peasant becomes a worker; a feudal lord is liquidated or becomes a businessman. When classes rise or fall, a man is employed or unemployed; when the rate of investment goes up or down, a man takes new heart or goes broke. When wars happen, an insurance salesman becomes a rocket launcher; a store clerk, a radar man; a wife lives alone; a child grows up without a father. (1959, p. 3)

According to Mills, neither a person's biography nor the history of a society can be understood unless we consider the influence of each on the other. The social forces of history—war, depression or recession, increases in population, changes in production and consumption, and many other social conditions—become the forces that influence individuals to behave in new ways. But those new ways of behavior themselves become social forces and, in turn, shape history.

To take just one example, the not-so-distant ancestors of many African Americans were brought to the Western Hemisphere in slave ships. African Americans have experienced slavery, war, emancipation, segregation, and rural and urban poverty. In reaction to the historical forces that deprived them of full citizenship in the United States, they developed a variety of behaviors, from the spirituals that expressed their deep feelings of religious faith and protest to boycotts and demonstrations against segregation. These protests and demonstrations, which often took the form of a special kind of parade, became powerful social forces that continue to shape the history of the American people.

By applying the sociological imagination to events such as the corporate scandals that rocked the U.S. economy in 2002 or to many of the episodes of tragedy and heroism that marked the war in Iraq in 2003, one can begin to "grasp history and biography and the relations between the two within society" (Mills, 1959, p. 6). Individual greed may explain why some executives manipulated company portfolios to enrich themselves beyond imagining, but in addition to these more psychological reasons, there were widespread failures of control and oversight in the accounting systems that made the excesses possible; in other words, failures at the sociological level were as important as individual motivations. In the case of the war in Iraq, the heroism of Private Jessica Lynch and her rescuers also can be explained only partially by individual characteristics. Private Lynch fully deserves to join the parade of American and British heroes who won the war, but her motivations for joining the army in the first place had a lot to do with sociological forces. She wanted to go to college and become a classroom teacher, but her family's limited resources made it desirable for her to first join the army, in the hopes of eventually going to college with support from the government based on her military service (Baker, 2003).

One of the main objectives of this book is to help you apply your sociological imagination to an understanding of the social forces that are shaping your own place in the parade—that is, the forces that are shaping your life and those of the people you care about. The sociological imagination can help us avoid blaming ourselves needlessly for the troubles we encounter in life. It can help us understand, for example, why some people are rich and powerful but many others are not; why the benefits of good health care or enriching education are available to some but not to others; or why women may find themselves resenting the men in their lives. The sociological imagination helps us sort out which facts about ourselves are explained by our place in society and which ones are a result of our own actions. Above all, the sociological imagination can suggest ways in which we can realistically effect change in our lives and in society itself.

SOCIOLOGY AND SOCIAL CHANGE

Sociology is the scientific study of human societies and human behavior in the many groups that make up a society. Sociologists must ask difficult, sometimes embarrassing questions about human life in order to explore the consequences of cataclysmic events such as those that shut down factories or enslave an entire people. To understand the possible futures of people who confront such drastic changes, sociologists are continually seeking knowledge about what holds societies together and what makes them bend under the impact of major forces such as war and migration.

We will see throughout this book that there are many ways in which sociologists can already predict the social changes that are likely to occur in coming years and decades. For example, as the proportion of elderly people in our society increases, we can predict how this important social change will bring about other changes in the need for health care or for improved retirement systems, or new definitions of the responsibilities of middle-aged children of the elderly. But there are also changes, such as the recent rise of terrorism directed against the United States, that might have been predicted and better anticipated but were not. Sociologists are trying to develop better knowledge about the causes of terrorism in order to help diminish the likelihood of terrorism in the future. To do so, we conduct research to better understand how different societies are changing or remaining stable, which groups are benefiting from social change, and which groups are being left behind.

The Social Environment

The knowledge sociologists gather covers a vast range. Sociologists study religious behavior; conduct in the military; the behavior of workers and managers in industry; the activities of voluntary associations such as parent–teacher groups and political parties; the changing relationships between men and women or between aging individuals and their elderly parents; the behavior of groups in cities and neighborhoods; the activities of gangs, criminals, and judges; differences in the behaviors of entire social classes—the rich, the middle classes, the poor, the down-and-out; the way cities grow and change; the fate of entire societies during and after revolutions; and a host of other subjects. But how to make sure the information gathered is reliable and precise, how to use it to build theories of social cohesion and social change—that is the challenge faced by the young science of sociology.

As in any science, there are many debates in sociology about the appropriate ways to study social life and about which theories or types of theories best explain social phenomena. Most sociologists, however, would agree with the following position:

> Human actions are limited or determined by "environment." Human beings become what they are at any given moment not by their own free decisions, taken rationally and in full knowledge of the conditions, but under the pressure of circumstances which delimit their range of choice and which also fix their objectives and the standards by which they make choices. (Shils, 1985, p. 805)

This statement expresses a core idea of sociology: Individual choice is never entirely free but is always determined to some extent by a person's environment. In sociology, *environment* refers to all the expectations and incentives established by other people in a person's social world. For the sociologist, therefore, the environment within which an individual's biography unfolds is a set of people and groups and organizations, all with their own ways of thinking and acting. Certainly each individual has unique choices to make in life, but the social world into which that person was born—be it a Native American reservation, an urban ghetto, a comfortable suburb, or an immigrant enclave in a strange city—determines to varying degrees what those choices will be.

Levels of Social Reality

In their studies of social environments, sociologists look at behaviors ranging from the intimate glances of lovers to the complex coordination of a space shuttle launch. For purposes of analysis, however, they often speak of social behavior as occurring at three different levels of complexity: micro, middle, and macro.

THE MICRO LEVEL   The **micro level** of sociological observation is concerned with the behaviors of the individual and his or her immediate others—that is, with patterns of interaction among a few people. One example is Erving Goffman's studies of the routine behaviors of everyday life. Goffman's research showed how seemingly insignificant ways of acting in public actually carry significant meanings. In a study titled "Territories of the Self" (1972), Goffman categorized some of the ways in which we use objects as "markers" to claim a personal space:

> Markers are of various kinds. There are "central markers," being objects that announce a territorial claim, the territory radiating outward from it, as when sunglasses and lotion claim a beach chair, or a purse a seat in an airliner, or a drink on a bar the stool in front of it. . . . There are "boundary markers," objects that mark the line between two adjacent territories. The bar used in supermarket checkout counters to separate one customer's batch of articles from the next is an example. (pp. 41–42)

The last time you placed your sweater or book on the empty seat next to you on a bus, you told yourself that when someone came for the seat you would take up your things. But you hoped that the stranger who was coming along the aisle would get your message and choose another seat; you would claim your extra space as long as possible. You communicated all this by the manner in which you placed your marker and the persistence with which, by your body language, you defended "your" space.

THE MACRO LEVEL   Some sociologists deal almost exclusively with a much larger-scale, or **macro**, level of analysis. The macro level of social life refers to whole societies and the ways in which they are changing—that is, to revolutions, wars, major changes in the production of goods and services, and similar social phenomena that involve very large numbers of people. One example of macrosociological analysis is the study of how the shift from heavy manufacturing to high-tech industries has affected the way workers earn a living. Another example is the study of how the invasion and settlement of the American West in the nineteenth and early twentieth centuries gave rise to the beliefs and actions that drove Native Americans onto reservations.

THE MIDDLE LEVEL   **Middle-level** social phenomena are those that occur in communities or in organizations such as businesses and voluntary associations. Middle-level social forms are smaller than entire societies but are larger and involve more people than micro-level social forms such as the family or the peer group, in which everyone involved knows everyone else or is in close proximity to the others (as on a bus or in a classroom). The drama that surrounds the firing of a coach on a sports team, and the reorganization of personnel that often follows, is an example of social change at the middle level of social analysis.

These three levels of sociological analysis can be helpful in understanding the experience of the immigrants from Asia, Africa, or Latin America who may be appearing in your town or community or in one nearby. Macro-level social forces such as war or overpopulation may account for the influx of immigrants. Middle-level social forces such as the availability of work at low wage and skill levels, or the presence of earlier arrivals from other nations, may help explain why certain immigrant groups become concentrated in particular communities within the

Each of these passengers in a railroad station waiting room has claimed a personal territory. Each has taken a separate bench and has chosen to sit at one end of the bench. If another person came to that bench, he or she would probably choose to sit as far away as possible.

© M. Dwyer/Stock, Boston

STUDY CHART

LEVELS OF SOCIOLOGICAL ANALYSIS

ANALYTICAL LEVEL	SOCIAL BEHAVIORS STUDIED	TYPICAL QUESTIONS
Macro	Revolutions; intercontinental migrations; emergence of new institutions.	How are entire societies or institutions changing?
Middle	Relations in bureaucracies; social movements; participation in communities, organizations, tribes.	How does bureaucracy affect personality? Do all social movements go through similar stages?
Micro	Interaction in small groups; self-image; enactment of roles.	How do people create and take roles in groups? How are group structures created?

United States. And at the micro level of analysis there will be, especially at first, important differences in the way immigrant and native-born people interact on a daily basis.

Note that the three levels of social reality are not defined according to fixed or standard measures. Instead, they are used in relative fashion. The social impact of a global corporation such as General Electric, for example, can be analyzed at the macro level of the entire corporation and its dealings on the world stage. In that case, its component factories, and the trade unions they often battle against, are middle-level forms, and specific groups within those factories operate at the micro level within the global corporation. How one uses and defines these levels of social reality often depends on the type of sociological analysis one is performing.

The Study Chart above presents the three basic levels of sociological analysis along with some examples of the types of studies conducted at each level. Throughout this book, we show how the sociological imagination can be applied at different levels of society. In this chapter, we set the stage by describing the basic perspectives from which modern sociologists approach the study of social conditions. In the next chapter, we outline the procedures and methods used by sociologists in conducting their research. We begin here with a brief description of the origins and development of the science of sociology.

FROM SOCIAL THOUGHT TO SOCIAL SCIENCE

Like all the sciences, sociology developed out of prescientific longings to understand and predict. The central questions of sociology have been pondered by the world's great thinkers since the earliest periods of recorded history. The ancient Greek philosophers believed that human societies inevitably arose, flourished, and declined. They tended to perceive the past as better than the present, looking back to a "golden age" in which social conditions were presumed to have been better than those of the degraded present. Before the scientific revolution of the seventeenth century, the theologians and philosophers of medieval Europe and the Islamic world also believed that human misery and strife were inevitable. As the Bible put it, "The poor always ye have with you." Mere mortals could do little to correct social conditions, which were viewed as the work of divine Providence.

The Age of Enlightenment

The roots of modern sociology can be found in the work of the philosophers and scientists of the Great Enlightenment, which had its origins in the scientific discoveries of the seventeenth century. That pivotal century began with Galileo's "heretical" proof that the earth was not the center of the universe; it ended with the publication of Isaac Newton's *Principia Mathematica*. Newton is often credited with the founding of modern science. He not only discovered the laws of gravity and motion but, in developing the calculus, also provided later generations with the mathematical tools whereby further discoveries in all the sciences could be made.

Hard on the heels of this unprecedented progress in science and mathematics came a theory of human progress that paved the way for a "science of humanity." Francis Bacon in England, René Descartes and Blaise Pascal in France, and Gottfried Wilhelm Leibniz in Germany were among the philosophers who recognized the social importance of scientific discoveries. Their writings emphasized the idea of progress guided by human reason and opposed the dominant notion that the human condition was ordained by God and could not be improved through human actions (Bury, 1932; Nisbet, 1969).

Today we are used to inventions crowding one upon another. Between the childhood of our grandparents and our own adulthood, society has undergone some major transformations: from agrarian to industrial production; from rural settlements and small towns to large cities and expanding metropolitan regions; from reliance on wood and coal as energy sources to dependence on electricity and nuclear power; from typewriters to computers. But in the seventeenth century, people were used to far more stability. Ways of life that had existed since the Middle Ages were not expected to change in a generation.

The rise of science transformed the social order. As was often said at the time, science "broke the cake of custom." New methods of navigation made it possible to explore and chart the world's oceans and continents. Applied to warfare, scientific knowledge enabled Europeans to conquer the peoples of Africa, Asia, and the Western Hemisphere. In Europe, those conquests opened up new markets and stimulated new patterns of trade that hastened the growth of some regions and cities and the decline of others. The entire human world had entered a period of rapid social change that continues today and shows no signs of ending.

The Age of Revolution

The vehicle of social change was not science itself since relatively few people at any level of society were practicing scientists. Rather, the modern era of rapid social change is a product of the many new ideas that captured people's imagination during the eighteenth century. The series of revolutions that took place in the American colonies, in France, and in England all resulted in part from social movements unleashed by the triumphs of science and reason. The ideas of human rights (that is, the rights of all humans, not just the elite), of democracy versus rule by an absolute monarch, of self-government for colonial peoples, and of applying reason and science to human affairs in general—all are currents of thought that arose during this period.

The revolutions of the eighteenth century loosed a torrent of questions that could not even have been imagined before. The old order of society was breaking down as secular (i.e., nonreligious) knowledge replaced sacred traditions. The study of laws and lawmaking and debates about justice in society began to replace the idea that kings and other leaders had a "divine right" to rule. Communities were breaking apart; courts, palaces, and great estates were crumbling as people struggled to be free. What would replace them? Would the rule of the mob replace the rule of the monarch? Would greed and envy replace piety and faith? Would there be enough opportunities in the New World for all the people who were being driven off the land in the Old World? Would the factory system become the new order of society, and if so, what did that imply for the future of society?

No longer could the Scriptures or the classics of ancient Greece and Rome be consulted for easy answers to such questions. Rather, it was becoming evident that new answers could be discovered through the **scientific method:** repeated observation, careful description, the formulation of theories based on possible explanations, and the gathering of additional data about questions arising from those theories. Why not use the same methods to create a science of human society? This ambitious idea led to the birth of sociology. It is little wonder that the French philosopher Auguste Comte thought of sociology, even in its infancy, as the "queen of sciences," one that would soon take its rightful place beside the reigning science of physics. It was he who coined the term *sociology* to designate the scientific study of society. Comte believed that the study of social stability and social change was the most important subject for sociology to tackle. He made some of the earliest attempts to apply scientific methods to the study of social life.

The Founders of Sociology

In the nineteenth century an increasing number of philosophers and historians began to see themselves as specializing in the study of social conditions and social change. They attempted to develop global theories of social change based on the essential qualities of societies at different stages of human history, and they devoted much of their attention to comparing existing societies and civilizations, both past and present. As Comte put it, the age of discovery had revealed such an array of societies that "from the wretched inhabitants of Tierra del Fuego to the most advanced nations of Western Europe" there is such a great diversity of societies that comparisons among them will yield much insight into why they differ and how they change (1971/1854, p. 48).

The early sociologists tended to think in macrosociological terms. Their writing dealt with whole societies and how their special characteristics influence human behavior and social change. Most sociologists would agree that the nineteenth-century social theorists who had the greatest and most lasting influence on the field were Karl Marx, Émile Durkheim, and Max Weber. All three applied the new concepts of sociology to gain an understanding of the immense changes occurring around them.

KARL MARX   German-born Karl Marx (1818–1883) became a radical philosopher as a young man and was embroiled in numerous insurrections and attempts at revolution in Germany and France. Forced to flee Germany after the abortive European revolution of 1848, he lived and worked in England for the rest of his life. Often penniless, Marx worked for hours on end in the library of the British Museum, where he developed the social and economic theories that would have a major influence on sociological thought. His famous treatise *Capital* is a detailed study of the rise of capitalism as a dominant system of production. In this work and elsewhere, Marx set forth an extremely powerful theory to explain the transformations taking place as societies became more industrialized and urbanized. He argued that those transformations would inevitably end in a revolution in which the workers would overthrow capitalism, but he also believed that revolution could be hastened through political action.

ÉMILE DURKHEIM   Émile Durkheim (1858–1917) was the founder of scientific sociology in France. His books, among which the best known are *The Division of Labor in Society, Rules of the Sociological Method,* and *Suicide,* were pioneering examples of the use of comparative data to assess the directions and consequences of social change. The first university professor with a chair in the "social sciences," Durkheim was soon surrounded by a brilliant group of academic disciples who were deeply interested in understanding the vast changes that occurred in societies as they became more populous, more urbanized, and more technologically complex. In 1898 Durkheim and his colleagues established the first scientific journal in sociology, *L'Année sociologique (The Sociological Year).* This journal and much of Durkheim's own writing were among the first examples of the application of statistics to social issues. (See the discussion of suicide in Chapter 2.)

MAX WEBER   Max Weber (1864–1920) was a German historian, economist, and sociologist. Weber's life, like Durkheim's, spanned much of the second half of the nineteenth century and the early decades of the twentieth. Like the other early sociologists, therefore, Weber witnessed the tumultuous changes that were bringing down the old order. He saw monarchies tottering in the face of demands for democratic rule. He observed new industries and markets spanning the globe and linking formerly isolated peoples. He saw and described the rise of modern science and jurisprudence and modern ways of doing business. The growing tendency to apply rational decision-making procedures, rather than merely relying on tradition, was for Weber a dramatic departure from the older ways of feudal societies and mercantile aristocracies. Weber compared many different societies to show how new forms of government and administration were evolving.

All three of these pioneers in sociology were scholars of great genius. They were also political activists. Marx, of course, was the most revolutionary of the three and devoted much of his energy to the international socialist movement. Durkheim was a lifelong socialist but was more moderate than Marx. Although he took stands on many political issues, Durkheim did not devote himself to political activities. As a young man, Weber had been involved in the movement to create a unified German nation, but as a mature scholar he developed a belief in "value-free" social science. A social scientist might draw research questions from personal political beliefs, but the research itself must apply scientific methods. This view, which Durkheim also shared, did much to advance sociology to the level of a social science rather than just a branch of philosophy.

To become a science, sociology had to build on the research of its founders. The twentieth century brought changes of such magnitude at every level of society that sociologists were in increasing demand. Their mission was to gain new information about the scope and meaning of social change.

The Rise of Modern Sociology

We credit the European social thinkers and philosophers with creating sociology, but nowhere did the new science find more fertile ground for development than in North

Karl Marx.

Émile Durkheim.

Max Weber.

THEN AND NOW   Women in Sociology

In the late nineteenth century, as it emerged from philosophy to become an independent scholarly field, sociology was dominated by male university professors. There were a few exceptions, such as W. E. B. Du Bois and the brilliant Muslim social thinker Ibn Khaldun, but for the most part the founders of sociology were European men.

A notable exception was Harriet Martineau (1802–1876), who is thought to have been the first woman to contribute to the emerging

Harriet Martineau by Richard Evans, by Courtesy of the National Portrait Gallery, London

Harriet Martineau.

field of sociology. Martineau wrote important sociological interpretations of the early phases of capitalism and modernity. She was also a social reformer whose writings on the plight of children and women in British

factories were highly influential (Hoecker-Drysdale, 1992).

In the United States as well, early female sociologists were usually barred from university positions, and their work was never accorded the intellectual respect it merited. An example is Ida B. Wells-Barnett (1862–1931), an African-American woman raised in the South after the Civil War. She wrote extensively about the new forms of discrimination and racism directed against her people and became a spokesperson for the civil rights of African Americans and women. Recent scholarship by feminist sociologists has drawn renewed attention to her work and that of other women founders of sociology (Lengermann & Niebrugge-Brantley, 1998).

Today sociology is far more diverse in every aspect, and women throughout the world are well represented among the field's most innovative minds. The photo of Manjula Giri shows a modern sociologist from a developing nation, Nepal, who is both a university-trained scholar and a dedicated social activist. Giri has written about the failure of revolution to improve the conditions of rural women in Nepal. In her own village she is using her sociological skills to help local women

Hulton/Archive/Getty Images

Ida B. Wells-Barnett.

develop a women's farming cooperative. She has also started literacy classes and is planning to expand her work to other villages in the region. Giri is an example of the scholar-activist, a dual role that is increasingly common throughout the poorer regions of the world.

Courtesy of Manjula Giri

Manjula Giri.

America. By the beginning of the twentieth century, sociology was rapidly acquiring new adherents in the United States and Canada, partly because of the influence of European sociologists like Marx and Durkheim, but even more because of the rapid social changes occurring in North America at the time. Waves of immigrants to cities and towns, the explosive growth of population and industry in the cities, race riots, strikes and labor strife, moral crusades against crime and vice and alcohol, the demand for woman suffrage—these and many other changes caused American sociology to take a new turn. There was an increasing demand for knowledge about exactly what changes were occurring and who was affected by them. In

North America, therefore, sociologists began to emphasize the quest for facts about changing social conditions—that is, the empirical investigation of social issues.

EMPIRICAL INVESTIGATION *Empirical* information refers to carefully gathered, unbiased data regarding social conditions and behavior. In general, modern sociology is distinguished by its relentless and systematic search for empirical data to answer questions about society. Journalists, for example, also seek the facts about social conditions, but they must cover many different events and situations and present them as "stories" that will attract their readers' interest. Because they usually cannot dwell on one subject very long, journalists often must content themselves with citing examples and quoting experts whose opinions may or may not be based on empirical evidence. In contrast, sociologists study a situation or phenomenon in more depth; when they do not have enough facts, they are likely to say, "That is an empirical question. Let's see what the research tells us. If the answers are inconclusive, we will do more research." Evidence based on measurable effects and outcomes is required before one can make an informed decision about an issue.

Among the chief goals of modern sociology are using the sociological imagination to ask relevant questions and seeking answers to those questions backed by evidence that can be verified by others. Anyone can make assertions about society or about why people behave the way they do. "I think it's human nature to act selfishly, no matter what kind of education people have" is a common assertion that is not backed up by any solid evidence. As you read this book, you will learn that to strengthen your sociological imagination you must learn how to apply evidence to your views and admit that your opinions can be modified by that evidence.

THE SOCIAL SURVEYS   The empirical focus of American sociology began largely as an outgrowth of the reform movements of the late nineteenth and early twentieth centuries. During this period, the nation had not yet recovered from the havoc created by the Civil War. Southern blacks were migrating to the more industrialized North in ever-increasing numbers, and at the same time millions of European immigrants were finding ill-paying jobs in the larger cities, where cheap labor was in great demand. By the turn of the twentieth century, therefore, the nation's cities were crowded with poor families for whom the promise of "gold in America" had become a tarnished dream. In this time of rapid social change, Americans continually debated the merits of social reform and proposed new solutions for pressing social issues. Some called for socialism, others for a return to the free market, a ban on labor organizations, an end to immigration, or the removal of black Americans to Africa. But where would the facts to be used in judging those ideas come from?

In order to gain empirical information about social conditions, dedicated individuals undertook numerous "social surveys." Jacob Riis's (1890) account of life on New York's Lower East Side; W. E. B. Du Bois's (1967/1899) survey of Philadelphia blacks; Emily Balch's (1910) depiction of living conditions among Slavic miners and steelworkers in the Pittsburgh area; and Jane Addams's famous *Hull-House Maps and Papers* (1895), which described the lives of her neighbors in Chicago's West Side slum area—these and other carefully documented surveys of the living conditions of people experiencing the effects of rapid industrialization and urbanization left an enduring mark on American sociology. The Sociological Methods box on

pages 12–13 presents an excerpt from the landmark survey conducted by Du Bois, the first black sociologist to gain worldwide recognition. Du Bois helped direct sociological research to racial and social issues in minority communities, using empirical data to provide an objective account of the dismal social conditions of northern blacks at the turn of the twentieth century.

THE CHICAGO SCHOOL AND HUMAN ECOLOGY   By the late 1920s, the United States had become the world leader in sociology. The two great centers of American sociological research were the University of Chicago and Columbia University. At these universities and others influenced by them, two distinct approaches to the study of society evolved. The Chicago school emphasized the relationship between the individual and society, whereas the major East Coast universities, which were more strongly influenced by European sociology, tended toward macro-level analyses of social structure and change.

The sociology department at the University of Chicago (the oldest in the nation) extended its influence to many other universities, especially in the Midwest, South, and West. At that time the department was under the leadership of Robert Park and his younger colleague Ernest Burgess. Park in particular is associated with the Chicago school. His main contribution was to develop an agenda for sociological research that used the city as a "social laboratory." Park favored an approach in which facts concerning what was occurring among people in their local communities (at the micro and middle levels) would be collected within a broader theoretical framework. That framework attempted to link macro-level changes in society, such as industrialization and the growth of urban populations, to patterns of settlement in cities and to how people actually lived in cities.

In one of his essays on this subject, Park began with the idea that industrialization causes the breakdown of traditional "primary-group" attachments (those of family members, age-mates, or clans). After stating the probable relationship between the effects of industrialization and high rates of crime, Park asked several specific questions:

> What is the effect of ownership of property . . . on truancy, on divorce, and on crime?
>
> In what regions and classes are certain kinds of crime endemic? In what classes does divorce occur most frequently? What is the difference in this respect between farmers and, say, actors?
>
> To what extent in any given [ethnic] group . . . do parents and children live in the same world, speak the same language, and share the same ideas, and how far do the conditions found account for juvenile delinquency in that particular group? (1967/1925a, p. 22)

W. E. B. Du Bois was one of the first American sociologists to publish highly factual and objective descriptions of life in American cities. An African American, Du Bois earned his doctorate in philosophy at Harvard before the turn of the twentieth century, when sociology was still regarded as a sub-field of that discipline. But, as can be seen in this excerpt from his account of black life in Philadelphia about a century ago, Du Bois was able to sharpen his arguments about the effects of racial discrimination with simple but telling statistics.

For a group of freedmen the question of economic survival is the most pressing of all questions; the problem as to how, under the cir-cumstances of modern life, any group of people can earn a decent living, so as to maintain their stan-dard of life, is not always easy to answer. But when the question is complicated by the fact that the group has a low degree of efficiency on account of previous training; is in competition with well-trained, eager and often ruthless competi-tors; is more or less handicapped by . . . discrimination; and finally, is seeking not merely to maintain a standard of living but steadily to raise it to a higher plane—such a

situation presents baffling problems to the sociologist. . . .

And yet this is the situation of the Negro in Philadelphia; he is trying to better his condition; is seeking to rise; for this end his first need is work of a character to engage his best talents, and remu-nerative enough for him to support a home and train up his children well. The competition in a large city is fierce, and it is difficult for any poor people to succeed. The Negro, however, has two especial difficulties: his training as a slave and freedman has not been such as make the average of the race as efficient and reliable workmen as the average [native-born] American or as many foreign immigrants. The Negro is, as a rule, willing, honest and good-natured; but he is also, as a rule, careless, unreliable and unsteady. This is without doubt to be expected in a people who for generations have been trained to shirk work; but an historical excuse counts for little in the whirl and battle of breadwinning. Of course, there are large exceptions to this average rule; there are many Negroes who are as bright, talented and reliable as any class of work-men, and who in untrammeled competition would soon rise high in the economic scale, and thus by

W. E. B. Du Bois.

the law of the survival of the fittest we should soon have left at the bottom those inefficient and lazy drones who did not deserve a better fate. However, in the realm of social phenomena the law of sur-vival is greatly modified by human choice, wish, whim and prejudice. And consequently one never knows when one sees a social outcast how far this failure to survive is due to the deficiencies of the individual, and how far to the accidents or in-justice of his environment. This is especially the case with the Negro. Every one knows that in a city like Philadelphia a Negro does not have the same chance to exercise his ability or secure work according to his talents as a white man. Just

---

This set of research questions, of which those quoted here are a small sample, inspired and shaped the work of hundreds of sociologists who were influenced by the Chicago school. To this day, Chicago remains the most systematically studied city in the United States, although similar research has been carried out in other large cities throughout the nation. From studies of the linguistic diversity of African peoples to attempts to un-derstand the subtle negotiations by which youth gangs divide up an urban "turf," the insights of the Chicago school remain a vital aspect of contemporary sociology (A.D. Abbott, 2001).

As you can see from the types of questions Park asked, the distinctive orientation of the Chicago school was its emphasis on the relationships among social order, social disorganization, and the distribution of populations in space and time. Park and Burgess called this approach

human ecology. With many modifications, it remains an important, though not dominant, perspective in con-temporary sociology.

Human ecology, as Park and others defined it, is the branch of sociology that is concerned with population growth and change. In particular, it seeks to discover how populations organize themselves to survive and prosper. Human ecologists are interested in how groups that are or-ganized in different ways compete and cooperate. They also look for forms of social organization that may emerge as a group adjusts to life in new surroundings.

A key concept for human ecologists is *community.* There are many ways of defining this term, just as there are many ways of defining most of the central concepts of sociology. From an ecological perspective, however, the term *commu-nity* usually refers to a population that carries out major life functions (e.g., birth, marriage, death) within a particular how far this is so we shall discuss later; now it is sufficient to say in general that the sorts of work open to Negroes are not only restricted by their own lack of training but also by discrimination against them on account of their race; that their economic rise is not only hindered by their present poverty, but also by a widespread inclination to shut against them many doors of advancement. . . .

What has thus far been the result of this complicated situation? What do the mass of the Negroes of the city at present do for a living, and how successful are they in those lines? And in so far as they are successful, what have they accomplished, and where are they inefficient in their present sphere of work, what is the cause and remedy? These are the questions before us, and we proceed to answer the first in this chapter, taking the occupations of the Negroes of the Seventh Ward first. . . .

Of the 257 boys between the ages of ten and twenty, who were regularly at work in 1896, 39 percent were porters and errand boys; 25.5 percent were servants; 16 percent were common laborers, and 19.5 percent had miscellaneous employment. The occupations in detail are as follows:

Total population, males 10 to 20	651	
Engaged in gainful occupations	257	
Porters and errand boys	100	39.0%
Servants	66	25.5%
Common laborers	40	16.0%
Miscellaneous employment		
Teamsters	7	
Apprentices	6	
Bootblacks	6	
Drivers	5	
Newsboys	5	
Peddlers	4	
Typesetters	3	
Actors	2	
Bricklayers	2	
Hostlers	2	51 19.5%
Typists	2	
Barber	1	
Bartender	1	
Bookbinder	1	
Factory hand	1	
Rubber worker	1	
Sailor	1	
Shoemaker	1	
	257	100.0%

Note: This simple table includes much useful information, but modern tables present data more efficiently. See Chapter 2 for a detailed discussion of the presentation of data in tables.
Source: Du Bois, 1967/1899, pp. 97–99.

territory. Human ecology does not assume that there will ever be a "steady state" or an end to the process of change in human communities. Instead, it attempts to trace the change and document its consequences for the social environment. What happens when newcomers "invade" a community? In what way are local gangs a response to recent changes in population or in the ability of members of a community to compete for jobs? Not only do populations change, but people's preferences and behaviors also continually change. So do the technologies for producing the goods and services we want. As a result, our ways of making a living, our modes of transportation, and our choices of leisure activities create constant change, not just in communities but in entire societies.

The Chicago school became known for this "ecological" approach, the idea that the study of human society should begin with empirical questions about population size, the distribution of populations over territories, and the like. The human ecologists recognized that society is shaped by many other processes, but their most important contribution to the discipline of sociology was to include the processes by which populations change and communities are formed.

Modern ecological theories also consider the relations between humans and their natural environment. We will see that the way people earn a living, the resources they use, the energy they consume, and their efforts to control pollution all have far-reaching consequences, not only for their own lives but also for the society in which they live. These patterns of use and consumption also have an increasing impact on the entire planet—so much so that ecological problems are becoming an ever more important area of sociological research. (See the Mapping Social Change box on pages 14–15.)

Worldwide Calorie Consumption and Areas of Famine

From a biological perspective, the success of any species is measured by how well it meets the broad requirements of population growth and maintenance. Every day the world's 6 billion people seek and obtain enough food to convert into bodily energy, a minimum of perhaps 1,500 calories a day for survival at starvation levels (although this varies greatly with climate and other factors). Over 70 percent of the world's population is inadequately nourished (that is, obtains fewer than 2,500 calories a day), often while engaging in hard physical labor. At the same time, a smaller proportion, including most (but by no means all) of the North American population, lives so comfortably and well above the daily minimum that overweight and obesity are a major health problem.

Ecological theories help explain malnutrition and starvation in some areas of the world. In Somalia, for example, the combination of a desert environment and warring political factions produces social instability that leads to persistent famine. The problem is not so much that food is unavailable as that supplies cannot be delivered or distributed effectively.

AP/Wide World Photos

These Iraqi children are searching in a dump for things to eat or sell. Scenes of children scavenging through garbage dumps are common throughout the world's poorest nations.

GLOBAL AND REGIONAL TRENDS IN THE ESTIMATED PREVALENCE OF PROTEIN-ENERGY MALNUTRITION IN UNDERWEIGHT CHILDREN UNDER 5, SINCE 1980

Region	1980 %	1980 Million	1990 %	1990 Million	1995 %	1995 Million	2000 %	2000 Million
Africa	26.2	22.5	27.3	30.1	27.9	34.0	28.5	38.3
Asia	43.9	146.0	36.5	141.3	32.8	121.0	29.0	108.0
Latin America	14.2	7.3	10.2	5.6	8.3	4.5	6.3	3.4
Developing countries	37.4	175.7	32.1	177.0	29.2	159.5	26.7	149.6

Source: WHO, 2000.

Since children are the most vulnerable segment of any society's population, they are usually affected most by adverse social conditions. This table shows that overall the percentages and numbers of underweight, malnourished children in the developing countries have declined from 37.4 percent (175.7 million) in 1980 to 26.7 percent (149.6 million) in 2000. The greatest improvements have occurred in Asia, where positive economic and social changes have brought higher levels of living to many. But in Africa, where civil strife in many regions blocks economic growth, the proportion of malnourished children is actually growing.

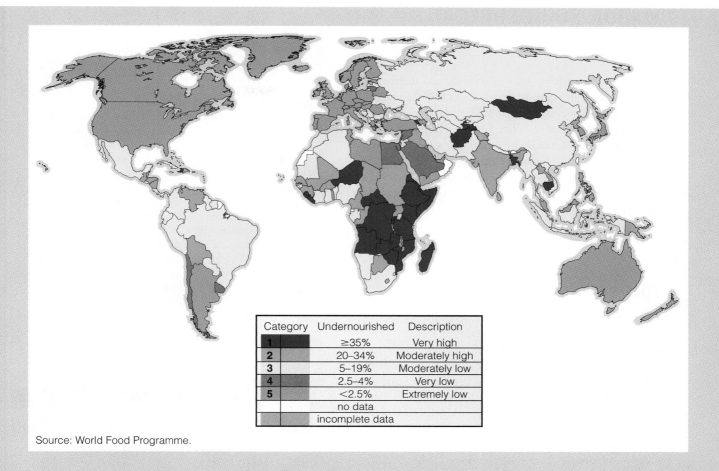

Category		Undernourished	Description
1		≥35%	Very high
2		20–34%	Moderately high
3		5–19%	Moderately low
4		2.5–4%	Very low
5		<2.5%	Extremely low
		no data	
		incomplete data	

Source: World Food Programme.

REGIONAL AND GLOBAL PREVALENCE AND NUMBERS OF OVERWEIGHT ADULTS AND CHILDREN UNDER 5, BY WHO REGION

WHO region	Children		Adults	
	% prevalence	Millions	% prevalence	Millions
Africa	3.4	3.3	2.9	8.2
The Americas	4.5	3.4	20.9	109.0
Southeast Asia	4.5	3.0	1.1	10.0
Europe	NA	NA	16.7	106.5
Eastern Mediterranean	1.8	3.0	10.0	24.9
Western Pacific	4.0	5.3	3.8	42.5
Global	**3.6**	**21.5**	**8.2**	**301.1**

Total for children includes an estimated 3.5 million overweight children in Europe, although Europe survey data not always adequate.
Source: WHO, 2000.

This table shows that overweight is more serious among adults than among children, especially in the more affluent regions of the world. Many measures of overweight are used throughout the world, making it difficult to compare nations, but for the most part, these figures are based on children and adults who would be more than two standard deviations above the average weight for their height.

MAJOR SOCIOLOGICAL PERSPECTIVES

Sociological *perspectives* are sets of ideas and theories that sociologists use in attempting to understand various problems of human society, such as the problem of population size, the problem of conflict between populations, the problem of how people become part of a society, and other issues that we will encounter throughout this book. Although human ecology remains an important sociological perspective, it is by no means the only one employed by modern sociologists. Other perspectives, to which we now turn, guide empirical description and help explain social stability and social change.

Interactionism

Interactionism is the sociological perspective that views social order and social change as resulting from all the immense variety of repeated interactions among individuals and groups. Families, committees, corporations, armies, entire societies—indeed, all the social forms we can think of—are a result of interpersonal behavior in which people communicate, give and take, share, compete, and so on. If there were no exchange of goods, information, love, and all the rest—that is, if there were no interaction among people—obviously there could be no social life at all.

The interactionist perspective usually generates analyses of social life at the level of interpersonal relationships, but it does not limit itself to the micro level of social reality. It also looks at how middle- and macro-level phenomena result from micro-level behaviors or, conversely, how middle- and macro-level influences shape the interactions among individuals. From the interactionist perspective, for example, a family is a product of interactions among a set of individuals who define themselves as family members. But each person's understanding of how a family ought to behave is a product of middle- and macro-level forces: religious teachings about family life, laws dealing with education or child support, and so on. And these are always changing. You may have experienced the consequences of changing values that cause older and younger family members to feel differently about such issues as whether a couple should live together before marrying. In sum, the interactionist perspective insists that we look carefully at how individuals interact, how they interpret their own and other people's actions, and the consequences of those actions for the larger social group (Blumer, 1969b; Frank, 1988).

The general framework of interactionism contains at least two major and quite different sets of issues. One set concerns the problems of exchange and choice: How can

The Sociological Observer

This is a well-known photo of a Nazi party rally in Nuremberg, Germany, that took place in 1934. Hitler is in the mid-foreground, facing the camera and flanked by two officers. He is leading a parade commemorating those who had died promoting the aims of his national socialist party, mainly in violent attacks on members of other German political parties.

As political propaganda, this photo expresses many aspects of what Hitler and his party were trying to convey to the German people and to the world. What do you think is the symbolic significance of the huge formation of men in this photo? How does physical space help convey the underlying aims of the parade? How does the organization of this parade contrast with that of a Mardi Gras parade? What other important differences are there between the two parades? (See page 21 for further insights into the sociological content of this photo.)

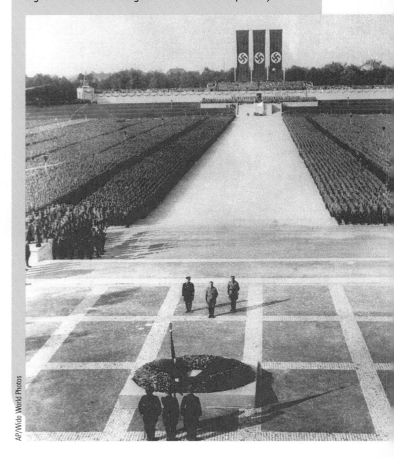

AP/Wide World Photos

social order exist and groups or societies maintain stability when people have selfish motives for being in groups—that is, when they are seeking to gain as much personal advantage as they can? The second set of issues involves how people actually manage to communicate their values and how they arrive at mutual understandings. Research and explanations of the first problem fall under the heading of "rational choice" (or exchange theory); the second issue is addressed by the study of "symbolic interaction." In recent years, these two areas of inquiry have emerged as quite different yet increasingly related aspects of the study of interaction.

RATIONAL CHOICE: THE SOCIOLOGICAL VIEW Adam Smith, whose famous work *The Wealth of Nations* (1965/1776) became the basis for most subsequent economic thought, believed that individuals always seek to maximize their pleasure and minimize their pain. If over time they are allowed to make the best possible choices for themselves, they will also produce an affluent and just society. They will serve others, even when they are unaware that they are doing so, in order to increase their own benefit. They will choose a constitution and a government that protects their property and their right to engage in trade. They will seek the government's protection against those who would infringe on their rights or attempt to dominate them, but the government need do little more than protect them and allow them to make choices based on their own reasoning.

You may have already encountered this theory, known as *utilitarianism,* in an economics or political science course. In sociology it is applied to a variety of issues. Often this rational-choice view of interaction is referred to as *exchange theory* because it focuses on what people seem to be getting out of their interactions and what they in turn are contributing to the relationship or to the larger group. In every interaction, something is being exchanged: It may be time or attention, friendship, material values (e.g., wages or possessions), or less easily calculated values such as esteem or allegiance. The larger the number of interacting members, the more complex the types of exchanges that occur among them. When people perceive an interaction as being one-way, they begin to feel that they are being exploited or treated unfairly and will usually leave the relationship or quit the group (Homans, 1961). In industry, for example, if workers feel that they are not being paid enough for their work, they may form a union, bargain collectively with the bosses, or even go on strike. But in doing so, each worker will weigh potential benefits against potential losses—losses in pay, in esteem, in friendship, and so forth. The choices are not always easy, nor are the motivations always obvious. When many values are involved, the rational calculation of benefits and costs becomes even more difficult.

Rational-choice models of behavior prompt us to look at *patterns* of behavior to see how they conform to and depart from normal expectations of personal profit and loss. But those models do not always identify the underlying values. How we learn what to value in the first place, how we communicate our choices and intentions, how we learn new values through interaction—all are subjects that

The players on opposing teams are paying their respects to one another after a game of soccer. Here is an example of social interaction that is highly structured—the players form opposing lines that walk past each other and touch hands—but the players are also free to add their own comments and perform the ritual with a bit of personal style.

require other concepts besides those found in rational-choice theories of behavior. Such questions lead us toward research about how human interaction is actually carried out and understood by people in their daily lives.

SYMBOLIC INTERACTIONISM When we make choices about our interactions with other people, we may be said to be acting rationally. But there are likely to be other forces shaping our behavior as well. For example, you may select a particular course because the instructor is rumored to be good. But what does "good" mean—clear and well organized? an easy grader? friendly? humorous? The dimensions of a choice can be complicated, and we may not be aware of everything that goes into our decisions. You may, without realizing it, choose a course as much to be with certain other people as to be in that particular course. Our choices tell other people about us: what we like, what we want to become, and so on. Indeed, the way people dress, the way they carry themselves (body language), the way they speak to each other, and the gestures they make convey a great deal of information that is not always intentional or expressed in speech. Some forms of communication give information without speaking it, or speak one thing and mean another. But words are of great importance too, and the content of communication is made explicit in words and sentences. Sociologists refer to all these aspects of behavior as *symbolic interaction.* From the symbolic-interactionist perspective, "society itself tends to be seen as a mosaic of little scenes and dramas in which people make indications to themselves and others, respond to those indications, align their actions, and so build identities and social structures" (Rock, 1985, p. 844).

Symbolic interactionists call attention to how social life is "constructed" through the mundane acts of social communication. For example, in all the choices students make—their joining of friendship groups, their learning of the informal rules of the school, their challenging and breaking of those rules—the social order of student society, or "college culture," is actually "constructed." Erving Goffman, whose work was mentioned earlier, is known for his research on these processes. Goffman applied the symbolic-interactionist perspective to the study of everyday interactions such as rituals of greeting and departure, of daily life in asylums and gambling houses, and of behavior in streets and public places. His work examines how people behave in social situations and how their "performances" are rated by others.

The power of symbolic interactionism lies in its ability to generate theories about how people learn to play certain roles and how those roles are used in the social construction of groups and organizations. However, if we want to think sociologically about more complex phenomena, such as the rise of bureaucratic organizations or the reasons why some societies experience revolutions, we also need the concepts developed by two other perspectives: functionalism and conflict theory.

Functionalism

Is society simply the sum total of countless micro-level exchanges and communicative interactions, or do the organizations within a society have properties independent of the actions of individuals? When we speak of the family, the army, the corporation, or the laboratory, we generally have in mind an entity marked by certain specific functions, tasks, and types of behavior. The army requires that

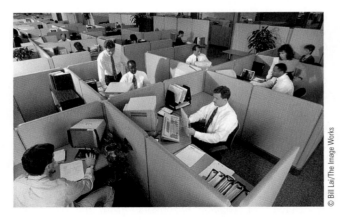

The cubicles of an open office space—whose occupants perform the specific duties required by their jobs—have become a visual metaphor for the functionalist arrangement of modern work life.

its members learn to engage in armed combat, even if that is not what they will be doing most of the time. The family requires that its members behave in nurturant ways toward one another. The farm requires that those who run it know how to plant and harvest. Individual interactions may determine how well a given person performs these various tasks; but it is the larger organization—the army, the family, the farm—that establishes specific ways of behaving and doing the work of that organization. In this sense the organization, which exists longer than any of its members, has its own existence.

The **functionalist** perspective asks how society manages to carry out the functions it must perform in order to maintain social order, feed large masses of people each day, defend itself against attackers, produce the next generation, and so on. From this perspective, the many groups and organizations that make up a society form the structure of human society. This social structure is a complex system designed to carry out the essential functions of human life. The function of the family, for example, is to raise and train a new generation to replace the old; the function of the military is to defend the society; the function of schools is to teach the next generation the beliefs and skills they will need to maintain the society in the future; and a major function of religion is to develop shared ideas of morality.

When a society is functioning well, all its major parts are said to be well integrated and in equilibrium. But periods of rapid social change can throw social structures out of equilibrium. Entire ways of life can lose their purpose or function. When that happens, the various structures of society can become poorly integrated, and formerly useful functions can become dysfunctional.

Consider an example: In agrarian societies, in which most people work the land, families typically include three generations, with many members in each generation living close to one another. Labor is in great demand; many hands are needed where there are no machines to perform work in fields and barnyards and granaries. Early marriage and large numbers of children in the agrarian family help such a society function optimally. But when the society industrializes and its agriculture becomes mechanized, families may continue to produce large numbers of children even though the demand for farmhands has decreased. When they grow up, those children may migrate to towns and cities. The migrants are likely to continue to value large families and to have numerous children, but if there are a limited number of jobs in the cities, they may join the ranks of the unemployed and their children may grow up in poverty. In this situation, the family can be said to be poorly integrated with the needs of the society; the value of large family size has become dysfunctional—it no longer contributes to the well-being of groups or individuals.

Conflict Theory

A major flaw in the functionalist perspective is that we have rarely seen anything approaching equilibrium in human societies. Inequalities of wealth and power, racism, religious intolerance, ethnic hatreds, grinding economic competition, and criminality constantly threaten peace and the smooth functioning of even the most affluent and stable societies (Barash, 2002). In the twentieth century alone, two world wars and many civil wars disrupted the lives of millions of people. Almost as devastating was the Great Depression of the 1930s, the most severe economic slump in modern history. Worst of all were the nightmares of the Nazi Holocaust and the purges of Stalinist Russia, in which more than 20 million people were exterminated.

The world wars, the Depression, and the Holocaust shocked and demoralized the entire world. They also called into question the optimism of the nineteenth- and early-twentieth-century social philosophers, many of whom believed in the promise of progress through modern science and technology. Between 1914 and the end of World War II, modern ideas and technologies were used for horrible purposes often enough to disillusion all but the most ardent optimists. Bewildered intellectuals and political leaders turned to sociology to find some explanation for those horrors.

One explanation was provided by Marxian theory. According to Marx, the rise of capitalism was the cause of conflict in modern times. Under capitalism, forms of exploitation and domination spread. For example, in the early period of industrial capitalism, workers were forced to work 12 hours a day, 6 days a week; in less developed

In Sarajevo, the physical and emotional scars of war will last long after the cessation of hostilities. As wars become more destructive, the study of social conflict and its solutions takes on even greater urgency.

areas of the world, large populations were virtually enslaved by the new colonial powers.

At the heart of capitalism, for Marx, is conflict among people in different economic classes, especially between those who control wealth and power and those who do not. Marx argued that the division of people in a society into different classes, defined by how they make a living, always produces conflict. Under capitalism, this conflict occurs between the owners of factories and the workers. Marx believed that class conflict would eventually destroy or at least vastly modify capitalism. His theory is at the heart of what has come to be known as conflict theory or the **conflict perspective.**

In the 1960s, when protests against racism and segregation, the Vietnam War, pollution of the environment, and discrimination against women each became the focus of a major social movement, the conflict perspective became more prominent. It clearly was not possible to explain the rapid appearance of major social movements with theories that emphasized how the social system would function if it were in a state of equilibrium. Even Marxian theory did not do a very good job of predicting the protest movements of the 1960s or their effects on American society. The environmental movement and the women's movement, for example, were not based on economic inequalities alone, nor were the people who joined them necessarily exploited workers. Sociologists studying the role of conflict in social change therefore had to go beyond the Marxian view. Many turned to the writings of the German sociologist Georg Simmel (1904), who argued that conflict is necessary as a basis for the formation of alliances. According to Simmel, conflict is one means whereby a "web of group affiliations" is constructed. The continual shifting of alliances within this web of social groups can help explain who becomes involved in social movements and how much power those movements are able to acquire.

The concept of *power* holds a central place in conflict theory. From the functionalist perspective, society holds together because its members share the same basic beliefs about how people should behave. Conflict theorists point out that the role of power is just as important as the influence of shared beliefs in explaining why society does not disintegrate into chaos. **Power** is the ability of an individual or group to change the behavior of others. A nation's government, as we will see in Chapter 4, usually controls the use of force (a form of power) to maintain social order. For sociologists who study conflict and power, the important questions are who benefits from the exercise of power and who loses. For example, when the government intervenes in a strike and obliges workers to return to their jobs, does the public at large or the corporation against which the workers were striking benefit

Text continues on page 22.

VISUAL SOCIOLOGY

All photography in this book is "visual sociology" in the sense that we have chosen pictures that highlight social situations, social relationships, and social institutions. But in assembling a group of photos we can communicate more subtle cues about what it feels like to be in a particular situation or relationship. Through photographs, we can convey a great deal about the culture, social structure, and patterns of interaction that characterize a particular social setting, while at the same time we leave the reader free to make his or her own judgments. Sociologists routinely use photography to focus on types of behavior, on the way people sort themselves out in space and time, on patterns of inequality, and much more. These are all aspects of visual sociology that appear in this book.

SOCIETY ON PARADE

Everybody loves a parade, and no one more than the sociologist. We see parades as events that intentionally display the people and the values we cherish. Parades also yield endless sociological insights into other people's social worlds. The way particular sociologists analyze a parade may tell us something about their concerns and values as well. Take the example of the Rose Bowl parade.

The Rose Bowl parade takes place in Pasadena, California, on New Year's Day. It is one of the most celebrated annual parades in the United States. It is both a local and a national event, and it attracts an immense television audience (which is also attracted by the promise of a major university football game). It is a celebration for the community and an opportunity for it to be in the national spotlight. A functionalist sociologist would argue that the parade affirms the society's values of competition and success and, in the process, helps the merchants of Pasadena. A sociologist with a more critical eye might call attention to the way the parade affirms values that perpetuate inequality and social injustices. The Rose Bowl Queen may be beautiful and talented, but a critical interpretation might emphasize how she is set on a pedestal and brought along to adorn the male field of combat. From this perspective the Queen symbolizes women as beautiful objects to be possessed by men with power and money. An interactionist analysis might see the parade and its viewers as a form of public theatre in which the symbols of American culture are displayed in endless variations as the different floats pass by.

© Crandall/The Image Works

© Zbigniew Bzdak/The Image Works

A saint's day parade in a devout Roman Catholic village of Central or South America offers another glimpse into the interactions that mark a special event in a village society. Who carries the village's patron saint? By what rules of social standing are people arranged in the parade? Simply by describing who's who in the parade, a local informant could offer many insights into the way the village is organized and how its people think and feel.

An ethnic parade such as those that honor Saint Patrick, the patron saint of Ireland, reveals how an ethnic group views itself. Its rituals, its food, and all the conflicts that threaten its solidarity can be observed from the sidelines. The spectator can also gain insights into how the group deals with relations between children and adults, men and women, adults and the elderly. By contrast, a small and somber parade of mourners can offer a version of the celebration of death that may jar observers into not taking for granted the meanings of their own death rituals.

A military parade may be a joyous or extremely ominous event, depending on whether one is on good terms with the generals or not. From a functionalist perspective, this is a display of force. Official communica-tions may portray it as a way of demon-strating that the nation has the capacity to defend itself against other nations. But in many parts of the world, military parades are also meant to let citizens know in no uncertain terms who con-trols the use of deadly force. From a conflict perspective, these parades reveal who has power in the society and how that power is used to favor some groups, who are usually featured in the parade, over others, who often are not included among the marchers.

The Sociological Observer
(See photo on page 16.)

The massed formation of Nazi party members in the Nuremberg parade grounds is clearly intended as political propaganda; its purpose is to show the

German people, and the world, that the Nazi party has strength in numbers and is highly disciplined in its allegiance to its leaders, particularly its supreme leader, Adolph Hitler, who occupies center stage. Everything in the photo, and especially the way physical space is used, is intended to convey a sense of overwhelming power. Note the extreme uniformity of the ranks, the open space separating Hitler and his aides from the massed ranks, and the way the ranks of men are standing so as to give an impression of almost infinite numbers reaching toward the horizon, where Nazi flags reach into the sky. All these effects are intended to reinforce the idea that the party is immensely powerful because it can cause such a grouping of men, and also that Hitler, the only person with space to move in, stands out as the leader, the central and only real individual in the photo. A Mardi Gras parade, by contrast, is highly disorganized, joyful rather than disciplined, and since everyone dresses differ-ently, it expresses the individu-ality of all members of the different groups that make up the parade.

© Alain Evrard/Photo Researchers, Inc.

AP/Wide World Photos

© Nour/Getty Images

STUDY CHART

MAJOR SOCIOLOGICAL PERSPECTIVES

PERSPECTIVE	DESCRIPTION	GENERATES QUESTIONS ABOUT . . .	APPLICATIONS
Interactionism	Studies how social structures are created in the course of human interaction.	How people behave in intimate groups; how symbols and communication shape perceptions; how social roles are learned and society is "constructed" through interaction.	Education practice, courtroom procedure, therapy.
Functionalism	Asks how societies carry out the functions they must perform; views the structures of society as a system designed to carry out those functions.	How society is structured and how social structures work together as a system to perform the major functions of society.	Study of formal organizations, development of social policies, management science.
Conflict Theory	Holds that power is just as important as shared values in holding society together; conflict is also responsible for social change.	How power affects the distribution of scarce resources and how conflict changes society.	Study of politics, social movements, corporate power structures.

most? And what about the workers themselves? What do they gain or lose? Such questions are central to conflict theory today (Fontana, 1993; Gramsci, 1971).

The Multidimensional View of Society

Each of the sociological perspectives leads to different questions and different kinds of observations. These are extremely powerful analytical tools. Anyone who masters them and learns to apply them in appropriate ways will have an immense advantage over more naive observers of the ever-changing parade of social life (Merton, 1998). From the ecological perspective come questions about how

populations can exist and flourish in various natural and social environments. From the interactionist perspective come questions about how people get along and behave in groups and organizations of all kinds. Functionalism asks questions about how society is structured and how it works as a social system. And the conflict perspective asks how power is used to maintain order and how conflict changes society. These different perspectives developed as sociologists asked different questions about society. In contemporary sociology, each continues to stimulate relatively distinct research based on the types of questions being asked. Yet a great deal of research combines the insights of different perspectives in ways that vastly increase the power of the resulting analysis. The Study Chart above summarizes the major sociological perspectives and the kinds of questions they ask.

SUMMARY

The Sociological Imagination

- *Sociology* is the scientific study of human societies and of human behavior in the groups that make up a society. It is concerned with how *social conditions* influence our lives as individuals.

- The ability to see the world from this point of view has been described as the *sociological imagination*.

Sociology and Social Change

- Sociologists study social behavior at three levels of complexity. *Micro-level* sociology deals with behaviors that occur at the level of the individual and immediate others. The *middle level* of sociological observation is concerned with how the social structures in which people participate actually shape their lives. *Macro-level* studies attempt to explain the social processes that influence populations, social classes, and entire societies.

From Social Thought to Social Science

- The scientific discoveries of the seventeenth century led to the rise of the idea of progress, as opposed to the notion of human helplessness in the face of divine Providence.

- In the eighteenth century, revolutions in Europe and North America completely changed the social order and gave rise to new perspectives on human social life.

- Out of this period of social and intellectual ferment came the idea of creating a science of human society. Sociology, as the new science was called, developed in Europe in the nineteenth century.

- During that formative period, several outstanding sociologists shaped and refined the new discipline. Among them were Karl Marx, Émile Durkheim, and Max Weber.

- In the twentieth century, sociology developed most rapidly in North America, spurred by the need for empirical information concerning social conditions. Numerous "social surveys" were conducted around the turn of the century; by the late 1920s, two distinct approaches to the study of society had evolved at American universities. The "Chicago school" focused on the relationship between the individual and society, while the major East Coast universities leaned toward macro-level analysis.

- Under the leadership of Robert Park and Ernest Burgess, the Chicago school developed the approach known as *human ecology.* This perspective emphasizes the relationships among social order, social disorganization, and the distribution of populations in space and time. Fundamental to this approach is the concept of *community,* meaning a population that carries out major functions within a particular territory.

Major Sociological Perspectives

- Modern sociologists employ other basic perspectives in addition to human ecology. *Interactionism* is a perspective that views social order and social change as resulting from all the repeated interactions among individuals and groups.

- One version of this approach is rational-choice or exchange theory, which focuses on what people seem to be getting out of their interactions and what they contribute to them. Another is the symbolic-interactionist perspective, which studies how social structures are actually created in the course of human interaction.

- *Functionalism,* in contrast, is concerned primarily with the large-scale structures of society; it asks how those structures enable society to carry out its basic functions.

- In the decades since World War II, functionalism has been strongly challenged by the *conflict perspective,* which emphasizes the role of conflict and *power* in explaining not only why societies change but also why they hold together.

- None of the major sociological perspectives is fully independent of the others. Each emphasizes different questions and different observations about social life. Used in combination, they greatly increase our ability to understand and explain almost any aspect of human society.

GLOSSARY

sociological imagination: According to C. Wright Mills, the ability to see how social conditions affect our lives. (p. 4)

social conditions: The realities of the life we create together as social beings. (p. 4)

sociology: The scientific study of human societies and human behavior in the groups that make up a society. (p. 5)

micro-level sociology: An approach to the study of society that focuses on patterns of social interaction at the individual level. (p. 6)

macro-level sociology: An approach to the study of society that focuses on the major structures and institutions of society. (p. 6)

middle-level sociology: An approach to the study of society that focuses on relationships between social structures and the individual. (p. 6)

scientific method: The process by which theories and explanations are constructed through repeated observation and careful description. (p. 8)

human ecology: A sociological perspective that emphasizes the relationships among social order, social disorganization, and the distribution of populations in space and time. (p. 12)

interactionism: A sociological perspective that views social order and social change as resulting from all the repeated interactions among individuals and groups. (p. 16)

functionalism: A sociological perspective that focuses on the ways in which a complex pattern of social structures and arrangements contributes to social order. (p. 18)

conflict perspective: A sociological perspective that emphasizes the role of conflict and power in society. (p. 19)

power: the ability to control the behavior of others, even against their will. (p. 19)

INTERNET RESOURCES

Virtual Society: The Wadsworth Sociology Resource Center
(http://sociology.wadsworth.com)

At Virtual Society you can access a wide range of enrichment material to aid your study of sociology. From the main page, click on the Student Resources link, and find your course and this textbook. Next, select the chapter you are presently studying from the pull-down menu. Among the useful options for each self-study chapter are online links and exercises, flashcards, practical study tips, and practice quizzes for each chapter.

MC   MicroCase Online

From the Virtual Society home page, click on MicroCase Online to access book-specific MicroCase exercises that allow you to further explore sociological issues and principles presented in the text.

InfoTrac College Edition

Another unique option available to you at the Student Resources section at Virtual Society is InfoTrac College Edition, an online library with access to hundreds of scholarly and popular periodicals. Below are suggested search terms for this chapter, but this resource also allows you to fit your study of sociology to your own interests by searching custom keywords.

Karl Marx

Functionalism

Conflict Theory

American Sociological Association
(www.asanet.org)

The official page of the American Sociological Association aims to serve sociologists in their work, advance sociology as a science and profession, and promote the use of sociology in society.

Sociological Timeline, University of Missouri
(www.missouri.edu/~socbrent/timeline.htm)

Provides a fascinating look at the development of sociology and its contributions to social change.

The SocioLog
(www.sociolog.com)

A private site endorsed by the American Sociological Association that offers links to numerous sociology departments, journals, and other resources.

The Tools of Sociology

© Mary Kate Denny/PhotoEdit

"Razors pain you;
Rivers are damp;
Acids stain you;
And drugs cause cramps.
Guns aren't lawful;
Noos
G
Yo

LISTEN
SAVE A LIF

Have you or any of your friends ever seriously considered committing suicide? This may not be the kind of question most people want to discuss openly, yet suicide is a serious social issue in the United States and many other nations. Perhaps the most tragic aspect of the phenomenon is the number of suicides committed by teenagers and young adults who have their entire adult lives ahead of them. What can a person do to counteract persistent thoughts about suicide? To whom can one turn when the urge to kill oneself becomes overwhelming? And what are the causes of suicide? These are all important sociological questions.

Most people who have not studied sociology assume that suicide is closely related to an individual's mental state. They will cite cases of people who ended their lives because of intense feelings of depression, or hopelessness, or shame due to crime, debt, loss of a career, or similar misfortunes. In other words, people who lack a sociological imagination will generally attribute suicide to personal problems that overwhelm the individual and make life seem intolerable. In some cases, they may also cite examples of groups of people who have committed suicide together, as members of the Heaven's Gate and People's Temple cults did. But these examples of mass suicide tend to be viewed as exceptions to the notion that suicide is an individual act based on an intense desire to "end it all."

FOCUS QUESTIONS:

• How are the questions sociologists ask about social life the same as, and yet different from, the questions people from all walks of life normally ask?

• What are the basic scientific methods that sociologists employ in their research?

Sociologists do not deny that people who kill themselves are suffering from intensely negative feelings, but they do not believe that all suicide is caused by intense mental states. There is too much evidence suggesting that other forces are operating on individuals who commit suicide. For example, in recent research on suicide in different nations, sociologists have found that the highest numbers of suicides occur in Russia, China, and the nations of the former Soviet Union. Among the Western democracies, numbers of suicides vary considerably. Finland, Austria, Denmark, and France have the highest levels of suicide. The United States is in the middle of the range, and Italy and Greece are at the bottom.

What explains these differences in how many people in a given society kill themselves? When sociologists ask a question like that, they are asking not why an individual commits suicide but why an entire society has a high level of suicides. This is an important question, because if you live in a society where suicide is more common, it may be more likely that you will consider this fatal option at some point in your life.

The study of suicide, like the study of any form of human behavior, raises many issues of scientific observation and interpretation. Consider this question: If in a given year 1,000 people kill themselves in a small nation and 1,000 people kill themselves in another nation with a far larger population, can we say that both nations have the same amount of suicide? Clearly, we need to consider the difference in population size when comparing the levels of suicide in these nations. Measurement of social phenomena like suicide is a vital aspect of understanding the behavior and possibly preventing it. This chapter, therefore, is devoted to the basic scientific methods that sociologists employ when trying to understand complex human behaviors.

APPLYING THE SOCIOLOGICAL IMAGINATION

As citizens of a democratic nation, we are encouraged to form opinions about the social issues of our time. Among the most troubling issues we face are many that involve life and death. Capital punishment, living wills, abortion, fertility drugs, suicide, assisted suicide—all pose extremely difficult ethical problems. These problems also indicate the rapid pace of social change in our lives. For the most part, our grandparents did not have to face many of these issues.

As in all democracies, candidates seeking our votes are eager to tell us what to believe about social issues and what society should do about them. But often the claims and recommendations we hear are contradictory. The explanations given for such problems as suicide, for example, may suggest very different solutions. How is an informed citizen to make decisions about the causes of social conditions or what should be done to remedy them? This is where sociology comes in. Sociology brings scientific methods to bear on these debates.

Most people associate social-scientific research with questionnaires, opinion surveys, and statistical reports. It is true that sociologists throughout the world use these research techniques, but they also use many other methods to explore social conditions. In this chapter, we review many of the most common research tools used by sociologists. We will show how sociological research conforms to the rules of the scientific method and how the findings lead to changes in theories and to new research.

Steps in the Research Process

In all research projects, certain basic steps must be completed, though not always in the order listed here:

1. *Deciding on the problem.* At first this may be simply a subject or topic of interest. Eventually, however, it must be worded in the form of a specific research question or questions to provide a focus for the rest of the work.

2. *Reviewing the literature.* Usually others have conducted research on the same topic. Find their reports and use them to determine what you can accomplish through your own research.

3. *Formulating research questions.* The work of others points to questions that have not been answered. Your own interest, time, resources, and available methods help determine what specific questions within your broad topic you can actually tackle.

4. *Selecting a method.* Different questions require different types of data, which in turn suggest different methods of data collection and analysis. Some of those methods are described in detail in this chapter.

5. *Analyzing the data.* Data are analyzed at each stage of the research, not just when preparing the final report.

In this chapter, we act as if this step-by-step procedure is always followed by researchers in the social sciences. But do not assume that this procedure can be applied to every research question. One does not always progress easily from one step to another, and often one must go back and repeat earlier steps. In addition, some research questions require that we devise new ways of conducting research or new combinations of existing research methods.

Formulating Research Questions

Émile Durkheim's study of suicide (1951/1897) provides a good example of the process by which a sociologist converts a broad question about social change into the specific questions to be addressed in an empirical study—one that gathers evidence to describe behavior and to prove or disprove explanations of why that behavior occurs. These explanations are often, but not always, stated in the form of a **hypothesis,** a statement that expresses an informed (or "educated") guess regarding the possible relationship between two or more phenomena.

In his study of suicide, Durkheim challenged the intellectuals and scientists of his day. Through the presentation of verifiable statistical evidence on suicide rates in different societies, he demonstrated that he could predict where and when suicides would be more numerous. Psychological reasons might account for why a particular individual committed suicide, but Durkheim showed that "social variables" such as religion or fluctuations in economic conditions could explain differences in the number of suicides from one society or region to another.

The question that eventually led Durkheim to his empirical study of suicide actually had nothing to do with suicide. Like many educated people of his time, he was troubled by the consequences of large-scale social change in Western nations. In particular, he believed that industrialization and the rapid growth of cities weakened people's attachments to their families and communities. As people became increasingly anonymous and isolated, they were more likely to engage in a variety of self-destructive acts, the most extreme being suicide. In Durkheim's view, the act of suicide could be explained as much by social variables like rates of marriage and divorce as by individual psychological variables like depression or despair. Thus

THEN AND NOW   Suicide in the Public Spotlight

The stock market crash of 1929 led to the suicides of people who had lost fortunes and faced immediate bankruptcy. More recently, the popular

© UPI/Bettmann/Corbis

AP/Wide World Photos

rock star Kurt Cobain killed himself. Both examples illustrate the key findings of Durkheim's pioneering studies of suicide. The suicide of an individual stockbroker or celebrity can be explained by the individual's state of mind at the time. However, the tendency for people to kill themselves when their fortunes change suddenly, or for celebrities to live out-of-control lives that often end in suicide, can be explained by social influences that cause people to feel lost or adrift. Durkheim labeled this feeling *anomie* and traced it to a lack of integration of the individual into social groups and communities.

for Durkheim the study of suicide was a way of exploring the larger concept of integration or lack of integration into society: He sought to discover whether people who were less well integrated into society (i.e., more isolated from other people) were more likely to commit suicide.

If this view was correct, Durkheim reasoned, the rates of suicide among various populations should vary along with measures of social integration. He therefore formulated these hypotheses, among others:

- Suicide rates should be higher for unmarried people than for married people.
- Suicide rates should be higher for people without children than for people with children.
- Suicide rates should be higher for people with higher levels of education (education emphasizes individual achievement, which weakens group ties).
- Suicide rates should be higher in Protestant than in Catholic communities (Protestantism places more stress on individual achievement than Catholicism does, and this in turn weakens group ties).

Each of these hypotheses specifies a relationship between two variables that can be tested—that is, proved true or false—through empirical observation. In sociology, **variables** are characteristics of individuals, groups, or entire societies that can vary from one case to another. In the hypotheses just presented, the suicide rate is a social variable. Religion, education, marital status, and number of children are other variables in these hypotheses. The techniques Durkheim used to establish a set of hypotheses became a model for modern social-scientific research.

Let us examine one of Durkheim's classic hypotheses about suicide to see what it can teach us about applying the scientific method to social issues. In the hypothesis stating that suicide rates should be higher for unmarried people than for married people, Durkheim was proposing that there is a relationship between two variables: incidence of suicide and incidence of marriage. The suicide *rate* is a measure of suicide that takes into account the size of the population. The marriage rate is also based on population size.

In this hypothesis, the suicide rate is referred to as the **dependent variable;** it is the variable that we are trying to explain. Our hypothesis suggests that variations in the suicide rate from one nation to another depend on the influence of another variable: marriage rates in different nations. Marriage rates are referred to as the **independent**

variable. An independent variable is a factor that the researcher believes causes changes in the dependent variable. It is independent of the variable we are trying to explain. (We cannot, for example, imagine explaining variations in marriage rates in terms of changes in suicide rates.)

Extreme care must be used in making statements about causality, however. All social phenomena are caused by interactions among several variables rather than by only one or two. Thus we may say that lower marriage rates are one cause of suicide in a society. We know that there are other causes as well. (We discuss the issue of causality more fully later in the chapter.)

But, clearly, the story is more complicated than that. Some people commit suicide even though they are married and loved. Today some people think about suicide as an alternative to a lingering hospital death. As Durkheim first showed a century ago, suicide can take many forms and have many causes in different societies. Since then, sociologists have argued that before anyone can develop a set of testable hypotheses about the causes of suicide (or any other complex social situation or behavior), it is necessary to know a great deal about the actual experiences of the people involved. (See the Popular Culture and Social Change box on page 30.) Thus even a sociologist who has never contemplated suicide or been part of a suicidal cult can attempt to see the world from the viewpoint of people in suicidal situations to find out what their daily lives are like. If they exist, such studies are usually the first ones consulted when the sociologist begins to conduct research on a particular problem.

Reviewing the Literature

Perhaps the insights one would need to understand the issues surrounding suicide are already available in "the literature"—in existing books or journal articles, published statistics, photos, and other materials. There is no need to conduct new research if the answers sought are already available. Most sociological research therefore begins in the library with a "review of the literature."

To stimulate our sociological imagination about suicide or any other social phenomenon, we need to look at a variety of studies that deal with this issue. But it takes some imagination just to think of the kinds of studies to look for. The various sociological perspectives described in Chapter 1 can help organize the search, especially when the perspectives are framed as questions.

WHO? HOW MANY? WHERE? Who are we talking about and where are they? This is a way of phrasing the ecological perspective, which suggests why that perspective is helpful in beginning research on an issue. In researching almost any subject involving human behavior, it is helpful to ask who is involved and in what numbers, and where the behavior in question occurs. In his pioneering research on suicide, Durkheim asked some very basic questions, including an important ecological one: Do suicide rates vary from one county to another within a nation? This question remains an active area of contemporary research, as we will see shortly.

The ecological perspective leads to two types of studies: community studies and demographic studies. *Community studies* are among the richest research traditions in sociology. They portray the typical day-to-day life of a particular population. An example of a community study of a suicidal group is John R. Hall's *Gone From the Promised Land: Jonestown in American Cultural History* (1987). Hall was not a member of the infamous People's Temple, but he had lived in several communes and religious communities, where he collected firsthand accounts of what it is like to be part of an intense community such as the one led by Jim Jones. If a student wanted to explore what led members of the Heaven's Gate community to commit mass suicide in March 1997, Hall's study would be an excellent resource for ideas and comparisons. A search of the literature on the Heaven's Gate suicide would also turn up many firsthand accounts about what it is like to live among people who are obsessed with extraterrestrials and UFOs.

Demographic studies are also useful in studying the magnitude of a major social phenomenon such as suicide. Such studies provide counts of people in various relevant population categories—in this case, people who are isolated in one way or another, or who have actually attempted or succeeded in committing suicide, or who may be considering assisted suicide because of advanced illness. Demographic studies of suicide offer a wealth of information about this drastic behavior from nations throughout the world. In a recent study, for example, the French National Institute for Demographic Studies reported that "France has the sad privilege to be classed among the nations of the world with the highest rates of suicide. If one eliminates the states of the old communist bloc and China, France, with a suicide rate in the neighborhood of 20 per 100,000, is in the fourth position behind Finland, Denmark, and Austria. All the other nations have a lower suicide rate: Japan (15 per 100,000), Sweden (15), Germany (14), Norway (13), Canada (13), the United States (12), the United Kingdom (7), Italy (7), Greece (3)" (Constantine & Huberman, 2000; Kremer, 1998).

HOW IS THE SITUATION DEFINED? Interactionist approaches to extreme phenomena such as suicide tend to look at how people who decide to take their own lives actually perceive their situation and how their interactions with others influence their behavior. In the case of

POPULAR CULTURE & SOCIAL CHANGE   Singing Out Against Anomie and Suicide

The term *popular culture* refers to the songs, dances, movies, and television shows that millions of people perform and consume as commercial products. Chapter 3 of this book presents formal definitions and examples of culture, including popular culture. For now it is enough to realize that popular culture is as varied as the human race and expresses all the hopes, fears, envy, lust, and other feelings we experience as social beings. Popular music, especially the various forms of rock, reggae, rap, country, and gospel, is among the most influential forms of popular culture among young people throughout the world because it directly addresses the feelings and challenges they face.

Bruce Springsteen sings about the feelings of loss that people experience when their factories are torn down. The murdered singer Selena captured the hearts of millions by singing popular Tejano songs that described her people's trials in coping with new social and economic conditions along the rapidly industrializing Texas–Mexico border. And in 1994 Susan Aglukark, a popular Eskimo singer from the frozen shores of Hudson Bay, became the first of her people ever to sign a major recording contract. EMI Music Canada signed her to produce more of her

Susan Aglukark.

haunting songs about the struggle of aboriginal people in the Eskimo-controlled region of Nunavut, which extends well above the Arctic Circle in the Northwest Territories.

Aglukark's Inuit, or Eskimo, name is Uuliniq, which means "scarred from burns." Although she is not literally scarred—the name is purely symbolic—the same symbolic name could easily be applied to all of Canada's 35,000 Eskimo people. Like people living at the edges of industrialization and urbanization throughout the world, they have experienced severe disruptions in their traditional way of life. They can no longer maintain their existence as a hunting-and-gathering people, not only because of depleted supplies of game but also because of the far-reaching effects of changing lifestyles and technologies. For example, their need for gasoline to power generators and snowmobiles and for televisions and prepared foods like coffee and sugar makes it impossible for them to maintain their traditional culture.

As a result of these social changes, many of Aglukark's people are experiencing *anomie,* or normlessness. Caught between the modern and the traditional, not knowing how to find work or where to go for advice, they often turn to alcohol and drugs, become angry and abusive, or even commit suicide. Aglukark's music has elements of rock and country gospel, but the words deal with subjects such as a girlhood friend who has taken her own life. She hopes that her songs will help young people everywhere deal with the feelings that lead them to despair and sometimes to suicide. Indeed, suicide rates are alarmingly high among indigenous young people, who often feel isolated and despair of ever seeing improvement in their lives. Popular music is one way of communicating with the alienated young people of the far north, which helps explain Susan Aglukark's popularity. It also explains why other Canadian rock groups, such as The Dreamcatchers, are touring the communities of the far north to

This high school student is wearing her version of "gothic" clothing. Just because she has chosen to adopt this particular uniform of a youth subculture does not automatically mean she is angry or expressing anomie. She is, however, sending a message to her schoolmates about which group she identifies with.

entertain young people and persuade them that suicide is not the only alternative to their bleak lives.

For sociologists who seek to help reduce suicide rates, especially among young people, these efforts are encouraging, but we naturally wonder how effective they are. Sociological research can show where these efforts are working and where they can be improved. Thus we ask questions such as "How many people attend the concerts? Are these numbers growing? When we speak to young people who attend the concerts, do they feel more hope for the future than they did before?" Even without ambitious surveys, we can learn a good deal about the impact of popular culture by counting audiences and listening carefully to the messages they are hearing.

suicide, such studies are not common, but sociological research can often draw on firsthand accounts. This is especially true of sensational suicides like the Heaven's Gate case: Since the 1997 mass suicide, there have been numerous testimonials by former cult members describing how followers surrender their personal autonomy to the will of the leader and accept the leader's extreme definition of the situation (Bearak, 1997; Brooke, 1997). For the Heaven's Gate cult, the definition of the situation was that all who killed themselves would be immediately transported to a better existence among the superior beings accompanying the Hale-Bopp comet. In fact, it was possible to follow the development of the deadly cult's beliefs on the Internet, which was also used to recruit new cult members (Levy, 1997).

WHAT GROUPS OR ORGANIZATIONS ARE INVOLVED? This question stems from the functionalist perspective. It asks how society is organized to deal with a social issue or problem. Functionalist sociologists are concerned with how social policies actually function, as opposed to how they are supposed to function. Studies of social interventions to prevent suicide, for example, would describe how community crisis hotlines are established and who operates them, and ideally would include some measures of how effective they are. These measures might include how many calls are received and the nature of the calls (e.g., actual suicide threats, people in need of counseling, parents or guardians of possible teenage suicides, and so on). There might also be some description of how many times the potential suicide victim was saved through the actual intervention of crisis center personnel.

WHAT DIFFERENCE DOES POWER MAKE? This question arises from the conflict perspective. Studies that take a conflict approach to suicide would be likely to compare suicide rates for men and women around the world. The differences would be striking. In many nations women are far more likely than men to kill themselves. Why this is so has a lot to do with men's power and women's lack of power in different societies. In remote parts of India, for example, a widowed woman is expected either to kill herself upon her husband's death or to submit herself entirely to the will of her husband's family—in which case she often serves essentially as a house slave, a condition that itself can drive a person to suicide. In some African and Latin American societies where there are arranged marriages or where women are routinely sexually exploited, we also find higher suicide rates for women than for men. In consequence, many sociologists argue that changes in the relative power of women, resulting from greater literacy, access to occupations, and basic protections under the law, would improve the balance of power between the sexes

and lead to more equal rates of suicide, in addition to many other benefits.

IS GENDER ADDRESSED ADEQUATELY? A problem with some social-scientific research literature is that the perspectives and experiences of men are assumed to apply to women as well. In fact, the same criticism applies to issues of race. The subjects of earlier research were often primarily white males, and their experience was often generalized to all others in the society, regardless of gender or race. But the most glaring problems occurred because male researchers tended to overlook the likelihood that women's experiences and perspectives would differ from those of their male subjects. As Sandra Harding, who has conducted extensive research on this problem, notes,

> Three decades ago women's movements around the globe were rigorously questioning the exclusion of women, their interests, and visions of the good life, from policy debates, including those of science ... What assumptions and processes had led male scientists and policy-makers to equate their own concerns and opinions with human perspectives in general? (1998, p. 1)

One such assumption, prevalent in mid-twentieth-century research, was that since women were subordinate to men, their membership in different social classes could be determined from the social class of their husbands. Men who were classified as members of the working class, for example, were assumed to have wives who were in the same class. Research on women who were not married or were working outside the home was extremely limited. But as women enter the labor force in ever-greater numbers and as far more women conduct sociological research, this situation has changed; one can more easily find research and develop research projects in which women are fully represented in the research design and the analysis of results (Maynard, 2002).

Today, when one searches the literature on suicide, there is quite an array of good literature on suicide among women as well as studies that compare suicide rates by gender. And these studies often relate directly to the classic work of Durkheim. For example, a recent study of suicide among women in North Carolina found that suicide rates for white women were three times higher than those for African-American women. The researchers explain their findings, in part, with a Durkheimian argument: They note that their data show that African-American women are more involved in extensive family kinship groups than are many white women. The latter often arrive in the state from elsewhere and are not surrounded by family and friends of long standing, and this sense of relative isolation may help explain why their despair is not diffused by participation in social groups. Because about 6,000 women commit suicide annually in the United States, making suicide the second leading cause of death for women under 50, research directed specifically at suicide among women is clearly important in developing more effective intervention strategies (*Women's Health Weekly,* 2003).

The foregoing are only a few of the studies one would find in a review of the sociological literature on suicide. They are not cataloged according to the basic sociological perspectives. Rather, one needs to know what questions each of the sociological perspectives raises about an issue. For any research subject, if you ask questions about who and where and how people interact, what organizations and policies guide their actions, and who has the power, you will be well on your way toward a thorough review of what is known about the issue you plan to study.

THE BASIC METHODS

Once the researcher has specified a question, developed hypotheses, and reviewed the literature, the next step is to decide on the method or methods to be used in conducting the actual research. Sociological research methods are the techniques an investigator uses to systematically gather information, or *data,* to help answer a question about some aspect of society. The variety of methods that may be used is vast, with the choice of a method depending largely on the type of question being asked. The most frequently used methods are observation, experiments, and surveys. These are summarized in the Study Chart on page 33.

Observation

PARTICIPANT OBSERVATION   Much sociological research requires direct observation of the people being studied. Community studies like Hall's work on the People's Temple are based on lengthy periods spent observing a particular group. This research method is rarely successful unless the sociologist also participates in the daily life of the people he or she is observing—that is, becomes their friend and a member of their social groups. Therefore, the central method of community studies is known as **participant observation.** The sociologist attempts to be both an objective observer of events and an actual participant in the social milieu under study—not an easy task for even the most experienced researcher. In such situations, the observer faithfully records his or her observations and interactions in *field notes,* which supply the descriptive data that will be used in the analysis and writing phases of the study.

An excellent example of a study based on participant observation is Donna Gaines's study *Teenage Wasteland* (1998). Gaines spent many months "hanging out" and speaking with teenagers in a relatively affluent suburban community adjacent to a large central city. Many of the teenagers lived lives devoted to school, family, and part-time jobs. But others became what Gaines called "suburbia's dead-end kids." They experimented with drugs, were attracted to satanism and heavy metal rock music, and flirted with violence and suicide, sometimes with tragic consequences. These young people, who often thought of themselves as "burnouts," described their lives to Gaines because she listened to them and showed that she could be trusted. In the beginning, they tested her by giving her information and telling her not to share it with other kids. Once they saw that she did not divulge secrets, she was able to learn much more about their behavior. And by listening carefully she also learned how some kids who seem to be at a dead end are actually struggling to create a better world for themselves, often against great odds.

This kind of research describes the quality of life of the people involved; therefore it is often called *qualitative* research to distinguish it from the *quantitative* research methods we will consider shortly. James Coleman observes that in qualitative research "we report a stream of action in which the interlinking of events suggests how the [social] system functions" (1964, p. 222).

Another excellent example of a study based on participant observation is Douglas Harper's classic, *Good Company* (1982). Harper spent many months riding on freight trains and living in hobo "jungles." His goal was to describe how hoboes, or tramps or bums as they are often called, actually live and how they learn to trust or distrust one another in a world considered deviant by members of "respectable" society. Harper had to learn how to live the nomadic and often dangerous life of the hobo, which meant that he needed to establish a relationship with someone in that life who could serve as his mentor. The successful participant observer usually finds at least one such person. In Harper's case, a hobo named Carl made it possible for him to participate in, and therefore to understand and write about, the hobo's world.

Qualitative research carried out "in the field" where behavior is actually occurring is the best method for analyzing the processes of human interaction. If Donna Gaines had not spent a good deal of time with suburban teenagers, she would not have obtained nearly as many insights into their behavior. A shortcoming of this approach, however, is that it is usually based on a single community, group, or social system, which makes it difficult to generalize the findings to other social settings. Thus community studies and other types of qualitative studies are most often used for exploratory research, and the findings serve as a basis for generating hypotheses for further research.

THE BASIC METHODS

METHOD	DESCRIPTION	EXAMPLE
Participant Observation	A form of field observation in which the observer participates to some degree in the lives of the people being observed.	Martin Sanchez-Jankowski spends many months with youth gangs, gaining their trust and learning gang norms regarding violence.
Unobtrusive Measures	Observational techniques that measure behavior but intrude as little as possible into actual social settings.	Media researchers find out what radio stations different types of cars are tuned to in order to learn about the listening tastes of different segments of the public.
Controlled Experiment	An experimental situation in which the researcher manipulates an independent variable in order to observe and measure changes in a dependent variable.	Judith Gerone of the Manpower Research and Development Corporation conducts controlled experiments to find out what types of training and job programs are most effective in reducing state welfare rolls.
Field Experiment	An experimental situation in which the researcher observes and studies subjects in their natural setting.	Milton Rokeach meets three delusional mental patients, each of whom believes he is Jesus Christ. He introduces them to each other to learn how they incorporate conflicting information into their self-presentations.
Survey	Research in which a sample of respondents drawn from a specific population respond to questions either in an interview or on a questionnaire.	A team of National Opinion Research Center sociologists survey the public about their sexual behavior and attitudes.

UNOBTRUSIVE MEASURES Observation can employ numerous other techniques besides direct participation. Among these are **unobtrusive measures,** observational techniques that measure the effects of behavior but intrude as little as possible into actual social settings. Here are some examples:

The floor tiles around the hatching-chick exhibit at Chicago's Museum of Science and Industry must be replaced every six weeks. Tiles in other parts of the museum need not be replaced for years. The selective erosion of tiles, indexed by the replacement rate, is a measure of the relative popularity of exhibits.

Chinese jade dealers have used the pupil dilation of their customers as a measure of the client's interest in particular stones. (Webb et al., 1966, p. 2)

To study changes in the diet of Americans, investigators sifted through more than 2,000 household trash collections to measure the amount of fat being trimmed from meat packages. (Rathje, 1993)

Observations like these can be transformed into useful measures of the variables under study. Their nature is limited only by the researcher's creativity, and they intrude far less into people's lives than do interviews or participant observation.

VISUAL SOCIOLOGY An increasingly popular set of observational techniques involves the use of photography and videotape, or *visual sociology.* These techniques can be just as obtrusive as interviewing, if not more so, but they can also be used in unobtrusive ways, depending on the questions being asked. A classic example of the use of photographic data is the work of the French anthropologist Claude Levi-Strauss. His extensive explorations in Brazil in the late 1930s provided priceless images of what life was like for the indigenous tribes of the Amazonian region before the most powerful effects of conquest and forced modernization began to be felt. Levi-Strauss created a photographic record of his interactions with the tribespeople; the results offer some rare glimpses of what social-scientific field research in simpler societies was like during the early part of the twentieth century. Many of his photos also show how rapid social change was altering the life of the Indians (Levi-Strauss, 1995).

Another powerful example of visual sociology is found in the work of Letizia Battaglia and Franco Zecchin

© Franco Zecchin

This photo by Letizia Battaglia of a murdered Mafia captain in Palermo, Sicily, is an excellent example of visual sociology because it shows that the violence of organized crime is also part of daily life. Here, three generations of the man's family—wife, daughter, and mother—mourn his death.

(1989), whose photographic studies of violence and Mafia influence in the Sicilian town of Palermo offer unique insights into the way organized crime pervades the life of a city. Their photos, such as the one shown here of women mourning for a loved but criminal family member, reveal how life is lived among people for whom organized crime and murder are a fact of daily existence in a world of poverty and relative lack of opportunity.

Applying your sociological imagination to visual material can be both interesting and informative. Levi-Strauss's work and the photos of Battaglia and Zecchin are only two examples of the rich vein of visual sociology that is captured in photographs, as well as in works of fine art. Similar examples are presented in the Visual Sociology and Art and the Sociological Eye boxes that appear throughout this book.

Experiments

Although for both moral and practical reasons sociologists do not have many opportunities to perform experiments, a large body of literature in the social sciences is based on experiments. There are two experimental models that social scientists use frequently. The first and most rigorous is the controlled experiment conducted in a lab-

The Sociological Observer

These two rescue workers are approaching a man who is threatening to commit suicide by jumping from the top of a suspension bridge. He seems to be warning them not to approach any closer. In the cupola of their cherry picker, the rescue workers are safe for the time being, but in order to remove the man from his suicidal position, they will have to risk their own lives.

What do you think the rescue workers are trying to communicate to the distraught man? What emotions does the photo evoke in you as you study it? What positive examples does the behavior you see in the photo offer to others in society? (See page 45 for further insights into the sociological content of this photo.)

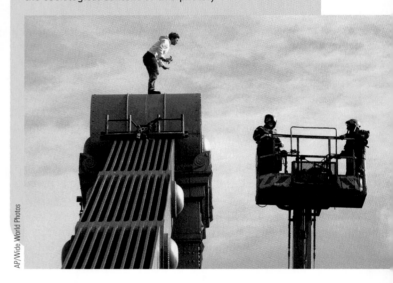

AP/Wide World Photos

oratory. The second is the field experiment, which is often used to test public policies that are applied to some groups but not to others.

CONTROLLED EXPERIMENTS   The **controlled experiment** allows the researcher to manipulate an independent variable in order to observe and measure changes in a dependent variable. The experimenter forms an **experimental group** that will experience a change in the independent variable (the "treatment") and a **control group** that will not experience the treatment but whose behavior will be compared with that of the experimental group. (The control group is similar to the experimental group in every other way.) This type of experiment is especially characteristic of studies at the micro level of sociological research.

Consider an example: Which line in Figure 2.1(b) appears to match the line in Figure 2.1(a) most closely?

Could anything persuade you that a line other than the one you have selected is the correct choice? This simple diagram formed the basis of a famous series of experiments conducted by Solomon Asch in the early 1950s. They showed that the opinion of the majority can have an extremely powerful influence on that of an individual.

Asch's control group consisted of subjects[1] who were seated together in a room but were allowed to make their judgments independently. When they looked at sets of lines like those in Figure 2.1, the subjects in this group invariably matched the correct lines, just as you no doubt have. But in the experimental group a different result was produced by the introduction of an independent variable: group pressure.

Asch's experimental group consisted of subjects who were asked to announce their decisions aloud in the group setting. Each subject was brought into a room with eight people who posed as other subjects but were actually confederates of the experimenter. When the lines were flashed on a screen, those "subjects" all chose a line that was not the matching one. When it was the real subject's turn to choose, he or she was faced with the unanimous opinion of a majority of "subjects" who had picked the wrong line. Thirty-two percent of the real subjects went along with the majority and chose the wrong line as well. And even among the subjects Asch called "independent" (the 68 percent of the real subjects who gave the correct response despite the pressure of the majority), there was a great deal of variation. Some gave the correct response at all times, whereas others gave it only part of the time. This conforming response was less likely when there was at least one other person in the group who also went against the majority. By varying the number of people who said that the shorter line was longer, Asch was varying the degree of group pressure experienced by the subject. Higher levels of the independent variable (group pressure) thus produced more "errors," or choices of the wrong line (Asch, 1966).

FIELD EXPERIMENTS **Field experiments** are used extensively in evaluating public programs that address specific social problems. In these experiments, there is usually a "treatment group" of people who participate in the program and a control group of people who do not. In one example of this type of experiment, Angelo Atondo, Mauro Chavez, and Richard Regua of California's Evergreen Valley College attempted to test the theory that if students at risk of failure are linked with adult mentors from their own communities, their chances of success will improve (Bashi, 1991). This popular theory stems in part from an influential arti-

Figure 2.1 Lines Used in the Asch Experiment on Conformity

Cards like these were used in the Asch experiment. Subjects were asked to judge the lengths of various lines by comparing them with the three lines on the bottom card. The line on the top card quite obviously matches line B on the bottom card; all of the judgments were this simple.

cle in the *Harvard Business Review* titled "Everyone Who Makes It Has a Mentor" (Collins & Scott, 1978). Many successful people from all walks of life, especially those who have escaped from impoverished backgrounds, say that they benefited greatly from the guidance of a mentor who steered them toward constructive goals. Most mentors do not actually tutor the individuals they spend time with; instead, they teach through conversation and example.

Researchers have found little evidence to prove that mentors actually make a difference. Unless one can compare students who had mentors with similar students who did not, it is impossible to say with any scientific certainty—that is, beyond individual stories of success or failure—whether the mentors made a difference. The Evergreen Valley College researchers therefore assigned 115 entering Latino students with low English proficiency to Latino mentors with excellent English skills. Their control group was composed of a comparable number of Latino students with similar characteristics; these students were not assigned to mentors. Both groups attended the same classes and took the same exams. At the end of the semester, 89 percent of the students with mentors passed the freshman English course, but only

---

[1]The term *subject* refers to a person who participates in a controlled experiment.

46 percent of the students in the control group passed the same course. Later, more of the students with mentors went on to 4-year colleges. Although much more controlled research of this nature needs to be done before we can fully understand how mentors help students overcome their educational problems, this example shows how a field experiment can advance our understanding of a social issue like success and failure in school (Bashi, 1991).

Sociologists can conduct "natural experiments" when two similar groups receive differing treatments and the results can be measured. An example of such an experiment deals with problems of teenagers, including early pregnancy, school failure, and suicide. Gregory J. Duncan and Jeanne Brooks-Gunn (1997) studied the lives of teenagers growing up in low-income neighborhoods. By comparing children from families with very similar social characteristics (e.g., income, race, ethnic background, education), they could identify the effects of certain characteristics of their surroundings (e.g., rates of poverty, crime, suicide, and drug abuse) on their behavior.

THE HAWTHORNE EFFECT   A common problem of experimental studies is that just by paying attention to people in an experimental group the researcher may be introducing additional variables. This problem was recognized for the first time in the late 1930s, when a team of researchers led by Elton Mayo conducted a famous series of experiments at Western Electric's Hawthorne plant. The purpose of the study was to determine the effects of various environmental and social conditions on the workers' productivity. One hypothesis was that improvements in the physical features of the workplace (such as better lighting) and improved social conditions (coffee breaks, different methods of payment, and so on) would result in greater productivity (the dependent variable). But it appeared that *no matter what the experimenters did,* the workers' productivity increased. When the experimenters improved the lighting, the workers' productivity increased over that of the control group. When they dimmed the lights, productivity went up again. This was true even when the workers were subjected to somewhat worse conditions or were returned to their original conditions.

At first this series of experiments was considered a failure, and the researchers concluded that the variables they were introducing had little to do with the changes in productivity that resulted. But on further reflection, they realized that the real independent variable was not better working conditions but, simply, *attention.* The workers liked the attention they were getting; it made them feel special, so they worked harder. This realization led the researchers to design experiments dealing with the effects of attention from supervisors and better communication between workers and their managers; those experiments led

to a new philosophy of worker–management relations, described in Chapter 19. Today the term **Hawthorne effect** is used to refer to any unintended effect that results from the attention given to subjects in an experiment.

The Hawthorne effect occurs in a variety of experimental situations. For example, in the Evergreen Valley College experiment described earlier, it is possible that the students with mentors were more successful than the students in the control group because they were getting extra attention from adults. Over time the effects of that attention may disappear, and the experimenters may conclude that once the novelty of the extra attention wears off, students with mentors do not do appreciably better than others. Sophisticated evaluations of educational change try to anticipate the Hawthorne effect by making sure that the experimental group does not get more attention than the control group.

Survey Research

A sociological *survey* asks people to give precise information about their behavior, their attitudes, and at times the behavior and attitudes of others (e.g., other members of their households). There is a world of difference between the modern sociological survey and the "social surveys" conducted around the turn of the twentieth century (see Chapter 1). Those surveys attempted to present an unbiased, factual account of the social conditions of a specific community; their findings could not be applied to other groups. In contrast, today's survey techniques make it possible to *generalize* from a small sample of respondents to an entire population. An example is election polls, in which a small sample of 1,000 or 2,000 respondents can be used to predict how the entire electorate will vote in a presidential election. Done properly, the modern survey is one of the most powerful tools available to social scientists.

NATIONAL CENSUSES   Surveys are the central method used in election polling, market research, opinion polling, television ratings, and a host of other applications. The most ambitious and most heavily used sociological surveys are national censuses. A *national census* is a full enumeration of every member of the society—a regular system for counting its people and determining where and under what conditions they live, how they work and gain income, their patterns of family composition, their age distribution, their levels of educational attainment, and related data. Without these measures, a nation cannot plan intelligently for the needs of its people. The United States conducts a national census every 10 years. The 2000 census, the 22nd in the nation's history, was the largest and most complex ever undertaken; it enumerated about 275 million people in about 115 million housing units.

SAMPLE SURVEYS   Once a national census has gathered the basic demographic and ecological facts about a nation's people, it is possible to add more information by using smaller and far less costly **sample surveys.** In the United States, this is done regularly through the Census Bureau's Current Population Survey (CPS). From the CPS we get monthly estimates of employment and unemployment, poverty, births, deaths, marriages, divorces, social insurance and welfare, and many other indicators of the social well-being and problems of the American people.

OPINION POLLS   Another type of survey research, pioneered by sociologists earlier in this century, is the *opinion poll.* Today opinion polling is a $3.5 billion industry. Opinion polls are used by marketing firms to help corporations make decisions about their products; political candidates and their staffs use them to measure the progress of their campaigns; and elected officials use polls to monitor public opinion on key political and economic issues.

A good example of an opinion poll is the Gallup Poll, conducted regularly by the Gallup Organization, one of the nation's oldest and most respected public opinion survey companies. In addition to this private polling corporation, research groups at a number of major universities conduct large-scale national opinion polls; an example is the National Opinion Research Center (NORC) at the University of Chicago.

The Gallup Poll illustrates how opinion surveys allow political leaders and the public to follow trends in the way people feel about social issues of all kinds. Table 2.1 shows how Americans rank different social issues and how these ratings changed between 2002 and 2003. Clearly, the greatest change has occurred in how Americans worry about the economy and unemployment. The threat of terrorism and fears about the availability or affordability of health care may worry more of the survey's respondents, but the greatest increase occurred in their worries about the state of the economy. These results are watched extremely carefully by political commentators and professional political consultants because they often indicate how voters will react to these issues in political campaigns or in their feelings about what government officials are doing, or not doing, about these issues.

Polls like these generalize from a sample of 1,500 respondents, on the average, to the entire U.S. population. How is it possible that a relatively small number of respondents can accurately represent the distributions of attitudes in a population of over 280 million people? The answer is found in the techniques used to choose a random **sample** of the population in question. The term *sample* refers to a set of respondents selected from a specific population. The first step in selecting a sample is to define the population to be sampled; in our example the population

TABLE 2.1

Percentage of Americans who Worry a "Great Deal" about Selected Problems, 2002 and 2003

	2002	2003	Change
The economy	37%	44%	+7%
Illegal immigration	33	37	+4
Unemployment	33	36	+3
Possibility of future terrorist attacks in U.S.	49	49	0
Hunger and homelessness	37	37	0
Availability and affordability of health care	56	55	−1
Quality of the environment	35	34	−1
Race relations	23	22	−1
Crime and violence	49	45	−4
Availability and affordability of energy	32	27	−5
Drug use	49	42	−7

Source: The Gallup Poll, 2003.

consists of adult American citizens. The next step is to establish rules for the *random* selection of respondents. The goal of this procedure is to ensure that within the specified population everyone has an equal chance, or *probability,* of being selected to answer the survey questions. A sample in which potential respondents do not all have the same probability of being included is called a *biased sample.* To avoid bias, respondents must be selected by some process of random sampling.[2] In other words, any form of "volunteering" to be interviewed must be eliminated. (For example, the researcher cannot intentionally select his or her friends to be part of the sample.) Only a random sample can be considered truly representative of the target population.

Surveys that are not based on random samples can be misleading. In a famous example from the early days of surveys, researchers predicted that candidate Alf Landon would defeat the incumbent president, Franklin D. Roosevelt, in the 1936 election. They based their prediction on data from a telephone survey, but at the time many low-income households did not have telephones. The survey therefore overrepresented the opinions of those with higher incomes, who were less likely to vote for Roosevelt. Roosevelt won by a landslide, and since then political pollsters have been much more alert to the problem of sample bias. But many contemporary surveys also produce biased results. Most mail

---

[2]Random sampling is accomplished by a variety of statistical techniques that are discussed in more advanced courses.

surveys and many telephone surveys that claim to be conducting research are actually marketing surveys designed to tap the opinions of particular subgroups rather than a representative sample of the entire population.

SAMPLING ERROR   Before leaving the subject of opinion polling, we should mention one additional point. Polls are subject to *sampling error.* A sampling error of plus or minus 3 percentage points, for example, would be normal in a national sample of 1,500 to 2,000 respondents. This is important information for anyone who reads and interprets poll data. It means that a difference of 3 percent or less between the percentages of American adults expressing certain opinions could be due to chance rather than to a real difference in the distribution of opinions. In other words, it is possible that just by chance a higher percentage of people with a certain opinion was included in the sample than is actually the case in the total population. The possibility of sampling error is more critical when there is a small difference between two sets of responses—for example, when 51 percent of the sample favors one presidential candidate and 49 percent favors another. In this example, the survey analysts would have to conclude that the election is "too close to call."

QUESTIONNAIRE DESIGN   Just as important as careful selection of the sample to be interviewed is the design of the *instrument,* or questionnaire, to be used in the survey. Questionnaire design is both a science and an art. Questions must be worded precisely yet be easily understood. Above all, the questions must be worded in such a way as to avoid biasing the answers. For example, the General Social Survey asked whether the United States was spending too much, too little, or about the right amount on "assistance to the poor." About 66 percent of the respondents answered "too little." But when "welfare" was substituted for "assistance to the poor," the findings were almost reversed, with slightly less than 50 percent responding that too much was being spent on welfare (Kagay & Elder, 1992). (See the Sociological Methods box on page 39.)

One of the first decisions to make in designing survey questions is whether they should be open or closed. **Closed questions** require respondents to select from a set of answers, whereas **open questions** allow them to say whatever comes to mind. The items in the Sociological Methods box are examples of closed questions. An example of an open question would be "Please tell me how you feel about your neighborhood." In answering this type of question, the respondent can say that he or she does not like the neighborhood at all or give one or more reasons for liking it. The interviewer attempts to write down the answers in the respondent's own words.

When researchers wish to include both forced-choice categories and freely given opinions in a single survey, the questionnaire usually begins with open questions and then shifts to closed questions on the same subject. Survey instruments that rely on open questions are often called *interview guides.* They guide the researcher's questions in certain directions and emphasize certain categories of information, but they also allow the interviewer to follow up respondents' comments with further questions.

Research Ethics and the Rights of Respondents

In asking any type of question in a survey or other type of sociological study, the researcher must be aware of the rights of respondents. Much sociological research deals with the personal lives and inner thoughts of real human beings. Although most of that research seems relatively innocent, there are many times when the questions asked or the behaviors witnessed may be embarrassing or even more damaging. In one famous example, Laud Humphreys (1970, 1975) studied interactions between men seeking casual sexual encounters in public restrooms. Many of his colleagues attacked him for invading the men's privacy. Others defended him for daring to investigate what had until then been a taboo subject (homosexuality and bisexuality). After all, they reasoned, Humphreys was careful to keep the men's identities secret. But he also followed some of the men home and conducted interviews with them there. They were not aware that he knew about their homosexual activities, and on reflection Humphreys admitted that he had deceived his subjects.

Sociologists continue to debate the ethical dilemmas raised by Humphreys's research and by studies like the Asch experiment (in which the subject is duped and may feel embarrassed). As a result of such controversies, the federal government now requires that research involving human subjects be monitored by "human subjects review panels" at all research institutions that receive federal funding. A research review must be undertaken before a study can be funded or approved for degree credit. To pass the review, the researcher must provide proof that he or she has taken precautions to protect the fundamental rights of human subjects. Those rights include privacy, informed consent, and confidentiality.

The right of **privacy** can be defined as "the right of the individual to define for himself, with only extraordinary exceptions in the interest of society, when and on what terms his acts should be revealed to the general public" (Westin, 1967, p. 373). **Confidentiality** is closely related to privacy. When a respondent is told that information will remain confidential, the researcher may not pass it on to anyone else in a form that can be traced to that respondent. The information can be pooled with information provided by other respondents, but extreme care must be taken to

SOCIOLOGICAL METHODS

Avoiding Bias in Survey Questions

In *Asking Questions: A Practical Guide to Questionnaire Design* (1982), survey researchers Seymour Sudman and Norman Bradburn of the National Opinion Research Center describe a common abuse of survey methods: the use of biased questions. In a questionnaire mailed to them by a lobbying group, the authors noticed questions like these:

1. Do you feel there is too much power concentrated in the hands of labor union officials?

   yes ___ no ___

2. Are you in favor of forcing state, county, and municipal employees to pay union dues to hold their government jobs?

   yes ___ no ___

3. Are you in favor of allowing construction union czars the power to shut down an entire construction site because of a dispute with a single contractor, thus forcing even more workers to knuckle under to union agencies?

   yes ___ no ___

These questions violate even the simplest rules of objectivity in questionnaire design. As the authors point out, they are "loaded with nonneutral words: 'forcing,' 'union czars,' 'knuckle under.'" Such questions are "deceptive and unethical, but they are not illegal" (p. 3).

To eliminate bias, one would have to begin by rephrasing the questions. For example, the first question could read something like this:

1. Which answer best sums up your feeling about the amount of power held by labor union officials today?
   a. too much power
   b. about the right amount of power
   c. too little power
   d. don't know

Fair questions avoid nonneutral words and give the respondent an opportunity to answer on either side of the issue or to say that he or she does not know. Whenever you read the results of a survey, ask yourself whether the questions are free of obvious bias, if they are specific or general, and if they are threatening or nonthreatening to the respondent. Such an evaluation can make a great difference in how you view the answers.

---

ensure that none of the responses can be traced to a particular individual.

Informed consent refers to statements made to respondents (usually before any questions are asked) about what they are being asked and how the information they supply will be used. It includes the assurance that their participation is voluntary—that is, that there is no compulsion to answer questions or give information. The respondent should be allowed to judge the degree of personal risk involved in answering questions even when an assurance of confidentiality has been given.

The ethics of social research require careful attention. Before undertaking research in which you plan to ask people questions of any kind, be sure you have thought out the ethical issues and checked with your instructor about the ethics of your methods of collecting data and presenting them to the public.

ANALYZING THE DATA

Survey research normally is designed to generate numerical data regarding how certain variables are distributed in the population under study. To understand how such data are presented and analyzed, refer to Tables 2.2, 2.3, and 2.4. We will use these tables as a framework for a discussion of some of the basic techniques of quantitative data presentation and analysis. Other types of sociological data

and analytical techniques are explained at appropriate points in later chapters.

In approaching a statistical table, the first step is to read the title carefully. The title should state exactly what information is presented in the table, including the *units of*

TABLE 2.2

Types of Households in the United States, 1970 and 2000 (in thousands)

Type of Household	1970	2000
All households	**63,401**	**105,480**
Nonfamily households	**11,945**	**33,693**
Family households	**51,456**	**71,787**
No own children under 18	22,725	37,199
With own children under 18	28,731	34,588
Married-couple family	44,728	54,493
No own children under 18	19,196	29,657
With own children under 18	25,532	24,836
Male householder	1,228	4,394
No own children under 18	887	2,179
With own children under 18	341	2,215
Female householder	5,500	12,900
No own children under 18	2,642	5,338
With own children under 18	2,858	7,562

Source: Adapted from *Statistical Abstract,* 2002.

TABLE 2.3

Types of Households in the United States, 1970 and 2000 (as percentage of total households)

Type of Household	1970	2000
All households	100.0	100.0
Nonfamily households	18.8	31.9
Family households	81.2	68.1
No own children under 18	35.8	35.3
With own children under 18	45.3	32.8
Married-couple family	70.5	51.7
No own children under 18	30.3	28.1
With own children under 18	40.3	23.5
Male householder	1.9	4.2
No own children under 18	1.4	2.1
With own children under 18	0.5	2.1
Female householder	8.7	12.2
No own children under 18	4.2	5.1
With own children under 18	4.5	7.2

analysis—that is, the entity (e.g., individual, family, group) to which a measure applies. In Tables 2.2 and 2.3, the units of analysis are households; in Table 2.4, they are married-couple families.

Also check the source of the information presented in the table. This is usually given in a source note at the end of the table. The source indicates the quality of the data (census data are considered to be of very high quality) and tells the reader where those data can be verified or where further information can be obtained.

Frequency Distributions

As you begin to study the table, make sure you understand what kind of information is being presented. The numbers in Table 2.2 are **frequency distributions.** For each year (1970 and 2000), they show how various types of households were distributed in the U.S. population. Frequency

TABLE 2.4

Married-Couple Families, by Number of Own Children Under 18, 1970 and 2000 (as percentage of total households)

	1970	2000
Married-couple families	100.0	100.0
No own children under 18	42.9	54.4
With own children under 18	57.1	45.6

distributions indicate how many observations fall within each category of a variable. Thus, within the category of "Married-couple family" for the variable "Type of Household," Table 2.2 indicates that there were 44,728,000 households in the United States in 1970 and that the total increased to 54,493,000 by 2000.

Table 2.2 can tell us a great deal about social change in the United States. For example, social scientists use the term *household* to designate all the people residing at a given address, provided that the address is not a hospital, school, jail, army barracks, or other "residential institution." A household is not necessarily a married-couple family, as is evident from the categories listed in Table 2.2. There are also many households in which a male, with or without his own children, or a female, with or without her own children, is the primary reporting adult. There are also millions of nonfamily households, in which the adults reporting to the census takers are not related. These include people who are roommates, people who are cohabiting, people who are sharing a house or apartment but do not consider themselves roommates, and many other possibilities.

In earlier times, it was considered unfortunate and a bit odd for a woman who was not a widow to head a household with children. It was assumed that a true family was composed of a male head, his wife, their children, and anyone related to them by blood who lived on their premises. The numbers in Table 2.2 show, however, that the number of female-headed households more than doubled between 1970 and 2000. The data also show that there was an increase in the number of family households (from 51.5 million in 1970 to 71.8 million in 2000), and almost as great a jump in the number of nonfamily households (from 11.9 million in 1970 to 33.7 million in 2000).

Percent Analysis

Comparing the numbers for 1970 and 2000 in Table 2.2 can be misleading. Remember that these are absolute numbers. They show that the number of nonfamily households has increased and that the number of female-headed and male-headed households has increased. However, the number of married-couple families has also grown, as has the total number of households. How, then, can we evaluate the importance of these various changes?

To compare categories from one period to another, we need a way of considering changes in the overall size of the population. This can be done through **percent analysis.** Here is an example:

Table 2.2 shows that between 1970 and 2000 the number of male-headed households with one or more children rose from 341,000 to 2,215,000—a sixfold increase. But how important is this increase in view of the increase in the total population between 1970 and 2000? By using the total number of households in each year as the base and calculating the percentage of each household type for that year, we can "hold constant" the effect of the increase in the total number of households. In the case of male-headed households with one or more children, we find that the increase as a percentage of all households (from 0.54 percent in 1970 to 2.10 percent in 2000) is not as important as the increase in absolute numbers would suggest. The calculation is as follows:

$$341,000/63,401,000 \times 100 = 0.54$$
$$2,215,000/105,480,000 \times 100 = 2.10$$

Table 2.3 presents each household type as a percentage of total households in that year. This way of presenting the data eliminates the effect of the increase in overall population size between 1970 and 2000. The percentages in Table 2.3 reveal some significant changes that would not be evident from a comparison of absolute numbers. For example, although Table 2.2 seems to indicate that there has been an increase in married-couple families, Table 2.3 shows that when we control for the overall increase in households, married couples actually declined as a proportion of the total, from 70.5 percent in 1970 to 51.7 percent in 2000. The proportion of female-headed families, especially those with children, increased during the period. So did the proportion of nonfamily households.

But we cannot yet view these findings as definite. We must examine them carefully to be sure we are making the right kinds of comparisons. Look again at Table 2.3. In the category of "Married-couple family," those with no children of their own decreased as a proportion of total households—from 30.3 percent in 1970 to 28.1 percent in 2000. But this apparent decrease is due to the overall increase in other types of households. It is still not clear whether, among married-couple families, those without children decreased in relation to those with children. Indeed, if we take only the category of "Married-couple fam-

ily" and compare subcategories within it, as shown in Table 2.4, we see that *as a percentage of married-couple households,* those without children actually increased from 42.9 percent to 54.4 percent.

This example should convince you to pay close attention to the comparisons made in numerical tables. In this example, we see that married couples with children accounted for a smaller percentage of all married-couple families in 2000 than in 1970, but we would not have seen this without making the additional comparison presented in Table 2.4.

Correlations

The term **correlation** refers to a specific relationship between two variables: As one varies in some way, so does the other. Figure 2.2 shows a correlation that people in Europe are particularly concerned about. The figure suggests that there is a correlation between the rate of suicide among men and the rate of unemployment among young people. We can observe from the graph that the two variables (rate of suicide and rate of unemployment) vary together: As one increases, so does the other. This correlation is another confirmation of Durkheim's original hypothesis that the rate of suicide in a society is related (correlated) to major changes in how people in the society behave (i.e., whether they marry, find jobs, have children, and so on). No wonder, then, that according to the French sociologists who gathered these data, the correlation between unemployment and suicide shows that suicide "is an expression of social distress, not only a matter of personal relationships" (quoted in Kremer, 1998, p. 8).

The search for correlations is a common strategy in many kinds of research. In market research, for example, the investigator seeks correlations between the use of certain products and other social variables. (Thus the consumption of beer correlates with the proportion of male consumers in

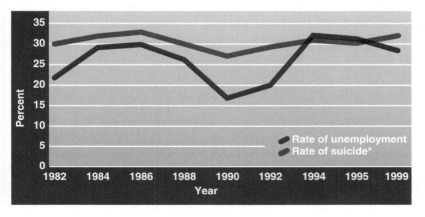

Figure 2.2 Rates of Youth Unemployment and Suicide in France, 1982–1995

*Male suicides per 100,000; male youth 2 years or less out of school, in percent.

a target population such as baseball fans; the consumption of light beer correlates with the proportion of older, more weight-conscious male consumers; and so on.)

If you take other courses in sociology and statistics, you will learn techniques for calculating the strength of correlations among variables and for sorting out the effects of different variables on the dependent variable you are studying. Although the calculation of correlation is covered in statistics courses, for our purposes it is helpful to know that the measure of correlation between two variables, termed the *correlation coefficient,* can vary between +1.0 and −1.0, with 0.0 representing no measured correlation at all. A correlation coefficient of +1 would indicate that the variables are positively and perfectly related—a change in one variable produces an equivalent change in the same direction (increase or decrease) in the other variable. A correlation coefficient of −1 would mean that the variables are perfectly inversely related—a change in one produces an equivalent change *in the opposite direction* in the other. In reality, most variables are not perfectly correlated, and correlation coefficients usually fall somewhere between these two extremes.

CORRELATION AND CAUSATION   Although correlation can be useful in the analysis of relationships among variables, it must not be confused with causation. For example, the French sociologists who studied the correlations presented in Figure 2.2 do not claim that unemployment causes suicide; they only point out that the two variables are closely related. They are cautious when making claims about causality because often a strong correlation that seems to indicate causality is in fact a spurious or misleading relationship. Take the example of storks and babies. The fable that storks bring babies seemed to be based on a statistical reality: In rural Holland, until recent decades there was a correlation between storks nesting in chimneys and the presence of babies in those households. The more storks, the more babies. In fact, however, the presence of babies in the home meant more fires in the fireplace and more heat going up the chimney to attract storks to nest there. Storks do not bring babies; babies, in effect, bring storks. But the real causal variable is heat, something that was not suggested in the original commonsense correlation. Correlations may suggest the possibility of causality, but one must be extremely careful in making the leap from correlation (or association) to causation.

Mapping Social Data

Data about individuals or households can be mapped in precise ways, providing a powerful tool for analyzing sociological data (Monnier, 1993). In a sense, the mapping of data is a form of correlation. The variable under study—it could be poverty, crime, educational achievement, an illness such as acquired immunodeficiency syndrome (AIDS), or any other variable—is mapped over a given geographic area, thereby correlating the variable with location.

When Émile Durkheim conducted his early research to demonstrate the social (rather than the individual psychological) causes of suicide, he used some basic mapping techniques. With some simple maps of France, he showed that if one identified counties with high suicide rates and high rates of single, unmarried individuals, the results revealed clusters of counties with high and low rates on both variables. He believed that this clustering offered support for his theory that lack of integration of the individual into society—through marriage, employment, and participation in social groups of all kinds—helps cause suicide (Durkheim, 1951/1897). But one of Durkheim's most important critics, Gabriel Tarde, proposed a more psychological explanation for the clustering. Tarde argued that the clusters that appeared on the map could be the result of imitation. He believed that where rates of suicide are high, people suffering from personal distress are likely to be imitating the suicidal behavior of others, which then explains why suicide rates appear in spatial clusters when one maps the incidence of suicide (Tarde, 1903).

Social scientists have been debating and seeking to test these competing theories ever since they were first stated. In their contemporary work on the problem, sociologists Robert D. Baller and Kelly K. Richardson have used some creative mapping techniques to tease out the relative contributions of integration versus imitation (Baller & Richardson, 2002). As shown in Figure 2.3, they rated each county in France on whether its suicide rate between 1872 and 1876 was high, low, or average. They also rated each county on whether the suicide rates of its neighboring counties were high, low, or average. This creates a ranking system for counties: They may be high-high (meaning that their suicide rate is high and so are those of their neighboring counties); low-low, meaning just the opposite; or high-low, meaning that while the county's suicide rate is high, its neighboring counties' rates are low. (Of course, the opposite pattern, low-high, can exist, and there can be counties that rate neither high nor low, which means that they are "not significant.") They carried out the same procedure for all the counties in the United States between 1989 and 1991 (Figure 2.4). In both cases they were seeking to test Durkheim's most basic hypothesis: that suicide rates will tend to cluster in regions with differing levels of social integration. But they were also seeking to test Tarde's hypothesis that the clustering is due to imitation and that therefore neighboring counties will have similar suicide rates.

The two maps show some striking results, and these results offer stronger evidence for Durkheim's hypothesis than for Tarde's. In both maps, there is evident clustering

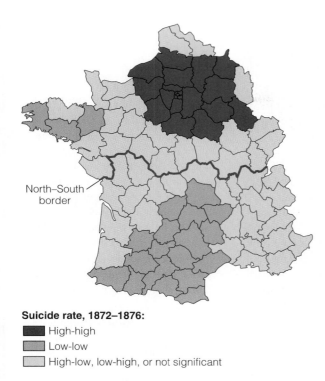

Suicide rate, 1872–1876:

■ High-high
▨ Low-low
▢ High-low, low-high, or not significant

Figure 2.3 Suicide Rates for French Departments (Counties), 1872–1876

Source: Baller, R. D., & Richardson, K. K. (2002). Social integration, imitation, and the geographic patterning of suicide. *American Sociological Review, 67,* pp. 873–888.

of high and low rates of suicide by counties. But both maps show many counties (those with no shading) that have high or low suicide rates but differ from their neighbors on these variables. If imitation is operating, as Tarde suggested in his hypothesis, it is certainly not uniform. There are clusters of counties with high suicide rates, which supports Tarde's imitation theory, but their locations offer far more support for Durkheim's integration theory.

As expected, suicide rates for France clustered in the region around Paris. In the late nineteenth century, the north of France was undergoing far more rapid urbanization than the south, with a great deal of new migration to Paris and surrounding towns. An exception that supports Durkheim's theory is Bretagne, in the northeastern corner, where traditional villages and high levels of social integration help explain the clustering of low suicide rates that one sees clearly on the map. Similarly, the major clustering of low-low counties in southern France is also largely explained by the persistence of traditional villages and higher levels of social integration there.

When they turn to analysis of the U.S. map, the sociologists note that "High rates of suicide are clustered in the American West, with the notable exception of the state of Utah. Other significant clusters of high suicide rates are located in the western tip of Virginia and in Northern Florida" (Baller & Richardson, 2002, p. 881). The authors go on to point out that the western and eastern sections of the United States differ greatly, with the West (again with the exception of Mormon Utah) displaying higher rates of single, unmarried residents, more recent settlement, and many other indicators of weaker social integration than either the South or the East. Note that this analysis does not deny that imitation may be associated with some cases of suicides or argue that lack of social integration is the main cause of most suicides. The analysis shows that the association among the variables offers more support for one theory than for the other, but, clearly, a phenomenon as complex as suicide has many explanations, and individual cases are always explained by psychological as well as social factors. Remember, Durkheim and Tarde were arguing

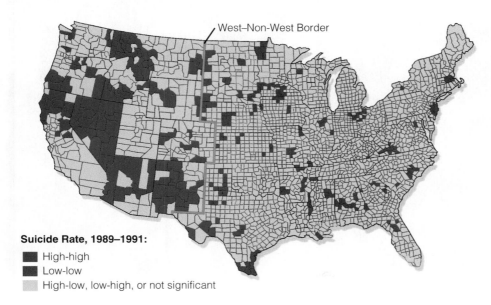

Suicide Rate, 1989–1991:

■ High-high
■ Low-low
▢ High-low, low-high, or not significant

Figure 2.4 Suicide Rates for U.S. Counties, 1989–1991

Source: Baller, R. D., & Richardson, K. K. (2002). Social integration, imitation, and the geographic patterning of suicide. *American Sociological Review, 67,* pp. 873–888.

VISUAL SOCIOLOGY

SUICIDE AS A FORM OF PROTEST

Suicide as a form of protest is one of the most profound and extreme acts imaginable. It is also a clear example of Durkheim's point that suicide can be a social as well as a psychological phenomenon. Any form of public death—be it an execution, a disaster, a brutal murder, or a suicide—sends shock waves through society and stimulates a great deal of emotion, especially among the witnesses. This has probably been true throughout history, but in our age of widespread mass media, sensational events are instantly visible to far greater numbers of people than ever before. A consequence of this change is that suicide deaths may have an immense impact on public feelings and opinions.

The suicide of a Buddhist monk by self-immolation during the Vietnam War was instantly broadcast around the world, not only as a photograph but also as a televised event. This act instantly conveyed the message that an important element of the South Vietnamese public opposed the actions of the U.S.-supported government then in power. For antiwar protesters in Europe and the United States, the event sent a clear moral message: Others who opposed the war must redouble their efforts to swing public opinion against the war.

Suicide bombings in public places by Palestinian militants are a central feature of the conflict in the Middle East. Without the power of a modern military with tanks and jet fighters, the Palestinians have relatively few means of striking out against the Israeli government. Fired by religious and political ideals, young Palestinians are sacrificing their lives to carry out bombing missions in much the same way that Japanese *kamikaze* pilots did during World War II. These bombings do nothing to ease the conflict between Muslim Palestinians and Jewish Israelis; in fact, they further escalate the bloodshed. But so far they have been an effective means of riveting world attention on the Palestinian struggle and the imbalance of power in the conflict.

The 1998 suicide of a prominent Catholic bishop in Pakistan is another example of the use of suicide as a form of political and moral protest. Bishop John Joseph killed himself in protest over the execution of a young Catholic villager named Ayub Masih, who was found guilty of blasphemy after praising Salman Rushdie's *Satanic Verses.* Here the issues involve not only the problems of the individual but also the rights of religious minorities (i.e., Catholics) in a society with one major religion (Islam). In this example, the bishop was distraught over his inability to influence events in Islamic Pakistan or to bring the problem to the attention of world leaders. His protest suicide did have the effect he desired; it embarrassed the Pakistani government. In the long run, however, more sustained protests by masses of people are usually necessary to bring about lasting political or social change.

From a sociological viewpoint, the foregoing examples represent a special type of suicidal behavior. These individuals, like all people who choose to end their lives, are no doubt motivated by many different feelings, notably suffering and despair. But their decision to link their death to a social cause raises many other sociological issues. Is the protest justified? Should the event be widely publicized? Is the person a hero for having made the supreme sacrifice for a cause? These are all examples of the moral and sociological issues raised by protest suicides.

AP/Wide World Photos

about why suicide rates might be high or low in a region, not about the causes of individual suicides. As we will see in the Mapping Social Change boxes in various chapters of this text, social scientists since Durkheim's time have found many new and creative ways to map social data.

THEORIES AND PERSPECTIVES

The material presented in Tables 2.2, 2.3, and 2.4 is valuable because it shows how the nation's most important survey, the census, reveals fundamental changes in the structure of the population. But how do these facts about household composition relate to larger trends and issues? The census reveals trends, but it does not explain those trends unless an investigator armed with a set of hypotheses goes to work on the facts to make them prove or disprove a theoretical point.

A **theory** is a set of interrelated concepts that seeks to explain the causes of an observable phenomenon. Some theories attempt to explain an extremely wide range of phenomena, whereas others limit their explanations to a narrower range. In physics, for example, Newton's theory of gravitation related the force of gravity to the mass and distance between objects, but it did not try to explain why the force of gravity existed in the first place or how it was related to other forces, such as electromagnetism, that could be observed in nature. Einstein's theory of relativity, on the other hand, attempted to explain the relationships among all natural forces, and it predicted forces that had not yet been observed, such as those released by nuclear fission.

It is often said that sociology lacks highly predictive theories like those of the physical sciences, but this is a debatable point. If theories are judged by their ability to explain observable phenomena and predict future events, then sociology has some powerful theories. At the beginning of the twentieth century, Émile Durkheim used his theory of social integration to predict the social conditions that would increase rates of suicide. The same theory of social integration predicted the conditions that would lead to the rise of totalitarian regimes such as that of the Nazis in Germany. Max Weber's theory of bureaucracy is valuable in explaining the experiences we are likely to have in organizations of all kinds. And Karl Marx's theory of class conflict is still the dominant explanation of the revolutions that occurred in feudal and early capitalist societies. No single sociological theory can explain all the complexities of human social life and social change, but in this respect sociology is not very different from other social and physical sciences. A variety of economic theories compete for the attention of

The Sociological Observer
(See photo on p. 34.)

We cannot know exactly what the rescue workers are saying as they approach the suicidal man, but they must be trying to calm him down and offer him assurances that they are not going to do anything that will further threaten his safety or theirs. The more they can speak to him, the greater the likelihood that they can convince him to let them help him.

The rescue workers are demonstrating the meaning of altruism and its importance for a society. While attempting such rescues is part of their job, their commitment to helping others in dangerous situations must have motivated them to take on this responsibility in the first place. Societies would be almost impossible to live in were it not for altruistic behavior like this and many other forms of prosocial behavior.

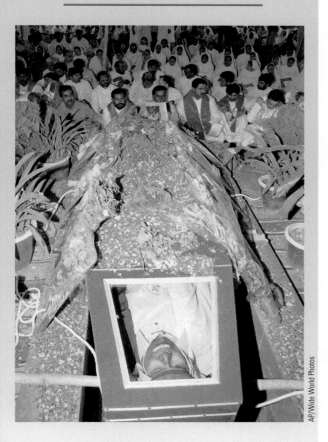

policymakers, and the theory of relativity has not fully explained the physical forces that produced the universe.

To cope with the many levels of social explanation, sociologists come to their work armed with **theoretical perspectives**: sets of interrelated theories that offer explanations for important aspects of social behavior. Like the methods of observation and analysis discussed in this chapter, theoretical perspectives are tools of sociological research. They provide a framework of ideas and explanations that helps us make sense of the data we gather. The basic theoretical perspectives are the ones discussed in Chapter 1: interactionism, functionalism, and conflict theory. We also rely on the ecological perspective for descriptive data about communities and populations. At times these perspectives offer competing explanations of social life; at other times they seek to explain different aspects of society; and at still other times they are combined in various ways.

Our knowledge about societies and how they change is advanced through scientific competition among sociologists who approach their subjects from different theoretical perspectives. Toward the end of most chapters of this book, you will find a feature that illustrates how practicing sociologists use questions and hypotheses derived from these perspectives in their research. To the extent possible, this feature will present cutting-edge, award-winning sociological research.

SUMMARY

Applying the Sociological Imagination

- In all scientific research, certain basic steps must be completed: deciding on the problem, reviewing the literature, formulating research questions, selecting a method, and analyzing the data. Not all researchers follow these steps in the order given, and often one or more steps must be repeated.

- The first step in designing sociological research is formulating the question—that is, asking a question about a social situation that can be answered through the systematic collection and analysis of data.

- Often the research question is expressed in the form of a hypothesis. A *hypothesis* states a relationship between two *variables* that can be tested through empirical observation. The variable that is to be explained is the *dependent variable.* The other variable, a factor that the researcher believes causes changes in the dependent variable, is the *independent variable.*

- Before collecting new data, a professional researcher reviews as much existing research and other data sources as possible. This "review of the literature" sometimes supplies all the data necessary for a particular study.

The Basic Methods

- The most frequently used research methods in sociology are observation, experiments, and surveys.

- Observation may take the form of *participant observation,* in which the researcher participates to some degree in the life of the people being observed. It may also take the form of *unobtrusive measures,* or observational techniques that measure behavior but intrude as little as possible into actual social settings. Visual sociology involves the use of photography and videotape to observe people in a variety of settings.

- Sociological experiments can take one of two basic forms: the controlled experiment and the field experiment. In a *controlled experiment,* the researcher establishes an *experimental group,* which will experience the "treatment" (a change in the independent variable), and a *control group,* which will not experience the treatment. The effect of the treatment on the dependent variable can be measured by comparing the two groups. *Field experiments* take place outside the laboratory and are often used in evaluating public programs designed to remedy specific social problems. The treatment group consists of people who experience a particular social program, and the control group consists of comparable people who do not experience the program.

- A common problem of experimental studies is the *Hawthorne effect,* which refers to any unintended effect resulting from the attention given to subjects in an experiment.

- The third basic method of sociological research, the survey, asks people to give precise information about their behavior and attitudes. The most ambitious surveys are national censuses; the data obtained in a census can be supplemented by smaller, less costly *sample surveys.* A *sample* is a selection of respondents drawn from a specific population. To ensure that everyone in the specified population has an equal chance of being selected, the respondents must be selected by some process of *random sampling.*

- Questionnaire design is an important aspect of survey research. Questions must be precisely worded, easy to understand, and free of bias. *Closed questions* require the respondent to select from a set of answers, whereas *open questions* allow respondents to say whatever comes to mind.
- Sociological researchers must always consider the rights of human subjects. *Privacy* is the right to decide the terms on which one's acts may be revealed to the public. *Confidentiality* means that the researcher cannot use responses in such a way that they can be traced to a particular respondent. For respondents to give *informed consent,* they must be told how the information they supply will be used and must be allowed to judge the degree of personal risk involved in answering questions.

Analyzing the Data

- The data gathered in a survey are usually presented in the form of statistical tables. In reading a table it is important to know what the units of analysis are and what kinds of data are being presented.
- *Frequency distributions,* given in absolute numbers, reveal the actual size of each category of a variable, but to compare the numbers for different years it is necessary to use *percent analysis.*
- Analyzing data often leads to the discovery of *correlations,* or specific relationships between two variables. Correlation should not be confused with causation.
- Mapping of data about individuals or households also provides a powerful tool for analyzing sociological data.

Theories and Perspectives

- Once data have been presented and analyzed, they can be used to generate new hypotheses. The types of hypotheses that might be developed depend on the researcher's *theoretical perspective*—a set of interrelated theories that offer explanations for important aspects of social behavior. The functionalist, interactionist, and conflict perspectives result in quite different hypotheses.

GLOSSARY

hypothesis: A statement that specifies a relationship between two or more variables that can be tested through empirical observation. (p. 27)

variable: A characteristic of an individual, group, or society that can vary from one case to another. (p. 28)

dependent variable: The variable that a hypothesis seeks to explain. (p. 28)

independent variable: A variable that the researcher believes causes a change in another variable (i.e., the dependent variable). (p. 28)

participant observation: A form of observation in which the researcher participates to some degree in the lives of the people being observed. (p. 32)

unobtrusive measures: Observational techniques that measure behavior but intrude as little as possible into actual social settings. (p. 33)

controlled experiment: An experimental situation in which the researcher manipulates an independent variable in order to observe and measure changes in a dependent variable. (p. 34)

experimental group: In an experiment, the subjects who are exposed to a change in the independent variable. (p. 34)

control group: In an experiment, the subjects who do not experience a change in the independent variable. (p. 34)

field experiment: An experimental situation in which the researcher observes and studies subjects in their natural setting. (p. 35)

Hawthorne effect: The unintended effect that results from the attention given to subjects in an experimental situation. (p. 36)

sample survey: A survey administered to a selection of respondents drawn from a specific population. (p. 37)

sample: A set of respondents selected from a specific population. (p. 37)

closed question: A question that requires the respondent to choose among a predetermined set of answers. (p. 38)

open question: A question that does not require the respondent to choose from a predetermined set of answers; instead, the respondent may answer in his or her own words. (p. 38)

privacy: The right of a respondent to define when and on what terms his or her actions may be revealed to the general public. (p. 38)

confidentiality: The promise that the information provided to a researcher by a respondent will not appear in any way that can be traced to that respondent. (p. 38)

informed consent: The right of respondents to be informed of the purpose for which the information they supply will be used and to judge the degree of personal risk involved in answering questions, even when an assurance of confidentiality has been given. (p. 39)

frequency distribution: A classification of data that describes how many observations fall within each category of a variable. (p. 40)

percent analysis: A mathematical operation that transforms an absolute number into a proportion as a part of 100. (p. 40)

correlation: A specific relationship between two variables. (p. 41)

theory: A set of interrelated concepts that seeks to explain the causes of an observable phenomenon. (p. 45)

theoretical perspective: A set of interrelated theories that offer explanations for important aspects of social behavior. (p. 46)

INTERNET RESOURCES

Virtual Society: The Wadsworth Sociology Resource Center
(http://sociology.wadsworth.com)

At Virtual Society you can access a wide range of enrichment material to aid your study of sociology. From the main page, click on the Student Resources link and find your course and this textbook. Next, select the chapter you are presently studying from the pull-down menu. Among the useful options for each self-study chapter are online links and exercises, flashcards, practical study tips, and practice quizzes for each chapter.

MC MicroCase Online

From the Virtual Society home page, click on MicroCase Online to access book-specific MicroCase exercises that allow you to further explore sociological issues and principles presented in the text.

InfoTrac College Edition

Another unique option available to you at the Student Resources section at Virtual Society is InfoTrac College Edition, an online library with access to hundreds of scholarly and popular periodicals. Below are suggested search terms for this chapter, but this resource also allows you to fit your study of sociology to your own interests by searching custom keywords.

Research Methods

Data Analysis

Census

Suicide

Sociology Department, Princeton University
(www.princeton.edu/~sociolog)

A good example of how modern sociology departments are using the Internet. Offers links with other sociology departments on each continent, domestic and international research institutes, data archives, and Web pages for academic journals.

Culture

© Dan Groshong/Corbis Sygma

For Native Americans, the coming of Europeans to the New World marked the beginning of a long-drawn-out disaster. This is how sociologist Russell Thornton, himself a Native American, describes it:

> In the centuries after Columbus these "Indians" suffered a demographic collapse. Numbers declined sharply; entire tribes, often quickly, were "wiped from the face of the earth." This is certainly true of the American Indians on the land that was to become the United States of America. . . . The fires that consumed North American Indians were the fevers brought on by newly encountered diseases, the flashes of settlers' and soldiers' guns, the ravages of "firewater," the flames of villages and fields burned by the scorched-earth policy of vengeful Euro-Americans. (Thornton, 1987, pp. xv–xvi)

Others have shown that even when Indians and settlers tried to live as neighbors it was difficult for them to do so (Cronon, 1983; Warhus, 1997). Seemingly simple differences could result in major conflicts. One major source of conflict could be found in the different ways in which Indians and settlers related to the land. The settlers tended to think of the bounty offered by their new environment as inexhaustible. They were not nearly as aware of the rhythms of nature as the Indians were, nor did they know how to live in harmony with nature without destroying its resources. So when they saw the Indians moving from one hunting or fishing ground to another as the seasons changed, they concluded that the Indians were not "improving the land" as proper farmers did. Over and over again, Europeans justified taking the Indians' forests and meadows by claiming that the Indians had no sense of ownership of the land because they did not clear it and farm it.

It would be difficult to overestimate the shock and confusion the Indians must have felt as they were continually driven from their traditional hunting and fishing grounds by the encroaching Europeans. The resulting conflicts were often bloody, with injuries and deaths on both sides, but the effects of the Europeans' technological superiority were especially devastating. The Europeans' cannon and rifles gave them the ultimate power to inflict their will on the Indians. No wonder that wherever they encountered the Europeans, the Indians began to covet the powerful new killing tools made of iron and steel. No wonder that the Europeans never doubted, even as they learned from the Indians how to survive in their new environment, that their own way of life was the only "true" civilization. Indeed, so powerful did the notion of European superiority become that even today we celebrate the "discovery" of the New World by European explorers. Too often we forget that what happened in 1492 was not the discovery of a new world but the establishment of contact between two worlds, both already old (Jennings, 1975; Marks, 1998).

FOCUS QUESTIONS:

• What are the many ways in which cultures guide and organize our social lives?

• How do cultures change to meet new social conditions and new patterns of contact among people with different cultures?

THE MEANING OF CULTURE

Was the European, or "Western," way of life really superior? This question remains a subject of stormy controversy throughout the world. Much of the resentment against Europeans and North Americans expressed by people in the Muslim world, for example, is based on the history of invasion, conquest, and domination by Western powers, a subject to which we return later in the chapter. For Native Americans in the Western Hemisphere, European invasion and settlement spelled the doom of some indigenous societies, but many others managed to survive and are struggling to maintain their way of life within the larger societies of Canada, the United States, Mexico, Bolivia, Brazil, and Peru. An example is provided by the Mayans of the Mexican highlands, as illustrated in the Visual Sociology section at the end of the chapter. And even when cultural contact occurs on a more equal basis, as it does when people from different modern cultures meet, it is difficult to achieve understanding and arrive at mutually beneficial forms of cooperation. Why is this so? Many of the answers may be found in the study of human culture.

In everyday speech, the word *culture* refers to pursuits like literature and music. But these forms of expression are only part of the definition of culture. To the social scientist, "a humble cooking pot is as much a cultural product as is a Beethoven sonata" (Kluckhohn, 1949, quoted in Ross, 1963, p. 96). Culture is a basic concept in sociology because it is what makes humans unique in the animal kingdom. All the familiar forms of social organization, from the simplest family to the most complex corporation, depend on culture for their existence. But although societies cannot exist without cultures, the two are not the same thing. *Societies* are populations that are organized to carry out the major functions of life. A society's *culture* consists of all the ways in which its members think about their society and communicate about it among themselves.

We can define **culture** as all the modes of thought, behavior, and production that are handed down from one generation to the next by means of communicative interaction—language, gestures, writing, building, and all other communication among humans—rather than by genetic transmission, or heredity. This definition encompasses a vast array of behaviors, technologies, religions, and so on—in other words, just about everything thought or made by humans. Among all the elements of culture that could be studied, social scientists are interested primarily in aspects that explain social organization and behavior. Thus, although they may analyze trends in movies and popular music (which significantly affect behavior in the modern world), they are even more likely to study aspects of culture that account for phenomena such as conflict between people with different languages and religions, or the conduct of people in different corporations that have their own ways of doing things ("corporate cultures").

Dimensions of Culture

The culture of any people on earth, no matter how simple it may seem to us, is a complex set of behaviors and artifacts. A useful framework for thinking about culture was suggested by Robert Bierstedt (1963). Bierstedt views culture as having three major dimensions:

1. **Ideas,** or ways of thinking that organize human consciousness;
2. **Norms,** or accepted ways of doing or carrying out ideas; and
3. **Material culture,** or patterns of possessing and using the products of culture.

Figure 3.1 presents some examples of these three dimensions, along with two aspects of culture—*ideologies* and *technologies*—that combine elements from more than one dimension.

IDEAS As indicated in Figure 3.1, theories about how the physical world operates (scientific knowledge), strongly held notions about what is right and wrong (values), and traditional beliefs, legends, and customs (folklore) are among the most important types of ideas found in any given culture. Of these, values are especially important because people feel so strongly about them and because they often undergo changes that result in social conflict (as we can see in contemporary debates about "a woman's right to control her reproductive life" versus "a fetus's right to life").

Values are socially shared ideas about what is important. Thus, for most people in North America, education is a value; that is, they conceive of it as a proper and good way to achieve social standing. Loyalty to friends and loved ones, patriotism, the importance of religion, the significance of material possessions—these and other values are commonly found in our culture and many others, but of course there are wide differences in how people interpret these values and in the extent to which they adhere to them. In small tribal and peasant societies, there tends to be far greater consensus on values than in large, complex industrial societies. In a large and diverse society such as ours, there is bound to be a good deal of conflict over values. Some people are satisfied with the way wealth and power are distributed, for example, while others are less satisfied with the status quo. Some people feel that it is desirable to attempt to improve one's own well-being and that society as a whole gains when everyone strives to be well-off. Others assert that the value of individual gain

Figure 3.1   Dimensions of Culture

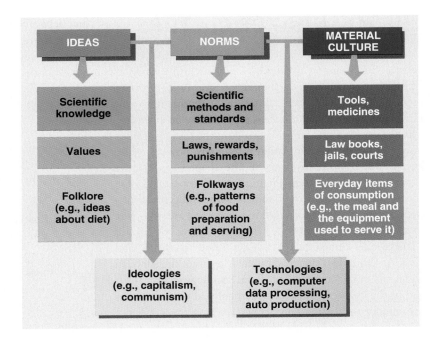

conflicts with the values of community and social cohesion; too great a gap between the well-off and the not-well-off creates suffering, envy, crime, and other problems.

In societies undergoing rapid and far-reaching social change, such as the United States, there is bound to be conflict over values. Controversies over "family values," the sanctity of marriage, obligations to children, and similar issues tend to be particularly intense because people's individual experiences differ greatly. The more diversity there is among the people who share a basic culture, the more conflict there is likely to be over certain aspects of that culture. Such disputes often turn on ideas about how to behave—that is, on the norms governing behavior in a society.

NORMS   From people's beliefs in what is right and good—that is, from their values—are derived the norms, or rules of behavior, of a society. Values are more abstract than norms; they are the ideas that support or justify norms. Norms are more specific. They are "the adjustments which human beings make to the surrounding environment. We may think of them as solutions to recurring problems or situations" (Nisbet, 1970, p. 225). But norms involve more than behavior. Any given norm is supported by the idea that a particular behavior is correct and proper or incorrect and improper. Norms known as *taboos,* such as the prohibition against incest, are widely shared throughout a culture and strictly enforced, even if they are sometimes violated. Other norms, such as dress codes, are enforced less strictly and are often violated.

If we think about a complex aspect of everyday life such as driving a car, it is evident that without norms life would be far more chaotic and dangerous than it already is. When we drive we keep to the right, obey traffic lights and speed limits, and avoid reckless behavior that could cause accidents. These are among the many norms that allow the automobile to be such an essential article of North American culture.

Examples of norms are easy to find. Take the college or high school classroom. The classroom is organized according to norms of educational practice: There should be a textbook or books; there should be class discussion; there should be assignments, exams, and grades. Note that these "shoulds" correspond to actual behavior. Norms usually refer to behavior that we either approve or disapprove of. However, members of a culture often disagree about how a particular norm operates. Thus, in the case of classroom organization, there is considerable debate about what educational practices are most effective. In Israel, for example, there is debate among orthodox and liberal Jews over whether boys and girls should be separated in classrooms, and similar debates divide fundamentalist and more secular Muslims in other Middle Eastern societies.

In societies where values are in conflict or where changes are occurring rapidly, norms are also subject to change. This can readily be seen in the case of smoking. The norms governing smoking are changing rapidly as a result of changing values regarding health. Until recent years, the norms governing smoking in the United States were very liberal. One could light up almost anywhere, and nonsmokers were expected not to complain. Recently, however, greater emphasis on fitness and health, as well as new knowledge about the dangers of secondhand smoke,

art *and the sociological eye*

"Reading" Art for Social Meaning

Drawing and painting give us our earliest evidence of human beings' desire to understand social life and to communicate that understanding to others. For instance, although we cannot know in much detail how the preliterate cave dwellers of southern Europe and northern Africa lived during the late Ice Age more than 10,000 years ago, cave paintings like the hunting scene shown here can give us glimpses into the way prehistoric humans felt about their lives. Note how carefully the artist rendered the scene, with special attention to the placement of the hunters before the onrushing antelope. In the very choice of the hunting subject, the ancient artist is communicating a message about what was uppermost in the minds of our early ancestors.

The art of any of the world's peoples, past or present, can likewise be "read" for evidence of how people organize their society, for the nature of interpersonal relationships, for what they value as sacred or simply enjoyable, and for what they despise. Thus the painted limestone carving of the Egyptian prince Rahotep and his wife Nofret, probably executed by an official artist of the pharaoh in about 2610 BC, reveals many details of the lives of people who lived more than three millennia ago. Look at how the couple's dress reveals differences in what must have been considered proper appearance for men and women of their social standing. Her breasts are covered, but his chest is bare; his only ornaments are a thin necklace

and an equally thin mustache, whereas her hair and jewelry are far more elaborate. The sculptures also suggest that the princely rulers of one of the world's first civilizations could have had either dark or light skin.

But let us not confuse sociology and fine art. These artists were not sociologists, nor were they necessarily seeking to make points about their society. Their goals were to use the forms of everyday life to create something that would please them and their patrons, to capture the nuances of shape and form, to convey the emotional quality of a scene. The task of the sociologist is to read their art for its social meaning, without detracting from the magic that makes art beautiful and timeless.

Cave painting from Los Caballos, Spain.

© Douglas Mazonowicz/Photo Researchers

Prince Rahotep and His Wife Nofret, artist unknown, about 2610 BC. Painted limestone, height 47 inches.

Egyptian Museum, Cairo

THEN AND NOW   The Once Glamorous Habit

How quickly norms can change, and how much confusion those changes can bring. Smoking is a fine example. In less than four decades, this behavior changed from a glamorous activity to an act that many people consider deviant.

For most of the twentieth century, smoking was extremely popular. Most Americans smoked, and smoking was even more popular in England and on the European continent. Humphrey Bogart and Lauren Bacall smoked, as did most other movie stars, as well as many athletes and famous journalists. Smoking reached its peak of popularity during and just after World War II. Children often began smoking steadily by age 14, encouraged to do so by ubiquitous advertising that associated smok-

ing with success, sensuality, and in the case of the famous Marlboro Man, masculinity.

Today much has changed. Smoking has been shown to be extremely dangerous to health—not only the health of the smoker but also the health of people exposed to secondhand tobacco smoke. In consequence, the norms and values associated with smoking are being challenged throughout most Western nations. New norms restricting smoking in public places and in most offices are creating a deviant group of smokers who must linger outside their offices to satisfy their craving and enjoy a cigarette.

have increased the value people place on clean air and have tipped the balance against the earlier norms. But the change has not occurred without conflict between smokers and nonsmokers and their representatives in courts and legislatures.

Laws are norms that are included in a society's official written codes of behavior. Laws are often developed by a specialized occupational group, such as priests in the ancient world and legislators, judges, and lawyers in the modern world. Some of the oldest examples of laws are the Code of Hammurabi, the ancient Babylonian code that specified punishments equal to the gravity of the crime (e.g., an eye for an eye, a tooth for a tooth); the Ten Commandments, written by God, according to the Old Testament, on stone tablets at least 1,600 years before the birth of Christ; and the codes of Confucius, written and interpreted by the royal scribes of the ancient Chinese empire. In our time, laws are the special province of professional lawmakers, but all citizens participate in a network of laws and other written regulations that govern daily life. Basic behaviors like driving, going to school, marrying, and investing are greatly influenced by laws governing these activities.

At times we may grumble or protest against laws that we find overly restrictive. And there is always some group planning to protest a law that is under consideration in a legislative body such as Congress. When we look beyond our own society, however, we see that the rule of law could save millions of lives if only it could be achieved in places like Guatemala, Rwanda, Bosnia, Cambodia, or many of the nations of the former Soviet Union. On the other hand, even in nations where the rule of law is generally accepted, social scientists often find that new laws have unintended consequences. For example, when extremely strict laws against adult drug-dealing were passed, the dealers began recruiting juveniles to sell drugs. The lawmakers never intended the new laws to encourage teenagers to become dealers, but in many states that is what happened (Bayer, 1991). Laws often have unintended consequences because they were created in response to vigorous efforts by people who espouse particular ideologies.

IDEOLOGIES   As indicated in Figure 3.1, **ideologies** comprise two dimensions of culture; they are sets or systems of ideas and norms. Ideologies combine the values and norms that all the members of a society are expected to believe in and act upon without question. A classic study of the emergence of an ideology was Max Weber's analysis of the link between Protestantism and capitalism, *The Protestant Ethic and the Spirit of Capitalism* (1974/1904). Weber noticed that the rise of Protestantism in Europe coincided with the rise of private enterprise, banking, and other aspects of capitalism. He also noticed that a majority of the most successful early capitalists were Protestants. Weber hypothesized that their religious values taught them that salvation depended not on good deeds or piety but on how they lived their entire lives and particularly on how well they adhered to the norms of their "callings" (occupations). As a result, the Protestants placed a high value on frugality and abstinence. To prove that they were worthy of salvation, they devoted themselves tirelessly to commerce and plowed their profits back into their firms. But Catholics, who did not share these values, were less single-mindedly dedicated to their business ventures. They often spent their profits on good deeds rather than investing them in their businesses. Weber attempted to show how a set of religious values and norms combined with economic norms to create the ideology of capitalism.

A contemporary example of an ideology may be found among religious fundamentalists. Christian fundamentalists in the United States generally share a set of ideas and norms of behavior that include the value of prayer, the value of family and children, the negative value of abortion and secular humanism (an ethical system based on scientific knowledge rather than on religious teachings), the belief in salvation and redemption for one's sins, and other values. In the Islamic world, conflict between religious fundamentalists and more secular people is especially widespread and bitter. And the fundamentalists often see the United States as a threat to their most cherished values. In part because of their prominence on global television, examples of life in the United States—especially those that feature sexual display, the consumption of alcohol, or gender equality (which is not permitted among orthodox Muslims)—become symbols of moral corruption.

VALUES AND IDEOLOGIES IN CONFLICT Most societies and regions of the world experience conflict among people with differing values and ideologies. At times this conflict can have serious outcomes, such as widespread violence among antagonistic factions or parties, as occurs in Northern Ireland between Protestants and Catholics, in Israel between ultra-orthodox Jews and more secular populations, and in Islamic nations like Egypt or Algeria, between extremely orthodox Muslims and those who seek to forge compromises between secular values and religious ones. We return continually to the subject of conflicting

values and resultant conflict among social groups because the subject is so important in understanding social life and social change. In discussing values and ideologies, however, it is important to point out that in almost every known society there are inherent conflicts in the values the society claims to support. In most democratic societies, for example, the values of liberty (freedom) and equality are cherished. But there is inherent conflict in these two central values. As Isaiah Berlin, one of the most influential social thinkers of the twentieth century, explained:

> Perfect liberty is not compatible with perfect equality. If man is free to do anything he chooses, then the strong will crush the weak, the wolves will eat the sheep, and this puts an end to equality. If perfect equality is to be attained, then men must be prevented from outdistancing each other, whether in material or in intellectual or in spiritual achievement, otherwise inequalities will result. (1998, p. 60)

We will see in later chapters that the desire of some groups to achieve total equality or freedom continues to produce ideologies in which the goals of action—that is, equality or freedom—lead people to assert that "the ends justify the means" used to achieve those ends, even if they include violating norms such as "Thou shalt not steal" or "Thou shalt not kill." Such ideologies led to some of the twentieth century's most atrocious episodes of mass violence and destruction. But the inherent conflict among values can also be a creative aspect of society. As we seek to decrease the gap between the haves and the have-nots in the United States and elsewhere, while attempting to preserve as much individual freedom as possible, we realize that a just society is one in which people are free to seek the best peaceful means of balancing their conflicting interests and values.

MATERIAL CULTURE The third dimension of culture identified by Bierstedt is material culture. Material culture consists of all the things a society produces. Mundane things, such as pots and pans or the wooden eating bowls of nonindustrial societies; immensely complex systems of things, such as the space shuttle; cherished items of religious worship, such as rosary beads or Indian fetish necklaces—all take their shape and purpose from the ideas of the culture that produces them. Members of societies that place a high value on science and efficiency are used to seeing these values expressed in material objects. For example, we design our houses to conserve energy and create desirable combinations of view and privacy. We may take older forms such as the ranch house or the Cape Cod bungalow and modify them to suit modern purposes; in this way our houses combine tradition with usefulness. The particular form that

© Chenault Photography Studio, Decatur, Alabama

Quilt making is a highly social folk art form. This quilt, created by University of Mississippi graduate student Patti B. Melton, is actually a sociology paper about quilt making reproduced on an original quilt. It blends ideas with material culture.

appeals to us is usually a result of many different ideas, including what we know from our own upbringing, what we can afford, how much space we require, and the environmental conditions we anticipate.

The same is true throughout the world. If one travels in Africa, for example, one will find large areas in which people build square houses with thatched roofs or roofs of corrugated metal. Suddenly one will pass into a region where the people build round houses with steeply pitched roofs. In another region, people may live in sprawling apartment-like complexes built of sand and mortar. When asked why they prefer a particular kind of dwelling, people usually say, "Because we have always built our houses this way." In other words, their answers are based on ideas of what is right for them. After further discussion, however, a traveler with a sociological imagination will discover that the different building forms also express functional ideas. The mud-walled "apartments" of the desert village seem cramped and dark to Western eyes, but the people of the village will explain that they often sleep outdoors and the dark, cool rooms are most useful on very hot days. On

the other hand, the tribespeople in a society that builds round houses may give a spiritual explanation for the shape of their dwellings; they may believe that corners are places where evil spirits can lurk. In sum, different cultures may give different reasons for the form and function of a material element such as a house, but in all cultures one will find a material culture that stems from the society's most important ideas (Kidder, 1985; Rybczynski, 1987).

TECHNOLOGIES   Technologies are another aspect of culture that spans two of Bierstedt's major dimensions. (Refer again to Figure 3.1.) **Technologies** are the things (material culture) and the norms for using them that are found in a given culture (Bierstedt, 1963; Ellul, 1964). Without the norms that govern their use, things are at best confusing and at worst useless or dangerous. In the United States, for example, new telecommunications technologies such as the Internet are a powerful means of communicating information across long distances. But norms for using these new technologies—such as norms about privacy, freedom of speech, and personal accountability—are only now developing. There is serious conflict, for example, about whether pornographic messages directed at juveniles or e-mail messages among colleagues in an office are protected under the norms of free speech or whether they are subject to public scrutiny and perhaps social sanction. Because the Internet is a relatively new form of communication, the norms (i.e., laws) that apply to print and TV communication have not yet been fully worked out and applied to this new communications medium.

Guns present another case in which norms governing use of the things themselves are very much in dispute. Most Americans agree that people should be free to own and use hunting weapons—but what about handguns, assault rifles, machine guns, and rocket launchers? What, if any, restrictions should there be on the distribution and use of such weapons? As we will see in later chapters, the debate about appropriate norms for controlling the distribution and possession of deadly firearms that are clearly not designed for hunting is an indication of a deeper cultural conflict over the right to bear arms versus the state's monopoly over the use of force.

Norms and Social Control

Norms are what permit life in society to proceed in an orderly fashion without violence and chaos. Shared norms contribute enormously to a society's ability to regulate itself without constantly resorting to the coercive force of armies and police. The term *social control* refers to the set of rules and understandings that control the behavior of individuals and groups in a culture. Park and Burgess (1921) noted that throughout the world there are certain basic norms that contribute to social control: "All groups have such 'commandments' as 'Honor thy father and mother,' 'Thou shalt not kill,' 'Thou shalt not steal'" (p. 787).

THE NORMATIVE ORDER   The wide array of norms that permit a society to achieve relatively peaceful social control is called its **normative order**. These norms create what Morris Janowitz has termed "the capacity of a social group, including a whole society, to regulate itself" (1978, p. 3). This self-regulation requires a set of "higher moral principles" and the norms that express those principles. The norms define what makes a person a "good" member of the culture and society.

The most important norms in a culture are often taught as absolutes. The Ten Commandments, for example, are absolutes: "Thou shalt not kill," "Thou shalt not steal," and so on. Unfortunately, people do not always extend those norms to members of another culture. For example, the same explorers who swore to bring the values of Western civilization (including the Ten Commandments) to the "savage Indians" of the New World thought nothing of taking the Indians' land by force. Queen Elizabeth I of England could authorize

This young woman has adopted a somewhat extreme version of a folkway that is fashionable among her crowd. Her supervisors at the bookstore where she worked insisted that she remove some of the piercings. She refused and was fired, the result of a clear difference in outlook about the significance of the norms involved.

agents like Sir Walter Raleigh to seize remote "heathen and barbarous" lands without viewing this act as a violation of the strongest norms of her own society (Jennings, 1975; Snipp, 1991). Protests by the Indians often resulted in violent death, but the murder of Indians and the theft of their land was rationalized by the notion that the Indians were an inferior people who would ultimately benefit from European influence. In the ideology of conquest and colonial rule, the Ten Commandments did not apply.

SANCTIONS   In the social sciences, punishments and rewards for adhering to or violating norms are known as **sanctions**. Cultural norms vary according to the degree of sanction associated with them. Rewards can range from a smile to the Nobel Prize; punishments may vary in strength from a raised eyebrow to the electric chair. During the period of European colonial expansion, the murder of a native was far less strongly sanctioned than was the murder of another European.

MORES AND FOLKWAYS   The most strongly sanctioned norms are called **mores**.[1] They are norms that people consider vital to the continuation of human groups and societies, and therefore they figure prominently in a culture's

This nineteenth-century painting shows a woman depositing her newborn infant in a "receptacle for foundlings" probably associated with a church or cathedral. Women who violated the norms of legitimate fertility by bearing children out of wedlock were often forced to give up their infants.

---

[1]This term, pronounced "morays," is the plural of the Latin word *mos,* meaning "custom."

SOCIOLOGICAL METHODS   Constructing a Typology of Norms

Typologies are ways of grouping observable phenomena into categories in order to identify regularities in what may appear to be a great variety of observations. For example, there are so many social norms that the average person has no hope of ever sorting them out without some kind of system for organizing them. In the chart presented here, the subject is norms of various types. The sociologist constructs the types by comparing various dimensions along which norms may differ. The norms listed in the Ten Commandments, for example, differ in many ways. The norm "Thou shalt not kill" not only is generally believed and passed along from one generation to the next but also is codified in laws. So is the commandment "Thou shalt not steal," which is an important part of the written laws of our society. But the commandment "Remember the Sabbath day, to keep it holy" is not a written law in the United States, at least not in the federal statutes.

In some states and communities, there are laws specifying that businesses must close on Sunday, but not all religious groups recognize Sunday as the Sabbath. In addition, ideas about what behaviors are appropriate on the Sabbath are changing, and laws governing those behaviors are being challenged. These differences indicate that norms may differ according to whether they are informally taught to new generations or whether they are formal, written "laws of the land."

Another dimension along which norms may differ is the degree to which they are sanctioned—that is, the degree to which adherence is rewarded and violation is punished. The norm that men do not wear hats indoors is relatively weak. On the other hand, the norm that men and women do not casually display (or "flash") their genitals is strongly sanctioned.

Using these two comparative dimensions—mode of development (formal versus informal) and degree of sanction (weak versus strong)—we can

A TYPOLOGY OF NORMS

		Degree of Sanction	
		Relatively Weak	Relatively Strong
Mode of Development	**Informal**	Folkways, fashions	Taboos, mores
	Formal	Misdemeanor laws, some rules, guidelines, civil rights laws	Capital-offense laws, felony laws

create four categories: (1) norms that are informal and are weakly sanctioned (e.g., table manners, dress fashions), (2) norms that are informal but are strongly sanctioned (e.g., adultery), (3) norms that are part of the formal legal code but are weakly sanctioned (parking regulations, antismoking laws, etc.), and (4) norms that are formal laws and are strongly sanctioned (e.g., capital offenses like murder of a police officer or treason in wartime).

By juxtaposing the two dimensions, each with its two categories,

we arrive at a fourfold classification of norms (see chart). But as Max Weber (1947) observed, such a classification is an "ideal-typical" arrangement of observations in a form that accentuates some aspects and neglects others. These ideal types (folkways, mores and taboos, misdemeanor laws, and felonies or capital offenses) are useful because they establish standards against which to compare the norms of other cultures. For example, not all cultures treat the norm about the Sabbath the way Americans do. In parts of Israel or the Islamic world, one could be arrested for violating the Sabbath laws. Typologies like this one also help identify areas of social change, as when one compares the way the Sabbath was treated in American laws early in the twentieth century, when stores were obliged to close on Sunday, with the way it is treated today, when Sunday is often viewed as another shopping day.

But the aspects of society described by ideal types are rarely so uncomplicated in real life. Even the norms that seem most formal and unambiguous, such as the prohibition against murder, become murky under some conditions, as in cases of self-defense or in war, or in arguments about the death penalty and abortion. Studies of how actual behavior departs from the ideal-typical version invariably offer insights into how cultures and social structures are changing in the course of daily life.

---

sense of morality. **Folkways,** on the other hand, are far less strongly sanctioned. People often cannot explain why these norms exist, nor do they feel that they are essential to the continuation of the group or the society. Both terms were first used by William Graham Sumner in his study *Folkways* (1940/1907). Sumner also pointed out that laws are norms that have been enacted through the formal procedures of government. Laws often formalize the mores of a society by

putting them into written form and interpreting them. But laws can also formalize folkways, as can be seen, for example, in laws governing the clothing worn in public places.

Sumner also pointed out that a person who violates mores is subject to severe moral indignation, whereas one who violates folkways is not. People who violate folkways such as table manners or dress codes may be thought of as idiosyncratic or "flaky," but those who violate mores are branded as morally reprehensible. Thus among prisoners there are norms for the treatment of fellow prisoners, based on the types of crimes they committed "outside." Rapists and child molesters are moral outcasts; their offenses are the most reprehensible. Such offenders are often beaten and tormented by other prisoners.

The Sociological Methods box on page 58 presents a typology of norms according to their degree of sanction and their mode of development—that is, whether they are formal or informal. Laws and other norms, such as company regulations or the rules of games and sports, are known as *formal norms.* They differ from *informal norms,* which grow out of everyday behavior and do not usually take the form of written rules, even though they too regulate our behavior. For example, when waiting to enter a movie theater, it is usually permissible to have one member of a small group save a place in line for the others, who may arrive later. And in a "pickup" basketball game a player can call a foul and the opposing player usually cannot contest the call. Of course, there are times when such norms are disputed, depending on how the people involved define the situation. In the case of the basketball game, when the player on whom the foul is called disagrees with the call—and the score is extremely close—different definitions of the situation can lead to conflict.

Culture and Social Change

Cultures in all societies change, and much of social science is devoted to trying to understand and predict those changes. Norms and values that once were thought to be odd or criminal may come to be shared by the majority of the society's members, and the opposite can occur as well. In recent Olympic Games, for example, American women have excelled in many events in which they previously were weak performers. In the past, American women were often reluctant to lift weights and increase their strength for fear of being considered unfeminine. As the level of world competition increased, Americans found ways to overcome the older values that said women had to be soft to be feminine. Star female athletes continue to demonstrate to the American public that a woman can be muscular and athletic and still project a "feminine" identity.

Emphasis on normative behavior can lead one to neglect all the ways in which norms are constantly being debated and how they are changing (Wrong, 1999). Figure 3.1 and the Sociological Methods box present some key aspects of human culture, but they leave out all the social processes whereby elements of culture are produced and changed and diffused from one society to another. An unsuspecting reader might even conclude that a society's norms and values are shared equally by all its members, which is hardly an ac-

When Gertrude Ederle (shown posing here in 1925) became the first woman to swim the English Channel, she was admired by other athletes but also became the butt of jokes about her supposed lack of femininity. Today female sports stars like Venus Williams are far more widely admired both on and off the sports field.

curate view of culture. Any given norm is likely to be obeyed to varying degrees by different people within a culture.

Consider the norms about marriage, fertility, and parenthood in the United States. All may agree that young couples should not have children out of wedlock. They may also agree that abortion is not a desirable means of birth control. Unmarried couples who are expecting a child resolve the conflict between these norms in different ways: Some obtain an abortion; others get married; still others decide to have the baby out of wedlock, perhaps giving it up for adoption. Some unmarried mothers decide to raise their children alone. One way or another, such events in people's intimate family lives require difficult choices among often contradictory norms.

CHANGING NORMS OF INTIMACY   Many critics of contemporary American society blame the rising divorce rate and the increase in single-parent families on changes in the norms of intimacy that occurred during the social movements and counterculture of the 1960s. They seek a return to "traditional" norms of intimacy, including premarital celibacy, monogamy, and heterosexuality. These and other critics of diversity in sexual norms view the 1950s as a "golden age" of traditional norms regarding the conduct of intimate relations.

Sociologists who study trends in American culture point out that the 1950s were by no means a golden age of traditional behavior. Changes in American culture brought on by mass advertising, television, the growing equality of men and women, and the increasingly widespread desire for individual happiness had been developing throughout the century. These longer-term changes, they reason, should be reflected in statistics on divorce rates. On the other hand, if changes in sexual norms were a result of the social movements of the 1960s, there should be evidence of such a connection in statistics on divorce rates over time.

Figure 3.2 shows that there is some justification for each of these positions, but it offers far more empirical support for the view that rising divorce rates are not a product of the tumultuous 1960s. Clearly, divorces have been increasing in frequency over a period going well back into the nineteenth century. These data call into question any "golden age" theory of stability in American couples.

But there is never a complete substitution of new norms for old ones in a large and diverse population like that of North America. In consequence, we will always see differences in how norms are understood and in how they guide actual behavior. And these differences, especially when they concern major areas of moral conduct, will continue to produce conflict over norms.

Another important issue in understanding culture and social change is the question of the extent to which human culture is determined by biological factors, if at all. Are there any features that all human cultures share—any norms, for example, that are found in all known societies? And what happens when two cultures exist within the same society or nation? The remainder of this chapter explores these questions, beginning with one that has long been a subject of lively debate: the connection between culture and biology.

CULTURE, EVOLUTION, AND HUMAN BEHAVIOR

Of all the species of living creatures on this planet, human beings are the most widely distributed. The early European explorers—Columbus, Magellan, Cook, da Gama, and many others—marveled at the discovery of human life thriving, more or less, in some of the earth's most inhospitable environments. Nevertheless, they were convinced that the "savages" they encountered were inferior to the more powerful Europeans; in fact, they had difficulty accepting the idea that the native peoples were fully human. In other words, they considered them biologically as well as culturally inferior.

Groups that are in conflict often accuse their enemies of being biologically inferior. The Nazis claimed that the Jews were a biologically inferior people. Serbian Orthodox

Figure 3.2   Divorce Rate, United States, 1860–2000

Figures for 1860–1920 represent the number of divorces per 1,000 existing marriages; figures for 1921–2000 represent the number of divorces per 1,000 married women age 15 and over.

Source: Cherlin, 1981; *Statistical Abstract,* 2002.

Christians think of the Muslim Kosovars as innately inferior, just as some highly prejudiced people in the United States believe that African Americans and other groups, such as Puerto Ricans, are inferior. These and other examples of racial and ethnic prejudice will be discussed more fully in later chapters. Here we need to emphasize that differences in culture often are wrongly viewed as innate biological differences between distinct peoples.

Students of sociology must see beyond this tendency to confuse cultural and biological differences. To do so, it is first necessary to understand how the famous naturalist Charles Darwin revolutionized modern thinking on these issues. Darwin's theory of natural selection is a starting point for scientific explanations of the differences among the animal species, including the human species (Eisley, 1961; Gould, 1996).

Darwin's Theory of Natural Selection

Darwin's theory of **natural selection** is the central explanation of how living species evolve to adapt to their changing environments. It is based on the observation that unexpected physical changes, or *mutations,* in organisms occur more or less randomly from one generation to the next. When those mutations improve an individual organism's ability to survive in its environment, the new traits are "selected for"; that is, an individual that possesses those traits is more likely to survive, and hence more likely to reproduce and pass on its traits to the next generation, than individuals that lack the new traits. Over a few generations such mutations can become so extensive that two species are created where formerly there was only one. This process of natural selection accounts for the great diversity of animal and plant life on the earth and for the ability of animals and plants to adapt to new environments.

Darwin's theory was based on his empirical observations of the natural world, especially those he had made as a scientist aboard the HMS *Beagle* during an extensive voyage of exploration in the early 1830s. On that voyage, Darwin had observed, in both fossils and living specimens, that some species of birds, turtles, and other animals had modified their physical form in ways that seemed to "fit" or "adapt" them to their environment. It took him almost two decades of study and reflection to make sense of his observations. After all, much of what he had observed directly challenged the fundamental beliefs of most of the religious and scientific leaders of his day. For when Darwin considered all the information, and especially his observations of similar species on different islands, it became clear to him that God had not created all the living things on earth at once—instead, they had been evolving through natural selection over many millions of years. And this theory could be applied to all other species, including humans.

The Social Darwinists

The theory of natural selection had a dramatic impact on biological science but an even greater effect on the prevailing views of human society. Among the social thinkers who were most profoundly influenced by Darwin was Herbert Spencer of England, whose writings in sociology and philosophy were to dominate intellectual life in much of the Western world from 1870 to 1890.

According to Spencer, the fact that humans, unlike other species, have remained similar even on different continents must be explained by the fact that we adapt to changes in our environment through the use of culture rather than through biological adaptation. This process, which can be termed **cultural evolution,** parallels biological evolution in that the most successful adaptations are handed down to the next generation (Geertz, 1973). Spencer had this process in mind when he coined the phrase "survival of the fittest." He meant that the people who are most successful at adapting to the environment in which they find themselves—that is, the better-educated, wealthier, more powerful people—are most likely to survive and to have children who will also be successful.

Spencer concluded that it is impossible, by means of intentional action, to improve on the course of cultural evolution. The task of sociology, as he saw it, is to discover that course through empirical observation and analysis. Sociologists should not engage in efforts to reform society—to aid the poor, for example. To do so would be futile, and it could have the damaging effect of violating the principle of survival of the fittest in favor of the "artificial preservation of those least able to take care of themselves" (Spencer, 1874, p. 343).

Spencer's view, which came to be known as **social Darwinism,** claimed to explain why some people prospered during the Industrial Revolution while others barely scraped by. The people who were being pushed off the land and into the factories and slums of the cities were less well equipped culturally to succeed in an urban environment than people who could innovate and invent. There was not much for government to do, according to Spencer's theory, besides keep the peace and let the most competitive groups in society flourish. In so doing, those groups would give less competitive groups a chance to survive, if not to thrive.

By the end of the nineteenth century, efforts to apply the theory of natural selection to human societies had reached their logical extreme. Largely as a result of the work of Spencer and his followers, early sociologists in the

United States and other Western societies favored the view that Western culture, with its emphasis on competition within the capitalist system, was clearly superior to all others and that the people who were most successful at competing within that system were to be considered superior human beings. The next generation of social scientists, who came to prominence around the turn of the twentieth century, rejected this theory. In Chicago and other U.S. cities where the Industrial Revolution was still occurring, they saw mounting evidence that wealth itself brings privilege to the children of the wealthy, regardless of whatever innate or learned traits they may possess. Cultural evolution, they argued, is a result of the development of more effective institutions and is not related to the innate qualities of individuals. Successful business firms, for example, are able to prosper in a highly competitive environment because of their superior organization. That is, their success can be explained without recourse to arguments about the genetic fitness of their leaders (Swedberg, 1994).

Sociobiology

The tendency to explain social phenomena in terms of biological causes such as physiology or genes is known as *biological reductionism*. For example, theories of crime proposing that there are genes that produce criminal behavior reduce the explanation of crime to biological causes. Some form of biological reductionism has emerged in every generation since Darwin's time.

The most recent version of biological reductionism is **sociobiology.** This term, coined by the Harvard biologist Edward O. Wilson (1975, 1998), refers to efforts to link genetic factors with the social behavior of animals. When applied to human societies, sociobiology has drawn severe criticism from both social scientists and biologists. Nevertheless, some sociologists support the sociobiological hypothesis that genes can explain certain aspects of human society and behavior (Caplan, 1978; Herlihy, 1995; Mascie-Taylor, 1990; Maxwell, 1991; Quadagno, 1979; Sahlins, 1976). Because this hypothesis is so controversial, it deserves a closer look.

Let us take as an example the incest taboo, one of the strongest and most widespread norms in human life. The social scientist tends to explain the incest taboo as a cultural norm that is necessary for the existence of the family as a social institution. The family is an organized group with a need for well-defined statuses and roles. If the different statuses within the family became confused, as would undoubtedly happen if sexual intimacy were permitted between children and their parents or between brothers and sisters, it would be difficult to maintain the family as a stable institution (Davis, 1939; Malinowski, 1927).

Sociobiology takes a different view. For the sociobiologist, the incest taboo evolved in response to biological conditions:

> . . . a deeper, more urgent cause, the heavy physiological penalty imposed by inbreeding. Several studies by human geneticists have demonstrated that even a moderate amount of inbreeding results in children who are diminished in overall body size, muscular coordination, and academic performance. More than 100 recessive genes have been discovered that cause hereditary disease . . . a condition vastly enhanced by inbreeding. (Wilson, 1979, p. 38)

Throughout most of the history of human evolution, sociobiologists point out, humans did not have any knowledge of genetics. Thus "the 'gut feeling' that promotes . . . sanctions against incest is largely unconscious" (Wilson, 1979, p. 40). Individuals with a strong predisposition to avoid incest passed on more of their genes to the next generation because their children were less likely to suffer from the illnesses that result from inbreeding. And over many centuries of natural selection of individuals who did not inbreed, humans developed "an instinct [to avoid inbreeding] which is based on genes" (Wilson, 1979, p. 40).

This leap, from the observation of a strong and persistent norm like the incest taboo to the belief that certain human behaviors are genetically programmed, is an example of the sociobiological hypothesis regarding human nature. Sociobiologists have proposed a hypothesis in which not only the incest taboo but also aggression, homosexuality, and religious feelings are genetically programmed, and they believe that future discoveries by geneticists will prove their hypothesis correct (Cecco & Parker, 1995).

Although it is true that genes set limits on human abilities and can be shown to influence many aspects of brain functioning, the hypothesis that genetic programming establishes complex forms of normative behavior is not supported by direct evidence: There is as yet no proof that such genes or sets of genes actually exist (Lewontin, 1995, 2003). Nevertheless, the rules of science require that we not reject the sociobiological hypothesis and that it remain an open area of investigation.

The counterargument to sociobiology is that the human brain and other physical attributes are products of cultural and biological evolution and that in the past 100,000 years of human evolution there has been relatively little organic change in our species. Instead, the important developments in human life have occurred as a result of social and cultural change. This widely accepted view of culture denies that humans have innate instincts such as an instinct to avoid incest. It argues instead that the great advantage of culture in human evolution is its creation of a basis for natural selection that would not depend on genes but would allow humans to adapt relatively quickly to any physical or social environment (Geertz, 1973; MacWhinney, 1998).

Archaeological evidence shows that humans were using tools for primitive agriculture and making jewelry and personal adornments more than 30,000 years ago (Stevens, 1988). No doubt they began using fire even earlier. Once humans could use fire and hand tools and simple weapons, the ability to make and use these items increased the survival chances of those who possessed these skills. This would create conditions for natural selection in which the traits being "selected for" were those that involved the manipulation of cultural and social aspects of life. These abilities (dexterity, linguistic ability, leadership, social skills, and so on) would in turn influence the further development of the human brain, again through the process of natural selection.

This view is supported by research on primate behavior showing that the higher primates use simple tools and that they teach this cultural technique to their young (Schaller, 1964). Jane Goodall (1968, 1994), for example, described how chimpanzees use sticks to probe for termites (see photo) and chew leaves to produce a pulp to be used as a sponge to draw water out of tree stumps. These and many other instances of rudimentary culture among animal species demonstrate that culture is not unique to humans; recent research on chimpanzees has demonstrated that their societies have cultures that are passed down from one generation to the next and can adapt to new conditions in the chimps' environments (Friend, 2000). What happened in the case of humans that did not happen (or at least has not happened yet) in any other species is that, at a certain stage in human prehistory, our ability to alter our cultures in response to changing conditions developed so quickly that the human species entered a new realm of social life. In other words, culture became self-generating. And once it had been freed from genetic constraints, culture had no limits.

LANGUAGE AND CULTURE

Perhaps the most significant of the inventions made possible by culture is language. In fact, the learning of culture takes place through language. From our enormous capacity to use language is derived our collective memory (myths, fables, proverbs, ballads, and the like), as well as writing, art, and all the other media that shape human consciousness and store and transmit knowledge. In 2001, scientists identified a gene that appears to have a direct influence on human linguistic ability (Lai et al., 2001). They believe that this gene triggers the action of many other genes that contribute to the development of language ability; however, it may also be influenced by external variables such as the particular language the person is exposed to. Thus, although the capacity to learn language appears to be innate (Chomsky, 1965; MacWhinney, 1998), language does not occur outside a cultural setting and indeed is the most universal dimension of human cultures.

To return to the example at the beginning of the chapter, as savage as they may have appeared to Europeans, the Native Americans had language. They could have learned Spanish, just as the explorers could have learned their language if they had made an effort to do so. But without a common language that they could use to communicate with each other, the Indians and the explorers misunderstood each other far more than they would have if they had possessed this powerful communication tool. Without language, neither side could explain to the other its strange behaviors and different ways of dealing with the physical world.

Research With Other Primates

What is unique about human language? Primatologists have shown that our closest evolutionary kin, the great apes (especially chimpanzees and pygmy chimpanzees), can learn language to some extent. Although their throats are not capable of producing the sounds that humans mold into language, apes do have the capacity to use language; that is, they can grasp the meanings of words as symbols for things and relationships. Through the use of sign language, or special languages using typewriters and other devices, apes can be taught a limited vocabulary.

Several examples of this capacity for learning have made headlines. Francine Patterson taught Koko, a female gorilla, American Sign Language. Koko learned more than 300 words. She also disproved the theory that apes can learn words but cannot invent new concepts. Koko invented sign words for *ring* ("finger bracelet") and *mask* ("eye hat") and was even able to talk in sign language about her feelings of fear, happiness, and shame (Hill, 1978). Subsequent research with a pygmy chimpanzee named Kanzi revealed that apes may actually be able to learn language through observation and imitation, the way a child does, rather than through long and difficult training (Eckholm, 1985). Sue Savage-Rumbaugh demonstrated that Kanzi could recognize English syntax, the patterns in the ordering of signs or words that give sentences different meanings. For example, Kanzi could distinguish between "Throw the potato at the ball" and "Throw the ball at the potato." Savage-Rumbaugh also showed that Kanzi could acquire new words simply by listening and watching as other chimps learn (Savage-Rumbaugh & Shanker, 1998). This kind of imitative language learning was formerly thought to be beyond the apes' mental capacities.

Fascinating as these experiments are, they only confirm the immense difference in communicative ability between humans and the apes. After months of training, an adult ape can use language with no more skill than an average 2½-year-old human infant (Bower, 2002; Dreifus, 1998). On the basis of the research conducted so far, primate researchers conclude that the apes' innate ability to learn language is severely restricted. No amount of training can produce in apes the more advanced uses of language, including complex sentences containing abstract concepts, that are found in all normal humans regardless of their culture (Eibl-Eibesfeldt, 1989). For example, every human language allows its speakers to express an infinite number of thoughts and ideas that can persist even after their originators are gone. This property of human language, which is not shared by any other known species (Eisley, 1970; Rymer, 1992a, 1992b), allows human groups to transmit elements of their culture from one generation to the next.

Does Language Determine Thought?

So complete is the human reliance on language that it often seems as if language actually determines the possibilities for thought and action in any given culture. Perhaps we are unable to perceive phenomena for which we have no nouns or to engage in actions for which we have no verbs. This idea is expressed in the **linguistic-relativity hypothesis.** As developed by the American linguists Edward Sapir and Benjamin Whorf in the 1930s, this hypothesis asserts that "a person's thoughts are controlled by inexorable laws or patterns of which he is unconscious. . . . His thinking itself is in a language—in English, in Sanskrit, in Chinese. And every language is a vast pattern-system, different from others" (Whorf, 1961, p. 135).

This observation was based on evidence from the social sciences, especially anthropology. For example, Margaret

Mead's field research among the Arapesh of New Guinea had revealed that the Arapesh had no developed system of numbers. Theirs was a technologically simple society, and therefore complex numbering systems were not much use to them. They counted only "one, two, and one and two, and dog" (dog being the equivalent of four and probably based on the dog's four legs). To count seven objects, the Arapesh would say "dog and one and two." Eight would be "two dog," and twenty-four would come out as "two dog, two dog, two dog." It is easy to see that in this small society one would quickly become tired of attempting to count much beyond twenty-four and would simply say "many" (Mead, 1971).

Other cultures have been found to have only a limited number of words for colors, and as a result they do not make some of the fine distinctions between colors that we do. And in a famous example, Whorf argued that many languages have ways of referring to time that are very different from those found in English and other Indo-European languages. In English, we have verb tenses, which lead us to make sharp distinctions among past, present, and future time. In Vietnamese, in contrast, there are no separate forms of verbs to indicate different times; the phrase *tôi đi về*, for example, could mean "I'm going home" or "I went home" or "I will go home." The language of the Hopi also lacks clear tenses, and it seemed to Whorf that this made it unlikely that the Hopi culture could develop the systems of timekeeping that are essential to modern science and technology.

Thus, in its most radical form, the linguistic-relativity hypothesis asserts that language actually determines the possibilities for a culture's norms, beliefs, and values. But there is little justification for this extreme version of the hypothesis. The Arapesh did not have a developed number system, but they easily learned to count using the Western base-10 system. Once they were exposed to the money economy of the modern world, most isolated cultures formed words for the base-10 number system or incorporated foreign words into their own vocabularies. They had no difficulty understanding the use of money, and this too became incorporated into so-called primitive cultures.

A more acceptable version of the linguistic-relativity hypothesis recognizes the mutual influences of thought and language. For example, someone living in Canada or the northern parts of the United States is likely to have a much larger vocabulary for talking about snow (*loose powder, packed powder, corn snow, slush,* and so on) than a person from an area where snow is rare. A person who loves to watch birds will have a much larger vocabulary about bird habitats and bird names than one who cares little about bird life. To share the world of birders or of winter sports fans, we will need to learn new ways of seeing and of talking about what we see. So although the extreme version of the linguistic-relativity hypothesis is incorrect, it has been a valuable stimulus toward the development of a less biased view of other cultures. We now understand that a culture's language expresses how the people of that culture perceive and understand the world and, at the same time, influences their perceptions and understandings.

CROSSING CULTURAL LINES

Global transactions of all kinds are a feature of the contemporary world. Success in such transactions often hinges on a person's ability to move comfortably among different cultures and subcultures. But unless we can see ourselves as others see us, we take for granted that our own cultural traits are natural and proper and that traits that differ from ours are unnatural and somehow wrong. Our ways of behaving in public, our food and dress and sports—all our cultural traits have become "internalized," so they seem almost instinctive. But once we understand another culture and how its members think and feel, we can look at our own traits from the perspective of that culture. This *cross-cultural perspective* has become an integral part of sociological analysis.

Ethnocentrism and Cultural Relativity

The ability to think in cross-cultural terms allows people to avoid the common tendency to disparage other cultures simply because they are different. However, most people live out their lives in a single culture. Indeed, they may go so far as to consider that culture superior to any other, anywhere in the world. Social scientists term this attitude *ethnocentrism*. Ethnocentrism refers to the tendency to judge other cultures as inferior in terms of one's own norms and values. The other culture is weighed against standards derived from the culture with which one is most familiar. The European explorers' assumption that the Native Americans could benefit from the adoption of European cultural traits is an example of ethnocentric behavior. But such obvious ethnocentrism is not limited to historical examples. We encounter it every day—for example, in our use of the term *American* to refer to citizens of the United States and not to those of Canada and the South American nations. Another example is our tendency to judge other cultures by how well they supply their people with the consumer goods we prize rather than by how well they adhere to their own values.

International study helps address problems of ethnocentrism by fostering cross-cultural contacts. In recent years, however, such exchanges have been hampered by the fear of terrorism.

To get along well in other parts of the world, a businessperson or politician or scientist must be able to suspend judgment about other cultures, an approach termed **cultural relativity**. Cultural relativity entails the recognition that all cultures develop their own ways of dealing with the specific demands of their environments. This kind of understanding does not come automatically through the experience of living among members of other cultures; it is an acquired skill.

LIMITS TO CULTURAL RELATIVITY   There are limits, however, to the value of cultural relativity. It is an essential attitude to adopt in understanding another culture, but it does not require that one avoid moral judgment entirely. We can, for example, attempt to understand the values and ideologies of the citizens who supported the Nazi regime, even though we abhor what that regime stood for. And we can suspend our outrage at racism in our own society long enough to understand the culture that produced racial hatred and fear. But as social scientists it is also our task to evaluate the moral implications of a culture's norms and values and to condemn them when we see that they produce cruelty and suffering (Mack, 2001). Consider the example of patriarchy.

A set of cultural values that appears widely throughout the world emphasizes that women should be subservient to men. Women may be influential in the home, but in the larger world of the village, the city, and the nation, men should dominate and rule. The set of values and norms that supports male dominance and the subordination of women is known as *patriarchy*, and societies that put the values of patriarchy into practice are known as patriarchal societies (Feldman, 2001).

Despite generations of struggle by women to break down the values and norms of patriarchy, in much of the world boys continue to be valued more highly than girls, a cultural value that leads to widespread suffering and neglect. Some patriarchal cultures forbid women to appear openly in public so that the honor of their fathers and husbands will not be put at risk. Other cultures set standards for women's appearance—small feet, for example, or large breasts and a small waist. Some cultures practice clitoridectomy, in which a woman's external genitalia are removed in order to reduce her desire for and enjoyment of sex. These and many similar practices are typical of patriarchal cultures or of cultures where patriarchal norms and values remain powerful despite women's assertion of their human rights.

A major feature of cultural change throughout the world is a movement by women to challenge the norms and values underlying patriarchy (Enloe, 2000). As women demand the right to determine how many children they bear; to read, drive, work in professions, and attend universities; and to enjoy other benefits often reserved for men, men perceive a threat to their power. And in many poor regions of the world, where men do not have much power or wealth themselves, the idea that women would challenge the status quo is seen by some as a direct threat to honor and male virtue and as a justification for many forms of violence against women. In such societies, women as well as men are often fearful of change and insist that traditional values must be upheld. Even in culturally diverse societies like those of the West, many women find themselves siding with men who want to return to the older values of patriarchy. But the dominant trend in the world, despite conflict and resistance, is for women to act as cultural innovators, challenge patriarchy, and assert their human rights.

Sociologists can be cultural relativists when they seek to understand the origins and strength of patriarchal norms in their own and other cultures. They can also recognize the limits of cultural relativity for understanding why many women reject values that insist on female subjugation. However, to argue that there are human values that transcend cultures, and that, for example, patriarchal cultures must change, is to risk imposing Western values on other cultures.

Cultural Hegemony: Myth or Reality?

When one culture's values, norms, and products become dominant and diminish the strength of another culture, the stronger culture is said to exert hegemony over the weaker one. The term *hegemony* refers to dominance or undue power or influence. A hegemonic culture is one that dominates other cultures, just as a hegemonic society is one that exerts undue power over other societies (Gramsci, 1992/ 1965, 1995). In Europe and parts of Asia, there is a lively debate about whether the culture of the United States endangers the continued existence of local cultures. English is the international language of business and science. American movies and popular music, fast food, and fashions are coveted around the world. Nations with less widespread languages and less powerful cultural institutions (e.g., media industries, universities, fashion industries) fear that their young people will lose interest in their own cultures and embrace the values, language, and norms of Americans. Discussions of the global influence of McDonald's or the Disney Company appear often in social-scientific essays and cultural critiques in nations where American culture is popular. These issues have only gained in prominence since the tragic events of September 11, 2001.

Within the United States, too, sociologists and others worry that the powerful commercial cultural institutions that make certain types of food, music, movies, fashions, and magazines popular throughout the nation endanger the existence of unique local subcultures. These critics fear that regional differences are decreasing and being replaced by a homogeneous culture that lacks diversity (Hardt & Negri, 2001; Oldenburg, 1997).

These movie billboards in Madras, India, capture some of the excitement that can always be felt outside theaters where "Bollywood" films are featured.

© Hans Georg Roth/Corbis

How realistic are these fears? Like all generalizations about social life, they contain some truth and much myth. Further research and more factual information are needed to understand whether American culture is indeed hegemonic, as its critics claim. But it is clear that in many regions of the world there are societies with extremely strong and distinct cultures that are able to produce their own adaptations of American commercial culture. India, for example, is the second leading producer of commercial movies in the world. There is a huge audience for Indian films, which combine the technology of Western films with the music, language, norms, and values of India's many subcultures (Palmer, 1995). And as Europe becomes more economically unified, it is likely that the strength of European cultural institutions will improve, despite the linguistic divisions that make some Europeans feel vulnerable to the influence of American culture.

At the same time, as the war in Iraq in 2003 demonstrated, there can be no doubt that on the world stage the United States is more than just another culture. It represents a powerful civilization whose cultural features have diffused across national boundaries to exert a lasting influence over the cultures of other societies. Does this mean that the United States exerts hegemony over other cultures? This question is a subject of continuing research and debate. Meanwhile, it is worth noting that much of what we think of as distinctive about American civilization originated in European, African, Asian, and Hispanic cultures. In consequence, we devote the rest of this chapter to a discussion of civilizations and cultural change.

The Sociological Observer

This photo portrays a ceremonial occasion in the Mayan Indian village of Chamula in Chiapas, Mexico. Careful study of the photo reveals a great deal about contemporary Mayan culture and society, in which the village is the most important unit of social structure (see Chapter 4 for a discussion of the elements of social structure). What do you think is growing on the hillside? What might the banners signify? What other observations about Mayan Indian culture can you glean from the photo? (See page 74 for further insights into the sociological content of this photo.)

JLFOX/XXX

CIVILIZATIONS AND CULTURAL CHANGE

Civilizations are advanced cultures. They usually have forms of expression in writing and the arts, powerful economic and political institutions, and innovative technologies, all of which strongly influence other cultures with which they come into contact. Some civilizations, like those of ancient Egypt and Rome, declined thousands of years ago and exist today mainly in museums and in the consciousness of scholars, artists, and scientists. Others are living civilizations with long histories, like those of China and India, which were conquered by other civilizations and are rising again in forms that combine the old with the new. As we will see shortly, Islamic civilization is an example of such a civilization; so are the dominant civilizations of North America, Europe, the former Soviet Union, and Japan.

They are dominant because they compete on a world scale to "export" their ideas and their technology—in fact, their entire culture or "blueprint for living."

The Concept of Civilization

Like most of the principal concepts in the social sciences, the concept of civilization can be elusive. It is used in many different contexts, in popular language as well as in social-scientific usage. In popular speech, the word *civilization* is often used to make negative comparisons between people who adhere to the norms of polite conduct, and are therefore said to be "civilized," and those who are "uncouth" and act like "barbarians" or "savages." This is how the word was understood by the explorers of Columbus's time, and colonial conquest was justified in part as an effort to civilize the barbarians.

In his effort to trace the origins of Western notions of what is civilized and what is barbaric behavior, the German sociologist Norbert Elias (1978/1939) showed that much of what we call "civilized" behavior is derived from the norms of the courts of medieval Europe. Elias based his study on accounts by medieval writers of the spread of "courtesy" (the manners of the court) to other levels of society. The following are some examples from a thirteenth-century poem on courtly table manners:

A man of refinement should not slurp his spoon when in company; that is the way people at court behave who often indulge in unrefined conduct.

It is not polite to drink from the dish, although some who approve of this rude habit insolently pick up the dish and pour it down as if they were mad.

A number of people gnaw a bone and then put it back in the dish—this is a serious offense. (p. 85)

Through his analysis of writings on manners, Elias demonstrated that Western norms concerning the control of bodily functions, from eating and sleeping to blowing one's nose, arose in the Middle Ages as the courts consolidated their power over feudal societies and exported the standards of courtly behavior to the countryside. Such behavior became a sign that a person was a member of the upper classes and not a serf or a savage.

In the social sciences, the most common use of the term *civilization* stems from the study of changes in human society at the macro level, which often requires comparisons among major cultures. In this context, a **civilization** is "a cultural complex formed by the identical major cultural features of a number of particular societies. We might, for example, describe Western capitalism as a civilization, in which specific forms of science, technology, religion, art, and so on, are to be found in a number of distinct societies" (Bottomore, 1973, p. 130). Thus Italy, France, Germany, the United States, Sweden, and many other nations that have made great contributions to Western civilization all have private corporations, and their normative orders, laws, and judicial systems are quite similar (Gramsci, 1995). Even though each may have a different language and each differs in the way it organizes some aspects of social life (European and North American universities define academic degrees differently, for example), they share similar norms and values and can all be said to represent Western civilization.

Islam is an outstanding example of a civilization that encompasses many distinct cultures and is still combining old and new cultural ways. The religion of Islam was founded by Mohammed, a prophet who was born in what is now Saudi Arabia in about 570 AD. Sometime between 610 and 612, outside the holy city of Mecca, Mohammed is said to have received a visit from the Archangel Gabriel, who brought him the word of God. Mohammed became a charismatic religious leader whose followers developed his sayings and writings into the Koran, the Islamic sacred text.

Mohammed and his followers were a small band who sought to spread the new religion to the people among whom they lived. Most of the early Muslims were nomadic Arabs, primarily members of the Bedouin tribes who tended flocks in the arid and semiarid regions of Arabia. During his lifetime, Mohammed and his followers met with limited success in converting the various Arab peoples to the new faith. However, his successor, Omar, a man of great piety and military prowess, summoned believers to join in efforts to convert the tribes of pagan unbelievers. In a series of outstanding victories, Islamic armies conquered Syria (636), Iraq (637), Iran (637), Mesopotamia (641), and Egypt (642). These were all distinct societies and cultures, those of the West part of the Greek and Byzantine civilization, with its written languages and highly developed cultures, while those of the East were influenced primarily by Persian civilization. For at least the next eight centuries, in fits and starts, Islamic civilization spread eastward and westward into the empires of India and China, over the old empires of Africa, and into Spain.

Compare the map of world cultures and civilizations in 1500 in Chapter 4 (Figure 4.4 on page 92) with the map of the Islamic world as it existed around the same time (Figure 3.3), after the wars between Christians and Muslims in what is now Israel and Jordan, and after the expulsion of the Islamic Moors from Spain. Both maps present some of the same facts, but Figure 3.3 suggests how important sea routes were in linking the far-flung regions of the Islamic world. Figure 4.4 emphasizes the many diverse societies, each with its own distinct cultures, encompassed by Islamic civilization. Tribal peoples in Africa and Indonesia, nomadic Bedouin and African societies, residents of older empires in India and China—all shared, with many variations, the basic tenets of Islam while contributing their own cultural forms to a great and diverse civilization.

Effects of Cultural Contact

Although sociologists do not distinguish among cultures in terms of how "civilized" they are, this standard is often applied by members of different cultures when they come into contact with one another. The contact between Christopher Columbus and his crew and the natives of the West Indies is typical of such episodes. The explorers represented the relatively advanced civilization of Europe,

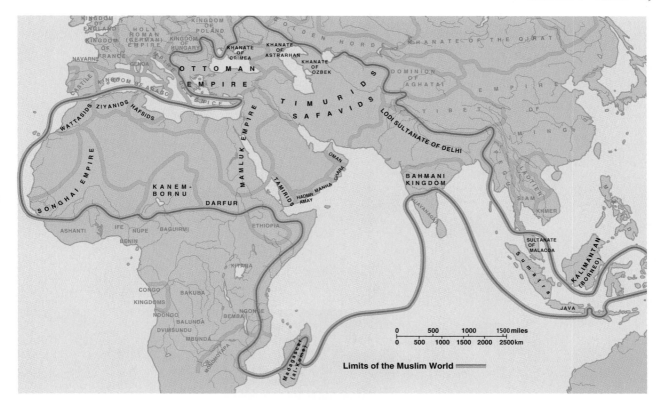

Figure 3.3   The Islamic World Around 1500

while the natives whom the Europeans first encountered represented a much simpler culture, one that seemed totally "uncivilized" to the explorers. Throughout the period of world exploration, from the late fifteenth to the early nineteenth centuries, explorers and traders brought back reports of "savages" living in every part of the globe. These episodes of cultural contact (and often conflict as well) shaped the history of the next two centuries and continue to influence human existence.

Through such processes as exploration and conquest, civilizations invariably spread beyond their original boundaries. Figure 3.4 shows how through much of the nineteenth century England spread its version of Western civilization throughout the world as it conquered tribal peoples and established colonies in Africa and Asia. Colonial rule brought *cultural imperialism,* the imposition of a new culture on the conquered peoples. This meant that colonial peoples had to learn the languages of their conquerors, especially English, Spanish, French, Portuguese, and Dutch (or Afrikaans). Along with language came the imposition of ideologies like Christianity in place of older beliefs and religions.

According to the historian Fernand Braudel, "The mark of a living civilization is that it is capable of exporting itself, of spreading its culture to distant places. It is impossible to imagine a true civilization which does not export its people,

its ways of thinking and living" (1976/1949, p. 763). In his research on the contacts and clashes between the great civilizations surrounding the Mediterranean Sea during the 1500s, Braudel uses three important sociological concepts to explain the spread of civilizations around the world: acculturation, assimilation, and accommodation. (See the Study Chart on page 71.)

ACCULTURATION   People from one civilization incorporate norms and values from other cultures into their own through a process called **acculturation.** Most acculturation occurs through intercultural contact and the borrowing or imitation of cultural norms. But there have been many instances of acculturation through cultural imperialism, in which one culture has been forced to adopt the language or other traits of a more dominant one. Thus people in societies that were colonized in the nineteenth century were forced to learn the language of the conquering nation.

Aspects of our culture that we take for granted usually can be shown to have traveled a complicated route through other cultures to become part of our way of life. For example, Braudel's study of the Mediterranean civilizations shows that many of the plants and foods that are commonly found around the Mediterranean Sea, and later were imported to

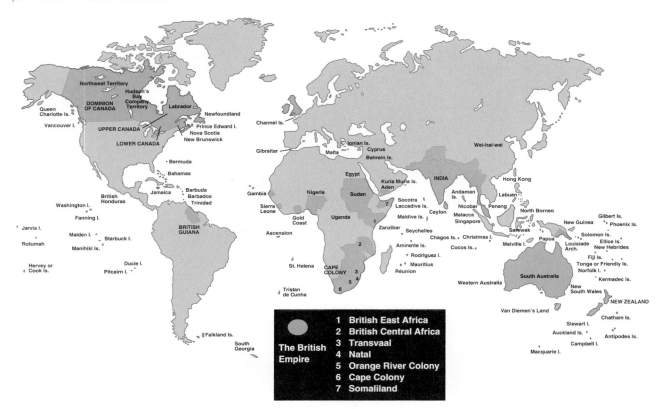

Figure 3.4   The British Empire in 1901

This map shows the extent of the British Empire in 1901. At the peak of its power, the empire had spread English civilization throughout the world. But its influence was strongest in peripheral, less industrialized lands. In a mere half-century, most of the empire would crumble, but the effects of English civilization on language and social institutions throughout the world would endure.

Source: Eldridge, 1978.

the New World, were borrowed from other cultures and incorporated into those of the Mediterranean societies. The process of acculturation can be traced in many other aspects of everyday life. As Ralph Linton has written:

> Our solid American citizen awakens in a bed built on a pattern which originated in the Near East. . . . He throws back covers made from cotton, domesticated in India. . . . He slips into his moccasins, invented by the Indians of the Eastern woodlands. . . . He takes off his pajamas, a garment invented in India, and washes with soap invented by the ancient Gauls. . . . He puts on garments whose form originally derived from the skin clothing of the nomads of the Asiatic steppes . . . and ties around his neck a strip of bright-colored cloth which is a vestigial survival of the shoulder shawls worn by the seventeenth-century Croatians. Before going out for breakfast he glances through the window, made of glass invented in Egypt, and if it is raining puts on overshoes made of rubber discovered by the Central American Indians and takes an umbrella, invented in southeastern Asia. (1936, p. 326)

The concept of acculturation can also be applied to how a newcomer people adopts the cultural ways of the host society. But acculturation is rarely a one-way process: At the same time that they are becoming more like their hosts in values and behavior, newcomers teach members of the host society to use and appreciate aspects of their own culture. Because of the cultural diversity of its population, examples of acculturation are especially prevalent in the United States. For example, even small towns in the interior of the country have at least one Chinese restaurant, but often the food served in those restaurants is a highly acculturated form of the cuisine of China. Indeed, most of the things we think of as part of

EFFECTS OF CULTURAL CONTACT

FORM OF CONTACT	DESCRIPTION	EXAMPLE
Acculturation	The process by which the members of a civilization incorporate norms and values from other cultures into their own.	Americans develop a taste for Italian, Chinese, and Mexican food, as well as other cuisines representing the cultures of the people who have joined their civilization.
Assimilation	The process by which culturally distinct groups within a civilization adopt the norms, values, and language of that civilization and gain equal statuses in its groups and institutions.	Spanish-speaking immigrants to the United States learn English and begin to move up the status hierarchy in education and jobs.
Accommodation	The process by which a smaller, less powerful society is able to preserve the major features of its culture even after prolonged contact with a larger, stronger culture.	Though conquered and forced onto reservations, Native Americans adapt by taking on many of the norms and values of the larger society while preserving aspects of their own culture.

the American way of life—from hamburgers, pizza, and baseball to democracy and free enterprise—originally were aspects of other cultures. That they have become incorporated into American culture through acculturation, and in the process have become changed from their original forms, does not deny the fact of their "foreign" origin (see the Global Social Change box on page 72).

ASSIMILATION AND SUBCULTURES When culturally distinct groups within a larger civilization adopt the language, values, and norms of the host civilization and their acculturation enables them to assume equal statuses in the social groups and institutions of that civilization, we refer to that process as **assimilation.** When groups become assimilated into American society, for example, people often say that they have been "Americanized." Assimilation has been a major issue for immigrant groups in North America, as it still is for immigrants all over the world. It is no surprise, then, that we continually see articles in the press that ask such questions as: Will the various Hispanic peoples in America give up their language over time? Will American Jews marry members of other groups and lose their distinct identity? Will Italian Americans gradually forget their cultural heritage and come to think of themselves as "100 percent Americans" (Brimelow, 1995)? These kinds of questions form the subject matter of racial and ethnic relations in pluralistic societies like the United States.

When a culturally distinct people within a larger culture fails to assimilate fully or has not yet become fully assimilated, we say that it is a **subculture** within the larger culture. (The term is also applied to groups that have had significantly different experiences from those of most members of the society.) People who maintain their own subculture generally share many of the values and norms of the larger culture, but they retain certain rituals, values, traditions, and norms—and in some cases their own language—that set them apart. Thus we speak of African American, Latino, Native American, and a host of other subcultures in the United States. As explained in Chapter 13, these are also known as *ethnic groups,* since their members have a sense of shared descent, a feeling of being "a people" with a history and a way of life that exists within a larger and more culturally diverse society.

Ethnic subcultures are created out of the experience of migration or invasion and subsequent adaptation to a host culture. But subcultures are also created out of the experience of people in complex societies who actively seek to create and maintain a way of life distinct from that of other members of their society (Fischer, 1987; Gans, 1976). For example, there are subcultures in large cities composed of artists and other people whose livelihood depends on the arts: theater people, rock musicians and record producers, visual artists, gallery owners, art critics, and curators. In many U.S. cities, and in some in Western Europe, there are quite distinct gay and lesbian subcultures. Because people who form homosexual relationships often experience hostility from heterosexuals, they tend to develop their own particular norms of communication and social behavior. When a subculture that challenges the accepted norms and values of the larger society establishes an alternative lifestyle, we call it a **counterculture.** The hippies of the 1960s, along with members of New Left political groups, activists in the women's movement, and environmental activists, formed a counterculture that had a significant influence on American politics and foreign policy during the Vietnam War years (Roszak, 1969).

GLOBAL SOCIAL CHANGE

North America's African Heritage

All the important streams of migration to North America have combined to produce the culture of the United States and Canada. Pizza (Italy), hamburgers (Germany), French fries—examples of the influence of immigrant groups on American material culture abound. Of all these cultural influences, perhaps the least well understood is the legacy of the people who were brought to North America from Africa as slaves, especially during the last three decades of the eighteenth century and the first half of the nineteenth.

One of the largest groups of slaves, captured in the region that is now Congo and Angola, was made up of people from many tribes who shared a common language system, Bantu. Many of these Bantu-speaking slaves were brought to the Carolinas. By the end of the Revolutionary War, the Carolinas had the largest concentration of people of African descent of any of the new states. In consequence, many of the names of towns and villages, rivers, streams, and other geographic features in those states are derived from Bantu words, often mixed with local Native American terms and transformed through long usage. Thus Pinder Town in South Carolina is derived from the Bantu word for peanut, *mpinda*. George

R. Stewart, an expert on place names, concludes that hundreds of small streams, swamps, and villages in the Carolinas, Mississippi, and Georgia received their names from the African slaves (Stewart, 1968; Vass, 1979).

The strongest evidence of African influence on contemporary American culture can be found in the Sea Islands along the Atlantic coast between Charlestown, South Carolina, and Savannah, Georgia. On the islands of Port Royal, Parris (famous for its Marine training base), Ladies, Hilton Head, and St. Helena reside the Gullah people. Also known as Geechi, they are descendants of slaves whose original tribes are believed to have lived in Angola (from which the word *Gullah* may be derived) and in the areas that are now Liberia and Sierra Leone. On the plantations, the Gullah slaves grew indigo and the

long-fiber cotton that made the region famous in the period before the Civil War. Some of them escaped to become leaders of slave rebellions. Others were arrested during the Civil War for singing spirituals like "Roll, Jordan, Roll" to which they had added verses about their dreams of freedom. To this

A Gullah woman of the Sea Islands in a photograph taken early in the twentieth century.

day, the religious practices, language, and place names of the Sea Island people bear witness to their African heritage (Creel, 1988).

Subcultures often are under intense pressure to conform to the society's most widely accepted norms and values or to adapt to new ways, new technologies, or the like. Social scientists often investigate the changing norms and values of such subcultures—the gay subcultures, the subculture of rock musicians and other celebrities, or the subcultures of occupational groups such as Appalachian miners, Wall Street lawyers, doctors, and construction workers, among others (Backer, 1982; Bosk, 1979; Eisenberg, 1998; Erikson, 1976; Millman, 1976; Smigel, 1964). This research is valuable in predicting trends in such areas as drug use, popular music, or patterns of labor–management conflict and cooperation (Boggs & Meyersohn, 1988; Flores, 1988; Nyden, 1984).

ACCOMMODATION AND RESISTANCE   Throughout history, many societies have withstood tremendous pressure to become assimilated into larger civilizations. But even greater numbers have been either wiped out or fully assimilated. Only a century ago, for example, one could still find many hundreds of hunter-gatherer societies throughout the world. Today there are probably fewer than 100, and these live in the most isolated regions of the earth.

Larger and smaller societies do not usually develop ways of living together without the smaller one becoming extinct or totally assimilated into the larger one. But when the smaller, less powerful society is able to preserve the major features of its culture even after prolonged contact, **accommodation** is said to have occurred. For example, in the

Islamic civilization of the Middle East before the creation of Israel in 1948, Jews and other non-Muslims usually found it rather easy to maintain their cultures within the larger Arab societies. Compare this pattern of accommodation with the experience of the Jews in Spain, who were forced to leave in 1492 in one of the largest mass expulsions in history.

Accommodation requires that each side tolerate the existence of the other and even share territory and social institutions. The history of relations between Native Americans and European settlers in the Western Hemisphere is a complex story of resistance and accommodation. Throughout the period of conquest, expansion, and settlement by the Europeans, there was continual resistance by the native peoples. This resistance took many forms, including refusal to adopt Christianity, to speak English or Spanish, to sell goods and services to the settlers, and to fight in the Europeans' wars. Resistance did not save Native Americans from death by disease, military conquest, or famine, but it did allow them to maintain their cultures and to borrow from the settlers the cultural customs that were most advantageous to them. For example, the Plains Indians adopted horses from the Spanish explorers, which completely changed their culture, and much later they borrowed trucks from American culture, which helped them adapt to modern ranching.

Most cultures in the world today have had to confront the influence of at least one expanding civilization. In some instances, the result has been prolonged conflict and the eventual annihilation of the smaller society. However, throughout the world, it is as easy to find examples of failures in accommodation as it is to find examples of sharing and cooperation among cultures. Many of the conflicts that lead to severe social unrest, such as the conflict between Islamic and Eastern Orthodox Bosnians, or among warring tribal peoples in Rwanda, are based on cultural differences. Such conflicts may also occur *within* a culture. In the United States, for example, cultural differences are becoming more visible, and so are cultural conflicts. In no area of contemporary life is this more true than in the realm of intimacy and sexual behavior.

CRITICAL SOCIOLOGY AND SOCIAL CHANGE

How American Values Are Perceived Outside the United States

"If you want to understand how America appears to the world today, consider the sport-utility vehicle. Over-sized and overweight, the SUV disdains negotiated agreements

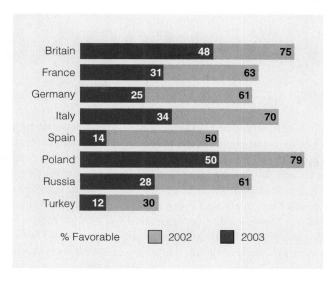

Figure 3.5 Proportion of Population With Favorable Image of United States, Selected Countries

Source: Pew foundation, Pew Global Attitudes Project, 2003.

to restrict atmospheric pollution. It consumes inordinate quantities of scarce resources to furnish its privileged inhabitants with supererogatory [greater than required] services. It exposes outsiders to deadly risk in order to provide for the illusory security of its occupants" (Judt, 2003, p. 24). This metaphor may seem unfair to many Americans, but experts on world opinion about the United States, such as Tony Judt, the author quoted here, use this image because they often hear it from people beyond the U.S. borders.

International polls show that anti-American feelings were increasing before 2003, although the events of 9/11 had brought widespread sympathy and support for the American people throughout the world. But anti-Americanism reached historic levels when the U.S. government declared its right to engage in preemptive wars, such as the invasion of Iraq, to combat terrorism and reduce the threat of "weapons of mass destruction." A majority of people in the United States saw these actions as representing American values of democracy, protection of human rights, and self-protection against terrorism. Throughout most of the world, however, attitudes were quite negative, as indicated in Figure 3.5.

The Pew Global Attitudes Project found that the image of the United States as a promoter of democracy around the world fell precipitously after the American and British invasion of Iraq.

The Pew survey measures the impact of globalization, modernization, rapid technological and cultural

VISUAL SOCIOLOGY

LIVING MAYA

The people in these photos are Mayans. They live in the mountains and jungles of Chiapas in southern Mexico and in part of Guatemala. They are descendants of the ancient Mayans, whose civilization flourished in Central America before 900 AD. The Mayan nobility was literate and, like the Egyptians, intensely interested in astronomy and the construction of calendars. The ancient noble palace and observatory of Palenque, deep in the Lacondon rainforest of Chiapas, was one of the most outstanding archaeological achievements of Mayan civilization. But the people in these photos are our contemporaries. They live in villages, each of which is clustered around a market and a small but much loved Catholic church. The men in one of the photos are holding a session of the village court. In the foreground a man occupies the time by plaiting palm fronds

to make a hat. The standing man is one of the parties to the dispute, as is the one arguing in the background. The seated men are civil officials.

Men's and women's lives are separated much of the time. In each village, the women engage in specialized crafts in addition to their other chores. In this highland region, most women are potters or weavers. Their crafts are an example of material culture passed from one generation to the next for centuries. The woven patterns and symbols on the cloth they are wearing can be seen in the clothing of ancient Mayans depicted on pottery and wall paintings.

These highlanders also believe in traditional spirits and powers. The shaman

with his back to the camera is searching the forest for flowers and branches that will become herbal cures and potions. Most Mayans can identify highland plants in stunning detail, but the shaman has experienced mystical dreams that have given him special knowledge of the magical powers of forest life. The botanical lore of the Mayans is legendary. In fact, the active ingredient in birth-control pills was discovered through the study of an herb well known to Mayan women.

Contemporary Mayans are extremely poor. Their subsistence agricultural and crafts economy is adequate to allow them to preserve their culture, but they crave access to better land. There are huge gaps in power and privilege between the Mayans and the wealthy, often absentee, landowners.

The Sociological Observer

(See photo on page 67.)

Chamula is a rather typical Mayan Indian village in the highlands of Chiapas, where the villagers' main subsistence crop is the corn seen

© Jeffrey Jay Foxx

growing on the hillside behind the church. Here is how Walter F. Morris, Jr., author (with photographer Jeffrey J. Foxx) of *Living Maya*, describes the photo:

> Strings of banners stretching from the bells of the church of Chamula to the walls of the atrium enclose the ritual space of the community, while a cloud of smoke rises behind the kiosk—the trail of a skyrocket shot off to announce the procession of religious officials emerging from the church. The patron of this festival stands before the church portal beside the two "bulls"—frameworks of fireworks carried over the heads of two dancing men. Black-robed civil officials [all males] holding their staffs of office watch the presentation from the kiosk. (Morris & Foxx, 1987)

© Jeffrey Jay Foxx

change, and the September 11 terrorist events on the values and attitudes of more than 38,000 people in 44 countries worldwide. Surveys conducted after the war found that, despite widespread hatred and condemnation of the tyrannical regime of Saddam Hussein, respondents blamed the American government for taking unilateral action and believed that it had acted out of selfish interests.

Although Americans tend to think of their government as a world leader and a generous partner on the international scene, the Pew survey finds that majorities in most countries view the policies of the U.S. government as contributing to the growing gap between rich and poor nations and believe that the United States does not do as much as it should to help solve global problems.

The global influence of the United States is felt very strongly, with some aspects of American values and culture warmly embraced and others just as strongly rejected. The United States is admired for its technological achievements, and people in most countries say that they enjoy American movies, music, and television programs. But the glimpses of the American way of life offered by these movies and programs often convince viewers abroad that the nation's leaders are in favor of maximizing private gain and minimizing public responsibility for others. In consequence, the spread of American ideas and customs is disliked by majorities in almost every country included in the survey. This sentiment is prevalent in friendly nations such as Canada (54%) and Britain (50%), and even more so in countries where America is broadly disliked, such as Argentina (73%) and Pakistan (81%). Aspects of globalization that show the wealth of Americans, as evidenced, for example, in their embrace of vehicles that reduce rather than increase fuel efficiency, highlight for the world's poor countries the widening gap between themselves and the wealthy Westerners. And for people in other Western nations, particularly in Europe, the widening gap between the wealthy and the poor in the United States itself, and the failure of the United States to provide basic health care for millions of its households, is a harsh reminder of the increasing differences between the United States and the welfare states of the European community (Kohut, 2002).

SUMMARY

The Meaning of Culture

- In the social sciences, *culture* refers to all the modes of thought, behavior, and production that are handed down from one generation to the next by means of communicative interaction. Sociologists are concerned primarily with aspects of culture that help explain social organization and behavior.
- Culture can be viewed as consisting of three major dimensions: ideas, norms, and material culture.
- *Ideas* are the ways of thinking that organize human consciousness. Among the most important ideas are *values,* socially shared ideas about what is right.
- *Norms* are specific rules of behavior that are supported or justified by values; *laws* are norms that are included in a society's official written codes of behavior.
- *Ideologies* combine ideas and norms; they are systems of values and norms that the members of a society are expected to believe in and act on without question.
- A society's *material culture* consists of all the things it produces.
- *Technologies* combine norms and material culture; they are the things and the norms for using them that are found in a given culture.
- *Social control* refers to the set of rules and understandings that control the behavior of individuals and groups in a culture. The wide array of norms that permit a society to achieve relatively peaceful social control is called its *normative order.*
- *Sanctions* are rewards and punishments for adhering to or violating norms. Strongly sanctioned norms are called *mores;* more weakly sanctioned norms are known as *folkways.*

Culture, Evolution, and Human Behavior

- One of the most hotly debated questions in the social sciences is how much, if at all, human culture is determined by biological factors.
- According to Darwin's theory of *natural selection,* mutations in organisms occur more or less randomly. Mutations that enable an individual organism to survive and reproduce are passed on to the next generation. This process permits animals and plants to adapt to new environments.
- Herbert Spencer and other social thinkers, who came to be known as *social Darwinists,* attempted to apply Darwin's theory to humans' ability to adapt to social environments. Spencer used the phrase "survival of the fittest" to describe this ability. People who were able to survive in the urban environment created by the Industrial Revolution were viewed as superior human beings.
- A more recent attempt to attribute social phenomena to biological processes is *sociobiology,* which refers to efforts to link genetic factors with the social behavior of animals. According to the sociobiologists, such behaviors as incest avoidance, aggression, and homosexuality may be genetically programmed in human beings. As yet there is no evidence that such genes or sets of genes actually exist.
- A more widely accepted view of culture denies that humans have innate instincts and states that at a certain stage in prehistoric times human culture became self-generating. Thus human evolution is not dependent on genes; instead, cultural techniques allow humans to adapt to any physical or social environment.

Language and Culture

- The learning of culture is made possible by language.
- Although apes have been taught to use language to some extent, human language is unique in that it allows its speakers to express an infinite number of thoughts and ideas that can persist even after their originators are gone.
- According to the *linguistic-relativity hypothesis,* language also determines the possibilities for a culture's norms, beliefs, and values. A less extreme form of that hypothesis recognizes the mutual influences of culture and language.

Crossing Cultural Lines

- The notion that one's own culture is superior to any other is called *ethnocentrism.*
- To understand other cultures, it is necessary to suspend judgment about those cultures, an approach termed *cultural relativity.*
- Throughout the world, women are at the forefront of cultural change, challenging norms of patriarchy that maintain the dominance of men over women.
- Recently there has been much debate over whether the culture of the United States is exercising undue dominance or *hegemony* over other cultures throughout the world. While more research is needed to answer this question, it is clear that in many regions of the world there remain extremely strong and diverse cultures that are able to maintain their own values and traditions.

Civilizations and Cultural Change

- Similarities among cultures have resulted from the processes by which cultures spread across national boundaries and become part of a larger, more advanced culture called a civilization. A *civilization* may be defined as a cultural complex formed by the identical major cultural features of a number of particular societies.
- A key feature of civilizations is that they invariably expand beyond their original boundaries. The spread of civilizations can be explained by three processes: acculturation, assimilation, and accommodation.
- When people from one civilization incorporate norms and values from other cultures into their own, *acculturation* is said to occur.
- The process by which culturally distinct groups within a larger civilization adopt the language, values, and norms of the host civilization and gain equal statuses in its institutions is termed *assimilation.* (If a distinct people fails to assimilate fully, it is referred to as a *subculture,* but if it challenges the accepted norms and values of the larger society, it may become a *counterculture.*)
- When a smaller, less powerful society is able to preserve its culture even after prolonged contact with a major civilization, *accommodation* has taken place.

GLOSSARY

culture: All the modes of thought, behavior, and production that are handed down from one generation to the next by means of communicative interaction rather than by genetic transmission. (p. 51)

ideas: Ways of thinking that organize human consciousness. (p. 51)

norms: Specific rules of behavior. (p. 51)

material culture: Patterns of possessing and using the products of culture. (p. 51)

values: The ideas that support or justify norms. (p. 51)

laws: Norms that are written by specialists, collected in codes or manuals of behavior, and interpreted and applied by other specialists. (p. 54)

ideologies: Systems of values and norms that the members of a society are expected to believe in and act on without question. (p. 54)

technologies: The products and the norms for using them that are found in a given culture. (p. 56)

social control: The set of rules and understandings that control the behavior of individuals and groups in a particular culture. (p. 56)

normative order: The array of norms that permit a society to achieve relatively peaceful social control. (p. 57)

sanctions: Rewards and punishments for abiding by or violating norms. (p. 57)

mores: Strongly sanctioned norms. (p. 57)

folkways: Weakly sanctioned norms. (p. 58)

natural selection: The relative success of organisms with specific genetic mutations in reproducing new generations with the new trait. (p. 61)

cultural evolution: The process by which successful cultural adaptations are passed down from one generation to the next. (p. 61)

social Darwinism: The notion that people who are more successful at adapting to the environment in which they find themselves are more likely to survive and to have children who will also be successful. (p. 61)

sociobiology: The hypothesis that all human behavior is determined by genetic factors. (p. 62)

linguistic-relativity hypothesis: The belief that language determines the possibilities for thought and action in any given culture. (p. 64)

ethnocentrism: The tendency to judge other cultures as inferior to one's own. (p. 65)

cultural relativity: The recognition that all cultures develop their own ways of dealing with the specific demands of their environments. (p. 65)

hegemony: Undue power or influence. (p. 66)

civilization: A cultural complex formed by the identical major cultural features of several societies. (p. 68)

acculturation: The process by which the members of a civilization incorporate norms and values from other cultures into their own. (p. 69)

assimilation: The process by which culturally distinct groups in a larger civilization adopt the norms, values, and language of the host civilization and are able to gain equal statuses in its groups and institutions. (p. 71)

subculture: A group of people who hold many of the values and norms of the larger culture but also hold certain beliefs, values, or norms that set them apart from that culture. (p. 71)

counterculture: A subculture that challenges the accepted norms and values of the larger society and establishes an alternative lifestyle. (p. 71)

accommodation: The process by which a smaller, less powerful society is able to preserve the major features of its culture even after prolonged contact with a larger, stronger culture. (p. 72)

INTERNET RESOURCES

Virtual Society: The Wadsworth Sociology Resource Center

(http://sociology.wadsworth.com)

At Virtual Society you can access a wide range of enrichment material to aid your study of sociology. From the main page, click on the Student Resources link and find your course and this textbook. Next, select the chapter you are presently studying from the pull-down menu. Among the useful options for each self-study chapter are online links and exercises, flashcards, practical study tips, and practice quizzes for each chapter.

MC   MicroCase Online

From the Virtual Society home page, click on MicroCase Online to access book-specific MicroCase exercises that allow you to further explore sociological issues and principles presented in the text.

InfoTrac College Edition

Another unique option available to you at the Student Resources section at Virtual Society is InfoTrac College Edition, an online library with access to hundreds of scholarly and popular periodicals. Below are suggested search terms for this chapter, but this resource also allows you to fit your study of sociology to your own interests by searching custom keywords.

Culture

Social Darwinism

Cultural Change

Ethnocentrism

Language

American Anthropology Association

(www.aaanet.org)

The home page for professional anthropologists. An excellent place to look for information about the social-scientific study of cultures, especially those in other parts of the world.

The United Nations

(www.un.org and www.unsystem.org)

The UN's home page and index page, presenting information about cultures and societies around the world.

Amnesty International

(www.amnesty.org)

A good place to start if you are looking for information about human rights and culture conflicts throughout the world. Information about the clashes between ethnic groups in Africa, the problems of leaders of opposition movements, and the like can be found here or through links from this site.

The Southern Institute at Tulane University

(www.tulane.edu/~so-inst/index.html)

Provides access to discussion groups, databases, and research publications, especially on issues of culture and race in the United States and elsewhere in the world.

Societies and Nations

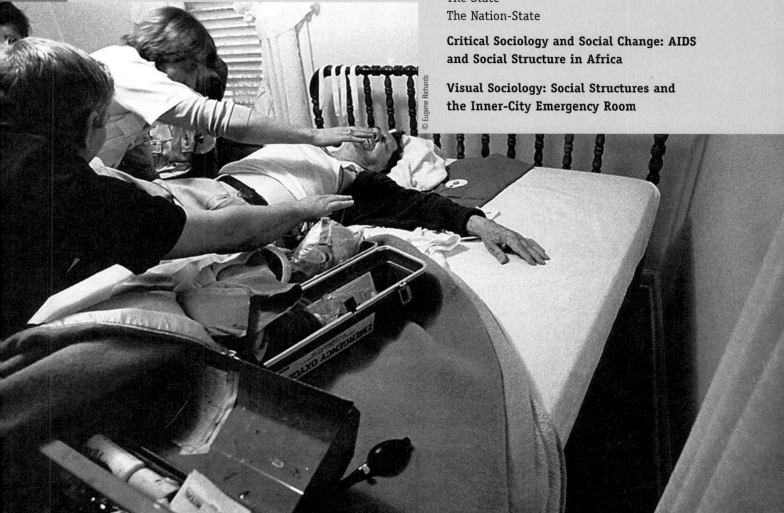

© Eugene Richards

It's almost 3 a.m. on a steamy summer Saturday. In the emergency room of Denver General Hospital, people of all ages and social types are slumped over chairs in the waiting room. Some are bent over in pain. Others are clutching injuries. Worried parents with a feverish child wait impatiently for their turn to finally pass through the doors where they will be seen by the medical staff. Outside the emergency room, incessant flashing lights signal the arrival of ambulances and police cars. They are bringing in the city's bloody harvest—its victims of speed, violence, and neglect. Those in danger of death or paralysis are rushed into treatment rooms for immediate, often heroic attention. Those with lesser injuries may sit in the corridors or even be shunted into the waiting room with the "walk-ins."

Clinical specialist Lori Jones often serves as the ER's triage nurse. Her job is to assess the gravity of patients' symptoms. "You cannot refuse care," she explains. "When you set a little sign outside with a light on it that says, 'Twenty-four-hour emergency room' you cannot refuse to see anybody. Then we turn around and teach everybody that in this day of limited resources and overcrowding, you can and must refuse care to those you don't believe need it" (Richards, 1989, p. 72). Jones has the unenviable job of deciding who gets care immediately, who gets it later, and who waits untreated through the long night. "The psych patient and the homeless person wants to stay in the ER to get seen immediately. He doesn't want to get put out in the waiting room or the walk-in clinic, where the wait could be two, four, five hours. And he knows from experience that the likelihood of getting a real bed upstairs is much greater if he comes in through the emergency room than the walk-in clinic" (p. 72). Most of the homeless street people who use the emergency room, Jones continues, "aren't bag people, don't have backpacks. Many of them don't push carts around and they don't carry big plastic garbage sacks of possessions around. They have only the clothes on their bodies. So if they can get into Denver General, it may be loud, but at least it's warm. At least we can't rob them. They will get a meal. Nobody will kick them or smash their head" (p. 73).

Inside the ER, the staff faces one crisis after another. Death lurks around the hospital gurneys, as many of us know from watching *ER*, one of the most popular programs in the history of American television. But Dr. Jim Rappaport has just witnessed the death of an elderly man with cardiac failure who he thought he might be able to save. "Death is a very nebulous thing sometimes. . . . At what point does he die? I don't know. The heart can stop working, yet each cell is still alive." Dr. Rappaport and his team fought to revive this patient, but at some point they knew it was hopeless. Yet they continued their efforts and finally said, "Okay, he's dead. . . . But at some time, at some point, maybe even hours ago when he was being carried over here in the ambulance, his soul left him" (p. 94).

For Dr. Paul Thurman, director of emergency medical services at Denver General, the threat to the quality of emergency care, and to the ultimate survival of the ER, is "without a doubt, selfishness. The reality is that about 20 percent of our society cannot or will not care for themselves. So the rest of society has got to make a decision about whether or not they're going to pick up the tab for that 20 percent." But as Dr. Thurman sees it, the society

FOCUS QUESTIONS:

• How are societies organized, and how has their organization evolved over time?

• How does social organization influence individual lives?

• To what extent can we intentionally change social structures, even those as complex as the nation-state, once we understand how they have evolved?

he lives in is increasingly indifferent to the needs of the poor and those who are otherwise incapable of caring for themselves. "So we have to decide what kind of society we want to live in. Do we want to live in a Calcutta where people die in the streets because there's nobody to help them and care for them? Or do we want to live someplace like Denver that has one of the finest indigent-care and trauma emergency systems in the country?" (p. 163).

The director and his staff of doctors, nurses, paramedics, ambulance drivers, and administrative personnel are struggling to provide care in the face of dwindling resources and budget cuts. The frustrations of trying to maintain an effective health care delivery organization in this negative environment weigh heavily on them. As Dr. Thurman says, "We're fighting desperately to keep alive, but I'm tired of working at a resource-poor hospital where we get punished for doing a good job."

Dr. Thurman and thousands of other health care professionals who serve less affluent segments of the U.S. population are now witnessing a relentless attack on public budgets. Federal tax cuts favoring more affluent citizens inevitably reduce the resources available for public health care and further erode the ability of hospitals to meet the health care needs of those who depend on their services (Higgins, 2003).

THE SOCIAL ORDER

Amid the chaos of incoming emergencies and frightened people, the emergency room staff maintain a definite social order. Despite the confusion and stress, all the professionals go about doing their jobs. As we see in the preceding vignette and in the Visual Sociology feature at the end of the chapter, these jobs are not always routine or easy. The triage nurse, for example, must watch as children and families wait anxiously for treatment while less deserving but more serious medical cases are placed ahead of theirs. The chief of medical services worries that even an effective social organization like that of the ER at Denver General is threatened by forces in the larger social environment within which the ER exists. Is the ER unique in facing these challenges? By no means. The members of every human social structure (organization, group, family, congre-

gation, etc.) experience different kinds of stress as they seek to carry out their functions. The larger social environment is always changing and exerting new forces that shape and alter the social structure, whatever its nature. One of the main goals of this chapter is to indicate the common features of the many different types of human social structures and to show how they influence individual behavior.

Of course, humans are not the only animals capable of social organization. We can learn a lot about life in human societies by comparing ourselves with other social animals. If you look closely at an ant colony or a beehive, for example, you can see a remarkable amount of organization. The nest or hive is a complete social world with workers, warriors, queen, drones, and so on. Each individual ant or bee has something to do and seems to do it quite well. But the differences between human societies and those of social animals like bees are even more important than the similarities. An individual social animal, such as a worker bee, is able to perform only a certain number of innate (inborn) tasks. A human, by contrast, can learn an infinite number of tasks. Thus Lori Jones, the clinical specialist in the ER, can be a mother, a voter, a taxpayer, a congregation member, a driver, a singer, and pretty much whatever else she sets her heart on becoming.

We often assume that we know how society works and how to steer our way through it. But there will be times—especially when we are learning to adapt to changing social environments—when we will be unsure of what is expected of us and how we should perform. Worse still, there may be times when it seems that society itself is threatened, that its continued existence as we know it is endangered. We catch glimpses of the breakdown of society during riots or wars or severe economic recessions.

At earlier times in human history, plagues and famines were frequent reminders that people had little control over their own destinies. Today plagues and famines still occur, but we are more often faced with real or potential crises of our own making: war, genocide, environmental disasters, drug addiction, criminal violence. Thus, if we are to continue to exist and thrive as a species, it is vital that we study societies and social structures—how they hold together, how they change, and why they sometimes seem to fall apart.

As in any science, we begin with some basic terms and definitions. The next few pages introduce the principal elements of social structure. (See the Study Chart on page 82.) Later sections of the chapter apply these and related concepts to an analysis of how societies have developed since the beginning of human history and how differences among societies affect the lives of individuals. We also discuss the important distinction between societies and nation-states.

ELEMENTS OF SOCIAL STRUCTURE

STRUCTURAL ELEMENT	DESCRIPTION	EXAMPLE
Group	Any collection of people who interact on the basis of shared expectations regarding one another's behavior.	A discussion group; a Bible study class; a local union.
Status	A socially defined position in a group.	Orderly, practical nurse, registered nurse, resident, chief resident (all statuses in a hospital ward).
Role	The way a society defines how an individual is to behave in a particular status.	The doctor diagnoses and treats illnesses; the nurse provides care to patients under the doctor's supervision.
Role Expectations	A society's expectations about how a role should be performed, together with the individual's perceptions of what is required in performing that role.	A major league center fielder is expected to have a batting average over .300, drive in more than 75 runs, and cover the field with a minimum of errors.
Institution	A more or less stable structure of statuses and roles devoted to meeting the basic needs of people in a society.	The military is the primary institution devoted to providing national defense.

Society and Social Structure

The term *society* refers to a population of people (or other social animals) that is organized in a cooperative manner to carry out the major functions of life, including reproduction, sustenance, shelter, and defense. This definition distinguishes between societies and populations. The notion of a population implies nothing about social organization, but the idea of a society stresses the *interrelationships* among the members of the population. In other words, a population can be any set of individuals that we decide to count or otherwise consider, such as the total number of people living between the Rio Grande and the Arctic Circle, whereas a society is a population that is organized in some way, such as the population of the United States or Canada, or the Amish people of Pennsylvania. In the modern world, most societies are also (but not always) nation-states.

Social structure refers to the recurring patterns of behavior that people create through their interactions, their exchange of information, and their relationships (Mark, 1998). We say, for example, that the family has a structure in which there are parents and children and other relatives who interact in specific ways on a regular basis. The larger society usually requires that family members assume certain obligations toward one another. Parents are required to educate their children or send them to schools; children are required to obey their parents until they have reached an age at which they are no longer considered dependent. These requirements contribute to the structure of rela-

tionships that is characteristic of the family. (The social scientist's method of diagramming family relationships, shown in the Sociological Methods box on page 83, creates a graphic depiction of family social structure.)

Throughout life, individuals maintain relationships in an enormous range of social structures, of which families are just one. There are many others. People may be members of relatively small groups like the friendship or peer group and the work group. They may also be members of larger structures like churches, business organizations, or public agencies. And they may participate in even more broadly based structures, such as political groups and party organizations, or interest groups like the National Rifle Association or Planned Parenthood. All these social structures are composed of groups with different degrees of complexity and quite different patterns of interaction. A military brigade, for example, is far more complicated than a barbershop quartet, and people behave quite differently in each, but both are social structures. In such structures, our time, our activities, and even our thoughts may be "structured" according to the needs and activities of the group.

Elements of Social Structure

GROUPS   The "building blocks" of societies are social groups. A **group** is any collection of people who interact on the basis of shared expectations regarding one another's behavior. One's immediate family is a group; so are a soft-

SOCIOLOGICAL METHODS   Using Kinship Diagrams to Portray Social Structure

Kinship diagrams like the one shown here provide a visual model of one type of social structure, that associated with family statuses extending over more than one generation. Such diagrams are used in both anthropology and sociology to denote lines of descent among people who are related by blood (children and their parents and siblings) and by marriage. To understand the chart, one must know the meanings of the symbols used; these are explained in the key to the chart. The chart applies these symbols to show how cross-cousin marriages between members of different bands link the bands together into a larger structure of kinship networks.

The chart illustrates the social structure of a hunter-gatherer group. One individual, Ego, is used as a point of reference, and kinship links are traced from Ego's offspring, parents, grandparents, and more distant relatives.

In most hunter-gatherer societies, it

is not possible for the entire society to travel and hunt within the same territory because of scarcities of game and edible vegetation. Instead, the society is divided into natal bands—in this example, those formed by the male line of descent (grandfather, father, Ego, Ego's son).

The striped coloring within the kinship symbols refers to another characteristic of hunter-gatherer societies: Marriages within the band cannot occur because of the incest taboo,

and there are specific rules governing marriage outside the band. Note that Ego has married his father's sister's daughter, or his first cousin on his father's side. Ego's wife's brother has married a woman from outside their band. This couple has come to live in the husband's natal band. Their daughter has married Ego's son, another cross-cousin marriage. Ego's daughter, on the other hand, will eventually marry someone from another band and live outside her natal

band. By means of this custom, the balance of women coming into and going out of the band is preserved.

Cross-cousin marriages, which are taboo in most Western societies, permit the hunter-gatherer band to develop a strong network of interfamily and interband kinship ties. This network widens over the generations and extends the ties of kinship throughout these small, mobile societies.

Source: Adapted from "The Origin of Society," by Marshall D. Sahlins. Copyright © September 1960 by Scientific American, Inc. All rights reserved. Reprinted with permission from Ikuyo Garber.

ball team, a seminar, a caucus, and so on. But a collection of people on a busy street—a crowd—is not a group unless for some reason its members begin to interact in a regular fashion. Usually a crowd is composed of many different kinds of groups—couples, families, groups of friends, and so on. They may be molded into a single group in response to an event that affects them all, such as a fire that creates the need for orderly evacuation of a building.

STATUSES   In every group there are socially defined positions known as **statuses**. Father, mother, son, daughter, teacher, student, and principal are examples of familiar statuses in the family and the school. There are an infinite number of statuses in human societies. In a corporation, for example, the statuses range from president and chief executive officer to elevator operator and janitor. Between these

two extremes there could be thousands of other statuses.[1] Moreover, the corporation can always create new statuses if the need arises. Thus, in the 1970s, when American society agreed to combat racism and sexism in business and government, many corporations invented the status of affirmative action director to provide equal opportunities for workers of both sexes and all racial and ethnic groups. In the 1990s, as the larger society became more deeply concerned about environmental pollution and drug abuse, corporations began to create new statuses like pollution control

[1]Like many other sociological terms, *status* has more than one meaning. It can refer to a person's rank in a social system and also to a person's prestige—that is, the esteem with which others regard him or her. The fundamental meaning is the one we use here.

manager, drug counselor, or ethics officer (Kelley, 1998). Each of these statuses then became part of the "corporate structure."

Human societies rely heavily on the creation of statuses to adapt to new conditions like environmental pollution and drug use, and one can often observe this adaptation occurring in daily life. In the family, for example, it is increasingly common (though not universally condoned) for young adults to cohabit before marriage or after divorce. As a large-scale phenomenon, this is a relatively recent trend in American society, so new that we have not defined very well the new status of the person who participates in such a relationship. Do we say *boyfriend* or *girlfriend, lover, mate, significant other,* or what? These terms seem awkward to us because this is an emerging status that our society has not yet fully accepted or defined.

This example highlights an essential point about human social structure: It is never fixed or perfectly formed but instead is always changing and adapting to new conditions. Often the process of change involves much conflict and uncertainty, and often there is little consensus about how one should perform in a given status. Should the president of a corporation be an aloof, aggressive leader who directs subordinates with little regard for their feelings? Or should the president show concern for employees' feelings and personal needs and perhaps thereby gain greater loyalty and motivation? This is just one of thousands of dilemmas arising from questions about how we should act in a given social status. To clarify our thinking about statuses in groups and the behaviors associated with those statuses, sociologists make a distinction between a *status* and a *role.*

ROLES AND ROLE EXPECTATIONS   The way a society defines how an individual is to behave in a particular status is referred to as a **role.** In the ER, for example, Lori Jones has several distinct roles to play. She specializes in giving care to homeless and psychiatric patients, but she also often serves as triage nurse, and then her role involves deciding which patients must wait while others receive care for more serious conditions. It bothers her that the ER offers care to all but has to turn some away, yet she manages to perform her role to the satisfaction of her superiors in the organization. Clearly, the ways in which people actually perform a role may vary widely. They are the product of **role expectations**—that is, the society's expectations about how a role should be performed, together with the individual's perceptions of what is required in performing that role.

To appreciate the importance of role expectations, you need only think of the mothers and fathers of your close friends: All hold the same statuses, but how different their behavior is! Part of that difference is caused by personality, but another part is determined by how those mothers and

fathers perceive what is expected of them in the statuses they hold. One mother and father may have been raised to believe that children should work to support the family. They will insist that their children get early job experience. Another couple may have been taught that childhood is too short and should be prolonged if possible. Other things being equal (e.g., adequate family income), that couple will not encourage their children to find jobs before they are more or less the same age the parents were when they went to work.

Social change makes for even more debate and anxiety about role expectations, a subject we discuss in more detail later in the chapter. For now, consider the example of a mother who is also an attorney (something that was rather rare before women gained greater access to professional training). Because of the demands of her profession, she may be unable to take on a leadership position in the school PTA. However, being active in the PTA may have been one of her role expectations for motherhood before the opportunity for a professional career (and the income it provides) became attractive. Now she may feel harried by the pressure of her conflicting statuses of mother and attorney—to say nothing of her other possible statuses, such as wife, daughter, citizen, consumer, committee member, and so on. She may demand that her spouse perform tasks not traditionally associated with the status of husband, and he may or may not modify his original role expectations about that status; in either case, there is likely to be some conflict in the family as it adjusts to these changes.

Another family, in which the mother is also in the labor force but there is no father in the home, has even more adjusting to do. The older children may take on parental roles far sooner than they might have in a two-parent family, but they may also resent this added responsibility and take out their anger on themselves and their siblings. In still another family, one that conforms to the tradition in which the mother is a homemaker and the father works outside the home, the pressures and conflict created by multiple role expectations may not occur in the early years. But what happens when the father retires and gives up his lifelong status of breadwinner? This is a time when traditional families often experience strain.

In sum, sociologists are interested in the way roles and statuses affect individual behavior. They also study how lack of roles—for example, in the form of jobs—can affect people's lives. They do not deny the importance of personality, but they place greater emphasis on the influence of social structure as an explanation of individual behavior.

ORGANIZATION IN GROUPS   Groups vary greatly in the extent to which the statuses of their members are well or poorly defined. The family is an example of a group in which statuses are well defined. Although parents carry out their roles in different ways, the laws of their society define many of the obligations of parenthood, placing certain limits on what they can and cannot do. Other groups are much more informal. We may form groups for brief periods in buses, hallways, or doctors' offices. These groups also have roles and statuses, but they are variable and ill defined. All of the people riding on a bus are passengers, but they do not interact the way the members of a family do. At most, we expect civility and "small talk" from other passengers on a bus, but we demand affection and support from other members of our family.

Social change is constantly making the structure of groups more varied and complex. To continue with our earlier example, the family may seem to have well-defined statuses, but high rates of divorce and remarriage have increased the proportion of families in which one parent is a stepparent (see Chapter 16). Consider the difference in role expectations for "mother" or "father" in a situation in which each spouse must interact with a new spouse, a new set of children, and a new set of in-laws, as well as an ex-spouse and children in the first family, plus the old in-laws, plus his or her own parents. Balancing role expectations among the often competing demands of these groups can be a daunting task, one that was far less common when the norms of society made it difficult to divorce.

Groups also vary greatly in the ways in which they are connected with other groups into a larger structure known as an *organization*. An army platoon, for example, includes the well-defined statuses of private, corporal, sergeant, and lieutenant, each with specific roles to play in training and combat. Platoons are grouped together under the leadership of higher officers to form companies; this pattern is repeated at higher levels to create the battalion and the brigade.

Figure 4.1 shows the formal structure of a typical army combat brigade. It does not show the brigade's informal organization, which consists of the ways in which its members actually relate to one another on the basis of friendships or animosities or mutual obligations of various kinds. (The importance of informal organization within larger groups, such as bureaucracies, is discussed more fully in Chapter 6.)

Social Institutions

The structure of most of the important groups in society is determined by shared definitions of the statuses and roles of their members. When such statuses and roles are designed to perform major social functions, they are termed **institutions**. In popular usage, the word *institution* generally refers to a large bureaucratic organization such as a university or hospital or prison (usually with cafeterias that serve "institutional food"). But although the word has this

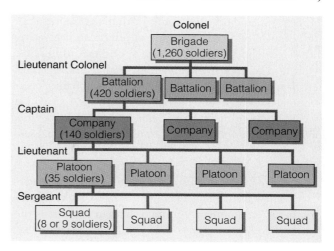

Figure 4.1 The Structure of a Typical Combat Brigade

meaning in everyday language, the sociological use of the term should not be confused with this meaning.

In sociology, an institution is a more or less stable structure of statuses and roles devoted to meeting the basic needs of people in a society. The family is an institution that controls reproduction and the training of new generations. The market is an institution that regulates the production and exchange of goods and services. The military is an institution that defends a society or expands its territory through conquest. Any particular family, corporation, or military unit is a group or organization within one of these institutions.

Within any given institution, there are norms that specify how people in various statuses are to perform their roles. Thus to be a general or a new recruit or a supplier of military hardware is to have a definite status in a military institution. But to carry out one's role in that status is to behave in accordance with a normative system—a set of mores and folkways that distinguish a particular institution from others. For example, in a classic research study about the process of becoming a military recruit, Sanford Dornbusch (1955) described how all the signs of a person's status in civilian life, from fashions in dress to the use of free time, are erased in boot camp. The new status of recruit must be earned by adhering to all the norms of military life. So it is with every social institution: Each has a specific set of norms to govern the behavior of people within that institution.

Institutions of religion, education, politics, and economics tend to become more complex over time as the society changes. It is helpful, therefore, to think of large-scale societies like the United States as having several institutional *sectors* (sets of closely related institutions). For example, the economy is an institutional sector that includes markets, corporations, and other economic institutions. Politics is an institutional sector containing legal, executive, legislative, and other political institutions. Each of these institutions, in turn, is composed of numerous groups and organizations. The Chicago Mercantile Exchange is a market organization; the U.S. House of Representatives is a legislative organization. In this book, as in much social-scientific writing, the term *institution* is used to refer to institutional sectors (e.g., religion) as well as to the institutions included within a sector (e.g., Buddhism or Christianity).

The history of human societies is marked by the emergence of new institutions like the university or the laboratory. In fact, a dominant feature of human societies is the continual creation of new social institutions, a feature that the social theorist Talcott Parsons (1951, 1966) labeled **differentiation.** By this term, Parsons meant the processes whereby sets of social activities performed by one social institution are divided among different institutions. In small-scale agrarian societies, for example, the family not only performs reproductive and training functions but is the primary economic institution as well. Over time the family gradually loses some of its functions to new institutions. The processes of differentiation result in the emergence of new institutions designed to manage economic production (corporations), train new generations (schools), develop new technologies (science), or perform other important social activities. (Many of those institutions are discussed in detail in Part 4.)

Why does this differentiation take place? One answer is provided by critical sociologists like Michel Foucault, who argue that new institutions in society, such as the prison, the insane asylum, and the public medical clinic, have evolved as a means by which the powerful members of society can control unruly or rebellious members whose behavior threatens their comfort (Baber, 2001; Foucault, 1977). This critical perspective on institutions appears often in the work of contemporary sociologists, and we return to it in more detail in later chapters. A more functionalist explanation for the emergence of new institutions highlights the importance of population growth, which creates a demand for new ways to coordinate the activities of groups and individuals and to carry out new social functions (e.g., education of large numbers of people or delivery of health care to people regardless of income). The need to perform these new functions for an ever-growing number of people places demands on existing institutions that they cannot fulfill, which leads to the development of new institutions—that is, new ways of performing important social functions (Halbwachs, 1960; Karnoe, 1997). We will see in the next section that new institutions are particularly likely to emerge when populations grow, the need for coordination of their activities increases, and new demands are placed on older institutions that they cannot entirely fulfill.

POPULATIONS AND SOCIETIES

The remarkable growth of the world's human population is the great biological success story of the last million years. Throughout most of the evolution of the human species, the world's population remained relatively small and constant. At the end of the Neolithic period, about 8000 BC, there were an estimated 5 million to 10 million humans, concentrated mainly in the Middle East, East Africa, southern Europe, and a few fertile river basins in India, China, Latin America, and Central America. The overall range of human existence was much wider—populations were moving north as the last Ice Age receded about 12,000 years ago—but the human population was nowhere near as widely distributed as it is today. By the time of Jesus there were an estimated 200 million people on the earth, and by the start of the Industrial Age, about the year 1650, there were an estimated 500 million. By 1945, however, the population had reached about 2.3 billion, and it is now more than 6 billion. This trend is illustrated in Figure 4.2.

What explains the shape of this population curve—the gradual rise in the world's population during the late Stone Age, the increasing rate of growth in the early millennia of recorded history, the explosive growth after 1650? The answers have to do with the changing production technologies of societies and their ever-increasing ability to sustain their populations, not only those directly involved in acquiring food but the ever-larger numbers of non-food-producers as well. In other words, human population growth is related to the shift from hunting and gathering to agriculture and, later, to industrial production as the chief means of supplying people with the necessities of life.

The First Million Years: Hunting and Gathering

A human lifetime is no more than a twinkling in time. What are 70 or 80 years compared with the billions of years of the earth's existence? What is one generation compared with the millions of years of human social evolution? Yet many of us hope to leave some mark on society, perhaps to change it for the better, to ease some suffering, to increase productivity, to fight racism and ignorance . . . what vaulting ambitions! And what a radical change from the worldview of our ancestors! The idea that people can shape their society—or even enjoy adequate shelter and ample meals—is widely accepted today. For most of human history, however, mere survival was the primary motivator of human action, and thus a fatalistic acceptance of

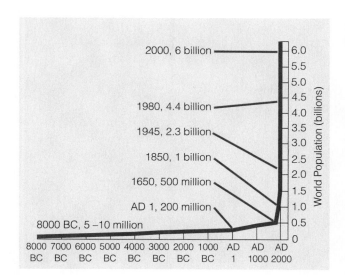

Figure 4.2 World Population Growth from 8000 BC to 2000 AD

This chart shows world population growth since 8000 BC. Note that the first, more gradual increase in world population is associated with the shift to agriculture but that its effects are dwarfed by the impact of the Industrial Revolution, which began in the eighteenth century.

Source: Data from Office of Technology Assessment.

human frailty in the face of overwhelming natural forces was the dominant worldview.

For most of the first million years of human evolution, human societies were developing from those of primates. Populations were small because humans, like other primates, lived on wild animals and plants. These sources of food are easily used up and their supply fluctuates greatly, and as a result periods of starvation or gnawing hunger might alternate with bouts of gorging on sudden windfalls of game or berries. Thus the hunting-and-gathering life that characterized the earliest human populations could support only extremely small societies; most human societies, therefore, had no more than about 60 members.

Archaeological evidence indicates that some hunting-and-gathering societies began to develop permanent settlements long before the advent of agriculture. The emergence of farming was one of the changes that accelerated human social evolution, but in parts of what is now Europe and the Middle East there were stable settlements of hunter-gatherers as early as 30,000 to 20,000 years ago. These rather large and complex societies were most firmly established in the area that is now Israel at the end of the last Ice Age, some 13,000 to 12,000 years ago (Henry, 1989; Stevens, 1988).

Despite the slow pace of human evolution until about 35,000 years ago, some astonishing physical and social changes occurred during that long period, changes that enabled human life to take the forms it does today. Among them were the following:

- The development of an upright posture (which freed the hands for eventual use of tools) and an enlarged cerebral brain, making possible vastly increased cognitive abilities and the development of language.
- Social control of sexuality through the development of the family and other kinship structures and enforcement of the incest taboo.
- The establishment of the band of hunter-gatherers as the basic territorial unit of human society, coupled with the development of kinship structures that linked bands together into tribes. Within the band, the family became the primary economic unit, organizing the production and distribution of food and other necessities.

The chart in the Sociological Methods box illustrates how kinship ties link hunting-and-gathering bands together into a larger society. Anthropologists and sociologists often represent social structures with diagrams of this type. They show how people are related to one another and what their status is in relation to any other person in the social structure.

By the end of the last Ice Age, many aspects of this evolutionary process were more or less complete. Human societies had fully developed languages and a social structure based on the family and the band. To be cast out of the band for some wrongdoing—that is, to be considered a deviant person (see Chapter 7)—usually meant total banishment from the society and eventual death, either by starvation or as a result of aggression by members of another society (Salisbury, 1962). But warfare and violence were not typical of early human societies, as the social anthropologist Marshall Sahlins has pointed out:

> Warfare is limited among hunters and gatherers. Indeed, many are reported to find the idea of war incomprehensible. A massive military effort would be difficult to sustain for technical and logistic reasons. But war is even further inhibited by the spread of a social relation—kinship—which in primitive society is often a synonym for "peace." Thomas Hobbes' famous fantasy of a war of "all against all" in the natural state could not be further from the truth. War increases in intensity, bloodiness, duration, and significance for social survival through the evolution of culture, reaching its culmination in modern civilization. (1960, p. 82)

On the other hand, one must not romanticize the hunter-gatherers. Their lives were far more subject to the pressures of adaptation to the natural environment than has been true in any subsequent form of society.

The "Ice Man," discovered in 1991 by hikers in the Italian Alps, is shown here with the hatchet and other items he was carrying when he died. These remains, among the oldest samples of human flesh and organs ever discovered, are providing a wealth of knowledge about daily life in hunting-and-gathering societies 5,000 years ago.

© Gerhard Hinterleitner/Getty Images

Individual survival was usually subordinated to that of the group. If there were too many children to feed, some were killed or left to die; when the old became infirm or weak, they often chose death so as not to diminish the chances of the others. Thus the frail Eskimo grandfather or grandmother wandered off into the snowy night to "meet the polar bear and the Great Spirit." Additional thousands of years of social evolution would pass before the idea that every person could and should survive, prosper, and die with dignity would even occur to our ancestors.

The Transition to Agriculture

For some time before the advent of plow-and-harvest agriculture in the Middle East and the Far East, hunting-and-gathering societies were supplementing their diets with foods acquired through the domestication of plants and animals. In this way, they were able to avoid the alternation of periods of feast and famine caused by reliance on animal prey. Karl Marx was the first social theorist to observe that social revolutions like the shift to agriculture or industrial production are never merely the result of technological innovations such as the plow or the steam engine. The origins of new forms of society are to be found within the old ones. New social orders do not simply burst upon the scene but are created out of the problems faced by the old order. Thus, as they experimented with domestication of animals and planting of crops, some hunting-and-gathering societies were evolving into nomadic shepherding or **pastoral societies** in which bands followed flocks of animals. Others were developing into **horticultural societies** in which the women raised seed crops and the men combed the territory for game and fish (Wilford, 1997).

Regarding this momentous change in the material basis of human survival, the historian William McNeill made the following observation:

> The seed-bearing grasses ancestral to modern cultivated grains probably grew wild eight or nine thousand years ago in the hill country between Anatolia and the Zagros Mountains, as varieties of wheat and barley continue to do today. If so, we can imagine that from time immemorial the women of those regions searched out patches of wheat and barley grasses when the seeds were ripe and gathered the wild harvest by hand or with the help of simple cutting tools. Such women may gradually have discovered methods for assisting the growth of grain, e.g., by pulling out competing plants; and it is likely that primitive sickles were invented to speed the harvest long before agriculture in the stricter sense came to be practiced. (1963, p. 12)

As a result of these and other innovations, agriculture became the productive basis of human societies. Pastoral societies spread quickly throughout the uplands and grasslands of Africa, northern Asia, Europe, and the Western Hemisphere, and grain-producing societies arose in the fertile river valleys of Mesopotamia, India, China, and—somewhat later—Central and South America. (See Figure 4.3.) Mixed societies of shepherds and marginal farmers wandered over the lands between the upland pastures and the lowland farms.

THE FIRST LARGE-SCALE SOCIETIES   We have reached the beginning of recorded history (around 4000 BC), which was marked by the rise of the ancient civilizations of Sumer, Babylonia, China and Japan, Benin, and the Maya, Incas, and Aztecs. The detailed study of these societies is the province of archaeology, history, and classics. But sociologists need to know as much as possible about the earliest large-scale societies because many contemporary social institutions (e.g., government and religion) and most areas of severe social conflict (e.g., class and ethnic conflict) devel-

Figure 4.3 Agricultural Origins

Source: From *The rise of the West: A history of the human community* by W. McNeill. © 1963 University of Chicago Press. Used with permission.

oped sometime in the agrarian epoch—between 3000 BC and 1600 AD.

From the standpoint of social evolution, the following dimensions of agrarian societies are the most salient (Braidwood, 1967):

- Agriculture allows humans to escape from dependence on food sources over which they have no control. Agrarian societies produce surpluses that do not merely *permit* but *require* new classes of nonfood-producers to exist. An example is the class of warriors, who defend the surplus or add to it through plunder.

- Agriculture requires an ever-larger supply of land, resulting in conflicts over territory and in wars with other agricultural or pastoral societies.

- The need to store and defend food surpluses and to house the nonagrarian classes results in new territorial units: villages and small cities.

NEW SOCIAL STRUCTURES   Freed from direct dependence on undomesticated species of plants and animals, agrarian societies developed far more complex social structures than were possible in simpler societies. Hunting-and-gathering societies divided labor primarily according to age and sex, but in agricultural societies labor was divided in new ways to perform more specialized tasks. Peoples who had been conquered in war might be enslaved and assigned the most difficult or least desirable work. Priests controlled the society's religious life, and from the priestly class there emerged a class of hereditary rulers who, as the society became larger and more complex, assumed the status of pharaoh or em-

peror. Artisans with special skills—in the making of armaments or buildings, for example—usually formed another class. And far more numerous than any of these classes were the tillers of the soil, the "common" agricultural workers and their dependents.

The process whereby the members of a society are sorted into different statuses and classes based on differences in wealth, power, and prestige is called **social stratification** and is described in detail in Chapter 11. In general, societies may be **open,** so that a person who was not born into a particular status may gain entry to that status, or **closed,** with each status accessible only by birth. A key characteristic of agrarian societies is that their stratification systems became extremely closed and rigid. Because most people were needed in the fields, there were few opportunities for people to move from one level of society to another. These therefore were closed societies.

The emergence of agrarian societies was based largely on the development of new, more efficient production technologies. Of these, the plow and irrigation were among the most important. The ancient agrarian empires of Egypt, Rome, and China are examples of societies in which irrigation made possible the production of large food surpluses, which in turn permitted the emergence of central governments led by pharaohs and emperors, priests and soldiers. Indeed, some sociologists have argued that because large-scale irrigation systems required a great deal of coordination, their development led to the evolution of imperial courts and such institutions as slavery, which coerced large numbers of agrarian workers into forced labor (Wittfogel, 1957).

THEN AND NOW   The Valley of Mexico

This detail from a famous mural in Mexico's Palacio Nacional shows what the Valley of Mexico looked like in 1519, when conquistador Hernán Cortés and a small band of Spanish soldiers began their conquest of the strife-weakened Aztec empire. The empire's social structure was that of an agrarian society in which great effort was devoted to organizing irrigation projects and building temples and tombs. Power resided in the hands of the emperor Montezuma and a priestly caste that ruled over extended families of farmers and warriors. The Aztec capital, Tenochtitlan, was carefully planned to allow its inhabitants to enjoy the temperate climate of the high valley and was served by a sophisticated irrigation system (Iglesia, 1990).

Today, less than 500 years after the conquest, the Valley of Mexico is blanketed by Mexico City and the many urban communities surrounding it. The social structure of Mexico City is extremely complex because the city is both Mexico's largest commercial

center and its national capital. The city is surrounded by ancient volcanoes, and the valley floor is prone to earthquakes. Despite the problems created by rapid growth in an environmentally sensitive area, Mexico City continues to grow and is now one of the largest metropolitan centers in the world.

By the fifteenth century, the world's population was organized into a wide variety of societies with many different types of cultures and civilizations. Figure 4.4 depicts the spread of human life over more than 150 million square kilometers of land in 1500, before the age of exploration and the Industrial Revolution. The 76 cultures and civilizations shown include hundreds of different societies, ranging from simple hunting-and-gathering societies to more advanced agrarian ones to civilizations that were already expanding and exporting their culture through conquest and trade. The areas numbered 1 to 27 on the map were inhabited by simple societies of hunters, gatherers, and fishers; those numbered 28 to 44 were inhabited by nomads and stockbreeders; areas 45 to 60 were inhabited by agricultural peoples, primarily peasants using hoes rather than plows; and the remaining areas were more advanced civilizations. With the exception of the Mayan and Incan civilizations, all of the latter were found in Asia, the Middle East, and parts of Europe.

The areas where the earliest civilizations emerged are to this day the most densely inhabited parts of the world. In 1500, these civilizations were marked by their ability to produce food surpluses through the use of the plow, domesticated animals, wheels, and carts. Above all, they are

marked by the importance of towns and cities as centers of administration and religious practice. Although the Mayan and Incan civilizations did not have the wheel or the plow, their advanced systems of astronomy, art, and writing make a strong argument for their inclusion as world civilizations.

The explorations led by Portugal, Spain, and England in the sixteenth and seventeenth centuries resulted in conquest and European settlement in many parts of the Western Hemisphere and Africa. Conquest caused radical disruptions in the internal development of the world's cultures and civilizations. But even more drastic would be the changes caused by the Industrial Revolution of the eighteenth and nineteenth centuries.

The Industrial Revolution

In 1650, when Holland, Spain, and England were the world's principal trading nations (Block, 1990), the population of England was approximately 10 million, of which about 90 percent earned a livelihood through farming of one kind or another. Just 200 years later, in 1850, the English population had soared to more than 30 million, with less than 20 percent at work in fields, barns, and granaries. England had become the world's first industrial society and the center of an empire that spanned the world.

A similar transformation occurred in the United States. In 1860, on the eve of the Civil War, there were about 30 million people in the United States. Ninety percent of that population, a people considered quite backward by the rapidly industrializing English, were farmers or people who worked in occupations directly related to farming. A mere 100 years later, in 1960, only about 8 percent of Americans were farmers or agricultural workers, yet they were able to produce enough to feed a population exceeding 200 million. Today less than 3 percent of Americans work on farms and ranches. These dramatic changes in England and America—and in other nations as well—occurred as a result of the Industrial Revolution.

The Industrial Revolution is often associated with innovations in energy production, especially the steam engine. But the shift from an agrarian to an industrial society did not happen simply as a result of technological advances. Rather, the Industrial Revolution was made possible by the rise of a new social order known as **capitalism.** This new way of organizing production originated in nation-states, which engaged in international trade, exploration, and warfare. Above all, the Industrial Revolution depended on the development of *markets,* social structures that would function to regulate the supply of and demand for goods and services throughout the world (Polanyi, 1944).

The transition from an agrarian to an industrial society affects every aspect of social life. It changes the structure of society in several ways, of which the following are among the most significant:

- The industrialization of agriculture allows many more people to be supported by each agrarian worker than ever before. Only a relatively small number of people live on the land; increasing numbers live in towns, cities, and suburbs.

- Industrial societies are generally far more receptive to social change than agrarian societies. One result is the emergence of new classes like industrial workers and scientific professionals (engineers, technicians) and new social movements like the women's movement and the movement for racial equality.

- Scientific, technical, and productive institutions produce both unparalleled wealth and unparalleled destructive capacities.

- The world "shrinks" as a result of innovations in transportation and communication. A "global society" develops, but at the same time the unevenness of industrialization leads to conflicts that threaten world peace.

These are only some of the important features of industrial societies. There are many others, which we analyze throughout this book. We will present research that shows how the types of jobs people find and the ways in which they spend their leisure time change as technology advances and their expectations change. We will also look into the ways in which other major institutions—especially the family—adapt to the changes created by the Industrial Revolution. In fact, we will continually return to the Industrial Revolution as a major force in our times.

THE THEORY OF POSTINDUSTRIAL SOCIETY The United States and most other societies that experienced industrialization in earlier periods are now considered by sociologists to be "postindustrial societies" (Bell, 1999). Even though these societies continue to be important producers of industrial goods like steel, glass, aluminum, and many other products, their industrial plants are highly automated and employment in manufacturing is no longer the largest sector of the economy. As sociologist Fred Block (1990) observes:

> [Ours is] a strange period in the history of the United States because people lack a shared understanding of the kind of society in which they live. For generations, the United States was considered as an industrial society, but that definition is no longer compelling. Yet no convincing alternative has emerged in its absence. (p. 1)

In this book, we continue to group the United States and the European nations among the world's industrial societies because they are major producers of manufactured goods. However, it should be noted that the businesses that produce those goods are dwindling in number because of the effects of the Industrial Revolution in other areas of the world. Also, for the first time in U.S. history, the number of jobs in services exceeds that of jobs in goods-producing industries. Far more jobs are created in restaurants and hotels each year than in steel mills and other kinds of factories (Kasarda, 1989). In addition, there is an ever-increasing demand for highly educated and trained workers in new industries that deal with high-speed transmission of information. Computers and telecommunications technologies are surely produced by "industries," but they are not the type of mass-employment "smokestack" industries that were the hallmark of earlier stages of the Industrial Revolution.

The theory of postindustrial society explores why these fundamental changes have come about and their impact, not only on postindustrial societies themselves but also on the cultures of other societies. There are also many questions about what will happen as the world's societies become ever

Figure 4.4   Civilization, "Cultures," and Primitive Peoples, ca. 1500

Source: Adapted from Hewes, 1954; Braudel, 1981.

1. Tasmanians
2. Congo Pygmies
3. The Vedda (Ceylon)
4. Andamanese
5. Sakai and Semang
6. Kubu
7. Punan (Borneo)
8. Negritos of the Philippines
9. Ciboneys (Antilles)
10. Gê-Botocudos
11. Gran Chaco Indians
12. Bushmen
13. Australians
14. Great Basin

15. Lower California
16. Texas and northeastern Mexico
17. Patagonia
18. Indians of the southern coast of Chile
19. Athabascans and Algonkin (northern Canada)
20. Yukaghir
21. Eastern and central Eskimos
22. Western Eskimos
23. Kamchadal, Koryak, Chukchi
24. Ainu, Gilyak, Gol'dy
25. Northwest coast Indians (United States and Canada)
26. Columbia Plateau
27. Central California

28. Reindeer-herding peoples
29. Canary Islands
30. Sahara nomads
31. Arabian nomads
32. Pastoral mountain peoples in the Near East
33. Pastoral peoples of the Pamir region and Hindu Kush
34. Kazakh-Kirghiz
35. Mongols
36. Pastoral Tibetans
37. Settled Tibetans
38. Western Sudanese
39. Eastern Sudanese
40. Somali and Galla of northeastern Africa

more interdependent and decisions made in metropolitan centers like Tokyo, Los Angeles, and London affect the lives of villagers in the most remote parts of the world (Giddens, 1984; Sassen, 1994). We will return to the issues raised by theories of industrialization and the emergence of postin-

dustrial society throughout this book. For it is clear that while the most advanced and powerful nations are undergoing an economic transformation, in many other parts of the world the Industrial Revolution is in full swing, and in still other, more remote areas, older forms of agrarianism and

41. Nilotic tribes
42. East African stock-rearing peoples
43. Western Bantu
44. Hottentots
45. Melanesian Papuans
46. Micronesians
47. Polynesians
48. American Indians (eastern United States)
49. American Indians (western United States)
50. Brazilian Indians
51. Chilean Indians
52. Congolese peoples
53. Lake-dwellers of East Africa
54. Guinea coasts

55. Tribes of the Assam and the Burmese highlands
56. Tribes of the Indonesian highlands
57. Highland peoples of Indochina
58. Mountain and forest tribes of central India
59. Malagasy
60. Caribbean peoples
61. Finns
62. Mexicans, Maya
63. Peru and the Andes
64. Caucasians
65. Ethiopia
66. Settled Muslims
67. Southwestern Europe

68. Eastern Mediterranean
69. Eastern Europe
70. Northwestern Europe
71. India (this map does not differentiate between Muslims and Hindus)
72. Lowlands of Southeast Asia
73. Indonesian lowlands
74. Chinese
75. Koreans
76. Japanese

tribalism continue to thrive. (See the Global Social Change box on page 94.)

The evolution of human societies continues at an ever more rapid pace. As we will see throughout this text, scientific and technological discoveries, wars, migration and immigration, disease, environmental change, and major social movements continually produce new social structures and ways of addressing social needs. Some of the major aspects of social evolution over the past 12,000 years are summarized in the Study Chart on pages 95–96,

Text continues on page 96.

GLOBAL SOCIAL CHANGE

Social Structures in a Changing World

Why all the noise about globalization, global influences on social change, and so on? Are these merely fashionable buzzwords, or are they central issues in our own lives and those of our neighbors and friends? To answer these questions, we need only think about some of the most important changes occurring in the social groups and structures around us and try to see what, if anything, these changes have to do with major social forces acting on a global, rather than merely national, level. Consider the following major areas of change, just for starters:

- *The revolution in information technologies.* Personal computers linked to worldwide information networks did not exist when your parents were children. They are making it possible for manufacturers to locate production facilities wherever in the world they can find low labor costs and a favorable business environment. This accelerates the trend whereby other parts of the world become specialized in manufacturing while in the United States there is a great deal of advanced technological production and many people work in service industries.
- *The rapid flow of information.* Through television, the Internet, modern long-distance phone systems, and jet travel, the globe "shrinks." Events that occur in once remote places like Kosovo or Afghanistan become subjects of dinner-table discussion in middle America. People in India and China read about American society and long for the kinds of opportunities Americans enjoy.

We hear so much about trends like these that there is a risk of becoming bored by them. Yet sociologists recognize these trends as the underlying causes of a great many fascinating and often heart-wrenching social phenomena. For example, if we look at two extremes of the recent wave of immigration to the United States, we see evidence of the powerful effects of these global social changes. At one extreme is the illegal immigration of the very poorest and most exploited workers. Labor shortages at the lowest levels of the pay scale make it attractive for unscrupulous entrepreneurs to "import" what is essentially slave labor. Sociologist Peter Kwong (1998) has studied this trend as it is experienced by unskilled Chinese workers. The most notorious example of the illegal importation of indentured or quasi-slave labor, according to Kwong, was the work of professional immigration criminals, known as "Dragons," who attempted to land a freighter, the *Golden Venture,* in New York harbor in 1994. Instead, the smugglers' ship grounded on the ocean shore, and many of the hapless immigrants were drowned as they attempted to swim through the surf to freedom. If they had been successfully smuggled into the city, the Dragons would have kept them in low-wage jobs in restaurants and illegal manufacturing concerns (sweatshops) for many years while they paid off the cost of their transport at exorbitant rates.

At the other extreme of responses to the forces of globalization is immigration by the most educated and highly trained elites of Third World nations. In India and China, for example, people with access to computers and the Internet are able to stay in touch with their kin and friends who have already immigrated to the United States, and to learn from them about areas of expanding educational and business opportunity (Mitra, 1997). For many years these nations have been exporting a significant proportion of their most highly educated and technically trained people to the United States, but this trend is changing in some important ways. There is still a steady stream of Chinese and Indian

© Rick Maiman/Corbis Sygma

university graduates who immigrate to obtain further training in U.S. universities. Many of these skilled immigrants seek careers in the U.S. telecommunications and computer industries. But this immigration, often known as a "brain drain," is no longer a one-way process. In fact, many skilled Chinese and Indian computer programmers and computer scientists are returning to their own nations to begin startup firms of their own (Das & Srinivasan, 1997). No wonder, then, that there is a regular circulation of Asian technicians and businesspeople between Silicon Valley in California and the rapidly expanding information technology centers in Delhi, Hong Kong, and elsewhere in China and India (Carnoy, Castells, & Benner, 1997).

© Paul De Maria/Corbis Sygma

TYPES OF SOCIETIES

TYPE OF SOCIETY	HISTORICAL PERIOD	ENERGY/ TECHNOLOGY	POPULATIONS SUSTAINED	SETTLEMENT PATTERN	SOCIAL ORGANIZATION	EXAMPLES
Hunting and gathering	Only type until about 12,000 years ago; a few examples remain but are threatened with absorption or extinction	Fire; crude weapons	Bands of 25–40 people	Nomadic	Family and clan centered; division of labor based on age and sex; little social equality	Eskimo; Pygmies of Central Africa; Aborigines of Australia
Horticultural and pastoral	From about 12,000 years ago, with rapidly decreasing numbers after about 4000 BC	Fire; hand tools for planting	Settlements of a few hundred, linked through clans and tribes to form societies with several thousand members	Horticulturists form small, relatively permanent settlements; pastoralists are nomadic, following herds of migrating animals (e.g., reindeer, caribou, buffalo) and engaging in some animal domestication	Family centered; religious systems encourage development of some specialized roles and statuses; emergence of social inequality based on prestige and wealth	Societies of the Fertile Crescent (now Iraq); Laplanders; Maasai
Agrarian	From about 7,000 years ago; large but decreasing numbers today	Fire; animal power for plowing; extensive irrigation systems	Millions of people	Cities become common, but the vast majority of people live on the agricultural lands outside them	Family remains strong but loses some power as extensive religious, political, and economic institutions emerge; extensive division of labor and increased social inequality based on power, wealth, and religious prestige	Egypt under the pharaohs; Medieval Europe; ancient China and India
Industrial (manufacturing)	From about 1750 to present	Steam, electricity, gasoline power; railroads and auto/truck transport	Millions of people	Cities; agriculture is mechanized, and manufacturing absorbs displaced workers	Distinct and specialized religious, political, economic, educational, and family institutions; extensive division of labor and interdependence; social inequality persists but is subject to social reform movements and revolutions	China; Brazil; Eastern European nations; Argentina; Philippines; South Korea

continued

TYPES OF SOCIETIES—CONT'D

TYPE OF SOCIETY	HISTORICAL PERIOD	ENERGY/ TECHNOLOGY	POPULATIONS SUSTAINED	SETTLEMENT PATTERN	SOCIAL ORGANIZATION	EXAMPLES
Postindustrial	From about 1960 to present	Electricity, gasoline power, nuclear energy; information technologies (computers, satellites)	Millions of people; high rates of immigration	Cities and suburbs, forming sprawling metropolitan regions	Distinct religious, political, economic, educational, and family institutions; service industries replace manufacturing although industrial production continues	United States; most nations of Western Europe; Japan

Source: Adapted from Lensky & Lenski, 1982; Bell, 1999.

which highlights important features of each type of society, from those of the hunter-gatherers to our own postindustrial society.

SOCIETY AND THE INDIVIDUAL

From Gemeinschaft to Gesellschaft

Imagine that you grew up in an agrarian village or a town in a slowly industrializing society and then came to live in the United States, as millions of people do each decade. A difficult part of that experience would be getting used to the impersonality of modern American society when compared with the close relationships you had with people you had known all your life in your native society. American society would seem to be composed of masses of strangers organized into highly impersonal categories. You would have to get used to being a shopper, an applicant, a depositor, a sports fan, a commuter, and so on, and it would be necessary to shift from one to another of these roles several times in a day or even within a half hour.

Sociologists often describe this experience as a change from **gemeinschaft** (the close, personal relationships of small groups and communities) to **gesellschaft** (the well-organized but impersonal relationships of modern societies). These are German terms taken from the writings of the social theorist Ferdinand Tönnies (1957/1887). Complex industrial societies, Tönnies argued, have developed gesellschaft social structures like factories and office bu-

reaucracies to such a degree that they tend to dominate day-to-day life in the modern world.

PRIMARY AND SECONDARY GROUPS   The American sociologist Charles H. Cooley applied this distinction to the micro level of society in his discussion of primary versus secondary groups. "By **primary groups**," Cooley wrote,

> I mean those characterized by intimate face-to-face association and cooperation. They are primary in several senses, but chiefly in that they are fundamental in forming the social nature and ideals of the individual. [Such a group] involves the sort of sympathy and mutual identification for which "we" is the natural expression. (1909, p. 23)

Secondary groups, in contrast, are groups in which we participate for instrumental reasons—that is, in order to accomplish some task or set of tasks. Examples are school classrooms, town committees, and political party organizations. We do not have intimate relationships with other members of secondary groups; at least, we do not normally expect to do so and are not concerned about the fact that our relationships in such groups involve only a limited range of emotions.

Of course, when we speak of intimacy in primary groups, we do not always refer to love and warm feelings. The intimacy of the members of a family refers to a highly charged set of emotions that can range from love to hate but rarely includes indifference. But in a secondary group, indifference, or lack of personal involvement, is the norm. We therefore do not usually develop strong feelings toward all the other members of the organizations for which we work or the associations to which we belong, even though we may have one or more close friends among our workmates. The idea that people do not have to form primary attachments in work organizations also protects people with less power from those with more. Women in subordinate positions, for example, often need protection from men in more powerful positions who make sexual advances. Modern laws dealing with sexual conduct in the workplace classify such behavior as illegal harassment. But the fact that we need such laws points out the degree of conflict we often experience in performing our roles.

Role and Status in Modern Societies

ROLES IN CONFLICT   Gesellschaft forms of social organization are more complex than gemeinschaft forms in terms of the number of statuses people hold and, thus, the number of roles they must perform. One result of this greater complexity is that roles in secondary groups or associations often conflict with roles in primary groups like the family. Much of the stress of life in modern societies is caused by the anxiety we experience as we attempt to balance the demands of our various roles. This anxiety is captured in the terms *role conflict* and *role strain*.

Role conflict occurs when, in order to perform one role well, a person must violate another important role. Parents who are also employees may experience this kind of conflict when their supervisors ask them to put in extra time, which cuts into the time they are able to spend with their children. The late Felicia Schwartz, a leader in research on women, work, and social policy, argued that many corporations informally classify their female employees into two categories: those who seem to make their career their primary life concern, and those who seek to balance career and family obligations. Often they reward the former and subtly discriminate against the latter by placing them on what some have called the "mommy track," in which the woman is allowed more flexibility to perform family roles at the cost of promotion to more demanding positions within the company. The 1993 Family and Medical Leave Act attempts to resolve this conflict between work and family roles by requiring corporations to provide options for family leave without penalties; nevertheless, role conflict stemming from the competing demands of family and work remains widespread, especially for working women but for men as well (Cramer & Boyd, 1995; Siegel, 1992).

Research on how people behave in disasters also illustrates some of the effects of role conflict. For example, a police officer or firefighter who is on duty during a disaster that affects his or her own family may leave an assigned post to see to the safety of loved ones, thereby violating one role in order to fulfill another (Killian, 1952).

The Sociological Observer

This woman is the widow of a Marine who died in a helicopter crash during the war in Iraq in 2003. As she places a rose on his casket, her role and status in society have changed forever. How will others now view her? What changes have occurred in her economic and social statuses? (See page 103 for further insights into the sociological content of this photo.)

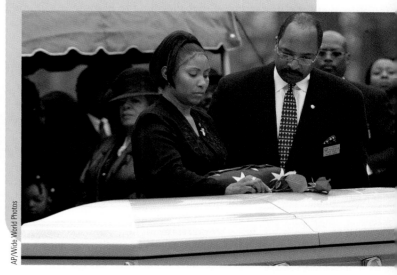

AP/Wide World Photos

Throughout the world, efforts are being made to train women in disaster-related skills so that some of the conflicts that male disaster workers experience may be eased through greater sharing of roles (Gramling & Krogman, 1997; Sapir, 1997).

Role strain occurs when people experience conflicting demands in an existing role or cannot meet the expectations of a new one. For example, when she performs the duties of a triage nurse, Lori Jones experiences severe role strain. She has been taught that care must be provided to those in need, but she must balance that role expectation against the fact that care is a scarce resource in a busy hospital and must be rationed (Chambliss, 1996; Goodman-Draper, 1995).

Role strain in the form of anxiety over poor performance is at least as common as role strain caused by conflicting expectations. For example, the unemployed head of a family feels severe stress as a result of inability to provide for the family's needs (Bakke, 1933; Jahoda, 1982; Jahoda, Lazarsfeld, & Zeisel, 1971). The mother of a newborn baby often feels intense anxiety over how well she can care for a helpless infant, a feeling that is heightened if she herself is young and dependent on others (Mayfield, 1984).

ASCRIBED VERSUS ACHIEVED STATUSES   Role conflicts may occur in simpler societies, but they are far more common in societies undergoing rapid change. One reason for the relative lack of role conflict in simpler, more stable societies is that in such societies a person's statuses are likely to be determined by birth or tradition rather than by anything the person achieves through his or her own efforts. These **ascribed statuses** (peasant, aristocrat, slave, and so forth) usually cannot be changed and hence are less likely to be subject to different role expectations. Such statuses are found in industrial societies too (statuses based on race or sex are examples), but they tend to become less important in modern institutions than **achieved statuses** like editor, professor, or Nobel Prize winner.

We expect to be able to achieve our occupational status, our marital and family statuses, and other statuses in the community and the larger society. Nevertheless, there is some tension in modern societies between the persistence of ascribed statuses and the ideal of achieved statuses. The empirical study of that tension and of efforts to replace ascribed with achieved statuses (e.g., through equality of educational opportunity) is another major area of sociological research. We will show in later chapters that many of the social movements studied by sociologists arose as different groups in a society (e.g., African Americans, wage workers, immigrants, and the poor) organized to press for greater access to economic and social institutions like corporations and universities.

MASTER STATUSES   One reason so many groups have had to organize to obtain social justice is related to the way statuses operate in many societies. Although any person may fill a variety of statuses, many people find that one of their statuses is more important than all the others. Such a status, which is termed a **master status,** can have damaging effects (Hughes, 1945). A black man, for example, may be a doctor, a father, and a leader in his church, but he may find that his status as a black American takes precedence over all of those other statuses. The same is often true for women. A woman may be a brilliant scientist and a leader in her community, and fill other statuses as well, but she may find that when she deals with men her status as a woman is more important than any of the others.

The effects of a master status are also felt by people who have been in prison, by members of various racial and ethnic groups, by Americans overseas (Smith, 1994, 1996), and by members of many other types of groups. For example, recent studies have shown that people who are noticeably overweight or obese often find that their status as a "fat person" is a master status that denies them opportunities to be appreciated for their performance in other statuses, such as student or worker.

Patterns of discrimination and prejudice stemming from the problem of master statuses are not easily corrected. We will see at many points in this book that a major source of social change is the efforts of some groups to eliminate those patterns. When changes actually occur, however, they often take the form of new national laws, such as laws against racial segregation or gender discrimination. This raises the question of the distinction between societies and nations.

SOCIETIES AND NATION-STATES

For most people in the world today, the social entity that represents society itself is the nation-state. The assumed correspondence between society and nation can be seen in the fact that expressions like "the United States" and "American society" are often used interchangeably. Moreover, most people think of their society in terms of national boundaries; thus, if you were asked to name the society of which you are a member, you would be more likely to say "the United States" than "California" or "Chicago" or "the University of Texas." Yet as we will see shortly, societies and nations are by no means the same thing.

The State

To understand the distinction between society and nation, we need to begin with the concept of the state. In a lecture at Munich University, Max Weber described a state as

> a human community that (successfully) claims the monopoly of the legitimate use of physical force within a given territory. . . . The right to use physical force is ascribed to other institutions or to individuals only to the extent to which the state permits it. The state is considered the sole source of the "right" to use violence. (quoted in Gerth & Mills, 1958, p. 78)

The **state** thus may be defined as a society's set of political institutions—that is, the groups and organizations that deal with questions of "who gets what, when, and how" (Lasswell, 1936). The **nation-state** is the largest territory within which those institutions can operate without having to face challenges to their sovereignty (their right to govern). Weber was careful to note that the state has a monopoly over the use of force, which under certain circumstances it grants to other agencies (e.g., state and municipal governments). But the state gains this right—the source of its power to influence the behavior of citizens—from the people themselves, from their belief that it is *legitimate* for the state to have this power. As we will see in later chapters, the concepts of power and legitimacy are essential to understanding the workings of the modern state; indeed, power is a basic concept at all levels of human social behavior. Here, however, we must examine the idea of a state as it operates in the concept of nation-state or, simply, nation.

The Nation-State

"One nation, under God, indivisible, with liberty and justice for all." We can say the words in our sleep, and often we do not bother to think about their meanings. After the tragic events of September 11, 2001, however, people of all ages began paying much greater attention to the significance of the Pledge of Allegiance. Repeating the pledge in schools and elsewhere is a highly significant action: It enhances the legitimacy of the state and thus helps create the nation—in this case, the nation known as the United States of America.

But do all the inhabitants of the United States of America think of themselves as members of one nation? To a large extent they do, and this is one of the greatest strengths of that nation. Yet at various times in American history, certain groups—African Americans, Native Americans, and the Amish, for example—have thought of themselves as separate peoples. And the idea of an "indivisible" nation was fought out in one of the bloodiest wars the world has ever known, the American Civil War of 1861–1865.

In the century since the Civil War, the United States has not experienced any real tests of its national solidarity. Countries like Lebanon, Zimbabwe, Afghanistan, Northern Ireland, and the nations that were formerly part of Yugoslavia or the Soviet Union—to name only some—have been far less fortunate. For them, the issue of creating a national identity that can unite peoples who think of themselves as members of different societies remains a burning question.

Between 1945 and 1970, as peoples all over the world adjusted to the breakup of the European colonial empires, more than 100 new states were created. In these new nations, as in many of the nation-states that existed before the 1950s, the correspondence between national identity and society is often problematic, a situation that frequently produces social upheavals. In Nigeria, for example, the stability—indeed, the very existence—of the nation-state is endangered by animosities among the various societies included within its boundaries. Although the nation has rich oil resources and is the largest of the sub-Saharan nations, its per capita income fell to $250 in 1993 from $1,000 in 1980. This decline is largely caused by conflicts among the major tribal groups and the failure of the nation-state's

leaders to overcome those conflicts. Although there are scores of tribal and ethnic groups in the nation's population, the largest are the Hausa (21 percent), the Yoruba (20 percent), the Ibo (17 percent), and the Fulani (9 percent), each of which is afraid that the others might gain power at their expense (Olojede, 1995). The political instability of the nation is worsened by the ever-present threat of military dictatorship, which is to some degree a consequence of these ethnic divisions. (See the Mapping Social Change box on page 100.)

South Africa provides another example of differing levels of national and social identity. In 1994, the minority white government ended its policy of apartheid (racial separation) and yielded political power to the black majority under the leadership of Nelson Mandela and the formerly banned African National Congress (ANC). But black South Africans themselves often experience conflicts derived from differing tribal identities. The larger tribal populations, such as the Zulus, have their own kings and political leaders. Some are afraid that the incorporation of their people into a modern nation-state will cause them to lose their identity and rights as Zulus. As a result, there have been numerous episodes of conflict and violence between Zulu separatists and the members of the ANC.

The lack of a clear match between society and nation can be seen in the case of entire groups who think of themselves as "a people" (e.g., the Ibo, the Jews, Native Americans, the Kosovars) as well as in smaller groups. You and your friends are part of "American society," by which we mean the populations and social structures found within the territory claimed by the nation-state known as the United States of America. But you are also part of a local community with smaller structures and more gemeinschaft, or primary, relationships. Indeed, this community level of society may have greater meaning for you in your daily life than society at the national level.

CRITICAL SOCIOLOGY AND SOCIAL CHANGE

AIDS and Social Structure in Africa

The global crisis of AIDS and HIV transmission has already accounted for more than 50 million deaths. This grim toll makes the AIDS epidemic far deadlier than the bubonic, or black, plague that ravaged European populations in the 1400s, with an estimated 20 million deaths, or the influenza epidemic of the early twentieth century, which also killed about 20 million people throughout the world (Caldwell, 2000). The extent of the death and suffering caused by the

Tribal Societies Within the Modern State of Nigeria

Nigeria is the largest nation of Africa south of the Sahara desert. It is also a nation where social change is extremely rapid and unpredictable, for tribal and religious differences make it difficult to create a Nigerian identity among citizens, and the influence of Western oil companies seeking to exploit the huge oil reserves in the impoverished coastal region creates opportunities for both development and corruption.

As the detailed map shows, it is composed of many societies with their own cultures and languages. Some, like the Hausa, are spread out over vast territories in the northern savannas; others, like the Tiv and Ibo, are clustered in the more densely populated coastal plains and on the delta of the mighty Niger River. Nigeria was once considered a leader in the development of democratic political institutions. It had a lively cultural and intellectual life and produced some of Africa's best novelists and playwrights. In 1998, after many years of dictatorship, the Nigerian military began to relinquish its harsh rule over the nation, but at this writing the persistence of regional and ethnic animosities continues to hamper the emergence of national leadership. Conflict between its many societies, often over the disposal of oil revenues from the Niger delta region, and rampant political and economic corruption continually threaten the viability of its democratic institutions.

Ken Saro-Wiwa, shown in the photo, was one of the leaders of the effort to create a modern Nigerian nation even as he fought for the well-being of his own region. He is now considered to be a martyr of Nigeria's democratic hopes. Despite protests throughout the world, this celebrated writer, environmental activist, and political dissident was executed by the Nigerian dictatorship in

1995. Saro-Wiwa was the founder and leader of the movement for the survival of the Ogoni people in Nigeria's oil-rich Niger delta region. Although the government and the Dutch Shell Corporation

have taken billions of dollars' worth of oil from their lands, the Ogoni, a small tribal society in the Cross River region, still live in mud huts and dig for yams with bamboo sticks. Acid rain and oil pollution have destroyed many productive farms. Saro-Wiwa was attempting to organize a peaceful social movement to protest these conditions. His arrest and execution is an example of how environmental issues increasingly become confounded with intergroup politics in this land of tribal conflict.

Since his murder, the new, more democratic government of Nigeria has cre-

ated a "Ken Saro-Wiwa Memorial Prize for Ethnic and Religious Tolerance." In a recent speech about this award, Nigeria's Nobel laureate, the world-famous playwright Wole Soyinka, said that "Since

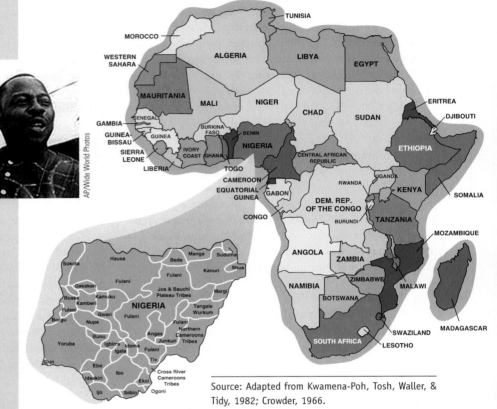

AP/Wide World Photos

Source: Adapted from Kwamena-Poh, Tosh, Waller, & Tidy, 1982; Crowder, 1966.

the death of Ken Saro-Wiwa . . . the state of ethnic consciousness has assumed a violent dimension." Worried that inequalities among Nigeria's different ethnic groups could result in civil strife, Soyinka issued an urgent call for a conference of "nationalities." Leaders around the world will be watching the Nigerian situation carefully because the problem of creating a sense of overarching national identity in a population divided by many different cultures and differing ideas of peoplehood is widespread (Africa News Service, 2000).

HIV virus is worse in Africa at the present time than in any other region of the world, so AIDS researchers and activists are particularly anxious to know more about why the disease is so prevalent in some African nations.

Research by AIDS researcher Helen Epstein shows some important links between AIDS transmission and the social structure of African societies. She notes that extensive migration from rural to industrial regions of Africa creates conditions that favor the virus's spread. Rates of infection have soared in regions that send large numbers of migrant workers to South Africa. Today about 300,000 migrants from other African nations in the southern cone of Africa work in the gold and copper mines of South Africa, about 40,000 of them from neighboring Mozambique, the site of much of Epstein's recent research. As she writes, "The migrant labor system in southern Africa has been blamed for many of the region's ills, including the disruption of family life and rural underdevelopment. Now it is also being blamed for the spread of HIV. The long absences from home, the tedious, dangerous work, the drab anomie of life in all-male miners' hostels, the gangs of prostitutes clinging to the chain link fences around the mines—are all believed to contribute to miners' higher risk of HIV infection" (2002, p. 43).

The connection between migrant labor and long-distance trucking, prostitution, and AIDS transmission is well documented, but Epstein's research team made some additional surprising discoveries. They measured HIV rates among miners and prostitutes in a South African mining area where there were large numbers of migrant workers. "Almost as an afterthought, the researchers also measured rates of HIV infection among ordinary women living in a township about fifteen miles away from the mines. The researchers were not surprised to find that 80 percent of the prostitutes were HIV-positive, or that 30 percent of the miners carried the virus as well. But what really surprised them was that nearly 60 percent of the women in the township between the ages of twenty and thirty were HIV-positive." Further research showed that these village women were not prostitutes, nor were they particularly promiscuous. Yet these more isolated women were almost as likely to be HIV-positive as the prostitutes, and they were more likely to be HIV-positive than the high-risk miners. "We were stunned," said one of the social scientists who worked on the study. "It turns out," Epstein explains, "that miners, not surprisingly, prefer long-term girlfriends in the more distant villages and townships to hasty tussles in the wet grass with prostitutes. When they do have sex with prostitutes, they know it's risky, so they usually use condoms. But they trust their longer-term township girlfriends, who trust them in return, and condoms are used far less often in these relationships" (2000, p. 44).

Armed with these new data, South African public health officials could revise their efforts to teach about safe sex and the use of condoms. But the research revealed other equally troubling aspects of the way social structures affect the course of the disease.

Deaths among the migrant miners are extremely high due to mine accidents—about one in thirty die before leaving the mines, and almost half become disabled by lung damage and die before age fifty. This leaves poverty-stricken women in the home villages. When they seek to claim their dead husbands' pensions or health benefits, they find that because they live across national boundaries, it is extremely difficult for them to make their claims. In desperation, they often seek the material and emotional support of other returned migrants, who are extremely likely to be HIV-positive. As in many studies of AIDS transmission, poverty and almost total lack of power are revealed as major contributors to the high rates of infection among African women. In this and many other cases, a knowledge of how social structures—the mines, the migrant camps, the nearby villages, the pension system, the public health system, and others—is vital to understanding the spread of disease and interventions that might reduce suffering.

By the time he died in 2001 at the age of 12, Nkosi Johnson was one of the best-known AIDS activists in the world. He called on people to overcome the stigma attached to HIV/AIDS, moving many to tears when he said, "You cannot get AIDS by hugging, you cannot get AIDS by kissing."

VISUAL SOCIOLOGY

SOCIAL STRUCTURES AND THE INNER-CITY EMERGENCY ROOM

After several years as a clinical specialist and triage nurse, Lori Jones knows that to be happy in her roles and balance all the conflicting demands they make on her she must do some serious soul-searching. As she explains it, "Actually, I've never done anything really great here, never saved anyone's life. The paramedics have. Yet patients have been lucky to have me as a nurse. No, I've never done things that are dramatic. I mean, I was happy because patients took their medicine as directed for 10 days. That's a feat in itself."

Jones also knows that the burdens of life in the ER are made even more difficult by the hospital's inner-city location, the need to provide services to so many poor people and minorities, and the fact that it is a public institution, dependent on a diminishing stream of tax revenues. "This is a city hospital on the edge," she observes, "losing money on indigent pa-

tients, and all around us is a massive system that has to raise more and more money, while politicians are threatening to close us down. So we are stretched incredibly thin, torn in so many different directions. It can be overwhelming."

The emergency room of a big-city hospital is not a place for the squeamish observer. The deadening calm of the night shift may suddenly be broken by the crackle of the paramedics' radio announcing that they are bringing in a severely wounded gunshot victim or a baby with a deadly high fever or three bleeding gang fighters. Immediately the routine work of the ER is suspended in a rush of activity. Even the less seriously ill or injured patients in the waiting room intuitively realize that their needs must be set aside for the life-threatening emergency.

Documentary photographer Eugene Richards (1989) spent many months conducting participant observation research in the emergency room of Denver General Hospital, known by local residents as the "knife and gun club." His photos capture the physically and emotionally draining work of the ER staff and the stark drama of the emergencies they deal with. In the text accompanying the

photos, he often refers to the social structure of the ER. The roles of the ER staff are well defined, so that even if the work stretches them to the limits of endurance, they know what they must do and how they must assist each other. Indeed, underneath its drama and emotion, the ER is a marvel of human social organization, without which it could not be effective.

A man and a woman are the only people in the waiting room. Their child, I was told, has spinal meningitis. I sit close to them, but I can't think of anything to say. The silence is deadening. I feel frozen in place. I hide my camera and sit there for a half hour, until I see an ambulance pull up the ramp.

It's early in the day, I'm told, for a suicide attempt. The woman is 35 years old, still alive. There really is something fishlike about her, naked on the table with all those lines attached to her skin. And her skin is pale as ice. And her mouth is gaping open. . . .

© Eugene Richards

© Eugene Richards

5:00 p.m. The patient is a big-bellied guy with an American eagle on his left arm and a tongue hanging out tattooed on his chest. Insensible and bloody now, he had crashed his car at 80 miles per hour.

5:30 p.m. A teenage boy, claiming to be a member of a gang, shows the doctors the scars on his belly. He brags that he had refused medical treatment when he was stabbed, though he now looks terribly frightened. When a doctor reaches for his arm, he grimaces and tries to slide off the table. As the IV needle is slid in, he bites down on a rubber bottle cap, imitating something he must have seen in a John Wayne movie.

The chief surgeon leans forward and begins the cut. He cuts through the skin, looks, touches, cuts again. The other doctors join in. I'm conscious of the clicking of scissors, and that I'm breathing way too fast. Then, my God, they split the breastbone and position a spreader to push the ribs apart. It's done. They get to her heart, a punctured, failing heart.

At 1:00 a.m. the surgeons straighten up and turn all together toward the clock. They agree as to the time of death and pronounce her. After shooting some Polaroid pictures, they hurry out the door, probably to another patient. The nurses left behind turn off the machines, cut loose the lines and drainage tubes, and toss the surgical instruments into a pile; the interns close the dead woman's chest.

The Sociological Observer

(See photo on page 97.)

Upon the death of her spouse, a woman is transformed, without choice, from her status as wife to the new status of widow. The photo shows a young woman whose husband lost his life in war. She can now be seen as representing the human face of that conflict and the losses suffered. The public nature of her pain brings sympathy from those who hear her story. Her status as a military wife has now been changed, and she can no longer count on her husband's salary as a source of family income. This sudden shift into widowhood also brings changes in her social status as she navigates life as a single woman.

© Eugene Richards

© Eugene Richards

SUMMARY

The Social Order

- A *society* is a population of people or other social animals that is organized in a cooperative manner to carry out the major functions of life.
- *Social structure* refers to the recurring patterns of behavior that create relationships among individuals and groups within a society.
- The building blocks of human societies are *groups*—collections of people who interact on the basis of shared expectations regarding one another's behavior. In every group, there are socially defined positions known as *statuses*. The way a society defines how an individual is to behave in a particular status is called a *role*.
- A social *institution* is a more or less stable structure of statuses and roles devoted to meeting the basic needs of people in a society. Within any given institution, there are norms that specify how people in various statuses are to perform their roles. New institutions continually emerge through the process of *differentiation*.

Populations and Societies

- The growth of the world's population is directly related to the evolution of human social structures, which in turn is related to changes in production technologies.
- The first million years of human social evolution were characterized by a hunting-and-gathering way of life. During that time, the family and other kinship structures evolved, and the band became the basic territorial unit of human society.
- The shift to agriculture is commonly linked with the invention of the plow, but for centuries human societies had been acquiring food through the domestication of plants and animals. Some became *pastoral societies* based on the herding of animals; others evolved into *horticultural societies* based on the raising of seed crops. However, the first large-scale agrarian societies evolved after the development of plow-and-harvest agriculture.
- Agrarian societies allow people to escape from dependence on food sources over which they have no control. In such societies, people produce surpluses that can be used to feed new classes of non-food-producers such as warriors. At the same time, these societies require increasing amounts of land, which may lead to conflicts over territory. The need to store and defend food supplies and to house non-food-producers results in the growth of villages and small cities.

- The next major change in human production technologies was the Industrial Revolution, the shift from agriculture to trade and industry. This began in England around 1650 and spread to the United States and other nations during the next two centuries. Its impetus came not only from technological advances but also from the rise of a new social order: *capitalism*.
- The shift to industrial production affects social structure in several major ways. As a consequence of the industrialization of agriculture, relatively few people live on the land, whereas increasing numbers live in cities and suburbs. Greater openness to change results in the emergence of new classes and social movements. Scientific and technical advances produce tremendous wealth, and the world "shrinks" as a result of innovations in transportation and communication.

Society and the Individual

- For the individual member of a human society, adaptation to a more modern society involves a shift from *gemeinschaft* (close, personal relationships) to *gesellschaft* (well-organized but impersonal relationships).
- In modern societies, *primary groups* like the family are supplemented, if not replaced, by *secondary groups* (organizations or associations) whose members do not have strong feelings for one another.
- Roles in secondary groups often conflict with roles in primary groups, a situation known as *role conflict*. *Role strain* occurs when a person experiences conflicting demands within a single role.
- Another difference between simpler and more advanced societies is that in the former almost all statuses are *ascribed* (determined by birth or tradition), whereas in the latter there is a tendency to replace ascribed statuses with ones that are *achieved* (determined by a person's own efforts).
- Sometimes a particular status takes precedence over all of an individual's other statuses; such a status is referred to as a *master status*.

Societies and Nation-States

- When they think of a society, most people in the world today think in terms of the nation-state, or nation, of which they are members. (A *state* is a society's set of political structures, and a *nation-state* is the territory within which those structures operate.) But although the members of a society often think of themselves as members of a particular nation, this is not always so, and in extreme cases the lack of a clear match between society and nation can result in a civil war.

GLOSSARY

society: A population that is organized in a cooperative manner to carry out the major functions of life. (p. 82)

social structure: The recurring patterns of behavior that people create through their interactions, their exchange of information, and their relationships. (p. 82)

group: Any collection of people who interact on the basis of shared expectations regarding one another's behavior. (p. 82)

status: A socially defined position in a group. (p. 83)

role: The way a society defines how an individual is to behave in a particular status. (p. 84)

role expectations: A society's expectations about how a role should be performed, together with the individual's perceptions of what is required in performing that role. (p. 84)

institution: A more or less stable structure of statuses and roles devoted to meeting the basic needs of people in a society. (p. 85)

differentiation: The processes whereby sets of social activities performed by one social institution are divided among different institutions. (p. 86)

pastoral society: A society whose primary means of subsistence is herding animals and moving with them over a wide expanse of grazing land. (p. 88)

horticultural society: A society whose primary means of subsistence is raising crops, which it plants and cultivates, often developing an extensive system for watering the crops. (p. 88)

social stratification: The process whereby the members of a society are sorted into different statuses. (p. 89)

open society: A society in which social mobility is possible for everyone. (p. 89)

closed society: A society in which social mobility does not exist. (p. 89)

capitalism: A system for organizing the production of goods and services that is based on markets, private property, and the business firm or company. (p. 91)

gemeinschaft: A term used to refer to the close, personal relationships of small groups and communities. (p. 96)

gesellschaft: A term used to refer to the well-organized but impersonal relationships among the members of modern societies. (p. 96)

primary group: A small group characterized by intimate, face-to-face associations. (p. 96)

secondary group: A social group whose members have a shared goal or purpose but are not bound together by strong emotional ties. (p. 96)

role conflict: Conflict that occurs when in order to perform one role well, a person must violate the expectations associated with another role. (p. 97)

role strain: Conflict that occurs when the expectations associated with a single role are contradictory. (p. 97)

ascribed status: A position or rank that is assigned to an individual at birth and cannot be changed. (p. 98)

achieved status: A position or rank that is earned through the efforts of the individual. (p. 98)

master status: A status that takes precedence over all of an individual's other statuses. (p. 98)

state: A society's set of political structures. (p. 98)

nation-state: The largest territory within which a society's political institutions can operate without having to face challenges to their sovereignty. (p. 98)

INTERNET RESOURCES

Virtual Society: The Wadsworth Sociology Resource Center *(http://sociology.wadsworth.com)*

At Virtual Society you can access a wide range of enrichment material to aid your study of sociology. From the main page, click on the Student Resources link and find your course and this textbook. Next, select the chapter you are presently studying from the pull-down menu. Among the useful options for each self-study chapter are online links and exercises, flashcards, practical study tips, and practice quizzes for each chapter.

MC MicroCase Online

From the Virtual Society home page, click on MicroCase Online to access book-specific MicroCase exercises that allow you to further explore sociological issues and principles presented in the text.

InfoTrac College Edition

Another unique option available to you at the Student Resources section at Virtual Society is InfoTrac College Edition, an online library with access to hundreds of scholarly and popular periodicals. Below are suggested search terms for this chapter, but this resource also allows you to fit your study of sociology to your own interests by searching custom keywords.

Social Structure

Capitalism

Primary Group

Role

From a helpless, entirely self-centered being, the human infant develops into a person capable of performing roles in a wide variety of social groups. Those groups, in turn, often develop and change—a small business founded by a few close friends, for example, may expand into a complex corporation with a structure far different from that of the original group. Likewise, the structure of an entire society may change as people find new ways of making a living and new ways of organizing to protect their interests. In response to such changes,

Social Dynamics

some people may turn to crime or other socially disvalued behaviors, and others may form protest movements that seek to change the social order.

In Part 2 of this book, we cover many of the processes that seem to account for social stability and change. In Chapter 5, we discuss socialization, the process by which individuals become fully participating members of their society. One major outcome of socialization is the ability to function in groups, the subject of Chapter 6. Chapter 7 discusses how and why people deviate from the norms of their culture, and Chapter 8 looks at collective behavior and social movements, phenomena that involve large numbers of people in a society and often produce major social change. Chapter 9 examines the changes in the nature of human settlements that have accompanied the growth of the world's population. Finally, Chapter 10 summarizes the ways in which sociologists think about and conduct research on the changes that affect the daily lives of people in societies throughout the world.

Socialization

© Richard Hutchings/PhotoEdit

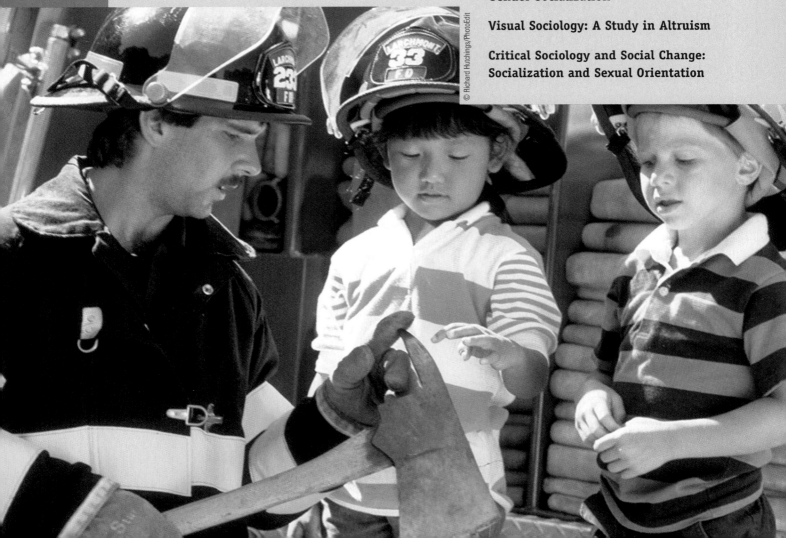

When the children at the Wee Care Preschool in Safety Harbor, Florida, saw a big red fire engine pull up in front of their school, they rushed to put away their toys and games. Chanting "The firemen are here!" they ran outside to greet the five men in blue fire uniforms, complete with white hats and gloves.

The firefighters were there to thank the children for the flag they had made and the $200 in pennies they had collected for the firefighters to take to New York City. "Our idea was to collect pennies because [young children] understand the value of a penny better than dollars," one of the teachers said. "They wanted to do what they could to help," said another teacher about the effort they named "Pennies for Peace."

The firefighters had gone to New York to attend the funerals of fellow firefighters and to help with the cleanup at Ground Zero. They had also made a contribution to the fund for the widows and children of those who lost their lives in the tragedy. "Everyone feels the pain, and it runs deep," the fire chief said. "So we tried to get involved."

The 50 white stars on the flag bore the names of the more than 80 children who attend school at Wee Care. Tiny red handprints made up the stripes that stretched across the cloth. When they were in New York, the firefighters, dressed in yellow rescue gear, took the flag to a spot on top of the rubble and took a picture of it.

As the firefighters told the students of their experiences, they became emotional, at times choking back tears. "The flag you all gave us to take to New York, we were going to leave it up there," the chief said. "But we decided to bring it back to you. This is something we will remember for a long, long time, so we want you guys to have it here at your school because it meant a lot to the guys we showed it to."

The firefighters stayed at the school for a while to speak with the teachers and children. Their gleaming red truck remained parked outside the school for about 30 minutes and became a playground for the children, who climbed onto the huge bumper and leaped off. "It really meant a lot to the kids," said one of the parents in attendance (Tucker, 2001).

After September 11, 2001, firefighters took center stage in a national drama. As horrible as the destruction and deaths on September 11 were, and the ensuing war and terrorism as well, the events focused attention on values such as courage, altruism, and patriotism. Children could identify with the heroes who rushed into burning buildings despite the risk of death. These were the same people they knew from their own neighborhoods, except now they were part of an event that everyone—from preschoolers to grandparents—could seek to understand and cope with together.

Before the tragedy, parents were worried about problems like school violence and wondering why some children could act like terrorists, as seen so vividly in the case of Columbine High School. But confronted by a hidden enemy, parents are reminded that qualities essential to the survival of societies, such as loyalty, bravery, and selflessness, are also communicated by examples like that of the New York Fire Department, and through the training and education we participate in throughout our lives.

FOCUS QUESTIONS:

- What are the major experiences that account for the way an individual becomes a "social being"?

- How does learning to take social roles occur throughout a person's lifetime?

- How much of the way people behave is determined by social learning and how much by genetic factors?

BECOMING A SOCIAL BEING

How do we become responsible members of our society? Why are some people endowed with qualities we admire, such as courage or altruism, while others display qualities we abhor, such as selfishness or cruelty? What are the influences of family, schools, peers, and other social groups on people's character and the way they behave toward others?

Socialization is the term sociologists use to describe the ways in which people learn to conform to their society's norms, values, and roles. People develop their own unique personalities as a result of the learning they gain from parents, siblings, relatives, peers, teachers, mentors, and all the other people who influence them throughout their lives (Corsaro, 1997; Handel, 2001). From the viewpoint of society as a whole, however, what is important about the process of socialization is that people learn to behave according to the norms of their culture. How people learn to behave according to cultural norms—that is, the way they learn their culture—makes possible the transmission of culture from one generation to the next. In this way the culture is "reproduced" in the next generation (Gonzalez-Mena, 1998; Roer-Strier & Rosenthal, 2001).

Socialization occurs throughout life as the individual learns new norms in new groups and situations. For purposes of analysis, however, socialization can be divided into three major phases:

1. *Primary socialization* refers to all the ways in which the newborn individual is molded into a social being— that is, into a growing person who can interact with others according to the expectations of society. Primary socialization occurs within the family and other intimate groups in the child's social environment.

2. *Secondary socialization* occurs in later childhood and adolescence, when the child enters school and comes under the influence of adults and peers outside the household and immediate family.

3. *Adult socialization* is a third stage, when the person learns the norms associated with new statuses such as wife, husband, journalist, programmer, grandparent, or nursing home patient (Elkin & Handel, 1989).

There are several unresolved and highly controversial issues in the study of socialization, and we will explore some of them in this chapter. Chief among them are the following:

- *Nature and nurture.* What is the relative strength of biological (i.e., genetic) versus social influences on the individual? This issue, often referred to as the nature-nurture problem, is raised most strikingly by the altruistic behavior of the firefighters and police officers who risked their lives attempting to rescue victims of the September 11 attacks. Was it some innate, biological aspect of their nature that made them act so selflessly ("nature"), or was their behavior a result of their home environment and professional training ("nurture")? Social scientists tend to lean toward explanations based on nurture, but as we will see in this chapter, biology plays a significant role in behavior and in forming an individual's personality. Neither biological nor sociological factors alone explain the complex behaviors involved in successful socialization (Steen, 1996; Wade, 2001).

- *The social construction of the self.* A second controversy in the study of socialization is the question of how a person's sense of self becomes established. We all learn to play many different roles, but how do the influences of others in our social world affect our role playing, and how do those experiences help form our sense of ourselves? How do people learn to conform to society's norms and to take the roles that society makes available to them?

- *Influences on socialization.* How do different social environments, such as the affluent suburban school or the slum neighborhood or the military boot camp, influence socialization? In other words, how do different social environments produce different kinds of people? What are the influences throughout life of different agencies of socialization and different experiences with other people?

- *Gender socialization and sexual identity.* Gender socialization refers to the ways in which we become the girls and boys and, gradually, the men and women of our society and culture. All the controversies over whether behavior is innate or learned are intensified when we consider the differences and similarities in the socialization of males and females. This is especially true in reference to the ways in which we are socialized to acquire a sexual identity.

In this chapter, we explore each of these questions in detail. We will be concerned primarily with the socialization of "normal" members of society—people who are able to perform roles, to feel empathy for others, to express emotions and yet control feelings that are antisocial, to nurture others and raise children who will also be able to nurture, and to take on new roles as they grow older. But the failures of socialization can also tell us a great deal about what is involved in creating the social being.

For instance, consider the case of Uday Hussein, who reportedly grew up watching his father, Saddam Hussein, punish political opponents as a way to control a large, diverse country. As a grown man, Uday, now 38, earned his own reputation for violent behavior. An Amnesty International report relates that when an Olympic Committee security guard was accused of stealing sports equipment, Uday ordered that his hand be cut off. The missing equipment was later found. Similar incidents tied to Uday were described in a United Nations report on human rights in Iraq (United Nations Commission on Human Rights, 1998). "The word that suits him is sadist," said Latif Yahia (2002), who, as Uday's former body double and a member of his entourage, claims to have witnessed the punishment of about 10 athletes. "I think Saddam's more human than Uday."

The issue in cases like Uday Hussein's is not whether we should excuse what such individuals have done due to their socialization but whether we can learn from those tragedies so that we can prevent others. And scientists, biological and social, still have a good deal to learn. Socialization is an extremely complex process. Some people who were abused and neglected can nonetheless become good parents, despite the odds. Others who seem to have experienced all the right influences can end up doing evil things, again despite the odds (Corsaro, 1997; Wrong, 1961). Even if we could trace all the social influences on a person's development, there would remain many unanswered questions about the combined influences of the person's genetic potential and his or her social experiences—that is, the relative importance of nature and nurture.

NATURE AND NURTURE

Throughout recorded history, there have been intense debates over what aspects of behavior are "human nature" and what aspects can be intentionally shaped through nurture or socialization. During all the centuries of prescientific thought, the human body was thought to be influenced by the planets, the moon, and the sun, or by various forces originating within the body, especially in the brain, heart, and liver. In the ancient world and continuing into the Middle Ages, blood, bile, phlegm, and other bodily fluids were thought to control people's moods and affect their personalities. Human behavior and health could also be affected by evil spirits or witches. While they are no longer dominant explanations of human behavior, none of these ideas has ever entirely disappeared.

In the eighteenth century, a new and radical idea of the "natural man" emerged. The idea that humans inherently possess qualities such as wisdom and rationality, which are damaged in the process of socialization, took hold in the imaginations of many educated people. Social philosophers like Jean-Jacques Rousseau believed that if only human society could be improved, people would emerge with fewer emotional scars and limitations of spirit. This

belief was based on the enthusiasm created by scientific discoveries, which would free humans from ignorance and superstition, and new forms of social organization like democracy and capitalism, which would unleash new social forces that would produce wealth and destroy obsolete social forms like aristocracy.

In the United States, Thomas Jefferson applied these ideas in developing the educational and governmental institutions of the new nation. Much later, in the nineteenth century, Karl Marx and other social theorists applied the same basic idea of human perfectibility in their criticisms of capitalism. A revolutionary new society, they predicted, would overturn the worst effects of capitalism and finally realize Rousseau's promise that a superior society could produce superior people. As these examples indicate, many of the most renowned thinkers of the last two centuries have rejected the belief that nature places strict limits on what humans can achieve.

The Freudian Revolution

Sigmund Freud was the first social scientist to develop a theory that addressed both the "nature" and "nurture" aspects of human existence (Nagel, 1994; Robinson, 1994). For Freud, the social self develops primarily in the family, wherein the infant is gradually forced to control its biological functions and needs: sucking, eating, defecation, genital stimulation, warmth, sleep, and so on. Freud shocked the straitlaced intellectuals of his day by arguing that infants have sexual urges and by showing that these aspects of the self are the primary targets of early socialization—that the infant is taught in many ways to delay physical gratification and to channel its biological urges into socially accepted forms of behavior.

ID, EGO, AND SUPEREGO   Freud's model of the personality is derived from his view of the socialization process. Freud divided the personality into three functional areas, or interrelated parts, that permit the self to function well in society.[1] The part from which the infant's unsocialized drives arise is termed the **id**. The moral codes of adults, especially parents, become incorporated into the part of the personality that Freud called the **superego**. Freud thought of this part of the personality as consisting of all the internalized norms, values, and feelings that are taught in the socialization process. In addition to the id

---

[1] Freud never expected that actual physical parts of the brain that correspond to the id, ego, and superego would be discovered. Instead, he was referring to aspects of the functioning personality that are observed in the individual.

and the superego, the personality as Freud described it has a third vital element, the **ego**. The ego is our conception of ourself in relation to others, in contrast with the id, which represents self-centeredness in its purest form. To have a "strong ego" is to be self-confident and able to accept criticism. To have a "weak ego" is to need continual approval from others. (The popular expression that someone "has a big ego" and demands constant attention actually signals a lack of ego strength in the Freudian sense.)

THE ROLE OF THE SAME-SEX PARENT   In the growth of the personality, according to Freud, the formation of the ego or social self is critical, but it does not occur without a great deal of conflict. The conflict between the infant's basic biological urges and society's need for a socialized person becomes evident very early. Freud believed that the individual's major personality traits (security or insecurity, fears and longings, ways of interacting with others) are formed in the conflict that occurs when parents insist that the infant control its biological urges. This conflict, Freud believed, is most severe between the child and the same-sex parent. The infant wishes to receive pleasure, especially sexual stimulation, from the opposite-sex parent and therefore is competing with the same-sex parent. To become more attractive to the opposite-sex parent, the infant attempts to imitate the same-sex parent. Thus for Freud, the same-sex parent is the most powerful socializing influence on the growing child, for reasons related to the biological differences and attractions between the child and the opposite-sex parent.

Contemporary sociologists who are influenced by Freud's biologically and socially based theories have used his concepts of same-sex attraction and imitation of the same-sex parent's behavior to explain differences between men and women. Alice Rossi (1977), for instance, argues that women's shared experience of menstruation and childbearing creates a strong bond between mothers and daughters. Nancy Chodorow (2002) claims that women's earliest experiences with their mothers tend to convince them that a woman is fulfilled by becoming a mother in her turn; thus women are socialized from a very early age to "reproduce motherhood." Research on socialization has shown that men also are strongly influenced by the same-sex parent. Fathers often serve as models of behavior whom boys will emulate throughout their lives.

Freud's theory includes the idea that the conflicts of childhood reappear throughout life in ways that the individual cannot predict. The demands of the superego ("conscience") and the "childish" desires of the id are always threatening to disrupt the functioning of the ego, especially in families in which normal levels of conflict are either exaggerated or suppressed. Note, however, that Freud focused on the traditional family, consisting of mother, father, and children. The more families depart from this conventional form, the more we need to question the adequacy of Freudian socialization theory.

Behaviorism

In the early decades of the twentieth century, Freud's theory was challenged by a different branch of social-scientific thought, known as **behaviorism.** In contrast to Freud and others who saw many human qualities as innate or biologically determined (nature), behaviorists saw the individual as a *tabula rasa,* or blank slate, that could be "written upon" through socialization. In other words, individual behavior could be determined entirely through social processes (nurture). Behaviorism asserts that individual behavior is not determined by instincts or any other "hardware" in the individual's brain or glands. Instead, all behavior is learned.

PAVLOV   Behaviorism traces its origins to the work of the Russian psychologist Ivan Pavlov (1927). Pavlov's experiments with dogs and humans revealed that behavior that had been thought to be entirely instinctual could in fact be shaped or **conditioned** by learning situations. Pavlov's dog, one of the most famous subjects in the history of psychology, was conditioned to salivate at the sound of a bell. The dog would normally salivate whenever food was presented to it. In his experiment, Pavlov rang a bell whenever the dog was fed. Soon the dog would salivate at the sound of the bell alone, thereby showing that salivation, which had always seemed to be a purely biological reflex, could be a conditioned, or learned, response as well.

WATSON   The American psychologist John B. Watson carried on Pavlov's work with an equally famous series of experiments on "Little Albert," an 11-month-old boy. Watson conditioned Albert to fear baby toys that were thought to be inherently cute and cuddly, such as stuffed white rabbits. By presenting these objects to Albert at the same time that he frightened him with a loud noise (i.e., a negative stimulus), Watson showed that the baby could be conditioned to fear any fuzzy white object, including Santa Claus's beard. He also showed that through the systematic presentation of white objects accompanied by positive stimuli, he could extinguish Albert's fear and cause him to like white objects again.

On the basis of his findings, Watson wrote:

> Give me a dozen healthy infants, well-formed, and
> my own specified world to bring them up in and
> I'll guarantee to take any one at random and train

him to become any type of specialist I might select—doctor, lawyer, artist, merchant-chief and, yes, even beggar-man and thief, regardless of his talents, penchants, tendencies, abilities, vocations, and race of his ancestors. (1930, p. 104)

For the behaviorist, in other words, nature is irrelevant and nurture all-important.

SKINNER Behaviorists who followed Watson—the most famous being B. F. Skinner—developed even more effective ways of shaping individual behavior. Skinner (1976) and his followers reasoned that in order to avoid failures in socialization it is necessary to completely control all the learning that goes on in the child's social environment. Sociologists are critical of the notion that it is possible to control the world of the developing person. They argue that while the behaviorists may show us how some types of social learning take place, psychological research often does not deal with real social environments. It has very little to say about what is actually learned in different social contexts, how it is learned (or not learned), and the influences of different social situations on the individual throughout life (Elkin & Handel, 1989). One type of situation that has been of interest to sociologists studying socialization processes is that of the child reared in extreme isolation.

Isolated Children

The idea that children might be raised apart from society, or that they could be reared by wolves or chimpanzees or some other social animal, has fascinated people since ancient times. Romulus and Remus, the legendary founders of Rome, were said to have been raised by a wolf. The story of Tarzan, a boy of noble birth who was abandoned in Africa and raised by apes, became a worldwide best-seller early in the twentieth century and has intrigued readers and movie audiences ever since. However, modern studies of children who have experienced extreme isolation cast doubt on the possibility that a truly unsocialized person can exist.

Throughout the nineteenth century and much of the twentieth, the discovery of a **feral** ("untamed") **child** always seemed to promise new insights into the relationship between biological capabilities and socialization, or nature and nurture (Davis, 1947). Social scientists looked on each case of a child raised in extreme isolation as a natural experiment that might reveal the effects of lack of socialization on child development. Once the child had been brought under proper care, studies were undertaken to determine how well he or she functioned. These studies showed that victims of severe isolation are able to learn,

but that they do so far more slowly than children who have not been isolated (Malson, 1972).

The case of Genie is representative of this line of research. Genie was born to a psychotic father and a blind and highly dependent mother. For the first 11 years of her life, she was strapped to a potty chair in an isolated room of the couple's suburban Los Angeles home. From birth she had almost no contact with other people. She was not toilet trained, and food was pushed toward her through a slit in the door of her room. When she was discovered by child welfare authorities after the mother told neighbors about the child's existence, the father committed suicide. Genie was placed in the custody of a team of medical personnel and child development researchers.

In the first few weeks after she was discovered, everyone who observed Genie was shocked. At first glance she looked like a normal child, with dark hair, pink cheeks, and a placid demeanor. Very quickly, however, it became clear that she was severely impaired. She walked awkwardly and was unable to dress herself. She had virtually no language ability—at most, she knew a few words, which she pronounced in an incomprehensible babble. She spit continuously and masturbated with no sense of social propriety. In short, she was a clear case of a child who had been deprived of social learning and in consequence was severely retarded in her individual and social development. She was alive, but she was not a social being in any real sense of the term. She had not developed a sense of self, nor had she the basic ability to communicate that comes with language learning.

For years, researcher Susan Curtiss (1977) studied Genie's slow progress toward language learning. Curtiss showed that Genie could learn many more words than a mentally retarded person would be expected to learn, but that she had great difficulty with the more complex rules of grammar that come naturally to a child who learns language in a social world. Genie's language remained in the shortened form characteristic of people who learn a language late in life. Most significant, Genie never mastered the language of social interaction. She had great difficulty with words such as *hello* and *thank you,* although she could make her wants and feelings known with nonverbal cues.

Although tests showed that in many ways Genie was highly intelligent, her language abilities never advanced beyond those of a third-grader. Genie gradually learned to adhere to social norms (e.g., she stopped spitting), but she never became a truly social being. Eventually the scientists who worked with her concluded that the most severe deprivation—the one that was the primary cause of her inability to become fully social and to master language—was her lack of emotional learning and especially her feelings of loss and lack of love. Genie expressed her inner

S. Curtiss, Genie: A Psycholinguistic Study of a Modern Day 'Wild Child' (Academic Press, 1977). Used by permission.

Genie drew this picture in 1977. First she drew the picture of her mother and labeled it "I miss Mama." Then she drew more. The moment she finished, she took the researcher's hand and placed it next to what she had just drawn. She motioned for the researcher to write and said, "Baby Genie." Then she pointed under her drawing and said, "Mama hand." The researcher wrote the corresponding letters. Satisfied, Genie sat back and stared at the picture. There she was, a baby in her mother's arms.

longings in the picture here, which she drew at the age of about 16. Never fully capable of independent living, Genie has spent her life in a home for developmentally disabled adults (Rymer, 1992a, 1992b).

The Need for Love

All studies of isolated children point to the undeniable need for nurturance in early childhood. They all show that extreme isolation is associated with profound retardation in the acquisition of language and social skills. However, they cannot establish causality because it is always possible that the child may have been retarded at birth. Despite their lack of firm conclusions, studies of children reared in extreme isolation have pointed researchers in an important direction: They suggest that lack of parental attention can result in retardation and early death. This conclusion receives further support from studies of children reared in orphanages and other residential care facilities, which have shown that such children are more likely to develop emotional problems and to be retarded in their language development than comparable children reared by their parents (Koler & Freeman, 1994; Spitz, 1945).

In a series of studies that have become classics in the field of socialization and child development, the primate psychologist Harry Harlow showed that infant monkeys reared apart from other monkeys never learned how to interact with other monkeys (Harlow, 1986; Harlow & Harlow, 1962); they could not refrain from aggressive behavior when they were brought into group situations. When females who had been reared apart from their mothers became mothers themselves, they tended to act in what Harlow described as a "ghastly fashion" toward their young. In some cases they even crushed their babies' heads with their teeth before handlers could intervene. Although it is risky to generalize from primate behavior to that of humans, these studies of the effects of lack of nurturance bear a striking resemblance to studies of child abuse in humans. This research generally shows that one of the best predictors of abuse is whether the parent was also abused as a child (Keniston, 1977; Ornish, 1998; Polansky et al., 1981; Talbot, 1998).

These findings confirm our intuitive knowledge that nurturance and parental love play a profound, though still incompletely understood, role in the development of the individual as a social being. These and related findings offer support for social policies that seek to enrich the socialization process with nurturance from other caring adults—for example, in early-education programs. Yet many researchers and policymakers remain convinced that biological traits place limits on what individuals can achieve, regardless of the kind of nurturance they receive. In recent years, proponents of this view have focused on the controversial question of whether such complex traits as intelligence and sexual orientation are the result of genetic predisposition or childhood socialization.

The Debate over Genetic Influences

The role of genes in shaping traits such as intelligence and sexual orientation is a subject of continual research and much controversy. In neither case is there any definitive evidence that specific genes determine these highly significant aspects of human behavior. Research on the human genome promises to increase our understanding of how genes contribute to many aspects of human development and behavior, including intelligence and sexual orientation. At this writing, however, it is perhaps more important to understand the nature of the controversy.

GENES AND INTELLIGENCE In an influential but flawed study titled *The Bell Curve*, biologist Richard Herrnstein and social psychologist Charles Murray (1994) attempted to show that IQ, one measure of intelligence, is an inherited trait that underlies inequality among different groups in the United States. Herrnstein and Murray do not believe that efforts to address inequalities through preschool programs, improvements in public education, and the like will ever successfully address the growing inequalities among individuals and groups in the United States or elsewhere. The real obstacle, they argue, is intelligence, or rather the lack of it in vast numbers of people. Since by their reasoning intelligence is an innate trait that is distributed unequally among various subgroups of the population, social intervention cannot do much to equalize the economic effects of differences in intelligence.

Like many traits that vary from one person to another, such as height and weight, scores on intelligence tests are distributed in the shape of a "normal" or bell curve. Most people's IQ scores fall near the center of the distribution, while some are at either extreme. About these facts there is no argument. Murray and Herrnstein further assert, however, that scores on the bell curve of intelligence are creating what they call "cognitive classes"—that is, categories of people whom they label "very bright," "bright," "normal," "dull," and "very dull" (see Figure 5.1). They note that 5 percent of the U.S. population falls within the left and right extremes of the curve, and another 20 percent are in Class II and Class IV. By this reasoning, approximately 50 million residents of the United States are classified in the lower cognitive classes.

Recent research on the human brain does indicate that the larger some regions of the brain are, the more intelligent an individual is (Thompson et al., 2001). Despite these findings, however, most social scientists continue to oppose Herrnstein and Murray's conclusions, for several reasons. First, there has been much criticism of IQ as a single measure of intelligence. Many experts believe that intelligence is far too complex to be represented by a single measure like IQ (Gardner, 1983). Second, there is evidence of cultural and middle-class biases in the questions used to test IQ; examination of the test items reveals that they would be far more familiar to middle-class test takers than to those from a disadvantaged background. Third, the authors of *The Bell Curve* have been criticized for asserting that correlation is the same as causality. Just because IQ and poverty are correlated does not mean that IQ causes poverty. In Northern Ireland, for example, Catholic Irish individuals score lower on IQ tests than do Protestant Irish, but these differences in IQ are not found in the United States, where there are no differences in wealth or advantage between the two groups as there are in Northern Ireland. In other words, socialization in an

Figure 5.1 Defining the Cognitive Classes

Caution: The labels imposed on this IQ curve and the score used as boundaries between "cognitive classes" are those of Herrnstein and Murray and do not represent the thinking of many other social scientists.

Source: Reprinted with the permission of Scribner, an imprint of Simon and Schuster Adult Publishing Group, from *Money: Who has how much and why*, by Andrew Hacker. Copyright © 1997 by Andrew Hacker.

impoverished environment could cause low IQ scores, rather than the other way around.

Most contemporary research on intelligence rejects narrow reliance on a single intelligence score like IQ in favor of a multidimensional conception of intelligence that corresponds far better to the great diversity of people we encounter in and outside of school. Howard Gardner (2002) has identified seven distinct types of intelligence, as follows:

- Visual/spatial intelligence
- Musical intelligence
- Verbal intelligence
- Logical/mathematical intelligence
- Interpersonal intelligence (ability to perceive other people's emotions and motivations)
- Intrapersonal intelligence (ability to understand one's own emotions and motivations)
- Bodily/kinesthetic intelligence (sometimes thought of in popular speech as "physical coordination" or natural athletic ability)

Once one begins to appreciate people for these multiple intelligences—for the intelligence that makes one a gifted artist or athlete, another a poet or someone with keen insights into people's feelings and motivations—it becomes impossible and even cruel to label people as average or dull on the basis of a far narrower definition of the highly complex set of natural and learned abilities known as intelligence. No doubt all these types of intelligence have a genetic basis, as well as the need for specific forms of socialization, but we are a long way from understanding how the complex interplay between nature and nurture produces people with the different intelligences that contribute so much to what we recognize as their personalities.

GENES AND SEXUAL ORIENTATION   *Sexual orientation,* an individual's preference for same-sex or different-sex partners, is another aspect of human behavior that is often claimed to be determined by genes rather than socialization. Over 20 years ago, Edward O. Wilson (1979), an influential biologist and pioneer in the field of animal behavior, argued that before long researchers would probably identify a gene, or genes, that determine whether an individual becomes heterosexual or homosexual. But to date genetic research has produced little evidence to support this hypothesis. Biologists know roughly which genes determine the development of different sexes in the human embryo, but they admit that many genes influencing sex determination are yet to be discovered (Vilain, 2000). They are even further from a scientific understanding of the contributions of genes, if any, to sexual orientation. Research by biologist Simon LeVay has found differences in the brains of gay and straight men, and research on identical twins shows that a person with a gay identical twin is at least 10 times more likely to be gay than a person without one. Further, research on the possible relationship between birth order and sexual orientation indicates that there is about a 2 percent chance that a firstborn male will grow up gay. That chance grows to at least 6 percent for males with four or more older brothers. But all the researchers who have reported these findings agree that while there are clear genetic influences, there are also many influences that appear to arise from aspects of socialization that are still poorly understood (Dahir, 2001).

Since sexual orientation is such a controversial topic among those who take a strong moral position about what is "natural" or "unnatural" in sexual behavior, these issues have moral aspects that extend far beyond the research community. Gay and lesbian writers and activists have tended to support the argument that sexual orientation is inborn and permanent and therefore cannot be a basis for discrimination. This stance has caused dramatic changes in the way heterosexuals and homosexuals alike think about the issues. Americans who say that they believe sexual orientation is either genetic or biological are much more likely to support gay and lesbian civil rights than those who take a moral stand against homosexuality. The latter tend to believe that it is a "lifestyle choice" determined primarily by environmental influences. This opinion now appears to be fading in importance. In a Gallup Poll conducted in May 2001, half of those surveyed said that they believe homosexuality is genetic, and half said it is environmental. This is a complete reversal of Gallup

Polls of the late 1970s, when respondents pointed to the environment over genetics by more than a 4-to-1 ratio. The Gallup researchers call this shift in perception "one of the more significant changes in American public opinion on gay and lesbian issues." It is accompanied by increasing tolerance toward gays and lesbians. In 2001, 52 percent of Gallup respondents said that homosexuality is an "acceptable alternative lifestyle," compared with 38 percent in 1977 (Dahir, 2001). On the other hand, 38 percent represents a sizeable minority who still believe that homosexuality is not an acceptable sexual orientation, indicating that there remains a good deal of conflict about the issue, as we will see again in the final section of the chapter.

A Sociological Summary

Neither extreme of the nature-nurture debate presents a complete picture of socialization. Nature may endow individuals with greater or lesser innate abilities, yet despite those differences most people learn to function as social beings. And although humans have an infinite capacity to learn behaviors of all kinds, through socialization they learn the particular behaviors required to function within their own culture and society. Nevertheless, the nature-nurture debate will endure and will continue to stimulate new research on the biological and psychological bases of behavior. In the meantime, most sociological research will focus on the following hypotheses:

1. *The social environment can unleash or stifle human potential.* Genetic and other biological traits establish broad boundaries for individual achievement, but the environment in which a person is raised can cause his or her potential to be realized more or less fully within those boundaries (Bronfenbrenner & Ceci, 1994). (This insight is found in numerous folktales and jokes. "Who was the greatest artist who ever lived?" a newly defunct art critic asked Saint Peter on his way into heaven. "Why, it was Lucius Cadmore," answered Saint Peter without a moment's hesitation. "But I never heard of him," said the sorely perplexed critic. "That's because he never had a chance to paint anything," Saint Peter explained.)

2. *The social environment presents an ever-changing array of roles and expectations.* Through socialization, people learn to perform roles as members of a particular culture and society. As the society and its culture change, so do definitions of what makes a person well socialized. These changing definitions create endless possibilities for misunderstandings and conflict within the groups and institutions in which socialization takes place.

THE SOCIAL CONSTRUCTION OF THE SELF

The self is the outcome of socialization; it may be defined as "the capacity to represent to oneself what one wishes to communicate to others" (Elkin & Handel, 1989, p. 47). Genie, an isolated, unsocialized child, did not develop a self in early childhood. She did not learn to formulate in her own mind the words that would express her feelings to others. Through socialization, most children learn to convert cries of discomfort, hunger, or fear into socially understandable symbols like "Want bottle" or "Go out now." These utterances show that the young child has learned to recognize his or her inner states and communicate them to others. "The child who can do this is on his or her way to becoming human, that is, to being simultaneously self-regulating and socially responsive" (Elkin & Handel, 1989, p. 47).

In sociology, the self is viewed as a social construct: It is produced or "constructed" through interaction with other people over a lifetime. Studies of how the self emerges therefore usually take an interactionist perspective.

Interactionist Models of the Self

The early American sociologist Charles Horton Cooley (1956/1902) was an astute observer of human interactions. As he watched young children interact with adults and other children, he saw that they continually pay attention to how others respond to their behavior. He realized that they are seeking cues in other people's behavior that reflect their own—that tell them how they look, how well they express themselves, how well they are performing a task, and so on. Cooley reasoned that as we mature, the overall pattern of these reflections becomes a dominant aspect of our identity—that is, of how we conceive of ourselves. He proposed that through these processes we actually become the kind of person we believe others think we are. He called this identity the "looking glass self." The looking glass self is the reflection of our self that we think we see in the behaviors of others around us.

LANGUAGE, CULTURE, AND THE SELF Cooley's insight into the role of others in defining the self was the foundation for the view of the self proposed by George Herbert Mead. Like Cooley, Mead believed strongly that the self is a social product. We are not born with selves that are "brought out" by socialization. Instead, we acquire a self by observing and assimilating the identities of others (Grodin & Lindlof, 1996; Nisbet, 1970). The vehicle for

this identification and assimilation is language. As Mead wrote, "There neither can be nor could have been any mind or thought without language; and the early stages of the development of language must have been prior to the development of mind or thought" (quoted in Truzzi, 1971, p. 272).

This view places culture at the center of the formation of the self. The kind of person we become is largely a result of the cultural influences that surround us during socialization. Through interaction with people who are Catholic, for example, one takes on the language, the jokes, and the style of a person of that religion. If the father is a firefighter and the mother a nurse, certain attitudes about service to society and about illness and danger will carry over to the child. If the same child plays on sports teams with children in the neighborhood, the norms and values of those children and their parents will become part of the child's experience and will be incorporated into his or her personality. Another child, growing up on a Sioux Indian reservation, would learn some of the same values—such as fair play, reward for achievement, and good citizenship—but would also learn the norms and values of the Sioux (e.g., reverence for one's ancestors and for the natural environment).

As each person learns the norms of his or her culture and its various ways of communicating—whether through language, dress, or gestures—and as each experiences the influences of a particular family and peer group, a unique self is formed. The self, thus, is a product of many influences and experiences; every person emerges with a personality of his or her own, and each has incorporated to varying degrees the values of the larger society and of a particular subculture.

ROLE TAKING: THE SIGNIFICANT OTHER AND THE GENERALIZED OTHER For Mead (1971/1934), two of the most important activities of childhood are play and games. In play, the child practices taking the roles of others. If you watch preadolescent children play, you will see them continually "trying on" roles: "You be the mommy and I'll be the teacher, and you'll come to school to find out why . . ." or "Pretend I'm Michael Jordan and you're Reggie Miller and the score is tied in the fourth quarter." They are reenacting the dramas of winning and losing, or calling into question the behaviors of the schoolroom, or trying to understand sickness and death.

This idea of **role taking** is central to the interactionist view of socialization. It refers to the way we try to look at social situations from the standpoint of another person from whom we seek a response. Mead believed that children develop this ability in three stages, during which they gain their sense of self and learn to act as persons in society. He labeled them the preparatory, play, and game stages. (See the Study Chart on page 119.)

art *and the sociological eye*

Graffiti—Art or Vandalism?

The teenagers who do it call it different things in different cities—writing, tagging, bombing, and even art. Most adults think of it as graffiti and consider it either a nuisance or, if it defaces their property, outright vandalism. Sociologists who study teenage behavior often explain that graffiti can send many kinds of signals. Gangs often use initials or symbols to mark their turf in an urban community. Aspiring young artists, influenced by hip-hop styles of dress and music, may become interested in graffiti as an art form. Sometimes this art is executed as a protest against the larger society, as when large graffiti murals are drawn at night on buses or trains or on public buildings. Part of the creative effort involves the daring exploit of producing art that is against the law. In some cities, youth who produce this underground or protest art are known as "bombers" because they make sudden, stealthy strikes on a building or a train. Bombers look down on mere "taggers," who scrawl their highly stylized initials ("tags") everywhere they go, even on the far more artistic bombers' work.

No matter how much we might understand and appreciate well-executed graffiti art, however, from the viewpoint of the larger society, graffiti art is a defacement of public property. Its removal

is costly; its effects can be demoralizing; and it can be read as a sign that a community's young people, or at least some of them, are alienated and angry. Realizing this, many youth workers and community leaders have found ways to reach out to graffiti artists and guide their energy and creativity into socially constructive or at least more acceptable channels. In New Orleans, for example, the Ya Ya Collective has made graffiti art into products that young people can reproduce and sell. This builds their self-esteem and provides funds for other

constructive youth activities. In New York City, where graffiti art is extremely popular, a sympathetic industrialist has hired graffiti artists to paint enormous murals on the walls of an old factory building in an industrial section of the city. In Philadelphia, Chicago, Cleveland, and many other U.S. cities, graffiti artists and their friends are applying their skills to the creation of public murals commemorating the victims of gang violence or the drug trade, and in so doing they are learning to use their art in positive ways.

Photo by Rich Puchalsky

In the *preparatory stage,* the child attempts to mimic the behavior of people who are significant in his or her life. **Significant others** are people who loom large in our lives, people who appear to be directly involved in winning and losing, achieving and failing. They tend to be people whose behavior we imitate—or whose behavior we seek to avoid. In the preparatory stage, the child's significant others are those who respond to calls for help and shape social behaviors such as language.

In Mead's second stage, the *play stage,* children play at being others who are significant in their lives:

> They play at being the others who are significant to them. They want to push the broom, carry the umbrella, put on the hat, and do all the other things they see their parents do, including saying what their parents say. The story is told of the four-year-old playing "daddy" who put on his hat

STAGES IN THE DEVELOPMENT OF ROLE TAKING

STUDY CHART

STAGE	DESCRIPTION	EXAMPLE
Preparatory	The child attempts to mimic the behavior of people who are significant in his or her life.	A toddler tries to walk in her mother's shoes.
Play	Children play at being people who are significant in their lives, such as parents.	Three children play house: "You be the mommy, I'll be the daddy, and Joey can be the baby."
Game	Each child is able to become, in a symbolic sense, all the other participants in the game.	A group of neighborhood kids gather at a playground to play baseball.

and his coat, said "good bye," and walked out the front door, only to return a few minutes later because he didn't know what to do next. He had taken as much of his father's work role as he could see and hear—the ritualized morning departure. (Elkin & Handel, 1989, p. 49)

As children grow in age and experience, they enter what Mead called the *game stage*. To take part in a game, a child must have already learned to become, in a symbolic sense, all the other participants in the game. Mead called this the ability to "take the role of the generalized other." Thus, in a baseball game:

[The child] must know what everyone else is going to do in order to carry out his own play. He has to take all of these roles. They do not have to be present in consciousness at the same time, but at some moments he has to have three or four individuals present in his own attitude, such as the one who is going to throw the ball, the one who is going to catch it, and so on. (Mead, 1971/1934, p. 151)

When we are able to take the role of the generalized other, we know that rules apply to us no matter who we are. We know, for example, that rules about not smoking in the school building apply equally to students, parents, and teachers, and that those who violate the rules will not be excused because of their status (Mead, 1971/1934).

The **generalized other** is a composite of all the roles of all the participants in the game. A person who participates in a game like baseball, for example, has developed the capacity for role taking and now (again using Mead's phrase) "takes the role of the generalized other." When little children play team games, they often have a difficult time taking specific roles. Watch them play basketball or soccer, for example, and you will often find them clumping together in an effort to get the ball. As children mature, their growing sense of the generalized other makes them better able to understand all the roles on a team and to learn their own specific roles and positions in games and team sports.

The generalized other represents the voice of society, which is internalized as "conscience." For some people, the generalized other demands perfection and strict adherence to every rule. For others, the generalized other may be extremely demanding where sports and other games are concerned but much more relaxed about achievement in school or adherence to the norms of property. For still others, the generalized other may insist on amassing large amounts of money as the primary indicator of success, or it may require community service and not value financial success at all. Within any given culture, such variations will be wide but will tend to follow certain easily recognized patterns.

Role Playing and "Face Work"

Why do Americans and Asians often have so much difficulty understanding each other even when they are playing the same role (e.g., student) and speaking the same language? Why are adolescents so "hung up" about their dealings with other kids? And why is it that in some communities seemingly small insults are treated as major signs of disrespect? These are all examples of the kinds of problems that arise when people actually play the roles for which they have been socialized. They can be analyzed according to the rules of interaction known as *face work*.

As Erving Goffman (1965) defines it, *face* is the positive social value a person claims for herself or himself by acting out a specific set of socially approved attributes (e.g., politeness, humor, strength, cuteness, sensitivity). Through his close observations of seemingly routine greetings, formulas of politeness, and the give-and-take of small talk, Goffman identified the rules of interaction whereby people seek to present a positive image of themselves, their "face." Once they have established a specific image, they seek to defend it against any possible threat that might cause them to "lose face." The concept of saving or losing face is found in cultures throughout the world. Indeed, in most Asian cultures, the rules of face work are even more elaborate than in the West. (The importance of such unwritten rules of interaction is explored more fully in Chapter 6.)

Most of us take it for granted that we want to maintain our self-respect and not lose face in social situations, but we do not give much thought to the actual interactions that serve to maintain face. Goffman explains:

> Just as the member of any group is expected to have self-respect, so also he is expected to sustain a standard of considerateness; he is expected to go to certain lengths to save the feelings and the face of others present, and he is expected to do this willingly and spontaneously because of emotional identification with the others and with their feelings. . . . The person who can witness another's humiliation and unfeelingly retain a cool countenance himself is said in our society to be "heartless," just as he who can unfeelingly participate in his own defacement is thought to be "shameless." (1965, p. 10)

The way we apply these rules of face work in performing our roles differs according to the prestige of the people involved. When firing a junior clerk, for example, the boss does not go to nearly the same lengths to take into account the employee's feelings as he does when firing a vice president. Recent studies of role playing among adolescents in inner-city communities draw on these insights. Where there is very little prestige of any kind for people to share, "fronting"—or pretending to play roles that one cannot really perform (e.g., great ballplayer, ladies' man)—is extremely common. So, therefore, are potential threats to one's face. Face work in such communities—among gang members, for example—can become a deadly business, especially in situations where one senses disrespect (i.e., feels that one is being "dissed") (MacLeod, 1995; Williams & Kornblum, 1994). Emotions play a strong part in these interactions. When people believe that they have seriously lost face, their feelings can run extremely high, especially if their peers do not hurry in to defend them.

Rapid social change tends to heighten the difficulties people have in playing the roles they have been socialized to perform. As Goffman points out:

> A person's performance of face-work, extended by his tacit agreement to help others perform theirs, represents his willingness to abide by the ground rules of social interaction. Here is the hallmark of his socialization as an interactant. If he and the others were not socialized in this way, interaction in most societies and most situations would be a much more hazardous thing for feelings and faces. (1965, p. 31)

As populations become more diverse through the processes of social change (e.g., immigration and migration), the possibilities for cultural confusion over the rules of successful role playing in school or on the street can multiply dramatically.

This interactionist perspective on socialization emphasizes how people become social actors and how they intuitively adopt the rules and rituals of interaction, such as face work, that exist in their cultures. But it does not address how people acquire their notions of morality. We know that people generally learn their values and ideas of morality as young children in the family, but research on child development shows that the acquisition of morality is not a simple matter.

Theories of Moral Development

Suppose that a friend asks you for help on an exam. Suddenly rules about cheating come into conflict with the norm that friends help each other. We face such moral conflicts all the time, and they often involve higher stakes or greater risk. Throughout life, we face a wide variety of moral dilemmas, which have a significant effect on our personalities. In consequence, social scientists have devoted considerable study to the processes through which people develop concepts of morality. Among the best-known students of moral development are the Swiss child psychologist Jean Piaget and the American social psychologists Lawrence Kohlberg and Carol Gilligan.

PIAGET Piaget stands with Freud as one of the most important and original researchers and writers on child development. In the 1920s, he became concerned with how children understand their environment, how they view their world, and how they develop their own personal philosophies. To discover the mental processes unique to children, he used what was then an equally unique method: He spent long hours with a small number of children, simply having conversations with them. These open-ended discussions were devoted to getting at how children actually think. In this way, Piaget discovered evidence for the existence of ideas that are foreign to the adult mind (Berman, 1997; Elkind, 1970). For example, the child gives inanimate objects human motives and tends to see everything as existing for human purposes. In this phase of his research, Piaget also described the egocentric aspect of the child's mental world, which is illustrated by the tendency to invent words and expect others to understand them.

In the later phases of his research and writing, Piaget devoted his efforts to questions about children's moral reasoning—the way children interpret the rules of games and judge the consequences of their actions. He observed that children form absolute notions of right and wrong very early in life, but that they often cannot understand the ambiguities of adult roles until they approach adolescence. This line of investigation was continued by the American social psychologist Lawrence Kohlberg, whose theory incorporates Piaget's views on the development of children's notions of morality.

KOHLBERG Kohlberg's theory of moral development emphasizes the cognitive aspects of moral behavior. (By *cognitive* we mean aspects of behavior that one thinks about and makes conscious choices about, rather than those that one engages in as a result of feelings or purely intuitive reactions.) In a study of 57 Chicago children that began in 1957 and continued until the children were young adults, Kohlberg presented the children with moral dilemmas such as the following:

> A husband is told that his wife needs a special kind of medicine if she is to survive a severe form of cancer. The medication is extremely expensive, and the husband can raise only half the needed funds. When he begs the inventor of the drug for a reduced price, he is rebuffed because the inventor wants to make a lot of money on his invention. The husband then considers stealing the medicine, and the child is asked whether the man should steal in order to save his wife. (Kohlberg & Gilligan, 1971)

On the basis of children's answers to such dilemmas at different ages, Kohlberg proposed a theory of moral development consisting of three stages: (1) *preconventional,* in which the child acts out of desire for reward and fear of punishment; (2) *conventional,* in which the child's decisions are based on an understanding of right and wrong as embodied in social rules or laws; and (3) *postconventional,* in which the individual develops a sense of relativity and can distinguish between social laws and moral principles. Subjects in the preconventional and conventional stages often immediately assume that stealing is wrong in the dilemma Kohlberg has posed, but postconventional thinking in older children causes them to debate the fairness of rules against stealing in view of the larger moral dilemma involved.

GENDER AND MORAL REASONING Kohlberg's studies have been criticized for focusing too heavily on the behavior of boys and men from secure American families and not exploring possible alternative lines of moral reasoning that may prevail among females or people from differing cultural and racial backgrounds (Dawson, 2002; Garcia, 1996; Gilligan et al., 1998). Pioneering work by social psychologist Carol Gilligan, an early collaborator of Kohlberg's, has produced an impressive body of evidence that demonstrates the propensity of females to make

The Dog in the Manger

A dog, looking for a comfortable place to nap, came upon the empty stall of an ox. There it was quiet and cool, and the hay was soft. The dog, who was very tired, curled up on the hay and was soon fast asleep.

A few hours later the ox lumbered in from the fields. He had worked hard and was looking forward to his dinner of hay. His heavy steps woke the dog, who jumped up in a great temper. As the ox came near the stall the dog snapped angrily, as if to bite him. Again and again the ox tried to reach his food, but each time he tried the dog stopped him.

Moral Orientation of Spontaneous Solution for the Dog in the Manger Fable, by Gender

Orientation	Female	Male
Rights (justice)	12	22
Response (caring)	15	5
Both	3	1

Source: Adapted from Johnston, 1988, p. 57.

Figure 5.2 The Dog in the Manger

moral choices on the basis of a somewhat different line of reasoning from that generally followed by males. Gilligan's research, and that of others who have followed her lead, shows that females are more likely than males to base moral judgments on considerations of caring as well as justice or law. More than their male counterparts, females tend to look for solutions to moral dilemmas that also serve to maintain relationships. Caring solutions that consider the needs of both sides are therefore more often invoked by females.

A good example of this difference appears in the work of D. Kay Johnston (1988), in which adolescent boys and girls were presented with dilemmas taken from Aesop's fables. The young people were read a fable that presents a moral dilemma and then asked what they understood the problem to be and how they would solve it. In the fable of the dog in the manger (see Figure 5.2), the problem is, clearly, that the dog has taken sleeping space from the deserving ox. Some adolescents judged the situation purely in terms of which animal had the right to the space, and made statements like "It's [the ox's] ownership and nobody else had the right to it." Others sought a caring solution that would take into consideration both animals' needs, and made statements like "If there's enough hay, well, this is one way, split it. Like, if they could cooperate."

The table in Figure 5.2 shows that boys were more likely than girls to give solutions based on rights, whereas girls were more likely than boys to choose solutions that emphasized caring. Some chose solutions that combined the two approaches. As Gilligan notes, "An innovative

TABLE 5.1

Skills of Emotional Competence

1. Awareness of one's emotional state, including the possibility that one is experiencing multiple emotions, and at even more mature levels, awareness that one might also not be consciously aware of one's feelings due to unconscious dynamics or selective inattention.

2. Skill in discerning others' emotions, based on situational and expressive cues that have some degree of cultural consensus as to their emotional meaning.

3. Skill in using the vocabulary of emotion and expression terms commonly available in one's subculture, and at more mature levels skill in acquiring cultural scripts that link emotion with social roles.

4. Capacity for empathic and sympathetic involvement in others' emotional experiences.

5. Skill in understanding that inner emotional state need not correspond to outer expression, both in oneself and in others, and at more mature levels understanding that one's emotional-expressive behavior may affect another and taking this into account in one's self-presentation strategies.

6. Skill in adaptive coping with aversive [negative] or distressing emotions by using self-regulatory strategies that ameliorate the intensity or temporal duration of such emotional states (e.g., "stress hardiness").

7. Awareness that the structure or nature of relationships is in part defined by both the degree of emotional immediacy or genuineness of expressive display and the degree of reciprocity or symmetry within the relationship; for example, mature intimacy is in part defined by mutual or reciprocal sharing of genuine emotions, whereas a parent-child relationship may have asymmetric sharing of genuine emotions.

8. Capacity for emotional self-efficacy: The individual views her- or himself as feeling, overall, the way he or she wants to feel. That is, emotional self-efficacy means that one accepts one's emotional experience, whether unique and eccentric or culturally conventional, and this acceptance is in alignment with the individual's beliefs about what constitutes desirable emotional "balance." In essence, one is living in accord with one's personal theory of emotion when one demonstrates emotional self-efficacy that is integrated with one's moral sense.

Source: Kagan et al., 2001.

aspect of Johnston's design lay in the fact that after the children had stated and solved the fable problems, she asked, 'Is there another way to think about this problem?' About half of the children . . . spontaneously switched orientation and solved the problem in the other mode" (from Gilligan et al., 1998, p. xxi). On the basis of this and much subsequent research, Gilligan concludes that by age 11 most children can solve moral problems both in terms of rights (a justice approach) and in terms of response (a caring approach). The fact that a person adopts one approach in solving a problem does not mean that he or she does not know or appreciate others.

Gilligan and others who study moral development and gender point out that adolescence is a critical time in the development of morality and identity. However, in schools and elsewhere in society, the message that comes across is that norms, values, and the most highly esteemed roles require that there be a "right way" to feel and think. Most often this right way is associated with the justice focus—and the caring focus is silenced, along with the voices of girls and others to whom it appears to be a valuable alternative mode of moral reasoning (Wren, 1997). In adolescent girls and many minority students, this form of silencing can be detrimental to the development of the self in social situations, a subject of immense importance to which we will return at many points in later chapters (Taylor, Gilligan, & Sullivan, 1995).

GENDER AND EMOTIONAL INTELLIGENCE   Women often complain that the men in their lives are "out of touch with their emotions." Men complain that women too often want to talk about feelings and are too quickly moved to tears. These differences in behavior are the subject of a good deal of research in psychology and sociology that attempts to help people understand why "men are from Mars [the warlike planet] and women are from Venus [the planet symbolizing love and the emotions]" (Gray, 1992; Tannen, 2001). Critics of such research point out that the evidence shows that both men and women can show great differences in their ability to understand and deal with their emotions and their interpersonal relations. Books that emphasize gender differences can make it seem as if there is nothing to be done about lack of emotional intelligence.

Jerome Kagan and others who study what Gardner identified as inter- and intrapersonal intelligence note that it can be found in both men and women, although in our society women are socialized to develop it more fully (Kagan, 2000; Kagan et al., 2001). Their research shows that—whether one is male or female—by better understanding what goes into emotional intelligence, one can vastly improve one's personal relationships and one's understanding of why others react as they do in different social situations. The basic dimensions of emotional intelligence as researchers are studying them appear in Table 5.1.

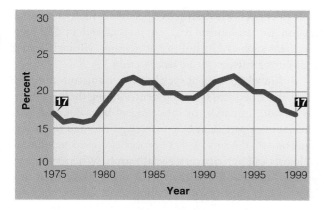

Figure 5.3   Percentage of Children in Poverty, 1975–1999

Source: Annie E. Casey Foundation, 2001; National Center for Children in Poverty, 2001.

Figure 5.4   Percentage of Families with Children Under 18 Headed by a Single Parent, 1975–2000

Source: Annie E. Casey Foundation, 2001; National Center for Children in Poverty, 2001.

These indicators are published annually by the Annie E. Casey Foundation of Baltimore, which is devoted to improving the quality of children's lives in the United States.

SOCIAL ENVIRONMENTS AND EARLY SOCIALIZATION

Socialization occurs in many different settings, some of which are more desirable than others. Children are born into relatively affluent homes in American suburbs, the squalid slums of Calcutta, the icy wastes of Siberia, the extreme poverty of the Somalian desert, and myriad other environments—yet in every case those who survive infancy are socialized to live and perhaps flourish in these diverse settings. Cross-cultural studies attempt to show how social-ization processes vary in different societies and how they are affected by demographic trends (trends in population size and composition) within societies. This comparative view of socialization attempts to bring together the often com-peting viewpoints of biological, psychological, and socio-logical explanations of developmental patterns.

Within the United States, important differences exist from one region or state to another in the degree of stress children experience in their home environment and in the "success" of their socialization. A crude but extremely useful measure of stress in children's socialization envi-ronment is the percentage of children living in house-holds with incomes below the official poverty line. Simi-larly, measures of the percentage of children living in single-parent households—which are more likely than other households to have below-average income and in which the parent may have less opportunity to interact with the child—are useful indicators of the outcomes of socialization. As shown in Figures 5.3 and 5.4, these in-dicators improved slightly during the boom years of the late 1990s, but unfortunately can be expected to worsen as a result of poor economic conditions after 2001.

In the early decades of the twentieth century, when children routinely worked in textile mills and coal mines, the environment in which they were socialized forced them to take on adult roles at an early age. For some children growing up in North America, this is still true, for different reasons.

The circumstances reflected in measures such as these have many causes and significant consequences for social change. For example, because teenage mothers are more likely than nonteenagers to be single mothers and to be living in poverty—two negative stresses on a child's socialization environment—teenage pregnancy becomes an important issue. A major consequence of the high rate of teenage fertility in the United States is that proportionately more babies are born into homes in which they will not receive the attention and material benefits that will help them realize their full genetic potential (Furstenberg, 1976, 2000). In other words, these children start off at a disadvantage in that their mothers have not yet reached maturity themselves and are likely to be single parents who may be unable to provide their children with economic security, love, and discipline.

Urie Bronfenbrenner, one of the nation's most respected and original researchers in the field of childhood socialization, summarizes the conclusions of numerous studies with these two propositions:

> *Proposition 1.* In order to develop normally, a child needs the enduring . . . involvement of one or more adults in care of and joint activity with the child.
> *Proposition 2.* The involvement of one or more adults in care of and joint activity with the child requires public policies that provide opportunity, status, resources, encouragement, example, and, above all, time for parenthood, primarily by parents, but also by other adults in the child's environment, both within and outside the home. (1981, p. 39)

No society can pass legislation requiring that a growing child experience love in the family or household. It can, however, formulate public policies that support the efforts of families to raise healthy children and socialize them well. It can do this, in part, by helping provide children with the attention of caring adults outside the family, especially in agencies of socialization such as schools.

Agencies of Socialization

Agencies of socialization are the groups of people, along with the interactions that occur within those groups, that influence a person's social development throughout his or her lifetime (Elkin & Handel, 1989; Gonzalez-Mena, 1998); **agents of socialization** are individuals, such as parents and teachers, who socialize others. The most familiar agencies of socialization are the family, schools, socializing agencies in the community, religion, the peer group, and the mass media. Later in life, adults may experience further socialization in the workplace, in universities, or in the military, to cite a few common examples. People who

wish to change self-destructive behaviors such as drug addiction or alcoholism may be resocialized in "12-step" programs such as Alcoholics Anonymous. (Resocialization is discussed further in the next section.)

Within all agencies of socialization, numerous processes shape the individual's development. Among these are direct instruction, imitation or modeling of behavior, and reinforcement of particular behaviors (e.g., through rewards or punishments). Many of these processes appear in what sociologists call **anticipatory socialization.** Whenever an individual plays at a role that he or she is likely to assume later in life, anticipatory socialization is taking place. By dressing up in adult clothing, for example, or by playing house, a child imitates the behavior of adults. The adolescent who attends a senior prom is being socialized in anticipation of a time when she or he will be expected to participate in formal social events. A worker in a corporate setting may rehearse before coworkers a presentation that he or she will later make to a potential client.

Another important aspect of agencies of socialization is that they must continually deal with social change. For example, as guns have become more readily available in large cities, peer groups have had to cope with the ever-present danger of violent death. As divorce and remarriage rates have risen, many families have had to deal with new structures that add much more complexity to family socialization patterns. As a result, the influence of social change on socialization patterns has become an important area of sociological research.

In the following pages, we briefly consider several agencies of socialization: the family, the schools, the community, the peer group, and the mass media. We will encounter many of these agencies in later chapters as well.

THE FAMILY   The family is the primary agency of socialization. It is the environment into which the child is born and in which his or her earliest experiences with other people occur—experiences that have a lasting influence on the personality. Family environments vary greatly, not only in terms of such key variables as parents' income and education but also in terms of living arrangements, urban versus rural residence, number of children, relations with kin, and so on. Much contemporary research centers on the effects of different family environments on the child's development (Berman, 1997; Gonzalez-Mena, 1998). For example, Michael Lewis and Candice Feiring's intriguing study of 117 families, "Some American Families at Dinner" (1982), shows that a typical 3-year-old child interacts regularly with a network of kin, friends, and other adults who may play a significant role in the child's early socialization. (See the Sociological Methods box on page 125.)

One of the most significant changes occurring in American society today is the increase in the proportion of

SOCIOLOGICAL METHODS

Measures of Central Tendency

When we say that the family is a primary agent of socialization, we mean not just the child's parents but all the people who make up the "family constellation"—that is, the people who are most often in the child's home and therefore capable of influencing his or her socialization. But how can we measure such a thing across many different families? In an innovative study of whom children interact with other than their parents, Lewis and Feiring observed ten very young children from different families and counted the number of people they saw each week. Here is an example of their data and the basic methodological tools they used to analyze it.

© Spencer Grant/PhotoEdit

The following table presents information from Lewis and Feiring's study of 3-year-old children's social networks:

The 3-Year-Old Child's Social Network (N = 117)*

	X	Range
Number of relatives other than parents seen at least once a week	3.20	0–15
Number of child's friends seen at least once a week	4.43	0–13
Number of adults seen at least once a week	4.38	0–24

*N refers to the number of subjects in a study.

Source: Lewis & Feiring, 1982, p. 116.

To understand this table, you must know something about the common measures of central tendency. The measure used here is the *mean,* represented by X. To arrive at this number, each child's total number of friends, relatives, and other adults seen at least once a week is added to the totals for the other children in the sample. The grand total is then divided by the number of children in the sample. The resulting number can be used to represent the entire sample.

The other common measures of central tendency are the *median* and the *mode.* The median is the number that divides a sample into two equal halves when all the numbers in the sample are arranged from lowest to highest. The mode is simply the score that occurs most often in the sample. Sociologists make a point of specifying which of these measures they are using. They try to avoid the term *average* in statistical tables because it can refer to any one of these measures.

To illustrate all three measures of central tendency, let us use the following data from 10 of the children in Lewis and Feiring's sample:

Child	Number of Friends Seen at Least Once a Week
1	2
2	3
3	3
4	7
5	12
6	2
7	3
8	1
9	0
10	5
	38

In this example, the mode would be 3 and the median would also be 3, but the mean would be 3.8.

children growing up in poor families (20 percent of all children under age 18) or in no family at all. In the early 1990s, nearly 10 percent of all children in the United States were growing up in households with no parent present. Most of these children (76 percent) were being socialized in the homes of grandparents and relatives; the remainder were living in group homes and with nonrelatives (Gross, 1992). There has also been a steady increase in the number of single-parent families, the vast majority of which are headed by women.

But changes in the way families are organized or how they cope with changing social conditions are not a new phenomenon. The values and ways of parents are never entirely valid for their children, although the degree to which this is true depends on how much social change is experienced from one generation to the next. Socialization creates the personalities and channels the behaviors of the members of a society, but that socialization is never entirely finished. Thus, in *Manchild in the Promised Land,* his masterpiece about growing up in Harlem during the period of rapid migration of blacks from the South, Claude Brown (1966) wrote that his rural-born parents did not "seem to be ready for urban life." Their values and norms of behavior made no sense to their son, who had to survive on Harlem's mean streets:

> When I was a little boy, Mama and Dad would beat me and tell me, "You better be good," but I didn't know what being good was. To me it meant that they just wanted me to sit down and fold my hands or something crazy like that. Stay in front of the house, don't go anyplace, don't get into trouble. I didn't know what it meant, and I don't think they knew what it meant, because they couldn't ever tell me what they really wanted. The way I saw it, everything I was doing was good. If I stole something and didn't get caught, I was good. If I got into a fight with somebody, I tried to be good enough to beat him. If I broke into a place, I tried to be quiet and steal as much as I could. I was always trying to be good. They kept on beating me and talking about being good. And I just kept on doing what I was doing and kept on trying to do it good. (p. 279)

Brown's story is that of a young man whose parents' experience with social change created a severe disjunction in their lives. This left them ill equipped to socialize their son for the demands of a new environment, so he learned to survive on the streets. He became a thief and a gang fighter. But by his own account, later in his life he was greatly influenced by people who had studied the social sciences and created well-functioning institutions, special schools in particular, that could bring out his talents and socialize him for a more satisfying and constructive life than he had led as a child.

THE SCHOOLS   For most of us, regardless of what our home life is like, teachers are generally the first agents of socialization we encounter who are not kin. In some cases, children are also influenced by agents of socialization in the church (e.g., priests or rabbis); for most children, however, the school is the most important agency of socialization after the family. Children experience many opportunities to perform new roles in school (e.g., student, teammate, friend). No wonder, then, that in these first "public" appearances they tend to be highly sensitive to taunts or teasing by other children. Even very young children can become distraught when they feel that they are not wearing the "right" clothes.

Schools are institutions where differences between the values of the family and those of the larger society come into sharp focus. In some families, for example, there may be great concern about any form of sex education in school.

Much of the conflict over educational norms—what ought to be taught, whether there should be prayer in school, and the like—stems from differences between the values of some families and the values that many educators wish to teach. Such conflicts point to the exceedingly difficult situation of schools in American society. Research on school–family and school–community relations has shown that the schools are expected to conserve the society's values (by teaching ideals of citizenship, morality, family values, and the like) and, at the same time, to play a major role in dealing with innovation and change (by expanding the curriculum to include new knowledge, coping with children's perceptions of current events, addressing past patterns of discrimination, and the like) (Goslin, 1965; Meier, 1995).

In Chapter 18, we return to questions of whether the schools help reproduce the status quo and maintain inequalities in society and whether they can actually affect the lives of disadvantaged students. Although many individuals credit schools (and even particular teachers) with helping them improve their lives in important ways, there is much debate on these questions in the social sciences.

THE COMMUNITY   Schools may be the most important agency of socialization outside the family, but there are other significant agencies of socialization in most communities, including day care centers, scout troops, churches, recreation centers, and leagues of all kinds. These agencies engage in many and varied forms of socialization. Parades on Memorial Day and the Fourth of July, for example, reinforce values of citizenship and patriotism. Participation in team sports instills values of fair play, teamwork, and competitive spirit. The uniforms and equipment required for these activities stimulate shopping trips to suburban malls and downtown department stores, and those trips prepare children and adolescents for the time when they will be consumers (McKendrick, Brewer, & Plump, 1982; Newman, 1988).

Of all these agencies of socialization, the day care center is perhaps the most controversial. Polls often show that Americans have doubts about the effects of day care on very young children, and scandals involving charges of child abuse by day care workers intensify those fears. But when both parents work outside the home, or when single parents must work to support their children, day care centers may play a critical role in socialization. Many studies have shown that high-quality centers are not harmful to children and in some cases may be beneficial, but the norm requiring that mothers stay home to care for young children remains strong in many communities (Kammerman, 1995).

The central question addressed by these studies is the quality of the care received. A recent longitudinal study of 1,153 children at 10 different child care centers revealed that in the better centers (as measured by indicators such

THEN AND NOW

The Indomitable Human Spirit

Blind and deaf as a result of a serious illness when she was only 19 months old, Helen Keller appeared incapable of learning. In the late nineteenth and early twentieth centuries, people like Helen were relegated to back wards of custodial care institutions or back bedrooms in affluent homes. However, through the patient instruction of a gifted teacher, Helen learned to understand the connection between objects and the words for them. Suddenly this profoundly handicapped girl had a future in the social world. Helen Keller became a world-famous symbol of the unconquerable human spirit, blazing a trail that other people with disabilities and special needs have followed ever since.

In a more recent example of the triumph of will over biological destiny, 19-year-old Craig Ludin is shown at his high school graduation. Craig was the first student with Down syndrome to graduate from a regular high school in his school district.

AP/Wide World Photos

© 1995 Newsday, Inc.

as the qualifications of the caregivers and the amount of individual attention received by the children), children actually made gains in language and thinking abilities that were superior to those made by children from similar backgrounds who were not enrolled in high-quality day care. This effect was especially strong for children from lower-income households (Garrett, 1997). On the negative side, however, the researchers found that the more time young children spent in centers with lower-quality care, the more likely they were to experience problems in forming close attachments with their mothers.

Conservative critics of day care often argue that mothers of young children should stay home and care for them. But about three of every five mothers with children under age three are in the labor force. They and their working spouses are dependent on various forms of child care. Whatever the reasons for this dependence, it is a reality of contemporary life. High-quality child care is becoming an increasingly pressing social need as a consequence of long-term changes in the economy that have resulted in large numbers of dual-earner families. At present, there are far too many low-quality day care facilities—as many as 40 percent of the total, according to one estimate—providing care to children in the United States (Population Reference Bureau, 1998).

RELIGION Religion may be involved in socialization in different ways throughout an individual's lifetime. For children and adults who attend church services, the shared expression of spirituality and the teaching of the religious leader can be an extremely powerful source of moral beliefs. These beliefs often shape one's behavior outside religious institutions. During World War II, for example, most of the people who risked their lives to rescue Jews, gypsies, gays, and political refugees had deep religious and moral convictions (Winik, 1996).

Recent sociological studies show, too, that among contemporary parents, those who attend religious services are half as likely to divorce as parents who never attend religious services. Again, the moral influence of religion, whether Christian, Muslim, Jewish, or other, is highly associated with moral beliefs that may help married couples endure hard emotional times. To the degree that religious behavior reduces the likelihood of divorce, it strengthens the family, the most important agency of socialization (Clydesdale, 1997). Finally, among elderly people, religion often becomes a major source of solace as they face the continual deaths of loved ones and their own eventual demise.

Despite its contributions to lifelong socialization, religion can also be the source of innumerable conflicts. Disputes

POPULAR CULTURE & SOCIAL CHANGE   Jocks, Nerds, Punks, Abercrombies, and Others

The rash of high school violence, culminating perhaps in the Columbine shootings in 1998, brought to national attention the subject of high school peer groups, sometimes pejoratively called *cliques*. But educators and sociologists have been concerned for many decades about the influence of teen peer groups, an influence that can be extremely constructive and prosocial or, in some cases, can lead to destructive behavior and conflict. To understand high school peer groups, it is vital to understand the way groups of teenagers adopt particular forms of popular culture as their own.

Here is an example of how a journalist described the different peer groups of a high school he visited in Illinois:

Jocks rule and nerds still struggle for acceptance just about everywhere. But many schools have their own unique cliques. A look at Illinois' Glenbrook South High:

- *Trophy-Case Kids.* Named for their hangout under the school awards case. They're punkish in black hooded sweatshirts.
- *Wall Kids.* Mostly seniors, mostly popular.

- Lots of preppies and "Abercrombies." Their turf: a wall outside the cafeteria.
- *Bandies.* Musicians, they stick to themselves outside rehearsal room. Not especially cool or uncool, just good friends.
- *Backstage People.* Theater and arts types (both genders) lounge on couches backstage to talk, do homework, and take naps.

- *Student-Council Kids.* Clean-cut, popular. Lunch-time hangout: the council office. (Adler & McCormick, 1999, p. 56)

Surely there were more groups in the high school that the journalist did not discover. Perhaps there were technology nerds who hung out in the computer labs or the AV room, and if it was a rural school, maybe there were farm kids involved in 4-H. And what about skateboarders or cheer-

over child rearing, sexual conduct, the role of prayer in education, and many more rancorous conflicts are brought to public awareness by people with differing religious backgrounds. Should gay men and women serve as spiritual leaders? Should same-sex marriages be performed in churches and synagogues? Is prayer in the classroom a violation of other people's right to the constitutionally guaranteed separation of church and state? These questions hardly begin to exhaust the list of controversies that are based on differences in the moral teachings of various religious communities. In an election held in Kansas in 2000, for example, voters rejected school board candidates committed to making creationism—the religious interpretation of the earth's creation in 7 days—stand on equal footing with the scientific theory of evolution over millions of years. We return to these issues in Chapter 17, but note here that, throughout the world, sociologists are among those in the forefront of efforts to find ways in which people with strong convictions on

either side of these disputes can come together peacefully to resolve their differences or work out compromises that prevent moral conflicts from worsening (Vondra, 1996).

THE PEER GROUP   In the United States, the peer group tends to be the dominant agency of socialization in middle and late childhood. **Peer groups** are interacting groups of people of about the same age. Among adolescents, peer groups exert a strong influence on their members' attitudes and values. Studies confirm the high degree of importance adolescents and adults alike attach to their friendship groups. Adolescents typically acquire much of their identity from their peers and consequently find it difficult to deviate from the norms of behavior that their peer group establishes (Gans, 1962, 1984; Homans, 1950; McAndrew, 1985; Whyte, 1943). In fact, the peer group may become even more important than the family in the development of the individual's identity.

leaders? If you think about your own high school and compare notes with friends, your lists of groups will bear many similarities, but the differences will reveal a lot about the particular social and cultural ways of the communities you come from. Many of us first realize that we have a sociological imagination when we begin to take an inventory of all the different peer groups in our immediate social world.

In the journalist's list, we can also see the outstanding importance of popular culture. In American society, the things we consume, most of which are aspects of popular culture, often help define whom we associate with and how we project our identities to others. This is particularly true among teenagers. The music a group listens to—is it heavy metal, rap, classic rock, Norteño, salsa?—is often used to define group identities. So are styles in clothing, cars, and participation in recreational

sports, which differentiate preppies, who often wear clothing from catalogs like Abercrombie & Fitch, from the hip-hop crowd, whose members wear baggy jeans.

But so what? What difference does it make that these different peer groups exist in a high school? What difference does it make if some groups embrace one form of popular culture, like skate-

© Will & Deni McIntyre/Photo Researchers, Inc.

boarding, and others are passionate about punk rock?

The answers are not universal; these groups are not everywhere the same. In some schools, the cliques may

be in conflict, as they seemed to be in Columbine High, where the Goths deeply resented the jocks. In other schools, the existence of different cliques may give students the freedom to choose their friends and to find a convivial social world for themselves. A love of particular forms of music and sports and clothing will always be one of the ways in which different groups define themselves. However, the ways in which such groups interact will depend on many other aspects of a community's social life, such as whether only the jocks and cheerleaders and preppies are rewarded in the school or whether other groups also feel that they are respected and that their feelings can be voiced. Here is where adults can make a big difference, for if they are oblivious to what is going on, if they have no knowledge of the ways in which teens use popular culture to define what they are thinking and doing, they will miss important cues about where school peer groups may be heading.

There is often a rather high level of conflict within families over the extent to which the peer group influences the adolescent to behave in ways that are not approved of by the family. Even where conflict is limited, the peer group usually provides the child's first experience with close friendships outside the family. The peer group becomes the child's age-specific subculture—that is, a circle of close friends of roughly the same age, often with shifting loyalties. (See the Popular Culture and Social Change box above.)

The peer group usually engages in a set of activities that are not related to adult society. The peer subculture may, for example, include games that adults no longer play and may have forgotten. British researchers Iona and Peter Opie (1969) conducted a classic study of the games children play. They identified hundreds of games that were known by children between the ages of 6 and 10 all over England. They also identified the common elements in

those games, such as chasing, pretending, or seeking, and found that in many of the games the central problem was to choose an "It," a seeker or chaser. The children's efforts to avoid being "It" seemed to express their desire to avoid roles that made them different from the others.

When children's peer groups are faced with conflict and social change—for example, in communities where there are high levels of poverty and demographic change, with groups of culturally distinct people moving in and out—the group often organizes itself in gangs for self-defense and aggression. There are many such gangs in large American cities characterized by rapid immigration, widespread drug use, and the ready availability of cheap handguns. Under these conditions, both male and female peer groups may become extremely dangerous environments for socialization, yet they exert a strong attraction on adolescents who seek protection and companionship in what they perceive as a hostile world (Sanchez-Jankowski, 1991; Williams, 1989).

THE MASS MEDIA The most controversial agency of social- ization in American society is the mass media. In debates about the effects of the media on socialization, television comes under the greatest scrutiny because of the number of hours children spend in front of the "electronic baby-sitter." Estimates of how much television children watch differ, depending on the methodology used to conduct the study (especially since simply having the set turned on does not mean that the children are actually watching). Many studies have shown that the amount of television viewed varies, depending on whether the child comes from a poor home with few alternatives or a more affluent one where other activities are available. Children from poor homes in urban communities often have the set turned on for 7 or more hours a day, as opposed to children from more affluent homes, where the set is turned on for 3 or 4 hours daily (Elkin & Handel, 1989; Wellins, 1990).

The effects of all this television viewing on children and adolescents are a subject of intensive research. In par- ticular, the effects of seeing violent acts on television or lis- tening to violent music like gangsta rap are hotly debated. There is no doubt that the amount of violence shown on TV is immense. George Gerbner, one of the nation's fore- most researchers on TV violence, has been monitoring the number of violent acts shown on TV. His data indicate that the average child will have seen about 100,000 acts of violence on TV before graduating from elementary school—and the number is far higher for children from poor neighborhoods (Gerbner, 1990).

It is important to recognize, however, that the effects of television on socialization are by no means all negative. Television, radio, and the movies provide windows onto social worlds that most people cannot otherwise enter. Children, adolescents, and adults in modern American so- ciety learn far more about current events, social issues, and the arts than people did before the advent of television.

SOCIALIZATION THROUGH THE LIFE COURSE

Childhood socialization is the primary influence on the individual. Whatever happens to a person later in life, the early childhood experiences that shaped the social self will continue to influence that person's attitudes and behavior. But people are also affected by their *life course:* the set of roles they play over a lifetime and the ways in which those roles change as a consequence of social change. The life course of a person who came of age just before World War II, for example, would typically have involved service in the armed forces for men (perhaps including combat

duty) and work in a factory (or noncombatant military service) for women. The life course of children born after the war is far less likely to include a long or intense expe- rience of warfare. Natural disasters, major changes in the educational system, shifts in the political stability of their society, and other changes can influence the roles people play during their life course.

Changes in the culture of a society can also significantly alter the roles people play during their lives. In the first half of the twentieth century, for example, the role of wife was less likely to include periods of single parenthood than it is now. Fifty years ago the role of an elderly person was far more likely to involve relative poverty and dependence on younger family members than it does now. The need to adjust to changes in society and culture, and the fact that so many people are able to make such adjustments (though often with great difficulty), are evidence that socialization is not finished in childhood but continues throughout the life course (Riley, Foner, & Waring, 1988; Sorenson, Weinert, & Sherrod, 1986).

Adult Socialization

Two of the influences that produce socialization after child- hood are significant others (especially new friends) and oc- cupational mobility (especially new jobs). When one moves into a new neighborhood, for example, one often makes new friends, and their influence may lead to new activities. A person who has always been uninvolved in politics may, through the influence of new friends, become committed to a social movement such as the women's movement. New friends can also introduce a person to dangerous or unlaw- ful activities such as drug use. One's *core identity*—the part of the self formed in early childhood that does not change easily—may prevent one from being overly influenced by a given peer group later in life, or it may actually cause that influence to be stronger (Elkin & Handel, 1989).

Such factors as stress and changing physical health may also have an influence on socialization. In a study of how people change their patterns of behavior later in life, Marjorie Fiske and David A. Chiriboga (1990) found that everyday hassles and the boredom of a rou- tine, predictable existence have a greater impact on the changes adults seek in their lives than was indicated by earlier research.

In any new activity, the newcomer or recruit must learn a new set of norms associated with the roles of the organi- zation. Socialization associated with a new job, for example, often requires that a person learn new words and technical terms. The individual also needs to interact with a new peer group, usually composed of people whose work brings them together for long hours. And in most jobs, the person will eventually be faced with choices between loyalty to peers and loyalty to those higher in the organizational hierarchy who can confer benefits such as raises and promotions. In these and most other adult socialization experiences, the choices people make will be highly influenced by the individual's core identity, which continually shapes his or her responses to new situations and challenges (Rosow, 1965).

Resocialization

Many adults and even adolescents experience the need to correct certain patterns of prior social learning that they and others find detrimental. This need usually cannot be met through the normal processes of lifelong socialization, especially since the individual's negative behaviors may be leading toward a personal crisis and causing immense pain for family members and friends. Such a condition often responds to specific efforts at resocialization.

Resocialization is a process whereby individuals undergo intense, deliberate socialization designed to change major beliefs and behaviors. It is often aimed at changing behaviors such as excessive drinking, drug use, and overeating, which are particularly common in affluent societies, where individuals are exposed to a great deal of choice and many pleasurable stimuli. Perhaps most widespread and pernicious among the addictions, alcoholism affects millions of people in North America and is involved in much of the marital strife that leads to family breakup. Alcoholics Anonymous (AA) is a voluntary group program that uses techniques of resocialization and peer example to help alcoholics reject old behaviors and learn new, more positive ones that do not involve drinking. The AA approach to voluntary resocialization, which emphasizes personal change and positive growth as the individual passes through 12 steps of recovery, has been successfully applied to problems of obesity and overeating (Overeaters Anonymous) and narcotic use (Narcotics Anonymous). Many other self-help support groups assist people in dealing with almost any kind of problem that they previously struggled with in isolation (Makela, 1996).

Much successful resocialization takes place in what are often called **total institutions** (Goffman, 1961). These are settings where people undergoing resocialization are isolated from the larger society under the control of a specialized staff whose members may have experienced the same process of resocialization. All aspects of the inmates' daily lives are controlled, and supervision is constant. Drug treatment centers, for example, are often set up as total institutions for the resocialization of addicts. Even the smallest rewards, like extra time alone or more freedom to walk around the grounds, are controlled by the staff and bestowed only on inmates who have made progress toward the resocialization goals.

The Sociological Observer

This photo shows a group of New York (Brooklyn) firefighters in the early twentieth century. They are posing around the dining table in their firehouse, looking proudly into the camera. What sociological observations can you make about this group? What do you think is the significance of the pets they are holding? Why are they not smiling at the camera? How might the age differences among the men affect the socialization of new firefighters? How can what we see in this photo help us understand how altruistically firefighters behave under conditions of extreme danger, such as those faced by their fellow New York City firefighters generations later in the World Trade Center towers? (See page 135 for further insights into the sociological content of this photo.)

Courtesy NYFD Photo Archives

In the resocialization process, the staff first attempts to tear down the individual's former sense of self. This stage may include various forms of degradation and abasement in which the individual is forced to reject the undesired thoughts and behaviors. In the next stage, the staff rewards the individual's attempts to build a new sense of self that conforms to the goals of the resocialization process (e.g., a sober person who accepts responsibility for previous wrongs and achieves new interests and new awareness of personal strengths). However, although total institutions can be extremely powerful environments for resocialization, they sometimes run the risk of creating people who need to remain in their controlling environment—that is, people who have developed a need to be "institutionalized."

TABLE 5.2

Erikson's View of Lifelong Socialization

Stage of Life	Conflict	Successful Resolution in Old Age*
Infancy	Trust vs. mistrust	Appreciation of interdependence and relatedness.
Early Childhood	Autonomy vs. shame in the development of the will to be a social actor	Acceptance of the cycle of life, from integration to disintegration.
Play Age	Initiative vs. guilt in the development of a sense of purpose	Humor; empathy; resilience.
School Age	Industry vs. inferiority in the quest for competence	Humility; acceptance of the course of one's life and unfulfilled hopes.
Adolescence	Identity vs. confusion; struggles over fidelity to parents or friends	A sense of the complexity of life; merger of sensory, logical, and aesthetic perception.
Early Adulthood	Intimacy vs. isolation in the quest for love	A sense of the complexity of relationships; value of tenderness and loving freely.
Adulthood	Generativity vs. stagnation in interpersonal relationships	*Caritas* (caring for others) and *agape* (empathy and concern).
Old Age	Integrity vs. despair	Wisdom and a sense of integrity strong enough to withstand physical disintegration.

*Erikson did not believe that elderly people necessarily resolve these conflicts entirely, but when they do, the results are as shown here.

Erikson on Lifelong Socialization

The theories of social psychologist Erik Erikson are especially relevant to the study of adult socialization and resocialization. Erikson agreed with Freud that a person's sense of identity is shaped by early childhood experiences. But Erikson also focused on the many changes occurring throughout life that can shape a person's sense of self and ability to perform social roles successfully. He demonstrated, for example, that combat experiences can produce damaged identities because soldiers often feel guilty about not having done enough for their fallen comrades (this is sometimes called "survivor guilt"). For Freud, in contrast, war-produced mental illness was always related to problems that the soldier had experienced in early childhood.

In *Childhood and Society* (1963), Erikson's central work on the formation of the self, the concept of identification takes center stage. **Identification** is the social process whereby the individual chooses other people as models and attempts to imitate their behavior in particular roles. Erikson noted that identification with these role models occurs throughout the life course. He pointed out that even older people seek role models who can help them through difficult life transitions.

For Erikson, every phase of life requires additional socialization to resolve the new conflicts that inevitably present themselves. Table 5.2 presents the basic conflicts that each person must resolve throughout life and indicates

how a positive role model can help in resolving those conflicts. (The major theories of socialization are summarized in the Study Chart on page 133.)

Resocialization at any age usually requires a strong relationship between the individual and the role model. In the military or in a law enforcement agency, for example, the new recruit is usually paired with a more experienced person who offers advice and can show the recruit the essential "tricks" of the new role—"how it's really done." Thus, in Alcoholics Anonymous, once the self-confessed "drunk" faces up to that negative identity, he or she is taught new ways of thinking, feeling, and acting that do not involve drinking. An important step in this process is the development of a relationship with a *sponsor,* a person who has been through the same experiences and has made a successful recovery. In fact, one of AA's aims is to enable the resocialized alcoholic to eventually perform as a sponsor—that is, as a role model—for someone else who is going through the same process.

GENDER SOCIALIZATION

No discussion of socialization would be complete without some mention of gender socialization. **Gender socialization** refers to the ways in which we learn our gender identity and develop according to cultural norms of "masculinity" or "femininity." Gender is not synonymous with biological sex; rather, "scholars use the word sex to refer to

STUDY CHART

THEORIES OF SOCIALIZATION

THEORIST	DESCRIPTION OF THEORY
Sigmund Freud	Through socialization, the infant is gradually forced to channel its biological urges into socially acceptable forms of behavior. Major personality traits are formed in the conflict between the child and its parents, especially the same-sex parent.
George Herbert Mead	Socialization is a process in which the self emerges out of interaction with others, not only in early infancy but throughout life. Role taking is central to socialization; role-taking ability develops through interaction during childhood in the preparatory, play, and game stages.
Jean Piaget	Children develop definite awareness of moral issues at an early age but cannot deal with moral ambiguities until they mature further. This insight is incorporated in Kohlberg's preconventional, conventional, and postconventional stages of moral development.
Erik Erikson	Throughout the life course, the individual must resolve a series of conflicts that shape the person's sense of self and ability to perform social roles successfully. Central to this process is identification, in which the individual chooses other people as role models.
Carol Gilligan	Children tend to develop different ways of resolving moral dilemmas. Some (more often male) tend to rely on strict rules of right and wrong, while others (most often but not always female) tend to make judgments based on notions of fairness and cooperation. In societies where male voices are dominant, issues of cooperation and fairness are passed over, to the detriment of female socialization for leadership and achievement.

attributes of men and women created by their biological characteristics and gender to refer to the distinctive qualities of men and women (or masculinity and femininity) that are culturally created" (Epstein, 1988, p. 6). By *gender identity* we mean "an individual's own feeling of whether she or he is a woman or a man, or a girl or a boy" (Kessler & McKenna, 1978, p. 10). Our ideas about what it means to be a man or a woman are different from our ideas about the anatomical definitions of *male* and *female.* These ideas are shaped by the values and socialization practices of our culture, but once they have become part of the self, they are usually extremely strong.

The strength and pervasiveness of gender socialization are illustrated by the case of Ron Kovic, the author of *Born on the Fourth of July* (played by Tom Cruise in the Oscar-winning movie directed by Oliver Stone). Kovic saw himself as a red-blooded American male, a typical product of socialization for boys raised in his community. He was taught to be patriotic, to want to defend his country, to want to prove his manhood in combat and sexual conquest. When he became paralyzed in Vietnam and lost his manhood (in the narrow, conventional sense of that term), he began to doubt everything—including himself, his country, and his friends. His story raises some important issues, not least of which is how we form our ideas of manliness and womanliness and whether those ideas are helpful in meeting the demands of a changing world.

The story of Ron Kovic is a striking example of how powerful gender socialization is and the effects it can have on a person's life. Elsewhere in this book (especially in Chapter 14), we present other examples of the importance of gender in explaining life chances. But here let us look at a more mundane example of the results of gender socialization: the way men and women view their own bodies. Men tend to think of their own bodies as "just about perfect," but women tend to think of themselves as overweight, at least when they compare themselves with a mental image of an attractive woman. These are the findings of a survey of 500 college-age men and women conducted by April Fallon and Paul Rozin (cited in Goleman, 1985a).

A striking indication of the role of agencies of socialization in the social construction of gender identity is the influence of the mass media in promoting ideal body types for men and women. These influences have a lot to do with why men tend to be happy with their bodies while many girls and women are extremely unhappy with theirs. Men dominate the media—radio, television, newspapers, and magazines—that communicate American culture to mass audiences. Girls and women are continually exposed to images of women created by men, and those images more often than not portray women as sex objects, to be judged by the shape and size of their breasts, the length of their legs, and the tightness of their skin (Chernin, 1981; Lurie, 1981). It is little wonder, then, that women feel

Text continues on page 136.

VISUAL SOCIOLOGY

A STUDY IN ALTRUISM

As thousands of people fled for their lives from the blazing World Trade Center towers, others rushed into the buildings to rescue those inside. Firefighters, emergency medical technicians, police officers, and civilians were the heroes of the tragedy. Theirs were acts of great altruism. They put their own survival at risk and sacrificed themselves to save others. We rightly honor anyone who displays such heroic altruism. The faces and acts of altruism that we see in this Visual Sociology feature are intended as a reminder of their bravery.

Surely some aspects of the ability to act in self-sacrificing ways on behalf of others are innate, but just as surely this behavior can be learned as well. In the case of firefighters, police officers, and others whose jobs require them to take risks to save others, much of what we understand as altruistic behavior is instilled during their rigorous training as recruits. A few weeks after the September 11 tragedy, the Fire Academy of New York City graduated 250 new firefighters. On the stage at the graduation ceremony were six empty chairs. Each was marked with an American flag or other symbol indicating that the seats were vacant because these probationary firefighters, or "probies" as they are called, were killed when the buildings collapsed. They were serving as trainees in firehouses that responded early to the alarms and thus had the greatest number of casualties. Like the more seasoned veterans who were killed in the collapse of the buildings, the probies were "just doing their jobs."

Another aspect of what we see as altruism comes from the intense bond of friendship that is formed by small groups who encounter highly dangerous situations. The self-sacrificing behavior that we understand as altruism also stems from each individual's belief that he or she must pitch in to help the group, not just to help strangers. The intensity of the peer bonds among firefighters, for example, helps explain the intense feelings they displayed when asked to withdraw from the Ground Zero site. The firefighters regard the area as sacred ground and did not want to be excluded from the search for the bodies of their missing comrades.

The altruistic behavior of so many on that day also provided a model of altruism for a generation of children throughout the world. The Halloween following the event saw a tremendous display of firefighter, nurse, and police costumes as children embraced and emulated the behavior of their new heroes.

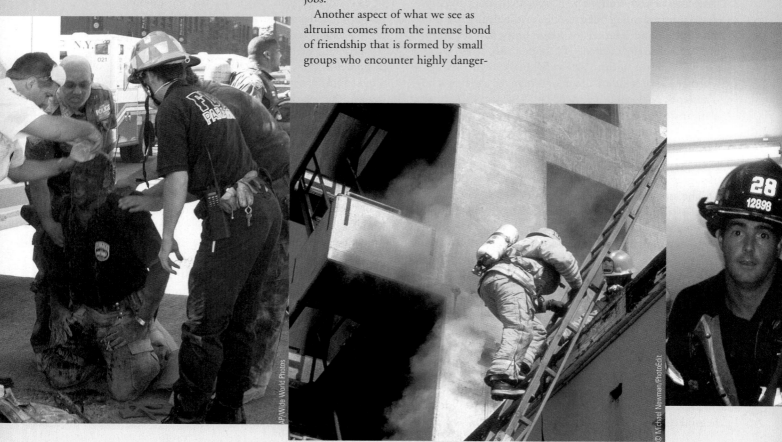

AP/Wide World Photos

© Michael Newman/PhotoEdit

The Sociological Observer

(See photo on page 131.)

The firefighters are demonstrating their attachment to each other and their affection for their firehouse pets. They are not smiling, largely because the idea that one should "smile for the camera" did not become a norm until later in the century. The way they are posing as a group and the obvious pride they take in their pets and their surroundings suggest the strong bonds of camaraderie and brotherhood among them. We see that there are older, veteran firefighters and younger, less experienced ones who are no doubt being socialized by the older men. Part of their socialization is that they take care of each other (and their pets) around the clock, not just when they face danger. The tight bonds of fellowship nurtured by this socialization process sustain the men as they assist each other and members of the public in situations of grave danger. But this same socialization into a tightly bonded fellowship can lead firefighters and others in occupational groups like theirs to believe that their solidarity is based on homogeneity of gender, race, or neighborhood of birth. In fact, however, when firefighters' groups are more diverse, as they increasingly are in New York and other cities today, there is no evidence that either their solidarity or their altruism is diminished.

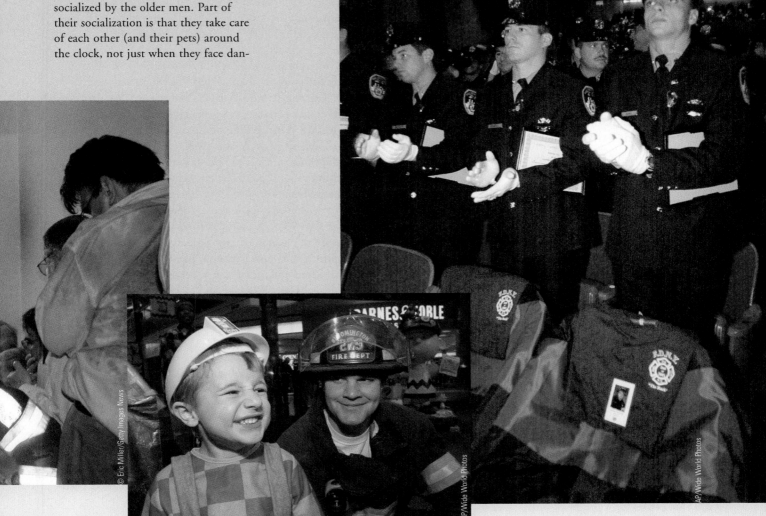

© Eric Miller/Getty Images News

AP/Wide World Photos

AP/Wide World Photos

worse about themselves than do men—about whom it has been said that it is sexy to be a sagging warrior or a somewhat wrinkled philosopher.

Among the many momentous changes that are occurring in the world today, those affecting gender socialization are among the most profound. Research on socialization in Asia and Africa, for example, shows how norms that favor boys over girls act to the detriment of female development. Studies from Bangladesh, India, Nepal, and Pakistan reveal that boys receive more food than girls, even though girls are often required to expend more calories on field and household work. In many poor nations, it is common for boys to be fed before girls and for the higher-quality nutrients, especially proteins, to be consumed before the girls are allowed to eat. So strong are gender norms in those countries that most mothers are convinced that this practice is necessary when food is scarce (Jacobson, 1992). As a result of this and other socialization practices that place females at a disadvantage, the health and learning capacities of women are imperiled from an early age in many parts of the world.

CRITICAL SOCIOLOGY AND SOCIAL CHANGE

Socialization and Sexual Orientation

Steve Lofton and Roger Croteau, shown in the photo below, currently reside in Portland, Oregon, and are the parents of five foster children: Frank and Tracy, both 14; Bert, 10; Wayne, 8; and Ernie, 5. As babies, Frank, Tracey, Bert, and a fourth child, Ginger (who died at age 6 from AIDS complications), were placed in the Lofton-Croteau home by Florida's Department of Children and Families. For several years, Lofton, Croteau, Frank, Tracey, and Bert lived in Miami; they then moved to Portland, where the state soon asked them to take in two HIV-positive children, Wayne and Ernie. Because Bert is under the age of 14 and no longer tests positive for HIV, he is considered "adoptable" by the

Courtesy Lofton-Croteau family

state of Florida, and since Florida bans gays from adopting, Bert could be taken away from the Lofton-Croteau family at any time.

It is impossible to know the percentage of gays and lesbians in the United States. Some estimates place it at approximately 10 percent of the population, although recent surveys suggest that the proportion is lower (Kornblum & Julian, 2004); this subject is considered more fully in Chapter 14. A study of 405 randomly selected gays and lesbians found that 8 percent had children under the age of 18 living with them in their home. The same study reported that 49 percent of the respondents wanted to have children. With more than half a million children currently in the foster care system in the United States and only 46,000 being adopted annually, restricting gays and lesbians from adopting or serving as foster parents can prove quite harmful for the children in the foster care system because they are being denied a potentially safe, loving, and stable home.

The American Civil Liberties Union (ACLU) was founded in 1920 to protect the liberties and rights of all Americans, regardless of race, gender, or sexual orientation. Over its long history, it has defended the rights of groups on the far right, the far left, and all ideological positions in between. For years, the ACLU, along with a number of other organizations, has been attempting to persuade Florida to repeal the ban against allowing homosexuals to adopt. Currently, Florida is the only state that explicitly prohibits any homosexual from adopting children; however, it does not prohibit homosexuals from being foster parents. Many reasons are given for barring gays from adopting; one of the most prevalent reasons cited is a fear that children exposed to such an environment will become gay themselves.

The ACLU has published a document titled *Too High a Price: The Case Against Restricting Gay Parenting,* which addresses the issues of gay parenting and the different perceptions and laws surrounding it, including the fear that children raised by gay parents would become gay themselves. The ACLU looked to social-scientific studies of children raised by gay parents. Although some policymakers may believe that these children will inevitably become gay, the opposite appears to be the case. Children raised by gay or lesbian parents are not more likely to identify themselves as gay or lesbian, although "children of lesbians were more likely to have considered the possibility of having a same-sex relationship and were more likely to have had a same-sex sexual experience" (p. 47). This suggests that children growing up in an environment in which gender norms are less restrictive will be more likely to view same-sex relationships as a viable option and to explore this option, regardless of their eventual sexual identity.

ACLU researchers interviewed Judith Stacey, a professor of sociology at the University of Southern California. When asked if heterosexual parents make better parents than gays, Stacey adamantly disagrees, and when asked if there are any reputable studies that suggest otherwise, she states: "There is not a single, highly regarded social scientist conducting and publishing research in this area

today who claims that gay and lesbian parents harm children . . . [many of those who have published such works] have been discredited and even expelled from the American Psychological Association and the American Sociological Association" (p. 49). She points out that "most gay adults, after all, were brought up by straight parents" (p. 50).

SUMMARY

Becoming a Social Being

- *Socialization* refers to the ways in which people learn to conform to their society's norms, values, and roles.
- Primary socialization consists of the ways in which the newborn individual is molded into a person who can interact with others according to the expectations of society. Secondary socialization occurs in childhood and adolescence, primarily through schooling, and adult socialization refers to the ways in which a person learns the norms associated with new statuses.

Nature and Nurture

- Among the most basic questions in the study of socialization is that of "nature" versus "nurture": To what extent does the development of the person depend on genetic factors, and to what extent does it depend on learning?
- The first social scientist to develop a theory that addressed this issue was Sigmund Freud. Freud believed that the personality develops out of the processes of socialization through which the infant is gradually forced to control its biological urges. He divided the personality into three functional areas: the *id,* from which unsocialized drives arise; the *superego,* which incorporates the moral codes of elders; and the *ego,* or one's conception of oneself in relation to others.
- In the growth of the personality, the formation of the ego or social self is critical. According to Freud, this takes place in a series of stages in which conflict between the demands of the superego and those of the id is always threatening to disrupt the functioning of the ego.
- *Behaviorism* asserts that all behavior is learned. It originated in the work of Ivan Pavlov, who showed that behavior that was thought to be instinctual could in fact be shaped or *conditioned* by learning situations. This line of research was continued by John B. Watson,

whose experiments revealed the ability of conditioning to shape behavior in almost any direction.
- Studies of *feral children,* who have experienced extreme isolation or have been reared outside human society, show that such children are able to learn but that they do so far more slowly than children who have not been isolated in early childhood.
- Other studies have found that normal development requires not only the presence of other humans but also the attention and love of adults. Children raised in orphanages and other nonfamily settings are more likely to develop emotional problems and to be retarded in their language development than comparable children reared by their parents.
- The role of genes in shaping traits such as intelligence and sexual orientation is a subject of continual research and much controversy. In neither case is there any definitive evidence that specific genes determine these highly significant aspects of human behavior.

The Social Construction of the Self

- Interactionist models of socialization stress the development of the social self through interaction with others.
- One of the earliest interactionist theories was Charles Horton Cooley's concept of the "looking glass self," the reflection of our self that we think we see in the behaviors of other people toward us.
- This concept was carried further by George Herbert Mead, who emphasized the importance of culture in the formation of the self.
- Mead believed that when children play, they practice *role taking,* or trying to look at social situations from the standpoint of another person. This ability develops through three stages. During the preparatory stage, children mimic the behavior of the *significant others* in their social environment. During the play stage, they play at being others who are significant in their lives. During the game stage, they develop the ability to take

the role of the *generalized other*—that is, to shape their participation according to the roles of other participants.

- In playing the roles for which they have been socialized, people adhere to rules of interaction known as "face work." They seek to present a positive image of themselves, their "face," and to avoid being embarrassed or "losing face."

- Lawrence Kohlberg proposed a three-stage sequence of moral development in which the child's moral reasoning evolves from emphasis on reward and punishment to the ability to distinguish between social laws and moral principles.

- Other sociologists, especially Carol Gilligan, have challenged Kohlberg's theory on the ground that it does not distinguish between moral reasoning based on rules and justice (most common in males) and moral reasoning based on fairness and cooperation (most common in females).

- Research on gender and emotion has shown that—whether one is male or female—by better understanding what goes into emotional intelligence, one can vastly improve one's personal relationships and one's understanding of why others react as they do in different social situations.

Social Environments and Early Socialization

- Studies of the environments in which socialization occurs have found that normal development requires the involvement of one or more adults in the care of the child, as well as public policies that promote such involvement.

- *Agencies of socialization* are the groups of people, along with the interactions that occur within those groups, that influence a person's social development.

- Within all agencies of socialization, one finds a great deal of *anticipatory socialization,* in which the individual plays at a role that he or she is likely to assume later in life.

- After the family, the most important agencies of socialization are the schools. Other socializing agencies include day care centers, churches, leagues, and other associations.

- Religion may be involved in socialization in different ways throughout an individual's lifetime.

- The dominant agency of socialization outside the family is the *peer group,* an interacting group of people of about the same age. Peer groups exert a significant influence on the individual from adolescence on.

- The mass media, especially television, are another significant agency of socialization in American society.

Socialization Through the Life Course

- The roles a person plays over a lifetime are influenced by social change and by changes in the culture of his or her society.

- Socialization after childhood often occurs as a result of occupational mobility and the influence of significant others.

- A person's core identity shapes that individual's responses to new situations and challenges.

- *Resocialization* may occur at any time during adulthood. Sometimes people undergo resocialization to correct patterns of social learning that they and others find detrimental.

- Erik Erikson focused on *identification,* the social process whereby the individual chooses adults as role models and attempts to imitate their behavior.

Gender Socialization

- An important aspect of socialization is *gender socialization,* or the ways in which we learn our gender identity and develop according to cultural norms of masculinity and femininity.

- Gender identity is an individual's own feeling of whether he or she is a male or a female.

GLOSSARY

socialization: The processes whereby we learn to behave according to the norms of our culture. (p. 110)

id: According to Freud, the part of the human personality from which all innate drives arise. (p. 111)

superego: According to Freud, the part of the human personality that internalizes the moral codes of adults. (p. 111)

ego: According to Freud, the part of the human personality that is the individual's conception of himself or herself in relation to others. (p. 112)

behaviorism: A theory stating that all behavior is learned and that this learning occurs through the process known as conditioning. (p. 112)

conditioning: The shaping of behavior through reward and punishment. (p. 112)

feral child: A child reared outside human society. (p. 113)

role taking: Trying to look at social situations from the standpoint of another person from whom one seeks a response. (p. 117)

significant other: Any person who is important to an individual. (p. 118)

generalized other: A person's internalized conception of the expectations and attitudes held by society. (p. 119)

agencies of socialization: The groups of people, along with the interactions that occur within those groups, that influence a person's social development. (p. 124)

agents of socialization: Individuals who socialize others. (p. 124)

anticipatory socialization: Socialization that prepares an individual for a role that he or she is likely to assume later in life. (p. 124)

peer group: An interacting group of people of about the same age that has a significant influence on the norms and values of its members. (p. 128)

resocialization: Intense, deliberate socialization designed to change major beliefs and behaviors. (p. 131)

total institution: A setting in which people undergoing resocialization are isolated from the larger society under the control of a specialized staff. (p. 131)

identification: The social process whereby an individual chooses role models and attempts to imitate their behavior. (p. 132)

gender socialization: The ways in which we learn our gender identity and develop according to cultural norms of masculinity and femininity. (p. 132)

INTERNET RESOURCES

Virtual Society: The Wadsworth Sociology Resource Center
(http://sociology.wadsworth.com)

At Virtual Society you can access a wide range of enrichment material to aid your study of sociology. From the main page, click on the Student Resources link and find your course and this textbook. Next, select the chapter you are presently studying from the pull-down menu. Among the useful options for each self-study chapter are online links and exercises, flashcards, practical study tips, and practice quizzes for each chapter.

MicroCase Online

From the Virtual Society home page, click on MicroCase Online to access book-specific MicroCase exercises that allow you to further explore sociological issues and principles presented in the text.

InfoTrac College Edition

Another unique option available to you at the Student Resources section at Virtual Society is InfoTrac College Edition, an online library with access to hundreds of scholarly and popular periodicals. Below are suggested search terms for this chapter, but this resource also allows you to fit your study of sociology to your own interests by searching custom keywords.

Behaviorism

Socialization

Peer Group

Gender Socialization

United Nations Children's Fund
(www.unicef.org)

Offers excellent resources and links to other Web sites dealing with child development throughout the world, including problems of child labor, slavery, and abuse.

Kaiser Family Foundation
(www.kff.org)

Contains features on many aspects of socialization, sexuality, health, and agencies of socialization, with links to other important sites.

Foster Parent Home Page
(http://fostercare.org/FPHP)

Includes debates on orphanages, surveys on child abuse and neglect, and analyses of media coverage of foster care.

Annie E. Casey Foundation
(www.aecf.org)

Publishes *Kids Count,* an annual review of the situation of children in the United States and elsewhere in the world. A valuable starting point for research on the problems of socialization.

Gender and Society, Trinity College
(www.trinity.edu/~mkearl/gender.html)

Features much current thinking on gender socialization and related topics, with links to fine sites with even more resources on gender socialization.

American Psychological Association
(www.apa.org/pubinfo)

Provides links to topics like work and family as they relate to recent study and research.

chapter

6

Interaction in Groups

Steve Hart © 2002

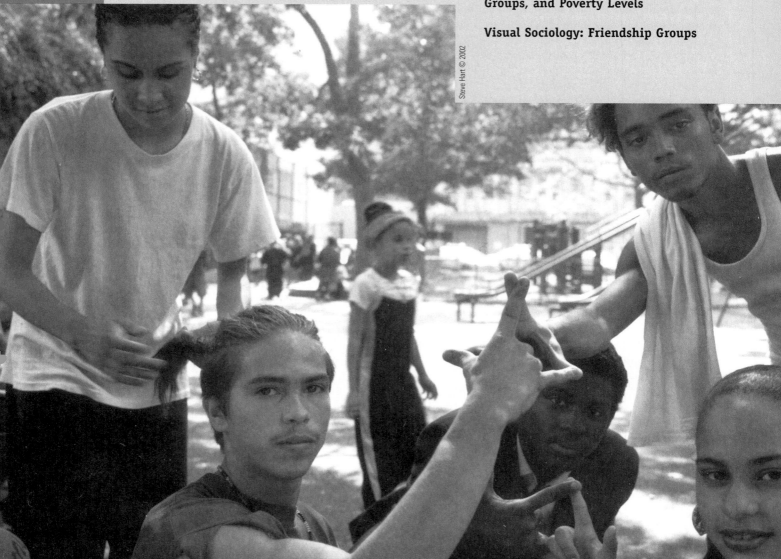

"What did being a gang member mean to you?" criminologist Dana Nurge recently asked a young woman from Boston. This is how she responded:

> I was always left out in some way and then when I met them (this was before I graduated from high school) I was more than part of the family . . . They had this need for me. Everyone wants to feel needed and I felt really at home with them. The other thing was I wasn't alone, anytime day or night, I could just pick up the phone and call someone. Financial-wise, also, I remember a couple times, like my first time moving out, I remember a couple times being worried about making rent and all the responsibilities. Guys would just come by with the groceries . . . They helped me be able to go to college . . . I couldn't have done it without them. (Nurge, 2003, p. 175)

When Nurge interviewed this young gang member a few years later, she had left the gang and explained her mixed feelings of gratitude and regret:

> There's a lot of things that I can't take back that I've done that I'll just have to live with for the rest of my life. Hurting people, losing a lot of friendships in order to do what the organization requires sometimes, you know . . . and a lot of these things, well, people say you're forgiven. It's not so much forgiveness from other people, it's forgiving myself. But one of the big things was . . . If I could've found the good in other places, I wouldn't have joined at all. That's about it. (p. 175)

In a parallel study of women members of the Latin Queens, termed a gang by the police but known to its members as a "street organization," sociologists David Brotherton and Camila Salazar-Atias (2003) observe:

> Most Queens come from backgrounds where racism, sexism, poverty, and limited opportunities are prevalent. They joined the nation in search of empowerment, identity, and support to compensate for a life in which they have often been left to fend for themselves as children and then left with minimal support to take care of their own children. (p. 205)

In the organization, they encountered new forms of sexism and double standards, which they often had to resist and struggle against, and like the women who spoke to Dana Nurge, they also wished there had been other alternatives for them. But the power of some of the friendships they made is something they have always cherished. This and much previous research emphasizes that gang peer groups have a strong and lasting influence on the men and women who pass through them (Moore, 1991). But gangs are only one of many types of friendship groups. For insights into other types of friendship groups, and glimpses of the strong emotions friends often express within them, see the Visual Sociology feature at the end of the chapter.

FOCUS QUESTIONS:

• What are some of the most common types of human groups?

• What are the benefits of bureaucracies to society, and what problems may arise in bureaucratic forms of social organization?

• How do various kinds of groups contribute to social change?

THE IMPORTANCE OF GROUPS

The study of gangs or "street organizations" is rich in examples of how people interact in groups. It also shows how the strong norms or values of a peer group often lead gang members to behave violently in particular situations (Horowitz, 1985; Hunt & Joe-Laidler, 2001). Martin Sanchez-Jankowski, who has conducted extensive comparative research on gangs throughout the United States, concludes that, contrary to what people often believe, most gang members do not enjoy fighting. Indeed, those who are not among the gang's leaders fear violence. However, as he reports, "Fear of physical harm . . . is not sufficient to completely deter gang violence, because most gang members . . . believe that if you do not attack, you will be attacked" (Sanchez-Jankowski, 1991, p. 177).

The social fabric of modern societies is composed of millions of groups. Gangs are only one example. Some groups are as intimate as a pair of lovers. Others, like the modern corporation or university, are extremely large and are composed of many interrelated subgroups. We need to perform well in all of these groups, and to have this ability is to be considered successful by others. But the knowledge needed for success in a group with a formal structure of roles and statuses is very different from the "smarts" needed for success in intimate groups.

In this chapter, we analyze some important aspects of the way people behave in groups. We begin by describing the most common types of groups and showing how they can be linked together by overlapping memberships. This first portion of the chapter illustrates the functionalist view of group interaction. It looks at the structure of groups and the way they function in society. It also provides typologies of groups and insights into how they are organized. However, simply describing categories of groups and their structure does not explain how groups maintain the commitment of their members or why they change. In the middle portion of the chapter, we examine these questions, focusing on the give-and-take that occurs in groups of different types and on how these interactions produce group norms. This section illustrates interactionist research on behavior in groups. In the final section of the chapter, we show how formal organization and bureaucracy operate to control conflict and cope with change in groups. The concepts introduced here will be used over and over again in other chapters, for, as we saw in Chapter 4, groups of all kinds are the building blocks of society.

CHARACTERISTICS OF SOCIAL GROUPS

We sometimes group people together artificially in the process of analyzing society (e.g., all the teenagers in a particular community). This results in a **social category**, a collection of individuals who are grouped together because they share a trait deemed by the observer to be socially relevant (e.g., sex, race, or age). But there are also groups in which we actually participate and in which we have distinct roles and statuses. These are **social groups.** A social group is a set of two or more individuals who share a sense of common identity and belonging and who interact on a regular basis. Group members are recruited according to specific criteria of membership and are bound together by a set of membership rights and mutual obligations. Throughout this chapter, unless indicated otherwise, when we refer to groups we mean social groups.

Group identity, the sense of belonging to a group, means that members are aware of their participation in the group and know the identities of other group members. This also implies that group members have a sense of the boundaries of their group—that is, of who belongs and who does not belong. Groups themselves have a social structure that arises from repeated interaction among their members. In those interactions, the members form ideas about the status of each and the role each can play in the group (Hare et al., 1994; Holy, 1985; Homans, 1950). A skilled member of a work group, for example, may become the leader, while an unskilled member may become recognized as the person whom others instruct and send on errands.

Through their interactions, group members develop feelings of attachment to each other. Groups whose members have strong positive attachments to each other are said to be highly cohesive, whereas those whose members are not strongly attached to each other are said to lack cohesion. Groups also develop norms governing behavior in the group, and they generally have goals such as performing a task, playing a game, or making public policy. Finally, because groups are composed of interacting human beings, we must also recognize that all groups have the potential for conflict among their members; the resolution of such conflicts may be vital to continued group cohesion.

Membership criteria, awareness and boundaries, a clear social structure, cohesion, norms and goals, and the possibility of conflict are among the dimensions that define different groups. If we briefly compare two types of groups—say, members of a computer chat group and a married couple—the importance of these dimensions becomes apparent. Membership in the couple is exclusive, and cohesion is based on intimacy and trust. If he comes home and says, "Honey, I brought a new woman into our relationship—I think you'll like her," she is likely to throw him out—unless they happen to come from a culture that practices polygyny, and even then the sudden introduction of a new woman into the household will disrupt the cohesion of the original marital group. Among members of the chat group, in contrast, the only criterion for membership may be ownership of the proper equipment and knowledge that the chat room exists. Not all the members will know each other, and new members can be added without any sense of reduced cohesion as would occur in the case of the married couple.

Group Size and Structure

If one walks along a beach on a nice summer day, the variety of groups one sees is representative of the range of social groups in the larger society. Many of the groups on the beach are composed of family members. Others are friendship groups, usually consisting of young men and women of about the same age. Some of these are same-sex groups; others include both males and females. Then there are groups that form around activities such as volleyball. Still other groups may be based on occupational ties; the lifeguards and their supervisors or the food service workers are examples of such groups.

PRIMARY AND SECONDARY GROUPS The distinction made in Chapter 4 between primary and secondary groups helps clarify some of the differences among the groups one encounters on a sunny beach or anywhere else in society. Charles Horton Cooley defined **primary groups** as "those characterized by intimate face-to-face association and cooperation. They are primary in several senses, but chiefly in that they are fundamental in forming the social nature and ideals of the individual" (1909, p. 25). Out on the beach, the family groups are, of course, examples of primary groups. So are the groups of friends one observes lying near each other on the sand. Among the food service workers or the lifeguards, there are probably some smaller friendship groups or cliques within the larger occupational group.

The occupational groups serving the beachgoers are examples of **secondary groups** (a concept we also introduced in Chapter 4 but need to use again here). The concept of a secondary group follows from Cooley's definition of primary groups, although he did not actually use the term (Dewey, 1948). Secondary groups are characterized by relationships that involve few aspects of their members' personalities. In such groups, the members' reasons for participation are usually limited to a few specific goals. The bonds of association in secondary groups are usually based on

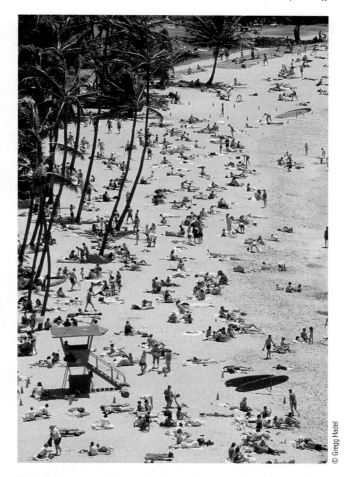

Beaches are excellent places to observe the way people group themselves in public. In this photo, note the way people cluster in primary groups and tend to leave as much space as possible between themselves and other groups.

some form of contract, a written or unwritten agreement that specifies the scope of interaction within the group. All organizations and associations, including companies with employers and employees, are secondary groups. (See the Study Chart on page 144.)

Within most secondary groups, one can usually find several primary groups based on regular interaction and friendship. Scottish clans and Native American tribes, for example, are secondary associations that link individuals together through a network of kin relations. But within the clan or tribe there are many primary groups, often composed of men or women of roughly the same age.

GROUP SIZE AND RELATIONSHIPS As the number of people in a group increases, the number of possible relationships among the group's members increases at a greater rate. When

SOCIOLOGICAL METHODS

Diagramming Group Structure

A variety of techniques, collectively known as *sociometry,* are used to study the structure of groups. The three most frequently used sociometric methods are basic group diagrams, diagrams that indicate the valence of group bonds, and sociograms, which chart individuals' preferences in groups.

At their simplest, group diagrams show the number of members in a group. Each member is represented by the same symbol, and the presence of a relationship between two members (a dyad) is shown by a line. The group diagrams in the figure labeled A show how the number of possible relationships increases geometrically as the number of members in the group increases arithmetically. (The formula for calculating the number of possible dyadic relationships in a group, where *R* is the number of relationships and *N* is the total number in the group, is $R = N(N - 1) / 2$.)

In a slightly more sophisticated type of diagram, a bond between group members is shown only if it actually exists in the group's interactions. Where there is no relationship between two members, no line is drawn between them. In a peer group it is usual for all the members to have a relationship, even if they do not all share the same strong feelings of friendship. In work groups, however, it is not uncommon for people to have relationships that are based on cooperation in carrying out specific tasks. If their work does not bring them together, they may not have any relationship at all.

Diagram B represents a group in a school where the third-grade (3G) and fourth-grade (4G) teachers who teach language arts are members of a com-

(A)

**2 people
1 relationship**

**3 people
3 relationships**

**4 people
6 relationships**

5 people • 10 relationships

6 people • 15 relationships

(B)

3G   4G

3G   AP   4G

3G   4G

STUDY CHART

PRIMARY AND SECONDARY GROUPS

TYPE OF GROUP	TYPE OF INTERACTION	CONTRIBUTIONS TO SOCIETY	EXAMPLES
Primary	Intimate, face-to-face; full range of emotions may be expressed	Help form individual's character and values	Family, peer group, gang
Secondary	Limited to specific roles (e.g., shopper, cashier); limited aspects of individuals' personalities and emotions are expressed	Carry out written and unwritten contractual relationships (e.g., buyer and seller)	PTA, teacher and students, hospital safety committee

mittee convened by an assistant principal (AP). The diagram shows that three of the teachers share relationships (either through cooperation in projects at work or through friendship), while the other teachers are linked to one another only through their work with the assistant principal.

Valence is the feeling that exists between any two people in a group. It refers to the value they place on their relationship. The most basic valence in a relationship is positive or negative—that is, like or dislike. In most friendship groups, there is a balance of valences; otherwise the group will likely break up. In diagram C, for example, Joe likes Dave and Marty and they reciprocate that liking, but Dave and Marty do not like each other. Joe must either convince the other two to like each other or choose between them.

A difference in valence between two people can be indicated with a

double line and two different signs. In diagram D, we see that Dave now likes Marty but Marty does not reciprocate. Perhaps he would like to have an exclusive relationship with Joe and views Dave as a threat. But now the pressure is all on Marty. If Joe can show him that Dave likes him and if Dave continues to try to get along with him, the group is likely to form a balanced triad, as shown in diagram E.

In a larger group, such as a school classroom or a club, the members express their preferences for each other in many ways. They call each other to talk about the events of the day or week; they gossip about each other; they give each other advice or criticism. These preferences result in a structure of cliques that exists within the larger group. When social scientists wish to chart such a structure, they simply ask all the members of the group to list the three or four individuals in the group with whom they would most like to spend time. By indicating each choice with a line, the researchers create a diagram known as a sociogram. Diagram F is a simple sociogram showing preferences among nine boys and girls. It reveals, among other things, that there is a clique centering on Dave and another centering on Latasha.

there are two people in the group, there is just one relationship; but when a third person is added, there are three possible relationships (A-B, B-C, A-C). When a fourth person joins the group, there are six possible relationships; a group of only six people includes fifteen possible relationships. The Sociological Methods box above describes this phenomenon in more detail.

When a group has more than six members, the relationships among the members become so complex that the group is likely to break up into smaller groups, at least temporarily. One often sees this behavior at parties or other social gatherings. Five or six people can carry on a

conversation in which all participate, but as more people arrive, the group tends to break up into several smaller groups of two, three, or four people. The difficulty of maintaining relationships as group size increases becomes greater when there are limited resources, such as seats in cars or at restaurants, and the group is forced to define the smaller groups that will interact more intimately. Intimacy and feelings of closeness to others decrease with increased group size.

The more possible relationships there are, the more likely it is that some of those relationships will be troubled by conflict and jealousy. In consequence, the larger the group, the more unstable it tends to be and the more likely it is to break up into smaller groups in which there are fewer possible relationships and a greater likelihood of positive bonds among all members. If a larger group devoted to specific goals is to maintain its cohesion in the face of the pressures created by primary attachments among its members, it will need a formal, agreed-upon structure of leaders and rules. Thus a group of friends who decide to meet regularly to play a favorite game (it could be golf, basketball, or any other activity) will find that as their numbers grow they need a formal structure—an elected or appointed leader, a calendar of events, a membership list, and written rules of conduct. In short, it will be transformed from a primary group into a secondary group or, more specifically, a formal organization.

DYADS AND TRIADS   The basic principles of group structure and size were first described by the pioneering German sociologist Georg Simmel (1858–1918). Simmel perceived the need to study behavior in small and larger groups because groups are the basic units of life in all societies. Among his other contributions, he pointed out the significance of what he termed **dyads**, groups composed of only two people, and **triads**, groups composed of three people. He recognized that the strongest social bonds are formed between two people, be they best friends, lovers, or married couples. But he saw that dyads are also vulnerable to breakup, since if the single relationship on which it is based ends, the dyad ends as well.

When the dyadic bond is strong (and the two who share it often jealously guard their intimacy), the introduction of a new person into the group often causes problems. Conventional wisdom has much to say about this matter ("Two's a couple, three's a crowd"), and if one observes children's play groups it soon becomes clear that much of the conflict they experience has to do with the desire to have an exclusive relationship with a best friend. In families, too, the shift from a dyad to a triad often creates problems. A couple who are experiencing a high level of conflict may believe that a baby will offer them a challenge they can meet together, thereby renewing their love for each other. At first this may seem to be the case, but as the infant makes more demands on the couple's energy and time, the father may feel that the baby is depriving him of attention from his wife, and he may become jealous of the newcomer. For some couples, the addition of a child can actually increase the chance of divorce, resulting in a stable mother–child dyad and a single male.

The instability of triads can also be seen among siblings. The third child often has a rough time of it. Not only is the third child "the baby" who imagines it impossible ever to perform as well as the older siblings, but he or she has committed the unintentional sin of breaking

The Sociological Observer

These men clearly have a close dyadic relationship, and it appears that something quite joyous is leading them to express their affection at this moment. But what else can we glean from this photo? Do you think these men are gay? Is it acceptable for men to embrace this way in public? (See page 165 for further insights into the sociological content of this photo.)

© Ken Heyman/Woodfin Camp & Associates

the bond between the two older children. Whenever one of the latter becomes intimate and loving toward "the baby," the other will demand attention and remind the third child that he or she is the newcomer. This point should not be exaggerated; sibling triads can be stable and happy. In general, however, the addition of a third child increases the possibility of conflict and coalitions within the family (Caplow, 1969; Deaux & Wrightsman, 1988).

Communities

At a level of social organization between the primary group and the larger institutions of the nation-state are communities of all descriptions. **Communities** are sets of primary and secondary groups in which the individual carries out important life functions such as raising a family, earning a living, finding shelter, and the like. Communities may be either territorial or nonterritorial. Both include primary and secondary groups. In general, **territorial communities** are contained within geographic boundaries, whereas **non-**

territorial communities are networks of associations that form around shared goals. When people speak of a professional community, such as the medical or legal community, they are referring to a nonterritorial community.

Territorial communities are populations that function within a particular geographic area, and this is by far the more common meaning of the term as it is used both in everyday speech and in social-scientific writing (Lowry, 1993; Suttles, 1972). Territorial communities are usually composed of one or more *neighborhoods*. The neighborhood level of group contact includes primary groups (particularly families and peer groups) that form attachments on the basis of proximity—that is, as a result of living near one another.

In studies of how people form friendship groups in suburban neighborhoods, both Herbert Gans (1976) and Bennett Berger (1961) found that proximity tended to explain patterns of primary-group formation better than any other variable except social class. Thus families that move into new suburban communities tend to find friends among others of the same social class who live near enough to allow ease of interaction and casual visiting; the same is true of students living in dorms on college campuses. On the international level, observers of the ethnic violence in Rwanda have reported that where members of the Hutu and Tutsi tribes live close to each other and cooperate in bringing in the harvest, they are far less likely to bear grudges and resort to violence than members of the same tribes who do not interact in their daily lives (Bonner, 1994).

That physical propinquity and social-class similarities explain how friendships form may seem self-evident to us. Moving into new neighborhoods or into dorms is a constant feature of life in a large urban society. But the idea that mere proximity, rather than kinship or tribal membership, can explain patterns of association would shock many people in simpler agrarian societies, where mobility is not a fact of everyday life. As Robert Park (1967/1926) noted, it is only under conditions of rapid and persistent social change that proximity helps explain why people form groups.

Networks

In modern societies, people form their deepest friendships in face-to-face groups, but these groups are, in turn, integrated into larger and more impersonal secondary-group structures that may extend well beyond the bounds of territorial communities. William F. Whyte opened *Street Corner Society* (1943), his classic study of street-corner peer groups, with this observation:

> The Nortons were Doc's gang. The group was brought together primarily by Doc, and it was built around Doc. When Doc was growing up, there was a kid's gang on Norton Street for every

significant difference in age. There was a gang that averaged about three years older than Doc; there was Doc's gang, which included Nutsy, Danny, and a number of others; there was a group about three years younger, which included Joe Dodge and Frank Bonilli; and there was still a younger group, to which Carl and Tommy belonged. (p. 3)

Like the gangs Joan Moore studies in contemporary Los Angeles, the Nortons were active in a network of neighborhood-level peer groups. They would compete against other groups of boys of roughly the same age in a yearly round of baseball, bowling, and occasional interneighborhood fights (the latter occurring mainly in their younger teenage years). But the Nortons were also integrated into the community through some of its secondary associations. For example, at election time they were recruited by the local political party organization, and some were recruited by the racketeers who controlled their low-income neighborhood. Party organizations and organized crime groups are examples of secondary associations that extend outside territorial communities.

IN-GROUPS AND OUT-GROUPS The "corner boys" studied by Whyte tended to be hostile toward similar groups from other street corners and even toward certain boys from their own territory. These distinctions between groups are common and are referred to as *in-group–out-group distinctions*. The **in-group** consists of one's own peers, whereas **out-groups** are those whom one considers to be outside the bounds of intimacy. Simmel observed that in-group–out-group distinctions can form around almost any quality, even one that many people would not consider meaningful at all. Thus, in a study of juvenile groups in a Chicago housing project, Gerald Suttles (1972) found that distinctions were made between boys who lived in lighter or darker brick buildings. Similarly, American children who have lived in foreign countries for several years may find themselves relegated to out-groups when they return to school in the United States (Smith, 1994, 1996).

In-group–out-group distinctions are usually based on such qualities as income, race, and religion. In "Cornerville," the community Whyte studied, group boundaries were based on educational background, particularly college versus noncollege education. One of Whyte's informants explained this distinction:

> In Cornerville the noncollege man has an inferiority complex. He hasn't had much education, and he has that feeling of inferiority. . . . Now the college man felt that way before he went to college, but when he is in college, he tries to throw it off. . . . Naturally, the noncollege man resents that. (Whyte, 1943, p. 79)

In-group–out-group distinctions often make it difficult for secondary associations to attract members from both groups. For example, when two ethnic or racial groups in a community make in-group–out-group distinctions, they often find themselves drifting toward different political parties or forming distinct factions within the same party rather than uniting to find solutions to common problems.

REFERENCE GROUPS   An important area of sociological research is the study of how the decisions we make are influenced by significant or relevant others—that is, by people we admire and whose behavior we try to imitate. The ways in which other people influence our attitudes and behavior are often discussed in terms of the **reference group,** a group that the individual uses as a frame of reference for self-evaluation and attitude formation (Deaux & Wrightsman, 1988; Merton, 1968). Some reference groups set and enforce certain values and norms, while others serve as a standard for comparison (Hare, 1992).

An example of the influence of reference groups can be seen in a study of students at Bennington College conducted by Theodore Newcomb (1958). Newcomb found that conservative students often joined groups of like-minded peers who would affirm the values they had brought with them from home. They also tended to go home for visits more often than liberal students did. By their senior year, however, they were likely to have shifted their attitudes to match those of a more liberal reference group because most of the students and faculty at Bennington were liberal or radical.

This pioneering research has been replicated in many later studies. For example, studies of how students' religious beliefs change in college show that the more a student's religious beliefs differ from those of other students interviewed, the more change there will be in his or her beliefs. Conversely, the more a student's parents' religious views coincide with the dominant views of other students at the college, the less change there will be in that student's beliefs (Roberts, Koch, & Johnson, 2001).

The concept of reference groups has many practical applications. In market research, for example, it is common practice to determine where potential customers tend to seek help in forming their attitudes—which magazines, writers, or television commentators they turn to for guidance. These *opinion leaders,* as they are sometimes called, are the customer's reference group in a particular area of consumption (Katz, 1957).

Note that a reference group is not the same thing as a primary group. The friends with whom you spend much of your time are a primary group and are likely to act as a reference group as well. But we can have numerous reference groups, each of which influences us in different areas. As you choose a profession or career, you will be influenced by the values and norms of reference groups in that field. As you gain new statuses, such as that of parent, voter, or supervisor, you will look to other reference groups: child care experts, political commentators, and the like. A reference group thus can be quite limited in its relationship to you as an individual—its influence may act on what you are to become rather than on what you are now.

SOCIAL NETWORK ANALYSIS   The study of whom people associate with, how those choices are made, and the effects of those choices on social structure and individual personality is known as *social network analysis.* The British social scientist Elizabeth Bott, one of the founders of this branch of sociology, describes a social network as follows:

> Each person is, as it were, in touch with a number of people, some of whom are directly in touch with each other and some of whom are not. . . . I find it convenient to talk of a social field of this kind as a network. The image I have is of a set of points, some of which are joined by lines. The points of the image are people, or sometimes groups, and the lines indicate which people interact with each other. (1977, p. 256)

The diagrams in the Sociological Methods box illustrate social networks.

Social network analysis grew out of studies of the choices people make in becoming members of various social groups. Today network analysis extends beyond this rather narrow subject to studies illustrating how the interconnectedness of certain members of a society can produce interaction patterns that may have a lasting influence on the lives of people both within and outside the network (Cochran et al., 1990). Sociologist Aubrey Bonnett (1981), for example, studied *susus,* the rotating credit associations formed by West Indian ethnic groups in New York and other American cities. These associations are actually networks composed of numerous small groups of neighbors and kin who join with other similar groups, pay an entrance fee, and take turns borrowing funds from the association at far lower interest rates than a bank would charge. Bonnett showed that these associations bring together members of immigrant groups with different histories and values. As one *susu* organizer told him, "In my *susu* I have had members from all the islands. . . . You would be amazed to know how it has helped to get ourselves together, yes, this is really a West Indian thing" (p. 67).

Sociologists who study the rich and powerful have described the networks that provide the social contacts essential for success in entering and climbing upward in the corporate hierarchy (Cookson, 1997). In their book *Preparing for Power,* for example, Peter Cookson and Caroline Persell (1985) describe how young men from elite social backgrounds develop strong attachments with others like them at prestigious prep schools, primarily (but not entirely) located in New England or Virginia, such as Phillips Academy in Massachusetts (founded in 1778) and Woodbury Forest

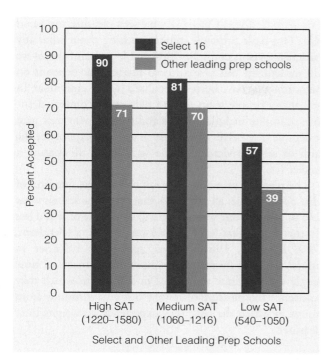

Figure 6.1 Acceptance at Highly Selective Colleges, by Prep School Status and SAT Scores

Source: Adapted from Cookson & Persell, 1985.

Figure 6.2 Achievement of High Corporate Position, by Manager's Class Background*

*Includes all college backgrounds.

Source: Adapted from Cookson & Persell, 1985.

School in Virginia (founded in 1889). Through attendance at these schools, the children of the wealthy acquire a great deal of "cultural capital." All students gain some forms of cultural capital by mastering a range of academic and social skills, but prep school students acquire a special form of cultural capital that prepares them for life among the elite. They learn how to speak; how to behave at formal social gatherings; how to behave as a guest at a country home; what colleges, clubs, companies, and communities one should seek to enter; and what kind of spouse one should marry. In short, prep schools "integrate new brains with old wealth to revitalize the upper classes" (Cookson & Persell, 1985, p. 187).

Prep school students' social networks come into play when they apply to elite colleges, particularly Ivy League institutions such as Harvard, Yale, and Princeton. Many of the administrators and admissions officers at the most prestigious colleges were former prep school students themselves and tend to show preference for applicants from those schools. Figure 6.1 shows that when graduates of elite prep schools apply to the most competitive colleges, even those with low SAT scores are highly likely to gain admission. Later in life they will continue to benefit from the social bonds formed at prep school. As can be seen in Figure 6.2, business managers from upper-class backgrounds (those who are most likely to have attended elite prep schools) are more likely to become chief executive officers or to hold seats on the boards of major corporations than those from other social-class backgrounds.

In other research on social networks, sociologists have demonstrated how the networks of individuals and groups within which people interact provide social support in times of stress or illness. Interestingly, this research often finds that people's social-support networks shrink as they become elderly and infirm and lose the ability to offer support or other resources in exchange (Fischer, 1982; Peek, Zsembik, & Cloward, 1997).

INTERACTION IN GROUPS

In the preceding section, we discussed the basic building blocks of social structure: the primary group and the secondary group. We saw that these groups are embedded in more complex structures of groups, such as communities and social networks. We also saw how reference groups act to confirm an individual's values and behavior, and how the distinctions we make between in-groups and out-groups help us maintain the boundaries of the groups in which we participate. But these descriptions do not tell us what principles of interaction operate to produce cohesion or instability in groups. In this section, therefore, we take a closer look at interaction in groups.

Simply to observe that a society is a fabric of groups is to neglect two important questions: How can groups stay together in the first place, and how can a fabric of groups produce a cohesive society? All around us we see evidence that groups constantly fall apart. Romantic ardor cools; marriages fail; friends argue and seek new friends; successful rock bands split up; businesses go bankrupt; entire nations are fragmented by social and economic upheavals. Certainly new groups are forming all the time, but others are continually breaking up.

When a group disintegrates, we often hear explanations like "I felt that I was only giving and not getting"; "We started to grow in separate directions"; "I no longer shared their values"; or "He [she, they] wanted too much of the [credit, money, power]." In short, when one listens to explanations of why groups fail to stay together, it sounds as if people are continually seeking more rewards for themselves or blaming others for taking too much of whatever rewards are available—too much attention, affection, approval, prestige, money, power, or whatever. If this is the case, it does not seem likely that groups could have much cohesiveness or stability.

One can imagine even more serious effects of human greed and self-serving behavior. The seventeenth-century English philosopher Thomas Hobbes was deeply concerned about the relationship between the individual and society. How is society, or any group within it, possible if every individual puts his or her own interests above those of everyone else? Hobbes warned that the sum total of everyone's selfish acts would be a "war of all against all." In *Leviathan,* his monumental treatise on this problem, he concluded that humanity needs an all-powerful but benevolent dictator to prevent social chaos.

Today people throughout the world reject this notion. We strive to create a social order based on individual freedom, democracy, and the rule of law. Nevertheless, wherever we look we see major threats to such a social order. Often such threats emerge when people feel that the groups they count on, such as political parties and legislatures, are not acting fairly. This brings us back to the question of how, given individual selfishness, humans can achieve order, cooperation, and trust in their associations rather than coercion, terror, and chaos.

Principles of Interaction

Social scientists have identified certain principles of interaction that help explain both stability and change in human groups. Among them are the pleasure principle, the rationality principle, the reciprocity principle, and the fairness principle.

THE PLEASURE PRINCIPLE   People seek pleasure and avoid pain. This basic principle implies nothing about what any particular person considers pleasurable or painful—as we will see shortly, this is a personal matter that depends on the norms that have been internalized by the individual. In fact, many people seem to find pain or discomfort desirable; examples include athletes and dieters, who seek pain or deprive themselves of pleasure in order to experience the thrill of athletic victory or the satisfaction of wearing a smaller size.

The pleasure principle does not address the question of what people value; all it states is that once one knows what kind of pleasure one wants, one will seek more of it and less of other values that yield less personal pleasure (Bentham, 1789; Homans, 1961). When applied to behavior in groups, the pleasure principle simply means that over time people will continue to interact in a group in which they experience the pleasure of reward but will withdraw from groups in which the pain they experience outweighs their pleasure.

THE RATIONALITY PRINCIPLE   In social life, a gain in pleasure may require some pain as well. For example, when two members of a group of friends become very close and find pleasure in their intimacy, the others may feel left out, and this causes some pain both to the two intimate friends and to those who feel left out. In larger groups, when a rule such as a ban on smoking is made, some members will derive more pleasure than others from the cleaner air. Those whose smoking pleasure is denied will experience an increase in pain. Consciously or not, people in groups calculate whether they think they will benefit personally from continued interactions with others in the group. Thus the smokers may decide that their loss of pleasure outweighs the gains they get by being in the group, and they may decide to withdraw. In the small friendship group, the other friends may feel that the pain of their jealousy outweighs the pleasure of their friendship with the intimate pair, and they may exclude them from the group.

The rationality principle means that people change their behavior according to whether they think they will be worse or better off as a consequence. In other words, in making decisions about their interactions with others, people tend to make rough calculations of costs and benefits.

Does the idea that people seek a net gain from their interactions mean that they are greedy or self-centered or lacking in motives other than materialism? Not at all. Of course, there are extremes: Hedonists are people who can enjoy only the pleasures of the body. Egotists are people who especially enjoy praise and have little capacity for giving to others. Altruists are people who enjoy giving to others, often at the expense of other pleasures. But most people strive to behave in ways that give them physical pleasure and ego gratification ("boosts" or "strokes") and also give them the satisfaction of helping others. How far they go in either direction depends on what other members of the group are doing (e.g., how giving the others are, how selfish, how self-sacrificing), which brings us to the principle of reciprocity in interaction.

THE RECIPROCITY PRINCIPLE In group interactions, people usually adhere to a norm stating that what others do for you, you should try to do for others. This is one of the world's most commonly followed rules of interaction; it is known as the norm of reciprocity (Homans, 1950). The Roman statesman Cicero recognized this principle when he wrote, "There is no duty more indispensable than that of returning a kindness. All men distrust one forgetful of a benefit." But it is not necessary to go back to ancient Rome for evidence that reciprocity is vital to continuing group interaction. Suppose that you and two classmates meet at a local pub. You pick up the check, and the other two agree to do so on future occasions. The next time, one of them pays the check. The third time, the third friend pleads a lack of cash and you each end up paying your own share. You and your second friend will feel that this is an embarrassing lapse on the part of your third friend. If such behavior continues, you will feel that the third friend takes more than he or she gives or thinks his or her company is worth the extra money paid by you. It is unlikely that this threesome will stay together very long if such imbalances continue.

Under what conditions could such a group continue despite the third friend's violation of the norm of reciprocity? One condition involves a loss of prestige for the third friend. You might ask him or her to make up the debt by doing something else for you. In that case, the third friend takes a subordinate position in the group, doing your bidding to make up for the inability to reciprocate on an equal basis (Homans, 1961; Mauss, 1966/1925). However, suppose that the nonreciprocator is a movie star or a powerful politician. Then the other two members of the threesome might continue to pay in the hope that the third member would continue to spend his or her valuable time with them and that there would be an even greater reward for them in the future. This kind of relationship is quite common in social life. Social climbers seek ways to flatter and please someone who can confer prestige on them. Power seekers do the same in order to gain positions in which they will have power over others. A suitor may forgo reciprocity for quite a while in the hope of eventual conquest. In these situations and others like them, the participants in the interaction have an intuitive sense of what they are giving and what they are receiving or hope to receive in the future.

In the Bible, the norm of reciprocity is stated in the form of the Golden Rule. "Do unto others as you would have others do unto you" in effect urges individuals to go beyond expectations of immediate reciprocity and set examples of higher moral behavior in the hope that others will follow them. In real life, however, people tend to prefer that their gains be as immediate as possible.

THE FAIRNESS PRINCIPLE We see ample evidence that people tend to expect certain kinds of treatment from others and that they tend to become angry when they do not receive it, especially when they feel that they have done what is expected of them in the situation. We want the rules to apply equally to everyone in the game, be it a friendly game of pool or the more complex game of corporate strategy. When we are not rewarded in the same ways as others, we say that we are being treated unfairly.

The unfair condition in which a person or group has come to expect certain rewards for certain efforts, yet does not get them while others do, is called *relative deprivation.* In times of economic depression, for example, all groups in society must make do with less, and all feel deprived in comparison to their previous condition. If the economy begins to improve and some groups begin to get higher wages or more profits while others experience only limited improvement, members of the less successful group will feel deprived relative to others and will likely become angry even though their own plight has actually improved somewhat (Merton & Kitt, 1950). The concept of relative deprivation is useful in explaining some aspects of group behavior and appears again in Chapter 8 when we discuss how major social changes like revolutions occur.

People's ideas about what is fair in their interactions with others often conflict with simple calculations of gain and loss. The fact that they might come out ahead in an interaction does not guarantee that they will feel good about it and continue the interaction. This was demonstrated in a series of studies by Daniel Kahneman and his associates (1986). A large number of respondents were asked to judge the fairness of this situation:

> A landlord rents out a small house. When the lease is due for renewal, the landlord learns that the tenant has taken a job very close to the house and is therefore unlikely to move. The landlord raises the rent $40 more than he was planning to.

An economist might argue that the tenant should think of the situation in terms of whether the rent increase is offset by the savings in the cost of travel to work (in terms of money, time, convenience, etc.). If the tenant still comes out ahead, it will make sense to sign the new lease (the rationality principle). But more than 90 percent of the respondents in Kahneman's survey said that the landlord was being unfair. In real life, when people feel that a transaction like this is unfair they often end the interaction, even at some cost to themselves. In this case, people intuitively felt that the landlord was unfairly taking advantage of a gain made by the tenant (the new job) without adding anything to the property to earn the right to raise the rent.

The pure-rationality model of behavior predicts that people will act in their own interests in order to maximize their profit. If we were simple profit takers, however, our feelings about fairness would not play such a strong part in explaining group interaction (Frank, 1988). But in fact these feelings are very powerful. Kahneman and his associates examined the strength of these feelings in an experiment in which they asked subjects to divide $20 with another player whom they could not see but were told was in the room. Only two choices were given: to give $10 to each player or to keep $18 and give the other player $2. Out of 161 subjects, 122—76 percent—offered the even split. From this the experimenters concluded that most people are motivated by their own ideas of fairness, presumably as a result of socialization over many years.

In real life there are many examples of situations in which notions of fairness outweigh the principle of rationality. Barbers and beauticians do not charge more for haircuts on Saturday, nor do ski resorts usually charge more for lift tickets on holidays. Although they might like to profit from the higher demand at those times, they are afraid that people would regard the higher prices as unfair (Frank, 1988). However, services are often offered at higher rates during peak seasons, or bargain offers such as early-bird specials or off-peak fares are used to encourage people to accept services at times other than those they might prefer.

Applications of the fairness principle can be seen in a great many group situations. In the classic study conducted by Elton Mayo and his associates at Western Electric's Hawthorne plant (see Chapter 2), the observers often noticed that workers used various forms of joking and sarcastic teasing to enforce the group's norms. They had a strong sense of how much work they should turn out, both individually and as a group, in order to merit their pay: a fair day's work for a fair day's pay. In the plant's Bank Wiring Room, where workers hand-wired electrical circuits, it was common to see the members of a work group gang up and in a joking way hit a fellow worker on the shoulder when he produced more than the other members of the group. This practice was called "binging." A worker was binged by his coworkers if he produced too much in a day or if he did not produce enough, according to their definition of a fair day's work.

The Hawthorne researchers quickly realized that binging was part of the work group's culture. That culture—the group's norms of conduct and the ways in which its members interpreted those norms—was unique to that group and applied only when the group was at work. The culture of this work group had evolved over many years, its norms functioning to control the workers' responses to the demands of the company's managers. Thus, in a later analysis of the Bank Wiring Room observations, George Homans (1951) made the following comments:

> [The workers] shared a common body of sentiments. A person should not turn out too much work. If he did, he was a "rate-buster." The theory was that if an excessive amount of work was turned out, the management would lower the piecework rate so that the employees would be in the position of doing more work for approximately the same pay. On the other hand, a person should not turn out too little work. If he did he was a "chiseler"; that is, he was getting paid for work he did not do. (p. 235)

The Economic Person Versus the Social Person

The four basic principles of interaction in groups—pleasure, rationality, reciprocity, and fairness—contain some obvious (and fortunate) contradictions. People calculate their individual gain and loss in interactions; they act according to their own interests in many situations. Does this mean that people will always act selfishly? Not always, for we have seen that people also have deeply ingrained notions of reciprocity and fairness, which often prompt them to act in favor of the needs of the group or of society as a whole. Indeed, many situations that arise in the social world demonstrate the "war of all against all" that would be created in a society whose members always acted in what they perceive as their self-interest.

Consider this example. It's the Friday evening rush hour. The streets downtown are crowded with cars, their drivers eager to get home. Although the light is about to turn red, some drivers move their cars into the intersection. They expect the traffic ahead of them to move forward so that they will be clear of oncoming traffic from the cross street. But alas, the traffic ahead does not move and the intersection is blocked. Now the cars on the cross street have a green light, but they cannot move. Fearing that they will miss their first opportunity to move, and amid much horn blowing and gnashing of teeth, some of these drivers also squeeze into the intersection. This chaotic and frustrating situation is known as "gridlock." It is the result of a number of drivers acting in what they perceive as their own interests and not thinking about the needs of all the drivers as a group. The gridlock example is one among many that could be cited in which it is actually advantageous for individuals to behave in a prosocial manner rather than attempt to maximize their

Taxi Gridlock, by Red Grooms, 2000, enamel on epoxy, 39³/₄ × 31 × 6 inches. Each taxi driver wants to collect as many fares as possible, which means moving as quickly as possible, even pushing into intersections when the traffic signals are changing. But as they attempt to maximize their individual advantage, they create a gridlock situation in which everyone actually does worse because so much time is lost.

immediate advantage (Hechter & Kanazawa, 1997; Sen, 1997; Shotland, 1985).

Situations like gridlock are made worse by problems of communication among individuals in groups. When people can freely share information about what they are experiencing, and when they trust each other's communications, positive outcomes are more likely than when information is not shared or communication is thwarted. It is not surprising, therefore, that communication and behavior in groups is an active area of sociological research.

Communication and Behavior in Groups

"Human interaction," Herbert Blumer observed, "is mediated by the use of symbols, by interpretations, or by ascertaining the meaning of one another's actions" (1969b, pp. 179–180). By "mediated" Blumer meant that we do not normally respond directly to the actions of another person. Instead, we react to our own interpretations of those actions. When we see other drivers moving into an intersection against the light, for example, we begin to feel that everyone is out for themselves and we would be fools to hold back. These interpretations are made in the interval between the stimulus (the other person's action) and the response (our own action). Thus, in the account at the beginning of the chapter, the gang member must frequently decide whether her honor is being attacked or, perhaps more important, whether her gang sisters and family members will demand that she defend her honor. Her decision to fight or not to fight will be guided by her interpretation and by her need to gain standing in the eyes of her peers.

What factors explain how people decide how to act and whether they should act for their own benefit or according to some notion of what is good for society? This question has been the subject of much research in the social sciences. Let us therefore take a brief look at some research on how people define their needs in social situations.

DEFINITIONS OF THE SITUATION "Situations we define as real, are real in their consequences" stated W. I. Thomas (1971/1921), a pioneer in the study of social interaction. By this he meant that our understandings or definitions of what is occurring around us—whether they are correct or not—guide our subsequent actions. Thus, in a study of how dying patients are treated by medical groups in hospital emergency rooms, David Sudnow (1967) found that when a patient was brought in with no heartbeat, the person's age had a great deal to do with what happened next. The arrival of a younger patient who seemed to be dying would produce a frenzy of attempts to restart the heart. At times the entire group of medical personnel would become involved. But an old person with no heartbeat was far more likely to be pronounced dead on arrival, with little or no mobilization of the medical group. The patient's aged appearance caused the members of the group to define the situation as one in which urgent and heroic efforts were not required.

In another study of medical groups, Charles Bosk (1979) found that surgeons developed subtle techniques for covering up the mistakes of residents in training, depending on how a particular situation was defined. They would invoke those techniques when they believed that a mistake was caused by lack of knowledge. But mistakes that they believed to be caused by carelessness would often be exposed. The guilty resident would be held up to public scorn, often at a high cost to the new surgeon's status among other doctors.

Both of the foregoing studies began by questioning how definitions of the situation account for the ways in which people interact. The emergency room teams that Sudnow observed were performing an unofficial cost–benefit analysis in deciding when to apply heroic measures to heart attack victims. The surgeons in Bosk's study were resolving a conflict between their teaching and medical functions: Young surgeons need to learn and practice, but patients need to receive the best possible care. The surgeon in training needs to maintain a good reputation among other doctors and nurses, even if he or she makes mistakes. Such conflicts are resolved by norms that define the legitimacy of mistakes in different situations.

As these examples show, the subtle cues that define each situation are communicated through phrases, gestures, and other symbolic behavior, as well as through explicit evaluations of what was good and bad about a particular operation. Several subfields of sociology and psychology study the intricacies of this micro-world of human interaction. Among the most powerful of these are ethnomethodology and the dramaturgical approach.

ETHNOMETHODOLOGY   Studies based on the interactionist perspective use a variety of techniques. One of these is **ethnomethodology,** the study of the underlying rules of behavior that guide group interaction. This approach was used by Harold Garfinkel (1967) in a classic series of studies of how we use verbal formulas to create a flow of communication that we feel is normal and that we can understand. Garfinkel asked his students to engage in conversations with friends and family members in which they violated some of the simple norms that most people follow in carrying on a conversation. Here is an example:

> **Victim:** [*waving cheerily*] How are you?
> **Student:** How am I in regard to what? My health, my finances, my schoolwork, my peace of mind, my . . . ?
> **Victim:** [*red in the face and suddenly out of control*] Look! I was just trying to be polite. Frankly, I don't give a damn how you are. (Garfinkel, 1967, p. 44)

As this brief example shows, when the norms of spoken interaction that "entitle" us to continue or maintain a conversation are violated, the conversation often cannot continue because there is no longer a mutual area of interaction within which both parties tacitly agree to make sense.

Such "experiments" reveal the taken-for-granted rules of interaction. For Garfinkel (1991), they show that social order is in fact the result of interactions in which people strive to create coherence, consistency, order, and meaning in their ordinary lives. Garfinkel's analysis of the case of Agnes is another important example of the contributions of ethnomethodology to our understanding of social behavior at the micro level.

Agnes participated in Garfinkel's research because she wanted to understand herself better and share her experience in life with professional researchers. Outwardly she was a woman; however, she had a penis, which she thought of as a mistake of biology. As a child she had suffered because her parents insisted on socializing her as a boy and required

her to play boys' sports. In her deepest feelings, however, she knew that she was a girl, and when during puberty she developed breasts, this new biological fact confirmed her beliefs about herself. You may be wondering what this has to do with how we behave in groups. Garfinkel noted that Agnes's gender, as opposed to her sex, was based on her feelings and behaviors, especially her choice of female friends, all of which Agnes viewed as "natural facts" but according to Garfinkel were also *social performances* that established her gender in the groups she joined (Garfinkel, 2000).

By recognizing that most roles, not just those of boy or girl, are performances, you will expand your sociological imagination. People often feel that when someone they know acts out a new role, they are being untrue to their original identity, or "phony." But even the most modest star athlete learns to perform as a star off the field because that is what many groups in the school and the community expect; and it is not easy to remain modest in this new role. Similarly, in interactions with others, the computer wizard learns to be a "computer nerd"; the homecoming queen adopts a socially defined way of behaving that she may adapt to her own personality but that she also borrows from others. We don't always realize the extent to which our behaviors in society are performances. Ethnomethodology helps us go beyond the limited notion of "phoniness" to see how we borrow many of our routines from the behaviors of others in groups of various kinds.

THE DRAMATURGICAL APPROACH   Another technique used in research on interaction in groups is the **dramaturgical approach.** This approach is based on the recognition that much social interaction depends on how we wish to impress those who may be watching us. For example, Erving Goffman (1965) observed that people change their facial expressions just before entering a room in which they expect to find others who will greet them. Couples who are fighting when they are "backstage" often present themselves as models of friendship when they are "frontstage"— that is, in the presence of other people. And many social environments, such as hotels, restaurants, and funeral parlors, are explicitly set up with a front and a back "stage" so that the public is spared the noisy and sometimes conflicted interaction occurring "behind the scenes." Using these and other strategies to "set a stage" for our own purposes is known as **impression management.**

In a well-known study that applied this dramaturgical view of group interaction, James Henslin and Mae Briggs (1971) drew upon Briggs's extensive experience as a gynecological nurse at a time when most gynecologists were men. Their research showed how doctors and nurses play roles that define the situation of a pelvic examination as unembarrassing and attempt to save each participant's "face," or self-image. According to Henslin and Briggs, the pelvic examination is carried out in a series of scenes. First the doctor and the patient discuss the patient's condition. If the doctor decides that the patient needs a pelvic examination, the doctor will leave the room; this is the end of scene 1. In scene 2 the nurse enters. Her role is to work with the patient to create a situation in which the body of the patient is hidden behind sheets and her depersonalized pelvic area is exposed for clinical inspection. Through these preparations, the patient becomes symbolically distanced from the doctor, allowing the next scene, the pelvic examination itself, to be desexualized. The props, the stage setting (the examining room), and the language used help define the situation as a nonsexual encounter, thereby saving everyone involved from embarrassment.

ALTRUISM AND THE BYSTANDER EFFECT Intentional efforts to set a stage for purposes of impression management are common in hospitals, restaurants, and many other social settings where patterns of behavior are predictable and regular. But in other public settings, especially streets, parks, and public transportation, people often try to hide behind their anonymity. They shy away from behavior that will be noticed, as illustrated in the following example of the *bystander effect.*

Late one night in 1964, Kitty Genovese was returning home from a social gathering when she was attacked by a man who had been following her. He caught up with her in front of a bookstore in the shadow of her apartment building. As she screamed for help, he stabbed her in the chest. Lights went on in some of the apartments, but no one intervened or called the police. One neighbor shouted from a window: "Let that girl alone." The stalker retreated and waited, and when the neighbor no longer seemed to be watching, he resumed his attack. He raped and stabbed the young woman to death in a stairwell of her apartment house, but the police did not receive a call for help from any of her neighbors until 30 minutes after she had first cried out. Interviewed later, the neighbors said things like "I was tired" or "I assumed others were helping" or "Frankly, we were afraid."

This incident is often cited to illustrate the callousness and indifference of urban dwellers (Frank, 1988). It might seem from this and similar incidents that when faced with danger and other costs of helping (e.g., time in court, dealing with the police, loss of time from work), people make fairly selfish calculations of gain and loss. But what about all the unselfish acts of heroism one reads about? Victims are dragged from fires and submerged cars and broken ice by self-sacrificing civilians, many of whom die in their efforts to help others. Did Kitty Genovese simply have a bad group of neighbors? Empirical evidence suggests that the situation is more complicated than that (Batson, Batson, & Todd, 1995).

Studies by Bibb Latané and John Darley (1970) have shown under many experimental conditions that bystanders are likely to offer help to victims. But their research also shows that the presence of other people who do not help increases the chances that no one will help. In one simple experiment, a graduate student begins interviewing the subject. The interviewer excuses himself or herself for a moment and enters an adjacent room. Suddenly the waiting subject hears cries for help: "Oh my God, my foot . . . I . . . I can't get this thing off!" In about 70 percent of the trials, the subject rushes into the room and offers help. But when there is another person in the first room who just sits there and seems to be associated with the experimenter in some way, only 7 percent of the subjects intervene to help the "victim."

In the experiment just described, the helper can see that no one else has offered help. In the Kitty Genovese case, however, people could conveniently assume that others must be helping. The point is that when responsibility seems to be diffused rather than falling on a particular individual, people are more likely to avoid helping others. But when people cannot avoid defining the situation as involving them, they are likely to throw the rationality principle to the winds and intervene altruistically despite the potential costs to themselves (Deaux & Wrightsman, 1988; McIntyre, 1995).

Interaction and Group Structure

The examples just discussed involve decisions and strategies that individuals use in deciding whether to behave more selfishly or more altruistically in a given situation. As members of groups, however, we often explain our actions on the basis of our status in the group rather than on the basis of our individual expectations. "I must do this because I'm expected to lead," we might say, or "I can't decide that without talking to the others and especially to [the group's leader]." These explanations suggest that the structure of groups is a major factor in explaining behavior. But the basic principles of interaction—pleasure seeking, rationality, reciprocity, and fairness—can be used to explain the emergence of group structure in the first place (Beebe, 1997; Pillari, 1998). In an early and now famous series of experiments, sociologist George Homans and others provided scientifically verifiable data on the emergence of group structure through interactions.

The procedure is as follows. Six college students of the same sex are hired to participate in a small-group experiment. All are unknown to one another before the experiment. The specific task they are asked to perform is of little importance except that it must involve all the members

TABLE 6.1

Aggregate Matrix for 18 Sessions of Six-Man Groups

		Initiated to Individuals					Total to Individuals	To Group as Whole	Total Initiated
	1	**2**	**3**	**4**	**5**	**6**			
1		1,238	961	545	445	317	3,506	5,661	9,167
2	1,748		443	310	175	102	2,778	1,211	3,989
3	1,371	415		305	125	69	2,285	742	3,027
4	952	310	282		83	49	1,676	676	2,352
5	662	224	144	83		28	1,141	443	1,584
6	470	126	114	65	44		819	373	1,192
Total Received	5,203	2,313	1,944	1,306	872	565	12,205	9,106	21,311

(Left side label for rows 1–6: **From Individuals**)

Note: Differences between the total number of interactions initiated and the number received result from the fact that some utterances are answered indirectly by means of utterances directed at the entire group. The diagonal cells are empty because the experiments did not count utterances by a subject to himself.

Source: *Social Behavior,* by George Caspar Homans. Copyright © 1961 by Harcourt Brace Jovanovich, Inc. Reprinted by permission of Wadsworth.

of the group in a cooperative effort and must not be so difficult that they become frustrated or so easy that they become bored.

Initially the group has no structure. All the subjects are peers, and all have come for the same reason: to earn some money for participating in the experiment. There are no predetermined statuses or roles. The students listen to a description of what they are to do and then are left alone to get the work under way. Actually they are being observed through a one-way mirror, and all their interactions are being recorded and counted.

Table 6.1 summarizes (or *aggregates*) the data obtained by counting all the interactions—including small utterances like "Oh" and "I see"—occurring in a group of six male subjects meeting for 18 one-hour sessions. This table shows who initiated each interaction and to whom it was directed, including interactions directed toward the group as a whole. The participants are ranked from high to low on this variable (i.e., initiating an interaction). Thus subject 1 spoke 1,238 times to subject 2, spoke 961 times to subject 3, and so on (Homans, 1961). Subject 1 initiated 3,506 utterances to specific individuals (e.g., "Why don't you . . . ?") and 5,661 utterances to the group as a whole (e.g., "Why don't we . . . ?"), for a total of 9,167 utterances over all the sessions—more than any of the other participants. You can see that subject 6 spoke only about one-ninth as often as subject 1 and that most of what he said was directed to subject 1 (470 utterances). In fact, subject 1 received the most interaction from all the other participants, illustrating that people who initiate interactions are more likely to receive them. In later interviews, the exper-

imenters also found that subject 1 was the most respected member of the group.

THE EMERGENCE OF GROUP LEADERS   What makes the person who initiates and receives the most communications the most respected member of the group? The reasons vary with the specific tasks the group is performing, but if we assume competence at those tasks, usually the person at the center of the communication is spending a lot of time helping others as well as helping the group accomplish its goals. That person not only is concerned with his or her own performance (the rationality principle) but also takes pleasure in helping the others—giving approval, voicing criticism, making suggestions, and so on (the pleasure principle). In exchange for this help, the other members of the group give approval, respect, and allegiance to the central individual (the reciprocity principle).

Is the person who initiates the most interactions respected simply because he or she talks a lot? Common sense tells us that this is far from true. People who talk a lot but have little to contribute soon find that no one is paying attention to them. Their rate of interaction then drops sharply. Table 6.1 cannot show such changes in interaction patterns, but they are often observed in small-group studies. Other patterns have also been identified. Robert F. Bales and Philip Slater (1955), for example, observed that the person who initiated the most interactions—both in getting tasks done and in supporting the suggestions of others—often came to be thought of as a leader. The group began to orient itself toward that person and to expect leadership from him or her. A second member of the group, usually the one who initiated the second-highest number of interactions, was often the best-liked person in the group.

Bales and his colleagues concluded that groups often develop both a "task leader" (or instrumental leader) and another leader, whom they called a "socioemotional leader" (or expressive leader). The former tends to adhere to group norms and to take the lead in urging everyone to get the work done, but this often leaves other members with ruffled feelings. The socioemotional leader is the person who eases the group over rough spots with jokes, encouragement, and attention to the group's emotional climate. Thus most classes have a class clown whose antics help release the tension of test situations, and most teams have a respected member who can also joke around and get people to relax under pressure. At times these roles are performed by the same person, but generally as the group settles into a given task there is an informal division of labor between the two kinds of leaders (Beebe, 1997).

Recall the Bank Wiring Room observations mentioned earlier. The workers at the equipment wiring tables are an example of small-group structure. Their leader was the person who could turn out the most work in the shortest time and could also help the others do their work. The workers with higher status in the group were those who showed greater competence at their jobs and stronger allegiance to the norms of the group. Newer workers with lesser skills and less shared experience with the others were spoken to less and were less central to the group's interactions. Over time, as these workers were "binged" for producing too little or too much, the other workers would see how they handled the criticism and would form opinions of them accordingly.

EFFECTS OF GROUP SIZE   One of the most striking aspects of the Hawthorne studies is that they revealed how norms about fairness in the work group are enforced through a particular kind of joking ritual (binging). But why are workers binged when they produce too much? That behavior points to the conflict between the norms of the small work group (which are based on fairness) and those of the larger corporation in which the group is embedded (which are based on rationality). The company would like to obtain greater productivity from the workers, but the workers have their own ideas about what is fair and their own ways of enforcing the group norm.

This example brings us to the principle that as group size increases, or as the number of groups in an organization increases, the leaders of the larger organization must invest in ways of controlling the behavior of groups within it (Hechter, 1987). This investment often takes the form of agents of control such as foremen, accountants, inspectors, and the like. These roles become part of the formal structure known as bureaucracy.

FORMAL ORGANIZATIONS AND BUREAUCRACY

Informal organizations are groups whose norms and statuses are generally agreed upon but are not set down in writing. The Bank Wiring Room observations are a classic example of the dynamics of informal organizations. The members of the work groups in the wiring room followed group norms that limited their output. Usually such groups have leaders who help create and enforce the group's norms but have no formal leadership position in the company.

Formal organizations have explicit (often written) sets of norms, statuses, and roles that specify each member's relationships to the others and the conditions under which those relationships hold. Organization charts and job descriptions are typical of such organizations. Formal organizations take a wide variety of forms. For example, the New England town meeting is composed of residents of a town who gather to debate and discuss any issues the members wish to raise. The tenants' association of an urban apartment building is also composed of people who reside in a specific place, but its scope of action is usually limited to housing issues. Both of these are formal organizations because there are rules defining who may participate and the scope and manner of that participation. As is true in many formal organizations, the members of town meetings and tenants' associations try to arrive at decisions through some form of democratic process—that is, by adhering to norms that allow the majority to run the organization but not to infringe on the rights of the minority.

VOLUNTARY ASSOCIATIONS   A familiar type of formal organization is the **voluntary association**. People join groups like the PTA or the Rotary Club to pursue interests they share with other members of the group. Voluntary associations are usually democratically run, at least in principle, and have rules and regulations and an administrative staff. Churches, fraternal organizations, political clubs, and neighborhood improvement groups are examples of voluntary associations often found in American communities. Sociologists study these associations in order to understand how well or poorly people are integrated into their society.

BUREAUCRACIES   Bureaucracies are another common type of formal organization. A **bureaucracy** is a specific structure of statuses and roles in which the power to influence the actions of others increases as one nears the top of the organization; this is in marked contrast to the democratic procedures used in other kinds of organizations. Voluntary associations, for example, usually have some of the elements of bureaucracies, but they are run as democratic

CHARACTERISTICS OF BUREAUCRACY

CHARACTERISTIC	EXAMPLE
Positions Clearly Defined	Job or position descriptions detail the responsibilities of each job, avoiding confusion about the duties of each jobholder.
Positions Ordered in a Hierarchy	Positions in the company or agency are ranked from top to bottom so that each position reports to another and supervisory responsibilities are clear.
Rules and Precedents	"The way we do things" in an organization is often written down, becoming "the book" of rules to be followed by its members.
Impersonality and Impartiality	At least in principle, actual performance on the job, rather than personal likes or favors, determines each individual's performance rating.
Career Ladder	New jobs are posted so that employees have a chance to move up in the organization on the basis of achievement, seniority, or both.
Norm of Efficiency	The company continually seeks to increase its efficiency by increasing productivity per employee; this can lead to layoffs or downsizing.

structures in which power is based on majority rule rather than on executive orders as is the case in pure bureaucracies like General Motors or the U.S. Army.

We owe much of our understanding of bureaucracies to the work of Max Weber, who identified the following typical aspects of most bureaucratic organizations:

1. *Positions with clearly defined responsibilities:* "The regular activities required for the purposes of the organization are distributed in a fixed way as official duties."

2. *Positions ordered in a hierarchy:* The organization of offices "follows the principle of hierarchy; that is, each lower office is under the control and supervision of a higher one."

3. *Rules and precedents:* The functioning of the bureaucracy is governed "by a consistent system of abstract rules" and the "application of these rules to specific cases."

4. *Impersonality and impartiality:* "The ideal official conducts his office . . . in a spirit of formalistic impersonality . . . without hatred or passion, and hence without affection or enthusiasm."

5. *A career ladder:* Work in a bureaucracy "constitutes a career. There is a system of 'promotions' according to seniority, or to achievement, or both."

6. *The norm of efficiency:* "The purely bureaucratic type of administrative organization . . . is from a purely technical point of view, capable of attaining the highest degree of efficiency" (Weber, 1958/1922). (See the Study Chart above.)

Weber believed that bureaucracy made human social life more "rational" than it had ever been in the past. Rules, impersonality, and the norm of efficiency are some of the ways in which bureaucracies "rationalize" human societies. By this Weber meant that society becomes dominated by groups organized so that the interactions of their members will maximize the group's efficiency. Once the group's goals have been set, the officials in a bureaucracy can seek the most efficient means of reaching those goals. All the less rational behaviors of human groups, such as magic and ritual, are avoided by groups organized as bureaucracies. But the people in a bureaucracy may not take full responsibility for their actions. For this and other reasons, therefore, Weber had some misgivings about the consequences of the increasing dominance of bureaucratic groups in modern societies.

Bureaucracy and Obedience to Authority

In Chapter 2 we discussed the experiments on conformity conducted by Solomon Asch. Asch's demonstration of the power of group pressure raised serious questions about most people's ability to resist such pressure. It also led to many other studies of conformity. None of those studies is more powerful in its implications and disturbing in its methods than the series of experiments on obedience to authority conducted by Stanley Milgram.

Milgram's study was designed to "take a close look at the act of obeying." As Milgram described it:

> Two people come to a psychology laboratory to take part in a study of memory and learning. One of them is designated as a "teacher" and the other as a "learner."
>
> The experimenter explains that the study is concerned with the effects of punishment on learning. The learner is conducted into a room, seated in a chair, his arms strapped to prevent excessive movement, and an electrode is attached to his wrist. He is told that he is to learn a list of word pairs; whenever he makes an error, he will receive electric shocks of increasing intensity.
>
> The real focus of the experiment is the teacher. After watching the learner being strapped into place, he is taken into the main experimental room and seated before an impressive shock generator. Its main feature is a horizontal line of 30 switches, ranging from 15 volts to 450 volts, in 15-volt increments. There are also verbal designations which range from SLIGHT SHOCK to DANGER— SEVERE SHOCK. The teacher is told that he is to administer the learning test to the man in the other room. When the learner responds correctly, the teacher moves on to the next item; when the other man gives an incorrect answer, the teacher is to give him an electric shock. He is to start at the lowest shock level (15 volts) and to increase the level each time the man makes an error, going through 30 volts, 45 volts, and so on. (1974, pp. 3–4)

The "learner" is an actor who pretends to suffer pain but receives no actual shock. The subject ("teacher") is a businessperson or an industrial worker or a student, someone who has been recruited by a classified ad offering payment for spare-time work in a university laboratory.

Milgram was dismayed to discover that many of his subjects were willing to obey any order given by the experimenter. In the basic version of the experiment, in which the "learner" is in one room and the "teacher" in another from which the "learner" is visible but cannot be heard, 65 percent of the subjects administered the highest levels of shock, while the other 35 percent were obedient well into the "intense shock" levels.

Milgram used a functionalist argument to explain the high levels of obedience revealed in his experiment: In bureaucratic organizations, people seek approval by adhering to the rules, which often absolve them of moral responsibility for their actions. But he also explored the conditions under which conflict will take place—that is, the conditions under which the subject will rebel against the experimenter. In situations in which subjects are forced to confront the consequences of their behavior, their ability to rely on

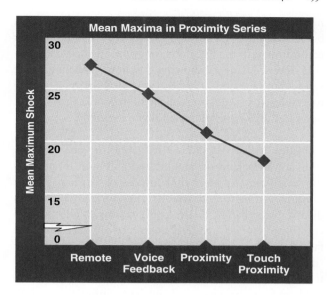

Figure 6.3 Mean Maximum Shocks in Four Variants of Milgram's Experiment

This graph illustrates the relationship between the maximum shocks administered and the four variants of proximity between the "teacher" and the "learner" in Milgram's experiment. The variants were: (1) remote (different rooms, in which the leaner could be seen but not heard); (2) voice feedback (different rooms, in which the learner could be seen and heard); (3) proximity (both in the same room); and (4) touch proximity (both in the same room, in which the teacher was told to force the learner's hand onto the electrode).

Source: *Obedience to Authority,* by Stanley Milgram. Copyright © 1974 by Stanley Milgram.

"duty" to justify that behavior seems to be diminished. This effect is presented in graphic form in Figure 6.3.

When Milgram published the results of these experiments, he was criticized for deceiving his subjects and, in some cases, causing them undue stress. The controversy created by this study was one of the factors leading to the establishment of rules to protect human subjects in social-scientific research (see Chapter 2).

Commitment to Bureaucratic Groups

Another question related to the impact of bureaucracy on individuals is how bureaucratic groups—which are based on unemotional and "rational" systems of recruitment, decision making, and reward—can sometimes attract strong commitment from their members. One possible answer is ideology: People believe in the goals and methods of the bureaucracy. Another explanation is that people within a bureaucracy form primary groups that maintain their commitment to the larger organization. There is considerable research evidence showing that both explanations are valid—both ideology and primary-group ties may operate to reinforce people's commitment to the organization. Several studies have addressed this question.

PRIMARY GROUPS IN BUREAUCRACIES   In one of those studies, Morris Janowitz and Edward Shils were assigned by the U.S. Army to study the attitudes of German soldiers captured during World War II. They were attempting to discover what had made the German army so effective and committed that isolated units continued to fight even in the face of certain defeat. As Shils explained it, he and Janowitz "discovered the influence of small, closely knit groups on the conduct of their members in the performance of tasks set them from the outside" (Janowitz & Shils, 1948, p. 48).

The soldiers of the German army behaved in this way not because of their ideological commitment to the Nazi cause but because of their loyalty to small combat units whose members had become so devoted to each other that to continue to fight even in the face of defeat, so as not to be dishonored as a group, seemed the only possible course of action. The close primary-group structure of the German army was one of the secrets of its success. The other was an extremely efficient organization. Ideology figured very little in its effectiveness.

IDEOLOGICAL PRIMARY GROUPS   Primary groups would seem to have no place in a "pure" bureaucracy, yet the study just cited, together with the Hawthorne experiments and other empirical studies, shows that no bureaucracy completely eliminates primary groups. In the case of the German army, it appears that the development of primary groups among combat troops increased the effectiveness of the organization as a whole. Another important study of this subject was Philip Selznick's (1952) analysis of what made the Bolsheviks so effective that they won out in the fierce competition for political dominance in Russia. Selznick's data show that the ideologically based primary group was the key element in the Bolsheviks' organization. Small, secret "cells" of devoted communists were organized in neighborhoods, factories, army units, farms, and universities. Through years of tense and often dangerous political activity, the members became extremely devoted to each other and to their revolutionary cause. According to Selznick, this doubling of ideological and primary-group cohesion made the Bolsheviks themselves an "organizational weapon."

In the contemporary world, we see many examples of ideological groups with extremely high levels of cohesion. These groups are often devoted to the leadership and teachings of a forceful and highly attractive leader whose ideas exert a powerful influence over the behavior of the group's members. We often focus on the extremes of such behavior, such as the suicidal terrorism of the Al Qaeda network or the mass suicide by the members of Heaven's Gate, but many ideological groups can have beneficial effects on their members. This is especially true of groups devoted to personal or spiritual growth and positive behavior change. Indeed, the ability of people to form groups freely and to leave them if they so desire is one of the distinguishing features of societies in which the rule of law protects the individual's right of association. A problem of some ideological groups, however, is that they may not grant their members this freedom (Elshtain, 1997).

GROUPS IN COMPLEX SOCIETIES

As we saw in Chapter 4, in simpler tribal or peasant societies all social structures are primary groups. The tribal village is usually so small that everyone knows everyone else. The family, the extended family, the age- and sex-segregated peer groups, and even the village itself all allow for everyone to know everyone else and to interact on an almost daily basis. Typically these societies lack a secondary-group level of life. In traditional peasant societies, for example, no associations existed to bring soldiers or farmers or artisans together in groups that extended beyond the limited bounds of the village. Yet that level of social life is what makes contemporary societies so efficient.

The differences between simpler and more complex societies can also make interactions among members of those societies confusing and frustrating (see the Global Social Change box on page 161. For example, when they were first assigned to peasant villages in Africa and Asia, American Peace Corps volunteers were unprepared to cope with situations in which villagers came to them with requests for money or help with marital and family problems. For the young Americans, such requests were appropriate only among members of primary groups—and the villagers did not know how to engage in interactions that are typical of secondary groups (Luce, 1964).

Effects of Bureaucratization

In his most famous theoretical work, *The Division of Labor in Society* (1964/1893), Émile Durkheim reasoned that as a society becomes larger and more complex, there is a vast increase in interdependence among its members as the

GLOBAL SOCIAL CHANGE

Communication and Interaction

Global social change continually produces waves of refugees and immigrants. For example, the new freedom to travel in the former Soviet satellite nations has produced thousands of ambitious immigrants. Civil strife in Central and Latin America, repression in some Asian societies (e.g., China and North and South Korea), growing poverty in the Philippines and Albania, and continuing turmoil in Cambodia and the Middle East have pushed families and individuals out of their homes and into the growing tide of worldwide migration. All of these changes are having profound effects on the linguistic diversity of North America and on how people in the Americas communicate and interact.

The United States continues to hold a global reputation as a place where immigrants can work to achieve success—and since it remains the nation with the most liberal immigration policies, it is no surprise that more than 500,000 legal immigrants and refugees (and an untold number of illegal entrants) seek to establish themselves in the "golden land" each year. In California alone, during the 1990s about 3.4 million immigrants brought their languages and cultural norms to the nation's most diverse state. But no part of the nation missed the increases in cultural and linguistic diversity that result from immigration. Between 1990 and 2000, for example, the number of foreign-language speakers in the state of Georgia (not known as a primary destination of immigrants) increased from 285,000 to 696,000. All told, by 2000 more than 45 million residents of the United States did not speak English in their homes (U.S. Census Bureau, 2000).

The need for English as a second language (ESL) courses in schools and community centers throughout the nation is only one indication of the kinds of demands increased linguistic diversity is placing on communities where immigration rates are high. In time most Americans come to appreciate the diversity of languages spoken in the United States as a great cultural resource. But the welter of different languages spoken in some communities can also be a source of conflict. The extreme rapidity of the change has created numerous controversies over how, and more specifically in what language, people should be expected to interact. For example, in 1989 a federal judge ruled that the Los Angeles suburb of Pomona had violated the civil rights of Korean and Chinese businesspeople by requiring them to place English signs on their shops. In the same community, however, Filipino nurses lost a suit against a hospital that would not allow them to speak their native language, Tagalog, among themselves at work.

Elsewhere in the nation, there is an active movement to make English the "official" language of the United States. This is accompanied by a crusade against the offering of bilingual education for children from other language groups. The problems of interaction across linguistic divides are greatest in states with large proportions of foreign-language speakers, such as New Mexico (37 percent), California (40 percent), Texas (32 percent), Hawaii (28 percent), and New York (29 percent). Conversely, these states benefit the most from the wealth of new phrases and styles of communication stemming from their growing linguistic diversity.

---

labor needed to feed, house, educate, communicate with, transport, care for, and defend them becomes more complex. Faced with more choices regarding what work to prepare for, whom to interact with, and how to live life, the individual gains much more freedom than is available to a member of a simpler society, who (for better or worse) is confined to a narrow set of village primary groups. But Durkheim also saw that the modern person could be overwhelmed by the choices open to him or her and might find it difficult to decide what groups to join and what norms to conform to.

Max Weber shared Durkheim's concern about the prospects for human happiness in the modern world. According to Weber (1958/1922), the fundamental paradox of modern society was the rise of bureaucracies, which greatly expanded the efficiency and rationality of society but "disenchanted the world." He meant that the modern formal organization, which is so effective in science, the military, the state (government), economic production, and almost every other aspect of modern life, at the same time deprives human life of a sense of magic and spirituality. The rise of fundamentalist movements in the Islamic world, for example, is in part a reaction against the influence of bureaucratic rationality in the institutions of secular states such as Egypt and Algeria.

Even in Western societies, where the process of bureaucratization is extremely advanced, people may feel overwhelmed by bureaucracy. The individual often feels like a tiny cog in a huge set of interlocking organizations. He or she fills specific statuses and enacts clearly defined roles yet feels more and more oppressed. Weber deplored the type of person that he felt was produced by the organizations of modern society: "a petty routine creature, lacking in heroism, human spontaneity, and inventiveness" (Weber, 1922, in Gerth & Mills, 1958, p. 50). In the United States, however, democracy was always linked with citizens' freedom of association and their tendency to join groups that could protect them against the excesses of

THEN AND NOW   From Haymarket Square to Waco

Although they occurred almost a century apart, the bombing in Chicago's Haymarket Square in 1886 and the

and 3 bystanders and wounding at least 100 others. Authorities immediately blamed the anarchists and their

The followers of David Koresh, known as the Branch Davidians, were a dedicated religious group, with little concern for destroying capitalism but firm ideas about the need to live a highly spiritual life apart from what they perceived as a corrupt society. They believed that they needed to arm themselves against a hostile world. Accusations of child abuse and felonies by their leader only confirmed the group's fears and desire to protect themselves. A long and sensational armed standoff between federal law enforcement agencies and the Branch

© Corbis

tragic assault and fire at Waco, Texas, in 1993 reveal many similarities in the way radical groups and agencies of the state become enmeshed in situations that lead to tragedy. The Haymarket bombing took place during a demonstration calling for an 8-hour workday held by a small, intensely cohesive group of committed anarchists, most of whom were immigrants from Europe, especially Germany. The anarchists were devoted to the destruction of the capitalist system of production and private property in the United States and elsewhere. Their leaders, including Albert Parsons, were speaking at the rally when Chicago police began forcing them to disperse. A bomb was thrown into the crowd, killing 7 police officers

AP/Wide World Photos

followers for the explosion, and their leaders were jailed. Four were hanged; one committed suicide. But their guilt was never well established, and after intense lobbying by labor groups and civil rights activists, Illinois Governor John Peter Altgeld pardoned the remaining anarchists in 1893.

Davidians ended in gunfire and the deadly fire pictured here. The Waco tragedy, like the Haymarket bombing, became symbolic both of the excesses of ideologically motivated and isolated extremist groups and of the blundering authoritarianism of law enforcement agencies (Niebuhr, 1995).

large bureaucracies, on the one hand, and offer them the intimacy of small-group sociability, on the other.

A Nation of Joiners

Early in the nineteenth century, the French aristocrat and social theorist Alexis de Tocqueville visited the United States. Like other European intellectuals, he considered the new nation a bold and controversial social experiment. He had doubts about the capacity of common people to govern themselves without the guiding hand of a strong aris-

tocracy. As he traveled through the former colonies, however, he was pleasantly surprised by what he observed. He was particularly impressed by the number of associations and small groups to which people belonged. Americans, he wrote, are "a nation of joiners" (1956/1840).

This phrase is often quoted in descriptions of democratic societies. Democratic theory states that when people are given the freedom to associate with whomever they choose, they will form a complex civil society—that is, a society characterized by a never-ending and always changing array of freely formed nongovernmental groups (see Chapter 8). In fact, as we will see in later chapters, dicta-

TABLE 6.2

Groups in the United States

	Estimated Numbers	
	Members	Groups
Sunday school classes	18–22 million	800,000
Bible study groups	15–20 million	900,000
Self-help groups	8–10 million	500,000
Special interest groups		
Political/current events	5–10 million	250,000
Book/discussion groups	5–10 million	250,000
Sports/hobby groups	5–10 million	250,000

Source: Reprinted with the permission of The Free Press, a division of Simon and Schuster Adult Publishing Group, from *Sharing the journey: Support groups and America's new quest for community* by Robert Wuthnow. Copyright © 1994 by Robert Wuthnow. All rights reserved.

tors who wish to curtail individual freedom invariably attempt to control the groups people can belong to.

The number of voluntary associations in the United States and other democratic nations has increased steadily since de Tocqueville's day. But what kinds of groups are people forming? What needs are they seeking to satisfy through their group interactions? A study by sociologist Robert Wuthnow directly addresses these questions. Wuthnow's findings, described in his book *Sharing the Journey* (1994), are based on a large survey carried out by the Gallup Poll in which respondents were asked about their group affiliations and the benefits they derived from them. Table 6.2 presents

Wuthnow's estimates of the major types of groups to which people in the United States belong. Religious groups engaging in Bible study and Sunday school classes are by far the largest category; self-help groups in which people attempt to resocialize themselves, to replace old and often destructive patterns of behavior with new and more desirable ones, are the second largest category.

Wuthnow's study revealed that people who join small groups are owning up to a deeply felt need to be part of a face-to-face primary group in which they attain a sense of community with others. Table 6.3 shows that there are often wide gaps between people's needs and the ability of group interactions to actually satisfy those needs. But these gaps do not seem to produce widespread disillusionment. In their search for a feeling of belonging and community, people continue to join groups of all kinds.

CRITICAL SOCIOLOGY AND SOCIAL CHANGE

Performance Expectations, Racial Groups, and Poverty Levels

Much of the research on interaction in groups has stemmed from theories about expectations, categorization, and inequality. One example is Penni Stewart and James Moore, Jr.'s "Wage Disparities and Performance Expectations" (1992), which provided evidence that income differences affect how one subjectively evaluates

Text continues on page 166.

TABLE 6.3

Meeting the Need for Community (percentage of group members who have [A] felt each need and [B] met each need fully)

	A	B
Having neighbors with whom you can interact freely and comfortably	93	43
Being able to share deepest feelings with someone	94	57
Having friends who value the same things in life you do	98	58
Having people in your life who give you deep emotional support	98	66
Being in a group where you can discuss your most basic beliefs and values	90	50
Having friends you can always count on when you're in a jam	97	64
Having people in your life who are never critical of you	83	29
Being part of a group that helps you grow spiritually	90	53
Having cooperation rather than competition with people at work	85	31
Having people you can turn to when you feel depressed or lonely	96	62
Knowing more people in your community	95	32

Source: Reprinted with the permission of The Free Press, a division of Simon and Schuster Adult Publishing Group, from *Sharing the journey: Support groups and America's new quest for community* by Robert Wuthnow. Copyright © 1994 by Robert Wuthnow. All rights reserved.

VISUAL SOCIOLOGY

FRIENDSHIP GROUPS

These photos capture some aspects of the universal experience known as friendship. They show friendship groups in societies throughout the world—from the young men and women in an urban street gang, to a group of wealthy English boarding school students, to scenes from African villages. They convey the emotional quality of interaction among friends, but to the sociological observer they also reveal some characteristic features of friendship groups.

First, note the size of the groups. None numbers more than six or seven members. As Georg Simmel first pointed out in his writing on friendship and intimacy, the larger a group is, the more opportunities there will be for conflict and schism. Increasing size brings with it a greater likelihood of jealousy, competition for attention, and conflicting values, and these tensions tend to break up larger friendship groups into smaller, more intimate ones like those shown here.

A second observation that we can draw from these photos has to do with gender differences in friendship groups. Children's friendship groups are involved in anticipatory socialization, in taking roles that will later be incorporated into adult statuses. Thus the girls are seen holding dolls and practicing the interactions that occupy so much of their mothers' time. And unlike the typical male friendship group, female groups often have the responsibility of caring for younger siblings, as we see in at least one of these photos. Males more typically engage in activities that involve physical prowess and changes in the environment. We also see in these photos that gender segregation is normally the rule in friendship groups, although there may be many exceptions, such as when games are played in school.

© Ken Heyman/Woodfin Camp & Assoc. Ltd-85

© Ken Heyman/Woodfin Camp & Associates

Finally, these photos remind us of the emotional complexity of friendship. Friends can fight and make up, but people who are less than friends often cannot fight without ending the relationship.

The Sociological Observer

(See photo on page 146.)

Is a scene like this one likely to occur in American culture? Perhaps today it is, but until recently such a show of emotion between men, even between a father and his son, was discouraged in our culture. Today this norm is changing. Male friends hug each other in public far more than they would have a generation ago. Still, in many other cultures it is far more acceptable for men to hug and kiss each other than it is in North America.

Figure 6.4 Poverty Rates
by Race and Hispanic
Origin, 1959–2001

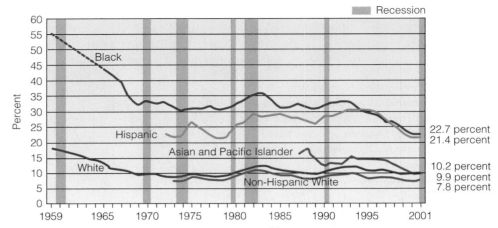

Note: The data points represent the midpoints of the respective years. The latest recession began in
March 2001. Data for Blacks are not available from 1960 to 1965. Data for the other race and
Hispanic origin groups are shown from the first year available. Hispanics may be of any race.
Source: U.S. Census Bureau, Current Population Survey, 1960-2002 Annual Demographic
Supplements.

one's own ability relative to others. Their findings indicate that higher pay is associated with expectations of greater ability—irrespective of the task's relevance—while lower pay is connected with less ability. These expectations are, obviously, shaped by interactions: One does not innately know that higher-paid work makes one more proficient to perform a task; instead, one learns by interacting with others that those who receive greater rewards for their work are thought to possess greater ability. Workers in a factory, for example, are often paid less than their supervisors even though they may have more technical skills and the ability to keep the factory running by doing their specific jobs. But because they earn less and have less authority, they tend to assume that they have less ability than the supervisors. As a result, they are more likely to accept the status quo—that is, to feel that their lower status is justified—and this tends to reinforce already existing patterns of inequality.

Stewart and Moore's findings could be used to explain trends like the one revealed by Figure 6.4, which presents poverty rates for different racial groups since 1959. The chart shows that black poverty rates decreased sharply with the rise of the civil rights movement in the 1960s. However, except during times of economic crisis, there was little fluctuation in the poverty rates for blacks between 1970 and 1990. Indeed, black poverty rates did not fall below 30 percent until the 1990s. Considerable fluctuation in Hispanic poverty rates appears in the 1970s, but the rates for the 1980s resemble those for blacks, and those for the 1990s are the highest of all racial groups. The poverty rate of non-Hispanic whites changed little throughout the entire time frame, never dipping below

roughly 7 percent or above 11 percent. Yet the most interesting and obvious aspect of this graph may be the differences *between* groups, as opposed to the historical change *within* one group over time. Those differences are fairly drastic, especially when one compares the poverty rates for non-Hispanic whites (roughly 10 percent) with those for blacks and Hispanics (always above 20 percent, and historically closer to 30 percent).

How would sociologists interested in interaction in groups analyze these differences in poverty levels? Racial categories are one way in which individuals within American society identify themselves—as white, black, and so forth. As Stewart and Moore's research shows, individuals develop expectations about their relative merit and capabilities, and these expectations affect their feelings about the social situations in which they find themselves. Moreover, these expectations are shaped by how much one is paid. This process is maintained as social roles and expectations are learned through interaction with others in families, work groups, and many other social groups.

If one takes this theory from the individual level to the group level, racial minorities that are paid less will develop performance expectations about themselves that are lower than those of racial groups that are paid more. As a result, it can be argued that racial groups that are rewarded less for their work will develop subjectively lower assessments of their own ability and become less likely to challenge the status quo. We will return to this theory in later chapters on inequalities of class and race. The important point here is that unequal expectations arising out of interactions in groups may lead to larger patterns of inequality that persist from one generation to the next.

SUMMARY
The Importance of Groups

- The social fabric of modern societies is composed of millions of groups of many types and sizes.
- Unlike a *social category,* a collection of individuals who are grouped together because they share a particular trait, a *social group* is a set of two or more individuals who share a sense of common identity and belonging and who interact on a regular basis. Those interactions create a social structure composed of specific statuses and roles.

Characteristics of Social Groups

- A *primary group* is characterized by intimate, often face-to-face, association and cooperation. *Secondary groups* are characterized by relationships that involve few aspects of the personality; the members' reasons for participation are usually limited to a small number of goals.
- As the number of people in a group increases, the number of possible relationships among the group's members increases at a faster rate. A group composed of only two people is known as a *dyad.* The addition of a third person to form a *triad* reduces the stability of the group.
- At the level of social organization between the primary group and the institutions of the nation-state are *communities. Territorial communities* are contained within geographic boundaries; *nonterritorial communities* are networks of associations formed around shared goals. Territorial communities are usually composed of one or more neighborhoods in which people form attachments based on proximity.
- Groups formed at the neighborhood level are integrated into networks that may extend beyond geographic boundaries.
- Key factors in the formation of networks are *in-group–out-group* distinctions. Such distinctions can form around almost any quality but are usually based on such qualities as income, race, or religion.
- Another type of group is the *reference group,* a group that an individual uses as a frame of reference for self-evaluation and attitude formation.
- The study of whom people associate with, how those choices are made, and the effects of those choices is known as *social network analysis.*

Interaction in Groups

- Social scientists have identified certain principles of interaction that help explain both stability and change in human groups. Among them are the pleasure principle, the rationality principle, the reciprocity principle, and the fairness principle.
- The balance among these principles varies from one situation to another, with economic motives dominating in some instances and social needs winning out in others.
- From an interactionist perspective, an important factor determining how people behave in a given instance is their definition of the situation.
- Studies of interaction in groups use a variety of techniques. *Ethnomethodology* is the study of the underlying rules of behavior that guide group interaction. The *dramaturgical approach* regards interaction as though it were taking place on a stage and unfolding in scenes.
- The strategies that people use to set a stage for their own purposes are known as *impression management.*
- Research on the bystander effect has shown that when responsibility seems to be diffused, people are more likely to avoid helping others. But when people define the situation as involving them, they will intervene despite the potential costs to themselves.
- Research on small groups has shown that they tend to develop two kinds of leaders: a "task leader" who keeps the group focused on its goals and a "socioemotional leader" who creates a positive emotional climate.

Formal Organizations and Bureaucracy

- *Informal organizations* are groups with generally agreed-upon but unwritten norms and statuses, whereas *formal organizations* have explicit, often written, sets of norms, statuses, and roles that specify each member's relationships to the others and the conditions under which those relationships hold.
- A *voluntary association* is a formal organization whose members pursue shared interests and arrive at decisions through some sort of democratic process.
- A *bureaucracy* is a formal organization characterized by positions with clearly defined responsibilities, the ordering of positions in a hierarchy, governance by rules and precedents, impersonality and impartiality, a career ladder, and efficiency as a basic norm.

- One effect of the increasing dominance of bureaucracies in modern societies is the possibility that individuals will not take full responsibility for their actions. A study of obedience to authority conducted by Stanley Milgram raised serious questions about people's ability to resist pressure to carry out orders for which they are not personally responsible. Milgram also found, however, that rebellion against authority is more likely when individuals who rebel have the support of others.

- Other studies have found that commitment to bureaucratic organizations is greatest when it is supported by ideology or by strong primary-group attachments.

Groups in Complex Societies

- As a society becomes larger and more complex, it tends increasingly to be characterized by secondary groups and organizations. These make the society more efficient, but they can also cause confusion and unhappiness.

- Durkheim pointed out that members of complex societies have greater freedom to choose what groups to join and what norms to conform to, but can be overwhelmed by the choices open to them.

- Weber examined the effects of the rise of bureaucracies in modern societies, finding that the individual often comes to feel like a tiny cog in a huge set of interlocking organizations.

- Democratic theory states that when people are given freedom of association they will form a complex civil society. This theory is supported by research on group membership in the United States. Religious and self-help groups are two types of groups that Americans join in large numbers.

GLOSSARY

social category: A collection of individuals who are grouped together because they share a trait deemed by the observer to be socially relevant. (p. 142)

social group: A set of two or more individuals who share a sense of common identity and belonging and who interact on a regular basis. (p. 142)

primary group: A social group characterized by intimate, face-to-face associations. (p. 143)

secondary group: A social group whose members have a shared goal or purpose but are not bound together by strong emotional ties. (p. 143)

dyad: A group consisting of two people. (p. 146)

triad: A group consisting of three people. (p. 146)

community: A set of primary and secondary groups in which the individual carries out important life functions. (p. 146)

territorial community: A population that functions within a particular geographic area. (p. 146)

nonterritorial community: A network of relationships formed around shared goals. (p. 146)

in-group: A social group to which an individual has a feeling of allegiance; usually, but not always, a primary group. (p. 147)

out-group: Any social group to which an individual does not have a feeling of allegiance; may be in competition or conflict with the in-group. (p. 147)

reference group: A group that an individual uses as a frame of reference for self-evaluation and attitude formation. (p. 148)

ethnomethodology: The study of the underlying rules of behavior that guide group interaction. (p. 154)

dramaturgical approach: An approach to research on interaction in groups that is based on the recognition that much social interaction depends on the desire to impress those who may be watching. (p. 154)

impression management: The strategies one uses to "set a stage" for one's own purposes. (p. 154)

informal organization: A group whose norms and statuses are generally agreed upon but are not set down in writing. (p. 157)

formal organization: A group that has an explicit, often written, set of norms, statuses, and roles that specify each member's relationships to the others and the conditions under which those relationships hold. (p. 157)

voluntary association: A formal organization whose members pursue shared interests and arrive at decisions through some sort of democratic process. (p. 157)

bureaucracy: A formal organization characterized by a clearly defined hierarchy with a commitment to rules, efficiency, and impersonality. (p. 157)

INTERNET RESOURCES

 Virtual Society: The Wadsworth Sociology Resource Center
(http://sociology.wadsworth.com)
At Virtual Society you can access a wide range of enrichment material to aid your study of sociology. From the main page, click on the Student Resources link and find your course and this textbook. Next, select the chapter you are presently studying from the pull-down menu. Among the useful options for each self-study chapter are

online links and exercises, flashcards, practical study tips, and practice quizzes for each chapter.

MC MicroCase Online

From the Virtual Society home page, click on MicroCase Online to access book-specific MicroCase exercises that allow you to further explore sociological issues and principles presented in the text.

InfoTrac College Edition

Another unique option available to you at the Student Resources section at Virtual Society is InfoTrac College Edition, an online library with access to hundreds of scholarly and popular periodicals. Search terms for this chapter are suggested in the following list, but this resource also allows you to fit your study of sociology to your own interests by searching custom keywords.

Primary Group
Communities
Reciprocity
Ethnomethodology

Bureau of Labor Statistics
(www.bls.gov)
Displays several pages and features on work and organizations in the U.S. economy, with links to international organizations like the International Labor Organization. Also provides links to many research reports and publications.

U.S. Department of Labor
(www.dol.gov)
Offers a great deal of information and data about people in organizations, especially companies and corporations, as well as a link to the Economics and Statistics Administration, the source of much of the statistical, economic, and demographic information collected by the federal government.

Deviance and Social Control

© Margaret Morton, author/photographer The Tunnel (Yale University Press, 1995)

I see them lining up for breakfast well before seven in the morning. They look exhausted and threadbare. Some have slept all night in chairs in the "day room." Others are drifting in from the street, where they have a secret hiding place to sleep—perhaps over a grate that in winter will blow warm air on them and keep them from freezing. Since the terrorist attack on New York City and the resulting loss of thousands of jobs, there is also a growing number of displaced workers, many of whom had recently struggled to get off the welfare rolls and into the labor market. But most of the homeless seeking help have been living on the streets for other reasons.

This morning, for example, I see Willie W. and his partner Samantha. They are crack addicts who roam the streets at night in search of soda and beer cans, which they will sell to other street folk for half of the 5-cent deposit price because they need immediate cash for a "hit" of cocaine. This morning I also spot the loan shark who waits outside the Drop-in Center to see if anyone who owes him money is around so he can collect on debts or threaten those who are delinquent in their loan payments.

As I climb the stairs to the Center, I am greeted by several staff members who were formerly homeless but are now on their way to work in the Center's kitchen or its various recycling and building maintenance programs. They greet me as "The Professor." The reason I appear so frequently in their midst is that I am the chair of the Center's board of directors. Its founder and executive director is a former doctoral student at my university. Two of my closest friends are also deeply involved in its programs. Although I have no shortage of responsibilities to occupy my time, I could hardly refuse when I was asked to serve on the board. It made sense for me to take my turn leading the board and participating in the Center's activities. Nor am I at all unusual in this regard. Most professional sociologists find that their research and writing leads to invitations to take active roles in organizations that seek to put into practice what they have recommended in their research. I chose to make a commitment of time and energy to the Grand Central Neighborhood Social Services Agency because I have been involved in research with the city's street population for almost three decades.

I believe that the problems of homeless adults in urban centers raise fascinating sociological issues about how a good society might deal with people who deviate from its norms and are "down and out." I find it sad that in one of the world's richest cities there are people living on the streets. Often they are mentally ill or addicted, or both. Equally often they are younger people who have been pushed out of crowded apartments after the breakup of a family. On the streets, they find many opportunities to make some money through various forms of hustling.

Race, ethnicity, and gender also play a part in the story. Two generations ago the city's homeless were primarily white males. Today most street people are black and Hispanic men from extremely poor backgrounds. An increasing number of street people are women; about 20 percent of those who come to the Center are female. All the people who spend time at the Center deviate from the norms of success that Americans value so highly. Many have served time in prison—but in fact they frequently come to the Center to escape from predatory felons on the streets. At the Center, we offer a helping hand, but we insist that everyone take responsibility for his or her behavior. Those who can do so often begin the long and difficult process of rehabilitation.

Like many other volunteers, I spend time at the Center because it gives me a sense of gratification to share my skills with those in need. As a professional sociologist, I also serve because it is a way to gain knowledge about society's outcasts and the approaches the city is developing to address their needs.

FOCUS QUESTIONS:

- How do societies define deviant behavior?

- How do sociologists explain patterns of punishment for deviant behavior?

- How is deviance prevented from threatening social stability?

WHAT IS DEVIANCE?

In this chapter, we look at some current trends in deviance and crime and examine issues of social control—that is, what societies do to attempt to curb deviance. Research on these and related issues is a major field within sociology. No one can offer definitive answers, but sociologists are frequently looked to for research on trends in deviance and criminal behavior and for explanations of these trends.

Deviance, broadly defined, is behavior that violates the norms of a particular society. But because all of us violate norms to some degree at some time or other, we must distinguish between *deviance* and *deviants*. Deviance can be something as simple as dyeing one's hair purple, wearing outrageous clothing, or becoming tipsy at a stuffy party. Or it may be behavior over which the individual has little control, such as being homeless and living on the street, or it may consist of more strongly sanctioned departures from the society's norms—such acts as rape, mugging, and murder. Not all deviance is considered socially wrong, yet it can have negative effects for the individual. For example, "whistle-blowers," who publicize illegal or harmful actions by their employers, deviate from the norms of bureaucratic organizations and are often threatened with the loss of their jobs. Yet at the same time they benefit the public by calling attention to dangerous or illegal activities (Stevenson, 1992b).

A deviant person, by contrast, is someone who violates or opposes a society's most valued norms, especially those that are valued by elite groups. Through such behavior, deviant individuals become disvalued people, and their disvalued behavior provokes hostile reactions (Davis, 1975; Goffman, 1963; Sagarin, 1975; Schur, 1984). *Deviant* may be a label attached to a person or group. Or the word may refer to behavior that brings punishment to a person under certain conditions.

The Social Construction of Deviance

Violations of social norms by people in powerful positions, such as influence peddling or extramarital sexual liaisons by government officials, raise an important question: What are the conditions under which violations of norms are punished? Here is an area of conduct in which there is often some uncertainty about what is legal and what is merely sleazy. Such questions reveal that deviance is not absolute. As sociologist Kai Erikson explains it, deviance "is not a property inherent in certain forms of behavior; it is a property conferred upon these forms by the audience which directly or indirectly witnesses them" (1962, p. 307). Some of

us may believe that influence peddling is deviant, whereas others may believe that it is acceptable. Which of our views become the norm—and which are to be enforced through rewards and punishments—is just as important as the behavior itself. This point is illustrated in Erikson's classic study of deviance among New England's Puritans during the infamous Salem witchcraft trials.

> No one knows how the witchcraft hysteria began, but it originated in the home of the Reverend Samuel Parris, minister of the local church. In early 1692, several girls from the neighborhood began to spend their afternoons in the Parris kitchen with a slave named Tituba, and it was not long before a mysterious sorority of girls, aged between nine and twenty, became regular visitors to the parsonage. (Erikson, 1966, p. 141)

The girls quickly drew the concerned attention of Salem's ministers and its doctor. Unable to understand much about their hysterical state or to deny their claim that they were possessed by the devil, the doctor pronounced the girls bewitched. This gave them the freedom to make accusations regarding the cause of their unfortunate condition.

Tituba was the first to be accused and jailed. She was followed by scores of others as the fear of witches swept through the community. Soon women with too many warts or annoying tics were accused, tried, and jailed for their sins. Then the executions began. In the first and worst of the waves of executions, in August and September of 1692, at least 20 people were killed, including one man who was pressed to death under piled rocks for "standing mute at his trial."

For the sociologist, the Salem witch-hunt of 300 years ago has meaning for today's world. Erikson showed that

The Trial of George Jacobs, August 5, 1692. Oil on canvas by T. H. Matteson, 1855. Jacobs was accused of witchcraft.

Essex Institute, Salem, Massachusetts

the punishment of suspected witches served as a defense against the weakening of Puritan society. By casting out the "witches," the Puritans were reaffirming their community values: strict adherence to religious devotion, fear of God, abstinence from the pleasures of secular society (e.g., drink, sex, music, dance), and the like.

For Erikson, the trial and punishment of the so-called witches illustrates Émile Durkheim's earlier discovery that every society creates its own forms of deviance and in fact needs those deviant acts. The punishment of deviant acts reaffirms the commitment of a society's members to its norms and values and thereby reinforces social solidarity. On the surface, Durkheim argued, deviant acts may seem to be harmful to group life, but in fact the punishment of those who commit such acts makes it clear to all exactly what deviations are most intolerable. By Durkheim's reasoning, the stark images of punishment—the guillotine, the electric chair, the syringe, the wretched life behind bars—become opportunities to let the population know that those who threaten the social order will be severely judged.

The historic 2003 Supreme Court decision that by a 6-3 vote overturned a Texas law forbidding homosexual consensual sexual behavior is another outstanding example of the way ideas of what is deviant change as the norms of a society change. In his majority opinion, Justice Anthony Kennedy wrote that most states had long abandoned criminal penalties for consensual sexual relations conducted in private because (1) such prohibitions encourage disrespect for the law by penalizing conduct that many people engage in, (2) such statutes regulate private conduct that is not harmful to others, and (3) such laws tend to be arbitrarily enforced and thus invite the danger of blackmail. Texas was one of 13 states that still had anti-sodomy laws on their books (Greenhouse, 2003).

The Court's historic decision came as a result of years of social change in which gay Americans had fought in the courts and in the streets, through social movement activities like those described in Chapter 8, to convince the public that such laws were an invasion of their privacy and their civil rights. "The state cannot demean their existence or control their destiny by making their private sexual conduct a crime," the Court's opinion stated (Greenhouse, 2003, p. 1; Mixner & Bailey, 2002). In a dissenting opinion, however, Justice Antonin Scalia warned that the Court had taken sides in a divisive "culture war" within American society and that the decision would open the way to legalization of same-sex marriages. Scalia's opinion reflects the fact that an important minority of Americans still believe that homosexual sex is immoral and will continue to argue that government should intervene in people's private lives for that reason.

As this example and that of the Puritans suggest, the study of deviance reveals a great deal about directions of social change in a society. Indeed, the study of deviance is

Tyrone Garner, left, and John G. Lawrence, right, who won their appeal in the Texas case, are greeted by a supporter at a rally.

central to the science of sociology, not only because deviance results in major social problems like crime, but also because it can bring about social change. The Puritans were a deviant group in England at the time of their emigration to the New World. They challenged the authority of the king and many of the central norms that upheld the stratification system of feudal England. In the Massachusetts Bay Colony, they created their own society, one in which they were no longer deviant. But, as Erikson showed, they also created their own forms of deviance, which reflected their unique problems as a society on a rapidly changing social frontier.

In fact, if you think about it, every aspect of daily life—driving, walking, going to a show, shopping, church attendance, political behavior, or sports—is controlled by the norms of a given culture. And thousands of deviant acts, such as cutting in front of someone in a line, are frowned on by people asserting their normative expectations ("Excuse me, I was ahead of you here"). All these norms and assertions constitute a system of informal social control without which society would dissolve into chaos, confusion, and hostility (Gibbs, 1994).

Forms of Social Control

The ways in which a society prevents deviance and punishes deviants are known as **social control**. As we saw in Chapter 3, the norms of a culture, the means by which they are instilled in us through socialization, and the ways in which they are enforced in social institutions—the family, the schools, government agencies—establish a society's system of social control. In fact, social control can be thought of as all the ways in which a society establishes and enforces its cultural norms. It is "the capacity of a social group, including a whole society, to regulate itself" (Janowitz, 1978, p. 3).

The means used to prevent deviance and punish deviants are one dimension of social control. They include the police, prisons, mental hospitals, and other institutions responsible for applying social control, keeping order, and enforcing major norms. But if we had to rely entirely on official institutions to enforce norms, social order would probably be impossible to achieve (Chwast, 1965). In fact, the official institutions of social control deal mainly with the deviant individuals and groups that a society fears most. Less threatening forms of deviance are controlled through the everyday interactions of individuals, as when parents attempt to prevent their children from piercing their tongues or wearing their hair in dreadlocks.

In this chapter, we look first at the dimensions of deviance and at how its meanings emerge and change as a society's values change. Then we explore the major sociological perspectives on deviance and social control. The final section deals with the ecology of deviance—its distribution among people in different subcultures and income categories—and ends with an introduction to the organization and functioning of institutions of social control such as prisons.

DIMENSIONS OF DEVIANCE

Deviance is an especially controversial topic: There is usually much disagreement not only about which behaviors are deviant and which are not but also about which behaviors should be strongly punished and which should be condoned or punished only mildly. The debate over whether abortion should be legal is a good example of such disagreement. As Erikson noted, "Behavior which qualifies one man for prison may qualify another for sainthood since the quality of the act itself depends so much on the circumstances under which it was performed and the temper of the audience which witnessed it" (1966, pp. 5–6).

Consider former South African president Nelson Mandela. Mandela was released from a maximum-security prison in 1990 after serving almost 30 years of a life sentence for his leadership of the movement to end apartheid, South Africa's racial caste system. The dominant white minority in South Africa regarded Mandela and other opponents of apartheid as criminals. But the black majority viewed him as a hero and a martyr; indeed, black South Africans revere Mandela the way people in the United

States revere George Washington. Until the black majority began to mobilize world opinion and other nations began to enforce negative sanctions against South Africa, the white minority was able to define Mandela's opposition to apartheid as a criminal activity.

The power to define which acts are legal and which are illegal is an important dimension of deviance. In the United States, the power of some groups to define certain acts as deviant helps explain why, for example, cultivating marijuana is a crime but influence peddling is not. In this connection it is interesting to note that during the 1960s, when the children of powerful members of society began smoking marijuana, legislators found themselves under pressure to relax the enforcement of marijuana laws.

The fact that people in power can define what behavior is deviant and determine who is punished fails to explain differences in definitions of deviance in societies with different cultures. Behavior regarded as normal in one society may be considered highly deviant in another. For example, in the United States, drinking alcoholic beverages is considered normal; in orthodox Islamic culture, it is forbidden. Even within a society, members of certain social groups may behave in ways that are considered deviant by others. Thus the official norms of the Catholic church do not permit the use of artificial methods of birth control, yet large numbers of Catholics use condoms, birth control pills, and other contraceptives. Similarly, the norms of Judaism require that the Sabbath be set aside for religious observance, yet many Jews work on the Sabbath and do not attend synagogue; in parts of Jerusalem they have occasionally been attacked by orthodox Jews for violating that norm. Clearly, differences in values are another important source of definitions of deviance and of disagreements about those definitions.

Ascribed Statuses

Another dimension of deviance concerns attributes that are ascribed unavoidably at birth (e.g., race or physical appearance) or that a person cannot control (e.g., having a convict as a parent), in contrast to statuses that are achieved through actual behavior, which is usually voluntary (see the discussion of ascribed versus achieved statuses in Chapter 4). A criminal is deviant in ways that a mentally ill person is not, and criminal behavior is more costly to society. In many situations, however, a mentally ill person is labeled as deviant, and this label may actually drive him or her toward criminality. A related issue is how people who deviate from generally accepted norms manage to survive in societies where they are considered outsiders. In fact, deviant people often form their own communities with their own norms and values, and these deviant subcultures sustain them in their conflicted relations with "normal" members of society.

An important point is that deviant subcultures, which engage in prostitution, gambling, drug use, and other deviant behaviors, could not exist if they did not perform services and supply products that people in the larger society secretly demand. It would be wise, therefore, not to draw the distinction between deviant and normal people too sharply. Many people deviate from the norm, and their deviations create opportunities for others whose identities and occupations are deviant.

In sum, three dimensions of social life—power, culture, and voluntary versus involuntary behavior—create the major forces operating in any society to produce the forms of deviance that are typical of that society.

Deviance and Stigma

To narrow the range of phenomena we must deal with in discussing deviance, let us keep in mind Erving Goffman's (1963) distinction between stigma and deviance. "The term *stigma*," Goffman stated, "refers to an attribute that is deeply discrediting" and that reduces the person "from a whole and usual person to a tainted and discounted one" (p. 3). People may be stigmatized because of ascribed statuses such as mental illness, eccentricity, or membership in a disvalued racial or nationality group. In some instances, the stigma is visible and obvious to all, as in the case of a disfigured person like John Merrick, commonly known as the Elephant Man. Suffering from a disease that grossly distorted his face, Merrick was rejected by society even though he was a highly intelligent person. In other cases, stigma is revealed only with growing acquaintance, as in the stigma attached to the children of convicts. For the stigmatized person, the disqualifying trait defines the person's master status (Becker, 1963; Scull, 1988) (see Chapter 4). A blind person, for example, may be an excellent musician and a caring parent, but the fact that he or she is blind will outweigh these achieved statuses except in unusual cases like that of Stevie Wonder.

Stigmatized people deviate from some norm of "respectable" society, but they are not necessarily social deviants. The term *deviant*, Goffman argued, should be reserved for people "who are seen as declining voluntarily and openly to accept the social place accorded them, and who act irregularly and somewhat rebelliously in connection with our basic institutions" (1963, p. 143). Among the people Goffman classified as social deviants are "prostitutes, drug addicts, delinquents, criminals, jazz musicians, bohemians, gypsies, carnival workers, hoboes, winos, show people, full time gamblers, beach dwellers, homosexuals, and the urban unrepentant poor." Goffman's list is somewhat whimsical and leaves out more recent groups that are considered so-

cially deviant, such as Internet pornographers; his point, however, is that these are examples of social groups that "are considered to be engaged in some kind of collective denial of the social order. They are perceived as failing to use available opportunity for advancement in the various approved runways of society" (1963, p. 144).

According to the definition of *stigma*, the population of social deviants is smaller than that of stigmatized individuals; only some stigmatized behaviors are socially deviant. Deviant behaviors are characterized by denial of the social order through violation of the norms of permissible conduct. This point should be kept in mind as we continue our discussion of criminals and other people who are considered social deviants.

Deviance and Crime

Much of the study of social deviance focuses on crime. *Crime* is usually defined as an act, or the omission of an act, for which the state can apply sanctions. Those sanctions are part of the criminal law, a set of written rules that prohibit certain acts and prescribe punishments to be meted out to violators (Kornblum & Julian, 2004). But the questions of which specific behaviors constitute crime and how the state should deal with them are often controversial.

In every society, there are some behaviors that almost everyone will agree are criminal and should be punished and other behaviors that some consider criminal but others do not. All societies punish murder and theft, for example, but there is far more variation in the treatment of adultery, prostitution, and pornography. Indeed, the largest number of "crimes" committed in the United States each year are so-called public order crimes such as public drunkenness, vagrancy, disorderly conduct, prostitution, gambling, drug addiction, and certain homosexual interactions. Many sociologists claim that these are "victimless crimes" because they generally cause no physical harm to anyone but the offenders themselves (Silberman, 1980; Thio, 1998). Not all social scientists agree with this view, however. Some point out that crimes like prostitution actually inflict damage on society because they are usually linked with an underworld that engages in far more serious and costly criminal activities (Wilson, 1977).

In the United States, crime is considered one of the nation's most serious social problems. According to the Federal Bureau of Investigation (FBI), one violent crime occurs every 22 seconds and one property crime every 3 seconds. The most serious, most common, and most likely to be reported crimes are called *index crimes* by the FBI because they are included in its Crime Index, a commonly used measure of crime rates. These categories of crime, along with crime rates, are shown in Table 7.1.

TABLE 7.1

The Crime Rate,* 1972–2001

	1972	1982	1996	2001
Crime Index, total	3,961	5,604	5,079	4,160
Violent crime	401	571	634	504
Property crime	3,560	5,033	4,445	3,656
Murder	9	9	7	6
Forcible rape	23	34	36	32
Robbery	181	239	202	149
Aggravated assault	189	289	388	319
Burglary	1,141	1,489	943	741
Larceny-theft	1,994	3,085	2,976	2,485
Motor vehicle theft	426	459	526	431

*Rate per 100,000 inhabitants, calculated on number of offenses before rounding.

Source: FBI, 2002.

For many decades, criminologists and other social scientists have criticized the FBI's crime statistics on the ground that they do not reflect differences in effectiveness among crime-reporting agencies. For example, a more professional law enforcement agency in one community could show higher crime rates than an agency in another community that has done a haphazard job of collecting the statistics. Another serious problem is that there is no way of knowing the crime rates for the total population (rather than just for those who actually reported crimes). Since 1973, therefore, the Census Bureau and the Law Enforcement Assistance Administration have conducted semiannual surveys in which respondents are asked whether they or their businesses have been victims of robbery, rape, assault, burglary, or other forms of theft. In general, these *victimization surveys* show that the overall rate of serious crime is actually between two and three times higher than the reported Crime Index.

Deviance and Changing Values

One of the factors that make it especially difficult to gather and interpret statistics on crime is that definitions of crime and deviance are constantly changing as the society's values change. Almost every week, for example, there are reports in the media of men who have battered and even killed their wives, often after serving brief prison sentences for previous attacks on their spouses. Why, many ask, are law enforcement agencies unable to prevent and punish spouse abuse? Advocates of new laws and greater investment in prevention point out that until fairly recently a married woman was viewed as the husband's household possession. Although both husband and wife had sworn to "love, honor, and cherish" their partner, these norms were applied far more forcefully to women than to men. This double standard is changing as men and women become more equal before the law, but in the minds of many judges and juries this change is not yet complete, and men who abuse their spouses often receive relatively light sentences (Heitzeg, 1996).

In any society, agreement on particular aspects of crime and deviance can range from weak (in cases in which there is much controversy) to strong (in cases in which there is little disagreement). Negative sanctions, or punishments, can also range from very weak to very strong. Capital punishment is the strongest sanction in the United States, followed by life imprisonment. Minor fines or the suggestion that a person undergo treatment for a behavior that is viewed as deviant are relatively weak sanctions. Nor are all sanctions formal punishments meted out according to law. Some deviance can be punished by means of shunning or the "silent treatment," and milder infractions can be controlled by simply poking fun at the person in an attempt to change his or her behavior.

Figure 7.1 uses these distinctions to construct a typology of deviance as it is generally viewed in the United States today. Figure 7.2 suggests what such a typology would have looked like before the Civil War. Together they highlight some of the continuities and changes in patterns

Figure 7.1   A Typology of Deviance in the United States

Figure 7.2 Deviance in the United States Before the Civil War

	STRENGTH OF SANCTION	
	Weak	**Strong**
DEGREE OF CONSENSUS — **Weak**	• Killing Native Americans • Lynching of African Americans • Prostitution • Wife or child beating	• Abortion • Indebtedness • Illegitimacy • Divorce • Adultery
DEGREE OF CONSENSUS — **Strong**	• Political corruption • Corporate crime	• Major felonies against whites • Treason • Homosexuality

of deviance in the United States over the last 150 years. You will probably find points in them to argue with—which is further evidence of the difficulty of classifying deviant behaviors in a rapidly changing society.

Driving while intoxicated (DWI) is classified as a deviant behavior, but only in the last two decades have DWI laws been enforced systematically. Why? We all fear the drunk driver and agree that driving while intoxicated is dangerous, but because so many people are social drinkers this norm is frequently violated. Consequently, we have placed relatively mild sanctions on DWI except when the outcome is a fatal accident. In recent decades, however, organized groups opposed to drunk driving have helped change public attitudes, and the sanctions against DWI have become stronger. In a study of this issue, Joseph Gusfield (1981) found that the highway death rate had steadily decreased after 1945, but that the public's perception of the relationship between highway deaths and drunk driving had sharpened as a result of media coverage and lobbying by citizens' groups.

Our perception and treatment of homosexuality are other examples of significant change in Americans' attitudes toward a deviant behavior and the strength of the sanctions invoked. A century ago, homosexuality was widely regarded as a serious form of deviance. Homosexuals were persecuted whenever they were exposed. Today there is far less agreement on this subject (Stolberg, 1997). A recent survey by the Kaiser Family Foundation (2001) found that 76 percent of lesbians, gays, and bisexuals believe there is greater acceptance of their sexual orientation, but almost equal numbers (74 percent) report that they have experienced prejudice and discrimination. About one-third (32 percent) report that they have been the target of physical violence because someone believed they were gay. The decision by the Walmart Corporation, the largest private employer in the United States, to accord gay and lesbian employees and their companions the same rights and benefits as other Walmart employees followed closely on the 2003 Supreme Court decision in *Garner v. Texas*. It, along with the earlier decision by the Disney Corporation to extend health benefits to same-sex part-

ners of its employees, is another indication of the increasing acceptance of gay rights.

Elsewhere in the world, the growing emphasis on religious orthodoxy in Islamic nations has led to attacks on writers and intellectuals who question Muslim norms. The Egyptian Nobel Prize winner Naguib Mahfouz, the Iranian novelist Salman Rushdie, and Bangladeshi physician, poet, and essayist Taslima Nasrin are among those who have experienced such attacks (Weaver, 1994). In the case of Nasrin, because she speaks and writes against the traditional norms that require women to remain in the

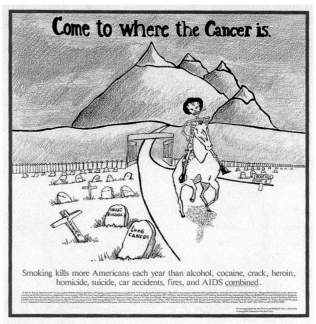

Changing Americans' views of smoking from an accepted to a deviant activity requires changes in the image of smoking. This public-service advertisement uses a child's prize-winning entry to turn the imagery used by tobacco companies to link smoking with outdoor activities into a negative representation.

Taslima Nasrin, a world-renowned feminist author, doctor, and poet from Bangladesh, is in hiding to avoid arrest or mob violence because of her criticism of Islamic gender norms. She is considered a courageous intellectual by many in the West but a deviant criminal by key political and religious authorities in her own country.

home, to be bought as brides, and otherwise to be treated as male possessions, fundamentalist religious leaders have offered a reward (about $2,500) to anyone who succeeds in killing her. Nasrin is now in hiding in Europe. "I know if I ever go back I'll have to keep silent, stay inside my house," she says. "I'll never lead a normal life in my country, until my death" (quoted in Weaver, 1994, p. 60).

Deviant Subcultures

Even when the majority of the population can be said to support a particular set of values, it will contain many subcultures whose lifestyles are labeled deviant by the larger population (Rubington & Weinberg, 1999). A deviant subculture includes a system of values, attitudes, behaviors, and lifestyles that are opposed to the dominant culture of the society in which it is found (Bucholtz, 2002). The members of the subculture are also members of the larger society; they have families and friends outside the subculture with whom they share many values and norms. Within the subculture, however, they pursue values that are opposed to those of the larger or "mainstream" culture. Subcultures evolve their own rather insulated social worlds or communities, with local myths ("X is a slick dealer who once beat the tables in Vegas and was asked to leave the casino"), ways of measuring people's reputations ("he's a

punk," "he's cool"), rituals and social routines, particular language or slang, formal and informal uniforms (e.g., the attire worn by bikers), and symbols of belonging such as tattoos (Simmons, 1985). (See the Popular Culture and Social Change box on page 179.)

Subcultures of drug users and dealers provide many illustrations of the ways in which people who engage in deviant activities often develop their own vocabulary and norms. In his fascinating accounts of the subculture of crack dealers and crack-cocaine addicts, urban sociologist Terry Williams (1989, 1992) shows how everyone in the crack subculture—addicts, dealers, and hangers-on—used the language of the famous TV series *Star Trek* in referring to the drug and its use. The drug itself was often called "Scotty," and smoking the drug was referred to as "beaming up." As addicts and dealers became more deeply enmeshed in the frantic world of crack-cocaine use, they spent increasing amounts of time in the company of people who spoke their language and saw the world as they did.

Similar examples of the power of the deviant subculture abound in the work of another sociologist, Janet Foster. Foster (1990) observed the lives of young criminal men in an English slum. In the following account of the feelings of a criminal's wife toward the police, Foster shows how the norms and attitudes of the criminals become assimilated into the thinking of women who have relationships with the men but are not themselves criminals:

> The two coppers came up that had nicked [arrested] him, and they said, "You all right, mate?" I thought how can you stand there and be so friendly? One of them looked at me and said, "Why don't you take a seat with the baby, love," and all this. I thought what are you being so nice for, you could be depriving my kid of a father here . . . I know it's not their fault and they're for doing what they're paid to do, and it was more fool Jim for doin' it, you know. It was just bad luck that he got caught. That must be the first time I felt any real resentment against the police. (quoted in Foster, 1990, p. 104)

Professional criminals—including major drug dealers, bookmakers and gamblers, hired killers, and loan sharks—who think of their illegal activities as occupations, often become part of secret crime organizations. The best known of these (but hardly the only one) is the Mafia. Originally a Sicilian crime organization, the Mafia spread to the United States via Sicilian immigration in the late nineteenth century. Today families associated with the Mafia are active in most large cities in North America and elsewhere and often extract millions of dollars from legitimate businesses in exchange for "protection." In recent years, some successful crusades have been waged against the Mafia, but competing crime organizations are always ready

POPULAR CULTURE & SOCIAL CHANGE   Rap and Deviance

"It's not music, it's ghetto babble," some complain. "It glorifies violence and criminality," others say. "It degrades women by calling them whores and bitches," still others claim. These are some of the common criticisms one hears of rap music. Such opinions are partly based in truth, but many others are motivated by racism or simply by fear of young people and their styles of dress and communication. Whatever their origins, they have made rap one of the most controversial genres of popular music to come along since the early days of rock-and-roll.

But rap music, like the "hip-hop" subculture it is part of, is also rich in insights into problems of deviance and crime, if one listens to the ideas and feelings rap artists express in their music. Like any aspect of popular culture, rap has evolved different styles that reflect various types of thought within the basic form.

Gangsta rap, as exemplified in the music of Death Row Records or Ice T or the murdered star Tupac Shakur, is an overtly deviant and aggressive rap style. Extremely contro-

Missy Elliot.

The late Tupac Shakur.

versial songs like "Cop Killer," by Ice T, which appeared around the time of the beating of Rodney King by the Los Angeles police, provoked the anger of the police and city legal authorities, but in the highly charged racial atmosphere of the time, that was the rappers' intent. For better or worse, they wanted to use rap as a weapon against the authorities.

Contemporary rap artists continue to comment on current events, and their lyrics, expressed as dramatic monologues, are a form of poetic social commentary. KRS1, for example, is a popular rap artist and political activist whose work is often directed against deviance and violence. Indeed, there are numerous currents in today's rap, and gangsta rap is no longer nearly as influential as it was. Singers or groups like Missy "Misdemeanor" Elliot, Jurassic Five, and A Tribe Called Quest celebrate the empowerment of stigmatized people. Their rap tunes often emphasize the joy of being alive and the pleasure of sharing good food and fun with loved ones. Outsiders may think of them as deviant, but they actually celebrate the many styles of popular music that they sample in their rap tunes.

to engage in lucrative criminal activities as the Mafia is weakened (Ianni, 1998).

The subculture of organized crime is not unique to North America. In Japan, rates of homicide and mugging are small fractions of those in U.S. cities, yet organized crime thrives there (Buruma, 1984; Kaplan, 1998). The Yakuza, as the crime gangs are called, control many illegal businesses, just as they do in other countries, and they often resort to violence to discipline their members. As in the United States, organized crime in Japan is most directly associated with behaviors that are considered deviant, such as prostitution, gambling, and drug use, and a distinct subculture has emerged among those who engage in such behaviors.

THEN AND NOW   Tattoos in Ritual and Fashion

Throughout history, as people from different cultures have come into contact with each other, norms that are part of the core culture of one society have been adopted by deviant subcultures in other societies. In time these deviant symbols tend to become less deviant, mildly acceptable, and even fashionable. A fascinating example of this process is the spread of tattooing into the cultures of Europe and the

© Bettmann/Corbis

Later, criminals and prostitutes in European cities took to tattoos as a way of signifying their allegiance to their trades. With almost endless time

Stock Montage, Inc.

United States, where tattoos are a major fashion statement.

European and American sailors who traveled through the Pacific islands and Oceania in the eighteenth century were impressed by the *tattaw* worn by people of high status like the Maori chief shown here. The sailors adopted tattoos as a subcultural symbol of their "exotic" experience.

© Patrick Ward/Stock, Boston

on their hands, prisoners made amateur tattoos (requiring hours of painful jabs with an inked pen) into symbols of their opposition to the "screws" and "pigs"—their jailors and tormentors. Soldiers of the colonial powers, such as the French legionnaire shown here, also adopted tattoos as a way of boasting of their various campaigns.

In the United States in recent decades, the tattoo has become a

© A. Ramey/PhotoEdit

sign of membership in certain subcultures, such as those of skinheads and bikers. But in the world of fashion, what was once thought of as deviant becomes daring and may eventually be fashionable, as can be seen in the contemporary use of the tattoo as a fashion statement among young people at almost all levels of society.

In sum, many deviant subcultures flourish because they provide opportunities to engage in behavior that is pleasurable to some people but is considered deviant in "respectable" (conventional) society. Clearly, therefore, the line between what is normal and what is deviant is not nearly as distinct as one might believe from official descriptions of the norms of good conduct. However, one must recognize that membership in a deviant subculture, especially for those without money and power, often leads to exploitation and early death. In view of these problematic aspects of deviant subcultures, sociological and other explanations of deviant behavior take on special importance.

This mother and child are standing in front of their makeshift home. Countless people in the Americas, Asia, and Africa are homeless in the sense that although they have somewhere to sleep, their shelter is grossly inadequate, cold in bad weather, boiling hot in the sun, unsanitary, unsafe, and "temporary."

Note the details of this family's "home." How is it constructed? How is the infant dressed? Where is the structure located? Do you think that this family would be considered as deviant in the region where they are living as they would were they living on the outskirts of a city in the United States? (See page 197 for further insights into the sociological content of this photo.)

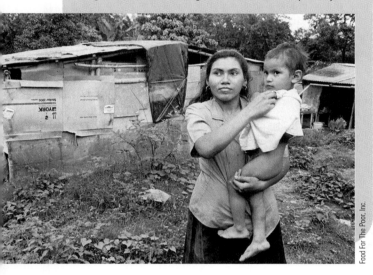

Food For The Poor, Inc.

THEORETICAL PERSPECTIVES ON SOCIAL DEVIANCE

Biological Explanations of Crime

Early in the twentieth century, the Italian criminologist Cesare Lombroso (1911) claimed to have proved that criminals were throwbacks to primitive, aggressive human types who could be recognized by physical features like prominent foreheads, shifty eyes, and red hair. Although Lombroso's theory has been thoroughly refuted by modern researchers, efforts to link body type with crime seem destined to reappear from time to time. In the 1940s, for example, the psychologist and physician William Sheldon announced that body type was correlated with crime. He believed that human beings could be classified into three types: *ectomorphs,* or thin people; *endomorphs,* or soft, fat people; and *mesomorphs,* or people with firm, well-defined muscles. The latter were most prone to crime, according to Sheldon, but he neglected to account for the possibility that mesomorphs simply might have led harder lives than less muscular individuals and therefore were better equipped to commit crimes that required strength (Glueck & Glueck, 1950).

The more modern biological view is represented in the influential work of social scientists Richard J. Herrnstein and James Q. Wilson. Their research has led them to conclude that both biology and social environment play important roles in producing criminals. In commenting on a recent study by researchers at the U.S. Department of Justice reporting that more than one-third of adult criminals in U.S. jails have at least one parent who is or was a criminal, Herrnstein argues that whatever determines criminality "is transmitted both genetically and environmentally. So kids brought up in criminal families get a double exposure" (quoted in Butterfield, 1992b, p. A16).

A study by Deborah W. Denno offers support for this view. In her research on 1,000 African-American boys from poor neighborhoods of Philadelphia, Denno (1990) found that a disproportionate number of individuals who had become criminals had histories of childhood hyperactivity. This genetically transmitted condition makes it difficult for children to concentrate and succeed in school. It also can make it hard for them to hold jobs. Thus Denno sees the causal chain as one of biological hyperactivity leading to social failure and then to crime.

But to many social scientists such studies are not convincing. Marvin E. Wolfgang, one of the nation's leading experts on criminality, points out that all the studies deal with people from poor neighborhoods, where a high proportion of people will be sent to jail whether they are related or not and whether they were hyperactive as children or not. Hyperactivity is also found in children from wealthier families but is not so often associated with criminal careers because the families can afford special schools and programs to deal with the condition (Butterfield, 1992b).

Social-Scientific Explanations of Deviance and Crime

Early sociological explanations of social deviance were also influenced by the biological concept of disease (Thio, 1998). The earliest of these explanations viewed crime as a form of social pathology, or social disease, that could be attributed to the evils of city life. Corruption, criminality, and depravity were thought to be bred in slums and to infect innocent residents of those grim communities, just as typhoid spread in unclean surroundings and was passed by contact from one victim to another (Bulmer, 1986). Thus many early juvenile training schools were built in rural areas where they would be isolated from the "corrupting" influence of cities (Platt, 1977).

The early sociological view of deviance and crime as resulting from "social pathologies" tended to rely on subjective terms and circular reasoning. To refer to crime or other forms of deviance as *pathologies,* for example, does not provide a theory of causality. It merely attaches a scientific-sounding term to behavior that the larger society finds wrong or offensive. It does not offer any insight into why the behavior occurs, what benefits it might provide for those who engage in it, and how it evolves from other behaviors or social conditions. In consequence, the view of deviance as a kind of disease was replaced by more objective and verifiable theories derived from the functionalist, interactionist, and conflict perspectives of modern sociology.

The Functionalist Perspective

The functionalist theorist Robert K. Merton (1938) developed a useful typology of deviance based on how people adapt to the demands of their society. Merton's aim was to discover "how some social structures *exert a definite pressure upon certain persons in society to engage in nonconformist rather than conformist conduct"* (p. 672). "Among the elements of social and cultural structure," Merton continued, "two are important for our purposes. . . . The first consists of culturally defined goals, purposes, and interests. . . . The second . . . defines, regulates, and controls the acceptable modes of achieving these goals" (pp. 672–673).

Merton's explanation of deviance is based on the concept of **anomie,** or normlessness. In his view, anomie results from the frustration and confusion people feel when what they have been taught to desire cannot be achieved by the legitimate means available to them. Merton believes that people in North America and other modern societies exhibit high levels of anomie because they are socialized to desire success in the form of material well-being and social prestige. For many, however, the means of attaining these culturally defined ends, such as hard work and saving, seem to be out of reach. This is especially true for people who experience rapid social changes, such as the closing of factories, and find themselves deprived of opportunities to attain what they have come to expect from life.

Consider some examples. Possession of money is a culturally defined goal. Work is a socially acceptable mode of achieving that goal; theft is not. Mating is also a culturally defined goal. Courtship and seduction are acceptable means of achieving it; kidnap and rape are not. But if theft and rape are unacceptable means of achieving culturally defined goals, why do they exist? According to Merton, the gap between culturally defined goals and acceptable means of achieving them causes feelings of anomie, which in turn make some people more likely to choose deviant strategies of various kinds.

Through socialization we learn the goals and acceptable means of our society. Most of us would love to be rich or powerful or famous. We accept these goals of our culture. We also accept the legitimate means of achieving them: education, work, the electoral process, plastic surgery, acting school, and so on. We are conformists. But not everyone accepts either the cultural goals or the accepted means of achieving them. Some become "innovators" in that they explore (and often step over) the frontiers of acceptable goal-seeking behavior; others (e.g., hoboes) retreat into a life that rejects both the goals and the accepted means; some rebel and seek to change the goals and the institutions that support them; and still others reject the quest for these precious values while carrying out the rituals of social institutions. (In many bureaucracies, for example, one can find ritualists who have given up the quest for promotion yet insist on receiving deference from people below them in the hierarchy.) Merton's typology thus is based on whether people accept either the cultural goals of their society, the acceptable means of achieving them, or neither. Figure 7.3 presents this typology, and Figure 7.4 gives examples of all the deviant types in Merton's framework.

You may be wondering how Merton's theory explains why some poor people resort to crime while so many others do not. The answer lies in the way people who experience anomie gravitate toward criminal subcultures. For example, adolescents who choose to steal to obtain things that their parents cannot afford must learn new norms—they must learn how to steal successfully and must receive some approval from peers for their conduct (Cloward & Ohlin, 1960; McNamara, 1994). As a result, they drift toward deviant peer groups. But this explanation presents a problem for the functionalist perspective: If there are deviant subcultures, the idea that there is a single culture whose goals and means are shared by all members of society is called into question. The presence of different subcultures within a society suggests another possible cause of deviant behaviors: conflict between groups.

Conflict Perspectives

CULTURAL CONFLICT   In an influential essay, "Crime as an American Way of Life," Daniel Bell (1962) observed that at the turn of the twentieth century, cultural conflict

MODE OF ADAPTATION		CULTURAL GOALS	INSTITUTIONAL MEANS
	Conformity	+	+
	Innovation	+	−
	Ritualism	−	+
	Retreatism	−	−
	Rebellion	+/−	+/−

Figure 7.3 The Merton Typology—Modes of Adaptation by Individuals Within the Society or Group

Merton explained that "+" signifies acceptance, "−" signifies elimination, and "+/−" signifies rejection and a substitution of new goals and standards. The line separating "Rebellion" from the other roles signifies that the individual no longer accepts the society's culture and structure; other individuals, though they may deviate, continue to accept the society's culture and structure.

developed between the "Big City and the small-town conscience. Crime as a growing business was fed by the revenues from prostitution, liquor, and gambling that a wide-open urban society encouraged and that a middle-class Protestant ethos tried to suppress with a ferocity unmatched in any other civilized society" (p. 128). This example of conflict between the official morality of the dominant American culture and the norms of subcultures that do not include strictures against gambling, drinking, prostitution, and the like encouraged the growth of criminal organizations. In the United States, as in many other societies, such organizations thrive by supplying the needs of millions of people who appear to be law-abiding citizens yet engage in certain deviant behaviors.

The prohibition of alcoholic beverages in the United States from 1919 to 1933 is an example of how cultural conflict can lead to situations that encourage criminal activity. Prohibition has been interpreted as an effort by the nation's largely Protestant lawmakers to impose their version of morality on immigrant groups for whom consumption of alcohol was an important part of social life. Once they were passed, however, laws against the production and sale of alcoholic beverages created opportunities for illegal production, bootlegging (smuggling), and illegal drinking establishments (speakeasies). These in turn

supported the rise of organized crime syndicates. The current laws against drugs like marijuana and cocaine have similar effects in that they lead to the clandestine production and supply of these illegal but widely used substances. Similar opportunities to make illegal profits arise when states pass laws raising the drinking age (Gusfield, 1966, 1996; Kornblum & Julian, 2004).

To recognize these effects of cultural conflict is not to condone the sale and use of illegal drugs. Rather, it is to be aware that whenever laws promoted by the powerful impose a set of moral standards on a minority, illegal markets are created that tend to be supplied by criminal organizations. Such organizations often act ruthlessly to control their markets, as can be seen in the murder of Mexican border guards who surprise drug smugglers, the killing of cocaine traffickers by rival dealers in Miami or Los Angeles, or the periodic "wars" that break out among organized crime families in many large cities.

MARXIAN CONFLICT THEORY For Marxian students of social deviance, the cultural conflict explanation is inadequate because it does not consider the effects of power and class conflict. Marxian sociologists believe that situations like Prohibition do not occur just because of cultural conflict (Felson, 1998). They happen because the powerful

MODE OF ADAPTATION		THE POOR	THE MIDDLE CLASS	THE RICH
	Conformity	The working poor	The suburban family	The wealthy civic leader
	Innovation	The mugger	The embezzler	The stock manipulator
	Ritualism	The chronic welfare recipient	The resigned bureaucrat	The hedonist
	Retreatism	The wino or junkie	The skidding alcoholic	The bohemian
	Rebellion	The bandit	The anarchist	The fascist

Figure 7.4 Examples of Social Roles Based on the Merton Typology

These examples are meant to illustrate possible outcomes, not stereotypes. Perceptions of approved goals and means may vary. In some cases, for example, the very rich, who feel that they could be even richer were it not for legal obstacles in their path, may choose to bend the rules. Also, a number of cultural values besides wealth shape the likelihood that a member of a given class will behave as he or she does.

classes in society (i.e., those who own and control the means of production) wish to control the working class and the poor so that they will produce more. From the Marxian perspective, as criminologist Richard Quinney (1980) points out, "crime is to be understood in terms of the development of capitalism" (p. 41), as it was in Marx's original analysis. From this perspective, most crime is essentially a form of class conflict—either the have-nots taking what they can from the ruling class, or the rich and their agents somehow taking what they can from the poor.

The economic "robber barons"—John Jacob Astor, John D. Rockefeller, J. P. Morgan, Leland Stanford, Andrew Carnegie, and many others—amassed huge fortunes in the period of booming industrial growth following the Civil War. But they often resorted to illegal means in pursuing the culturally approved goal of great wealth. Among other tactics, they used violence to drive settlers off land they had purchased or to break strikes by workers, and they were not above manipulating prices in order to drive out competitors and monopolize the markets for steel, oil, coal, precious metals, food products, and numerous other goods (Chernow, 1998). In Merton's typology of deviance, their actions would classify them as "innovators" (see Figure 7.4), but from a Marxian viewpoint they were merely carrying out "the logic of capitalism," which was based on the exploitation of the poor by the rich and powerful.

Marxian students of deviance point out that legal definitions of deviant behavior usually depend on the ability of the more powerful members of society to impose their will on the government and to protect their actions from legal sanctions. Thus the crimes of the robber barons almost always went unpunished. Definitions of what is criminal and who should be punished are generally applied more forcefully to the poor and the working class than to the middle and upper classes (Quinney, 1978; Reiman, 2002).

Marx and his collaborator Friedrich Engels recognized that the working class (or *proletariat*, as they called it) would resort to individual crimes like robbery when driven to do so by unemployment and poverty, but they believed that the workers would be more likely to form associations aimed at destroying capitalism. The chronic poor, however, would form a class that Marx called the *lumpenproletariat*, people who were unable to get jobs in the capitalist system or were cast off for not working hard enough or for being injured or sick. Marx did not believe that members of this class would join forces with the proletariat. Instead, they would act as spies, informers, and thugs whose services could be purchased by the rich to be used against the workers. Marx agreed with other thinkers of his time who called the lumpenproletariat the "dangerous class" created by capitalism; from its ranks came thieves, prostitutes, gamblers, pickpockets, con artists, and contract murderers.

It can be helpful to think of crime and deviance as symptoms of the class struggles that occur in any society and to show that laws that define and punish criminal behaviors are often imposed by the powerful on those with less power. But to attribute crime as we know it to the workings of capitalism is to suggest that if capitalism were abolished, crime would vanish. This clearly is not the case. In China, for example, there are thousands of prisoners in a vast chain of prison camps. Many of those prisoners were convicted of the deviant act of opposing the dominant regime (Ning, 1995; Wu & Wakeman, 1995). And in Cuba homosexuality is considered a serious crime. It is severely punished because the society's leaders think of it as an offense against masculinity and a symbol of a "decadent" subculture. As these examples indicate, societies with Marxian ideologies are hardly free from their own forms of deviance and crime.

The Interactionist Perspective

Functionalist theories explain deviance as a reaction to social dysfunctions; conflict theories explain it as a product of deviant subcultures or of the type of class struggle that occurs in a society in a particular historical period. Neither of these approaches accounts very well for the issues of recruitment and production (Rubington & Weinberg, 1999). *Recruitment,* in this context, refers to the question of why some people become deviants while others in the same social situation do not. *Production* refers to the creation of new categories of deviance in a society.

RECRUITMENT THROUGH DIFFERENTIAL ASSOCIATION   In 1940, the sociologist and criminologist Edwin H. Sutherland published a paper, "White-Collar Criminality," in which he argued that official crime statistics do not measure the many forms of crime that are not correlated with poverty. Outstanding among these are *white-collar crimes*—that is, the criminal behavior of people in business and professional positions. In Sutherland's words:

> White-collar criminality in business is expressed most frequently in the form of misrepresentation in financial statements of corporations, manipulation in stock exchange, commercial bribery, bribery of public officials directly or indirectly in order to secure favorable contracts and legislation, misrepresentation in advertising and salesmanship, embezzlement and misapplication of funds, short weights and measures and misgrading of commodities, tax frauds, misapplication of funds in receiverships and bankruptcies. These are what Al Capone called "the legitimate rackets." These and many others are found in abundance in the business world. (1940, pp. 2–3)

Sutherland was pointing out that an accurate statistical comparison of the crimes committed by the rich and the poor was not available. But his paper on white-collar crime also set forth an interactionist theory of crime and deviance:

> White-collar criminality, just as other systematic criminality . . . is learned in direct or indirect association with those who already practice the behavior; and . . . those who learn this criminal behavior are segregated from frequent and intimate contacts with law-abiding behavior. Whether a person becomes a criminal or not is determined largely by the comparative frequency and intimacy of his contacts with the two types of behavior. This may be called the process of differential association. (pp. 10–11)

The concept of **differential association** offered an answer to some of the weaknesses of functionalist and conflict theories. Not only did it account for the prevalence of deviance in all social classes, but it also provided clues to how crime is learned in groups that are culturally distinct from the dominant society. For example, in the 1920s sociologist Clifford Shaw (1929) observed that some Chicago neighborhoods had consistently higher rates of juvenile delinquency than others. These were immigrant neighborhoods, but their high rates of delinquency persisted regardless of which immigrant groups lived there at any given time. Sutherland's theory explained this pattern by calling attention to the culture of deviance that had become part of the way of life of teenagers in those neighborhoods. According to Sutherland, the teenagers became delinquent because they interacted in groups whose culture legitimated crime. It was not a matter of teenage delinquents deviating from conventional norms because the approved means of achieving approved goals were closed to them. Rather, they acted as they did because the culture of their peer group made crime an acceptable means of achieving desired goals.

In an empirical study that tested Sutherland's theory, Walter Miller (1958) found that delinquency in areas with high rates of juvenile crime was in fact supported by the norms of lower-class teenage peer groups. In three years of careful observation, Miller found that delinquent groups had a set of well-defined values: *trouble, toughness, smartness, excitement, fate,* and *autonomy.* Whereas other groups felt that it was important to stay out of trouble, the delinquent groups viewed trouble—meaning fighting, drinking, and sexual adventures—as something to brag about, as long as they didn't get caught. Toughness as shown by physical prowess or fearlessness; smartness as evidenced by the ability to con or outsmart gullible "marks"; the excitement to be found in risking danger successfully; one's fate as demonstrated by luck or good fortune in avoiding capture; and the autonomy that crime seemed to provide in

the form of independence from authorities—all were values of delinquent groups that distinguished them from nondelinquent groups in the same neighborhoods.

A study undertaken by the criminologist Donald R. Cressey (1971/1953) supported the theory of differential association with the finding that embezzlers generally had to learn how to commit their crime by associating with people who could teach them how to commit it with the greatest likelihood of avoiding suspicion. Moreover, Cressey also found that people who became embezzlers often had serious personal problems (marital difficulties, gambling, and the like) that directed them toward people who would influence them to commit this form of white-collar crime. When bank officials had problems of this sort, they were vulnerable to suggestions of deviant means of gaining money and solving personal problems while maintaining the outward signs of respectability.

Not all deviants are people whose means of achieving success have been blocked or who are acting out some form of class struggle or have associated with a deviant group. For example, many alcoholics and drug users are not thought of as deviant, either because their behavior is not considered serious or because it is not witnessed by other people. From an interactionist perspective, the key question about such people is how their behavior is understood by others (Rubington & Weinberg, 1999). The central concepts that attempt to answer this question are *labeling* and the *deviant career.*

LABELING According to symbolic-interactionist theory, deviance is produced by a process known as **labeling,** meaning a societal reaction to certain behaviors that labels the offender as a deviant. Most often, labeling is done by official agents of social control like the police, the courts, mental institutions, and schools, which distribute labels like "troublemaker," "hustler," "kook," or "blockhead" that stick to a person, often for life (Becker, 1963; Erikson, 1962; Gusfield, 1981; Lerman, 1996). Here is what occurs in the labeling process, according to Howard Becker:

> Social groups create deviance by making the rules whose infraction constitutes deviance and by applying those rules to particular people and labeling them as outsiders. From this point of view, deviance is not a quality of the act the person commits, but rather a consequence of the application by others of rules and sanctions to an "offender." The deviant is one to whom that label has been successfully applied; deviant behavior is behavior that people so label. (1963, p. 9)

In a famous experiment that tested the effects of labeling, David Rosenhan (1973) and eight other researchers were admitted to a mental hospital after pretending to "hear voices." Each of these pseudopatients was diagnosed as schizophrenic. Before long, many of the patients with whom the pseudopatients associated recognized them as normal, but the doctors who had made the diagnosis continued to think of them as schizophrenic. As the pseudopatients waited in the lunch line, for example, they were said to be exhibiting "oral-acquisitive behavior." Gradually the pseudopatients were released with the diagnosis of "schizophrenia in remission," but none was ever thought to be cured.

Rosenhan and his researchers also observed that not only did the diagnosis of schizophrenia label the patient for life, but the label itself became a justification for other forms of mistreatment. The doctors and hospital staff disregarded the patients' opinions, treated them as incompetent, and often punished them for infractions of minor rules. The hospital's social atmosphere was based on the powerlessness of the people who were labeled mentally ill.

Rosenhan's study accelerated the movement to reform mental institutions and to deinstitutionalize as many mental patients as possible. But studies of deinstitutionalized mental patients (many of whom are homeless), together with research on the problems of released convicts, have shown that the labels attached to people who have deviated become incorporated into their definitions of themselves as deviant. In this way, labeling at some stage of a person's development tends to steer that person into a community of other deviants, where he or she may become trapped in a *deviant career* (Bassuk, 1984).

DEVIANT CAREERS   "There is no reason to assume," Becker (1963) points out, "that only those who finally commit a deviant act actually have the impulse to do so. It is much more likely that most people experience deviant impulses frequently. At least in fantasy, people are much more deviant than they appear" (p. 26). Becker suggests that the proper sociological question is not why some people do things that are disapproved of, but rather, why "conventional people do not follow through on the deviant impulses they have" (p. 26). According to Becker and other interactionists, the answers are to be found in the individual's commitment to conventional institutions and behaviors.

Commitment means adherence to and dependence on the norms of a given social institution. The middle-class youth's commitment to school, which has developed over many years of socialization in the family and the community, often prevents him or her from giving in to the impulse to play hooky. "In fact," Becker asserts, "the normal development of people in our society (and probably in any society) can be seen as a series of progressively increasing commitments to conventional norms and institutions" (p. 27).

Travis Hirschi studied how people become committed to conventional norms. Such commitment, he found, emerges out of the interactions that create our social bonds to others.

When we are closely tied to people who adhere to conventional norms, we have little chance to deviate. And as we grow older, our investment in upholding conventional norms increases because we feel that we have more to protect. This process of lifetime socialization in groups produces a system of social control that is internalized in most members of the society (Hirschi & Gottfredson, 1980, 1994). (See Chapter 5 for more on socialization over the life course.)

By the same token, a person who once gives in to the impulse to commit a deviant act and is caught, or who becomes a member of a deviant group because it has recruited him or her, gradually develops a commitment to that group and its deviant culture. The reasons for taking the first step toward deviance may be many and varied, but from the interactionist perspective, "one of the most crucial steps in the process of building a stable pattern of deviant behavior is likely to be the experience of being caught and publicly labeled as deviant" (Becker, 1963, p. 31).

In a well-known empirical study of youth gangs, William J. Chambliss (1973) applied both the conflict and interactionist perspectives. For 2 years, Chambliss observed the Saints, a gang of boys from rather wealthy families, and the Roughnecks, a gang of poor boys from the same community. Both gangs engaged in car theft and joyriding, vandalism, dangerous practical jokes, and fighting—and in fact the Saints were involved in a larger overall number of incidents. But the Roughnecks were more frequently caught by authorities, described as "tough young criminals headed for trouble," and sent to reform school. The wealthier youths were rarely caught and were never labeled delinquent.

Chambliss observed that the Saints had access to cars and could commit their misdeeds in other communities, where they were not known. The Roughnecks hung out in their own community and performed many of their antisocial acts there. A far more important explanation, according to Chambliss, pertained to the relative influence of the boys' parents. The parents of the Saints argued that the boys' activities were normal youthful behavior; the boys were just "sowing their wild oats." Their social position enabled them to influence the way their children's behavior was perceived, an influence the Roughnecks' parents did not have. Thus the Roughnecks were caught and labeled and became increasingly committed to deviant careers, while the Saints escaped without serious sanction.

In commenting on Chambliss' study, sociologists often note that members of both gangs engaged in deviant acts, referred to as **primary deviance,** but that only the Roughnecks were labeled delinquent by the police and the juvenile courts. As a result of that labeling, many of the Roughnecks went on to commit acts that sociologists call **secondary deviance**—that is, behaviors appropriate to someone who

THEORETICAL PERSPECTIVES ON DEVIANCE

PERSPECTIVE	DESCRIPTION	CRITIQUE
BIOLOGICAL THEORIES	Crime and other forms of deviance are genetically determined.	There is evidence of effects of socialization.
SOCIOLOGICAL THEORIES		
Social Pathology	The deviant or criminal person is a product of a "social sickness" or social disintegration.	A popular notion, but discredited among professionals because it suggests no real theory of causality.
Functionalism	Deviance and crime result from the failure of social structures to function properly. Every society produces its own forms of deviance.	Does not explain why some people drift into deviant subcultures.
Conflict Theories		
Cultural conflict	Cultural conflict creates opportunities for deviance and criminal gain in deviant sub-cultures (e.g., prohibitions create opportunities for organized crime).	Explains a narrow range of phenomena.
Marxian theory	Capitalism produces poor and powerless masses who may resort to crime to survive. The rich employ their own agents to break laws and enhance their power and wealth.	Crime exists in societies that have sought to eliminate capitalism.
Interactionist Theories		
Differential association	Criminal careers result from recruitment into crime groups based on association and interaction with criminals.	Excellent explanation of recruitment but not as effective in explaining deviant careers.
Labeling	Deviance is created by groups that have the power to attach labels to others, marking particular people as outsiders. It is extremely difficult to shed a label once it has been acquired, and the labeled person tends to behave in the expected manner.	Not always supported by empirical evidence. People can also use labels (e.g., drunk) to change their behavior.

has already been labeled delinquent. (For example, in juvenile detention centers, teenage offenders often learn deviant skills such as drug dealing.) The distinction between primary and secondary deviance is useful because it emphasizes that most of us deviate from cultural norms in many ways; but once we are *labeled* deviant, we tend to commit additional deviant acts in order to fulfill the negative definitions that society has attached to us (Goode, 1994; Rubington & Weinberg, 1999).

Reasonable as the labeling perspective appears, it has not always been borne out by empirical research. Some studies have found that people who have been labeled delinquent after being caught and convicted of serious offenses go on to commit other deviant acts, but other studies have found that labeling can lead to decreased deviance and a lower proba-

bility of further offenses (Rubington & Weinberg, 1999). (The various theoretical perspectives on deviance that we have discussed are summarized in the Study Chart above.)

CRIME AND SOCIAL CONTROL

We have seen that crime as defined by a society's laws is only one aspect of the range of behaviors included in the study of deviance. But the general public and policymakers in government are most concerned with crime and its control. In this section, therefore, we touch on some of the most hotly debated issues in the control of crime and the treatment of criminals.

TABLE 7.2

The Crime Rate,* by Region of the United States, 2001

	Northeast	Midwest	South	West
Crime Index, total	3,007	3,981	4,761	4,355
Violent crime, total	430	432	580	520
Murder	4	5	7	6
Forcible rape	23	35	34	33
Robbery	150	128	160	150
Aggravated assault	253	263	380	332
Property crime, total	2,577	3,549	4,181	3,835
Burglary	470	678	927	736
Larceny-theft	1,788	2,492	2,827	2,519
Motor vehicle theft	319	380	428	580

*Offenses known to the police, per 100,000 population.

Source: FBI, 2002.

At the beginning of the chapter, we defined social control in broad terms as all the ways in which a society establishes and enforces its cultural norms. Certainly it is true that without socialization and the controlling actions of social groups like the family, schools, the military, and corporations there would be much more anomie, crime, and violence. But in considering a society's means of controlling crime, sociologists most often study what might be called "government social control"—that is, the society's legal codes; the operation of its judicial, police, penal, and rehabilitative institutions; and the ways in which its most powerful members promote their views of crime, deviance, and social control (Black, 1984; Scull, 1988). The rates of crime and the ways in which crime affects communities in different parts of the society establish the need for these institutions of social control, as we will see in the following analysis.

Ecological Dimensions of Crime

Table 7.2 shows that the incidence of different types of crime varies from one region of the country to another, with homicides highest in the southern states and rape and assault lowest in the northeastern states. Ecological data like these are an essential starting point in research on the incidence of crime and provide some insights into why such regional differences exist. In the South, for example, high rates of gun ownership contribute to higher homicide rates. The higher average age of the population in the Northeast contributes to lower rates of rape and assault in that region, while greater disparities between rich and poor lead to a higher rate of robbery.

Another contribution of ecological analysis can be seen in data on the relationship between crime and the age composition of a population. Some political leaders and social scientists favor larger police forces and tougher law enforcement, and they argue that these policies are responsible for the decrease in the U.S. crime rate over the past several years. However, it must not be forgotten that the age composition of the U.S. population is changing rather quickly. Among other things, the baby boom generation has moved out of the young-adult years, those in which people are most likely to commit crimes. (About half of all reported violent crimes are committed by males between the ages of 15 and 24.) Thus, before taking credit for reducing crime rates, law enforcement agencies and advocates of tough anticrime measures must determine whether lower crime rates are not simply the result of a reduction in the most crime-prone portion of the population.

Still another variable that lends itself to ecological analysis is the effect of possession of firearms on homicide rates. The United States far outpaces other industrialized nations in number of homicides. No other nation even comes close. This fact is often thought to reflect a greater overall level of violence in the United States than in other comparable nations. However, in a study comparing rates of violent crime in Denmark and northeastern Ohio, investigators found that rates of assault did not differ in the two areas. What did differ were rates of homicide using firearms; such crimes were much more frequent in Ohio. In Denmark, the possession of handguns is banned, whereas in the United States, "50 percent of all households have guns and one in five has a handgun" (Mawson, 1989, p. 239). (See the Mapping Social Change box on page 189.)

Worldwide Homicide Rates

Although homicide rates in the United States have declined in the past few years, there is little likelihood of a decline to levels characteristic of the European democracies. There are nations with higher homicide rates, such as Ecuador, the Bahamas, and perhaps Russia. All are undergoing rapid social change, but none enjoy the degree of affluence found

often include stops in this island nation, are an important influence. In Russia, the abrupt changes accompanying the transition from communism to capitalism have produced an increase in homicide rates.

The United States shares certain characteristics with each of these nations. Like Ecuador and other Latin American

ing the use of guns. It also has a widening gap between rich and poor, with the poor often concentrated in ghetto slums. Drug activity contributes significantly to homicide rates, as in the Bahamas. And as in Russia, much of the deadly violence occurring in the United States stems from the activities of criminals in organized gangs.

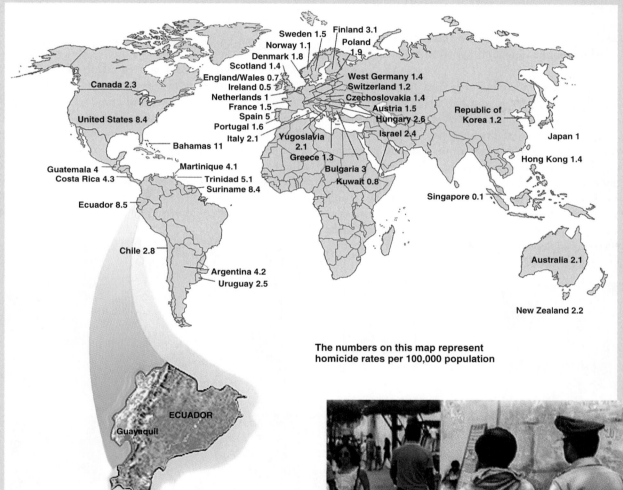

Sweden 1.5
Finland 3.1
Norway 1.1
Poland 1.9
Denmark 1.8
Scotland 1.4
England/Wales 0.7
Ireland 0.5
Netherlands 1
France 1.5
Spain 5
Portugal 1.6
Italy 2.1
West Germany 1.4
Switzerland 1.2
Czechoslovakia 1.4
Austria 1.5
Hungary 2.6
Yugoslavia 2.1
Greece 1.3
Israel 2.4
Republic of Korea 1.2
Japan 1
Hong Kong 1.4
Canada 2.3
United States 8.4
Bahamas 11
Guatemala 4
Costa Rica 4.3
Martinique 4.1
Trinidad 5.1
Suriname 8.4
Bulgaria 3
Kuwait 0.8
Singapore 0.1
Ecuador 8.5
Chile 2.8
Argentina 4.2
Uruguay 2.5
Australia 2.1
New Zealand 2.2

ECUADOR
Guayaquil

The numbers on this map represent homicide rates per 100,000 population

in the United States. In Ecuador, high homicide rates are associated with rapid urbanization in cities like Guayaquil, where murders occur at extremely high rates in sprawling slums. In the Bahamas, the international drug markets, which

nations, the United States has a frontier tradition that fosters and still maintains norms of rugged individualism, includ-

As mentioned earlier in the chapter, studies of criminal victimization, which ask people about their actual experiences with crime, have provided a major breakthrough in our understanding of crime in complex societies. Of every 1,000 crimes, slightly more than half are reported to the police. Of those, about 15 percent result in arrests. Twenty-five years ago, less than half of all arrests led to convictions, and less than half of those convicted were sentenced to custody. Today, with more forceful law enforcement strategies, including tougher sentencing guidelines and mandatory jailing of third-time offenders in California and other states, these figures have improved. Nevertheless, the probability that a criminal who is arrested will be sentenced to prison remains low. On the other hand, while the probability of arrest for a single property crime, such as theft of an automobile, is low, criminals who commit many crimes do tend to be arrested eventually; this is especially true for those who commit violent crimes (Butterfield, 1998b).

RECIDIVISM   Most sociological studies of **recidivism** (the probability that a person who has served a jail term will commit additional crimes and be jailed again) indicate that there is an overall probability of 50 percent that recidivism will occur. Recidivism is most frequent among young minority males from poor backgrounds who are drug and/or alcohol addicts and have been imprisoned on numerous previous occasions for crimes against property (Land, 1989). In recent years, there have been forceful efforts to reduce the types of recidivism that pose the greatest threat to society. People who have been convicted of violent of-

fenses and people who have served prison sentences for sex crimes are especially likely to be refused parole. In the case of sex offenders, community notification policies, in which neighbors are informed that a former sex offender has moved into their community, are being implemented in many states (Zonana, 1997). The high crime rates of recent decades, together with public support for longer sentences and less lenient parole policies, have resulted in record high rates of imprisonment, as we will see shortly. Despite the decline in crime rates in the last few years, states are finding it necessary to build new prisons even as corrections professionals search for alternatives to imprisonment, especially for nonviolent offenders.

Institutions of Coercive Control: Courts and Prisons

When the United States consisted mainly of small agrarian communities, there were jails and courts, but a great deal of social control of deviance and crime was carried out by the local institutions of the family or the church. Parents, for example, were expected to control their children; if they did not, they would lose the respect of other members of the community. But as the size, complexity, and diversity of societies increase, the ability of local institutions to control all of the society's members is diminished (Wirth, 1968/1938). Societies therefore develop specialized, more

In earlier periods of history, executions were public spectacles and often considered a form of entertainment. In modern societies that still practice execution, there is much less emphasis on public spectacle and much more on the technology employed to perform the execution.

or less coercive institutions to deal with deviants. Courts, prisons, police forces, and social-welfare agencies grow as the influence of the community on the behavior of its members declines.

CAPITAL PUNISHMENT: THE GLOBAL DEBATE Capital punishment provides an illustration of the issues raised by the use of coercive forms of social control. Only recently (during the twentieth century in some nations) has there been ongoing debate about the morality of capital punishment (Phillips, 1998). In simpler societies and earlier civilizations, execution was more than a penalty carried out on an individual; it was also an occasion for a public ceremony. People attended beheadings and hangings, and hawkers sold food and other goods as the crowd waited for the bloody pageant. The villain's death reaffirmed their common values, their solidarity as a people who could purge evil elements from their midst.

Today, by contrast, the value of capital punishment is a matter of heated debate, as we have seen recently in the case of Timothy McVeigh, who was executed on June 11, 2001, for the Oklahoma City bombing in which 168 people were killed. Although many people believe that the death sentence is necessary as a means of discouraging some individuals from committing terrible crimes, others are convinced that there is no justification for putting another person to death, the more so because it is always possible that the person did not commit the crime for which he or she was executed. One study of this grim possibility provides evidence of as many as 18 wrongful executions in the United States since 1900 (Radelet & Bedau, 1992).

In one of a series of studies of the equity of capital punishment, criminologists Marvin Wolfgang and Marc Riedel (1973) found that blacks were more likely than whites to be executed for the same crimes and that people who could afford good lawyers were far more likely to escape execution than those who lacked the means to hire the best legal defenders. As we see in Figure 7.5, although the absolute number of white inmates on death row is higher than that of African Americans by about 500, in proportional terms—that is, relative to their proportion of the overall population—African Americans are extremely overrepresented on death rows in the United States. The graphs also show that since capital punishment was reinstated in many states, the overall number of inmates on death row has increased dramatically.

In 1972, swayed by evidence like that gathered by Wolfgang and Riedel and by arguments that capital punishment could be considered "cruel and unusual punishment" according to the Constitution (most other Western nations had already banned the death penalty), the Supreme Court ruled in a 5-to-4 decision that, in the absence of clear specifications for when it might be used, the

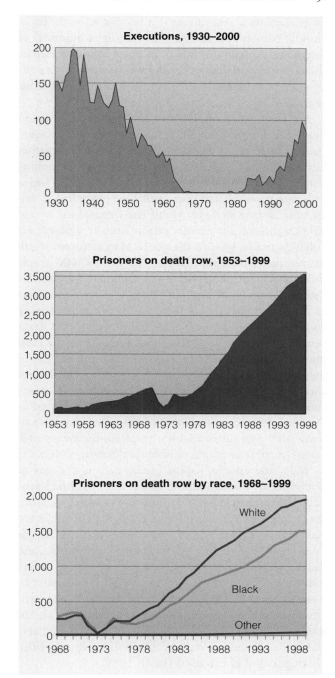

Figure 7.5 Executions and Prisoners on Death Row, United States

Source: Bureau of Justice Statistics.

death sentence violated the Eighth Amendment to the Constitution. But Congress has since passed new legislation that legalized the death sentence, and the Court has not overruled it. As a result, capital punishment has been reinstated in many states; there are now between 15 and

30 executions a year in the United States, with Texas, Florida, Mississippi, and Arizona leading in numbers of executions carried out. Indeed, in many states, the debate about capital punishment has shifted away from its morality to questions about technology, such as the use of lethal injections versus the electric chair.

But does capital punishment have the effect of deterring people from committing murder, as its advocates claim? Much of the evidence on this subject is negative. Little encouragement is found in comparisons among states that have the death penalty, states that have had it with interruptions, and states that have never had it. For example, despite its highly visible and frequent use of capital punishment, the murder rate in Texas is almost 6 per 100,000 people, whereas the rate in Massachusetts, which has not had capital punishment, is 2 per 100,000 people (FBI, 2002). Yet in interviews with criminals charged with robbery, James Q. Wilson (1977) found evidence that fear of the death penalty discouraged them from carrying guns. There is still considerable opposition to the death penalty among people who feel that it represents cruel and unusual punishment, but surveys indicate that the tide of public opinion has turned toward support for it. Surveys also show, for better or worse, that the public's increased concern about crime has led to greater emphasis on use of the death sentence as retribution for murders that have already been committed and less emphasis on the possible deterrent effect of capital punishment (Koretz, 2003).

Today the value of capital punishment is a matter of heated debate throughout the world. In 1998, 1,625 prisoners were executed in 37 countries, 4 of which—China, the Democratic Republic of the Congo, the United States, and Iran—accounted for 80 percent of the total. All the European nations have abolished capital punishment, and Russia has placed a moratorium on executions. Many countries decided to suspend or abolish capital punishment as a way of turning over a new leaf after long periods of political repression. This is true of South Africa, the former communist countries of eastern Europe, and several Latin American nations (Argentina, Brazil, Peru, Nicaragua, and El Salvador) (Jacot, 1999).

PLEA BARGAINING: A REVOLVING DOOR?   Capital punishment addresses a small but sensational part of the crime problem. Many more criminals will commit other types of crimes, and for them, too, the issue of punishment and rehabilitation is controversial. At present, judges and police officers feel hampered by the relatively limited array of treatments for criminal offenders, as well as the backlogs in the courts and the overcrowding of prisons. One means of reducing the pressure on the judicial system is **plea bargaining,** in which a person who is charged with a crime agrees to plead guilty to a lesser charge and thereby free the courts from having to conduct a lengthy and costly

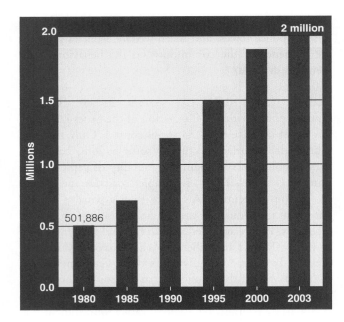

Figure 7.6   Adult Correctional Populations, 1980–2003

Source: Bureau of Justice Statistics.

jury trial. The shorter sentences that result from this system diminish somewhat the size of prison populations. Plea bargaining has been criticized as "revolving-door justice"; however, criminologists estimate that an increase of only 20 percent in the number of offenders who are tried and imprisoned would place an intolerable burden on the correctional system (Reid, 1993).

PRISONS: SCHOOLS FOR CRIME?   Despite the small proportion of crimes resulting in arrest and imprisonment, prisons remain the social institution with the primary responsibility for dealing with criminals. From 1980 to 2003, the total number of Americans in prisons of all kinds almost quadrupled (see Figure 7.6). In addition to the prison population, there are more than 4.5 million people on probation or parole. It is estimated that within a decade more than 7.5 million people will be under some form of law enforcement surveillance in the United States (Butterfield, 1998a).

The largest proportion of new prisoners were arrested for the sale or possession of felonious quantities of narcotics and were imprisoned under mandatory sentencing laws that were passed as part of the national war on drugs. But the arrests were by no means equally distributed among drug users and dealers. According to researchers with the Federal Sentencing Project, for young Americans from ghetto communities and many other impoverished areas "going to prison has become as inevitable . . . as going to college is for middle-class kids" (quoted in Butterfield, 1992a, p. E4). While there is widespread agreement on the need to punish

JUSTIFICATIONS FOR PUNISHMENT

STUDY CHART

JUSTIFICATION	FUNCTION	CRITICAL ISSUES
Deterrence	To prevent crime and protect society from criminal predation	Does prison, as a dominant form of punishment, deter crime or socialize criminals?
Rehabilitation	To resocialize the criminal so that he or she can reenter society	What forms of rehabilitation actually work to prevent recidivism?
Retribution	To take revenge on the criminal and make punishment show society's anger about the crime	Do extreme punishments reduce all members of society to the level of the criminal?

drug dealers and users, there is growing debate over the desirability of sending them to prison, since it is highly likely that a young person who is imprisoned will learn from fellow inmates more diverse and devious ways of breaking the law.

FELONY DISENFRANCHISEMENT Another serious concern about the way inequalities in imprisonment affect specific groups in the society is the denial of voting rights to some ex-felons, a situation known as *felony disenfranchisement*. Most states do not allow imprisoned felons to vote, but 14 states bar ex-offenders who have fully served their sentences from voting throughout their lifetime.

The scale of felony disenfranchisement in the United States is greater than anywhere else in the world. Approximately 3.9 million U.S. citizens are disenfranchised, including more than 1 million who have fully completed their sentences. In its research report on the issue, the Sentencing Project of the Human Rights Watch reported that

> The racial impact of disenfranchisement laws is particularly egregious. Thirteen percent of African American men—1.4 million—are disenfranchised, representing just over one-third (36 percent) of the total disenfranchised population. In two states, our data show that almost one in three black men is disenfranchised. In eight states, one in four black men is disenfranchised. If current trends continue, the rate of disenfranchisement for black men could reach 40 percent in the states that disenfranchise ex-offenders.
>
> Disenfranchisement laws in the United States are a vestige of medieval times when offenders were banished from the community and suffered "civil death." Brought from Europe to the colonies, they gained new political salience at the end of the nineteenth century when disgruntled whites in a number of southern states adopted them and other ostensibly race-neutral voting restrictions in an effort to exclude blacks from the vote. (Human Rights Watch, 1998)

While they are partly a holdover from the era of enforced racial segregation, particularly in southern states like Florida, it is unlikely that these laws will be changed soon, since they benefit many incumbent political leaders.

Functions of Prisons

The arguments used to support reliance on prison as the central institution of punishment and reform are mainly functionalist in nature. The functions of prisons are said to be *deterrence, rehabilitation*, and *retribution* (i.e., punishment) (Goode, 1994; Hawkins, 1976). As Bruce Jackson, a well-known student of prison life, explains it, a prison is supposed to deter criminals from committing crimes ("its presence is supposed to keep those among us of weak moral strength from actions we might otherwise commit"); it is supposed to rehabilitate those who do commit crimes ("within its walls those who have, for whatever reason, transgressed society's norms are presumably shown the error of their ways and retooled so they can live outside in a more acceptable and satisfactory fashion"); and it is supposed to punish criminals—the only function that it clearly fulfills (1972, p. 248). (See the Study Chart above.)

Sociologists who study prisons note their similarity to other kinds of total institutions—social environments in which every aspect of the individual's life is subject to the control of authorities. In these institutions, inmates are deprived of their former statuses through haircuts, uniforms, and the like (Goffman, 1961). (See Chapter 5.) The goal of this process is to socialize the inmates to behave in ways that suit the organization's needs. But in most such organizations there is also a strong inmate subculture consisting of norms that specify ways of resisting the officials in favor of such values as mutual aid and loyalty among the inmates (Rubington & Weinberg, 1999). Thus, in Bruce Jackson's (1972) collection of case histories of criminals and prison inmates, a seasoned convict summed up the world of the total institution as follows: "A penitentiary is like a prisoner of war camp. The officials are the enemy and the inmates are captured. They're on one side and we're on the other" (p. 253). But the same prisoner also described another aspect of life in total institutions. Often, as the following passage reveals, the inmates develop "institutional personalities." As they try to conform to the norms of the organization, they become dependent on the routines and constraints of minimal freedom and, hence, minimal responsibility:

> I like things to be orderly. You might say I'm a conservative, I like the status quo. If something's going smooth I like that. . . . Some people . . . kind of like it. Get institutionalized. You know, there's a lot of security in a place like this for a person. . . . They'll tell you when to get up, they'll tell you when to go to bed, when to eat, when to work. They'll do your laundry for you. You don't have to worry about anything else. (p. 253)

Only relatively recently, beginning mainly in the second half of the twentieth century, has the goal of rehabilitation—the effort to return criminals to society as law-abiding citizens—been taken seriously as a function of prisons. Critics of the prison system, many of whom argue from a conflict perspective, often claim that far from rehabilitating their inmates, prisons in fact function as "schools for crime" (Califano, 1998). As early as 1789, the English philosopher and economist Jeremy Bentham wrote that "prisons, with the exception of a small number, include every imaginable means of infecting both body and mind. . . . An ordinary prison is a school in which wickedness is taught by surer means than can ever be employed for the inculcation of virtue" (pp. 351–352). In the intervening years, many studies have attempted to show under what conditions this is true and what can be done to increase the deterrent effects of prison and prevent it from becoming a community that socializes criminals.

Yet there is much sociological research that defends prisons as a means of deterrence and a necessary form of retribution (Allen, 1997). James Q. Wilson (1977) holds to the functionalist position: Societies need the firm moral authority they gain from stigmatizing and punishing crime. He believes that prisoners should receive better forms of rehabilitation in prison and be guaranteed their rights as citizens once they are outside again. But, he states, "to destigmatize crime would be to lift from it the weight of moral judgment and to make crime simply a particular occupation or avocation which society has chosen to reward less (or perhaps more) than other pursuits" (p. 230). Some states have taken the desire to get tough on crime to the extreme of reinstating chain gangs.

Whatever their sociological perspective, all students of the American prison system agree that by far the least successful aspect of prison life is rehabilitation. Research conducted in the 1970s consistently found that the only effec-

tive rehabilitation programs in prisons, measured by lower rates of recidivism, involve job training and education (Martinson, 1972). Indeed, during the 1980s, as prison populations more than doubled, sociologists and criminologists found that men from very poor and minority backgrounds were beginning to regard prison as the only way they could obtain job training, health care, and other social services. Prisons, after all, provide more adequate housing than the large urban shelters for the homeless, and in prison one gets three meals a day and, in some cases, a chance to improve one's skills and self-confidence.

The conservative mood of the United States has had a profound impact on rehabilitation programs in federal and state prisons. Throughout the United States, legislative and administrative actions reduced educational opportunities for offenders, especially by limiting federal and state funding for prison post-secondary education programs (Koretz, 2003; Tewksbury & Taylor, 1996). Some legislators, showing far more interest in punishment than in rehabilitation, supported a proposal that would void all court-ordered efforts to correct inhumane conditions in prisons (Kunen, 1995). As one of the nation's leading researchers on crime and prisons has observed, in our society "we have an exaggerated belief in the efficacy of imprisonment. The real problem is that we make life really terrible for some people and then blame them when they become dangerous" (Norval Morris, quoted in Butterfield, 1992a).

CRITICAL SOCIOLOGY AND SOCIAL CHANGE

Corporate Crime

A wave of corporate crime swept through American business in 2001–2003, and it included some of the most spectacular losses of shareholder value in American history (Rosoff, Pontell, & Tillman, 2002). Major companies that have gone bankrupt, with subsequent losses of thousands of jobs, include Enron, Arthur Andersen, Global Crossing, and others; some of the most important are shown in Table 7.3.

When sociologists ask people about their attitudes concerning these scandals, they often get cynical responses like "What else is new?" or "The system is filled with corruption," or "The politicians and the corporate types are in bed together." But such answers are not adequate explanations for what amounted to a crime wave among some of the nation's most respected business leaders. Nor do responses like these lead in a direction that can decrease the likelihood of such scandals in the future and protect jobs and investments. A more sophisticated approach would be to ask some questions about what has occurred that are based on the major sociological perspectives.

TABLE 7.3

Corporations Embroiled in Scandal and Fees Paid to Accountants

Fees in millions ($)	2000	% of fees for consulting 2000	2001	% of fees for consulting 2001	Accountant	Scandal in brief
Adelphia Communications	$ 3.5	62%	n/a	n/a	Deloitte & Touche	Investigations by the SEC and 2 grand juries.
Auditing	1.3		n/a			
Non-audit and consulting	2.2		n/a			
Enron	52.0	52%	n/a	n/a	Arthur Andersen	Took advantage of lax regulations to defraud consumers & investors.
Auditing	25.0		n/a			
Non-audit and consulting	27.0		n/a			
Global Crossing	14.2	84%	n/a	n/a	Arthur Andersen	Under investigation by the FBI and SEC for accounting fraud.
Auditing	2.3		n/a			
Non-audit and consulting	12.0		n/a			
Halliburton	51.5	86%	26.5	73%	Arthur Andersen	In May the SEC began investigating Dick Cheney's role in $100 million in questionable accounting reports when he was the company's CEO.
Auditing	7.4		7.2			
Non-audit and consulting	44.1		19.3			
IMClone Systems	0.2	63%	0.4	58%	KPMG	CEO arrested for insider trading, Martha Stewart also under investigation.
Auditing	0.1		0.2			
Non-audit and consulting	0.1		0.2			
Kmart	12.8	91%	Filed for bankruptcy 8 days before they would have been required to disclose for 2001		Pricewaterhouse Coopers	Under investigation by the SEC for accounting fraud.
Auditing	1.1					
Non-audit and consulting	11.7					
Lucent Technologies	Did not disclose for 2000		62.6	88%	Pricewaterhouse Coopers	Under investigation by the SEC for accounting fraud.
Auditing			7.6			
Non-audit and consulting			55.0			
Martha Stewart Living Omnimedia	1.0	69%	0.8	64%	Arthur Andersen	Martha Stewart is under investigation by the SEC for insider trading.
Auditing	0.3		0.3			
Non-audit and consulting	0.7		0.5			
Merck & Co	6.3	33%	6.5	34%	Arthur Andersen	Shareholder lawsuits concerning accounting problems.
Auditing	4.2		4.3			
Non-audit and consulting	2.1		2.2			
Tyco	n/a	n/a	34.9	62%	Pricewaterhouse Coopers	Under investigation by the SEC for accounting fraud.
Auditing	n/a		13.2			
Non-audit and consulting	n/a		21.7			
WorldCom	26.7	86%	16.8	74%	Arthur Andersen	Under investigation by the SEC for accounting fraud.
Auditing	3.8		4.4			
Non-audit and consulting	22.9		12.4			
Xerox	18.8	40%	n/a	n/a	KPMG	Paid a $10 million fine to the SEC for accounting fraud.
Auditing	11.3		n/a			
Non-audit and consulting	7.5		n/a			

Source: www.citizen.org/documents/scandalappendixa.pdf.

THE CONFLICT PERSPECTIVE Rich and powerful corporate leaders are granted many privileges in American society, and this is widely accepted. So what is unusual about the recent episodes of corporate greed? This question seeks to determine how corporate crime differs from crimes committed by people without great wealth or easy access to political influence.

A low-level drug user and dealer convicted of selling small quantities of a drug is typically sentenced to a long prison term and then, as a felony offender, in many states is deprived forever of the right to vote. A high-level and prestigious corporate leader who bilks his employees and the public out of millions of dollars is extremely unlikely ever to do jail time. So differences in power and the likelihood of eventual punishment may make it attractive for corporate leaders to take liberties with the public trust and with stockholders' funds (Fortunato, 2002). Recent corporate scandals, however, require that we ask further questions about

Text continues on page 198.

VISUAL SOCIOLOGY

THE TUNNEL PEOPLE

During the first few decades of the twentieth century, homeless people, especially homeless men, were shunted into the "skid row" areas of cities in the United States. Skid row was, and in some cities still is, a downtown area where there were cheap hotels and cafeterias and religious missions, all of which served the needs of homeless men, day laborers, migrant workers, chronic alcoholics, and other destitute people who sought to survive in the city while maintaining socially disapproved lifestyles. But skid row areas have been no more immune to major social change than other parts of cities. Changes in the need for cheap labor in seaports and regional shipment centers have decreased the demand for day-rate workers. The population of hoboes has decreased as well, and so has the propensity for some men to go on drunken binges for weeks at a time, drifting into skid row to enjoy its cheap bars and anonymous hotels. Most recently, the rising value of downtown real estate has driven out the older skid row institutions. So where can homeless, alcoholic, drug-addicted, mentally ill, or destitute men and women live in the contemporary city?

Very often these people still live in the downtown area, under boxes, or on the periphery of the city, in vacant lots or alleys. In the largest cities, however, these people are often driven from such visible spots. Some find shelter underground, in railroad tunnels and abandoned water tunnels. Photographer Margaret Morton and sociologist Terry Williams have conducted extensive studies of the lives of homeless people underground. These photos are from Morton's photo essay about the tunnel people of midtown Manhattan. They show how desperately people strive to create the semblance of a "normal" life under the most discouraging conditions.

© Margaret Morton, author/photographer The Tunnel (Yale University Press, 1995)

© Margaret Morton, author/photographer The Tunnel (Yale University Press, 1995)

You get to meet some weird people coming through the tunnel. We met young graffiti artists. In fact we met one of the best graffiti artists—his name was Freedom-Chris. He just did a mural down in our place. It must be something like sixty-foot by thirty-foot. Then we had a fellow by the name of Sane. He died recently—fell off a bridge. And he did a piece right on our wall about the mind, intellectuality, that man is screwing up the whole world. And it really looked nice.

I take medication for asthma and epilepsy. It doesn't matter where you live, what you're doing. If it comes, it comes. There's nothing you can do about it. I go out every day. I have friends. I go to the bar to see my friends and stuff like that. I don't hide. But everybody doesn't know everything about me either because it's none of their business. I don't ask them about them, and they don't ask me about me. So, that's the way it is. Because some of them are my friends, they know where I live. But then there are others who are just acquaintances that I see when I see, and that's it. And they don't know nothing. They don't have to.

The Sociological Observer

(See photo on page 181.)

While homeless people are often considered deviant outcasts in American cities and frequently find themselves shunted into places like tunnels or public shelters, in much of the Third World, homelessness is far more common. Homeless people are often recent arrivals to urban regions who are living in makeshift shelters on the city's edges. As bad as their living situation might be, it is also likely that they have come from even more impoverished conditions in their home villages. Although the rich in their societies may see them as a nuisance, they can hardly be considered deviant since so many are in similar situations.

Coke and amphetamines started coming back to me because I had an unlimited supply [as a cook in a hospital] .... And I gave up everything, gave up everything that I had. And I moved into a place called the Amtrak Tunnel.

I have always done most of the cooking. In most cases, people will heat up stuff down there. But cooking stews, soups—I'm an excellent cook. I love to cook. People say, "That was amazing!" I've never cooked professionally, I've never had a job as a cook. They thought I was in the military or something, which I wasn't.

I got my little family [18 cats], and that's enough. I don't need any more. They are all different, and if you're feeling bad they make you feel better. They're not like people, they're not two-faced. They don't have one side and then have another the next time. So that's why I love my animals. And they know they can depend on me.

why some corporations and corporate leaders acted in such scandalous ways while others did not.

THE FUNCTIONALIST PERSPECTIVE   Were there structural problems that encouraged behavior in particular situations that led to the scandals? Indeed there were. This question takes a functionalist perspective. It probes the ways in which specific companies were functioning in their business environments that might have encouraged the commission of crimes in those corporations and not in others.

One example was the system, applied in companies like Enron, WorldCom, and many others, that awarded company stock and stock options to employees as part of their pension plans. Top corporate officials, however, often received huge amounts of stocks and options (which permit the owner to buy the stocks at a set price). If the stocks rose in value due to increased profits, everyone in the company benefited, especially those at the top who received the most stocks or options. But lower-level employees often were not permitted to sell their company stocks. And by rewarding top executives with enormous sums of company stock, the directors were creating incentives whereby the same top executives would be rewarded even more liberally if the stock kept rising. That, in turn, created incentives for executives to influence the company's auditors to accept questionable accounting practices that would hide losses and magnify profits. And when this coverup was accomplished, some company officials sold their stocks even as they failed to warn lower-level employees that the company's losses would soon become public knowledge. In other words, the corporate leaders traded on insider information, the knowledge that the stock's price would soon go down.

Audits of corporate earnings are carried out by separate accounting firms whose analysis is used by the company to report its profits and losses to the public. When a company's audits show large profits, the company's stock becomes more attractive to investors and its price goes up. But the auditors were often being paid not only to do the audits but also to give the corporation advice about how to improve its business. Table 7.3 shows that in 2000 the Enron Corporation paid its accounting firm, Arthur Andersen, $52 million

in fees, of which 52 percent was for consulting services. The structure of this relationship created a major conflict of interest for the Andersen auditors. They felt pressure to use faulty accounting to magnify Enron's profits because their consulting relationships had led them to suggest questionable practices in the first place.

Structural changes in response to this corporate crime wave—based on legislation either passed or pending in Congress—include greater flexibility for employees to sell their company stocks in their pensions, and rules that require that accounting firms not provide consulting services to companies for which they are the official auditors.

THE INTERACTIONIST PERSPECTIVE   Many corporate leaders had the same incentives to influence their auditing companies to inflate profits. Why did it occur in some companies and not in others? The interactionist perspective is particularly helpful in understanding the most flagrant episodes of corporate crime, such as what occurred at Enron.

Enron's top executives made a great deal of money quite rapidly and began spending lavishly. Top executives like Kenneth Lay, the firm's chief executive, developed high profiles in Houston and became well known for their political donations and their philanthropy. Lay and his associates were considered generous bosses and community leaders. But their lavish lifestyles, with many houses in different parts of the nation, required that they continually increase their own salaries and perks. Under these conditions, the executives found it extremely difficult to resist the temptation to collude with their corruptible auditors in "cooking the books" and reporting false profits, which eventually led to their downfall. For the interactionist, the key aspect of the Enron executives' behavior, and that of other corporate leaders caught in the recent wave of false reporting, is that they began to interact with one another in ways that made them feel that their illegal actions would eventually be justified by their successes and by the adulation they had become used to. Opportunities to buy power and influence, and the sense that they were entitled to be rich beyond imagining, led them, in turn, to lose their "core values" (Etzioni, 2002; Simpson & Piquero, 2002).

SUMMARY

What Is Deviance?

- *Deviance,* broadly defined, is behavior that violates the norms of a particular society. The deviant label is attached to a person who violates or opposes a society's most valued norms.

- The ways in which a society encourages conformity to its norms and prevents deviance are known as *social control.*

- There is usually much disagreement not only about which behaviors are deviant but also about which ones should be condoned or punished only mildly.

Dimensions of Deviance

- An important dimension of deviance is the power of some groups in society to define which acts are legal and which are illegal.

- Deviance should be distinguished from *stigma*. A stigmatized person has some attribute that is deeply discrediting, such as a disfiguring disease, but is not necessarily a social deviant.

- The study of deviance is concerned with social deviants—that is, people who voluntarily violate the norms of their society. In particular, the study of deviance focuses on criminal deviance: acts or omissions of acts for which the state can apply sanctions.

- As a culture's values and norms change, so do its notions of what kinds of behavior are deviant and how they should be sanctioned.

- The extent to which the members of a society agree on whether a particular behavior is deviant can range from weak (in cases in which there is much controversy) to strong (in cases in which there is little disagreement). Negative sanctions, or punishments, can also range from very weak to very strong.

- A deviant subculture includes a system of values, attitudes, behaviors, and lifestyles that are opposed to the dominant culture of the society in which it is found. Many deviant subcultures are harmful to society because they sustain criminal occupations. Others provide opportunities to engage in behavior that is pleasurable to many people but is considered deviant in "respectable" society. The boundaries between what is normal and what is deviant are not distinct.

Theoretical Perspectives on Social Deviance

- Biological explanations of deviance relate criminality to physical features or body type.

- These explanations influenced the earliest sociological theories of deviance, which viewed crime and other forms of social deviance as varieties of "social pathology" that could be attributed to the evils of city life. This view has been replaced by more objective and verifiable theories drawn from the basic perspectives of modern sociology.

- Functionalist theories of deviance include Robert Merton's typology based on how people adapt to the demands of their society. In this view, through socialization people learn what goals are approved of in their society and the approved means of achieving those goals. Individuals who do not accept the approved goals and/or the legitimate means of achieving them are likely to engage in deviant behaviors.

- Functionalist theories have been criticized for assuming that there is a single set of values shared by all the members of a society. Conflict theorists stress the relationship between cultural diversity and deviance.

- The two main types of conflict theories are cultural conflict theories and Marxian theories. Cultural conflict theories concentrate on the ways in which conflicting sets of norms result in situations that encourage criminal activity. Marxian theories place more emphasis on class conflict, explaining various types of crime in terms of the social-class position of those who commit them.

- Interactionist theories of deviance focus on the issues of recruitment (the question of why some people become deviant whereas others do not) and production (the creation of new categories of deviance in a society).

- Edwin H. Sutherland's theory of *differential association* holds that whether a person becomes deviant is determined by the extent of his or her association with criminal subcultures.

- Interactionists believe that deviance is produced by the process of *labeling,* in which the society's reaction to certain behaviors is to brand or label the offender as a deviant. Once acquired, such a label is likely to become incorporated into the person's self-image and to increase the likelihood that he or she will become committed to a "deviant career."

Crime and Social Control

- Studies of the incidence of crime often start with ecological data on crime rates.

- Studies of criminal victimization, which ask people about their actual experiences with crime, have made a major contribution to the understanding of crime in complex societies.

- The methods used to control crime change as societies grow and become more complex. In larger, more diverse societies, the ability of local institutions to control all of the society's members is diminished. Such societies tend to develop standardized, more or less coercive institutions to deal with deviants. Among the most prominent institutions of social control in modern societies are courts and prisons.

- The primary functions of prisons are said to be deterrence, rehabilitation, and punishment. However, prisons do not seem to deter crime, and only recently has the goal of rehabilitation been taken seriously. Numerous studies have found that prisons are not successful in rehabilitating their inmates and in fact often serve as "schools for crime." The only rehabilitation programs that appear to be effective are those that give inmates job training and work experience.

GLOSSARY

deviance: Behavior that violates the norms of a particular society. (p. 172)

social control: The ways in which a society encourages conformity to its norms and prevents deviance. (p. 173)

stigma: An attribute or quality of an individual that is deeply discrediting. (p. 175)

crime: An act, or omission of an act, that is prohibited by law. (p. 175)

anomie: A state of normlessness. (p. 182)

differential association: A theory that explains deviance as a learned behavior determined by the extent of a person's association with individuals who engage in such behavior. (p. 185)

labeling: A theory that explains deviance as a societal reaction that brands or labels people who engage in certain behaviors as deviant. (p. 185)

primary deviance: An act that results in the labeling of the offender as deviant. (p. 186)

secondary deviance: Behavior that is engaged in as a reaction to the experience of being labeled as deviant. (p. 186)

recidivism: The probability that a person who has served a jail term will commit additional crimes and be jailed again. (p. 190)

plea bargaining: A process in which a person charged with a crime agrees to plead guilty to a lesser charge. (p. 192)

INTERNET RESOURCES

Virtual Society: The Wadsworth Sociology Resource Center
(http://sociology.wadsworth.com)
At Virtual Society you can access a wide range of enrichment material to aid your study of sociology. From the main page, click on the Student Resources link and find your course and this textbook. Next, select the chapter

you are presently studying from the pull-down menu. Among the useful options for each self-study chapter are online links and exercises, flashcards, practical study tips, and practice quizzes for each chapter.

MC   MicroCase Online
From the Virtual Society home page, click on MicroCase Online to access book-specific MicroCase exercises that allow you to further explore sociological issues and principles presented in the text.

InfoTrac College Edition
Another unique option available to you at the Student Resources section at Virtual Society is InfoTrac College Edition, an online library with access to hundreds of scholarly and popular periodicals. Below are suggested search terms for this chapter, but this resource also allows you to fit your study of sociology to your own interests by searching custom keywords.

Subculture
Deviance
Social Control
Stigma

Federal Bureau of Investigation
(www.fbi.gov)
Provides several sources of information about current and historical investigations; provides links to many other information sources.

U.S. Department of Justice
(www.usdoj.gov)
A regularly updated home page with links to various agencies and projects.

Violence Against Women Office
(www.ojp.usdoj.gov/vawo)
Offers information about the National Domestic Violence Hotline, copies of federal legislation and regulations, ongoing research reports and studies, and a Domestic Violence Awareness Manual.

Federal Bureau of Prisons
(www.bop.gov)
Provides statistics on the federal prison population.

The National Gay and Lesbian Task Force
(www.ngltf.org)
A "progressive civil rights organization" with a home page that tracks political issues of concern to lesbians and gays and suggests activities for those who want to advance their civil rights.

Collective Behavior, Social Movements, and Mass Publics

Photo courtesy Kaiser Foundation

What do the soft drink Sprite and the South African anti-AIDS organization loveLife have in common? The answers reveal a great deal about such matters as public opinion, fashion and fads, rumor and gossip, and social movements against plagues such as violence and AIDS.

The AIDS epidemic is ravaging much of the African continent below the Sahara Desert, where many think the virus began its spread. AIDS in Africa, and especially in South Africa, continues to infect millions of young people each year and is the leading cause of death among adults below age 50. In South Africa, about half a million people become infected with HIV each year, and about half of these individuals are under age 25. Although anti-retroviral drug "cocktails" have been effective against the disease in the wealthy nations of the West and North, they are not a cure, they are expensive, and they do not prevent new infection. While much of the politics of the AIDS crisis focuses on making these drugs more widely available and at a far lower cost in Third World nations, there is also growing recognition of the need for effective public awareness campaigns in Africa and elsewhere. This is where the comparison between a soft drink and the loveLife anti-AIDS awareness campaign in South Africa comes in.

The loveLife campaign encourages young people and parents to talk about sex and HIV/AIDS. This may not seem to be anything startling, but in South Africa the subject of AIDS and AIDS-related illnesses is almost a taboo. Young people are afraid to talk about it, partly because the government has been harsh in its attitude toward people with AIDS and reluctant to allow open discussions of

AIDS and sexuality. In consequence, the loveLife campaign sponsors youth groups in which discussions of safe sex are encouraged. The campaign also includes billboards and television commercials, which appear all over the nation and emphasize the need to "be cool" in thinking about sex and AIDS. Two other important aspects of the loveLife program are the loveTrain—a sexual health center and clinic on rails—and loveTours—a mobile outdoor broadcast unit. Their purpose is to promote sexual responsibility and healthy living to young people.

The loveLife campaign is modeled on Sprite's highly successful marketing campaign in the United States. When sales of the soft drink were declining in the 1990s, the company began an aggressive campaign to "embed Sprite in youth culture, by sponsoring hip-hop concerts and planting attractive, popular kids in Internet chat rooms or college dormitories and paying them to praise or distribute Sprite in an unobtrusive way" (Epstein, 2003, p. 46). Sprite is now one of the most profitable drinks in the world because of the company's success in recruiting influential young "opinion leaders" who can help shape norms and behavior among other youth.

The theory that a small number of trendsetters among South African young people can change complex behavior such as sexuality remains to be proven, although the loveLife campaign is garnering a great deal of international support. Its critics point out that it still does not directly confront the problems faced by people with AIDS. The campaign's emphasis on being cool and avoiding unsafe sex is extremely important for those who remain uninfected, but it skirts the need for frank discussion among children and their parents, for example. Smaller anti-AIDS organizations that attempt to confront the extreme discrimination and prejudice faced by families in which some members are suffering from AIDS are being ignored by the government and by international organizations, which are attracted by the glitzier images and slogans of campaigns like loveLife.

At present, the most successful interventions to change sexual behavior in Africa have occurred in the East African nation of Uganda, where the rate of infection has decreased from over 18 percent in the 1990s to about 6 percent today. Years of civil war and extremely high rates of AIDS infection have brought tragedy to innumerable Ugandan homes. Sociologists have found that what has helped the most are frank conversations in homes and villages that deal with the frightening and calamitous effects of AIDS. People are persuaded to understand and avoid risky sex on the basis of these conversations among loved ones and neighbors, which do a great deal to negate the effects of malicious gossip and rumors filled with misinformation. In Uganda, people feel free to talk about the disease in highly personal ways, about "my mother, my father, my brother. And this is not the case yet in South Africa" (Low-Beer & Stoneburner, 2004). Despite the high profile of the loveLife campaign, unless South Africans also begin talking frankly about all the aspects of AIDS as it affects people in families and villages, the ravages of the disease may continue to worsen.

THE MEANINGS OF DISORDER

In the early years of the AIDS epidemic, many people panicked. They were afraid that they could contract the disease by kissing or even by being in the same room with a person infected with HIV. In this chapter, we look closely at various types of collective behavior, many of which are far more violent than the AIDS panic, while others are far more benign and even playful. Momentous episodes, like the riots in Los Angeles after the trial of the police officers accused of beating Rodney King, are the most severe form of collective behavior. The race riots that occurred during the civil rights movement in the United States, the huge rallies and demonstrations that ushered in the Nazi regime in pre–World War II Germany, the strikes and picketing that spurred the labor movement, the demonstrations that enlivened the women's movement in the 1970s, the demonstrations and riots that occurred during the global trade talks in Seattle in 2000, and most recently, the outburst of patriotic feeling and anger among masses of Americans after the events of September 11, 2001, and the beginning of the war against the Taliban in

Afghanistan—these are all examples of episodes of collective behavior that have shaped history in our own time.

But there are less extensive and less dangerous incidents of collective behavior in modern societies that are nonetheless important. Think of the panic that occurs when a local bank or savings and loan association is rumored to be short of funds, or the joyful anticipation of the crowds that form outside ticket offices when a popular rock star announces a concert. These events also have economic and social significance: Banks fail when panicked depositors suddenly withdraw their savings; rock promoters wait in gleeful anticipation of full houses as the lines of ticket buyers form. The huge slump in the tourism industry throughout the world since the terrorist attacks of 2001 is another example of how collective behavior can have profound effects on societies.

Many sectors of the American economy profit from the behavior of large numbers of people. The fast-food industry, for example, depends on the behavior of the millions of Americans who stop for burgers and fries as they stream home from beaches or concerts or movies. Every year the toy industry produces gimmicks like Beanie Babies, and fortunes are made and lost on the accuracy of predictions about whether the public will embrace such notions. The computer industry also has profited from fads and crazes, and it has also seen what happens when crazes wane rapidly. During the economic boom of the 1990s, the hottest stocks were those of Internet startup companies like iVillage.com and major computer equipment suppliers like Cisco Systems. But many of these companies were benefiting from a classic stock "bubble" in which people with little knowledge of the stock market were rushing to buy in the hope of instant profits. As all stock bubbles do, this one burst as the world economy began to slide into recession and war in 2001. Millions of people who were still holding highly overvalued stocks lost their investments.

The study of mass or collective behavior encompasses a wide range of phenomena and presents many problems of classification and explanation. Yet this subject deserves our attention because of its influence on social change. The student occupation of Beijing's Tiananmen Square; the strikes and protests in Poland, Czechoslovakia, Hungary, and Romania that toppled communist dictatorships; the antitax movements occurring throughout the United States—all attest to the immense power of people who are moved to engage in collective action for social change.

In our attempt to understand the nature and importance of these behaviors, we turn first to the concepts that define their similarities and differences. Then we turn to theories regarding why these episodes occur, how social movements mobilize, and with what consequences. Finally, we discuss the concept of mass publics, especially the leisure and consumption behavior of large populations.

THEN AND NOW   Collective Behavior in Time of War

In democratic societies, citizens have the right to speak out in protest against policies that they do not support. Even in times of war, this right is precious, but it often becomes more controversial, as we saw in 2001 when Attorney General John Ashcroft stated that those who criticized the U.S. government were threatening the war effort and giving comfort to enemies of the United

AP/Wide World Photos

States. But unlike the situation in the Vietnam era, when sizable minorities— and eventually the majority—opposed the war, there has been far more solidarity and collective behavior in favor of the U.S. war against terrorism, as witnessed by the massive outpouring of patriotic feeling in the months following the September 11 terrorist attacks.

© Ted Streshinsky/Corbis

The Nature of Collective Behavior

The term *collective behavior* refers to a continuum of unusual or nonroutine behaviors that are engaged in by large numbers of people. At one extreme of this continuum is the spontaneous behavior of people who react to situations they perceive as uncertain, threatening, or extremely attractive. The violence that occurred in race riots in Los Angeles and Cincinnati is one example of spontaneous collective behavior. Another is the sudden action of coal miners who decide that conditions in the mines are unsafe and walk off their jobs in a sudden and unplanned wildcat strike. Such behaviors are not governed by the routine norms that control behavior at the beach or on the job (Smelser, 1962).

At the other extreme of the continuum of collective behaviors are rallies, demonstrations, marches, protest meetings, festivals, and similar events. These involve large numbers of people in nonroutine behaviors, but they are organized by leaders and have specific goals. When workers in a union plan a strike, for example, their picketing and

rallies are forms of organized collective behavior whose purpose is to demonstrate their solidarity and their determination to obtain their demands. When blacks marched in commemoration of those who died in the 1919 race riot in Chicago, the event was organized to build solidarity and publicize a new determination to resist racism. In such cases, the organization that plans the event and uses collective behavior to make its feelings or demands known is a social movement.

Social movements are intentional efforts by groups in a society to create new institutions or reform existing ones. Such movements often grow out of more spontaneous episodes of collective behavior; once they are organized, they continue to plan collective events to promote their cause (Blumer, 1978; Genevie, 1978). Some movements, like the antiabortion movement, resist change; others, like the civil rights movement and the labor movement, have brought about far-reaching changes in social institutions. Still others, like the gay and lesbian movement, seek to gain the rights other groups have won. In this sense, they are movements for full inclusion in society by people who believe they are discriminated against. We will see in later chapters that many social movements in a multiethnic and culturally diverse society challenge discrimination and deviant labels (Tarrow, 1994).

The American labor movement provides many examples of the ways in which spontaneous episodes of collective behavior and the social movements associated with them can change the course of a society's development. During the nation's stormy transition from an agrarian to an industrial society, workers fought against the traditional right of employers to establish individual wage rates and to hire and fire workers as they pleased. They demanded instead the right to organize unions that could negotiate a collective wage rate (collective bargaining) for each category of workers. They also demanded better working conditions and benefits. Mass picketing, sit-down strikes, and pitched battles between workers and company agents or the police were everyday events in the 1890s.

Often the workers joined in walkouts, rioting, or other spontaneous collective actions when faced with mine disasters or intolerable working conditions. From these episodes of bitter conflict emerged the modern labor movement. In the ensuing decades, culminating in the period of New Deal legislation in the 1930s, the workers' demand for collective bargaining was institutionalized. By this we mean that the right to join unions and to bargain collectively was incorporated into the nation's laws. Labor unions thereby became recognized organizations and collective bargaining the recognized means of settling labor disputes. The unions, in turn, had to discipline their workers by specifying in labor agreements the conditions under which collective behavior such as strikes and other actions could be used.

By the end of World War II, labor unions and collective bargaining had become legitimate social institutions. In recent decades, however, drastic declines in industrial employment in North America and Europe, combined with renewed attacks on labor unions by employers, have led to a decrease in the ranks of organized labor. But major social movements that affect the lives of millions of people often go through cycles of growth and decline followed by a rebirth of activity. It remains to be seen whether this will be true of the labor movement (Geoghegan, 1991).

Spontaneous collective behavior, from which social movements often arise, can take many forms. Such behaviors range from the demonstrations and riots that mark major revolutions to the fads, fashions, crazes, and rumors that sweep through modern societies with such rapidity that what is new and shocking one day will be a subject of nostalgia the next. Some of these types of collective behavior become associated with social movements, but many do not. Each of them, however, can result in extremely important changes in behavior among large numbers of people, with consequences that can dramatically alter thousands or even millions of lives.

FADS AND FASHIONS Fads and fashions are closely related forms of spontaneous collective behavior. They tend to be somewhat short-lived, but they may also result in more permanent changes in behavior.

Fads are new forms of behavior that are pursued with enthusiasm by large numbers of people once they are said to "catch on," but then fade as people begin to see them as "not the newest thing." Fads are often disparaged by adults—which makes them quite popular among the young, who are often casting about for new ways of expressing themselves and asserting their unique identities. There are language fads (with music exerting a strong influence on the emergence of new slang); dress and adornment fads; fads in toys, recreation (scooters, yo-yos, hula hoops), food, and much more. Some fads may have important lasting effects, such as the unprecedented popularity of the Harry Potter books, which are influencing millions of young people around the world to become more interested in reading for pleasure. Fads tend to rise in popularity and then decline in predictable ways once they become so widespread in the population that it appears that "everyone is doing it" (Meyersohn & Katz, 2004).

Fashions are currently accepted styles of appearance and behavior that are thought of as temporary in that they will soon be replaced by new fashions. In small-scale, simpler societies people wear traditional garb and otherwise tend to behave in the same ways most of the time, so fashion is unknown to them. Fashion is one of the defining characteristics of modern societies, where people are often more concerned about the future than the past, where dress and other behaviors mark one's status relative to others, and where powerful commercial interests want to stimulate the creation of new desires at all times. Marketing and advertising are major industries devoted to manipulating fashion, but they are not always successful, a fact that makes the study of fads and fashion particularly important in modern economies (Berger, 2000).

RUMOR AND GOSSIP Rumor and gossip are common and closely related forms of communication in modern societies. *Rumor* is information from an anonymous source that is transmitted informally—that is, from person to person—at least initially, although it may later be "picked up" by formal channels of communication such as newspapers and television.

Gossip is information spread informally that usually centers on other people whom one knows or knows about (in the case of gossip about celebrities). While people often sneer at gossip, especially of the malicious variety, English social scientists who study interpersonal communication have found that about 65 percent of conversations—whether the speakers are men or women, neighbors, coworkers, homemakers, or executives—can be categorized as gossip about others. The research shows that gossip is a way for people to develop relationships, establish trust and social status, and create a community based on inclusion and exclusion (Karras, 2003). In modern societies like the United States, gossip can also become a commodity that is collected by specialists (gossip columnists) and disseminated in specialized publications such as *People* Magazine, which are part of the contemporary "celebrity industry" (see the Critical Sociology section at the end of the chapter).

In the post-9/11 world, governments are trying with renewed vigor to understand and control the spread of rumors that might cause panic or lead to needless endangerment of large numbers of people. Through its Department of Homeland Security, for example, the U.S. federal government tries to monitor rumors concerning terrorism and related subjects so as to be in a position to provide confirmation or refutation of the information they contain. By posting the latest information on public-access web sites, and through its color-coded system for warning the public about the danger of possible terrorist activities, the Department of Homeland Security seeks to remain in control of public opinion and public awareness rather than let unverified rumors develop into panic and mass hysteria.

PANIC AND MASS HYSTERIA   *Panic* is a form of collective behavior in which people respond to a perceived threat in uncoordinated and unpredictable ways, usually involving fear, flight, rage, or other emotions and irrational behaviors as well. Cooperative social relationships break down under panic, and behavior is uncoordinated, as in a surge of people toward exits when they smell fire. Delays at the doorways may cause further panic and result in trampling and suffocation. Panics also occur among people who are not in contact with one another, as we see in the case of stock market panics, in which people begin selling their stocks to protect their own interests, but their mass behavior results in further panic selling and a possible market crash (Bodenhorn, 2002).

Mass hysteria is a form of widespread collective anxiety, often caused by an unfounded belief, that results in panic behaviors of various kinds. The Salem witch-hunt discussed in Chapter 7 is a famous example of mass hysteria, and there were isolated outbreaks of mass hysteria and panic directed against Arab and Indian Americans (mistaken for Arabs) after the 2001 attacks on the Pentagon and the World Trade Center. In fact, a goal of terrorism is to create mass fear, anxiety, and hysteria that results in panic. The better prepared communities are to quickly address public fears, through effective forms of communication and early intervention by skilled law enforcement agents and educated citizens, the more difficult it is for terrorism to succeed in fomenting mass hysteria and panic (Coates, 2002).

A Typology of Spontaneous Collective Behaviors

Sociologists who study collective behavior try to discover the conditions under which different types of spontaneous collective behavior occur and why these events do or do not become linked to social movements. Typologies that classify these phenomena are an important first step toward understanding why collective behavior assumes particular forms and develops through recognizable stages.

CROWDS AND MASSES   Students of spontaneous forms of collective behavior often begin by examining the structure of such behavior—that is, by discovering whether the people who engage in a particular kind of behavior are in close proximity to one another or whether they are connected in a more indirect way. In this regard, it is useful to distinguish between crowds and masses. A **crowd** is a large number of people who are gathered together in close proximity to one another (e.g., at a demonstration or a football game). A **mass** is more diffuse; it does not occur in a physical setting. A mass is a large number of people who are all oriented toward a set of shared symbols or social objects (Lofland, 1981); an example is the audience for a particular television program. Collective behavior can occur in crowds, in masses, or in both at once.

MOTIVATING EMOTIONS   The actual behavior a crowd or mass generates depends largely on the emotions the people involved feel are appropriate to express in a particular situation. They may be motivated by many desires—for excitement, for a change, for material gain, and so on—but outwardly most will express an emotion that the norms of the event suggest is appropriate. In the witch-hunt described in Chapter 7, the people involved expressed fear and hysteria (although, as is true of all such events, some were "just going along with the crowd"). Hostility aroused by anger, desire for revenge, or enraged hatred is another common motivating emotion in episodes of collective behavior. Lynch mobs are one kind of hostile crowd. The crowd of angry strikers that violently opposes "scabs" trying to cross a picket line is another. At the mass level, the outbreak of animosity toward Islamic people immediately after the suicide attacks on the World Trade Center and the Pentagon in 2001 is an example of collective behavior provoked by hostility.

Joy is a third important emotion that motivates crowds and masses. The Mardi Gras celebrations in Latin America and New Orleans involve large, joyful crowds that create a "moral holiday" in which behaviors that would not be acceptable at other times are tolerated. At the mass level, the immense interest and joy that spread through the U.S. population during the 1998 baseball

	SETTING	
BASIC EMOTION	**Crowd**	**Mass**
Fear	• Panic exodus from burning theater • Hostages taken by terroist groups aboard an airliner	• Natural calamities • Red scares • Crime waves • Three Mile Island • Salem witch-hunts
Hostility	• Political rallies, marches • Lynch mobs • Race riots	• Scapegoating of public figures • Waves of cross burnings
Joy	• Revival meetings • Rallies in Nazi Nuremberg • Mardi Gras carnival • Rock concerts • Sports events	• Gold rushes • Punk fashion • Jogging • Disco • Star Wars, Star Trek • Pokémon

Figure 8.1 Lofland's Typology of Spontaneous Collective Behaviors

Source: Adapted from *Social Psychology: Sociological Perspectives,* edited by Morris Rosenberg and Ralph H. Turner. Copyright © 1981 by The American Sociological Association.

season, when Mark McGwire and Sammy Sosa were locked in a battle to break the single-season home run record, raised the sport to new levels of popularity and stimulated many examples of joyful collective behavior, especially in St. Louis and Chicago.

By cross-classifying the most significant emotions that motivate collective behavior (fear, hostility, and joy) with the structural dimensions of crowd and mass, sociologist John Lofland created a typology that includes a wide range of spontaneous collective behaviors. This typology is presented in Figure 8.1. Can you think of examples of your own for the various types? Where, for example, would you place the Boston Tea Party, the riots that often occur during spring break in Florida, or the crowds who came out to pay last respects to firefighters and police officers killed in the line of duty on September 11, 2001?

The Lofland typology is useful as a means of classifying some types of collective behavior, but remember that often there are interactions among these categories: Mass behavior may turn into crowd behavior; spontaneous collective behavior may generate a social movement. For example, when the stock market crashed in 1929 at the beginning of the Great Depression, crowds of panic-stricken investors spilled onto the streets of the financial districts of New York, Chicago, and San Francisco. There, within sight of one another, people found their fears magnified. And those fears quickly spread through the mass of Americans. The panic started among people who had made investments on credit, but it spread to people who merely had savings in local banks. Crowds of terrified savers descended on the banks, which were unable to handle the sudden demand for withdrawals because they also had been investing in

stocks that were suddenly worthless. As a result, millions of Americans lost all their savings.

In the aftermath of the stock market crash and the resulting mass panic, social movements arose to seek reforms like investment insurance that would protect investors against similar episodes in the future. During the depression that followed the crash, citizens' fears about their lack of retirement or pension savings led to the development of new institutions like Social Security and deposit insurance. Today AARP, an organization that represents the interests of older people who once protested as an unorganized mass, is the largest single lobbying group in American politics.

Dimensions of Social Movements

There are as many types of social movements as there are varieties of spontaneous collective behavior. Just think of how many "causes" can motivate people to take organized action. We have a social-welfare movement, an antitax movement, a civil rights movement, a women's movement, a gay rights movement, an environmental protection movement, a consumer movement, an animal rights movement, and on and on. Within each of these movements, numerous organizations attempt to speak for everyone who supports the movement's goals. Actually, within any large social movement there are likely to be several different social movement organizations (sometimes referred to as SMOs) that may have different, and at times competing, ideas about how to achieve the movement's goals (Goode,

This is a photo from the NAMES Project, in which people make panels for a giant quilt. Each panel tells something about a person who has died of AIDS. In this photo, taken when the quilt was on display in the Washington Mall, a man and a woman kneel at the edge of a quilt panel. What emotions do you detect in this photo? What social phenomena do you think brought these individuals to the Mall on this occasion? (See page 222 for further insights into the sociological content of this photo.)

© Matt Herron 1987

the institutions of capitalism—the market and private property—must be replaced with democratic worker groups, or soviets, whose efforts would be directed by a central committee. Meanwhile certain other existing institutions, especially religion and the family, had to be either eliminated or drastically altered.

2. *Reformist movements* seek partial changes in some institutions and values, usually on behalf of some segments of society rather than all. The labor movement is basically reformist. It seeks to alter the institutions of private property by requiring the owners of businesses to bargain collectively with workers concerning wages and working conditions and to reach an agreement that will apply to all the workers in the firm. Collective bargaining replaces the old system of individual contracts between workers and employers, but it does not eliminate the institution of private property.

3. *Conservative movements* seek to uphold the values and institutions of society and generally resist attempts to change them, unless their goal is to undo undesired changes that have already occurred. The conservative movement in the United States seeks to reinforce the values and functions of capitalist institutions and to support the traditional values of such institutions as the family and the church.

4. *Reactionary movements* seek to return to the institutions and values of the past and, therefore, to do away with some or all existing social institutions and cultural values (Cameron, 1966; McAdam, McCarthy, & Zald, 1996). The Ku Klux Klan is part of a reactionary social movement that seeks a return to the racial caste system that was supported by American legal institutions (laws, courts, and the police) until the 1954 Supreme Court decision that declared the "separate but equal" doctrine unconstitutional.

1992). As we will see shortly, the way such organizations operate and the goals they seek depend largely on the characteristics of the social movement itself.

CLASSIFYING SOCIAL MOVEMENTS   Social movements can be classified into four categories based on the goals they seek to achieve, as follows:

1. *Revolutionary movements* seek to overthrow existing stratification systems and institutions and replace them with new ones (McAdam, McCarthy, & Zald, 1996). The Russian Bolsheviks who founded the Communist party were a revolutionary social movement that sought to eliminate the class structure of Russian society. They also believed that

OTHER TYPES OF MOVEMENTS   Although they cover some of the movements that have had the greatest impact on modern societies, the preceding four categories do not include all the possible types of movements. Herbert Blumer (1969a), for example, identified a fifth category: *expressive social movements,* or movements devoted to the expression of personal beliefs and feelings. Those beliefs and feelings may be religious or ethical or may involve an entire lifestyle, as in the case of the punk movement of the 1980s. An important aspect of expressive social movements is that their members typically reject the idea that their efforts should be directed at changing society or the behavior of people who do not belong to their movement. Their quest is for personal expression, and if others choose to "see the

TYPES OF SOCIAL MOVEMENTS

TYPE	DESCRIPTION	EXAMPLE
Revolutionary	Seeks to overthrow and replace existing stratification systems and institutions.	Bolsheviks
Reformist	Seeks partial changes in some institutions and values, usually on behalf of some segments of society rather than all.	Labor movement, civil rights movement
Conservative	Seeks to uphold the values and institutions of society and resists attempts to change them.	Antitax, antigovernment movements
Reactionary	Seeks to return to the institutions and values of the past and do away with existing institutions and values.	Ku Klux Klan
Expressive	Devoted to the expression of personal beliefs and feelings.	Punk movement
Millenarian	Combines elements of revolutionary and expressive movements.	People's Temple

light," that is welcome. Expressive social movements often peter out when aspects of self-expression are adopted in the larger society (e.g., when people copy styles of fashion or language) and the original adherents must use new means of identification. For this reason, among others, the slang expressions that groups use are always changing as the original slang terms become part of everyday speech.

Some of the various New Age groups and organizations now popular in the United States fit well into the expressive social movement category. Non–Native Americans who appropriate some aspects of Native American spirituality (including the use of sweat lodges or the practice of vision quests), but do not proselytize, are examples of people involved in an expressive social movement. So are men who follow the teachings of poet Robert Bly, practicing collective drumming to bond together and express suppressed emotions. But, like the followers of any social movement, there can be those in expressive social movements whose extreme beliefs lead to tragedy, as in the 1996 case of the 7-year-old pilot whose parents encouraged her to follow her vision at all costs. Such advice resulted in her death, as well as the deaths of her father and her flight instructor.

Other social scientists who study social movements identify still more categories or develop subcategories that combine elements of those just presented. (See the Study Chart above.) For example, in his classic study *The Pursuit of the Millennium* (1961), Norman Cohen analyzed what are known as *messianic* or *millenarian* movements, which are both revolutionary and expressive. A millenarian movement promises its followers total social change by miraculous means. These movements envision a perfect

society of the future, "a new Paradise on earth, a world purged of suffering and sin, a Kingdom of the Saints" (p. xiii). Most millenarian movements are secular, but the term is derived from the Christian concept of the millennium, the return of Christ as the messiah who would save the world after a thousand years. Often millenarian movements begin as small movements with a charismatic leader (someone who seems to possess special powers) and a few devoted followers.

An example of a millenarian movement is the People's Temple, whose 900 members committed suicide by drinking cyanide-laced Kool-Aid in Jonestown, Guyana, on November 18, 1978. In his insightful study of the events leading up to the tragedy, sociologist John Hall (1987) demonstrates that popular interpretations of this shocking story are inadequate. The conclusion reached in most previous accounts is that the movement's leader, Jim Jones, was a deranged personality who acted as the Antichrist and led his misguided followers to their deaths. Such accounts, according to Hall, may be comforting expressions of moral outrage, but by exaggerating the influence of an individual personality, they lead to wrong ideas about how such tragedies can occur.

In his analysis of the Jonestown tragedy, Hall shows that the members of the People's Temple were part of a cohesive social movement. Many were of modest means, some quite poor; in addition, most were black. They felt alienated from the larger society and saw the Temple as their community and often as their family. It is only by understanding the strength of their attachments to one another and to their belief in Jones's vision of a better world to come that one can make sense of what appears to be a senseless, insane episode of collective behavior. Faced with what they perceived as imminent attacks on the religious community they were building in the jungle, some Temple members worked themselves into a frenzy in which they became convinced that by drinking the poison they were "stepping over" into a better world. Others may or may not have felt these emotions; we cannot ever know. Probably some people thought the occasion was a practice suicide. In any case, Hall's study shows that Jones planned the act of "collective martyrdom" but that most of the Temple members followed to the end because of their unshaken belief in the goals of their social movement.

SOCIAL MOVEMENT THEORY

Early theories of collective behavior were derived from the notion that hysteria or contagious feelings such as hatred or fear could spread through masses of people. One of the first social thinkers to develop a "mass contagion" theory of collective behavior was Gustave LeBon. An aristocratic critic of the emerging industrial democracies, LeBon believed that those societies were producing "an era of crowds" in which agitators and despots are heroes, "the populace is sovereign, and the tide of barbarism mounts" (1947/1896, pp. 14, 207). In its usual definition, he pointed out, "the word 'crowd' means a gathering of individuals of whatever nationality, profession, or sex, and whatever be the chances that have brought them together." From a psychological viewpoint, however, a crowd can create conditions in which "the sentiments and ideas of all the persons in the gathering take one and the same direction, and their conscious personality vanishes" (quoted in Genevie, 1978, p. 9).

LeBon attributed the strikes and riots that are common in rapidly urbanizing societies to the fact that people are cut off from traditional village social institutions and jammed into cities, creating a mass of strangers. This view of early industrial societies was clearly exaggerated; research has shown that urban newcomers seek to form new social attachments, often drawing on networks of people who came to the city from the same rural area or small town. But more important, research on crowds and riots has shown that despite the appearance of a "mob mentality" and psychological "contagion," people who participate in riots, demonstrations, and other forms of collective behavior actually have many different motivating emotions and may only *appear* to be following along blindly as if they were part of a herd. Also, the contagion theories of LeBon and others are not useful in understanding the full range of collective behaviors and social movements that arise from the strains and conflicts characteristic of rapidly changing industrial societies (Rochon, 1998).

A Continuum of Collective Behavior

Collective behaviors and social movements can be placed along a continuum according to how much they change the societies in which they occur. At one end of the continuum are revolutions; at the other are fads or crazes. In the twentieth century, three major revolutions occurred: the communist revolutions in Russia and China and the fascist revolution that brought Hitler to power in 1933. These can be placed at the high end of the continuum. At the low end are fads and crazes that may excite us for a while but usually do not bring about lasting change in the major structures of society (Turner, 1974). Some people become so completely involved in a fad or craze (as has occurred, for example, among collectors of Beanie Babies) that they devote all their energies to the new activity.

Between the two extremes of revolutions and fads are social movements that capture the attention of masses of people and have varying effects on the societies in which they occur. The women's movement, the civil rights movement, and the environmental protection movement are examples of movements with broad membership in many nations and the continuing power to bring about social change. The gay liberation movement, the antiabortion movement, the evangelical movement, and the hospice movement (see Chapter 15) are examples of more narrowly focused movements that are concerned with a single issue or set of issues but also exert powerful pressure for change in the United States and other societies.

There are also movements that attract large numbers of people for a brief time but then begin to falter and have a limited impact. An example is the men's spiritual and social renewal movement, which found expression in the Million Man March by African Americans and the mass rallies held by the Promise Keepers. The latter was a social movement organization led by a former University of Colorado football coach. It called on Christian men to become "promise keepers, not promise breakers" and promoted racial reconciliation, family values, and male leadership within the family. After much initial success in attracting large crowds of men to stadiums throughout the United States, in 1998 the group faltered as its leaders tried to find other ways of raising money besides charging high admission prices for its rallies. Unable to cover expenses, the organization was forced to fire at least two-thirds of its staff as its leaders struggled to attract donations (Sahagun & Stammer, 1998; Wheeler, 1998).

Theories of collective behavior and social movements often seek to explain the origins and effects of revolutionary and reform movements (Crosley, 2002; McAdam, McCarthy, & Zald, 1988). In the remainder of this section, we discuss several such theories. We begin by examining the nature of revolutions and revolutionary movements. Then we consider theories that attempt to explain why major revolutions and revolutionary social movements have arisen and what factors have enabled them to succeed. Note that these are macro-level theories: They explain revolutions and the associated social movements as symptoms of even larger-scale social change.

Theories of Revolution

Sociologists often distinguish between "long revolutions," or large-scale changes in the ecological relationships of humans to the earth and to one another (e.g., the rise of capitalism and the Industrial Revolution), and revolutions that are primarily social or political in nature (Braudel, 1984; Wolf, 1984a, 1984b). The course of world history is shaped by long revolutions, whereas individual societies are transformed by social revolutions like those that occurred in the United States, France, and Russia (Bobrick, 1997).

POLITICAL AND SOCIAL REVOLUTIONS Sociologist Theda Skocpol (1979) makes a further distinction between political and social revolutions. **Political revolutions** are transformations in the political structures and leadership of a society that are not accompanied by a full-scale rearrangement of the society's productive capacities, culture, and stratification system. **Social revolutions,** on the other hand, sweep away the old order. They not only change the institutions of government but also bring about basic changes in social stratification. Both political and social revolutions are brought about by revolutionary social movements as well as by external forces like colonialism.

The American Revolution, according to Skocpol's theory, was a political revolution. The minutemen who fought against British troops at the Battle of Concord were a political revolutionary group that did not at first seek to change American society in radical ways. On the other hand, the revolutions that destroyed the existing social order in Russia and China in the twentieth century were social revolutions. Their goal was to transform the class structure and institutions of their societies.

Skocpol's analysis further shows that the actual outcomes of social revolutions depend on the kinds of coalitions formed among revolutionary parties and larger social classes. The communist revolutionaries in Russia, for example, did not join forces with the peasants as the Chinese communist revolutionaries did. One consequence was that in the former Soviet Union the peasants were persecuted during the revolution; their land was taken from them, and many were forced to live on collective farms. These disruptions of the society's agrarian base severely weakened the economy. In China, however, while there were many disruptions of rural life after the communists took power, food production continued to be carried out in villages and small landholdings. Peasant communist leaders replaced feudal landowners, but agricultural production did not suffer as it did in the former Soviet Union.

Why do revolutionary social movements arise, and what makes some of them content mainly with seizing power while others call for a complete reorganization of society? For most of the twentieth century, the answer was some version of Marxian conflict theory. This theory uses detailed knowledge of existing societies to predict the shape of future ones. According to Marx, the world would become capitalist; then capitalist markets would come under the control of monopolies; impoverished workers and colonial peoples would rebel in a generation of mass social movements and revolutions; and a new, classless society would be created in which the workers would own the means of production. (Marx's theory of class conflict leading to revolution is discussed in Chapters 7 and 11.)

RELATIVE DEPRIVATION The idea that the increasing misery of the working class would lead workers to join revolutionary social movements was not Marx's only explanation of the causes of revolution. He also believed that under some conditions, "although the enjoyments of the workers have risen," their level of dissatisfaction could rise even faster because of the much greater increase in the "enjoyments of the capitalists, which are inaccessible to the worker" (Marx & Engels, 1955, vol. 1, p. 94). This is a version of the theory known as **relative deprivation** (Stouffer et al., 1949). According to this theory, the presence of deprivation (i.e., poverty or misery) alone does not explain why people join revolutionary social movements. Instead, it is the feeling of deprivation relative to others. We tend to measure our own well-being against that of others, and even if we are doing fairly well, if they are doing better we are likely to feel a sense of injustice and, sometimes, extreme anger. This feeling of deprivation relative to others may result in revolutionary social movements.

Alexis de Tocqueville came to the same conclusion in his study of the causes and results of the French Revolution. He was struck by the fact that the revolution did not occur in the seventeenth century, when the economic conditions of the French people were in severe decline. Instead, it occurred in the eighteenth century, a period of rapid economic growth. Further, Tocqueville concluded that "revolutions are not always brought about by a gradual decline from bad to worse. Nations that have endured patiently and almost unconsciously the most overwhelming oppression often burst into rebellion against the yoke the moment it begins to grow lighter" (1955/1856, p. 214). The Zapatista rebellion in the Mexican state of Chiapas is an

Figure 8.2   Need Satisfaction and Revolution

Source: Davies, 1962.

example of a revolutionary movement that began among very poor Indian peasants but became a broader movement during a time of relative economic prosperity (Preston, 1998; Vilas, 1993).

Revolutions are most likely to occur when a period of improvement in economic and social conditions is followed by a sudden reversal. Figure 8.2 expresses this relationship in terms of expectations that rise steadily over time. When expectations are rising, people do not generally rebel, either through outbreaks of mob action or through organized social movements. But when their situation begins to improve and their expectations continue to rise as well, the extent to which their expectations are actually satisfied takes a sharp downturn. Then the conditions for rebellion are enhanced. At some point, the affected population can no longer tolerate the gap between what it expects and what it is getting, and rebellion breaks out.

Think of Figure 8.2 as applying to any form of collective protest, not just to revolutions. For example, the unrest and revolutionary sentiments in many Islamic nations, which had been developing for decades but were brought home most clearly after the terrorist attacks on the United States in 2001, lend themselves to analysis using the "J-curve" model of Figure 8.2. Growing populations of educated males in nations like Pakistan, Saudi Arabia, and Algeria create rising expectations. The failure of these nations' economies to continue to grow and to provide careers for more educated young people creates a gap between needs and their satisfaction. Those who feel the greatest resentment and are most likely to join radical movements are not the impoverished people from the countryside but those in cities who feel that the gap between their expectations and their prospects is intolerable. They may blame forces outside their nation, such as Israel, the United States,

or Western culture in general, but the J-curve model helps explain who joins the radical movements and why.

Clearly, the theory of relative deprivation can help us identify the conditions that lead to collective behavior. However, it cannot tell us when the gap between expectations and reality will become intolerable or what kinds of collective behavior will actually occur. To know those things, we must be far closer to the actual situation and be skilled at observing and interpreting it.

Valuable as they are as broad theories of revolution, neither Marxian theory nor Tocqueville's analysis can fully explain the rise of revolutionary movements throughout the contemporary world, nor do they help much in understanding the changes major social movements go through as their goals and organizations evolve. These and related questions are analyzed more directly in recent theories of protest cycles and changes within social movements, to which we now turn.

Protest Cycles, Collective Action Frames, and Charisma

In analyzing the revolutions that have occurred during the past 500 years, sociologist Charles Tilly concludes that there are no "neat formulations of standard, recurrent conditions for forcible transfers of state power" (1993, p. 237). However, he agrees with other social scientists who have pointed out that revolutionary social movements and other forms of protest often occur in cycles or waves of unrest. He cites the waves of protest that swept through Europe and North America in the late 1960s and the current wave of fundamentalist movements in much of the contemporary world. During such waves, he observes:

> One set of demands seems to incite another, social movement organizations compete with each other for support, demands become more extreme for a while before subsiding. As this happens, activists often experiment with new ways of organizing, framing their demands, combating their enemies and holding on to what they have. (1993, p. 13)

PROTEST CYCLES   No theory adequately explains why particular waves of protest sweep through societies. But Sidney Tarrow (1994), another astute student of protest cycles, argues that waves of protest often result from major social shocks such as an international economic recession, the end of a period of warfare, or hasty actions by one or more governments. Such an episode occurred in Poland in the early 1980s when the communist regime announced large increases in the price of bread. The movement that ensued, known as Solidarity, demonstrated the weakness of that regime (McAdam, Tarrow, & Tilly, 2001).

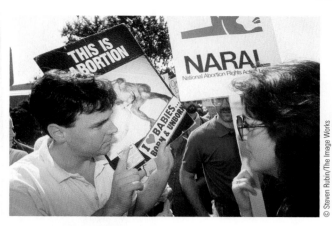

Antiabortion and pro-choice activists confront each other at a demonstration outside a clinic in Wichita, Kansas. At least in this example the two are speaking rationally to each other, each from his or her own action frame based on his or her stance on the issue.

During cycles of protest, social conflicts of all kinds increase dramatically, often resulting in violent episodes of collective behavior—riots, demonstrations, and counterdemonstrations. The heightened sense that change is in the air, often brought on by the activities of a few "early risers" among protest leaders (e.g., Lech Walesa and Mahatma Gandhi), triggers a variety of processes, including imitations of the protest elsewhere (e.g., Martin Luther King, Jr., and Nelson Mandela, who followed the example set by Gandhi). The wave of protest may also build momentum through diffusion, often spreading from larger cities to smaller towns and rural areas. New ideologies arise to justify collective action and help the movement mobilize a following (Meyer & Tarrow, 1998).

COLLECTIVE ACTION FRAMES The old saying that "the pen is mightier than the sword" refers to the power of ideas to shape our view of society and why it needs to be changed. In the twentieth century, we saw the revolutionary power of ideas embodied in *The Communist Manifesto* of Karl Marx and Friedrich Engels, Hitler's *Mein Kampf* ("My Struggle"), and the "Little Red Book" containing the sayings of Chairman Mao Ze-dong. In our own time, such books as Newt Gingrich's *To Renew America* and William Bennett's *Book of Virtues* have presented ideas that motivate various conservative movements in the United States. Millions of people latch on to these concepts, not because they are incapable of forming their own ideas, but because all of us are continually trying out ideas that seem to explain our times and help us make sense of our experiences in society. When faced with quandaries about what to do, what actions we should take or support, we often seek out concepts that

are phrased as *collective action frames,* sets of beliefs and interpretations of events that inspire and justify social movements (Snow & Benford, 1992). There are many examples of collective action frames in the seminal work of William Gamson on this subject.

Gamson (1992) is one of the leading students of political activism in the United States. His research on social movements focuses on the mental frameworks people develop in their thinking about social issues. He notes that social movements strive to offer one or more collective action frames. These are ways of thinking that justify the need for and desirability of a particular course of action. After studying the writings and speeches of activists in many different social movements, Gamson concluded that collective action frames have three important components:

1. *An injustice component,* which includes a sense of moral indignation or outrage against a perceived injustice and the people who are said to be responsible for the condition.

2. *An agency component,* which embodies the idea that not only is there injustice, but together "we" can do something about the condition.

3. *An identity component,* which defines who "we" are, usually in opposition to a "they" with different tastes and values.

Gamson studies collective action frames by recording conversations in which people discuss social issues. In exploring the injustice component, for example, he listened carefully for statements like "That is just wrong," "That's unfair," "That really burns me up," or "That pisses me off." Such statements are marked by "explicit moral condemnation, unqualified by offsetting arguments and unchallenged by other group members," as in this example:

Characters:
Marjorie, a waitress, in her forties.
Judy, a data entry clerk, in her thirties.
Several others who don't speak in this scene.
(The group is near the end of a discussion of nuclear power.)
Marjorie: They shouldn't have taken all that money to nuclear power and everything—and you've got kids starving in America.
Judy: Yeah.
Marjorie: You've got homeless people. Where's your values? *[pause]* They suck. They really do suck.
Judy: You're on tape.
[laughter]
Marjorie: I don't care what I'm on. Still—it's obvious—when you pay millions and millions of dollars in nuclear plants when people in America are starving—
Judy: Right.

Marjorie: And you've got homeless people, no matter what they are—whether they're drunks or they're—whatever they are. Mentally ill people and you've got them living on a street. And you've got a family of five people—I worked for Legal Services of Greater Boston and I had people in the Milner Hotel, mothers with five kids in one room. Living. And we don't have places for them, but we have places to build nuclear plants. That's garbage. That's garbage! (Gamson, 1992, pp. 48–49)

Sociologists listen carefully to the way people like Marjorie frame issues. In this case, the frame is injustice, and the point being made is that too much money is being spent on nuclear plants while other, more pressing human needs go unmet. In this dialogue, Marjorie is outspoken and not afraid of having her opinions recorded, whereas Judy is far more passive and concerned about voicing her opinions. The sociologist would probably conclude that within her circle of friends and coworkers Marjorie is a leader who often frames issues for others. As you listen to conversations like this one, observe how the leaders frame issues for the other participants. (Remember, however, that leaders do many other things in addition to creating or modifying collective action frames.)

CHARISMA   Leadership plays an extremely important part in the success or failure of revolutionary social movements. The leaders of such movements are often said to have almost supernatural powers to inspire and motivate masses of followers. Max Weber (1968) called this ability **charisma**. A charismatic leader appears to possess extraordinary "gifts of the body and spirit" that mark him or her as specially chosen to lead. The voices that Joan of Arc heard, which convinced her to take up arms to save France, gave her the inspired commitment to her cause that is a central feature of charisma. Mahatma Gandhi, probably the twentieth century's greatest example of a charismatic leader, swayed the Indian masses with his almost supernatural spirituality and courage. Similarly, the extraordinary gifts of oratory, faith, and energy displayed by Martin Luther King, Jr., allowed him to emerge as the most influential leader of the American civil rights movement.

A movement's followers also may attribute special powers to their leader. This process may produce additional myths about the leader's powers and add to whatever personal magnetism the leader originally possessed. For example, Hitler was no doubt a fiery orator, but his followers' frenzied reception of many of his ideas contributed to the perception that he possessed exceptional charisma.

INSTITUTIONALIZATION OF CHARISMA   The charisma of the leader may eventually pose problems for the movement. Every social movement must incorporate the goals and gifts

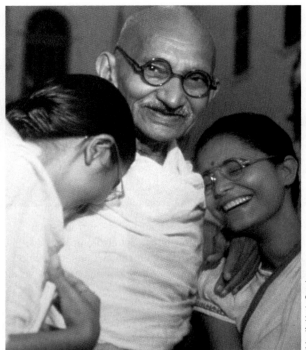

Mahatma Gandhi, probably the most revered and charismatic political figure of the twentieth century, is shown here during a light moment with his granddaughters. Gandhi's techniques of nonviolence and passive resistance inspired Martin Luther King, Jr., and other leaders of political protest movements. But his followers often endured great personal sacrifice and physical danger, for his political strategies called for nonviolent civil disobedience in the name of higher moral values.

of its leaders into the structure of the movement and eventually into the institutions of society. But how can this be done without losing track of the movement's original purpose and values? Scholars who follow Weber's lead in this area of research have termed this problem the *institutionalization of charisma* (Shils, 1970). Weber recognized that the more successful a movement becomes in taking power and assuming authority, the more difficult it is to retain the zeal and motivation of its charismatic founders. Once the leaders have power and can obtain special privileges for themselves, they tend to resist continued efforts to eliminate inequalities of wealth and power. Perhaps the most instructive example of this problem is the institutionalization of the ideals of Marx and Lenin in the organization of the Bolshevik party in Russia after the revolution of 1917.

"Workers of the world, unite," Marx urged in *The Communist Manifesto;* "you have nothing to lose but your chains" (Marx & Engels, 1969/1848). The vision of a society in which poverty, social injustice, repression, war, and all the evils of capitalism would be eliminated formed the core of Marxian socialism. The founders of the Bolshevik party realized, however, that revolutions are not made with slogans and visions alone (Schumpeter, 1950). The unification of the workers required an organization that not only would carry forward the revolution but also would take the lead in mobilizing the Russian masses to work for the ideals of socialism. The charismatic leader who built this organization was Vladimir Ilyich Lenin.

Under the leadership of Lenin (and far more ruthlessly under his successor Josef Stalin), any Bolshevik who challenged party discipline was exiled or killed. Because the goals of the Bolsheviks were so radical and the need for reform so pressing, Lenin and Stalin argued that the party had to exert total control over its members in order to prevent spontaneous protests that might threaten the party's goals. By the same logic, other parties had to be eliminated and dissenters imprisoned. Such efforts by an elite to exert control over all forms of organizational life in a society are known as *totalitarianism*. All social movements that believe the ends they seek justify the means used to achieve them risk becoming totalitarian because they sacrifice the rule of law and the ideal of democratic process to gain power (Harrington, 1987; Howe, 1983).

CO-OPTATION Weber's theory predicts that social movements will institutionalize their ideals in a bureaucratic structure. Moreover, the more successful they are in gaining the power to change society, the more they will be forced to

control the activities of their members. In fact, once a movement is institutionalized, with an administration and bureaucratic rules, its leaders tend to influence new charismatic leaders to become part of their bureaucracy, a process known as *co-optation.* In the labor movement, for example, maverick leaders who demand reform and instigate protests in their plants are often given inducements such as jobs in the union administration to keep them under control (Geschwender, 1977; Kornhauser, 1952). In politics, local party leaders may identify and co-opt a local leader who they think might pose a threat in the future, offering inducements such as support in an election campaign in return for loyalty to the party. In this way, an outspoken environmentalist and history professor named Newt Gingrich was co-opted by the Republican leaders of Carrollton, Georgia, early in his political career.

SOCIAL MOVEMENTS AND CIVIL SOCIETY

Most of us will probably never belong to a revolutionary social movement, at least not one devoted to the violent overthrow of a government or society. Nor will many of us experience the deadening force of totalitarian rule. Most of us therefore will not find ourselves helping to rebuild the voluntary associations and communities, the leagues, the hobby groups, the unions and auxiliaries of our societies, as the people of many Eastern European nations are doing today. But many readers of this book will become members of organizations and groups of all kinds, which in turn may become affiliated with broader social movements.

In contemporary societies, an ever-growing and changing array of groups and organizations are formed in the public sphere of social activity. Known as **civil society,** this sphere of nongovernmental, nonbusiness social activity is composed of millions of church congregations, sports leagues, amateur arts groups, charitable associations, ethnic associations, and much more. The Mexican sociologist Carlos M. Vilas explains it as follows:

> Civil society refers to a sphere of collective actions distinct from both the market and "political society"—parties, legislatures, courts, state agencies. Civil society is not independent of politics, but clearly, when people identify themselves as "civil society," they are seeking to carve out a relatively autonomous sphere for organization and action. (1993, p. 38)

In parts of the world where the gap between rich and poor is widening, people who participate in civil society are often recruited into movements calling for social and

This famous photo from the Holocaust shows Jewish families being rounded up for transport to concentration camps. Under Hitler, the National Socialists (Nazis) often resorted to public acts of terror to establish their absolute rule over German society. Such totalitarian regimes often use terror to destroy mutual trust among citizens.

economic justice. Vilas observes, for example, that in Latin America, activity in social movements "creates a confluence of the poor and middle classes . . . to confront the traditional alliance of the rich and powerful with the state" (1993, p. 41).

In more affluent regions of the world, civil society also flourishes and provides a rich source of recruits for social movements. As noted in Chapter 6, increasing membership in voluntary associations appears to be a long-term trend in the United States. National surveys conducted in the 1950s found that about one-third of adult citizens were members of voluntary associations; today more than two-thirds of American adults say that they belong to a voluntary association (Caplow et al., 1991). Since 1980, the number of registered nonprofit associations of all kinds has increased from 14,726 to 22,449 (*Statistical Abstract,* 2002). While a significant minority of Americans are not members of any voluntary organizations or congregations, the majority are active members. From the standpoint of social movements, the importance of these facts is that many of the activists in social movements are recruited from the ranks of voluntary associations (e.g., through mailing lists or membership meetings).

Even people who never join social movements will surely find that their lives are changed by them. The social critic H. L. Mencken once said that if three Americans are in a room together for more than an instant, two of them will try to change the morals of the third. Campaigns against smoking, drinking, rock lyrics, violence on television, wearing of furs, abortion, and many other behaviors would seem to confirm this notion. So too would patterns in the growth of different types of voluntary associations. Since 1980, the number of nonprofit voluntary associations devoted to educational and cultural issues has increased by 33 percent, and the number devoted to public affairs has risen by 74 percent (*Statistical Abstract,* 2002).

Resource Mobilization and Free Riders

What is the relationship between civil society and social movements? In sociology, this is known as the *resource mobilization* question, referring to the fact that social movements need to mobilize existing leaders and organizations rather than simply relying on the participation of people who happen to be moved to action (Klandermans, 1997; Zurcher & Snow, 1981). A second, related issue is known as the *free rider problem.* This refers to the tendency of many people not to lend their support and resources—time, money, and leadership—to social movements but to reap the benefits anyway (Marwell & Ames, 1985; Olson, 1965).

Are these issues important? One need only think of all the American workers who have benefited from the gains won by the labor movement. Or consider the rapid growth of the environmental protection movement in the late 1960s and early 1970s. What explains the speed with which that movement captured a central place in public policy debates? In studying the growth of the movement for environmental quality, sociologist Carol Kronus (1977) found that out of a sample of 209 existing organizations in a midwestern city, more than half gave material and moral support to the new movement. She also found that the groups that did link up with the movement were ones whose goals agreed with those of the movement and whose members believed in taking action to improve the quality of life in their community. Free rider groups, on the other hand, agreed that "something should be done about pollution" but felt that other groups should take action before they were able to do so.

The free rider hypothesis predicts that some proportion of the potential members of a social movement will not lend their energies to the movement but will nonetheless hope that the movement will provide them with the benefits they desire. But how extensive will the free rider problem be? How many people will act out of self-interest and try to reap the rewards of the movement's activities without making any personal sacrifices? A growing body of research findings addresses these empirical questions.

One study of the free rider problem is Edward J. Walsh and Rex H. Warland's (1983) study of the social movement that emerged after the near-meltdown of a nuclear reactor on Three Mile Island (TMI) near Middletown, Pennsylvania, in 1979. After the accident, antinuclear organizations grew in strength throughout the TMI area. Many of them opposed efforts to start up a second reactor at TMI, which had not been damaged. Walsh and Warland found that of those who opposed the start-up of the undamaged reactor, 87 percent were free riders in that they had not contributed in any way to the organizations opposing the start-up. Of those in favor of the start-up, 98 percent were free riders. Only a very small percentage—6 percent of those in opposition and 1 percent of those in favor—actually participated. Although this proportion is small, it does show that there are people who are ready to be mobilized as activists on an important social issue. Not everyone is an apathetic or alienated free rider.

The TMI research suggests that most people will be free riders and will not join a social movement even when they strongly desire it to succeed and to win victories that will benefit them directly. Other research, however, indicates that the tendency to be a free rider is far less prevalent than the TMI study suggests (Garner & Tenuto, 1997). Data show that more than 85 percent of American households make charitable contributions of some kind.

And public television and radio stations do succeed, after much persuasion, in raising the funds they need to continue operating, even though many people who enjoy listening or viewing would just as soon be free riders. Findings from thousands of laboratory experiments conducted since the early 1970s also contradict the free rider hypothesis, showing instead that many people make commitments and sacrifice individual gain in order to advance a cause. Still, the relatively low proportion of people who join a cause, vote in elections, or voluntarily support institutions like National Public Radio promises to make the free rider problem a subject of continuing social-scientific research (Frank, 1988; Hechter, 1987).

In predicting the success of any given social movement, resource mobilization theory points to the need to consider how well a movement enlists or mobilizes the resources available to it—for example, how well it deals with gender differences in recruiting members or how well it keeps recruits actively committed. Research by Doug McAdam (1992) on the experience of men and women in the civil rights movement during the early 1960s shows that organizations in the movement were constantly struggling with the problem of gender. White women who volunteered as civil rights workers often had more experience in organizations and civil rights activities than white male applicants but were less likely to be selected to participate. Those who were selected were often assigned jobs that were considered "women's work" unless they protested against such treatment. Indeed, McAdam found that many of the women who participated in the civil rights movement later became active in the women's movement, in part because of the discrimination they had encountered in the earlier movement. Studies of participation in other social movements during the 1960s have yielded similar findings: Women are available to be mobilized by social movements, but once they become involved they often find themselves faced with issues of gender inequality (McAdam, Tarrow, & Tilly, 2001).

Mobilization of the law is another aspect of resource mobilization theory that has been studied extensively in recent years (Hoffman, 1989). For example, in his research on how activists attempt to use laws and the courts to advance their cause, sociologist Robert Burstein (1991) shows that activists seeking to end discrimination against minorities in the labor force are increasingly petitioning the courts under the Equal Employment Opportunity (EEO) laws. Burstein and other researchers have found that social movements are more likely to use the tactics of protest and demonstration when they are outside the framework of the law, but when laws have been passed in response to their demands, they become more likely to initiate lawsuits to achieve their goals. Burstein shows that the more a group has mobilized its resources as a protest movement, the more it will be able to mobilize the law in

its favor as well. Thus racial minorities and women's groups, two well-mobilized civil rights groups, do much better at winning enforcement of EEO laws than religious or ethnic minorities, which have less experience organizing and mobilizing members and money for their causes.

MASS PUBLICS AND PUBLIC OPINION

Most of the examples of social movements discussed in this chapter have had a lasting impact on the societies in which they occurred. In this section, we apply the insights gained from earlier sections to some of the less world-shaking, yet still exciting, aspects of collective behavior in American life.

Over the past century, North America has been transformed from a continent of wide-open spaces and agrarian settlements to the earth's technologically most advanced and socially most mobile region. For the rest of the world, North America is synonymous with both the best and the worst aspects of what has come to be known as "modern" society.

According to Reinhard Bendix (1969), **modernization** consists of all the political and economic changes that accompanied industrialization. Among the indicators of modernity are urbanization, the shift from agricultural to industrial occupations, increasing literacy, and the demand for greater political participation by the masses. Bendix is quick to point out that his definition does not necessarily apply everywhere in the world. Modernization may not always mean what it has meant in Western societies. It is probable, however, that despite setbacks in some nations, modernization will always involve the extension of rights, values, and opportunities from the elites to the masses in a society.

None of these changes in the organization of societies came about without collective protests and social movements. For every radical movement there was a reactionary one; for every revolution there was a counterrevolution or at least an attempt at one. Social movements continue to exert pressure for change in our norms and institutions. The extension of voting rights to women and blacks had to be won through political struggle. Nor did the benefits of new technologies come automatically to American workers; they had to be won by the labor movement. Likewise, the rapidly expanding cities of North America became scenes of collective protest as new populations of immigrants and new occupational groups fought for "a piece of the pie" (Lieberson, 1980). It is hardly surprising, therefore, that so much sociological research is devoted to studying how modern society came about, discovering

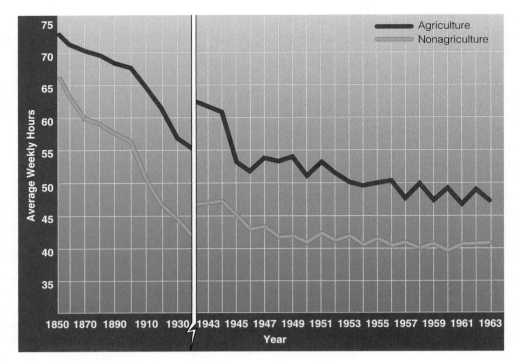

Figure 8.3   Average Weekly Work Hours, 1850–1963

There was a brief increase in average hours of work between 1940 and 1943 (not shown on the chart), due to the labor shortages that occurred during World War II.

Source: Data from Bureau of Labor Statistics; adapted from Dankert, Mann, & Northrup, 1965.

how much further some groups have to go to gain their share of the benefits of modernity, and analyzing the role of collective behavior in these major social changes.

Consider just one important consequence of the labor movement of the late nineteenth and early twentieth centuries: the change in the length of the workweek. "Our lives shall not be sweated, from day until night closes," went the famous refrain of the Industrial Workers of the World (known as the Wobblies). "Hearts starve as well as bodies; give us bread but give us roses." Figure 8.3 shows how the demand for enough leisure to enjoy the finer things of life produced dramatic changes in the hours of work. Today we take the 8-hour day and the 5-day week as the standard for full-time employment, but in 1919 American steelworkers shut down the entire industry in protest against the 12-hour day and the 6-day week (Brody, 1960). The concessions won by them and other workers were an essential part of the extension of the benefits of modernity to working people (McAdam & Snow, 1997). The increase in leisure created by these changes in hours and days of work, along with greater social mobility as a result of increased affluence, contributed to the development of mass publics, as illustrated in the Popular Culture and Social Change box on page 219.

Mass Publics

Mass publics are large populations (regional or national) of potential spectators or participants who engage in collective behavior of all kinds. Typically this behavior consists of the formation of crowds, audiences, or streams of buyers and voters, but it can also include crazes, panics, and the spreading of rumors. Thus a massive traffic jam can turn into a dangerous panic; a joyful victory celebration can become a violent riot like the one that occurred after the Chicago Bulls won the National Basketball Association championship in 1992. The panic selling that occurred on Wall Street in 1987 and again in 1998, resulting in a massive loss of investors' capital, is a reminder that mass publics continue to exert important effects even when supposed safeguards are in place. For this reason alone, social scientists, urban planners, and governmental leaders increasingly recognize the need to cooperate in anticipating the behaviors of mass publics.

This recognition has come after some painful experiences. A famous case of failure to anticipate the possible reaction of mass publics occurred with the 1938 radio dramatization of H. G. Wells's novel *The War of the Worlds*. This broadcast, which vividly described an inva-

POPULAR CULTURE & SOCIAL CHANGE   Amusing the Millions

The idea that the United States is becoming "a nation of spectators" was a popular sociological notion in the 1950s. A contemporary version of this "spectatoritis" thesis is the claim that greater affluence and increased access to television and other media have transformed Americans into a nation of overweight "couch potatoes." A more sophisticated analysis of these issues is provided by the study of leisure in the United States and other advanced industrial nations. Indeed, the study of leisure is an important frontier of sociological research.

Since the 1940s, the pursuit of leisure activities of all kinds has become a passion for those who can afford the time. This is true throughout most of the industrial world, not just in the United States and Canada (Machlis & Tichnell, 1985). People are spending more money on leisure pursuits and engaging in more diverse pleasures than ever before. In ancient Rome and feudal Europe, only the nobility had leisure; everyone else toiled ceaselessly in the fields or at their crafts. The limited leisure available to the masses took the form of religious festivals and games. The notion that common people could enjoy leisure in specified blocks of time—weekends, holidays, vacations, retirement— would have been viewed as revolutionary.

The rise of modern social movements changed the expectations of "common folk" about many values, including leisure. For example, at the turn of the twentieth century, the labor movement called for an end to the 12-hour workday. At around the same time, the conservation movement was pressing for preservation of the nation's virgin forests and the creation of national parks. The suffrage movement marched for women's right to vote, which would eventually lead to demands by women for more leisure time.

One consequence of the increase in leisure time in North America has been the steady growth of institutions devoted to leisure and recreation. It is estimated that more than 350 million visits are paid to national parks in the United States each year and that approximately 700 million visits are made to state parks. More than 45 million tickets to major league baseball games are sold each year, and about 15 million people attend NFL football games. About 415 million rounds of golf are played each year, more than 60 million people go bowling, and at least 9 million people own an outboard motor. There are some 1,100 opera companies in the nation; they perform for at least 14 million people a year (Gorn & Goldstein,

© Jeff Greenberg/Photo Researchers

1993). Try maneuvering through the traffic jam caused by a college football game when 60,000 fans are trying to get home for dinner. Imagine the same scene repeated simultaneously at thousands of other locations, some smaller and some larger, and you can begin to grasp the impact of leisure pursuits.

Data like those just presented tell only part of the story of leisure's impact on a modern society. In the United States, people's leisure preferences increasingly shape the landscape itself. Highways extend to beaches and mountain recreation sites. Large portions of states like Florida, Montana, Wyoming, Arizona, and California are managed as leisure and recreation areas by powerful state and national land management agencies. Private vendors of recreation services (motels, tennis courts, restaurants, shops, etc.) crowd the tourist gateways to major attractions like Yellowstone Park or the Great Smokies. In major cities, leisure institutions like theaters, symphony orchestras, museums, sports complexes, and parks are vital to the local economy and culture. Without them, cities would become dark ghost towns after business hours. Urban planners and city leaders therefore compete to attract talent and develop such institutions into tourist and cultural centers. Leisure for the millions translates into jobs for hundreds of thousands of people in every region of the country.

sion of the earth by Martians, was presented to the radio audience in documentary fashion, beginning with a fictitious news flash and continuing with reports of a spacecraft landing in a New Jersey field and descriptions of the invading Martian army. Not realizing that the broadcast was only a dramatic presentation, hundreds of thousands of Americans began gathering in panicky crowds, while thousands of others jammed telephone lines in efforts to reach loved ones.

A few years later, when the dramatization was broadcast by Radio Quito using Ecuadorian place names, "the initial reaction was the same as in the United States. Multitudes poured out of the city in all directions, running and driving as far and as fast as they could" (Klass, 1988, p. 48).

art *and the sociological eye*

Images of Collective Behavior

Artists often capture for future generations the feelings and images associated with collective behavior and social movements. We see many examples of this in famous paintings in museums throughout the world. People's daily lives are being severely disrupted, for better or worse, by great social movements or far-reaching changes in the fate of entire social classes. There is a dynamism in these paintings; the people they portray are being swept up in the great events of their time.

Simone Martini's depiction of *The Road to Calvary* portrays a scene in which Christ, the Virgin and saints, and the Roman soldiers and commoners all are caught up in a chaotic and violent event. The artist sets the scene against the backdrop of a fortified town, suggesting the strains in the medieval social order of Europe that were occurring as a result of the accelerating renaissance in art, science, and commerce. The

Renaissance threatened the long-standing dominance of the church and the feudal state. Thus the painting makes a strong connection between the changes that occurred in Jesus' time and those that were occurring in Europe during the fourteenth century.

Revolutions, civil wars, and invasions of the weak by the powerful are often either consequences or causes of lasting social change. It is no wonder, then, that scenes of war are so often portrayed in paintings. Francisco de Goya's *The Executions of the Third of May* is a fierce rendering of the brutality of the Napoleonic conquest of Spain. Firing

Cliches des Musees Nationaux

The Road to Calvary, by Simone Martini, about 1340. Panel, 10" x 6".

Museo del Prado, Madrid

The Executions of the Third of May, by Francisco de Goya, 1808. Oil on canvas, 8' 8³/₄" x 11' 3⁷/₈".

squad executions like these took place in Madrid after the weak Spanish monarchy had refused to resist the invasion. But it is not necessary to know the details of this moment in history. Goya's painting gains its impact from the way the artist portrays the behavior of individuals under extreme conditions. The soldiers' faces are hidden. The soldiers are presented as automatons following orders rather than as humans. The dying civilians, in contrast, are all too human in their reactions. Some stare defiantly at their executioners while others cower with their faces covered.

When listeners found out that the program had been a dramatization, they were so angry at the radio station that they burned it to the ground. As a result of experiences like these, broadcasters became far more careful in presenting fictitious accounts on the radio (Cantril, 1982/1940).

The availability of more time for leisure pursuits, the development of a mass market for automobiles, and the technological revolution in communications and the mass media have all exerted an immense influence on the lifestyles of mass publics, who in turn shape the society in which they live. For example, through their demands for roads, leisure facilities, and services that cater to a highly mobile lifestyle, Americans have transformed the physical landscape. Rural scenes of farms and small towns still exist, but throughout the nation they are being enveloped by networks of suburbs, shopping malls, and pleasure grounds (stadiums, amusement parks, etc.) linked together by a labyrinth of highways (Carter, 1975; Flink, 1975; Thomas, 1956).

Mass publics have also created the conditions that make whole new industries possible. The hot dog, for example, was an innovation that allowed large numbers of people to eat while strolling along the boardwalk at Coney Island. But fast food soon became an industry and even, as McDonald's founder Ray Kroc (1977) described it, an art form:

> Consider, for example, the hamburger bun. It requires a certain kind of mind to see beauty in a hamburger bun. Yet, is it any more unusual to find grace in the texture and softly curved silhouette of a bun than to reflect lovingly on the hackles of a favorite fishing fly? Or the arrangement of textures and colors in a butterfly wing? . . . Not if you regard the bun as an essential material in the art of serving a great many meals fast. (p. 99)

The thousands of teenagers and young adults who work in the fast-food industry may not sing rhapsodies to buns and burgers; nevertheless, their industry owes its existence to the behavior of hungry, mobile multitudes—that is, mass publics.

Public Opinion

The presence of mass publics sets the stage for the emergence of public opinion as a powerful force in modern societies. **Public opinion** refers to the values and attitudes of mass publics. The kinds of behavior that develop out of public opinion include fads, fashions, demands for particular goods and services, voting behavior, and much more.

Public opinion is shaped in part by collective behavior, especially social movements. An example is the rise of the conservative movement in the United States in the 1980s. The impact of this movement can be seen in the contrast between the results of the 1964 and 1984 presidential

elections. In 1964, Barry Goldwater, who espoused many of the ideals of the current conservative movement, was overwhelmingly defeated by Lyndon Johnson, an outspoken proponent of liberal social-welfare policies. Twenty years later, the pendulum of public opinion had swung to the other extreme, and the staunchly conservative Ronald Reagan defeated a liberal candidate, Walter Mondale, by an even greater percentage of the electoral vote than Johnson had won in 1964.

During the 1992 presidential election campaign, there seemed to be a backlash against extreme conservatism, reflected in the voters' rejection of Republican emphasis on "family values" as code words for disapproval of homosexuals, single parents, and other people with unconventional lifestyles. But then, Republican victories in the 1994 congressional elections showed that conservative values were at least temporarily in ascendance once again. Supported by active social movements, particularly the antiabortion forces and those promoting Christian conservative causes, the Republicans faced the problem of satisfying the demands of those movements while persuading others that the party could accommodate their often conflicting needs. Democrat Bill Clinton's reelection in 1996, the small but surprising Democratic gains in the 1998 off-year elections, and the strength of conservative support for George W. Bush in 2000 indicate how difficult it can be to predict public opinion and to satisfy mass publics.

Public opinion is also shaped by more fleeting shifts in the national mood as citizens respond to experiences that are shared by all, especially through the mass media. For example, no one knows for sure whether the severe droughts that burned crops in the United States and Canada in 1987 and 1988 were a symptom of global warming, but scientists' warnings about this possibility, and their explanations of the "greenhouse effect" caused by high levels of carbon dioxide and other gases in the atmosphere, were made far more vivid by media coverage of the drought. Public support for environmental protection was stimulated still further by media coverage of the oil spill by the Exxon *Valdez* in Alaska in 1989.

CRITICAL SOCIOLOGY AND SOCIAL CHANGE

The Celebrity Industry

Americans are hooked on fame. Famous people, or *celebrities,* are so much in demand, so much the focus of attention, so widely discussed that everywhere we turn—at the supermarket, on television, in the press—gossip about the rise and fall of celebrities crowds in on us. No

Text continues on page 224.

VISUAL SOCIOLOGY

THE NAMES PROJECT QUILT

Many people have come to understand the personal meaning of the AIDS epidemic through an extraordinary social movement—the NAMES Project—and the famous quilt it has produced. This movement uses visual sociology in the most creative way one can imagine. As AIDS activist Elizabeth Taylor writes:

The quilt is a moving depiction of stories of the loved ones of human beings who have died of AIDS. It reflects the true spirit of America. In their tragedy and grief over loss immeasurable, contributors to the quilt have used art and love to keep the spirit of their loved ones alive. (quoted in Ruskin, 1988, p. 7)

The NAMES Project and the quilt are the inspiration of Cleve Jones (2002). When the actor Marvin Feldman, his dear friend of 14 years, died of AIDS at age 33, Jones went to his backyard with

paint, stencils, and a sheet to create a memorial. He remembers spending the entire day thinking about Marvin: "I thought about why we were best friends and why I loved him so much. By the time I finished the piece, my grief had been replaced by a sense of resolution and completion." Jones realized that if people got together to make quilts as memorials to lost loved ones, the activity could be a redeeming and mobilizing way of confronting the AIDS epidemic.

A Quaker with years of political activism in his background, Jones became a gay activist when he was 18. In 1986, he appeared on *60 Minutes* and discussed his reactions to the discovery that he was HIV positive. Shortly thereafter, in Sacramento, he was attacked by two men who stalked him, calling him "faggot," and stabbed him in the back. During his convalescence, he thought more about the idea of the NAMES Project and the quilt, and after his recovery he joined with AIDS activists throughout the world to advertise the project. Before long, hundreds of groups of friends and family members were producing quilt panels to commemorate the loss of their loved ones.

On October 11, 1987, the quilt was displayed on the Mall in Washington, D.C.; it covered an area larger than two football fields. It was subsequently ex-

hibited throughout the United States, focusing attention on the need for increased funding for research and the allocation of additional medical resources to the AIDS epidemic. Today the quilt is constantly on display around the world, especially on December 1 of each year, which has been designated World AIDS Day by the United Nations and the World Health Organization. For much more information about the project, see www.aidsquilt.org/Newsite/natwaddisplays.htm.

The Sociological Observer

(See photo on page 208.)

Although the most obvious emotion these two people are displaying is grief, they are also sharing their feelings in a way that will help each of them cope better with their grief than they could if they were alone; this is why in times of grief we so often reach out to others with whom we can share deep emotions. Although these individuals no doubt came to Washington to express their feelings together, they are also there because of a social movement, the NAMES Project, which created the opportunity to use their personal experience in a larger public setting to make millions of other Americans aware of the ravages of AIDS.

© Matt Herron 1987

"There is nothing beautiful about AIDS. It is a hideous disease. . . . With the Quilt, we're able to touch people in a new way and open their hearts so that they no longer turn away from it but rather understand the value of all those lost lives."

© Matt Herron 1987

H. D.C.
2,1983

"I CAME HERE TODAY TO ASK THAT THIS NATION WITH ALL ITS RESOURCES AND COMPASSION NOT LET MY EPITAPH READ HE DIED OF RED TAPE"

Roger Gail Lyon

"The saddest thing, I believe, for Roger Lyon," says his devoted friend, Cindy McMullin, "was how unfair it was to have to die without knowing how it—AIDS—is going to end."

These quilt panels are typical of the thousands that now make up the NAMES Project quilt. Sixty-year-old homemaker Marian Mosner of Lincoln, Nebraska, made Neil Patchek's panel for a man who worked with her son in Denver. She did not know her son's friend well but says, "I thought that there would be no recognition from his family. I felt bad about that. I feel bad about all the people who die of AIDS that nobody knows."

surprise, then, that sociologists who study collective behavior and public opinion are seeking to better understand the origins of this explosion in the public's appetite for stories about stars and celebrities.

Sociologist Josh Gamson (1994) shows in detail how celebrity is constructed by a thriving "fame industry." But Gamson admits that he became fascinated by fame and celebrities just the way other Americans do, by watching television, often instead of studying. "I became interested in exploring the peculiarities of celebrity culture in graduate school," he says, "through my evening encounters with *Entertainment Tonight,* a television program that can generously be called lightweight." Gamson was amazed to read that *Entertainment Tonight's* anchor, Mary Hart, "whose celebrity derives from a chipper reading of teleprompted words about entertainers," had received a star on the Hollywood Walk of Fame. But trivial as Gamson thought her fame was, he could not help watching the show and thinking about the celebrities. Trained to analyze collective behavior and fads, he realized that he needed "to tap into the weird world of what for many people in this country, including myself, had become the stuff of everyday life" (1994, p. 4).

Gamson's study examines what is done in the entertainment industry to "manufacture" celebrity, and it also looks at the audience for fame by analyzing "how people actively encounter celebrities and interpret and use celebrity images" (p. 5). Like all professional researchers, however, Gamson drew many of his research questions and investigative leads from a thorough study of the historical and sociological literature about fame.

A question that is often raised in the literature on celebrity is this: If people like Mary Hart and other television celebrities are famous, what is that fame in comparison with "the famous of the past, those names that echo in our minds—Alexander, Caesar, Cleopatra, Jesus, Mohammed, Joan of Arc, Shakespeare" (Braudy, 1997)? In the past, our heroes tended to be people of great achievement with admirable qualities that set them apart from the rest of us. In premodern societies, however, word of the deeds of heroes spread relatively slowly. It could take weeks for the details of a general's actions in a great battle to spread, even through the elites of a population. With the rise of modern and more democratic societies, equipped with ever more rapid forms of communication, names and faces arise and fall with stunning rapidity. The important differences between actions and image, between truth and fiction, between deserving and undeserving, are blurred in the rush of information and the seductive power of the media.

Gamson found plenty of critical writing about fame in the modern world. Most of this literature emphasizes how visibility becomes its own reward and artificial images replace real-life ones so that people become unable to distinguish between truth and fiction and, more important, are uninterested in doing so. But Gamson found more balanced evaluations of the fame phenomenon in the work of historians and sociologists who wonder how deep the frenzy for fame actually goes in contemporary societies. From sociologist Michael Schudson, for example, Gamson learned to question how seriously consumers take the fleeting fame of many celebrities. There are probably many gradations in consumers' ability to distinguish among celebrities whose fame is purely a matter of television exposure and those, like Mark McGwire or Michael Jordan, who more clearly merit their fame because of their achievements.

These insights led Gamson to narrow the focus of his study to the entertainment industry. "Entertainment," he argues, "is clearly the dominant celebrity realm in this century; it is also the most fully rationalized and industrialized. It is therefore typically used as a model for the development of celebrity in other realms (politics, for example). . . . Understanding entertainment celebrity promises to help us comprehend celebrity as a general cultural phenomenon: its particular dynamics, its place in everyday lives, its broader implications" (1994, p. 5).

Gamson sees in the rise of mass entertainment the technological possibilities for more instant renown. Today's celebrities are the "products" of an efficient fame industry. No doubt many of the older generation of movie stars, like Elizabeth Taylor and John Wayne, actually developed their fame over long careers of outstanding acting. They and hundreds like them seem different from television personalities whose fame appears to be based on mere exposure in the mass media. But Gamson's research shows that the rise of the mass entertainment industries earlier in the twentieth century also spurred the rise of the modern fame industry. The need for movie studios to maintain the fame of their actors helped account for the emergence of occupations designed to keep important names and faces before the public: the agent, the publicist, the celebrity photographer. As more media channels have developed, the pressure to attract viewers by showing them people who are famous has also increased, and the meaning of fame has been watered down.

Through extensive interviews and observations in the Los Angeles and New York celebrity industries, Gamson shows just how fame is manufactured. The entertainment industry is "much like other commodity-production systems." People working in it "speak primarily in the language of commerce and machinery," and "marketing plays a key role in marching products to distributors and consumers, depending especially on strategies of product transformation and the building of consumer loyalty" (1994, p. 58). Over and over again, those whose job is to make and evaluate, buy and sell famous people described to Gamson the ins and outs of creating and, sometimes more difficult, maintaining celebrity. The photo of Cher, which Gamson includes in his study, is one of many he analyzes to reveal the processes of "celebrity making." In this photo, which is designed to show the often frenetic Cher in a serene mood, we get a glimpse of the artificiality of the situation she was in at the time. In the photo of "Two Actors," Gamson points out that humorous commentary on celebrity itself can be used in the "hype" of stardom.

SUMMARY

The Meanings of Disorder

- The term *collective behavior* is used to refer to a continuum of unusual or nonroutine behaviors that are engaged in by large numbers of people. At one end of the continuum is the spontaneous behavior of people reacting to situations they perceive as uncertain, threatening, or extremely attractive; these behaviors include fads and fashions, rumor and gossip, and panic and mass hysteria. At the other end are events that involve large numbers of people in nonroutine behaviors but are organized by leaders and have specific goals.

- The set of organizations that plan such events is a *social movement.*

- The study of spontaneous forms of collective behavior often begins by distinguishing between crowds and masses. A *crowd* is a large number of people who are gathered together in close proximity to one another. A *mass* is a large number of people, not necessarily in close proximity, who are all oriented toward a set of shared symbols or social objects.

- Collective behavior can occur in crowds, in masses, or in both at once. The actual behavior that a crowd or mass generates depends largely on the emotions people involved in the events feel are appropriate to express in those situations.

- The most significant categories of emotions that motivate collective behavior are fear, hostility, and joy.

- Social movements have been classified into four types based on the goals they seek to achieve: (1) revolutionary movements aim to overthrow existing stratification systems and social institutions; (2) reformist movements seek partial changes in some institutions and values; (3) conservative movements attempt to uphold the existing values and institutions of society; and (4) reactionary movements seek to return to the institutions and values of the past.

- In addition, there are expressive social movements, or movements devoted to the expression of personal beliefs and feelings, and millenarian movements, which are both revolutionary and expressive.

- Within any large social movement there are likely to be several different social movement organizations, or SMOs.

Social Movement Theory

- Early theories of collective behavior were based on the notion that hysteria or contagious feelings like hatred or fear could spread through masses of people. Gustave LeBon attributed the strikes and riots that are common in rapidly urbanizing societies to a mob mentality created by the presence of large numbers of strangers in crowded cities.

- Sociologists often distinguish between "long revolutions," or large-scale changes in the ecological relationships of humans to the earth and to one another, and revolutions that are primarily social or political.

- *Political revolutions* are transformations in the political structures and leadership of a society that are not accompanied by a full-scale rearrangement of the society's productive capacities, culture, and stratification system.

- *Social revolutions* not only change the institutions of government but also bring about basic changes in social stratification.

- According to Marx, revolutions would occur as a result of the spread of capitalism: Impoverished workers and colonial peoples would rebel against the capitalists and create a new classless society.

- Also, Marx and Tocqueville pointed to the role of *relative deprivation*, noting that the feeling of deprivation relative to others—not the presence of deprivation itself—may result in revolutionary social movements.

- More recent analyses have shown that revolutionary social movements often occur in cycles or waves. Waves of protest may result from major social shocks. During such periods social conflicts increase dramatically, often motivated by collective action frames, or sets of beliefs and interpretations of events.

- Successful leaders of social movements are often said to have almost supernatural powers to inspire and motivate their followers. Max Weber called this ability *charisma.*

- Over time, however, those leaders' goals must be incorporated into the structure of the movement, a process that is referred to as the institutionalization of charisma.

- However, the more successful the movement, the more difficult it is to maintain the zeal of its founders. In extreme cases, the process can end in totalitarianism, or efforts by an elite to control all forms of organizational life in a society.

Social Movements and Civil Society

- The sphere of public nongovernmental, nonbusiness social activity is termed *civil society.*

- People who participate in civil society are often recruited into social movements. The resource mobilization question refers to the need to mobilize existing leaders and organizations to achieve a movement's goals.

- A related issue is the *free rider problem,* the tendency of many people not to lend their support and resources to social movements but to reap the benefits anyway.

- In recent years, activist groups have made increasing use of laws and the courts. Social movements are more likely to use the tactics of protest when they are outside the framework of the law; when laws have been passed in response to their demands, they become more likely to initiate lawsuits to achieve their goals.

Mass Publics and Public Opinion

- *Mass publics* are large populations of potential spectators or participants who engage in collective behavior.

- Such factors as increased leisure time, the almost universal use of automobiles, and the technological revolution in communications and the mass media have had an immense influence on the lifestyles of mass publics, which in turn shape the society in which they live.

- The presence of mass publics makes possible the emergence of *public opinion,* or the values and attitudes of mass publics.

- The behavior that develops out of public opinion can take a variety of forms, including fads, fashions, and demands for particular goods and services.

- Public opinion is shaped in part by collective behavior, especially social movements. It is also affected by experiences that are shared by all the members of society through the mass media.

GLOSSARY

collective behavior: Nonroutine behavior that is engaged in by large numbers of people responding to a common stimulus. (p. 204)

social movement: Organized collective behavior aimed at changing or reforming social institutions or the social order itself. (p. 204)

crowd: A large number of people who are gathered together in close proximity to one another. (p. 206)

mass: A large number of people who are all oriented toward a set of shared symbols or social objects. (p. 206)

political revolution: A set of changes in the political structures and leadership of a society. (p. 211)

social revolution: A complete transformation of the social order, including the institutions of government and the system of stratification. (p. 211)

relative deprivation: Deprivation as determined by comparison with others rather than by some objective measure. (p. 211)

charisma: A special quality or "gift" that motivates people to follow a particular leader. (p. 214)

civil society: The sphere of nongovernmental, nonbusiness social activity carried out by voluntary associations, congregations, and the like. (p. 215)

modernization: A term used to describe the changes that societies and individuals experience as a result of industrialization, urbanization, and the development of nation-states. (p. 217)

mass public: A large population of potential spectators or participants who engage in collective behavior. (p. 218)

public opinion: The values and attitudes held by mass publics. (p. 221)

INTERNET RESOURCES

Virtual Society: The Wadsworth Sociology Resource Center
(http://sociology.wadsworth.com)

At Virtual Society you can access a wide range of enrichment material to aid your study of sociology. From the main page, click on the Student Resources link and find your course and this textbook. Next, select the chapter you are presently studying from the pull-down menu. Among the useful options for each self-study chapter are online links and exercises, flashcards, practical study tips, and practice quizzes for each chapter.

MicroCase Online

From the Virtual Society home page, click on MicroCase Online to access book-specific MicroCase exercises that allow you to further explore sociological issues and principles presented in the text.

InfoTrac College Edition

Another unique option available to you at the Student Resources section at Virtual Society is InfoTrac College Edition, an online library with access to hundreds of scholarly and popular periodicals. Below are suggested search terms for this chapter, but this resource also allows you to fit your study of sociology to your own interests by searching custom keywords.

Collective Behavior

Revolution

Social Movement

Charisma

Project on Social Research for Social Change, Cornell University
(www.cornell.edu)
Provides information about grassroots social movements, with links to many related sites.

The AFL-CIO Home Page
(www.aflcio.org)
An example of an older social movement organization that is adapting to new conditions and technologies.

U.S. Census Bureau: The Official Statistics
(www.census.gov)
The official site for the U.S. Census Bureau continually updates labor and social statistics. The current U.S. population count and current economic indicators are popular features of the site.

Population and Urbanization

© Liba Taylor/Corbis

The peasant families with many children were asked to come sit in front of the gathering. The huge crowd watched as hundreds of parents and children filed toward the front of the throng of people seated in a grain field, sweating in the afternoon sun. They were waiting to see and hear Chandrababu Naidu, one of India's most powerful political leaders.

When the families were settled in the front, Naidu began speaking, but his words were not designed to make the large families happy. He criticized them for having too many children. They could not provide adequate education and health care for so many children, he warned, and the government could not afford to help them either. He urged the parents to immediately make appointments for voluntary sterilization. The parents seemed embarrassed. Many people in the crowd could not suppress their nervous laughter. They knew that the subject was one of great importance, but it was also one that they preferred to whisper about in the privacy of their homes.

Summoning all his courage, a peasant farmer named Nara Singh, a father of four with another baby on the way, stood up in front of the crowd, took the microphone, and firmly but with great conviction insisted that he needed even more children to help work his small farm. The politician listened to him respectfully, but when the farmer was finished, he asked the crowd, "Is this man on the right path?" Very few of the listeners raised their hands in agreement with the farmer. He had won their respect for speaking his mind, but they knew that he represented the old, and now discredited, idea that having as many children as possible was desirable for rural people.

After years of public discussion on radio and television and in sweaty gatherings like this one, many of the people in the crowd understood that India needed to control its population growth. The nation had added more than 180 million new mouths to feed in the previous decade alone. At current growth rates, India's population, which recently passed the billion mark, will surpass China's by the middle of the century, making India the world's most populous nation. But the idea of vasectomies for men or tubal ligations for women still struck many as a drastic measure.

Those in the crowd with more education and the ability to read the newspapers also knew that the politician's policies were controversial. Their state had the highest rate of voluntary sterilizations in India, and it appeared that the policy had had some success in decelerating the region's population growth rate. But other states of India had shown even more success by instituting programs to dramatically increase female literacy, health care, and contraception. In their state, men and women with no more than two children who underwent voluntary sterilization were given a small cash payment and preference in the distribution of small farm lots or building plots. These were powerful incentives, but they were not making nearly as much progress in raising literacy levels, and low literacy rates could be an obstacle to economic development over the long term.

A combination of tactics, including education, health care, and incentives for sterilization, would be even more effective, some of the educated listeners argued. But the need for urgent measures was clear even to the least educated in the crowd. Growing populations were threatening to exhaust available supplies of wood for cooking fires. Water resources were being stretched to their limits. The landless were being forced into the nearby cities, where they often had to resort to begging and life in the streets. The political leaders of their state were making sterilization attractive enough to the small landholders that it was beginning to become a common practice. Clearly, the peasants, and especially the women, wanted to control their fertility, which was a good sign for the future of their society and its natural environment (Dugger, 2001).

FOCUS QUESTIONS:

• How do sociologists measure and predict population changes?

• Is there a "population explosion," and what are some of the effects of population growth on natural resources?

• How does the growth of cities affect population, and what specific challenges does urbanization pose to social organization?

PEOPLE, RESOURCES, AND URBAN GROWTH

This story about the reproductive dilemmas poor people face in India only begins to touch on the many issues that population growth raises throughout the world. Stress created by the struggle to make ends meet, degradation of the natural environment, and massive migrations to crowded cities are not limited to the developing regions of the world. More affluent nations have their own versions of these dilemmas.

The human population continues to spread throughout the world. Although most of the world's people live in rural villages, in modern societies they typically live in cities or metropolitan areas rather than on farms or in small towns. In fact, 90 percent of Americans live within 25 miles of a city center (Anderton, 1997; Berry, 1978). This means that they live in the human-built environment of cities and suburbs; relatively few live in the "country" environment of rural areas. It also means, among many other things, that settlement occurs in unstable places that invite disaster.

The study of population growth and the growth of cities as centers of demographic and social change has long been a central field in sociology. In this chapter, therefore, we see how increasing population size and other important changes in populations are connected with the rise of cities and metropolitan areas throughout the world. At the end of the chapter, we turn to the study of natural and social disasters.

The Population Explosion

For many decades, sociologists have been conducting research on the impacts of population growth, on how such growth places stresses on the earth's natural resources, and on the rapid growth of cities throughout the world. This chapter highlights some of the main issues addressed by this research. First, however, we must note that the most basic facts about how many people there are on the earth and how fast their numbers are growing (and will grow in the future) are surprisingly complicated. In Chapter 4, we described the extremely rapid growth of the world's population in the past three centuries. If you refer back to Figure 4.2, you can readily see that the *rate* of population growth increased dramatically in the twentieth century, giving rise to the often-used term *population explosion*. The world's population is currently estimated at 6.8 billion (*Statistical Abstract*, 2002), and according to recent United Nations forecasts, it is likely to increase to about 8.8 billion by 2025 (O'Neill & Balk, 2001). This would represent

growth over a 30-year period that is roughly equal to the entire world population in 1965 (Mitchell, 1998).

At present about 90 million new people are added to the world's population each year. Most forecasts predict that this rapid growth will begin to decline by midcentury, but by then there could be many as 10.7 billion people on a very crowded planet. Demographers point out, however, that crop production, famine and war, contraception, economic development, and many other variables affect population. The potential effects of these variables make it extremely difficult to predict trends in population growth. It is certain, though, that rapid population growth, especially in the poorer regions of the world, will continue in coming decades and will pose severe challenges to human survival and well-being (Sanderson & Scherbov, 1997). The pressures of population growth on resources of food, space, and water have produced changes in economic and social arrangements throughout history, but never before have those changes occurred as rapidly or on as great a scale as they are occurring today (Cohen, 1998; Smil, 2001).

CATASTROPHISTS VERSUS CORNUCOPIANS   Is there a danger that the earth will become overpopulated? The debate over population growth is not new. For almost two centuries, social scientists have been seeking to determine whether human populations will grow beyond the earth's capacity to support them. *Catastrophists* believe that it is possible that rapid population growth may lead to increasing social and environmental disasters: famines; wars driven by people desperate to expand into others' lands; and extreme depletion of water and soil resources (Brown, 1995; Ehrlich & Ehrlich, 1990). The far more optimistic *cornucopians* believe that there are endless possibilities for humans to control populations and devise solutions to environmental and social problems. Many argue that population growth is necessary for economic growth and is not an obstacle to development (Simon, 1996; Singer, 1999).

The earliest and most forceful theory of overpopulation appeared in Thomas Malthus's *An Essay on Population* (1927–1928/1798). Malthus attempted to show that population size normally increases far more rapidly than the food and energy resources needed to keep people alive. Couples will have as many children as they can afford to feed, and their children will do the same. This will cause populations to grow *geometrically* (2, 4, 8, 16, 32, . . .). Meanwhile, available food supplies will increase *arithmetically* (2, 3, 4, 5, 6, . . .) as farms are expanded and crop yields increased. As a result, population growth will always threaten to outstrip food supplies. The resulting poverty, famine, disease, war, and mass migrations will act as natural checks on rapid population growth.

History has proved Malthus wrong on at least two counts. To begin with, we are not biologically driven to

TABLE 9.1

Population Growth and Doubling Time, Selected Countries

Country	Population (millions)	Annual Growth Rate* (percent)	Doubling Time* (years)
India	1,002.1	1.8	39
China	1,264.5	0.9	79
Brazil	170.1	1.5	45
Bangladesh	128.1	1.8	38
Nigeria	123.3	2.8	24
Pakistan	150.6	2.8	25
Indonesia	212.2	1.6	44
Russia	145.2	−0.6	—
Mexico	99.6	2.0	36
United States	275.6	0.6	120

*Annual rate of natural increase.

**Number of years in which the population will double at current rate of increase.

Source: Population Reference Bureau, 2000.

multiply beyond the capacity of the environment to support our offspring; Malthus himself later recognized that people could limit their reproduction through delay of marriage or celibacy. The second fault of Malthusian theory is its failure to recognize that technological and institutional change could expand available resources rapidly enough to keep up with population growth. This has occurred in the more affluent regions of the world, where improvements in the quality of life have tended to outstrip population growth. Improvements in agricultural technology have also increased the yield of crops in some of the less developed parts of the world, such as India. But rates of population growth and exhaustion of environmental resources (firewood, water, grazing land) are highest in the poorest nations (Furedi, 1997). Will reductions in population growth rates and increases in available resources also occur there? Or will the fears of the catastrophists prove correct in the long run? The theory known as the *demographic transition* provides a framework for studying this question, but before we explore this theory we need to know more about measuring population change.

RATES OF POPULATION CHANGE Populations change as a consequence of births, deaths, out-migration, and in-migration. The most basic measures of population change are *crude rates,* or the number of events of a given type (e.g., births or deaths) that occur in a year divided by the midyear population (Bogue, 1969). Thus the **crude birthrate** (CBR) is the number of births occurring during a year in a given population divided by the

midyear population, and the **crude death rate** (CDR) is the number of deaths occurring during a year divided by the midyear population. These fractions are usually expressed as a rate per thousand persons. They are "crude" because they compare the total number of births or deaths with the total midyear population, when in fact not all members of the population are equally likely to give birth or to die.

The **rate of reproductive change** is the difference between the CBR and the CDR for a given population. It is a measure of the natural increase of the population; that is, it measures increases caused by the excess of births over deaths and disregards in- and out-migration. At present there are several nations in which the rate of reproductive change is zero or less, meaning that there is no natural population growth. Germany, for example, had a CBR of 9 and a CDR of 10 in 2001, for an annual rate of increase of −0.1. In Greece, the CBR was 10 and the CDR 10, for an annual rate of increase of 0. In the United States, the rate of population growth is about 0.6 percent, representing an increase of about 1.65 million people per year. These rates are in dramatic contrast with the annual growth rates of countries like Liberia and Nicaragua, which are above 3 percent. Rates of population growth in selected countries are listed in Table 9.1.

The last column in Table 9.1 shows the time it would take for the population of each nation to double if existing growth rates continued without change. A growth rate just under 1 percent, such as China has achieved, will double the population in 79 years, but a growth rate of

TABLE 9.2	
Relationship of Population Growth per Year and per Century	
Population Growth per Year (percent)	Population Growth per Century (percent)
1	270
2	724
3	1,922

Source: Data from Worldwatch Institute.

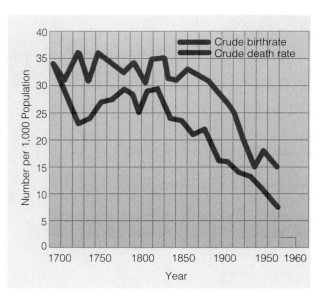

Figure 9.1 The Demographic Transition: Sweden, 1691–1963

The peaks in birth and death rates in the early 1800s were a result of social unrest and war. The drop in deaths and simultaneous rise in births in the early 1700s was a result of peace, good crops, and the absence of plagues.

Source: Judah Matras, *Population and Societies*, Englewood, Cliffs, NJ: Prentice Hall, © 1973. Permission of Armand Éditeur.

almost 3 percent, such as we see in Nigeria, doubles the population in 24 years. In contrast, in the United States an annual growth rate of 0.6 percent doubles the population in 120 years.

We can easily see from Table 9.2 that an annual rate of population growth of only 1 percent will lead to an increase of almost 270 percent in a century, and growth rates of 2 percent or more, such as we find in many of the poorer nations of the world, would yield populations of over 16 billion within a century. But current estimates for the end of this century, based on declining fertility rates, indicate that the world's population is likely to cease its rapid growth and level off somewhat below 10 billion (O'Neill & Balk, 2001). The reasons for these changes are summarized in the phenomenon known as the demographic transition.

THE DEMOGRAPHIC TRANSITION The **demographic transition** is a set of major changes in birth and death rates that has occurred most completely in urban industrial nations in the last 200 years. We saw in Chapter 4 that the rapid increase in the world population in the past 150 years resulted largely from rapid declines in death rates. Beginning in the second half of the eighteenth century and continuing until the first half of the twentieth century, death rates in the countries of northern and western Europe declined significantly. Improvements in public health practices were one factor in that decline. Even more important were higher agricultural yields because of technological changes in farming methods, as well as improvements in the distribution of food as a result of better transportation, which made cheaper food available to more people (Bacci, 1997; Vining, 1985). At the same time, however, birthrates in those countries remained high. The resulting gap between birth and death rates produced huge increases in population. It appeared that the gloomy predictions of Malthus and others would be borne out.

In the second half of the nineteenth century, however, birthrates began to decline as couples delayed marriage

and childbearing. As a result of lower birthrates, the gap between birth and death rates narrowed and population growth slowed. This occurred at different times in different countries (Figure 9.1 graphs the demographic transition in Sweden), but the general pattern was the same in each case and consisted of three stages:

1. A stage of high birthrates and death rates (the *high growth potential* stage).

2. A stage of declining death rates (the *transitional growth* stage).

3. A stage of declining birthrates (called the stage of *incipient decline* because it is possible for population growth rates to decrease at this point).

These three stages are summarized in the Study Chart on page 233.

In the second, or transitional growth, stage of the demographic transition, the population not only grows rapidly but also undergoes changes in its age composition. Because people now live longer, the proportion of elderly people increases slightly. There is also a marked increase in the proportion of people younger than age 20 as a result of significant decreases in infant and child mortality. This is the stage in which many less developed countries find them-

STUDY CHART

DEMOGRAPHIC TRANSITION AND DEVELOPMENT

STAGE OF POPULATION GROWTH	TYPE OF SOCIETY	MAIN DEVELOPMENTAL FEATURES
High Growth Potential	Most types of preindustrial societies.	High death rates due to infant mortality and low life expectancy; high rates of fertility; relatively low rates of increase.
Transitional Growth	Most societies in early stages of urban and industrial development where basic public health measures are being introduced (e.g., safe drinking water systems).	Decreasing mortality rates; continuing high rates of fertility. High rates of female illiteracy and limited protection of women's rights.
Incipient Decline	Societies in more advanced stages of urban and industrial development where people are delaying marriage and are more likely to use birth control.	Decreasing rates of mortality and fertility, with low or even negative rates of increase. High rates of female literacy and high levels of medical care for women in their reproductive years.

selves today: Death rates dropped in the twentieth century because of improved medical care and public health measures, as well as increased agricultural production. Yet in these societies birthrates have remained high, causing phenomenal increases in population, especially in the younger, more dependent age groups.

No population has entered the third stage of the demographic transition without limiting its birthrate. This can be achieved by encouraging couples to marry later and postpone childbearing or by preventing pregnancies or births through various birth-control techniques. In advanced industrial societies, many couples use both approaches, making their own decisions about whether and when to have children. In other societies, such as China and India, the state has attempted to limit population growth by promoting birth control through educational programs or, in the case of China, imposing penalties on couples who have more than a prescribed number of children. Such measures have had some transitory success, but often at a high political cost to national leaders. In China, for example, the strict one-child rule is not being enforced rigorously in areas undergoing rapid industrial and commercial development, where labor is in demand (Faison, 1997). We will see in more detail in the next chapter that guarantees of education for women, protection of their reproductive rights, and guarantees of their safety and right to vote are all highly correlated with decreases in fertility rates (Dasgupta, 2000).

Note that economic and social development is essential if the demographic transition is to occur. Death rates cannot decrease, or food supplies increase, without progress in social institutions such as public health, medicine, and transportation. People in more developed societies tend

to limit their family size because they seek economic advancement and wish to delay marriage and childbearing until they can support a family.

In many highly industrialized nations, on the other hand, population growth rates have fallen below the rate necessary to maintain the population at the existing level. If a fertility rate of two children or less per couple became the norm for an entire population, the growth rate would slow to zero or even a negative rate. The United States, New Zealand, Japan, Australia, and Canada all have total fertility rates of 2.1 or less (Population Reference Bureau, 2001). Similar low rates are appearing in many European nations. This development is highly significant; if it continues over a generation or more, it could result in negative rates of natural increase and, possibly, other consequences such as slower economic development and labor shortages. Continued low fertility could also result in increased immigration from countries with high birthrates to countries with lower birthrates.

A related issue is the rapid aging of populations in Europe and the United States as the proportion of elderly people increases while the proportion of children declines. This is somewhat less of a problem in the United States than in Europe because of continuing high rates of immigration, but as we will see in more detail in Chapter 15, the entry of the large baby boom cohort into its retirement years represents a major challenge for social policy in the United States (Koretz, 2003).

A full exposition of the processes and politics of population control is not possible here. Suffice it to say that most sociologists would agree with the demographer Philip Hauser (1957) that low population growth rates are caused primarily by a combination of delay of marriage,

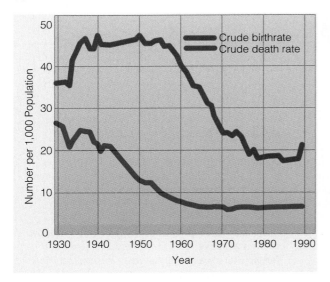

Figure 9.2   Crude Birth and Death Rates: Singapore, 1930–1988

Source: Davis, 1991.

celibacy, and use of modern birth-control techniques. This trend is beginning to occur in many less developed nations (Furedi, 1997; Ofosu-Amaah, 1998). Figure 9.2 illustrates the demographic transition in Singapore, a nation in Southeast Asia that has undergone this important population change more recently. Note that the decline in deaths, which took almost 150 years in Western industrial nations, took less than 50 years in Singapore. The decline in births began in the late 1950s, spurred by rapid economic development, the new desire for smaller families, and widespread availability of contraceptives. Whereas in Western nations like Sweden this phase of declining births unfolded over more than 100 years, in Singapore this phase occurred in only about 20 years (between about 1955 and 1975). Although world population growth remains a serious problem, the demographic transition in formerly poor nations like this one shows that population control efforts along with economic development can have dramatic effects (Davis, 1991).

LIFE EXPECTANCY IN GLOBAL CONTEXT   *Life expectancy*—usually defined as the number of years one can expect to live—is one of the most important indicators of how well a society cares for its population. Highly developed societies with advanced systems of health care and well-developed public health systems (sewage, drinking water, shelter, hospitals) have resulted in average life expectancies well up in the 70s (see Table 9.3). Societies that are in the earlier stages of industrialization and urbanization, such as Brazil and China, have lower average life expectancies, but impover-

TABLE 9.3

Infant Mortality and Life Expectancy for Selected Countries, 2002

Country	Infant Mortality*	Life Expectancy**
Angola	191.7	38.9
Australia	4.9	80.0
Canada	5.0	79.7
China	27.3	71.9
Egypt	58.6	64.0
Finland	3.8	77.8
France	4.4	79.0
Germany	4.7	77.8
Guatemala	44.5	66.8
India	61.5	63.2
Iran	28.1	70.2
Japan	3.8	80.9
Kenya	67.2	47.0
Mexico	24.5	72.0
Mozambique	138.5	35.5
Pakistan	78.5	61.8
Peru	38.2	70.6
Russia	19.8	67.5
South Africa	61.8	45.4
Sweden	3.4	79.8
United Kingdom	5.5	78.0
United States	6.7	77.4
Zimbabwe	63.0	36.5

*Infant deaths per 1,000 live births.

**Life expectancy at birth, in years, both sexes.

Source: U.S. Census Bureau, International Database.

ished, war-torn societies like Angola and Zimbabwe have life expectancies that are extremely low and may be declining, largely due to extremely high rates of infant mortality.

Infant mortality and life expectancy are closely related indicators of how well societies care for their populations. Newborn infants are extremely susceptible to infections and diseases, often the result of failures in basic sanitation and unclean drinking water. When poor societies make improvements in their public health systems, even before making more lasting improvements in health care and hospitals, life expectancy increases because far fewer infants die in the first year or so after birth. This is the period when death rates are falling but birthrates remain high, so populations can increase quite rapidly in this phase of the demographic transition. This is the situation in much of India at present.

HEALTHY LIFE EXPECTANCY It is one thing to life a long life, and quite another to live a long and healthy life. Standard measures of life expectancy, such as those given in Table 7.3, are based only on measures of mortality. Recently the World Health Organization has developed a more sophisticated measure that takes into account how long the average person in a nation can expect to live without severe and disabling illness. This *disability-adjusted life expectancy (DALE)* summarizes the average number of years a person can expect to live in "full health." According to this measure, Japan has the world's best healthy life expectancy at 74.5 years, and Sierra Leone, which has suffered years of civil war and rampant corruption, has the world's lowest at 26 years. Under this system of measurement the United States falls to 24th in the world with a disability-adjusted life expectancy for newborn babies of 70.0 years.

The WHO cites various reasons for why the United States ranks relatively low among wealthy nations. Those reasons include the following:

- In the United States, some groups, such as Native Americans, rural African Americans, and the inner city poor, have extremely poor health, which is more characteristic of a poor developing country than of a rich industrialized one.
- The proportion of young and middle-aged people suffering death or disability due to HIV is higher in the United States than in most other advanced countries. HIV-AIDS cut 3 months from the healthy life expectancy of male American babies born in 1999, and 1 month from that of female babies.
- The United States has one of the highest rates of cancers relating to tobacco use, especially lung cancer. Tobacco use also causes chronic lung disease.
- The United States has a high rate of coronary heart disease; this rate has dropped in recent years but remains high.
- The United States has fairly high levels of violence, especially homicides, compared to other industrial countries. (Murray, 2000)

Environmental Impacts

The growth of the human population in the past two centuries has begun to exert major stresses on the earth's resources of arable soil, clean air, and fresh water for drinking and irrigation, as well as on its sources of fuels. Three thousand years ago, when the total population was less than 100 million, the impact of human activities like cooking and mining was negligible. Today, however, the combined impact of more than 6 billion people is enormous,

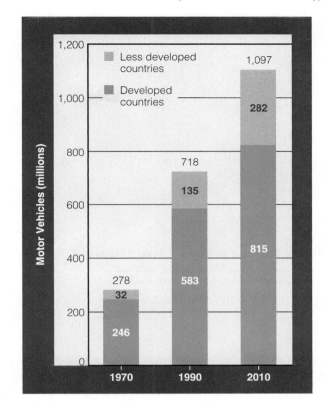

Figure 9.3 Increase in Motor Vehicles, 1970–2010

Source: Livernash & Rodenberg, 1998.

and it is especially severe because of the extremely high use of fossil fuels and high levels of consumption of steel and other durable goods in the richest nations of the world.

The United States, for example, with less than 5 percent of the earth's population, consumes more than 20 percent of its energy resources and, in consequence, puts far more than its share of pollutants and earth-warming gases into the atmosphere. Much of this consumption and pollution is directly related to the high rate of automobile ownership and use in the United States, where there are about 132 million private autos on the road, or 488 per 1,000 people. In Germany, there are 508 autos per 1,000 people, perhaps the highest rate of auto ownership in the world, but the total number of autos (42 million) is far lower than in the United States (*Statistical Abstract,* 2001). Figure 9.3 shows that by 2010 there will be more than 1 billion automobiles operating globally, with about 26 percent in the developing nations. Low incomes in those nations prevent ever-higher rates of auto acquisition, but ownership of less expensive two- and three-wheeled motor vehicles is increasing rapidly. In India, for example, motorcycle ownership is increasing by about 17 percent annually. All growth in the use of internal combustion engines contributes to the production of

Figure 9.4 World Marine Harvest, 1950–1995

Note: Excludes marine production from aquaculture.

Source: Livernash & Rodenberg, 1998.

carbon dioxide, the most prevalent "greenhouse gas" associated with the growing problem of global warming. Overall, however, industrialized nations produce 90 percent of the world's hazardous wastes (Livernash & Rodenburg, 1998).

Increases in population in poor regions of the world place additional pressures on critical resources, especially soil for crops, water for irrigation, forests for lumber and firewood, and fish species in nearby lakes and oceans. As noted earlier, the catastrophist view of these resources, especially land and arable soils, is that they will be exhausted and incapable of supporting rapid increases in population. But this gloomy view has proven, so far, to be overstated. According to one analysis, "despite the unprecedented population growth in the second half of the twentieth century, the world's farmers produce enough food to feed the current population and will probably be able to feed several billion more people in the next century" (Livernash & Rodenberg, 1998, p. 19). On the other hand, most of the available soil resources in the world are being used, and each year a small proportion of those resources is lost to urban expansion and degradation through overuse. Still, improvements in irrigation, fertilization, and crop rotation continue to produce increased yields (Boserup, 1965; Dasgupta, 2000). The same is not true, however, of world marine harvests, which have been increasing steadily and have resulted in widespread overfishing of wild fish stocks such as salmon, herring, and others (see Figure 9.4). In theory, therefore, agriculture and fishing can continue to feed growing populations, but in practice this may not be true for all regions of the world, particularly those most subject to dire poverty and political unrest.

In coming decades, many of the answers to the problems of poverty, resource depletion, and political unrest currently experienced in poor regions of the world will emerge from the rapidly growing cities of those regions. Rapid urbanization can worsen social conditions, but over time the growth of cities usually signifies that societies are moving into stages of development marked by greater emphasis on education, invention, and economic modernity.

Population Growth and Urbanization

Studies of the demographic transition in Europe (Bacci, 1997; Laslett, 1972, 1983) have concluded that its specific course in any given society depends on a complex combination of factors: higher age at marriage and fewer couples marrying, use of birth-control techniques, increased education, migration to other countries, and rural-urban migration. In each case, however, the bulk of the population growth was absorbed by the cities. Thus, rapid urbanization is partially an outgrowth of the demographic transition.

Urbanization refers to the proportion of the total population that is concentrated in urban settlements. Although urbanization and the growth of cities have occurred together, it is important to distinguish between the two. Cities can continue to grow even after most of the population is urbanized and the society's dominant institutions (e.g., government agencies, major markets, newspapers, television networks) are located in its urban centers.

Urbanization contributes to the lower birthrates that are characteristic of the third stage of the demographic transition. As Louis Wirth pointed out, "The decline in the birthrate generally may be regarded as one of the most significant signs of the urbanization of the Western world" (1968/1938, p. 59). In the city, a variety of factors lead to postponement of marriage and childbearing. For one thing, living space is limited. For another, newcomers to the city must find jobs before they can even think about marrying, and often they lack the ties to family and kin groups that might encourage them to marry and have children.

Despite declining birthrates in many non-Western countries, the populations of some cities in Asia and Africa are increasing faster than those of rural areas. The reason seems to be that rapid change in rural areas, especially the mechanization of agriculture, pushes rural people to the cities, where they often live in shantytowns and villagelike settlements. In those settlements, the rural tradition of large families is not quickly altered. In addition, because they have greater access to health care during pregnancy and childbirth, the infant death rate may be lower among the migrants than in rural villages. However, when these populations become part of the urban economy, they too begin to limit their family size (Gugler, 1997; Lowey, 1990). (See the Global Social Change box on page 238.)

In sum, urbanization is closely linked with rapid increases in population, yet the nature of life in cities tends to limit the size of urban families. Cities grow primarily as a result of migration, but new migrants do not find it easy to form families. Thus, in his research on the changing populations of Western industrial cities, Hauser (1957) showed that birthrates were lowest in the areas of the city that had the highest proportions of new migrants. Mounting evidence from archaeology also suggests that child sacrifice in ancient cities may have helped control urban populations (Browne, 1987). The eventual result of large-scale migration to cities may be a slowdown in population growth: As an increasing proportion of a society's population lives in cities, the rate of growth of the population as a whole tends to drop.

The Growth of Cities

In Chapter 4, we noted that cities became possible when agricultural populations began to produce enough extra food to support people who were not directly engaged in agriculture, such as priests, warriors, and artisans. Changes in the technology of food production made it possible for increasingly larger populations to be supported by the same number of agricultural workers. This has been a central factor in the evolution of cities, but as we will see shortly, the most dramatic increases in urban populations have occurred only in the past 200 years.

THE URBAN REVOLUTION   The increasing tendency of people throughout the world to live in cities has been referred to as the *urban revolution*. The extent of this "revolution" can be grasped by comparing a few figures. In 1800, only 3 percent of the world's people lived in cities with populations of over 5,000, and of this proportion a mere 2.4 percent lived in cities with populations of over 20,000. Between 1800 and 1970, a period during which the world's population increased fourfold, the percentage of people living in cities with 5,000 or more inhabitants increased elevenfold, whereas that of people living in cities with 100,000 or more inhabitants increased almost fourteenfold. By 1970, fully one-third of the world's population lived in cities (Gugler, 1997; Vining, 1985).

These data indicate not only that increasing percentages of the world's population are living in cities but also

The Sociological Observer

Wendy Ewald is a teacher and documentary photographer who is dedicated to social change and children's issues. She has taught in Appalachia, Colombia, Mexico, South Africa, and India and is currently a research associate at the Duke University Center for Documentary Studies. This photo illustrates her work in the 2000-year-old village of Vichya in the state of Gujarat in northwestern India (Ewald, 1996), in which she encouraged the villagers to use photography to better understand their own lives. Some of that work is featured in the Visual Sociology section of this chapter. This photo is one of the few in which Ewald actually appears.

As you study this photo, you may wonder why there are no boys and men in the group. Also, in this era of computers and the World Wide Web, what is so special about learning how a simple camera works? (See page 256 for further insights into the sociological content of this photo.)

that the cities themselves are larger than ever before. The growth of cities in this century has given rise to the concept of the **metropolitan area,** in which a central city is surrounded by several smaller cities and suburbs that are closely related to it both socially and economically. Most people in the United States live in large metropolitan areas, as the Sociological Methods box on page 239 demonstrates.

GLOBAL SOCIAL CHANGE

The Power of Rural-Urban Migration

Immigration and migration are social forces that continually bring about change of all kinds. In Eastern Europe, for example, the animosities among nationality groups that periodically erupt in violence can often be traced to earlier periods of immigration and resettlement of populations resulting from war and conquest. In the United States as well, immigration continually produces social change, especially in the major cities that serve as the gateways for newcomers.

Migration, which includes both immigration from a foreign nation and movement within national boundaries, is, along with birth and death rates, a key factor affecting population size. People have migrated from one region or country to another throughout history, compelled to seek new homes because they have exhausted their food supplies or been driven out by invaders or because they believe they will find a better life in the new land. Although people have migrated from rural areas to the city throughout history, rural-urban migration has become especially pronounced in the last two centuries.

The forces that impel residents of rural areas to migrate to cities are not fully understood. There is continual debate over whether rural people are "pushed" into cities by conditions beyond their control or "pulled" to cities by the attractions of city life. Of course, both push and pull factors affect rural-urban migration, but it is not clear exactly how they interact. It appears, however, that "it is the push of existing rural circumstances which suggests to the rural resident that things might be better in the urban area" (Breese, 1966, p. 80).

Several factors may be responsible for pushing people out of rural areas. Chief among these is overpopulation, which reduces the amount of food and work available per rural resident. Others include lack of opportunities to obtain farmland (e.g., as a result of *primogeniture,* in which only the oldest son inherits land) and the seasonal nature of employment in agriculture. When rural people who are experiencing these conditions become aware of higher living standards in urban places, they may develop a sense of relative deprivation (see Chapter 8). "They view with great interest the reported higher income, access to education, and other rumored facilities of the urban area" (Breese, 1966, pp. 80–81). The feeling of relative deprivation is intensified by improvements in communication and transportation that provide rural people with more feedback about the advantages of life in the city.

A significant pull factor is the presence of relatives and friends in the city. These individuals can be called on for help when the rural migrant arrives in search of a new home and a job. This factor produces what is known as *chain migration,* a pattern in which a network of friends and relatives is transferred from the village to the

city over time. The result is the formation of a small, homogeneous community within the city.

Chain migration operates across national boundaries as well as between rural and urban areas in the same country. (For example, a large proportion of the immigrants to American cities in the twentieth century were rural people from European and Asian countries.) Once a few hardy souls establish a foothold, their families and friends can join them. In this way, small ethnic communities are formed within the city—like the Chinatowns of New York and San Francisco, the Slovenian community in Cleveland, or the Mexican community in Chicago. Recently this pattern has been established in suburban portions of metropolitan areas as well as in central cities. Thus the suburbs of metropolitan areas in the South and West have become home to large numbers of immigrants from Vietnam (Portes & Rumbaut, 1996).

A U.S. Border Patrol agent marches a group of illegal immigrants across a portion of the Yuha Desert after they were found hiding in the brush near El Centro, California.

Large-scale urbanization is a relatively recent development in human history. As Kingsley Davis (1955) pointed out:

Compared to most other aspects of society—such as language, religion, stratification, or the family— cities appeared only yesterday, and urbanization,

meaning that a sizable proportion of the population lives in cities, has developed only in the last few moments of man's existence. (p. 429)

Although there were a few cities as early as 4000 BC, they were very small and were supported by large rural

SOCIOLOGICAL METHODS — Defining Metropolitan Areas

Formal definitions of urban places changed considerably in the twentieth century. Traditionally, an urban place had been defined as any incorporated area with 2,500 or more inhabitants, but this definition became highly unsatisfactory as cities expanded and their surrounding areas became increasingly urbanized, especially after World War II. As early as 1910, the U.S. Census Bureau introduced the concept of the *metropolitan district,* or metropolitan area. This concept has been refined often as urban growth has engulfed the rural areas adjacent to cities. Moreover, as cities and their suburbs have begun to run into each other, it has become necessary to distinguish between central cities and the surrounding metropolitan areas.

In 1984, the Census Bureau established new definitions of urban areas that remain in effect today. The basic types of urban areas are the metropolitan statistical area, the primary metropolitan statistical area, and the consolidated metropolitan statistical area. A *metropolitan area* is a geographic area with a population of at least 100,000, consisting of a nucleus with a population of at least 50,000 together with adjacent communities that have a high degree of economic and social integration with that nucleus. The term *statistical areas* refers to the fact that these definitions are used to organize numerical data about urban regions. Federal, state, and local government agencies use these geographic and statistical definitions to monitor social change and carry out essential planning functions.

A *metropolitan statistical area (MSA)* is a metropolitan area that is not closely associated with other metropolitan areas and typically is surrounded by nonmetropolitan counties. A *primary metropolitan statistical area (PMSA)* is defined as a large urbanized county or cluster of economically interdependent counties with a population of at least 100,000 that is part of a metropolitan area with more than 1 million inhabitants. A metropolitan area that contains two or more PMSAs is a *consolidated metropolitan statistical area (CMSA).* A CMSA therefore is equivalent to what sociologists often call a "megalopolitan region," such as the Dallas–Fort Worth area or the Greater Los Angeles area.

Central cities are the officially designated largest and most densely populated places in metropolitan areas.

There are central cities that are not included in a metropolitan area.

The accompanying graph shows the proportions of the U.S. population living in rural, urban, metropolitan, and nonmetropolitan areas. The organization of data shown in the graph is useful because the curve above the area for each category shows its relative trend in population growth. In order to find out how many millions of people lived in a metropolitan area in 1980, for example, subtract the reading at the bottom of the area for that year from the reading at the top of the area for the same year. For 1980, the line at the bottom of the area falls at about 50 million and the line at the top at about 225 million; thus there were about 175 million residents of metropolitan areas in the United States in that year.

Source: Council on Environmental Quality; Census Bureau.

populations. The famous cities of ancient times were minuscule by modern standards: Babylon covered roughly 3.2 square miles, Ur some 220 acres (Davis, 1955).

Preindustrial cities like Ur and Nineveh, early Athens and Rome, and the ancient Mayan cities were vastly different from the cities we know today. They did not grow around a core of office buildings and retail outlets the way industrial cities do. Instead, they were built around temples or other ceremonial buildings (e.g., Notre Dame in Paris). Close by the temple, one could find the palaces of the rulers and the courtyards of the royal families. Parade grounds and public shrines made the core of the ancient city a spacious place where the city's population could meet on special occasions. On the outskirts of these ancient cities, one found not the rich, as in contemporary cities with well-developed transportation networks, but the poor, who lived in hovels and were often pushed from one location to another according to the whims of those with more wealth and power (Gugler, 1997; Sjoberg, 1968).

A variety of factors limited the size of cities. Among them were farming methods that did not produce enough surplus food to feed many city dwellers, the lack of efficient means of transporting goods over long distances, inadequate technology for transporting water in great quantities, and the lack of scientific medicine. Not until about 1800 did large-scale urbanization become possible.

The speed with which urbanization has changed the size and layout of cities is remarkable: "Before 1850 no society could be described as predominantly urbanized,

© Peter Menzel/Stock, Boston

Urban sociologists have always looked at the relationship between the planned and unplanned aspects of urban growth and the social groups that represent each aspect. Usually the poor and the immigrants represent unplanned additions to the city, while the rich and the powerful guide the processes of urban planning and organization to suit their interests.

and by 1900 only one—Great Britain—could be so regarded. Today . . . all industrial nations are highly urbanized, and in the world as a whole the process of urbanization is accelerating rapidly" (Davis, 1968, p. 33). By 1990, over 45 percent of the world population lived in urban areas, and by 2000 this figure was nearly half—40 percent of the population in developing countries and 78 percent in developed countries (*Statistical Abstract,* 2000). Africa now has the fastest rate of urbanization, and about 70 percent of the population of Latin America lives in urban areas—a rate of urbanization comparable to that of North America and Europe.

As shown in Table 9.4, many metropolitan regions in older advanced nations like the United States (especially Greater New York), Great Britain (Greater London), and Germany (Rhein-Ruhr) reached their peak of growth decades ago and are now growing slowly if at all. In many parts of Latin America and Asia, in contrast, metropolitan regions are experiencing explosive growth and attracting vast populations of urban newcomers, many of whom are living as squatters on vacant land.

Rapid urbanization occurring throughout the world brings together diverse groups of people in cities that often are not prepared to absorb them. The problems caused by such urbanization are immense. They include housing, educating, and caring for the health of newcomers; preventing gang violence and intergroup hatred; and many other difficult tasks. Moreover, as the world becomes ever more urbanized, populations become increasingly interdependent. Urban populations are supported, for example, by worldwide agricultural production, not just by the produce grown in the surrounding countryside. In the same way, the problems of one major city or one large urbanizing region can no longer be thought of as isolated from the problems of the older, more affluent urbanized regions.

URBAN SOCIETIES   Urbanization produces *urban societies.* By this we mean not only that cities are the cultural and institutional centers of a society but also that urban life has a pervasive influence on the entire society (Durkheim, 1964/1893; Weber, 1962/1921; Wirth, 1968/1938). Today the United States is spanned by interstate highways that link the nation's rapidly growing urban and suburban places and carry traffic through rural areas at high speeds. Waterways, forests, hills, and valleys are channeled and cut and bulldozed to make way for expanding settlements. Once considered far from the urban scene, national parks and forests now receive millions of visitors from the metropolitan centers. And in an urban society, more and more people, even those living in isolated rural communities, share in the mass culture of that society—the television and radio programs, the movies, the books and magazines, all of which stress themes that appeal to people who are

TABLE 9.4

Populations of the World's Largest Urbanized Areas, 1950–2000

Rank in 2000	Country	Urbanized Area	Thousands of Inhabitants		
			1950	1975	2000
1	Mexico	Mexico City	3,050	11,610	25,820
2	Japan	Tokyo–Yokohama	6,736	17,668	24,172
3	Brazil	São Paulo	2,760	10,290	23,970
4	India	Calcutta	4,520	8,250	16,530
5	India	Bombay	2,950	7,170	16,000
6	United States	New York–N.E. New Jersey	12,410	15,940	15,780
7	Rep. of Korea	Seoul	1,113	6,950	13,770
8	Brazil	Rio de Janeiro	3,480	8,150	13,260
9	China	Shanghai	10,420	11,590	13,260
10	Indonesia	Jakarta	1,820	5,530	13,250
11	India	Delhi	1,410	4,630	13,240
12	Argentina	Buenos Aires	5,251	9,290	13,180
13	Pakistan	Karachi	1,040	4,030	12,000
14	Iran	Tehran	1,126	4,267	11,329
15	Bangladesh	Dhaka	430	2,350	11,160
16	Egypt	Cairo–Ginza–Imbaba	3,500	6,250	11,130
17	Iraq	Baghdad	579	3,830	11,125
18	Japan	Osaka–Kobe	3,828	8,649	11,109
19	Philippines	Manila	1,570	5,040	11,070
20	United States	Los Angeles–Long Beach	4,070	8,960	10,990
21	Thailand	Bangkok–Thonburi	1,400	4,050	10,710
22	United Kingdom	London	10,369	10,310	10,510
23	Russia	Moscow	4,841	7,600	10,400
24	China	Beijing	6,740	8,910	10,360
25	Germany	Rhein–Ruhr	6,853	9,311	9,151
26	Peru	Lima–Callao	1,050	3,700	9,140
27	France	Paris	5,525	8,620	8,720
28	Nigeria	Lagos	360	2,100	8,340
29	Italy	Milan	3,637	6,150	8,150
30	India	Madras	1,420	3,770	8,150

Note: The urban places listed above are areas of dense contiguous settlement whose boundaries do not necessarily coincide with administrative boundaries; they usually include one or more cities and an urbanized fringe.

Source: UNDP, 2002.

familiar with metropolitan living. In an urban society, not everyone lives in the cities, but no one can escape the pervasive influence of urban centers.

The concept of an urban society may become clearer if we look at a society that has not become fully urbanized, such as India. Until the early twentieth century, the rate of city growth in India was relatively slow. Beginning in the 1920s, however, the populations of India's cities increased dramatically, and by 1960 seven Indian cities had popula-

tions surpassing 1 million. Yet India has not become an urban society. It remains, in the words of Noel P. Gist (1968), "a land of villagers." Because of persistently high birthrates and declining death rates in the villages, India's rural population is growing almost as fast as its urban population. Moreover, although the growth of the cities has affected village life, especially through the efforts of city-trained teachers, health officials, administrators, and storekeepers, it has had little effect on the social structure of rural India. Thus, as a whole, Indian society exhibits the extremes of rural isolation and urban dynamism, with all the chaos and poverty that are characteristic of societies undergoing major social change (World Bank, 1997).

Throughout the twentieth century, sociologists devoted considerable study to urbanization and the changes that accompany it. The ways in which the growth of cities and metropolitan regions alters the surface of the planet are part of the sociological study of urbanization. So are questions about how cities change our experience of community and our relationships with others. Finally, sociologists continue to focus on the changing patterns of inequality and conflict that occur in metropolitan regions. The remainder of this chapter explores these issues in greater detail.

THE URBAN LANDSCAPE

Urban Expansion

The effects of urbanization began to be felt in American society in the mid-nineteenth century. As growing numbers of people settled in the West, waves of immigrants from Ireland, Germany, Italy, and many other parts of central and southern Europe streamed into the cities of the East. In the 1840s and 1850s, for example, approximately 1.35 million Irish immigrants arrived in the United States, and in just 12 years, from 1880 to 1892, more than 1.7 million Germans arrived (Bogue, 1985). In other chapters, we have more to say about the impact of the great migrations from China and Korea and Latin America, the importation of slaves from Africa, and the large numbers of people of all races and ethnic groups who continue to arrive in U.S. cities. The point here is that for 150 years, North American cities have been a preferred destination of people from all over the world; as a result, they have received numerous waves of newcomers since their period of explosive growth in the nineteenth century.

The science of sociology found early supporters in the United States and Canada partly because the cities in those nations were growing so rapidly. It often appeared that North American cities would be unable to absorb all the newcomers who were arriving in such large numbers. Presociological thinkers like Frederick Law Olmsted, the founder of the movement to build parks and recreation areas in cities, and Jacob Riis, an advocate of slum reform, urged the nation's leaders to invest in improving the urban environment, building parks and beaches, and making better housing available to all (Cranz, 1982; Kornblum & Lawler, 1999). As we saw in Chapter 1, these reform efforts were greatly aided by sociologists who conducted empirical research on the social conditions in cities. In the

early twentieth century, many sociologists lived in cities like Chicago that were characterized by rapid population growth and serious social problems. It seemed logical to use empirical research to construct theories about how cities grow and change in response to major social forces as well as more controlled urban planning.

The founders of the Chicago school of sociology, Robert Park and Ernest Burgess, attempted to develop a dynamic model of the city, one that would account not only for the expansion of cities in terms of population and territory but also for the patterns of settlement and land use within cities. They identified several factors that influence the physical form of cities. Among them are "transportation and communication, tramways and telephones, newspapers and advertising, steel construction and elevators—all things, in fact, which tend to bring about at once a greater mobility and a greater concentration of the urban populations" (Park, 1967/1925a, p. 2). The important role of transportation is described in one of Park's essays:

> The extent to which . . . an increase of population in one part of the city is reflected in every other depends very largely upon the character of the local transportation system. Every extension and multiplication of the means of transportation connecting the periphery of the city with the center tends to bring more people to the central business district, and to bring them there oftener. This increases the congestion at the center; it increases, eventually, the height of office buildings and the values of the land on which those buildings stand. The influence of land values at the business center radiates from that point to every part of the city. (1967/1926, pp. 57–58)

THE CONCENTRIC-ZONE MODEL   Park and Burgess based their model of urban growth on the concept of *natural areas*—that is, areas in which the population is relatively homogeneous and land is used in similar ways without deliberate planning. In Park's words:

> Every great city has its racial colonies, like the Chinatowns of San Francisco and New York, the Little Sicily of Chicago. . . . Most cities have their segregated vice districts . . . their rendezvous for criminals of various sorts. Every large city has its occupational suburbs, like the Stockyards in Chicago, and its residential enclaves, like Brookline in Boston. (1967/1925a, p. 10)

Park and Burgess saw urban expansion as occurring through a series of "invasions" of successive zones or areas surrounding the center of the city. For example, migrants from rural areas and other societies "invaded" areas where housing was cheap. Those areas tended to be close to the

THEN AND NOW

Street Urchins and Trailer Kids

A century ago, as millions of new-comers from throughout the world crowded into U.S. cities in search of opportunity, rapid social change produced some of the world's most notorious urban slums. Jacob Riis, a photojour-nalist and amateur sociologist, brought the harsh living condi-tions in those slums to the attention of the world in his famous photos of "how the other half lives." Children who spent much of their time on the streets and survived by their wits were called "street urchins" (or, as Riis called them, "Street Arabs").

In today's world, the central city is no longer viewed as a place to find new opportunities. Mobile families and individuals travel long distances, seeking manufacturing and service jobs outside major city centers. They often find what they hope will be tem-porary lodging in trailer parks. Poor and lacking health insurance and other

forms of social security, residents of trailer parks tend to be stigmatized by those who are more fortunate. They and their children are sometimes called "trailer trash," a term that reveals the deep prejudices that con-tinue to divide Americans, even in a society that is far more affluent than the one described by Riis.

places where they worked. In turn, people who could af-ford better housing and the cost of commuting "invaded" areas farther from the business district, and these became the Brooklines, Gold Coasts, and Greenwich Villages of their respective cities.

Park and Burgess's model, which has come to be known as the *concentric-zone model,* is portrayed in Figure 9.5. (Figure 9.6 applies the model to Chicago.) Because the model was originally based on studies of Chicago, its cen-ter is labeled "Loop," the term that is commonly applied to that city's central commercial zone. Surrounding the central zone is a "zone in transition," an area that is being invaded by business and light manufacturing. The third zone is inhabited by workers who do not want to live in the factory or business district but at the same time need to live reasonably close to where they work. The fourth, or residential, zone consists of higher-class apartment build-ings and single-family homes. And the outermost ring, outside the city limits, is the suburban or commuters'

zone; its residents live within a 30- to 60-minute ride of the central business district (Burgess, 1925).

Studies by Park, Burgess, and other Chicago school sociologists showed how new groups of immigrants tended to become concentrated in segregated areas within inner-city zones, where they encountered suspi-cion, discrimination, and hostility from ethnic groups that had arrived earlier. Over time, however, each group was able to adjust to life in the city and to find a place for itself in the urban economy. Eventually many of the immigrants were assimilated into the institutions of American society and moved to desegregated areas in outer zones; the ghettos they left behind were promptly occupied by new waves of immigrants (Kasarda, 1989).

Note that each zone is continually expanding outward. Thus, Burgess wrote, "If this chart is applied to Chicago, all four of these zones were in its early history included in the circumference of the inner zone, the present business dis-trict. The present boundaries of the [zone in transition] were

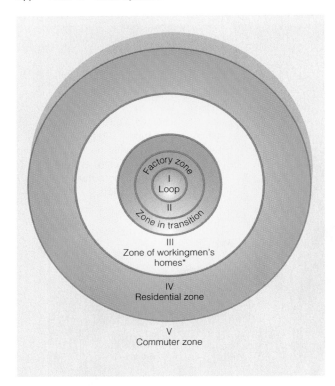

Figure 9.5 The Concentric-Zone Model

*Workers' homes ("workingmen" was the accepted terminology of the time).

Source: From The City: Suggestions for the investigation of human behavior in the urban environment, in R. E. Parks and E. W. Burgess (eds.), *The City.* © 1967 University of Chicago Press. Used by permission.

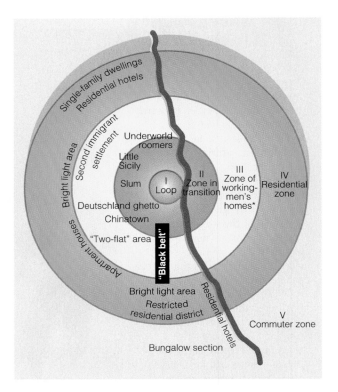

Figure 9.6 The Concentric-Zone Model Applied to Chicago

*Workers' homes ("workingmen" was the accepted terminology of the time).

Source: From The City: Suggestions for the investigation of human behavior in the urban environment, in R. E. Parks and E. W. Burgess (eds.), *The City.* © 1967 University of Chicago Press. Used by permission.

not many years ago those of the zone now inhabited by independent wage-earners" (1925, p. 50). Burgess also pointed out that "neither Chicago nor any other city fits perfectly into this [model]. Complications are introduced by the lake front, the Chicago River, railroad lines, historical factors in the location of industry, the relative degree of the resistance of communities to invasion, etc." (pp. 50–51).

The Park and Burgess model of growth in zones and natural areas of the city can still be used to describe patterns of growth in cities that were built around a central business district and continue to attract large numbers of immigrants. But this model is biased toward the commercial and industrial cities of North America, which have tended to form around business centers rather than around palaces or cathedrals, as is the case in so many other parts of the world. Moreover, it fails to account for other patterns of urbanization, such as the rise of satellite cities and the rapid urbanization that occurs along commercial transportation corridors.

SATELLITE CITIES Outside the city of Detroit lies the town of River Rouge, long famous as a center of steel and automobile production. Outside the city of Toronto lies Hamilton, also a smoky manufacturing town where much

of Canada's steel is produced. And outside Chicago is Gary, Indiana, another major center of heavy industrial production. Outside New York City, there are many other *satellite cities,* some devoted to heavy industries whose needs for space, rail and water service, and energy make it impossible to locate them in the central business districts.

Other satellite cities are devoted to less environmentally stressful industries. Fort Worth, Texas, for example, is becoming a major center for white-collar industries that are leaving older central-city locations in search of cheaper space and a well-educated labor force. Still others, like Tysons Corner, Virginia, near Washington, D.C., have grown around large shopping centers and mall complexes. In the second half of the twentieth century, the growth of these and other satellite cities was accelerated by public investment in the interstate and metropolitan highway systems, a point to which we will return shortly in discussing the rise of metropolitan urban systems (Baldassare, 1986; Clay, 1994; Fishman, 1987).

STRIP DEVELOPMENT The growth of satellite cities specializing in the production of a particular commodity or product is typical of the period of rapid industrial growth

Figure 9.7 Strip Development and Sprawl

Source: Clay, 1980.

that occurred before World War II. A more current model of urbanization is known as *strip development;* it is shown in schematic form in Figure 9.7. Strip I represents a typical nineteenth- or early twentieth-century farming area bisected by a road and a stream. In time the bridge over the stream and the path along the stream became a road that intersected the original road (Strip II), creating an intersection that stimulated the growth of a village with a mill; families living in the village depended on wages from the mill. As the village grew into a town, population growth and increasing automobile traffic created the need for wider roads and bypass roads, as shown in Strips III and IV. Specialization as an "automobile-convenient" strip, with the development of more motels, a drive-in theater, and drive-in businesses, can be seen in Strip V. At this time, the residential functions along the strip began to disappear and the area assumed an increasingly commercial character.

Strip VI shows the strip's present stage of development. A spur of the limited-access highway system creates new growth around a cloverleaf (including a new community college situated between the artificial lake and the shopping center). Note that along the original main road are office buildings and a modern industrial park rather than the smaller retail businesses that once defined the town

center. Indeed, as the strip has developed and surrounding roads have been enlarged to form part of the metropolitan highway system, the town center itself has largely disappeared (Clay, 1980). The strip development model thus describes the incorporation of smaller communities and towns into a larger metropolitan area.

Metropolitan Areas

MEGALOPOLIS After 1920, new metropolitan areas developed largely as a result of the increasing use of automobiles and the construction of a network of highways covering the entire nation (Flink, 1988). The shift to automobile travel brought former satellite cities within commuting distance of the major industrial centers, thereby adding to the size of those metropolitan areas. In the South and Southwest, new metropolitan areas developed. In fact, in recent years these have become the fastest-growing urban areas in the nation.

Since World War II, sociologists have been studying an increasingly important urban phenomenon: the emergence of large multinuclear urban systems. The term *megalopolis* is used to describe these vast complexes, whose total population exceeds 25 million. Jean Gottmann (1978)

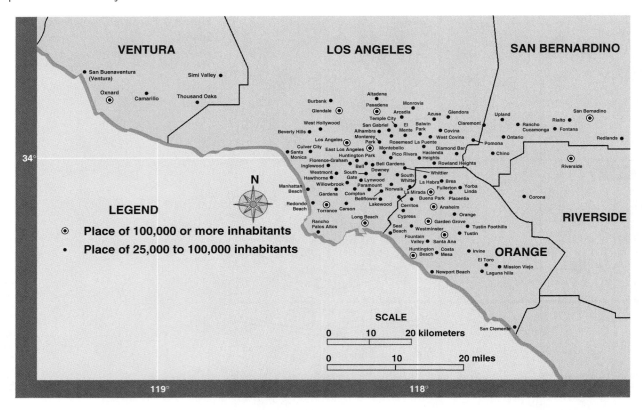

Figure 9.8   The Los Angeles–Anaheim–Riverside Megalopolis

Source: U.S. Census Bureau.

pointed out that a megalopolis is not "simply an over-grown metropolitan area"; rather, it is a system of cities distributed along "a major axis of traffic and communication" (p. 56). Gottmann identified six megalopolises: the American Northeastern megalopolis, the Great Lakes megalopolis, the Tokaido megalopolis in Japan, the megalopolis in England (the London area), the megalopolis of northwestern Europe (extending from Amsterdam to the Ruhr), and the Urban Constellation in China (centered on Shanghai). Four others are developing rapidly: the Rio de Janeiro–São Paulo complex in Brazil, the Milan-Turin-Genoa triangle in northern Italy, the Valley of Mexico, and the urban swath extending from San Diego to the San Francisco Bay area.

A megalopolis is characterized by an "intertwined web of relationships between a variety of distinct urban centers . . . expressed partly in a physical infrastructure consisting of highways, railways, waterways, telephone lines, pipelines, water supply, and sewage systems criss-crossing the whole area, and partly in more fluid networks, such as the flows of traffic, the movement of people and goods, the flows of telephone calls [and] of mail" (Gottmann, 1978, p. 57). Despite their interdependence, however, "the sizes and specializa-

tions of the various . . . components [of a megalopolis] are extremely varied, as demonstrated by the diverse characteristics of the cities, towns, villages, suburban and rural areas that form the vast system" (p. 57). Therefore a megalopolis can best be described as a huge social and economic mosaic.

Los Angeles provides a good example of the development of a megalopolis (see Figure 9.8). Between 1960 and 1970, the population of Los Angeles increased by more than 2 million, double the growth of Chicago and more than that of New York and San Francisco put together (Smith, 1968). Today the Los Angeles metropolitan area continues to grow, although at a somewhat slower rate. As a result of its extraordinary growth, the region must struggle to control the effects of air pollution from more than 3 million automobiles. It must also struggle to furnish adequate supplies of water for its residents. In a review of conflicts between Angeleno leaders and the residents of smaller towns near water sources, sociologist John Walton (1992) has shown that control over water and other natural resources, especially by powerful groups that dominate the regional real estate markets, is a key to understanding the history not only of the Los Angeles metropolitan region but of the entire desert West as well.

Another problem affecting many of the world's megalopolitan regions is the possibility of major disasters. Many are located in disaster-prone areas—either on coastal shorelines, as in the case of the Boston–Washington corridor, or worse, along major fault lines of earthquake activity, as in the case of Los Angeles (Davis, 1998).

DECENTRALIZATION One effect of the growth of megalopolitan areas is *decentralization,* in which outlying areas become more important at the expense of the central city. This trend is not new. In the 1960s and 1970s, large numbers of middle-income city dwellers moved to suburban areas while the poor remained in the central cities. Business and industry also moved to the suburbs, creating widespread speculation that vibrant central cities would become a thing of the past. Over the past generation, however, the central cities of some metropolitan areas—such as New York, Philadelphia, Chicago, and Baltimore—have shown renewed vitality. Far from decaying, they have become major financial and cultural centers serving the needs of huge populations. On the other hand, medium-sized cities like Gary, Indiana, and Paterson, New Jersey, have suffered because their central business districts have little to offer suburban dwellers in the way of financial services like banking and insurance or cultural attractions like theaters and symphony orchestras (Kasarda, 1988).

An important feature of megalopolitan areas—especially as they become more decentralized—is their diversity. These huge urban regions include many different kinds of communities: ethnic communities in both central cities and suburbs, middle-class "bedroom" suburbs, industrial towns, areas devoted to truck gardening or dairy farming, "second home" communities (e.g., beachfront areas), and so on. Each meets the economic and cultural needs of a specific urban population. Sociologists have devoted considerable study to these urban communities, and we discuss their findings in the next section.

URBAN COMMUNITIES

"The city," wrote Robert Park, is more than a set of "social conveniences—streets, buildings, electric lights, tramways, and telephones, etc.; something more, also, than a mere constellation of . . . courts, hospitals, schools, police, and civil functionaries of various sorts. The city is, rather, a state of mind, a body of customs and traditions. . . . It is a product of nature, and particularly of human nature" (1967/1925a, p. 1).

The connection between the city and human nature has been a recurrent theme in literature throughout history. Many literary images of the city are negative. In the Bible, for example, the cities of Sodom and Gomorrah are symbols of the worst aspects of human nature. The poet Juvenal complained that Rome produced ulcers and insomnia and subjected its residents to burglars and dishonest landlords. American literature also contains many negative images of the city. Thomas Jefferson, for instance, wrote, "I view great American cities as pestilential to the morals, health, and the liberties of man." And Henry David Thoreau escaped from the city to Walden Pond in an effort to "rediscover his soul" (Fischer, 1976).

Social scientists who study cities have devoted a great deal of attention to the tension between "community" and "individualism" as it relates to life in cities (Lofland, 1998). Country dwellers have been thought of as "happily ensconced in warm, humanly rich and supportive social relationships: the family, neighborhood, town," whereas city dwellers are "strangers to all, including themselves. They are lonely, not emotionally touching or being touched by others, and consequently set psychically adrift" (Fischer, 1976, p. 19). On the other hand, country dwellers are sometimes viewed as "stifled by conventionality, repressed by the intrusion and social control of narrow-minded kin, neighbors, and townsmen," whereas city dwellers are "free to develop individual abilities, express personal styles, and satisfy private needs" (p. 20). These views of the city are obviously contradictory, and much research has been devoted to the question of how urban life affects individuals and communities. In this section, we look at some of the findings of that research and the theories of urban life that have been proposed on the basis of those findings.

The Decline-of-Community Thesis

Early studies of the nature and effects of urban life were dominated by efforts to evaluate the differences between rural and urban societies. They tended to reach rather gloomy conclusions. We have already noted (see Chapter 4) that Ferdinand Tönnies described the process of urbanization as a shift from *gemeinschaft* (a community based on kinship ties) to *gesellschaft* (a society based on common interests). Émile Durkheim reached a similar conclusion: Small rural communities are held together by ties based on shared ideas and common experiences, whereas urban societies are held together by ties based on the interdependence of people who perform specialized tasks. Both Tönnies and Durkheim believed that urban life weakens kinship ties and produces impersonal social relationships.

In a 1905 essay, "The Metropolis and Mental Life," Georg Simmel focused on the effects of urban life on the minds and personalities of individuals. According to

In urban societies, where there are large numbers of people who are strangers to one another, sociologists have noted a propensity to wear identifying "uniforms" that indicate the kind of person one wishes to know and interact with.

Simmel, cities bombard their residents with sensory stimuli: "Horns blare, signs flash, solicitors tug at coattails, polltakers telephone, newspaper headlines try to catch the eye, strange-looking and strange-behaving persons distract attention" (quoted in Fischer, 1976, p. 30). The urban dweller is forced to adapt to this profusion of stimuli, which Stanley Milgram (1970) termed *psychic overload.* The usual way of adapting is to become calculating and emotionally distant, hence the image of the city dweller as aloof, brusque, and impersonal in his or her dealings with others.

This view of the effects of urban life found further expression in the work of Louis Wirth, especially in his essay "Urbanism as a Way of Life" (1968/1938). Wirth began by defining the city as "a relatively large, dense, and permanent settlement of socially heterogeneous individuals" (p. 28). He then attempted to show how these characteristics of cities produce psychological stress and social disorganization. The primary psychological effect of urban life, according to Wirth, is a weakening of the individual's bonds to other people. Without such bonds, the individual must deal with the crises of life alone, and often the result is mental illness.

In other cases, the city dweller, again because of the absence of close ties to friends or kin, lacks the restraints that might prevent him or her from engaging in antisocial behaviors.

Wirth linked social disorganization to the diversity that is characteristic of cities. Unlike rural residents, city dwellers work in one place, live in another, and relax in yet another. They divide their social lives among coworkers, neighbors, friends, and kin. Their jobs, lifestyles, and interests are extremely varied. As a result, no single group—be it the family, the friendship group, or the neighborhood—controls their lives. In Wirth's view, this absence of social control produces anomie or normlessness (see Chapter 7). Urban dwellers often do not agree on the norms that should govern their lives, and hence they are likely to either challenge existing norms or ignore them. Consequently, instead of being controlled by the norms of primary groups, the lives of city dwellers are controlled by impersonal agencies such as banks and police forces.

One consequence of the impersonality of urban life, some argue, is greater callousness among city dwellers. An often-cited example is the case of Kitty Genovese, discussed in Chapter 6. After that episode, in which a young woman was murdered while 38 residents of nearby apartments—who heard her cries—did nothing, many commentators called attention to the callous character of city dwellers. Subsequent research on bystander apathy revealed that the presence of many other people tends to diffuse the sense of responsibility. We are less likely to take action if we have reason to believe that someone else will do so (Hunt, 1985; Latané & Darley, 1970). In this sense, the bigger the city and the more one is surrounded by strangers, the more likely it is that such behavior will occur—but this does not mean that city dwellers are alienated from one another when they are among people they know, or that when alone they would not help someone in trouble.

On the basis of many years of research on urban social interaction, together with an extensive review of the literature, urban sociologist Lyn Lofland (1998) concludes that city dwellers adhere to a set of norms that govern behavior among strangers in the city. These norms stress civility along with inattention, concern along with avoidance of any appearance of prying. To some observers, the urban dweller's behavior might seem hostile or unconcerned, but according to Lofland, this is largely a misunderstanding. Moreover, although urbanites may feel less responsibility for others when surrounded by strangers, this condition of city life is hardly evidence for the decline-of-community thesis.

The Persistence of Urban Communities

The idea that urbanization leads to the decline of community has been criticized on several grounds. Rural life is nowhere near as pleasant as some urban sociologists have assumed it to be; evidence of this is the almost magical attraction that cities often have for rural people. On the other hand, urban social disorganization is not as extensive as the early urban sociologists believed. Many city dwellers maintain stable, intimate relationships with kin, neighbors, and coworkers. Moreover, urban life is not necessarily stressful or anomic.

SUBCULTURAL THEORY   A more recent view of urban life sees the city as a "mosaic of social worlds" or intimate social groups. Numerous studies have shown that the typical urban dweller does not resemble the isolated, anomic individual portrayed by Simmel and Wirth. In fact, communities of all kinds can be found in cities. Many urban dwellers, for example, are members of ethnic communities that have not become fully assimilated into the melting pot of American

society and are unlikely to do so. They may be the children or grandchildren of immigrants who formed ethnic enclaves within large cities in the late nineteenth and early twentieth centuries, or they may be recent immigrants themselves, trying to build a new life in a strange culture.

But group ties among urban dwellers are not based solely on ethnicity. They may be based on kinship, occupation, lifestyle, or similar personal attributes (Fischer, 1976; Hummin, 1990; Lofland, 1998). Thus many cities contain communities of college students, elderly people, homosexuals, artists and musicians, wealthy socialites, and so on. Although the members of any given group do not always live in the same neighborhood, they are in close touch with one another much of the time. Their sense of community is based not so much on place of residence as on the ability to come together by telephone, in special meeting places like churches or synagogues, or even in restaurants and bars (Duneier, 1992; Fischer, 1976; Oldenburg, 1997).

An example of this point of view, known as *subcultural theory*, is Illsoo Kim's (1981) detailed study of the Korean community in New York City. This growing ethnic community has developed since the passage of the Immigration Act of 1965, which eliminated the nationality quotas established earlier in the twentieth century. Largely because of population pressure in South Korea (which has led to overcrowded cities and high rates of unemployment), more than 750,000 Koreans have immigrated to the United States since 1970, with at least 100,000 finding new homes in the city of New York.

Like all immigrants, the Koreans have had to create a new way of life. They have had to find new ways of making a living, and they have had to adapt to a new culture. The first problem has been solved mainly by opening small businesses, the second by establishing neighborhoods where the immigrants can maintain their own culture while they and their children learn the values and norms of Western culture. Kim explains the Koreans' inclination to open small businesses (mainly grocery stores) in this passage:

> Old-timers frequently tell newcomers that "running a jangsa (commercial business) is the fastest way to get ahead in America." The language barrier partly explains this inclination. . . . This is an insuperable barrier to most Korean immigrants; it deprives them of many opportunities. . . . This fact, combined with differences in both the skills demanded and the system of rewards in the United States, means that occupational status cannot be transferred from the homeland to the new land. A high proportion of Korean immigrants were thus forced to turn to small retail businesses. (1981, pp. 102–103)

Many of the businesses established by Korean immigrants are geared to Korean ethnic tastes and cultural needs. For example, Korean immigrants are often unwilling to change their diet and will buy most of their food from Korean-owned food stores. Other shops import books, gifts, magazines, and other items from South Korea. Numerous Korean travel agencies satisfy the immigrants' strong desire to visit their homeland. But Korean small businesses are not limited to serving the needs of the immigrant population. A growing number cater to all racial and ethnic groups and supply typically American goods and services.

In summing up the situation of Korean immigrants in New York, Kim points out that "until they completely master the American language, education, and culture, Koreans will be forced to rely on one another" (p. 319). For this reason, they are likely to maintain their own community within the city for at least two generations. However, in time their commitment to education and a better life will cause them to become more fully assimilated into American society, and their ties to the Korean community will be weakened.

The case of the Koreans echoes that of many other immigrant groups, both past and present, as well as that of other groups, such as homosexuals and artists. The details may differ somewhat, but the tendency to establish ethnic or cultural enclaves in large cities is universal. In a well-known study titled *The Urban Villagers,* Herbert Gans (1984) described an Italian neighborhood in Boston. This community was a long-established one with many of the characteristics that are typical of ethnic communities everywhere. At the time that Gans did his research, however, the neighborhood was being destroyed by an urban renewal project. Its residents were forced to find new homes in other parts of the city, to join new churches, attend new schools, seek out new places to buy food and clothes. For some, the upheaval was so great that it produced depression and anomie (Fried, 1963).

It seems reasonable to conclude that the effects of urban life on communities and individuals are more complex than Durkheim, Simmel, and Wirth suggested. Certainly, social disorganization occurs in cities, but so does social *re*organization. Communities that are uprooted by urban renewal eventually may be re-formed in other parts of the city or its suburbs. The new community may be less homogeneous than the old one, but it is a community nonetheless.

THE SUBURBS   Like city dwellers, suburban dwellers have been said to lack the close attachments that are thought to characterize rural communities. In fact, before the late 1960s, most social scientists had a rather dismal view of suburban life. Suburbs had grown rapidly after World War

II as large numbers of middle-class Americans left the central cities in search of a less crowded, more pleasant lifestyle. Many suburban dwellers were corporate employees, and in the 1950s and early 1960s, they became the subject of a widely held stereotype. The suburbs, it was said, were "breeding a new set of Americans, as mass-produced as the houses they lived in, driven into a never-ending round of group activity ruled by the strictest conformity. Suburbanites were incapable of real friendships; they were bored and lonely, alienated, atomized, and depersonalized" (Gans, 1967, pp. xxvii–xxviii).

In *The Levittowners,* a classic study of a new suburban community in Pennsylvania, Gans (1967, 1976) challenged this stereotype. He found that the residents of Levittown lost no time in forming attachments to one another. At first they associated only with their neighbors, but before long they formed more extensive associations based on shared interests and concerns. Moreover, far from being bored and isolated, most of the Levittowners were satisfied with their lives and felt that Levittown was a good place to live. Gans concluded that "new towns are merely old social structures on new land" (1967, p. vii). In other words, the contrasts between central-city and suburban life are generally exaggerated. Other researchers have reached similar conclusions. They note that as suburban communities age and newcomers buy homes from people whose children are grown, these neighborhoods go through ethnic, racial, and generational changes that are not so different from the patterns occurring inside the cities (Jackson, 1985).

Some comparative research has focused on women born in suburban communities after the 1950s who never lived in other types of communities (Stimson, 1980; Wekerle, 1980). For example, Sylvia Fava (1985) found that younger women born in suburban communities do not think of suburban life as stifling or as limiting their opportunities. They may prefer to live in older, more diverse suburban communities within easy commuting distance of the jobs and nightlife of the central cities, but they normally do not feel that their suburban lifestyle is unsatisfactory. Indeed, as conditions continue to deteriorate in some inner-city communities—with increasing homelessness, exposure to drug markets, and violence—both older and newer suburban areas become more attractive to people seeking to escape the dangers they perceive in urban life (Lofland, 1998).

For the past few decades the phenomenon of "white flight" from older inner-city communities to newer and presumably safer suburban communities has been a subject of concern among urban sociologists and policymakers (Wilson, 1987). Recent data show, however, that African Americans and other minority groups are also fleeing the central cities at an accelerating rate. Demographer William

Frey notes that "minority suburbanization took off in the 1980s both as the black middle class came into its own and as more assimilated Latinos and Asians translated their moves up the socioeconomic ladder into a suburban life style" (quoted in De Witt, 1994, p. A1). This outward migration threatens to leave central-city communities with even greater concentrations of poor people. In cities with large numbers of immigrants, this discouraging trend is countered by increasing racial, ethnic, and class diversity (Huang, 1994), but in other cities the trend toward greater concentration of poor people inside the city and more affluent people in the suburbs is a growing problem. Recent research by Paul Jargowsky (1997) on ghettos and barrios (predominantly Latino neighborhoods) shows that middle-class migration, combined with the flight of industries from central cities, has produced dramatic increases in the number of people living in city neighborhoods with household poverty rates of 40 percent or more. Figure 9.9 demonstrates this disturbing trend, whose implications will become evident in later chapters on social inequality.

PRIVATE COMMUNITIES   The growth of private communities throughout the United States is another indication of the widespread fear of urban life (Garreau, 1991; McKenzie, 1994). Recent data indicate that about 4 million Americans live in private communities where public through-traffic is prohibited. For those who can afford to live there, these heavily patrolled and regulated communities represent a decision to place individual comfort and family safety above more social efforts to create communities. An even larger number of Americans, about 28 million, live in communities represented by private community associations. These include condominiums and cooperatives that require all residents to be members of the association, obey its rules, and pay fees to support its operations. Although they are less restrictive than private communities, these community associations also seek to control public access.

These private and quasi-private communities are the fastest-growing types of communities in the United States, and there is some concern about what this growth implies. Supporters of such communities dwell on their safety and their ability to maintain property values. Critics like Gerald Frug, an expert on local government, believe that people are trying to capture the feeling of life in a village without many other qualities of village life. "The village was open to the public," Frug observes. "The village did not have these kinds of restrictions. The village had poor people, retarded people. Somebody could hand you a leaflet. These private communities are totally devoid of random encounters" (quoted in Egan, 1995, p. A22). Frug and other critics of the trend toward private communities fear that as people choose to live

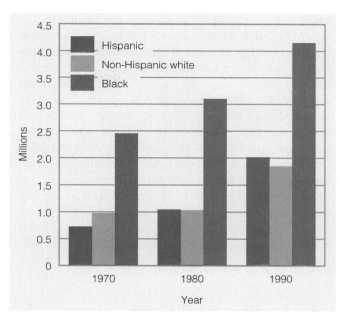

Figure 9.9   Residents of High-Poverty Neighborhoods, by Race/Ethnicity, 1970–1990

Source: Jargowsky, 1997.

only with others like themselves, "they will become less likely to support schools, parks or roads for everyone else" (p. A22).

CITIES AND SOCIAL CHANGE

In the preceding section, we stressed the presence of a wide variety of communities and subcultures within cities. We noted that contemporary social scientists see the city as a place where many different communities coexist and thrive rather than as a place where people are isolated and do not have a feeling of belonging to a particular social group or community. At the same time, however, there is no escaping the fact that various urban communities are often in conflict. For example, ethnic and racial communities may clash in violent confrontations over such issues as busing children to achieve school integration. In this section, we examine the origins and implications of such conflicts.

Social change in an urban society is likely to be felt most deeply by city dwellers because people are most densely congregated in cities. In recent decades, this has been the case in North America as manufacturing jobs have been "exported" to Asia and Latin America. As a result of this shift, American cities are undergoing massive social change. "America's major cities are different places today from what they were in the 1960s," concludes John Kasarda (1989, p. 28), one of the nation's foremost urban sociologists. New modes of transportation, new communication technologies such as satellites and computers, and new industrial technologies (e.g., automation and recycling) are transforming our cities from production and distribution centers to administrative, financial, and information centers. "In the process," writes Kasarda, "many blue-collar jobs that once constituted the economic backbone of cities and provided employment opportunities for their poorly educated residents have either vanished or moved." Many of those jobs have been replaced by "knowledge-intensive white-collar jobs with educational requirements that exclude many with substandard education" (p. 28).

Inequality and Conflict

As noted earlier, American cities and metropolitan regions have always attracted streams of migrants and immigrants. Migrants arrive from other parts of the nation—blacks from the rural South, Chicanos from the Southwest. Immigrants come from foreign lands—Haiti, Poland, China, Korea, Italy, and elsewhere. Until the 1970s, except during economic depressions or recessions, the new arrivals had no difficulty finding work in the mills and factories that produced textiles, clothing, steel, rubber, glass, cars, and trucks. And much of their education was gained while working. Formal schooling was not as crucial to job success as it is today.

Today, although there are still many manufacturing jobs, it is much more difficult to make a good living at such a job. Within the cities, where the decline in manufacturing jobs has been greatest, the number of low-status jobs, especially in restaurants and other low-paying services, has increased. So has the number of highly paid jobs in management and the professions, positions that require high levels of education. At the same time, more than 20 million legal immigrants have entered the country since 1970, usually settling in the cities. The result, often, has been fierce competition between immigrants and more established residents.

The net effect of these trends is a growing gap between the "haves" and the "have-nots," especially in large cities (Silk, 1989). The study of *social stratification*—of patterns of inequality and how they produce entire classes of people with differing opportunities to succeed in life—is at the core of sociology and is discussed in detail in later chapters. Certainly the gap between those who enjoy the good things in life and those who spend their lives simply trying to survive is not unique to cities. Small towns and villages also have affluent and poor residents. But the conflicts and social problems associated with social inequality are most visible in the cities. In many poor urban neighborhoods, for example, wealthier city dwellers are buying the buildings in which the poor live, forcing them to move elsewhere. In neighborhoods where this occurs, the shops and stores that once catered to lower-income residents cannot afford the higher rents paid by stores that serve the wealthy newcomers and are forced out of business. This process, whereby poor and dilapidated neighborhoods are renovated by higher-income newcomers while poor residents and merchants are pushed out, is known as *gentrification*.

STATUS CONFLICT   In the last section, we noted that an urban renewal project had dislocated large numbers of Italian Americans from their Boston neighborhood. Such projects have sometimes been labeled "urban removal" because they remove poor people from decaying neighborhoods and force them to find homes elsewhere. Recently urban renewal has fallen into disfavor and *redevelopment* has become popular. Redevelopment does not involve the destruction of entire neighborhoods, but it may have similar effects. For example, the redevelopment of New York City's Times Square by the Walt Disney Company and other powerful groups, both public and private, is restoring a sleazy area to its former glory as an entertainment center. The explicit goal is to make the area attractive to "decent" people and to eliminate the prostitutes, drug and pornography dealers, and petty criminals that have made Times Square a symbol of vice throughout the world (Kornblum, 1995; McNamara, 1995; Mollenkopf, 1985). This is a typical instance of *status conflict,* in which different groups (e.g., theater and restaurant owners versus owners of "adult" establishments) vie for territory, occupational advantages, and other benefits that will enhance their prestige in the neighborhood or community.

Some urban sociologists see the city as divided into "defended neighborhoods" or territories (Lofland, 1998; Suttles, 1972). This concept was originally developed by Park and Burgess, who viewed such neighborhoods as a type of "natural area" within the city. The defended neighborhood is a territory that a certain group of people consider to be their "turf" or base, which they are willing to defend against "invasion" by outsiders. Neighborhood defense is a common element of urban conflict, although the means used to defend neighborhoods may differ. For example, in wealthy suburban neighborhoods it may take the form of zoning regulations that establish minimum lot sizes of an acre or more. Such regulations effectively defend the neighborhood against invasion by people who cannot afford the large lots or by developers who would like to erect apartment buildings (Perin, 1977). In less affluent neighborhoods, defense is often conducted by neighborhood improvement groups, which sometimes engage in vigilante action when they fear racial "invasion" (Hamilton, 1969). In poor neighborhoods, defense is often the province of street-corner gangs.

GENDER CONFLICT   In the nineteenth century, many social commentators were dismayed at the increasingly frequent sight of women walking alone or with other women in city streets. Women unaccompanied by men were thought to be either immoral or innocently risking their honor or their lives in a world of predatory males. As Lyn Lofland observes, "The increasing presence of 'respectable' women in urban public space served as especially vivid and provocative evidence of women's unnatural and undesirable abandonment of hearth and home" (1998, p. 128). Of course, Lofland realizes that "poor women had rarely, in the earliest cities, been barred from the streets," whereas the "spatial freedom of privileged women has been culturally and historically quite variable." What moralists were protesting against was the presence of middle-class or "respectable" women in public places.

Today, too, one can find many examples of the conflicts experienced by women in urban public places. On their lunch breaks, for example, women are routinely harassed by ogling men and then accused of inviting such behavior by wearing provocative clothing. In Islamic cities, especially in more orthodox nations like Pakistan, women are prohibited from appearing in public at all; if they must be out on the streets, they are required to hide their faces and completely cover their bodies. Conflicts that result from efforts by men to "keep women in their place" thus take many forms and are a widespread form of status conflict, one that is especially visible in cities. It may be true that racial conflict is more strident and violent, but for a person with a sociological imagination, gender conflicts are easy to spot.

RACIAL CONFLICT   Perhaps the most common source of intergroup conflict in American cities has been racial tension. In the belief that the presence of black residents reduces the prestige of a neighborhood and lowers the value of real estate there, whites have resisted efforts by blacks to obtain housing in "their" neighborhoods. This resistance has taken a wide variety of forms, ranging from discrimination by real estate agents to outright violence against black families moving into white neighborhoods. When blacks have succeeded in gaining a foothold in previously all-white neighborhoods, many white families have sold their homes and moved to the suburbs (Massey & Denton, 1993).

For racial and ethnic minorities, the desire to move out of segregated ghettos is based on the need to establish or maintain a residential community while pursuing opportunities to build a better life. This is among the key findings of studies of immigrant groups in South Florida. In looking at the difficulties that Haitian and Cuban refugees encounter in finding jobs in the Miami area, Alejandro Portes and Alex Stepick (1985) found that Cubans could draw on kin and ethnic networks in Miami neighborhoods in looking for jobs, but that the Haitians had no such networks to help them adapt to their new environment.

The riots that took place in 1992 in Los Angeles, Atlanta, and other major U.S. cities were a tragic example of the relationship between social change and racial violence in urban centers. Although the conditions of life had been deteriorating in central-city ghettos throughout the 1980s, it was not until televised bloodshed brought this situation to the attention of the public that significant numbers of people began to demand that the federal government take action. But this is by no means a new phenomenon in American social life. As we saw in Chapter 8, conflict between racial and other groups often raises public consciousness and contributes to major social change (Rothenberg, 1992).

CRITICAL SOCIOLOGY AND SOCIAL CHANGE

Coping with Disasters in Urban Communities

Riots, epidemics, earthquakes, terrorist bombings, wars, floods, tornadoes, and hurricanes are among the many kinds of disasters that may strike densely populated human settlements. Of course there are important differences in the causes and outcomes of purely social disasters like riots and purely natural ones like earthquakes (see Figure 9.10). But from a sociological vantage point, social and natural disasters have a great deal in common. Moreover, because we can expect both natural and social disasters to occur with increasing frequency on our urbanizing planet, the study of disasters is a thriving area of sociological theory and research.

Recent sociological research on disasters has focused on the longer-term consequences for the victims. In this area of research, the work of sociologist Kai Erikson is particularly noteworthy. Erikson's powerful descriptions of responses to disasters and his development of the sociological theory of trauma are having significant and positive impacts on victims' lives. In several precedent-setting cases, Erikson has convinced juries and judges that victims have suffered sociological damage, especially in the form of loss of community.

Erikson's recent work on social disasters focuses on the consequences of what he calls "a new species of trouble"

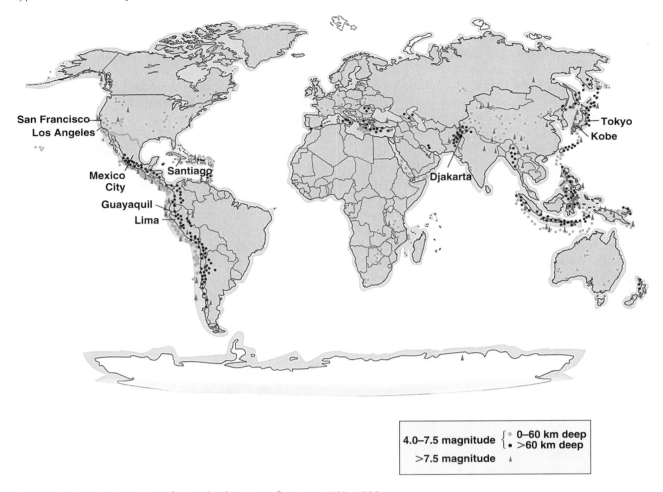

Figure 9.10   Earthquakes of Magnitude 4.0 or Greater, 1960–1989

This map shoes the regions of the world where earthquake activity is greatest and where major urban disasters are likely to occur because metropolitan regions are located on fault lines.

that is particularly common in urban industrial societies. The trouble may take the form of toxic spills, nuclear accidents, mercury poisoning, or many other disasters attributable to human negligence, greed, or combinations of both. The result is often an abrupt and shattering loss of community. Erikson and other sociologists who do similar research point out that disasters, especially those caused by the negligence or criminal behavior of corporations, are not distributed randomly across societies. On the contrary, they occur with far greater frequency in low-income and minority communities because dangerous facilities, dump sites, and tank farms are often located on the boundaries of those communities. This ecological pattern has been labeled "environmental racism" (Bullard, 2003).

In one such case, Erikson interviewed the residents of East Swallow Drive in Fort Collins, Colorado. This middle-income neighborhood of private homes with middle-aged or elderly residents was the site of a gasoline spill with devastating consequences. The local service station had been experiencing "inventory losses" for several years and had finally replaced three "incontinent" fuel tanks with new ones. Not long afterward, nearby residents began smelling gasoline fumes in their homes. An investigation revealed that there were large pools of gasoline in the ground under the homes along East Swallow Drive. One house near the service station was condemned, and in the months that followed, as Erikson describes it, "waves of concern began to radiate in slow-motion ripples down East Swallow Drive as people began to understand that a plume of petroleum was moving eastward with the sureness of a glacier" (1994a, pp. 99–100).

A group of homeowners brought suit against the companies involved in the spill. As is often the case, however, the companies were able to hire teams of lawyers who could delay the suit for months. Eventually lawyers for the residents asked Erikson to prepare testimony on the sociological damage caused by the spill. He and an assistant conducted observations in the neighborhood and interviewed the residents. Later Erikson shared transcripts of the interviews with the residents and asked them for additional comments. This method, it turned out, had powerful effects. As one resident noted, "I was greatly relieved to see what other people said. . . . Seeing this report gives me a little reassurance that I wasn't feeling something that other people were not feeling" (quoted in Erikson, 1994a, p. 138).

In his report, Erikson argued that the personal distress the residents were experiencing—in the form of anxiety, sleeplessness, anger, and other emotions—was not only a sign of psychological suffering but also a symptom of sociological trauma caused by the loss of their attachments to the neighborhood. As one resident said, "Well, we feel that the value of our property has taken a nose dive. It is our only security. We don't feel that it's salable. If we can't sell it, we can't relocate, we can't move, we can't expand or change. We feel that we're sort of stuck" (quoted in Erikson, 1994a, p. 232).

Erikson convinced the court not only that the residents had lost property value in terms of dollars but also that they had suffered a greater loss in a sociological sense. He noted that they had invested a great deal more than money in their homes:

> It is well understood by social and behavioral scientists who are familiar with accidents of this

kind that the loss of a home can be profoundly traumatic. I wrote in my report on the Buffalo Creek flood of 1972 [in West Virginia], for example, that a home in which a person has made a real personal investment "is not simply an expression of one's taste; it is the outer edge of personality, a part of the self itself." (1994a, p. 233)

Similarly, a well-known study of the impact of a tornado in Texas reported that people who had lost their homes felt as if they had lost part of themselves (Moore, 1958). And an equally well-known study of an urban relocation project in Boston's East End was titled simply "Grieving for a Lost Home" (Fried, 1963). In the East Swallow Drive case, the residents benefited from Erikson's sociological insight: Eventually the corporations responsible for the damage had to settle with the residents and pay not only for the damage to their property but for their loss of community as well.

Erikson and other sociologists who study disasters hope that as a consequence of their research—and their successes in court—there will be more safeguards against negligence and more emphasis on anticipating the risks of natural disasters. In the near term, however, Erikson fears that the balance of power is shifting toward corporations and other powerful actors, to the disadvantage of the victims or potential victims of community disasters.

Contamination and pollution of the earth and water beneath these houses, caused by the criminal dumping of toxic wastes, forced the residents to abandon their homes. Sociologist Kai Erikson has identified such disasters as a "new species of trouble" that has profound consequences for its victims.

VISUAL SOCIOLOGY

WOMEN'S EDUCATION AND FERTILITY CONTROL

Feminist sociologists and most experts on population issues agree that none of the approaches to fertility control attempted to date—contraception, abstinence, celibacy, sterilization, or delay of marriage—can have much success if women are not able to control their own reproductive lives. And they cannot do this if they remain illiterate and powerless in societies with rapidly growing populations. When given a chance to express their feelings on the matter, women and girls throughout the poor regions of the world usually agree with this crucial point. Consider as an example the outstanding visual sociological work of photographer Wendy Ewald in Vichya, in the state of Gujarat in northwestern India near the Pakistani border.

Ewald's method is to bring inexpensive cameras to the people she works with. She teaches them to take photos and to develop and print the results. Then they discuss what the photos reveal. As Ewald explains, "I gave the children assignments to expand their ideas of picture-making while staying close to what they knew. I asked them to photograph their festivals, their families, themselves, their village, and their animals" (1996, p. 14).

Tidi, the girl shown here, was 10 years old when Ewald came to her village. In her reflections on her photos, note especially her desire to go to school:

I have a mommy, father, two brothers, and three sisters. One brother is married and the other is going to marry. My father laughs a lot, but I don't like him when he beats us. My small brother and cousin are at home. One younger brother and sister got smallpox right after they were born. When they died, we buried them on the roadside and marked the grave with a red cloth. I can't find it now. The sweepers must have taken it away.

I get enough food to eat—even during the drought. We went to the city then and lived in our uncle's house for six months. . . . My father did construction work. My mother helped him and washed dishes and clothes for a rich family. I don't mind washing dishes, but I'd like to go to school.

I had to leave my studies because of the housework. Anyhow, soon we have to marry. I'll be happy then. My husband will get me a scooter. I'll get on it and wander. I want sons, as many as God wants to give me—two, three, or four. I'll play with my children and scold them when they're mischievous. When I'm older I'll look after my husband's house. (quoted in Ewald, 1996)

Tidi and her neighbors.

SUMMARY

People, Resources, and Urban Growth

- Populations change as a consequence of births, deaths, out-migration, and in-migration.

- Since World War II, the world population has been increasing at a rate of more than 1.5 percent, surpassing 6 billion in 2000.

- The *crude birthrate* is the number of births occurring during a year in a given population divided by the midyear population.

The Sociological Observer

(See photo on page 237.)

Ewald does not appear in many of the photos because either she is behind the camera taking the shot or, even more often, the photos she selects are those taken by the villagers themselves. Their photos reveal their own unique insights into village life, and the feelings and memories their photos elicit as Ewald converses with them enrich our understanding of a culture far different from our own. In most of the photos, men and women, boys and girls, are engaged in same-gender activities. There are times when males and females of different ages come together in family activities such as weddings and funerals, and in religious ceremonies, but much of daily life in rural Indian cultures involves people in gender-segregated activity. So when Ewald wanted to make sure that the girls learned to use the camera, she naturally taught boys and girls separately. Taking pictures when one has never held a camera can be an empowering experience because the photos allow the individual to make his or her own sense of village life and to comment on that life as one whose voice is listened to and respected.

"Hasmukh, Chandrakant, Harshad, and Dasrath learning to use the camera."

"Grandfather is sitting on the ledge with the dog."

- The *crude death rate* is the number of deaths occurring during a year divided by the midyear population.
- The *rate of reproductive change* is the difference between the crude birthrate and the crude death rate for a given population.
- The *demographic transition* is a set of major changes in birth and death rates that has occurred most completely in urban industrial nations in the past 200 years. It takes place in three stages: (1) high birth and death rates, (2) declining death rates, and (3) declining

birthrates. These stages are accompanied by changes in the age composition of the population.

- Life expectancy is highest in societies with advanced systems of health care and well-developed public health systems. A more sophisticated measure, disability-adjusted life expectancy (DALE), takes into account how long a person can expect to live without severe and disabling illness. On this measure, the United States ranks relatively low among wealthy nations.
- The growth of the human population in the past two centuries has begun to exert major stresses on the earth's resources of arable soil, clean air, and fresh water for drinking and irrigation, as well as on its sources of fuels.
- Urbanization is closely linked with rapid increases in population, but at the same time the nature of life in cities tends to limit the size of urban families.
- Cities grow primarily as a result of migration (which is often caused by population increases in rural areas), but new migrants do not find it easy to form families.
- Not only are increasing proportions of the world's population living in cities, but the cities themselves are also larger than ever before.
- The growth of cities in the twentieth century gave rise to the concept of the *metropolitan area,* in which a central city is surrounded by several smaller cities and suburbs that are closely related to it both socially and economically.
- The growth of cities should be distinguished from *urbanization,* which refers to the proportion of the total population that is concentrated in urban settlements. The end result of urbanization is an "urban society." Not only do cities serve as the cultural and institutional centers of such societies, but urban life has a pervasive influence on the entire society as well.

The Urban Landscape

- Sociologists have devoted a great deal of study to the processes by which cities expand and to patterns of settlement within cities. An early model of urban expansion was the concentric-zone model developed by Park and Burgess. In this model, a central business district is surrounded by successive zones, or rings, devoted to light manufacturing, workers' homes, higher-class apartment buildings and single-family homes, and a commuters' zone.
- This model is limited to commercial and industrial cities that formed around business centers and does not account for the rise of satellite cities and the rapid

urbanization that occurs along commercial transportation corridors. The growth of satellite cities was especially rapid before World War II.

- A more current model of urbanization is known as *strip development* and describes the incorporation of smaller communities and towns into a larger metropolitan area.
- Metropolitan areas have expanded greatly since the mid-twentieth century, largely as a result of the increasing use of automobiles and the construction of a network of highways covering the entire nation. In some areas, this growth has created large multinuclear urban systems that are described by the term *megalopolis.*
- One effect of the development of such areas is decentralization, in which outlying areas become more important at the expense of the central city.

Urban Communities

- Social scientists who have studied the effects of urban life have been particularly concerned with the tension between community and individualism as it relates to life in cities.
- Early studies of urban life tended to conclude that it weakens kinship ties and produces impersonal social relationships. Urban life was also thought to produce "psychic overload" and anomie.
- More recently these conclusions have been criticized by researchers who have found that many city dwellers maintain stable, intimate relationships with kin, neighbors, and co-workers and that urban life is not necessarily stressful or anomic.
- Subcultural theory sees the city as a mosaic of social worlds or intimate social groups. Communities of all kinds can be found in cities. Those communities may be based on ethnicity, kinship, occupation, lifestyle, or similar personal attributes.
- Suburban dwellers also have been found to be far less bored and isolated than was once supposed.

Cities and Social Change

- Occasionally various communities within cities come into conflict. Such conflict may arise out of different class interests or the conflicting goals of different groups within the city.
- Some urban sociologists see the city as divided into "defended neighborhoods" or territories whose residents attempt to protect them from "invasion" by outsiders.

GLOSSARY

crude birthrate: The number of births occurring during a year in a given population, divided by the midyear population. (p. 231)

crude death rate: The number of deaths occurring during a year in a given population, divided by the midyear population. (p. 231)

rate of reproductive change: The difference between the crude birthrate and the crude death rate for a given population. (p. 231)

demographic transition: A set of major changes in birth and death rates that has occurred most completely in urban industrial nations in the past 200 years. (p. 232)

urbanization: A process in which an increasing proportion of a total population becomes concentrated in urban settlements. (p. 236)

metropolitan area: A central city surrounded by several smaller cities and suburbs that are closely related to it both socially and economically. (p. 237)

megalopolis: A complex of cities distributed along a major axis of traffic and communication, with a total population exceeding 25 million. (p. 245)

INTERNET RESOURCES

Virtual Society: The Wadsworth Sociology Resource Center
(http://sociology.wadsworth.com)

At Virtual Society you can access a wide range of enrichment material to aid your study of sociology. From the main page, click on the Student Resources link and find your course and this textbook. Next, select the chapter you are presently studying from the pull-down menu. Among the useful options for each self-study chapter are online links and exercises, flashcards, practical study tips, and practice quizzes for each chapter.

MC MicroCase Online

From the Virtual Society home page, click on MicroCase Online to access book-specific MicroCase exercises that allow you to further explore sociological issues and principles presented in the text.

InfoTrac College Edition

Another unique option available to you at the Student Resources section at Virtual Society is InfoTrac College Edition, an online library with access to hundreds of scholarly and popular periodicals. Below are suggested search terms for this chapter, but this resource also allows you to fit your study of sociology to your own interests by searching custom keywords.

Urbanization

Decentralization

Subculture

Inequality

The Population Council
(www.popcouncil.org)

One of the best places to begin looking at the wealth of resources on the Internet that deal with population growth, population control, and studies of population processes.

The Urban Institute
(www.urban.org)

One of the nation's premier think tanks concerned with urban problems. Its Web site contains many of its publications.

Popexpo
(www-popexpo.ined.fr/eMain.html)

An excellent source of information about world population growth and its effects on other aspects of social life. The site is developed and maintained by the prestigious Museé de l'Homme in Paris and is available in English as well as other languages.

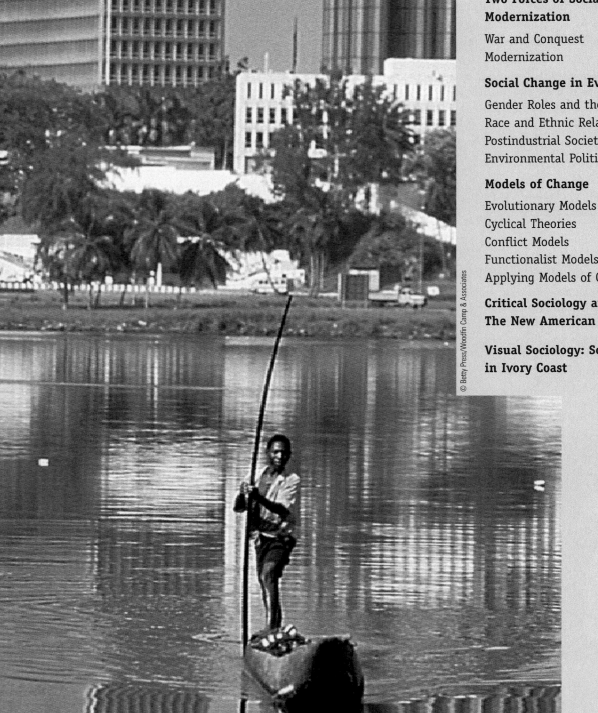

chapter 10

Global Social Change

One sultry African night, as the people of Blokosso were sleeping, a band of thieves crept into their houses and ransacked them. They stole radios, jewelry, and expensive articles of ceremonial clothing. But as the villagers assessed the damage early the next morning, they mourned a far greater loss. Never before in anyone's memory had a robbery like this occurred in the village. It was not the goods themselves they missed, for these could be replaced. It was the loss of a way of life, a social world, that they lamented. "We loved to sleep outside on the very hot nights," said Mr. Joseph, one of the most respected men in the village—"the women by this palm grove in the soft sand along the lagoon, the men under the lamp a bit. We like to talk and sleep with each other. We are not used to sleeping with our things."

Throughout history, theirs had been a village society. Blokosso was one of several fishing villages inhabited by the Ebrié tribe. For as long as they could remember, the Ebrié people had made their living by fishing in the quiet waters of the lagoon, which was protected from the huge ocean swells by a long barrier island. But in recent decades the village had been engulfed by the rapidly growing city of Abidjan, the capital of Ivory Coast and a booming port. More and more of the tribesmen were now working in the city. The women continued to tend their garden plots, but they too were increasingly drawn into the economy of the city and felt an ever-increasing need for spending money, which they earned by renting rooms to migrant workers and selling their extra produce.

Gradually, in the time before the robbery occurred, Blokosso had ceased to be a self-sustaining village with its own economy and tribal culture. Instead, it was becoming a "village enclave," a little island of cultural homogeneity in an urban society. The robbery was a blunt statement to the villagers about how much change had occurred in a short time and how much more was likely to come.

For me, the experience of living in Blokosso at that time (during 1962 and 1963) was as much of a revelation as the robbery was to the villagers.

I had been trained as a biologist and was living in Blokosso while teaching physics and chemistry in a junior college. During the day I delighted in opening up to students the secrets of matter and energy. In the evenings, however, the villagers taught me about living in a totally different social world, one that was experiencing even more rapid social change than my own.

Mr. Joseph, my best friend in the village, was a middle-level executive in one of Abidjan's insurance agencies. He commuted across the lagoon in a motorized dugout canoe. During the day, his mind was entirely devoted to business. In the evenings, he dealt with the problems of a traditional African family. His three wives became increasingly jealous of one another as new wealth and their rising expectations led to new opportunities for better health and more leisure and also to new sources of conflict. I watched him and his family deal with the impact of change on their lives. I saw the villagers attempt to invoke their ancestral spirits and to use witchcraft to cope with new phenomena like robberies. The entire colony had become independent from France only 2 years before, and I saw the villagers—now citizens of a new nation called Ivory Coast—becoming interested in politics and current events.

During that time, my own interests shifted from the physical to the social sciences. Nothing has ever interested me more than the villagers' questions about what social change brought to them and what it caused them to lose. When I began to study sociology, I discovered that such questions are at the core of this young science.

FOCUS QUESTIONS:

• What are some of the most important examples of social change in the contemporary world?

• What forces have produced the greatest social changes throughout human history?

• How do sociologists create and apply models of social change?

THE NATURE OF SOCIAL CHANGE

Throughout this book, we deal with social changes of all kinds. The term *social change* refers to variations over time in the ecological ordering of populations and communities, in patterns of roles and social interactions, in the structure and functioning of institutions, and in the cultures of societies. We have seen that such changes can result from social forces building within societies (**endogenous forces**) as well as from forces for change exerted from the outside (**exogenous forces**).

Ebrié is not a written language. The villagers speak their history to each other and to their children as they gather in the evenings around their home fires. When I was living with them, they often told stories about how, in the distant past before the whites came, a tribal village sometimes grew too large. When that happened, severe conflict would result. Factions would form and there would be fighting over land or other resources. Soon there would be a major split: The stronger faction would stay and keep the existing village while the less powerful faction would establish a new village on unused land along the lagoon. This is an example of people adjusting to endogenous change caused by population increase, a very common cause of social change.

The Ebrié also told stories about recent changes in their lives, changes brought on mainly by colonial conquest and, more recently, by their own efforts to create a new nation and maintain its social and economic growth. Colonial rule and rebellion against it are examples of social change produced by exogenous forces, particularly the influence of a powerful conquering society attempting to impose its culture on conquered peoples.

Social change affects people's lives all over the world, sometimes for the better, sometimes for the worse. As I sat under the palm trees with my Ebrié friends, we endlessly debated issues of social change. In many ways, our debates were about the difference between change and progress. "Before the white man came," my friends told me, "we had time but no watches. Now we have watches but no time." The village primary school was known in Ebrié as the "paper house" where children struggled to master the three R's in order to be able to earn money, or "white man's paper." But there was also general agreement that many of the technologies introduced by the Europeans were of immense value. Health care innovations that could prevent debilitating diseases like malaria or schistosomiasis were considered a great blessing. Yet the most prestigious Western invention from the villagers' viewpoint was the camera, for with it, they exclaimed, "our children can see their ancestors."

The people of Ivory Coast and other societies that are undergoing rapid social change do not see the future as a matter of becoming Westernized. Their struggle to maintain aspects of their traditional way of life as they build a modern national state is documented in the Visual Sociology section at the end of the chapter. They are aware of a decline in their sense of community and mourn the weakening of their culture, but they actively embrace the aspects of modernity that will permit more of them to lead longer and perhaps more enjoyable lives. For my Ebrié friends, there is no question of returning to an earlier state. Change is inevitable. They want to help make the change, however, and to do this they understand that they must compete in modern social institutions like schools and businesses while attempting to preserve their village life as best they can.

Dilemmas of Social Change

Social change is a dominant theme of this book because it exerts such powerful influences on every aspect of our lives. Macro-level changes in the way the entire society is organized, such as the organization of metropolitan regions around automobile transportation, are relatively rapid. Our great-grandparents traveled in railroad sleeping cars and never imagined vast shopping malls with acres of automobile parking. Global social change accounts for the decline of whole sectors of the U.S. economy and the rise of new ones. At the middle level of social organization—in our communities and workplaces—social change can have drastic and immediate impacts. The September 11, 2001, terrorist attacks, for example, accelerated an economic downturn that caused many communities to lose the revenue surpluses they had counted on to rebuild schools and parks, and employers began cutting back on hiring and sending layoff notices to their workers.

At the micro level, social change also has dramatic impacts. Changing norms of sexuality, for example, may create new and unexpected situations. As gay people realize their need to express their sexuality, they also wish to "come out" and speak frankly about their lifestyle with family members. Issues like abortion, interracial marriage, divorce, and drug abuse create similar conflicts and pressures. When we argue about norms within our intimate circle of family or friends, the result may be even greater confusion. Today no aspect of life seems secure and free from conflict. (More comparative examples of social change at different levels of the social order are presented in Table 10.1.)

Wars and acts of terrorism, rampant political corruption and international bickering, famines and epidemics of AIDS and SARS—these are some of the current events

TABLE 10.1

Examples of Effects of Social Change

		Tribal Society (Ebrié)	Metropolitan Society (United States)
Macro-Level Changes	Population growth	Creates new markets for Ebrié real estate; adds newcomers to villages.	Causes new conflicts and need for social control in increasingly congested regions.
	Globalization: economic and cultural	Gives tribe members jobs at branches of multinational companies; threatens forests and waters if environmental controls are not established.	Encourages manufacturing concerns to move their production overseas; forces people to find more jobs in services and high-tech manufacturing.
Middle-Level Changes	Urbanization	Surrounds villages with new neighborhoods and nontribal strangers.	Enmeshes most residents in metropolitan regions, where their community boundaries are blurred and diversity becomes an issue.
	Increased crime	Causes villagers to distrust strangers.	Engenders efforts to control crime and encourages privatization.
Micro-Level Changes	Rising material expectations	Leads village women to rebel against polygyny.	Pushes more women into the labor force, creating the need for child care.
	Changing norms of conduct	Creates a sense of anomie, confusion over expectations.	Increases the level of conflict in communities over sexuality, public conduct, and the like.

that are shaking the stability of nations throughout the world. They are also changing much sociological thinking about social change. In the post–World War II period, when hundreds of former colonial nations like Ivory Coast were becoming independent, most sociologists and political leaders in the West regarded modernization as a process that would gradually but inevitably produce healthier societies and accelerated economic and social development in the poor regions of the world, just as it had in the wealthier regions. There would be new frontiers of democracy, new levels of international understanding through world bodies like the United Nations, and a decline in ethnic and religious intolerance due to increased trade, communication, and guarantees of people's rights under the rule of law (Zakaria, 2003).

But many nations are not progressing toward the bright future envisioned for them after colonialism and the end of the world wars. Some have made great gains, but others are mired in poverty, corruption, and lawlessness (Kagan, 2003). Conflict among adherents of major world religions now threatens to replace conflict between the Soviet Empire and the American-led capitalist nations as a major cause of terrorism and war. Even in the most well-off and stable regions of the world, there are new conflicts and anxieties. In the United States, there is a widening gulf between the rich and the middle and lower classes, just as there is a poten-

tially widening gap between the beliefs of the religious and less religious segments of the population. Some of these changes were predicted by sociological models of social change developed in the mid-twentieth century, but others were not.

In revising their models of social change, sociologists ask a basic set of questions: Is social change universal? Is social change the same as progress? Can we intervene and control social change? And finally, can we predict social change better than we have in the past?

IS SOCIAL CHANGE UNIVERSAL?   It would seem that ever since the Industrial Revolution about three centuries ago social change has been occurring throughout the world. For thousands of years, people had lived in simpler societies that might or might not have been experiencing social change as a consequence of such processes as population growth, factional conflict, war, and disease. But with the advent of industrialization, urbanization, colonial conquest, and global warfare, all the societies of the earth were increasingly brought into what sociologist Immanuel Wallerstein (1974) has called the capitalist world system. Trade and markets, often dominated by the more powerful nations, enmesh all the world's people in a network of relationships and interdependencies that make self-sufficiency and social equilibrium ever more difficult to attain. As we have noted in earlier chapters, perhaps no change in human history has been as far-reaching and universal in its consequences as the transition from an agrarian to an urban, industrial way of life brought about by the Industrial Revolution. In sum, social change may be more or less rapid in different societies and in different parts of the world, but the forces of global social change are felt everywhere. Thus, at least in our own era, it can be said that social change is universal.

IS SOCIAL CHANGE PROGRESS?   Those who promote social change of one kind or another often equate change with progress, but in fact much social change is extremely difficult and disruptive for the people who live through it. In Iraq, for example, the U.S. government claims to bringing democracy to that embattled nation, but it is extremely wary of allowing free elections in which fundamentalist Shiite leaders might win public office, even though the Shiites are a majority of the nation's population (Berman, 2003). In Russia, the fall of communism and the rise of the new capitalist economy have created many newly rich and many more newly poor Russians, and how the average citizen feels about progress often depends on how he or she is doing in the new economy.

"Progress" is defined differently, depending on the values of those who are trying to assess whether a particular change constitutes progress (Harper, 1993). In some instances, social change has positive consequences for many people, and perhaps even for an entire society. Fifty years ago, for example, the United States was a highly segregated society, unable to claim that it was realizing the democratic vision of its founders. Today, after decades of struggle, many aspects of segregation remain, but many of the worst aspects of racism have been reduced or eliminated through protest, compromise, new laws, and other forms of social change. However, for every instance of positive social change, there will be others that people do not agree on or that are seen as negative or too complicated to assess. When factories close and communities lose vital jobs, that is a form of social change that most people in the affected communities do not think of as progress. Yet when the same jobs become available in Mexico, people there rejoice at their good fortune. Similarly, when political leaders persuade local police forces to protect the rights of homosexuals, gay people may feel that progress has been made. Yet in the same communities there will be conservative residents who wish to return to a past in which homosexuals were considered sinners who did not deserve equal rights.

CAN WE CONTROL SOCIAL CHANGE?   The examples of the American and British occupation of Iraq and changing race relations in the United States raise a fundamental question about social change: Is it something we can control intentionally, or is it a result of powerful social forces that are be-

yond our ability to shape or modify? The answer is that some social change is intentional and some is far beyond our power to control. In a society governed by laws and democratic processes, it appears possible to reduce injustice and even to reduce some of the worst forms of inequality. But global forces of social and economic change are extremely difficult to shape even if we can learn to accommodate and adjust to them (Etzkowitz & Glassman, 1991).

Even when we engage in intentional social change, the results are often surprising and unanticipated. Before the Social Security and Medicare systems were created, the elderly experienced extremely high rates of poverty and untreated illness. These intentional and hotly debated programs changed that situation dramatically. However, it is impossible to control the rapid rise in the number of elderly people who will be covered by these programs in coming decades. This threat to the financial stability of the system may result in a weakening of the scope of Social Security and Medicare coverage in the future.

CAN SOCIAL CHANGE BE PREDICTED?   Social science has had mixed success in predicting social change. The master trends of our era, such as economic globalization, population growth, urbanization, technological change, and the rising expectations of oppressed people, are well known. Their consequences can be understood and predicted, to a degree. Demographers can predict with reasonable certainty the major population trends that will affect societies over a 20- or 30-year period. Survey researchers can predict the outcomes of election campaigns or referenda on major social issues like immigration or crime. But we have limited ability to predict technological changes or to anticipate the outbreak of wars or the appearance of new social movements or new diseases. Yet these are some of the most important sources of social change. In fact, one difference between the "pop" sociology books sold in supermarkets and the sociological research conducted at universities is the caution with which the university researchers discuss social change (Chirot, 1994a).

Sociological researchers usually make projections based on current trends, with carefully stated assumptions about what will happen if those trends continue into the future. For example, we know that as members of the huge U.S. "baby boom" grow older and face death, the media will pay more attention to issues involving aging, death, and dying, just as they paid more attention to issues such as day care when the baby boomers were forming families. But other aspects of social change, especially those caused by technological innovations, are far more difficult to predict. We have difficulty predicting their appearance and limited success predicting their consequences.

Consider an example: For decades sociological writers who produce forecasts for popular media have been predicting that computers and telecommunications networks would spell the end of the central city as a place of work and entertainment for masses of people (Naisbitt & Aburdene, 1990; Toffler, 1970). However, research exploring this prediction shows that the new technologies have very mixed consequences for urban downtown areas. In large cities like Los Angeles, Chicago, New York, and Baltimore, there is an unpredicted renaissance of central-city business and entertainment and an explosion of new small businesses, often based on applications of computer and communications technologies. But it is also true that the new communications technologies make it easier for employers in the information industries to distribute work among employees at many different locations. Hence, the future of central cities as employment-generating environments is extremely difficult to predict.

In sum, we can study major trends and use them to predict some important aspects of continuing social change, but others are still far beyond the power of any social scientist to actually predict. The breakup of the Soviet empire in 1989, the outbreak of war in the Balkans, the dramatic changes in U.S. social policies after the conservative sweep of the 1994 congressional elections, the impact of terrorism in 2001—none of these events was actually predicted, even though there were some indications that they might occur.

organization, the devastation caused by war has increased. The wars fought by so-called primitive societies were frequently ritual affairs; the combatants often withdrew from the field after a single skirmish. Although not all preindustrial warfare was so ritualistic, relatively few combatants were killed because the technologies for killing were so limited compared with those available today.

In the Middle Ages, often viewed as a warlike time because of the influence of knights and Crusaders, the rate of fatalities among warriors in battle was about 2 percent. In World War I, in contrast, the proportion was 40 percent. Modern warfare is increasingly dangerous not only for the combatants but for civilians as well. In the Vietnam War, more than 75 percent of those who died were civilians (Galtung, 1985; McNeill, 1982). In Afghanistan, civilians know the terror of war—in the form of buried land mines or unexploded bombs—long after the warring armies have withdrawn from the field.

Although warfare is as old as human societies, the forms and conduct of war are always changing. New technologies, such as biological weapons delivered in missiles or dirty bombs that might spread a cloud of radioactive poisons, causing panic and hysteria in unprotected urban populations, or even the use of hijacked airplanes as flying bombs, are examples of current changes that may permit weaker forces to mount devastating attacks on stronger nations.

TWO FORCES OF SOCIAL CHANGE: WAR AND MODERNIZATION

War and modernization are among the most powerful and pervasive forces that produce social change at every level of social life. As we have noted, social change is caused by many other social forces, especially technological innovation and population growth or mobility, but we will see in this section that war and modernization also stimulate these other forces of change. Many of the most significant technological innovations of the twentieth century were developed in response to the crisis of war. And many of the greatest movements of people over the planet were first set in motion by the disruptions caused by warfare or modernization (Chirot, 1986, 1994a, 1994b; Kagan, 2003).

War and Conquest

War is among the greatest and certainly the most violent of the forces that produce social change. Ironically, the deadliest forms of warfare are associated with the rise of modern civilizations. As societies have become more advanced in their command of technology and their social

American Marines pulled down this statue of Saddam Hussein after the conquest of Baghdad, but fear of the deposed ruler and his henchmen remained high among Iraqis for many months as Hussein's loyalists resorted to tactics of asymmetrical warfare (guerrilla ambushes and terrorism).

Terrorism, using conventional weapons like mortar shells or unconventional ones like suicide bombs, is a form of *asymmetrical warfare* because the terrorist organization, whether sponsored by a nation or by a faction like Al Qaeda, is militarily far weaker than the force it attacks (Vest, 2001).

In *symmetrical warfare*, such as occurred in the 2003 Iraq war, two or more conventional armies confront each other. In the case of Iraq, however, conventional symmetrical warfare soon gave over to terrorism and asymmetrical warfare once the U.S.-British coalition had prevailed on the conventional battlefield. The need for the occupying armies to quickly transform themselves from an invading force into a policing force capable of restoring order and tracking down war criminals highlighted the difficulties of adapting conventional armed forces for new roles in bringing about positive social change under hostile and chaotic conditions. In the contemporary world, it is clear that asymmetrical warfare and difficult peacekeeping assignments will be ever more common forms of war and the response to war.

Any evaluation of the place of war in social change must consider four broad questions: (1) What are the ecological effects of war on human populations? (2) How do wars help shape the consciousness and culture of a people? (3) How does warfare affect the roles of women in society? (4) How does war change the institutions of societies?

THE ECOLOGICAL IMPACT OF WAR   Casualties and conquest are the major ecological effects of war. People all over the world were shocked by televised scenes of oil fires and polluted coastlines during the 1991 Persian Gulf War, but the most significant ecological impacts of the Gulf War were felt by human populations. Like an epidemic of cholera or bubonic plague, war accounts for extraordinary and rapid declines in population. Pitirim Sorokin (1937) estimated that between AD 1100 and 1925 about 35.5 million people died in European wars alone. World War I claimed the lives of about 8.4 million soldiers and about 5 million civilians, and in World War II about 17 million military personnel and about 34 million civilians died. It is estimated that the Soviet Union lost about 15 million people during World War II and that in China about 22 million perished. Germany lost 3.7 million, Japan about 2.2 million, and the United States slightly under 300,000 (Beer, 1981).

When millions of soldiers are killed, entire populations are unbalanced for more than a generation. Many women remain single or become widows and either do not have children or raise children alone. The effect may be to reduce population pressure on food and other resources, but the loss of so many skilled workers also causes labor shortages and economic disarray.

War also results in large-scale shifts in population and rapid acceleration of economic change. For example, the

Source: AMAR International.

In the aftermath of the 1991 Iraq war, Saddam Hussein's forces took revenge against the Shiite Arabs who lived in the great marshes of southern Iraq and who he believed were disloyal to his regime. In one of the worst examples of the ecological effects of warfare against a civilian population, the regime ordered the marshes drained in an effort to destroy them and with them the Marsh Arabs' 5,000-year-old way of life. By the time of the 2003 war, only an estimated 20,000 of the original 500,000 inhabitants of the marshes remained. About 200,000 had fled to refugee camps in Iran.

TABLE 10.2

U.S. Respondents' Rank Ordering of Important Events as They Perceive Them

Event/Change	Age					
	18–29	30–39	40–49	50–59	60–69	70 Plus
World War II (265)	14	16	24	29	30	23
Vietnam (144)	18	18	13	2	4	1
Space exploration (93)	8	6	8	10	6	8
Kennedy assassination (62)	3	8	10	3	1	1
Civil rights (77)	7	7	5	7	6	3
Nuclear war, threat of (55)	6	5	6	4	2	3
Communication/transportation (46)	1	4	4	5	3	9
Depression (43)	3	3	2	5	7	13
Computers (23)	2	1	2	3	2	0
Terrorism (43)	4	2	0	1	1	0
Moral decline (28)	2	2	2	2	4	1
Women's rights (20)	1	2	3	0	2	1
Other event/change (357)	30	26	22	29	33	37
	100	100	100	100	100	100
	(289)	(312)	(200)	(167)	(165)	(110)

Source: Schuman & Scott, 1989.

western parts of the United States and Canada experienced their most rapid growth as a result of mobilization for war during the first half of the twentieth century. New dams, new electric power plants, and new factories to produce all kinds of goods were built. San Diego, Los Angeles, San Francisco, Portland, Seattle, and Vancouver all experienced massive population growth, as did many inland centers of industry and agriculture. The end of the war saw continued growth in the western states as young families who had come west during the war decided to settle there permanently.

For the losers in war, the ecological consequences of defeat are usually far more dramatic. Population loss, economic subjugation, the imposition of a foreign language and culture, and forced movement to new towns and industrial areas are common. During more than a century of genocidal wars waged by whites against Native Americans in the nineteenth and early twentieth centuries, the consequences for the losers were death, expulsion, and banishment to reservations. For tribal peoples of Africa, invasion, war, and conquest led to colonial rule and rapid social change, often imposed through taxation, labor gangs, military draft, and similar means. In areas of the world that are torn by war today—such as Iraq, Afghanistan, Kashmir, the former states of Yugoslavia (especially Bosnia and Kosovo), and African countries like Congo, Liberia, and Somalia—war has brought genocidal ethnic conflicts, mass expulsions ("ethnic cleansing"), and years of abject poverty in squalid refugee camps.

THE CULTURAL IMPACT OF WAR   War changes a society's culture by stamping the memories of chaos and cruelty, heroism and camaraderie on entire generations. Years after a major war, its effects on values and norms continue to be felt (Schuman & Scott, 1989). One need only think of the impact of the American Civil War on the former Confederate states, an impact that remains strong today and can be seen in Civil War memorials, rebel yells, the conduct of interracial relations, and North–South animosities. Recent sociological research shows that even for generations that did not experience war firsthand, the memory or threat of warfare is perceived as extremely important. Table 10.2 shows that people will cite specific wars first among "national events or changes that seem especially important to you"—even if they were not alive during the wars they mention.

No doubt far more respondents would list terrorism at or near the top of the list if this study were repeated today. As evidence, note the Gallup Poll results shown in Table 10.3. On the evening just after the September 11, 2001, terrorist strikes, Americans were still hoping to learn more about the probable perpetrators before they committed themselves to a war against terrorism. But only a few days later, there was such a high level of approval of the war that it is quite clear

TABLE 10.3

Opinions on U.S. Response to Terrorist Attacks

Opinion	Percentage in Favor
September 11, 2001	
Should conduct immediate strikes	21
Should wait until identify those responsible	71
Should not conduct strikes	4
No opinion	4
September 14–15, 2001	
Do you think the United States should—or should not— take military action in retaliation for Tuesday's attacks on the World Trade Center and the Pentagon?	
Should	88
Should not	8
No opinion	4

Source: Gallup Poll.

that this event will occupy a major place in the memory of the present generation of teenagers and young adults.

The impact of a major war can also be seen in the damage done to the minds and bodies of the survivors. In addition to the thousands who are maimed and mutilated, thousands more suffer from *post-traumatic stress disorder,* in which the shock of war continues to haunt the victim; others experience *survivor guilt,* the feeling of shame that many survivors feel because they escaped the fate of their comrades. These effects, which occur at the micro level of interpersonal relations, have been described by the Italian social observer Primo Levi, who was imprisoned at Auschwitz and liberated by Russian soldiers. When the soldiers encountered the piles of dead and the groans of the dying, Levi reports, they felt shame: "They did not greet us, nor smile; they seemed oppressed. . . . It was the shame which the just man experiences when confronted by a crime committed by another, and he feels remorse because of its existence" (1989, p. 72).

This kind of shame and guilt pervades a culture that has been torn by war. People feel that those who died were the best, the

most valorous of society's members. Levi describes the shame he felt at the deaths of Chaim, a watchmaker who tried to teach him how to survive in the camp, and Szabo, a tall, silent Hungarian peasant who needed more food than others yet never failed to help his weaker companions. He tells of his guilt over the fact that Robert, a professor at the Sorbonne, died even though he "spread courage and trust all around him," and that Baruch, a longshoreman from Livorno, died on the first day because he hit back when the guards beat him. "These, and innumerable others, died not despite their valor but because of it" (p. 83).

WAR AND GENDER RELATIONS Throughout history, women and girls have suffered particular cruelties during wars and conquest. As refugees from warfare, or as civilians in the midst of deadly battle, women are often abused, degraded, raped, and killed, sometimes along with their children. Thousands of Albanian women were forced to flee to the mountains of Kosovo, knowing that to stay in the path of their Serbian attackers was to risk rape, torture, and the possible violent death of their children. In Afghanistan, the defeat of the Taliban in 2001 ended a regime that had brought untold suffering for women. They were subjected to the strictest possible religious rules, which denied them even the most basic opportunities for education and health care. In these examples, and many others that could be cited, women have been caught in the middle of vicious local conflicts that have developed largely as a consequence of the end of the cold war and its uneasy equilibrium of competing superpowers. But all wars in the modern age have taken an extremely high toll on women, as thousands of war widows can attest.

Women are by no means merely passive victims of warfare. Sociologist Suzanne Staggenborg, a researcher on gender, family, and social movements, notes that "Women's peace movements had existed in many countries since the early twentieth century and included international organi-

During World War II, American GIs brought their culture to places throughout the world where they lived and fought. Here the orchestra of the First Cavalry Division takes time out for a jam session on Los Negros Island.

THEN AND NOW

Two Images of the Warrior

When the Plains Indians and the U.S. Cavalry fought bloody battles during the period of westward expansion in the nineteenth century, warfare was brutal and deadly, especially for the less well-equipped Indian warriors. But as deadly as it was, war was not nearly as devastating for noncombatant populations as it is today. A century ago, warfare required guns and bayonets, cannons, and a great deal of organization and logistical support, but it did not involve sophisticated technologies like those represented by the modern fighter or bomber plane. As combat has become less a matter of brute force and more dependent on brains and technology, the possibility that well-trained women can compete as warriors has become a reality. This change in the conduct of war would have been inconceivable to General Custer or Sitting Bull.

© Traver/Getty Images

© Traver/Getty Images

zations such as the Women's International League for Peace and Freedom, which was founded in 1915" (1998, p. 45). Women's opposition to war is nothing new, however; the ancient Greek playwright Aristophanes dealt with the subject in *Lysistrata,* a semiserious comedy in which the women of Athens go on strike in an effort to avert war with Sparta. During the twentieth century, the massive mobilizations of the two world wars—in which the vast majority of women and men had their lives disrupted and their careers dramatically altered by wartime industrial mobilization, military service, civilian defense, and the untimely death of loved ones who were also parents and breadwinners—had lasting effects on gender relations. These experiences increased the desire of women to enjoy the same rights and responsibilities as men, including the right to serve in the military. We return to this major aspect of social change later in this chapter and in Chapter 14.

WAR'S IMPACT ON SOCIAL INSTITUTIONS   The structure of a society, especially its major social institutions, may be drastically changed by war and preparation for war. The mobilization of large numbers of people and the marshaling of new technologies for military purposes have a cen-

tralizing effect on social institutions. In the United States, for example, the growth of large research universities in the 1960s was accelerated by huge investments in applied science and technology after the Soviet Union became the first nation to launch a space satellite. Universities that were capable of developing new science programs grew rapidly, and their administrations gained greater power. The power and influence of the national government have also grown, often at the expense of local governmental institutions, as a consequence of the two world wars and the arms race. Providing for national defense is extremely expensive and requires that the central government be granted increased taxing powers.

The French sociologist Raymond Aron (1955) has called the twentieth century "the century of total war" because of the capacity of warfare to shape the destiny of entire regions and because of the unprecedented power of nuclear and other weapons. Aron's phrase also captures the transforming power of modern war, its ability to alter societies. In the United States, for example, there is no doubt that the mobilization necessary to fight two world wars, major regional wars in Korea and Vietnam, and innumerable smaller skirmishes in Africa, Latin America, and Asia contributed to

TABLE 10.4

Trade-Offs Between Military and Social or Environmental Priorities

Military Priority	Cost	Social/Environmental Priority
Trident II submarine and F-18 jet fighter programs	$108,000,000,000	Estimated cost of cleaning up the 10,000 worst hazardous waste dumps in the United States.
Stealth bomber program	$73,440,000,000	Two thirds of estimated costs to meet U.S. clean water goals.
2 weeks of world military expenditure	$32,400,000,000	Annual cost of the UN Water and Sanitation Decade.
3 days of global military spending	$7,200,000,000	Cost to fund Tropical Forest Action Plan over 5 years.
Development cost for Midgetman ICBM	$6,480,000,000	Annual cost to cut sulfur dioxide emissions by 8–12 million tons/year in the United States to combat acid rain.
2 days of global military spending	$5,184,000,000	Annual cost of UN Action Plan to halt Third World desertification over 20 years.
10 days of European Economic Community military spending	$2,160,000,000	Annual cost to clean up hazardous waste sites in ten European Union countries.
1 Trident submarine	$1,512,000,000	Global 5-year child immunization program against six deadly diseases, preventing 1 million deaths a year.
2 months of Ethiopian military spending	$54,000,000	Annual cost of UN Anti-Desertification Plan for Ethiopia.
1 nuclear weapon test	$12,960,000	Cost for installation of 80,000 hand pumps to give Third World villages access to safe water.
1-hour operating cost, B-1B bomber	$22,680	Cost of community-based maternal health care in ten African villages for 10 years.

Source: Adapted from Renner, 1989; *Statistical Abstract*, 2000.

the controversial growth of the federal government during the twentieth century. The impetus for creating many of the institutions of the welfare state, such as Aid to Families with Dependent Children (the former national welfare program), was the need to care for war widows and their children. The massive growth of the federal budget deficit during the latter part of the century is largely attributable to the expenditure of billions of dollars on military institutions (Galbraith, 1995).

Elsewhere in the world, the dominance of military institutions and the fragility of legal and governmental institutions produce "garrison states" in which economic growth and the rule of law are subordinated to the needs of the military (Lasswell, 1941). The end of the cold war has led to political instability in middle Europe, parts of Africa, and many areas once dominated by the former Soviet Union. It has also caused unprecedented economic and social changes in Western Europe. Political instability in many regions of the world is used to justify continued military spending; in the United States, military spending still exceeds $250 billion annually. Environmentalists and other opponents of high levels of military expenditures argue that individuals cannot comprehend the magnitude of military spending unless it is presented in terms of trade-

offs indicating what alternative social choices would cost. Table 10.4 presents some examples of such trade-offs.

Modernization

A second major source of social change is the set of trends that are collectively known as **modernization**. This term encompasses all the changes that societies and individuals experience as a result of industrialization, urbanization, and the development of nation-states. These processes occurred during a period of two or more centuries in the Western nations and Japan, but they are taking place at a far more rapid rate in the former colonial societies that are today's new nations.

The term *modernization* should be used cautiously, in its sociological sense rather than as a value judgment about different societies. It does not mean that we can judge life in modern societies as better or more satisfactory or more humane than life was for people in societies like the one the Ebrié once knew. As noted earlier, modern societies have developed the capacity to cause more destruction and human suffering than any simpler society could possibly have caused. And we have seen in other chapters that many of the advantages enjoyed by the most modern nations have come at a high cost to simpler, less modern societies.

The concept of modernization does not assume that change is irreversible. For example, the rise of nation-states throughout the world during the past few centuries does not imply the end of loyalties based on a sense of "peoplehood" that conflict with the sense of shared citizenship in a nation (see Chapter 4). The bloodshed in the former Yugoslavia and in many places on the African continent bears heartrending witness to the strength of feelings about peoplehood as opposed to loyalty to the modern nation-state with its laws and governments.

Nevertheless, the term *modernization* summarizes most of the major changes, for better or worse, that societies throughout the world are experiencing, albeit at differing rates and with varying amounts of social disruption (Chirot, 1994a). Neil Smelser (1966) associates modernization with the following set of changes:

1. In the realm of technology, a developing society is changing from simple and traditionalized techniques toward the application of scientific knowledge.

2. In agriculture, the developing society evolves from subsistence farming toward the commercial production of agricultural goods. This means specialization in cash crops, purchase of nonagricultural products in the market, and often agricultural wage labor.

3. In industry, the developing society undergoes a transition from the use of human and animal power toward industrialization proper, or men working for wages at power-driven machines, which produce commodities marketed outside the community of production.

4. In ecological arrangements, the developing society moves from the farm and village toward urban concentrations. (pp. 110–111)

These processes can take place simultaneously, but this is not always the case. Many societies mechanize their agriculture and begin to produce cash crops for foreign markets before their cities and urban forms of employment have begun to grow rapidly. This was the case, for example, in Sri Lanka (formerly Ceylon), Indonesia, and many of the newer African nations.

Smelser and others who study modernization have shown that "technical, economic, and ecological changes ramify through the whole social and cultural fabric" (1966, p. 111). In the political sphere of life, we see the authority systems of the village yielding to domination by the institutions of nation-states. In the area of education, as societies attempt to produce workers who can meet the needs of new industries, new educational institutions are established. In the area of religion, the strength of organized religions has decreased. Families change as traditional extended families adapt to new economic institutions that demand greater mobility.

Patterns of inequality in societies also change. Older patterns of gender inequality are modified (and often replaced by new forms of inequality) as women are in greater demand to fill positions in new economic institutions. The emergence of a new class, the wage workers, increases the power of the common people, usually adding to their determination to become better educated and to participate more fully in political life. None of these changes is inevitable or irreversible; workers, for example, may see their unions "busted" in times of recession or economic change. In the long run, however, all of these trends are likely to appear in a modernizing society.

MODERNITY, TECHNOLOGY, AND "CULTURAL LAG" The central part that technology plays in modern societies has led some sociologists to view it as a basic principle of social change. The classic statement of this view is that of William Fielding Ogburn (1942). Ogburn hypothesized that inventions affect the size of populations, which in turn influences the course of history. (For example, overpopulation often leads to wars and migrations.) Some inventions affect population directly: Improvements in sanitation, the development of cures for fatal diseases, and more effective contraceptive techniques are examples. But inventions can also have indirect effects on population. For example, techniques that improve crop yields or permit long-term storage of food surpluses make it possible to support a larger population with a given amount of farmland. And improvements in military technology (e.g., the use of horses in warfare, the invention of gunpowder, and the development of the armored tank) have had dramatic effects on the conduct of war and hence on population size.

Ogburn also proposed the theory known as **cultural lag**. In his words, "A cultural lag occurs when one of two parts of culture which are correlated changes before or in greater degree than the other part does, thereby causing less adjustment between the two parts than existed previously" (1957, p. 167). This theory is most often applied to the adaptation of social institutions to changing technologies. For example, the Industrial Revolution gave birth to many kinds of machines, often with moving parts that made them dangerous to use. The rates of injury and death resulting from industrial accidents climbed rapidly in the decades following the introduction of the new machines to the United States around 1870. Such accidents spelled disaster for workers and their families because it was hard to prove that the employer was responsible for the accident. Not until around 1910 were the concepts of employer liability and workers' compensation adopted, a lag of about 40 years.

One problem with the cultural lag theory is that it fails to account for the effects of social power. For example, workers who sought compensation for the costs of industrial accidents did not have nearly as much power as the owners of the machines. When this power imbalance changed as a result of the labor movement, it became possible to enact legislation that would protect the workers.

THE POSTMODERNIST CRITIQUE   For more than two centuries, the forces of modernity have been changing societies throughout the world. In fact, all species of life on the earth are affected by these broad-ranging changes in the way humans exist. It is not surprising, then, that the forces of modernity also stimulate a wide variety of countertrends and reactions. The desire for gender and racial equality that accompanies modernity is countered by antifeminist and racial supremacy movements. The increasing influence of scientific thought is countered by revivals of fundamentalist religious beliefs and opposition to scientific education. The demand by some Christian conservative groups that public schools teach an anti-Darwinian view of creation, sometimes called "creation science," is an example of this trend in the United States.

Many other social movements are direct attacks on modernity itself or on specific aspects of modern thought. One of those aspects is *rationality*, which Max Weber viewed as a central principle of modernity (see Chapter 6). When applied to economic and governmental affairs, rationality fosters the development of bureaucracies, which, at least in principle, apply rational codes and regulations to the conduct of their affairs. The modern emphasis on rationality in scientific thought has been accompanied by an increase in *secularism*—separation of church and state, abolishment of state religions, and protection of free speech (including agnosticism and atheism). However, many critics point out that along with the bounty provided by scientific rationality have come the destructiveness of the nuclear age and the erosion of religious and ethical values.

In recent decades, the critique of modernity in the older developed nations has given rise to a diffuse school of thought known as *postmodernism* (Foucault, 1973, 1984; Lash, 1992). Postmodernism can be defined as a critique of modern societies and cultures. It argues that science, rationality, and all the "isms" of the modern world—capitalism, socialism, behaviorism, to name only a few—deprive human lives of spirituality, mystery, myth, and diversity of expression. Modern economic institutions transform popular forms of music and art into mass-produced products. Postmodernist critics also believe that the major institutions of modern societies, including markets, laboratories, clinics, the military, and

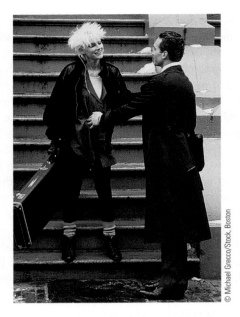

According to postmodernist theories, styles of dress and grooming and preferences for particular lifestyles and tastes in music will become ever more diverse. At the same time, there will be less and less consensus on what the norms of society should be.

other bureaucratically controlled administrations, have become instruments of social control by powerful elites (Harper, 1993). According to postmodernist theories (which in some ways resemble New Age ideas), this control is weakening as people feel increasingly estranged from modern institutions and turn to new expressions of fantasy, myth, sexuality, and styles of dress and architecture. In health care, for example, disillusionment with some aspects of modern medicine leads people to try a wide range of alternatives, such as folk healing, holistic medical practices, and remedies that have not been scientifically tested (Deierlein, 1994).

Postmodernism remains influential as a critique of modernity and an explanation for the proliferation of often zany styles and behaviors in today's world. It is especially popular in academic circles, but aside from stimulating the development of some new cultural products (e.g., styles of architecture that refer to many different periods), it has not had any perceptible influence on modern corporations or other bureaucracies. The postmodernist critique is an important reminder that modernization has many negative effects, but it has not stimulated social movements that seriously challenge the growing influence of modern social institutions such as global corporations. The same cannot be said for other antimodernist cultural movements, such as fundamentalism, as we will see shortly.

MODERNIZATION IN DEVELOPING NATIONS Social scientists often use the term *Third World* to refer to nations that have won independence from colonial dominance in the decades since World War II. If the "first world" is that of the capitalist nation-states and the "second world" that of the former communist nations, the Third World nations are those that are not aligned with either of these "worlds" but are united in their need to survive in an environment dominated by more politically or economically powerful nations.

But the term *Third World* can be misleading, since in the past 30 years many of these nations have made strides toward modernity. Moreover, trends in global social and economic change have produced impoverished areas—sometimes called the "fourth world"—in affluent nations where illegal immigrants or stigmatized minorities work under conditions similar to those found elsewhere in the Third World (Sassen, 1991, 1998). Therefore, we prefer to use the term *developing nations* or *modernizing nations*. A **developing nation** is undergoing a set of transformations whose effect is to increase the productivity of its people, their health, their literacy, and their ability to participate in political decision making. These transformations occur at different rates in different nations and different regions of the world. To measure modernization and compare rates of change in different nations or regions, sociologists use a variety of quantitative indicators, as explained in the Sociological Methods box on pages 274–275.

ANTIMODERNIST MOVEMENTS The theory of modernization as we have described it implies that modernization will occur in a similar fashion in every society. But the differing experiences of the developing nations call this view into question. Not only do we often see the industrialization of agriculture (i.e., the growth of huge mechanized farms) without the rise of industrial cities, or the growth of cities without a decline in the strength of organized religions or the emergence of modern educational institutions, but we also see the rise of antimodernist social movements in some of these nations (Randall, 1998). Events in the Islamic world are a case in point. In Algeria, Pakistan, Iran, Saudi Arabia, Libya, Sudan, and other Islamic nations, a fundamentalist religious movement has been gaining strength in the past quarter century. This resurgence of traditional Islamic beliefs and practices denies that modernization must be accompanied by the rejection of religious faith, by the separation of religion and government, or by more democratic political participation. These and other aspects of the Western version of modernity are being strongly challenged by the Islamic fundamentalist movement (Ashmawi, 1998; Naipaul, 1998; Rejwan, 1998).

Studies of these antimodernist movements are being conducted throughout the world. For example, in her studies of Algerian women confronting the antimodernist movement sweeping through the Arab nations, the Algerian-American sociologist Marnia Lazreg (1994) found that these movements are misnamed. In reality, she concludes, they are actually radical attempts to seize political power in which the movement's leaders use the religious fervor of the masses to achieve their goal.

The rise of antimodernist movements is not limited to the Islamic nations. Similar movements can be seen in the United States. Conservative groups plead for a return to more traditional values, and some radical groups advocate a return to self-sufficient communities that would engage in farming on a small scale. The effects of such movements on a society's institutions show that modernization does not necessarily follow a single direction or imply a single set of changes (e.g., the decline of religious faith, the rise of science, or the growth of industrial cities).

Another challenge to this view of modernization is posed by the fact that the world's resources of raw materials, water, and energy are far less plentiful than they once were. Today there are serious doubts about whether those resources are adequate to permit the poor nations to become developed to anywhere near the extent that the Western nations have, or whether the rich nations can continue to grow as they have in the past.

MODERNIZATION AND DEPENDENCY Some sociologists argue that the development of the more advanced modern nations actually impedes development in the newer nations, or at least channels it in directions that are not always beneficial. In a general statement of this theory, André Gunder Frank (1966) questioned the idea that the less developed societies are merely at an earlier stage of modernization than the advanced nations. He cited the development of one-crop economies in many parts of Latin America as evidence of how social forces in the developed nations actually transform the tropical countryside. According to Frank, when peasants give up subsistence agriculture and trading in local markets because their land has been absorbed into huge banana or coffee plantations, the result is a form of underdevelopment that did not exist before, one in which the peasantry is transformed into a class of landless rural laborers.

Immanuel Wallerstein (1974; Hopkins & Wallerstein, 1996) has proposed a more general theory that he calls *world system theory*. In this theory, he divides the world into core states, semiperipheral areas, and peripheral areas. The **core states** include the United States, England, France, Russia, Germany, and Japan, which are the most technologically advanced nations and which dominate the banking and financial functions of the world economy. The

SOCIOLOGICAL METHODS   Indicators of Social Change and Modernization

The basic measures of a nation's level of development and modernization are quite varied; there is no single set of indicators. But social scientists generally agree that population size and growth rate, population health, urbanization, and literacy, especially for females, are among the most important measures with which one can compare change over time among nations and regions.

1. **Population Change.** The preceding chapter introduced some of the basic measures of population growth, such as doubling time and crude rates. Another important rate is the *total fertility rate* (TFI), the average number of children a women would have, assuming that current age-specific birthrates remain constant throughout her childbearing years (ages 15–49). When the TFI reaches 2—that is, the average number of children per woman is two—the couple is said to just "replace themselves with two children." Populations with this low fertility rate will soon stabilize, meaning that they will not be growing as a result of "natural" increases. In

the United States, the TFI is 2.1, representing an extremely slow rate of natural increase, but the U.S. population is growing far more rapidly because of immigration. As we saw in the preceding chapter, a region or nation's population doubling time is a convenient measure of growth because it indicates how quickly extremely large numbers of people will be added to a population. Note that the doubling time for the world's population was about 51 years in 2000, but for the world's more developed nations it was 809 years.

2. **Population Health.** *Infant mortality,* the annual number of deaths of infants under age 1 per 1,000 live births, is an extremely important measure of a population's relative health. Most infants who die before they are 1 year old do so because of malnutrition, poor or absent pre- and postnatal care, infections caused by poor public health systems (especially contaminated drinking water), and other preventable illnesses. We will return in other chapters to this essential measure, but note

for now that in North America the rate is 7 (5.5 for Canada and 7.0 for the United States), while in very poor nations like Nigeria or Sudan, it is over 70.

3. **Life Expectancy.** *Life expectancy,* the number of years a newborn infant can expect to live, assuming current mortality levels, ranges from 79 years among women in more developed nations to a low of 60 years for men in less developed nations (excluding China).

4. **HIV/AIDS.** The percentage of adults aged 15 to 49 with HIV/AIDS is a measure of how well a region's or nation's health care system is doing in the face of a worldwide epidemic. High rates of AIDS infection will exert immense burdens on the economies, cultures, and social structures of nations and regions for decades to come.

5. **Economic Indicators.** A nation or region's *gross national product per capita* includes the value of all domestic and foreign output divided by total population. It is a quick measure of how much wealth per person an economy generates, but it does not indi-

---

semiperipheral areas are places like Spain and Portugal, the oil-producing nations of the Middle East, and Brazil and Mexico. In these areas, industry and financial institutions are developed to some extent, but they remain dependent on capital and technology provided by the core states. The **peripheral areas** include much of Africa, Asia, and Latin America. They supply basic resources and labor power to the core states and the semiperipheral areas. This world system, Wallerstein asserts, is based on various forms of economic domination and does not require political repression.

Wallerstein's theory has the drawback of suggesting that the so-called core states do not include any areas of production that may resemble the peripheral, dependent regions more than they do the fully modernized nations. Evidence suggests that even the most modern nations contain such regions. For example, in a study of share-

cropping in California, Miriam Wells (1996) showed that large California berry growers have been dividing their land into small plots and renting them to low-income farm laborers. Wells contends that the growers have adopted this strategy as a means of avoiding the higher costs of unionized farm labor. "The sharecropper is responsible for maintaining the plots, for harvesting and packing the fruit, and for hiring and paying whatever labor is necessary to accomplish these tasks" (p. 17). In return, the sharecropper receives from 50 to 55 percent of the proceeds minus the costs of handling, loading, hauling, and marketing the crop. Wells points out that modernization theory views sharecropping as an obsolete form of production, yet it can reappear even in the most advanced societies under certain conditions, such as lack of machinery for harvesting. Once again, therecate how well that wealth is actually distributed.

6. *Urbanization.* The percentage of a nation or region's population that is urbanized is a crude measure of how much of the rural–urban transition has occurred. This is not to say that urbanization should occur every-where because much urbanization is not accompanied by actual economic growth, but it does offer a quick comparative view of development, for better or worse.

The accompanying table presents these measures for the world as a whole and for selected regions of the world. Note the huge differences between the less developed and more developed nations. At the same time, it is important to recognize that, despite some reversals (due, for example, to the impact of AIDS), there have been significant improvements in these measures in many parts of the world.

INDICATORS OF SOCIAL CHANGE AND MODERNIZATION

	Total Fertility Rate	Doubling Time	Infant Mortality Rate	Life Expectancy		Percent with HIV	Percent Urban	GNP per Capita
				Male	Female			
World	1.3	51	56	65	69	1.1	46	$4,890
More Developed	0.1	809	8	72	79	0.3	75	19,480
Less Developed	1.6	42	61	63	66	1.4	40	1,260
Less Developed (excluding China)	1.9	36	67	61	64	1.9	30	1,450
Sub-Saharan Africa	2.5	27	94	49	52	8.6	30	520
North America	0.5	124	7	74	80	0.6	75	28,230
South America	1.6	42	31	67	73	0.5	79	4,270
South Central Asia (including India)	1.8	37	72	60	62	0.5	30	510
East Asia (including China)	0.8	85	30	70	74	0.1	42	3,880

Source: Data from Population Reference Bureau, 2000, 2001.

fore, we see that modernization is not a unilinear process with inevitable outcomes for every society or nation. People in all societies, including our own, experience social change in an infinite number of ways, as we see in the next section.

SOCIAL CHANGE IN EVERYDAY LIFE

People often experience social change as highly problematic, and they often blame themselves for not coping with it more effectively. But as we saw in Chapter 1, the sociological imagination requires that we ask how our own troubles are related to larger social forces. And we have seen that modernity brings with it many contradictions. In seeking new opportunities in education, leisure pursuits, intimate relationships, and political participation, we also create new problems for ourselves. Thus, according to social theorist Ralf Dahrendorf (1990), anomie has become an element of the lives of many people, especially those who are still on the way to attaining full membership in their societies. The Ebrié felt such anomie when their peaceful habit of sleeping outside their houses was shattered by a robbery.

In many parts of the world, the experience of anomie is even stronger and has stimulated extremely violent attacks on what are perceived as threats to traditional values and ways of life. An example is the anger against the United States and other Western nations that accompanied the

Gender Roles and the Family

The Sociological Observer

Will this Iranian child survive the vaccination experience? No doubt she will, and for her and billions of children throughout the world, the slight pain they suffer is a small price to pay for the eradication of devastating illnesses like polio and smallpox. But what other sociological observations can you make about this photo? What does the women's dress tell us about them? How does their dress compare with that seen in typical photos of women in Saudi Arabia or in Afghanistan under the Taliban? As you study the photo, what other questions or hypotheses about gender relations in Iranian society come to mind? (See page 287 for further insights into the sociological content of this photo.)

© Shepard Sherbell/Corbis Saba

attacks of September 11, 2001. Although the immediate political context of the terrorism was the Arab–Israeli conflict in the Middle East, many demonstrators voiced the belief that Western ways—including materialism, secularism, feminism, and other traits believed to be distinctly Western—were also being attacked.

Like most social theorists, Dahrendorf does not believe that we can or should attempt to reverse the course of modernization. Instead, he suggests, we need flexible institutions that can be adjusted without disruption. We are far from achieving such flexibility, however. When we look at the range of problems we encounter in our daily lives, we can readily see how much more change is needed. To appreciate this point more fully, it will be helpful to review some of the dilemmas of modern life that result from rapid social change. These and related topics are discussed in more detail in later chapters.

Clearly, one of the most significant social changes in Western societies in the past 30 years has been the changing definition of women's roles. The entry of women into the labor force is only one indicator of this aspect of social change. Today over 70 percent of all married women with children are at work in offices, factories, and other workplaces, compared with only about 4 percent in 1890 (*Statistical Abstract*, 2002). But it should be noted that there have always been subgroups in the population, especially African Americans and immigrants, for whom women's wages were necessary to the family's survival. Even among women who "kept house" a century ago, some 20 percent took in lodgers and earned cash in this fashion (Aldous, 1982; Modell & Hareven, 1973).

For both women and men, these changes often produce feelings of guilt and stress. One writer on the subject (Fallows, 1985) urged young mothers to reject career goals so that they could raise their children themselves. On the basis of observations of day care centers, she had concluded that day care is a poorly developed institution that cannot substitute for maternal care. Arguments of this nature are common. Other studies show, however, that high-quality day care does not impede a child's development. Moreover, advocates of gender equality question the assumption that child rearing should remain the primary role of women. This assumption has the effect of depriving women of opportunities to contribute their skills and talents to society. If day care is inadequate, a more practical response would be to improve it through public funding, education of child care workers, and the like, rather than forcing women to return to their traditional role as homemakers (Bergmann & Hartmann, 1995; Wrigley, 1995).

These arguments call attention to the need for more research on the future of families and other intimate groups in which children are reared. Some sociologists attempt to show how day care can be improved. Others conduct research on how people actually cope with changes in the household division of labor. Are we moving toward a "symmetrical society" in which men and women share equally in household and occupational pursuits? If so, the evidence suggests that we still have a long way to go. In an analysis of data from 555 couples, Carmi Schooler, Joanne Miller, and their associates (1985) found that typically the husband's sphere of household work "tends to be limited to household repairs, whereas wives are responsible for and actually do a vastly wider range of the household tasks" (p. 112).

Research on time use conducted by John Robinson confirms these findings. Robinson's analysis of detailed diaries of how men and women use their time each day shows that, on average, women spend about 30 hours per week on child care, housework, and family care, whereas

art *and the sociological eye*

Impressions of Social Change

Pierre-Auguste Renoir's painting of a gala scene in a nineteenth-century Parisian café is considered a masterpiece of impressionist modern art, but it also affords a glimpse into the immense changes that were occurring among Europe's middle classes in the late nineteenth century.

The impressionists, among whom Renoir was a pioneer, were rebelling against the strict rendering of pompous historical subjects that constituted "establishment art." They wanted to bring art outdoors, into the shimmering light of the everyday world. The impressionists were fascinated by the play of light on their subjects. They reveled in the freedom they felt to paint personal impressions of a scene rather than rendering it as if the canvas were a photographic plate. The scenes they captured, like this one in a café, were indicative of the social changes occurring around them. Here were women and men dancing in public. The women, especially, were exhibiting their dress and their emotions freely and in doing so were asserting their right to be full citizens of the modern city. No wonder the impressionists' art was considered daring and even dangerous by the cultural conservatives of their day.

Bal au Moulin de la Galette, by Pierre-Auguste Renoir, 1876. Oil on canvas, 51½" x 69".

Musee d'Orsay, Paris/Cliche des Musees Nationaux

men spend less than 10 hours per week on such activities. While men often assume other responsibilities for the family, including putting in extra time at work, the data show that they are not yet close to sharing equally in family chores (Robinson, 1988; Robinson & Godbey, 1997). Women who have young children and work full-time are the most harried segment of the population; they have only an average of 31 hours per week of free time, as opposed to 36 hours per week for women who stay home with their children.

Another major issue related to changes in the family is the requirement that welfare recipients work at paid jobs in order to remain eligible for welfare benefits. This policy also involves the matter of day care: Single parents must have adequate care for their children while they gain the skills and experience needed to enter the labor force. Are we willing, as a society, to invest in social-welfare institutions like day care? The answer awaits further debate and political conflict. So too does the question of what, if anything, we can do about problems like teenage pregnancy, sexually transmitted diseases, or high rates of divorce. Changes in values give us more choices and more opportunities to realize our potential as individuals, but at what cost to society (Rochon, 1998)?

Race and Ethnic Relations in a Postindustrial Society

Another significant area of social change is race relations. When we look at the bitter ethnic strife occurring in Rwanda or Kosovo, we often congratulate ourselves on the progress our society has made toward racial and ethnic equality. Racial discrimination in the United States, which until fairly recently was supported by laws in many parts of the nation and by informal norms elsewhere, has decreased a great deal as a result of the civil rights movement of the 1960s. Since that stormy decade, blacks have made gains in all of our society's major institutions. Voting rights, greater access to education and jobs, achievement in sports, and full civil rights for blacks are often taken for granted. Yet as the 1992 Los Angeles riots (prompted by the acquittal of the police officers who beat Rodney King) clearly demonstrated, much needs to be done to address racial inequality. In the words of philosopher and sociologist Cornel West:

> The verdict that sparked the incidents in Los Angeles was perceived to be wrong by the vast majority of Americans. But whites have often failed to acknowledge the widespread mistreatment of black people, especially black men, by law-enforcement agencies, which helped ignite the spark. The Rodney King verdict was merely the occasion for deep-seated rage to come to the surface. This rage is fed by the "silent" depression ravaging the country—in which real weekly wages of all American workers since 1973 declined nearly 20 percent, while at the same time wealth has been upwardly distributed.
>
> The exodus of stable industrial jobs from urban centers to cheaper labor markets here and abroad, housing policies that have created "chocolate cities and vanilla suburbs," white fear of black crime and the urban influx of poor Spanish-speaking and Asian immigrants—all have helped erode the tax-base of American cities just as the federal government has cut its supports and programs. The result is unemployment, hunger, homelessness, and sickness for millions. (1992, p. 24)

In the chapters that follow we delve far more deeply into the causes and consequences of inequalities of income, race, gender, and age, as well as their importance for social change. It is worth noting here, however, that West's critical observations signal some of the ways in which inequalities of wealth and opportunity overlap with inequalities of race and tend to exacerbate the problem of race relations in American society.

Changes in the economic structure of society supply the main explanation for the growing divergence between the haves and the have-nots. Manufacturing jobs and many kinds of blue-collar service jobs are becoming far less numerous, while the number of jobs in white-collar service industries like finance, insurance, and banking is growing rapidly. Despite high overall levels of employment during the 1990s, higher levels of production of high-technology items like computers have not yet made up for the loss of well-paid jobs in heavy manufacturing industries like steel, autos, glass, and rubber. Blacks and Hispanics are more severely affected by these changes because they have long depended on heavy industry as a source of jobs.

Environmental Politics and Policies

A third area in which social change touches the individual is public policy. *Public policies* are laws and administrative regulations that are formulated by governments to control, regulate, or guide behavior. What public policies are likely to emerge as the United States is transformed into a postindustrial society and as other regions of the world industrialize? Clearly, one area of policy that will gain in urgency involves measures to safeguard the earth's environment. The contemporary exploration of space, applying the most advanced technologies, has allowed us to see the planet as a whole, which in turn has stimulated the development of environmental thinking and efforts to develop policies that will reduce problems such as global warming. However, to the extent that environmental policies impinge on people's livelihoods and on their reproductive behavior, these policies are bound to be extremely controversial and difficult to formulate (Perutz, 1992).

Environmental issues like the exhaustion of food resources, the spread of deserts, the destruction of forests by acid rain, and the denuding of large tracts of land for fuelwood are fast gaining a high place on the agenda of world politics. Figure 10.1 shows that population growth in excess of food-producing capacity is occurring in the Middle East and many parts of Africa; that fuelwood is scarce in India, Africa, and eastern Brazil; and that deserts are expanding on all the continents. Victims of "food insecurity" (people who lack sufficient food for normal health and physical activity) now total more than 100 million (Brown, Flavin, & French, 1997).

What are the political implications of these physical and social conditions? Gro Harlem Brundtland, former chair of the World Commission on Environment and Development, answers that "to secure our common future, we need a new international ethic based on the realization that the issues

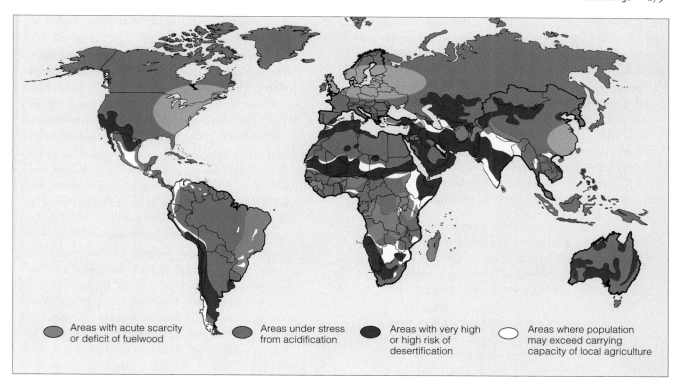

Figure 10.1   Worldwide Patterns of Environmental Stress

Land degradation results from a variety of human activities. Shown are regions threatened by overharvesting of firewood, acid rain, desertification, and stress induced by efforts to feed more people than the land is actually able to support.

Source: *World Watch*, 1998.

with which we wrestle are globally interconnected." The only way different nations can pursue their own self-interest, she adds, is for the United Nations or a similar world political body to become the institution in which environmental policy is made. And that policy cannot "insult the poor and tell them that they must remain in poverty to 'protect the environment'" (1989, p. 190). Clearly, the wealthy nations must make equal sacrifices to achieve a stable environment.

As the worldwide environmental crisis worsens, citizens of the United States and Canada will increasingly be faced with the need to regulate their economies and to end practices that contribute to pollution. This will be a costly and politically wrenching process, as evidenced by the difficulties encountered in developing policies for solid-waste disposal or the abatement of acid rain. A divided society, in which many people wish to be responsive to the environmental crisis but many others do not wish to think about it, is certain to produce conflict for years to come—unless a crisis such as flooding caused by global warming creates such an obvious threat that unity of purpose is achieved overnight. Thus we face a dilemma brought on by great changes in the environment coupled with slower changes in the ability of political institutions to deal with them. This situation points to the

need to look more closely at the models that sociologists use in assessing social change and predicting its course.

MODELS OF CHANGE

"We are such stuff as dreams are made on, and our little life is rounded with a sleep." These words from Shakespeare's *The Tempest* capture one of the basic difficulties of studying social change. In one short lifetime, we catch glimpses of our ability to create a better world, but we can never realize all our ambitions, nor can we know what will become of our achievements or the problems we leave to later generations. Terrorists may strike again; prices may shoot up again if inflation rates rise; long lines may form at gasoline pumps during a new oil shortage; or we may be faced with new medical problems like AIDS or dengue fever. To cope with these changes, we may join new social movements and attempt to build new institutions or work to improve the ones we already have. We may also record our desire for a better society in cultural products of all kinds—in poetry and plays and novels, in film and music, and perhaps in social-scientific studies. Yet we know that social change will continue after we are gone, and we wonder whether it is possible to foresee what will happen to our society and civilization in the distant future.

Sociologists have often attempted to develop models of social change that span many generations and predict the future of whole societies or civilizations. Of course, none of these theories can be tested using data from actual experience. As Robert Nisbet has observed, "None of us has ever seen a civilization die, and it is unimaginable, short of cosmic disaster or thermonuclear holocaust, that anyone ever will" (1969, p. 3). Instead, he continues:

> We see migrations and wars, dynasties toppled, governments overthrown, economic systems made affluent or poor; revolutions in power, privilege, and wealth. We see human beings born, mating, child-rearing, working, worshiping, playing, educating, writing, philosophizing, governing. We see generation succeeding generation, each new one accepting, modifying, rejecting in different proportions the works of preceding generations. We see, depending upon our moral or esthetic disposition, good and evil, greatness and meanness, tragedy, comedy, and bathos, nobility and baseness, success and failure. (p. 3)

Nisbet's point is that we can trace trends in all of these areas, but it is extremely difficult to develop theories that can explain them all and, more important, predict the decline of existing societies and civilizations or the rise of new ones. Even when we believe we are witnessing the birth of a new society out of the chaos of revolution or war, it takes many generations to distinguish what is truly new, in terms of culture and social structure, from what has been carried over from the past. Despite these difficulties, models of change that seek to predict the future of entire societies or civilizations can be helpful. They allow us at least to compare new ideas about social change with those that have been in use for many decades. In this section, therefore, we review the most significant models of large-scale social change that have been proposed by sociologists in the past two centuries.

Evolutionary Models

UNILINEAR MODELS   Many of the founders of sociology were strongly influenced by evolutionary views of social change even before Darwin's theory seemed to offer an analogy between biological and social evolution (Chirot, 1994a; Nisbet, 1969). The main components of the nineteenth-century evolutionary model are as follows:

1. *Social change is natural and constant.* Social order exists even while change occurs; social change, on the other hand, is the means of attaining higher levels of social order.

2. *Social evolution has a direction.* Societies become increasingly complex. Émile Durkheim, for example, viewed societies as evolving from simpler forms based on similar segments like villages into more complex forms based on division of labor and the resultant interdependence among ever-larger numbers of people.

3. *Social evolution is continuous.* Change occurs as a result of social forces acting within a society, even without exogenous influences like colonialism. This happens through a steady series of stages. Many, but not all, evolutionary theories interpret social change as progress toward better conditions of life.

4. *Change is necessary and proceeds from uniform causes.* Because social change occurs naturally, continuously, and from within, it must be necessary. In other words, whether or not we want change, it will occur because of the logic of social evolution. And social evolution will be similar in all societies because all societies are similar in their ways of dealing with the dilemmas of human existence.

Two assumptions implicit in the nineteenth-century model of social evolution have been strongly criticized by twentieth-century social scientists. The first is that all of the world's societies would eventually resemble those of Western Europe in their institutions and even in their cultural values and ideologies. The second is that social evolution represents progress.

Modern evolutionary theorists refer to earlier models as *unilinear* because they predict that all societies will inevitably come to resemble Western societies. A less ethnocentric version of evolutionary theory is found in *multilinear* models of social change. These models do not assume that large-scale change in a society represents progress, and they attempt to account for the values that are lost as well as for those that are gained.

MULTILINEAR MODELS   Multilinear models also emphasize that one must study each society separately in order to discover the evolutionary stages that are unique to a particular society as well as those that have been experienced by other societies (Lenski & Lenski, 1982; Sahlins, 1960; Steward, 1955). Thus societies like Ivory Coast, where the Ebrié live, have not developed much heavy industry and may never do so. On the other hand, Ivory Coast has a relatively advanced agricultural base that provides the surpluses needed for modernization to take place in other areas of social life.

Multilinear models can be useful in accounting for the erratic course of modernization in the Islamic world, or in helping the Ebrié in their attempts to understand what aspects of their village culture might remain viable even as their tribe becomes incorporated into a modern African state. But such models do not tell us why societies like Great Britain have declined from the heights of imperial power or why the ancient civilizations of Egypt and Rome flourished, declined, and are now known primarily through courses in ancient history and classics. An alternative viewpoint is found in cyclical theories of social change, which attempt to explain such phenomena by placing the possibility of decline at the same level as that of growth and "progress."

Cyclical Theories

OSWALD SPENGLER   In 1918, when Europe had been devastated by World War I, Oswald Spengler, a German schoolteacher turned historian, published a controversial book titled *The Decline of the West.* Spengler's gloomy thesis was that all societies pass through stages that are roughly equivalent to the life stages of human beings: infancy, youth, adulthood, and old age. The West, he argued, had passed through its maturity in the eighteenth century and was now experiencing a long period of decline. This process was inevitable and irreversible. There was nothing anyone could do to change its course.

ARNOLD TOYNBEE   A similar but more positive "rise and fall" theory of social change was developed by the British historian Arnold Toynbee (1972). In his "challenge and response" model, Toynbee suggested that all societies grow and decline as they respond to the challenges posed by their physical and social environments. For example, England needed to solve basic ecological problems, such as the fact that it is a small island nation with a limited supply of farmland. It responded by emphasizing foreign trade and using its superior naval power to protect its trade routes. When its naval power declined, it had to find new ways of meeting its challenges or face further decline. Thus, for Toynbee, the rise and fall of a society is accounted for by continual innovation in response to changes in its environment. However, although this theory is quite convincing as an explanation of history, it says little about what any particular society may expect in the way of challenges in the future.

PITIRIM SOROKIN   Pitirim Sorokin (1937), a Russian immigrant who greatly influenced American social theory in the early twentieth century, also developed a cyclical theory of social change. His theory attempted to account for why a society or civilization might change in a particular way. All societies, he wrote, are continually experiencing social change, and such change originates in their cultures because cultures are not unified but are marked by opposing sets of values, norms, and lifestyles. At one extreme of

a society's cultural system is its "ideational culture," so named because it stresses spiritual values, hard work, self-denial, and a strong moral code. At the other extreme is its "sensate culture." This set of cultural traits encourages sensory experiences, self-expression, and gratification of individual desires. Neither of these extremes can produce a stable society. Ideational culture results in benefits that are enjoyed by pleasure seekers in later generations, and the society will decline until this trend is reversed and ideational traits are emphasized once again. At some point in its history, a society may combine these two cultural tendencies. Then, according to Sorokin, it has reached its "idealistic point." But such a golden age is not likely to last forever.

Conflict Models

Cyclical theories of social change, with their cycles of rise and fall and their brief golden ages, may seem to confirm the common notion that history repeats itself (Chirot, 1994a). This notion is erroneous, however. Societies may experience similar events, such as wars or revolutions, at different times in their history, but the actual populations and issues involved are never exactly the same. More important, cyclical theories fail to deal with changes in social institutions or class structures. This is where conflict models of social change are most useful. They argue that conflict among groups with different amounts of power produces social change, which leads to a new system of social stratification, which in turn leads to further conflict and further change.

KARL MARX AND FRIEDRICH ENGELS   "The history of all hitherto existing societies," wrote Karl Marx and Friedrich Engels in *The Communist Manifesto* (1969/1848), "is the history of class struggles." As we see in the next chapter, social classes are defined by how people make their living or gain their wealth. Marx argued that struggles between classes (e.g., workers versus managers and company owners) are the source of social change in every period of history. In any society, the main conflicting classes will be the exploiters and the exploited: those who control the means of production and those whose labor power is necessary to make those means of production actually produce. The exploited workers could become a revolutionary class—that is, one that could bring about an entirely new social order. But this can occur only when changes in the means of production—for example, new technologies like the factory system—make older classes obsolete.

We know that revolutionary class conflict has not occurred in many capitalist societies, nor did the former communist societies of Eastern Europe or the Soviet Union succeed in eliminating worker exploitation. Yet as we look around the world at the struggles between the haves and the have-nots, the rulers and the ruled, the rich nations and the poorer nations, we cannot help but apply Marxian categories and test Marx's theory of social change over and over again.

RALF DAHRENDORF   Some modern conflict theorists depart from the Marxian view of social change, finding conflict among many different kinds of groups and in every social institution. For Ralf Dahrendorf (1990, 1997), this conflict produces social change at all times, but the change is not always revolutionary. We cannot change our laws, our bureaucracies, or even our families, for example, without first experiencing conflicts among various group and individual interests. An example of such a conflict is the controversy aroused by a statement by the Rev. Jerry Falwell, speaking on Pat Robertson's national television broadcast directly after the terrorist attacks of September 11, 2001. Falwell said that the American Civil Liberties Union, abortion providers, proponents of gay rights, and federal courts that had banned school prayer and legalized abortion had so weakened the United States spiritually that it was left exposed to terrorist attacks (Niebuhr, 2001). These comments were widely condemned in the United States and throughout the world, but they are a succinct statement of the resentment that a minority of people feel about changes that appear to them to be amoral. In most cases, however, only when severe anger or deprivation is experienced by whole classes or other major population groups are violent unrest and revolutionary social change likely to occur.

Functionalist Models

From a functionalist perspective, social change occurs as a result of population growth, changes in technology, social inequality, and efforts by different groups to meet their needs in a world of scarce resources. There is no prediction of rise and fall or unilinear changes like those we find in early evolutionary theory or even in classical Marxian theory. Instead, the functionalist model sees change as occurring on so many fronts that it seems incredible that society can exist at all.

One of the dominant figures in functionalist social theory, Talcott Parsons (1960), developed a *homeostatic* model of society. As change occurs, said Parsons, a society's institutions attempt to restore it to something approaching equilibrium. Conflict is minimized through the emergence of legitimate governing institutions; decisions are made about who governs and with what form and degree of authority. Adjustments are also made in economic institutions: New occupational roles develop; old roles decline; wages and status rankings such as occupational prestige ex-

plain who gets what rewards. Cultural institutions, schools, the arts, the media, and religious institutions maintain the shared values that support our feeling that our government is legitimate, that a certain amount of inequality is required to maintain individual initiative, and that opportunities are distributed as well as can be expected.

Parsons and other functionalist theorists do not contend that efforts to adapt to change, to create an integrated, well-functioning social system, always work. The integrated functioning of social institutions can be disrupted, sometimes severely, when some institutions experience rapid change while others are slow to adapt. Technological innovations in health care, for instance, make longer lives for some individuals possible at great expense, but other economic and political institutions have been slow to develop norms for distributing these costly benefits among the members of society and finding ways of paying for them. (All the models and theories of social change discussed in this section are summarized in the Study Chart on page 283.)

Applying Models of Change

The last two models we described—the conflict and functionalist models—clearly reflect two of the theoretical perspectives that are among the basic conceptual tools of sociology. They are most useful at the global or macro level of analysis, but they can also be used, along with the interactionist perspective, to explain social change at the micro and middle levels of social analysis.

How can we apply the basic sociological perspectives to understand what is happening to the Ebrié as they become part of a bustling West African city? Starting from an ecological viewpoint, we must ask how the Ebrié are managing to make the transition from rural to urban life. We see them becoming more dependent on a worldwide economy. Changes in the value of their nation's currency, for example, affect them now just as much as the failure of a yam crop might have in an earlier time. The interactionist perspective helps us listen as they speak about how these changes affect them. It lets us see how they are adapting to a life led largely among strangers. Functionalism helps us understand how some of their tribal institutions can survive in a modern society. We see new roles emerging, and at the same time we see old ones declining in the face of new values like those regarding the place of women in society. Finally, the conflict perspective tells us that a good part of the answer to how much of Ebrié culture will persist and how much will be lost depends on the extent to which the Ebrié resist assimilation into the national culture. Their struggle to maintain their language, their forms of worship, and their worldview will continue, even if it produces some conflict among themselves.

STUDY CHART

MODELS OF CHANGE

MODEL	DESCRIPTION
Evolutionary	
Unilinear	Social change is natural and constant, has a direction, and is continuous. Change is necessary and proceeds from uniform causes.
Multilinear	Large-scale change in a society does not represent progress. Each society must be studied separately to discover the evolutionary stages unique to it.
Cyclical	
Oswald Spengler	All societies pass through stages like the life stages of humans and eventually decline.
Arnold Toynbee	Societies grow and decline as they respond to the challenges posed by their physical and social environments.
Pitirim Sorokin	Social change originates in a society's culture, which alternates between "ideational" and "sensate."
Conflict	
Karl Marx	Social change results from conflict between social classes, which are defined by how people make their living or gain their wealth.
Ralf Dahrendorf	Social change results from conflicts among many different kinds of groups and in every social institution.
Functionalist	
Talcott Parsons	As change occurs, a society's institutions attempt to restore equilibrium.

CRITICAL SOCIOLOGY AND SOCIAL CHANGE

The New American Reality

Reynolds Farley is one of the leading demographers and students of social change in the United States. He is a master at using census data to chart the course of major social changes in U.S. society and culture. For Farley, the censuses conducted every 10 years "reveal social and economic trends in a uniquely rich and detailed matter . . . they reveal how people are now adapting—some with great success and others not well at all—to the massive social and economic trends that will make the United States of 2000 extremely different from what it was in generations past" (Farley, 1996, p. 1). Farley also uses large national surveys and opinion polls to supplement his demographic analyses of social trends. His analyses show how different generations of Americans have experienced the major events that have shaped their actions and values.

For social scientists who look at the effects of long-term and short-term trends, "social change occurs largely—but not entirely—on a cohort basis. The word *cohort* refers to all persons born in a specified time span" (Farley, 1996, p. 24). Generations differ most according to the social

forces and cultural values that influence their life decisions in their late adolescent and young adult years. People who were young adults at the outbreak of World War II, for example, were likely to have had their adult lives disrupted by military service or early widowhood; on the other hand, they benefited from the array of programs created to help veterans and their families after the war, including education scholarships (the GI bill) and subsidized housing loans. The early baby boomers, who became adults during the late 1960s, experienced major upheavals in sexual mores and attitudes about military service and gender and race relations. "Generation X" (as it is often called) includes some of the readers of this text, or their older siblings. This cohort "grew up after social values had changed, but they entered a competitive job market, one in which those with specialized training would do well, but those lacking it would have a much tougher time finding a high paying job than did their parents. Their standard of living will, quite likely, fall below that of their parents—the early baby boomers" (Farley, 1996, p. 24). Perhaps the generation of Americans who are now in their late teens and early twenties will be thought of as the "millennium generation." They will share many of the same opportunities and concerns as Generation X, but perhaps they will be more open to new political and cultural ideas, or, depending on the economic conditions they experience or their exposure to war and civil strife, their values may be channeled in directions that we cannot anticipate.

TABLE 10.5

Twentieth-Century Birth Cohorts

Years of Birth	Name of Cohort	Became Young Adults	Key Events at That Time	Ages in Census of			
				1960	1970	1980	1990
1966–1975	Generation X	Mid-1980s through 1990s	Era of economic polarization			5–14	15–24
1956–1965	Late baby boom	Mid-1970s through 1980s	Era of employment restructuring		5–14	15–24	25–34
1946–1955	Early baby boom	Mid-1960s through 1970s	Era of civil rights and sexual revolutions	5–14	15–24	25–34	35–44
1936–1945	World War II	Mid-1950s through 1960s	Post–World War II boom	15–24	25–34	35–44	45–54
1926–1935	Parents of the baby boom	Mid-1940s through 1950s	Post–World War II boom	25–34	35–44	45–54	55–64
1916–1925	Parents of the baby boom	Mid-1930s through 1940s	World War II	35–44	45–54	55–64	65–74
1906–1915	Grandparents of the baby boom	Mid-1920s through 1930s	Depression	45–54	55–64	65–74	75–84

Source: Farley, 1996.

In consequence, the cohort analysis of social change ends, for now, with Generation X (see Table 10.5).

For Reynolds Farley and other students of social change, cohorts are often identified by decade. The adult behavior of these cohorts has been influenced by many different events and changes, but few are more vivid than the civil rights movement and the gender revolution. The two oldest twentieth-century cohorts, the grandparents and parents of the baby boom generation (refer again to Table 10.5), are now in their advanced years. In their youth and early adulthood, the United States remained a racially segregated society—and thus it is no surprise that earlier in the century, when these older cohorts were coming of age, it was far more common than it is today for people to approve of segregation in jobs, transportation, neighborhoods, and education. Later cohorts, born after the civil rights era of the 1960s, are far more likely to express the antisegregationist opinions of their time (see Figure 10.2).

With regard to gender relations, women in the pre–baby boom cohorts were expected to become homemakers while their husbands worked outside the home. Even though millions of families did not conform to this cultural ideal, it remained the ideal, especially among more affluent Americans. In consequence, women were not expected to

Figure 10.2   Percentage of Whites Giving the Equal Opportunity Response to Questions About Principles of Racial Equity, 1940–1995

Source: Farley, 1996.

TABLE 10.6

Attitudes About Roles of Employed Women (by Birth Cohort)*

	Generation X Less Than 25	Late Baby Boom 25–34	Early Baby Boom 35–44	World War II 45–54	Parents of Baby Boom 55 and Over
It is more important for a wife to help her husband's career than to have one herself (% agree)					
Women	13	13	16	24	51
Men	20	17	17	29	47
It is better for everyone involved if the man is the achiever outside the home and the woman takes care of the home and family (% agree)					
Women	18	24	23	36	63
Men	29	28	32	42	67
A preschool child is likely to suffer if his or her mother works (% agree)					
Women	27	30	34	41	56
Men	47	42	46	55	69
A working mother can establish just as warm and secure a relationship with her children as a mother who does not work (% agree)					
Women	80	77	79	79	53
Men	69	64	61	55	43

*Column heads reflect cohort members' age in 1990.

Source: Farley, 1996.

aspire to the same levels of social, economic, intellectual, or artistic achievement as men. Table 10.6 and Figure 10.3 show the dramatic changes in these norms that occurred during the twentieth century, especially since the 1970s. We see significant change beginning with the World War II cohort, and the rate of change accelerates for the two baby boom cohorts and levels off in Generation X, in which there is a discernible return to more traditional attitudes among men. A comparison of Figures 10.2 and 10.3 also shows that there is far more consensus among white respondents on attitudes about race than on attitudes about gender.

No doubt cultural change along the critical dimensions of race and gender will continue, but what will the direction and magnitude of these changes be? Because of the uncertainties of global political and economic conditions, we cannot predict the answers to these questions. However, thanks to analyses of census and survey data by Farley and others, we have a good understanding of the behavior of earlier cohorts, making possible intelligent comparisons in the future.

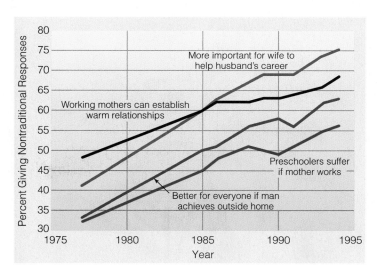

Figure 10.3   Percentage of National Sample Giving Liberal Responses to Questions About Women Combining Home and Labor Market Activities, 1975–1995

Source: Farley, 1996.

VISUAL SOCIOLOGY

SOCIAL CHANGE IN IVORY COAST

The Ebrié people with whom I lived and worked many years ago are now almost fully incorporated into the sprawling modern metropolis of Abidjan, the capital of Ivory Coast. But as these photos show, the Ebrié continue to maintain many aspects of their traditional way of life even as they continually adapt to the demands of an urban environment. Men and women who have become educated often commute across the lagoon from Blokosso to the commercial center of the city, where they work as managerial and professional employees. But other Ebrié, like the young women shown walking past a modern building, commute from the village to engage in commerce in one of the city's many open-air markets. These women are likely to wear the traditional sarong or pagne and gracefully carry their wares balanced on their heads.

Blokosso men still ply some of their traditional trades; outstanding among them is goldsmithing. Like many of the ethnic groups of this region of West Africa, including the Ashanti people of neighboring Ghana, the Ebrié culture has a rich tradition of jewelry making. Men and women proudly wear gold ornaments on feast days, and many of these highly ornate gold pieces are cast in the Ebrié villages of the Abidjan region, including Blokosso. When I left the village, one of my friends, Mr. Robert, gave me a gold elephant as a symbol of our years spent together.

The Ebrié people are mainly Christian, although many Muslims live in their villages as well. The village of Blokosso is home to one of the region's finest Harrist churches, shown here. Harris was an African missionary who preached an African form of Protestantism that became extremely popular earlier in the twentieth century among the lagoon peoples of Liberia, Ivory Coast, and Ghana. Harrist church ceremonies are lively and colorful, with many aspects of

© Betty Press/Woodfin Camp & Associates

Photograph by Eliot Elisofon, 1972. Slide no. HEBR 2, Eliot Elisofon Photographic Archives, National Museum of African Art

Independent Picture Service

traditional African music and dance incorporated into the Protestant service.

Over decades, as cities have developed around them, many of the Ebrié villages have become hemmed in by the crush of poorly housed urban migrants. Adjame, shown here, was once a peaceful Ebrié village but has become an urban slum. Does the same fate await Blokosso? Perhaps. But that village is fortunate to be located along the lagoon, along with luxury hotels and villas. It is unlikely that migrants to the region will crowd this part of the city. Thus the people of Blokosso are able to maintain their delicate balance between traditional and modern African ways of life, at least for the time being.

This lighthearted sculpture by a traditional African artist shows a missionary or colonial administrator being ferried around in a dugout canoe. Colonial regimes were a major exogenous source of social change.

The Sociological Observer
(See photo on page 276.)

The women are both wearing scarves that cover their hair, but their faces are fully visible, making it easier for them to get their work done. The mother and the physician are both women, and both appear from their dress to be from moderate Islamic religious backgrounds. Many Iranian women have attained relatively high levels of educa-

tion and are a major influence on the nation's democratic reform movement. Women like the doctor shown here often call for changes in the laws that will allow women to contribute fully to the development of their society and nation.

SUMMARY

The Nature of Social Change

- *Social change* refers to variations over time in the eco-logical ordering of populations and communities, in patterns of roles and social interactions, in the structure and functioning of institutions, and in the cultures of societies.

- Such changes can result from forces building within societies *(endogenous forces)* as well as from forces exerted from the outside *(exogenous forces)*.

- Changes at the micro, middle, and macro levels of social life usually are interrelated.

- No social change in human history has been as far-reaching and universal in its consequences as the transition to an urban, industrial way of life. However, not all people who are experiencing such changes think of them as progress. Nor can all forms of social change be controlled, although some changes are intentional. Similarly, while social scientists can understand and predict the master trends of their era, they have limited ability to anticipate major forms of change such as wars, social movements, or technological changes.

Two Forces of Social Change: War and Modernization

- One of the major forces that produce social change is war. The primary ecological effects of war are casualties and conquest. War also results in large-scale shifts in population and rapid acceleration of economic change. It can affect a society's culture in a variety of ways, and it may drastically change the structure of a society, especially its major social institutions.

- A second major source of social change is *modernization*—the changes that have taken place in societies throughout the world as a result of industrialization, urbanization, and the development of nation-states.

- These changes include a shift from simple techniques toward the application of scientific knowledge; an evo-lution from subsistence farming toward the commercial production of agricultural goods; a transition from the use of human and animal power toward the use of power-driven machines; and a movement from the farm and village toward urban concentrations. These processes may or may not take place simultaneously.

- Some sociologists view technology as a basic principle of social change. They recognize, however, that social institutions are often slow to adapt to changing tech-nologies. This recognition forms the basis of the theory known as *cultural lag*.

- Postmodernist critics argue that technology and rationality deprive human lives of spirituality; they also believe that major institutions of modern societies have become instruments of social control by powerful elites.

- The so-called Third World nations are those that have won independence from colonial dominance in the decades since World War II. Such nations are also called *developing nations* or modernizing nations. They are undergoing a set of transformations whose effect is to increase the productivity of their people, their health, their literacy, and their ability to participate in political decision making.

- Wallerstein's world system theory divides the world into *core states, semiperipheral areas,* and *peripheral areas.*

Social Change in Everyday Life

- People often experience social change as highly prob-lematic. In pursuing new opportunities in education, leisure activities, intimate relationships, and political participation, they may find themselves without a clear set of norms to guide their lives and hence may experience anomie.

- The entry of large numbers of women into the labor force, for example, has upset the traditional norms of family life.

- Similarly, the civil rights movement has greatly re-duced racial discrimination in the United States, but for a large proportion of the black population these gains have been offset by changes in the structure of the economy.

- A third area in which social change touches the indi-vidual is public policy, which may involve trade-offs between conflicting goals such as eliminating poverty and protecting the environment.

Models of Change

- Sociologists have often attempted to develop models of social change that can be used to predict the future of whole societies or civilizations.

- Many of the founders of sociology favored an evolu-tionary model in which social change is seen as nat-ural and constant; all societies inevitably become in-creasingly complex through a steady series of stages. Modern evolutionary theorists refer to such models as unilinear because they predict that all societies will undergo the same process of change.

- Multilinear models emphasize that one must study each society separately to discover the evolutionary stages that are unique to a particular society.

- A variety of theories have taken a cyclical view of social change, in which civilizations rise and fall, respond to a series of challenges, or alternate between two opposing sets of cultural values.

- Conflict theorists argue that conflict among groups with different amounts of power produces social change, which leads to a new system of social stratification, which in turn leads to further conflict and further change.

- From a functionalist perspective, social change occurs as a result of population growth, changes in technology, social inequality, and efforts by different groups to meet their needs in a world of scarce resources. The latter two perspectives can be applied to change at the micro and middle levels of social life as well as to macro-level changes.

GLOSSARY

social change: Variations over time in the ecological ordering of populations and communities, in patterns of roles and social interactions, in the structure and functioning of institutions, and in the cultures of societies. (p. 262)

endogenous force: Pressure for social change that builds within a society. (p. 262)

exogenous force: Pressure for social change that is exerted from outside a society. (p. 262)

modernization: A term used to describe the changes experienced by societies and individuals as a result of industrialization, urbanization, and the development of nation-states. (p. 270)

cultural lag: The time required for social institutions to adapt to a major technological change. (p. 271)

developing nation: A nation that is undergoing a set of transformations whose effect is to increase the productivity of its people, their health, their literacy, and their ability to participate in political decision making. (p. 273)

core state: A technologically advanced nation that has a dominant position in the world economy. (p. 273)

semiperipheral area: A state or region in which industry and financial institutions are developed to some extent but that remains dependent on capital and technology provided by other states. (p. 274)

peripheral area: A region that supplies basic resources and labor power to more advanced states. (p. 274)

cohort: All persons born in a specified time span. (p. 283)

INTERNET RESOURCES

Virtual Society: The Wadsworth Sociology Resource Center
(http://sociology.wadsworth.com)
At Virtual Society you can access a wide range of enrichment material to aid your study of sociology. From the main page, click on the Student Resources link and find your course and this textbook. Next, select the chapter you are presently studying from the pull-down menu. Among the useful options for each self-study chapter are online links and exercises, flashcards, practical study tips, and practice quizzes for each chapter.

MicroCase Online
From the Virtual Society home page, click on MicroCase Online to access book-specific MicroCase exercises that allow you to further explore sociological issues and principles presented in the text.

InfoTrac College Edition
Another unique option available to you at the Student Resources section at Virtual Society is InfoTrac College Edition, an online library with access to hundreds of scholarly and popular periodicals. Below are suggested search terms for this chapter, but this resource also allows you to fit your study of sociology to your own interests by searching custom keywords.

Social change
Modernization
War
Cultural lag

National Association of Community Action Agencies

Social Science Research Council
(www.ssrc.org)
A professional social science organization that has sponsored research on social change for many decades.

Sage Publications
(www.sagepub.com)
An online catalog of books and research monographs dealing with all aspects of social change, including works by sociologists in many nations.

An American who was born in the second half of the twentieth century has lived through events that dramatically changed the fortunes of many groups in the U.S. population. The economic growth and prosperity of the 1950s brought the promise of relative affluence for all, or almost all, Americans. Blue-collar workers and their families were encouraged to buy houses and cars, to take trips on the new interstate highway system, and to send their children to college. Blacks and other minority groups won major advances in civil rights and economic security. Women, too, increasingly rejected their status of cultural and economic inferiority. We will see in this

Social Divisions

part of the book, however, that these and other victories are incomplete. Social divisions remain, even though in some instances they are becoming less severe.

The next five chapters look in more detail at social inequality, particularly in American society. Chapter 11 shows how the members of a society are sorted into social layers, or strata, and how a society's stratification system changes as its economic and political structure changes. Chapter 12 deals with inequalities of social class. After a discussion of how inequalities are defined and measured, the chapter moves on to an analysis of how social inequalities caused by lack of wealth, education, prestige, and other rewards affect people's chances of achieving success and "the good life." Chapter 13 examines how present patterns of racial and ethnic inequality have evolved from historical patterns of intergroup hostility, conflict, and cooperation. In Chapters 14 and 15, we will see how the roles a culture defines as appropriate for women and men of different ages are related to patterns of inequality in that society.

chapter

11

Stratification and Global Inequality

© Miguel Rio Branco/Magnum Photos, Inc.

Sebastião Salgado, a Brazilian with training in the social sciences, is widely recognized as one of the world's foremost photographers. He travels throughout the world taking powerful photographs of people who are experiencing the wrenching consequences of changes in their traditional way of life. He has received awards for his photographic coverage of droughts in Africa and poverty throughout the world, but he may be best known for his global photo studies of the Industrial Revolution. Indeed, he terms his photos of women and men at work throughout the world "an archaeology of the industrial age." In Salgado's words: "Concepts of production and efficiency are changing, and, with them, the nature of work. The highly industrialized world is racing ahead and stumbling over the future. In reality, this telescoping of time is the result of the work of people throughout the world, although in practice it may benefit few" (1993, p. 7).

The developed world, of which the United States is the recognized superpower, contains one-fifth of the world's population but enjoys a far greater proportion of the world's wealth. As Salgado sees it: "The remaining four-fifths, who could theoretically benefit from surplus production, have no way of becoming consumers. They have transferred so many of their resources and wealth to the prosperous world that they have no way of achieving equality." Thus Salgado sees the world divided in many ways, especially on the basis of unequal access to wealth and power: "the first world in a crisis of excess, the third world in a crisis of need, and, at the end of the century, the second world—that built on socialism—in ruins" (1993, p. 7).

Although the affluent nations are undergoing rapid social change resulting from automation, the technological revolution in information processing, and the export of industrial jobs overseas, many of the world's poorer regions are still experiencing the first shocks of the Industrial Revolution. People who are desperate for income are forced out of their villages and into the industrial labor market. In consequence, since the beginning of the 1990s Salgado has followed the migrations of poor people all over the world as they seek better opportunities and living conditions outside their villages of birth (Loke, 2002). In Gujurat, India, for example, Salgado finds a dam being built that will irrigate an area of 185 million acres: "And in place of a desert, cotton and grain will grow." A large number of women are working on the dam. The men do the hardest physical work as "human bulldozers, tearing at the earth with the shoulders, legs, and hands. But the women carry the earth away" (1993, p. 19). They do this six days a week; "on the seventh day they stay home preparing food for the week ahead." Nevertheless, these workers, like so many of the others whom Salgado photographs, maintain their inner strength and their dignity.

This dignity and grace under severe conditions is the subject of some of Salgado's best photography, as illustrated in the Visual Sociology feature later in this chapter. Coal miners in India, working in temperatures of 120°F, descend daily into the mines while their wives, mothers, and daughters toil equally long hours under the hot sun. In Bangladesh, the Industrial Revolution centers on textile production, and Salgado finds scenes reminiscent of the "satanic" mills of the early nineteenth century that so shocked British reformers and socialists like Karl Marx and Friedrich Engels. In Spain, Salgado spends time photographing women working in the canning factories. Usually they are the wives of the fishermen he has also photographed as they tend nets in the face of storms and

FOCUS QUESTIONS:

• How are a society's patterns of inequality structured so that they are reproduced from one generation to the next?

• In what ways have individuals and societies attempted to change these structured forms of social inequality?

• What are some of the most important indicators of inequality among the world's nations?

declining catches. "The fish-freezing plants," Salgado writes, "are putting the canning industry out of business. . . . Fishing is no longer what it was, the old canning industry is dying, ancient factories are in a state of abandonment" (1993, p. 8).

Salgado succeeds in overcoming the "compassion fatigue" that many people in affluent nations experience when confronted by scenes of harsh working conditions, exploitation, and the faces of the "working poor." He does this by spending so much time with his subjects that his photographs transcend their woes and capture their dignity and indomitable spirit.

THE MEANING OF STRATIFICATION

Numerous social-scientific studies have demonstrated that all human societies produce some form of inequality (Bendix & Lipset, 1966; Harris, 1980; Murdock, 1949; Sen, 1992). In the simplest societies, this inequality may exist because one family's fields produce more than another's do, because one family has accumulated a greater herd than others have, or because one family has produced more brave warriors and thus has received more esteem from the other families in the tribe. In other societies, periods of scarcity caused by droughts, famines, or changes in the migration patterns of game animals may allow some clans or large families who were already relatively well-off to become wealthier and more powerful. These advantages may then be passed on to the next generation and become part of the society's social structure (Nussbaum & Sen, 1993; Temkin, 1993). But as societies become increasingly complex, encompassing ever-larger populations and more elaborate divisions of labor, these simple forms of inequality are replaced by more clearly defined systems for distributing rewards among members of the society. And those systems result in the classification of families and other social groups into rather well-defined layers, or *strata*. In each society, the various strata are defined by how much wealth people have, the kinds of work they do, whom they marry, and many aspects of life.

In this chapter, we will see how inequality in societies results in systems of social stratification that are a major feature of every society's social structure. Stratification is nonrandom in that each infant is born into a family that already has a particular place in the society's system of in-

equality, although some societies provide more opportunities than others for that same infant to move upward in the hierarchies of wealth, power, and honor (prestige). We will also see that while issues of poverty are especially important in the study of stratification, many other values besides wealth and poverty are distributed unequally in societies.

Social stratification is a society's system for ranking people and distributing rewards according to such attributes as income, wealth, power, prestige, age, sex, ethnicity, race, religion, and even celebrity. These ranking systems correspond to actual social structures, such as castes or classes, and they account for a great deal of what people experience in life—their pleasures and pains, their patterns of health and illness, their level of education, and much more. In this chapter, we will deal primarily with stratification by wealth, power, and prestige. The final section of the chapter is devoted to global stratification, with an emphasis on global poverty.

Caste, Class, and Social Mobility

In every society, people are grouped into different categories according to how they earn their living. This produces an imaginary set of horizontal social layers, or *strata*, that are more or less closed to entry by people from outside any given layer. Societies that maintain rigid boundaries between social strata are said to have **closed stratification systems;** societies in which the boundaries are easily crossed are said to have **open stratification systems.**

SOCIAL MOBILITY   In open societies, it is possible for some individuals and their families, and even entire communities, to move from one stratum to another; such movement is termed **social mobility.** A couple whose parents were unskilled workers may become educated, learn advanced job skills, and be able to afford a private house instead of renting a modest apartment as their parents did. Such a couple is said to experience **upward mobility.** If they have enough wealth to make their parents comfortable and to help other family members, the entire family may enjoy upward social mobility. If everyone with the same education and skills and the same occupation experiences greater prosperity and prestige, the entire occupational community is said to be upwardly mobile. But a family or community's fortunes can also decline. People with advanced skills—in engineering or higher education, for example—may find that there are too many of them around. They may not be able to afford the kind of housing, medical care, education for their children, and other benefits that they have come to expect. When this occurs, they are said to experience **downward mobility.**

CASTES   The best examples of closed societies are found in caste societies. **Castes** are social strata into which people are born and in which they remain for life. Membership in a caste is an **ascribed status** (a status acquired at birth) rather than an **achieved status** (one based on the efforts of the individual). Members of a particular caste cannot hope to leave that caste. Slaves and plantation owners formed a caste society in the United States before the Civil War. The slaves were captives; runaway slaves were pursued and returned to their masters. Their children were born into slavery. Plantation owners, on the other hand, had amassed great wealth, especially in the form of land, and this wealth was passed on to their children. On occasion a plantation family might lose its wealth, or another family might acquire a plantation and the wealth and prestige that went with it, but this form of social mobility was rather infrequent and did not alter the caste nature of the plantation system.

Today much of modern India remains influenced by caste-based inequalities. South Africa, on the other hand, is an example of a society that is moving away from a rigid caste system. Under apartheid, blacks in South Africa were a racially defined caste that was kept at the bottom-most rungs of the stratification order by violent repression and laws mandating racial segregation. Although this situation has been changing since the remarkable transition to majority African rule, the extreme poverty of the black population indicates that most aspects of the caste system are far from ended.

During the Persian Gulf War in 1991, many Americans discovered that Kuwait and other nations of the Middle East have strong ruling castes. In Kuwait, the ruling caste is composed mainly of members of a single large, immensely wealthy family—the Al-Sabahs—many of whom live on the Italian and French rivieras for much of the year. The Al-Sabahs rule Kuwait as a closed leadership caste, and after the Gulf War they were careful to reimpose their rule and forestall any democratic movement that could challenge their authority.

In India, the caste system remains extremely strong, but it is changing. The lowest castes are defined by the types of work they are assigned, usually work that is thought of as particularly unclean or shameful, like preparing the dead for cremation or cleaning toilets. Formerly known as the untouchables, these castes are now termed "scheduled" castes to signify their rights to affirmative action under the Indian constitution. In the more egalitarian and open society India is trying to establish, the scheduled castes are to gain rights and opportunities previously denied to them, but in the old India that persists in thousands of rural villages and even in the cities, the old notions of untouchability remain strong (De Zwart, 2000; Deshpande, 2000).

The Sociological Observer

Using mobile phones to communicate has become a norm in the developed world. In Bangladesh, which has one of the lowest telephone penetration rates in the world (three land lines per 1,000 people), the possession of modern communication technology can be significant. What are some possible ways in which this Bangladeshi villager's mobile phone might represent stratification in his society? How could it reflect his social mobility? (See page 316 for further insights into the sociological content of this photo.)

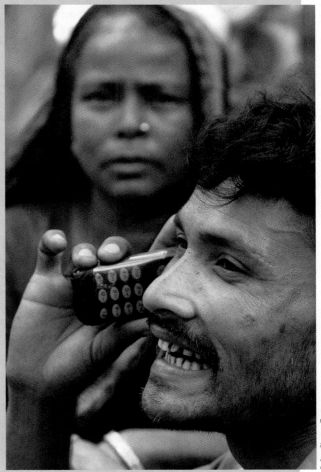

Rafiqur Rhaman/Reuters

CLASSES AND STATUS GROUPS   **Classes**, like castes, are social strata, but they are based primarily on economic criteria such as occupation, income, and wealth. England is famous for its social classes and for the extent to which social class defines how people are thought of and how they think of themselves. George Orwell, the author of

Animal Farm and *1984,* also wrote about the English class system earlier in the twentieth century, when he lived among the homeless and the migrant workers at the very bottom of the class system, and among miners whose lives were sacrificed to the dangers and diseases of the coal mines. In the following passage, he described how class affected his own life:

> All my notions—notions of good or evil, of pleasant and unpleasant, of funny and serious, of ugly and beautiful—are essentially middle class notions; my taste in books and food and clothes, my sense of honour, my table manners, my turns of speech, my accent, even the characteristic movements of my body, are the products of a special kind of upbringing and a special niche halfway up the social hierarchy. (quoted in Campbell, 1984)

Classes are generally open to entry by newcomers, at least to some extent, and in modern societies there tends to be a good deal of mobility between classes. Moreover, the classes of modern societies are not homogeneous—their members do not all share the same social rank. Within economically defined social classes, there are wide variations in social status—that is, in how much prestige individuals or groups are accorded in the wider society. Among very rich people, for example, one can identify different **status groups** such as the Kennedys, organized crime families, and the families of film stars or professional athletes.

The concept of status groups is illustrated by "high society." The nobility of England is one of the world's most prestigious status groups, despite the well-publicized marital troubles of the royal family. In the United States, people with names like Rockefeller, du Pont, Lowell, Roosevelt, Harriman, and many others, who are of Western European Protestant descent, often have more prestige than people with just as much wealth who are of Italian or Jewish or African-American descent. In cities throughout the United States, these very rich and prestigious families, who form a status group as defined by wealth and reputation, also tend to form groups that interact among themselves and play significant roles in their communities. The society pages of metropolitan newspapers devote most of their gossip to the philanthropic activities and private affairs of these families. Yet most of the old wealthy families in North America came from quite modest origins, as revealed by the underlying meanings of their names. Rockefeller, for example, means "a dweller in rye fields"; du Pont, "one who lives near the bridge"; Harriman, "a manservant"; Roosevelt, "one living near a rose field." Moreover, people with prestigious family names typically enjoy fortunes gained from activities that were once considered too lowly to permit entry into high society. Thus the Fords were looked down on by high society because their fortune was linked to "smelly gasoline"; the Whitneys, whose fortune a century ago spread over five states and 36,000 acres of palatial homes, were looked down on by older millionaire families because their funds were derived from 5-cent trolley fares rather than from railroad freight charges. In sum, both money and family prestige—gained by living expensively and engaging in public philanthropy—are required for entry into the highest levels of upper-class society (Domhoff, 1983; Hacker, 1997).

Life Chances

Rankings from high to low are only one aspect of social stratification. The way people live (often referred to as their *lifestyle*), the work they do, the quality of their food and housing, the education they can provide for their children, and the way they use their leisure time are all shaped by their place in the stratification system.

The way people are grouped with respect to access to scarce resources determines their **life chances**—that is, the opportunities they will have or be denied throughout life: the kind of education and health care they will receive, the occupations that will be open to them, how they will spend their retirement years—even where they will be buried. The place in a society's stratification system into which a person is born (be it a comfortable home, with access to good schools, doctors, and places to relax, or a home that suffers from the grinding stress of poverty) has an enormous impact on what he or she does and becomes throughout life. A poor child may overcome poverty and succeed, but the experience of struggling out of poverty will leave a permanent mark on his or her personality. And most people who are born poor will not attain affluence and leisure even in the most open society.

More than any other social condition, poverty has the greatest impact on people's life chances throughout the world. Figure 11.1 shows that, as measured by the number of people living on less than $1 a day, the level of poverty in the world rose rapidly during the twentieth century, reaching a peak after World War II. During the global economic boom of the 1990s, world poverty began to decline. Even with the recent improvements, however, there remain at least 1.2 billion people in the world who must subsist on less than $1 a day. Imagine trying to live on such a small amount! Even in the most impoverished regions of the world, where most people have relatively little, this is difficult. To subsist on so little means that one's life chances are greatly diminished, especially because of lack of medical care, schooling, and an adequate diet. Income is by no means the only indicator of life chances, but as people have more money at their disposal, their daily

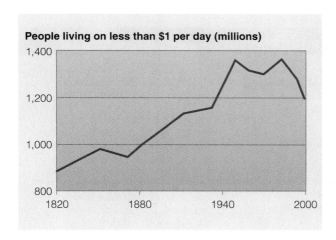

Figure 11.1 World Poverty, 1820–2000

Source: World Bank, 2003.

lives improve, as do their chances of mobility in their societies. People living in abject poverty, however, must spend most of their waking hours securing the bare necessities to remain alive.

STRATIFICATION AND THE MEANS OF EXISTENCE

The principal forces that produce stratification are related to the ways in which people earn their living. In the nonindustrial world, most people are small farmers or peasants. When they look up from their toil in the fields, they see members of higher social strata—the landlords, the moneylenders, the military chiefs, the religious leaders. These groups control the peasants' means of existence: the land and the resources needed to make it produce. Even when farmers or peasants are citizens of a modern nation-state

with the right to vote and to receive education, health care, and other benefits, when harvests are poor the landowners still take their full share while the peasants must make do with less. The system of stratification that determines their fate depends on how much the land can yield. In contrast, in the stratification systems of industrial societies, whether capitalist or socialist, most people are urban wage workers whose fates are determined by the managers of public or private firms. If the firms are no longer productive or consumers no longer desire their products, urban workers may lose their jobs and suffer economic hardship.

The stratification systems of the United States and Canada, where less than one-twentieth of the population works the land, are most relevant to understanding people's life chances in modern industrial societies. To understand the conditions of life for most of the world's population, we must study inequalities in rural villages, where more than two-thirds of the earth's people till the soil and fish the rivers and oceans (see Figure 11.2).

Stratification in Rural Villages

In 2000, the poorest 20 percent of the world's population earned a miserable 1.05 percent of the world's income, down from 1.4 percent in 1991 (UNDP, 2003). Although Figure 11.1 shows that there were important decreases in the number of people living in extreme poverty (less than $1 per day), income increased far faster among the more affluent than among the world's poorest (and we will see in Chapter 12 that the growing gap between the haves and the have-nots is also becoming more severe in the United States). Throughout the world, most impoverished people live in rural villages. Of course, not all rural agriculturists are impoverished, but in most of the developing world their situation is extremely difficult. In India and China, more than 1.2 billion people spend their lives coaxing an existence from the soil. Millions of other rural villagers squeeze a modest livelihood from the land in Central and

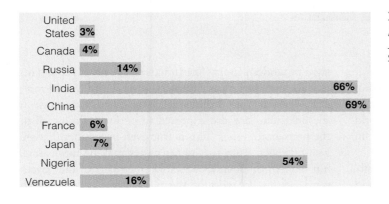

Figure 11.2 Percentage of Workforce Engaged in Agriculture, Various Countries

Source: Lye, 1995; World Bank, 2000.

GLOBAL SOCIAL CHANGE   Sweetness and Power

Sugar, tobacco, tea, coffee, cocoa, pepper—these and other substances derived from plants that thrive in tropical climates were once unknown in the colder regions of the earth. Of them all, sugar has had perhaps the greatest influence. Sugar can be combined with cocoa to produce chocolate, fermented to produce rum, refined and sold in its pure form, or baked in candy and confections of all kinds. An exotic crop known mainly to European royalty in the fifteenth century, sugar had become an addiction of the masses by the eighteenth century. The craving for sugar and rum stimulated the growth of slavery in the New World and the transformation of entire Caribbean islands into sugar plantations (Mintz, 1985).

Most people do not realize that even today the production of sugar requires extremely dangerous and debilitating labor. This is especially true in Florida, where soft soils prohibit mechanized

harvesting of the cane. Let a Jamaican sugar harvester who was brought to Florida as a contract worker continue the description:

In America, we work the roughest way to make a living. Coming over, they ask if you're willing to work seven days a week, willing to wash your own clothes, willing to eat poor, willing to obey, work in all style of weather, eat rice seven days. . . .

A lot of accident happen in the cane. When you working, your hand is sweaty, maybe the bill [cane knife] slip and fly up, maybe take your hand or your foot. Maybe take your partner. . . . Your hand become like part of a machine. Look at my palm, the bill rest here—it make a channel for its shape. When you go home, that one hand you have been cutting with you can't use. It's no good for anything else; you got to use the other one until it heal. . . .

We got to watch dangerous things . . . snake, bobcat, ants climbing up your pants leg to sting you, the cane stalk strike you in the eye, pierce your eardrum. Sometime to make money we got to eat no lunch, we got no time for it, sick and still working. . . . You got to be wise and understand yourself and be quiet, otherwise they send you home. It is very disappointing, the way we are treated. We are slaves. They pay us money, but really they buy us. (quoted in Wilkinson, 1989, pp. 56–57)

Investigations of working conditions for contract labor in Florida and other cane-producing areas of the United States have spurred sporadic efforts to improve conditions on the plantations, but little has changed. In fact, the officials of the cane-producing companies make free use of arbitrary firings and deportations, and they prefer foreign workers who can be easily controlled and summarily dismissed and sent home. A section of a report published by the Florida Fruit and Vegetable Growers Association, "Why Foreign Workers Are More Productive," explains how raw power maintains the flow of sugar:

The "unique and awesome form of management power" that sugar cane growers exert over their foreign workers provides a supermotivated workforce. As a Vice President of U.S. Sugar once said, "If I had a remedy comparable to breaching"— that is, firing and deporting—"an unsatisfactory worker which I could apply to the American worker, they'd work harder too." (quoted in Wilkinson, 1989, p. 64)

AP/Wide World Photos

South America, Africa, and Southeast Asia. Social divisions in these villages are based largely on land ownership and agrarian labor. Yet even in rural villages, inequalities of wealth and power are increasingly affected by world markets for agricultural goods and services, as shown in the Global Social Change box above.

In peasant societies, the farm family, which typically works a small plot of land, is the basic and most common productive group. Such families can be found in the vil-

lages of modern India. The Indian village reveals some important dimensions of stratification in Third World societies. For example, women are assigned to hard work in the fields and are also expected to perform almost all of the household duties. This is true even in families that are well-off. Men from the higher castes may be innovators, but women of all castes and male members of the "backward" castes do most of the productive work (Myrdal, 1965; Redfield, 1947).

In China before the communist revolution of the late 1940s and early 1950s, a feudal system of stratification organized the lives of peasants and gentry alike. Among the peasants, there were four broad strata (Tawney, 1966/1932). The rich peasants had enough land to meet their basic needs and to produce a surplus that could be converted into cash at local markets. They usually had one or more draft animals, and they often hired less fortunate villagers to help in their fields. The "middle peasants" were the second stratum of Chinese village life. They had a small plot of land, barely adequate shelter, and enough food and fuel to get through the winter. A small surplus in good years allowed them to own their own houses and even to have a few animals to provide meat on feast days. Only a very few of these "luxuries" were available to the third stratum, the poor peasants, and virtually none were to be had by the fourth and worst off, the tenants and hired laborers. Most Chinese peasants were in this impoverished stratum.

At the top of the stratification system of prerevolutionary China (i.e., above the rich peasants) were the gentry, the class of landowners whose holdings were large enough to allow them to live in relative comfort and freedom from labor:

> What made the lives of the gentry so enviable to the working peasants was the security they enjoyed from hunger and cold. They at least had a roof over their heads. They had warm clothes to wear. They had some silk finery for feast days, wedding celebrations, and funerals. . . . The true landlords among them did no manual labor either in the field or in the home. Hired laborers or tenants tilled the fields. Servant girls and domestic slaves cooked the meals, sewed, washed, and swept up. (Hinton, 1966, p. 37)

As our examples from contemporary India and prerevolutionary China show, in rural villages the facts of daily life are determined largely by one's place in the local system of agricultural production. The poor peasant family, with little or no land, hovers on the edge of economic disaster. Work is endless for adults and children alike. Meals are meager; shelter is skimpy; there is not much time for play. Among the gentry, who have large land holdings and hired help to ease the burdens of work, there are "the finer things of life": education, ample food and shelter, music and games to pass the time. Of course, wealth brings additional responsibilities. Participation in village or regional politics takes time away from pleasure, at least for some. So does charity work. But the power that comes with such activities provides opportunities to amass still more wealth. Thus, with few exceptions, the poor remain poor while the rich and powerful usually become richer and more powerful. And between the rich and the poor there are other strata—the middle peasants, the middle castes with skills to sell—whose members look longingly at the

pleasures of the rich and console themselves with the fact that at least they are not as unfortunate as the humble poor in the strata below them.

How does this scheme of social stratification compare with that found in industrial societies? We will see that there is more mobility in industrial societies but that, just as in rural societies, to be born into the lower strata is to be disadvantaged compared with people who are born into higher strata.

Stratification in Industrial Societies

STRUCTURAL MOBILITY The Industrial Revolution profoundly altered the stratification systems of rural societies. The mechanization of agriculture greatly decreased the number of people needed to work on the land, thereby largely eliminating the classes of peasants and farm laborers in some societies. This dimension of social change is often called **structural mobility:** An entire class is eliminated as a result of changes in the means of existence. As noted in Chapter 4, the Industrial Revolution transformed the United States from a nation in which almost 90 percent of the people worked in farming and related occupations into one in which less than 10 percent did so. Similar changes took place in England and most of the European nations and are now taking place in many other parts of the world.

But structural mobility did not end with the Industrial Revolution. Today automation, foreign competition, and technological advances are creating new patterns of structural mobility. Older smokestack industries like steel and rubber have been steadily losing factories and jobs; newer industries based on information and communication technologies have been creating plants and jobs, but the people who have become superfluous as a result of the closing of their plants are not always willing to move to new jobs and often are not trained to meet the demands of such jobs. Thus structural mobility often leads to demands for social policies like job training programs and unemployment insurance (Bluestone, 1992).

SPATIAL MOBILITY A second major change brought on by the Industrial Revolution was a tremendous increase in **spatial mobility** (or geographic mobility). This term refers to the movement of individuals, families, and larger groups from one location or community to another. The increase in spatial mobility resulted from the declining importance of the rural village and the increase in the importance of city-centered institutions such as markets, corporations, and governments. Increasingly one's place of work became separate from one's place of residence; people's allegiance to local communities was weakened by their need to move, both

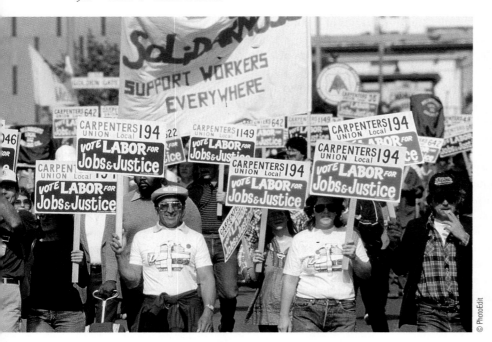

These men and women from the Carpenters Union are marching to demonstrate their solidarity with workers in other parts of the world. Labor unions like this one are organized to represent the social-class interests of workers.

their situation. But lack of power does not prevent people from rebelling against inequality. Many people also believe that their inferior place in the system is justified by their own failures or by the accident of their birth. If people who have good cause to rebel do not do so and instead support the existing stratification system, those who do wish to rebel may feel that their efforts will be fruitless.

Another reason people accept their place in a stratification system is that the system itself is part of their culture. Through socialization, we learn the cultural norms that justify our society's system of stratification. The rich learn how to act like rich people; the poor learn how to survive, and in so doing they tacitly accept being poor. Women and men learn to accept the places assigned to them, and so do the young and the old. Yet despite the powerful influence of socialization, at times large numbers of people rebel against their cultural conditioning. To understand their reasons for doing so, we need to examine the cultural foundations of stratification systems.

within the city and to other parts of the nation; and as a result social strata began to span entire nations. Working-class people created similar communities everywhere, as did the middle classes and the rich (Janowitz, 1978; Seligson & Passe-Smith, 1993).

Despite these immense changes, our relationship to the means of existence is still the main factor determining our position in our society's stratification system. We continue to define ourselves to one another first and foremost in terms of how we make a living: "I am a professor; she is a doctor; he is a steelworker." Once we have dealt with the essentials of our existence—essentials that say a great deal about the nature and the quality of our daily lives—we go on to talk about the things we like to do with our lives after work or after educating ourselves for future work.

STRATIFICATION AND CULTURE

Why do people accept their "place" in a stratification system, especially when they are at or near the bottom? One answer is that they have no choice; they lack not only wealth and opportunities but also the power to change

The Role of Ideology

You will recall from Chapter 3 that an ideology is a system of ideas and norms that all the members of a society are expected to believe in and act on without question. Every society appears to have ideologies that justify stratification and are used to socialize new generations to believe that existing patterns of inequality are legitimate. In the United States, for example, most people embrace the ideology of the American dream, the idea that in America anyone who works hard can achieve success and wealth. At the same time, we know that the odds of achieving great wealth are very low. This is one reason people love to hear stories about poor or hard-working people of modest means whose lives are transformed by sudden lottery winnings. In the nineteenth and early twentieth centuries, the "rags-to-riches" stories of Horatio Alger were extremely popular. In Alger's first novel, *Ragged Dick,* the central character is a poor but honest boy who comes to the city looking for work. As he walks the streets, he sees a runaway carriage; he leaps onto the horses and stops them. In the carriage is a beautiful young woman who turns out to have a rich father. The father takes Dick into his business, where he proves his great motivation and becomes highly successful.

The people of prerevolutionary China were also guided by ideology; they believed in the teachings of Confucius

(551–479 BC), which emphasized the need to accept one's place in a well-ordered, highly stratified society (McNeill, 1963). Similarly, the castes of Hindu India are supported by religious ideology. The *Rig-Veda* taught that Hindu society was, by divine will, divided into four castes, of which the Brahmins were the highest because they were responsible for religious ceremonies and sacrifices (Majundar, 1951; McNeill, 1963). Over time, other castes with other tasks were added to the system as the division of labor progressed and new occupations developed. Still another powerful ideology had its origins in Europe before the spread of Christianity. Tribal peoples in what is now France and Germany associated their kings with gods, and that association became stronger in the feudal era (Dodgson, 1987).

Religious teachings often serve as the ideologies of civilizations, explaining and justifying the stratification systems associated with them. But this relationship has not held in every historical period or for every religious movement. Originally, for example, the teachings of Jesus opposed the stratification systems of both the Roman Empire and the Jewish people. Jesus preached a gospel of love and claimed that "The last shall be first" and "It is easier for a camel to pass through the eye of a needle than for a rich man to enter heaven." He showed sympathy for prostitutes and outcasts such as moneylenders. No wonder his teachings appealed to the poor and downtrodden and enraged the wealthy and powerful. Over many centuries, however, Christ's teachings were incorporated into church doctrine and organization, and by the Middle Ages, Christianity was the ideology underlying the stratification system of kings, lords, merchants, and peasants. The vicars of the church upheld that system by affirming its legitimacy in coronations and royal weddings. They also presided over the execution of heretics who challenged the system, which was viewed as divinely ordained.

In our own era, the civil rights movement in the United States, the movement to end apartheid in South Africa, the struggle of the Northern Irish Catholics for independence from Britain, and other social movements often invoke the ideology of radical Christianity. "We Shall Overcome," the theme song of the civil rights movement, was borrowed from an African-American Baptist spiritual, "I Shall Overcome," and transformed into a moving song of hope and protest with religious overtones.

Stratification at the Micro Level

These relationships between religious ideologies and the stratification systems of civilizations are macro-level examples of how culture maintains stratification systems from one generation to the next. But we can also see the connection between culture and stratification in the micro-level interactions of daily life. The way we dress—whether we wear expensive designer clothes, off-the-rack apparel, or second-hand clothing from the Salvation Army—says a great deal about our place in the stratification system. So does the way we speak, as anyone knows who has been told to get rid of a Southern or Brooklyn accent in order to "get ahead." Our efforts to possess and display **status symbols**—material objects or behaviors that convey prestige—are encouraged by the billion-dollar advertising industry. Many other examples could be given, but here we will concentrate on two sets of norms that reinforce stratification at the micro level: the norms of *deference* and *demeanor* (Goldhamer & Shils, 1939).

DEFERENCE By **deference** we mean the "appreciation an individual shows of another to that other" (Goffman, 1958, pp. 488–489). In popular speech, the word *deference* is often used to indicate how one person should behave in the presence of another who is of higher status. Formulas for showing deference differ greatly within different subcultures. Among teenage gang members, for example, deference is shown through greeting rituals. Not performing those rituals properly may cause a gang member to feel

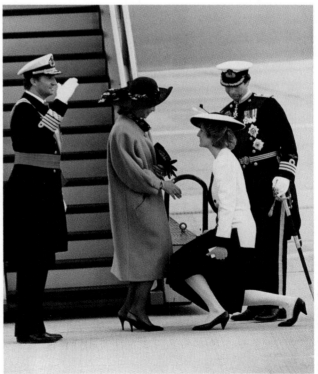

In this display of deference, the late Diana, Princess of Wales, curtsies to Queen Sofia and King Juan Carlos of Spain as she is introduced by Prince Charles.

"dissed" (disrespected), which can lead to violence. (Recall the discussion of "face work" in Chapter 5.) These formulas for showing deference illustrate how our society's stratification system is experienced in everyday life. In the United States, for example, we learn to address judges as "Your Honor" and feel embarrassed for the plaintiff who begins a sentence with "Excuse me, Judge." In most European countries, with their histories of more rigid stratification, people who want to show deference go further and address the judge as "Your Excellence."

But deference is not a one-way process. Erving Goffman has pointed out that the act of paying deference to someone in a higher status often obligates that other person to pay some form of deference in return: "High priests all over the world seem obliged to respond to offerings [of deference] with an equivalent of 'Bless you, my son'" (Goffman, 1958, p. 489). The point here is that deference is often symmetrical, in that both participants defer according to their place in the stratification system. Through deferent behavior and the appropriate response, both parties affirm their acceptance of the stratification system. Intuitively we all know this. When we are stopped by a police officer, we may become deferential, using the most polite forms of address ("Yes, sir," "No, sir," and the like) in order to avoid embarrassment. The officer, in turn, may attempt to find out our place in the stratification system and use the appropriate forms of address in speaking to us.

DEMEANOR   Our **demeanor** is the way we present ourselves—our body language, dress, speech, and manners. It conveys to others how much deference or respect we believe is due us. Here again the interaction can be symmetrical. The professor must make the first move toward informality in relations with students, for instance, but among professors of equal rank there is far more symmetry. The move toward informal demeanor, such as the use of first names, can be initiated by whomever feels most comfortable in his or her status. On the other hand, asymmetry in the use of names can be used to reinforce stratification, as in an office where the secretaries are addressed by their first names but address their supervisor by his or her last name plus a title such as Mr., Dr., or Professor.

STRATIFICATION AND SOCIAL INTERACTIONS   These largely taken for granted aspects of how we carry out or "construct" social stratification in our social interactions can have far-reaching effects. Maya Angelou, Richard Wright, and other African-American writers describe vividly the extreme shuffling and obsequious deference demanded of their parents in the era of segregation. Even to lift one's eyes to admire a white woman could cause trouble for a black man in the Jim Crow regions of the United States. And as we saw in Chapter 7, failure to carry out the rules of demeanor—to

twitch, to have a runny nose, to encroach on another person's space—can cause a person to be labeled deviant and to be cast out of the "acceptable" strata of society.

Deference, demeanor, and other ways in which we behave according to the micro-level norms of stratification further reinforce our sense of the correctness of those norms. Thus, in times of rebellion against a society's stratification system, those norms are explicitly rejected. During the 1960s, for example, students from wealthy families often wore jeans and tie-dyed shirts in social situations that would normally call for suits or dresses. Long hair and beards, refusal to wear a bra, and other symbolic acts in violation of generally accepted norms of demeanor were intended to communicate rejection of the society's stratification system.

POWER, AUTHORITY, AND STRATIFICATION

When the macro dimensions of social stratification change, the changes may be reflected in the behavior of people at the micro level, and those changes, in turn, accelerate change throughout the entire society. Thus, for example, the civil rights and women's movements have altered the norms of demeanor for blacks and women. Blacks insist on being referred to as blacks or African Americans if their ancestors were of African origin, rather than as Negroes. Women refuse to be called "girls" by men and especially by their supervisors, although some women continue to use the term among themselves. These may seem to be trivial matters, but when people demand respect in everyday interactions, they are demonstrating their determination to create social change at a more macro level—in other words, to bring about a realignment of social power.

Max Weber defined **power** as "the probability that one actor within a social relationship will be in a position to carry out his own will despite resistance" (1947, p. 152). This is a very general definition; it applies equally to a mugger with a gun and to an executive vice president ordering a secretary to get coffee for a visitor. But there is a big difference between the types of power used in these examples. In the first, illegitimate power is asserted through physical coercion. In the second, the secretary may not want to obey the vice president's orders yet recognizes that they are legitimate; that is, such orders are understood by everyone in the company to be within the vice president's power. This kind of power is called **authority**.

Even when power has been translated into authority, there remains the question of how authority originates and is maintained. This is a basic question in the study of stratification. As we saw earlier, the fact that people in lower strata accept their place in society requires that we examine not only the processes of socialization but also how power and authority are used to maintain existing relations among castes or classes.

A brief review of the causes of the French Revolution of 1789 provides a case study in the relationship between power and authority on one hand and stratification on the other: Why did the French people accept the rule of absolute monarchs for so long before they finally ended that rule in a bloody revolution? In answering this question, we can apply all the aspects of stratification discussed so far. We will begin with the feudal stratification system.

The major strata of French society, called *estates,* were the nobility, the clergy, the peasantry, and the bourgeoisie (merchants, shopkeepers, and artisans). Each estate had its own institutions and culture, causing its members to feel that they were part of a unified community with its own norms and values. The estates were linked together by the time-honored norms of feudalism: vassalage and fealty. A *vassal* was someone who received a grant of land from a lord. In return he swore *fealty,* an oath of service and loyalty, to that lord. The lord, in turn, swore fealty to a more powerful lord, until one reached the highest level of society, the king. (The feudal stratification system is described in detail in the Global Social Change box on page 304.) In such a well-ordered and legitimate system, where were the seeds of revolution? The answer lies in how power, authority, and changing modes of production combined to shake the foundations of feudal France.

In any system of stratification, there are likely to be conflicts. Those conflicts may be caused by the ambitions of a particular leader or group, but sometimes the characteristics of the system—and especially of the way its powerful members try to cope with change—create conflict. Both types of conflict existed in prerevolutionary France. In order to compete with the other major European powers, the king had to raise armies and send fleets abroad, both of which cost huge sums of money and required thousands of men. But the vow of fealty extended only from the king to the highest level of the nobility. The nobles, in turn, were responsible for seeing that their vassals provided more money and men. This system placed severe constraints on the king, who could not easily make direct demands on all his subjects. The king was dependent on the nobles and, through them, on the lesser lords. In return, the lesser lords often demanded more power, thereby challenging the king's authority. In order to reduce the power of the lords, the king went to the clergy and the bourgeoisie for assistance.

As the cities grew and the trading and manufacturing capacities of the bourgeoisie expanded, the king was increasingly successful at drawing on the wealth of the bourgeoisie and undermining the power of the feudal lords.

This engraving from prerevolutionary France depicts the bourgeoisie, or Third Estate, as a woman being forced to support the burden of the clergy and the nobility, the dominant "estates" before the revolution.

The court flourished; in fact, it seemed that the king's power had become absolute. Beneath the pomp and display of the court, however, the feudal stratification system was in ruins. The weakened nobility could no longer hold the fealty of the peasants. Throughout the countryside, the peasants groaned under the heavy debts imposed by their feudal masters, and they began to question the right of the nobility to tax them.

Meanwhile, in the cities and towns, the rapidly growing bourgeoisie, along with the new social stratum of urban workers, clearly understood that the king's power derived from their productive activities. They felt that they were not adequately rewarded for their support. At the same time, another new stratum, the intellectuals—people who had been educated outside the church and the court—was creating a new ideology and promoting it through new institutions like the press. This new ideology—"liberty, equality, fraternity"—helped spur revolutionary social movements, but the underlying cause of the revolution was a drastic change in the stratification system, in which the new middle class of wealthy business owners (the bourgeoisie) eventually challenged the ancient aristocracy.

In our own era, revolutions, social upheavals, and the wars often associated with them continue to occur in response to extremes of social stratification. In the early 1990s, for example, peasants in the impoverished province of Chiapas, Mexico, staged an uprising that shook the

GLOBAL SOCIAL CHANGE   **Feudal Relationships**

Imagine a peasant in a feudal society whose daughter wishes to marry a young man from another village. (The society could be medieval England in the time of King Arthur or present-day Afghanistan, where daily life for many people in rural areas is still governed by feudal relationships.) She cannot marry without the permission of the lord of the manor, who controls the destiny of everyone dwelling on his land. The peasant must wait for the day when the lord holds court, settling disputes and hearing petitions. Finally the day arrives. The peasant waits nervously until the reeve signals him to come forward. He approaches timidly, his wife following close behind. With the utmost humility he bows, pressing the knuckles of both hands against his forehead, while his wife makes the deepest possible curtsy. He makes his

request as briefly as possible and silently awaits the lord's reply.

Feudalism is a form of social organization that has appeared throughout the world as societies have experienced the so-called agrarian revolution. It took somewhat different forms in China, Africa, Japan, and Europe, but it has always been characterized

by a fundamental principle: the subordination of one person to another. As social historian Marc Bloch (1964) wrote, the essence of feudalism is "to be the 'man' of another man. . . . The Count was the 'man' of the king, as the serf was the 'man' of his manorial lord" (p. 145). In this system, known as *vassalage,* it was understood that women shared the loyalties of their male masters.

The swearing of *homage* signified and cemented the relationship of vassalage. In Bloch's words:

Imagine two men face to face; one wishing to serve, the other willing or anxious to be served. The

former puts his hands together and places them, thus joined, between the hands of the other man—a plain symbol of submission, the significance of which was sometimes further emphasized by a kneeling posture. At the same time, the person proffering his hands utters a few words— a very short declaration—by which he acknowledges himself to be the "man" of the person facing him. The chief and subordinate kiss each other on the mouth, symbolizing accord and friendship. Such were the gestures—very simple ones, eminently fitted to make an impression on minds so sensitive to visible things—which served to cement one of the strongest bonds known in the feudal era. (1964, pp. 145–146)

The basic relationship of feudalism, signified in the act of homage, is shown in the accompanying diagram. In essence, the vassal exchanges independence for protection, but this relationship can also entail more material exchanges: The lord can give his vassal a manor with the associated land and villagers, and the vassal can provide wealth and soldiers when the lord requires them.

Sociologists study feudalism and its relationships not only because some institutions derived from feudalism still exist today, but also because the exchange of independence for protection continues to appear in modern social institutions. For example, organized crime "families" often resemble feudal systems, as do many political party organizations and some business corporations. As people in contemporary societies like Afghanistan fight for greater equality in economic and legal institutions, they often demand an end to what they describe as - "paternalistic, feudal relations" in those institutions.

These Afghan men, members of the Hazara society, are loyal followers of Muhammed Karim Khalili, who led them in the fight against the Taliban. Each has sworn a vow of fealty to his lord. They are listening in rapt attention to his homecoming speech after he participated in the formation of a new government in Afghanistan in December 2001.

© Carolyn D. Smith

Although feudalism is no longer dominant, its former strength is reflected in the villages of southern France that date from that era. In those villages, perched amid the foothills of the Maritime Alps, the houses of commoners were clustered around a large chateau that dominated not only the village but also the surrounding agricultural fields.

political and economic institutions of Mexican society. The Chiapas peasants and their rebel leaders continue to press for reforms in the regional economy and government.

STRATIFICATION IN THE MODERN ERA

We saw in the preceding section that under the leadership of the bourgeoisie a new social order known as *capitalism* largely destroyed the feudal system. Capitalism is a form of economic organization based on private ownership and control of the means of production (land, machines, buildings, etc.). Whereas under feudalism land was viewed as belonging to a family as a matter of birthright, under capitalism land can be bought and sold like any other commodity. And whereas feudal labor systems were based on institutions like serfdom, in which peasants were bound to a particular lord, in capitalist systems workers are free to sell their labor to the highest bidder and to endure unemployment when work is unavailable. Capital-

ism is also an ideology based on the value of individual rights; the ideology of feudalism, in contrast, stressed the reciprocal obligations of different strata of society.

In descriptions by Karl Marx and other observers of nineteenth-century society, capitalism seemed almost to explode onto the world scene. Capitalism made possible the dramatic change in production methods that we call the Industrial Revolution, which transformed England and Europe from a world of towns and villages, courts and cathedrals to a world centered on markets, factories, and crowded cities. A few places where the physical structures of feudalism remain, such as Mont-St.-Michel in France or Dubrovnik in Croatia, continue to illustrate the contrast between the old order and the new.

The Industrial Revolution began in England and other parts of Europe in the late seventeenth century. Today it is still occurring in other parts of the world, including China, India, and Africa. The former colonial outposts of England, France, and Germany are only now undergoing the transformation from rural agrarian societies to urban industrial states in which an ever-decreasing portion of the population is engaged in farming. Although not all of these industrializing societies have capitalist economies, they all are developing a class of managers, entrepreneurs, and political power brokers who resemble the bourgeoisie of early capitalism.

The Great Transformation

It is not enough, however, to describe the Industrial Revolution in terms of the spread of industrial technology and urban settlement. Technological innovations such as the steam engine, the railroad, the mechanization of the textile industry, and new processes for making steel and mining coal were accompanied by equally important innovations in social institutions.

In the words of sociologist and historian Karl Polanyi (1944), the Industrial Revolution was a "Great Transformation." For the first time in human history, the market became the dominant institution of society. By *market* we do not refer only to the places where villagers sold produce or traded handicrafts. Rather, the market created by the Industrial Revolution was a social network that gradually extended over the entire world and linked buyers and sellers in a system that governed the distribution of goods of every imaginable type, services of all kinds, human labor power, and new forms of energy like coal and fuel oil.

Among other key elements of the Great Transformation were these:

- Goods, land, and labor were transformed into commodities whose value could be calculated and translated into a specific amount of gold or its equivalent—

that is, money (Marx, 1962/1867; Schumpeter, 1950; Weber, 1958/1922).

- Relationships that had been based on ascribed statuses were replaced with relationships based on contracts. A producer hired laborers, for example, rather than relying on kinship obligations or village loyalties to supply workers (Polanyi, 1944; Smith, 1910/1776).
- The business firm or corporation replaced the family, the manor, and the guild as the dominant economic institution (Weber, 1958/1922).
- Rural people, displaced from the land, began selling their labor for wages in factories and commercial firms in the cities (Davis, 1955).
- In the new industrial order, demands for full political rights and equality of opportunity, which originated with the bourgeoisie, slowly spread to the new class of wage workers, to the poor, and to women. This was especially true in societies in which revolutions created more open stratification systems (Bendix, 1969; de Tocqueville, 1980/1835; Mannheim, 1941).

The last point deserves further comment. The demand for full political rights originated with the bourgeoisie, which was to become the capitalist class in industrial societies—the owners of the factories, heavy equipment, and other means of producing wealth. To enhance their ability to do business and make profits, members of the bourgeoisie were interested in removing various feudal barriers to economic activity. They therefore called for an end to feudal restrictions on the sale of land, greater freedom for workers to move from one employer to another, the elimination of aristocratic privileges like the right to charge tolls for the use of roads and waterways that happened to cross a lord's property, and an end to voting rights based solely on aristocratic birth. These demands for economic and political rights then spread to the new class of wage workers and to other groups in society. Although the bourgeoisie originally sought rights for itself, it had to form alliances with workers and professionals in order to topple the feudal aristocracy. (Note that these demands originally applied only to men. As we will see in Chapter 14, similar movements for equal participation by women have taken many more generations to develop and gain influence.)

Class Consciousness and Class Conflict

The Great Transformation had a profound impact on the stratification systems of modern societies. It produced new and powerful social classes and thereby changed the way people thought about their life chances and the legitimacy of their society's institutions. As Marx wrote in the last chapter of *Capital,* "The owners merely of labor-power, owners of capital, and landowners, whose respective sources of income are wages, profit, and ground rent . . . constitute the three big classes of modern society based upon the capitalist mode of production" (1962/1867, pp. 862–863). Here, as elsewhere, Marx defined classes in terms of the "modes of production" that are characteristic of a society in a given historical period. The workers, by far the largest class in modern societies, must sell their labor to a capitalist or landowner in return for wages. The capitalists and landowners are far less numerous than the workers, but because they own and control the means of production, they command more of everything of value than the workers do.

Of course, Marx recognized that in societies that had not yet undergone the Great Transformation there were classes that were very different from those of capitalist societies. The peasants of Russia, the slaves of America, and the exploited Indians of Latin America were "precapitalist" classes. Marx predicted that these strata would eventually be transformed into what he termed the *proletariat,* workers who did not own the means of production and had to survive by selling their labor.

Marx believed that the class of wage workers created by capitalism would inevitably rise up against the capitalist class and create a classless socialist society. As noted earlier, this prediction was proved wrong: Proletarian revolutions never occurred in the most industrialized nations. Yet Marx's description of how members of the working class become conscious of their situation as a class remains an important subject in the study of stratification.

SOURCES OF CLASS CONFLICT   "The history of all hitherto existing societies is the history of class struggles," wrote Marx and his collaborator Friedrich Engels in *The Communist Manifesto* (1969/1848, p. 11). In the modern era, "society as a whole is more and more splitting up into two great hostile camps, into two great classes directly facing each other, bourgeoisie and proletariat" (p. 11). Why did Marx and other observers of the capitalist system believe that conflict between the bourgeoisie and the proletariat was inevitable? The answer can be found by taking a closer look at Marx's analysis of the evolution of capitalism.

To begin with, Marx observed the misery of industrial workers (many of whom were children) in the smoky factories of industrial England. He saw that however wretched the workers were, there would always be what he called a "reserve army" of unemployed people who were willing to work for lower wages than those who already had jobs. He noticed that the capitalists (and the intellectuals they paid to argue in their defense) always blamed the workers themselves for the miserable conditions in which they were forced to exist. If they were hungry, the capitalists claimed, it was because they did not work hard enough or spent their pay on too much alcohol or could not curb their sexual passions and bore too many children. Thus the capitalists refused to accept blame for the misery of the working class under capitalism.

Marx also argued that business competition would eliminate less successful firms and result in monopolies, which would control prices and wages and thereby contribute still more to the impoverishment of the workers. Moreover, the capitalists had the power to determine who ran the government and who controlled the police and the army. If the workers were to rebel, the armed forces and police would intervene as agents of the capitalists. Through these means, the workers and the unemployed would be forced to remain a huge, helpless population that could be manipulated by the capitalists. Over time, according to Marx and his followers, these masses of people would become increasingly conscious of their plight and would unite in a revolution that would destroy the power of the capitalists and their allies.

But why would workers become more conscious of their situation as a class, rather than merely remaining miserable in their impoverished families and communities? This problem of class consciousness became a central issue in Marxian thought. The study of changing patterns of class consciousness remains a major subject in sociology to this day.

OBJECTIVE AND SUBJECTIVE CLASSES In thinking about how a social class might be able to take collective action, revolutionary or otherwise, Marx distinguished between *objective* and *subjective* classes. All capitalist societies, according to Marx, have **objective classes**—social classes that an observer can identify by simply looking at people's visible, specific relationships to the means of production in their society. The workers, for example, are easily identified as an objective class that does not own the means of production and sells its labor power in return for wages. The capitalists are the objective class that owns the means of production—the machines and property and railroads—and buys the labor power of the working class.

These facts would be visible to an observer equipped with an understanding of what makes a social class, but they might not always be evident to the members of those classes themselves. Thus Marx identified **subjective class** as the extent to which the people in a given stratum of society actually perceive their situation as a class. For example, if the workers in the chicken processing industry in the southern United States are not aware that their low wages and miserable working conditions are similar to the conditions faced by millions of workers in other industries elsewhere in the world, and if they do not understand that

they can improve their fortunes only by taking some of the power of another class (the capitalists), they are not yet a subjective class. Without this awareness of their situation, the workers are said to lack **class consciousness.** And without class consciousness, they cannot form the political associations that will allow them to fight effectively against the capitalists.

In an often quoted passage, Marx described the peasants of France as an objective class because of their shared experience as agriculturists with small landholdings, but he was doubtful about their ability to form a subjective class:

> A small holding, a peasant and his family; alongside them another small holding, another peasant and another family. A few score of these make up a village, and a few score of villages make up a Department. In this way, the great mass of the French nation is formed by simple addition of homologous magnitudes, much as potatoes in a sack form a sack of potatoes. . . . In so far as there is merely a local interconnection among these small holding peasants, and the identity of their interests begets no community, no national bond and no political organization among them, they do not form a class. (1963/1869, p. 124)

The working class, Marx believed, would be different from the peasantry because its members would become conscious of their shared interests as a class.

THE CLASSLESS SOCIETY Marx and other observers of early capitalism believed that the growing conflict between the working class, or proletariat, and the capitalist class, or bourgeoisie, would produce revolutions. In those revolutions, the proletariat and its allies would depose the bourgeoisie and establish a new social order known as socialism. Under socialism, the key institutions of capitalism—private ownership of the means of production, the market as the dominant economic institution, and the nation-state controlled by the bourgeoisie—would be abolished. The new society would be classless because the economic institutions that produced classes would have been eliminated and all the members of society would collectively own the means of production.

In fact, Soviet-style socialism as it developed under the Bolshevik dictatorship of Lenin and then Joseph Stalin did not produce a classless society. After the revolution of 1917, a new class of Communist party officials, military generals, and government bureaucrats, known as the *nomenklatura,* replaced the older aristocratic ruling class. As the communist elite used its power to secure privileges that were not granted to those in the lower classes, the Marxian dream of a classless society gave way to cynicism. And in the years since the demise of the Soviet Union, the

THEN AND NOW   Bolsheviks and Capitalists

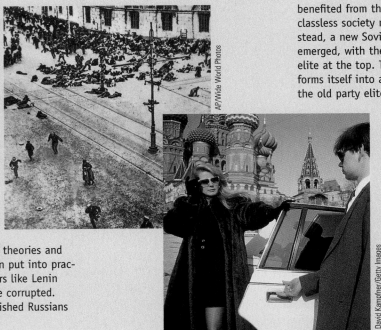

Much of the social thought and ideology of the twentieth century was shaped by the Russian Revolution. The Bolsheviks, shown here storming the Winter Palace, put an end to the reign of the Russian czars and kindled hopes for a classless society not just among their own followers but among impoverished and politically repressed people throughout the world. However, the theories and ideals of socialism, when put into practice by dictatorial leaders like Lenin and Stalin, soon became corrupted. Although many impoverished Russians benefited from the revolution, the classless society never emerged. Instead, a new Soviet class system emerged, with the Communist party elite at the top. Today, as Russia transforms itself into a capitalist nation, the old party elite and the newly rich class of entrepreneurs are combining to form a powerful new class at the top of Russian society. Other classes, especially blue-collar workers who were protected under Soviet socialism, are experiencing downward mobility, at least during the painful transition to a new social order.

extremely rapid conversion of the economy from socialism to capitalism has created an entirely new class of self-made millionaires. Elsewhere in the world, however, in societies that did not experience the abuses and rigidity of Soviet communism, the Marxian view of class struggle remains one of the powerful forces generating social movements to reduce inequality.

Social Mobility in Modern Societies: The Weberian View

Well before the failure of Soviet communism, Max Weber took issue with Marx's view of social stratification. Marx had defined social class in economic terms; classes are based on people's relationship to the means of production. Weber challenged this definition of social class. People are stratified, Weber reasoned, not only by how they earn their living but also by how much honor or prestige they receive from others and how much power they command. A person could be a poor European aristocrat whose lands had been taken away during a revolution, yet his prestige could be such that he would be invited to the homes of

wealthy families seeking to use his social status to raise their own. Another person could have little money compared with the wealthy capitalists, and little prestige compared with the European aristocracy, yet could command immense power. The late Mayor Richard J. Daley of Chicago (the father of the present mayor) was such a person. He was born into a working-class Irish-American family, and although he was rather well-off he was not rich. Yet his positions as mayor and chair of the Cook County Democratic party organization made him a powerful man. Indeed, Mayor Daley's fame as a politician who led a powerful urban party organization but did not enrich himself in doing so helped his son continue the family tradition of political leadership: In 1989 his son, Richard M. Daley, was elected mayor of Chicago.

For Weber and many other sociologists, therefore, wealth or economic position is only one of at least three dimensions of stratification that need to be considered in defining social class. Prestige (or social status) and power are the others. We need to think of modern stratification systems as ranking people on all of these dimensions. A high ranking in terms of wealth does not always guarantee a high ranking in terms of prestige or power, although they often go together.

STUDY CHART

MARX AND WEBER ON STRATIFICATION

	ORIGINS OF STRATIFICATION	HOW IS STRATIFICATION MAINTAINED?	WHAT CHANGES STRUCTURES OF STRATIFICATION?
Karl Marx	Economic: based on different populations' relationship to means of production in a given society	By the power of dominant castes or ruling classes over all other groups and institutions	Class conflict and revolution due to the rise of new classes (e.g., the bourgeoisie in feudal or aristocratic societies) or conflict between the proletariat and the bourgeoisie in capitalist societies
Max Weber	Economic and cultural: based on relationship to the dominant means of production and degree of honor and power given to one's occupation or family in the community or culture	By the power of ruling castes and classes, as well as by the honor and prestige conferred on the rich and powerful in religion and politics	Not just class conflict but also social mobility and new means of gaining power (e.g., through party politics in democracies)

Other challenges to Marx's view of stratification focus on social mobility in industrial societies. Contrary to Marx's prediction, modern societies have not become polarized into two great classes, the rich and the poor. Instead, there is a large middle class of people who are neither industrial workers nor capitalists (Wright, 1989, 1997), and there is considerable social mobility, or movement from one class to another. (See the Study Chart above.)

FORMS OF SOCIAL MOBILITY   Social mobility can be measured either within or between generations. These two kinds of mobility are termed *intragenerational* and *intergenerational* mobility. (See the Study Chart on page 310.) **Intragenerational mobility** refers to one's chances of rising to or falling from one social class to another within one's own lifetime. **Intergenerational mobility** is usually measured by comparing the social-class position of children with that of their parents. If there is a great deal of stability from one generation to the next, one can conclude that the stratification system is relatively rigid.

Unfortunately, not all mobility is upward. Downward mobility involves loss of economic and social standing. It is a problem for families and individuals at all levels of the class structure in the United States and elsewhere. In its broadest sense, downward mobility can be defined as "losing one's place in society" (Newman, 1988, p. 7). In fact, the term encompasses many different kinds of experiences. The married woman who works part-time and then is divorced, loses the family house, and must move with her children to a small apartment and work full-time is experiencing downward mobility. The couple who have been living with the wife's mother in public housing and are forced out during a check of official rosters and must

seek refuge in a homeless shelter also experience downward mobility. The affluent young couple living in a downtown condominium experience downward mobility when he loses his job at a brokerage firm and she must go on maternity leave while he is looking for a new job. Often entire groups of people experience downward mobility, as happened to U.S. citizens of Japanese descent when their property was confiscated during World War II, and to people of Indian descent when they were expelled from Kenya and Uganda in the 1970s.

The General Social Survey, conducted annually by the National Opinion Research Center (NORC), charts changes in people's opinions about their prospects for mobility in either direction, using questions like these:

> Compared to your parents when they were the age you are now, do you think your own standard of living now is much better, somewhat better, about the same, somewhat worse, or much worse than theirs was?
>
> When your children are at the age you are now, do you think their standard of living will be much better, somewhat better, about the same, somewhat worse, or much worse than yours is now? (NORC, 2000)

Fear of downward mobility weighs heavily on the minds of many Americans. A central feature of the American dream is that our standard of living, and that of our children, will continue to improve. But that vision is challenged by the realities of global competition and the "export" of jobs to lower-wage regions of the world (Block, 1990; Harrison, Tilly, & Bluestone, 1986). Indeed, the findings of the General Social Survey show

TYPES OF SOCIAL MOBILITY

TYPE	DESCRIPTION	EXAMPLE
Structural	Entire occupations emerge and grow rapidly while others decline because of technological or other major changes.	Workers in high-tech industries (e.g., computers); farmers.
Individual or Family *Intergenerational*	Children experience mobility in either direction in comparison with their parents.	Upward—father a blue-collar worker, son a lawyer; daughter a professor, mother a factory worker. Downward—parents professionals, children waiters and aspiring actors.
Intragenerational	A person experiences an upward or downward shift in economic and social status.	A steelworker becomes a janitor, earning less; his wife goes to work to help make ends meet.

that more respondents claim to have experienced an improvement in their standard of living compared to their parents than believe their children will also enjoy such mobility. These results are presented in Figure 11.3. We will see in later chapters that this doubt about future opportunities for one's children is an extremely powerful force in contemporary politics.

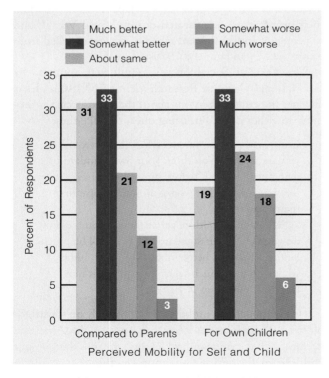

Figure 11.3   Perceptions of Mobility Opportunities (Respondent's Own and Children's)

Source: NORC, 2000.

THEORIES OF STRATIFICATION

"The first lesson of modern sociology," wrote C. Wright Mills in his study of white-collar workers, "is that the individual cannot understand his own experience or gauge his own fate without locating himself within the trends of his epoch and the life-chances of all the individuals of his social layer" (1951, p. xx). We have examined the concepts of stratification and life chances and have seen that they are related to the way people earn their living in different societies. But what about the origins of "social layering" or stratification? That subject will be discussed in the next chapter with specific reference to the social-class system of the United States and other nations. In this section, we examine some of the basic theories of social stratification. Each of the major sociological perspectives continues to generate important insights into how stratification and inequality emerge and operate in different societies.

Conflict Theories

As mentioned earlier, Marx's theory of stratification asserts that capitalist societies are divided into two opposing classes, wage workers and capitalists, and that conflict between these two classes will eventually lead to revolutions that will establish classless socialist societies. However, Marx's prediction was not borne out in any society that attempted to implement his ideas on a large scale. Deny it as they might, all of those societies developed well-defined systems of social stratification (Aronowitz, 2003; Djilas, 1982; Szelenyi, 1983). Each had an elite of high party officials; an upper stratum of higher professionals, scientists, managers of economic enterprises, local party officials, and high police officials; a middle level of well-educated technical workers and lower professionals; a proletariat of industrial and clerical workers and military personnel; and a bottom layer of people who were disabled, criminals, or political outcasts.

No persuasive evidence shows that class conflict is heightening the division between workers and owners of capital in capitalist societies. Conflict does exist, but the industrial working class is shrinking and the new occupational groups do not always share the concerns of the industrial workers. Moreover, reforms of capitalist institutions have greatly improved the workers' situation, thereby reducing the likelihood that the revolution predicted by Marx will occur.

Modern conflict theorists agree with Marx's claim that class conflict is a primary cause of social change, but they frequently debate both the nature of the class structure and the forms taken by class conflict. Thus Erik Olin Wright (1979, 1997) notes that Marxian theorists agree that workers who are directly engaged in the production of goods are part of the working class. However, he makes the following observation:

> There is no such agreement about any other category of wage-earners. Some Marxists have argued that only productive manual workers should be considered part of the proletariat. Others have argued that the working class includes low-level, routinized white-collar workers as well. Still others have argued that virtually all wage-laborers should be considered part of the working class. (1979, p. 31)

This disagreement stems, of course, from the fact that there is far greater diversity within all the classes of modern societies than Marx or his contemporaries imagined there would be. In addition to the bourgeoisie (the owners of large amounts of capital) and the petit bourgeoisie (the owners of small firms and stores), there is a constantly growing professional class, a class of top managers and engineers, another class of lower-level managers, and a class of employees with special skills (e.g., computer specialists, nurses and other medical personnel, and operating engineers). Perhaps many of these people should think of themselves as part of the working class, but they normally do not because they are earning enough to enable them to live in middle-class communities.

Some conflict theorists focus on other aspects of social stratification besides class conflict. Melvin Tumin (1967), for example, pointed out that stratification systems "limit the possibility of discovery of the full range of talent available in a society"; that they create unfavorable self-images that further limit the expression of people's creative potential; and that they "function to encourage hostility, suspicion, and distrust among the various segments of a society"

(p. 58). Problems like wasted talent and poor self-image are among what Richard Sennett and Jonathan Cobb (1972) term "the hidden injuries of class," meaning the ways in which a childhood of poverty or economic insecurity can leave its mark on people even after they have risen out of the lower classes. In the next chapter, we look more specifically at social stratification in the United States and examine its consequences in human terms.

The Functionalist View

The functionalist view of stratification was originally stated by Talcott Parsons (1937, 1940) and Kingsley Davis and Wilbert Moore (1945). This theory holds that social classes emerge because an unequal distribution of rewards is essential in complex societies. Such societies need to reward talented people and channel them into roles that require advanced training, personal sacrifice, and extreme stress. Thus the unequal distribution of rewards, which allows some people to accumulate wealth and deprives others of that chance, is necessary if the society is to match the most talented individuals with the most challenging positions.

Research by sociologists in the former Soviet Union often provided support for the functionalist idea that extreme "leveling" deprives people of the motivation to achieve more than a minimum of skills. On the basis of extensive surveys of workers in Russia and other former Soviet republics, sociologist Tatyana Zaslavskaya (cited in Aganbegyan, 1989) argues that unless incentives are provided in the form of high wages and other advantages (such as better housing in areas where good housing is in short supply), engineers and scientists will resent their situation and will not work hard. In the United States, the same arguments are used to justify higher salaries for doctors, lawyers, and other professionals. Too much equality, it is said, reduces the incentive to master difficult skills, and as a result the entire society may suffer from a lack of professional expertise.

Critics of the functionalist view of inequality and stratification point to many situations in which people in positions of power or leadership receive what appear to be excessive benefits. For example, the late Roberto Goizueta, former chief executive officer of the Coca-Cola Company, was criticized for taking home more than $10 million in salary and bonuses. Many other executives were earning equally high salaries even when their companies were not doing as well as they might in international competition. With the annual pay of top Japanese executives often running 5 to 10 times less than that of their American counterparts, it became difficult for the American corporate elite to argue that these enormous rates of executive compensation are "functional." And in 2000, when the "dot-com" stock market bubble burst and small stockholders lost money while many company executives and insiders reaped huge profits by selling before the market declined, it was again difficult to show that this behavior was justified by the functional need for creative business entrepreneurs.

From the point of view of those who are critical of social inequality, the large sums paid to a few people seem wrong, especially when so many others are struggling just to survive. Indeed, the heads of large corporations in the United States often earn more than 50 times as much as the average employee of those corporations. Conflict theorists argue that such great disparity is not "functional" when it produces enormous gaps between the very rich and the working classes. Functionalist theory claims that the disparity is functional because in a capitalist system of free enterprise top executives will seek the firms that are most willing to reward them for their talents. Those firms will benefit, and so will their workers.

The Interactionist Perspective

Conflict theory explains stratification primarily in economic terms. So does functionalist theory. Both trace the existence of certain classes to the central position of occupation, income, and wealth in modern life. But neither goes very far toward explaining the prestige stratification that occurs *within* social classes. Among the very rich in America, for example, people who have stables on their property tend to look down on people with somewhat smaller lots on which there is only a swimming pool. And rich families who own sailing yachts look down on equally rich people who own expensive but noisy powerboats. The point is that within economic classes people form status groups whose prestige or honor is measured not according to what they produce or how much wealth they own but according to what they buy and what they communicate about themselves through their purchases. Rolex watches and BMW cars are symbols of membership in the youthful upper class. Four-wheel-drive vehicles equipped with gun racks and fishing rods are symbols of the rugged and successful middle- or working-class male. Armani suits are symbols of urbane professionalism; tweed suits and silk blouses are signs that a woman is a member of the "country club set." All of these symbols of prestige and group membership change as groups with less prestige mimic them, spurring a search for new and less "common" signs of belonging (Dowd, 1985).

Our tendency to divide ourselves up into social categories and then assert claims of greater prestige for one group or another is of major significance in our lives. The interactionist perspective on stratification, therefore, may not be very useful in explaining the emergence of eco-

nomic classes, but it is essential to understanding the behaviors of the status groups that form within a given class. Those behaviors, in turn, often define, reinforce, or challenge class divisions. The stratification system, in this view, is not a fixed system but is created over and over again through the everyday behaviors of millions of people.

STRATIFICATION AND GLOBAL POVERTY

Today it is no longer possible to think of a society's stratification system separately from those of other societies. More than ever before, the life chances of people in the United States and other highly developed nations are influenced by changes in the structure of industrial employment and the worldwide distribution of jobs. At the end of the 1990s, for example, many nations of Southeast Asia were struck by economic crises. Indonesia experienced widespread social unrest in the wake of financial instability. Japan's economy, one of the strongest in the world, faltered badly. In 2001, the war against terrorism led by the United States began at the same time that another global economic turndown was occurring; this further impeded the recovery of many economies in poorer nations. These crises worsened the plight of millions of impoverished people in the developing nations and throughout the world.

Globalization opens new regions to increased trade and investment, to increased communications from other parts of the world, and to greater movement of people across national boundaries. But the benefits of these trends are not shared equally. The richest 20 percent of the world's nations command far more than their proportional share of wealth, information, and the energy needed to fuel development. The graphs in Figure 11.4 demonstrate that greater progress has come in developing new ways of doing business and enhancing the growth of world trade than in developing the human potential of poor populations (UNDP, 2003). These trends become even more evident when we consider the implications of world poverty for human health.

Inequality, Poverty, and Health

Differences in income and wealth can sometimes mean the difference between life and death. In some developing nations, health conditions are changing for the better as public health measures such as improved water supply and sewage systems take effect. Nevertheless, the correlation between poverty and death remains extremely high in many nations, and in the United States it has increased in recent years. These trends are so important that social scientists and international planning experts often use health statistics as a barometer of how well a nation is doing in improving the gap between the haves and the have-nots in its population.

Three indicators—mortality of children younger than age 5, the adult illiteracy rate, and the incidence of income poverty—are often used as primary measures of social change when comparing different nations (UNDP, 2003). We see in Figure 11.5 that some nations and regions have made progress toward reducing these indicators of severe ill health, illiteracy, and poverty but that the needs remain immense. An estimated 1.3 billion people must survive on the equivalent of less than $1 a day. Nearly 1 billion people, of whom most are women, are illiterate, and more than 1 billion face severe health threats because they lack access to safe water (UNDP, 1997). And as we see in Figure 11.6, infant mortality rates are two or three times higher in families in which the mother has no education than in families in which the mother has secondary or higher education.

Figure 11.7 compares mortality rates for developed and less developed nations, and also indicates how much greater risk males face (compared with females) of dying before age 60.

The single most important factor in determining survival, however, is income. At the extreme of poverty, in Africa, with annual per capita income of US$800, life expectancy is 52 years. At the other end of the income spectrum, in the United States, with annual per capita income of US$20,000, average life expectancy is 75 years. Some low-income regions, however, have invested in the health and safety of their populations (e.g., some states of India), and some affluent regions still rank relatively low on measures of health and survival (Mosley & Cowley, 1991; Sen, 1993).

In impoverished nations like Ethiopia and Bangladesh, the primary causes of death before old age are diseases such as amoebic dysentery (severe diarrheal diseases), which result from contaminated water supplies and poor sewage systems. In more affluent nations, the rate of death before age 60 increases for adolescents and young adults, especially males, because of the greater risks they take in their leisure activities (dangerous sports, drug use, etc.) and the higher rates of interpersonal violence in some of these nations (especially the United States).

Studies of health and inequality in the United States show that over the past four decades the health and mortality gap between the rich and the poor has widened

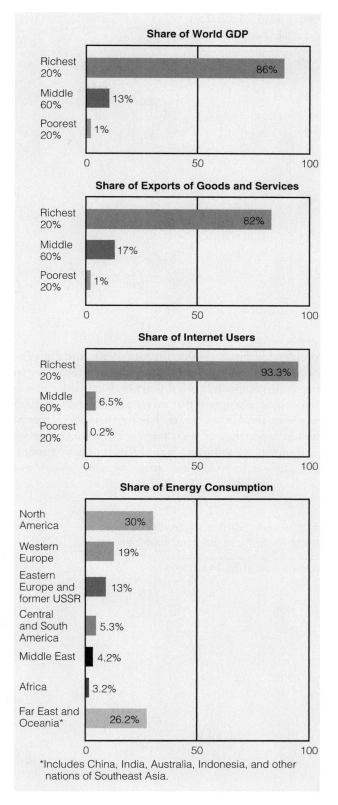

Figure 11.4 Disparities Among Rich and Poor Nations

Source: UNDP, 2003; Statistical Abstract, 2000.

Figure 11.5 Indicators of Social Change

Source: UNDP, 2003.

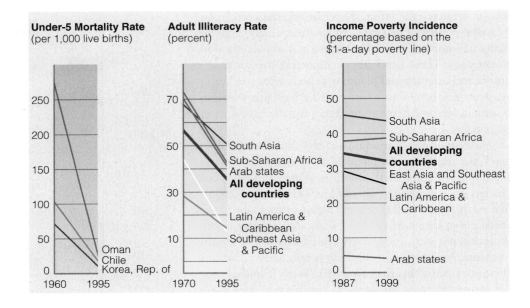

considerably. From 1960 to the mid-1980s, the degree of inequality in mortality rates more than doubled. Racial inequality compounds this difference. Medicaid, the federal insurance program that serves more than 30 million people in the United States, has significantly improved the life expectancy of poor people, but poor diet, poor environmental conditions, high risk of contracting contagious diseases (especially new strains of tuberculosis), and

high rates of interpersonal violence have helped widen the mortality gap. Because similar trends have been occurring in affluent nations of Europe, where universal health insurance is the norm, medical sociologists warn that better insurance systems for the United States will not automatically narrow the gap in the absence of improvements in eating and smoking habits and other lifestyle changes among the poor (Pear, 1993).

Figure 11.6 Mother's Education and Infant Mortality in Selected Countries

Source: Gelbard, Haub, & Kent, 1999.

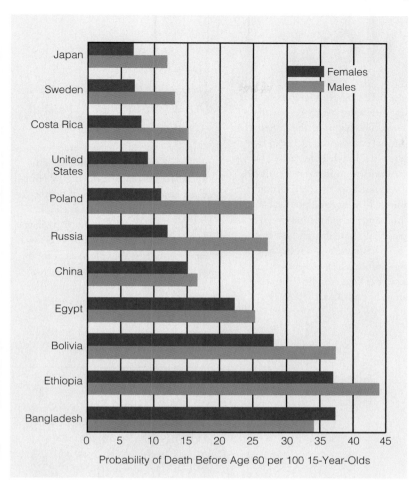

Figure 11.7 Risk of Dying Before Age 60 for 15-Year-Old Males and Females, Selected Countries

Note: The following example shows how the information in this chart can be interpreted: In the United States, a woman has about 9 chances out of 100, or a 9 percent probability, of dying before age 60, whereas in Ethiopia or Bangladesh a woman has about 37 chances out of 100, or a 37 percent probability, of dying before age 60.

Source: Feachem et al., 1993.

Gender Disparities

No contemporary society treats its women as well as its men. The United Nations Development Programme's annual *Human Development Report* summarizes the situation as follows:

> In developing countries there are still 60% more women than men among illiterate adults, female enrollment even at the primary level is 13% lower than male enrollment, and female wages are only three-fourths of male wages. In industrial countries unemployment is higher among women than men, and women constitute three-fourths of the unpaid family workers. (1997, p. 39)

In the world's poorest nations, women face double deprivation: Human development problems such as lack of medical care, lack of clean water, extreme poverty, and unemployment affect all but the comfortable elite, but women in these countries face even higher levels of risk and deprivation. On the other hand, some developing nations outperform much richer nations in achieving gender equality in political, economic, and professional activities: "Barbados is ahead of Belgium and Italy, Trinidad and Tobago outranks Portugal, and the Bahamas leads the United Kingdom. France lags behind Suriname, Colombia, and Botswana and Japan behind China, Guatemala, and Mexico" (UNDP, 1997, p. 41).

Achieving Greater Equality

The *Human Development Report* points out that in most societies some members of the upper classes have a vested interest in perpetuating poverty. The poor form "a mobile pool of low-paid and unorganized workers" who are useful for doing the dirty, dangerous, and difficult work that others often refuse to do. In industrial nations like the United States, many such jobs are taken by people from the poorest backgrounds and often by immigrants, legal and illegal. In many nations—including Russia and Nigeria, to mention two notable examples—patterns of corruption among

Text continues on page 318.

VISUAL SOCIOLOGY

EXTREME POVERTY

Sebastião Salgado spends long periods living with the people he photographs and using his camera to document their work and their efforts to overcome extreme poverty. "Salgado photographs from the inside," claims the Uruguayan writer Eduardo Galeano. "He remained in the Sahel desert for fifteen months when he went there to photograph hunger. He traveled in Latin America for seven years to garner a handful of photographs" (Salgado, 1990, p. 11).

The photos included in this sample of Salgado's "concerned photography" document the agony of extreme poverty. The great pit shown in one of the photos is a gold mine in the province of Paras, Brazil, where more than 50,000 mud-covered men carry heavy bags of dirt up slippery ladders in the hope that now and then one of the bags will yield a nugget of gold.

These haunting photographs capture two very different poverty-producing conditions. The plight of the miners is a result of the exploitation of cheap human labor in a jungle gold rush. The photos of starvation in the Sahel document the conditions of severe drought compounded by extreme political anarchy. Thousands of people have died in Ethiopia, Mali, Somalia, and other drought-stricken areas—not because food was unavailable but because violence and war kept supplies from those without guns and power.

The Sociological Observer
(See photo on page 295.)

This Bangladeshi villager's mobile phone is a status symbol and as such can reflect his place at the higher levels of the stratification system of his society. In a country where communication technology is not the norm, this villager can communicate only with others who own telephones; this allows him to interact with others of a similar status. His possession of a status symbol like a mobile phone in one of the world's poorer regions could also reflect his upward social mobility and possible achieved status in his society.

Tens of thousands of refugees from the great drought in Brazil's northeast gather near cities. Often the only way to survive is to fight with the vultures for the spoiled food in garbage dumps. (Fortaleza, Brazil, 1983)

Children's ward in the Korem refugee camp. (Ethiopia, 1984)

© Sebastiao Salgado/Contact Press Images

Overall view of the Sierra Pelada gold mine, where more than 50,000 workers were employed. (Brazil, 1986)

Women carry ground rock for road repair near Jaipur, India.

Able-bodied men have left for town looking for work and food. They leave behind them their families and the "drought widows." Here people are walking on what used to be Lake Faguibine. (Mali, 1985)

TABLE 11.1

Cost of Achieving Universal Access to Basic Social Services

Need	Annual Cost (in U.S. dollars)
Basic education for all	$6 billion
Basic health and nutrition	$13 billion
Reproductive health and family planning	$12 billion
Low-cost water supply and sanitation	$9 billion
Total for basic social services	$40 billion

Source: UNDP, 1997.

the elites make it even more difficult to narrow the gap between rich and poor.

Reports about worldwide inequality and poverty often seem to suggest that the problems are so great that improvements are unlikely. But despite the magnitude of the challenge, skepticism and cynicism are unwarranted. After all, the report notes that since the 1990 World Summit on Children, the first-ever summit on human issues, rates of child mortality have declined in all regions of the world. Seven million more children's lives are being saved each year than in 1980. Immunization against major diseases like polio now cover over 80 percent of the world's children. On other fronts, such as reducing poverty among the aged or ensuring greater access to medical care, efforts to improve conditions are having demonstrable success. Although AIDS and other major diseases continue to wreak havoc in many regions, the record shows that when the world's nations make concerted efforts to address social ills related to poverty and disease, they can have major successes.

What is the price tag for poverty eradication? The *Human Development Report* estimates the cost of achieving basic social services for all people in the developing countries at about $40 billion per year over the 10-year period between 1995 and 2005 (see Table 11.1). However, as the report concludes: "Lack of political commitment, not financial resources, is the real obstacle to poverty eradication. Eradicating absolute poverty is eminently affordable" (1997, p. 112).

CRITICAL SOCIOLOGY AND SOCIAL CHANGE

Fighting to Learn

What can a single person do to address the harsh realities of inequality? One answer that sociologists often give to this question is: "Try teaching, at least for a while, and

teach somewhere where people are desperate for dedicated teachers."

In the face of extreme poverty and injustice, and against the systematic exploitation of those who have little by the few who seem to have everything, what can a teacher accomplish? We can never fully answer this question, but there are teaching situations around the world and in our own country where it will be obvious, once you are doing the work, that teaching the basics of reading and writing is a primary route to social change. Consider, for example, the research of sociologist John L. Hammond among the peasants of El Salvador, where literacy instruction was a key element in the struggle for equality and democracy.

Hammond's focus was on the nation's teachers, particularly those known as "popular teachers." Unlike the teachers in the regular schools, who relied on traditional methods of rote memorization and drill and taught only students enrolled in the official schools, the popular teachers worked among the peasants and taught basic literacy. As Hammond (1998) observes: "Popular educators endorsed participatory, liberating teaching and criticized the authoritarian, rote-learning classes of traditional education" (p. 141). They threw themselves with great energy into their work among the children and adult peasants who came to them after their work in the fields. The pop-

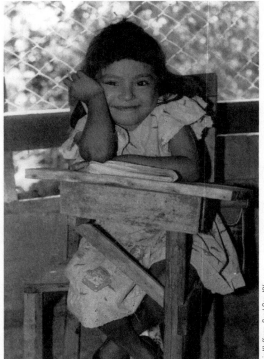

Popular school, El Sitio del Lago, Cuscatlán.

ular teachers relied on people like Hammond, with extensive university educations, to help them train other teachers who could go to the fields and the refugee camps to teach basic literacy. By teaching illiterate children to read and write, they were giving them the tools needed to begin to understand the social conditions that made them poor and prevented them from taking a full part in building the democratic institutions of their societies.

As the accompanying illustration suggests, popular education in Central America was often critical of the status quo, and therefore at times it became the target of oppression by those in power. But teaching literacy, whether to rural children and adults in Central America, women in the Islamic world, or people in poor communities in our own

LEAMOS Y PLATIQUEMOS

El analfabetismo nos aprieta.

En nuestro país hay injusticia social

Pocos tienen mucho: grandes casas, haciendas, comida abundante, trabajan cuando quieren, sólo se la pasan ordenando.

En fín, viven como reyes.

La mayoría de nosotros tenemos poco, ni siquiera podemos estudiar.

HAY ANALFABETISMO por que HAY INJUSTICIA SOCIAL

Reprinted with permission of Funcionamiento CIAZO.

This page from a literacy manual offers people in rural El Salvador a political analysis for why they are illiterate. "Illiteracy is squeezing us," it says. "A few have much: big houses, ample food, work when they wish—and live like kings. The majority of us have little, and cannot pursue learning. There is illiteracy because there is social injustice."

society, always entails some controversy and risk. That is what makes it such a valuable endeavor and such a unique learning experience for students and teachers as well.

SUMMARY

The Meaning of Stratification

- *Social stratification* refers to a society's system for ranking people hierarchically according to various attributes such as wealth, power, and prestige.
- Societies in which there are rigid boundaries between social strata are said to have *closed stratification systems,* whereas those in which the boundaries are easily crossed are said to have *open stratification systems.*
- Movement from one stratum to another is known as *social mobility.*
- Most closed stratification systems are characterized by *castes,* or social strata into which people are born and in which they remain for life.
- Membership in a caste is an *ascribed status* (a status acquired at birth), as opposed to an *achieved status* (one based on the efforts of the individual).
- Open societies are characterized by *classes,* which are social strata based primarily on economic criteria.
- The classes of modern societies are not homogeneous; within any given class there are different groups defined by how much honor or prestige they receive from society in general. Such groups are sometimes referred to as *status groups.*

- The way people are grouped with respect to their access to scarce resources determines their *life chances—* the opportunities they will have or be denied throughout life.

Stratification and the Means of Existence

- The principal forces leading to social stratification are created by the means of existence in a given society.
- For small farmers or peasants (the majority of the world's population), social strata are based on land ownership and agrarian labor, with the members of the lowest strata doing the hardest work and those at the top of the stratification system living in relative comfort.
- Modern industrial societies are characterized by *structural mobility* (the elimination of entire classes as a result of changes in the means of existence) and *spatial mobility* (the movement of individuals and groups from one location to another).

Stratification and Culture

- People accept their place in a stratification system because the system itself is part of their society's culture.

- The facets of culture that justify the stratification system are learned through the processes of socialization. The system is often justified by an ideology.
- At the micro level, the norms of everyday interactions, especially *deference* and *demeanor,* reinforce the society's stratification system.

Power, Authority, and Stratification

- Changes in stratification systems may have as much to do with realignments of social power as with economic or cultural changes.
- *Power* has been defined as "the probability that one actor within a social relationship will be in a position to carry out his own will despite resistance."
- Legitimate power is called *authority* and is a major factor in maintaining existing relationships among castes or classes.

Stratification in the Modern Era

- According to Karl Marx, capitalism divided societies into classes based on ownership of the means of production. The largest of these classes, the workers, must sell their labor to capitalists or landowners in return for wages.
- In time, the workers would become conscious of their shared interests as a class and would rebel against the capitalist class. The outcome of the revolution would be a classless society.
- Marx defined social class in economic terms. Max Weber took issue with this definition and pointed out that people are stratified not only by wealth but also by how much honor or prestige they receive from others and how much power they command.
- Marx's view of stratification is also challenged by studies of social mobility in industrial societies, which have shown that there is considerable movement between classes.

Theories of Stratification

- Modern conflict theorists, like Marx, believe that class conflict is a primary cause of social change. They disagree, however, on the nature of the class structure of capitalist societies.
- Functionalist theorists believe that classes emerge because an unequal distribution of rewards is necessary in order to channel talented people into important roles in society.
- This view has been criticized because it fails to account for the fact that social rewards in one generation tend to improve the life chances of the next generation; nor does it explain why talented people from lower-class families often are unable to obtain highly rewarded positions.
- From the interactionist perspective, the stratification system is not a fixed system, but rather, one that is created out of everyday behaviors.

Stratification and Global Poverty

- Globalization opens new regions to increased trade and investment, to increased communications from other parts of the world, and to greater movement of people across national boundaries, but the benefits of these trends are not shared equally.
- Social scientists and international planning experts often use health statistics as a barometer of how well a nation is doing in narrowing the gap between the haves and the have-nots in its population.
- In the world's poorest nations, women face double deprivation: Human development problems such as lack of medical care, lack of clean water, extreme poverty, and unemployment affect all but the comfortable elite, but women in these countries face even higher levels of risk and deprivation.

GLOSSARY

social stratification: A society's system for ranking people hierarchically according to such attributes as wealth, power, and prestige. (p. 294)

closed stratification system: A stratification system in which there are rigid boundaries between social strata. (p. 294)

open stratification system: A stratification system in which the boundaries between social strata are easily crossed. (p. 294)

social mobility: Movement by an individual or group from one social stratum to another. (p. 294)

upward mobility: Movement by an individual or group to a higher social stratum. (p. 294)

downward mobility: Movement by an individual or group to a lower social stratum. (p. 294)

caste: A social stratum into which people are born and in which they remain for life. (p. 295)

ascribed status: A position or rank that is assigned to an individual at birth and cannot be changed. (p. 295)

achieved status: A position or rank that is earned through the efforts of the individual. (p. 295)

class: A social stratum that is defined primarily by economic criteria such as occupation, income, and wealth. (p. 295)

status group: A category of people within a social class, defined by how much honor or prestige they receive from society in general. (p. 296)

life chances: The opportunities an individual will have or be denied throughout life as a result of his or her social-class position. (p. 296)

structural mobility: Movement of an individual or group from one social stratum to another caused by the elimination of an entire class as a result of changes in the means of existence. (p. 299)

spatial mobility: Movement of an individual or group from one location or community to another. (p. 299)

status symbols: Material objects or behaviors that indicate social status or prestige. (p. 301)

deference: The respect and esteem shown to an individual. (p. 301)

demeanor: The ways in which individuals present themselves to others through body language, dress, speech, and manners. (p. 302)

power: The ability to control the behavior of others, even against their will. (p. 302)

authority: Power that is considered legitimate both by those who exercise it and by those who are affected by it. (p. 302)

objective class: In Marxian theory, a social class that has a visible, specific relationship to the means of production. (p. 307)

subjective class: In Marxian theory, the way members of a given social class perceive their situation as a class. (p. 307)

class consciousness: A group's shared subjective awareness of its objective situation as a class. (p. 307)

intragenerational mobility: A change in the social class of an individual within his or her own lifetime. (p. 309)

intergenerational mobility: A change in the social class of family members from one generation to the next. (p. 309)

INTERNET RESOURCES

Virtual Society: The Wadsworth Sociology Resource Center
(http://sociology.wadsworth.com)
At Virtual Society you can access a wide range of enrichment material to aid your study of sociology. From the main page, click on the Student Resources link and find

your course and this textbook. Next, select the chapter you are presently studying from the pull-down menu. Among the useful options for each self-study chapter are online links and exercises, flashcards, practical study tips, and practice quizzes for each chapter.

MC MicroCase Online
From the Virtual Society home page, click on MicroCase Online to access book-specific MicroCase exercises that allow you to further explore sociological issues and principles presented in the text.

InfoTrac College Edition
Another unique option available to you at the Student Resources section at Virtual Society is InfoTrac College Edition, an online library with access to hundreds of scholarly and popular periodicals. Below are suggested search terms for this chapter, but this resource also allows you to fit your study of sociology to your own interests by searching custom keywords.

Social stratification

Social mobility

Class consciousness

Refugee

International Sociological Association
(www.ucm.es/OTROS/isa)
Provides a fine introduction to global sociological work by professional researchers.

Population Reference Bureau
(www.prb.org)
Provides demographic data and links to other sources of useful demographic statistics.

The World Bank
(www.worldbank.org)
An excellent source of comparative global statistics on indicators of social stratification in different nations and regions of the world, with particular emphasis on the developing nations.

Inequalities of Social Class

© Jose More

"What I always wonder," he says with a slight shrug, "is how the young people are going to find a way to get ahead now that the mills are gone." Ed Sadlowski is standing in the economically depressed streets of South Chicago, the neighborhood where he was born, where he raised his five children, and where most of them are now living and raising their own children.

"You know, Bill," he continues as we walk slowly past the deserted mill gates, "the United States makes as much steel as we did back when these plants had thousands of workers in them. It's just that we make it so much more efficiently. The productivity of the individual workers is so much greater because of the new technologies, computer control of machines, robotization, and all the rest. So the old system of mass employment in industries like steel is never going to return. The industrial proletariat that Marx wrote about is gone, at least in this country, but not elsewhere in the world where industry is newer."

Edward Sadlowski is among the nation's leading experts in industrial history and the sociology of labor–management relations. We met many years ago when I was working in a local steel mill while gathering material for a book about this famous industrial community. Sadlowski's grandfather came to Chicago as an immigrant from Poland, drawn like millions of others by the chance to use his strong back and hands in the search for a new and better life in America. His father worked in the mills too. He was one of the union's early organizers. From an early age, Ed was taught that the unions in steel, railroads, and mining were responsible for bringing workers a fairer share of the profits of their industries. To do so they had to constantly struggle against the mill owners, who often seemed ready to kill them rather than relinquish their control or share the wealth.

When Sadlowski was 18, he too entered the mills, but he was able to join an apprenticeship program in which he learned a skilled trade as a machinist. He immediately became active in the union and was elected to represent his workmates as their grievance officer. This meant that he was a shop floor lawyer who assisted workers when they were disciplined or fired. Their union contract afforded the workers a common pay scale and scheduled increases in their hourly wages, as well as health and other benefits they had not had before the unions gained legal recognition in the 1930s. Overtime pay and the right to a semblance of due process in disciplinary matters were also among the union's achievements.

Eventually Sadlowski was elected president of the union at U.S. Steel's South Works, Chicago's largest steel mill until it was torn down in the late 1980s. Later in his career, he ran unsuccessfully for president of the U.S. and Canadian steelworkers' union, but for his entire working life he has remained a staunch union supporter.

As we walk through the "brownfields"—acre after acre of abandoned railroad tracks and ore docks on the shore of Lake Michigan—Sadlowski wonders about the future of manufacturing in the United States. There are so many groups whose mobility depended until very recently on well-paid jobs in plants with union contracts. In Chicago, there are thousands of African Americans and Chicanos whose progress toward greater economic security has been stymied by plant closings. And from his travels throughout industrial America, Sadlowski understands only too well the consequences of rapid deindustrialization—consequences that are reflected in the harsh realities faced by the workers who appear in the Visual Sociology section of this chapter. "Too many people are looking for too few good jobs," he comments. "You know, the kind that pay a decent wage you can raise a family on, and that pay for adequate health care."

FOCUS QUESTIONS:

• How is inequality structured in the United States?

• What kinds of social classes are found in the United States, and how do they compare to classes in other societies?

• How are social classes changing, and what effects do the changes have on members of these classes?

DIMENSIONS OF SOCIAL INEQUALITY IN AMERICA

The Sadlowskis and other families in South Chicago are struggling to adapt to a set of social changes that are global in scope. People in different parts of the world are experiencing these changes in differing ways. South of the U.S. border, for example, parents in hundreds of communities miss their children, who have migrated to manufacturing towns along the border. In the industrial centers of North America, people mourn the loss of jobs to countries or regions where labor costs are lower. These changes are forcing many people to go back to school and gain new skills and credentials so that they can be more competitive in changing labor markets. Union members in manufacturing industries are being forced to end strikes and go back to work to avoid losing their jobs to "replacement workers." But these are only some of the realities of life in a stratified and rapidly changing industrial society. The U.S. economy also generates immense wealth and a growing number of jobs. The society boasts an enormous middle class, many of whose members are far more affluent than their parents and grandparents ever dreamed of becoming. Thus social mobility and class conflict, the subjects of this chapter, remain important aspects of life in the United States and elsewhere in the world. No wonder they are central issues in contemporary sociology.

In the United States, inequalities of class and status have worsened despite rates of employment that are generally higher than those of other Western industrialized nations (Shapiro & Greenstein, 2001). In the nation's poorest communities—in urban ghettos and on Indian reservations and in the hill country of the South—many people doubt whether the conditions of poverty and depression in which they live can ever be improved. Sociological research has shown that the rich are doing better than ever and that the gap between the haves and the have-nots is widening. In different regions of the nation, the details of social inequality differ, but the basic patterns of wealth, prestige, and power are the same (Aronowitz, 2003; Gans, 1995).

This chapter further develops many of the terms and concepts defined in the preceding chapter and applies them to the study of inequality and stratification in the United States. First we discuss the ways in which sociologists measure inequality and their changing views of how inequalities result in the formation of social classes. Then we examine social classes and life chances in the United States today and analyze the influence of social-class position on opportunities for upward mobility. We will see that there is nothing static about social inequality in the United States; changes in the class structure of North America are occurring even as this chapter is being written.

Measures of Social Inequality

The basic and most readily available measures of inequality in any society are income, wealth, occupational prestige, and educational attainment. Of these measures, income is most often used to give an initial view of social-class inequality.

INCOME INEQUALITY   A common method of comparing incomes in a large population like that of the United States is to divide the entire population into equal fifths, or *quintiles,* on the basis of personal or household income. The researcher starts at the lowest level of reported income and continues upward until one-fifth of the population has been accounted for. This establishes the upper and lower income boundaries for that quintile. The same procedure is used to identify each of the other four quintiles; the average income for each quintile can then be compared with the average incomes for the other four quintiles. Table 12.1 shows that between 1970 and 2000 income inequality was increasing, and that the income gap between the highest income quintile and the lowest grew most rapidly in the last 5 years of that 30-year period. In 2000, the table shows, households in the top 20 percent of the income range enjoyed almost 50 percent of all income, while those in the lowest and next-to-lowest quintiles received income shares of 3.6 percent and 8.9 percent, respectively. Although not all the data are available yet, there can be little doubt that the combined effects of income tax reductions favoring those with high incomes and decreased earnings among the lower quintiles due to recession will widen this gap further. The table also demonstrates that households whose earnings put them in the top 5 percent gained income most dramatically, from 16.6 percent of all income in 1970 to 21.9 percent in 2000.

By comparing the average incomes of quintiles at different points in time, social scientists and policymakers can see how changes in income over time are distributed among different strata of the population. For example, Figure 12.1 allows us to chart actual income changes for households in the U.S. income quintiles. During the economic boom years of the 1990s, all U.S. households experienced income growth, but those at the top saw their incomes grow much faster than those in the bottom three quintiles. By 2001, the average pretax household income for the top 20 percent was almost $100,000, and it was almost $170,000 for the average household in the top 10 percent. But for the bottom quintile, although income rose by over 14 percent, it does not exceed $10,000 for the average household in this quintile.

Note that Table 12.1 reports income share while Figure 12.1 documents growth in average dollar income. The second quintile—households in the middle income range—experienced an 11.7 percent increase in income, from less than $50,000 to over $60,000 before taxes, but

TABLE 12.1

Share of Aggregate Income Received by Each Quintile and Top 5% of Households

Year	Quintiles					
	Lowest	Fourth	Third	Second	Highest	Top 5%
1970	4.1	10.8	17.4	24.5	43.3	16.6
1975	4.4	10.5	17.1	24.8	43.2	15.9
1980	4.3	10.3	16.9	24.9	43.7	15.8
1985	4.0	9.7	16.3	24.6	45.3	17.0
1990	3.9	9.6	15.9	24.0	46.6	18.6
1995	3.7	9.1	15.2	23.3	48.7	21.0
2000	3.6	8.9	14.9	23.0	49.6	21.9

Source: Stewart, 2002.

its share of income actually decreased from 24 percent in 1990 to 23 percent in 2001. In fact, an analysis by the Congressional Budget Office indicates that the top fifth of the population received 50.4 percent of all after-tax income in 1999, up from 44.2 percent in 1977—a new record. In other words, the top 20 percent of U.S. households are receiving more income than the remainder of all households (Shapiro & Greenstein, 2001).

WEALTH INEQUALITY If one studies the distribution of wealth rather than income, the picture is even more skewed in favor of the rich. If we measure wealth in terms of the net financial worth of households—that is, their total assets—only about 6 percent of American households have a net worth of $250,000 or more, whereas over 25 percent have

a net worth of less than $5,000. Figure 12.2 shows that wealth is even more unequally distributed than income. The top 1 percent of Americans enjoy almost 40 percent of all wealth (real estate, possessions, stocks, businesses, etc.). The top fifth have 84 percent of the total, leaving the remaining 80 percent of the population with about 16 percent of assets (Shapiro & Greenstein, 2001).

Recent studies show that the United States has replaced Great Britain and Ireland as the Western industrial nation with the largest gap between rich and poor (Hacker, 1997; Stewart, 2002). The percentage of total private wealth owned by the richest 1 percent of the U.S. population is rising quickly, but the opposite is true in Great Britain, which, unlike the United States, has never been thought of as an egalitarian society.

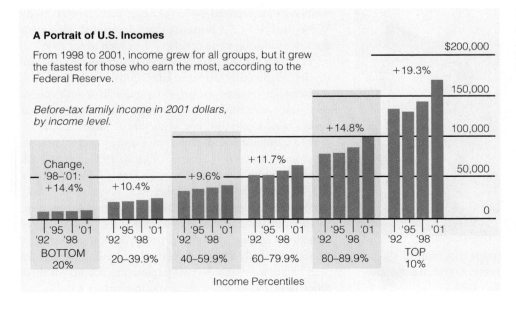

A Portrait of U.S. Incomes

From 1998 to 2001, income grew for all groups, but it grew the fastest for those who earn the most, according to the Federal Reserve.

Before-tax family income in 2001 dollars, by income level.

Figure 12.1   A Portrait of U.S. Incomes

Source: Andrews, 2003.

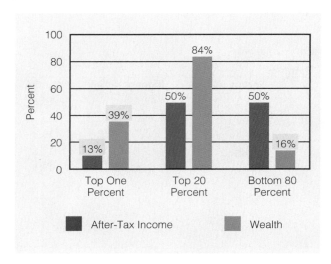

Figure 12.2   Shares of After-Tax Income Versus Shares of Wealth

Source: Shapiro & Greenstein, 2001.

In the United States, the richest 10 percent of families own homes valued at about 35 percent of the total worth of all homes. The same 10 percent, however, own almost 80 percent of other real estate, more than 90 percent of securities (stocks and bonds), and about 60 percent of the money in bank accounts (Hacker, 1997). Remember, too, that inequality expressed in dollars of income or possession of property and stocks translates into large differences in what people can spend on health care, shelter, clothing, education, books, movies, trips to parks and museums, vaca-

For the upper classes, food becomes a symbol of status; its cost and the artistry of its presentation assume an importance well beyond mere nutrition.

tions, and other necessities and comforts. These advantages and enjoyments are only likely to increase for the rich as decreases in federal taxes on wealth and income passed in 2003 take effect. At the same time, however, decreased tax revenues are causing increases in the costs of college tuition and decreases in public education budgets in many states, and these trends are likely to result in wider gaps in educational attainment.

INEQUALITY IN EDUCATIONAL ATTAINMENT   The distribution of educational attainment and occupational prestige is more nearly equal than the distribution of wealth and income. **Educational attainment,** or number of years of school completed, has become more equal among major population groups in the United States, but important inequalities remain. The educational attainment of the nation's black population, for example, has risen dramatically in the past generation. In 1960, only 20 percent of African Americans (who were age 25 or older at the time) had completed 4 years of high school or more, while the comparable figure for whites was 43 percent. Today, 78.5 percent of African Americans have completed 4 years of high school or more, compared to 85 percent of whites; however, only 16.5 percent of African Americans have completed 4 years or more of college, compared to about 26 percent of whites. And for Latinos the gap remains far wider. Approximately 57 percent of Latinos in the U.S. population (age 25 or older) have completed 4 years of high school or more, and 10.6 percent had completed 4 years of college or more in 2000 (*Statistical Abstract,* 2002).

Women, on the other hand, have nearly attained parity with men in terms of educational attainment. Eighty-four percent of adult women and 84.2 percent of men in the U.S. population had completed high school or beyond in 2000. Almost 28 percent of men and 23.6 percent of women had completed 4 years of higher education or more. We see in Table 12.2, however, that educational attainment does not yield the same benefits for women as for men.

The past two decades have seen an important increase in the relationship between educational attainment and income. The advantage enjoyed by individuals with college educations over those with only high school diplomas has always been significant, but as shown in Table 12.2, it increased by almost 16 percent for men and by over 22 percent for women between 1975 and 1995. In 1975, a man with a college diploma could expect to earn $1,510 for every $1,000 earned by a male worker with only a high school diploma. These averages were somewhat lower for women. In 1995, by contrast, a female worker with a college degree earned, on average, $1,658 for every $1,000 earned by a woman with only a high school diploma, and the figures are even higher for males. We will explore the reasons for these differences later in this chapter and in Chapter 14.

TABLE 12.2

Payment by Degrees: 1975 vs. 1995 *(average earnings of full-time workers, age 35 to 44 in the years' actual dollars)*

1975	Men	Women
High school diploma only	$14,007	$7,774
Bachelor's degree only	21,152	10,560
Bachelor's per $1,000 high school earnings	1,510	1,358
1995	**Men**	**Women**
High school diploma only	$32,689	$22,257
Bachelor's degree only	57,196	36,901
Bachelor's per $1,000 high school earnings	1,750	1,658
Advantage for bachelor's degree (change from 1975 to 1995)	+15.8%	+22.1%

Source: Reprinted with permission from Scribber, An Imprint of Simon and Schuster Adult Publishing Group, from *Money: Who Has How Much and Why*, by Andrew Hacker. Copyright © 1997 by Andrew Hacker.

In a rapidly changing economy like that of the United States, educated people are in increasing demand, and education thus becomes a more common route to upward mobility. Improvements in **educational achievement**—in basic reading, writing, and computational skills—are increasingly vital to individual careers. For the entire society, improvements in educational achievement represent improvements in the nation's "human capital," the wealth-producing capacity of its people (Harbison, 1973). But educational attainment and educational achievement are not always correlated. When students are moved through the school system without meeting certain minimum achievement criteria, attainment figures mask significant gaps in achievement. As a result, large segments of the population are unable to achieve nearly as much as they might, either for themselves or for their society.

INEQUALITY IN OCCUPATIONAL PRESTIGE   Another aspect of social inequality, **occupational prestige**, is measured using surveys of how people throughout a society rate different jobs. Such surveys find that the prestige people attach to an occupation is heavily influenced by the education required for the job or the authority it offers its holder, as well as by income (Blau & Duncan, 1967; Bose & Rossi, 1983; NORC, 1998). Thus many occupations that do not pay extremely high salaries are nonetheless

highly rated. Table 12.3 shows how selected occupations are ranked according to their prestige.

There are many other types of prestige or honor that people or groups seek besides occupational prestige. One can attain prestige through a family name or reputation, or achievement in a sport, or service to one's community, to name only a few other types of prestige. But occupational prestige is especially important because along with income, wealth, and education, it figures prominently in the way people think about their position and that of others in their society's system of social-class rankings.

These measures of wealth, income, education, and occupational prestige indicate that not all Americans share equally in "the good life." But what are the larger consequences of these patterns of inequality, both for individuals and for society? Do they combine to form an identifiable system of social-class stratification in the United States? Do marked patterns of inequality contradict the American dream, the vision of the United States as a place where hard work and sacrifice will lead to success and material comfort? We explore these questions in the rest of this chapter, but before doing so it is helpful to look at how views of inequality have changed over the past 150 years, as the United States was transformed from an agrarian society to an urban industrial society and, finally, to a postindustrial society.

INEQUALITY, THE AMERICAN PARADOX   Why does the richest, most powerful nation on earth exhibit the highest measures of inequality and the highest rates of poverty of all the urban industrial nations with which it is often compared? And why do so many Americans tolerate and even defend these inequalities? The seeming contradiction between the nation's achievements—its productivity, its liberties, its entrepreneurial risk taking, its scientific leadership, to name a few (see Figure 12.3 for others)—and its growing inequality (and worsening health indicators like child mortality and homicide) is often called *the American paradox* (Halstead, 2003). In their attempts to understand the origins of this paradox, sociologists have conducted studies of how Americans' views of inequality have developed and changed in different historical periods and different types of communities. They also conduct research on how individuals and groups perceive inequality and how it affects their life chances, subjects to which we turn in the next section.

Changing Views of Social Inequality

The dominant view of American society before the Industrial Revolution was the Jeffersonian view, which envisioned a society in which most families lived on their own farms or ran small commercial or manufacturing enterprises (Lipset,

TABLE 12.3

Prestige Scores of Selected Occupations

Occupation	Prestige	Occupation	Prestige
Physician	95.8	Beautician	42.1
Mayor	92.2	Piano tuner	41.0
Lawyer	90.1	Landscape gardener	40.5
College professor	90.1	Truck driver	40.1
Architect	88.8	House painter	39.7
City superintendent of schools	87.8	Hairdresser	39.4
Owner of a factory employing 2,000 people	81.7	Pastry chef in a restaurant	39.4
Stockbroker	81.7	Butcher in a shop	38.8
Advertising executive	80.8	Washing machine repairman	38.8
Electrical engineer	79.5	Automobile refinisher	36.9
Building construction contractor	78.9	Someone who sells shoes in a store	35.9
Chiropractor	75.3	Cashier	35.6
Registered nurse	75.0	File clerk	34.0
Sociologist	74.7	Dress cutter	33.3
Accountant	71.2	Cattledriver, working for own family	33.0
High school teacher	70.2	Cotton farmer	32.4
Manager of a factory employing 2,000 people	69.2	Metal-container maker	31.1
Office manager	68.3	Hospital aide	29.5
Administrative assistant	67.8	Fireman in a boiler room	29.2
Grade school teacher	65.4	Floor finisher	28.8
Power house engineer	64.5	Assembly-line worker	28.3
Hotel manager	64.1	Book binder	28.2
Circulation director of a newspaper	63.5	Textile machine operator	27.9
Social worker	63.2	Electric-wire winder	27.6
Hospital lab technician	63.1	Vegetable grader	27.4
Artist	62.8	Delivery truck driver	26.9
Electrician	62.5	Shirt maker in a manufacturing plant	26.6
Insurance agent	62.5	Person who repairs shoes	26.0
Private secretary	60.9	Fruit harvester, working for own family	26.0
Floor supervisor in a hospital	60.3	Blacksmith	26.0
Supervisor of telephone operators	60.3	Housekeeper	25.3
Plumber	58.7	Flour miller	25.0
Police officer	58.3	Stock clerk	24.4
Manager of a supermarket	57.1	Coal miner	24.0
Car dealer	57.1	Boardinghouse keeper	23.7
Practical nurse	56.4	Warehouse clerk	22.4
Dental assistant	54.8	Waitress/waiter	22.1
Warehouse supervisor	54.2	Short-order cook	21.5
Assembly-line supervisor in a manufacturing plant	53.8	Baby-sitter	18.3
Carpenter	53.5	Rubber mixer	18.1
Locomotive engineer	52.9	Feed grinder	17.8
Stenographer	52.6	Garbage collector	16.3
Office secretary	51.3	Box packer	15.1
Inspector in a manufacturing plant	51.3	Laundry worker	14.7
Housewife	51.0	Househusband	14.5
Bookkeeper	50.0	Salad maker in a hotel	13.8
Florist	49.7	Janitor	12.5
Tool machinist	48.4	Yarn washer	11.8
Welder	46.8	Maid (F)/household day worker (M)	11.5
Wholesale salesperson	46.2	Bellhop	10.6
Telephone operator	46.2	Hotel chambermaid (F)/hotel bedmaker (M)	10.3
Auto mechanic	44.9	Carhop	8.3
Typist	44.9	Person living on welfare	8.2
Typesetter	42.6	Parking lot attendant	8.0
Postal clerk	42.3	Rag picker	4.6

Source: Adapted from Bose & Rossi, 1983; NORC, 1998.

This list of "bests" and "worsts" is based on a variety of sources—including statistics from the United Nations, the Organization for Economic Cooperation and Development, and a number of other groups and experts—but the basic criteria are consistent. Among advanced democracies, the United States had to rank in the top three for a category to be listed under "bests," and in the bottom three for a category to be listed under "worsts." (Where applicable, all rankings were determined on a rate basis or as a percentage of population.)

Figure 12.3   The American Paradox: Two Faces of the United States

Source: Halstead, 2003.

Bests	Worsts
Gross domestic product	Poverty
Productivity	Economic inequality
Business start-ups	Carbon-dioxide emissions
Long-term unemployment	Life expectancy
Expenditure on education	Infant mortality
University graduates	Homicide
R&D expenditure	Health-care coverage
High-tech exports	HIV infection
Movies exported	Teen pregnancy
Breadth of stock ownership	Personal savings
Volunteerism	Voter participation
Charitable giving	Obesity

1979; Pyle, 1996; Wright, 1997). This view emphasized the value of economic self-sufficiency through hard work—a value that has persisted to the present time. Yet even in Jefferson's time, the pattern of agrarian and small-town independence was not universal. In the early nineteenth century, American society was already developing a rather complex and diverse set of stratification systems. In New England and the Middle Atlantic states, the Jeffersonian ideal of rural farmers and town-dwelling tradesmen, all with similar degrees of power and prestige, was reflected in reality. But in the larger cities a landless wage-earning class was emerging, as was a class of factory owners, bankers, and entrepreneurs. Throughout most of the southern states, in contrast, the major classes were the plantation owners and their families and staffs, the town merchants and tradesmen, and the marginal "poor white" farmers; in addition to these classes there was a caste: the slaves.

Native Americans were not included in any of these stratification systems. By the 1830s, they were already a *pariah group*—excluded from the stratification system and considered too different or inferior to be eligible for citizenship. As a consequence of their pariah status in many parts of the nation, together with the settlers' desire to inhabit their lands, most Native Americans were steadily pushed west of the Mississippi.

THE IMPACT OF THE DEPRESSION   A century later, in the mid-1930s, a different view of inequality had emerged. In the midst of the most severe economic and social depression in world history, President Franklin D. Roosevelt claimed that "one third of the nation [was] ill-housed, ill-clad, and ill-nourished." Faced with mass poverty and unemployment, with able-bodied workers selling apples on street cor-

ners, the grandparents of many of today's college students questioned the reality of the American dream. Many observers saw heightened conflict between workers and the owners of capital. To many intellectuals, it seemed that the dire predictions of Karl Marx were coming true and that only a communist revolution could save millions of people from starvation. Largely as a result of the Depression and fear of social disorder, legislators in the United States passed reform measures like the Social Security Act to alleviate the worst effects of poverty.

Muncie, Indiana, made famous by Helen and Robert Lynd in their books *Middletown* (1929) and *Middletown in Transition* (1937), provided numerous examples of the gap in income and lifestyle between the working class and the owners or managers of capital. In the decades since 1880, industrialization had transformed Muncie from an agricultural trade center with 6,000 inhabitants into a bustling city of more than 36,000. According to the Lynds (1937), Muncie's businessmen "lived in a culture built around competition, the private acquisition of property, and the necessity for eternal vigilance in holding on to what one has" (p. 25). Below them was a middle class of managers, teachers, and clergymen who believed in the right of the business class to control wealth and power. In contrast, "across the railroad tracks from this world of businessmen [was] the other world of wage earners—constituting a majority of the city's population" (p. 25).

When the Lynds first studied Middletown, they became convinced that social-class divisions, especially those between the working class and the owners of local firms, were reaching a state of crisis. When they returned during the Great Depression, they continued to find evidence that the business class dominated the city's social institutions. In

art *and the sociological eye*

Picturing the Consequences of Social-Class Inequality

In two famous paintings from the mid-twentieth century, we see artists offering their own personal insights into the consequences of class inequalities in the United States. Reginald Marsh's view of Depression-era Chicago, *Tattoo and Haircut*, depicts the life of single men living on Skid Row, the term still used for inner-city areas that cater to the needs of migrant laborers, alcoholics, and people who are "down on their luck." Marsh conveys the sense of boredom and resignation that is common among residents of Skid Row.

Tattoo and Haircut, by Reginald Marsh, 1932. Tempera on masonite, 46½″ x 48″.

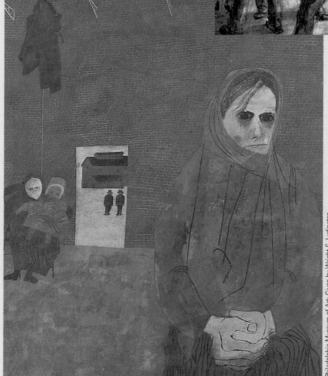

Miners' Wives, by Ben Shahn, 1948. Egg tempera on board, 48″ x 36″.

Ben Shahn's painting, *Miners' Wives*, depicts the anxiety and suffering of women in a poor working-class community. Their grief is made more vivid by the distance between the doorway of their home and the mine and its owners, who appear in the background. What explains the grim face of the woman in the foreground and her tightly clenched hands? Without being explicit about it, Shahn may be suggesting that the women are awaiting news of the fates of their absent husbands. Mining is one of the world's most dangerous occupations. Too often the wives of miners find themselves holding anxious vigils in the hope that their husbands and sons will return after an explosion or sudden cave-in deep underground.

one famous passage, a local factory worker described the influence of the "X family": "If I'm out of work I go to the X plant; if I need money I go to the X bank, and if they don't like me I don't get it; my children go to the X college; when I get sick I go to the X hospital" (Lynd & Lynd, 1937, p. 74).

The X family (actually the Ball family) owned the large glassworks in Middletown. The Ball brothers had built a fortune making glass jars and then had expanded into real estate, railways, banking, and retail stores. They worked so hard that they had little time to enjoy the pleasures their wealth could obtain. But their children appeared to be creating a distinctive upper class with exclusive country clubs, farms where their horses could be maintained, and private planes.

As a result of the Depression, there was more hostility between economic classes in Muncie in the late 1930s than there had been when the Lynds first studied Muncie's class system a few years before the Depression. The workers and their families were far less likely to believe that the business class had a right to its wealth, and they were increasingly drawn to social movements, especially the labor movement, that challenged the power of the business class. The business class itself was far less unified because the managers of the large corporations moving into the city did not feel obligated to join the clubs and churches of the established elite.

YANKEE CITY AND THE BLACK METROPOLIS   In the mid-twentieth century, several studies of inequality in American communities refined our knowledge of how income and prestige combine to produce stratification in modern communities. The research of William Lloyd Warner on social class in a New England town and Drake and Cayton's classic study of the caste system in an urban ghetto are important examples because they describe class relations more clearly than earlier studies did.

Warner's study was conducted in the seaside town of Newburyport, Massachusetts. Once famous for its whaling fleet and Yankee sea captains, Newburyport had become a small city with 17,000 inhabitants. It had several textile and shoe factories and had managed to hang on to many of its Yankee families, descendants of the hardy seafarers of the nineteenth century. For this reason, Warner dubbed the community "Yankee City."

Here is how Warner began his description of the class structure of Yankee City:

> Studies of communities in New England clearly demonstrate the presence of a well-defined social-class system. At the top is an aristocracy of birth and wealth. This is the so-called "old family" class. The people of Yankee City say the families who belong to it have been in the community for a long time—for at least three generations and preferably many generations more than three. "Old family" means not only old to the community but old to the class. (Warner, Meeker, & Calls, 1949, p. 12)

The new families of Yankee City's upper class, who possessed wealth but had not gained "old family" status, "came up through the new industries—shoes, textiles, silverware—and finance" (p. 12). Below this upper class, people in Yankee City identified an upper-middle class of highly respectable people who "may be property owners, such as storekeepers, or highly educated professionals, but they do not have the wealth or family status to be included in the upper class" (p. 13).

Below these classes, Warner's respondents identified three "common man" levels. These made up the lower-middle class, which was composed primarily of clerks, skilled tradesmen, other white-collar workers, and some skilled manual workers. Directly below this class, and most difficult for the respondents to separate from those above and below it, was the "upper-lower class," or the people Yankee City residents identified as "poor but honest workers, who more often than not are only semi-skilled or unskilled" (p. 14).

In Yankee City the lowest class, which Warner called the "lower-lower class," was described as the "low-down Yankees [and immigrants] who live in the clam flats" and have a bad reputation among the classes above them. "They are thought to be improvident and unwilling or unable to save money . . . and therefore often dependent on the philanthropy of the private or public agency and on poor relief" (p. 14). The six "prestige classes" that Warner identified on the basis of the Yankee City interviews are listed in Table 12.4, along with the percentage of the city's population in each class and the proportion of income spent on necessities by members of each class. It is interesting that Warner's terms, such as *upper-middle class* and *lower-middle class,* have become part of our everyday vocabulary.

At about the same time that Warner was conducting his study, other social scientists were attempting to describe stratification in larger, more complex communities. Among those efforts was the first full-scale study of Chicago's African-American community. It was carried out by St. Clair Drake and Horace Cayton in the 1940s and published under the title *Black Metropolis.*

Studies of inequality in southern communities had already documented the existence of a racially based caste system in the South (Dollard, 1937). But did this racial caste system also operate in northern cities like Chicago? At the time of Drake and Cayton's study, Chicago's black population was almost entirely concentrated in a single

TABLE 12.4

Prestige Classes in "Yankee City" and Proportion of Income Spent on Necessities of Life, 1941*

Prestige Class	Percent of Total Population	Percent Spent on Necessities
Upper-upper	1.4	33
Lower-upper	1.6	35
Upper-middle	10.2	51
Lower-middle	28.1	59
Upper-lower	32.6	66
Lower-lower	25.2	75

*"Necessities of life" include food, shelter, and clothing.

Source: The Social Life of a Modern Community, by W. Lloyd Warner and Paul S. Lunt, copyright © 1941. Reprinted by permission of Yale University Press.

urban ghetto. A **ghetto** is a section of a city that is segregated either racially or culturally (e.g., by race, religion, or ethnicity). Large numbers of blacks worked outside the ghetto, but even those who could afford housing elsewhere were excluded from other neighborhoods by long-established patterns of residential segregation. In addition, despite the integration of workers in industrial occupations, especially steel and meatpacking, Drake and Cayton (1970/1945) showed that Chicago's blacks were barred from more comfortable, better-paying jobs in other fields. They called this pattern of occupational segregation, in which blacks could rise only so far, the *job ceiling*. In their view, the job ceiling, together with the segregation of blacks in the ghetto, constituted a northern form of the racial caste system (see Figure 12.4). Many of the persistent racial inequalities in contemporary U.S. society have their origins in this urban job ceiling and the ways in which blacks and other people of color adapted to this form of stratification early in the twentieth century. We return to this subject in the next chapter.

MIDDLETOWN REVISITED   In the late 1970s, Theodore Caplow, Howard Bahr, Bruce Chadwick, and their collaborators returned to Middletown to see how the community had changed over more than 40 years. They found that the city's stratification system had changed a great deal since the Depression. The population had increased from about 40,000 to more than 80,000. This size increase brought new patterns of mobility:

> The local dominance of a handful of rich families that looked so threatening in 1935 quietly faded away during the decades of prosperity that fol-

lowed World War II. Hundreds of fortunes were made in the old ways and new—building subdivisions and shopping centers; trading in real estate; selling insurance, advertising, farm machinery, building materials, fuel oil, trucks and automobiles, furniture. . . . Middletown's new rich . . . lived much less ostentatiously than their industrial predecessors, and much of their money was spent away from Middletown (for yachts in Florida, condominiums in Colorado, boarding schools for their children, and luxury tours to everywhere for themselves). . . . The handful of families whose wealth antedated World War II adopted the same style. The imitation castles of the X, Y, and Z families were torn down or converted for institutional uses. (1983, p. 12)

The distinctive upper class that the Lynds saw emerging in Middletown in the 1930s had vanished by the 1970s:

> Meanwhile, at the lower end of the socioeconomic scale, life-styles were becoming more homogeneous. The residential building boom that began after World War II continued, year after year, to submerge the flat, rich farmlands at the edge of town under curved subdivision streets bordered by neat subdivision houses with various exteriors but nearly identical interiors. They all had central heating, indoor plumbing, telephones, automatic stoves, refrigerators, and washing machines. (pp. 12–13)

By the 1970s, the factory workers of Middletown were much better off than they had been in 1935. They enjoyed job security, health insurance, and paid vacations, and their average incomes were higher than those of many white-collar workers. These changes had come about largely as a result of the activities of labor unions, which had been excluded from Middletown's factories in 1935 but were accepted soon afterward (Caplow et al., 1983). But in the 1980s, the tide turned again, and Middletown, like many other industrial cities, began losing manufacturing jobs and gaining more low-paying service jobs.

Today the community of Middletown is far less self-contained than it was in the early decades of the twentieth century (Caccamo, 2000). It is subject to the influence of outside forces such as the shift of manufacturing jobs to other regions and even to other countries. Members of all social classes are more dependent on impersonal institutions such as corporations, national labor unions, and international markets. As a result, the old upper class has less influence, and the class structure is less cohesive and much less clear-cut than it was in the 1930s.

Figure 12.4 The Job Ceiling in Government and Private Industry Before the Civil Rights Movement

Source: *Black Metropolis,* copyright © 1945 by St. Clair Drake and Horace R. Cayton; renewed by Susan C. Woodson. Reproduced by permission of Harcourt Brace.

SOCIAL CLASSES IN POSTINDUSTRIAL SOCIETY In the decades since these studies were conducted, stratification in the United States has been strongly affected by technological and social changes. As we saw in Chapter 10, the study of these changes, which are thought to be producing a "postindustrial" society, is a lively area of sociological theory and research. The black workers whose struggles for dignity and economic security are described in *Black Metropolis,* the auto workers whom the Lynds encountered in Middletown, the members of Ed Sadlowski's family who worked in the steel mills—all were part of an earlier form of industrial society in which masses of workers were employed in large-scale manufacturing enterprises. By 2000, however, over three-quarters of all workers were en-gaged in providing services rather than producing goods of any kind (*Statistical Abstract,* 2002). According to Daniel Bell (1973), the principal theorist of "postindustrial society," this change represents a "revolution taking place in the structure of occupations and, to the extent that occupation determines other modes of behavior . . . it is a revolution in the class structure of society as well" (pp. 125–126). Bell and other sociologists believe that we now live in a postindustrial society in which what counts is not "raw muscle power" but scientific, technical, and financial information. The dominant person in this new order of society is the professional, who is equipped by education and training to supply the skills and information that are in most demand.

Although Marx argued that social-class divisions in industrial societies would become sharper and that class conflict would become more bitter, many American sociologists find evidence to the contrary. Their research shows that changes in the structure of the American economy, and especially in the types of jobs it produces, have resulted in a blurring of class lines and an easing of class conflict between industrial workers and the owners and managers of the means of production. More people work in offices, fewer in factories. More people live in metropolitan suburbs, fewer in industrial communities surrounding large factories. The union electrician or plumber wears a work shirt but maintains a home in a suburb with neighbors who work in offices. The computer operator wears a white shirt and has graduate training in computer science but may receive an hourly wage. The social-class membership of these employees and many others appears to be more than a simple matter of worker versus owner. Some sociologists argue, therefore, that the various dimensions of stratification—educational attainment, occupational prestige, income, wealth, and family status—overlap in complicated ways that make it difficult for people to form well-defined ideas about social-class membership (Hodge & Treiman, 1968; Wolf, 1998). Moreover, such factors as race, ethnicity (national origin), religion, and lifestyle crisscross economic class divisions and further blur what may once have been clearly defined class boundaries (Jackman & Jackman, 1983; NORC, 2002).

Other sociologists, however, are convinced that inequalities in income, wealth, and family status still produce clear social-class divisions in the American population (Piven, 1997). Although industrial workers make up a declining proportion of the labor force, they are still a large segment of the population, as are the poor below them. And these populations continue to demand social-welfare policies like unemployment insurance and medical benefits, in keeping with their interests as less-advantaged classes. Members of the more affluent middle and upper classes also recognize the interests they share; they may demand such benefits as tax reductions or aid to college students (Hacker, 1997; NORC, 1998). Thus some sociologists contend that the American public does recognize class divisions and that class inequalities do play an important role in determining life chances. Although this debate continues, the empirical evidence shows that people in the United States have a good idea of the social class to which they belong.

Class Awareness in America Today

As mentioned in the preceding chapter, Marx reasoned that social class has both subjective and objective dimensions. In his view, objective social class depends on a person's relationship to the means of production (whether the person owns capital or land, sells his or her labor power, engages in a profession, etc.). Subjective social class is determined by how a person thinks about his or her membership in a social class. In Marx's view, many people who objectively are members of the working class because they sell their labor power and do not own capital in fact identify with the concerns of the owners of capital because they help run the businesses that employ them; in other words, they think of themselves as members of a higher class (subjective class), but their occupation places them in a lower class (objective class).

SUBJECTIVE VERSUS OBJECTIVE MEASURES   Research on class awareness distinguishes between these two views of social class. The *subjective method* of measuring social-class membership uses interviews in which respondents give their opinions about their class rankings. This method of assigning people to classes is based on personal opinions. The *objective method* uses indicators of rank such as occupational prestige (see Table 12.3), place of residence and type of home, level of education, and income, which are combined to form a composite index. These measures are not affected by the respondents' opinions. Researchers have found high correlations between the data generated by both methods (Hollingshead, 1949; Kahl, 1965). However, there is a tendency for people who work in blue-collar occupations, and therefore are in the working class by objective measures, to identify themselves as members of the middle class (NORC, 1998; Vanneman & Cannon, 1987).

Sociologists often use opinion surveys when they study subjective perceptions of class membership, but they use the objective method when they are interested in the effects of class membership on other aspects of a person's life, such as political views or access to health care.

Over the last 25 years, the National Opinion Research Center's (NORC's) General Social Survey has found that an average of about 5 percent of Americans perceive themselves as being in the lower class (NORC, 1998). In contrast, sociologists Robert and Mary Jackman found that a higher proportion of respondents perceive themselves as poor. This difference probably occurs because the term *lower class* has a negative connotation for many people.

The NORC measures subjective social class by asking thousands of respondents this question: "People talk about social classes such as the lower class, the working class, the middle class, and the upper class. Which of these classes would you say you belong to?" Most people in the survey—at least 97 percent—assign themselves to a social class. The data in Table 12.5 show that almost 45 percent of men and 46 percent of women classify themselves as members of the middle class, whereas far

TABLE 12.5

Social Class by Sex and Race

Social Class by Sex

	Lower Class	Working Class	Middle Class	Upper Class	No Class	Total
Male						
Percent	4.5	47.4	45.0	3.1	0	100
N	607	6,423	6,087	425	0	13,542
Female						
Percent	5.7	45.0	46.2	3.1	0.01	100
N	977	7,681	7,899	524	1	17,082

Social Class by Race

	Lower Class	Working Class	Middle Class	Upper Class	No Class	Total
White						
Percent	4.1	44.2	48.7	3.0	0	100
N	1,049	11,380	12,537	783	1	25,750
Black						
Percent	11.6	58.6	28.2	3.6	0	100
N	482	2,350	1,170	150	0	4,152
Other						
Percent	7.3	51.8	38.6	2.2	0	100
N	53	374	279	16	0	722
Total number of cases	30,624					

Source: NORC, 1998, 2000.

fewer black Americans (28 percent) do so. And even though the category "lower class" has a negative connotation for many people, we see in the table that almost 6 percent of women rank themselves in this social class and almost 12 percent of African Americans do so. These and many similar survey studies led the Jackmans to conclude that "at their basis, classes take shape in the public awareness as clusters of people with similar socioeconomic standing" (1983, p. 217).

SOCIOECONOMIC STANDING   The term *socioeconomic standing* (usually referred to as **socioeconomic status** or **SES**) requires further definition. When people think of social-class divisions in American society, they first assign various occupations to broad class ranks. When there is confusion about how an occupation is ranked, people tend to think of other aspects of social class, such as family prestige, education, and earned income. And as they think about these factors, they tend to reach a consensus about what social class they belong to and what classes others should be assigned to.

But that consensus is by no means perfect. Some blue-collar occupations (e.g., many skilled trades, such as plumber and electrician) are relatively well paid; in fact, they are better paid than many office jobs. This leads

people to classify the holders of such jobs as members of the middle class, while they may assign holders of jobs in offices and stores to the working class. Remember also that the distinction between the lower-middle and upper-middle classes was the most difficult one for Warner's respondents in Yankee City and the other communities he studied.

SOCIAL CLASS IN RURAL AREAS   In addition to this ambiguity in how people distinguish among social classes, there is the problem of how classes are perceived in rural, as opposed to urban, areas. Most studies of social inequality in America exclude the farm population, which is relatively small—about 6 million people, or less than 2.2 percent of the total population (Smiley, 1992; *Statistical Abstract,* 2002). But since the early years of the nation's history, farmers have occupied a special place in American culture and the U.S. economy. The problems faced by farmers in a society that is steadily eliminating family farms have caused them to develop a strong class identity despite differences in their actual wealth. Hence, in the next section, which describes America's major social classes, we will include farmers and people living in rural areas dominated by agriculture, forestry, and mining.

SOCIAL CLASS AND LIFE CHANCES IN THE UNITED STATES

The rich have far more money than the poor, and they tend to have more education and a great deal more wealth, as measured by the value of homes, cars, investments, and much else. These facts are clear from the tables presented earlier in the chapter. But what differences do these inequalities make in people's lives? Social scientists often answer this question by analyzing the life chances of people born into different social classes. By *life chances* they mean the relative likelihood that individuals will have access to the opportunities and benefits that the society values. Compare, for example, the life chances of a child born into a family in which the mother and father earn slightly more than the minimum wage by working in restaurants and supermarkets with the life chances of a child born into the home of a police officer and a teacher, and compare both of these with the life chances of a child born into the home of a successful banker. Will these differences in the circumstances of birth affect the quality of education each child is likely to receive? Will the children's access to quality health care differ? Will the differences in the social class of their families influence who they are likely to marry? Will it make a difference in the likely length of their lives? The answer to all of these questions is, emphatically, yes. But being born into a given social class does not determine everything about an individual's life chances. The more a society attempts to equalize differences in life chances—by improving health care for the poor, for example, or by creating high-quality institutions of public education—the more it reduces the impact of social class on life chances.

Numerous social-scientific studies have shown that one's social class tells a great deal about how one will behave and the kind of life one is likely to have. Later in this section, we will discuss specific social classes, but first we present some typical examples of the relationship between social class and daily life. These examples apply primarily to American society, but many of the same conditions can be found in other societies as well.

Social Class in Daily Life

CLASS AND HEALTH   A child born into a rich upper-class family or a comfortable middle-class family is far less likely to be premature or have a low birthweight than one born into a working-class or poor family. And a baby born into a family in which the parents are working at steady jobs is far less likely to be born with a drug addiction or AIDS or

fetal alcohol syndrome than a child born to parents who are unemployed and homeless. These and many other disparities contribute to what is often called "the socioeconomic status (SES) gradient in health" (Sapolsky, 1998).

The SES gradient in health exists in all of the world's nations and is based on a complex combination of social class and culture, but the gradient is particularly marked in the United States:

> For example, in the United States the poorer you are, the more likely you are to contract and succumb to heart disease, respiratory disorders, ulcers, rheumatoid disorders, psychiatric diseases, or a number of types of cancer. And this is a whopper of an effect: In some cases disease or mortality risk increases more than fivefold as you go from the wealthiest to the poorest segments of our society, with things worsening each step of the way. (Sapolsky, 1998, p. 46)

Among adults, a salaried member of the upper class who directs the activities of other employees is less likely to be exposed to toxic chemicals or to experience occupational stress and peptic ulcers than wage workers at their machines and computer terminals. Those workers, in turn, are more likely to have adequate health insurance and medical care than the working poor—dishwashers, migrant laborers, temporary help, low-paid workers, and others whose wages for full-time work do not elevate them above the poverty level (Ellwood, 1988). The working poor are the largest category of poor Americans, and like those who lack steady jobs, they often depend on local emergency rooms for medical care and report that they have neither family doctors nor health insurance. The same poor and working-class population is also more likely to smoke, consume alcohol, and be exposed to homicide and accidents—while receiving less police protection—than members of the classes above them.

EDUCATION   Children of upper-class families are more likely to be educated in private schools than children from the middle or working classes. Sociologists have shown that education in elite private schools is a means of socializing the rich. As we saw in Chapter 5, Cookson and Persell's (1985) study of socialization in elite American prep schools found that "preppies" develop close ties to their classmates, ties that often last throughout life and become part of a network they can draw on as they rise to positions of power and wealth. The segregation of upper-class adolescents in prep schools also limits dating and marriage opportunities to members of the same class.

Although middle-class parents are more likely than rich parents to send their children to public schools, they tend to select suburban communities where the schools are known to produce successful college applicants. The public

THEN AND NOW

From Food Baskets to Food Stamps

The late nineteenth-century drawing and the modern photograph shown here represent two quite different approaches to aiding the poor. The drawing depicts a well-off family bringing a basket of food to the poor. This form of individual charity, which the rich often thought of as their responsibility and obligation, frequently engendered hostility rather than gratitude. The modern welfare system replaces the individual gift with "entitlements" (i.e., payments and other

services to poor people who qualify for them). But the modern system is inadequate to provide a dignified quality of life. And as evidenced by the antiwelfare sentiment prevailing in the United States in recent years, the notion of entitlement to welfare is an easy political target because many middle- and working-class voters are persuaded that the welfare system unfairly takes money from them to sustain "undeserving" poor people.

schools that serve the middle classes spend more per pupil than the schools attended by working-class and poor children, and they offer a wider array of special services in such areas as music, sports, and extracurricular activities. Children in the middle and upper classes also tend to have parents who insist that they perform well in school and who can help them with their schoolwork. Moreover, children from working-class and poor families are more likely to drop out of school than children from upper-class families.

POLITICS   The poor and members of the working class are more likely to vote for Democratic party candidates, whereas upper- and middle-class voters are more likely to choose Republican candidates. Throughout the industrialized world, voters with less wealth, prestige, and power tend to vote for candidates who promise to reduce inequalities, whereas voters with higher SES tend to choose candidates who support the status quo. Thus in their studies of social-class identification, the Jackmans (1983) found that 48.5 percent of poor respondents and 43 percent of respondents who assign themselves to the working class believe the federal government should be doing more

to achieve full employment and job guarantees, as opposed to only 24 percent of upper-middle-class respondents. They also found that about 48 percent of working-class respondents believe that "some difference" in levels of income (though less than currently exists) is desirable to sustain people's motives to achieve, whereas almost 50 percent of upper-middle-class respondents believe that a "great difference" is desirable. The most recent survey data (NORC, 1998) confirm the Jackmans' findings. Members of all classes tend to agree that whatever differences there are ought to be based on individual achievement rather than on advantages inherited at birth. Members of the working class and the poor, however, are more likely than members of other classes to vote for candidates who propose measures that would increase equality of opportunity.

Many other examples could be presented to illustrate the influence of social class on individuals in American society. But social-class divisions also affect the society as a whole. Let us turn, therefore, to an examination of some key characteristics of the major social classes in the United States, and to some of the consequences of the different life chances experienced by these classes.

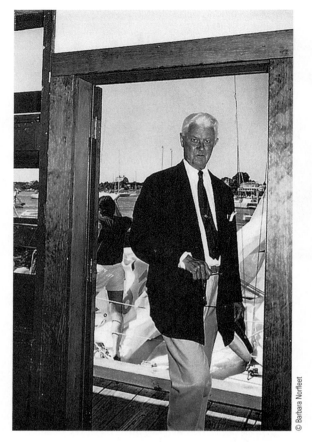

Photographer Barbara Norfleet was studying the lifestyles of the very wealthy in the United States when she caught this patrician gentleman stepping off his yacht on a summer day in Massachusetts.

TABLE 12.6

The 20 Largest Family Fortunes

Family	Fortune Founded	1996 Worth (in billions)
Walton (retailing)	1962	$24.8
du Pont (chemicals)	1802	13.9
Mars (candy)	1911	12.0
Rockefeller (oil)	1870	9.9
Newhouse (publishing)	1922	9.0
Haas (jeans)	1873	8.6
Bass (oil)	1930s	8.1
Cox (newspapers)	1898	8.0
Cargill (grain)	1865	7.9
Dorrance (soup)	1876	7.7
Pritzker (finance)	1902	6.0
Mellon (banking)	1869	5.8
Lauder (cosmetics)	1946	4.1
Scripps (newspapers)	1870s	3.6
Upjohn (pharmaceuticals)	1885	3.2
Ziff (publishing)	1927	3.0
Smith (machinery)	1889	2.8
Davis (groceries)	1925	2.3
Chandler (newspapers)	1894	2.1
Gund (food, banking)	1919	2.1

Source: Reprinted with permission from Scribber, An Imprint of Simon and Schuster Adult Publishing Group, from *Money: Who Has How Much and Why,* by Andrew Hacker. Copyright © 1997 by Andrew Hacker.

The Upper Classes

For the past 15 years, the General Social Survey has found that approximately 4 percent of Americans classify themselves as members of the upper class (NORC, 2002). And as we saw at the beginning of the chapter, the richest members of the upper class, about 1 percent of the total population, control almost 40 percent of all personal wealth in the United States. However, sociologists regard the upper class as divided roughly into two subgroups: the richest and most prestigious families, who constitute the elite or "high society" and tend to be white Anglo-Saxon Protestants, and the "newly rich" families, who may be extremely wealthy but have not attained sufficient prestige to be included in the communities and associations of high society.

At the beginning of the twentieth century, families whose wealth came from railroads and banking looked down on "upstarts" like Rockefeller and Ford, whose money came from oil and automobiles. More recently, the great manufacturing families—the du Ponts (chemicals),

the Rockefellers (oil), the Carnegies and Mellons (steel and coal)—have questioned the upper-class status of families like the Kennedys, whose wealth originally came from merchandising and whose Irish descent marked them off from the rich Protestant families.

Throughout much of the twentieth century, the number of family-owned fortunes declined as large corporations like General Motors, Boeing, and IBM gained greater economic power. But as we see in Table 12.6, the major family fortunes still represent billions of dollars of capital controlled by the members of immensely wealthy families, many of whom are not descended from earlier Yankee families. (Other familiar names, such as Bill Gates of Microsoft, Michael Dell of Dell Computers, or even Oprah Winfrey, certainly one of the best-known and richest women in the United States, do not appear on the list because this compilation of family fortunes includes only those that have been active for more than one generation.)

Members of the upper class tend to create special places in which to live and relax. They often maintain apartments in exclusive city neighborhoods and country estates in se-cluded communities. They send their children to the most expensive private schools and universities, maintain mem-berships in the most exclusive social clubs, and fly through-out the world to leisure resorts frequented by members of their own class. Examples of these resorts and enclaves of great wealth include Vail and Aspen in Colorado, Palm Springs in California, Palm Beach in Florida, and large stretches of the New England coastline.

IS THERE A "RULING CLASS"?   A question that sociologists continually debate is whether the upper class in America is also the society's ruling class. The hit film *Titanic* presents a vision of the social-class system in which the wealthy are in-deed a ruling class, but in reality the question of whether great wealth also confers the ability to rule by controlling political actors is open to empirical research and debate. Elite theorists like C. Wright Mills and William Domhoff argue that the upper class not only holds a controlling share of wealth and prestige, which it can pass along to its chil-dren, but also maintains a virtual monopoly over power in the United States (Zweigenhaft & Domhoff, 1998). A rul-ing class, Domhoff states, "is socially cohesive, has its basis in the large corporations and banks, plays a major role in shaping the social and political climate, and dominates the federal government through a variety of organizations and methods" (1983, p. 1). Mills (1956) attempted to show that this ruling class produces a *power elite* composed of its most politically active members plus high-level employees in the government and the military. The power elite, these sociol-ogists claim, is the leadership arm of the ruling class.

Other sociologists and political scientists contend that there is no single, cohesive ruling class with an identifiable power elite that carries out its bidding. This is known as the *pluralist* concept (Polsby, 1980; Sullivan, 1998). These researchers agree that there is a readily identifiable upper class in American society. However, its power is not ex-erted in a unified fashion because there are competing centers of wealth and power within the upper class; more-over, its members' viewpoints on social policy are often opposed to one another. (We return to the debate between the power elite and pluralist theories in Chapter 20.)

The Middle Classes

Unlike the upper classes, in which family status establishes who is included in the highest stratum and who is not, the middle class includes far more varied combinations of wealth and prestige. As we saw in Table 12.5, subjective measures of social class show that about 45 percent of Americans classify themselves in the middle class, although this figure is lower for African Americans (28 percent). But this large proportion of Americans who identify themselves as members of the middle class is by no means a homoge-neous population. The middle class is often referred to as the "middle classes" to emphasize the existence of strata with differing income, education, and access to wealth.

One group of Americans who usually identify them-selves as members of the middle class are highly educated professionals. Most often they have attended graduate schools and built successful careers as engineers, lawyers, doctors, dentists, stockbrokers, or corporate managers. But their comfortable incomes, often much more than $100,000 a year, may also be derived from family-owned businesses. Members of this class typically live in the sub-urbs. They join expensive country clubs, are active in community affairs, and spend a good deal of time trans-porting their children to "enriching" activities.

Another segment of the middle class is composed of peo-ple whose income is derived from small businesses, espe-cially stores and community-oriented enterprises (in con-trast with large corporations that have offices at many locations). Often referred to as the *petit bourgeoisie* or inde-pendent small-business owners, the members of this class may be found among the leaders of local chambers of com-merce and other business associations that advocate local economic growth. Erik Olin Wright and his colleagues (1982, 1997) found that of the 9 percent of Americans who employ other workers, most are members of the petit bour-geoisie and employ fewer than 10 people.

The American concept of the middle class is based far more on patterns of consumption and the American dream of shared affluence than on the kinds of economic realities that Marx used to describe social classes. Americans have always believed that they could achieve individual affluence and become part of a great middle class. Thus in subjective terms the middle class is the largest single class in American society, but in cultural terms it is highly diverse because so many different lifestyles are represented within it.

The dominant image of the middle class from the end of World War II until the mid-1970s was of a suburban population living in relatively new private homes (Scott, 1998). The culture of the suburban middle class was thought to be shaped by the experience of frequent changes of residence and long-distance commuting, to-gether with status symbols like "the ranch house with its two car garage, lawn and barbecue, and the nearby church and shopping center" (Schwartz, 1976, p. 327). The sub-urban middle class was said to be oriented toward family life and suspicious of the offbeat (Fava, 1956; Riesman, 1957). However, empirical research by several sociologists, including Bennett Berger (1961), Herbert Gans (1967, 1976), and M. P. Baumgartner (1988), has shown that suburban communities are far from homogeneous, that many people who think of themselves as members of the working class can be found in them, and that there is no easily identified middle-class suburban culture.

Another change in the nature of the middle class has to do with education. In the 1950s and 1960s, a college diploma was often viewed as a passport to the American middle-class way of life. But we will see later that, although education remains the primary route to upward mobility for people without inherited wealth, the college diploma has lost some of its power to open the door to middle-class prestige.

The most general points that sociologists can make about the middle class are that its members tend to be employed in nonmanual occupations and that they usually have to work hard to afford the material things that are more easily acquired by the upper-middle class. Identification with the middle class is likely to be highest among teachers, middle- and lower-level office managers and clerical employees, government bureaucrats, and workers in the uniformed services.

EFFECTS OF ECONOMIC INSECURITY   Political candidates attempt to win the support of the middle class because they recognize that large numbers of voters think of themselves as members of that class, rather than as rich or poor. But as we have seen, the idea of an all-inclusive American middle class is more a myth than a reality for increasing numbers of working Americans. Between the extremes of poverty and wealth are, instead of a unified middle class, two increasingly distinct groups that think of themselves as middle class but face far different life chances and economic realities.

In the more secure segment of the middle class are highly skilled, highly educated professionals and managerial women and men who are doing rather well, although they increasingly experience income stagnation and must find ways to supplement their incomes. But below this segment there is a larger stratum of less skilled and less educated people who are experiencing ever-greater economic insecurity resulting from stagnant incomes and declining living standards. Appealing to this growing insecure middle-class stratum is a central goal of political leaders.

Politics aside, it is doubtful that the problems of the middle class can be solved through social policy. Recent figures released by the Department of Labor show that people in the middle income quintile are now spending almost half their incomes on three basic necessities of life: housing (approximately 32 percent), utilities (approximately 8 percent), and health care (approximately 7 percent). A generation ago these expenditures accounted for only one-third of a typical middle-class income. (Spending on food has remained fairly constant.) Also, during the period from 1975 to 1995, the average price of a house rose by nearly 330 percent while the consumer price

TABLE 12.7

Where Americans Live

	1970	1990
Detached single-unit homes	66.3%	59.0%
Trailers or mobile homes	3.1	7.2
Apartments and other housing	30.6	33.8

Source: Reprinted with permission from Scribber, An Imprint of Simon and Schuster Adult Publishing Group, from *Money: Who Has How Much and Why*, by Andrew Hacker. Copyright © 1997 by Andrew Hacker.

index increased by 220 percent. As a result, fewer young people can afford to buy a private home, perhaps the central symbol of membership in the American middle class (Cassidy, 1995). The difficulties Americans are experiencing in realizing the dream of owning their own home are clearly shown in Table 12.7. The proportion of Americans who live in detached single-family homes declined from 1970 to 1990, while the proportion living in mobile homes and in apartments increased. These indicators point to some of the most far-reaching aspects of social change in our nation and others like it, and in later chapters we will have many reasons to examine their consequences for adults and children in all social classes.

The Working Class

Forty-four percent of white Americans and almost 57 percent of African Americans identify themselves as members of the working class (NORC, 1998). This class is undergoing the most rapid and difficult changes in America today. Indeed, as with the middle class, those who classify themselves as members of the working class are extremely diverse. There are skilled craftspeople, plumbers, carpenters, machinists, and others who earn wages protected by strong unions, and factory workers whose class interests may or may not be protected by labor unions and whose plants may be threatened with closings or layoffs resulting from automation and the globalization of manufacturing. And there are people in the working class who work long hours yet cannot earn enough income to lift them very far above the poverty threshold. These struggling working people and their families are sometimes referred to as the "working poor."

The most important characteristic of the working class is employment in skilled, semiskilled, or unskilled manual occupations. Another distinguishing feature of this class is union membership; in fact, labor unions refer to their members as "working people." However, the proportion of workers who are union members is declining. In the mid-1970s,

The Sociological Observer

What observations can you make about the kind of work this woman may do? In what ways are she and the equipment she works with representative of "the changing landscape of labor in advanced industrial societies"? (See page 350 for further insights into the sociological content of this photo.)

These hotel workers, proudly showing off the luxurious accommodations they help maintain, are part of the working class. In fact, far more people are now employed in restaurants and hotels than in metal, automobile, and textile production combined.

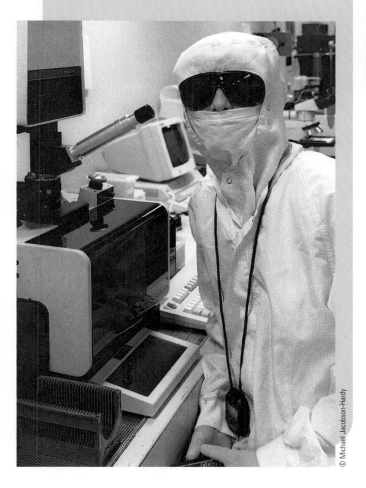

approximately 23 percent of the American labor force belonged to labor unions. Today that proportion has declined to less than 16 percent, largely as a result of the decline in factory employment. One result of this trend is that many workers have less protection against arbitrary changes in their working conditions and earnings (Aronowitz, 1998). Another is that the wages of working people are decreasing, especially in semiskilled and unskilled blue-collar jobs. This controversial issue has been thoroughly documented in the research of Richard Freeman (1994), who has shown that the decreases in union membership and hourly wages ac-

count for as much as half of the increase in income inequality referred to in Table 12.1.

There are two major divisions within the American working class. The first is often known as the industrial working class and consists of blue-collar workers who work in large manufacturing industries and are members of industrial unions. The United Automobile Workers, the United Steelworkers, the International Ladies' Garment Workers' Union, the United Mine Workers, and the International Brotherhood of Teamsters are examples of such unions (Aronowitz, 1998; Aronowitz & DiFazio, 1994; Burawoy, 1980). The second major division of the American working class is composed of workers employed in skilled crafts, especially in the construction trades (Halle, 1984; LeMasters, 1975).

Sociologists have found that the industrial working class is more conscious of its class identity and more prone to believe that its fortunes as a class depend on its ability to win in labor–management conflicts. Members of the skilled trades, by contrast, are more likely to be uncertain about their class identity or to think of themselves as members of the middle class. For both segments of the working class, financial worries are a routine fact of life (Halle, 1984). The situation of women in this class is especially problematic because they are often the first to suffer the effects of layoffs and plant closings (Rosen, 1987), an issue that is discussed further in Chapter 14.

More racial and ethnic diversity exists in the working class than in other classes. White workers in the working class are far more likely to work alongside black and Hispanic workers, for example, than are white members of other classes. This situation often brings workers of different races and ethnic backgrounds into competition when jobs are in short supply or an industry is shrinking as a result of automation. The animosity produced by such competition results largely from the fear of losing one's job and skidding downward into the ranks of the poor.

The Poor

Studies of subjective class membership usually underestimate the poor population because many people in this class think of themselves as working people who are underpaid or "down on their luck." This may be particularly true of the NORC measures of subjective social class (see Table 12.5), which use the term "lower class" instead of "poor." In an earlier study by Mary and Robert Jackman (1983), almost 8 percent of Americans classified themselves as poor. In the NORC study, about 5 percent of the sample said that they were in the "lower class." Whichever term one uses, however, these measures greatly underestimate the number of poor people in the United States. Official census statistics show that approximately 11 percent of Americans—about 31 million people—are living in poverty (*Statistical Abstract*, 2002). These figures count only people whose household incomes are below the poverty threshold income of about $348 a week for a family of four. As shown in Table 12.8, African Americans, Hispanics, and children (the majority of whom live in female-headed families) are disproportionately represented among the poor (O'Hare, 1996).

POVERTY: A RELATIVE CONCEPT   Social scientists often point out that poverty is not an absolute concept but must be measured relative to the standards of well-being in particular societies. A family of four in the United States with an annual income of $17,000 is poor by official standards, yet compared with equivalent families in India or Africa it is doing quite well. The U.S. family probably has permanent shelter, even if it is in a slum or a run-down neighborhood. It probably receives some form of government income supplement, if only in the form of food stamps and federal medical insurance (Medicaid). The poor family in Africa or India, by contrast, may be living without permanent shelter, forced to beg and sift through scraps to obtain enough food to survive. Although some poor families and individuals in the United States live under similar conditions, most of the U.S. poor are not yet in immediate danger of starvation.

Does this mean that the poor in the United States are better off? In absolute terms (i.e., in comparison with the poor in very poor nations), they are not deprived of the necessities of life. In relative terms (i.e., in comparison with the more affluent majority in the United States), they are severely deprived. This distinction between absolute

TABLE 12.8

Which Americans Are Poor?

Number and Percent in Each Group Who Are Poor

Group	Number (millions)	Percent
In total population	36.1	13.8
Children younger than 18	14.7	20.8
Men 18–64	7.5	9.5
Women 18–64	10.9	13.3
Men 65 and older	0.8	6.2
Women 65 and older	2.5	13.6
White	16.3	8.5
Black	9.9	29.3
Hispanic	8.6	30.3
Asian	1.4	14.6

Americans Below the Poverty Line, 1960–1995

Year	All Families	Persons Older Than 65	Children Younger Than 18
1960	18.1%	35.2%	26.9%
1970	10.1	24.6	15.1
1980	10.3	15.7	18.3
1990	10.7	12.2	20.6
1995	10.8	10.5	20.8

Source: Reprinted with permission from Scribber, An Imprint of Simon and Schuster Adult Publishing Group, from *Money: Who Has How Much and Why*, by Andrew Hacker. Copyright © 1997 by Andrew Hacker.

and relative deprivation is important in explaining how people feel about being poor. It is no comfort to a child in a poor family in the United States whose parents cannot afford fancy sneakers or a color TV that people are starving in Africa. In short, people feel poor in comparison with others around them who have more.

THE WORKING POOR   One of the chief causes of poverty is that people who are working full-time are not being paid wages that provide enough income to raise them above the poverty line. Two-thirds of American children living in poverty have a parent who works full-time for wages that are too low to lift the household out of poverty (Tucker, 1998). Of course, many of these households are one-parent families, but in a study of two-parent families living in poverty, David Ellwood found that 44 percent had at least one member who was working full-time. Low wages, Ellwood states, are a major cause of poverty:

Work does not always guarantee a route out of poverty. A full-time minimum-wage job (which pays $5.15 per hour) does not even come close to

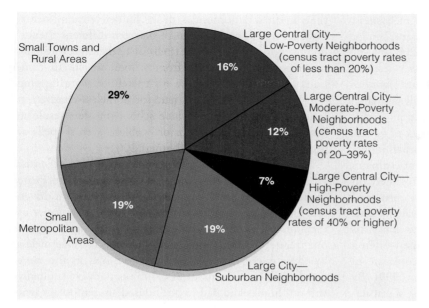

Figure 12.5 Geographic Distribution of the Poor (percent of total below poverty line)

Figures from the 2000 census indicate that the percentages in this chart have changed somewhat since Ellwood conducted his study, but the basic distribution remains the same (the percentages do not add up to 100 because of rounding).

Source: Ellwood, 1988; U.S. Census Bureau, 2001.

supporting a family of three at the poverty line. Even one full-time job and one half-time job at the minimum wage will not bring a family of four up to the poverty line. (1988, p. 88)

Because so many of the jobs created during the economic expansion of the 1980s and 1990s were low-wage jobs, rates of employment and poverty have risen simultaneously.

Another reason for the increase in poverty is the increase in the number of single-parent, female-headed families. The breakup of marriages or long-term relationships leaves women alone with the responsibility for raising small children and earning the income to do so. Such families often become poor because it is more difficult for a woman to support a family alone than it is for a man. As we will see in Chapter 15, one result of this trend toward the "feminization" of poverty is that a rising proportion of the nation's children are growing up in poor female-headed families and are deprived of the advantages enjoyed by children from more affluent homes.

A common stereotype of the poor in the United States is that they are heavily concentrated in inner-city minority ghettos. Ellwood's study of poverty shows this notion to be false, as can be seen in Figure 12.5. The poor in large central cities (those living in moderate- or high-poverty neighborhoods) account for just 19 percent of the total poor population, with only about 7 percent concentrated in high-poverty neighborhoods. Fully 29 percent of the poor reside in rural and small-town communities, and 19 percent live in the affluent suburbs of large cities. In short, the poor live everywhere and are not concentrated in a single type of community.

One reason for this pattern is that the poor are an extremely diverse population. A large portion of the poor are aged people living on fixed incomes (Social Security or very modest savings or pensions). Other categories of poor people include marginally employed rural workers and part-time miners in communities from Appalachia to Alaska; migrant farm workers in agricultural areas throughout the United States; chronically unemployed manual workers in the industrial cities; disabled workers and their families; and people who have been displaced by catastrophes like hurricanes, drought, or arson. For all of these groups, poverty brings enormous problems of insecurity and instability. Many poor people do not even know where they will be living next month or next year. This problem is especially acute for farm families who have been driven from their land.

THE HOMELESS AND INDIGENT Homelessness is one of the most visible effects of severe poverty. In a relatively affluent nation like the United States, homelessness can be defined simply as a social condition in which people do not have regular housing and are forced to sleep in public places, public shelters, or other facilities designed for homeless individuals and families. From a global perspective, the situation is somewhat more complicated. In India, for example, millions of people live on the street, but they are not homeless because they consider the spot they occupy—under a makeshift awning against a building, for example—as home. They may be indigent beggars, new arrivals to the city or town, or people with extremely low-paying work, none of whom can afford more adequate shelter. In Europe and North America, the fact that they live on the street would qualify them as homeless, but in their own societies they may be considered to have homes despite their poverty. In sociological analyses of homelessness, therefore, we must always consider local and regional definitions of the phenomenon. In the following discussion of homelessness, we will draw examples from the United States and similar urban industrial nations (Kornblum & Julian, 2004).

The recession of 2001 and 2002 brought homelessness back to national attention when individuals and families crowded food lines, soup kitchens, and all available church beds and homeless shelters. But it is extremely difficult to arrive at good estimates of the number of homeless people in the United States or any other urban industrial society. A major part of the problem is that estimates for different cities and states are most often based on counts taken at a given point in time. These measures of the homeless population are called "point prevalence estimates" because they are based on street surveys and visits to shelters at a given moment or point in time—often a day in midwinter when large numbers of people are in shelters and can be counted (Phelan & Link, 1999). By combining all such point prevalence estimates, social scientists come up with estimates that generally range from a very conservative 600,000 to more than 1 million.

Point prevalence counts underestimate the number of people who are homeless for one or more periods during a year, which includes far more adults and children who become homeless because of family disputes, fires, unemployment, and other social and economic disasters. If one considers the number of people who report that they have ever been homeless in a given year, the number of people who experience homelessness is estimated to be approximately 3 million, of whom 38 percent are children and parents (Nuñez, 2001).

Two of the leading researchers on homelessness in the United States, Martha Burt and Barbara Cohen, describe the social characteristics of the homeless as follows:

> The homeless population is extremely heterogeneous. The main population is single men, but the fastest growing group appears to be homeless families, generally headed by a single woman. Two constraints most often cited for the failure of people to leave homelessness and become completely self-sufficient are mental illness and drug or alcohol abuse. However, homelessness is not just a problem of mental illness or substance abuse; it is also a consequence of severe poverty and a lack of adequate housing. The effects of poverty and inadequate housing are exacerbated by such problems as mental illness and substance abuse. (Cohen & Burt, 1990, p. 1)

This description is most apt for the homeless encountered in large cities. In rural areas of North America, and in many communities outside the central cities, homelessness is a form of nomadism. Families and individuals who are experiencing periods of homelessness may live for a time in their automobiles or in hidden encampments. Others may go back and forth between different friends' homes. For children, these spells of homelessness usually mean periods of absence from school, which, in turn, leads to school failure and a high likelihood of dropping out. This last point is also true for homeless children in inner-city communities, where school transfers resulting from homelessness are a major problem even if spells of homelessness are not long (Nuñez, 2001).

Throughout the world, homelessness touches the most vulnerable populations. Poor people who have inadequate shelter in the first place tend to be those who are driven into homelessness by natural disasters like hurricanes or earthquakes. In 2001 in El Salvador, for example, almost one-quarter of the nation's population was made homeless by three major earthquakes and mudslides in the same two-month period. About 200,000 people were suddenly without homes and had to be "housed" in temporary tent cities (*Economist,* 2001). Recent political disasters in Afghanistan and parts of Africa have created immense numbers of homeless people who populate refugee camps. These homeless populations tend to be made up of people from rural areas who normally make their living in agriculture. On a global scale, they are a small minority of the poor population, but their dire needs and suffering, especially grave among women and children, make them extremely significant from a moral and political standpoint.

Farmers and Farm Families

In analyzing the situation of the poor in America, it is helpful to look at what is occurring in rural areas, where a large proportion of the poor live. Although many rural communities are experiencing renewed economic growth as factories relocate to areas where the costs of energy, space, training, and wages are lower, in communities based on agricultural production poverty rates continue to increase. A survey of 1,700 American farmers (Robbins, 1985) indicated that approximately 36 percent owed more than 40 percent of their assets (land and equipment, livestock, and crops in the ground) to lending institutions. Within this category of heavily indebted farmers, 15 percent (or more than 5 percent of all farmers) owed 70 percent or more of their total assets. The consequences of these debt pressures can be seen in the changing demographics of farm families. Figure 12.6 shows that the proportion of young farmers is decreasing while that of farmers older than age 65 is increasing; the average age is 54.5 years. Overall, the number of farmers is decreasing steadily each year.

This situation repeats a condition that has been part of American social life for more than a century as the nation has been transformed from a rural to an urban society

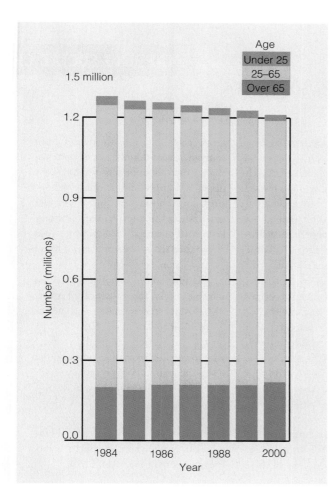

Figure 12.6 Number of Farmers, by Age, 1984–1990

Source: Bureau of Labor Statistics, 2003.

(Dyer, 1996). Although the dream of owning a family farm, or keeping one in the family, has always been an important part of American culture, the rising cost of farm technology, together with the need for ever-larger amounts of land to make farms profitable, has steadily pushed farm families off the land. Very large farms devoted to the production of a narrow range of crops and farm products now dominate North American agriculture. In the United States, more than half of total farm production comes from only about 4 percent of the nation's farms. In consequence, more farmers are employed by large agribusiness operations, and each decade a smaller percentage own family farms (Albrecht, 1997; Strange, 1988).

Larger farms are typically owned by corporations that may also can, freeze, package, or otherwise prepare the crop for sale in supermarkets. These agribusinesses may be highly efficient producers, but they have some negative social consequences for rural counties. Studies by rural sociologists have shown that communities dominated by large farms are characterized by a declining population, a decreasing number of local businesses and civic associations, and an increase in poverty. One study conducted for the U.S. Congress in 200 of the richest agricultural counties in the United States found that the more farm size increases, the more the poverty rate in the county also increases as people are displaced from the land and must search for marginal employment (Office of Technology Assessment, 1986). In 1998, as a consequence of low grain prices and extreme heat in the Great Plains, family farmers in some Plains states were experiencing the kind of severe crisis that often makes their existence precarious. In North Dakota, for example, it was estimated that some 2,000 family farmers (out of about 30,000) would be forced out of business (Clairborne, 1998).

As a social class, farmers still take pride in the fact that the United States has the highest level of agricultural production in the world, but this does little to alleviate their difficulties. Moreover, as a class, American farmers are continually at the mercy of a fickle world economy, a condition that they increasingly share with farmers in Europe and other industrialized regions.

One method farmers have traditionally used to hold on to the land they love is for some family members to find work in a nearby town while others continue to work the land. In fact, about half of all farmers farm part-time and work at wage-paying jobs full-time. A growing number of women in farm families work full- or part-time in rural factories. Many also work at home producing knitwear and other apparel on a piecework basis or performing electronic data processing via computer networks. Still others have service jobs.

The strategy of trying to maintain the household's economic position by adding more wage earners is increasingly common in other social classes as well. This trend has far-reaching implications, not only for the way Americans think about social class but for all of the society's institutions. For farmers, however, the numbers are discouraging. As an economic class, they are diminishing steadily, especially as young people leave farming for other occupations. (See Mapping Social Change box on pages 346–347).

MORE EQUALITY?

A large proportion of the world's people are extremely poor. India, China, Bangladesh, the Philippines, Malaysia, most of sub-Saharan Africa, the mountain regions of Latin America, and many other parts of the world are inhabited by large numbers of people with drastically limited incomes and only the most rudimentary health care, education, and other resources. If poverty continues to increase

Poor Counties in the United States

This map shows all of the counties of the United States, grouped by average income. The extremes of wealth and poverty in U.S. society are apparent. Or are they? Actually, such a map is more useful in revealing areas of poverty outside central cities than within them. This is because impoverished inner-city communities usually constitute only a portion of a densely urban county that may also include affluent and middle-class communities. Their incomes raise the average so that the pockets of inner-city poverty do not appear on the map.

This map still reveals a great deal about the places where poor people live. For example, along the Mississippi River, especially in Arkansas and Mississippi, we see groups of counties whose residents' average income is in the lowest range. The same is true in parts of the arid Southwest. Why are there such high concentrations of poor residents in these counties?

The Mississippi delta region has rich agricultural land, but most of it is owned by a few white families and agricultural corporations. The land is farmed by African-American and poor white workers who earn extremely little. Thus the delta region has a pattern of agrarian stratification that results in high rates of poverty. In the impoverished counties of the Southwest, the land often contains mineral and water resources that are controlled by a few wealthy individuals and corporations; Chicanos, Native Americans, and poor whites do not share in the wealth created by these resources, and the counties in which they live have low average incomes.

The isolated poor counties of the mountain states in the West often suffer from a newer form of poverty. In these areas, economic growth results from tourism, second-home developments, skiing, and other pursuits of the affluent upper and upper-middle classes. Farms, small-town businesses, and the trailer parks where the resort workers live may be located in a nearby valley, which may be part of a separate county with a lower average income.

Classification of counties by median income masks the existence of many high-poverty communities and neighborhoods in urban areas. The red zones on the map, which denote the counties with the highest median incomes, do not reveal the high rates of poverty in neighborhoods in and around New York City, Philadelphia, and Baltimore, or Chicago and Detroit, or the Los Angeles–San Diego corridor, to name only a few of the most outstanding areas in which poverty is concentrated (Jargowski, 1997).

in those areas and the hopes of impoverished millions for a better life are frustrated, it will become increasingly difficult to maintain peace, achieve slower population growth, and prevent massive environmental damage.

Poverty is reduced through better health care, more schools, more food and shelter, and more jobs, all of which require economic and social development. The experience of the more affluent nations indicates that such development is likely to produce larger working and middle classes and reduce the rate of poverty. But the persistence of poverty and near-poverty in the United States and other industrialized nations shows how difficult it is to promote greater equality elsewhere in the world.

Two Types of Equality

The presence of millions of poor people in a country as affluent as the United States is a major public policy issue as well as a subject of extensive social research. However, policy debates on this issue are often clouded by problems of definition. Most Americans will say that they believe in equality, citing the claim of the nation's founders that "all men are created equal." When pressed to define equality, however, they often fail to distinguish between **equality of opportunity** (equal opportunity to achieve material well-being and prestige) and **equality of result** (actual equality in levels of material well-being and prestige). Americans

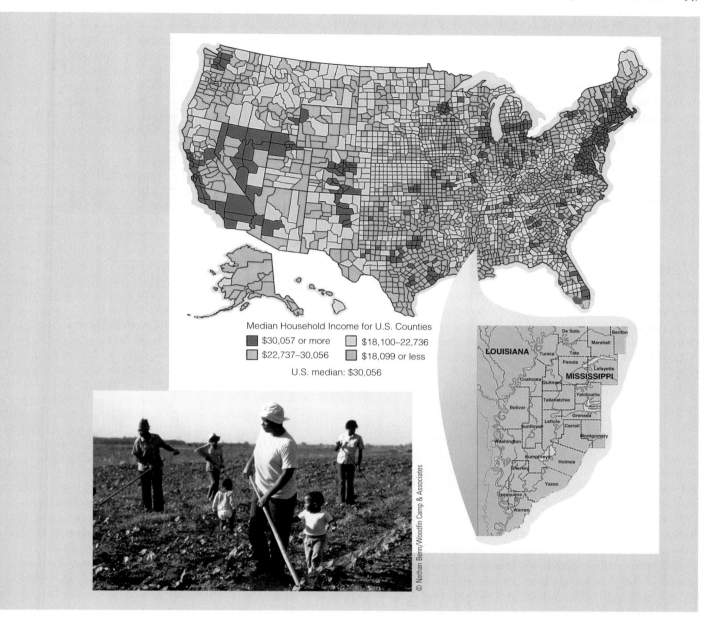

Median Household Income for U.S. Counties

- ◼ $30,057 or more
- ◻ $22,737–30,056
- ◻ $18,100–22,736
- ◻ $18,099 or less

U.S. median: $30,056

© Nathan Benn/Woodfin Camp & Associates

may believe that opportunities to succeed should be distributed equally and that the rules that determine who succeeds and who fails should be fair. But their commitment to the ideal of equality falters in the face of their belief that hard work and competence should be rewarded and laziness and incompetence punished. Thus many Americans believe that poverty is proof of personal failure. They do not stop to ask whether poor Americans have ever been given equality of opportunity, nor do they stop to notice how hard many poor people work (Jencks, 1994; Liebow, 1967).

Sociologists who study inequality in modern societies usually ask how equality of opportunity can be increased and the gaps between the haves and the have-nots decreased. Yet they are also highly aware of how difficult it is to narrow that gap in the United States or any other society. In response to those who believe that government can do nothing effective in its efforts to reduce poverty, sociologists point to the kinds of hard facts presented in Table 12.8. The table clearly shows that poverty among people older than age 65 has been reduced dramatically, from 35.2 percent in 1960 to 10.5 percent in 1995, largely as a consequence of Social Security legislation and Medicare. Poverty among children, on the other hand, was greatly reduced between 1960 and 1980 but has been increasing rapidly since the 1980s.

The role the government should play in alleviating poverty is a major issue in American society today. It is frequently asserted, both in government and in the social sciences, that government has no business engaging in large-scale redistribution of income in the interests of the lower classes. This viewpoint, which is represented in the writings of conservative social scientists like Milton Friedman (1962), George Gilder (1982), and Charles Murray (1984, 1988), as well as in current social policies, agrees that public funds must be spent to provide the poor with a "safety net" of programs to prevent suffering, but it also holds that programs to redistribute wealth infringe on individual freedom and the right of private property.

Welfare Reform

The extent to which declines in the income and well-being of poor children in the United States are a consequence of changes in the welfare system is an extremely controversial subject. In 1996, Congress enacted historic changes in the nation's welfare laws, which now require each state to ensure that a rising percentage of its adult aid recipients engage in approved work. The head of each family on government financial assistance ("welfare") is required to find a job within 2 years after assistance payments begin. Most families may receive benefits for no longer than 5 years, and states may impose even shorter time limits if they choose to do so. The new law has dramatically reduced the welfare population, from about 5 percent of the total U.S. population in 1994 to about 2.6 percent in 2000 (Beneckson et al., 2000). This reduction, due largely to "welfare to work" programs in the states, is considered successful by the Bush administration, which has proposed even greater efforts to oblige recipients to move into the labor market. But one may ask whether this new policy actually improves the well-being of children. That question, in turn, leads to many different empirical questions, especially about the actual job experience and earnings of former welfare recipients (Burtless, 1998).

An excellent study conducted in Pinellas County, Florida, examined the earnings of former welfare recipients to determine how many have earnings that raise them and their children above the poverty level. Figure 12.7 shows the percentage of blacks, Hispanics, and whites that left welfare and whether their earnings, once they had done so, were adequate to raise them out of poverty. Although there are minor differences among the groups, the figure shows that for each group, the large majority did not earn enough to get themselves out of poverty. Similar research done in Wisconsin tracked 18,000 former recipients who found work, but noted that job turnover was so

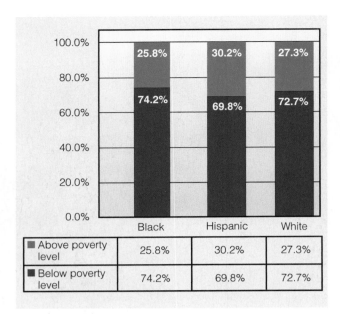

Figure 12.7   Percentage of Successful Welfare Leavers Above and Below the Federal Poverty Level for Pinellas, February 1997–February 1998

Source: Beneckson et al., 2000.

	Black	Hispanic	White
Above poverty level	25.8%	30.2%	27.3%
Below poverty level	74.2%	69.8%	72.7%

high that they actually held a total of 42,000 different jobs over a 1-year period. More than half of these jobs were obtained from temporary help agencies.

Another disturbing fact is that welfare reforms were implemented during a period of sustained economic growth and record high demand for entry-level workers. The downturn in the U.S. economy will likely make it even more difficult for former welfare recipients, most of whom have limited educational credentials, to find work that will sustain their families or offer reasonable income stability.

Recent studies also point out that the children of former welfare recipients who find jobs are more likely to receive inadequate supervision at home, which also increases the likelihood that these vulnerable workers will temporarily leave the labor force. Figure 12.7 illustrates the "multiple jeopardy" faced by single mothers: It compares those who never received welfare benefits with those who received benefits for 1 to 24 months and those who were longer-term welfare recipients (more than 60 months). Workers in the latter group have fewer resources at home and on the job that would enable them to work through children's illnesses or other household difficulties. These and many other indicators point to the need for the United States to make greater investments in quality child care institutions and early-childhood education programs, a subject to which we return in later chapters.

Is There a War Against the Poor?

Many sociologists who study welfare reform are highly critical of the new policies—not because they require people to work rather than receive benefits, but because they seem to increase the number of children living in poverty. Some also argue that the new policies are essentially designed to promote competition for low-wage jobs, which will ensure that the working poor remain poor. Under both past and present policies, sociologist Herbert Gans observes, poverty is so persistent that one can well ask whether it might have positive social functions. With large doses of irony, he goes on to list why he believes that legislators are waging a "war against the poor." He describes several "positive" functions of poverty:

- The existence of poverty ensures that society's dirty work will be done. . . . Society can fill these jobs by paying higher wages than for "clean" work, or it can force people who have no other choice to do the dirty work.

- Because the poor are required to work at low wages, they subsidize a variety of economic activities that benefit the affluent. For example, domestics subsidize the upper-middle and upper classes, making life easier for their employers.

- Poverty creates jobs for occupations and professions that serve or "service" the poor, or protect the rest of society from them. . . . Penology would be minuscule without the poor, as would the police.

- The poor can be identified and punished as alleged or real deviants in order to uphold the legitimacy of conventional norms. (1985, pp. 155–161)

These and other hidden functions of poverty, Gans argues, are far outweighed by its dysfunctions—suffering, violence, and waste of human and material resources. And they could be eliminated by "functional alternatives," such as higher pay for doing dirty work, or by the intentional redistribution of income. He believes welfare payments and tax credits for the poor should be increased so they can qualify for the housing and other subsidies available to better-off Americans (Gans, 1995).

Other sociologists offer proposals that focus on education or local and regional economic development. We saw earlier that success in the job market is directly related to educational attainment. In fact, in today's economy, the lack of a high school diploma puts a job seeker at a tremendous disadvantage. And when the job seeker has limited education and is also African American or Hispanic and a young mother, the disadvantages she faces can be overwhelming. (See Chapters 13 and 14 for more on this sub-

ject.) But sociologists like William J. Wilson (1998) point out that many poor people are poor because they happened to be born into households in very poor communities. If public policies were directed toward improving job prospects in these communities, they argue, the gap between the haves and the have-nots would be narrowed as well. In the final section of the chapter, therefore, we turn to issues of poverty and place.

CRITICAL SOCIOLOGY AND SOCIAL CHANGE

The Working Poor: Nickel and Dimed

Sometimes it takes a special kind of courage and dedication to be a sociological pioneer. Barbara Ehrenreich has a Ph.D. in biology, but for many years she has been a leading political activist, feminist, and sociological researcher. In 1998, during the boom economy, she asked herself how people at the bottom of the labor market were doing in these flush years. She had studied the statistics and census data about the working poor, but her method was to spend time working at minimum-wage jobs in different U.S. cities. Well into her 50s and not used to physical labor, she knew that her choice would be difficult, but she underestimated just how many difficulties she would face as a woman in the low-wage sector (Ehrenreich, 2001).

Ehrenreich knew that many women work in the "pink-collar ghetto" as secretaries, store clerks and cashiers, beauticians, waitresses, telephone operators, and nursing-home and hospital attendants. Those who do the most exhausting and backbreaking jobs tend to get the lowest pay and the least fringe benefits. Often unable to make ends meet and forced to remain in jobs that allow them little opportunity for self-improvement, these women workers were far removed, Ehrenreich soon realized, from "boom-time America."

Ehrenreich worked as a cleaning woman, a nursing-home aide, a store clerk, a waitress, and other jobs that women often perform. Here are a few of her perceptions of the experience:

> I guess I was confirmed in my expectation that it would be difficult, in some cases impossible, to make a living. That was not so surprising. But one of the big shocks for me, almost from the beginning, was how little privacy or rights you have in the workplace. Very early, the first or second day of my life as a waitress, I was warned by a coworker that my purse could be searched at any time. I just didn't believe that could be legal. But I

Text continues on page 352.

VISUAL SOCIOLOGY

THE CHANGING LANDSCAPE OF LABOR

Michael Jacobson-Hardy's photographs contrast the work environment in traditional, basic industries such as paper mills, foundries, textile mills, and shipyards with that in newer, high-technology industries such as computer manufacturing and aircraft production. In addition to examining the physical environment in which industrial production occurs, his images give visibility and voice to the workers themselves—the men and women whose lives and livelihoods have been affected most directly by the social and economic transformations now under way. The photographer explains his approach as follows:

In 1989 I decided to seek out the effects of capitalism on workers and to record their stories through photography. The division of labor in a factory mirrors society as a whole. I sought out the impact of class oppression on different ethnic, racial, and gender groups. I became enamored with creating dignified portraits of entry-level workers. Images of the rich and famous are plentiful. It is the factory worker who needs visibility and a voice. One worker I met told me, "I've been working in this factory for forty years and nobody's ever asked to take my picture." (Jacobson-Hardy, 1995, p. 43)

The photos shown here are part of an exhibition titled "The Changing Landscape of Labor: Workers and Workplace." Although the focus of the exhibition is New England, the issues addressed are relevant to the United States as a whole, as can be seen in the accompanying comments by workers.

The Sociological Observer
(See photo on page 341.)

Work in technologically sophisticated industries often requires workers to wear protective suits and to be extremely conscious of cleanliness. This woman could be working in a dangerous environment, dealing with radiation or toxic chemicals, for example, or she could be working in the computer industry, perhaps testing computer chips, which requires a dust-free environment. In either case, the technical requirements of her work impose strict limitations on her physical freedom and comfort.

It's a very dirty job [extracting oil from metal shavings]. When you walk downstairs, it's a . . . big cloudy mist of oil. Sometimes you come home and you're oil from head to toe.

The plan is to do away with manufacturing. A lot of good people have been laid off. Both of my parents once worked here and lost their jobs. We can't compete. I like it here. I like the people I work with. Three and a half years ago we had about 32,000 employees—now, there are about 6,000. Every 3 or 4 months, more people get laid off. It's a slow process.

When I started in the paper industry, it was still . . . a trade. You had to fight to get to be a machine tender. . . . It would take you sometimes 15 or 20 years to get to that position. . . . You had to wait. You had to grow into your job.

When the mills shut down some workers never even bothered to return to pick up their pay. . . . We just lost track of them. . . . What people got, if they were old enough, wouldn't be enough money to last for a week. . . . They had the worst pension plans you ever saw in your life. It wouldn't amount to a pot of beans.

I'm tired. I want to quit. . . . I have to work until I'm 65. Maybe I'll never make it.

AP/Wide World Photos

© Chapman/The Image Works

Barbara Ehrenreich, a sociologist and social activist whose research and writing call attention to the way workers are exploited in low-paying jobs like that of supermarket checkout clerk.

have since, of course, checked with labor lawyers, and it's true. At work, you have no privacy as to your personal effects, purse or backpack, in any state that I know of.

There were all these rules I was not prepared for, things like no talking or "no gossiping," meaning no chatting with coworkers, which doesn't mean that you don't chat, it means that you chat stealthily. At the housecleaning job, we couldn't drink anything, even water, or eat anything, during the time period we were in each house. We were in little teams of four, and we could be in a house for four hours, but we were not to have a sip of water. I'm one of those yuppie types who always carries a plastic bottle of water with her everywhere, in case I feel the slightest twinge of thirst. I would be sweating, the sweat would be just pouring down my face, and the only thing to do would be to try to sneak into a bathroom in one of these houses and drink from the faucet now and then. I was

astonished by the degree of micro-management and absurd rules, which seemed to have no function except to assert the authority of management.

It really changed the way I saw the world. . . . I began to see all the invisible people. . . . I became aware of a world of discomfort and pain all around me: in the grocery store, at restaurants.

Reflecting on her experiences, and on what she would wish for the people she worked with and wrote about, Ehrenreich makes these points:

First, think about how they vote and influence the political process. Ask themselves what's the difference between the candidates on these issues, learn more about what's at stake and vote accordingly. Second, I'd like to see people honor union-organizing drives and not cross picket lines. There comes a time when most of us face a choice about those things. Third, I'd like more people to see low-paid working people as interesting human beings and to treat them with respect. That was one of the things that really hurt me when I was in those jobs—the invisibility, and the contempt I felt from the people I was serving. (quoted in Abbott, 2001)

SUMMARY

Dimensions of Social Inequality in America

- The basic measures of inequality in any society are income, wealth, *occupational prestige,* and *educational attainment.*

- In U.S. society, the distribution of educational attainment and occupational prestige is more nearly equal than the distribution of wealth and income.

- Sociological views of inequality in America have changed as the nation has been transformed from an agrarian society to an urban industrial society and then to a postindustrial society.

- The Jeffersonian view of America envisioned a society in which most families lived on their own farms or ran small commercial or manufacturing enterprises. However, this view did not apply to the larger cities, the southern states, or Native Americans.

- During the Great Depression, the effects of industrialization tended to increase hostility between workers and the owners of businesses.

- In the mid-twentieth century, several important studies of inequality in American communities revealed the existence of a complex social-class system as well as a racial caste system.

- The shift from an economy based on manufacturing to one based on services has resulted in a blurring of class lines and an easing of class conflict between industrial workers and the owners and managers of the means of production. Nevertheless, some sociologists argue that Americans continue to recognize social-class divisions.

- When people are asked what social class they belong to, the largest proportion say that they are members of the middle class. They base their class assignments on *socioeconomic status,* which is derived primarily from occupation but also takes into account family status, education, and earned income.

Social Class and Life Chances in the United States

- Social-class position has important consequences for the daily life of individuals and households. Members of the upper classes tend to have better health and more adequate health care than people in the lower classes. They are also likely to receive more and better education. In politics, the poor and members of the working class generally support the Democratic party, whereas those in the middle and upper classes support the Republican party.

- The upper class is estimated at about 1 percent of the U.S. population but controls 40 percent of all personal wealth in the United States. This class may be divided into the wealthiest and most prestigious families, who make up the elite or "high society," and families that have acquired their money more recently.

- Sociologists continually debate whether the upper class in America is also the society's ruling class.

- The middle class, the largest class in American society, is culturally extremely diverse and hence is often referred to as the "middle classes." In the past, it was thought to be associated with a family-oriented, conservative, suburban lifestyle, but recent studies have shown that no easily identified middle-class suburban culture exists.

- The working class, which accounts for 44 percent of white Americans and almost 57 percent of African Americans, is undergoing rapid and difficult changes as production technologies change and industrialization spreads throughout the world. Members of this class are employed in skilled, semiskilled, or unskilled manual occupations, and many are union members. The working class can be divided into industrial workers and those employed in skilled crafts. More racial and ethnic diversity exists in the working class than in other classes.

- Estimates of the proportion of the population living in poverty vary widely, depending on the standard used to define poverty. According to official statistics, about 12 percent of Americans are living in poverty. A significant proportion of the poor have jobs that do not pay enough to support their families. Another large percentage of poor families are single-parent families headed by women. Other categories of poor people include aged people with fixed incomes, marginally employed rural workers and part-time miners, chronically unemployed manual workers, and disabled workers and their families. Another group of people in danger of becoming poor are farmers.

More Equality?

- Policy debates on the issue of poverty are often clouded by problems of definition. Although many Americans believe in *equality of opportunity,* they are less committed to the ideal of *equality of result.*

- Most sociologists agree that it is impossible to achieve a completely egalitarian society; instead, they concentrate on how much present levels of inequality can and should be reduced.

- In 1996, Congress enacted major reforms in the welfare laws, which now require that adult aid recipients engage in approved work. Data on the effects of the reforms indicate that they have had mixed results and may actually have worsened conditions for poor children.

GLOSSARY

educational attainment: The number of years of school an individual has completed. (p. 326)

educational achievement: Mastery of basic reading, writing, and computational skills. (p. 327)

occupational prestige: The honor or prestige attributed to specific occupations by adults in a society. (p. 327)

ghetto: A section of a city that is segregated either racially or culturally. (p. 332)

socioeconomic status (SES): A broad social-class ranking based on occupational status, family prestige, educational attainment, and earned income. (p. 335)

equality of opportunity: Equal opportunity to achieve desired levels of material well-being and prestige. (p. 346)

equality of result: Equality in the actual outcomes of people's attempts to improve their material well-being and prestige. (p. 346)

INTERNET RESOURCES

Virtual Society: The Wadsworth Sociology Resource Center
(http://sociology.wadsworth.com)

At Virtual Society you can access a wide range of enrichment material to aid your study of sociology. From the main page, click on the Student Resources link and find your course and this textbook. Next, select the chapter you are presently studying from the pull-down menu. Among the useful options for each self-study chapter are online links and exercises, flashcards, practical study tips, and practice quizzes for each chapter.

MC   MicroCase Online

From the Virtual Society home page, click on MicroCase Online to access book-specific MicroCase exercises that allow you to further explore sociological issues and principles presented in the text.

InfoTrac College Edition

Another unique option available to you at the Student Resources section at Virtual Society is InfoTrac College Edition, an online library with access to hundreds of scholarly and popular periodicals. Below are suggested search terms for this chapter, but this resource also allows you to fit your study of sociology to your own interests by searching custom keywords.

Socioeconomic status

Middle class

Ghetto

Educational attainment

U.S. Census Bureau
(www.census.gov)

Includes useful demographic data. Click on "Subjects A-Z" and then, for example, on "P" to look up Poverty or on "W" to look up Wealth.

The National Center for Children in Poverty
(http://cpmcnet.columbia.edu/dept/nccp)

Has updated information and ongoing research on the effects of changes in welfare policy on the lives of poor children and their communities.

Institute for Research on Poverty
(www.ssc.wisc.edu/irp)

Offers access to the most recent research on the causes and consequences of poverty and social inequality in the United States.

Cato Institute
(www.cato.org)

A conservative research institution devoted to criticism of the welfare state. Advocates market alternatives rather than government-driven policies to address problems of social stratification and inequality.

Inequalities of Race and Ethnicity

AP/Wide World Photos

25·APR·1959   MACK CHA
AND LYNCH

24·SEP·1957

PRESIDENT EISENHOWER ORDERS
FEDERAL TROOPS TO ENFORCE SCHOOL
DESEGREGRATION·LITTLE ROCK, AR

G·1957   CONGRESS PASSES FIRST CIVIL RIGHTS ACT
SINCE RECONSTRUCTION

LIE EDWARDS JR·KILLED BY KLAN
ONTGOMERY, AL

23·JAN

SUPREME COURT BANS SEGREGATED SEATING
ON MONTGOMERY BUSES

13·NOV·1956

MONTGOMERY BUS BOYCOTT BEGINS

C·1955

ROSA PARKS ARRESTED FOR REFUSING TO
GIVE UP HER SEAT ON BUS TO A WHITE
MAN·MONTGOMERY, AL

DEC·1955

E·SLAIN BY NIGHTRIDERS
CHOOL   VER·TX

When she was only 20 years old and still an undergraduate architecture student at Yale University, Maya Lin had an astounding experience. The young Asian American's design for a monument to commemorate the 58,156 Americans killed in the Vietnam War was chosen from more than 1,500 entries in an international competition. Earlier in the semester, she had submitted the design as a project in her architecture course, but the professor did not like the concept very much. However, Lin had a strong vision of how the polished black granite monument would offer people a chance to reflect on the meaning of the war and remember those who died in it. She believed in her work.

After spending many weeks revising a one-page statement describing the intent of her design, Lin submitted the drawings to the competition's jury, never expecting to win. The rest is history. The Vietnam Veterans Memorial has become the most popular and moving piece of commemorative sculpture in the nation. Visitors run their fingers along the wall and often place bouquets, photographs, poems, or other items below the spot where their loved one's name is in-

FOCUS QUESTIONS:

• In what way is race a "social construct" rather than a distinctively biological trait of different populations?

• What are some of the most common patterns of inter-group relations?

• How do social scientists explain the existence of racial and ethnic inequalities?

Maya Lin.

AP/Wide World Photos

scribed. "I knew people would have a personal experience as they searched for the names of those they knew," Lin (1995) explains, "but I never expected that they would leave things there. That was a surprise to me."

Although the monument commemorates the Vietnam War and does not directly address racism or ethnic conflict, Lin had to deal with a fair amount of racial abuse as the monument was being constructed. Mingled with the praise were letters that said, among other hateful things, that "a gook should not have been chosen to design a Vietnam War memorial." Even at the dedication, which Lin attended with her family, there were racial slights that wounded her deeply. But the popularity of the monument, and the way it brings together Americans of all races to contemplate death and heroism, more than compensate for the hurt. And as described in the Visual Sociology section of this chapter, the universal appeal of her vision has resulted in other commissions.

THE MEANING OF RACE AND ETHNICITY

How can we explain prejudice and racial discrimination and the inequalities they engender? And how can we measure their effects on individuals and social institutions? Many social scientists focus their research on why some groups in a society have been subordinated and the consequences of that subordination for them and their children. The effects of various forms of subordination, such as slavery, expulsion, and discrimination, on a society's patterns of inequality are at the center of the study of race and ethnicity.

Given the ever-changing diversity of the population, racial and ethnic relations in the United States are always complex and sometimes marked by overt conflict. No sooner does the society appear to be making some progress in combating prejudice and discrimination than new issues and problems appear. After the terrorist attacks on the World Trade Center and the Pentagon, for example, Arab Americans experienced the same kinds of discriminatory searches and questioning, known as racial profiling, that African Americans have struggled against in recent years.

The United States is not unique in the extent to which inequality and hostility among its ethnic and racial groups result in severe social problems. In Canada, conflict between Anglo and French Canadians in Quebec periodically threatens national unity. In Germany, there have been severe riots as native-born Germans have pressed for limits on the nation's acceptance of refugees from Eastern European nations that were formerly dominated by the Soviet Union. In what used to be Yugoslavia, hostility among Croats, Serbs, Bosnians, and Albanians has produced the bloodiest ethnic wars in recent history. More recently, in Iraq after the U.S. invasion, conflict among that nation's main ethnic and religious groups—ethnic Kurds, Sunni Muslims, and Shiite Muslims—vastly complicated the development of a new government (Lippmann, 2003).

In view of its importance throughout the world, it is no wonder that the study of racial and ethnic relations has always been a major subfield of sociology. Most societies include minority groups, people who are defined as different according to the majority's perceptions of racial or cultural differences. And in many societies, as the ironic song from the musical *South Pacific* goes, "You've got to be taught to be afraid/of people whose eyes are differently made/or people whose skin is a different shade./You've got to be carefully taught." Sociologists try to get at the origins of these fears and groundless distinctions that categorize people as different and influence their life chances, often in dramatic ways.

In this chapter, we first look at how race and ethnicity lead to the formation of groups that have a sense of themselves as different from the dominant group. In the second section of the chapter, we analyze patterns of inequality and intergroup relations; in the third section, we discuss cultural consequences, particularly in American society. This is followed by a presentation of social-scientific theories that seek to explain the phenomena of intergroup conflict and accommodation. Rather than discussing each of the major racial and ethnic groups in American society in turn, throughout the chapter we present examples from the experience of blacks, Hispanic Americans, Native Americans, and other ethnic groups that have played an important part in American history.

Race: A Social Concept

Of the millions of species of animals on earth, ours, *Homo sapiens,* is the most widespread. For the past 10 millennia, we have been spreading northward and southward and across the oceans to every corner of the globe, but we have not done so as a single people. Rather, throughout our history we have been divided into innumerable societies, each of which maintains its own culture, thinks of itself as "we," and looks upon all others as "they." Through all the millennia of warfare, migration, and population growth, we have been colliding and competing and learning to cooperate. The realization that we are one great people despite our immense diversity has been slow to evolve. We persist in creating arbitrary divisions based on physical differences that are summed up in the term *race.*

In biology, **race** refers to an inbreeding population that develops distinctive physical characteristics that are hereditary. Such a population therefore has a shared genetic heritage (Graves, 2001; Marks, 1994). But the choice of which physical characteristics to use in classifying people into races is arbitrary. Skin color, hair form, blood type, and facial features such as nose shape and eyefolds have been used by biologists in such efforts. In fact, however, the distribution of these traits overlaps considerably among the so-called races. Human groups have exchanged their genes through mating to such an extent that any attempt to identify "pure" races is bound to be fruitless (Gould, 1981; Graves, 2001). Thus, biologist Joseph Graves points out:

> As far as distinct lineages, throughout history, we have had too much gene flow between so-called races. If sub-Saharan Africans only mated with sub-Saharan Africans and Europeans only mated with Europeans, then there might be unique lineages. But that hasn't occurred, particularly in America. Here, because of our history of chattel slavery, individuals are still classified as black by means of the "rule of hypodescent," whereby one drop of black blood makes one black. However, there is no biological rationale for this rule. (quoted in Villarosa, 2002, p. 5)

Yet doesn't common sense tell us that there are different races? Can't we see that there is a Negro, or "black," race of people with dark skin, tightly curled hair, and broad facial features; a Caucasian, or "white," race of people with pale skin and ample body hair; and a Mongoloid, or "Oriental," race of people with yellowish or reddish skin and deep eyefolds that give their eyes a slanted look? Of course these races exist. But they are not a set of distinct populations based on biological differences. The definitions of race used in different societies emerged from the interaction of various populations over long periods of human history. The specific physical characteristics that we use to assign people to different races are arbitrary and meaningless—people from the Indian subcontinent tend to have dark skin and straight hair; Africans from Ethiopia have dark skin and narrow facial features; American blacks have skin colors ranging from extremely dark to extremely light; and whites have facial features and hair forms that include those of all the other supposed races. There is no scientifically valid typology of human races; what counts is what people in a society define as meaningful. In short, race is a social concept that varies from one society to another, depending on how the people of that society feel about the importance of certain physical differences among human beings. In reality, as Edward O. Wilson (1979) has written, human beings are "one great breeding system through which the genes flow and mix in each generation. Because of that flux, mankind viewed over many generations shares a single human nature within which relatively minor hereditary influences recycle through ever-changing patterns, between the sexes and across families and entire populations" (p. 52).

Racism

Throughout human history, many individuals and groups have rejected the idea of a single human people. Tragic mistakes and incalculable suffering have been caused by the application of erroneous ideas about race and racial purity. They are among the most extreme consequences of the attitude known as *racism*.

Racism is an ideology based on the belief that an observable, supposedly inherited trait, such as skin color, is a mark of inferiority that justifies discriminatory treatment of people with that trait. In their classic text on racial and cultural minorities, Simpson and Yinger (1953) highlighted several beliefs that are at the heart of racism. The most common of these is the "doctrine of biologically superior and inferior races" (p. 55). Before World War I, for example, many of the foremost social thinkers in the Western world firmly believed that whites were genetically superior to blacks in intelligence. However, when the U.S. Army administered an IQ test to its recruits, the results showed that performance on such tests was linked to social-class background rather than to race. And when investigators controlled for differences in social class among the test takers, the racial differences in IQ disappeared (Kleinberg, 1935).

Since that time, there have been other attempts to demonstrate innate differences in intelligence among people of different races. The most recent of these efforts is Herrnstein and Murray's controversial study, *The Bell Curve* (1994), which we discussed in Chapter 5. This study argues that because scores on intelligence tests are distributed along a "normal" bell curve, many people will have scores that fall well below the mean, and these individuals will not be capable of performing well in situations requiring reasoning ability or other academic skills. Because the bell curves for African Americans and whites are different, with that of blacks peaking at a somewhat lower mean score, the authors argue that group differences in IQ establish biological limits on ability. This conclusion, in turn, leads them to argue that programs intended to correct differences in educational opportunities, such as Head Start, are doomed to failure.

Critics of these conclusions argue that studies like *The Bell Curve* merely dredge up old academic justifications for the status quo of racial and class inequality (Gould, 1995; Graves, 2001). There is much evidence that IQ tests are biased against members of minority groups and that something as complex and elusive as intelligence cannot be summarized by a single score on a test. The history of efforts to address inequalities in education shows that when they have access to high-quality educational programs, minority students quickly begin to achieve at the same levels as white students.

RACE MATTERS   Race is not a biologically meaningful concept, but that does not mean it is not a significant aspect of life in societies all over the world. In the United States, as a result both of misunderstandings about race and of overt racism, African Americans, Asian Americans, Native Americans, and other population groups with physical features that set them apart have endured prejudice, discrimination, and economic exploitation. One result is persistent forms of inequality and injustice (West, 1996; Wilgoren, 2003). But there are also more positive outcomes. To survive and to cope with life in a society in which they are considered different and inferior, these groups have developed their own subcultures and a strong sense of themselves as distinct peoples within the larger society. This process occurs among groups that are not considered racially distinct, such as the Irish or Jews, who have struggled against prejudice and discrimination and have also developed strong subcultures.

THEN AND NOW

Reaching Higher Ground

"Do you know the hymn that goes, 'The great trees are bending/The Good Lord is sending/His people up to higher ground'?" The speaker is Polly Heidelberg, a founder of the Civil Rights movement in Meridian, Mississippi. Among the events that have burned themselves into her memory are the murders of three civil rights workers—James Chaney, Michael Schwerner, and Andrew Goodman—who worked together in Mississippi during the "Freedom Summer" of 1964. Chaney was an African-American resident of Meridian; Schwerner and Goodman were volunteers from northern colleges. And Polly Heidelberg was one of the last people the young men saw before they set out for the little village of Philadelphia, Mississippi, where they were murdered and hastily buried in an earthen dam. (Their murder, one of the pivotal moments of the Civil Rights movement, is the subject of the 1988 film *Mississippi Burning*.) "Miz" Heidelberg, as she is known in Meridian, was Chaney's neighbor, and she feels responsible for "bringing him into the movement." She knew all three men, and even now when she thinks of them her eyes cloud over and she prays for their souls.

As she speaks, Heidelberg and I are sitting in a white-owned coffee shop in a white neighborhood of Meridian. One of her granddaughters, a child of about 4, has finished eat-

ing and is playing quietly on the floor. I am scribbling Heidelberg's words on a notepad while attempting to eat an ample southern breakfast. An interview with Polly Heidelberg is fun. She often slips riddles into her speech to gently tease the listener. She is also a deeply religious and patriotic person, and her speech is filled with allusions to God and country.

Heidelberg tells me about the movement to integrate the armed forces during World War II, about the bitterness of racial strife during the 1950s, and about the exhausting, exhilarating years of the 1960s. There is no end to the movement as she sees it. Civil rights was only one aspect of the struggle for true equality of opportunity. Now there must be more progress toward economic equality.

We have finished our breakfast and the child is becoming restless. Heidelberg asks me, "That line in the hymn that mentions higher ground, what do you think higher ground is?"

Stammering a bit, I begin by saying something about "loftier values, greater spirituality, . . ." but Miz Heidelberg gently interrupts me.

"Sure, you could think about it that way. But to me 'higher ground' is right where we are now. It's you and me and the child having breakfast in this coffee shop here in Meridian, Mississippi."

SOCIAL CHANGE AND RACISM: CONFRONTING HATE Attacks on Arab storekeepers and turban-wearing Sikhs in the aftermath of 9/11, the brutal dragging murder of William Byrd by three white men in Texas, "ethnic cleansing" in Kosovo, continual strife between Palestinians and Jews in Israel . . . where will it strike next? Will it ever end? Perhaps more to the point, what can we as individuals do in the face of the seemingly overwhelming racial and ethnic divisions in our society and the world?

One answer is that we can try not to tolerate racism and bigotry and not fail to speak out when confronted by

these forms of ignorance and hatred. This goes as much for the victims of these behaviors as it does for those who witness them. An example of a person who refused to accept racism is Earl G. Graves, Jr., a senior executive at *Black Enterprise* magazine. Graves was mistakenly detained and frisked by detectives on a railroad platform in New York City's Grand Central Terminal. The detectives were seeking an alleged perpetrator who was reported to be African American, 5 feet 10 inches tall, with a moustache, and carrying a concealed weapon. Graves is an African American but is 6 feet 4 inches tall and has no

Metro-North wants its riders and Mr. Graves's neighbors and fellow commuters to know that Mr. Graves was not the subject its detectives were looking for and that Metro-North detectives were wrong in making the decision to detain and pat down Mr. Graves.

Metro-North deeply regrets this most unfortunate and insensitive incident, and seeks by this notice to apologize publicly to Mr. Graves and his family.

Metro-North wants to assure its ridership that it is committed to taking the steps necessary to reduce the risk of future such incidents and to assure that all of its riders are treated with respect and sensitivity, without regard to their race, color, or national origin.

Donald Nelson

Donald N. Nelson
President

METRO-NORTH COMMUTER RAILROAD COMPANY

moustache. Mortified at having been victimized in front of fellow commuters with whom he rides every day, Graves protested to railroad officials, who then published the accompanying apology in local newspapers.

What can we as individuals do when we witness hostility directed against people just because they are different? We may find it difficult to confront racism or ethnic prejudice in people who are our peers and with whom we must interact on a daily basis. Often we look away or pretend to "go along," hiding our feelings of shame and confusion. Another strategy is to confront the problem head-on, as Graves did. It may take courage, but we can tell someone that their behavior is racist or prejudiced. Of course, this could result in the loss of a friend, but perhaps that is not the end of the world. We can befriend others who are not hampered by racism or ethnic bigotry.

It can also help to try to understand the origins of prejudice in people we know and love. Try to see how their attitudes have been affected by social changes such as new forms of competition with recently arrived ethnic or racial groups, or appeals to fear and prejudice by political leaders who stand to benefit from divisions among working people. You won't get very far by giving sociological lectures to those close to you, but by applying your sociolog-

ical imagination, you may come up with some strategies for changing their minds—or at least giving them an opportunity to see things a bit differently.

Racist beliefs in the innate inferiority of populations that are erroneously thought of as separate races remain one of the major social problems of the modern world. And this tendency to denigrate socially defined racial groups often extends to members of particular ethnic groups as well (Conley, 1999; Duster, 2001).

Ethnic Groups and Minorities

Ethnic groups are populations that have a sense of group identity based on a distinctive cultural pattern and, usually, shared ancestry, whether actual or assumed. Ethnic groups often have a sense of "peoplehood" that is maintained within a larger society (Kornblum, 1974; Teitelbaum & Weiner, 1995). Their members usually have migrated to a new nation or been conquered by an invading population. In the United States and Canada, a large proportion of the population consists of people who either immigrated themselves or are descended from people who immigrated to the New World or were brought there as slaves. If one traces history back far enough, it appears that everyone living in the Western Hemisphere can trace his or her origins to other continents. Even the Native Americans are believed to have crossed the Bering Strait as migrant peoples between 14,000 and 20,000 years ago.

European conquests of the Americas in the sixteenth and seventeenth centuries resulted in people of Iberian (Spanish and Portuguese) origins becoming the dominant population group in Central and South America. People of English, German, Dutch, and French origins became the dominant population groups throughout much of North America. By the late 1770s, almost 80 percent of the population of the 13 American colonies had been born in England or Ireland or were the children of people who had come from those countries. A century later, because of the influence of slavery and large-scale immigration, the populations of the United States and Canada were far more diverse in terms of national origins, but people from England were still dominant.

According to sociological definitions of the term *dominance*, a dominant group is not necessarily numerically larger than other population groups in a nation. More important in establishing dominance is control or ownership of wealth (farms, banks, manufacturing concerns, and private property of all kinds) and political power—especially control of political institutions like legislatures, courts, the military, and the police. Thus, by the beginning of the twentieth century, white Anglo-Saxon Protestant males (or WASPs, as they are sometimes called) had established dominance over U.S. society even though they no longer constituted a clear majority of the population.

Between 1820 and 1960, approximately 42 million people immigrated to the United States. Since 1960, an average of at least 300,000 immigrants have arrived each year, with the number increasing to more than 900,000 in the past few years. Since its earliest history, the United States has had one of the most liberal immigration policies of any nation, partly because many of its inhabitants can trace their origins to other countries. And except in the case of the Native Americans, who were expelled from their ancestral lands and forced to resettle on reservations, no area of the nation is seen as the ancestral homeland of a particular people. Unlike many nations, the United States is a multiethnic society where notions of "blood" (descent) do not coincide with claims to ancestral land. In the United States, therefore, there are no separatist movements that claim territory and threaten national unity. However, severe inequalities affect particular populations, especially Native Americans, African Americans, Latinos, and Appalachian whites. Many of these inequalities date back to major periods of settlement and ethnic group formation, which are summarized in the Global Social Change box on pages 362–363.

MINORITY GROUPS Immigrant groups that are distinct because of racial features or culture (language, religion, dress, etc.) are often treated badly in the new society and hence develop the consciousness of being a minority group. Louis Wirth (1945), a pioneer in the study of racial and ethnic relations, defined a **minority group** as a set of "people who, because of their physical or cultural characteristics, are singled out from the others in the society in which they live for differential and unequal treatment, and who therefore regard themselves as objects of collective discrimination" (p. 347). The existence of a minority group in a society, Wirth explained, "implies the existence of a corresponding dominant group with a higher social status and greater privileges. Minority status carries with it exclusion from full participation in the life of the society" (p. 347).

In the United States, the term *minority* often suggests "people of color," meaning African Americans, American Indians, Mexicans (many of whom have the darker coloring of Amerindian ancestry), and Asians. But the term can also be applied to people with lighter skin coloring. In Great Britain, for example, the Irish were a conquered people who were subjected to economic and social discrimination by the English. It is not surprising, therefore, that when the Irish began immigrating to the United States in the nineteenth century, they were treated as an inferior minority by Americans of English ancestry. This attitude was especially prevalent in cities like Boston and New York, to which the Irish came in large numbers.

It should also be noted that the term *minority* does not always imply that the population is numerically inferior to the dominant group. There are counties in some states in the South, and entire cities in the North, in which African Americans constitute a numerical majority yet cannot be considered the dominant group because they lack the power, wealth, and prestige enjoyed by the white population. Wealth, rather than income, is especially important in allowing families to pass advantages on to their children. As sociologist Dalton Conley (1999) notes, the median wealth of white families in the United States is seven times higher than that of nonwhite families. See the Sociological Methods box on page 364 for further analysis of how these differences are measured and why these measures are so important.

ETHNIC GROUP FORMATION Ethnic groups often form in cities or metropolitan regions for reasons of choice as well as necessity. In fact, the identity of a group is often defined through the experience of coping with life in the new society as well as through the group's desire to hold on to its language, food, and other cultural ways (Handlin, 1992; Rodriguez, 1992). In one of the first and best studies of ethnic group formation, W. I. Thomas (1971/1921) described how in the early decades of the twentieth century Italian immigrants settled in small neighborhoods in Manhattan where they could live with people who had come from the same region and spoke the same dialect of Italian. At first these immigrants identified themselves as Calabrians or Sicilians or Piedmontese, the way they had before leaving their home regions. Thomas found that they identified with those home regions rather than with the nation of Italy. In New York, however, they could speak to each other and appreciate each other's food, and they had reason to join together to compete with other ethnic groups for jobs and homes. They were also called Italians by people outside their neighborhoods. Gradually, therefore, they began to think of themselves as Italians or Italian Americans, but this identity was forged out of their experience in the United States and did not mean the same thing as being an Italian in Italy.

Most ethnic populations have had similar experiences that caused them to develop a group consciousness and create organizations to represent their interests. Homosexuals and other populations that are defined in terms of their behavior and cultural traits may become organized into cultural minority groups, but they differ from true ethnic groups because they do not trace their ancestry to another society.

Today sociologists are interested in knowing whether a similar process of ethnic group formation is occurring in regions where there are large Spanish-speaking populations.

In 1790, when the republic was newly formed, the vast majority of U.S. citizens and resident foreigners (77 percent) had come from Great Britain and the counties that are now included in Northern Ireland. People from Germany (7.4 percent), Ireland (4.4 percent), the Netherlands (3.3 percent), France (2 percent), Mexico (1 percent), and other countries were present in the population, but with the exception of the Irish, they were also primarily white Protestants. Blacks—involuntary immigrants—and their children actually accounted for 19 percent of the total population, but neither they nor Native Americans were citizens.

1820–1885: The "Old" Northwest European and Asian Migration

By about 1830, the mass migration of different groups into the new nation was under way. The largest inflows of immigrants came from Ireland and Germany, with more than 1 million people from each of these countries coming to the United States to escape political or economic troubles. Smaller waves of immigrants originated in the northern European nations of Sweden, Norway, and Denmark.

Although people from northern Europe made up the most important immigrant groups, far exceeding the continuing influx from Great Britain, 1885 marked the beginning of an inflow of immigrants from China that continued at high rates for the next 30 years. Chinese immigrants settled primarily in the West and contributed immensely to the development of the western states, although they met with sporadic and often violent hostility.

1885–1940: The "Intermediate" Migration from Southern and Eastern Europe and the Beginning of Heavy Immigration from Mexico

From 1880 to 1900, the inflow of immigrants from Italy, Poland, Russia, the Baltic states, and southern Europe (Serbs, Croats, Slovenes, Romanians, Bulgarians, Greeks, etc.) exceeded the inflow of people from older immigrant groups by about 4 to 1. In 1907 alone, more than 250,000 Italians and 338,000 Poles and other central Europeans were admitted through New York's Ellis Island. Many of these immigrants were Jewish, Roman Catholic, or Orthodox Christian. The newcomers' tendency to live in neighborhoods known as "Little Italy" or "Little Poland" convinced more established Americans that the immigrants would never learn English or become fully American. The mass arrival of physically distinctive groups such as Mexicans and Japanese during this period also aroused fear and hostility among those who disliked the newcomers.

During World War I, thousands of impoverished black southerners were attracted to the cities of the North and the Midwest. This began a trend that would continue throughout the twentieth century whenever wars or economic booms made it possible for blacks to overcome discrimination and get factory jobs.

1921–1959: Immigration by Quota and Refugee Status

Agitation against the "new" immigrants and demands for "Oriental exclusion" led Congress to establish a quota system that drastically altered the inflow of newcomers into the nation after 1920. At first the quotas were fixed at 3 percent of the number of people from each country who had been counted as U.S. residents in the 1910 census. But because that formula still allowed large numbers of "new" immigrants to enter the nation, in 1924 the law was changed so that quotas would be based on the national origins of the foreign-born population as of the 1890 census. This biased the quota system in favor of northern Europeans; in fact, Asians were explicitly excluded.

World War II and the Cold War produced millions of homeless and stateless refugees, especially from Germany, Poland, and the Soviet Union. Almost half a million of these displaced persons arrived in the United States between 1948 and 1950; another 2 million came between

---

They seek to discover whether Mexicans, Puerto Ricans, Colombians, and Dominicans are beginning to think of themselves as Latinos in cities where they are all present in large numbers, or whether their allegiance to their nationality of origin will prevent them from taking on the more inclusive Latino identity. Likewise, researchers are asking questions about whether a new Asian ethnicity will be forged out of the experience of various Asian immigrant groups, especially the Koreans and Chinese, in American cities (Moore & Pachon, 1985; Portes & Rumbaut, 1996).

WHEN WORLDS COLLIDE: PATTERNS OF INTERGROUP RELATIONS

Throughout history, when different racial and ethnic groups have met and mixed, the most usual outcome has been violence and warfare. In fact, the desire for peaceful and cooperative relations among diverse peoples has emerged only relatively recently. In this section, we explore

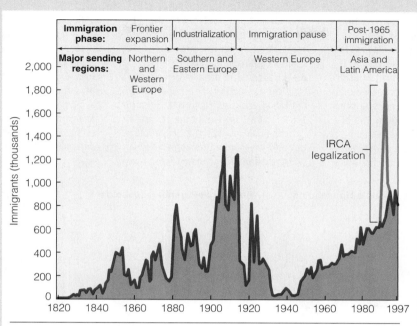

Immigration phase:	Frontier expansion	Industrialization	Immigration pause	Post-1965 immigration
Major sending regions:	Northern and Western Europe	Southern and Eastern Europe	Western Europe	Asia and Latin America

Note: IRCA refers to the amnesty provisions of the Immigration Reform and Control Act of 1986, under which 2.7 million unauthorized foreign residents were transferred to legal immigrant status.

Source: INS, 1997, 1999.

1950 and 1957. Their arrival swelled the populations of ethnic enclaves in America's industrial cities.

1960 to the Present: Worldwide Immigration

In the 1960s, national quotas were replaced with a system based on preference for skilled workers and professionals, regardless of country of origin, as well as refugees and people with families already in the United States. Gradually Congress increased the number of immigrants who may enter the country legally. Today the United States is once again the foremost immigrant-receiving nation in the world. The largest streams of immigrants are from Mexico, other Central American and Caribbean nations, Asia (especially Korea, China, India, and Pakistan), and South America. Untold numbers of undocumented, or illegal, immigrants also arrive each year—especially from Mexico, Canada, and the Dominican Republic—but studies show that a high proportion of these newcomers eventually become legal residents or return to their country of origin (Lee, 1998; Portes & Rumbaut, 1996).

a continuum of relations between dominant and minority groups that extends from complete intolerance to complete tolerance, as shown in Figure 13.1. At one extreme is extermination or genocide; at the other is assimilation.

Genocide and Mass Killing

In a study of the Siane tribe of New Guinea, anthropologist Richard Salisbury (1962) found that the members of this isolated highland tribe believed that anyone from another tribe wanted to kill them. Therefore, the Siane believed that they must kill any member of another tribe they might encounter. (Fortunately, they excluded the anthropologist from this norm.) We often think of such behavior as primitive, savage, or barbarous. Yet barbarities on a far greater scale have been carried out by supposedly advanced societies. The most extreme of these is **genocide**, state-sponsored mass killing explicitly designed to completely exterminate a population deemed to be racially or ethnically different and threatening to the dominant population.

SOCIOLOGICAL METHODS   Measuring Inequality of Wealth Versus Income

The accompanying illustrations from Melvin Oliver and Thomas Shapiro's study *Black Wealth/White Wealth* (1995) make an important point. If we look at African-American households consisting of a married couple and their children and compare them to similar white households, the black family has somewhat less income (almost $5,000 a year) but far less wealth. On average, the black house-

In Oliver and Shapiro's study, *net worth* is defined as "the straightforward value of all assets less any debts." The term *net financial assets* "excludes equity accrued in a home or vehicle from the calculation of a household's available resources" (Oliver & Shapiro, 1995, p. 58). *Income* is the stream of cash that comes into the household through jobs and earnings of all who participate in the economy in any way.

single major survey of income and wealth among American households, the Survey of Income and Program Participation (SIPP). It contains data on income and, more to the point, extensive data on assets (e.g., checking accounts, savings accounts, equity in homes and other property, mutual funds, stocks, and much more) and debts (e.g., credit cards, medical bills, home mortgages, personal debts, and so on). Like all

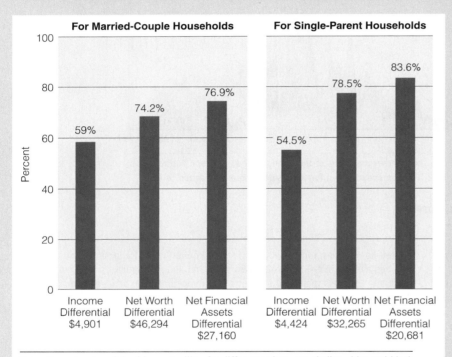

Note: Percent not explained by controlling for differences between similar white and black households.

Source: Oliver & Shapiro, 1995.

surveys, the SIPP tends to undersample populations that are difficult to reach, such as unemployed young males and the very rich. In consequence, the differences in income and wealth reported are conservative. The disparities would be even wider if the extremes of poverty and wealth were accurately represented. In any case, when one looks at middle-class segments of the survey, such as married-couple families, the errors are less important.

Why do these differences in wealth matter? Clearly, when a family can pass a home or its value to succeeding generations, that represents an advantage (Conley, 1999). When there is wealth in the household, the family is better able to withstand economic shocks or sudden reversals of fortune. When there is some wealth accumulating, the family is in a far better position to afford higher-quality educational opportunities for its young people. Recognizing these and many other advantages, Oliver and Shapiro argue that all forms of discrimination that prevent African Americans and others from accumulating wealth (e.g., discrimination in mortgage assistance and other lending policies) are especially pernicious and must be corrected immediately.

hold's net worth is about $46,000 less, and its net financial assets are lower by an average of $27,000. In other words, income inequality is not nearly as severe as inequality of wealth. But how are these differences measured? And why bother making such measurements?

But most income is spent quickly, as we all know too well, and it is much more difficult to divert income into more stable forms of wealth such as homes, savings accounts, mutual funds, and the like.

Most of the data on which Oliver and Shapiro base their analysis come from a

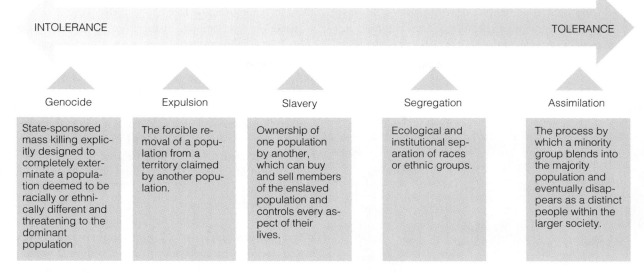

Figure 13.1   A Continuum of Intergroup Relations

Note: The placement of slavery to the right of expulsion is not meant to imply that slavery is less severe than expulsion. The reason for the placement is that slaves and slave masters are interdependent populations within a single society, whereas expulsion excludes the subordinated population from any form of membership in the society.

There have been numerous instances of mass killings and fewer explicit policies of genocide in recent history. Those incidents have been characterized by a degree of severity and a level of efficiency unknown to earlier civilizations. Consider the following:

• The Native American populations of North, Central, and South America were decimated in mass killings by European explorers and settlers between the sixteenth and twentieth centuries. Millions of Native Americans were killed in one-sided wars and through intentional starvation, forced marches, and executions. The population of Native Americans in North America was reduced from more than 4 million in the eighteenth century to less than 600,000 in the early twentieth century (Thornton, 1987).

• Mass killings during European colonial conquests: When England, France, Germany, Portugal, and the Netherlands were engaged in fierce competition for colonial dominance of Africa during the nineteenth and early twentieth centuries, millions of native people were exterminated. The introduction of the Gatling machine gun made it possible for small numbers of troops to slaughter thousands of tribal warriors.

• State-sponsored genocide: Six million Jews and 400,000 gypsies were systematically killed by the Nazis during World War II; thousands of Tutsis living in Rwanda were exterminated by the Hutus in the 1990s.

Mass executions and other forms of genocide are almost always rationalized by the belief that the people who are being slaughtered are less than human and in fact are dangerous parasites. Thus the British and Dutch slaughtered members of African tribes like the Hottentots in the belief that they were a lower form of life, a nuisance species unfit even for enslavement. The Nazis rationalized the extermination of Jews and gypsies by the same twisted reasoning (Chalk & Jonassohn, 1990).

Expulsion

In many societies, extended conflicts between racial or ethnic groups have ended in **expulsion**, the forcible removal of one population from territory claimed by the other. Thus, on the earliest map of almost every major American city, there appears a double line drawn at the edges where the streets end. This is the Indian Boundary Line, and it symbolizes the expulsion of Native Americans from lands that were taken from them in order to create a city in which they would be strangers.

Expulsion was the usual fate of North America's native peoples, who also experienced massacres, deadly forced marches, and other genocidal attacks. These actions were rationalized, in part, by the nineteenth-century doctrine of "manifest destiny," which asserted the inevitability of the westward expansion of Europeans across the territories of the Southwest and West (Davis, 1995). As white settlement expanded westward, Native Americans were continually expelled from their tribal lands. After the 1848 gold rush and the rapid settlement of the West Coast, the pressure of white settlement pushed the Indian tribes into the high plains of the West and Southwest. Between 1865 and the

Dorothea Lang

Dorothea Lang

These two photos by the documentary photographer Dorothea Lang only begin to capture the way expulsion shattered the lives of Japanese Americans during World War II. A commemorative plaque at one of the internment camps conveys the feelings of many who experienced those events: "May it serve as a constant reminder of our past so that Americans in the future will never again be denied their constitutional rights and may the remembrance of that experience serve to advance the evolution of the human spirit."

1890 massacre of Sioux Indians at Wounded Knee, South Dakota, the remaining free tribes in the West were forced to settle on reservations. In the process, the Indians lost more than their ancestral lands. As the famous Sioux chief Black Elk put it: "A people's dream died" (quoted in Brown, 1970, p. 419).

The forced settlement of Native Americans on reservations is only one example of expulsion. Asian immigrants in the American West also suffered as a result of intermittent attempts at expulsion referred to as the Oriental exclusion movement. In an effort to prevent the large-scale importation of Chinese laborers into California and other states, Congress passed the Chinese Exclusion Act of 1882, which excluded Chinese laborers from entry into the United States for 10 years. But this legislation did little to relieve the hostility between whites and Asians. Riots directed against Chinese workers were common throughout the West during this period, and Chinese immigrants were actually expelled from some towns. In 1895, for example, a mob killed 28 Chinese immigrants in Rock Springs, Wyoming, and expelled the remaining Chinese population from the area (Lai, 1980).

The most severe example of expulsion directed against Asians in the United States occurred in 1942 after the Japanese attack on Pearl Harbor and the American entry into World War II. On orders from the U.S. government, more than 110,000 West Coast Japanese, 64 percent of whom were U.S. citizens, were ordered to leave their homes and their businesses and were transported to temporary assembly centers (Kitano, 1980). They were then assigned to detention camps in remote areas of California, Arizona, Idaho, Colorado, Utah, and Arkansas. When the U.S. Supreme Court declared unconstitutional the incarceration of an entire ethnic group without a hearing or formal charges (*Endo* v. *United States,* 1944), the Japanese were released, but by then many had lost their homes and all their possessions. In 1989, after many years of pressing their claim of human rights violations, Japanese Americans finally succeeded in persuading Congress to create a reparations program for families who had been imprisoned during the war. Although the amounts paid—generally about $20,000—do not come close to restoring their material or emotional losses, the apology they received from President Reagan, along with the symbolic value of having won their claim, created an important precedent for other groups that have been victims of racism. As Amy Hiratzka, a survivor of the Gila River prison camp, told an interviewer: "I just want to work toward the fact that this doesn't happen to anyone again. I accepted the $20,000 for my daughter. I think of the blacks. I think of the American Indians. Their plight has been just a chronic series of ups and downs and unfair treatment, lack of justice" (quoted in Dymski, 2000, p. 6).

Figure 13.2 The Transatlantic Slave Trade

From the end of the sixteenth century to the early decades of the nineteenth, approximately 11 to 12 million Africans were imported to the New World (Patterson, 1982). The thickness of the arrows shows the approximate volume of the slave trade to each region.

Source: Adapted from Curtin, 1969.

Slavery

Somewhat farther along the continuum between genocide and assimilation is slavery. **Slavery** is the ownership of a population, defined by racial, ethnic, or political criteria, by another population that not only can buy and sell members of the enslaved population but also has complete control over their lives. Slavery has been called "the peculiar institution" because, ironically, it has existed in some of the world's greatest civilizations. The socioeconomic systems of ancient Greece and Rome, for example, were based on the labor of slaves. And the great trading cities of late medieval Europe, such as Venice, Genoa, and Florence, developed plantation systems in their Mediterranean colonies that were based on slave labor. In fact, the foremost student of slave systems, Orlando Patterson, makes the following comment:

> There is nothing notably peculiar about the institution of slavery. It has existed from before the dawn of human history right down to the twentieth century, in the most primitive of human societies and in the most civilized. . . . Probably there is no group of people whose ancestors were not at one time slaves or slaveholders. (1982, p. vii)

Figure 13.2 indicates the magnitude of the transatlantic slave trade; the widths of the arrows represent the relative size of each portion of that terrible traffic in humanity. The arrows do not show, however, that for the Americas to acquire 11 million slaves who survived the voyage on the slave ships and the violence and diseases of the New World, approximately 24 million Africans had to be captured and enslaved (Fyfe, 1976; Patterson, 1982, 1991). The chart demonstrates that the United States imported a proportionately small number of slaves. However, although somewhat less than 10 percent of all slaves

were sold in the United States, by 1825 almost 30 percent of the black population in the Western Hemisphere was living in the United States (Patterson, 1982) because of the high rate of natural increase among the American slaves. In Brazil, by contrast, the proportion of slave imports was relatively high, but there was also a high mortality rate among the slaves as a result of disease and frequent slave revolts.

At the time of the first U.S. census in 1790, there were 757,000 blacks in the overall population. By the outbreak of the Civil War, the number had increased to 4.4 million, of whom all but about 10 percent were slaves. In the southern states that fought in the war, one-third of white families owned slaves, the average being nine "chattels" per owner (Farley & Allen, 1987). (The term *chattels* refers to living beings that are considered property, including slaves and, in some cultures, women.)

It can be inferred from the great increase in the U.S. slave population that slaveholders in the United States treated their slaves less badly than did slaveholders in other parts of the Western Hemisphere. This does not mean, however, that slaves in the Americas did not bitterly resent their condition and struggle against it. Slave revolts were extremely common in the Caribbean and elsewhere in the New World. Even when slaves could not rebel openly, they carried out many forms of resistance. Patterson points out that the slave has always striven, against all odds, "for some measure of regularity and predictability in his social life. . . . Because he was considered degraded, he was all the more infused with the yearning for dignity" (1982, p. 337). Patterson concludes that one of the chief ironies of slavery throughout history has been that "without [it] there would have been no freedmen" (p. 342). In other words, the very idea of freedom developed in large part from the longing of slaves to be free.

The Sociological Observer

This striking photo
of fugitive slaves
during the Civil War
was taken at Cumberland, Virginia, on May 14, 1862.
Look carefully at the faces of the people in the photo.
What feelings do you read in their gaze at the camera?
What do you notice about the material condition of the
people in the group? (See page 387 for further insights
into the sociological content of this photo.)

LEGACIES OF SLAVERY   Groups that have endured slavery (and this is true of expulsion and genocide as well) typically experience its effects for generations after gaining freedom. Their history of slavery, emancipation, and dealing with slavery's consequences becomes a central aspect of their shared culture. Jews, for example, celebrate the holiday of Passover to commemorate their liberation from Egyptian slavery over 25 centuries ago. For African Americans, the memories of slavery and the failures of the U.S. government to make good on promises of land after emancipation in 1863 are far more recent and vivid. Scholars of race relations argue that just as the Indian reservations are a continuing legacy of expulsion and genocide, so, too, are the nation's areas of segregated rural and urban poverty a continuing legacy of slavery (Conley, 2003).

Does this historical legacy justify such policies as affirmative action, official apologies, or material reparations to the descendants of the enslaved or excluded? In the case of affirmative action, the courts have agreed that it does. And the possibility of some form of reparations is a subject of serious discussion (Robinson, 2003). Yet there is also the question of whether present generations of people should

be required to give up money or opportunity to correct the wrongs of the past. These are momentous moral and political questions.

Sociological research, both past and present, provides empirical evidence to inform debates over these issues. It shows that racially distinct groups that have been subjected to the continuing effects of slavery and other extreme treatment do experience long-term disadvantages in their ability, as a group (with many individual exceptions), to gain wealth and income, educational status, physical and mental health, occupational prestige, and social mobility (Burdman, 2003; Ogbu, 1994). These disadvantages and efforts to address them are discussed more fully in later sections of the chapter.

Segregation

Although African-American slaves gained their freedom during the Civil War and became citizens of the United States, this did not mean that they became fully integrated into American society. A long period of segregation followed. **Segregation** is the ecological and institutional separation of races or ethnic groups. The segregation of racially or ethnically distinct peoples within a society may be voluntary, resulting from the desire of a people to live separately and maintain its own culture and institutions. The Amish, the Hutterites, and the Hasidic Jews are examples of groups that voluntarily segregate themselves. But segregation is often involuntary, resulting from laws or other norms that force one people to be separate from others. Involuntary separation may be either **de jure** (created by laws that prohibit certain peoples from interacting with others or place limits on such interactions) or **de facto** (created by unwritten norms that result in segregation, just as if it were "in fact" legally required).

During the 1990s, South Africa underwent a stunning reversal of its system of de jure segregation. Known as *apartheid,* South Africa's racial laws insisted that blacks, whites, and "coloreds" (people of mixed ancestry) remain separate. Intermarriage and integrated schools and communities were forbidden. In 1991, after years of struggle and violence, the white-dominated government agreed to repeal the apartheid laws. A constitutional convention—at which all segments of the population were represented—created a democratic regime in which all citizens' votes count equally. The African majority, led by Nelson Mandela and the African National Congress, assumed power in a relatively peaceful transition. Nevertheless, whites continue to hold most of the nation's wealth, whereas most South African blacks are trapped in dire poverty and illiteracy, just as the former slaves were in the United States after the Civil War.

JIM CROW In the United States, legally sanctioned segregation no longer exists, but this has been true only in recent decades. Before the Civil Rights movement of the 1960s, de jure segregation was common, especially in the southern states. The system that enforced segregation was supported by **Jim Crow** laws. This term refers to laws that enforced or condoned segregation, barred blacks from the polls, and the like. (Jim Crow was a nineteenth-century white minstrel who performed in blackface and thereby reinforced black stereotypes.) The system was in effect for about 100 years, from just after the Civil War until the early 1970s. During that period, the so-called color line was applied throughout the United States to limit the places where blacks could live, where they could work and what kinds of jobs they could hold, where they could go to school, and under what conditions they could vote.

At first the color line was an unwritten set of norms that barred or restricted black participation in many social institutions. By the turn of the twentieth century, however, segregation had become officially sanctioned through legislation and court rulings. This official segregation was rationalized by the "separate but equal" doctrine set forth by the Supreme Court in *Plessy* v. *Ferguson* (1896). Under this doctrine, separate facilities for people of different races were legal as long as they were of equal quality. In addition, de facto segregation and the existence of a "job ceiling" based on race kept blacks in subordinate jobs and segregated ghettos, as we saw in Chapter 12 in the case of Chicago's "black metropolis."

Only after years of struggle by opponents of de jure segregation did the U.S. Supreme Court finally decide, in the landmark case of *Brown* v. *Board of Education, Topeka* (1954), that "separate but equal" was inherently unequal. The *Brown* ruling put an end to legally sanctioned segregation of schools, hospitals, public accommodations, and the like. But it took frequent, often violent demonstrations and the mobilization of thousands of citizens in support of civil rights to achieve passage of the Civil Rights Act of 1964. That act mandated an end to segregation in private accommodations, made discrimination in the sale of housing illegal, and initiated a major attack on the job ceiling through the strategy known as *affirmative action*. Despite these judicial and legislative victories, however, de facto segregation remains a fact of life in the United States, especially in large cities (Massey & Denton, 1993).

THE SEGREGATION INDEX Ecological studies of racial segregation show that residential segregation persists in almost all U.S. cities. Table 13.1 is based on a measure known as the *segregation index.* It shows "the minimum percentage of nonwhites who would have to change the block on which they live in order to produce an unsegregated distribution—one in which the percentage of non-

TABLE 13.1

Trends in Black–White Segregation in 20 Metropolitan Areas With Largest Black Populations, 1970–1990

Metropolitan Area	1970	1980	1990
Northern Areas			
Boston	81.2	77.6	68.2
Chicago	91.9	87.8	85.8
Cleveland	90.8	87.5	85.1
Detroit	88.4	86.7	87.6
Kansas City	87.4	78.9	72.6
Los Angeles–Long Beach	91.0	81.1	73.1
Milwaukee	90.5	83.9	82.8
New York	81.0	82.0	82.2
Philadelphia	79.5	78.8	77.2
St. Louis	84.7	81.3	77.0
San Francisco–Oakland	80.1	71.7	66.8
Northern average	84.5	80.1	77.8
Southern Areas			
Atlanta	82.1	78.5	67.8
Baltimore	81.9	74.7	71.4
Birmingham	37.8	40.8	71.7
Dallas–Fort Worth	86.9	77.1	63.1
Houston	78.1	69.5	66.8
Memphis	75.9	71.6	69.3
New Orleans	73.1	68.3	50.3
Washington, DC	81.1	70.1	66.1
Southern average	75.5	68.3	66.5

Note: New indexes of segregation are not available for 2000 census data, but readers can find a wealth of detail in Maps of the African American and White Populations (2000) in the 100 Largest Metro Areas, The University of Wisconsin-Milwaukee Employment and Training, at www.uwm.edu/Dept/ET/integration/maps.htm.

Source: Adapted from Massey & Denton, 1993.

whites living on each block is the same throughout the city (0 on the index)" (Taeuber & Taeuber, 1965, p. 30). A value of 100 on the index would mean that all nonwhite people live on segregated blocks (i.e., the city is 100 percent segregated). In 1970, for example, 81.2 percent of the nonwhite population in Boston would have had to move to another block to produce an unsegregated distribution of whites and nonwhites. By 1990, that proportion had declined to 68.2 percent, clearly an improvement.

Despite such improvements in many metropolitan regions, Table 13.1 shows that most cities, especially in the North, continue to be highly segregated. Although segregation in some regions has fallen below the 70 percent level, high segregation indexes remain a fact of American life. Urban ecologists point out that most changes in segregation patterns are a result of the movement of blacks into newer suburban communities and older white neighborhoods in the cities (Jaynes & Williams, 1989; Massey & Denton, 1993).

SEGREGATION AND POVERTY One effect of racial and ethnic segregation is to further concentrate poverty. Because African Americans and some Latino groups are at an economic disadvantage and hence are more likely to be poor than other groups in the United States, residential segregation tends to create neighborhoods that are poor as well as segregated. In their studies of the impacts of residential segregation, Douglas Massey and his colleagues note that the growing income and wealth gaps that we discussed in Chapter 12 have been accompanied by increasing spatial separation between classes: "As income inequality rose, so did the degree of class segregation, as affluent and poor families increasingly came to inhabit different social spaces. These trends undermined the socioeconomic well-being of all racial and ethnic groups in the United States" (Massey & Fischer, 2000, p. 670). And although all low-income groups were affected by this widening of class inequalities, African Americans, the most segregated population, were most negatively affected.

An analysis of the 2000 census by sociologist John Logan and others (see Figure 13.3) shows that while the average white or black person in an urban or suburban neighborhood is less likely to live in a racially homogeneous neighborhood than was true a decade ago, Hispanics and Asians are slightly more segregated. Perhaps more important is the fact that a large majority of whites and a smaller majority of blacks still live in segregated neighborhoods. "The average white person," Logan observes, "continues to live in a neighborhood that looks very different from those neighborhoods where the average black, Hispanic, and Asian live." In sum, the United States is more racially and ethnically diverse than ever, but its citizens still either choose or are obliged to live in segregated neighborhoods (Schmitt, 2001).

Other problems of inequality follow from these persistent patterns of racial segregation. It is extremely difficult, for example, to have integrated schools, especially in the primary grades, when children live in segregated neighborhoods. And it is difficult to establish tolerance and understanding among racial and ethnic groups whose members have grown up in segregated neighborhoods and schools.

Assimilation

One of the factors that led to segregation was fear of racial intermarriage; the ideology of white supremacy held that intermarriage would weaken the white race. As late as 1950, 30 states had laws prohibiting such marriages, and even after racist sentiments began to diminish in the 1950s, 19 states (17 of them in the South) maintained

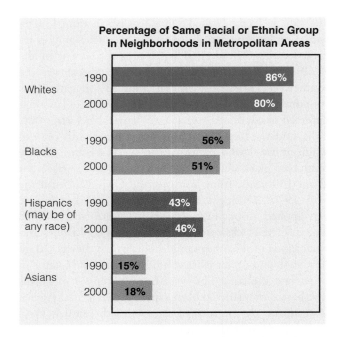

Figure 13.3 Residential Segregation in Metropolitan Areas

Source: John Logan, Lewis Mumford Center for Comparative Urban and Regional Research, State University of New York at Albany.

such laws until the Supreme Court declared them unconstitutional in 1967 (Holt, 1980). Today interracial marriages account for about 2 percent of all marriages, but as we see in Figure 13.4, this represents a dramatic rise since 1960. And the popularity of Tiger Woods, Mariah Carey, and other celebrities from multiracial backgrounds suggests that the old norms against interracial families will continue to erode.

Intermarriage between distinct racial and ethnic groups is an important indicator of **assimilation**, the pattern of intergroup relations in which a minority group is forced or encouraged or voluntarily seeks to blend into the majority population and eventually disappears as a distinct people within the larger society. (We saw in Chapter 3 that assimilation refers to the process by which a culturally distinct group adopts the language, values, and norms of a larger society. Here we are using the term in a broader sense to include social as well as cultural blending.) Needless to say, it makes a great deal of difference whether an ethnic or racial group has been the victim of forced assimilation or has been allowed to absorb the majority culture at its own pace. Many Latin-American societies offer examples of peaceful, long-term assimilation of various racial and ethnic groups. For example, as a result of generations of intermarriage, Brazilians distinguish among many shades of skin color and other physical features

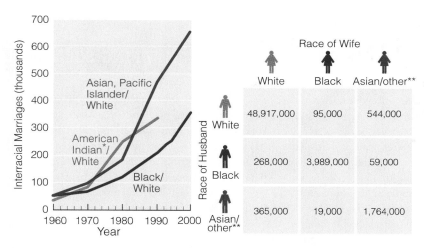

Figure 13.4 Interracial Marriages, United States, 1960–2000

*Includes Eskimo and Aleut for 1980–1992.

**Race includes Asian, American Indian, and Pacific Islanders; Hispanics may be of any race.

Source: Data from *Statistical Abstract,* 2002.

	Race of Wife		
Race of Husband	White	Black	Asian/other**
White	48,917,000	95,000	544,000
Black	268,000	3,989,000	59,000
Asian/other**	365,000	19,000	1,764,000

rather than relying on crude black–white distinctions (Fernandes, 1968).

In the United States, assimilation has had a more troubled history. In an influential treatise on this subject, Milton Gordon (1964) identified three "ideological tendencies" that have affected the treatment of minority groups at various times. These ideologies specify how ethnic or racial groups should change (or resist change) as they seek acceptance in the institutions and culture of American society. They can be summarized as follows:

1. *Anglo-conformity*—the demand that culturally distinct groups give up their own cultures and adopt the norms and values of the dominant Anglo-Saxon culture
2. *The melting pot*—the theory that there would be a biological merging of ethnic and racial groups, resulting in a "new indigenous American type"
3. *Cultural pluralism*—the belief that culturally distinct groups can retain their communities and much of their culture even though they participate in the institutions of the larger society

Because these ideological tendencies have played an important role in intergroup relations in the United States, we will examine them in some detail.

ANGLO-CONFORMITY   The demand for Anglo-conformity rests on the belief that the persistence of ethnic cultures, ethnic and racial communities, and foreign languages in an English-speaking society should be aggressively discouraged. The catchword of this ideology is *Americanization,* the idea that immigrants and their children must become "100 percent American" by losing all traces of their "foreign" accents, abandoning their ethnic cultures, and marrying nonethnic Americans. This demand is reflected

in the movement to make English the official language of the United States, along with opposition to bilingual education. In some cases, discrimination against members of certain ethnic groups is rationalized by the statement that they are not yet fully American. (See the Mapping Social Change box on pages 372–373.)

THE MELTING POT   In an 1893 paper, a young historian named Frederick Jackson Turner challenged the notion that American culture and institutions had been formed by the nation's original Anglo-Saxon settlers. Turner's essay argued that the major influences on American culture were the experiences of the diverse array of people who met and mixed on the western frontier. Turner held that "in the crucible of the frontier the immigrants were Americanized, liberated, and fused into a mixed race" (1920/1893, pp. 22–23).

Turner's "crucible" became widely known as the "melting pot," a term taken from a play by Israel Zangwell about a Russian immigrant. David, the play's hero, makes the following declaration:

> America is God's crucible, the great Melting Pot where all the races of Europe are melting and reforming! Here you stand, good folk . . . in your fifty groups, with your fifty languages and histories, and your fifty blood hatreds and rivalries. . . . Germans and Frenchmen, Irishmen and Englishmen, Jews and Russians—into the Crucible with you all! God is making the American. (1909, p. 37)

The melting-pot view of assimilation attracted many scholars, artists, and social commentators, but sociologists were not convinced that it was an accurate view of what actually happens to ethnic groups in American society. Their research showed that certain ethnic groups have not been fully assimilated, either through intermarriage or

Text continues on page 374.

Receptivity to Immigrants

How welcoming is the United States to new immigrants? We hear a great deal about the increasing presence of immigrants in the "gateway cities"—Los Angeles, New York, Miami, Houston, and Chicago—and somewhat less about the increasing dispersion of new immigrants to smaller metropolitan areas like Charlotte, North Carolina. What kind of reception do immigrants receive in these and other areas of the United States? The question is being addressed by sociologists Gordon F. De Jong and Quynh-Giang Tran, who use data from the General Social Survey to compare how Americans respond to new immigrants in metropolitan and nonmetropolitan regions. The accompanying maps from their research show that there are major differences in opinions about immigrants in different parts of the United States.

The greatest number of immigrants are found in 20 major metropolitan areas, but clearly there are important differences in how well immigrants are received in these areas. Dallas, San Diego, San Francisco, and Tampa appear to be the least receptive, while Chicago, Minneapolis, Seattle, and to a somewhat lesser degree New York, Pittsburgh, and St. Louis are generally warm and welcoming. Note within Florida the difference between Miami (receptive) and Tampa (less so).

Americans in smaller metropolitan areas, especially in the Midwest, are quite receptive to immigrants, whereas those in small metropolitan areas in the Atlantic states are much less so. And it appears that people in smaller cities and metropolitan regions of Texas and California are somewhat more receptive to immigrants than people in the major metropolitan regions.

The third map looks at nonmetropolitan areas. Here we see that receptivity to immigrants tends to be far lower overall than it is in more historically diverse metropolitan regions. Only nonmetropolitan residents in the industrial Midwest tend to express positive attitudes toward immigrants.

What explains these differences? The sociologists note that, first, much of the reception of immigrants is based on people's previous experience with immigration in their communities. Miamians are familiar with Cuban and other immigrants, whereas immigration to Tampa is more recent and the residents have less experience in accommodating newcomers. A second explanation has to do with border issues: With the exception of Phoenix, most of the metropolitan areas near the nation's borders, where immigration is often clandestine and is associated with hardship and poverty, are relatively negative toward immigrants. Finally, where residents perceive immigrants as economic competitors, especially where there is high unemployment or a high proportion of low-wage jobs that immigrants often compete for, hostility is higher, and this is often the case in nonmetropolitan areas in the South and Southwest. Unfortunately, these data were gathered at a period of high employment. Any prolonged increase in unemployment is likely to engender greater hostility toward immigrants in specific areas, which makes the assimilation of immigrant newcomers more problematic.

AP/Wide World Photos

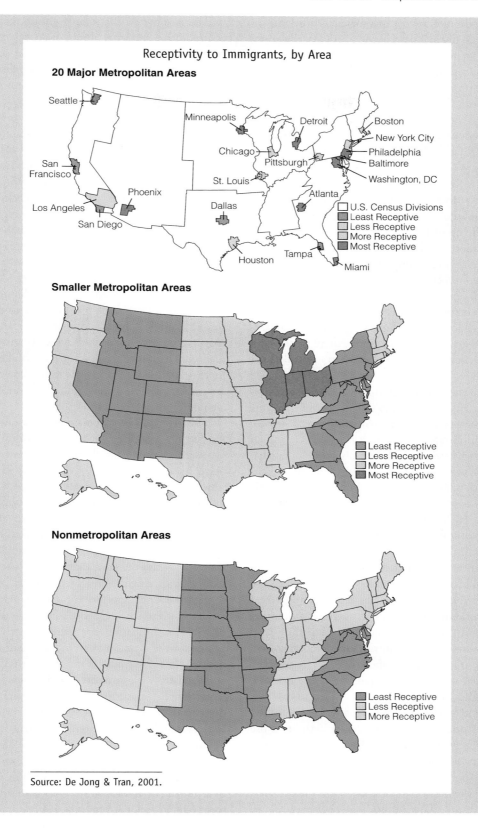

Receptivity to Immigrants, by Area

20 Major Metropolitan Areas

Seattle
Minneapolis
Detroit
Boston
New York City
Chicago
Philadelphia
Pittsburgh
Baltimore
San Francisco
St. Louis
Washington, DC
Phoenix
Atlanta
Los Angeles
Dallas
San Diego
Houston
Tampa
Miami

☐ U.S. Census Divisions
■ Least Receptive
☐ Less Receptive
☐ More Receptive
■ Most Receptive

Smaller Metropolitan Areas

■ Least Receptive
☐ Less Receptive
☐ More Receptive
■ Most Receptive

Nonmetropolitan Areas

■ Least Receptive
☐ Less Receptive
☐ More Receptive

Source: De Jong & Tran, 2001.

through integration into the nation's major institutions. Instead, there remain distinct patterns of **ethnic stratification;** that is, different groups are valued differently depending on how closely they conform to Anglo-Saxon standards of appearance, behavior, and values. People of Scandinavian or northern European descent, for example, are more readily accepted into the top levels of corporate management than are people of Mediterranean descent, who in turn are more readily accepted than black, Hispanic, and Asian minorities.

Even among groups that have been fully assimilated into U.S. society, there remain many differences that can be traced to their diverse backgrounds. In fact, the term **diversity** is often used to refer to the heterogeneous nature of a society made up of numerous different racial, ethnic, religious, and other population groups.

In an early empirical study of assimilation, Ruby Jo Reeves Kennedy (1944) analyzed rates of ethnic intermarriage in New Haven, Connecticut. She found that intergroup marriages increased in frequency between 1870 and 1940, but that while there was a growing tendency for people to marry outside their *ethnic* group, there remained a very strong tendency for people not to marry outside their own *religious* group. From this finding, Kennedy developed the hypothesis of the "triple melting pot," the idea that assimilation occurs first among groups that share the same religion and later among groups with different religions. More recently, in *Beyond the Melting Pot* (1970), Nathan Glazer and Daniel Patrick Moynihan also concluded that ethnic and racial assimilation is far from inevitable. Ethnicity does not disappear as a result of assimilation; ethnic subcultures are continually being created and changed. Thus *Beyond the Melting Pot* pointed to the emergence and significance of cultural pluralism in American life.

CULTURAL PLURALISM   As new waves of immigrants from all over the world have streamed into the United States—Jews fleeing religious intolerance in Russia, Italians and Poles fleeing economic depression in their communities, Central and Latin Americans fleeing dictatorships and poverty, refugees from Asian countries torn by conflict—all have tended to join other members of their nationality group who settled in the United States in earlier decades. Although the influx of new immigrants has led to conflicts between older and newer residents of some communities, in many cases it has resulted in new growth in those communities—in new ethnic businesses such as restaurants and grocery stores, and new social institutions such as churches and social clubs. It has also reinforced pride in ethnic identity as expressed in language and other aspects of ethnic subcultures. This infusion of new energy into ethnic communities confirms Glazer and Moynihan's thesis that the emergence of cultural pluralism is a significant aspect of life in American society.

The recognition that ethnic groups maintain their own communities and subcultures even while some of their members are assimilated into the larger society supported the concept of cultural pluralism. A **pluralistic society** is one in which different ethnic and racial groups are able to maintain their own cultures and lifestyles even as they gain equality in the institutions of the larger society. Michael Waltzer's (1980) comparative research on pluralism in the United States and other societies has shown that although white ethnic groups like the Italians, Jews, and Scandinavians may have the option of maintaining their own subcultures and still be accepted in the larger society, blacks and other racial minorities frequently experience attacks on their subcultures (e.g., opposition to bilingual education or African studies courses) and, at the same time, are discriminated against in social institutions. Waltzer concludes that "racism is the great barrier to a fully developed pluralism" (p. 787). In his study of Latinos in the United States, Earl Shorris (1992) essentially agrees with Waltzer. He finds that despite intense pressure to assimilate, many people from Spanish-speaking nations continue to speak their native language and are using their growing influence in some parts of the country to promote bilingualism. Shorris also notes, however, that Latinos are embracing their own version of the American dream and are not advancing separatist claims.

The problems of pluralism are illustrated by the case of the French-speaking Quebecois minority in Canada. The Quebecois account for almost 28 percent of the Canadian population and constitute the majority in the province of Quebec. This leads to a situation in which a group with its own culture and language seeks protection against pressure to assimilate into the dominant culture and yet demands equal access to the society's political, economic, and cultural institutions. The resulting tensions and hardships have led to the demand that Canada become a bilingual nation, with English and French given equal status. Although the Canadian government has taken firm steps to ensure that French is Quebec's first language, the memory of past discrimination has generated a social movement calling for the creation of an independent French-speaking nation. This movement is especially strong in small towns and rural areas whose entire population is French-speaking. This population strongly backed the separation referendum held in Quebec in 1995. However, the referendum was defeated by an extremely narrow margin, largely because of voters in the more multicultural districts of Montreal, Quebec's largest and most diverse city.

As this example shows, a truly pluralistic society is difficult to achieve. The various ethnic and racial subgroups within a society often feel a strong sense of cultural identity, which they wish to preserve. They also demand equal access to the society's institutions: access to better schools, opportunities to obtain jobs in every field, opportunities to hold important

How many ethnic groups can you spot in this photo? Crowded neighborhoods of new immigrants often display signs in the language of people's origin. But the effects of assimilation are powerful, and it is likely that the immigrants' children will prefer to read signs in English when they are adults. This loss of linguistic ability is a mixed blessing for the larger society, which gains new English speakers but loses some of its linguistic diversity.

positions—in short, a fair share of the wealth and power available in the society. These desires sometimes conflict, with the result that some groups may be tempted to "go it alone"—that is, form their own cultural and political institutions (their own businesses, newspapers and other media, labor unions, etc.)—or else give up their ethnic identity in order to gain greater access to the society's major institutions.

CULTURE AND INTERGROUP RELATIONS

Why do ethnic stratification and inequality persist in societies that are becoming increasingly pluralistic, like those of the United States and Canada? Sociologists have proposed a variety of theories to explain racial and ethnic inequality. Before we explore them, however, we need to understand the cultural basis of ethnic diversity and intergroup hostility—that is, the underlying values and attitudes that shape people's consciousness of other groups and, hence, their behavior toward members of those groups. Chief among these are the tendency to view members of other groups in terms of stereotypes and to use those stereotypes to justify differential attitudes (prejudice) and behaviors (discrimination) toward such individuals.

Stereotypes

People often express the opinion that specific traits of members of certain groups are responsible for their disadvantaged situation. Thus, in South Africa, it was common for whites to assert that blacks were not ready for full citizenship because "they remain childlike and simple." In the United States, the fact that Hispanics are more likely to be found in low-paying jobs is explained by the assertion that "they don't want to learn English." And the fact that black unemployment rates are generally twice as high as white unemployment rates is explained by the statement that "they don't want to work; they like sports and music, but not hard work, especially in school." These explanations are **stereotypes**, inflexible images of a racial or cultural group that are held without regard to whether they are true.

Sociologist William Helmreich (1982) conducted a study of widely held stereotypes regarding America's major ethnic and racial groups. He found that "every single stereotype discussed turns out to have a reason, or reasons" (p. 242). Those reasons usually stem from earlier patterns of intergroup relations. For example, jokes about stupid Poles stem from a period in the nineteenth century when uneducated Polish peasants immigrated to the United States. The idea that blacks are good at music or sports also has some basis, not because blacks are naturally superior in those areas but because when blacks were barred from other avenues to upward mobility they were able to succeed in entertainment and sports; as a result, many young blacks have developed their musical and athletic talents more fully than whites have. But even though stereotypes usually have some basis, they never take account of all the facts about a group. As the famous social commentator Walter Lippmann once quipped, "All Indians walk in single file, at least the one I saw did."

Prejudice and Discrimination

The fact that many people hold stereotypical ideas about other groups may be an indication that they are ignorant or prejudiced, but it does not imply that they will actually discriminate against people whom they perceive as different. In a classic study of prejudice, social psychologist Richard LaPiere (1934) traveled throughout the United States with a Chinese couple, stopping at about 250 restaurants and hotels. Only one of the establishments refused them service. Six months later, LaPiere wrote to each establishment and requested reservations for a Chinese couple. More than 90 percent of the managers responded that they had a policy of "nonacceptance of Orientals." This field experiment was replicated for blacks in 1952, with very similar

Figure 13.5 Merton's Typology
of Prejudice and Discrimination

Source: Adapted from pp. 99–126 of *Discrimination and National Welfare*, edited by R. M. MacIver. Copyright © 1948 by the Institute for Religious and Social Studies. Reprinted by permission of Harper & Row Publishers, Inc.

		PREJUDICE	
		Yes	**No**
DISCRIMINATION	**Yes**	TRUE BIGOT: does not believe in the American creed and acts accordingly	WEAK LIBERAL: not prejudiced, yet afraid to go against the bigoted crowd
	No	CAUTIOUS BIGOT: does not believe in the American creed but is afraid to discriminate	STRONG LIBERAL: not prejudiced and refuses to discriminate

results (Kutner, Wilkins, & Yarrow, 1952; Shibutani & Kwan, 1965).

The purpose of such experiments is to demonstrate the difference between prejudice and discrimination. **Prejudice** is an attitude that prejudges a person, either positively or negatively, on the basis of real or imagined characteristics (stereotypes) of a group to which that person belongs. **Discrimination**, on the other hand, refers to actual unfair treatment of people on the basis of their group membership.

The distinction between attitude and behavior is important. Prejudice is an attitude; discrimination is a behavior. As Robert Merton (1948) pointed out, there are people who are prejudiced and who discriminate against members of particular groups. There are also people who are not prejudiced but who discriminate because it is expected of them. With these distinctions in mind, Merton constructed the typology shown in Figure 13.5.

INSTITUTIONAL DISCRIMINATION Merton's typology is valuable because it points to the variety of attitudes and behaviors that exist in multicultural and multiracial societies. However, it fails to account for situations in which certain groups are discriminated against regardless of the attitudes and behaviors of individuals. This form of discrimination is part of the "culture" of a social institution; it is practiced by people who are simply conforming to the norms of that institution; hence, it is known as *institutional discrimination*.

At its simplest, **institutional discrimination** is the systematic exclusion of people from equal access to and participation in a particular institution because of their race, religion, or ethnicity. Over time, however, this intentional exclusion leads to another type of discrimination, which has been described as "the interaction of the various spheres of social life to maintain an overall pattern of oppression" (Blauner, 1972, p. 185). This form of institutional discrimination can be quite complex.

The conditions that led to the riot that broke out in South Central Los Angeles in 1992 after the acquittal of

the police officers who beat a black motorist, Rodney King, conform very well to what sociologists have observed in similar communities where blacks or other minority groups are trapped in a self-perpetuating set of circumstances caused largely by historical patterns of discrimination (Blauner, 1989; Tuch & Martin, 1997). Blocked educational opportunities result in low skill levels, which together with job discrimination limit the incomes of minority group members. Low income and residential discrimination force them to become concentrated in ghettos. The ghettos never receive adequate public services such as transportation, thus making the search for work even more difficult. In those neighborhoods, also, the schools do not stimulate achievement, thereby repeating the pattern in the next generation. The young often grow up bitter and angry and may form violent gangs that engage in vandalism and other activities that the outside world sees as antisocial. At the same time, the police patrol ghettos to the point of harassment, with the result that young blacks are more likely to be arrested—and to be denied jobs because of their arrest records. Researchers have found that dark-skinned African-American males with criminal records have a jobless rate of 54 percent, compared with 41.7 percent for light-skinned African-American males and 25 percent for white males with similar records (Johnson & Farrell, 1995). When these conditions are combined with a precipitating event such as the savage beating of a black person and the acquittal of the police officers responsible for the beating, the results often take the form of violence like that which erupted in South Central Los Angeles.

All of the institutions involved—employers, local governments, schools, real estate agencies, agencies of social control—may claim that they apply consistent standards in making their decisions: They hire the most qualified applicants; they sell to the highest bidder; they apply the law evenhandedly; in short, they do not discriminate. Yet in adhering to its institutional norms, each perpetuates a situation that was created by past discrimination.

Ethnic and Racial Nationalism

The conditions that contributed to the Los Angeles riot are an example of the pervasive and discouraging effects of institutional discrimination. In the face of such discrimination, racial and ethnic groups frequently organize their members into movements to oppose social inequality. Those social movements often appeal to ethnic or racial nationalism—that is, to the "we feeling" or sense of peoplehood shared by the members of a particular group.

Ethnic (or **racial**) **nationalism** is the belief that one's ethnic group constitutes a distinct people whose culture is and should be separate from that of the larger society. Feelings of nationalism among America's ethnic and racial groups have often been strongly affected by nationalist movements outside the United States. American Jews, for example, were deeply influenced by Zionism, a movement that arose in the late nineteenth century with the goal of creating a Jewish homeland in the holy land of Palestine (now Israel). Similarly, Irish Americans have been influenced by the struggle of the Catholic minority in Northern Ireland to gain independence from England. Nationalist movements often produce a new or renewed ideology of pluralism that replaces the goal of complete assimilation into the larger society. We can see this very clearly among African Americans.

In his famous study *An American Dilemma* (1944), the Swedish social scientist Gunnar Myrdal noted that African Americans were in fact "exaggerated Americans." Myrdal believed that blacks had assimilated American values and norms more than any other ethnic or racial group and that

they had no distinctive subculture of their own. This theme was repeated in the influential work of E. Franklin Frazier (1957/1939), the leading black sociologist of his generation. Frazier, like Myrdal, believed that African Americans had no distinctive culture. They had the same religions, language, and values as white Americans, and the folkways they had developed (e.g., musical forms like jazz and the blues) had become part of mainstream American culture.

Events of the late 1950s and 1960s drastically changed these views of black cultural assimilation. Along with the Civil Rights movement of the 1960s came a wave of nationalism. Black intellectuals and community leaders began calling not merely for integration but for cultural pluralism. Leaders like Stokely Carmichael of the Student Nonviolent Coordinating Committee (SNCC) and Malcolm X, the charismatic Black Muslim leader, preached that "black is beautiful" and that African Americans should drop the term *Negro* in favor of *black*. In Carmichael's words, "They oppress us because we are black and we are going to use that blackness. . . . Don't be ashamed of your color" (quoted in Bracey, Meier, & Rudwick, 1970, p. 471). In recent years, many black Americans have gone further and adopted the term *African American* in order to emphasize their common heritage and to deemphasize the racial character of their shared background.

People in the United States are not alone in struggling with issues of nationalism. Now that the Cold War between the former Soviet Union and the United States has ended, ethnic and religious nationalism is the primary threat to peace throughout the world. Although North

Chicago Historical Society

© C. Simonpietri/Corbis Sygma

Racial violence and rioting invariably disrupt neighborhoods, often for long periods. During the 1919 Chicago race riots, many African Americans were evicted from their homes in integrated working-class neighborhoods and forced back into the ghetto. During the 1992 Los Angeles riots, so many stores and businesses were burned that people like this mother and child felt severe disorientation long after the rioting had ended.

America is relatively free of the extreme nationalism that results in bloodshed, at various times in North American history ethnic or racial nationalism has strained the social fabric. Entire populations, such as African Americans, Puerto Ricans, or French Canadians, have yearned to become entirely separate from the larger culture and society.

At other times, nationalism has been a creative social force, welding a racial or ethnic group into a more politically conscious community able to struggle more effectively for its rights. As the Native American sociologist Russell Thornton notes, there are some highly positive aspects of nationalism or, in the case of Native Americans, tribalism:

> Research shows that American Indians make considerable efforts to reaffirm tribalism in urban areas by living in Indian neighborhoods, by maintaining contacts with reservation areas and extended families, and by creating urban American Indian Centers. Frequent results are a new tribalism for urban American Indians and, sometimes, "bicultural" individuals, that is, American Indians who live successfully in Indian and non-Indian worlds. (1987, p. 239)

A key to Indian survival, Thornton concludes, is the ability to maintain an Indian identity while interacting with non-Indians in an urban environment. The same point is often made by Hispanic and African-American sociologists. One difficulty in maintaining a bicultural existence is that it requires assertion of the minority group's values, its ways of expression, its history, and its demands for greater equality. The demand for greater equality is often expressed in terms of the need for affirmative action.

Affirmative Action

What separates relatively peaceful multiethnic and multiracial nations from those in which racial, ethnic, or religious hatreds result in war and massacres? One important answer is the rule of law. When minority populations believe that their rights can be protected by government and laws, when they feel that their past grievances will be corrected in time, they will lend their support to the government and laws of their nation. However, in too many countries—even in the United States at times—minorities do not hold these beliefs. As a result, the quest for racial and ethnic equality is a persistent issue in national affairs (Hacker, 1995; Shuck, 2001).

Our society's foremost governmental and economic institutions are besieged with demands for *affirmative action*— that is, policies designed to correct persistent racial and ethnic inequalities in promotion, hiring, and access to other opportunities. Even more forceful in many parts of the country are the demands to do away with affirmative action policies. Conservatives bitterly oppose affirmative action (Glazer, 1975; Sowell, 1972), whereas liberals feel that such policies are necessary if our society is to undo the effects of past discrimination (Ezorsky, 1991; Horowitz, 1979).

At present, the conservative view is in the ascendance. Congress has done away with preferential treatment for minority-owned firms in awarding small government contracts. In California, steps have been taken to eliminate affirmative action policies in the state's universities and colleges. It is likely that efforts to eliminate affirmative action will continue and will be increasingly successful. But it is also true, as Martin Kilson points out, that affirmative action has been essential to the advancement of African Americans and, increasingly, Latinos in job markets that were formerly out of bounds to minorities. In 1970, for example, "barely 2 percent of the officers in the armed forces were black; twenty years later, thanks (partly) to affirmative action, 12 percent of officers were African Americans" (Kilson, 1995, p. 470).

We saw earlier that the Supreme Court struck down the doctrine that "separate but equal" facilities and institutions did not violate the constitutional rights of African Americans. It did so largely because social-scientific evidence showed that separate institutions are inherently unequal. Similar arguments have been advanced in affirmative action cases that have reached the Court. If a fire department in a city whose inhabitants are 30 percent black and Hispanic has no firefighters from those minority groups, it can be demonstrated that there is a pattern of discrimination that can be changed only if the department is required to hire a certain number of minority applicants—a quota—within a designated time. However, members of the majority may then feel that they are victims of "reverse discrimination," in which they are being penalized for the wrongs of earlier generations. Thus, difficult choices remain: Should employers mix or replace hiring decisions based on experience and merit with decisions based on race and ethnicity? In essence, the courts have said that they must.

Affirmative action remains an extremely controversial issue in American life. Table 13.2 shows that blacks and whites hold widely divergent views on government efforts to narrow the gaps in achievement by race. In fact, both whites and blacks tend to favor race-targeted policies that offer compensatory programs, such as job training and education, but the majority of whites and a significant minority of blacks oppose employment and educational programs that require preferential treatment in hiring and college admissions decisions (Tuch, Sigelman, & Martin, 1997). The divisions revealed by these attitude data confirm that Americans remain divided along racial lines over how much government should be doing to correct the cumulative impact of slavery and racial discrimination.

TABLE 13.2

Blacks' and Whites' Opinions on Racial Policy Issues (in percent)*

Should federal spending programs that assist blacks be increased, decreased, or kept about the same?

	Blacks	Whites
Increased	69.5	18.4
Kept the same	28.8	56.5
Decreased	1.7	25.2

Some people say that, because of past discrimination, blacks should be given preference in hiring and promotion. Others say that such preference in hiring and promotion of blacks is wrong because it gives blacks advantages they haven't earned. What about your opinion—are you for or against preferential hiring for blacks?

	Blacks	Whites
Strongly favor	53.4	6.2
Favor	10.1	7.9
Oppose	4.9	18.3
Strongly oppose	21.6	67.6

*N = 5,012

Source: Tuch, Sigelman, & Martin, 1997.

It should be noted that affirmative action applies to women as well as to racial and ethnic minorities (Epstein, 1995). The effects of institutional discrimination against women are explored in the next chapter.

THEORIES OF RACIAL AND ETHNIC INEQUALITY

For large numbers of people, a dominant aspect of life in American society is racial or ethnic inequality and, often, hostility. How can we explain the persistence of these patterns of hostility and inequality? The first thought that comes to mind is that many people are prejudiced against anyone who is different from them in appearance or behavior. This may seem to explain phenomena like segregation and discrimination, but it fails to explain the variety of possible reactions to different groups. Social-psychological theories that focus on prejudice against members of out-groups find the origins of racism and ethnic inequality in individual psychological processes, but there are also more sociological theories that view prejudice as a symptom of other aspects of intergroup relations.

Social-Psychological Theories

The best-known social-psychological theories of ethnic and racial inequality are the frustration-aggression, projection, and authoritarian personality theories. All of these see the origins of prejudice in individual psychological orientations toward members of out-groups, but they differ in important ways.

FRUSTRATION-AGGRESSION   The frustration-aggression hypothesis, which is associated with the research of John Dollard, Neil Miller, and Leonard Doob (1939), holds that the origin of prejudice is a buildup of frustration. When that frustration cannot be vented on the real cause, the individual feels a "free-floating" hostility that may be taken out on a convenient target, or **scapegoat.** For example, in the case of workers in eastern Germany who have lost jobs in antiquated factories as a result of unification with western Germany, with its far more modern industries, a convenient scapegoat may be found in gypsies, Turks, or even Jews—all groups that have historically been accused of causing negative conditions for native-born Germans. To justify the hostility directed at the out-group, the prejudiced individual often grasps at additional reasons (usually stereotypes) for hating the "others," such as "Gypsies steal children"; "Jews are usurers"; or "Turks will work for almost nothing."

PROJECTION   The concept of projection is also used to explain hostility toward particular ethnic and racial groups. **Projection** is the process whereby we attribute to other people behaviors and feelings that we are unwilling to accept in ourselves. John Dollard (1937) and Margaret Halsey (1946) applied the concept of projection to white attitudes toward black sexuality. Observers had noted that southern whites frequently claimed that black males were characterized by an uncontrollable and even vicious sexuality. The theory of projection explains this claim as resulting from the white males' attraction to black females, an attraction that was forbidden by strong norms against interracial sexual contact. Thus the white male projected his own forbidden sexuality onto blacks and developed an attitude that excused his own sexual involvement with black women.

THE AUTHORITARIAN PERSONALITY   The frustration-aggression and projection explanations of prejudice are general in nature in that anyone can develop pent-up frustrations that will engender hostility under certain conditions, and anyone can project undesirable traits onto others. A more specific explanation of prejudice is the theory of the authoritarian personality, which emerged from attempts to discover whether there is a particular type of person who is likely to display prejudice.

In 1950, a group of social scientists led by Theodor Adorno published an influential study titled *The Authoritarian Personality*. Their research had found consistent correlations between prejudice against Jews and other minorities and a set of traits that characterized what they called the authoritarian personality. Authoritarian individuals, they found, were punished frequently as children. Consequently, such individuals feel an intense anger that they fail to examine (Pettigrew, 1980). They submit completely to people in positions of authority, greatly fear self-analysis or introspection, and have a strong tendency to blame their troubles on people or groups whom they see as inferior to themselves. Unfortunately for Jews, blacks, and other minorities that have been subordinated in the past, the anger and hostility of the authoritarian personality is often directed against them.

Interactionist Theories

Not far removed from these social-psychological theories of intergroup hostility are theories derived from the interactionist perspective in sociology. But instead of locating the origins of intergroup conflict in individual psychological tendencies, interactionists tend to look at how hostility or sympathy toward other groups, or solidarity within a group, is produced through the norms of interaction and the definitions of the situation that evolve within and between groups. A few examples illustrate how the interactionist perspective is applied.

From his analyses of interaction in different groups, Georg Simmel concluded that groups often find it convenient to think of nonmembers or outsiders as somehow inferior to members of the group. But why does this familiar in-group–out-group distinction develop? Simmel explained it as arising out of the intensity of interactions within the group, which leads its members to feel that other groups are less important. Once they have identified another group as inferior, it is not a great leap to think of its members as enemies, especially because doing so increases their sense of solidarity (Coser, 1966; Simmel, 1904).

Conflict and hostility between racial or ethnic groups can be overcome by creating situations that require the groups to cooperate to achieve a common goal. Such situations occasionally occur—for example, when people from different ethnic and racial backgrounds compete in sports or when they work side by side in school and in industry. Unfortunately, the integration and friendship found in such settings are not sufficient to overcome the more deep-seated prejudices and fears of many racist individuals. As film director Spike Lee has observed, racists place all black people in one of two categories: "entertainers and niggers." By this he means that people with racist sentiments tend to exclude famous entertainers and sports figures from their negative feelings about blacks as a group, thereby accentuating their failure to see all blacks as individual human beings.

Functionalist Theories

The difficulty of reducing racism and discrimination through interaction leads to the question of whether racial and ethnic inequalities persist because they function to the advantage of certain groups. One answer was provided by the functionalist theorist Talcott Parsons (1968), who wrote that "the primary historic origin of the modern color problem lies in the relation of Europeans to African slavery" (p. 366). Parsons was not denying that racism is produced through interactions. Rather, he was pointing out that the specific form taken by those interactions— oppression, subordination, domination of blacks by whites—is directly related to the perceived need of white colonialists and traders to use blacks for their own purposes. The whites could abduct, enslave, and sell Africans because their societies had developed technologies (e.g., oceangoing ships and navigational instruments) and institutions (e.g., markets and trading corporations) that made them immensely more powerful than the Africans.

From the functionalist perspective, inequalities among ethnic or racial groups exist because they have served important functions for particular societies. Thus, in South Africa, it was functional for the white government to insist on maintaining apartheid because to do otherwise would mean that whites would become a minority group in a black-dominated society. But as world opinion continued to condemn the white regime and blacks continued to build group solidarity and challenge that regime, it became less and less "functional" for the white government to insist on complete apartheid. Indeed, some have speculated that the nation's white rulers released Nelson Mandela and took steps to legalize the formerly banned African National Congress as a way of showing the world that they were willing to begin negotiations toward some form of shared power. Their move incurred the wrath of many South African whites, who feared the consequences of majority black rule under a new constitution. Similarly, the Israeli government's negotiations with the Palestine Liberation Organization enraged many Jewish settlers living in areas that would be placed under the control of Palestinians. This rage resulted in the shocking assassination of Israeli prime minister Yitzhak Rabin in November 1995 and continues to dominate politics in the Middle East.

In both Israel and South Africa, it appears that the status quo of intergroup relations had become dysfunctional. Change had to come either through peaceful negotiations or through bloodshed. The processes whereby power is redistributed and new social relations develop are often best understood with the help of conflict theories.

Conflict Theories

Conflict theories do a better job than functionalist theories of explaining why groups with less power and privilege, like the South African blacks or the Palestinians in the Middle East, do not accept their place in the status quo. Conflict theories try to explain why these groups often mobilize to change existing intergroup relations (Blauner, 1989). Conflict changes societies, as we see clearly in the case of South Africa, where many years of conflict waged by the disenfranchised blacks led to the creation of a new constitution and majority black rule. But conflict can also destroy societies and nations, as we see all too clearly in the war-torn nations of the former Yugoslavia, where a long history of ethnic conflict has prevented the achievement of a stable, well-functioning society.

Conflict theories trace the origins of racial and ethnic inequality to the conflict between classes in capitalist societies. Marx believed, for example, that American wage earners were unlikely to become highly class conscious because ethnic and racial divisions continually set them against one another and the resulting strife could be manipulated by the capitalist class. Thus, in American history, we see many examples of black and Mexican workers being brought in as strikebreakers by the owners of mines and mills, especially during the 1920s and 1930s. Strikebreakers from different racial and ethnic groups often absorbed the wrath of workers, anger that might otherwise have been directed at the dominant class. To forge class loyalties despite the divisions created by racial and ethnic differences, Marx believed, it would be necessary for workers to see that they were being manipulated by such strategies.

INTERNAL COLONIALISM   Conflict perspectives on racial inequality also include the theory of **internal colonialism**. According to this theory, many minority groups, especially racial minorities, are essentially colonial peoples within the larger society. Four conditions mark this situation:

1. The "colonial" people did not enter the society voluntarily.
2. The culture of the "colonial" people has been destroyed or transformed into a version of the dominant culture that is considered inferior.
3. The "colonial" population is controlled by the dominant population.

4. Members of the "colonial" people are victims of racism; that is, they are seen as inferior in biological terms and are oppressed both socially and psychologically (Blauner, 1969; Davidson, 1973; Hechter, 1974). This is why African Americans, Native Americans, and Jewish Americans react with such anger to suggestions that they may be different from other populations on measures of intelligence or any other biological trait. They have seen such notions used to rationalize slavery or genocide and hence are not willing to let them pass as harmless speculation or "value-free" science.

Although these characteristics describe colonial peoples everywhere, the theory of internal colonialism asserts that they also apply to subordinated ethnic and racial groups in societies like England, the United States, Canada, and the nations of the former Soviet Union. Michael Hechter (1974) extended the theory to show that societies that have created colonial or "ghettoized" populations within their boundaries also develop a "cultural division of labor" in which the subordinated group is expected to perform types of work that are considered too demeaning to be done by members of the dominant population. The South African institution of *Baaskop* was (and in some parts of the nation still is) an example of this phenomenon. It is a set of norms specifying that lower-status, physically exhausting work is appropriate for blacks and higher-status work is appropriate for whites, and that whites should never accept "black" work nor allow themselves to be subordinate to blacks.

Ecological Theories

Are the segregated ghetto communities of black and Hispanic Americans a product of internal colonialism? The answer to this question depends on whether the residents of those communities are able to achieve upward mobility. According to ecological theories of intergroup relations, such mobility should occur naturally in the course of a group's adaptation to the culture and institutions of the larger society. The eventual outcome should be the existence of racially and ethnically integrated communities.

Ecological theories explore the processes by which conflict between racial or ethnic groups develops and is resolved. Along these lines, Robert Park (1914) devised a cyclical model to describe intergroup relations in modern cities. That model consisted of the following stages:

1. *Invasion.* One or more distinct groups begin to move into the territory of an established population.
2. *Resistance.* The established group attempts to defend its territory and institutions against newcomers.

THEORIES OF RACIAL AND ETHNIC INEQUALITY AND PREJUDICE

THEORY	KEY VARIABLES	EXAMPLES
Social-Psychological Theories		
Frustration-Aggression	Prejudice stems from a buildup of frustration and aggressive feelings toward stereotyped victims.	Scapegoating of minority groups such as gypsies or Jews.
Projection	Displaces feelings about ourselves onto others and justifies mistreatment.	Attribution of one's own sexual desires to others.
Interactionist Theories	Intensity of interactions within a group leads in-group members to disparage other groups, but when groups include racially or ethnically distinct others, friendship can supersede hostility.	Groups that need to cooperate (e.g., sports teams) often find ways to reduce racial or ethnic tensions.
Functionalist Theories	Racism and prejudice exist because they bring benefits of some kind to some individuals or group members.	Inequalities derived from prejudice help maintain a supply of low-wage workers.
Conflict Theories	Racial and ethnic inequalities emerge in class conflict under capitalism, but change occurs when subordinated groups resist and rebel.	African Americans were treated as a colonial people until they mobilized to fight back.
Ecological Theories	Helpful in explaining the process of settlement and segregation that often results from prejudice.	People in racial or ethnic ghettos seeking upward mobility.

3. *Competition.* Unless the newcomers are driven out, the two populations begin to compete for space and for access to social institutions (housing, jobs, schooling, recreational facilities, etc.); this extends to competition for prestige in the community and power in local governmental institutions.

4. *Accommodation and Cooperation.* Eventually the two groups develop relatively stable patterns of interaction. For example, they arrive at understandings about segregated and shared territories (Suttles, 1967).

5. *Assimilation.* As accommodation and cooperation replace competition and conflict, the groups gradually merge, first in secondary groups and later through cultural assimilation and intermarriage. They become one people. A new group arrives, and the cycle begins again.

Of course, this is an abstract model. It represents what Park and other human ecologists believe are the likely stages in intergroup relations. The Korean-American sociologist Ilsoo Kim (1981) found that Korean merchants in New York City met resistance both from white merchants and from black residents of ghetto communities when they purchased stores in those communities, but eventually they reached an accommodation with those groups. This finding tends to support Park's model, although the extent to which

assimilation will occur remains an open question. On the other hand, critics point out that there is not always a steady progression from one of these stages to the next. Moreover, accommodation, cooperation, and assimilation do not occur in every case. The ecological model fails to explain why and how groups compete for power and under what conditions they eventually come to cooperate. Nevertheless, the model presents a general picture of the stages that culturally distinct groups often (but by no means always) go through over time. (See the Study Chart above.)

A PIECE OF THE PIE

Up to this point, we have explored the patterns of intergroup relations, the cultural basis of those patterns, and some of the theories that have been proposed to explain them. But we have not discussed how groups actually win, or fail to win, a fair share of a society's valued statuses and other rewards—that is, a piece of the social pie. In particular, the persistence of racial inequality in the United States requires more attention.

How can we explain the fact that so many social problems in the United States today are associated with race? As William Julius Wilson (1984) has stated: "Urban crime,

As a result of their unsuccessful resistance to the European invasion, Native Americans were segregated on reservations, many of which lacked adequate resources to permit them to share in the "American dream."

drug addiction, out-of-wedlock births, female-headed families, and welfare dependency have risen dramatically in the last several years and the rates reflect a sharply uneven distribution by race" (p. 75). Wilson and others doubt that racial prejudice and discrimination adequately account for the severity of these problems because the period since the early 1970s has seen more antidiscrimination efforts than any other period in American history. The answers are to be found, Wilson argues, in how older patterns of racism and discrimination affect the present situation.

In an important study of this issue, sociologist Stanley Lieberson (1980) asked why the European immigrants who arrived in American cities in the late nineteenth and early twentieth centuries have fared so much better, on the whole, than blacks. Sociologist Marta Tienda asks similar questions about people of Latino ancestry (Tienda & Singer, 1995; Tienda & Wilson, 1992). Wilson, Lieberson, and Tienda all agree that the problem of lagging black mobility is a complex one. For African Americans, the situation can be summarized as follows:

1. African Americans have experienced far more prejudice and discrimination than any immigrant group, partly because they are more easily identified by their physical characteristics. As a result of the legacy of slavery, which labeled blacks as inferior, they have been excluded from full participation in American social institutions far longer than any other group.

2. Black families have higher rates of family breakup than white families. The problems of the black family are not part of the legacy of slavery, however. As Herbert Gutman (1976) has shown, slavery did not destroy black families to the extent that earlier scholars believed it did. Nor did the migration of blacks to the North during industrialization. A comprehensive review of the status of black Americans

(Jaynes & Williams, 1989) notes that "there was no significant increase in male-absent households even after the massive migration to the urban North." Until the 1960s, three-quarters of black households with children younger than age 18 included both husband and wife. "The dramatic change came only later, and in 1986, 49 percent of black families with children under age 18 were headed by women" (Jaynes & Williams, 1989, p. 528). The report reasons that if black two-parent families remained the norm throughout slavery, the Great Depression, migration, urban disorganization, and ghettoization, then it appears unlikely that there is a single cause for the dramatic decline in two-parent families during the last two decades.

3. Structural changes in the American economy—first the shift from work on farms to work in factories and then the shift away from factory work to high-technology and service occupations—have continually placed blacks at a disadvantage. No sooner had they begun to establish themselves as workers in these economic sectors than they began to suffer the consequences of structural changes in addition to job discrimination.

Recent research by social scientists points to the decrease in manufacturing jobs and the increase in service-sector jobs as contributing to the sharp decline in the fortunes of black males. (Black females also suffer, but they are more readily recruited into clerical employment.) Throughout the second half of the twentieth century, the unemployment rate for black males was twice that for white males. The situation is even worse for black men who do not have high school diplomas. Their unemployment rate is more than three times higher than that for white males (Oliver & Shapiro, 1990). A great deal of research shows that difficulty in securing adequate employment contributes to the problems young couples experience in forming lasting relationships (Danziger & Gottschalk, 1993; Garfinkel & McLanahan, 1986).

It is significant that among Hispanic groups in the United States, Puerto Ricans have experienced northward migration and problems of discrimination that are similar to those experienced by African Americans in northern cities. Still a dependent territory of the United States, since World War II Puerto Rico has sent hundreds of thousands of working people to cities like New York, Philadelphia, and Chicago, which have been rapidly losing manufacturing jobs. The status of Puerto Ricans in the population is similar to that of blacks. There is a growing Puerto Rican middle class and an even more rapidly growing number of Puerto Ricans among the poor. This situation is largely a result of changes in the types of jobs available to unskilled blacks and Puerto Ricans (Sandefur & Tienda, 1988).

It is worth noting that social mobility is more available to blacks today than it was before the Civil Rights movement. Today there are millions of middle-class African Americans, and the earnings of black males who have completed college are about 85 to 90 percent of those of whites with comparable education. But although the black middle class is growing, most black workers remain dependent on manual work in industry or lower-level service jobs—types of jobs that are in decreasing supply and in which unemployment is common. Another important segment of black workers, male and female, are employed in the public sector. Drastic cuts in public budgets in the 1990s drove down their earnings as well. Chronic unemployment is associated with family breakup, alcohol and drug addiction, and depression. These social problems, in turn, severely hamper the ability of individuals to learn the attitudes and skills they need for entry into available jobs (Oliver & Shapiro, 1990; Wilson, 1987).

Nor is the life of middle-class blacks free from the continuing consequences of racism and prejudice. In interviews with a sample of middle-class black Americans in 16 cities, sociologist Joe R. Feagin found that "they reported hundreds of instances of blatant and subtle bias in restaurants, stores, housing, workplaces, and on the street" (1991, p. A44). And in recent years the number of crimes against minority individuals of all social classes has increased.

CRITICAL SOCIOLOGY AND SOCIAL CHANGE

Migrating to Achieve Greater Equality

A surprising finding of the 2000 census was the rapid growth of the Hispanic population—from 22 million to 35 million—between 1990 and 2000. In 2000, the Hispanic population surpassed the non-Hispanic African-American population for the first time. The Asian population also increased rapidly, though less so than the Hispanic population. Among Asians, however, Indians and Pakistanis were the fastest-growing group during the decade. Where these new immigrants are settling, and why, will have a major influence on patterns of inequality, mobility, and ethnic diversity in the United States, as the following discussion of research on internal migration demonstrates.

Reynolds Farley, one of the nation's most knowledgeable experts on the sociology of population change in the United States, has combed through U.S. census data for information about Americans' efforts to achieve greater equality. His recent research shows that more and more Americans of African-American and Latino descent are migrating out of the older industrial states to the more rapidly growing states of the South and West. The data also show that whites, especially those in their retirement years, are continuing to move away from the Northeast and Midwest, but the flow of African Americans and Latinos is especially notable because it reverses the historic south-to-north migration pattern.

For 18 decades after the American Revolution, Farley explains, the population of the South grew far more slowly than the national average. The South relied on agriculture, whereas the most rapid growth of manufacturing was centered in the Northeast and the Midwest. By 1970, the South's share of the nation's total population had dropped to 30 percent. Now, Farley writes: "The drop has ended.

Marta Tienda, a leading scholar of poverty among Latino Americans, chose this research area in part because she herself came from a Mexican-American family of modest means.

TABLE 13.3

Interregional Exchange of Migrants, 1985–1990

Region	Net Gain or Loss of Interregional Migrants (in thousands)	Net Migrants per 1,000 Residents
Total Migrants		
Northeast	−1,116	−23
Midwest	−847	−15
South	+1,425	+18
West	+538	+11
Migrants Age 65 or Older		
Northeast	−217	−30
Midwest	−118	−15
South	+276	+26
West	+59	+10
Migrants with Complete College Educations		
Northeast	−108	−18
Midwest	−196	−34
South	+133	+17
West	+171	+30
Non-Hispanic Black Migrants		
Northeast	−153	−32
Midwest	−63	−12
South	+181	+13
West	+35	+14
Hispanic Migrants		
Northeast	−94	−31
Midwest	−9	−7
South	+61	+1
West	+42	+5

Source: From Farley, Reynolds. "The Interregional Exchange of Non-Hispanic Black Migrants, 1985–1990 (in thousands)." In *The New American Reality: Who We Are, How We Got Here, Where We Are Going,* © 1996 Russell Sage Foundation, 112 East 64th St., New York, NY 10021. Reprinted with permission.

The restructuring of employment and the growth of the service sector mean that many jobs are no longer bound to mines, deepwater ports, or rail lines. And three southern metropolises—Houston, Miami, and Washington—are now major ports of entry for immigrants, so the South grows rapidly" (Farley, 1996, p. 281).

Since the era of rapid development just before and during World War II, the West, with California in the lead, has been growing extremely rapidly, but as Table 13.3 shows, the South leads all regions. (The figures in the table show each region's net gain or loss of migrants: the difference between the flow of migrants into the region and the flow out to other regions.) Figures 13.6 and 13.7 on page 388 show the volume of migrant flows between regions. The differences between inflow and outflow on these and similar maps (for total migrants, migrants with college educations, and migrants older than age 65) are indicated in Table 13.3. The right-hand column of the table is a rate of

migration per 1,000 people, which allows us to compare these migration streams independently of the region's original population.

The changes shown in the maps and table have enormous consequences for racial and ethnic inequality. With the exception of migrants in their retirement years, most people on the move are seeking to relocate in areas of the nation where they hope to find better employment opportunities. Over the past 15 or 20 years, employers in the South have been most successful in attracting new plants and new businesses from all parts of the world. This success stimulates the migration of younger wage earners and educated job seekers from other regions. Their movement to growing metropolitan areas of the South, in turn, further stimulates the service, real estate, government, and health care sectors of those areas' economies.

African Americans are moving from the North to the South in record numbers, largely in order to benefit from

Text continues on page 389.

VISUAL SOCIOLOGY

MAYA LIN: A STRONG, CLEAR VISION

What measures can a society take to heal the wounds of civil strife and bloodshed? This question is being raised throughout the world as nations seek to diminish intergroup hatreds and cope with the corrosive memories of civil war and genocide. In the United States, one of the strongest examples of successful efforts to address painful memories in a healing fashion is found in the commemorative sculpture of Maya Lin.

Commemoration, in the sense in which it is used to speak about Lin's work, refers to the effort a society makes to officially remember the major events that have marked its history. In the case of the Vietnam Veterans Memorial, the names of all U.S. military personnel who were killed in the war are carved into the shiny black granite of a long, gracefully proportioned wall. People from around the nation come to the wall to remember their loved ones or simply to remember the war and its many consequences for American society. As they stand in contemplation, their own images are reflected by the sheen of the polished stone. Few people leave this monument without being deeply affected by the experience.

Commemorative sculpture for major public sites is never the work of a single person. A committee usually selects from several possible approaches and artists. Thus, in the case of the Vietnam Veterans Memorial, much of the credit for the success of the monument must also go to the committee members who were able to recognize the power of Lin's vision. The same must be said for the committee representing the Southern Poverty Law Center, which commissioned Lin to design the Civil Rights Memorial in Montgomery, Alabama.

The Civil Rights movement was characterized by a great deal of heroism and martyrdom, as well as the kind of hatred and violence that became too familiar in photos like this famous one of anti–civil rights demonstrators pouring food and abuse onto civil rights workers seeking to integrate a lunch counter. A commemorative monument that focused on the heroism and the brutality, however, would not be as likely to result in emotional uplift as a quieter, more contemplative installation. On the other hand, a commemorative monument must also give clear recognition to the movement's heroes and martyrs. Lin seems to have solved this problem brilliantly.

Like the Vietnam Veterans Memorial, the Civil Rights Memorial draws the viewer into a personal meditation. Water from a deep pool on the monument's upper level:

> spills down in even sheets across the face of the wall, on which is a gold-leafed inscription of Martin Luther King's inspiring statement that the fight will continue (in the words of the Bible) "until justice rolls down like waters and righteousness like a mighty stream." An elliptical table, on which are engraved the landmark events in the civil rights era from 1955 to 1968, including the names of 40 people who died in the struggle, glistens with a film of

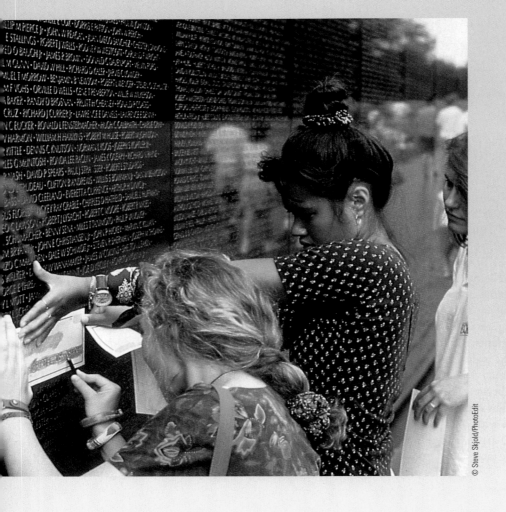

© Steve Skjold/PhotoEdit

water from above. People walk slowly around the monument reading the engraved text, and as they do so many feel compelled to run their fingers across the wet surface in an "act of communion." (Stein, 1994, p. 70).

The Sociological Observer
(See photo on page 368.)

The African-American men and women of the civil rights movement, who are commemorated in Maya Lin's fountain, are the descendents of the men, women, and children shown in this famous photo of fugitive slaves. Some of the quiet resolve and determination that marked the civil rights struggles a century after this photo was taken is evident in the faces of the escaped slaves. They also appear tired, as might be expected given their perilous flight. One notes that the children and some of the adults are shoeless. All are wearing the only clothes they possess, and there are no other possessions shown in the photo, most likely because they had almost nothing with them besides the clothes on their backs. No group ever to come to the shores of America began their American journey in as destitute a condition as did former African-American slaves, a fact that is highly important in understanding how many obstacles successful African Americans have overcome and how many remain to be overcome.

© William Johnson/Stock, Boston

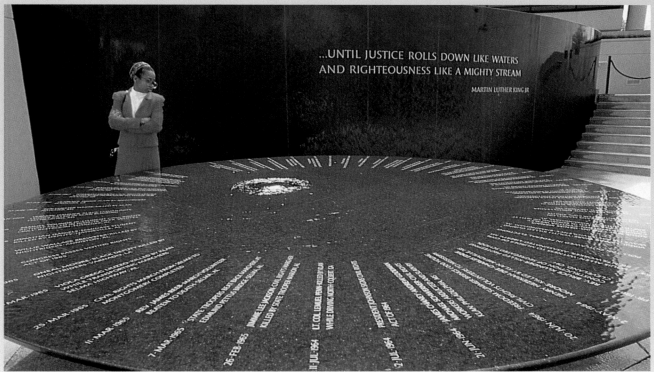

...UNTIL JUSTICE ROLLS DOWN LIKE WATERS AND RIGHTEOUSNESS LIKE A MIGHTY STREAM

MARTIN LUTHER KING JR

© William Johnson/Stock, Boston

Figure 13.6 Interregional Exchange of Hispanic Migrants, 1985–1990 (thousands)

Source: From Farley, Reynolds. "The Interregional Exchange of Non-Hispanic Black Migrants, 1985–1990 (in thousands)." In *The New American Reality: Who We Are, How We Got Here, Where We Are Going*, © 1996 Russell Sage Foundation, 112 East 64th St., New York, NY 10021. Reprinted with permission.

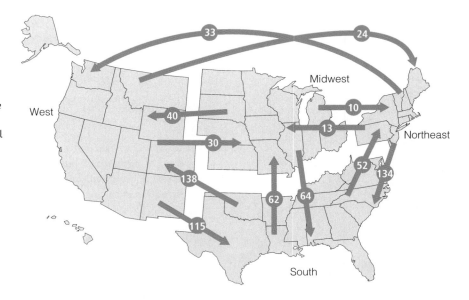

the economic growth occurring in cities like Atlanta, Birmingham, and Houston, to name only the largest. Latinos are moving to the West in larger numbers but are also making their presence felt in southern states, especially Florida and Texas. The data in Table 13.3 show, however, that the Midwest and the Northeast are "exporting" college-educated migrants, many of whom are Latinos and African Americans, to the South and West. This migration pattern is worsening the situation of less educated, less skilled blacks and Latinos in the older manufacturing regions, where more secure manufacturing jobs and better service sector jobs are scarce. In short, the regional patterns of migration revealed by Farley's analysis are widening the gap between the haves and the have-nots. As more affluent and educated minority group members leave metropolitan areas, it is increasingly difficult for the "sending" areas to come up with the funds to continue investing in education, health care, and other services for their disproportionately poor inner-city populations. At the same time, many of the cities of the Midwest and Northeast, Chicago and New York in particular, continue to receive large inflows of black and Hispanic immigrants, especially from Latin America and Africa, who require education, health services, and employment training. As these immigrants gain experience and skills and improve their socioeconomic status, they or their children will likely join the

Figure 13.7 Interregional Exchange of Non-Hispanic Black Migrants, 1985–1990 (thousands)

Source: From Farley, Reynolds. "The Interregional Exchange of Non-Hispanic Black Migrants, 1985–1990 (in thousands)." In *The New American Reality: Who We Are, How We Got Here, Where We Are Going*, © 1996 Russell Sage Foundation, 112 East 64th St., New York, NY 10021. Reprinted with permission.

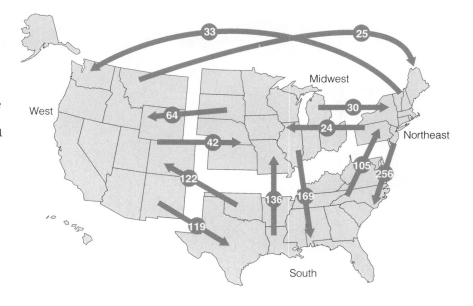

net outflow of migrants to more rapidly growing metropolitan areas. The states of the Midwest and Northeast that "export" these migrants have a legitimate claim on the national government to compensate investments made in the migrants' "human capital" (education, health care, and so on). But along with losses in population go losses in political power, leaving the "sending" regions at a disadvantage in pressing their claims for help from Congress. On the other hand, the influx of a more racially and ethnically diverse population into the South is having important consequences for southern politics, a subject to which we will return in Chapter 20.

SUMMARY

The Meaning of Race and Ethnicity

- In biology, the term *race* refers to an inbreeding population that develops distinctive physical characteristics that are hereditary. However, the choice of which physical characteristics to consider in classifying people into races is arbitrary. And human groups have exchanged their genes through mating to such an extent that it is impossible to identify "pure" races.

- The social concept of race has emerged from the interactions of various populations over long periods of human history. It varies from one society to another, depending on how the people of that society feel about the importance of certain physical differences among human beings.

- *Racism* is an ideology based on the belief that an observable, supposedly inherited trait is a mark of inferiority that justifies discriminatory treatment of people with that trait.

- *Ethnic groups* are populations that have a sense of group identity based on a distinctive cultural pattern and shared ancestry. They usually have a sense of "peoplehood" that is maintained within a larger society.

- Ethnic and racial populations are often treated as *minority groups*—people who, because of their physical or cultural characteristics, are singled out from others in the society for differential and unequal treatment.

When Worlds Collide: Patterns of Intergroup Relations

- Intergroup relations can be placed on a continuum ranging from intolerance to tolerance, or from genocide through assimilation.

- *Genocide* is state-sponsored mass killing explicitly designed to completely exterminate a population deemed to be racially or ethnically different and threatening to the dominant population. It is almost always rationalized by the belief that the people who are being slaughtered are less than human.

- *Expulsion* is the forcible removal of one population from territory claimed by another population. It has taken a variety of forms in American history, including the expulsion of Native Americans from their ancestral lands, the Oriental exclusion movement of the nineteenth century, and the detention of Japanese Americans during World War II.

- *Slavery* is the ownership of a population, defined by racial, ethnic, or political criteria, by another population that has complete control over the enslaved population. Slavery has been called "the peculiar institution" because it has existed in some of the world's greatest civilizations, including the United States.

- Although African-American slaves gained their freedom during the Civil War, a long period of segregation followed. *Segregation* is the ecological and institutional separation of races or ethnic groups. It may be either voluntary or involuntary. Involuntary segregation may be either *de jure* (created by laws that prohibit certain groups from interacting with others) or *de facto* (created by unwritten norms).

- *Assimilation* is the pattern of intergroup relations in which a minority group is forced or encouraged or voluntarily seeks to blend into the majority population and eventually disappears as a distinct people within the larger society.

- In the United States, three different views of assimilation have prevailed since the early nineteenth century. They are Anglo-conformity, the demand that culturally distinct groups give up their own cultures and adopt the dominant Anglo-Saxon culture; the melting pot, the theory that there would be a social and biological merging of ethnic and racial groups; and cultural pluralism, the belief that culturally distinct groups can retain their communities and much of their culture and still be integrated into American society.

Culture and Intergroup Relations

- *Stereotypes* are inflexible images of a racial or cultural group that are held without regard to whether they are true.

- They are often associated with *prejudice,* an attitude that prejudges a person, either positively or negatively, on the basis of characteristics of a group to which that person belongs.
- *Discrimination* refers to actual behavior that treats people unfairly on the basis of their group membership; *institutional discrimination* is the systematic exclusion of people from equal participation in a particular social institution because of their race, religion, or ethnicity.
- Social movements whose purpose is to oppose institutional discrimination are often supported by *ethnic nationalism,* the belief that one's ethnic group constitutes a distinct people whose culture is and should be separate from that of the larger society.
- Policies designed to correct persistent racial and ethnic inequalities in promotion, hiring, and access to other opportunities are referred to as *affirmative action.*

Theories of Racial and Ethnic Inequality

- Social-psychological theories of ethnic and racial inequality argue that a society's patterns of discrimination stem from individual psychological orientations toward members of out-groups.
- Interactionist explanations go beyond the individual level to see how hostility or sympathy toward other groups is produced by the norms of interaction that evolve within and between groups.
- The functionalist perspective generally seeks patterns of social integration that help maintain stability in a society.
- Conflict theories trace the origins of racial and ethnic inequality to the conflict between classes in capitalist societies.
- The conflict perspective includes the theory of *internal colonialism,* which holds that many minority groups are essentially colonial peoples within the larger society.
- Ecological theories of race relations explore the processes by which conflict between racial or ethnic groups develops and is resolved.

A Piece of the Pie

- The persistence of racial inequality in the United States is a source of continuing controversy. This complex problem is a result of several factors besides racial prejudice and discrimination. Other factors are high rates of family breakup and the effects of structural changes in the American economy.

- Although social mobility is more available to blacks today than it was before the Civil Rights movement, most blacks are in insecure working-class jobs or are unemployed.

GLOSSARY

race: An inbreeding population that develops distinctive physical characteristics that are hereditary. (p. 357)

racism: An ideology based on the belief that an observable, supposedly inherited trait is a mark of inferiority that justifies discriminatory treatment of people with that trait. (p. 358)

ethnic group: A population that has a sense of group identity based on shared ancestry and distinctive cultural patterns. (p. 360)

minority group: A population that, because of its members' physical or cultural characteristics, is singled out from others in the society for differential and unequal treatment. (p. 361)

genocide: State-sponsored mass killing explicitly designed to completely exterminate a population deemed to be racially or ethnically different and threatening to the dominant population. (p. 363)

expulsion: The forcible removal of one population from a territory claimed by another population. (p. 365)

slavery: The ownership of one racial, ethnic, or politically defined group by another group that has complete control over the enslaved group. (p. 367)

segregation: The ecological and institutional separation of races or ethnic groups. (p. 368)

de jure segregation: Segregation created by formal legal sanctions that prohibit certain groups from interacting with others or place limits on such interactions. (p. 368)

de facto segregation: Segregation created and maintained by unwritten norms. (p. 368)

Jim Crow: The system of formal and informal segregation that existed in the United States from the late 1860s to the early 1970s. (p. 369)

assimilation: A pattern of intergroup relations in which a minority group is absorbed into the majority population and eventually disappears as a distinct group. (p. 370)

ethnic stratification: The ranking of ethnic groups in a social hierarchy on the basis of each group's similarity to the dominant group. (p. 374)

diversity: A term used to refer to the heterogeneous nature of a society made up of numerous different racial, ethnic, religious, and other population groups. (p. 374)

pluralistic society: A society in which different ethnic and racial groups are able to maintain their own cultures and lifestyles while gaining equality in the institutions of the larger society. (p. 374)

stereotype: An inflexible image of the members of a particular group that is held without regard to whether it is true. (p. 374)

prejudice: An attitude that prejudges a person on the basis of a real or imagined characteristic of a group to which that person belongs. (p. 376)

discrimination: Behavior that treats people unfairly on the basis of their group membership. (p. 376)

institutional discrimination: The systematic exclusion of people from equal participation in a particular institution because of their group membership. (p. 376)

ethnic (or racial) nationalism: The belief that one's own ethnic group constitutes a distinct people whose culture is and should be separate from that of the larger society. (p. 377)

scapegoat: A convenient target for hostility. (p. 379)

projection: The psychological process whereby we attribute to other people behaviors and attitudes that we are unwilling to accept in ourselves. (p. 379)

internal colonialism: A theory of racial and ethnic inequality that suggests that some minorities are essentially colonial peoples within the larger society. (p. 381)

INTERNET RESOURCES

Virtual Society: The Wadsworth Sociology Resource Center
(http://sociology.wadsworth.com)

At Virtual Society you can access a wide range of enrichment material to aid your study of sociology. From the main page, click on the Student Resources link and find your course and this textbook. Next, select the chapter you are presently studying from the pull-down menu.

Among the useful options for each self-study chapter are online links and exercises, flashcards, practical study tips, and practice quizzes for each chapter.

MC MicroCase Online

From the Virtual Society home page, click on MicroCase Online to access book-specific MicroCase exercises that allow you to further explore sociological issues and principles presented in the text.

InfoTrac College Edition

Another unique option available to you at the Student Resources section at Virtual Society is InfoTrac College Edition, an online library with access to hundreds of scholarly and popular periodicals. Below are suggested search terms for this chapter, but this resource also allows you to fit your study of sociology to your own interests by searching custom keywords.

Racism

Ethnic nationalism

Genocide

Assimilation

The National Fair Housing Advocate
(www.fairhousing.com)

Keeps track of legal cases concerning housing discrimination throughout the nation, links organizations that advocate fair housing practices, and provides updated information on federal guidelines, job openings, articles, news, and so forth.

International Sociological Organization

European Research Centre on Migration and Ethnic Relations (ERCOMER)
(www.ercomer.org)

A university-based research institute in the Netherlands that promotes "peaceful coexistence, justice, and harmony in inter-ethnic relations." Offers access to research papers and important research findings on ethnic and racial relations.

Inequalities of Gender

© Chenault Studios/Decatur, AL

For most people the word *safari* conjures up images of wild animals—lions, elephants, and rhinos roaming the savannahs. I wanted to go and experience all that Kenya had to offer, and yet there was something more that tugged at me. I felt a calling from deep within me to go to East Africa, to go and see the beginnings of all humankind.

The writer of this passage is sociologist Carol Chenault of Calhoun Community College in Decatur, Alabama. She and her husband, Ellis Chenault, traveled to Kenya to observe the way of life of the Maasai people. "I am confident," she says, "that the teaching of culture in college sociology classes for 15 years is a major source of my interest in the Maasai." For her and for the students with whom she now shares her experiences, this sociological voyage was an eye-opening one.

What I observed was an extremely independent people whose entire lives revolve around the care and herding of their cattle. They truly believe that all of the cattle on earth are their gift from God (Engai). One Maasai warrior asked me if I had any cows. When I told him no, he said, "Good, because we would come get them if you did."

For Chenault, some of the most challenging aspects of life among the Maasai centered on the differences between the roles of men and women. "The Maasai culture has a very traditional division of labor between men and women," she writes.

Women are nurturing, loving mothers who spend a great deal of their time hugging, holding, and kissing their children. However, care of the children is a responsibility that is also shared with the fathers. Early childhood has few responsibilities; time is spent learning the ways of the adults, the language skills and play. The girls gradually begin to learn the tasks of the women, such as care of the animals, making clothing, food preparation, and doing beadwork. Girls are initiated into womanhood through circumcision; however, their attitude toward this is not one of fearful anticipation and bravery. The young women see this as a time when they have to give up their freedom for a strict married life. No longer will they be free to choose their lovers as they once did. Circumcision occurs in the mother's house and does not require the public demonstration of courage and bravery that is required of the males in their circumcision rituals. An elderly Maasai woman told me that it is unclean not to be circumcised.

Maasai girls are betrothed during infancy, or in some cases before they are born. A young couple may be approached and asked if their firstborn is a girl, then may she become the wife of their son. The wedding ceremony is a simple one in which the bride's head is shaved and then adorned with bands of beadwork. Her clothing at the wedding is very colorful in that it is all new and dyed with the familiar red ochre. Both the bride and groom are washed with milk at the time of the wedding. (Chenault, 1996, pp. 1–3)

FOCUS QUESTIONS:

• How do inequalities of gender operate in different societies to prevent women from realizing their full potential?

• What are the costs to societies of patriarchy and male dominance?

• How are women mobilizing to challenge inequalities of gender, and in what way does feminist sociology assist in their effort?

GENDER AND INEQUALITY

Many women in the nations of Asia and Africa are confronting the cultural norms that keep them in subservient positions and prevent them from asserting their own choices about their futures. The Maasai are unusual in the contemporary world. They are pastoralists who are relatively isolated from the powerful social forces that are rapidly changing other tribes in Kenya and elsewhere in Africa. In consequence, the Maasai insist on the necessity of continuing to adhere to the norms of their own tribal culture. For the sociologist, the example of the Maasai is extremely useful because it challenges assumptions about gender and society.

As observant sociologists like Carol Chenault travel to other cultures, they invariably recognize that despite cultural differences, the differences in the life chances of men and women remain one of the major dimensions of inequality in human societies. This chapter therefore begins by presenting some of the key patterns of gender inequality in the United States and throughout the world. Then the second section examines the social and biological concepts of gender and sex that are essential to understanding the inequalities people experience as a consequence of their gender or sexual orientation. Gender stratification and gender roles are discussed in the third section.

The fourth section of the chapter explores cultural norms and ideologies dealing with gender inequality, especially as they are manifested in industrial societies. The next two sections explore the women's movement and the situation of women in the workplace, where some of the most exciting and difficult changes in patterns of gender inequality are occurring today. The final section highlights current research being conducted at the grassroots level to identify and address the problems of women in the world today.

Patterns of Gender Inequality

Gender inequality stunts women's social and economic development throughout the world. It also impedes the development of entire societies, although it often takes different forms in developed and less developed nations. No wonder the subject has become a central theme of global social science. Throughout most of the last century and continuing today, the struggle for female emancipation has been a distinctive characteristic of urban industrial nations of the West (Burum & Margalit, 2002). But even in the West, the notion of equal rights for women has been under attack, especially from extreme conservatives who support the status quo of male superiority and dominance. The Nazi regime in Germany, for example, was bitterly opposed to female emancipation. In the United States as well, certain segments of the population view gender equality as a threat to traditional family values.

TABLE 14.1

Ratio of Median Weekly Earnings for Full-Time Wage and Salary Workers, Selected Occupations, 1983 and 2001

Occupation	Women-to-Men Earnings Ratio (percent)	
	2001	1983
Financial managers	70.0	63.8
Physicians	62.8	81.6
Securities and financial services sales	62.9	NA
Marketing, advertising, and public relations managers	64.5	60.1
Production coordinators	64.6	75.7
Miscellaneous managers and administrators	64.6	58.4
Sales supervisors and proprietors	65.7	61.6
Supervisors, cleaning and building service workers	67.2	NA
Designers	67.6	53.0
Total	**76.2**	**66.7**

NA = Not available; no estimates for occupations of 50,000 or less.

Source: Bureau of Labor Statistics, Current Population Survey, unpublished tables, 2003.

For those who feel most threatened by female emancipation, women's assertion of control over their own bodies and any public display of their sexuality are forms of provocation. For example, some Muslims believe that gender equality strips men of their manhood. But the oppression of women under extremely orthodox Islamic rule does not represent a "clash of civilizations." All the world's monotheistic religions include factions with varying degrees of influence that consider female emancipation a form of decadence and sin. Nevertheless, the emancipation of women remains one of the most far-reaching aspects of social change in the world. It will continue even in the face of severe and often violent reactions against it.

The United Nations International Conference on Population and Development, held in Cairo, Egypt, in 1994, concluded that "the empowerment of women and improvement of their status are important ends in themselves and are essential for the achievement of sustainable development" (United Nations, 1995). Some graphic examples of how gender inequality differs in the developed and less developed regions of the world are presented in Table 14.1 and Figure 14.1.

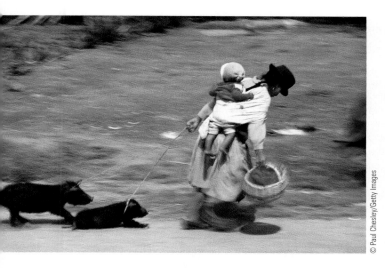

© Paul Chesley/Getty Images

Women and children make up 70% of the world's poor.
Women and children account for 80% of the world's refugees.
Women comprise over 2/3 of the world's illiterate population.
Women in developing countries are victims of violence in 1/3 of
    all families.
Women perform 2/3 of the world's work.
Women produce, process, and market 3/5 of all the world's food.
Women own 70% of all small businesses.
Women in developing countries repay their loans promptly 97%
    of the time.
YET
Women receive only 10% of the world's income.
Women own less than 1% of the world's property.

Figure 14.1 Essential Facts of Global Gender Inequality

Source: Based on data from the United Nations Human Development
Report and UNIFEM (the United Nations Development Fund for Women).

Table 14.1 shows changes in the ratio of women's earnings to men's for major occupations between 1983 and 2001. If earnings were equal, the ratio, expressed as a percentage, would be 100, but clearly the figures show a continuing gap (which in some cases is worsening) between what women and men earn in the same occupational categories. The table shows, for example, that in 2001, for every $100 earned by male financial managers, women in the same occupation earned $70. While this is a distinct improvement over the ratio in 1983, there is still a significant gender wage gap in this and most other occupations. We will see later in the chapter that even as increasing numbers of women join the labor force and compete for jobs and careers in ways that were almost unheard of just a few decades ago, men still tend to move into the higher-paying jobs in each occupation.

Figure 14.1 shows dramatically that in many parts of the world women shoulder a far greater number of domestic burdens than do men. Much of the difference may seem to occur because women take primary responsibility for bearing and nurturing children. And one might argue that in a developed country like the United States, the differences in men's and women's incomes could be attributed to the fact that so many women take time out from work and careers to bear and raise children. These familiar (and flawed) arguments raise further questions about biological versus social causes of gender inequality, which, in turn, may create confusion about the differences between sex and gender and the role of sexuality and sexual orientation in defining an individual's life chances. Before exploring the contours of gender inequality further, therefore, we turn to a discussion of the basic concepts of sex and gender.

SEX VERSUS GENDER

Masculine and *feminine* are among the most confusing words used both in everyday speech and in the social sciences. The confusion stems largely from the fact that our ideas of what is male and female in human individuals are based on overlapping influences from biology and culture. As in all such situations, it is difficult to sort out the relative contributions of each source of influence. But the underlying concepts are not hard to grasp: One's sex is primarily a biological quality, whereas one's gender is formed largely (but not entirely) by the cultural forces we experience through socialization from infancy on (Connell, 1995).

Sex refers to the biological differences between males and females, including the primary sex characteristics that are present at birth (i.e., the presence of specific male or female genitalia) and the secondary sex characteristics that develop later (facial and body hair, voice quality, and so on). Note that these biological qualities differ considerably among individuals, so that the differences between the sexes are not always as marked as the male–female distinction suggests. Moreover, some people are born as **hermaphrodites;** their primary sexual organs have features of both male and female organs, making it difficult to categorize the person as male or female. Hermaphrodism is uncommon, but it occurs in societies throughout the world.

Another ambiguous sexual category consists of the many thousands of **transsexuals,** people who feel strongly that the sexual organs they were born with do not conform to their deep-seated sense of what their sex should be. Transsexuals sometimes undergo a course of endocrine hormonal treatments to change their secondary sex

THEN AND NOW   Women Under the Taliban

Few regimes in recent history have been as oppressive for women as the Taliban of Afghanistan. Deprived of the ability to teach or to practice medicine and other professions, forced to wear full-body veils or *burquas,* deprived of medical care and the ability to work outside the home, Afghan women were often essentially imprisoned in their homes. They could venture out on the streets only if they conformed to strict Taliban rules. Deviance from those rules could lead to violent attack and execution. The defeat of the Taliban in 2002 and the formation of a new government, with two women included in the cabinet, made it possible once again for Afghan women to resume something like their normal lives.

At this writing, however, many Afghan women still live under conditions of oppressive rule and extreme male dominance. In rural areas of the nation, women still do not appear outside the home without *burquas,* and the idea that women could assert their rights or press for more liberal interpretations of strict religious codes is almost unthinkable. Indeed, many uneducated rural women do not challenge the severe forms of gender inequality that they consider an essential feature of their culture.

Fariba, 19, stands in her cell in a women's prison as a Northern Alliance soldier looks on. She was imprisoned by the Taliban for not fulfilling an arranged marriage agreement.

Afghan women register as teachers at a high school in Kabul. After the city was freed from Taliban rule, women teachers rushed to register before the next school term.

characteristics and may eventually have irreversible sex-change operations. Most such operations are performed to change the individual from a male to a female.

One of the most famous transsexuals in the contemporary world is the writer Jan Morris. As a male, James Morris reported on an expedition to Mount Everest and engaged in many activities that are associated with masculinity. But as Morris explains it: "I was born with the wrong body, being feminine by gender but male by sex, and I could achieve completeness only when the one was adjusted to the other" (quoted in Money & Tucker, 1975, p. 31). In making this distinction, Morris is calling attention to the difference between her biologically determined sex and her socially and emotionally influenced gender.

Gender refers to the culturally defined ways of acting as a male or a female that become part of an individual's personal sense of self. Most people develop a "gut-level" sense of themselves as male or female, boy or girl, early in life; however, as we will see shortly, some people's gender identities are more ambiguous. It is not entirely clear exactly how a person's gender identity is formed, but much of the research done to date suggests that the assignment of a gender at birth has a strong influence during the early years of life. In other words, children's feelings of being a boy or a girl are defined more by how they are treated by their parents than by their actual biological sex characteristics (Stockard & Johnson, 1992).

The Lenses of Gender

"Throughout the history of Western culture," Sandra Bem writes,

> three beliefs about women and men have prevailed: that they have fundamentally different psychological and sexual natures, that men are inherently the dominant or superior sex, and that both male-female difference and male dominance are natural. Until the mid-nineteenth century, this naturalness was typically conceived in religious terms, as part of God's grand creation. Since then, it has typically been conceived in scientific terms, as part of biology's—or evolution's—grand creation.
>
> Consequently, most Americans did not see any inconsistency between commitment to equality and denial of political rights to women until the appearance of the women's rights movement in the mid-nineteenth century. This first wave of feminist advocacy not only established women's basic political rights; it also made the inconsistency between ideology and the treatment of women widely visible for the first time in U.S. history.
>
> Beginning in the 1960s, the second major wave of feminist advocacy raised social consciousness still further by exposing—and naming—the "sexism" in all policies and practices that explicitly discriminate on the basis of sex. This second feminist challenge gradually enabled people to see that restricting the number of women in professional schools or paying women less than men for equal work was not a natural requirement of a woman's biological and historical role as wife and mother but an illegitimate form of discrimination based on outmoded cultural stereotypes. Even political reactionaries began to espouse the principle of equal work. (Bem, 1993, p.1)

Despite the major changes that have taken place over the past century and a half, Bem and other feminist scholars point out that we still cling to deeply ingrained assumptions about gender. As a result, we "systematically reproduce male power in generation after generation" (Bem, 1993, p. 2). Bem calls these often unquestioned assumptions "lenses of gender." Her purpose in identifying them and writing about how they shape our lives is to render them visible and thus subject to positive change.

ANDROCENTRISM   The first of the three lenses of gender she identifies is *androcentrism,* or male-centeredness. This is the "historically crude perception that men are inherently superior to women," which leads to the even more insidious perception that male experience is the natural standard or norm and that "female experience is a sex-specific deviation from that norm."

GENDER POLARIZATION   The second "lens" that Bem analyzes in her research is *gender polarization.* This is the crude idea that men and women are fundamentally different from each other, which leads to the pervasive use of that perceived difference "as an organizing principle for the social life of the culture." Modes of dress, speech, social roles, "and even ways of expressing emotion and experiencing sexual desire" are subject to gender polarization.

BIOLOGICAL ESSENTIALISM   The third lens of gender in our culture is that of *biological essentialism,* "which rationalizes and legitimizes both other lenses by treating them as the natural and inevitable consequences of the intrinsic biological natures of women and men." Of course, Bem does not deny that there are obvious biological differences between men and women, but she and other feminist

The Kobal Collection

Here we literally see the lenses of gender at work. Note that all the production crew members are male. This 1919 photo of a film star on a studio set is clearly a study in gender polarization.

scholars argue that "these facts have no fixed meaning independent of the way that a culture interprets and uses them, nor any social implications independent of their historical and contemporary context" (Bem, 1993, p. 2).

Bem realizes that eradication of these lenses of gender would require almost revolutionary changes, especially in the way boys and girls are socialized. But the first step toward this revolution is to open your imagination to a future in which the distortions caused by existing gender lenses are absent.

Gender Socialization and Gender Separation

In Chapter 5, we introduced the concept of gender socialization and discussed its powerful influence on how men and women develop as members of society. We showed, for example, that the values of beauty and youth, especially as they are applied to women by the media, have a strong and often negative influence on how women feel about their bodies and about themselves (Wolf, 1991). Current research on gender inequality is focusing increasing attention on these issues, not only for women but for men as well. Social scientists who are critical of cultures that produce and perpetuate gender inequality point to the many ways in which these inequalities are justified by values, norms, and the workings of major social institutions.

According to many comparative studies and international population reports, a central problem of gender socialization throughout the world is that the traditional separation of men and women in socializing agencies leads to the failure of men to recognize their responsibilities as sexual partners and fathers later in life. As a recent United Nations report states:

> It is clear that women cannot adequately protect their sexual and reproductive health in the context of power imbalances with their male partners. . . . Men must be involved because they share the responsibility of reproductive health, and both men and women do not understand their own and each other's bodies. (Sadik, 1995, p. 23)

In the United States, a major theme in social-scientific research is the way gender socialization, particularly in schools, tends to separate males and females into different social worlds with their own forms of activity and language. The theory that boys and girls are socialized to perform in more or less separate worlds receives a great deal of support in the sociological literature (Fine, 1987; Gilligan, 1982; Lever, 1978; Tannen, 1990). However, we will see shortly that the "separate worlds" thesis also has many limitations (Thorne, 1993, 2000).

A broad version of the gender separation theory as experienced in urban industrial societies is that children absorb ideas about their gender identities from their parents and the media. By the time they are preschoolers, they have strong ideas about what types of dress are appropriate. Boys especially are mortified if they are caught wearing something they feel is inappropriate for their gender. But children's expressions of gender identity are also shaped through interactions in play groups throughout many years of schooling. From their separate, gender-segregated interactions with peers in school, it is argued, boys and girls develop different values, different ways of bonding with each other, different types of conflict and ways of resolving conflict. In many ways, they develop separate cultures with their own norms, values, and languages. These differences are thought to persist through life and to exert a lasting influence on how the individual fares in the job market (Kanter, 1977).

In their insightful observation of preadolescent boys' interactions on Little League baseball teams, sociologist Gary Allen Fine and popular writer Stephen King were struck by the depth of male bonding that occurs as the boys undergo the pressure of competition and support each other through their successes and failures on the playing field (Fine, 1987; King, 1994). Fine notes that adult males often want their sons to join teams so that they can "teach their preadolescent boys to see the world from their perspective," which includes teaching what the men consider core values as these values emerge in sports competition. However, "whereas adults focus on hustle, teamwork, sportsmanship, and winning and losing"—as desirable moral behaviors developed through team sports—"the preadolescent transforms these concerns" (Fine, 1987, p. 78). The team members respect the adults' teachings, but they are more concerned with their self-presentation, which includes some of the adult values and some of those that are part of the preadolescent moral code—learning to be tough or fearful under the appropriate conditions; learning to control aggressions, fears, and tears; not being a "rat" (telling on others); and hustling in order to help the team win games. The boys engage in a great deal of sexual talk, much of which expresses their ambivalence about relationships with girls, in which their desire to have sexual experiences is offset by their fears of embarrassment and loss of male friends. The boys' banter with each other also expresses their fear of not being masculine enough. Although they have little or no experience with homosexuality, they use words like *faggot* or *gay* to tease each other or denigrate other boys.

Sociologists who study gender and socialization often point out that the strong same-sex bonds formed by boys in preadolescence and during their teen years may prove invaluable in the corporate world. In their research on life in American corporations, Rosabeth Moss Kanter and her associates found that sports analogies are commonplace. The male business leader typically thinks of those he works with as members of a team, and as a result of his early socialization experiences, he is more comfortable with male team members than with females (Kanter & Stein, 1980).

Studies of girls' play groups note that although boys and girls are increasingly likely to play some games together, the separation of the genders in playgrounds and schoolyards remains a norm (Sutton-Smith & Rosenberg, 1961; Whiting & Edwards, 1988). These studies confirm that girls' games are likely to involve small groups, rather than large ones with more complex structures and hierarchies of status. They are interrupted not by arguments over rules or specific plays but by emotional issues, feelings of being slighted, or other hurts—which the girls repair in private conversations rather than in public protests to umpires or other adults. In addition, girls tend to engage in turn-taking games that emphasize cooperation, whereas boys more often engage in competitive team sports in which they become extremely concerned with establishing hierarchies of skill and success (e.g., batting averages, win–loss records) (Lever, 1976, 1978).

Of course, children learn many other social distinctions besides gender from their parents and playmates. Barrie Thorne, who observed children's peer interactions in two primary schools, makes this observation:

> In the lunchrooms and on the playgrounds of the two schools, African-American kids and kids whose main language was Spanish occasionally separated themselves into smaller, ethnically homogeneous groups. . . . I found that students generally separate first by gender and then, if at all, by race or ethnicity. (1993, p. 33)

Problems with the Gender Separation Theory

How fully are men and women socialized into separate social worlds with separate cultures? As mentioned earlier, a great deal of popular and social-scientific writing supports this thesis. The immense success of Deborah Tannen's analysis of men's and women's spoken communication in her popular book *You Just Don't Understand: Women and Men in Conversation* suggests that men and women do feel separate and different in their everyday lives. But recent research on gender differences is critical of the idea of separate gender cultures (Thorne, 1993).

Although there is an undeniable tendency for boys and girls to be socialized in gender-segregated peer groups, they are also raised together in families and often spend a

great deal of time together. Boys and girls are increasingly participating in the same types of activities in their schools and communities. In some communities, these changes are controversial, but in many others, teachers, parents, and administrators seek to avoid the worst effects of gender separation (Meier, 1995). Girls' and women's team sports, for example, are undergoing rapid and steady growth. And as they review the literature on separate gender cultures or conduct new research, students of gender often find that the previous emphasis on gender separateness was based on what they refer to as "the Big Man bias"—the tendency to observe only the activities of the most powerful and socially successful individuals. More isolated, less successful children are less likely to be subjects of research, yet their experiences are important because they do not adhere strictly to the norms of gender separation. Finally, as Thorne (1993) argues, generalizations about "girls' culture" are based primarily on research with upper-class white girls, while the experiences of girls from other class, racial, and ethnic backgrounds tend to be neglected.

Gender and Sexuality

Sexuality refers to the manner in which a person engages in the intimate behaviors connected with genital stimulation, orgasm, and procreation. Like most areas of human behavior, sexuality is profoundly influenced by cultural norms and social institutions such as the family and the school, as well as by social structures like the class system of a society. Sociologists and historians believe that there have been major changes in sexuality as a result of changes in the economy, politics, and the family. Over the past 300 years, for example, the meaning and place of sexuality in American life have changed: from a family-centered system for ensuring reproduction and social stability during the colonial period; to a romantic and intimate sexuality in nineteenth-century marriage, with many underlying conflicts; to a commercialized sexuality in the modern period, when sexual relations are expected to provide personal identity and individual happiness apart from reproduction (D'Emilio & Freedman, 1988; Rossi, 1994).

These changes are important and controversial, but they hardly begin to exhaust the range of sexual norms in cultures throughout the world. Polygyny (the practice of having more than one wife), which is illegal in North America and Europe, is condoned throughout much of the Islamic world. Marriage between adult men and preadolescent girls is practiced in some Asian cultures but would be considered a form of child abuse in the West. Women bare their breasts on the beaches of Europe but may be issued summonses for the same behavior on the beaches of North America. On

American television screens, women and men expose their bodies in a fashion that is horrifying to people in many parts of Asia. Catholic priests and nuns are expected to remain celibate, whereas Protestant ministers are encouraged to have families, as are Jewish rabbis. With all of these contrasting cultural norms governing sexuality, can it be said that there are any universal sexual norms?

Universal cultural norms exerting social control over sexuality include the *incest taboo, marriage,* and *heterosexuality,* but even these norms include variations and differing degrees of sanction. As noted in Chapter 3, the incest taboo is known in every existing and historical society and serves to protect the integrity of the family. Incest norms prohibit sexual intimacy between brothers and sisters and between parents and children, and usually specify what other family relatives are excluded. However, the specific relatives involved vary in different cultures; for example, sex between first cousins is permissible in some societies and strictly taboo in others.

Every society also has marriage norms that specify the relationships within which sexual intimacy is condoned. Marriage norms protect the institution of the family, confer legitimacy on children, and specify parental rights and obligations. But while marriage norms are found in all cultures, there are vast differences in how they operate. In addition to variations having to do with polygyny, there are some important variations with regard to the strength of sanctions on adultery (sexual intimacy outside marriage). Most cultures prohibit adultery, but the sanctions vary widely. Former French President François Mitterrand, who died in 1996, specified in his funeral instructions that both his wife and his mistress were to be present at his funeral. Although adultery is not openly condoned in France, it is far less strongly sanctioned than in the United States, where evidence that a presidential candidate may have had an extramarital affair often becomes a major issue in the campaign (Stockard & Johnson, 1992).

Heterosexuality refers to sexual orientation toward the opposite sex, in contrast to **homosexuality,** which refers to sexual orientation toward the same sex, and **bisexuality,** which refers to sexual orientation toward either sex. Heterosexuality is a norm in every society, but it too is subject to wide variations. Norms of heterosexuality function to ensure that genital sexual intercourse occurs between men and women in the interest of population replacement and growth. The Shakers of colonial North America were an example of a society that attempted to curtail or eliminate heterosexuality in favor of celibacy in the interest of religious piety. Because Shaker society could continue only through recruitment of new members, it eventually declined and essentially disappeared.

Although heterosexuality is practiced in some form in all societies, about one-third of them actively ban homo-

sexual practices, while many other societies tolerate them in some form (Murdock, 1983). Historically, the best-known examples of heterosexual societies that condoned some forms of homosexuality and bisexuality were ancient Greece, Confucian China, and Hawaii before it was colonialized by Europeans (Connell, 1995). In most Western cultures, the norm of heterosexuality is strong, but older taboos against homosexuality and bisexuality are changing as well.

HOMOSEXUALITY AND BISEXUALITY   The intensity of debate over homosexuality in the United States is an indication, on one hand, of how controversial the behavior remains and, on the other, of the growing, if grudging, acceptance of alternatives to traditional norms of heterosexuality. In the mid-twentieth century homosexuality was a taboo subject. Homosexual men and women remained secretive or "in the closet" about their true sexual feelings. Today there is at least one homosexual member of Congress and many other openly homosexual elected officials and public figures. At the same time, fear and loathing of homosexuals—gay men and lesbian women—is a major social problem that continues to cause immense human suffering.

Estimates of the incidence of homosexuality—that is, the proportion or number of women and men in a population who are sexually attracted to people of the same sex—raise several social-scientific and political problems. In his pathbreaking and courageous studies of male and female sexual behavior, Alfred Kinsey interviewed thousands of Americans about their sexual preferences and behavior. Kinsey described sexuality as a continuum extending from exclusive heterosexuality to equal attraction for the same and the opposite sex (bisexuality) to exclusive homosexuality. By his estimates, about 4 percent of men and 2 percent of women were exclusively homosexual, while far more, perhaps as many as one-third of men and about 12 percent of women, said that they had had a homosexual experience leading to orgasm at least once in their lives (Kinsey, Pomeroy, & Martin, 1948, 1953). Subsequent reinterpretations of Kinsey's data led social scientists to estimate that 10 percent of the population was homosexual or had strong homosexual tendencies. This estimate became a commonly cited statistic in the politics of the gay rights movement. However, the most recent major study of sexuality in the United States, conducted by the National Opinion Research Center (NORC), finds this estimate to be too high. For instance, in the NORC sample, about 4 percent of men and about 1.4 percent of women said that they were exclusively homosexual, but only about 10 percent of men (not the 30 to 35 percent cited by Kinsey) admitted to having had prior homosexual experiences even if they did not claim to be homosex-

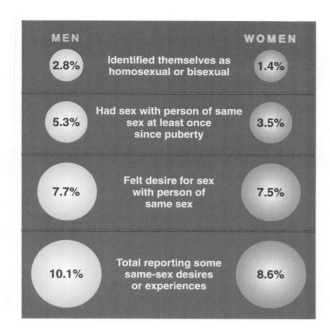

MEN		WOMEN
2.8%	Identified themselves as homosexual or bisexual	1.4%
5.3%	Had sex with person of same sex at least once since puberty	3.5%
7.7%	Felt desire for sex with person of same sex	7.5%
10.1%	Total reporting some same-sex desires or experiences	8.6%

Figure 14.2 Defining "Gay"

Source: From Laumann et al., *The Social Organization of Sexuality*. Copyright © 1994 University of Chicago Press. Reprinted with permission.

ual in their daily lives (see Figure 14.2). Data from the NORC study also indicate that there are wide differences among men and between men and women in how sexual pleasure is defined and derived (see Table 14.2) (Laumann et al., 1994).

Given the anxiety that many people feel about discussing their sexual orientation and behavior, however, some people believe that the NORC study may underestimate the incidence of homosexuality in the population (Gould, 1995). It should also be noted that the ambitious study would have included a far larger sample and somewhat greater scientific accuracy if the federal funds that had been scheduled for its budget had not been withdrawn by conservative members of Congress opposed to research on sexuality.

Only about 0.8 percent of men and 0.9 percent of women in the NORC sample said that they were bisexual. But when they were asked more indirectly whether they were sexually attracted to both sexes, the proportions who said yes increased to 4.1 percent of women and 3.9 percent of men. Martin S. Weinberg observes that many people "would say that the person who feels the sexual attraction to both sexes but never acts on it is not bisexual, but in my definition they are" (quoted in Gabriel, 1995b, p. A12). The findings of Weinberg's recent study of bisexuality refute the common assumption that bisexuality is a stage leading to eventual homosexual orientation. His sample included women and men who had come to their bisexuality

from both heterosexual and homosexual orientations and for whom bisexuality appeared to be a stable lifestyle.

Many homosexuals, along with an increasing number of biologists and social scientists, believe that homosexuality will be shown to have genetic origins (Rosario, 2001; Tobach & Rosoff, 1994). In accounts of their earliest sexual feelings, homosexual men, and to a lesser degree lesbian women, recount their experiences of sexual attraction to members of the same sex. These experiences convince many gay people that their sexual orientation is not merely a "lifestyle choice," as critics often claim. However, as yet there is insufficient evidence from genetic studies to resolve this issue (Kemper, 1990; Kluger, 2001).

HOMOPHOBIA   Most of the young boys in Barrie Thorne's study of gender play used negative images of homosexuals well before they ever encountered a gay person. Fear of homosexuals and same-sex attraction is known as *homophobia*. Although it is common in the United States, its causes are not entirely clear. Most social-scientific (as opposed to religious or ideological) explanations of homophobia hinge on an analysis of the problems of masculinity and the male role in Western societies.

Identification with the male gender and the ability to take male roles, as these are defined for young boys and later for men, are two different aspects of what it means to "be a man." Every society has its notions of what distinguishes men from women, and seeks to teach boys and girls how to perform the roles assigned to their gender. In Western societies, the male role is often depicted in movies, on television, and in advertising as distinct from that of the female and imbued with more strength, power, and rationality—a subject to which we return later in the chapter. Because as children they lack the power and strength they admire in images of masculinity, young boys typically become concerned about being seen as lacking in masculinity and the ability to take on male roles. Thus their vocabulary is rich with terms of abuse for anyone they believe to be lacking in masculinity: wimp, nerd, turkey, sissy, lily liver, yellowbelly, candy ass, ladyfinger, cream puff, mama's boy, dweeb, geek, and so on (Connell, 1995). As they grow older, a small but socially significant proportion of boys may become violently homophobic and go out of their way to abuse males whom they consider effeminate or "queer."

Girls may also develop homophobic attitudes early in life, often through identification with their male siblings, but homophobia among females often occurs during the teenage years. Female socialization stresses the ability to attract men, to appear feminine, and anxiety over these aspects of the female role may lead young women to reject other women whom they do not regard as feminine enough.

TABLE 14.2

The Appeal of Various Sexual Practices (percentages of respondents)

	Appealing to Men Ages 18–44				Appealing to Women Ages 18–44			
	Very	Somewhat	Not Really	Not at All	Very	Somewhat	Not Really	Not at All
Vaginal intercourse	83%	12%	1%	4%	78%	18%	1%	3%
Watching partner undress	50	43	3	4	30	51	11	9
Receiving oral sex	50	33	5	12	33	35	11	21
Giving oral sex	37	39	9	15	19	38	15	28
Active anal intercourse	5	9	13	73	—	—	—	—
Passive anal intercourse	3	8	15	75	1	4	9	87
Group sex	14	32	20	33	1	8	14	78
Same-sex partner	4	2	5	89	3	3	9	85
Sex with a stranger	5	29	25	42	1	9	1	80
Forcing someone to do something sexual	0	2	14	84	0	2	7	91
Being forced to do something sexual	0	3	13	84	0	2	6	92

Source: From Laumann et al., *The Social Organization of Sexuality*. Copyright © 1994 University of Chicago Press. Reprinted with permission.

These early patterns can have lasting consequences. Throughout their lives, the early habit of avoiding emotions for fear of seeming effeminate tends to make men in the United States and other Western societies wary of expressing their feelings and of admitting vulnerability: "Men are thus denied an important part of their . . . well-being when they cannot touch and cannot express their tender feelings for other men. Needless to say, gay men are damaged by the negative implications of homophobia" (Blumenfeld, 1992, p. 37). And of course homophobia causes untold suffering for gay men and women (Richmond-Abbott, 1992).

Fundamentalist religious beliefs are another important source of negative attitudes and strong disapproval of homosexuality, including vehement homophobia. For example, 77 percent of fundamentalist Baptists disagree or strongly disagree with the statement "Even if homosexuality is wrong, the civil rights of gays should be protected." They believe that homosexuality is immoral and inimical to the propagation of the species. In the United States, it is common for prominent fundamentalist Christian leaders to state that AIDS is God's punishment for the homosexual lifestyle (Ammerman, 1990). Despite the vehemence of such religiously motivated attacks, gay men and women in smaller towns and communities with fundamentalist congregations are increasingly asserting their right to live as they choose as long as they do not violate the rights of others (Lampman, 2001; Miller, 1989).

Controversies over male and female roles, homosexuality, norms of sexual conduct, and the origins of sexual orientation all point to the extent to which these central areas of social life are subject to change and reactions to change. In the study of gender inequalities, the origins and patterns of change in the condition of women and the continuing inequalities between the sexes are a central focus, to which we now turn.

GENDER STRATIFICATION

After class and race, the most important dimensions of inequality in modern societies are gender and age. As stated earlier, gender refers to a set of culturally conditioned traits associated with maleness or femaleness. There are two sexes, male and female; these are biologically determined ascribed statuses. There are also two genders, masculine and feminine; these are socially constructed ways of being a man or a woman. **Gender roles** are the sets of behaviors considered appropriate for individuals of a particular gender. Controversies over whether women in the armed forces can serve in combat or whether men with children ought to be eligible for family leave from work are examples of issues arising out of the definition of gender roles.

All human societies are stratified by gender, meaning that males and females are channeled into specific statuses and roles. "Be a man"; "She's a real lady"—with these familiar expressions we let each other know that our behavior is or is not conforming to the role expectations associated with our particular gender. When women's roles are thought to require male direction, as is the case in many households and organizations, the unequal treatment of men and women is directly related to gender roles. The roles assigned to men and women are accorded differing amounts of income, power, or prestige, and these patterns of inequality contribute to the society's system of stratification.

Gender Roles: A Cultural Phenomenon

Until recently, it was assumed that there were two spheres of life, one for women and the other for men. The chief agents of socialization—church, family, and school—worked effectively together to transmit and legitimize the notion that boys would grow up to be leaders in the world outside the home whereas girls would become wives and mothers whose involvement in the world outside the home would be more indirect. Out of this gender-based division of labor, which defined the activities that were appropriate for men and women, grew the notion of differences in men's and women's abilities and personalities. These differences were thought to be natural—an outgrowth of biological and psychological differences between males and females (Epstein, 1985). Behaviors that did not fit these patterns were viewed as deviant and in some cases as requiring severe punishment.

In the twentieth century, evidence from the social sciences called into question the assumption that there are innate biological or psychological reasons for the different roles and temperaments of men and women. Margaret Mead's famous research in New Guinea directly challenged this assumption. Mead was one of the first social scientists to gather evidence to show that gender-specific behavior is learned rather than innate. In her study of gender roles in three tribes, Mead (1950) found that different tribes had different ways of defining male and female behavior. In one tribe, the Mundugumor, men and women were equally aggressive and warlike, traits that Westerners usually associate only with men. In a second tribe, the Tchambuli, the men spent their time gossiping about women and worrying about their hairdos, while the women shaved their heads and made rude jokes among themselves. In the third tribe, the Arapesh, both men and women behaved in sympathetic, cooperative ways and spent a great deal of time worrying about how the children were getting along, all behaviors that Westerners traditionally associate with women.

Mead's research has been criticized in that she may have been actively looking for gender-role patterns that differed from those that Westerners usually associate with males and females. Nevertheless, her study was highly significant

because it began a line of inquiry that established that gender roles are not innate. Nor are gender roles wholly determined by a society's relationship to its environment. Although hunting-and-gathering societies sent men out to hunt while women cared for the home, in early agrarian societies there was a less rigid division of labor. In early horticultural societies, women had more power than they did in hunting-and-gathering societies or in later feudal societies. Women maintained the grain supply and knew the lore of cultivation, and they were priestesses who could communicate with the harvest and fertility gods (Adler, 1997; Balandier, 1971/1890).

The lesson of this cross-cultural research is that gender roles are heavily influenced by culture. Although the relationship of earlier societies to their natural environment often required that women tend the hearth and home while men went out to hunt for big game, women were also hunting for small game around the encampment and experimenting with new seeds and agricultural techniques. The division of labor by gender was never fixed; it could always be adapted to new conditions. In industrial societies, as the greater strength of males became less important as a result of advances in technology, it made less sense to maintain the earlier divisions of labor. Indeed, modern societies have demanded more involvement of women in a broader range of tasks. Women are now competing with men as military and police officers, engineers, scientists, judges, political leaders, and the like; they may be found in many roles that were assumed to be unsuitable for women less than half a century earlier.

GENDERED ORGANIZATIONS   Recent research, especially that of feminist sociologists, has expanded our understanding of gender in society by demonstrating that gender stratification is a feature of organizations of all kinds, and not merely an attribute of individuals and their roles (Lorber, 1994; Staggenborg, 1998). The concept of "gendered organizations" encourages researchers to study how assumptions about gender are ingrained in the culture of organizations ranging from the family to corporations and universities. Many law firms, for example, strongly suggest that success is based on long hours of time spent in the office. This assumption distinctly favors male workers whose wives have chosen to be homemakers. And as we will see in Chapter 16, the family is often a highly gendered organization as well.

Especially in the second half of the twentieth century, women have organized in social movements to remove barriers to their employment based on the gendered nature of organizations and the assumption that they could not do certain types of work (e.g., policing, fire fighting, or construction). Table 14.3 shows that women have increased their share of employment in many occupational groups that were formerly male "turf." The proportions of

TABLE 14.3

Percentage of Women in Major Occupational Groups, 1970–2001

Major Occupational Group	1970	2001
Executive, administrative, and managerial	18.5%	46.0%
Professional specialty	44.3	53.7
Technicians and related support	34.4	53.4
Sales occupations	41.3	49.4
Administrative support, including clerical	73.2	78.7
Private household	96.3	96.2
Protective service	6.6	20.4
Other service	61.2	65.4
Farming, forestry, fishing	9.1	20.8
Precision production, craft, and repair	7.3	8.7
Machine operators, assemblers, and inspectors	39.7	36.4
Transportation and material-moving occupations	4.1	10.4
Handlers, equipment cleaners, helpers, and laborers	17.4	20.5
Total	38.0	46.6

Source: Data from Bianchi & Spain, 1986; and *Statistical Abstract*, 2003.

The Sociological Observer

This group of Maasai women and children are shown interacting as people do across the generations throughout the world. What observations can you make about the generations represented here? What aspects of gender relations do you see in the photo? (See page 419 for further insights into the sociological content of this photo.)

© Chenault Studios/Decatur, AL

female executives and managers have increased dramatically, as have those of technicians and professionals. But older barriers and assumptions continue to stand in the way of equal access to male-dominated occupations such as precision production. Conversely, women continue to be disproportionately represented in "pink-collar" occupational sectors such as clerical and administrative support and domestic service (Bianchi & Spain, 1986).

Historical Patterns of Gender Stratification

In preindustrial societies, gender often plays a greater role in social stratification than wealth and power. Fewer members of such societies are wealthy or powerful than is true in modern societies, but all are male or female. Cross-cultural research has provided some insight into the development of gender-based stratification in such societies. Among the main findings of that research are the following:

- Preindustrial societies are usually rigidly sex-segregated. Males and females tend to pass through life in cohesive peer groups. Even after marriage, women and men tend to spend more time with their same-sex peers than they do with their spouses.
- As societies increase in size and complexity, women usually become subordinated to men. There have been few, if any, societies in which women as a group controlled the distribution of wealth or the exercise of power (Harris, 1980; Leacock, 1978).

Larger, more complex societies also exhibit distinct patterns of gender-role stratification, but these are more likely to be part of a multidimensional system of stratification in which class, race, ethnicity, gender, and age are intertwined.

The origins of gender inequality in most modern societies can be traced to their feudal periods. Most industrial societies developed out of feudal societies, either as a result of revolutions (in Europe) or through changes brought about by colonialism (in North and South America, Asia, and parts of Africa). Although they are no longer as easily justified, many of the norms that specify separate spheres of activity for males and females, as well as the subordination of women to men, were carried over into modern societies.

In some feudal societies, these norms were far more repressive than those found in modern societies; in others, the subordination of women was disguised as reverence or worship. In European feudal societies, for example, the norms of chivalry and courtly love seemed to elevate women to an exalted status, but in reality they reinforced practices that kept women in undervalued roles. These practices resulted in a set of norms that specified that women do not initiate sexual activity, do not engage in warfare or politics but wait for men to resolve conflicts, and do not compete with men in any sphere of life beyond those reserved for women.

The situation of Guinevere in the tales of King Arthur aptly illustrates this point (de Rougemont, 1983; Elias, 1978/1939). Courtly love applied only to women of the nobility. It specified that a woman must be chaste—either a virgin or entirely faithful to her husband at all times. Like Guinevere, she could be worshiped from afar by a noble knight (Lancelot), but she could not be touched or even spoken to without the consent of her male guardian (King Arthur). Figuratively she was set upon a pedestal. In reality, however, she was imprisoned—kept forever separate from the knightly suitor who worshiped her from a distance and engaged in chivalrous acts in her name. Adultery and the subordination of women were common in the lower orders of feudal society, but the women of the nobility were more likely to be constrained by the norms of chastity.

As feudal societies developed and changed, the norms of courtly love were extended to the new middle classes, and they still exist today in greatly modified forms. They can be seen, for example, in the traditions of courtship that persist in Spanish-speaking nations, in which a man serenades a woman (or hires someone to do it on his behalf) and the woman is never without a chaperone. It should be noted that courtly (or romantic) love eventually elevated the status of women from that of property to that of significant other, a change that had far-reaching implications for the position and influence of women in the family. At the same time, in many Western cultures norms derived from medieval notions of courtly love continue to justify the notion that there are "good women," whom one reveres and protects, and "bad women," who are available for sexual exploitation. This denial of normal female

This medieval illustration depicts the norms of chivalry in action. Notice the women standing on the battlements, aloof from the fray. Their lot is to watch the combat and hope that their hero will not be skewered by his opponent.

sexuality and the assertion of the male's sexual needs is associated with a host of psychological and social problems, including the conflict that some women feel about their sexuality and the inability of some men to relate to their wives as sexual partners.

GENDER INEQUALITY IN INDUSTRIAL SOCIETIES

In modern industrial societies, age and gender interact to shape people's views of what role behavior is appropriate at any given time. Before puberty, boys and girls in the United States tend to associate in sex-segregated peer groups. Because they model their behavior on what they see in the home and on television, girls spend more of their time playing at domestic roles than boys do; boys meanwhile play at team sports more than girls do. These patterns are changing at different rates in different social classes, but they remain generally accepted norms of behavior. And they have important consequences: Women are more likely to be socialized into the "feminine" roles of mother, teacher, secretary, and so on, whereas men are more likely to be socialized into roles that are considered "masculine," such as those of corporate manager or military leader. It is expected that men will concern themselves with earning and investing while women occupy themselves with human relationships (Rossi, 1980; Witt, 1997).

Childhood socialization explains some of the inequalities and differences between the roles of men and women, but we also need to recognize the impact of social structures. In the United States, for example, it was assumed until fairly recently that boys and girls needed to be segregated in their games. Boys were thought to be much stronger and rougher than girls, and girls were thought to need protection from unfair competition with boys. This widespread belief translated into school rules that did not permit coeducational sports. Those rules, in turn, reinforced the more general belief that girls' roles needed to be segregated from those of boys. Such patterns have significant long-term effects. As sociologist Cynthia Epstein points out, human beings have an immense capacity "to be guided, manipulated, and coerced into assuming social roles, demonstrating behavior, and expressing thoughts that conform to socially accepted values" (1988, p. 240). Through such means, gender roles become so deeply ingrained in many people's consciousness that they feel threatened when women assert their similarities with men and demand equal opportunity and equal treatment in social institutions.

In their adult years, men enjoy more wealth, prestige, and leisure than women do. Working women earn less than men do, and they are often channeled into the less prestigious strata of large organizations. Even as executives, they are often shunted into middle-level positions in which they must do the bidding of men in more powerful positions. Similar patterns are found in all advanced industrial nations.

The Feminization of Poverty

Earlier in the chapter (see Table 14.1) we showed that women earn less than men in the same occupations. Coupled with existing patterns of gender inequality, these income disparities mean that women are more likely to be living at or below the poverty line. The U.S. Census shows that about 16 percent of women and about 12 percent of men are officially classified as poor. "The ratio of women to men's poverty—the gender poverty ratio—was 1.30 in 1991, which means that

women are 30 percent more likely to be poor than men" (Casper, McLanahan, & Garfinkel, 1994, p. 594). To compare this gender poverty gap to that in other industrial nations, sociologists use an international study of income and poverty known as the Luxembourg Income Study. That study classified people as poor if they "live in a household whose disposable income (after taxes and government cash transfers) is less than 50 percent of the median disposable income for all households in that country" (Casper, McLanahan, & Garfinkel, 1994, p. 595). This definition (with adjustments for differing household size) is based on a relative measure rather than the absolute income standard used to determine the official "poverty line" in the United States. It allows investigators "to examine differences in poverty between men and women in different countries relative to the common standard of living in those countries" (Casper, McLanahan, & Garfinkel, 1994, p. 596).

Some findings of this international comparison are presented in Figures 14.3 and 14.4. Although the figures show that the United States lags behind other industrial nations in reducing the gender poverty gap, an analysis of the findings reveals that the causes of these differences are varied (Pressman, 1998). Disparities in employment, with women concentrated in lower-paying jobs, are a major factor in explaining the situation in the United States, but some nations do not have high rates of female labor force participation. In those nations (e.g., Italy), female poverty is reduced by the tendency of women to marry men who can support them, and to remain married. In still other nations, social policies play an important role. In "social democratic" nations like Sweden, there is less gender integration in occupations than in the United States. Single women with young children are not obliged to work but are given generous subsidies through income support, child care, education, and other policies (Kammerman & Kahn, 1993). As a result, rates of female poverty are low.

In sum, comparative research indicates that gender inequality and female poverty rates are very much related to the specific workings of other social institutions—particularly those of the economy and government—and that they can be reduced when the society has the resources and will to do so.

Sexism

Gender stratification is reflected in attitudes that reinforce the subordinated status of women. The term *sexism* is used to refer to an ideology that justifies prejudice or discrimination based on sex. It results in the channeling of women into statuses considered appropriate for women and their exclusion from statuses considered appropriate for men. Sexist

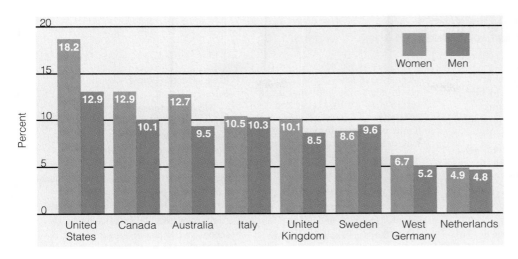

Figure 14.3 Poverty Rates of Women and Men (percentages)

Source: Reprinted from *The Social Science Journal,* vol. 35, S. Pressman, "The Gender Poverty Gap in Developed Countries: Causes and Cures," p. 275–287, Copyright 1998, with permission from Elsevier Science.

attitudes also tend to "objectify" women, meaning that they treat women as objects for adornment or sex rather than as individuals worthy of a full measure of respect and equal treatment in social institutions. This can be seen in the case of beautiful women. Such women receive special treatment from both men and women, but their beauty is a mixed blessing. The beautiful woman is often viewed as nothing more than an object for admiration. Being a woman is a master status (see Chapter 4) in that gender tends to outweigh the person's achieved statuses. This is even more painfully true for beautiful women. Someone like Marilyn Monroe is thought of only in terms of her beauty; the person beneath the surface is ignored. (See the Sociological Methods box on pages 408-409.)

The objectification of women can be seen in the beauty contest, which came into being in the United States in the summer of 1921 when the first Costume and Beauty Show

Men are often compelled by gender norms to behave in stereotypically "masculine" ways in public.

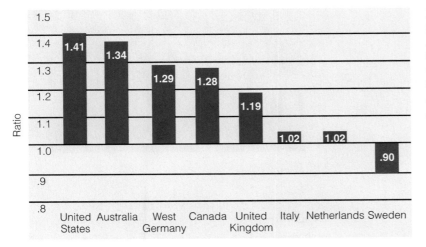

Figure 14.4   Ratio of Women's to Men's Poverty Rates

Source: From Casper, McLanahan, & Garfinkel, "The Gender–Poverty Gap: What We Can Learn from Other Countries," *American Sociological Review,* vol. 59. August 1994. Copyright 1994 American Sociological Association.

Text continues on page 410.

SOCIOLOGICAL METHODS

The Beauty Ideal and Women's Self-Image

Recent news articles reveal that employers increasingly seek to hire women whose looks and figures conform to an ideal of beauty, and that major sales corporations like Abercrombie & Fitch and L'Oreal are using standards of female beauty that are possibly discriminatory and may result in charges of racial and age discrimination (Greenhouse, 2003). For feminist sociologists and critics, however, this is old news. For decades, they have been arguing that the images of female beauty presented in the media help maintain gender inequality by promoting an ideal that few women can attain.

In her influential study *The Beauty Myth*, Naomi Wolf argues that

> The more legal and material hindrances women have broken through, the more strictly and heavily and cruelly images of female beauty have come to weigh upon us . . . During the past decade, women breached the power structure; meanwhile, eating disorders rose exponentially and cosmetic surgery became the fastest-growing specialty . . . pornography became the main media category, ahead of legitimate films and records combined, and thirty-three thousand American women told researchers that they would rather lose ten to fifteen pounds than achieve any other goal . . . More

women have more money and power and scope and legal recognition than we have ever had before; but in terms of how we feel about ourselves physically, we may actually be worse off than our unliberated grandmothers. (Wolf, 1991, p. 3)

Recent studies of the impact of media images on women confirm Wolf's argument. They also demonstrate some useful methods of exploring these issues. The first of these methods is what is known as *meta-analysis*—that is, analysis of previous studies of a similar subject to determine the degree to which their findings are similar or different. For example, in a meta-analysis of 25 studies on the effects of viewing thin images in magazines and television, researchers found overwhelming evidence in all the studies that women felt more negative about their bodies after viewing thin media images than after viewing images of either average-size models, plus-size models, or inanimate objects. The effects were strong for all age groups, but young women below age 19 felt the strongest neg-

ative effects (Groesz, Levine, & Murnen, 2002).

What difference does it make if women tend to feel bad about their bodies after viewing media representations of thin models? Unfortunately, these negative feelings are also associated with eating disorders like anorexia and bulimia, and with lowered self-esteem, which in turn lowers women's confidence and ability to compete in school and in the economy (Clarke, 2002).

Another research method sheds further light on these issues. It is a form of comparative research over time periods that looks at the differences between the bodies of women who are valued in society as models, pin-ups, or beauty pageant winners and the actual bodies of young women in the larger society. The researchers com-

The heirs to the Hilton Hotel fortune, Nicky, 18, and Paris, 21, are darlings of the media. Impossibly rich and slender, they are shown going out to all the hottest spots with movie stars as their escorts. Research shows that, to the detriment of many women in modern societies, the popular media in the United States and elsewhere are fixated on celebrities who display the idealized thin woman's body.

AP/Wide World Photos

pared data on the height and weight of Miss America Pageant winners, Playboy playmates, fashion models, and young women in general from the 1920s through the 1990s. The results are shown in the accompanying table. We see that the average height of young women in the general population increased from an average of 63.2 inches in the 1930s to 64.1 inches in the 1990s, but that of models went from over 67 inches to over 69 inches. The changes were even more dramatic for body weight. As the average weight of young women rose from 120.3 pounds to 141.7 pounds over the period studied, that of models actually decreased (Byrd-Bredbenner & Murray, 2003).

As Americans were enjoying the fruits of affluence—driving more, walking less, and responding to advertising that promotes consumption of high-calorie foods—average body weight was increasing. The epidemic of obesity in the United States and other Western nations is one consequence (see Chapter 21). Another consequence is the growing "disconnect" between idealized images of the attractive, super-thin woman one sees in the media and real women, who increasingly feel oppressed by these images but respond by trying new diets or by giving up and bingeing. A countertrend, however, is taking hold among some women, who are exercising more, learning how to eat sensibly, and taking control of their own bodies, but unfortunately they are still a minority.

COMPARISON OF MEAN MEASUREMENTS (MEAN ± SD) WITHIN DECADES OF MISS AMERICA PAGEANT WINNERS (MAPW), PLAYBOY PLAYMATES OF THE YEAR (PMOY), FASHION MODELS, AND YOUNG WOMEN IN GENERAL (YWIG)

		Decade							
		1920s	1930s	1940s	1950s	1960s	1970s	1980s	1990s
Height (inches)	MAPW	64.9 ± 1.9	66.3 ± 0.9	67.3 ± 2.6	66.9 ± 1.9	66.5 ± 1.1	67.3 ± 1.9	67.2 ± 2.2	66.5 ± 2.8
	PMOY				64.7 ± 1.5	64.7 ± 1.6	66.3 ± 1.3	68.7 ± 1.7	67.7 ± 2.5
	Models	67.1 ± 1.6	67.5 ± 1.8	68.0 ± 1.6	67.4 ± 1.8	67.8 ± 1.4	68.7 ± 1.8	69.4 ± 1.2	69.1 ± 2.6
	YWIG	63.2	63.1	64.0	64.3	63.8	64.3 ± 2.5	64.3 ± 2.6	64.1 ± 0.1
Weight (lb)	MAPW	125.9 ± 11.9	120.0 ± 6.3	128.0 ± 8.0	125.1 ± 9.2	120.8 ± 6.3	117.4 ± 7.4	116.7 ± 7.8	120.1 ± 10.7
	PMOY				115.0 ± 5.1	115.2 ± 8.2	116.1 ± 7.7	119.7 ± 8.4	121.2 ± 10.6
	Models	121.6 ± 8.3	118.7 ± 9.1	116.4 ± 6.8	115.1 ± 8.0	115.9 ± 9.5	124.5 ± 10.6	123.0 ± 9.7	120.2 ± 9.6
	YWIG	120.3	123.0	124.9	128.5	127	132.0 ± 27.4	133.6 ± 26.3	141.7 ± 1.25
BMI	MAPW	21.0 ± 1.2	19.3 ± 0.6	19.9 ± 1.3	19.6 ± 0.7	19.2 ± 0.6	18.3 ± 0.3	18.2 ± 0.7	19.2 ± 0.7
	PMOY				19.4 ± 0.5	19.4 ± 0.7	18.6 ± 1.0	17.9 ± 0.7	18.6 ± 0.6
	Models	19.0 ± 1.0	18.4 ± 1.0	17.8 ± 0.9	17.9 ± 1.4	17.7 ± 1.2	18.6 ± 1.7	18.0 ± 1.4	17.8 ± 1.8
	YWIG	21.2	21.8	21.5	21.9	22.0	22.5	22.6 ± 4.2	24.3

Source: Adapted from Byrd-Bredbenner & Murray, 2003.

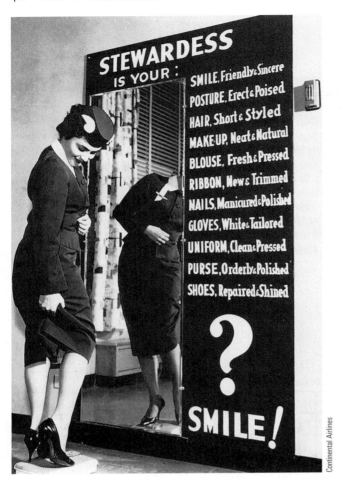

This photo from the 1950s shows the degree of explicit sexism in the airlines industry at the time. We have not found an equivalent photo for male flight crews. Although female airline employees still must conform to dress codes, they have formed unions and have won more stable careers and greater job security.

was held at a bathing beach on the Potomac River. There the women wore tunic bathing suits and hats, but later that year a similar contest was held at Atlantic City, New Jersey, that eventually developed into the Miss America Pageant. In that contest, women wore one-piece bathing suits that showed their calves and thighs and created a sensation in the tabloid newspapers. These contests and the publicity they generated made beauty a way for women to gain celebrity and wealth, but they also reflected the dominant male view that the most extraordinary women are those with the most stunning faces and the shapeliest figures (Allen, 1931). Women have been struggling against this view throughout the modern era, a struggle that has frequently been opposed not only by men but also by women who feel threatened by changes in their traditional statuses.

Sexual Harassment

Sexism is also expressed in violence and harassment of women, often intended to "keep women in their place" and maintain male power. In some extremely patriarchal societies, women who have been raped may be beaten or killed by their own husbands, fathers, or brothers, who feel dishonored by the violation of "their" woman. These "honor killings" are merely an extreme example of the violence (physical and emotional) that is routinely directed at women throughout the world.

Two million American women are severely beaten in their homes every year, and 20 percent of visits by women to hospital emergency rooms are caused by battering (Kornblum & Julian, 2004). In popular American culture, especially movies, television, and some popular music, violence against women may not be condoned but is often presented as a form of thrilling entertainment. Films like *Nightmare on Elm Street* and *Looking for Mr. Goodbar* suggest that the brightest and most independent women are most likely to be victimized. Rap lyrics referring to women as "bitches" and "hos" degrade women and in fact degrade the men who express such sexist sentiments. Examples like these hardly exhaust the overt types of sexism that exist in many areas of social life in the United States. In fact, sexual harassment in the workplace is a continual subject of conflict and social change.

Many definitions of sexual harassment at work rely on the woman's perceptions of the situation. Louise Fitzgerald, one of the foremost researchers in this field, and her colleagues defined sexual harassment as "an unwanted sex-related behavior at work that is appraised by the recipient as offensive, exceeding her resources, or threatening her well-being" (Fitzgerald, Swan, & Magley, 1997, p. 20). This and similar definitions rely on an appraisal of the victim's perceptions, which makes sense because harassment can include sexist joking, sexual innuendo, and unwanted flirting in addition to more direct sexual contact. But the courts have resisted subjective definitions of harassment and have insisted that definitions of sexual harassment focus more attention on the work environment itself (Sbraga & O'Donohue, 2000). The U.S. Equal Employment Opportunity Commission's (EEOC's) guidelines define sexual harassment as "verbal or physical conduct of a sexual nature that unreasonably interferes with the employee's work or creates an intimidating, hostile, or offensive working environment" (EEOC, 1993, p. 1). This widely accepted legal definition requires the victim to show that harassment made it difficult or impossible for her to do her work as required.

Most researchers in the field of gender relations at work observe that far more sexual harassment occurs than is ever reported (Sbraga & O'Donohue, 2000). Many women are fearful of losing their jobs, of incurring the wrath of super-visors, or simply of "rocking the boat." In a recent study of this aspect of sexual harassment at work, Beth Quinn interviewed women and men in a variety of work environments to find out how women perceive and deal with sexual harassment, especially the common forms of sexual bantering and teasing. She found that women often know that they are being harassed but go along with male co-workers' claims that they should "not take it personally" (Quinn, 2000). Here is how one respondent described her perceptions of her work environment:

> I believe there really is sexual harassment. . . . But I also think women abuse it. [pause] Because back there [in my department] they, they comment all the time, you know, about my breasts, or whatever. But I know that they're doing it in the context of a joke, and like I say, it rolls off my back. . . . If I thought they really meant it, then maybe it would bother me.
>
> —Peggy (quoted in Quinn, 2000, p. 2)

Quinn describes Peggy as "friendly, hardworking, and funny. In her mid-40s, she is divorced, has taken a few college classes, and works a blue-collar job that pays fairly well." The researcher notes that she is typical of the many women who are regularly subjected to sexual harassment by their coworkers. Peggy refuses to publicly label any of their behavior "sexual harassment," even though just talking about it during the interview brings tears to her eyes.

Other women in similar situations resort to counter-joking, also with sexual connotations, and may jokingly insult their male's coworkers' sexual prowess as a way of getting back and showing that their taunts and jokes are "not taken personally." But Quinn and others point out that like the strategy of silence, joking counterattacks by victims allow males to perpetuate a culture of harassment in the workplace. This socially constructed culture of everyday harassment deprives women of control over their own work life and can be corrected only by encouraging women to speak out about their true feelings to their male coworkers and, when necessary, to their supervisors.

VIOLENCE IN INTIMATE RELATIONSHIPS Sociologist Claire Renzetti is one of the nation's foremost experts on violence against women. As editor of the influential journal *Violence Against Women,* she tracks the most recent research on the subject. She continually seeks ways to help women speak out more effectively against violence in their intimate relations.

"If most young women do not believe they are at risk for date rape," Renzetti writes, "it is not surprising . . . that when they are raped—as defined by law—they do not label the event as rape. It is also not surprising that they place

Sociologist Claire Renzetti, activist and expert on violence against women.

Courtesy of Daniel J. Curran

most of the blame for the 'bad date' on themselves: It wasn't supposed to happen; therefore, they must have done something that helped make it happen" (1999a, p. 227). Renzetti knows that many women rationalize violence against them on dates as a consequence of drinking and drunkenness, but she observes that "even women who were not drunk at the time of the rape, even women who were raped by force or the threat of force, often blamed themselves for the rape." Ashamed and hurt, they are most often "deeply, negatively affected by what happened to them" (1999a, p. 227).

Renzetti believes that

> feminists must take the lead in "news making" about violence against—and by—women. We must call press conferences to release our research findings to the public, hold book launches in popular or attention-getting venues and invite the media, write op-ed pieces for local newspapers, and volunteer as consultants or commentators for local radio and television stations—in short, be seen and heard, not after the fact, but proactively. (1999b, p. 1235)

Difficult as it may be, by taking a stand, women may ultimately be avoiding the painful next steps that involve formal legal complaints. Unfortunately, in too many situations women may be required to take such steps if harassment—even of the joking, "don't-take-it-personally" kind—continues. From a feminist viewpoint, the women's movement must continue to strive to educate women about their rights and their need to speak out against sexual harassment.

THE WOMEN'S MOVEMENT

In the 1950s, the women's movement was dormant. In the late nineteenth and early twentieth centuries, women had organized social movements to gain full citizenship rights and greater control over reproduction (e.g., through family planning and birth control). In the United States, they were known as suffragettes because they campaigned vigorously for woman suffrage—the right of women to vote. But in 1920, after the Nineteenth Amendment to the Constitution extended suffrage to women, the movement faded.

Stock Montage, Inc.

Early in the twentieth century, women in the suffrage movement were fighting for the right to vote. Their movement often met with organized resistance from men.

The victory of the suffragettes did not change the patterns of gender stratification, however. For example, in their famous studies of Middletown, Helen and Robert Lynd (1929, 1937) found that women who had worked their way into good factory jobs and professional occupations were severely set back during the Great Depression. Like blacks and members of other minority groups, women were the last to be hired and the first to be fired when times were bad. And although women were hired as factory workers in unprecedented numbers during World War II, they often faced discrimination and harassment and were usually "bumped off" their jobs by returning GIs after the war (Archibald, 1947). Nor did this situation change greatly when women began entering the professions and the corporate world in the 1950s. Women still tended to be limited to roles that were either subordinate to those of men or part of an entirely separate sphere of "women's work."

In her review of the origins of the modern women's movement, Jo Freeman (1973) wrote that even in the mid-1960s the resurgence of the women's movement "caught most social observers by surprise." After all, women were widely believed to have come a long way toward equality with men. Their average educational level was rising steadily, and they were gaining access to the better professions and even to positions in the top ranks of corporate management. Freeman suggested that the movement developed out of an existing network of women's organizations that made many women aware of the inequality still prevailing in American society and encouraged them to organize to demand equal rights. Influ-

ential writing by women activists, such as Betty Friedan's *The Feminine Mystique* (1963), and studies of gender inequality by social scientists like Alice Rossi (1964) and Jessie Bernard (1964) played a major part in this growing awareness.

Meanwhile another, less formal network of women was developing. Women who were experiencing sexism within other social movements—the antiwar movement, the civil rights movement, the environmental protection movement, and the labor movement—began to form small "consciousness-raising" groups (Morgan, 1970). By questioning traditional assumptions and providing emotional and material support, these groups attempted to develop a sense of "sisterhood." Their members formed a loosely connected network of small groups that could mobilize resources and develop into a larger and better-organized movement.

The women's movement achieved significant victories during the 1960s and 1970s. In 1963, Congress passed "equal pay for equal work" legislation, and Title VII of the 1964 Civil Rights Act prohibited discrimination against women. In the 1970s, the federal Equal Employment Opportunity Commission began to enforce laws barring gender-based discrimination in employment. Lawsuits filed under the Civil Rights Act and other federal laws forced many employers to pay more attention to women's demands for equality in pay and promotion and an end to sexual harassment on the job. Research shows that men very slowly began to accept roles that had previously been considered "women's work" (Rosen, 1987), and at work they were more likely to have women as supervisors than was true only a decade earlier. Throughout American society, the attitudes of both men and women were becoming more favorable toward a more equal allocation of political and economic roles (NORC, 1998).

Despite these changes, gender equality is far from complete. Some survey data indicate that there is greater sharing of household tasks, with men doing more of what was once viewed as "women's work" around the home (Gallup, 1997). However, a closer analysis shows that it is premature to assume there have been far-reaching decreases in the sexual division of labor within the average American household. Studies that ask men and women whether the men are doing more housework, and what kinds of work they are actually doing, tend to come up with optimistic figures compared to those obtained in similar surveys a generation ago. But studies based on detailed time-use diaries find far less actual participation by men in housework chores than is reported in the opinion polls. This indicates that men and women may be embarrassed to admit that men are not taking on a fair share of responsibilities for housework and child care, and hence may inflate their estimates in response to pollsters'

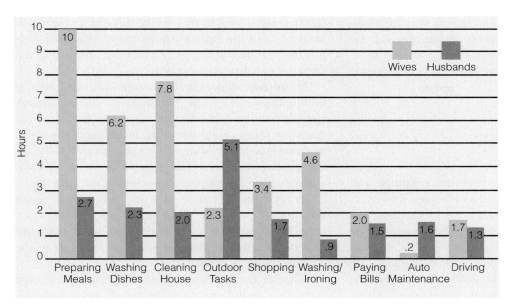

Figure 14.5 Average Hours per Week Wives and Husbands Spend Doing Household Tasks

Source: Chadwick & Heaton, 1999.

questions. Time diaries call for detailed information about how time is actually used, and in these diaries people tend to report their time use more accurately (Press & Townsley, 1998).

The Second Shift

Sociologist Arlie Hochschild (1989) coined the term *the second shift* to describe the extra time working women spend doing household chores after working at a job outside the home. This term emphasizes the expectation that women who work will also perform the bulk of domestic and child care duties. This is an example of the persistence of **patriarchy**, the dominance of men over women. Although women often attempt to influence their male partners to share household chores that were formerly considered "women's work," the men continue to resist despite slow changes—especially in two-career families in which both partners are highly educated. As we see in Figure 14.5, the household division of labor is still significant. Men still tend to do chores involving outside work and the family car, but women spend far more time per week than men do on the basic household tasks of shopping, cleaning, washing, and preparing meals. These topics are discussed further in Chapter 16.

Some sociologists have proposed that as women gain greater parity with men in occupations, the disparities between men's and women's roles will diminish, and gender roles in the household will become more symmetrical (Bernard, 1982; Willmott & Young, 1971). But as Hochschild (1989) and others report, this remains a speculative hypothesis despite the exceptions one might cite here and there. On the average, data on time budgets show that working women in the United States have at least 10 hours a week less leisure time than their husbands or partners because they shoulder far more of the domestic responsibilities (Press & Townsley, 1998). The same disparities do not exist in all industrial nations. France and Holland, for example, incorporate gender equality into national social policies. These nations provide excellent universal child care, family leave, and longer vacations than do lagging nations like the United States, and these policies ease the burdens of dual-earner families in coping with the demands of work and family life (Hacker, 1997).

Outside the home, patterns of gender inequality are also proving to be extremely persistent. The pattern of wage inequality described earlier in the chapter, together with the tendency for women to be segregated in such occupations as secretary, bank teller, and elementary school teacher, has led activists in the women's movement to call for new policies designed to reduce inequality. Increasingly they have pressed for "comparable worth"—that is, for increases in the salaries paid in traditionally female occupations to levels comparable to those paid in similar, but traditionally male, occupations (Reid, 1998). A recent study by the federal government's General Accounting Office (GAO) found that during the boom years between 1995 and 2000 some of the worst gender disparities in salaries occurred at the top levels of the corporate hierarchy. Women's executive salaries worsened in comparison with those of men at the same levels of responsibility. And not surprisingly, the gap widened most for working executives who were mothers—they earned 66 percent of what fathers in similar positions earned. One consequence of this clear pattern of discrimination against working mothers in the executive ranks is that 60 percent of female executives said that they were deferring motherhood, whereas 60 percent of men at the same levels were already fathers (Becker, 2002).

WOMEN AT WORK

In the industrial nations of North America, Europe, and Oceania, the increasing proportion of women who are in the labor force as paid employees is one of the most important aspects of social change in those societies. At midcentury, for example, 34 percent of U.S. women were in the labor force, but in subsequent decades that proportion increased steadily. By 2001, about 60 percent of women considered themselves to be employees, either at work or looking for work (*Statistical Abstract,* 2002). Among women with children over age 20 the trends are similar. In 1960, just over 20 percent of these older women had jobs or were looking for jobs; by 2001, this figure had more than doubled, to almost 55 percent (*Statistical Abstract,* 2002).

In fact, women assumed an important economic role well before industrialization created a sharp distinction between work in the paid labor force and work at home or in the fields. When the United States was an agrarian society, women planted and harvested crops, including extensive household gardens, and were also expected to take responsibility for housework and child rearing, both of which were highly labor intensive in the pre-electricity era. And because women have higher life expectancies than men, widows routinely ran farms or businesses after their husbands died, and many middle-class women gained additional income by taking in lodgers and selling handicrafts or other products of their labor. With the Industrial Revolution came growing demand for factory workers. Although male workers were often preferred, thousands of women and children also swelled the ranks of the new industrial working class. A recent study has shown that many of the working women in the early years of the Industrial Revolution were immigrants or poor single women from rural backgrounds. Large numbers of African-American women were also working for wages in fields and factories and as domestic servants (Hacker, 1997).

World War II marked a significant turning point in women's labor force participation. Although returning servicemen "bumped" women (and minority men) from jobs in factories and offices, thousands of war widows and single women had to continue earning wages whether they wanted to or not. As a result, although in the 1950s women's labor force participation was still far lower than it is today, in fact female employment was increasing at a far faster rate than male employment.

At the same time, the 1950s were a time of relative economic prosperity. The middle classes were expanding, and a suburban home became a central feature of the American dream. Popular culture, including the powerful new medium of television, emphasized the ideal norms of the middle-class nuclear family in which the mother was a homemaker and the father worked in the labor force. This "feminine mystique" asserted that women would find fulfillment as wives and mothers. In reality, thousands of women were entering the labor force in a trend that would continue throughout the second half of the century (Epstein, 1988).

Whether they worked outside the home because they wanted to or because necessity forced them to do so, women in the labor force encountered problems of gender segregation and discrimination. In a survey of 150,000 working women conducted during the mid-1980s by the National Commission on Working Women, the most frequently cited problems were low wages, differentials in fringe benefits, dead-end jobs with little opportunity for training or advancement, sexual harassment on the job, lack of child care or difficulty obtaining it, stress over multiple roles, and lack of leisure time (Richmond-Abbott, 1992).

An enduring problem for women in the labor force is segregation into what are known as "pink-collar ghettos." Secretarial and clerical work especially remain heavily gender segregated, but child care, nursing, and dental assistants also remain largely female occupations despite some increases in the proportions of males in these fields in recent decades. Largely as a result of antidiscrimination laws and women's efforts to break into occupations that previously were more or less closed to them, women have made considerable gains in some areas. Occupations like bus driver, psychologist, and others show significant gains in female employment, but clerical occupations remain a pink-collar ghetto: Clerical work employs one in five working women, a figure that has not changed since the 1950s (Roberts, 1995).

Throughout the world, new occupations are emerging in professional and technical fields, and as women achieve greater educational parity with men, the comparative statistics show that they are sharing these positions more equally with men. Figures 14.6 and 14.7 show that this is the case in Latin America, the Caribbean, and the economically developed regions of the world, but that in much of Asia and Africa, where women still lag in education, there are wide disparities.

art and the sociological eye

Feminism and Art

Each day thousands of visitors crowd into the museums of major European and American cities. By far the majority of the artists whose works they come to view are white males. Is this because white males have so much more talent than women or people from minority backgrounds? Obviously the answer is no. It was not until the late nineteenth century that women began to have the opportunity to study art and display their talents—but once they did, they proved themselves just as capable of artistic expression as men. The same is true of African Americans and members of other minority groups, who were once excluded from access to careers in art.

After entering the museums, visitors often spend time looking at male representations of the nude female form, works that are usually explained (through the unacknowledged "lens" of androcentrism) as expressing a universal vision of beauty. But if people visit the city's more innovative museums and galleries, the works they view are just as likely to have been created by women as by men. And whether the artists are white women or women of color, their work is likely to express strong feminist themes. The art of Barbara Kruger, shown here, is one of many examples one might offer. Kruger's work appropriates the everyday techniques of newspaper headlines and photos to make strong but slightly ambiguous statements about the situation of people, especially women, confronted by institutional sexism, racism, or bureaucratic power. And like that of other feminist artists in the United States today, Kruger's work often challenges stereotypes about powerlessness, submission, sexuality, and other androcentric representations of women in society.

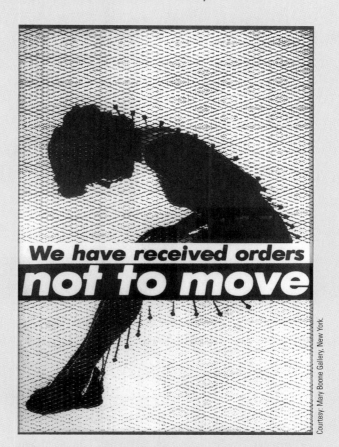

"Untitled" (We have received orders not to move), by Barbara Kruger, 1982. Photograph, 72" x 48". Courtesy Mary Boone Gallery, New York.

In administrative and managerial positions, the situation is far less favorable for women. Recent research shows that the United States ranks highest among industrialized nations in promotion of women to managerial positions, and this is in large part the result of affirmative action policies in American business. In contrast to the United States, where 46.0 percent of such positions are held by women, and Sweden (30.5), Japan (8.9%) has done extremely little to promote women to managerial roles. Social scientists believe that this failure to enlist the leader-

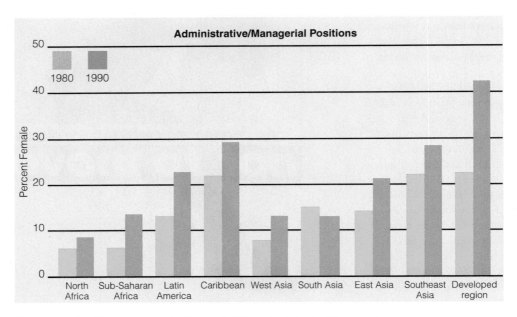

Figure 14.6   Improvement in Women's Share in Selected Occupations

Source: Sadik, 1995.

ship talent of women is one reason why the Japanese economy continues to stagnate (French, 2003).

Elsewhere in the world, competition for these desirable positions in management is even more intense. Promotion to management is often based not only on education but also on access to social networks and political power. Because women are far less likely than men to have such access, their entry into the managerial ranks is stymied. An exception is found in the island nations of the Caribbean, where women have had access to education and training in business schools longer than in many other regions. Caribbean women often accumulate money and power through their own business activities, which enable them to become owners, managers, and administrators at a greater rate than in the more affluent regions of the world.

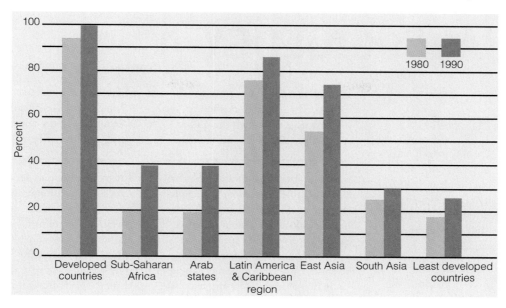

Figure 14.7 Growth in Female Literacy Levels

Source: Sadik, 1995.

CRITICAL SOCIOLOGY AND SOCIAL CHANGE

Empowering Women

The term *empowerment* is often used in discussions of women and development. The term refers to the process whereby relatively powerless people of any gender, race, ethnicity, or social class organize to assert their needs and overcome obstacles to their full participation in the institutions of their societies. The term can also refer to the processes whereby people gain the ability to assert their needs in more personal contexts—in their families, work groups, schools, or communities.

Empowerment of women is a major global issue because such a large proportion of the world's females are trapped in patriarchal societies. Indeed, the extent to which different nations move toward greater parity between male and female holders of elective office (as shown in Figure 14.8) is an international measure of relative progress in dealing

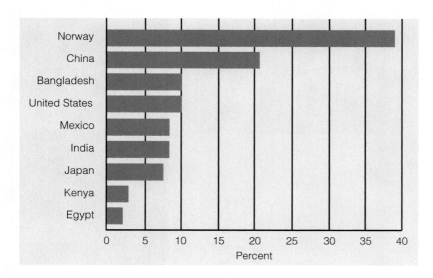

Figure 14.8 Women's Share of National Legislatures in Selected Countries

Source: UNDP, 2000.

Text continues on page 420.

VISUAL SOCIOLOGY

GENDER ROLES AMONG THE MAASAI

When sociologist Carol Chenault and her photographer husband, Ellis, spent time with the Maasai people in 1995, they sometimes felt as if they had wandered back in time to the biblical era. For, as Carol Chenault explains, the Maasai are true pastoralists:

The people are Nilotic, migrating from the Nile regions of North Africa into the Great Rift Valley of Kenya and Tanzania. Myth has it that they lived in a deep crater where life was plagued with drought, famine, and discouragement. The only ray of hope for them was to follow the birds that kept bringing green grass and twigs. Scouts went up and over the steep escarpment and found green, fertile valleys with rivers and streams, and this is where they made their home. The language they speak is Maa; hence the term Maasai, meaning Maa-speaking people. The only transmission of the language is through the spoken word; their language is not written.

As we saw at the beginning of the chapter, gender role distinctions are significant among the Maasai. But unlike Western industrial societies (where women are expected to spend more time on personal adornment), among the Maasai attention to beauty is a preoccupation of both males and females:

Even the smallest of children are dressed with necklaces and anklets. Ear piercing is done during childhood, well before circumcision. A slit is cut in the earlobe and a green stick is placed in it. Over time this is replaced with successively larger [sticks] until the opening is large enough to be decorated with an earring and leather-beaded strands.

Chenault notes that despite their relative lack of acculturation to Western ways, she saw a Maasai man wearing a 35 mm plastic film canister as an ear adornment, a vivid reminder of the spread of Western culture. The Maasai were extremely open and willing to share their culture with the visiting sociologist. "They are a proud people," Chenault concludes, "committed to passing their culture on to their future generations. I think this is the quality that I admire most about them."

These photos provide some clues about social status and gender roles among the Maasai. Notice that the elderly woman with close-cropped hair wears a limited number of personal adornments. Like most elderly women in traditional societies, she seems to feel no need to impress the viewer with her physical appearance. Not so for

© Chenault Studios/Decatur, AL

© Chenault Studios/Decatur, AL

the woman with the distinctive head-piece and gorgeous array of necklaces. She is dressed in the fashion of the Maasai warrior herdsmen, but only the women wear these headpieces. In another photo, the same woman, the wife of a prominent warrior, is shown with her children. The Maasai women bear children almost as long as they are physically capable of doing so.

The man with a shawl over his shoulders looking quizzically into the camera was one of a group who conducted their own "interview" with the sociologist. They thought it was terrible that the American sociologist was no longer having babies. The women also asked whether American women were circumcised. "When we told them we were not," said Chenault, "they clapped their hands down at their sides, indicating their disapproval."

The Maasai man playing the flute also makes sandals out of old tires. These are called "thousand milers" because the Maasai walk endlessly and need tough, cheap footwear. Making musical instruments and footgear are examples of tasks that are specifically "men's work" among the Maasai. The man wearing the distinctive feathered headdress and smiling at the sociologist is a professional guide. He has a high school education and moves easily between Westerners and Maasai. With one foot in the traditional world and another in the tourist industry, his role allows the Maasai people to remain culturally distinct while benefiting from their contact with interested visitors.

The Sociological Observer
(See photo on page 404.)

As in many other cultures throughout the world, women interact most with children, particularly female children. The group shown here is gender segregated. There are no little boys among them because most likely the boys, once they can walk, tend to spend their time among other boys of their age and slightly older. The norm of heterosexual couples spending much of their time together is largely a Western one.

with patriarchy. In the United States, which tends to lag behind other Western democracies in electing women to federal office, the empowerment of women is also a major sociological subject because so many women are victims of abuse, violence, poverty, gender discrimination, and other effects of patriarchy.

The empowerment of women is of particular concern to feminist sociologists, both male and female. Ever since the nineteenth-century movement to gain the vote for women, feminist social scientists and activists have been struggling to use theoretical reasoning, objective evidence, and persuasive argument to convince other citizens of the need for women to share political power at all levels of society, from the family to the community to the state and nation. An excellent recent example of feminist empirical sociology is Nancy Naples's research on the empowerment of women through community politics.

Naples (1998) uses a "biographical narrative approach" to explore the experience of women who became community activists in the late 1960s and remained active in politics over the next 20 or more years. This method is a form of qualitative research in which a "panel" of representative subjects are reinterviewed periodically over a period long enough to trace their development through different stages of life. The sociologist encourages each subject—in this case, mothers from low-income, predominantly minority communities in Philadelphia and Boston—to recount her biography, focusing on specific themes. In particular, Naples was interested in recording their stories (narratives) of how they began to become active in local movements to address poverty and racism in their communities. She also wanted to find out how they managed to juggle the often conflicting demands of motherhood, marriage, and jobs while maintaining their commitment to improving life in their communities. She selected the women from existing community action projects that had hired them to perform a variety of jobs. In 1995, she reinterviewed about one-third of the 60-plus women she had included in her panel more than 20 years earlier. She also interviewed the daughters of some of the women in order to "explore some unintended and rarely acknowledged intergenerational effects of mothers' community work" (1998, p. 8).

The women who told their stories to Naples were representative of the communities she visited. For the most part, they were working-class women of African-American, Puerto Rican, or white European descent. As mothers in low-income households—some with husbands, some without—they faced a variety of daunting

challenges to their ability to be effective mothers and homemakers while also becoming active in the social movements that were developing in their communities. In the following passage, Wilma North, one of the women in Naples's study, describes how she became involved in her community:

> Well, see the PTA was not my kind of thing. Back in those days the only thing PTAs did was have teas and sell candy. . . . [Well] that's the way I saw it anyway. There was too much to be done to be sitting around gossiping and having tea parties, and I never had time for that kind of stuff. I didn't then and I don't now. And there were things to be done like . . . [closing] a pinball parlor across the street from the school. Somebody needs to take some action. Or if you need crossing guards, or if there are dilapidated houses, or if you're not getting the kind of response from the police department that you feel the community needs to get. . . . And we did get it! (Naples, 1998, p.19)

North and other young mothers were recruited into what became known as *community action projects*. These organizations were funded by the federal government during the Johnson administration's War on Poverty. They used federal funding to provide training and jobs to people from low-income backgrounds, especially minorities and women, who would be paid to develop programs like day care, elder care, and preventive health services. North was trained in office management and administration, a career she has pursued ever since.

The community action projects were extremely controversial. Designed to give "maximum feasible participation" to residents of impoverished inner-city and rural communities, they often came into conflict with local political leaders. They were also favorite targets of critics who were opposed to government intervention in job creation and early education. But Naples's extensive interviews with women like North, whose lives were changed by their participation in the projects, yields a far more detailed account of the actual experience of the War on Poverty. Above all, Naples finds that the women almost always developed a sense of empowerment as mothers, with rights and responsibilities to help build better local institutions—day care centers, preschools, public schools, after-school centers, and the like—that would help them raise their children well despite economic deprivation in their communities and households.

SUMMARY

Sex Versus Gender

- *Sex* refers to the biological differences between males and females, including the primary sex characteristics that are present at birth and the secondary sex characteristics that develop later.

- Some people are born as *hermaphrodites;* their primary sexual organs have features of both male and female organs, making it difficult to categorize the person as male or female.

- Another ambiguous sexual category consists of *transsexuals,* who feel strongly that the sexual organs they were born with do not conform to their deep-seated sense of what their sex should be.

- *Gender* refers to the culturally defined ways of acting as a male or a female that become part of an individual's personal sense of self.

- Gender socialization in the family and in schools tends to separate males and females into different social worlds with their own forms of activity and language. However, boys and girls are increasingly participating in the same types of activities in their schools and communities, and many teachers, parents, and administrators seek to avoid the worst effects of gender separation.

- *Sexuality* refers to the manner in which a person engages in the intimate behaviors connected with genital stimulation, orgasm, and procreation. It is profoundly influenced by cultural norms and social institutions like the family and the school, as well as by social structures like the class system of a society.

- Universal cultural norms exerting social control over sexuality include the incest taboo, marriage, and heterosexuality, but even these norms include variations and differing degrees of sanction.

- *Heterosexuality* refers to sexual orientation toward the opposite sex, in contrast to *homosexuality,* which refers to sexual orientation toward the same sex, and *bisexuality,* which refers to sexual orientation toward either sex.

- Norms of heterosexuality function to ensure that genital sexual intercourse occurs between men and women in the interest of population replacement and growth.

- Fear of homosexuals and same-sex attraction is known as homophobia.

Gender Stratification

- All human societies are stratified by gender, meaning that males and females are channeled into specific statuses and roles.

- Until recently, it was assumed that there were two separate spheres of life for men and women. Out of this gender-based division of labor grew the notion of differences in men's and women's abilities and personalities. These differences were thought to be based on biological and psychological differences between males and females.

- In the twentieth century, however, evidence from the social sciences established that *gender roles* are not innate but are strongly influenced by culture.

- Preindustrial societies are usually rigidly sex-segregated. As societies increase in size and complexity, women usually become subordinated to men.

- The origins of gender inequality in most modern societies can be traced to their feudal periods. In Europe, for example, the norms of courtly love specified that women do not engage in warfare or politics or compete with men in any sphere of life beyond those reserved for women.

Gender Inequality in Industrial Societies

- In modern industrial societies, boys and girls are socialized into "masculine" and "feminine" roles. In their adult years, men enjoy more wealth, prestige, and leisure than do women.

- Gender stratification in modern societies is reflected in attitudes that reinforce the subordinate status of women.

- *Sexism* refers to an ideology that justifies prejudice or discrimination based on sex.

- Sexism is also expressed in violence and harassment of women, often intended to "keep women in their place" and maintain male power.

The Women's Movement

- The modern women's movement arose in the mid-1960s out of an already existing network of women's organizations, together with a less formal network of women in consciousness-raising groups.

- The movement won significant victories during the 1960s and 1970s and began to change the way men and women think about gender roles.

- Women who work outside the home are also expected to perform the bulk of domestic and child care work. This "second shift" is an example of the persistence of *patriarchy,* the dominance of men over women.

Women at Work

- The most frequently cited problems of women in the workplace are low wages, differentials in fringe benefits, dead-end jobs, sexual harassment, lack of child care, stress over multiple roles, and lack of leisure time.

- Another problem is the segregation of women into the pink-collar ghettos of secretarial and clerical work.

GLOSSARY

sex: The biological differences between males and females, including the primary sex characteristics that are present at birth (i.e., the presence of specific male or female genitalia) and the secondary sex characteristics that develop later (facial and body hair, voice quality, etc.). (p. 395)

hermaphrodite: A person whose primary sexual organs have features of both male and female organs, making it difficult to categorize the individual as male or female. (p. 395)

transsexuals: People who feel strongly that the sexual organs they were born with do not conform to their deep-seated sense of what their sex should be. (p. 395)

gender: The culturally defined ways of acting as a male or a female that become part of an individual's personal sense of self. (p. 396)

sexuality: The manner in which a person engages in the intimate behaviors connected with genital stimulation, orgasm, and procreation. (p. 399)

heterosexuality: Sexual orientation toward the opposite sex. (p. 400)

homosexuality: Sexual orientation toward the same sex. (p. 400)

bisexuality: Sexual orientation toward either sex. (p. 400)

gender role: A set of behaviors considered appropriate for an individual of a particular gender. (p. 402)

sexism: An ideology that justifies prejudice and discrimination based on sex. (p. 406)

patriarchy: The dominance of men over women. (p. 413)

INTERNET RESOURCES

Virtual Society: The Wadsworth Sociology Resource Center
(http://sociology.wadsworth.com)

At Virtual Society you can access a wide range of enrichment material to aid your study of sociology. From the main page, click on the Student Resources link and find your course and this textbook. Next, select the chapter you are presently studying from the pull-down menu. Among the useful options for each self-study chapter are online links and exercises, flashcards, practical study tips, and practice quizzes for each chapter.

MC MicroCase Online

From the Virtual Society home page, click on MicroCase Online to access book-specific MicroCase exercises that allow you to further explore sociological issues and principles presented in the text.

InfoTrac College Edition

Another unique option available to you at the Student Resources section at Virtual Society is InfoTrac College Edition, an online library with access to hundreds of scholarly and popular periodicals. Below are suggested search terms for this chapter, but this resource also allows you to fit your study of sociology to your own interests by searching custom keywords.

Gender

Sexism

Gender roles

Patriarchy

National Organization for Women
(www.now.org)

Features calls for action, press releases, and the NOW newspaper, all of which exemplify the activities of a mainstream feminist organization.

The Eagle Forum
(www.eagleforum.org)

A conservative political organization that speaks out on issues of gender and inequality.

Inequalities of Youth and Age

The Imogen Cunningham Trust

Imogen Cunningham.

Like many of the world's urban industrial nations, the United States has an aging population. Consider this simple fact: In 1960, the number of centenarians, or people older than age 100, in the United States was slightly more than 3,200. Today it is more than 28,000. Does this momentous change mean that the United States is becoming a society in which to be old is to be respected and appreciated? Most experts on aging would say no. Our culture, as judged by the messages we continually receive on TV or in other media, values youth, vitality, strength, speed, and youthful beauty. No wonder the Irish poet William Butler Yeats wrote in his declining years that an aged person is:

> . . . but a paltry thing,
> a tattered cloak upon a stick, unless
> soul clap its hands and sing, and louder sing
> for every tatter in its mortal dress.

FOCUS QUESTIONS:

• How have youth and old age, both important phases in the life course, changed as societies have developed?

• How are these changes reflected in major indicators of well-being among the young and the elderly?

• How do patterns of inequality based on class, race and ethnicity, and gender influence the conditions experienced by the young and the old?

But how can an elderly person's soul sing in the face of declining health and the gnawing isolation that many elderly people experience? Some answers can be found in the efforts of people with strong sociological imaginations to change our perceptions of the elderly. One of the best examples of this approach may be seen in the photographic work of Imogen Cunningham.

Cunningham, one of the twentieth century's most influential photographers, spent most of her long life in San Francisco. In her later years, she devoted much of her work to photographing people who were more than 90 years old but "still alive and kicking." Her photographs of elderly people, some of which appear in the Visual Sociology section of this chapter, are studies of dignity and courage in the face of advanced age and imminent death.

Ironically, despite the high value placed on youth, young people are another age class that is experiencing severe social stress. This is true in affluent societies like the United States as well as in many developing nations. The specific causes may differ widely from one region to another, but wherever mothers of children and young people are under stress because of poverty and violence, the children suffer as well. Of course, people in other age categories also experience inequalities based on age, but as we will see in this chapter, the young and the aged are particularly subject to age-based inequality.

SOURCES OF AGE STRATIFICATION

In many societies, age determines a great deal about the opportunities open to a person and what kind of life that person leads. Only a little more than 50 years ago, for example, becoming old in the United States almost automatically meant becoming poor. Today children are the most impoverished and vulnerable population group in many nations, including the United States. This chapter examines how age stratification—the roles assigned to young people, adults, and the elderly—contributes to inequality. From a discussion of the life course and age structure of societies, the chapter proceeds to a closer examination of the situation of young people. The remainder of the chapter is devoted to the growing sociological subfield known as **gerontology,** the study of aging and the elderly in this and other societies.

The Life Course: Society's Age Structure

All societies divide the human life span into "seasons of life" (Bengston & Schaie, 1999; Neugarten, 1996). This is done through cultural norms that define periods of life, such as adulthood and old age, and channel people into **age grades**—sets of statuses and roles based on age. These systems of age grades create predictable social groupings and turning points that everyone in a society can easily recognize. Graduations, communions, weddings, retirements, and funerals are among the ceremonies that are used to mark these turning points.

Age strata are rough divisions of people into layers according to age-related social roles. We speak of infants, preschoolers, elementary school children, teenagers, young adults, and so on; these categories form a series of younger-to-older layers, or strata, in the population. People in different age strata command different amounts of scarce resources like wealth, power, and prestige (Moody, 1998). Numerous laws establish inequalities between youth and adults; they include laws governing the rights to vote, to purchase alcoholic beverages, to incur debt, and the like. In theory, a person who lacks the rights of adult citizenship will be protected by adults, who are responsible for providing him or her with adequate food, shelter, and education (and are presumed to have the resources to do so). In practice, however, hundreds of thousands of children and teenagers do not receive the care that is intended to offset their unequal status under the law.

Social scientists often refer to the **life course,** which may be defined as a "pathway along an age-differentiated, socially created sequence of transitions" (Hagestad & Neugarten, 1985, p. 36; see also Cain, 1964; Clausen, 1968; Elder, 1981). The cultural norms that specify the life course and its important transitions create what is thought of as the normal and predictable life cycle (Neugarten, 1996). We expect that we will go to school, find a job, get married, have children, and so on at certain times in our lives, and we consider it somewhat abnormal not to follow this pattern. Social scientists often refer to ceremonies that mark the transition from one phase of life to another as **rites of passage** (Van Gennep, 1960/1908). The confirmation, the bar mitzvah, the graduation, and the retirement party are examples of rites of passage in modern societies.

In the United States and other Western cultures, the life course is constructed from categories like childhood, adolescence, young adulthood, adulthood, mature adulthood, and old age. But our definitions of these categories lack the stability and uniformity of the age grades found in many traditional societies. For example, the French historian Philippe Ariès (1962) showed that in Western civilization the concept of childhood as a phase of life with distinct characteristics and needs did not develop until the late seventeenth century. Before that time, children were treated as small adults. They were expected to perform chores and to conform to adult norms to the extent possible. When they reached puberty, they were usually married, often to spouses to whom they had been promised in infancy. Today many studies of childhood argue that there is again a blurring of the cultural definitions of childhood and adulthood because children are exposed to adult themes in the media and many children are prosecuted for adult crimes (Applebome, 1998).

Norms regarding gender are closely linked to the life course established by a society. Thus Ariès's study of the emergence of childhood revealed that ideas about the appropriate forms of play and education for boys, and indeed the very concept of boyhood, developed at least a century before the concept of girlhood emerged. In eighteenth-century European societies, boyhood was conceived of as a time when male children could play among themselves and receive education in the skills they would need as adults. Girls, in contrast, were treated as miniature women who were expected to work alongside their mothers and sisters.

Cohorts and Age Structures

When we think about age, we tend to think in terms of **age cohorts,** or people of about the same age who are passing through the life course together (Bosworth & Burtless, 1998). We measure our own successes and failures against the standards and experiences of our own cohorts—our schoolmates, our workmates, our senior circle—as we pass through life.

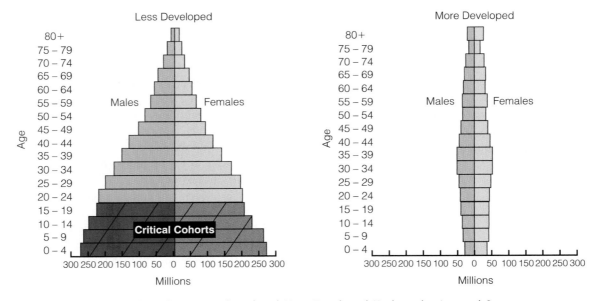

Figure 15.1   Population of Less Developed and More Developed Nations, by Age and Sex

Source: Population Reference Bureau, 1998.

Demographers use the cohort concept in studying how populations change. If we divide populations into 5-year cohorts, grouped vertically from age 0 to 100+ and divided into male and female, we can form a *population pyramid,* a useful way of looking at the influence of age on a society. Figure 15.1 compares the age structure of the population of developing nations with that of the more developed ones, including the United States. The base of the population structure of the developing nations is wide because of high birthrates. But the structure narrows in each cohort because of high rates of mortality, largely because of lack of access to up-to-date medical care and lack of preventive health care. High mortality rates for people older than age 40 result in the pyramidal form that is characteristic of the age structure of developing nations.

The developed nations have a more cylindrical population age structure, a consequence of far lower birthrates and, hence, smaller early-childhood and youth cohorts. For example, the 0–4 age cohort is smaller than the 5–9 cohort, reflecting the continuing decrease in birthrates in the industrialized and urbanized regions of the world. Note also that death rates are far lower in affluent countries than they are in developing nations, so that in the absence of war or deadly epidemics, the age cohorts pass through the age structure with little attrition until well into middle age, when increasing rates of mortality produce slightly smaller age cohorts.

In developing nations, the age cohorts from birth to age 19 are termed the "critical" cohorts because the reproductive behavior of these cohorts will largely determine the future size of the world's population. There are about 2 billion people younger than age 20 living in less developed nations, of which more than 400 million are already in their early child-bearing years (ages 15–19) (UNDP, 2003). In some industrialized nations, about 1 percent of teenagers in these cohorts give birth, but in parts of Africa and Asia, the rate can be as high as 24 percent. Overall, in Africa below the Sahara and above the nations of southern Africa, 18 percent of teenagers give birth each year. Were that rate to continue, the region's population would double in 23 years. In Latin America, where 8 percent of teenagers give birth each year, the population doubling time would be 42 years. Concerned about these statistics, representatives of more than 180 nations agreed in 1994 to rapidly increase investments in health care, family planning, and education for young women in the less developed regions of the world in the hope of stabilizing world population growth.

THE BABY BOOM   When a population experiences marked fluctuations in fertility, there are bulges in its population pyramid that have important effects. Perhaps nowhere in the world has this phenomenon been more thoroughly studied than in the United States. The "baby boom" cohorts, which were produced by rapid increases in the birthrate from about 1945 through the early 1960s, have profoundly influenced American society and will continue to do so for the next three decades.

Throughout Europe and North America, the baby boom generations did not have nearly as many children as their parents had. A mean family size of 2.1 children per

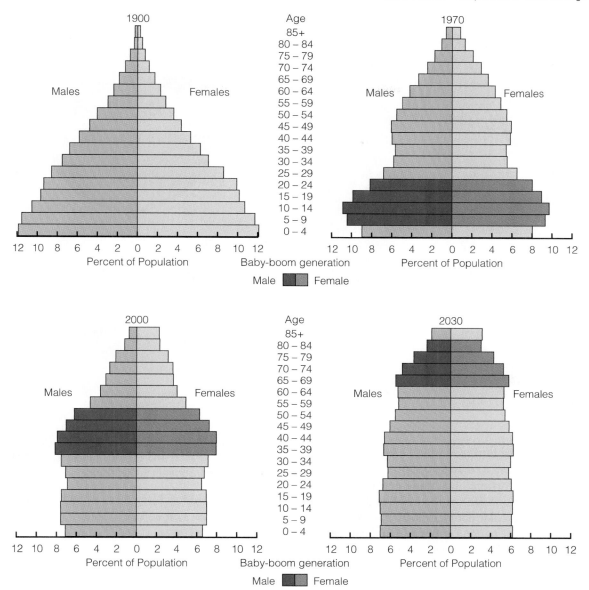

Figure 15.2   U.S. Population by Age and Sex, 1900, 1970, 2000, and 2030

Source: Population Reference Bureau, 2001.

couple is required for a population to remain constant over time (rapid growth requires a mean number of children closer to 3.0 per family). Since the 1970s, however, the mean number of children per family in industrial societies has been about 1.85 (and much lower in nations like Japan and Germany); as a result, the baby boom has been followed by a relative shortage of children known as the "baby bust" (Himes, 2001; Morgan, 1998). One way to visualize the impact of the baby boom and baby bust is to compare the population pyramids in Figure 15.2. The first of the four pyramids represents the U.S. population in 1900. It is

the classic shape for a population, with relatively high birthrates and thus high proportions of people younger than age 20. The next three pyramids show the large baby boom cohorts born between 1945 (the end of World War II) and the mid-1960s. Note the relatively smaller size of the cohorts just above the baby boomers, which is a result of war and delay of marriage. The 2000 and projected 2030 pyramids show the baby boom cohorts moving through the society's age structure until they are the most elderly segments of the population. Note also the changing shape of the pyramids as a result of the aging of the population

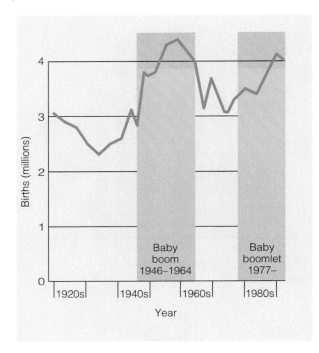

Figure 15.3   Number of Births in the United States Each Year, 1920–1993 (in millions)

Source: Data from U.S. Census Bureau.

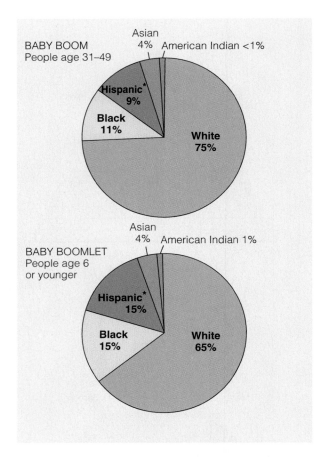

Figure 15.4   Racial and Ethnic Composition of the Baby Boom and Boomlet Generations

Note: Because of rounding, figures do not add up to 100 percent.

*Hispanic people can be of any race.

Source: Data from U.S. Census Bureau.

and the relatively low birthrate, which keep the youngest cohorts small compared to those of 1990.

As these cohorts mature, they make new demands on the society's institutions. During the 1960s and 1970s, for example, when the baby boom cohorts passed through their college years, the nation's universities and colleges expanded; the slogan of the day was "Never trust anyone over 30." Now the baby boom cohorts are moving into the dominant age groups of the population. The Clintons, Tipper and Al Gore, the Bush brothers (George W. and Jeb), and many other well-known political leaders are in these cohorts. Their succession to national leadership during the 1990s represents a transfer of power from the generation that fought in World War II and is now in its 70s and 80s, to the generation that experienced the Vietnam War and the social movements of the 1960s. But sociologists note that the baby boom cohorts are quite diverse and cannot be easily categorized as liberal or conservative, religious or secular, and so on (Brauss, 1995).

THE BABY BOOM ECHO   Sometimes referred to as the "baby boomlet" or the "baby boom echo," the children of parents who were part of the original baby boom are themselves an important demographic phenomenon. Note in Figure 15.3 that in the late 1980s the number of births exceeded 4 million per year, a threshold reached over a longer period dur-

ing the original baby boom, which extended from the 1940s to the 1960s. Like any "bulge" in a society's age structure, the wave of children born during the 1980s and early 1990s promises to have significant effects on social institutions like schools and businesses (Himes, 2001).

Figure 15.4 shows that a sizable proportion of the "second wave" or "boomlet" children are members of minority groups. This trend, combined with high rates of immigration, will increase the proportion of minority children moving through the nation's schools and colleges in coming decades. Between 1988 and 2000, for example, kindergarten enrollments rose by over 8 percent and preschool enrollments by 16 percent, both trends that presage increasing enrollments in many school districts. This demographic effect, in turn, increases debate over the investment of public funds in schools versus other uses, such as medical care for the poor and elderly (Wise, 2001).

Figure 15.5 Population Age 65 and Older, by World Regions, 1995 and 2025

Source: Data from United Nations.

* Projected.

AGING IN GLOBAL PERSPECTIVE As fertility decreases in most regions of the world and fewer babies are born, and as improvements in health care are extended to poorer regions, the proportion of older people in most nations rises accordingly. This "graying" of populations occurs at different rates, and with differing consequences, in developed and less developed regions, as do rates of change in life expectancy. But population aging will affect every man, woman, and child in the world. The steady increase of older age groups will have a direct bearing on relationships within families, inequality across generations, changes in lifestyles, and family solidarity (United Nations Department of Public Information, 2002). In regions with increasing elderly populations and continuing high rates of fertility, especially in Asia and Africa, high proportions of dependent children and increasing proportions of dependent elderly people increase the burden on working adults. We turn, therefore, to a discussion of population aging, or "graying," increased life expectancy and longevity, and their consequences for dependency in the near future.

Europe, North America, and Oceania have "graying" populations, in contrast to regions where the proportions of people age 65 and older remain relatively small. These differences are shown in Figure 15.5. Remember, however, that the figure shows proportions of older people in each region and not absolute numbers. Since Asia has the largest share of the world's population, it also has the highest number of elderly people. Rapidly expanding numbers of very old people represent a social phenomenon without historical precedent. Today the

number of persons aged 60 years or older is estimated to be 629 million. That number is projected to grow to almost 2 billion by 2050, when the population of older people will be larger than that of children (0–14 years) for the first time in human history. Fifty-four percent of the world's older people live in Asia. Europe has the next largest share, with 24 percent (United Nations Department of Public Information, 2002; U.S. Department of Commerce, 2001).

The dramatic increase in the proportion of elderly people in the industrialized nations projected for 2025 is largely attributable to the aging of the baby boom cohorts. This increase, often referred to as the "graying of America," is already resulting in greater concern about the needs of the elderly and will augment the influence of the aged on American culture and social institutions. (See the Mapping Social Change box on pages 430–431.)

Demographers and biologists disagree over estimates of how many very elderly people there will be in the U.S. population during the twenty-first century. Most Census Bureau demographers estimate that the population older than age 85 will increase from about 3.3 million persons (mainly women) in 1990 to about 18.7 million in 2080. But demographers working with the U.S. Institute of Aging argue that there may be no biological limits on life expectancy. With advances in medicine and better prevention of disease, more people may live into their 90s. If that happens, there could be as many as 70 million people over age 85 in the U.S. population late in this century—a change that would have enormous effects on all aspects of social life (Himes, 2001).

Text continues on page 432.

The Age Structure of Sun City, Arizona

MAPPING SOCIAL CHANGE

The aging of the U.S. population is creating major migration streams and new patterns of urban and suburban growth. The accompanying map, which shows the percentage of the U.S. population age 65 or older by county, offers a detailed view of the ecology of aging. We are used to thinking of Florida, Arizona, and now Nevada as destinations for retired people, but why are there such high proportions of elderly people in the Great Plains states? In the Dakotas, Nebraska, and Minnesota, cold weather is a severe deterrent to in-migration by the elderly, so what is the reason for the projected growth of this population

there? The answer has more to do with the movement of young people out of these states. As young people leave the Great Plains in search of opportunities in California and the rapidly growing states of the Southeast and Southwest, older people constitute a greater proportion of the remaining population.

In many of the Plains states, the elderly must be extremely vigorous in order to survive in the harsh environment and must be highly dedicated to their communities in order to maintain them in the absence of enough younger people to fill available positions, especially in unpaid volunteer work.

The migration patterns of the elderly also create some unusual inversions of the normal age pyramid in places where they become the most numerous population segment. The age pyramid for Sun City, Arizona, a retirement community in the Sun Belt, is a case in point. In this retirement community, only 0.1 percent of the population is younger than age 15 and nearly 85 percent is older than age 65. Note also that women outnumber men, as would be expected considering their greater life expectancy.

© Kevin Moloney/NYT Pictures

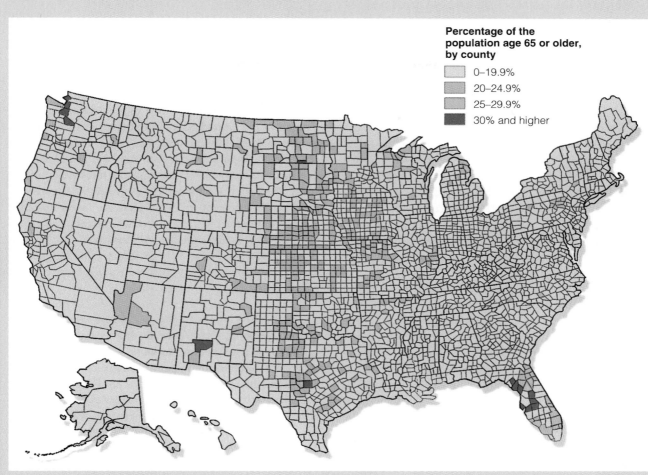

Percentage of the
population age 65 or older,
by county

0–19.9%
20–24.9%
25–29.9%
30% and higher

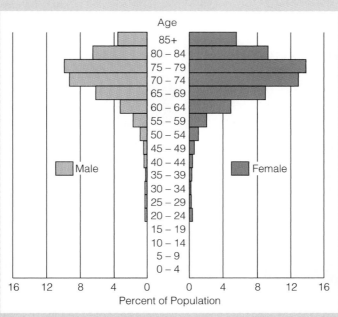

Longevity and Life Expectancy

As people live longer lives—that is, as *longevity* increases—due especially to better nutrition, more medical care, and improved economic and political stability—there are both positive and negative consequences, or risks, for societies and nations. More older people means that more people will live to be grandparents capable of helping their adult children care for their kids. Older people in good health have opportunities to travel and continue to develop their human potential. But greater longevity also means that there will be more "frail" elderly and greater incidence of illnesses such as cancer and Alzheimer's disease, which families and entire societies must learn to cope with. Despite these and other risks, increased life expectancy, as noted in earlier chapters, is a measure of social development because the overwhelming majority of people wish to live longer and more productive lives.

At age 65 and beyond, over 50 percent of North American women are widowed, whereas only 13.6 percent of men have lost their wives. This difference is due to the fact that the life expectancy of females is at least 7 years longer than that of males. (By **life expectancy** we mean the average number of years a member of a given population can expect to live beyond his or her present age.) Typically, men die before their wives do. Older men also tend to marry younger women, making widows the single largest category in the elderly population.

In the future, if male and female roles become more similar and women experience the stresses and risks that are thought to cause earlier death in men, the gap between the life expectancies of the sexes may narrow. Research on sex differences in the causes of death indicates that women may be less vulnerable to death for genetic reasons, but it is extremely difficult to prove this scientifically. The research of Lois M. Verbrugge and colleagues (Verbrugge, Gruber-Baldini, & Fozard, 1996) on health trends among males and females indicates that the lifestyles of men and women in the United States have become similar; in particular, women's lives are more like men's. This change has unfortunate implications for women's health and longevity. For example, women are now smoking almost as much as men. Smoking among men declined from 50.2 percent in 1965 to 25.9 percent in 1998, while the rate for women decreased from 31.9 percent to 22.1 percent (*Statistical Abstract,* 2001). Among older smokers, men were twice as likely to quit as women. It is no surprise that lung cancer now almost equals breast cancer as a leading cause of death for women.

AGE AND DEPENDENCY   People in the working adult cohorts—that is, those between the ages of 18 and 64 (although many continue to work well after age 64 and may start before age 18)—contribute disproportionately to the well-being of the young and the elderly. Of course, societies justify this pattern of dependency by recognizing that adults are merely doing in their turn what was done for them as children or will be done for them when they are among the frail elderly. Institutions of modern societies, such as public education and Social Security, ensure that a share of wealth passes to the dependent cohorts.

When there are very large numbers of children in a society, as is the case in the developing nations, or increasing numbers of elderly people, as is the case in the older nations of western Europe and North America, working adults may shoulder an increased burden. Figure 15.6 vividly illustrates the dependency problem. It charts the ratio of workers in the U.S. labor force to people receiving Social Security benefits. That ratio has been decreasing sharply with the aging of the U.S. population, so that now there are close to three workers for every retired person drawing on the Social Security fund. The graph also projects the ratio well into the twenty-first century in order to demonstrate that the dependency situation will continue to worsen as population aging accelerates. According to these projections, by the end of the second decade of this century, more funds will be drawn out of the Social Security system than are being paid

Social movements among the elderly are increasing in strength as the older population grows in numbers. Older Americans have taken an active interest in recent efforts to reform the nation's health care system.

© Terry Ashe/Getty Images

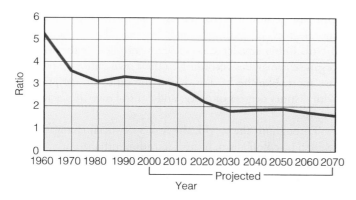

Figure 15.6 Ratio of U.S. Workers to Social Security Benficiaries

Source: Social Security Administration.

into it by active workers. In consequence, there is a lively debate among legislators about how to modify the system in the face of these changing demographics. Should the retirement age increase? Should Social Security taxes rise? Should the system be changed so that wealthier people receive lower benefits than less affluent citizens? These are all extremely controversial issues that need to be addressed to ensure that the major gains in well-being made by elderly people since the 1930s are not eroded in coming decades.

AGE STRATIFICATION AND INEQUALITY

In urban industrial societies, there are distinct patterns of stratification in which age defines the roles one plays and the rewards one can expect. We speak of the "age of majority"—the age at which a person crosses the legal boundary between childhood and adulthood. In fact, this age is not always clearly defined. A person can vote at age 18 but cannot legally consume alcohol until age 21. In addition to the age of majority, there are other distinct ages that mark the passage toward the full rights of adulthood. At age 18, one can join the armed forces without parental permission. At age 16, in many states, one is no longer obliged by law to attend school, even though parents still share responsibility for the behavior of the school dropout. Teenagers can drive at age 16 in many U.S. counties, but their parents remain responsible, through insurance systems, for their actions and can be held liable for the consequences. We also make clear distinctions between children in the primary grades and teenagers in high school, and in most homes a child's passage through

these age grades is accompanied by various privileges and responsibilities. So although the passage to full adult status may be somewhat vague, it is clear that to be young is to be less equal.

Later in life, as people become elderly, they may yield some of their autonomy to their grown children—either willingly through trusts and wills, or unwillingly as they are committed to nursing homes because their care has become too great a burden for their children. Thus, at the early and late extremes of youth and age, the relationship between age and inequalities of power and material resources are most evident.

Age-based inequalities may also affect the life chances of nonelderly adults. As corporations downsize (i.e., lay off employees in order to increase profit margins), higher-paid people in their 50s may find that their jobs are combined with other work and offered to younger, less well-paid replacements. These changes in the economy are producing major changes in the mature labor force. By the end of the 1990s, some 66 percent of males between the ages of 55 and 64 were active workers, a decrease of about 20 percent

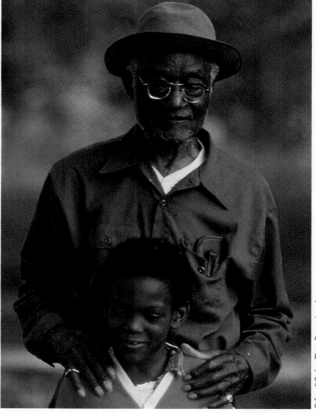

Given the opportunity, elderly men and women can have a profound influence on the lives of children in their families and neighborhoods.

since the mid-twentieth century. But the opposite was true for women. Among women in the same age group, the proportion of active workers increased to 49 percent in 1998 from only 27 percent in 1950 (Himes, 2001). More men are leaving full-time work in their fifties in order to pursue other interests, while more women are taking up the slack by finding full-time employment, often after working most of their lives at home as well as in the labor force.

Race and Gender: The Double and Triple Binds of Aging

Inequalities of age are compounded by those of race and gender to produce particular forms of inequality among the aged in industrial societies, especially the United States. If being elderly is a disadvantage, being an elderly woman often places one at a double disadvantage. Being elderly, female, and black or Hispanic places one in triple jeopardy for being isolated, ill, and impoverished (Himes, 2001; Holden, 1996). Women of advanced age, especially those older than age 85, are three times more likely than older men to be living in poverty. The situation is worse for elderly black and Hispanic women. Because large numbers of these women either were never married or experienced divorce (a subject to which we return in the next chapter), in their later years higher proportions live alone and have lower incomes than their white counterparts.

As we have seen, age influences life chances in important ways and helps produce the patterns of inequality that we often take for granted, especially among the young and the old. And age compounded by race and gender often entails further inequality. But if we study age stratification and inequality from a comparative perspective, we find some surprising differences. In smaller-scale, more traditional agrarian or pastoral societies, age stratification works in different ways than in urban industrial societies. For example, among the Maasai, whom we met in the preceding chapter, there are fixed age grades for males and females that strictly define an individual's roles and opportunities throughout life. Children and adolescents have no individual status in Maasai society. It is not until their passage through circumcision and other rituals during puberty that they achieve status as autonomous individuals.

Initiation into adult status occurs for a group of Maasai of roughly similar age, who then constitute an age grade. There are four age grades in the Maasai system, each covering about 15 years and involving a mandatory set of activities, especially for males. Young initiates engage in military activity. Young elders are married adults with family and economic responsibilities. Elders have political decision-making power, and senior elders have religious ritual power. Each of these age grades has a name in the Maasai language,

and passage into it is marked by rituals that convey differing degrees of authority and responsibility (Chenault, 1996). Other smaller-scale societies throughout the world organize age grades according to their own cultural norms, but most, like the Maasai, invest the different age grades with distinct degrees of power and control over the society's wealth.

Throughout the world, the forces of social change unleashed by colonialism, industrialization, urbanization, and population growth have tended to disrupt the formal age grade systems of smaller, more isolated societies. Often the loss of their traditional ways of commemorating the passage from one age to another has been among the more disorienting aspects of social change for people in those societies. The passage into old age is a good example. In most small-scale tribal and peasant societies, the elderly are revered as guardians of moral values, rituals, and religious beliefs. In urban industrial societies, by contrast, they are typically treated as dependents with little status and few rights. The situation of children is similar. In traditional societies, children have well-defined roles. The young girls are typically helpers while the boys are expected to play games that teach them the skills they will need as adult males. But all this changes in urban industrial societies. In those societies, the status of children is extremely fluid and subject to many conflicting ideas and rapid changes in norms (Ariès, 1962).

The Challenge of Youth

In *The Challenge of Youth* (1965), his seminal work on youth in Western societies, Erik Erikson observed that in societies with high levels of youth rebellion, deviance, and even suicide, the problem often lies in the failure of adults to provide young people with clear goals and paths toward a constructive future. Kenneth Keniston (1965), another expert on the problems of growing up in modern societies, adds that the challenges young people face are further complicated by such rapid and far-reaching changes that they are often bewildered about such questions as what careers to pursue, what standards to apply to personal relationships, and how much to devote to oneself and how much to the community and the society. Many young people have parents or other adults in their lives who can help them solve these dilemmas, but many others do not. As we saw in Chapter 7, young people may react to the problems and failures of those around them (e.g., alcoholism or divorce) by withdrawing into a world of anomic, alienated youth that explicitly rejects the values of the larger society, sometimes through gang violence.

In this regard, one of the most fascinating unanswered questions in the social sciences is why some children growing up under extremely adverse social conditions appear to work in fields and factories, but the stereotypical image of women's work was the homemaker. Far smaller numbers of boys, and even fewer girls, could be expected to complete high school, and even fewer went on to colleges and universities. Contrast this with the contemporary situation, in which most young men and women continue into postsecondary studies.

One effect of this major change in the social organization of youth is the emergence of an ever-greater variety of subcultures among young people. Because teenagers and young adults spend far more time in educational institutions making themselves ready for an ever-more-demanding labor market, adolescence—the phase of life considered to be relatively free from full adult responsibilities—often lasts well into the young-adult years. And during those years young people have increased freedom to try out different identities and associate with different kinds of peer groups.

At the beginning of the twentieth century, youth peer groups that developed their own subcultures were common, especially in the cities among boys who spent time in the streets and joined gangs, or among elite young men who joined the secret societies and fraternities of universities and colleges. But with the increasing racial and ethnic diversity of the North American population and the greater freedom young people have to make choices about friends and activities, the range of youth subcultures is far greater. The existence and behaviors of identifiable groups in any high school—the nerds, skateboarders, surfer dudes, cheerleaders, and on and on—are well known to most teenagers but often far more mysterious to parents, who find it difficult to communicate with their children about sensitive issues of sexuality and substance abuse.

In the 1960s, as the baby boom generation entered its teenage years, the marketing of music, clothes, films, and food to young people became extremely lucrative. Youth marketing became a major industry, and it in turn began to play a significant role in shaping what young people do, how they dress, and how they display their allegiance to different youth subcultures. For example, a popular Canadian Web site is designed to attract the attention of teenagers and young adults and simultaneously attract businesses that want to market goods and services to them. Its "Trendscan" survey uses sociological research techniques to track trends in youth cultures in Canada and show businesses how to better attract teenage buyers, as the following statement shows:

> Understanding the uniqueness of the 12–13 year old experience versus 14–15, 16–17 and 18–19, male versus female, and the regional variances is essential for developing thoughtful marketing strategies. Further, active brands can profile their specific youth consumers.

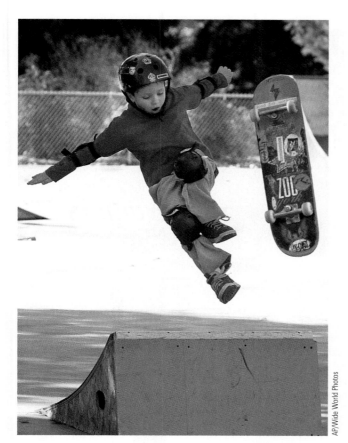

AP/Wide World Photos

Although he lost his skateboard in this jump, this young athlete went on to win in his event class. Skateboarding is part of a youth subculture that attracts young boys and may lead to their participation in extreme forms of the sport as they develop their skills.

be resilient, to be able to succeed in school and in other social settings, while so many others are set back and defeated by the same adverse conditions (Conger, Ge, & Elder, 1994; Garmezy, 1993; Williams & Kornblum, 1994). On a broader sociological level, however, Keniston and others note that changing norms of childhood and youth, on one hand, and the decreasing well-being of young people in industrial nations, on the other, strongly influence the fortunes of youth everywhere.

YOUTH CULTURES AND SOCIAL CHANGE At the beginning of the twentieth century, when the United States and Canada were still largely agrarian societies (though with booming population growth in their major urban centers), adolescents typically went to work, often in their father's agricultural or industrial workplace. "A son follows his father's trade," was the common expression, and teenage girls were expected to learn to do domestic work in preparation for unpaid careers as homemakers. Girls from working-class and poor families typically went to

THEN AND NOW

From Adulthood in Miniature to Childhood—and Back?

These photos offer versions of ideal behavior among children in the eighteenth century, the mid-twentieth century, and the present. They raise questions about the ever-shifting norms and expectations of childhood. In the eighteenth century, as depicted in the famous Gainsborough portrait known as the *Blue Boy,* the ideal of childhood was one of adulthood in miniature. By age 7 or 8, children "were dressed and treated as little adults. They dressed the same, did the same work, and entered into the sexual community of adults. . . . Even in the United States, the age of sexual consent was under 10 in half the states until the end of the 19th century" (Applebome, 1998, p. 3). The idea that children are different and have their own rights to education and protection under the law emerged in the early twentieth century. By mid-century, the idea of healthy childhood was solidly reinforced in the mainstream culture, as the *Saturday Evening Post* illustration from the 1950s clearly demonstrates. Today, experts on childhood worry that cultural understandings about childhood have again become blurred. The public's fascination with another "miniature adult," JonBenet Ramsey (the winner of the 1995 Little Miss Colorado beauty pageant, who was murdered in 1996 at the age of 6), is only a small part of the story. Perhaps more ominous is the fact that by 2000 almost all states had passed laws allowing the prosecution and sentencing of 14-year-olds as adults.

Do these and many other examples of the blurring of the boundaries of childhood mean that childhood is disappearing? Most experts would disagree. They note that children "usually prove more resilient than grown-ups expect" and that survey research shows "American teenagers to be worldly in ways previous generations were not, but sharing most of the values and sensibilities of earlier times" (Applebome, 1998, p. 3).

THE SATURDAY EVENING POST

April 20, 1940   5c. the Copy

COUNTRY DOCTOR GOES TO TOWN
By J. C. FURNAS

YOUR MOM WAS A LADY
By R. ROSS ANNETT

© The Curtis Publishing Company

The Huntington Library, Art Collections, and Botanical Gardens, San Marino, California/SuperStock

© Dave Sartin/Getty Images

Our Early Style Adopter (ESA) Teen is a core component of the Trendscan survey. These youth have been earmarked as the style and opinion leaders within the Canadian youth population. Understanding ESAs can be an essential factor in successfully marketing to a consumer group heavily influenced by "the cool kids." (www.youthculture.com)

Understanding the rapid change occurring in youth cultures and young people's consumer behavior, including their consumption of illegal substances, is the subject of innumerable TV ads and Web sites, but the intensity of communications about young people is also an indicator that the social changes we have discussed are associated with widespread debate and uncertainty about norms and expectations for children and teenagers in most of the world's nations.

VARIATIONS IN THE VALUE PLACED ON CHILDREN   Social definitions of childhood—what we expect of children, how we value the child and treat the child—differ immensely throughout the industrial world as well as between modern and traditional societies. In her study of the changing meanings of childhood, sociologist Viviana Selizer shows that in the United States there occurred a "profound transformation in the economic and sentimental value of children—fourteen years of age or younger—between the 1870s and the 1930s" (1985, p. 3). During that period, child labor laws ended a common practice, at least among poorer families, of requiring children to work for wages. Earlier in the nineteenth century, the incomes of the middle classes had risen enough so that they could keep their young ones out of the labor force; by the 1930s, this became the norm for all classes.

As a result of this transformation, Selizer points out, children became economically "worthless" but emotionally "priceless"—and this is true today as well. We think of our children as priceless beings to be nurtured, protected, socialized, and gradually introduced to the world of work and careers—not forced into that world abruptly after a brief period of innocent childhood, as was the case in the early years of industrialization. Studies of children's responsibilities in the home find that people justify giving their children chores to do on the grounds that doing so builds character, discipline, responsibility, and so on, not because it contributes to the economic well-being of the family. In fact, in many middle-class homes the allowance system operates in lieu of any form of wages; the allowance is seen as a form of token money that the child has a right to receive but must also learn to spend responsibly.

But Selizer also shows that this transformation in the value placed on children was surrounded by a great deal of social conflict as the institutions of the larger society, especially courts and schools, were given the responsibility for enforcing the new norms about child protection. Debates over definitions of childhood and the proper roles of children continue today. For example, the home schooling movement has arisen among people who reject the values of the public schools and wish to maintain the absolute authority of parents over their children by educating them in the home.

More important than these conflicts are the class contradictions inherent in the value placed on childhood. Many families are not able to give their children the array of goods and opportunities that are available to children in more affluent families. The worst situations of material deprivation experienced by children and young people, along with their parents, are often hidden from view in racial and ethnic ghettos and class-segregated communities "across the tracks" or in isolated trailer parks (Kozol,

1995). Overall trends in child welfare show that there is a widening gap between "priceless" children and children who bear a heavy burden of poverty and deprivation.

INDICATORS OF WELL-BEING AMONG YOUTH   There is a growing consensus among social scientists on the need for a quantitative measure of well-being among youth. In recent years, as ideological debates over social problems like teenage fertility have become more rancorous, this need has become even more pressing (Zill, 1995). Toward this end, a group of eminent sociologists has been working to create a set of data books titled *Kids Count*. These data books provide an invaluable and up-to-date array of indicators of trends in child well-being in the United States. They are available for use by local officials, scholars, and those who work with the youth of their communities (Annie E. Casey Foundation, *Kids Count 2000*, www.aecf.org).

Although in many communities most children are healthy and well cared for, the *Kids Count* data indicate that increasing numbers of young people are experiencing poverty and near-poverty conditions. The late Senator Daniel Patrick Moynihan of New York, himself a skilled social scientist, noted that "a child in America is almost twice as likely to be poor as an adult. This is a condition that has never before existed in our history" (1988, p. 5).

Table 15.1 presents some indicators of well-being among American youth. Measures of children in poverty, rates of violent death, infant mortality, teenagers not in school, and births to single teenagers are among the most important ways of looking at the proportion of children and young people whose well-being is questionable and whose daily lives are fraught with risk of further trouble. Perhaps the most controversial of these indicators are those dealing with births to teenagers. In the United States and other urban industrial societies, there is a great deal of debate about increasing rates of teenage childbearing. But the facts show that, contrary to what many people believe, rates of births to teenagers decreased from 1960 through 1980, when they began increasing again but never reached the same levels as those prevailing at the end of the 1950s. Figure 15.7 demonstrates that U.S. teenagers are much more likely to become pregnant unintentionally than teenagers in other developed countries. They are also more likely to want to become mothers (intentional pregnancies) and to have abortions.

It should be noted that some of the indicators presented in Table 15.1, such as the rate of violent death among teenagers, have actually improved in the last year or two. Others, however, such as the percentage of low-birthweight babies, have worsened. These indicators are sensitive to changes in society (e.g., declining use of crack cocaine, efforts to reduce truancy, dropout prevention

TABLE 15.1

Indicators of Child Well-Being

	Trend Data	
	1990	2000
Percent low-birthweight babies	7.0%	7.6%
Infant mortality rate (deaths per 1,000 live births)	9.2	6.9
Child death rate (deaths per 100,000 children ages 1–14)	31	22
Rate of teen deaths by accident, homicide, and suicide (deaths per 100,000 teens ages 15–19)	71	51
Teen birthrate (births per 1,000 females ages 15–17)	37	27
Percent of teens who are high school dropouts (ages 16–19)	10%	9%
Percent of teens not attending school and not working (ages 16–19)	10%	8%
Percent of children living with parents who do not have full-time, year-round employment	30%	24%
Percent of children in poverty (data reflect poverty in the previous year)	20%	17%
Percent of families with children headed by a single parent	24%	28%
Teenage violent death rate*	62.8	54.0

*Deaths per 100,000 teenagers ages 15–19, 1985 and 1998.

Source: Annie E. Casey Foundation, 2003.

programs). The low-birthweight indicator is especially sensitive to changes in the economic situation of low-income households. But of all the indicators, the infant mortality rate—the proportion of infants who die in early infancy—is the most universally recognized measure of how well societies are doing in providing healthy environments for mothers and young children.

INFANT MORTALITY: A GLOBAL MEASURE OF INEQUALITY Throughout the world, the infant mortality rate is considered the single most important indicator of the relative well-being of a nation's people (see Chapter 21). It measures the extent and efficacy of a nation's investment in the health of its people. The infant mortality rate in the United States—6.8 per 1,000 live births—ranks among the world's best, but it is higher than those in Japan (3.9), the Netherlands (4.4), or Australia (5.0), while it is much lower than that in Russia (20.1) and far lower than those in relatively impoverished nations like India (63.2) (*Statistical Abstract*, 2002). Thus the United States, one of the world's most affluent nations, actually ranks on the lower

end of the scale of infant mortality among the developed nations with which it is often compared. Much of the difference is attributable to the large number of underweight babies born in the United States.

The infant mortality rate for African Americans in the United States (14.6) is more than twice the rate for whites (5.8) (*Statistical Abstract*, 2002). Much of this disparity is attributable to the high percentage of babies with low birthweights among members of minority groups, especially those in poverty. Birthweights below 5.5 pounds are a cause of infant death and are associated with higher rates of illness in later years as well as a higher incidence of neurological and developmental handicaps and poor academic performance (Partin & Palloni, 1995). Figure 15.8 shows that the incidence of low-birthweight babies among African Americans declined from over 14 percent in 1970 to a little over 12 percent in the mid-1980s, but began climbing again after 1984.

In explaining these trends, sociologists Melissa Partin and Alberto Palloni (1995) point out that while poverty is always associated with low birthweight, a woman's access to prenatal care in her community combined with her decision not to have an abortion are important factors. As more poor minority women choose not to have abortions and find it more difficult to obtain adequate care during pregnancy, the risk of low birthweight increases. Neither side in the abortion debate wishes to see more abortions among poor women. The central implication of these findings is that the rate of low-birthweight babies would be reduced by improved access to health care for young mothers and more education about the need to decrease behaviors such as smoking during pregnancy.

Age and Inequality

At the turn of the twentieth century, the largest segment of the U.S. population living in poverty or near-poverty conditions was the elderly (Preston, 1984). This was also true throughout much of Europe. Until the development of modern systems of employee pensions, Social Security, and basic health insurance (both private insurance systems and public systems like Medicare), people older than age 60 were highly likely to be poor. Although poor and working-class elderly people without substantial wealth or savings might receive assistance from adult children and other family members, even those relatively fortunate individuals often felt deep resentment about having worked all their lives only to end up powerless and dependent.

The Social Security Act of 1935 established federal old-age pensions based on employee and employer contributions, as well as unemployment insurance and other anti-poverty programs. The results of these programs, and the

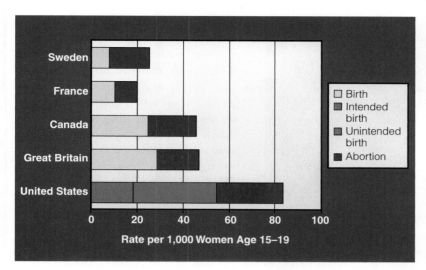

Figure 15.7 Intended and Unintended Pregnancies and Abortions, Among Teenagers in Selected Western Nations

Source: Data from Alan Guttmacher Institute, 2001.

Medicare system instituted in 1965, have been dramatic. Rates of poverty among the elderly, which were close to 40 percent in the early decades of the twentieth century, declined to about 28 percent in the early 1960s and then to about 14 percent after Medicare went into effect. At present, 10.2 percent of people age 65 and older in the United States live at or below the poverty line, compared to 11.3 percent of the population as a whole (*Statistical Abstract*, 2002).

Among elderly members of minority groups, however, the situation is not nearly so positive. Over 22 percent of African Americans and about 19 percent of Hispanics older than age 65 are living in poverty (*Statistical Abstract*, 2002). These differences often result because elderly people who previously worked at lower-paying jobs, which contributed little or nothing to private pension plans, may be forced to live almost exclusively on their federal Social Security payments, which by themselves are not enough to raise them above the official poverty line. And elderly blacks and Hispanics are especially likely to have had jobs that did not provide pensions.

As more people join the ranks of the elderly, concern about their economic situation becomes an ever-more-powerful theme in American life. Many Americans in their early 60s are subject to mandatory retirement. Once they are forced into retirement, they are limited in what they can earn without experiencing cuts in their Social Security payments and decreases in Medicare support. Matilda White Riley, a leading authority on the sociology of aging, asserts that there is a growing gap between the number of skilled and energetic elderly people in the population and the availability of "meaningful opportunities in work, family, and leisure" (Riley, Kahn, & Foner, 1994). We return to this theme shortly.

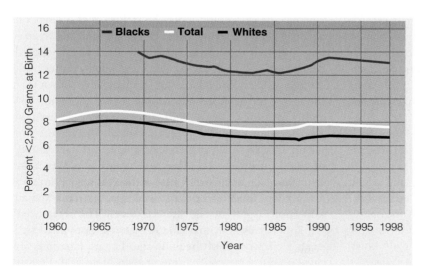

Figure 15.8 Percent of Low-Birthweight Babies, by Race, 1960–1998

Source: Partin & Palloni, 1995; *Statistical Abstract*, 2000.

Robert Frost, shown here in his advanced years, was far more than a poet of rural America. Among other things, he promoted the idea that people need to remain passionate participants in the world around them throughout their lives.

AGE AND DISABILITY   As life expectancies have increased throughout the world, so have the numbers of people with major disabilities that seriously impair their ability to function effectively in their daily lives. In the United States, the average life expectancy for people age 60 is 19 years for women and 15 years for men. On the average, women who live that many years after their 60th birthday can expect to experience major disabilities for 5 of those years (4 years for men). In Germany, another affluent industrial nation, life expectancies for women and men age 60 are 22 years and 18 years, respectively, and the chances of experiencing major disabilities are the same as those in the United States. In Egypt, a developing nation, the comparable figures are 13 years of life expectancy for women after age 60 and 12 years for men, but because of less advanced health care, the average Egyptian woman can expect to experience 6 years of disability (4 years for men) (Haber & Dowd, 1994). People who live longer do not automatically suffer major disabilities. As they age and become more frail, however, the experience of living with disability inevitably affects higher proportions of women because of their greater life expectancy.

The problems of health and disability among the elderly are compounded by inequalities of socioeconomic status. The more affluent and educated people are as they enter their 60s, the healthier they tend to be. In their last years, however, the effects of socioeconomic status diminish (House et al., 1994). People who have worked for decades tending machines in factories, often in polluted and stressful conditions, are more likely to have health problems and to have difficulty obtaining regular medical care than people who have worked in more physically and emotionally favorable conditions. Moreover, data on aging and health show that people from poor and working-class backgrounds are more likely to engage in **psychosocial risk behaviors** like smoking and heavy drinking (90 or more drinks per month). They also tend to experience a higher than average number of **lifetime negative experiences** (e.g., the death of a child or spouse, divorce, physical assault), which cause long-term stress. Even when risk behaviors and sources of chronic stress are considered, however, quantitative studies show a strong positive relationship between higher socioeconomic status and better health in elderly people (Himes, 2001; House et al., 1994).

LOSS OF SOCIAL FUNCTIONS WITH AGE   As people age, they experience more medical problems and disabilities—but does this mean that they must inevitably withdraw from social life? Can anyone deny the biological facts of aging and death? Isn't it only natural for the elderly to perform less important roles as their physical capacities diminish? The answer, of course, is that it is not obvious at all. The increasing participation of elderly widows in securities investment clubs throughout the nation is a good example of how elderly people may perform socially important roles even as their physical strength diminishes. It is not uncommon for members of these clubs to impress far younger stockbrokers with their skill as players in the volatile securities market.

Sexual behavior among the elderly is another area in which popular notions about the influence of biology on age roles have been disproved. In the late nineteenth century and well into the twentieth, it was widely believed that people lose their sexual desire and potency after middle age. In fact, however, several studies have shown that the image of the elderly as lacking sexual desire and the ability to enjoy sex is an ageist stereotype. For example, in a pioneering study, Eric Pfeiffer, Adrian Verwoerdt, and Glenn Davis (1972) gathered data from several samples of elderly people—including individuals as old as 94—that showed conclusively that although sexual interest and activity tended to decline with age, sex remained an important aspect of the subjects' lives. The researchers also found, however, that elderly men are more interested in sex than women of the same age. The explanations for this difference are cultural rather than biological. Elderly men are in short supply. They tend to be married to women with whom they have had a long-standing relationship that includes an active sex life. If they are not married, they are in such great demand that they have less difficulty than women of the same age in finding a sexually compatible partner (Greeley, Michael, & Smith, 1990; Kornblum & Julian, 2004).

CARING FOR THE ELDERLY: WHOSE RESPONSIBILITY? As noted earlier, social scientists who study the situation of the elderly increasingly recognize that longer life spans need to be accompanied by new concepts of social roles in more advanced years. The well-known gerontologists Matilda White Riley and John W. Riley, Jr., believe there is a growing mismatch between the strengths and capacities of older people and their roles in society. As people live longer, they often find themselves living alone with few constructive roles that demand their time and attention. Neglect of the elderly further reduces their mental and physical strength. The Rileys believe that "increasing numbers of competent older people and diminishing role opportunities cannot long coexist" (1989, p. 28). In their view, there is an urgent need for many small-scale programs that create work and volunteer opportunities in which older people can use their skills and feel needed (Riley, Kahn, & Foner, 1994).

Shifts in age statuses can have dysfunctional effects for society as well. A research project of the Carnegie Foundation attempted to assess the impact of an aging society (i.e., one in which the median age is increasing) on social roles. For example, whose responsibility is it to pay for long-term care of the elderly? A family may have to pay $40,000 per year or more to provide nursing home care for a disabled elderly mother or father. Should the sons and daughters take on this responsibility? Most of us would say yes, if we are able to do so. The Carnegie study found, however, that an increasing proportion of people say, in effect, "No sir, that's a public responsibility; let them go on Medicaid." In that case, however, we would force the elderly to sell all their assets in order to qualify for government aid because Medicaid is available only to people who have exhausted their own funds before applying to the government for assistance (Pifer & Bronte, 1986).

The question of responsibility for caring for the frail elderly is a controversial policy issue. The conservative position is that family members or close relatives should be required to pay for such care until funds are no longer available. The liberal position is that individuals should not have to be dependent on possibly reluctant family members; moreover, the high costs of long-term care for the elderly are an especially heavy burden for households with low incomes. The elderly themselves, who form a major segment of the U.S. voting population, are increasingly concerned about threats to their economic and social security, especially as represented by efforts to reduce the extent of health coverage under the Medicare system. They also are increasingly sensitive to any slights or discriminatory behavior based on their age.

AGEISM The attitude known as **ageism** is similar to sexism (see Chapter 14). The term refers to an ideology that justifies prejudice or discrimination based on age. Ageism limits people's lives in many ways, both subtle and direct. It may label the young as incapable of learning. It labels the elderly as mentally incapable or asexual or too frail to get around. But people of all ages increasingly reject these notions. In their everyday lives in families and communities, for example, older people continually struggle against the debilitating effects of ageism. "Just because I need help crossing the street doesn't mean I don't know where I'm going," an elderly woman said to community researcher Jennie Keith (1982, p. 198).

Gerontologist Robert Butler observes that "ageism allows the younger generation to see older people as different from themselves; thus they subtly cease to identify with their elders as human beings" (1989, p. 139). Butler, a physician and social scientist, has found that as the proportion of older people in a society increases (as is occurring in the United States and Europe), the prevalence of ageism also increases. The younger generations, he notes, tend to fear that the older, increasingly frail and dependent generations will deprive them of opportunities for advancement. This fear is expressed in demands for reduced spending on Medicare and other programs that assist the elderly, as well as in the belief that the elderly are affluent and do not need social supports.

STEREOTYPING OF THE ELDERLY A form of ageism that can be corrected through greater sociological knowledge about aging is the tendency to view all old people as frail, dependent, incapable, and asexual. But as this proportion of the population increases, older people will be found doing many things that are viewed as inappropriate for their age. A woman in her 80s recently set the age record for solo sailing across the Atlantic. Just before reaching the age of 100, George Burns dedicated a book "to his past five doctors."

Just as other groups in the population reject labels that deprive them of their individuality and self-esteem, elderly people reject ageist labels that relegate them to dependent, unequal status. There will of course be large numbers of dependent older people, but there will also be large numbers of vigorous people of advanced age who need and demand encouragement and support in maintaining their vitality and in continuing to live life to its fullest. Younger people who can apply their sociological imagination to these issues will be highly valued (Kornblum & Julian, 2004).

THEORIES OF AGING

Although they have been less far-reaching than the women's movement, social movements among the elderly—led by organizations like the Gray Panthers and AARP—have had a significant impact on American society. And as the population continues to age, we can expect to see more evidence of the growing power of the elderly. Consider, for instance, how changes in the consciousness and political activity of elderly people themselves are altering the way sociologists formulate questions about old age.

Disengagement Theory

Until the social movements of the 1960s prompted the elderly to form movements to oppose ageism and fight for their rights as citizens, the most popular social-scientific view of aging was *disengagement theory.* Numerous empirical studies had shown that old people gradually disengage from involvement in the lives of younger people and from economic and political roles that require responsibility and leadership. In a well-known study of aging people in Kansas City, Elaine Cumming and William Henry (1971) presented evidence that as people grow older, they often gradually withdraw from their earlier roles, and that this process is a mutual one rather than a result of rejection or discrimination by younger people. From a functionalist viewpoint, disengagement is a positive process both for society as a whole (because it opens up roles for younger people) and for the elderly themselves (because it frees them from stressful roles in their waning years).

Activity Theory

The trouble with disengagement theory is that, on one hand, it appears to excuse policymakers' lack of interest in the elderly and, on the other, it is only a partial explanation of what occurs in the social lives of elderly people. An alternative view of the elderly is that they need to be reengaged in new activities. Known as *activity theory,* this view states that the elderly suffer a sense of loneliness and loss when they give up their former roles. They need activities that will serve as outlets for their creativity and energy (Binstock & George, 2001).

Theories of aging are not simply abstract ideas that are taught in schools and universities. The disengagement and activity theories lead to different approaches that often impose definitions of appropriate behavior on people who do not wish to conform to those definitions. Today gerontologists and elderly activists tend to reject both theories. They see older people demanding opportunities to lead

The Sociological Observer

Two old friends are enjoying a game of chess at the public chess tables in Manhattan's Greenwich Village. Why are the men sitting on the same side of the table? During what time of the year might this game be occurring? In what ways does this photo provide support for "activity theory"? (See page 446 for further insights into the sociological content of this photo.)

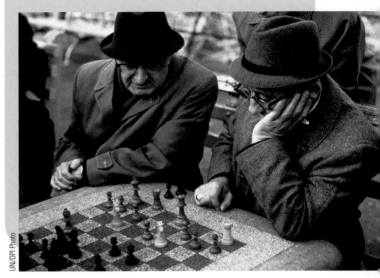

UN/DPI Photo

their lives in a variety of ways based on individual habits and preferences developed earlier in life. Elderly people themselves express doubt that activity alone results in successful adjustment to aging or happiness in old age. For example, in her study of a French retirement community, Jennie Keith (1982) made this observation:

> The residents . . . seem to offer support to the gerontologists who have tried to mediate the extreme positions, disengagement vs. activity, by introducing the idea of styles of aging. . . . Some people are happy when they are very active, others are happy when they are relatively inactive. From this point of view, life-long patterns of social participation explain the kinds and levels of activity that are satisfying to different individuals. (p. 59)

In sum, for the elderly as well as for women, there is a growing tendency among social scientists to emphasize individual needs and capabilities. The social movements for gender and age equality also advance the needs of individuals, but in a collective manner, by asserting the needs of entire populations and rejecting preconceived notions of what is best for all women, all youth, all men, or all the elderly.

DEATH AND DYING

As members of the large baby boom generation move through the adult years and approach middle age, their parents enter the ranks of the elderly. This demographic change has led to increased concern about the quality of life of the elderly and about death and the dying process. The questions of how best to prepare to die and whether one can have a "good death" might have seemed strange to Americans of an earlier time, when so many people died as a result of sudden, acute illnesses like pneumonia or tragic accidents in mines and mills. Today almost two-thirds of the people who die each year experience long struggles with chronic illnesses like cancer and heart disease and are often "sequestered" from the rest of society in hospital intensive-care units. The proportion of deaths occurring in hospitals, nursing homes, and other institutions has risen rapidly since the 1930s and now exceeds 80 percent of deaths. Sociologists who study death and dying believe that this change is a major reason for poll results showing that most Americans support the right of patients to receive a lethal overdose from their doctors (Horgan, 1997). It is also a reason why so many health care experts and activists are seeking alternatives to hospital care for dying loved ones (Perls & Silver, 1999).

People who are dying often experience a period between life and death known as the *living–dying interval* (Kübler-Ross, 1969). For many dying people and their loved ones, this an extremely important time. During this time, there may be reconciliations, clarifications, expressions of love and understanding, and, under the best circumstances, a sense of closure and repose for the dying person. But most people die in hospitals. Nurses, doctors, and orderlies may intrude on these emotional scenes to minister to the patient. The hospital is dedicated to prolonging life, even in a dying patient. As the Rileys express it: "The hospital is geared for treatment and cure, it func-

tions according to standards of efficiency and bureaucratic rules, its environment is sterile and unwelcoming to those who would visit patients *in extremis*" (1989, p. 27).

The Hospice Movement

In recent decades, first in Great Britain and later in the United States, a social movement has emerged that is known as the hospice movement. The term *hospice* refers to a place, a set of services, or both; increasingly it refers to a service that can be brought into the dying person's home. The purpose of the hospice is to offer palliative care, which makes the patient as comfortable as possible so that all concerned can use the living–dying interval effectively and humanely. In a hospice, the patient and his or her surrounding social group are viewed as the relevant social unit. Medical personnel and other professionals, such as social workers, are available to help everyone involved.

Although many people still die in hospitals, hospice care is available in most parts of the United States and is an increasingly popular alternative to hospital death (see Figure 15.9). This change is a result of modifications in the insurance laws, which now allow Medicare reimbursements for home hospice care. Since 1983, when these rule changes were made in response to pressure from the hospice movement, the number of people who choose to die at home has more than doubled, and it continues to increase despite the additional sacrifices that home hospice care requires from loved ones (Belkin, 1992; Horgan, 1997).

Dying is never an easy experience, and the hospice movement cannot make it so. Nevertheless, the hospice movement is providing opportunities for new definitions of the last social role in the life course—the dying role—as well as the roles of those who will remain behind to continue their own life course. (See the Popular Culture and Social Change box on page 444.)

Figure 15.9 Number of Patients in U.S. Hospices, 1985–1995

Source: From "Number of Patients in Hospices, United States, 1985–1995," by J. Hogan. Copyright © 1995 by Scientific American, Inc. All rights reserved.

POPULAR CULTURE & SOCIAL CHANGE   "Death Ends a Life, Not a Relationship"

Who would have predicted that sociologist Morrie Schwartz would become a media star, and especially after his retirement from active research and teaching? But that is just what happened. The story is partly about the way television helps create the heroes of our popular culture, partly about a teacher who was a hero to his students and colleagues, and partly about one of his former students, who went back to learn from his dying mentor and wrote one of the greatest nonfiction best-sellers in publishing history.

Morrie Schwartz was a sociologist at Brandeis University who had been an inspiring teacher and had written some important research papers about mental health and American society. In 1995, now retired from teaching, he was paralyzed by ALS (Lou Gehrig's disease) and confined to a wheelchair.

But his spirit and intellectual curiosity were so strong that his illness only stimulated his mind further, and he refused to be depressed. He wrote down all his thoughts and began listing them as short bits of wisdom from a dying person to the living: "Learn to forgive yourself and to forgive others"; "Don't assume that it's too late to get involved." He shared this wisdom with his colleagues, and one of them, Maurice Stein, sent them to the *Boston Globe,* which ran a story with the headline "A Professor's Final Course: His Own Death."

A producer of Ted Koppel's "Nightline" TV show read the article and convinced Koppel to do a show about Professor Schwartz. The show became a sensation; it was viewed nationwide and rebroadcast numerous times. One of Schwartz's former students, Mitch

Albom, a sportswriter with the *Detroit Free Press,* saw the broadcast and was stunned to see his old professor talking as if from the grave, but very much alive. Albom had had a close relationship with his mentor and had promised to stay in touch with him after graduation, but he had not done so. Now he resolved to visit him. They resumed their friendship, and Albom visited his dying professor on Tuesdays for the remaining months of his life, recording his sayings and writing about his courage and wisdom in a short book titled *Tuesdays With Morrie.*

The book became a sensation, and although professor Schwartz died in 1999, it remains on the *New York Times* best-seller list, where is has been (at this writing) for more than 220 weeks, longer than any other book on the list. Before Schwartz died, Koppel returned to do two more shows and to share the sociologist's wisdom about life, dying, and death with the viewing public. Schwartz's last words on the last show were, "Be compassionate, and take responsibility for each other." Then he told Koppel, "Ted, this disease is knocking at my spirit, but it will not get my spirit. It'll get my body. It will *not* get my spirit" (quoted in Albom, 1997, p. 163).

Throughout the world, dying people and their families are taking comfort from the sayings of a sociologist who made understanding death and life his final work. With the immense help of a former student, the professor's prediction about his spirit has come true.

photograph by Heather Pillar

Morrie Schwartz and Mitch Albom.

CRITICAL SOCIOLOGY AND SOCIAL CHANGE

Youth and the Future of Civic Service

AmeriCorps, like the Peace Corps of the Kennedy years, has become a model of service for an entire generation. Yet despite promises to expand it beyond the 50,000 vol-

unteers serving today, current proposals in Congress would cut its size in half, a major step toward its elimination (Eggers, 2003). Thousands of deserving children will lose tutors, mentors, and motivated young teachers if these programs disappear. But sociological research shows that failure to expand projects like AmeriCorps also sends a negative message to the nation's teenagers and young adults. The volume of applications to volunteer programs like Teach for America and AmeriCorps shows that young Americans want to meet the challenges of a rapidly changing society by serving those who are less advantaged. But what happens when the larger society fails to harness their energies and talents? Critical research on youth and community service by James Youniss and Miranda Yates provides some of the answers.

Youniss and Yates (1997) have investigated Erik Erikson's thesis that societies that "fail to harness the services of youth in their historical aims" leave young people "to seek their own combinations, in small groups occupied with serious games, good-natured foolishness, cruel prankishness, and delinquent warfare. In no other stage of the life cycle, then, are the promise of finding oneself and the threat of losing oneself so closely allied" (Erikson, 1965, p. 11). This view implies that societies need to create opportunities for young people to interact with adults as they jointly seek to address society's problems and, in this fashion, to realize their society's "historical aims."

The Research Background

Youniss and Yates examined all the available research on participation in youth groups such as Girl and Boy Scouts, 4-H Clubs, Future Farmers of America, YMCA and YWCA, and many more. Social-scientific evaluations of young people's experiences offer evidence that they encourage involvement in the community and inhibit anti-social activities. Research on young people's participation in more focused efforts to deal with social problems, however, show even deeper and more lasting influences over the individual's life. For example, a major follow-up study of men and women who joined the Civil Rights movement during the Freedom Summer of 1964 and went to Mississippi to volunteer in Freedom Schools and help in voter registration found that more than 20 years later "the volunteer alumni continued to devote their energies to work that changes society in contrast to the no-shows [volunteers who decided not to go to the South], who took up more conventional occupations" (McAdam, 1988, quoted in Youniss & Yates, 1997, p. 33).

The Empirical Study

To explore their thesis, Youniss and Yates found a program in a Catholic high school whose student body consisted largely of African Americans from middle-class backgrounds. In their senior year, the students took a required course in "social justice." They read sociological studies and critical analyses of social institutions, studied examples of Christian activism, and worked one day a week at a local soup kitchen that served meals to 300 to 400 people each day. Most of those who came for meals were "black men in their 30s and 40s. Some had served in the military. Many looked physically ill. Drug abuse was a

pervasive problem, and there were difficulties on several occasions during the year in trying to keep the dining room free of drugs and alcohol" (Youniss & Yates, 1997, p. 44). The students often met adult volunteers with whom they conversed, but the adults who came to the kitchen on court-mandated "community service" sentences were usually far more isolated and reticent than the students. Back in the classroom, the students held lively discussions about their experiences and about the sociology of social class, poverty, and homelessness.

As part of their required work for the semester, the students were required to write four short essays about their experiences in the soup kitchen and with the homeless people and the adults who worked among them. The researchers collected and analyzed these essays. Through them, they were able to see how the students' experiences were (and sometimes were not) actually changing their feelings about themselves and about social issues in small but gratifying ways.

By no means did the social justice course produce uniform political thinking or uniformly high levels of social commitment among the students. The researchers revisited the students during and after their college years and asked them to again write essays or letters about their ideas of service. Some retained the idealism they had gained in the religion class. Others had shed their idealism, and some had become somewhat cynical about social activism. The most important finding from the researchers' viewpoint, however, is that all the students agreed that the experience had "jarred them out of a passive acceptance of society as it is and started them on a path of critical thinking about society and what it might be" (Youniss & Yates, 1997, p. 126). Here is how two of the most committed students summed up the experience:

> I am currently working (volunteer) to help the homeless find jobs and homes. My lifelong aspiration is to be able to start a program where all homeless can be helped in some way. My expectation is that if this program can catch on and a bill—like the health bill—is passed, we can eliminate this plague.

> Right now I have the world in my hand. I am three months from a Harvard degree. I will be attending either Harvard or Yale law school in the fall. I am almost guaranteed more money, success, and material goods than any black kid from northeast DC could ever imagine. However, I plan to dedicate myself to creating the same opportunities for other kids in the inner city that I had. Social Justice class did this. The impact of that class was immeasurable. (quoted in Youniss & Yates, 1997, p. 126)

Text continues on page 448.

VISUAL SOCIOLOGY

AFTER 90

Imogen Cunningham's life spanned almost a century, and she spent it making loving photographic portraits of people in the cities where she lived. Born in Scranton, Pennsylvania, at the end of the nineteenth century, she learned photography in its early days, when camera equipment was extremely cumbersome and unpredictable. With the encouragement of her artistic and thoughtful father, shown here in a photo she took when he was 90, Cunningham built her own darkroom and learned every aspect of the fledgling art of photographic portraiture.

In her adult years, Cunningham lived and worked mainly in Seattle and San Francisco, but her career gave her opportunities to take photographs of people all over the world. During the period before World War II, she was one of the most celebrated photographers working for the innovative magazine *Vanity Fair*. The subjects of her portraits range from world-famous artists and scientists to unknown but singular characters such as the tattooed woman who spent her life in the carnival.

At the end of her life, Cunningham became interested in a sociological question: What ideas and activities occupy the minds of very old people? The photos shown here are a representative sample from a collection of stirring portraits she made of people who were, as she put it, "alive and kicking." She photographed many people in their 90s, like Old Norton in his shack and the nursing home resident feeling forgotten and forlorn, for whom the main challenge of life was merely to live through each day. She also photographed people who, like Cunningham herself, had the good fortune to have a passion for work and ac-

tivity and felt little concern about their physical deterioration because they were absorbed in their creative efforts.

Cunningham died at the age of 93, just as the volume containing these photographs was about to be published. Although she missed the chance to celebrate the appearance of her book about the very old, she herself lived long enough to have the pleasure (denied to many artists) of seeing her work honored during her lifetime. Even from the few photos presented here, we can readily see that her work captures the mystery of the human spirit and demonstrates that extreme age does not extinguish the love of life.

The Sociological Observer

(See photo on page 442.)

Since the friends are playing chess outdoors while wearing overcoats, we can assume that the game is taking place in

She said to me, "When you come here nobody knows where you are."

This woman had been at the carnival all her life, but I found her in the hospital. It looks like lace, doesn't it?

the colder months of the northeastern fall or early spring. And since the men are on the same side of the table, either they are partners against a third person or one of the friends is simply an observer. If they are motivated to sit outdoors in overcoats to concentrate on a game of chess, we can infer that the activity is highly rewarding to them. Indeed, activity theory argues that abandoning mentally and physically challenging activities can lead to despondency and debility. Recent medical research supports sociological theories that emphasize the need to engage in stimulating activities as we age. The research shows that mentally stimulating activity is associated with lower rates of Alzheimer's disease and other forms of senile dementia (*Neurology*, 2002).

She is a distinguished radiobiologist who asked me to photograph her. I wasn't taking on commissions anymore, but I did it because she didn't care if she looked old and she didn't hate her face.

Old Norton lives by himself in his shack.

My father at 90.

Research like that of Youniss and Yates does not provide direct support for the AmeriCorps and Teach for America programs or for the thousands of internships and community projects that enlist the idealism of America's young adults. But it does support the argument that when a society eliminates opportunities for public service it discourages a generation of its young people from participating in the process of extending equality of opportunity beyond the neighborhoods of the comfortable and affluent. Such discouragement, in turn, increases cynicism, selfishness, and the growth of socially destructive youth cultures.

SUMMARY

Sources of Age Stratification

- In many societies, age determines a great deal about the opportunities open to a person and what kind of life that person leads.
- The study of aging and the elderly is termed *gerontology*.
- All societies channel people into *age grades,* or sets of statuses and roles based on age. The transitions among these age grades create a *life course* and are often marked by ceremonies known as *rites of passage.*
- *Age cohorts* are people of about the same age who are passing through life's stages together.
- The baby boom cohorts, which were produced by rapid increases in the birthrate from about 1945 through the early 1960s, have profoundly influenced American society.
- A sizable proportion of the children of the baby boom generation, the "baby boom echo," are members of minority groups.
- By *life expectancy* we mean the average number of years a member of a given population can expect to live beyond his or her present age.
- As life expectancy in a population increases, the proportion of the population that is dependent on the adult cohorts also increases.

Age Stratification and Inequality

- In urban industrial societies, there are distinct patterns of stratification in which age defines the roles one plays and the rewards one can expect.
- The forces of social change unleashed by colonialism, industrialization, urbanization, and population growth have tended to disrupt the formal age grade systems of smaller, more isolated societies.
- Social definitions of childhood differ immensely throughout the industrial world as well as between modern and traditional societies. As a result of in-

creasing incomes and the passage of child labor laws, children became economically "worthless" but emotionally "priceless." However, there is a growing gap between "priceless" children and children who bear a heavy burden of poverty and deprivation.

- A century ago, the largest segment of the U.S. population living in poverty or near-poverty conditions was the elderly. As a result of programs such as Social Security and Medicare, rates of poverty among the elderly have decreased dramatically. However, the situation is not nearly so positive for elderly members of minority groups.
- As people age, they experience more medical problems and disabilities, but this does not mean that they must inevitably withdraw from social life. Social scientists who study the situation of the elderly point out that longer life spans need to be accompanied by new concepts of social roles in more advanced years.
- *Ageism* is an ideology that justifies prejudice or discrimination based on age. As the proportion of older people in a society increases, as is occurring in the United States and Europe, the prevalence of ageism also increases.

Theories of Aging

- As the population as a whole has aged, the impact of the elderly on American society has increased. This is changing the way sociologists view old age. Before the 1970s, the most popular social-scientific view of aging was disengagement theory, the belief that as people grow older they gradually disengage from their earlier roles. An alternative view of the elderly, known as activity theory, states that the elderly need activities that will serve as outlets for their creativity and energy. Today gerontologists tend to reject both of these theories, seeing older people demanding opportunities to lead their lives in a variety of ways based on individual habits and preferences.

Death and Dying

- The growing proportion of elderly people in the population has led to increased concern about the quality of life of the elderly and about death and the dying process.

- One outcome of this concern is the hospice movement, which attempts to provide dying people and their loved ones with a comfortable, dignified alternative to hospital death.

GLOSSARY

gerontology: The study of aging and older people. (p. 425)

age grade: A set of statuses and roles based on age. (p. 425)

life course: A pathway along an age-differentiated, socially created sequence of transitions. (p. 425)

rite of passage: A ceremony marking the transition to a new stage of a culturally defined life course. (p. 425)

age cohort: A set of people of about the same age who are passing through the life course together. (p. 425)

life expectancy: The average number of years a member of a given population can expect to live. (p. 432)

psychosocial risk behaviors: Behaviors that are detrimental to health, such as smoking and heavy drinking. (p. 440)

lifetime negative experiences: Experiences that cause long-term stress, such as the death of a child or spouse. (p. 440)

ageism: An ideology that justifies prejudice and discrimination based on age. (p. 441)

INTERNET RESOURCES

Virtual Society: The Wadsworth Sociology Resource Center
(http://sociology.wadsworth.com)
At Virtual Society you can access a wide range of enrichment material to aid your study of sociology. From the main page, click on the Student Resources link and find your course and this textbook. Next, select the chapter you are presently studying from the pull-down menu. Among the useful options for each self-study chapter are online links and exercises, flashcards, practical study tips, and practice quizzes for each chapter.

MC   MicroCase Online
From the Virtual Society home page, click on MicroCase Online to access book-specific MicroCase exercises that allow you to further explore sociological issues and principles presented in the text.

InfoTrac College Edition
Another unique option available to you at the Student Resources section at Virtual Society is InfoTrac College Edition, an online library with access to hundreds of scholarly and popular periodicals. Below are suggested search terms for this chapter, but this resource also allows you to fit your study of sociology to your own interests by searching custom keywords.

Life course

Baby boom

Ageism

Life expectancy

Sociometrics
(www.socio.com)
The Web site for the journal *Sociometrics*. It is devoted to the study of social groups and networks and how they are related to social issues of all kinds (e.g., adolescence, health, disability).

READ ALL ABOUT IT

93 PIKE ST.   624-0140

Change is occurring all the time in every major institution of society: The family must adapt to high rates of divorce and remarriage; markets are continually introducing new products and new methods of production; governments must constantly adjust to pressures from opposing interest groups—the list could be made much longer. The processes of institutional change are endless and often complex, but increasingly they can be understood and even predicted through the application of sociological concepts and research.

Social Institutions

In this set of chapters, the concepts and perspectives discussed earlier in the book will be applied to an analysis of several major social institutions. Chapter 16 explores the changing nature of the family, and especially research on the ways in which family statuses and roles are changing and the social forces that seem to account for these changes. The other chapters in Part 4 explore other institutions—proceeding from an analysis of how each is typically organized to a discussion of how it is changing. Chapters 17 and 18 discuss two major cultural institutions—religion and education—whose role is to transmit and reinforce a society's most cherished values. Chapter 19 deals with the roles and statuses that generate jobs and income. Chapter 20 shows how political institutions determine "who gets what, when, and how." It also deals with the grave difficulties facing nations attempting to institute the rule of law. Finally, in Chapter 21 the institutions of science and technology are analyzed, with special attention to their role in health care.

The Family

© Eugene Richards

The two photos shown here of "the birth of a family" convey much of the joy of family intimacy: the young couple just before she gives birth and the new father thrilled by his first experience with their child as the mother lays the baby on his chest. In the first photo, we see a couple about to become a family. They will quickly take on a host of new roles with new demands and gratifications that will challenge their love in ways that they can hardly anticipate. In the second photo, our eyes linger on the baby's tiny, perfect fingers and toes and the rapt gaze of the new mother. Is there the slightest hint in the man's somewhat rigid fingers that the crying newborn's vulnerability may tinge his joy with feelings of awkwardness? We cannot know this for sure, but the early days and months of parenthood are filled with many emotions—and love, awkwardness, joy, anxiety, and fatigue are prominent among them.

If we examine these photos from a historical perspective, we will surmise that this is a contemporary couple. There are few clues in the scenes themselves. Her flannel nightgown could be from any decade of the last two centuries. The plain gold band on his left hand is a timeless symbol of matrimony. What reveals them as people of our time is the photographer's choice of them as subjects. No doubt couples in earlier decades behaved in exactly similar ways, but they were not often encouraged to display their joy and intimacy in public. In the early twentieth century, it was more common for photographers to capture the gender-specific aspects of childbirth. The woman's joy at receiving the baby, often with adoring grandmothers or nurses in the background, expressed the heavily gender-specific quality of the childbirth scene. The man was portrayed in a stereotypical fashion, pacing in the hospital corridor, perhaps with one cigarette in hand and another still burning in a nearby ashtray, symbols of his ineffectual nervousness. Other photos of early family moments would focus on the father's first glimpse of the baby through the windows of the hospital nursery. Contemporary approaches to childbirth encourage more direct involvement of the father in the birthing process. They advocate more immediate contact between the new parents and the infant. For thousands of couples, going through the experience of childbirth together provides some of life's most thrilling memories.

As we gaze at these most personal glimpses into family life, we may also be reminded of the mystery of human love and attraction. We come back to these mysteries in the Visual Sociology section of the chapter, which captures people in a variety of intimate embraces, all of which convey the power of love and intimacy. Between this intimate chapter opening and the return to intimacy at the chapter's end, however, we will be dealing with many of the challenges to love and intimacy that arise in today's world. The risk in taking this sociological journey into the institutions of family and marriage is that we may forget to what extent love—between a couple, or among siblings, or between parents and children—is a force that can overcome many of the shocks and strains of modern life. On the other hand, we will learn that there are ways in which society makes love of various kinds possible and even inevitable.

FOCUS QUESTIONS:

• How has the family been changing as an institution of modern societies?

• What are the most significant trends in marriage, divorce, and remarriage, and how does divorce affect family members?

• What explanations do sociological perspectives offer for the causes and consequences of changes in family structure and family relations?

© Eugene Richards

THE NATURE OF FAMILIES

We continually hear warnings about the "death of the family" in modern societies. As early as 1934, sociologists like William Fielding Ogburn were writing about the decline of the family. "Prior to modern times," according to Ogburn, "the power and prestige of the family was due to . . . functions it performed. . . . The dilemma of the modern family is caused by the loss of many of these functions in recent times" (Ogburn & Nimkoff, 1934, p. 139). More recent commentators have pointed to the so-called sexual revolution as a threat to this basic social institution. Others insist that even in the face of trends toward single parenthood, cohabitation without marriage, divorce and remarriage, and smaller family size, the family is "here to stay." Recent surveys of how Americans view the future of marriage and the family confirm this conclusion. The overwhelming majority of Americans value marriage, children, and family. Yet they also believe that their commitments to marriage and family are more voluntary and less obligatory than was the case in previous generations. The same changes are true in all other urban industrial nations. The family as we know it will not disappear, but it will take on new forms and functions, as we will see throughout this chapter (Bianchi & Casper, 2000; Thornton & Young-DeMarco, 2001).

In this chapter, we will see that there are so many variations in family form, even within a single society, that it has become increasingly difficult to speak of "the family" as a single set of statuses, roles, and norms. Nevertheless, it remains true that in all known societies almost everyone is socialized within a network of family rights and obligations known as *family role relations* (Goode, 1964). In the first section of this chapter, therefore, we examine the family as an institution and show how family role relations have changed in the twentieth century. The second section focuses on how the basic sociological perspectives explain changes in family roles and functions and in the interactions between parents and children. In the third section, we look at the dynamics of family formation—especially mate selection, marriage, divorce, and remarriage.

The Family as an Institution

There is a big difference between a particular family and the family as a social institution. Your family, for example, has a particular structure of statuses (mother, father, sister, brother, grandmother, etc.), depending on who and where its members are. Your immediate family is also part of an extended kinship system (aunts, uncles, cousins, grandparents, etc.) that also varies according to how many branches you and your immediate family actually keep

track of. The family as a social institution, however, comprises a set of statuses, roles, norms, and values devoted to achieving important social goals. Those goals include the social control of reproduction, the socialization of new generations, and the "social placement" of children in the institutions of the larger society (colleges, business firms, and so forth).

SOCIAL PLACEMENT   "Social placement" refers to the ways in which parents and relatives work to ensure that their children will achieve the same or higher social-class positions as their parents. When teachers comment about young children "coming from good families" or when others comment on how "well brought up" a child appears to be, they are referring to the ways in which the parents have developed the child's *cultural capital,* all the knowledge and norms of behavior valued by higher-class people. Reading books to children, listening to classical music with them, teaching them how to be polite, being concerned with how they dress, spending time visiting their schools, pushing them to succeed in school—these are all ways in which parents help place their children socially by developing their cultural capital (Bourdieu, 1993; Coleman, 1994). Extensive research on families and social mobility documents how family background and behavior influence the way children and adolescents are perceived and treated in school. For example, a recent study of primary-school teachers in England found that teachers expect higher achievement from children whose parents have good spoken language skills and seem to read a lot to their children. These expectations, even at a very early age, can help determine how much children enjoy school and how well they learn (Feiler & Webster, 1999).

THE FAMILY AND INSTITUTIONAL DIFFERENTIATION These are not the only goals that the family is expected to fulfill. In many societies, especially tribal or peasant societies, the family performs almost all the functions necessary to meet the basic needs of its members. Those needs are listed in Figure 16.1, which compares less differentiated *gemeinschaft* or village-type societies with more differentiated *gesellschaft* societies like that of the United States. It shows that most of the functions that were traditionally performed by the family are now performed either partly or wholly by other social institutions that are specially adapted to performing those functions.

Figure 16.1 only begins to illustrate the institutional complexity of modern societies. Not only are there many more separate institutions in modern societies, but basic social functions are often divided among several institutions. Thus the institutions that meet protective and social-control needs include governments at all levels, the military, the judiciary, and the police. Replacement needs are met by the family through mating and repro-

TYPE OF SOCIETY

SOCIAL FUNCTION	Less Differentiated (gemeinschaft)	More Differentiated (gesellschaft)
Communication among members: first through language alone and then through specialized institutions devoted to communication	Family, kin networks	Mass media
Production of goods and services: from the basic items required for survival to items designed to satisfy new, more diverse needs created by increasing affluence	Family groups	Economic institutions
Distribution of goods and services: within societies at first, and later, with the rise of trade and markets, between societies as well	Extended family, local markets	Markets, transportation institutions
Protection and defense: including protection from the elements and predators and extending to defense against human enemies	Family, village, tribe	Armed forces, police, insurance agencies, health care institutions
Replacement of members: both the biological replacement of the deceased and the socialization of newcomers to the society	Family	Family, schools, religious institutions
Social placement: to establish roles and status of children in society as they mature by developing their cultural capital	Family	Family, schools, religious institutions, civic voluntary associations
Control of members: to ensure that the society's institutions continue to function and that conflict is reduced or eliminated	Family	Family, religious institutions, government in all forms

Figure 16.1 The Family: Institutional Differentiation

Source: Adapted from Lenski & Lenski, 1982. *Human Societies,* 7 ed. © 1982 McGraw-Hill Companies. Reprinted with permission.

duction. In addition to the family, religious institutions, education, and other cultural institutions meet the need to socialize new generations.

The family's ability to meet the goals society expects it to meet is often complicated by rapid social change. For example, many families in industrial communities throughout the United States were quite good at preparing their children for blue-collar manufacturing jobs, but those jobs have been eliminated as a result of automation and the globalization of the economy. For many families, therefore, it is no longer clear how they can equip their offspring to compete in the new job market.

When there are major changes in other institutions in a society, such as economic institutions, families must adapt to those changes. Similarly, when the family changes, other institutions will be affected. As an example, consider the impact of the "sexual revolution" that began in the 1920s. During that decade, often called the Roaring Twenties, young adults began to upset the moral code that had regulated the behavior of couples for generations, at least among people who considered themselves "respectable." According to this traditional set of norms, women were the guardians

of morality. Men were more likely to give in to sexual desire, "but girls of respectable families were supposed to have no such temptations" (Allen, 1931, p. 74). After World War I, however, "respectable" young women began to reject the **double standard,** by which they had to adhere to a different and more restrictive moral code from that applied to men. They began smoking cigarettes, wearing short skirts, and drinking bootleg gin in automobiles or at "petting parties." These changes in the behavior of couples produced far-reaching changes in other institutions. Women demanded more education and more opportunities to earn income. This in turn led to demands for new institutions such as coeducational colleges and integrated workplaces, as well as greater access by women to existing institutions such as medicine, law, and science. These changes in women's expectations and behavior, along with the increasing educational and occupational mobility of men after the world wars, contributed immensely to changes in traditional family roles—especially the weakening of the role of the father as the central and most powerful authority figure in the family. The consequences of these fundamental changes in family roles are still felt today.

Changes in the institutions in one area of social life can place tremendous pressure on those in other sectors. This is especially true in the case of the family, as will be evident throughout this chapter. But before we examine the ways in which families have changed in the twentieth century, it is necessary to define some terms that are often used in discussing the family.

Defining the Family

The family is a central institution in all human societies, although it may take many different forms (Bianchi & Casper, 2000; Cherlin, 1996). A **family** is a group of people related by blood, marriage, or adoption. Blood relations are often called *consanguineous attachments* (from the Latin *sanguis,* meaning "blood"). Relations between adult persons living together according to the norms of marriage or other intimate relationships are called *conjugal relations.* The role relations among people who consider themselves to be related in these ways are termed **kinship.**

The familiar kinship terms—*father, mother, brother, sister, grandfather, grandmother, uncle, aunt, niece, nephew, cousin*— refer to specific sets of role relations that may vary greatly from one culture to another. In many African societies, for example, "mother's brother" is someone to whom the male child becomes closer than he does to his father and from whom he receives more day-to-day socialization than he may from his father. It must be noted that biological or "blood" ties are not necessarily stronger than ties of adoption. Adopted children are usually loved with the same intensity as children raised by their biological parents. And many fam-

ily units in the United States and other societies include "fictive kin"—people who are so close to members of the family that they are considered kin despite the absence of blood ties (Stack, 1974). Finally, neither blood ties nor marriage nor adoption adequately describes the increasingly common relationship between unmarried people who consider themselves a couple or a family (Medalie & Cole-Kelly, 2002).

The smallest units of family structure are usually called **nuclear families.** This term is usually used to refer to a couple and their children, if any. Nowadays one frequently hears the phrase "the traditional nuclear family" used to refer to a

© Paul Conklin/Monkmeyer

These photos show a conventional nuclear family, with a father, mother, and two children, and an extended family, with three generations of family members, including aunts, uncles, and cousins. Although these may once have been the most common forms of traditional and modern family structures, the numbers of single-parent families and families that share custody of the children after divorce are increasing.

© Stephanie Maze/Woodfin Camp & Associates

SOCIOLOGICAL METHODS

Kinship Diagrams

Kinship diagrams are used in both anthropology and sociology to denote lines of descent among people who are related by blood (children and their parents and siblings) and by marriage. Kinship terms are often confusing because families, especially large ones, can be rather complex social structures. It may help to devote a little time to the kinship diagram shown here.

To understand the chart, one must know the meanings of the symbols used; these are explained in the key to the chart. "Ego" is the person who is taken as the point of reference. You can readily see that Ego has both a family of orientation and a family of procreation. So does Ego's spouse. Ego's parents become the in-laws of the spouse, and the spouse's parents are Ego's in-laws.

Kinship diagrams like this one provide a visual model of family statuses extending over more than one generation. They are a very useful way of analyzing the social structure of families. We can quickly see the generations in the family, from Ego's grandparents to Ego's children. We can also compare the nuclear and extended families of Ego's parents and cousins.

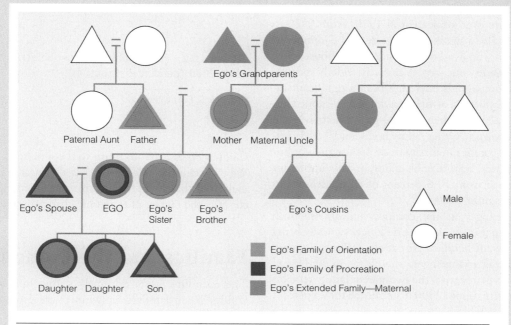

This diagram shows the family relationships of a hypothetical individual, Ego. Ego (a female in this example) was born and socialized in what sociologists call the family of orientation. Ego formed a family of procreation through marriage or cohabitation.

married mother and father and their children living together. But as we will see throughout this chapter, there is no longer a "typical" nuclear family structure. Increasingly, therefore, sociologists use the term *nuclear family* to refer to two or more people related by consanguineous or conjugal ties or by adoption who share a household; it does not require that both husband and wife be present in the household or that there be any specific set of role relations among the members of the household (Benokraitis, 1996).

The nuclear family in which a person is born and socialized is termed the **family of orientation.** The nuclear family a person forms through marriage or cohabitation is known

as the **family of procreation.** The relationship between the two is shown in the Sociological Methods box above.

By studying the chart in the box, we can identify Ego's family of orientation and family of procreation. But like most people, Ego also has an **extended family** that includes all the nuclear families of Ego's blood relatives—that is, all of Ego's uncles, aunts, cousins, and grandparents. Ego's spouse also has an extended family, which is not indicated in the chart, nor is it defined as part of Ego's extended family. But relationships with the spouse's extended family are likely to occupy plenty of Ego's time. Indeed, as the chart shows, the marriage bond brings together far more than two individuals. Most married couples have extensive networks of kin to which they must relate in many ways throughout life.

Variations in Family Structure

For the past several years, sociologists have been demonstrating that the traditional household consisting of two parents and their children is no longer the typical American family. This is not a value judgment that sociologists applaud or deplore, but a matter of demographic fact that needs to be carefully assessed. Figure 16.2 shows that the so-called traditional family of mother, father, and children accounts for somewhat less than one-fourth of all households, down from over 40 percent in 1970. From 1970 to 2000, there was also a significant increase in the number of men and women who live alone, outside family households. These are primarily but not exclusively elderly people. Among family households, there has been a significant increase in the proportion of married couples without children (although their children may be grown and living in families of their own). "Other family households" refers primarily to single-parent families with no spouse present but with other relatives, who may be children. This important category increased from 10.6 percent of all households in 1970 to 16 percent in 2000.

Do these changes in the composition of American households mean that children are no longer typically being raised in two-parent families? Not at all. Table 16.1 shows trends in the living arrangements of children in the United States. From this perspective, the two-parent family remains the dominant form, but in 2000 it accounted for 73 percent of families with children, down from 93 percent in the 1950s. The difference is accounted for by the rapid increase since the 1950s of single-mother and, more recently, single-father families.

These trends point to a growing diversity of family types, including far more people living alone and far more women raising children alone. There are also more households composed of unrelated single people who live together not just because they are friends but because only by doing so can they afford to live away from their families of orientation. Thus, when they discuss family norms and roles, sociologists must be careful not to represent the traditional nuclear family, or even the married couple, as typical. As an institution, the contemporary family comprises a far greater array of household types than ever before.

Sociologists are divided on the meaning and implications of these facts. For some, the trend toward greater diversity of family forms means that the family as an institution is adapting to change. For others, the decline of the family composed of two married parents living with their biological

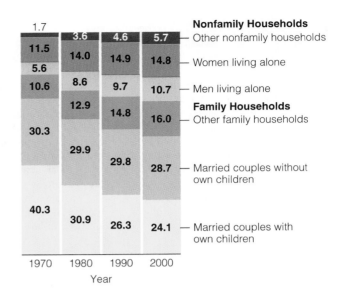

Figure 16.2   Households by Type: Selected Years, 1970–2000 (percent distribution)

Source: U.S. Census Bureau.

children poses a serious threat to the well-being of children. We will return to this debate over the meaning (and explanation) of changes in family form and function, but first we consider the impact of economic change on the family.

Families and the Economy

The economy exerts extremely strong influences on the family. When family breadwinners are promoted and income increases, there may be more vacations, better food, or a greater chance that the children will be able to go to

TABLE 16.1

Trends in Single-Parent and Two-Parent Families with Children Under Age 18, 1950–2000

	Percentage distribution of families		
Year	Single mother	Single father	Two parents
1950	6	1	93
1960	8	1	91
1970	10	1	89
1980	18	2	80
1990	20	4	76
2000	22	5	73

Source: U.S. Census Bureau.

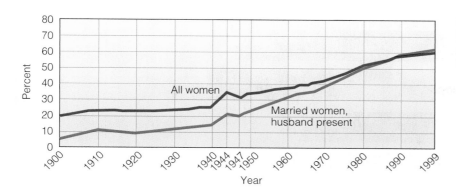

Figure 16.3 Percentage of Women in the Labor Force

Source: Moen, 2001.

college, to name only a few possibilities. When income decreases, perhaps because of recession and layoffs or because one of the breadwinners leaves the family, parents and children usually must lower their expectations and spend less. Economic mobility, upward or downward, often means that the family will move to another neighborhood or community, perhaps to another part of the nation, and this uprooting can be extremely difficult for all concerned—especially adolescents, for whom peer relations count so heavily. These examples hardly begin to account for the influence of work and the economy on family life. Think, for example, about how your own family's daily schedules are based on the need to cope with the sometimes conflicting demands of work and family activities.

In the United States and most urban industrial nations, increasing numbers of married women with children are in the labor force (Moen, 2001). This striking social change has occurred because families need the income women earn and, in a smaller proportion of families, because women with high-level skills wish to pursue professional careers. Whatever the specific reasons, the trends over the past century have all been in the same direction: toward more families in which both parents work. Figure 16.3 shows that during World War II there was a strong upsurge in the number of women in the labor force. After the war ended, employment of married women declined, but the decline was temporary; the trend over the entire century, which accelerated after the war, was upward. Figure 16.4 shows that dual earners are so important in allowing contemporary families to make ends meet that only 13 percent of married couples now conform to the older norm of the "traditional family" with children in which only the husband is in the labor force.

In families in which both parents work, time pressures on the family increase. As family members work longer hours, role conflicts and stresses within the family also increase. Most couples argue most often about money, but allocation of time within the family is another source of constant tension. Figure 16.5 shows that most workers are working longer hours but that the increase is greatest for men and women in their child-rearing years.

FAMILIES AND POVERTY   Economic conditions can produce drastic changes in the number of families that experience deprivation and poverty. At this writing, the recession following the end of the technology "bubble" and in the aftermath of the terrorist attacks is reducing working hours and income for thousands of low-wage workers and for thousands of others in the middle classes. Although it is too soon to know how long the recession will last, the last major economic downturn in the U.S. economy drove an additional 500,000 white families, 250,000 black families, and 230,000 Hispanic families below the official poverty line.

In the mid-1990s, the United States ended the system of Aid to Families with Dependent Children, which allowed single mothers to collect benefits for their children, and replaced it with a variety of state programs funded by

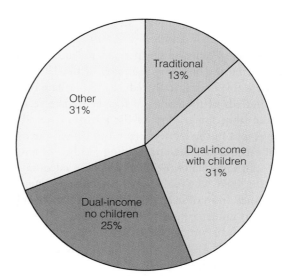

Note: Traditional households include married-couple households with children in which only the husband is in the labor force.

Figure 16.4 Types of U.S. Married-Couple Households

Source: Population Reference Bureau, 2003.

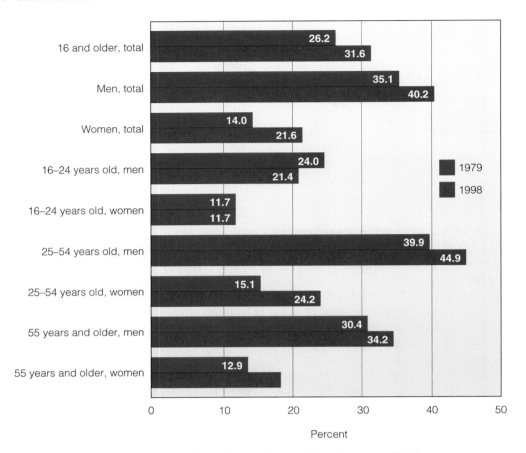

Figure 16.5 Percentage of Workers Who Work 41 or More Hours per Week

Source: Moen, 2001.

the federal government under the heading of Temporary Assistance of Needy Families (TANF). These programs encourage or require single parents to enter the labor force. During the booming economy of the 1990s, most states were able to drastically reduce their welfare rolls and help hundreds of thousands of former welfare recipients enter the labor force. Most of the jobs they found were low-level jobs in the service sector, but overall the experience of earning incomes and holding steady jobs has been positive. In some states, women have been encouraged to marry the men who fathered their children, men who were banned from official residence in households receiving benefits under the old system (Harden, 2001).

FAMILY POVERTY AND FOOD INSECURITY   Recent research on welfare-to-work programs in the United States shows that it is extremely difficult for single parents, especially women, to lift their families out of poverty with the incomes they earn at work. Success in lifting single-parent families out of poverty varies from one state to another, depending on local rates of employment and the quality of

job training offered, but most jobs available for former welfare recipients are at the low end of the wage scale, and less than half of those who gain jobs are able to escape from poverty. More disturbing, however, is the growing number of extremely poor families (approximately 16 percent in the pilot studies) whose incomes are less than half of the poverty threshold income. While they have been widely hailed as a successful new policy, mandatory work programs and deep cuts in other forms of assistance to poor families with children appear to be increasing the problem of food insecurity (Cancian et al., 2003).

Food security—the assured access to enough food for a healthy and active life—is widely acknowledged as an essential component of well being. But national and regional studies suggest that a startlingly high number of American families are considered "food insecure"; these families experience persistent anxiety about their ability to afford food, eat inadequately, or skip meals because they lack the money to buy food. (Barfield, 2003, p.19)

Increasing numbers of families with wage earners—the working poor—are finding it necessary to visit food pantries to cope with food insecurity. The *Current Population Survey* (2002) estimates that there are 32,000 food pantries nationwide, which distribute almost 3 billion pounds of food a year, the equivalent of 2.2 billion meals. It reports that 11 percent of American families are not always sure where they will obtain their next meal. A far smaller proportion—3.3 percent—of families actually experience food insecurity with bouts of hunger. But food insecurity is a more serious problem among single-parent families. A Wisconsin study found that 39 percent of single mothers who visited food pantries had experienced food insecurity with hunger. (See Table 16.2.) Another striking finding is that 48 percent of single mothers who had jobs were visiting food pantries.

The table includes "income-to-poverty ratios" for food pantry clients and food stamp recipients. The income-to-poverty ratio is a measure of how a family's actual income compares to the official poverty threshold for a family of that size. A ratio of 50 percent, for example, means that the family's actual income is less than half of the official poverty income for families of that size; a ratio between 50 percent and 100 percent means that the family's actual income falls between half and all of the official poverty income. The table shows that 41 percent of single mothers who used food pantries and 49 percent of those who received food stamps earned less than half of the official poverty income for their family size. But only 12 percent of food pantry clients and 11 percent of food stamp recipients were earning 100 percent to 130 percent of the poverty level income. Thus, use of these vital safety net institutions increases markedly with extreme poverty (Barfield, 2003).

Female single parents who are not in the labor force remain at the bottom of the society's stratification system and constitute the most vulnerable segment of the population. Their children are at risk of severe health, emotional, and legal difficulties, and face the possibility of joining the approximately 312,000 children who have been removed from their parents' supervision and placed in foster care (*Statistical Abstract*, 2002). Poverty makes family life far more difficult than it might otherwise be, but even for many families above the poverty level, adjusting to changes in the family can be difficult, as we see in the following sections.

Parenting, Stepparenting, and Social Change

It has never been easy to be a parent. Keeping a family intact and raising children who are confident and capable and will become loving, capable parents themselves is a

TABLE 16.2

Profiles of Single-Mother Food Pantry and Food Stamp Participants

	Food Pantry Clients (% of total)	Food Stamp Recipients (% of total)
Age		
25 or younger	16	25
26–35	41	41
36–45	33	27
46+	10	7
Number of Children		
1	31	29
2	35	33
3 or more	34	38
Child under 6	50	58
Labor Force Status		
Employed	48	46
Unemployed & looking for work	15	13
Disabled—out of labor force	12	10
Out of labor force—other	24	30
Education		
Less than high school	30	37
High school/GED	34	39
More than high school	35	24
Food Security Status		
Food secure	19	46
Food insecure without hunger	42	36
Food insecure with hunger	39	18
Income-to-Poverty Ratio		
<50%	41	49
50%–100%	38	36
100%–130%	12	11
130%–185%	9	4

Source: Adapted from Barfield, 2003.

domestic miracle. For better or (sometimes) worse, most people learn to be parents by following the examples set by their own parents when they were children. Much as we may swear that when our turn comes we will improve on the way our parents performed their roles, we often find ourselves acting toward our children much as our parents acted toward us. In fact, many parents seek help from family counselors because they are shocked to find themselves doing and saying the same things to their children that their parents did to them (Scarf, 1995).

Many other adults and children will experience major reorganizations of their families as couples divorce and remarry. When stepfamilies are formed, family members must adapt to new role relations as stepchildren and stepparents, often while maintaining many of their obligations in the original family. Sharon L. Hanna, an expert on stepfamilies, notes that there are more than 20.6 million stepparents in the United States and estimates that in the early years of the twenty-first century, almost 50 percent of all Americans will be part of a stepfamily (Hanna, 1994).

"Stepfamilies," sociologists Frank Furstenberg and Andrew Cherlin point out, "are a curious example of an organizational merger; they join two family cultures into a single household" (1991, p. 83). While this joining of family cultures also occurs in first marriages, in those marriages the couple usually has time to work out differences before children are born. In the case of stepfamilies, the task of working out a mutually acceptable concept of the family may be more stressful than the partners anticipated.

Sociologists point out that positive relationships in any family do not just happen but are worked on consciously through much learning and discussion. These efforts are particularly necessary in stepfamilies (Ganong & Coleman, 1999). Some studies of stepfamilies show that new stepparents often conceive of themselves as "healers," people who can use the force of love to form strong bonds of attachment between two sets of children. Very often, however, the children cling to the fantasy that their original parents will get back together, and the stepparents' efforts may meet with frustration. Stepparents who manage to reorganize the family successfully tend to be diplomatic and sensitive and to avoid competing with biological parents. They gain the support of their spouses and wait for opportunities to gain the acceptance of their stepchildren (Papernow, 1988).

However, resolving the complexity and ambiguity of roles in reorganized families is no simple matter. Many factors come into play when a new family is formed. For example, Furstenberg and Cherlin point out that legal norms "reinforce the second-class status of stepparents" as nonbiological partners (1991, p. 80). A biological father is held responsible for child support even if he has never lived with the child, whereas a stepfather incurs no financial responsibility for a child even if he has lived with that child for many years. "The only legal recourse for stepparents who want to claim rights and responsibilities is to adopt their stepchildren, an act that seems to symbolize a deeper and more permanent tie, more like a biological relationship" (Furstenberg & Cherlin, 1991, p. 80).

Members of all kinds of families experience particular stress in times of economic hardship or when other social changes influence the family. Stress and change in the larger society may cause parents to feel unable to perform their roles as providers of material and emotional support. In the early decades of the twentieth century, for example, the combination of frequent severe recessions, high rates of industrial accidents, and lack of adequate health care had a significant impact on families. Fathers were often forced to leave their families in search of work; infection often claimed the lives of mothers during childbirth. Demographers estimate that at the beginning of the twentieth century, when divorce rates were still extremely low, almost 25 percent of all children lost at least one parent through death before reaching the age of 15 (Uhlenberg, 1980).

By midcentury, improvements in health care had reduced this proportion to 5 percent, but divorce rates had increased to 11 percent, and another 6 percent of children were born to unmarried parents. Thus, even in the 1950s—the most stable decade for families and children—demographers estimate that 22 percent of children were being raised in families that had only one parent as a result of death, separation, divorce, or single parenthood (Bumpass, Raley, & Sweet, 1995). Even this relative stability lasted only a decade. By the end of the 1950s, divorce rates had begun their precipitous rise, and so had rates of births to unmarried parents. By 2000, almost 30 percent of births in the United States were to unmarried mothers (National Center for Health Statistics, 2000).

These profound changes in family composition have many causes and many consequences. As families age, children move through the school years, adolescence, and young adulthood while parents pass through adulthood to their senior years. Throughout this period, all families seek to accomplish certain basic socialization goals. As the diversity of families increases, the ways in which they attempt to reach these goals differs, but the goals themselves do not change nearly as much.

The Family Life Cycle

Sociologist Paul Glick, an innovator in the field of family demography and ecology, developed the concept of the *family life cycle,* the idea that families pass through a sequence of five stages:

1. Family formation: first marriage
2. Start of childbearing: birth of first child
3. End of childbearing: birth of last child
4. "Empty nest": marriage of last child
5. "Family dissolution": death of one spouse (Glick & Parke, 1965)

These are typical stages in the life cycle of conventional families. Although other stages could be identified within each of these—such as retirement (the years between leaving the workforce and the death of one spouse) or the "baby" stage (during which the couple is rearing preschool-age children)—the ones that Glick listed are most useful for comparative purposes.

Figure 16.6   Estimated Median Age at First Marriage, United States, 1890–2000

Source: Data from U.S. Census Bureau.

As the "typical" family structure becomes increasingly difficult to identify because of changes in family norms, the stages of family development also vary. In fact, the stages of the family life cycle have become increasingly useful as indicators of change rather than as stages that all or most families can be expected to experience. The Census Bureau estimates, for example, that there are almost 4.9 million heterosexual couples in the United States who are cohabiting. This number represents an almost tenfold increase since 1970, when an estimated 500,000 cohabiting couples were counted (*Statistical Abstract,* 2002). (Note that the census figures include only heterosexual couples and therefore vastly underestimate the total number of cohabiting couples.) Although most cohabiting couples will eventually marry, about half will break up or continue to live together without marrying (Farley, 1996).

When sociologists look at the median age at which people experience the various stages of the family life cycle, significant trends emerge. Consider age at first marriage: In 1890, the median age of Americans at first marriage was 26.1 years for men and 22 years for women; in the 1950s and 1960s, it reached the historic lows of 22.8 and 20.3. Then it began rising again slowly, until by 2000 it was 26.7 for men and 25.0 for women (see Figure 16.6). Age at first marriage tends to be somewhat higher for males than for females and is associated with educational attainment; more highly educated people are more likely to delay marriage. There is also a tendency for members of minority groups to marry later because of the proportionately lower income levels of these populations. People with lower incomes tend to delay marriage or not to marry because they lack the material means to sustain a marital relationship (Farley, 1996).

As it passes through the family life cycle, every family experiences changes in its system of role relations. In analyzing these changes, social scientists often modify Glick's stages in order to focus more sharply on interactions within the family. An example is the set of developmental stages shown in Figure 16.7. There are major emotional challenges at each of these stages. For example, families with adolescent children must adapt to the children's growing independence. This may involve going through a stage of negotiation over such issues as money, cars, and dating. But researchers who study family life note that parents are often confused about how to interact with their adolescent children. They may assume that it is normal for adolescents to leave the family circle and to become enmeshed in their own peer groups, which often get into trouble. However, as Carol Gilligan (1987) has pointed out, adolescents also want the continuing guidance and involvement of adults.

Social changes that create hardships for young people—especially declines in less-skilled manufacturing jobs, increases in low-wage service-sector jobs, and shortages of low-rent housing—have a major impact on the transition from dependence to independence for many young adults in the United States and elsewhere in the world. The Population Reference Bureau reports that "compared with the 1970s, more young adults (ages 18 to 24) are living at home with their parents. . . . Over half (54 percent) of all 18–24 year olds lived with their parents in 1991" (Ahlburg & De Vita, 1992, p. 9). Sociologist Paul Attewell, who is conducting research on what he terms "incompletely launched young adults," observes that continuing difficulties in finding work will oblige many young adults to live with their family of orientation, a situation that often frustrates family members' expectations about "normal" movement through the life course (cited in Lehman-Haupt, 1999).

In later stages of family life, the parents must be willing to watch their grown children take on the challenges of family formation while they themselves worry about maintaining their marital roles or caring for their own parents. The latter issue is taking on increasing importance in aging societies like the United States. And because women are

Stage	Emotional Process	Required Changes In Family Status
1. Between families: The unattached young adult	Accepting parent–offspring separation	a. Differentiation of self in relation to family of origin b. Development of intimate peer relationships c. Establishment of self in work
2. The joining of families through marriage: The newly married couple	Commitment to new system	a. Formation of marital system b. Realignment of relationships with extended families and friends to include spouse
3. The family with young children	Accepting new generation of members into the system	a. Adjusting marital system to make space for children b. Taking on parenting roles c. Realignment of relationships with extended family to include parenting and grandparenting roles
4. The family with adolescents	Increasing flexibility of family boundaries to include children's independence	a. Shifting of parent–child relationships to permit adolescents to move in and out of system b. Refocus on midlife marital and career issues c. Beginning shift toward concerns for older generation
5. Launching children and moving on	Accepting a multitude of exits from and entries into the family system	a. Renegotiation of marital system as a dyad b. Development of adult-to-adult relationships between grown children and their parents c. Realignment of relationships to include in-laws and grandchildren d. Dealing with disabilities and death of parents (grandparents)
6. The family in later life	Accepting the shifting of generational roles	a. Maintaining own and/or couple functioning and interests in face of physiological decline; exploration of new familial and social role options b. Support for a more central role for middle generation c. Making room in the system for the wisdom and experience of the elderly; supporting the older generation without overfunctioning for them d. Dealing with loss of spouse, siblings, and other peers, and preparation for own death; experiencing life review and integration

Figure 16.7 Stages of the Family Life Cycle

Source: Adapted from McGoldrick & Carter, 1982.

still expected to be more nurturing and emotionally caring than men, it often falls to women to worry about the question of "where can Mom live?" (Hochschild, 1989). According to Elaine Brody, a leading researcher on this issue: "It's going to be primarily women for a long time. Women can go to work as much as they want, but they still see nurturing as their job." Moreover, "with many more very old people, and fewer children per family, almost every woman is going to have to take care of an aging parent or parent-in-law" (quoted in Lewin, 1989, p. A1).

As if these stages were not stressful enough, consider the complications resulting from divorce, remarriage, and the combining of children of different marriages in a new family. It is increasingly common, for example, for teenagers and young adults to have parents who are dating and marrying, and for children to have four parental figures in their lives instead of two. These and many other changes in the family pose profound problems for sociologists who seek to develop theoretical perspectives on the family as a central institution in contemporary societies, as we will see in the next section.

PERSPECTIVES ON THE FAMILY

High divorce rates do not indicate that the family is about to disappear as an institution in modern societies. Even though many marriages end in divorce and increasing numbers of young adults postpone marriage or decide not to marry at all, most do marry, and most of those who divorce will eventually remarry. Far from disappearing, the family is adapting to new social values and to changes in other institutions, especially economic ones. But one need only listen to an hour or two of talk radio or read a newspaper to find fierce debates about whether it is morally justified for single people to have children or for members of same-sex unions to be legally married or for unmarried adults to live together outside of wedlock, along with many other issues involving "family values." Most sociologists leave the moral debates to people with ideological commitments to one or another concept of the ideal family. Social scientists devote more thought

PERSPECTIVES ON THE FAMILY

PERSPECTIVE	EMPHASIS	CENTRAL ISSUES	RESEARCH ISSUES
Functionalist	The family is a critical institution in societies but must continually adapt to major social changes.	The family has lost many functions as societies have become more complex, particularly its economic and political roles. Socialization and advancement of children in society remains a major function.	Are societies developing new institutions to support family cohesion and resolve opposing demands of work and home? How well do different families support their children's achievement (e.g., through involvement in schools, aid with schoolwork at home, etc.)?
Conflict	Family cohesion can be threatened by stresses and challenges occurring within the family group and coming from larger social forces in the society.	Conflict within families is often the result of struggles for power among family members and of individuals' efforts to gain more attention and love.	Do abrupt changes in family structure, due to divorce or separation, for example, result in more internal conflict? How do larger social forces, such as loss of work, heavy debt, or the necessity to move the home due to changing economic fortunes, relate to family conflict?
Interactionist	The family is a system of interacting personalities who must also cope with continual changes in family roles and composition as individuals mature.	Many interactions center on individual needs versus those of the family as a group. Sibling rivalry, for example, can stem from competition for a parent's attention.	How do parents learn skills that help them avoid stress and conflict? How do patterns of interaction change and adapt to new family forms after divorce or death in the family?

to theoretical issues and to conducting research designed to obtain factual information about the changing family in the United States and elsewhere in the world. In this section, therefore, we review the basic sociological perspectives on family roles and relationships, as well as research that applies those perspectives. (See the Study Chart above.)

The Interactionist Perspective

Interactions within the family cover a wide range of emotions and may take very different forms in different families. Families laugh and play together, work together, argue and bicker, and so on. All of these aspects of family interaction are important, but the arguing and bickering often drive family members apart. Studies of family interaction therefore often focus on the sources of tension and conflict in the family's interactions, but they are equally concerned with understanding family rituals, how family members help make each other feel better, and how they interact as a family with other groups in society.

Observe any normal family with young children, and before long there will be some whining and complaining

of this sort: "Mom, he's teasing me." "Mom, she's taking up too much room." "Dad, you said we were going to stop for ice cream. We want ice cream." The parents may argue with each other about how to deal with these demands, or they may present a unified parental front with a consistent message such as, "You need to stop teasing each other and share the seat. We'll have ice cream after dinner." Such typical family interactions often stem from competition for attention, but they are also caused by the simple fact that children depend so much on their parents for satisfaction of their wants. When children appeal to their parents to address wrongs they feel have been committed by other siblings against them, the underlying cause can be normal sibling rivalry. Skillful parents often develop techniques to diffuse rivalry by devising family games or by singing together, or any number of cooperative techniques that can transform angry interactions into more pleasant ones. But when parents are under stress themselves due to lack of time or resources (especially money), it becomes more difficult for them to develop the interactive skills of more effective parents (Lachs & Boyer, 2003).

The context within which family life occurs can affect family interactions in profound ways. At the lower levels of a society's stratification system, for example, money (or the lack of it) is often a source of conflict between parents or between parents and children. But the rich are by no means immune to problems of family interaction. Because they do not have to be concerned about the need to earn a living as adults and because their parents can satisfy any desires they may have, the children of the very rich often develop a sadness that resembles anomie (Wixen, 1979). Their lack of clear goals, which sometimes expresses itself in a compulsion to make extravagant purchases, may create conflict between them and their parents.

In order to study these situations, either to help a family resolve its problems or to understand the nature of family conflict more thoroughly, the social scientist must interact with and observe the family, either at home, in a laboratory, or in a therapy setting (Minuchin, 1974; Satir, 1972; Whitchurch & Constantine, 1993). For instance, consider the case described by two family therapists, Augustus Napier and Carl Whitaker (1980), in which the parents are deeply troubled by the behavior of their 17-year-old daughter, the oldest of their three children. The father is a prominent attorney, the mother a college-educated woman who has devoted herself to homemaking. The parents' definition of the situation that has brought them into therapy is that they are worried about their daughter. She disobeys, is delinquent, and is depressed enough to make them fear that she might commit suicide. The mother and daughter fight bitterly, but usually the mother retreats. The father often attempts to defend the daughter, but eventually he sides with the mother.

After a few sessions, Napier and Whitaker begin to challenge the parents' assumption that it is the daughter who is "the problem." They guess that her depression, anger, and delinquent behavior are symptoms of larger problems in the family. After some gentle probing, they identify a triangle of family conflict in which "two parents are emotionally estranged from each other and in their terrible aloneness they overinvolve their children in their emotional distress" (p. 83). The children blame themselves for their parents' problems and develop a low sense of self-worth. The therapists help the couple face the issues that divide them and that motivate their children to offer themselves as scapegoats or intermediaries who divert attention from the parents' basic problems.

Families like the one just described need to resolve a contradiction inherent in the institution of the family: the need to maintain the *individuality* of each member while providing love and support for him or her within a set of *interdependent* relationships. Many families never succeed in developing ways of encouraging each member to realize his or her full potential within the context of family life. Research shows that the core problem is usually the failure of the adult couple, even in intact families, to understand and develop their own relationship. Such a couple may

become what John F. Cuber and Peggy B. Haroff (1980) term "conflict-habituated" or "devitalized." Couples of the first type have evolved ways of expressing their hostility toward each other through elaborate patterns of conflict that persist over many years. In contrast, the devitalized or "empty-shell" marriage may have begun with love and shared interests, but the partners have not grown as a couple and have drifted apart emotionally. Each has the habit of being with the other, a habit that may be strongly supported by the norms of a particular ethnic or religious community. Neither partner is satisfied by the relationship, but neither feels that he or she can do anything to change the situation. Thus the conflicts that might have produced change are reduced to indifference.

Today social scientists who study family interaction must deal with family structures that are more complex than the traditional nuclear family. Divorce and remarriage create many situations in which children have numerous sets of parental figures—parents and stepparents, grandparents and surrogate grandparents, and so on. These changes in family form result in new patterns of family interaction. For example, in a study of 2,000 children conducted over a 5-year period, sociologist Frank Furstenberg found that 52 percent of children raised by their mothers do not see their fathers at all—partly because some fathers are absent by choice but also because opportunities for visits decrease as parents remarry or move away (cited in Aspaklaria, 1985). This produces situations in which parents strive to maintain long-distance relationships with their children and occasionally have brief, intense visits with them. Although this specific type of relationship may not be the most desirable, it appears that if parents and children can express love and affection even when the parents are divorced, the children's ability to feel good about themselves and to love others in their turn may not be impaired.

The Conflict Perspective

The conflict perspective on families and family interactions assumes that "social conflict is a basic element of human social life." Conflict exists "within all types of social interaction, and at all levels of social organization. This is as true of the family as it is of any other type of social entity" (Farrington & Chertok, 1993, p. 368). From this perspective, one can observe actual family interactions (the micro level) and ask why conflict occurs, what the issues are, and how they are resolved. At a more macro level, one can ask how conditions of inequality and class conflict influence actual families or the laws and policies governing the family as a central institution in society.

At the micro level of internal family affairs, the conflict perspective points to ways, for example, in which the subordination of women often results in particular forms of powerlessness and anger. The familiar complaint that a parent, particularly a mother, does a lot of nagging is a common one, but it is often a signal that the parent feels relatively powerless to change a situation. In family groups in which power is shared equally and parents have the means to withhold favors or desired rewards from children who do not meet their expectations, nagging is far less frequent. But when the mother is clearly subordinated and does not share equally in the resources the family has at its disposal, conflict in various forms is worsened (Boxer, 2002). Similarly, when problems of alcohol or substance abuse weaken parental authority, all the nagging, cajoling, or punishment meted out by parents can be ineffective in reaching angry children who feel, often without understanding it, that their own needs for love and attention are not being met. Such problems are often influenced by macro problems of unemployment, stress at work, lack of health insurance, and many other external social influences that conflict theorists focus on in their analysis of family issues.

"FAMILY VALUES" AND CLASS CONFLICT As mentioned earlier, citizens of the United States are engaged in a major public debate over issues related to the family, including homosexual marriage, freedom to obtain abortions, enforcement of child support and child abuse laws, and a host of other controversies that have a direct bearing on the family as an institution in society. The federal budget battles of the past decade also represent an arena of conflict over family policies, for they centered on the social safety net of welfare agencies, payments to families with dependent children, and many other spending categories that transfer money from more affluent families and individuals to those with fewer resources and, often, great need.

There are approximately 6.2 million families in the United States living at or below the official poverty line, and 8.9 million living at or below 125 percent of the poverty line (*Statistical Abstract*, 2002). Poverty affects a far greater proportion of black and Hispanic families than white families, even though most poor families are white.

Sociologists who study poverty argue that most families are poor for the obvious reason that they do not earn or receive enough income. But critics of liberal social-welfare policies argue that self-destructive behaviors of family members themselves, such as dropping out of school, drug use, and out-of-wedlock childbearing, are causes of poverty. Social-welfare policies that are too generous or take the form of entitlements that do not have to be earned are said to encourage behaviors that cause poverty.

Social scientists who study class conflict and poverty policies, notably Herbert Gans (1995) and Christopher Jencks (1993), point out that class conflict helps explain the views of different population groups on family poverty. In the early decades of the twentieth century, they note, a large proportion of impoverished families consisted of elderly couples who did not have Social Security or Medicaid, two programs that have drastically reduced poverty among elderly Americans. Yet at the time that these policies were being debated, many members of the upper classes opposed them, viewing them as undemocratic transfers of wealth to less deserving members of society. The situation today is similar in that members of the upper classes oppose adequate funding for day care and other policies that can help move adult family members from poverty and dependence on public support to employment at decent jobs.

Functionalist Views of the Family

From a functionalist perspective, the family evolves in both form and function in response to changes in the larger social environment. As societies undergo such major changes as industrialization and urbanization, the family must adapt to the effects of those changes. Functionalist theorists like Talcott Parsons and William Goode have called attention to the loss of family functions that occurs as other social institutions like schools, corporations, and social-welfare agencies perform functions that were previously reserved for the family. We have discussed numerous examples of this trend in earlier chapters (e.g., the tendency of families to have fewer children as the demand for agricultural labor decreased, the changing composition of households as people were required to seek work away from their families of orientation, and the increasing number of dual-income households). The functionalist explanation of these changes is that as the division of labor becomes more complex and as new, more specialized institutions arise, the family, too, must become more specialized. Thus modern families no longer perform certain functions that used to be within their domain, but they do play an increasingly vital part in early-childhood socialization, in the emotional lives of their members, and in preparing older children for adult roles in the economic institutions of industrial societies (Cherlin, 1996; Parsons & Bales, 1955).

A good example of empirical studies of how family functioning adapts to social change is research on the effects of child care on infant development. Figure 16.8 shows that there is a wide array of child care arrangements. For very young children, day care is far less common than care by other relatives or care by nonrelatives outside an institution. But by the time children of working parents reach the age of 5, day care centers account for fully 75 percent of child care arrangements. An often-cited study (Belsky, 1988; see

Percentage of children in each age group*

	less than 1	1 year old	2 years old	3 years old	4 years old	5 years old
Children in relative care	24%	24%	19%	21%	18%	15%
Children in nonrelative care	17%	19%	20%	19%	15%	17%
Children in center-based program	7%	11%	19%	41%	65%	75%

*Columns do not add up to 100 because some children participated in more than one type of day care.

Figure 16.8   Child Care Arrangements

Source: U.S. Department of Education, National Center for Educational Statistics.

also Belsky & Steinberg, 1991) offered some evidence that infants who are given over to a nonparent early in life may suffer developmental problems. This finding has been widely challenged. More recent research using more sophisticated methods shows that with quality care there are no discernible disadvantages for children of working mothers. Of course, the larger issue is how to provide high-quality care while parents are away working (Eckholm, 1992).

Researchers who approach the issue of child care from a functionalist perspective ask how societies cope with the dilemma faced by families in which both parents work outside the home. In an influential study, Kammerman and Kahn (1981) found that advanced industrial societies are struggling with the question: "Can adults manage productive roles in the labor force at the same time as they fulfill productive roles within the family—at home?" (p. 2). Many European nations answered this question by developing policies to assist working parents, including the development of high-quality child and infant care services (e.g., universal day care and school meal programs), paid parental leave, and family allowances that ease the financial burden on families with several children. In the United States, however, there is a great deal of debate about whether such policies are appropriate functions of government or whether they lead to higher taxes, forcing more mothers into the labor force (Pittman, 1993). (See the Global Social Change box on page 469.)

In related studies, sociologist Arlie Hochschild (1989, 1997) asked how adult family members adjust to what she calls the "second shift" (see Chapter 14). Only a few decades ago, housework and child care were viewed as primarily the mother's duty even if she worked outside the home. Today, many working parents cooperate and share domestic roles and responsibilities, but it is often difficult to achieve such cooperation. Hochschild found that "most egalitarian women—those with strong feelings about sharing—did one of two things. They married men who planned to share at home or they actively tried to change their husband's understanding of his role at home" (1989, p. 193). Many of the

women Hochschild interviewed were like Adrian Sherman, who "took the risky step of telling her husband 'It's share the second shift or it's divorce.' She staged a 'sharing showdown' and won" (p. 193). Other women do not go so far as to stage a showdown. They may make incremental efforts to change their husbands' attitudes. Still others discuss the issue with their husbands, but the process is not an easy one. More than half of the working women Hochschild interviewed had tried in one way or another to change domestic roles. As Hochschild notes, "If women lived in a culture that presumed active fatherhood, they wouldn't need to devise personal strategies to bring it about" (p. 193).

In sum, research from all the major sociological perspectives supports the view that the family is a resilient institution; it adapts to changing economic conditions and changing values. As Napier observes:

> Every family is a miniature society, a social order with its own rules, structure, leadership, language, style of living. . . . The hidden rules, the subtle nuances of language, the private rituals and dances that define every family as a unique microculture may not be easy for an outsider to perceive at first glance, but they are there. (Napier & Whitaker, 1980, p. 78)

At the macro level, the strength of the family as an institution does not mean the divorce rate will decrease rapidly or families that experience severe stress caused by unemployment, ill health, and the like will have an easier time remaining intact. Whatever the perspective from which they study the family, sociologists recognize that problems such as family violence and family breakup are pervasive and require more effective intervention techniques to protect vulnerable family members and strengthen the family as an institution. We turn, therefore, to examples from contemporary research that show how the basic sociological perspectives on the family can help us understand and intervene more successfully in different situations of family violence.

Looking to France for Models of Child Care

An unintended consequence of efforts to "end welfare as we know it" has been increased pressure on existing child care services. Inadequate to meet the demand before welfare reform, day care and other child care services for working parents in the United States are under even more pressure today. This situation makes it more difficult for low-income parents, who need subsidized day care, to balance work and family obligations. Because early-childhood language and social learning experiences are immensely important to later learning and school achievement, lack of high-quality affordable child care for working parents can lead to higher social and economic costs in the long run.

The shortage of child care services is also a good example of "structural lag." Existing day care institutions (social structures dealing with child care) lag behind the demand created by new norms—that is, the expectation that low-income single mothers must work to receive additional benefits (health care, supplemental income, and the like).

Many American child care experts look to France and other European nations for examples of how to address this problem of structural lag in the provision of day care services. Children are born into poverty in France and the United States at virtually the same rate—25 percent in the United States and 24 percent in France. But by age 6 the rate of child poverty in France drops to 7 percent, while in the United States

Allison Shelley/Education Week

it hovers around 17 percent. Social scientists believe the greater improvement in France is largely a result of greater public support of high-quality child care. All French infants are born into a system that guarantees universal health care and financial support for families. The new mother immediately qualifies for 14 weeks of paid maternity leave, which parents often combine with several weeks of paid vacation, all of which enable French citizens to stay at home with newborns far longer than low-income American parents can. In the United States, there are no requirements for paid maternity leave. Only very recently have parents in companies employing 50 or more workers gained the right to take unpaid maternity leave (a maximum of 12 weeks) and still return to their jobs.

The French system offers numerous benefits that are not available in the United States except for employees in the most family-supportive firms or at the higher levels of the salary scale. Children in France are screened for any health problems in infant child care centers (known as *crèches*) before they

enter preschool. These health screenings continue regularly throughout the public school years. When American child care experts toured French child care centers, they noticed "that they had never before seen so many toddlers and preschoolers wearing eyeglasses, and they realized that it was probably because more French children are screened for vision problems earlier than is the case for American youngsters." All child care workers receive extensive professional training in child care and human development. While new French parents, like their American counterparts, might wish to be at home with their infants, they can at least be confident in the level of care their children are receiving outside the home.

From a critical sociological viewpoint, this comparison indicates that in France there is greater commitment in the society as a whole to raising healthy children than there is in the United States. American families do not value their children less, but they are much more individualistic about such issues—more likely, that is, to believe that child care arrangements are the responsibility of individual families. This makes Americans far more susceptible to claims by employers that universal high-quality child care is too expensive and a detriment to profitability. It also makes many Europeans wonder about the social priorities of Americans (Jacobson, 2001).

Family Violence: Applying the Perspectives

Family researchers Jeffrey L. Edleson and Ngoh Tiong Tan (1993) describe cases of family violence that can be analyzed in terms of each of the main sociological perspectives on the family. Their research compares Chinese and North American families in which the wives have experienced incidents of abuse by their husbands.

SPOUSE ABUSE IN A CHINESE FAMILY   Mrs. Lee is referred to a social worker after seeking aid at a police station when she was struck in the face by her husband. In Chinese and other Asian cultures, the wife is expected to leave her family of orientation to take up residence with her husband and his extended family. Mrs. Lee's husband's family is dominated by her mother-in-law, a powerful widow who treats Mrs. Lee as the person with the lowest status in the family. Mrs. Lee wishes her mother-in-law would be less autocratic and complains about her dictatorial behavior to her own parents and to her husband. Her husband, on the other hand, believes his wife should conform to the ancient norms of Chinese family life and obey his mother. He and his mother consider Mrs. Lee a "traitor" because she has appealed to authorities outside the family.

From a functionalist perspective, the police and social workers are representatives of institutions in the larger society that seek to help families avoid violence. But they cannot simply impose a new form of power on this complex extended family. Instead, they apply an interactionist perspective to the conflict as they understand it. The social worker convenes a meeting of the family, to which Mrs. Lee's older brother is also invited. Together the group works out a detailed understanding of the roles of all the family members. The social worker explains that Mrs. Lee is not seeking to challenge her mother-in-law. In fact, however, the social worker has demonstrated to the extended family that Mrs. Lee has a support network and resources outside the family—a new notion for a traditional Chinese family. No doubt there will be further conflict, but power relations within the family have been subtly altered as a result of this intervention.

A NORTH AMERICAN FAMILY COPES WITH VIOLENCE   Susan was a regular victim of her husband Bob's violent anger. The beatings began on their honeymoon and ended 20 years later when he struck her with a baseball bat, almost killing her. During those years, their children suffered emotionally from the violent interactions they witnessed and the unhappiness their mother experienced. But Susan loved Bob and struggled to make the marriage work. Now the couple are in court because after the last assault Bob was arrested. He faces a jail sentence, and Susan has abandoned hope of making the marriage work. She understands that she must make a new life for herself. She is seeking opportunities to do so but knows that she also needs protection from possible future assaults.

Unlike Mr. and Mrs. Lee, neither Bob nor Susan lives near an extended-family network. Many Americans do not live in close contact with relatives; on the average, "extended families do not figure as prominently in the lives of Caucasian Americans as they do in other subcultures and in many Asian societies" (Edleson & Tan, 1993, p. 384). Bob and Susan had left their extended families in search of economic opportunity. Susan now has nowhere to turn for help except the police and social-welfare agencies. This social safety net will act to protect her so that she and her children can live in peace. From a functionalist perspective, Susan will also have to rely on these agencies to enforce Bob's responsibilities toward his children. The functionalist sociologist argues, therefore, that it is of vital importance that the agencies function effectively in this and similar cases.

Susan needs the help of outside agencies to gain relief from the deadly conflict that has destroyed her family. Yet these very agencies came into being as a result of conflict in the larger society. They emerged after decades of protests and demands by women and social activists for ways to protect innocent family members from their abusers. But as we learn almost daily from reports of incidents of spouse and child abuse, it is never easy to ensure that the agencies created by society will intervene effectively. Even if they have the necessary resources, there is no guarantee that they will always act wisely to balance the conflicting values of individual rights and preservation of the family.

Domestic abuse is the most frequently reported issue in American policing (Defina & Wetherbee, 1997). These cases only touch the surface of an immense social problem, but they offer some insight into how sociologists contribute to understanding these extremely complex instances of violence at the micro level. Contemporary law enforcement officers are trained in the basic sociology and psychology of family violence. They understand that the batterer and the domestic victim are often caught in a cycle of repeated hostility and violence. Too often the violent spouse, usually the husband or male partner, expresses contrition after the violent act and is forgiven, and so the cycle resumes. The authorities and the neighbors believe the household is a troubled one but do not believe they can do very much about it.

In many communities, however, new policies require more stringent approaches to domestic violence. The norms and sanctions are changing to prevent fatalities and trauma to children and spouses. Gradually the focus is shifting from merely "maintaining the peace" to arresting offenders, protecting victims, and referring battered women to shelters and other community resources available to help victims of domestic violence. Better understanding of the dynamics of violent family interactions, more forceful demands by women and community residents for protection from batterers, and more effective techniques for creating protective organizations are all applications of the basic perspectives of sociology.

Of course, all the training in the world does not explain why so many loving relationships become violent. On the other hand, with so much stress and such great economic, social, and emotional demands placed on husbands and wives, an even better question might be why, despite high rates of divorce and family breakup, so many unions are successful and so many individuals crave love and a stable relationship more than almost any other cherished value. We turn, therefore, to a sociological consideration of romance and marriage.

DYNAMICS OF MATE SELECTION AND MARRIAGE

We may think of mate selection and marriage as matters that affect only the partners themselves, but in reality the concerns of parents and other family members are never very far from either person's consciousness. As we will see shortly, the values of each partner's extended family often have a significant impact on the mate-selection process.

Marriage as Exchange

People in Western cultures like to think that interpersonal attraction and love are the primary factors in explaining why a couple forms a "serious" relationship and eventually marries. But while attraction and love are clearly important factors in many marriages, social scientists point out that in all cultures the process of mate selection is carried out according to basic rules of bargaining and exchange (Daniel, 1996). Sociologists and economists who study mate selection and marriage from this exchange perspective ask who controls the marriage contract, what values each family is attempting to maximize in the contract, and how the exchange process is shaped by the society's stratification system.

Among the upper classes of China and Japan before the twentieth century, marriage transactions were controlled by the male elders of the community—with the older women often making the real decisions behind the scenes. In many societies in the Middle East, Asia, and preindustrial Europe, the man's family negotiated a "bride price" with the woman's family. This price usually consisted of valuable goods like jewelry and clothes, but in some cultures it took the form of land and cattle. Throughout much of Hindu India, in contrast, an upper-class bride's family paid a "groom price" to the man's family.

Although such norms appear to be weakening throughout the world, arranged marriages remain the customary pattern of mate selection in many societies. The following account describes factors that are often considered in arranging a marriage in modern India:

> Every Sunday one can peruse the wedding ads in the classifieds. Many people still arrange an alliance in the traditional manner—through family and friend connections. Caste is becoming less important a factor in the selection of a spouse. Replacing caste are income and type of job. The educational level of the bride-to-be is also a consideration, an asset always worth mentioning in the ad. A faculty member at a college for girls has estimated that 80–90 percent of the students there will enter an arranged marriage upon receiving the B.A. Perhaps 10 percent will continue their studies. In this way, educating a daughter is parental investment toward securing an attractive, prosperous groom. (Smith, 1989)

In all of these transactions, the families base their bargaining on considerations of family prestige within the community, the wealth of the two families and their ability to afford or command a given price, the beauty of the bride and the attractiveness of the groom, and so on. Different cultures may evaluate these qualities differently, but in each case the parties involved think of the coming marriage as an exchange between the two families (Goode, 1964). But do not get the idea that only selfish motives are involved in such marriages. Both families are also committing themselves to a long-standing relationship because they are exchanging their most precious products, their beloved young people. Naturally, they want the best for their children (as this is defined in their culture), and they also want a climate of mutual respect and cooperation in their future interfamily relationships.

Changing Norms of Mate Selection

ENDOGAMY/EXOGAMY   All cultures have norms that specify whether a person brought up in that culture may marry within or outside the cultural group. Marriage within the group is termed *endogamy;* marriage outside the group and its culture is termed *exogamy.* In the United States, ethnic and religious groups normally put pressure on their members to remain endogamous—that is, to choose mates from their own group. These rules tend to be especially strong for women. Among Orthodox Jews, for example, an infant is considered to have been born into the religion only if the mother is Jewish; children of mixed marriages in which the mother was not born a Jew are not considered Jewish. The conflict between Orthodox and Reform Jews over the status of children born to non-Jewish mothers—even when the mothers have converted to Judaism and the children have been raised as Jews from birth—is an example of conflict over endogamy/exogamy norms. Many African tribes have developed norms of exogamy that encourage young men to find brides in specific villages outside the village of their birth. As noted in Chapter 4, such marriage systems tend to promote strong bonds of kinship among villages and strengthen the social cohesion of the tribe while breaking down the animosity that sometimes arises between villages within a tribe.

art *and the sociological eye*

Symbols of Marriage

The famous wedding portrait painted by Jan van Eyck in 1434 can be interpreted on several levels. On the surface, it is simply a painting of a bride and groom, people of obvious wealth and social standing, in their bedroom. But at a deeper level of meaning, the painting is a study in the symbols associated with marriage in Europe during the fifteenth century. The wedding bed was understood as a symbol of marital fidelity, the dog as a symbol of trust; and the couple have removed their shoes to show that they stand on the holy ground of matrimony. These and other symbols in the painting could not be understood, however, without some study of the way people of that time thought about marriage and its relationship to religious belief.

A contemporary artist would use other symbols and perhaps try to convey other emotions in depicting a newly married couple, just as the photographer captures a few very telling symbols in the portraits of the young couple and their new baby at the beginning of this chapter. But the van Eyck painting is considered a great work of art because of the timeless and universal quality of the married couple's expression as they gaze out on an approving society.

The National Gallery, London

The Marriage of Giovanni Arnolfini and Giovanna Cenani, by Jan van Eyck, 1434. Panel, 33″ x 22½″.

HOMOGAMY   Another norm of mate selection is **homogamy,** the tendency to marry a person from a similar social background. The parents of a young woman from a wealthy family, for example, attempt to increase the chances that she will associate with young men of the same or higher social-class standing. She is encouraged to date boys from "good" families. After graduating from high school, she will be sent to an elite college or university, where the pool of eligible men is likely to include many who share her social-class background. She may surprise her parents, however, and fall in love with someone whose social-class, religious, or ethnic background is con-

siderably different from hers. When this happens, however, she will invariably have based her choice on other values that are considered important in the dating and marriage market—values like outstanding talent, good looks, popularity, or sense of humor. She will argue that these values outweigh social class, especially if it seems apparent that the young man will gain upward mobility through his career. Often the couple will marry and not worry about his lower social-class background. On the other hand, "the untalented, homely, poor man may aspire to a bride with highly desirable qualities, but he cannot offer enough to induce either her or her family to choose him, for they can find a groom with more highly valued qualities" (Goode, 1964, p. 33).

Homogamy in mate selection generally helps maintain the separateness of religious groups. Because the Census Bureau does not collect systematic data on religious preferences, it is extremely difficult to obtain accurate data on religious intermarriage. Yet sociologists and religious leaders agree that although parents continue to encourage their children to marry within their religion, there is a trend away from religious homogamy, particularly among Protestants and Catholics (Scanzoni, 1995). This trend may affect rates of divorce and separation. Research shows that families who maintain an active religious life tend to have lower divorce rates than those who do not participate in religious worship together (National Commission on America's Urban Families, 1993). Similarly, a study by Howard Weinberg (1994) found that shared religion has the strongest effect on the likelihood that couples will be able to overcome a period of separation and achieve a successful reconciliation.

INTERRACIAL MARRIAGE   The norm of homogamy also applies to interracial marriage. Before 1967, when the U.S. Supreme Court struck them down as unconstitutional, many states had laws prohibiting such marriages. After that decision, the number of marriages between blacks and whites began to increase rapidly, reaching almost 4 million in 2000. Intermarriage of Hispanic and non-Hispanic whites also increased during the same period, from about 500,000 marriages in 1960 to 1.7 million in 2000 (*Statistical Abstract*, 2002). Both of these trends are signs that more people are choosing to marry across racial and ethnic lines, but because most marriages are within racial categories, it is clear that the norm of racial homogamy remains strong in the United States.

Romantic Love

Although exchange criteria and homogamy continue to play significant roles in mate selection, for the past century romantic attraction and love have been growing in importance in North American and other Western cultures. Indeed, the conflict between romantic love and the parental requirement of homogamy is one of the great themes of Western literature and drama. "Let me not to the marriage of true minds/Admit impediments," wrote Shakespeare in a famous sonnet. The "star-crossed lovers" from feuding families in *Romeo and Juliet*—like the lovers who have forsaken family fortunes to be together in innumerable stories and plays written since Shakespeare's time—attest to the strong value we place on romantic love as an aspect of intimate relationships between men and women (Cancian, 1994).

In his classic study of worldwide marriage and family patterns, William J. Goode (1964) found that compared with the mate-selection systems of other cultures, that of the United States "has given love greater prominence. Here, as in all Western societies to some lesser degree, the child is socialized to fall in love" (p. 39). Yet although it may be taken for granted now that people will form couples on the basis of romantic attachment, major changes in the structure of Western societies had to occur before love as we know it could become such an important value in our lives. In particular, changes in economic institutions as a result of industrialization required workers with more education and greater maturity. These changes, in turn, lengthened the period of socialization, especially in educational institutions. This made it possible for single men and women to remain unattached long enough to gain the emotional maturity they needed if they were to experience love and make more independent decisions in selecting their mates.

However familiar it may seem to us, love remains a mysterious aspect of human relationships. We do not know very much—from a verifiable, scientific standpoint—about this complex emotional state. We do not know fully what it means to "fall in love" or what couples can do to make their love last. But two theories that have stimulated considerable research on this subject are Winch's theory of *complementarity* and Blau's theory of *emotional reciprocity*.

COMPLEMENTARY NEEDS AND MUTUAL ATTRACTION   Robert F. Winch's (1958) theory of complementary needs, based on work by the psychologist Henry A. Murray, holds that people who fall in love tend to be alike in social characteristics such as family prestige, education, and income but different in their psychological needs. Thus, according to Winch, an outgoing person often falls in love with a quiet, shy person. The one gains an appreciative audience, the other an entertaining spokesperson. A person who needs direction is attracted to one who needs to exercise authority; one who is nurturant is attracted to one who needs nurturance; and so on.

Winch and others have found evidence to support this theory, but there are some problems with this research. It is difficult to measure personal needs and the extent to which they are satisfied. Moreover, people also show a variety of patterns in their choices of mates. Some people, in fact, seem to be attracted to each other because of their similarities in looks and behavior rather than because of their differences.

ATTRACTION AND EMOTIONAL RECIPROCITY   Peter Blau's (1964) theory of emotional reciprocity as a source of love is based on his general theory that relationships usually flourish when people feel satisfied with the exchanges between them. When people feel that they are loved, they are more likely to give love in return. When they feel that they love too much or are not loved enough, they will eventually come to feel exploited or trapped and will seek to end the relationship. In research on 231 dating couples, Zick Rubin (1980; see also Peplau, Hill, & Rubin, 1993) found that among those who felt this equality of love, 77 percent were still together 2 years later, but only 45 percent of the unequally involved couples were still seeing each other. As Blau explained it, "Only when two lovers' affection for and commitment to one another expand at roughly the same pace do they mutually tend to reinforce their love" (quoted in Rubin, 1980, p. 284).

Blau's exchange approach confirms some popular notions about love—particularly the ideas that we can love someone who loves us and that inequalities in love can lead to separation. And yet we still know little about the complexities of this emotion and how it translates into the formation of the most basic of all social groups: the married couple. This is ironic because books, movies, and popular songs probably pay more attention to love than to just about any other subject.

Francesca M. Cancian (1994), a leading researcher on love in a changing society, notes that when men and women place a high value on individuality, the price may be "a weakening of close relationships." As people spend time enhancing their own lives, they may become more self-centered and feel less responsible for providing love and nurturance. Cancian's research on loving relations among couples of all kinds has convinced her that people are increasingly seeking a form of love that "combines enduring love with self-development." She regards this kind of relationship as based on interdependencies in which each member of the couple attempts to assist the other in realizing his or her individual potential and simultaneously seeks to strengthen the bond between them. But she finds that in order to foster a loving interdependent relationship, couples often need to sacrifice a certain amount of independence and career advancement—not a simple matter in a culture that places a high value on individual achievement.

Marriage and Divorce

More than any other ritual signifying a major change in status, a wedding is a joyous occasion. Two people are legally and symbolically joined before their kin and friends. It is expected that their honeymoon will be pleasant and that they will live happily ever after. But about 20 percent of first marriages end in annulment or divorce within 3 years (Cherlin, 1996). Of course, divorce can occur at any time in the fam-

ily life cycle, but the early years of family formation are the most difficult for the couple because each partner experiences new stresses that arise from the need to adjust to a complex set of new relationships. As Monica McGoldrick and Elizabeth A. Carter (1982) point out: "Marriage requires that a couple renegotiate numerous personal issues that they have previously defined for themselves or that were defined by their parents, from when to sleep, have sex, or fight, to how to celebrate holidays and where and how to live, work, and spend vacations" (p. 178). For people who were married before, these negotiations can involve former spouses and shared children, resulting in added stress for the new couple.

In the United States and other Western societies, the rate of divorce rose sharply after World War II, accelerated even more dramatically during the 1960s and 1970s, and has decreased only slightly since then. These statistics often lead sociologists to proclaim that there is an "epidemic" of divorce in the United States. But demographer Donald Bogue has concluded that "the divorce epidemic is not being created by today's younger generation. It has been created by today's population aged thirty or more, who married in the 1960s and before" (1985, p. 190). This generation was noted for its search for self-realization, often at the expense of intimate family relationships. It is not yet clear whether subsequent generations, who appear to be somewhat more pragmatic, will continue this trend. If they do, we can expect high divorce rates to continue.

Most states in the United States now have some form of no-fault divorce that reduces the stigma of divorce by making moral issues like infidelity less relevant than issues of child custody and division of property. While the growing acceptance of divorce helps account for why divorce rates are so much higher in the United States than in other nations with highly educated populations, Americans today also place a higher value on successful marriage than their parents may have. This means that they often divorce in the expectation of forming another, more satisfying and mutually sustaining relationship (Ahlburg & De Vita, 1992).

TRIAL MARRIAGE   In the 1980s, it was widely believed that the practice of "trial marriage," or cohabitation before marriage, would result in greater marital stability: Couples who lived together before marriage would gain greater mutual understanding and a realistic view of marital commitment, and this would result in a lower divorce rate among such couples after they actually married. By the 1990s, however, it had become evident that these expectations were unfounded; in fact, the divorce rate among couples who had lived together before marriage was actually higher than the rate for couples who had not done so.

Within 10 years of the wedding, 38 percent of those who had lived together before marriage had divorced, compared to 27 percent of those who had married without cohabiting beforehand.

On the basis of an analysis of data from a federal government survey of more than 13,000 individuals, Larry Bumpass and James Sweet (1989; see also Bumpass & Raley, 1995; Bumpass, Raley, & Sweet, 1995) concluded that couples who cohabit before marriage are generally more willing to accept divorce as a solution to marital problems. They also found that such couples are less likely to be subject to family pressure to continue a marriage that is unhappy or unsatisfactory. In addition, cohabitation has become a predictable part of the family life cycle, not only before marriage but also in the interval between divorce and remarriage. Once again, these changes in families mean that family life has become more variable and uncertain for children. Thus, while some advocate a return to traditional family norms and values, others urge greater tolerance for a variety of family types and accommodation to their needs. This conflict is most evident in discussions of same-sex relationships.

last few decades, so that today at least 60 percent of Americans say that they condone same sex relationships (Herek, 2002). However, among Christian conservatives there remains a great deal of opposition to gay rights and to acceptance of gay marriages. After the Supreme Court ruling, President Bush, who depends on the support of conservatives, said he continues to believe that "marriage is between a woman and man" and that he would seek legal advice about how to prevent gay marriages from becoming legal. But in the population at large, and among many of the nation's most important corporations, there is diminishing support for this view.

In 1995, the Walt Disney Company, long viewed as a defender of traditional family values, shocked many conservative Americans by announcing that it would provide spousal benefits (health insurance, pension rights, etc.) for its employees who were part of a same-sex relationship or marriage. In taking this action, Disney was simply acknowledging that norms are changing and it is becoming less acceptable for companies to impose their definitions of the family on their employees.

Gay and Lesbian Relationships

In 2003, in a stunning 6-3 decision, the U.S. Supreme Court struck down laws banning homosexual sex in Texas and 12 other states. In its ruling, the Court declared that a Texas law banning what some states have called deviate sex acts, or sodomy, was an unwarranted government violation of the right to privacy. Scholars and gay and lesbian activists said that the decision would make their efforts on behalf of gay rights easier. They also believed that it would add new credibility to their struggle to legitimate same-sex marriages, adoptions, and parental benefits. Critics, both among the minority on the Court and among opponents of gay rights, argued that the ruling would open a floodgate of efforts to legalize forms of sexuality such as prostitution and bestiality. In its ruling, however, the Court recognized that its decision follows legal precedents already established in many other democratic nations.

For sociologists who study these issues, it was clear that the Court was responding to important changes in the norms of sexuality in the American population. As noted elsewhere, attitudes toward same-sex relationships have been becoming more tolerant for the

The Sociological Observer

This photo, titled "Proud of Vermont!," appears at a Web site devoted to information about Vermont's gay and lesbian community and their efforts to convince their fellow citizens to pass the state's historic civil union bill. When you look at this photo, can you make any observations about the sexual orientations of any of the people in the photo? The crowd is celebrating the first anniversary of the civil union bill. What is the difference between civil union and marriage? Why are even civil unions among gays and lesbians still regarded as controversial? (See page 480 for further insights into the sociological content of this photo.)

Courtesy of the Vermont Freedom to Marry Task Force from their website www.vtfreetomarry.org, photographer Jordan Silverman

CURRENT RESEARCH ON GAY AND LESBIAN FAMILIES   It is difficult to know exactly how many gay and lesbian households there are in the United States because respondents still hesitate to reveal this information to census takers. However, the 2000 Census included data on 601,209 gay and lesbian families, of which 304,148 were gay male families and 297,061 were lesbian families. These families were found to be living in 99.3 percent of all U.S. counties, with the greatest concentration found in major metropolitan regions across the nation. These figures must be considered extremely conservative estimates of the total number of same-sex families currently living in the United States because other surveys find higher numbers of respondents who say they are in such relationships. The official census figures are likely to be only half the actual number (Smith & Gates, 2001).

There is now a substantial body of evidence showing that growing up in a lesbian or gay family does not have a negative influence on child development (Goode, 2001). In fact, in a review of this research, sociologists Judith Stacey and Timothy Biblarz (2001) found that some studies indicate that children growing up in lesbian and gay families may be more open-minded about relationships, far less homophobic, and more willing to consider careers that cross traditional gender barriers than children growing up in heterosexual families. This research has been attacked by those who believe that same-sex families should be illegal, but there is no empirical support for this ideological position.

Sources of Marital Instability

Because it generally causes a great deal of emotional stress and pain for everyone involved, to say nothing of its financial costs, divorce is a subject of intense study by social scientists (Amato & Sobolewski, 2001; McManus & DiPrete, 2001). Space does not permit a full treatment of this subject here, but we can discuss some of the major variables associated with divorce.

Age at marriage is one of the leading factors in divorce. It seems that it is best not to marry too young or to wait too long before marrying. Women who marry while still in their teens are twice as likely to divorce as women who tie the knot in their 20s. But those who marry in their 30s are half again as likely to divorce as those who marry in their 20s (Ruggles, 1997). How can we explain these differences?

In a study of age and marital instability, Alan Booth and John N. Edwards (1985) examined data obtained from a national sample of more than 1,700 couples. Among the younger couples, a pattern that the authors identified as inadequate role performance—especially not being attuned to the other partner's sexual needs and not being comfortable with the role of husband or wife—seemed to explain much of the instability in their relationships. Among those who married at an older age, another pattern appeared. These couples were more likely to engage in bitter disputes over the division of labor within the family—that is, over the definition of gender roles. Women who marry at older ages, for example, are more likely to demand that both partners share equally in the housework.

It appears that until about the middle of the twentieth century, when women were more likely to assume the role of homemaker, marriages had a higher probability of lasting. The demand by women for sharing of household roles—what sociologists often call the demand for a "symmetrical family" in which partners share equally in the roles of provider and homemaker—creates new opportunities for both men and women, but it also places more stress on the family in its early stages. Symmetrical families are not necessarily more dissatisfied with their marriages than nonsymmetrical families, nor do they necessarily encounter more marital problems. It appears, however, that the greater ability of both partners to be economically independent may allow them to consider divorce sooner than would a couple in which the wife is not in the labor force (Bittman, 1993).

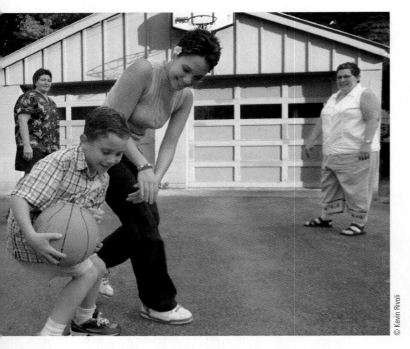

© Kevin Rivoli

Jamie Bergeron, with her brother, Casey, and parents, Sharon Trinkl, left, and Lynette Bergeron, says she is more open-minded because she has grown up with two mothers.

Even when a couple is doing well economically, researchers find that the husband's role in the couple's problem-solving efforts is a key predictor of whether the couple will divorce. Couples in which the husband "stonewalls," withdraws from arguments, and fails to make an effort to work things out are more likely to divorce (Brody, 1992).

Several other factors have also been found to be correlated with marital instability and divorce. They include the following:

- The couple met "on the rebound" (i.e., after one or both partners had recently experienced a great loss or hurt), and the new relationship may be flawed as a result.

- One of the partners wants to live far away from his or her family of orientation, suggesting that feelings of hostility toward family members may complicate the relationship.

- The spouses' family backgrounds are markedly different in terms of race, religion, education, or social class, which may result in differences in values that can cause conflict between the spouses.

- The couple is dependent on one of the extended families for income, shelter, or emotional support.

- The couple married after an acquaintanceship of less than 6 months or after an engagement of more than 3 years.

- Marital patterns in either spouse's extended family were unstable.

- The wife became pregnant before or within the first year of marriage (McGoldrick & Carter, 1982; Bumpass, Raley, & Sweet, 1995).

These correlates of marital instability do not, of course, necessarily mean that marriages that occur under these conditions are doomed to break up. They merely suggest that on the basis of statistical probabilities such marriages have a higher chance of ending in divorce.

The Impact of Divorce

At midcentury, it was still considered almost impossible for a divorced man to run for the presidency. Ronald Reagan was the first president who had previously been divorced. Senators Robert Dole and Phil Gramm, candidates in the 1996 presidential election, had each been divorced. Divorce is much more prevalent today. Nevertheless, it remains a significant event in people's lives—as significant as marriage itself. But unlike a wedding, a divorce is not a happy event. Although some divorces turn out well for both partners, most do not.

Research on divorce has shown that many of the most disruptive consequences are due to its economic impact. Women suffer an average decline of about 30 percent in their income in the year after separation, while men experience a 10 percent increase (McManus & DiPrete, 2001). In fact, most women who apply for various forms of public support do so because they have recently experienced a drastic decline in income as a result of divorce, separation, or abandonment. In addition, almost 40 percent of divorced mothers (and the children in their custody) move within the first year after divorce, and another 20 percent move after a year, a rate far higher than that for married couples (Cherlin, 1996; Furstenberg & Cherlin, 1991). And as if the breakup of their families is not stressful enough, many children also experience the loss of friends and familiar neighborhoods.

Beyond the material effects of divorce, there are the longer-term effects on family roles and the feelings of family members. In an important longitudinal study, Wallerstein and Blakeslee (1989) tracked 60 families with a total of 131 children for a period of 10 to 15 years after divorce. Both parents and children were interviewed at regular intervals. The data from those interviews show that the turmoil and stress of divorce may continue for a year or more. Many divorced adults continue to feel angry, humiliated, and rejected as much as 18 months later, and the children of divorced parents tend to exhibit a variety of psychological problems. Moreover, both men and women have a diminished capacity for parenting after divorce. They spend less time with their children, provide less discipline, and are less sensitive to their needs. Even a decade after the divorce, the parents may be chronically disorganized and unable to meet the challenges of parenting. Instead, they come to depend on their children to help them cope with the demands of their own lives, thereby producing an "overburdened child"—one who, in addition to handling the normal stresses of childhood, also must help his or her parent ward off depression (Wallerstein & Blakeslee, 1989; Wallerstein, Lewis, & Blakeslee, 2000).

There is a silver lining to the dark cloud of divorce, however. Because so many adults who are now marrying for the first time come from families that have experienced divorce, they are likely to take more time in selecting their mates in an effort to make sure that their choice is best for both partners; in addition, they try to become economically secure before marrying, thereby eliminating a major source of stress in a new marriage (Cherlin, 1996). Thus the recent modest downturn in the divorce rate may be expected to continue in the future. In any case, the data on the effects of divorce on adults and children suggest that societies need to do more to ease the stress experienced by young families—for example, by providing more day care facilities, establishing more flexible work schedules, and offering opportunities for family leave so that they can care for family members in times of need.

Research on the problems of African-American families adds emphasis to the relationship between poverty and problems of family dissolution. Research on black families also confirms the basic need for family-oriented social policies.

CRITICAL SOCIOLOGY AND SOCIAL CHANGE

The Black Family

The headlines announced a stunning new research finding: "Birth Rate Falls to a 40-Year Low Among Unwed Black Women: Education and Contraception Are Seen as Crucial" (Holmes, 1998). The news came from a research project headed by demographer Stephanie J. Ventura of the National Center for Health Statistics. Her most recent research shows that during the 1990s, fertility rates for unmarried black teenagers fell more steeply (31 percent) than those for any other U.S. population group—from 115.5 births per 1,000 unmarried women in 1990 to 79.2 in 2000. This decline appears to be part of a decrease in fertility among all black women—teenagers and adults, married and unmarried. In fact, births to unmarried women of any race or ethnicity declined during the decade, but not as rapidly as births to African-American teenagers. As Figures 16.9 and 16.10 indicate, fertility rates for unmarried African-American (and Hispanic) teenagers remain substantially higher than those for white teenagers, but they are declining at a faster rate. It should also be noted that while overall rates of teenage childbearing in the United States have been decreasing, they are still the highest rates for any urban industrial nation (Ventura et al., 2001).

In seeking explanations for this significant shift in births to unmarried black women, Ventura and others point to increases in education programs in African-American communities, which encourage teenagers and younger adults to stay in school and to use contraception. Donna E. Shalala, former secretary of health and human services, pointed out that increased condom use is associated with greater awareness of the risk of AIDS. "We really did scare people," she commented, and of course AIDS is a matter worthy of fear and great precaution (Holmes, 1998).

Encouraging news about declines in births to unmarried teenagers and young adults is only part of the larger and far more complex picture that describes the strengths and problems of African-American families. Poverty rates

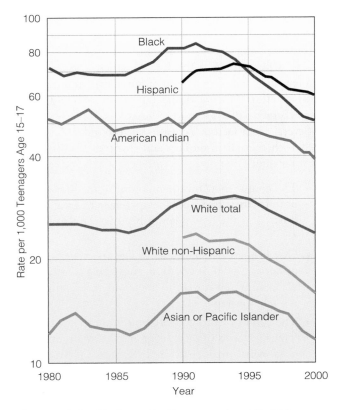

Figure 16.9 Birthrate for Teenagers Age 15–17 by Race and Hispanic Origin: United States, 1980–2000

Source: Ventura et al., 2000.

are higher for black and other minority families than for white families, even though in absolute terms there are many more poor white families. Adding to the confusion is the controversy over "family values." In the case of the black family, the central issue is whether high rates of poverty, crime, and school failure in low-income, segregated black communities are a cause or a consequence of the large number of black single-parent families.

This issue is not a new one. More than half a century ago, the eminent African-American sociologist E. Franklin Frazier argued in *The Negro Family in the United States* (1957/1939) that the violence of the Middle Passage, in which Africans were captured, shipped in chains, and sold into slavery, had wiped out their previous family ties. Frazier believed that as a result of that experience, the only enduring family form among blacks was the bond between mother and child. He urged black Americans to emulate the white middle-class family. In 1965, his views were endorsed by the famous *Moynihan Report,* which attributed the higher rates of social problems found in poor black communities to inadequate family functioning and the "tangle of pathology" that results from fatherlessness.

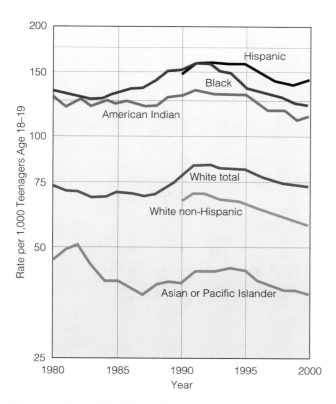

Figure 16.10 Birth Rate for Teenagers Age 18–19 by Race and Hispanic Origin: United States, 1980–2000

Source: Ventura et al., 2000.

Critics of this theory argue that it neglects the effects of both past and present discrimination, which have been particularly severe for black men in America. The extreme difficulty experienced by black men in gaining the economic security necessary to sustain a family, it is argued, becomes a formidable obstacle to marriage (Bumpass, Raley, & Sweet, 1995). Focusing on the problems of the black family suggests that there is something wrong with poor black people rather than with the larger society (Miller, 1993).

Demographer Valerie Kincade Oppenheimer (1994) notes that the number of men between the ages of 20 and 35 who are not in the labor force has been rising since the 1950s and has accelerated since 1970. This trend is particularly evident among black men, especially those with no college education. In 1960, approximately 26 percent of this group were not in school or in the labor force; by 1990, that figure had risen to more than 50 percent. (The comparable figures for white men are 11 percent and 23 percent, respectively.) One consequence of this trend has been a marked increase in delay of marriage and in rates of nonmarriage.

Oppenheimer observes that among black women, "there seems little doubt that, in addition to greater delays in marriage, the proportion who will never marry has been rising significantly and is historically unprecedented. It is unclear whether this represents a rejection of marriage or is indicative of the difficulties blacks have been experiencing in making a satisfactory marriage" (p. 306).

Most sociologists agree that the rapid rise in female-headed African-American families was attributable mainly to the difficulties faced by young black men with limited education when seeking jobs. Harriet P. McAdoo, a specialist in the study of disadvantaged women and children, makes the following point:

> The tradition used to be that if a woman got pregnant, they were expected to get married, if not forced to get married, to supply income and a name for the child. But if the man has no job, there's no impetus for them to get married. Her parents would have three people to support instead of just two. The boy would become an additional burden on the family. Parents feel: "Why should I force her to marry him? He'll be a drain." (quoted in Cummings, 1983, p. 56)

Other sociologists believe that the problem is multidimensional. As family sociologist Bonnie Thornton Dill points out: "Poverty, unemployment, welfare programs that penalize families: these things explain a major portion of the variance between blacks and whites in the number of female-headed households, not all of it." She notes that changes in the nature of urban poverty that increasingly isolate poor people from quality education and employment opportunities also deprive them of the opportunity to marry. "Teen-age pregnancy among blacks has not increased so much," Dill concludes, "but the rate of marriage among teen-agers has dropped and the number of children born to married couples has dropped. These things are related to perceptions of opportunity" (quoted in Suro, 1992, p. A12).

Even though the data show that the phenomena of teenage pregnancy, female-headed families, and children being raised in poverty are related to social class rather than to race, the fact that more blacks than whites are found in the lower income levels of society means that these problems are proportionally more serious for blacks. In the words of sociologist Joyce Ladner (1973), "Life in the black community has been conditioned by poverty, discrimination, and institutional subordination" (p. 425). Under these conditions, she concludes, the black family has shown surprising resilience. Although within a given black family there may be households headed by single women, the extended family often provides substantial support for its less fortunate members.

VISUAL SOCIOLOGY

INTIMATE RELATIONSHIPS

At the beginning of the chapter, we saw a young couple become a family of three as they shared the intimate experience of childbirth. In closing the chapter, we return to some emotional photos of intimate relationships. All the photos come from a book titled *Life and Love: A Book of Embraces*. They were created by professional photographers trying to capture moments of love and its expression in a diverse social world.

The prom night, the wedding scene, the gay lovers expressing their deep devotion and sadness, the rapturous young couple lost in their intimacy—all convey something of the joy of human love. But each of the photos may also make one wonder about the particular story behind it. Will the relationship of the lovers at their prom last through the subsequent phases of life as each partner continues to grow and meet new people? Will Alicia and Buddy learn to adapt to the shocks and stresses with which life confronts love at every turn? If these questions sound as if they could be from a soap

opera, there is a good reason for that. After all, love stories are featured on daytime television because, of all subjects, love is closest to our hearts, our desires, and our doubts. So often, when it seems to be within our grasp, it takes wing. But once we know it at all, we seek it forever.

The Sociological Observer

(See photo on page 475.)

It is impossible to tell from the photo anything about the sexual preferences of the people in the group. We may be able to see children and people here and there with their arms around each other, but what does that prove? Most gay and lesbian individuals and couples lead lives that are not very different from other

Person with AIDS being comforted by a friend.

© 1994 Frank Fournier/Contact Press Images

Vietnamese wedding banquet.

people's lives, and their desire to preserve their rights and privacy is extremely important to them.

Vermont is the only state in the United States that has passed a civil union act, which confers on gay and lesbian unions some of the same legal rights that married heterosexual couples enjoy, although the unions are not officially termed marriages. Recent nationwide polls indicate that about half of Americans continue to oppose gay and lesbian marriages, and conservative political leaders continue to mobilize to stop any laws that will allow such marriages, but public opinion is rapidly changing toward greater tolerance of almost all aspects of homosexual life.

© Jeanne Strongin, 1990

Alicia and Buddy.

© Donna Ferrato, 1994

© Dan Habib/Impact Visuals

Prom night.

SUMMARY

The Nature of Families

- In all known societies, almost everyone is socialized within a network of family rights and obligations that are known as family role relations.

- In simple societies, the family performs many other functions as well, but in modern societies, most of the functions that were traditionally performed by the family are performed partly or entirely by other social institutions.

- A *family* is a group of people related by blood, marriage, or adoption, and the role relations among family members are known as *kinship* relations.

- The smallest unit of family structure is the *nuclear family,* consisting of two or more people related by consanguineous ties or by adoption who share a household.

- The nuclear family in which a person is born and socialized is the *family of orientation,* and the nuclear family a person forms through marriage or cohabitation is the *family of procreation.*

- An *extended family* includes an individual's nuclear family plus all the nuclear families of his or her blood relatives.

- The traditional household consisting of two parents and their children is no longer the typical American family. Since the 1940s, there has been a dramatic increase in female-headed single-parent families and in nonfamily households, as well as in the numbers of women and men living alone and in the numbers of unmarried same-sex couples.

- The economy exerts extremely strong influences on the family and can produce drastic changes in the number of families that experience deprivation and poverty.

- These changes are often complicated by divorce, remarriage, and the combining of children of different marriages in stepfamilies.

- The typical stages of the family life cycle are family formation, start of childbearing, end of childbearing, empty nest, and family dissolution (i.e., the death of one spouse).

- As it passes through this cycle, every family experiences changes in its system of role relations.

Perspectives on the Family

- The structural context within which family life occurs can affect family interactions in a variety of ways. Problems may arise in connection with the demands placed on the family by institutions of the larger society, or as a result of its position in the society's stratification system.

- A basic contradiction inherent in the institution of the family is the need to maintain the individuality of each member while providing love and support for him or her within a set of interdependent relationships.

- From a conflict perspective, changes in the family as an institution cannot occur without conflict both within the family and between the family and other institutions. Such conflict is illustrated by public debates over family policies and "family values."

- Functionalist theorists have called attention to the loss of family functions that occurs as other social institutions assume functions that were previously reserved for the family. At the same time, they note that modern families play a vital part in early-childhood socialization, in the emotional lives of their members, and in preparing older children for adult roles.

Dynamics of Mate Selection and Marriage

- In all cultures, the process of mate selection is carried out according to basic rules of bargaining and exchange.

- In many societies, the customary pattern of mate selection is the arranged marriage, in which the families of the bride and groom negotiate the marriage contract.

- All cultures also have norms that specify whether a person brought up in that culture may marry within or outside the cultural group. Marriage within the group is termed *endogamy;* marriage outside the group is termed *exogamy.*

- In societies in which marriages are based on attraction and love, individuals tend to marry people similar to themselves in social background, a tendency that is referred to as *homogamy.*

- Homogamy generally helps maintain the separateness of religious and racial groups.

- Compared with the mate selection systems of other cultures, that of the United States gives love greater prominence. Yet from a scientific standpoint, little is known about this complex emotional state. It appears that people who fall in love tend to be alike in social characteristics but different in their psychological needs; however, this is not always the case. There is also considerable evidence that love relationships are more lasting when the partners' affection for each other is roughly equal.

- In the United States and other Western societies, the rate of divorce has risen sharply since World War II.

- In the 1980s, it was widely believed that the practice of cohabitation before marriage would result in greater marital stability, but in fact the divorce rate among couples who lived together before marriage is higher than the rate for couples who have not done so.

- There is substantial evidence showing that growing up in a lesbian or gay family does not have a negative influence on child development.

- Age at marriage has been found to be one of the leading factors in divorce. Marriages that take place when the woman is in her teens or in her 30s are much more likely to end in divorce than marriages that take place when the woman is in her 20s.

- Among other factors that have been found to be correlated with divorce are marked differences in the family backgrounds of the spouses, dependence on either spouse's extended family, patterns of marital instability in either spouse's extended family, and early pregnancy.

- Studies of the impact of divorce have found that the turmoil and distress of divorce may continue for a year or more. Both men and women have a diminished capacity for parenting after divorce and may come to depend on their children to help them cope with the demands of their own lives.

GLOSSARY

double standard: The belief that women must adhere to a different and more restrictive moral code than that applied to men. (p. 455)

family: A group of people related by blood, marriage, or adoption. (p. 456)

kinship: The role relations among people who consider themselves to be related by blood, marriage, or adoption. (p. 456)

nuclear family: Two or more people related by blood, marriage, or adoption who share a household. (p. 456)

family of orientation: The nuclear family in which a person is born and raised. (p. 457)

family of procreation: The nuclear family a person forms through marriage or cohabitation. (p. 457)

extended family: An individual's nuclear family plus the nuclear families of his or her blood relatives. (p. 457)

endogamy: A norm specifying that a person brought up in a particular culture may marry within the cultural group. (p. 471)

exogamy: A norm specifying that a person brought up in a particular culture may marry outside the cultural group. (p. 471)

homogamy: The tendency to marry a person who is similar to oneself in social background. (p. 472)

INTERNET RESOURCES

Virtual Society: The Wadsworth Sociology Resource Center
(http://sociology.wadsworth.com)
At Virtual Society you can access a wide range of enrichment material to aid your study of sociology. From the main page, click on the Student Resources link and find your course and this textbook. Next, select the chapter you are presently studying from the pull-down menu. Among the useful options for each self-study chapter are online links and exercises, flashcards, practical study tips, and practice quizzes for each chapter.

MC   MicroCase Online
From the Virtual Society home page, click on MicroCase Online to access book-specific MicroCase exercises that allow you to further explore sociological issues and principles presented in the text.

InfoTrac College Edition
Another unique option available to you at the Student Resources section at Virtual Society is InfoTrac College Edition, an online library with access to hundreds of scholarly and popular periodicals. Below are suggested search terms for this chapter, but this resource also allows you to fit your study of sociology to your own interests, by searching custom keywords.

Nuclear family
Extended family
Marriage
Double standard

American Sociological Association
(www.asanet.org)
Includes references to sociologists doing original research on the family.

Administration for Children and Families of the U.S. Government

Anthropology Department at the University of Manitoba
(www.umanitoba.ca/anthropology/kintitle.html)
Offers "Kinship and Social Organization," an online interactive tutorial that is engaging and informative and will reinforce or greatly expand your knowledge of family systems.

U.S. Census Bureau
(www.census.gov/population/socdemo)
Offers an array of statistical information, including information about the estimated median age at first marriage, the number of interracial couples, the number of young adults living at home, and language preferences within homes.

Religion

The months following the terrorist attacks on the United States saw innumerable acts of cowardly revenge as well as neighborly tolerance and generosity. Vandals in Columbus, Ohio, for example, stole into that city's oldest mosque, drilled holes in the floor, broke water pipes, flooded the building, and tore apart copies of the Koran, the Muslim sacred text. The mosque's president, Mohammed Shareef, said that the sanctuary would not be usable for many months. Non-Muslim groups in the community immediately offered space, money, and other support. A local Jewish congregation and the Rotary Club of Columbus offered to share facilities while the mosque was closed (AP, 2002).

Elsewhere in Ohio, as in many other parts of the United States, there were attacks on Islamic institutions and individual Muslims, but there were also intense efforts by officials, from President Bush to local leaders in hundreds of communities, to reach out to Arab Americans and followers of Islam and assure them that Americans know that Islam is not a religion of terror.

One of the worst effects of terrorist attacks, however, is to destroy trust among different groups and weaken the guarantees of civil liberties. Despite efforts to allay fears, U.S. government actions against Islamic organizations and against individuals suspected of affiliations with terrorist networks inevitably caused increased fear and sadness in communities like Columbus, where Muslims and non-Muslims live side by side. "The Koran is very clear: Your neighbors are those where you live. America is our neighborhood, so we have to be loyal to America," said Professor Muqtedar Khan of Adrian College in Michigan (quoted in Lampman, 2002, p. 15).

Educated American Muslims often feel most strongly the dilemmas of trying to be loyal citizens while witnessing increased surveillance of their behavior and questions about their trustworthiness. "Rather than treating American Muslims as assets—using their knowledge of the Muslim world for diplomacy and even for intelligence—the govern-

ment is treating them as suspects," Khan continued (p. 15). The domestic antiterrorism campaign seeks to reassure the majority of Americans that it is safe to travel and lead normal lives. Frequently it has the opposite effect on Muslims who are caught up in searches aimed at finding violent criminals, which many experience as understandable but extremely unsettling. "Who has the most to lose from a terrorist act?" asks a young Muslim businessman in Ohio. "It's Muslim Americans. So we are probably more interested than anyone in ending terrorist activity in the world" (quoted in AP, 2002, p. 14).

Non-Muslim Americans flocked to bookstores to buy copies of the Koran and learn more about Islam and the religious feelings of their Muslim neighbors. But small groups of haters also continued to spread fear and ill will.

All of the world's religions espouse peace and understanding among neighbors. All disavow terrorism. But some aspects of religious belief work against tolerance and, in the minds of zealots, bar the acceptance of differences in belief and behavior. All of these phenomena make the sociology of religion one of the most urgently needed and fascinating subfields within sociology.

FOCUS QUESTIONS:

- What features are common to all religions, no matter what their beliefs or how they are organized?

- Do religions defend the status quo at all times, or have they been involved in lasting social change?

- What are some characteristics of the world's major religions?

- Why is it so difficult for people of different religions to live together peacefully?

RELIGION IN SOCIETY

Religion, one of the oldest human institutions, is also among the most changeable and complex. On the one hand, religion expresses our deepest yearnings for spiritual enlightenment and understanding; on the other, conflicts over religious beliefs and practices have resulted in persecution, wars, and much human suffering, as can be seen, for example, in the violence between Muslims and Jews in the Middle East, between Hindu Indians and Muslim Pakistanis, and between Catholics and Protestants in Northern Ireland. Little wonder, therefore, that the founders of sociology—including Émile Durkheim, Karl Marx, and Max Weber—all wrote extensively about the power of religion and the great changes religion has undergone as societies have evolved.

Defining Religion

Religion is not easy to define. One could begin with a definition that has a concept of God as its core, but many religions do not have a clear concept of God. One could define religion in terms of the emotions of spirituality, oneness with nature, awe, mystery, and many other feelings, but that would not be a very helpful definition because emotions are extremely difficult to capture in words. Taking another tack, one might think in terms of

Throughout most of human history, until the past century or two, religion dominated all cultural life, as it still does in many societies. This photo shows Muslim worshippers praying outdoors in Mecca, Saudi Arabia, the most sacred site of the Islamic faith.

organized religion—churches, congregations, ministers, rabbis, and so on—but clearly the organizational aspect of religion is just one of its many dimensions. It is frustrating to have to work so hard to define something that seems so commonplace, yet without a good working definition of religion, it is impossible to compare different religions or refer to particular aspects of religion.

We can approach a working definition of religion by saying that **religion** is any set of coherent answers to the dilemmas of human existence that makes the world meaningful. From this point of view, religion is how human beings express their feelings about such ultimate concerns as sickness, death, or the meaning of life. An outstanding function of religion is to reduce personal insecurities and anxieties by providing answers to the unknown and incomprehensible (Hunt, 1999). Almost all religions involve their adherents in a system of beliefs and practices that express devotion to the supernatural and foster deep feelings of spirituality. In this sense, we say that religion functions to meet the spiritual needs of individuals.

But religion has also been defined in terms of its social function: It is a system of beliefs and rituals that helps bind people together through shared worship, thereby creating a social group. **Rituals** are formal patterns of activity that express symbolically a set of shared meanings; in the case of religious rituals such as baptism or communion, the shared meanings are sacred. The term *sacred* refers to phenomena that are regarded as extraordinary, transcendent, and outside the everyday course of events—that is, supernatural. That which is sacred may be represented by a wide variety of symbols, such as a god or set of gods; a holy person, such as the Buddha; various revered writings, such as the Bible, the Torah, or the Koran; holy objects, such as the cross or the star of David; holy cities, such as Jerusalem or Mecca; and much else. The term *profane* refers to all phenomena that are not sacred (Kurtz, 1995).

Religion as an Institution

Religion is a major social institution because it carries out important social functions and encompasses a great variety of organizations (e.g., churches, congregations, charities), each with its own statuses and roles (e.g., ministers, priests, rabbis, parishioners, fundraisers) and specific sets of norms and values (e.g., the Ten Commandments, the Golden Rule, the Koranic rules). As an institution, religion helps people express their feelings of spirituality and faith. Religion is often said to be a cultural institution because it guides a society's mental life, especially its ideas about morality, goodness, and evil. Of course, religion is not alone in performing these functions, but it remains a powerful source of moral precepts (Dudley, 2002; Gilbert, 1997).

Religion also confers legitimacy on a society's norms and values. Families seek the "blessing of holy matrimony" in wedding ceremonies. Baptisms, bar mitzvahs, confirmations, and other religious ceremonies mark the passage of children through their developmental stages and are occasions for statements about proper behavior and good conduct. Swearing on a Bible is common in courtrooms and on other occasions when norms of truth and fairness are being enforced. The political institutions of society also often look to religion for legitimation. The monarchs of eighteenth-century Europe invoked the will of God in their activities and sometimes claimed to rule by "divine right." The Pledge of Allegiance includes the phrase "under God" to reinforce the feeling that the destiny and unity of the nation and the values of liberty and justice are human efforts to carry out an even higher purpose.

CHURCH AND STATE   Most Western nations are characterized by separation of church and state. For the most part, this means that these societies, including the United States, prohibit the establishment of an official state religion. The First Amendment to the U.S. Constitution states: "Congress shall make no law respecting an establishment of religion, or prohibiting the free exercise thereof; or abridging the freedom of speech, or of the press; or the right of the people peaceably to assemble, and to petition the government for a redress of grievances." But there are ambiguities in this law. While the government clearly is prohibited from doing anything that might seem to favor one religion, such as Christianity, over another, neither can it prohibit the voluntary or free exercise of prayer or other forms of religion. Does this mean, for example, that children cannot pray in school? No, but it does mean that anything that even hints of mandatory prayer in school is contrary to the separation doctrine. Controversies over issues like school prayer are an indication of even more basic conflicts about exactly what separation of church and state means (Whittle, 2003). We return to this issue later in the chapter.

Many nations do not separate church and state; instead, they have chosen an official state religion, which usually conforms to the beliefs of the vast majority of the citizens. Israel, where Judaism is the official state religion, other nations of the middle East, where Islam is the official state religion, and Greece, where Orthodox Christianity is the state religion, are examples of societies that do not practice separation of religious and governmental institutions. Other religions in these societies are, in principle, protected under the law, but a particular religion is chosen as the national religion and its clerics are granted powers that those of other religions do not have. Nations with some form of state religion often experience conflict when religious minorities fear that their rights will not be protected equally under the law, as occurred, for example, in parts of the former Yugoslavia in the 1990s.

THEOCRACY   A more extreme form of church involvement in a society's politics is *theocracy*. In Iran, for example, religious leaders actually have the power to control elected officials, especially through their control of the judicial branch of government and of the media. Although the voting population has voiced its desire for more secular government, the hold of the Islamic leaders over civil politics remains quite strong (Kazemipur & Rezaei, 2003). In the ancient world, theocracies were far more common, and many of the societies described in the Old Testament, including Israel, were theocracies. With the secular revolutions of the modern age, from the American and French Revolutions of the eighteenth and nineteenth centuries to the Russian Revolution in the early twentieth, it appeared that secular states that excluded clerics from official power would become the norm. But events in the Muslim world and elsewhere, in which religious leaders have taken power from secular ones, cast doubt on the theory that secularization is inevitable. Even in the United States, which is far from being a theocracy, the growing power of fundamentalist Christian religious leaders over elected political leaders shows that the separation of church and state is not complete.

The Power of Faith

Until comparatively recent times, religion dominated the cultural life of human societies. Activities that are now performed by other cultural institutions, particularly education, art, and the media, used to be the province of religious leaders and organizations. In hunting-and-gathering bands and in many tribal societies, the holy person, or shaman, was also the teacher and communicator of the society's beliefs and values. In early agrarian societies, the priesthood was a powerful force; only the priests were literate and, hence, able to interpret and preserve the society's sacred texts, which represented the culture's most strongly held values and norms. For example, in ancient Egypt, where the pharaoh was worshiped as a god, his organization of regional and local priests controlled the entire society.

Today religion continues to play an important part in the lives of people throughout the world, even though the influence of organized religions is diminishing in many societies. In the United States, for example, the Gallup Poll routinely asks Americans whether they believe in God. In 1944, 96 percent of the population said they were believers; in the 1990s, the proportion of believers remains over 90 percent (National Opinion Research Center, 2000). The strength of religious attitudes and the influence of some religions can also be seen in the conflict over abortion, which plays such a prominent role in American politics, and in the controversies generated by Christian fundamentalists who believe in the literal interpretation of the Bible and may therefore deny the validity of evolutionary theory. Outside the United States, the Islamic world is torn by religious strife between liberals and fundamentalists, and Northern Ireland and Lebanon remain deeply divided largely because of conflict between Protestants and Catholics or between Christians and Muslims.

At the same time that religion is a source of division and conflict, however, it can also be a force for healing social problems and moving masses of people toward greater insight into their common humanity. This occurs at the micro level of interaction—for example, in groups like Alcoholics Anonymous, in which spirituality is an essential part of the recovery program. At the macro level, the power of faith can be seen in impoverished rural and urban communities throughout Latin America. In those communities, Catholic church leaders, parish priests, and lay parishioners have embraced the ideals of a "social gospel" that seeks the liberation of believers from poverty and oppression. These "base Christian communities," as they are often called, have become a powerful force in the movement for social justice and other far-reaching changes in their societies (Tabb, 1986).

SECULARIZATION AND ITS LIMITS   Despite the great power of spirituality, since medieval times the traditional dominance of religion in many spheres of life has been greatly re-

duced. The process by which this has occurred is termed *secularization.* This process, according to Robert A. Nisbet (1970), "results in . . . respect for values of utility rather than of sacredness alone, control of the environment rather than passive submission to it, and, in some ways most importantly, concern with man's present welfare on this earth rather than his supposed immortal relation to the gods" (p. 388). Secularization usually accompanies the increasing differentiation of cultural institutions—that is, the separation of other institutions from religion. In Europe during the Middle Ages, for example, there were no schools separate from the church. The state, too, was thought of as encompassed by the church or at least as legitimated by the official state religion and church organization. Laws and courts were guided by religious doctrine, and clerical law could often be as important as civil law—indeed, to be tried as a heretic often meant torture and death. Churches engaged in large-scale economic activity, owned much land and property, and often mounted their own armies.

The Renaissance, the Enlightenment, and the revolutions of the eighteenth and nineteenth centuries all speeded the process of differentiation in which schools, science, laws, courts, and other institutions gained independence from religious control. However, this process has not occurred at the same rate throughout the world. For example, the removal of education from the control of religious institutions has occurred more slowly in some societies than in others. In Eastern Europe, all education was controlled by the state until recently. In most coun-

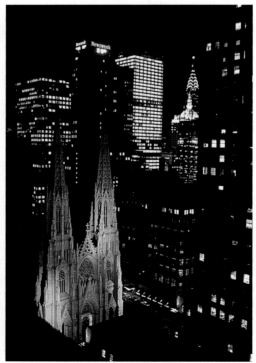

These two pictures of cathedrals provide a graphic illustration of secularization. In the medieval town, the cathedral dominated the landscape; it was the highest, and symbolically the most important, building. In the modern city, even the great cathedral is dwarfed by the greater scale and importance of the commercial buildings that surround it.

© David Moore, Black Star

© Robert Goldwitz/Photo Researchers, Inc.

tries of Western Europe and the Americas, there are religious schools, but these are separate from and overshadowed by the state-run educational system (Kurtz, 1995).

The emergence of cultural institutions like the secular public school and the weakening of the influence of religion on government do not result in complete secularization. People who are free to determine their own religious beliefs and practices may attend church less often or not at all, but total secularization does not occur (Finke & Stark, 1992). Moreover, in almost every society that has experienced secularization, one can find examples of religious revival. Indeed, modern communication technologies, especially television, have contributed immensely to the revival of interest in religion, as witnessed by the popularity of "televangelists" like Oral Roberts and Pat Robertson (Iannaccone, Stark, & Finke, 1998).

FAITH AND TOLERANCE: UNEASY TOGETHER People who believe that theirs is the "one true faith" are found in every religion. For such true believers, it can be extremely difficult, if not impossible, to practice tolerance and accept other beliefs and other religions. Thus the Taliban's destruction of ancient Buddhist statues in Afghanistan in 2001 was widely viewed as an act of extreme religious intolerance. So were some extremely anti-Islamic statements

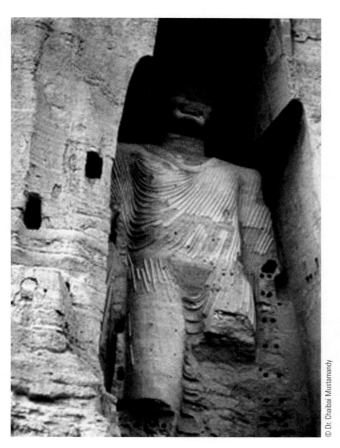

made by a few Christian and Jewish religious leaders in the United States after the events of September 11. But is Islam more or less intolerant than Christianity, Judaism, Hinduism, or any other major religion?

Adherents of all the major religions have at times acted as if theirs were the one true faith, and they have used this claim as a basis for persecuting those who deviated from their beliefs, both within their own religion and in other religions. In our own time, the assassination of peacemaker Yitzhak Rabin by fanatical Jewish fundamentalists is an example of extreme intolerance within a religion. In Christianity, for centuries before the Enlightenment it was common practice to harass and kill people who practiced pagan religions and to attack believers in other monotheistic faiths (particularly Judaism and Islam), who were called "infidels" or nonbelievers. During the same historical period, far more tolerance for other religions was practiced in the Islamic world. Jews expelled from Spain during the Catholic Inquisition in the 1490s, for example, were often given safe havens in Islamic societies. So from a historical perspective, we see that all major religions pass through phases during which they are more or less tolerant of other religions.

The separation of church and state, a hallmark of American culture and society as well as many other democracies, negates the idea that there is only one true faith. Instead, it promotes the idea that "you may believe what you like, and so may I, and neither can impose belief on the other." Thus Thomas Cahil, a scholar of religion and an expert on religious tolerance, writes:

> Each of the great religions creates, almost from its inception, a colorful spectrum of voices that range from pacifist to terrorist. But each religion, because of its metaphorical ambiguity and intellectual subtlety, holds within it marvelous potential for development and adaptation. This development will be full of zigzags and may sometimes seem as slow as the development of the universe, but it runs—almost inevitably, it seems—from exclusivist militancy to inclusive peace. (Cahil, 2002, p. 4)

These Afghan statues of the Buddha, carved into a mountainside over 1500 years ago, were destroyed by the Taliban, the intensely fundamentalist Islamic government that was disposed in 2001 by a United Nations–sanctioned invasion. The Taliban rules Afghanistan according to its own interpretations of Islamic and tribal Pashtun law. Islamic leaders throughout the world condemned the destruction as "un-Islamic" and "an act of cultural genocide against humanity."

VARIETIES OF RELIGIOUS BELIEF

Religious sentiments and behavior persist even in highly secularized societies like the United States. As sociologist Robert Wuthnow (1988) points out:

> The assumption that religion in modern societies would gradually diminish in importance or else become less capable of influencing public life was once widely accepted. That assumption has now become a matter of dispute. . . . Modern religion is resilient and yet subject to cultural influences; it does not merely survive or decline, but adapts to its environment in complex ways. (p. 474)

Many of the adaptations that religions make to social change become evident when one examines the varieties of religious belief in the world today, and especially when one studies the major world religions.

Major World Religions

In a 1913 essay, Max Weber commented that "by 'world religions' we understand the five religions or religiously determined systems of life-regulation which have known how to gather multitudes of confessors around them" (1958/1913, p. 267). Among these Weber included, in addition to Christianity, "the Confucian, Hinduist, Buddhist, and Islamic religious ethics." He added that despite its small population of adherents, Judaism should also be considered a world religion because of its influence on Christianity and Islam as well as on Western ethics and values even outside the religious sphere of life.

In discussing religion, sociologists often refer to the "Islamic world" of the Middle East, the "Roman Catholic world" of Latin America and southern Europe, the "Hindu world" of the Indian subcontinent, and the "Buddhist world" of the Far East. The United States, northern Europe, and Australia are among the societies in which Protestantism is strongest. There are also, of course, the nations of Eastern Europe and the former Soviet Union, where until recently communism as a civil religion was the only legitimate belief system (although millions of people resisted the state's efforts to eradicate traditional religious faiths) (Robertson, 1985).

Figure 17.1 shows the distribution of the world's major religions. Note that in many parts of the world, particularly in Asia and Africa, large numbers of people practice other religions. Many are indigenous peoples whose religious practices may be influenced by the major world religions but continue to be based on beliefs and ways of

NORTHERN AMERICA	(296)
Roman Catholic	75 (25%)
Protestant	121 (41%)
Other Christian	58 (20%)
Jewish	6 (2%)
(All other)	36 (12%)

LATIN AMERICA	(490)
Roman Catholic	409 (83%)
Protestant	35 (7%)
Other Christian	12 (2%)
(All other)	34 (7%)

EUROPE	(728)
Roman Catholic	269 (37%)
Protestant	80 (11%)
Other Christian	21 (3%)
(All other)	370 (51%)

AFRICA	(748)
Muslim	309 (41%)
Christian	361 (48%)
Ethnic Religionist	70 (9%)
(All other)	8 (1%)

THE WORLD	(5,804)
Christian	1,955 (37%)
Muslim	1,126 (19%)
Hindu	793 (14%)
Buddhist	325 (6%)
(All other)	1,605 (28%)

ASIA	(3,513)
Christian	303 (9%)
Muslim	778 (22%)
Hindu	707 (20%)
Buddhist	322 (9%)
(All other)	1,403 (40%)

OCEANIA	(29)
Christian	24 (82%)
(All other)	5 (17%)

Note: Percentages may not add up to 100 because of rounding.
Source: Data from *Britannica Book of the Year*, 2002.

MAJOR RELIGIONS OF THE WORLD, RANKED BY SIZE (MILLIONS OF MEMBERS)

1. Christianity	2,000	7. primal-indigenous	190	15. Shinto	4
2. Islam	1,300	8. Sikhism	23	16. Cao Dai	3
3. Hinduism	900	9. Yoruba religion	20	17. Tenrikyo	2.4
4. Secular/Nonreligious/ Agnostic/Atheist	850	10. Juche	19	18. Neo-Paganism	1
		11. Spiritism	14	19. Unitarian-Universalism	0.8
5. Buddhism	360	12. Judaism	14	20. Scientology	0.75
6. Chinese traditional religion	225	13. Baha'i	6	21. Rastafarianism	0.7
		14. Jainism	4	22. Zoroastrianism	0.15

Figure 17.1   Estimated Religious Membership, by Continent (millions)

worship that are unique to that culture. For example, in her sociological portrait of Mama Lola, a Haitian priestess, Karen McCarthy Brown notes that many Haitians practice voodoo, which is derived from African religious beliefs. Some of Mama Lola's followers may worship in Catholic churches yet continue to practice the traditional rituals of voodoo as well (Brown, 1991, 1992).

Classification of Religious Beliefs

The religions practiced throughout the world today vary from belief in magic and supernatural spirits to complicated ideas of God and saints, as well as secular religions in which there is faith but not God (Bowker, 1997). With such a wide range of religious beliefs and practices to consider, it is useful to classify them in a systematic way. One often-used system classifies religions according to their central belief. In this scheme, the multiplicity of religious forms is reduced to a more manageable list consisting of five major types: simple supernaturalism, animism, theism, abstract ideals, and civil religion. (See the Study Chart below.) In this section, we describe each type briefly. Be warned, though, that not all religions fit neatly into these basic categories.

SIMPLE SUPERNATURALISM   In less complex and rather isolated societies, people may believe in a great force or spirit, but they may not have a well-defined concept of God or a set of rituals involving God. Studies by anthropologists have found that some isolated peoples (e.g., South Pacific island cultures and Eskimo tribes) believe strongly in the power of a supernatural force but do not attempt to embody that force in a visualized conception of God. In this form of religion, called **simple supernaturalism**, there is no discontinuity between the world of the senses and the supernatural; all natural phenomena are part of a single force. Consider these remarks by an Inuit Eskimo:

> When I was small I knew a man who came from the polar bears. He had a low voice and was big. That man knew when he was a cub and his bear mother was bringing him to the land from the ocean. He remembered it. (quoted in Steltzer, 1982, p. 111)

STUDY CHART

FORMS OF RELIGION

FORM	DESCRIPTION	EXAMPLE
Simple Supernaturalism	A form of religion in which there is no discontinuity between the world of the senses and the supernatural; all natural phenomena are part of a single force	Some Inuit Eskimo cultures
Animism	A form of religion in which all forms of life and all aspects of the earth are inhabited by gods or supernatural powers	Native American culture; some African tribal cultures
Theism	A form of religion in which gods are conceived of as separate from humans and from other living things on the earth, although the gods are in some way responsible for the creation of humans and for their fate	
Polytheism	A form of theism in which there are numerous gods, all of whom occupy themselves with some aspect of the universe and of human life	The pantheon of gods of the ancient Greeks and Romans
Monotheism	A form of theism that is centered on belief in a single all-powerful God who determines human fate and can be addressed through prayer	Christianity, Islam, Judaism
Abstract Ideals	A form of religion that is centered on an abstract ideal of spirituality and human behavior	Buddhism, Confucianism
Civil Religion	A collection of beliefs, and rituals for communicating those beliefs, that exists outside religious institutions	Marxism-Leninism; some versions of humanism

ANIMISM   More common among hunting-and-gathering societies is a form of religion termed **animism,** in which all forms of life and all aspects of the earth are inhabited by gods or supernatural powers. Most of the indigenous peoples of the Western Hemisphere were animists, and so were many of the tribal peoples of Africa before the European conquests. Europeans almost invariably branded American Indians "heathens and barbarians" because, among other things, the Indians believed that "people journeyed into supernatural realms and returned, animals conversed with each other and humans, and the spirits of rocks and trees had to be placated" (Jennings, 1975, p. 48). The same can be said of European attitudes toward African religions. Determined to subjugate nature and make the earth yield more wealth for new populations, the Europeans could not appreciate the meanings of animism for people who lived more closely in touch with nature.

Yet if one takes some time to read about the perceptions of animistic religions, it becomes clear that they contain much wisdom for our beleaguered planet. In one beautifully written account, an Oglala Sioux medicine man, Black Elk, speaks "the story of all life that is holy and is good to tell, and of us two-leggeds sharing in it with the four-leggeds and the wings of the air and all green things;

for these are children of one mother and their father is one Spirit" (Neihardt, 1959/1932, p. 1). Black Elk's prayer continues:

> Grandfather, Great Spirit, lean close to the earth that you may hear the voice I send. You towards where the sun goes down, behold me; Thunder Beings, behold me! You where the White Giant lives in power, behold me! You where the sun shines continually, whence come the day-break star and the day, behold me! You in the depths of the heavens, an eagle of power, behold! And you, Mother Earth, the only Mother, you who have shown mercy to your children! (p. 5)

Traces of animism can also be seen in the religious beliefs of the ancient Egyptians, Greeks, and Romans. The Greeks, for example, spoke of naiads inhabiting rivers and springs, and of dryads inhabiting forests. These varieties of nymphs were believed to be part of the natural environment in which they dwelled, but sometimes they took on semihuman qualities. They thus bridged the gap between a quasi-animistic religion and the more familiar theistic systems that evolved in Greece and Rome.

THEISM   Religions whose central belief is **theism** usually conceive of gods as separate from humans and from other living things on the earth, although these gods are in some way responsible for the creation of humans and for their fate. Many ancient religions were **polytheistic,** meaning that they included numerous gods, all of whom occupied themselves with some aspect of the universe and of human life. In the religion of the ancient Greeks, warfare was the concern of Ares; music, healing, and prophecy were the domain of Apollo; his sister Artemis was concerned with hunting; Poseidon was the god of seafaring; Athena was the goddess of handicrafts and intellectual pursuits; and so on. A similar division of concerns and attributes could be found among the gods of the Romans and, later, among the gods of the Celtic tribes of Gaul and Britain.

The ancient Hebrews were among the first of the world's peoples to evolve a **monotheistic** religion—one centered on belief in a single all-powerful God who determines human fate and can be addressed through prayer. This belief is expressed in the central creed of the Jews: "Hear O Israel, the Lord our God, the Lord is One." Jewish monotheism, based on the central idea of a covenant between God and the Jewish people (as represented in the written laws of the Ten Commandments, for example), helped stimulate the codification of religious law and ritual, so that the Jews became known as "the people of the book." As they traveled and settled throughout the Middle East, the Jews were able to take their religion with them and hold on to the purity of their beliefs and practices (Johnson, 1987; Kurtz, 1995).

Among the Quechua-speaking Indian peoples of the Andes, Christianity and older religious practices often coexist. Shown here is a ritual in which guinea pigs, believed to possess magical powers, are sacrificed for the well-being of the community.

© Edmundo Morales

art *and the sociological eye*

Sister Gertrude Morgan, Religious Folk Artist

As we experience other societies and cultures, it is remarkable how much of our time is spent looking at and thinking about the expression of spiritual feelings in their art, literature, and architecture. Anyone traveling through the capitals of Europe or Asia or any other continent will find that the greatest examples of a culture's achievements are often inspired by religious feelings and institutions. Michelangelo's breathtaking sculptures and frescos in the Vatican's Sistine Chapel, the great mosques of Istanbul, the prayer wheels on Tibetan mountain crags, the processions of carved saints in a Mexican Indian village festival, and the whimsically spiritual work of American religious folk artists are only a few of the thousands of examples of expressions of faith that form the heart of so many of the world's cultures.

Sister Gertrude Morgan is considered one of the most distinctive religious artists in the United States. Born in 1900 to a devoutly Christian African-American family in Lafayette, Alabama, Morgan experienced a series of religious visions that shaped her life and led her, at the age of 23, to begin drawing and painting. In an unschooled but inspiring and highly personal style, she portrays the religious life of her society in the form of a spiritual "autobiography." Her work is an outstanding example of how religious feelings and thoughts find expression in artistic works by people who did not necessarily have artistic training and did not necessarily think of themselves as artists.

Morgan, for example, regarded her art as a form of private communication between herself and her God. The images and the words she wrote on them came pouring out of her in response to the experience of religious inspiration. But she never exhibited her work or had any intention of selling it. In the 1970s, art lovers in New Orleans, her adopted hometown, discovered her work and began featuring it in exhibitions. Much against her will, Morgan became something of an artistic celebrity. This acclaim disturbed her; she felt that it distracted her from her devotion and dedication to good works. As a result, she stopped producing art, believing that she had been so ordered by God.

After her death in 1980, Morgan's art became even more highly acclaimed. In 1982, it was prominently featured in a historic exhibition titled "Black Folk Art in America" at Washington's Corcoran Gallery. Its simple beauty and evidence of saintly devotion

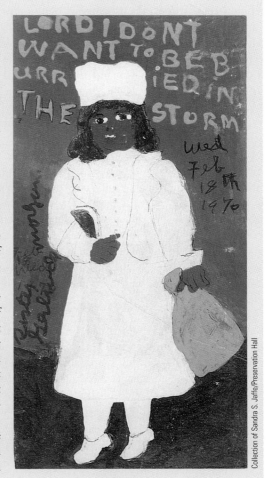

Collection of Sandra S. Jaffe/Preservation Hall

Lord I don't want to be buried in the storm, by Sister Gertrude Morgan, 1970. Acrylic and ink on cardboard, 1912 cm x 912 cm.

continue to inspire. Morgan's story is not dissimilar to that of many other folk artists whose religious vision seems unquenchable.

Sister Morgan is but one of many well-known religious folk artists. Somewhere in your area there may be undiscovered folk artists creating similar works, and it is likely that even if their work is largely secular, some of it expresses their deepest spiritual feelings.

Collection of the Museum of American Folk Art, New York. Gift of Mr. And Mrs. Edwin C. Braman. 1983.14.4.

The Barefoot Prophetesses, by Sister Gertrude Morgan, New Orleans, Louisiana, © 1971. Watercolor on paper, 11½" x 16".

Christianity and Islam are also monotheistic religions. The Roman Catholic version of Christianity envisions God as embodied in a Holy Trinity consisting of God the Father, Christ the Son, and the Holy Spirit of God, which has the ability to inspire the human spirit. The fundamental beliefs of Islam are similar in many respects to those of Judaism and Christianity. Islam is a monotheistic religion centering on the worship of one God, Allah, according to the teachings of the Koran as given by Allah to Mohammed, the great prophet of the Muslim faith. In his early preachings, Mohammed appears to have believed that the followers of Jesus and the believers in Judaism would recognize him as God's messenger and realize that Allah was the same as the God they worshiped. The fundamental aim of Islam is to serve God as he demands to be served in the Koran.

Another basically monotheistic religion, Hinduism, is difficult to categorize. On the one hand, it incorporates the strong idea of an all-powerful God who is everywhere yet is "unsearchable"; on the other hand, it conceives of a God who can be represented variously as the Creator (Brahma), the Preserver (Vishnu), and the Destroyer (Shiva). Each of these personifications takes several forms in Hindu ritual and art. Of all the great world religions, Hinduism teaches most forcefully that all religions are roughly equal "paths to the same summit."

ABSTRACT IDEALS   In China, Japan, and other societies of the Far East, the dominant religions are centered not on devotion to a god or gods but on an abstract ideal of spirituality and human behavior. The central belief of Buddhism, perhaps the most important of these religions, is embodied in these thoughts of Siddhartha Gautama, the Buddha:

> Life is a Journey
> Death is a return to the Earth
> The universe is like an inn
> The passing years are like dust

Like all the world's major religions, Buddhism has many branches. The ideal that unifies them all, however, is the teaching that worship is not a matter of prayer to God but a quest for the experience of godliness within oneself through meditation and awareness.

Another important religion based on abstract ideals is Confucianism, which is derived from the teachings of the philosopher Confucius (551–479 BC). The sayings of Confucius are still revered throughout much of the Far East, especially among the Chinese, although the formal study of Confucius's thought has been banned since the communist revolution of the late 1940s and early 1950s. The central belief of Confucianism is that one must learn and practice the wisdom of the ancients. "He that is really good," Confucius taught, "can never be unhappy. He that

is really wise can never be perplexed. He that is really brave can never be afraid" (quoted in McNeill, 1963, p. 231).

In Confucianism, the central goal of the individual is to become a good ruler or a good and loyal follower and thus to carry out the *tao* of his or her position. *Tao* is an untranslatable word that refers to the practice of virtues that make a person excellent at his or her discipline. As is evident even in this brief description, Confucianism is a set of ideals and sayings that tend toward conservatism and acceptance of the status quo, although the wise ruler should be able to improve society for those in lesser positions. Little wonder that under communism this ancient and highly popular set of moral principles and teachings was banned in favor of what sociologists call a civil religion.

CIVIL RELIGION   In the last few decades, some social scientists, notably Robert Bellah (1970), have expanded the definition of religion to include so-called **civil religions.** These are collections of beliefs, and rituals for communicating those beliefs, that exist outside religious institutions (Swift, 1998). Often, as in the former Soviet communist societies, they are attached to the institutions of the state. Marxism-Leninism can be thought of as a civil religion, symbolized by the reverence once paid to Lenin's tomb. Central to communism as a civil religion is the idea that private property is evil, but property held in common by all members of the society (be it the work group, the community, or the entire nation) is good. The struggle against private property results in the creation of the socialist personality, which values all human lives and devalues excessive emphasis on individual success, especially success measured by the accumulation of property. Although the communist regimes of the Soviet Union and Eastern Europe have fallen, there are millions of people in those nations and in China who were socialized to believe in these principles.

In the United States, certain aspects of patriotic feeling are sometimes said to amount to a civil religion: reverence for the flag, the Constitution, the Declaration of Independence, and other symbols of America is cited as an example. Thus most major public events, be they commencements, political rallies, or Super Bowl games, begin with civil-religious rituals such as the singing of the national anthem or the recitation of the Pledge of Allegiance, in which a nonsectarian God is invoked to protect the nation's unity ("one nation under God").

Although there is no doubt that Lenin's image and the American flag may be viewed as sacred in some contexts, neither communism nor American patriotism can compete with the major world religions in the power of their central ideals and their spirituality. In consequence, sociologists tend to concentrate on religions in the traditional sense—that is, on the enactment of rituals that represent the place of sacred beliefs in human life. In the remainder of this chapter, we discuss the structure of religious institutions and the processes by which new ones arise.

RELIGION AND SOCIAL CHANGE

Now that the nations behind the former "Iron Curtain" are enjoying new freedoms, the role of religion in bringing about social change is an important aspect of life in those societies. Indeed, in many parts of the world, religion is one of the primary forces opposing or supporting change. However, it is not always a simple matter to predict whether religion will encourage change or hinder it. In Israel, for example, highly orthodox Jews, although they account for a small minority of the electorate, often hold the votes necessary to keep the ruling party in power. The orthodox political parties favor continued Jewish settlement on the West Bank of the Jordan River and oppose the creation of a Palestinian state near Israel's borders.

In the United States, the Catholic church plays an active role in seeking social change. The church strongly opposes women's right to obtain abortions legally. Instead, it supports a return to the traditional view of abortion as a crime, which is based on the belief that humans must submit to the will of God and not use their technological skills to achieve power over life and death. In this instance, therefore, although the church is promoting social change, the change represents a return to an earlier moral standard. Throughout much of Latin America, in contrast, the Catholic church is fighting in support of the masses of urban and rural poor who seek social justice and equitable economic development. In Brazil, for example, the typical Catholic priest or nun favors the political left, which seeks a more egalitarian distribution of wealth and income and is highly critical of the rich.

We could add many other examples of the role played by religion and religious organizations in social change. But in attempting to generalize about the relationship between religion and social change, it is useful to return briefly to classic sociological theories.

MARX AND WEBER ON RELIGION AND SOCIAL CHANGE

The pioneering European sociologists, particularly Karl Marx and Max Weber, noted the prominent role of religion in social change. But they wondered whether the influence of religious faith is a determining force in social change or whether religious sentiments and the activities of religious organizations are an outgrowth of changes in more basic economic and political institutions.

Marx, as we have seen, believed that economic institutions are fundamental to all societies and that they are the source of social change. In his view, religion and other cultural institutions are shaped by economic and political institutions; they are a "superstructure" that simply reflects the values of those institutions—of markets, firms, the government, the military, and so on. The function of cultural institutions, especially religion, is to instill in the masses the values of the dominant class. In this sense, they can be said to shape the consciousness of a people, but they do so in such a way as to justify existing patterns of economic exploitation and the existing class structure. Religion, in Marx's words, is "the opium of the people" because it eases suffering through prayer and ritual and deludes the masses into accepting their situation as divinely ordained rather than organizing to change the social system.

For Marx, the French Revolution represented a major example of what would happen to religious institutions in a time of revolutionary change. The French Revolution eventually established democracy and capitalism as dominant systems in many Western nations in the eighteenth and nineteenth centuries. It stripped power and privilege from the landowning aristocracy and the church officials who used their religious authority to justify the status quo of rule by kings and their allies in the aristocracy.

For Weber, on the other hand, religion can be the cause of major social change rather than the outcome or reflection of changes in other institutions. Weber set forth this thesis in one of his most famous works, *The Protestant Ethic and the Spirit of Capitalism* (1974/1904). Noting that the rise of Protestantism in Europe had coincided with the emergence of capitalism, Weber hypothesized that the Protestant Reformation had brought about a significant change in cultural values and that this was responsible for the more successful development of capitalist economic systems in Protestant regions.

As Weber explained it, Protestantism instilled in its followers certain values that were conducive to business enterprise, resulting in the accumulation of wealth. Because the early Protestants believed that wealth was not supposed to be spent on luxuries or "the pleasures of the flesh," the only alternative was to invest it in new or existing business enterprises—in other words, to contribute to the rapid economic growth characteristic of capitalist systems (Kurtz, 1995). This view was reinforced by the belief—also part of the Protestant ethic—that a person who worked hard was likely to be among those predestined for salvation.

Some have questioned the validity of Weber's thesis regarding Protestantism and early capitalism, but there can be no doubt that religious institutions are capable of assuming a major role in shaping modern societies. Throughout the Islamic world, there are currents of orthodoxy and reform that threaten to cause both civil and international wars. And as noted earlier, in many Latin American communities the Catholic church leads the movement for large-scale social change. So Marx was wrong in his claim that religion functions largely to maintain the existing values of more basic social institutions. On the contrary, religion can often lead to new ways of organizing societies—to new political and economic institutions as well as whole new lifestyles.

The Marxian view of religion is still relevant to those who are critical of the influence of religious institutions. These critics assert that religion, along with other cultural institutions such as education, reaffirms and perpetuates inequalities of wealth, prestige, and power. When the poor are encouraged to pray for a better life, for example, they are further oppressed by a religion that prevents them from realizing that they need to marshal their own power to challenge the status quo. Thus there is still some question about whether (and how much) religious institutions change society in any fundamental way.

To make informed judgments about this and related issues, we need to have a better understanding of the nature of religious organizations and how they function in modern societies. In the next section, therefore, we describe the main types of religious organizations. We then focus on trends in religious belief and practice in the United States.

STRUCTURE AND CHANGE IN MODERN RELIGIONS

Religion today is a highly structured institution, with numerous statuses and roles within a variety of organizations as well as many kinds of smaller, less bureaucratic groups. This was not always so. The religions of tribal peoples were not highly institutionalized; that is, there were no separate organizations like churches or interfaith councils or youth fellowships. It is true that the occupational status of holy person or priest might exist.

Thus most Native American peoples had spiritual leaders who specialized in the rituals and symbols through which the members of the tribe could address the Great Spirit and the sacred spirits of their ancestors. But even in societies that had spiritual leaders or priests, religious practice was intertwined with tribal and family life. There was no concept of the church as a separate institution specializing in religious rituals.

Religion as a fully differentiated institution developed in agrarian societies, and formal religious organizations first appeared in such societies. As we saw in Chapter 4, agrarian societies produce enough surplus food to support a class of priests and other specialists in religious rituals. In those less complex societies, religion was incorporated into village and family life; it had not yet become differentiated into a rec-

ognized, separate institution with its own statuses and roles (Warner, 1998). Over time, however, the development of religious institutions resulted in a wide variety of organizations devoted to religious practice. Today those organizations include the church, the sect, and the denomination.

Forms of Religious Organization

CHURCHES AND SECTS   A **church** may be defined as a religious organization that has strong ties to the larger society. Often in its history it has enjoyed the loyalty of most of the society's members; indeed, it may have been linked with the state itself (Weber, 1963/1922). An example is the Church of England, or Anglican church.

A **sect,** by contrast, is an organization that rejects the religious beliefs or practices of established churches. Whereas the church distributes the benefits of religious participation to anyone who enters the sanctuary and stays to follow the service, the sect limits the benefits of membership (i.e., salvation, fellowship, common prayer) to those who qualify on narrower grounds of membership and belief (McGuire, 1987; Weber, 1963/1922).

Sects require strong commitment on the part of their members and usually are formed when a small group of church members splits off to form a rival organization. The sect may not completely reject the beliefs and rituals of the church from which it arose, but it changes them enough to be considered a separate organization. Most "storefront churches" are actually sects that have developed their own particular interpretations of religious ritual.

An important difference between churches and sects is that churches draw their adherents from a large social environment (i.e., from a large pool of possible members), whereas the size of the population from which a sect draws its members tends to be small (Iannaccone, Stark, & Finke, 1998). Also, churches make relatively limited demands on their members, whereas sects make heavy claims on their members' time, money, and emotional commitment. As Robert Wuthnow (1988) writes: "Churches attempt to regulate or fulfill a few of the activities or needs of large numbers of people; sects attempt to regulate or fulfill many of the activities or needs of small numbers of people" (p. 495).

DENOMINATIONS   A third type of religious organization is the **denomination.** Unlike a sect, a denomination is on good terms with the religious institution from which it developed, but it must compete with other denominations for members. An example of a denomination is the United Methodist Church, a Protestant denomination that must compete for members with other Protestant denominations such as Presbyterians, Episcopalians, and Baptists. Denominations sometimes evolve from sects. This occurs when the sect is

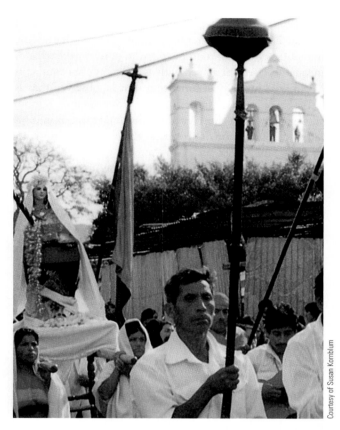

Courtesy of Susan Kornblum

This photograph of a religious festival in the province of Chiapas in Mexico clearly shows the social organization of the village church. The male officials of the church (visible in the background) march with banners and candles while the women bear the saint through the village.

successful in recruiting new members and grows in both size and organizational complexity (Wuthnow, 1994b).

In a recent study of the strength of attachments to denominations (e.g., Lutheranism, Congregationalism, or Presbyterianism), sociologist Nancy Ammerman (2000) and her colleagues interviewed people about the importance of denominational differences in Christian congregations. They visited more than 500 churches, which included 91 different denominational and other religious groups, including 51 congregations that were nondenominational or interdenominational and another 22 that were part of more informal networks.

Although many people change congregations one or more times during their lives and some churches are less attached to their parent denomination than others, Ammerman found that denominational differences are hardly about to disappear. Her main finding was that:

A congregation's sense of identification with a particular denominational tradition is closely tied to how many of its members grew up in the tradi-

tion. Relatedly, individuals who themselves have "switched" are less likely to say that denomination is important to them. Which is the chicken and which the egg is hard to say. But congregations full of "switchers" are much less likely to report that denomination is an important part of the way they "do church" (49 percent versus 69 percent of congregations with few switchers).

The phenomenon of "switching" is relevant to a lot of congregations. Indeed, nearly three-quarters of the white Protestant congregations we studied reported that half or more of their members grew up in another denomination. African-American Protestants are much less denominationally mobile. Only 11 percent of the ones in which we interviewed people had similar numbers of switchers in their pews. Similarly, almost all the Catholic parishes contain mostly people who grew up Catholic. (Ammerman, 2000, p. 3)

CULTS   Still another type of religious body, the **cult,** differs in significant ways from the organizations just described. Cults are usually entirely new religions whose members hold beliefs and engage in rituals that differ from those of existing religions. Some cults have developed out of existing religions. This occurred in the case of early Christianity, which began as a cult of Jews who believed that Jesus of Nazareth was the Messiah and who practiced rituals that were often quite different from those of Judaism. Cults may also be developed by people who were not previously involved in a church or sect, such as individuals who become active in pagan cults like those based on ancient forms of witchcraft (Barrett, 1996). Most major religions began as seemingly insignificant cults, but new cults are formed every day throughout the world, and few of them last long enough to become recognized religions. The Mormons, who began as a cult in 1830 with six members, grew into a large religious organization with more than 60,000 members by 1850. Today the Mormon church is one of the fastest-growing Christian churches in the world (Finke & Stark, 1992).

In a study of trends in church, sect, and cult membership, sociologists Roger Finke and Rodney Stark found that, contrary to common assumptions, the rate at which cults are formed is no higher today than it was in earlier historical periods. Moreover, compared to some of the earlier cults, contemporary cults often have less success in gaining members:

No cult movement of the sixties or early seventies seems ever to have attracted more than a few thousand American members, and most of even the well-publicized groups counted their true membership in the hundreds, not the thousands. For example, after more than thirty years of missionizing, it is estimated that there have never been more than 5,000 followers of the Unification Church (the Moonies) in the United States, and some of them are from abroad. (Finke & Stark, 1992, p. 241; see also Melton, 1989)

In a similar example, Barry Kosmin and his colleagues (1991) estimate, on the basis of the largest sample survey of religious beliefs ever conducted in the United States, that actual membership in the Church of Scientology very likely does not exceed 45,000, despite the cult's claims that its domestic membership is more than 450,000. On the basis of findings such as these, Finke and Stark conclude that cults have always interested some relatively small proportion of U.S. citizens and still do. Despite sensational media accounts of the activities of cults like the Branch Davidians, the rate of cult formation in the United States has not increased appreciably in recent decades, nor are cults more successful in gaining members than they were before.

One reason cults and sects do not always grow in numbers or influence is that established religions often absorb them through the process known as *co-optation.* This term is not limited to religious institutions; we encountered it in Chapter 8 in connection with social movements. It refers to any process whereby an organization deals with potentially threatening individuals or groups by incorporating them into its own organizational structure (Selznick, 1966). For example, over the centuries the Roman Catholic church has been particularly successful at co-opting regional Catholic sects by including their leaders in the panoply of lesser saints, thereby allowing people to worship a holy person of their own culture while remaining true to the world church.

stratification because they must appeal to people of all classes. Sects, on the other hand, may be led by charismatic individuals who appeal to people who have felt the sting of inequality. Niebuhr agreed with Weber that class conflict is a primary cause of sect formation. But he observed that as a sect becomes more successful and better organized, it becomes more like a church and begins to justify existing systems of stratification. This creates the conditions in which new sects may emerge.

Another motivation for the formation of sects or cults is dissatisfaction with the interactions that occur in more established organizations. In church rituals, for example, prayer is often led by a priest or other religious professional and is relatively restrained, whereas in sects and cults communication between God and the individual is more direct and typically allows the individual to express deep emotions. The differing styles of interaction in different types of religious organizations can be illustrated by the contrast between the hierarchy of statuses and roles that characterizes the Catholic church (with its pope, cardinals, bishops, priests, and other well-defined statuses) and the seemingly greater equality and looser structure of a cult like Krishna Consciousness or the Unification Church.

People who are attracted to cults are often influenced by a charismatic leader who inspires them to new and very personal achievements, such as ecstatic experiences, a sense of salvation, or a release from physical or psychological suffering. Some become cult members simply because they are lonely; others are born to cult members and are socialized into the cult.

Some, but by no means all, cults are extremely authoritarian and punitive. Their leaders may demand that mem-

Religious Interaction and Change

Sects and cults are a major source of change in religious organizations. People who are not satisfied with more established churches and denominations, or are otherwise alienated from society, often form or join a cult or sect (Barrett, 1996). One of the most convincing explanations of the emergence of sects was suggested by H. Richard Niebuhr (1929), borrowing from Max Weber's (1922) pioneering analysis of churches and sects. According to Weber, churches tend to justify the presence of inequality and

The Ghost Dance religion spread rapidly in the 1890s and was based on the belief that through the dance, all Native Americans, living and dead, would be reunited on an earth restored to its original natural state.

National Anthropological Archives

bers cut themselves off entirely from family and friends and sacrifice everything for the sake of the cult. The leaders may also insist that they themselves are above the moral teachings to which their followers must adhere. Under these conditions of isolation and submission to a dominant authority, cult members may be driven to incredible extremes of behavior—even mass suicide, as occurred in the case of the followers of Heaven's Gate in 1997. However, not all cults are so dangerous or so easily condemned, and there is an ongoing conflict between norms that protect the right of individuals to belong to cults and efforts to protect people from the harm that can occur when cult leaders place themselves above morality and the law.

SOCIOLOGICAL INSIGHTS INTO WACO AND WOUNDED KNEE

The confrontation that took place in Waco, Texas, on February 28, 1993, between the Branch Davidians and agents of the Bureau of Alcohol, Tobacco, and Firearms (BATF) revealed the need for greater understanding of alternative religious groups (Foster et al., 1998). Among sociologists who study religion and social change, there is growing consensus that the term *cult* can be dangerous when it is applied as a pejorative label to all religious groups that are outside the mainstream of religious organizations.

Nancy Ammerman, one of the foremost authorities on Protestant religious groups in the United States, notes that "One of the primary interpretive lenses through which the general public views groups such as the Branch Davidians is the lens supplied by 'cult awareness' groups and 'exit counselors.' Namely, most people think members of a group like the Branch Davidians must have been 'brainwashed' into joining" (Foster et al., 1998, p. 27). Analyses of the Waco tragedy now place greater emphasis on the deep misunder-

standings that existed between the government agencies, primarily the FBI and the BATF, that laid siege to the Branch Davidian community, and the members of the community—especially its leader, David Koresh. These misunderstandings appear to have been deepened by hysterical press and television coverage during the episodes of violence and siege (Bates, 1999).

Sociologist Joel Martin observes that the Branch Davidians were not newcomers but an established alternative religious group that had lived in the Waco area since the mid-1930s. The group did believe in an unconventional variant of Seventh-Day Adventist millenarianism and that Armageddon and the end of time were close at hand. They also had some unorthodox and disturbing sexual practices, but these charges, and the charge that they were stockpiling weapons, could have been addressed by quietly apprehending the group's leader for questioning rather than engaging in the large-scale operation that resulted in an armed standoff and the eventual death of the entire group in a blaze of fire and bullets.

Many sociologists point to the similarities between the Waco disaster and the tragedy at Wounded Knee, South Dakota, in 1890. In both cases (and many others like them), a new religion attracts men and women with visions of a new heaven and earth. As they seek to live in accord with these visions, they withdraw into their own community, altering their behavior in ways that may seem strange and even threatening to others. People outside the community begin to spread rumors about them. Government authorities get nervous and plan to move against the group. Journalists congregate, anticipating a big story. When a confrontation takes place, gunfire erupts and a few of the authorities are killed. In the end, the millenarian community is destroyed. After the tragedy, officials, scholars, historians, and journalists interpret what happened. Many conclude that the community's members had been caught up in a "messiah craze." Thus the dead are blamed for their own deaths.

Such was the case with the Lakota Indian Ghost Dancers who were killed at Wounded Knee in 1890. In the Ghost Dance religion, some Indians began to believe they might be invulnerable to white attackers. In a sense, they courted death at the hands of white men. Many believed

Big Foot, leader of the Sioux, lies frozen on the battlefield of Wounded Knee, South Dakota. Photograph ca. 1890.

© Bettmann/Corbis

that if the Ghost Dance did not protect them, they would at least achieve speedy transport to a happier existence than the one they led among the conquering white people (Hackett, 1995). The situation of the Branch Davidians killed outside Waco a century later was similar. The issue is not whether either group was right or wrong, but how people in a position to bring understanding to these tragic situations can help prevent similar events from occurring over and over again.

TRENDS IN RELIGION IN THE UNITED STATES

In studying religion in the United States, sociologists are unable to use census data because the Census Bureau does not collect information on religious affiliation. However, some statistics are available from smaller sample surveys such as those conducted by the National Opinion Research Center (NORC). The available data indicate that more than half of Americans older than age 18 identify themselves as Protestant, about one-quarter are Roman Catholic, and about 2 percent identify themselves as Jewish. All other religions combined account for about 7 percent of the population. The remaining 8 percent say that they have no religious affiliation; they constitute the third-largest category of religious preference in the United States (*Statistical Abstract,* 2002). (See Figure 17.2.)

The religious preferences of Americans have been changing slowly but steadily over the last two generations. The Protestant majority has gradually declined, partly as a result of upward mobility and the tendency of more affluent and educated people to be less active in religious institutions. Meanwhile the proportion of the population who identify themselves as Catholics has been growing, primarily as a result of the large numbers of Hispanic immigrants who have entered the United States in recent years. Also, since the mid-1960s there has been an increase in the percentage of people who express no religious preference. Thus it is possible that as the twenty-first century begins, less than half of all Americans will be Protestant (Iannaccone, Stark, & Finke, 1998; National Opinion Research Center, 2000).

Membership in a religious organization is different from identification with a religious faith, and this is reflected in statistics on Christian church membership in the United States. Because data on membership are obtained from the organizations themselves, there are significant differences in who is included. (Some churches, for example, count all baptized infants, whereas others count only people above a certain age who are enrolled as members.) The Mapping Social Change box on pages 502–503 illustrates the geographic distribution of reported church

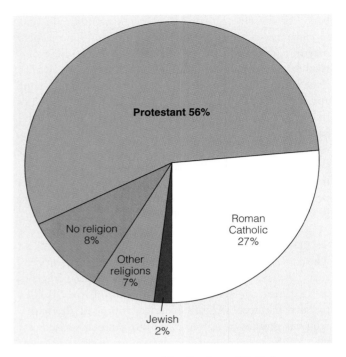

Figure 17.2 Percentage Distribution of Religious Preference in the United States (persons 18 years of age and older)

Source: Data from *Statistical Abstract,* 2001.

membership in the United States. As can readily be seen, various regions of the country differ with respect to the church membership of most of their residents. Protestants outnumber members of all other religions in the South, for example; in the West and Southwest, the Roman Catholic church is dominant.

There are also significant differences in church membership by size of place: Protestants are most likely to live in rural places, small cities, and suburbs of smaller cities, while native-born Catholics are found in medium-sized cities and suburbs of larger cities. Much of the rapid growth of Catholic congregations in the United States is accounted for by immigrants to major cities such as Miami, Los Angeles, and New York (Niebuhr, 1995). Jews, who originally migrated to the nation's largest cities, are most numerous in major metropolitan regions such as New York, Los Angeles, Chicago, and Miami (National Opinion Research Center, 2000).

Religion has always had an especially important place in the lives of African Americans, and a major proportion of the black population is deeply religious. Many of the functions of religion as a central cultural institution— meeting the spiritual needs of individuals, binding together the members of social groups, and sometimes engendering social change—are illustrated by the history of the black church in America.

The Black Church in America

The respected black sociologist E. Franklin Frazier was a firm believer in the principles of the Chicago school of ecological research and an astute student of race relations. He specialized in two of the most basic social institutions—the family and the church—as they affected and were affected by the situation of black Americans.

Frazier's (1966) study of the history of the black church in America emphasized the role of religion in the social organization of blacks ever since they were imported from Africa to the New World to be sold as slaves. Few aspects of the slaves' African culture were able to survive the experience of abduction and slavery, but one of those that did was dancing, which Frazier refers to as the most elemental form of religious expression. Although the slaves were encouraged to dance, the religious beliefs expressed in their dances were not permitted to flourish in America.

With the coming of Baptist and Methodist missionaries, the slaves found a form of religion in which they could express their most intense feelings. The religious services in which they participated helped bind them together into close-knit groups, replacing the bonds of kinship and tribal membership they had lost when they were sold into slavery. However, the freed slaves resented the subordinate status of blacks in the white-dominated churches. They left those churches and established all-black churches.

Out of these black churches, Frazier noted, other forms of black organizational activity emerged. The churches began to play an important role in the organization of the black community in such areas as economic cooperation and the building of educational institutions. The church also became the center of political life for black Americans, the arena in which they learned how to compete for power and position.

The large-scale urbanization of blacks that began in World War I transformed the black church. In particular, the church became more secular, placing less emphasis on salvation and turning its attention to the serious problems of blacks in the here and now. Changes in the class structure of the black community have also been reflected in the black church, with many middle-class blacks shifting to the Presbyterian, Episcopalian, and Congregational churches. A countertrend may be seen in the emergence of "storefront churches" (i.e., sects) that satisfy the spiritual needs of those who prefer a more intimate and expressive form of worship. And some blacks have joined so-called holiness cults that seek to return to an earlier form of expressive Christianity.

At the same time, blacks have become more fully integrated into American society. This has naturally affected the organization of black communities and the black church. Today the church is no longer the dominant institution for blacks that it once was (Patterson, 1999). Nevertheless, as Frazier pointed out, the black church has

Internationally acclaimed singer Aretha Franklin attributes her success to the vitality and inspiration of the black church in the United States.

left its imprint on most aspects of African-American life. And it is clear that the black church (including the Black Muslims and other Islamic sects) provides much of the leadership and many of the rank-and-file supporters of movements for political and economic justice among minority groups in the United States.

Unofficial Religion

Religion in the United States is increasingly voluntaristic. People are less likely to practice a religion simply because their parents did so. They are more likely than ever to join a religious group that appeals to their desire for membership in a community of like-minded peers and that upholds their particular moral standards (Swift, 1998). People in the United States and Canada are also more likely to engage in what sociologists term *unofficial religion*—a set of beliefs and practices that are "not accepted, recognized, or controlled by official religious groups" (McGuire, 1987, p. 89). Sometimes called folk or popular religion because it is practiced by ordinary people rather than by religious professionals in formal organizations, unofficial religion takes many forms. It is engaged in by people who purchase religious books and magazines, follow religious programs on television, make religious pilgrimages, or practice astrology, faith healing, transcendental meditation, occult arts, and the like—and who may belong to organized churches at the same time. Contrary to older sociological theories that viewed these practices as holdovers from rural folk cultures, research has shown that urban societies continually produce their own versions of popular religion (Fischer, 1987).

Religious Pluralism in the "Bible Belt"

The wide swath of states in the South and Southwest where Baptist church congregations predominate is often known as the "Bible Belt." This term refers to the strong religious convictions of many of the region's residents and to the powerful influence of Baptist churches in thousands of small communities. On the accompanying map, the Bible Belt stands out clearly. But maps showing the distribution of religious beliefs often mask the changes occurring in regions that appear more homogeneous than they are. Migration, urbanization, and differences in the growth of specific religious groups can lead to more religious pluralism (or less, depending on the region), even though a map shows a static distribution.

When we look closely at communities in west Texas, at the western end of the area of heavy Baptist church membership, we find higher levels of Catholic church membership. This is largely a result of the growing presence of Latino residents. Wherever there are changing patterns of church membership (represented here by photos of Catholic and Baptist congregations in this region), there is also likely to be more interfaith communication and more frequent discussion of the need for religious tolerance.

Similar evidence of pluralism can be found in other regions of the United States. In the heavily Catholic Northeast, for example, the map of Christian congregations does not indicate non-Christian, particularly Jewish, congregations, which are concentrated in the larger cities of this region. Catholic–Jewish interfaith dialogues are strongest in these urban centers. So while ecological maps like this one are useful, they only begin to suggest the important sociological facts that will be revealed by further research.

Muslims and Hindus in the United States

Largely as a consequence of recent waves of immigration from Asia and the Near East, membership in Islamic and Hindu religious groups is growing rapidly. By 2000, it was estimated that there were about 5 million Muslims in the United Sates and Canada, and more than 1,000 Islamic centers with about half a million Muslims attending mosque services as official members. The largest numbers of Muslims are found in Chicago, Washington, New York, Toronto, and southern California. The largest ethnic groups among North American Muslims are African American and Indo-Pakistani, with Arab Americans ranked third. The oldest continuously functioning mosque in the United States is located in Cedar Rapids, Iowa, and is known as the Mother Mosque of America.

Most Muslims in the United States belong to the Sunni sect, but membership in the more fundamentalist and militant Shiite sect is also increasing. Muslims, particularly those of the first immigrant generation, tend to hold views on moral issues that are similar to those of conservative Jews and Christians, and to oppose abortion, pornography, and extramarital sex. First-generation Muslim immigrants, like other first-generation immigrants, tend to be con-

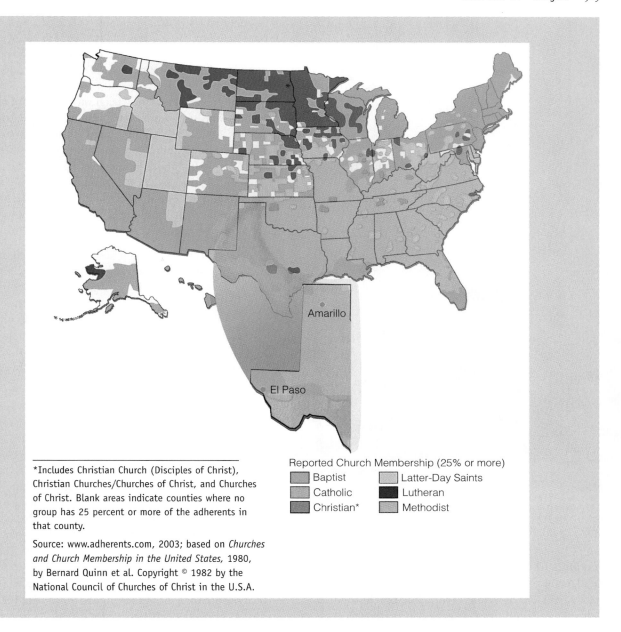

*Includes Christian Church (Disciples of Christ),
Christian Churches/Churches of Christ, and Churches
of Christ. Blank areas indicate counties where no
group has 25 percent or more of the adherents in
that county.

Source: www.adherents.com, 2003; based on *Churches
and Church Membership in the United States,* 1980,
by Bernard Quinn et al. Copyright © 1982 by the
National Council of Churches of Christ in the U.S.A.

Reported Church Membership (25% or more)
Baptist   Latter-Day Saints
Catholic   Lutheran
Christian*   Methodist

cerned about whether their children will marry within the faith and continue to share their Islamic beliefs and values (Swift, 1998).

Immigration from Pakistan, India, and nations of Africa and the Caribbean that were formerly part of the British Empire has caused a rapid increase in the number of Hindus in North America in the past decade or so. An estimated 400,000 Hindus now reside in the United States, most of them concentrated in southern California, New York, and Washington, D.C. Most Hindus worship at home, but Hindu temples have recently been established in several major U.S. cities. A far smaller proportion of practicing Hindus in the United States are native-born Americans who are at-

tracted to the religion's values of inner peace and enlightenment and have studied with Indian gurus like Bagwan Shree Rajneesh (Swift, 1998).

Pagans

Another trend, while not strictly a result of immigration, nonetheless reflects the influence of other cultures on contemporary religious practices. Sociologists studying religion in the United States note the small but significant increase in rates of participation in pagan religions, witchcraft, or Wicca. Wicca is particularly attractive to

The Sociological Observer

This photo shows Muslim Americans praying in a mosque in New York City. As in all religious ceremonies, much of what the faithful do and say under the sacred roof of their place of worship is proscribed in holy scriptures, in this case the Koran. What do you think is the significance of the fact that the worshippers are all kneeling, and in the same direction? (See page 513 for further insights into the sociological context of this photo.)

feminists who reject what they perceive as the patriarchal tendencies of Judaism and Christianity. Pagan holy days and rituals are associated with, but not limited to, the solstices and equinoxes. Pagans believe that women participate in the divine nature of the Goddess, the source of human life and of all nature. Many pagans are reluctant to reveal their religious beliefs and practices because of the history of Christian suppression of paganism (Adler, 1997).

Religiosity

Neither church membership figures nor self-reports of religious identification are accurate indicators of the aspect of religious behavior known as **religiosity.** This term refers to the depth of a person's religious feelings and how those feelings are translated into religious behavior. Responses to questions about whether one believes in God and how

strongly, whether one believes in a life after death, whether one's religious beliefs provide guidance in making major decisions, and the frequency of one's church or temple attendance all can be used to measure religiosity (Smith et al., 2002).

When sociologists study religiosity as opposed to church membership, some important results emerge. Although a common stereotype of Americans describes them as materialistic, individualistic, pleasure seeking (hedonistic), and secularized, data on their religious faith and behavior do not confirm the stereotype. Compared with citizens of other urban industrial nations, Americans are more religious. In fact, the most recent World Values Survey of the University of Michigan reports that:

> Fully 44 percent of Americans attend church once a week, excluding funerals and christenings, compared with 27 percent of Britons, 21 percent of the French, 4 percent of Swedes, and 3 percent of Japanese. Not only do they go to church, but 53 percent of Americans say religion is very important in their lives, compared with just 16 percent of the British, 14 percent of the French, and 13 percent of Germans. (Reese, 1998)

Of course, these figures mask major variations among Americans in their commitment to religious practice, and in fact sociologists are engaged in a lively debate about the meaning of the survey data. Closer examinations of church attendance statistics have found that a sizable proportion of Americans who say they attend church or synagogue regularly actually exaggerate their estimates. Analysis of their responses suggests that the figures for American church attendance are inflated, in some instances by 50 percent or more (Hadaway & Marler, 1998). But other sociologists note that successful congregations have a core group of regular attenders who tend to be most active in all of the congregation's activities. Those on the margins of this core group tend to be those who also overestimate their attendance (Ploch & Hastings, 1995; Reese, 1998).

There is far less disagreement over what the poll data reveal about other aspects of religiosity, particularly about beliefs as opposed to behavior. About 90 percent of Americans believe in the existence of God, and 86 percent express certainty in a life after death. Adults in the Pacific states, which tend to have the lowest rates of church membership, do not differ very much on these measures from those in other regions. The lower rates of church membership on the West Coast are correlated with the greater spatial mobility and lower median age of the populations of those states. People who move often tend to sever their attachments not only to churches but to all organizations in the community. Yet people who do

TABLE 17.1

Percentage of Adults Attending Services Last Week, by Religion and Year, United States, 1939–1990

Year	Religion				
	Protestant	Catholic	Jewish	Other	None
1939	40	64	12	—	1
1969	39	64	8	18	0
1979	40	53	19	40	5
1990	47	50	30*	31*	6*

*Small sample size accounts for large fluctuations in these percentages.

Sources: Hout & Greeley, 1987; National Opinion Research Center, 2000.

Religious Pluralism

Differences in the distribution of religious belief are important because they show how religion helps account for cultural differences among populations within a society. Thus we use the expression "Bible Belt" to refer to the most strongly Protestant areas of the nation—the South and Midwest. The large Catholic populations in some cities make them quite different in cultural terms from the Protestant-dominated suburbs. And the large Jewish populations in New York and Miami are reflected in the cultural life of those cities—in joint Hanukkah/Christmas celebrations in offices and schools, for example, and in the incorporation of Jewish holidays into the school calendar.

The United States is an example of a society in which the state protects religious pluralism. The First Amendment to the Constitution guarantees freedom of religion, which in turn allows different religions to exist and to compete for adherents if they wish to do so. Religious pluralism is also protected in most European nations today, although before the Protestant Reformation of the sixteenth century, many European states made Roman Catholicism the official state religion and attempted to force all citizens to convert to Catholicism. And in the early 1990s the religious diversity and tolerance of the former Yugoslavia dissolved into a genocidal religious and nationalist war.

In societies in which religious pluralism is protected, one usually can observe the continual formation of new religious organizations. New religious groups tend to arise either out of schisms within existing organizations or as a result of the teaching of charismatic leaders who attract people to new religious movements. Many new religious movements are also stimulated by severe inequalities and the widening gap between rich and poor. Whether it originates in schisms within existing religious organizations, as

not belong to organized churches can nevertheless hold deeply cherished religious beliefs.

Data on church attendance do not support the notion that the United States is becoming an increasingly secular society. In fact, as can be seen in Table 17.1 and Figure 17.3, for some major religions, church attendance has been increasing since 1950 (Hout & Greeley, 1987; Ploch & Hastings, 1995). There are no clear patterns in rates of church attendance. Although Catholics have the highest weekly attendance rates and Jews the lowest, those rates can change considerably from one year to the next, for reasons that are not fully understood. Nevertheless, it is clear that the data do not bear out the secularization hypothesis. It should also be noted that increases in immigration during the 1980s and 1990s are significantly increasing the diversity of religious practice in the United States. As noted earlier, Muslims, Hindus, Buddhists, and others are well represented among the new immigrants.

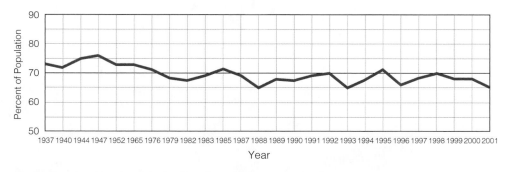

Figure 17.3 Membership in Church or Synagogue, 1937–2001

Most Americans say that they belong to a church or synagogue (or mosque), and this proportion has not changed substantially over the past half century.

Source: Data from Gallup Poll, 2001.

a result of the emergence of charismatic religious leaders, or in response to severe inequalities, religious pluralism presents many personal questions and challenges. Two examples of these challenges are found in movements for social change within the Catholic church and the rise of fundamentalism in the United States and elsewhere.

SOCIAL CHANGE AND THE CATHOLIC CHURCH It is a striking fact that throughout the world one finds deeply devout individuals involved in movements for social change. Religious workers were killed in El Salvador because they advocated greater democracy and equality. In Poland before the fall of the Soviet empire, the Catholic church was a leader in the movement to democratize that nation. American bishops speak out against poverty and inequality in the United States. The Civil Rights movement has tended to be led by members of the clergy and bases many of its appeals on biblical principles of justice and equity. Yet, on the other hand, we could cite many examples of religious intolerance and an apparently high correlation between devotion to religious faith and resistance to social change.

Support for and resistance to social change are relative ideas—relative, that is, to the position of their advocates. If one supports a woman's right to choose whether to have an abortion, the social change in question is tolerance for abortion rights (which does not necessarily mean that one favors abortion). If one is opposed to abortion rights, the change one seeks is a return to a situation in which abortion is illegal. As noted earlier in the chapter, by opposing abortion rights, the Catholic church stands for social change in a conservative direction.

In religious life, the same institution can stand for conservative social change in one place and for more radical change in another. For example, the conservative Episcopalian (Anglican) church in Northern Ireland favors the continuation of British colonial rule there, while the Episcopalian church in the United States supports liberal causes such as abortion rights and environmental action. The relationship between the Catholic church and social change is even more complex. In the United States, the church is accused by some of its own leaders of having too conservative a view of social change. In Brazil, by contrast, the church is accused of being too liberal. How can a single institution be perceived so differently in two societies?

Part of the answer is that a church that is so large and embraces so many separate organizations can never be free from internal politics. Many Catholic theologians agree with Father Richard P. McBrien of Notre Dame University that "since his election in 1978, Pope John Paul II has been determinedly appointing a certain type of cleric to important archdioceses and dioceses all around the world" (1990, p. A17). According to McBrien and others, these bishops and cardinals tend to be "uncritically loyal to the Pope" and "rigidly authoritarian and solitary" in their leadership style. They are unlikely to take their parishioners' views into account when they differ from those of the pope and his curial associates. For their part, high church officials argue that their function is to keep the church on the right track in defending the sanctity of life while seeking constructive social change where possible. Hence, on many social issues (e.g., abortion rights, the rights of homosexuals, treatment of AIDS patients, ordination of women, economic reform), the leadership of the Catholic church (although not always its rank-and-file adherents) tends to act as a conservative force in the United States and other industrial nations.

The pope, shown here mingling with a crowd of devout followers, often takes a conservative position on social issues like abortion and women's roles. In many parts of Latin America, however, the Catholic church is a significant force for social change, and its leaders play an important part in the struggle against severe economic inequality.

© A. Keler/Corbis Sygma

CHAPTER 17 Religion 507

The opposite is true in Brazil and other Latin American nations, where the Catholic church is identified with movements for radical social reforms. In Brazil, theologian Leonardo Boff and Bishop Dom Helder Camara have developed and taught the idea that spiritual salvation is not possible without action to liberate the oppressed. Religion itself could help transform the miserable conditions of the peasantry and the Indians and the impoverished working people (Schubeck, 1995). This view has come to be known as "liberation theology."

As liberation theology took hold during the 1960s and 1970s, church leaders began to develop what they called "the preferential option for the poor." Recognizing that the so-called miracle of Brazilian economic growth had not helped most of the nation's poor people, they proposed to correct this situation even at the expense of the spiritual needs of the affluent. Church leaders and lay activists organized thousands of small groups known as Communidades Eclesial de Base, or CEBs. These 30- to 40-person groups were the building blocks of a powerful social movement to bring both spiritual comfort and economic uplift to the nation's poor masses. Never a very popular strategy in Rome, the CEBs seem nevertheless to have had a real impact in moving Brazil's elite classes toward the realization that if they do not do more to distribute the benefits of economic development, they might be swept out of power in coming elections.

At this writing, it is not clear what the future holds either for liberation theology or for the liberal–conservative dispute among Catholics in the United States. During his visit to Mexico and the United States in 1999, the pope made the growing gap between rich and poor throughout the world a major issue in his addresses. Within the church hierarchy, however, there are ongoing efforts to ban the teaching of liberation theology, as well as criticism of the preferential option for the poor (*National Catholic Reporter,* 1997). It is clear, however, that like all the major religions of the world, Catholicism will continue to face the challenges of social change. Among the most severe of those challenges is the rise of fundamentalist religious movements, which pose major threats to religious pluralism in Islamic nations, among Indian Hindus, among Jews in Israel, and in many congregations throughout the United States.

THE CHURCH AND SEXUALITY   At this writing, the Catholic church in the United States is coping with one of the worst scandals in its history. Accusations of sexual abuse of children by priests, and longstanding patterns of cover-up of such abuses by prominent bishops in Boston, New York, and elsewhere, have caused inordinate conflict among parishioners and church leaders. Gradually, however, through new appointments of bishops and progress

in addressing legal claims by injured families, the church is beginning to address the conflict and trauma among its faithful. Whether this means that the church will reconsider its traditions of priestly celibacy or its staunch opposition to the legitimation of homosexuality remains an open question (Loseke, 2003; Scheper-Hughes & Devine, 2003). The crisis in the church over sexual abuse demonstrates that issues of sexuality among priests and laypeople continue to produce diverse attitudes and behaviors. While no one involved condones abuse of children in any form, open discussion of how the church deals with sexuality remains highly controversial.

Other major religions and Christian denominations in the United States are also facing conflict and controversy over issues of sexuality among church leaders and parishioners. The Episcopal Church in America is divided over the appointment of an openly gay bishop to be the leader of the church in New Hampshire. While the majority of Episcopalians do not oppose this move, a strong and vocal minority do, and this conflict threatens to divide the church into two separate organizations if calmer voices do not prevail (Goodstein, 2003).

FUNDAMENTALISM   Religious *fundamentalists* are believers (and their leaders) who are devoted to the strict observance of ritual and doctrine. They hold deep convictions about right and wrong in matters of faith and lifestyle, with little tolerance for differences in belief and practice, and they are fiercely opposed to astrology, magic, unorthodox conceptions of religion, and any form of civil religion. In all the world religions, there are divisions between liberal and conservative approaches to the religious norms that guide daily life. Among fundamentalists, however, there is a belief in the

> basic, intrinsic, essential, inerrant truth about humanity and deity; that this essential truth is fundamentally opposed by forces of evil which must be vigorously fought; that this truth must be followed today according to the fundamental, unchangeable practices of the past; and that those who believe and follow these fundamental teachings have a special relationship with the deity. (Hunsberger, 1995, p. 9)

Clearly, these beliefs, passionately held as they are, present enormous challenges for societies in which there is considerable religious diversity. (The consequences of Islamic fundamentalism, particularly for the lives of women, are presented in the Global Social Change box on pages 508–509.) In the United States, fundamentalist believers may be found in every major religion, but fundamentalism is especially strong among some Protestant churches and sects.

GLOBAL SOCIAL CHANGE   Women in Islam

More than 1 billion people adhere to the Islamic faith. Most of them live in the Arab states of the Middle East and North Africa, but Muslims may be found in growing numbers in every corner of the globe, including the United States.

Relations between the Islamic world and Western societies are colored by a great deal of misinformation and bias. An example from the social sciences is the theory that social changes do not affect the Islamic world in the same way that they do, or did, affect the Western nations. In particular, it is argued that because of the subordinate status of women in the Islamic religion, the movements for gender equality, limiting of family size, and greater equality in politics that have brought about such dramatic change in the West will not occur in the Islamic world (Caldwell & Caldwell, 1988). This hypothesis attributes the slow pace of demographic change in many Islamic nations to orthodox Islam's traditional values, such as polygyny, which permits men to father many children with as many as four wives. The tradition of female submission in orthodox Islam is also said to account for the persistence of gender inequalities in those nations. Islamic sociologists point out, however, that there are significant differences among the various Islamic societies and that some have long-standing norms

supporting birth control and education for women.

When we examine empirical data about the Islamic nations, many ironies become apparent. There are nations where traditional Islamic norms are quite powerful and women cannot hope for educational or occupational equality with men, and there are others where these differences are diminishing rapidly. For example, in Saudi Arabia patriarchal norms are in effect and the subordination of women is strictly enforced. Women are not allowed to drive, yet that nation is the world's foremost producer of petroleum. As shown in the accompanying table, in Saudi Arabia only 65 percent of girls of primary school age are enrolled in school, among the lowest rates in the Arab world. Extremely poor, peripheral Islamic nations like Somalia (with only 13 percent female primary school

© Tony Savino/The Image Works

attendance) are even less advanced, but in these nations it is usually the challenge of day-to-day survival rather than religious orthodoxy that prevents children from attending school. In Iraq, on the other hand, orthodoxy is less powerful and women's average level of education is among the highest in the Islamic world.

Many other differences among the Arab nations in the heart of the Islamic world show up clearly in the table. (Note that Iran is not included in this list because, although it is an Islamic nation, its culture is Persian, not Arab.) There are major differences among these nations in basic social and demographic indicators. All have high fertility rates, but in more urbanized Arab nations like Kuwait—where education for women is more easily available and polygyny is waning— rates of fertility and child mortality are closer to those of other more developed nations. In more agrarian societies like Egypt, which also tend to have larger populations, fertility remains extremely high, as does child mortality. Sociologists from these societies find, however, that Islamic teachings themselves do not account for these disparities so much as economic conditions such as poverty and concentration of the population in rural villages and farms (Obermeyer, 1992).

Historically, the influence of religious fundamentalism on the culture and politics of American life reached its height in 1919, when the Eighteenth Amendment to the U.S. Constitution prohibited the manufacture, sale, or transportation (and hence the consumption) of "intoxicating liquors," regardless of whether one supported the fundamentalist view of alcohol consumption. The repeal

of Prohibition in 1933 represented a defeat for religious fundamentalism in American culture and politics.

Another famous episode involving fundamentalism was the so-called "monkey trial" of 1925, in which John T. Scopes, a biology teacher in Tennessee, was charged with teaching the then-forbidden theory of evolution, which many religious fundamentalists oppose because it contra-

DEMOGRAPHIC AND SOCIOECONOMIC INDICATORS IN ARAB COUNTRIES

	Population (millions)	Gross National Product per Capita (US$, 1989)	Percent Urban	Percent of Age Group Enrolled in Primary School*		Total Fertility Rate 1985–1990	Infant Mortality Rate 1985–1990	Life Expectancy 1985–1990 (years)	
				Male	Female			Male	Female
Algeria	24.9	2,230	51.7	105	87	5.4	74	63	65
Bahrain	0.5	6,340	82.9	111	110	4.1	16	69	73
Egypt	52.4	640	46.7	100	79	4.5	65	58	60
Iraq	18.9	—	71.3	105	91	6.4	69	63	65
Jordan	4.0	1,640	68.0	98	99	6.2	44	64	68
Kuwait	2.0	16,150	95.6	95	92	3.9	18	71	75
Lebanon	2.7	—	83.7	105	95	3.8	48	63	67
Libya	4.5	5,310	70.2	128	119	6.9	82	59	63
Mauritania	2.0	500	46.8	61	42	6.5	127	44	48
Morocco	25.1	880	48.0	85	56	4.8	82	59	63
Oman	1.5	5,220	10.6	103	92	7.2	40	62	66
Qatar	0.4	15,500	89.4	121	121	5.6	31	67	72
Saudi Arabia	14.1	6,020	77.3	78	65	7.2	71	62	65
Somalia	7.5	170	36.4	26	13	6.6	132	43	47
Sudan	25.2	480	22.0	59	41	6.4	108	49	51
Syria	12.5	980	50.4	115	104	6.8	48	63	67
Tunisia	8.1	1,260	54.3	126	107	4.1	52	65	66
United Arab Emirates	1.6	18,430	77.8	98	100	4.8	26	69	73
Yemen, YAR (North)	9.2	640	25.0	141	40	8.0	120	50	50
Yemen, PDRY (South)	2.5	430	43.3	96	35	6.7	120	49	52

*Enrollment ratios are expressed as a percentage of the total population of primary school age. For countries with universal education, the gross enrollment ratio may exceed 100 percent because some pupils are above or below the official primary school age.

Sources: Obermeyer, 1992; UNDP, 2000.

dicts the account of creation presented in the Bible. The prominent lecturer and religious fundamentalist (and former presidential candidate) William Jennings Bryan prosecuted the controversial case, which received worldwide attention. Despite a strong defense by Scopes's lawyer, Clarence Darrow, Scopes was convicted and fined $100. (Although courts later reversed the conviction on a techni-

cality, it would be more than 30 years before the Tennessee legislature repealed the law that prohibited teaching evolution theory in state-supported schools.) Despite the conviction, the Scopes trial is seen as a turning point for the intellectual opponents of fundamentalism. Although fundamentalism continued to pose a challenge to mainline Baptist, Methodist, and Presbyterian denominations, after the Scopes trial it lost influence—until recently—as a religious ideology (Simpson, 1983; Swift, 1998).

Sociologists of religion tend to view the rise of fundamentalist religious movements as part of a larger effort by people in modern societies to make moral and spiritual sense of their lives. In the Islamic world, fundamentalism is also associated with the failure of elites to deliver on their promises of well-being for the masses of people in their societies (Hussein, 1994). In more affluent nations like the United States, however, the appeal of fundamentalism seems to be more often based on rejection of moral relativism, racial integration, and cultural pluralism, and on the desire to find moral absolutes that can guide people through complex and ambiguous social environments.

This fact is reflected in the remarks of Robert Bellah, a well-known commentator on American culture. For several centuries, he writes, Americans "have been embarked on a great effort to increase our freedom, wealth, and power. For over a hundred years, a large part of the American people, the middle class, has imagined that the virtual meaning of life lies in the acquisition of ever-increasing status, income, and authority, from which genuine freedom is supposed to come" (Bellah et al., 1985, p. 284). Yet many Americans seem uneasy about their lives despite their material comfort. They seem to yearn for spiritual values without necessarily wanting to return to traditional religious practices. They adhere to the values of individualism, but they also long for the stronger sense of community and commitment that one finds in religious congregations.

Bellah predicts that Americans will continue to seek self-actualization as individuals, but that increasingly they will express their desire for community attachments and higher values, either in traditional religions or in civil-religious practice. Research on the challenges faced by Southern Baptists, however, suggests that the divisions between more secular and more fundamentalist believers will continue to strain the institutions of pluralistic societies like the United States.

CRITICAL SOCIOLOGY AND SOCIAL CHANGE

Social Change and the Southern Baptists

Fundamentalist Christian church leaders in the United States were appalled by the Supreme Court ruling that struck down state laws against consensual sex among same-sex partners. Many believe that the decision would open the way toward more campaigns in the states to legalize same-sex marriage. President Bush himself, who depends heavily on conservative Christian support in the South and Southwest, promised that he would continue to oppose any such changes in marital laws. While the climate of American public opinion is moving toward greater acceptance of homosexuality, Christian conservatives are not ready to accept what they see as an extreme form of pluralism that threatens their own "family values." But does this conflict suggest that differences between fundamentalists and others threaten social stability in the United States? The answer depends in large part on the future of fundamentalist denominations themselves.

Sociologist Nancy Tatom Ammerman views issues of pluralism and social change as central to understanding the split between fundamentalist and moderate Southern Baptists. She writes:

> The disruption against which fundamentalists struggle is often labeled "modernity." Whatever else that label may mean, the "modern" world is one in which change is a fact of life, in which people of multiple cultures live side by side, and in which religious rules have been largely relegated to a private sphere of influence. (1990, p. 150)

To assess differences among Baptists in the way they view social change and diversity, Ammerman surveyed more than 900 Baptist leaders in congregations throughout the United States. Her survey sample included men who were pastors and church deacons and women who were presidents of their local Baptist women's organizations. After examining their responses to key questions about their beliefs, Ammerman developed categories (or "theological parties") with labels corresponding to the terms respondents often used to describe themselves (e.g., *fundamentalist, conservative, moderate*). She also developed a scale for measuring individuals' degree of opposition to modernity. The questions on which the scale is based and the method of scoring responses are discussed in the Sociological Methods box on page 511. Table 17.2 shows that "among those who disapprove of pluralism, fundamentalists outnumber moderates nearly ten to one" (Ammerman, 1990, p. 151). But the data in the table and the box also show that Baptists classified as "conservative," whose views fall somewhere between those of the fundamentalists and moderates, are the most numerous category and are quite divided in their views of pluralism.

When she examined how respondents felt about modernity in relation to such variables as education, occupation,

Text continues on page 514.

SOCIOLOGICAL METHODS

Scales and Composite Scores

When analyzing questionnaire responses, sociologists often create *scales* in order to arrive at a composite score for a particular variable. Nancy Tatom Ammerman created scales to measure the strength of a person's fundamentalist beliefs and opposition to modernity. (See the accompanying tables.) A scale is a set of statements that fit together conceptually in that they deal with aspects or examples of the same attitude or behavior. For each statement, the respondent may be asked to choose among responses ranging, for instance, from 1 ("Strongly disagree") to 5 ("Strongly agree"), with "Unsure" in the middle. The statements in a particular scale

(e.g., fundamentalist beliefs) are scattered throughout the questionnaire to avoid *response set,* the tendency to answer all such items similarly without giving them much thought; response set is a frequent problem when similar items are grouped together. To ensure that the statements in a scale actually measure the behavior or attitude the researcher is studying, great care must be taken in their selection and wording.

Once the questionnaires have been completed and the data entered into a computer, the researcher can arrive at a simple composite score by adding up the scores on all the items in a scale. Then the researcher can either use each

respondent's composite score as a continuous variable or establish cutoff points that will create categories for analysis, as Ammerman did. In her measurement of opposition to modernity, for example (see table), Ammerman decided that those who agreed or strongly agreed with all the items (i.e., whose scores ranged from 5 to 9) could be classified as "strongly agreeing with pluralism." Those who agreed with most of the items but not all of them (i.e., scored from 10 to 14) were classified as showing "moderate approval." Those who scored 15 or above—in other words, those who disagreed as often as they agreed—were classified as "disapproving."

FUNDAMENTALIST BELIEFS

Items	Scoring
The Scriptures are the inerrant Word of God, accurate in every detail.	Strongly agree = 5
God recorded in the Bible everything He wants us to know.	Strongly agree = 5
The Genesis creation stories are there more to tell us about God's involvement than to give us a precise "how and when."	Strongly disagree = 5
The Bible clearly teaches a premillennial view of history and the future.	Strongly agree = 5
It is important that Christians avoid worldly practices such as drinking and dancing.	Strongly agree = 5

Distribution

Range	Percent
5–10	5
11–15	14
16–20	47
21–25	34

OPPOSITION TO MODERNITY

Items	Scoring
I like living in a community with lots of different kinds of people.	Very untrue = 5
Public schools are needed to teach children to get along with lots of different kinds of people.	Strongly disagree = 5
I sometimes learn about God from friends in other faiths.	Very untrue = 5
One of the most important things children can learn is how to deal creatively with change.	Strongly disagree = 5
Children today need to be exposed to a variety of educational and cultural offerings so they can make informed choices.	Strongly disagree = 5

Distribution

Range	Percent
5–9	29
10–14	52
15–19	17
20–25	2

VISUAL SOCIOLOGY

THE CHANGING FACE OF ISLAM

Can American Muslim women and men like those shown in these photos play a role in transforming the Islamic world? That might seem like a far-fetched question to many, but if one studies the sociology of religious and ethnic groups in the United States, it becomes less so. After all, Jews in the United States greatly aided in creating the modern state of Israel after World War II, and American Catholics, who often take a relatively liberal stance in disputes about issues such as birth control or the use of local languages in the mass, have influenced Vatican policies on these issues over the years. It is quite likely, then, that American Islamic women who seek to reconcile the demands of their religion with those of living as modern women with careers and families will have some influence on debates about these issues elsewhere in the Islamic world.

Here, for example, is a statement about women in Islam from the Southern California Islamic Center, which represents the desire of some Muslims in the United States to address the critical question of the future of women in Islam:

Contrary to widespread erroneous belief,

Contrary to widespread negative stereotyping, and

Contrary to regrettable practices in some Islamic societies where anti-Islamic culture traditions have won over Islamic teachings and where women are subdued (and men even more so).

This information has been written with the objective of briefing you on the true Islamic teachings regarding women laid down by the Quran and prophet Mohammad over 14 centuries ago.

- Islam declared women and men equal.
- Islam condemned pre-Islamic practices degrading and oppressing women.
- The same injunctions and prohibitions of Islam equally apply to both sexes.
- Islam gave women the right of inheritance and the right of individual independent ownership unhampered by father, husband, brother, son or anyone else.

- Islam gave women the right to accept or reject a marriage proposal free from pressure, and by mutual agreement to specify in the marriage contract that she has the right to divorce (if she misses that option she has the right to seek court divorce if she deems the marriage to have failed beyond repair).
- Islam does not require a woman to change her name at marriage.
- Islam protects the family and condemns the betrayal of marital fidelity. It recognizes only one type of family: husband and wife united by authentic marriage contract.

(Published by Islamic Center of Southern California and reproduced with permission.)

American Muslims share basic religious beliefs with Muslims throughout the world, but compared with the leaders of Islam in Saudi Arabia, where an especially patriarchal form of Islam prevails, they are far more liberal and tolerant of others and more receptive to the claims of women for equal treatment.

For better or worse, the events following the terrorist attacks on the United States have brought American Muslims to the forefront of public scrutiny, and as these photos suggest, they are a diverse people who share the American dream of success, security, and

© Beryl Goldberg

AP/Wide World Photos

freedom. A recent poll sponsored by the American Muslim Council confirms this perception and adds useful information like the following:

Who Are America's Muslims?

A snapshot from a poll of U.S. Muslims in November 2002:

- 50% earn more than $50,000 annually.
- 58% are college graduates.
- 69% are married.
- 36% were born in the United States; the rest come from 80 other countries.
- 32% are South Asian, 26% Arab, 20% African-American, 7% African, and 14% "other."
- One-fifth are converts to Islam.

Politics:

- 79% are registered to vote.
- 40% are Democrats, 23% Republicans, and 28% Independents.
- 36% are moderate, 27% are liberal, and 21% are conservative.
- They are liberal on some issues—93% favor both universal health care and more generous government assistance to the poor—and conservative on many social issues: They support

the death penalty (68%); oppose physician-assisted suicide (61%); support a ban on pornography (65%); and favor making abortions harder to obtain (57%).

- They support prayer (53%) and the display of the Ten Commandments in schools (59%), and favor vouchers for private schools (68%) (Lampman, 2002).

The Sociological Observer

(See photo on page 504.)

Islamic mosques like this one can be seen in scores of American communities, from coast to coast. The worship-

pers are all kneeling as they pray, one of the universal norms of Islamic religious practice. They are also turned toward the holy city of Mecca, in contemporary Saudi Arabia, another universal practice among all the world's Muslims.

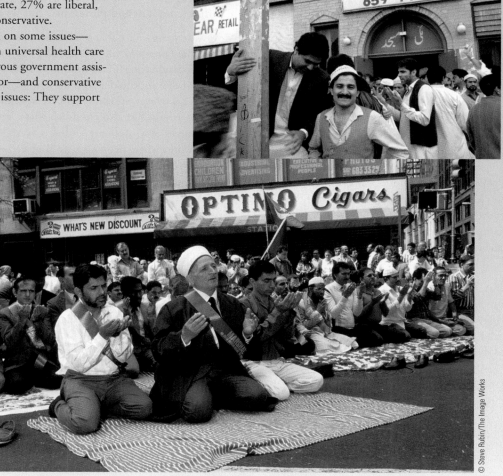
© Steve Rubin/The Image Works

TABLE 17.2

Percentage in Different Theological Parties, by Responses to Pluralism

Theological Party	Strong Approval of Pluralism	Moderate Approval of Pluralism	Disapproval of Pluralism	Total
Self-Identified Moderate	21%	5%	3%	9%
Moderate Conservative	16	8	3	9
Conservative	38	55	43	48
Fundamentalist Conservative	18	24	27	23
Self-Identified Fundamentalist	8	9	23	11
Total	101%	101%	99%	100%
(Number of Cases)	(256)	(500)	(187)	(944)

Note: Difference statistically significant at p <.001. Some percentages do not total 100 due to rounding.

Source: Ammerman, 1990.

and rural versus urban residence, Ammerman found some surprising results. Although people often think of individuals who hold strong fundamentalist beliefs and reject modernity as uneducated people living in remote farming hamlets, and of individuals who approve of modernity as educated middle-class urban dwellers, Ammerman's results challenge this conventional wisdom:

> Those among Southern Baptists who were the most skeptical of change, choice, and diversity were blue collar workers, those with middle incomes, people who had moved from farm to city, and those who had been to college, but did not have a degree. And combinations were important: people who had moved from farm to city *and* had some college or people with middle income *and* blue collar households, for instance. These were people who knew exactly what the modern world was all about, and they were less enthusiastic about embracing it than were any other Southern Baptists. And the less enthusiasm they had for modern attitudes, the more likely they were to adopt fundamentalist beliefs and identity. (1990, p. 155)

Eventually, Ammerman believes, these differences in outlook may lead to an irremediable schism in which moderates may form a new Baptist denomination. She is not convinced that religious fundamentalism poses dire threats. The rise of Christian fundamentalism does, in her

view, challenge widespread beliefs about the inevitable progression of modern societies toward ever-greater "differentiation, individualism, and rationalism as 'the way things are'" (1997, p. 202). Modern frameworks for understanding the social world, she argues, emphasize the "individualized 'meaning system' that would be carved out of differentiation and pluralism." But we live in a world

> where organizational boundaries are more fluid, where mergers and out-sourcing and flextime and telecommuting are as common as the time clock and the stockholder corporation. We live in a world where rationality and the scientific method are valued, but also critiqued, where multiple sources of wisdom are finding a voice. We live in a world where people are both more rooted in particularistic ethnic and religious communities that refused to melt and more aware of the larger world and the choices that have brought them to their current practices. (1997, p. 202)

A clear implication of Ammerman's brilliant empirical research, and the conclusions she draws from her findings, is that fundamentalist communities are the result of unquestioned religious socialization of some people and the rational choices of others. These congregations may present severe challenges to religious pluralism, but in the long run, it is in pluralistic societies that they will eventually find a secure, though limited, place.

SUMMARY

Religion in Society

- *Religion* is among the oldest and most changeable and complex of human social institutions. It has been defined as any set of coherent answers to the dilemmas of human existence that makes the world meaningful.

- It has also been defined as a system of beliefs and rituals that helps bind people together into a social group.

- *Rituals* are formal patterns of activity that express a set of shared meanings; in the case of religious rituals, the shared meanings are *sacred*, pertaining to phenomena that are regarded as extraordinary, transcendent, and outside the everyday course of events.

- Most Western nations practice some form of separation of church and state, but many other nations have chosen an official state religion. A few nations are theocracies, in which the government is controlled by religious leaders.

- Until comparatively recent times, religion dominated the cultural life of human societies. Since medieval times, however, the traditional dominance of religion over other institutions has been reduced by a process termed *secularization*. This process is never complete; religion continues to play an important role in the contemporary world.

- Adherents of all the major religions have at times acted as if theirs were the one true faith, and they have used this claim as a basis for persecuting those who deviated from their beliefs.

Varieties of Religious Belief

- In simpler and rather isolated societies, people may believe in a great force or spirit, but they do not have a well-defined concept of God or a set of rituals involving God. This form of religion is called *simple supernaturalism*.

- More common among hunting-and-gathering societies is *animism*, in which all forms of life and all aspects of the earth are inhabited by gods or supernatural powers.

- *Theism*, in contrast, comprises belief systems that conceive of a god or gods as separate from humans and from other living things on the earth.

- Many ancient religions were *polytheistic*, meaning that they included numerous gods.

- The ancient Hebrews were among the first of the world's peoples to evolve a *monotheistic* religion, one centered on belief in a single all-powerful God.

- In China, Japan, and other societies of the Far East, the dominant religions are centered not on devotion to a god or gods but on an abstract ideal of spirituality and human behavior.

- Some social scientists have expanded the definition of religion to include *civil religions*, or collections of beliefs and rituals that exist outside religious institutions.

Religion and Social Change

- A major controversy in the study of religious institutions has to do with the role they play in social change.

- Karl Marx believed that cultural institutions like religion are shaped by economic and political institutions and that they function to instill in the masses the values of the dominant class.

- Max Weber, on the other hand, argued that religion can cause major social change by instilling certain values in the members of a society, in turn causing changes in other institutions.

Structure and Change in Modern Religions

- Religion today is a highly structured institution, with numerous statuses and roles within a variety of organizations as well as many kinds of smaller, less bureaucratic groups.

- The three main types of religious organizations are the church, the sect, and the denomination.

- A *church* is a religious organization that has strong ties to the larger society and has at one time or another enjoyed the loyalty of most of the society's members.

- A *sect* rejects the religious beliefs or practices of an established church and usually is formed when a group of church members splits off to form a rival organization.

- A third type of religious organization is the *denomination*, which is on good terms with the religious institution from which it developed but must compete with other denominations for members.

- A *cult* is an entirely new religion. Along with sects, cults are a major source of change in religious organizations.

- People who are not satisfied with more established churches and denominations may form or join a cult or sect. New religious movements arise when a "religious innovator" attracts followers. This is particularly likely when traditional religions fail to meet the needs of their members or when a society is undergoing rapid secularization.

Trends in Religion in the United States

- The black church has left its imprint on most aspects of African-American life and provides much of the leadership and many of the rank-and-file supporters of movements for political and economic justice.
- Membership in a religious organization is quite different from identification with a religious faith, and this is reflected in trends in religion in the United States. Among those trends are a growing tendency to practice unofficial or "folk" religion and an emphasis on religiosity as opposed to church membership.
- *Religiosity* refers to the depth of a person's religious feelings and how those feelings are translated into religious behavior.
- Studies of religiosity find high percentages of Americans believing in the existence of God and in a life after death.
- In societies characterized by religious pluralism, one usually can observe the continual formation of new religious organizations.

GLOSSARY

religion: Any set of coherent answers to the dilemmas of human existence that makes the world meaningful; a system of beliefs and rituals that helps bind people together into a social group. (p. 486)

ritual: A formal pattern of activity that expresses symbolically a set of shared meanings. (p. 486)

sacred: A term used to describe phenomena that are regarded as extraordinary, transcendent, and outside the everyday course of events. (p. 486)

profane: A term used to describe phenomena that are not considered sacred. (p. 486)

secularization: A process in which the dominance of religion over other institutions is reduced. (p. 488)

simple supernaturalism: A form of religion in which people may believe in a great force or spirit but do not have a well-defined concept of God or a set of rituals involving God. (p. 491)

animism: A form of religion in which all forms of life and all aspects of the earth are inhabited by gods or supernatural powers. (p. 492)

theism: A belief system that conceives of a god or gods as separate from humans and from other living things on the earth. (p. 492)

polytheistic: A term used to describe a theistic belief system that includes numerous gods. (p. 492)

monotheistic: A term used to describe a theistic belief system centered on belief in a single all-powerful God. (p. 492)

civil religion: A collection of beliefs and rituals that exist outside religious institutions. (p. 494)

church: A religious organization that has strong ties to the larger society. (p. 496)

sect: A religious organization that rejects the beliefs and practices of existing churches; usually formed when a group leaves the church to form a rival organization. (p. 496)

denomination: A religious organization that is on good terms with the institution from which it developed but must compete with other denominations for members. (p. 496)

cult: A new religion. (p. 497)

religiosity: The depth of a person's religious feelings. (p. 504)

INTERNET RESOURCES

Virtual Society: The Wadsworth Sociology Resource Center
(http://sociology.wadsworth.com)

At Virtual Society you can access a wide range of enrichment material to aid your study of sociology. From the main page, click on the Student Resources link and find your course and this textbook. Next, select the chapter you are presently studying from the pull-down menu. Among the useful options for each self-study chapter are online links and exercises, flashcards, practical study tips, and practice quizzes for each chapter.

MicroCase Online
From the Virtual Society home page, click on MicroCase Online to access book-specific MicroCase exercises that allow you to further explore sociological issues and principles presented in the text.

InfoTrac College Edition
Another unique option available to you at the Student Resources section at Virtual Society is InfoTrac College Edition, an online library with access to hundreds of

scholarly and popular periodicals. Below are suggested search terms for this chapter, but this resource also allows you to fit your study of sociology to your own interests by searching custom keywords.

Religiosity

Theism

Cult

Secularization

Islam

Boston College Center for International Higher Education
(www.bc.edu)
Provides links to research centers and international news and library information dealing with the Catholic religion throughout the world.

The Anti-Defamation League
(www.adl.org)
Monitors hate activities in the United States and throughout the world; includes addresses of other useful research sites.

Ontario Consultants on Religious Tolerance
(www.religioustolerance.org)
Explores many religions and states; does not promote or denounce a specific belief. The site does list religious beliefs and news topics among more than 20 denominations.

Andrew Greeley: Author, Priest, Sociologist
(www.agreeley.com)
Offers insights into Andrew Greeley's recent writings. The site includes previews of his recently published works and articles addressing recent issues in Catholicism and other religious groups.

Education

Courtesy of Jonas Chartock

Wendy Kopp.

Wendy Kopp was an idealistic American college senior, about to graduate and filled with the desire to make the world a better place. In her senior thesis, she proposed a plan to develop a corps of new teachers who would go into communities where too many children were failing. That was in 1989. Today Kopp is president of Teach for America, one of the most successful teacher recruitment efforts for underserved communities in the nation's history.

Only days after her graduation, Kopp secured a seed grant and began working tirelessly to put her thesis into practice. Her central idea was that young people like herself would respond with enthusiasm to the chance to be trained for teaching assignments in poor urban and rural schools. She recruited some influential educators and foundation and business executives to her cause. Under her leadership, they raised the first $2.5 million to begin Teach for America as a nonprofit corporation. They received 2,500 applications, from which they selected the first 500 recruits for their new training institute. School districts in six states were prepared to hire recruits who successfully completed the training.

By 1999, more than 5,000 corps members had taught for at least 2 years in classrooms in needy schools all over the United States, and at any time of the school year there are at least 1,000 corps members in the classroom. Perhaps most impressive, about 4,000 of 5,000 Teach for America veterans continue to work for educational equality and social justice. Many have gone on to start their own schools, become principals, develop innovative teaching methods and programs, or become doctors and lawyers who practice in disadvantaged communities. Wendy Kopp remains president of the original corporation, which is linked to the federal Americorps program, whose recruits receive modest incomes for 2 years of national service.

All this success came after an enormous amount of work and struggle. Teach for America had—and still has—critics, who believe that putting underprepared teachers in classrooms does no one a service. Some professional educators fault the program for promoting what they say is the danger-ous myth that "anybody can teach." The 1994 attack on a wide range of social programs in the Republicans' Contract for America would have ended Americorps and severely stunted the growth of Teach for America. But Congress was not about to scuttle a program that was so appealing to the nation's young graduates and so needed in disadvantaged regions. In fact, the program's measurable success has made Teach for America more secure. Surveys show that 77 percent of principals in the schools where the recruits teach feel that the recruits do better than the first-year teachers usually assigned to them. Eighty-five percent of recruits complete their full 2-year commitment, a rate far higher than those most school systems in poor communities report for their entering teachers (Chaddock, 1999).

Teach for America has won such high marks from educators and policymakers, with more than 8,000 recruits now in service or having completed their service, that in the 2002 State of the Union Message to Congress, President Bush asked for an expansion of Americorps and

FOCUS QUESTIONS:

• Why are schools, especially public schools, so often at the center of bitter controversy in democratic societies?

• What questions about education in society are typically studied by sociologists using one or another of the major theoretical perspectives?

• What are the major educational barriers to realizing the goal of equality of opportunity?

the teacher corps with it. Wendy Kopp has been honored with many awards, but no doubt she is proudest of the testimony of Teach for America recruits like Jonas Chartock:

> There is not another job that would bring me back to work excited day in and day out as teaching does. I enjoy my life as the 23-year-old chief executive officer of the nonprofit organization known as Room 104B. I have a responsibility matched by few. The potential for "growth" and "increasing shareholder value" and "opening new markets" in my industry cannot be quantified.

EDUCATION FOR A CHANGING WORLD

Teach for America is one among many current initiatives in North America and throughout the world that address the need for more effective education. In the poorer regions of the world, there is a dire need for universal access to schools; in the more developed regions, serious issues of educational equity need to be addressed. And amid the clamor for school reform in the United States, there is also concern that new standards and new pressures for higher performance will not be matched by the necessary resources of money and talent. Although critics of public schooling abound, there is little consensus about how to achieve better student performance (Torres & Mitchell, 1998). But why are schools and education so often at the center of controversy and debate? To begin answering this question, we turn to basic concepts in educational sociology.

Efforts to change the goals and methods of education are not new. One of the most famous trials in history took place in ancient Greece when Socrates was accused of corrupting the morals of Athenian youth with his innovative ideas and educational methods. Today, the fact that proposals for educational reforms are receiving so much hopeful attention is evidence of the importance of education in modern societies. There is great concern with the need to improve education in order to train new generations of workers. We will see at many points in this chapter that there is a widespread desire to reform schools without significantly increasing school funding. However, although critics of the public schools abound, there is little consensus about how to achieve better student performance (Torres & Mitchell, 1998).

Education may be defined as the process by which a society transmits knowledge, values, norms, and ideologies and in so doing prepares young people for adult roles and adults for new roles; in other words, it transmits the society's culture to the next generation. Education thus is a form of socialization that is carried out by institutions outside the family, such as schools, colleges, preschools, and adult education centers. Each of these is an educational institution because it encompasses a set of statuses and roles designed to carry out specific educational functions—it is devoted to transmitting a specific body of knowledge, values, and norms of behavior. A particular school or college may be referred to as an *institution* in everyday language, but in sociological terms it is an *organization* that exemplifies an educational institution. Thus, El Centro College in Dallas, Texas, is an organization that exemplifies the institution of higher education. The high school you attended was also an organization, but its curriculum and norms of conduct were those of the institution known as secondary education.

Educational institutions have a huge effect on communities in the United States and other modern societies. Upwardly mobile couples often base their choice of a place to live on the quality of the public schools in the neighborhood. Every neighborhood has at least an elementary school, and every large city has one or more high schools and at least one community college or 4-year college. Cities usually also have a variety of school administrations—public and private—and some owe their existence, growth, and development to the presence of a college or university (Ballantine, 1997).

Education and Social Change

If education is so desirable, why are there so many controversies about how best to educate new generations? Educational institutions, like those of religion, seem to be always under intense scrutiny and ideological attack. And the level of controversy over education and schools seems to be particularly high in democratic nations like the United States. Here are some basic sociological explanations for why education and schooling draw so much fire:

1. *High stakes*—Everyone wants what they feel is the best education for their children. Educational success counts a great deal in explaining later patterns of success and failure, not only for individuals but for entire social groups and communities (Kingston et al., 2003).

2. *Class and cultural diversity*—Schools, especially public schools, bring together extremely diverse groups of students, parents, and educators, whose values and attitudes about what should be learned and how it should be learned are often in conflict (Arnot, 2002).

3. *Citizen involvement*—In democratic societies, people expect to speak freely about their beliefs and values and exert political influence to create changes in the institutions they pay for and are involved in; this is particularly true of schools and other educational institutions (Bowles & Gintis, 2000).

4. *Rapid change in knowledge*—Our expectations about what education can and must achieve for the society is always changing as scientific and humanistic knowledge changes. School curricula therefore are always open to revision, which leads to further ideological debate about how best to teach and study, and the value of particular levels of education (Moore & Muller, 2002).

These and other, more specific issues—such as how people think reading should be taught, or whether they believe teachers should lead children in prayer, or whether the schools in a community are failing—account for much of the daily debates about education and schooling in America and elsewhere. How can one go beyond these debates and gain a more sophisticated understanding of educational quality? Social scientists, and especially sociologists, conduct systematic research on a host of educational questions. Sociological theory and research cannot resolve debates among people with widely differing values, but it can contribute in extremely important ways to our factual knowledge about how students, teachers, schools, and other educational organizations are actually working or not working in this and other societies. Application of the major sociological perspectives to education and schooling provides an overview of major areas of research on education.

CHANGING FUNCTIONS OF EDUCATION AND SCHOOLING   To the sociologist, the most common educational institution, the school, is a specialized structure with a special function: preparing children for active participation in adult activities. In simpler societies, however, education of the young is everybody's task in the village or settlement. Children learn through direct demonstration around the hearth or in pastures or fields. For example, among the Maasai, whom we encountered in Chapter 14, boys learn to hunt from their uncles and fathers; girls learn their roles by helping their mothers perform their tasks. But in urban industrial societies with a great deal of division of labor and highly developed social institutions, schools of all kinds, including universities, have become highly specialized institutions designed to teach young people the skills and values the society wishes to foster. The typical school has a clearly defined authority system and set of rules. In fact, sociologists often cite schools as examples of bureaucratic organizations (Ballantine, 1997; Mulkey, 1993).

From this functionalist perspective, another primary function of schools is to help assimilate the children of immigrants into U.S. society. Through language instruction and socialization of students into "the American way of life," schools have been active agents in the assimilation of waves of immigrants over the past 150 years of U.S. history. But debates over bilingual education and interpretations of American history (e.g., the treatment of Native Americans by the U.S. government) in school curricula are indications that the assimilation function is also subject to controversy.

INTERACTION IN SCHOOLS   A more interactionist viewpoint sees the school as a set of behaviors; that is, the central feature of the school is not its bureaucratic structure but the

kinds of interactions and patterns of socialization that occur there. From this perspective, we need to examine all the roles involved and see how they interact—how they mesh or fail to mesh. For example, homework is assigned, but who besides the student is involved in completing the assignment? Are the parents involved? In what ways—as helpers or merely as disciplinarians? Do the parents ever ask what the teacher did with a homework assignment? The interactionist perspective thus insists on examining all the factors involved in learning, often in an effort to determine how they may be strengthened or challenged so as to create more effective learning environments (Torres & Mitchell, 1998).

Interactionist sociologists ask questions about what actually goes on in the daily life of schools and classrooms. Their research focuses on the interactions among students, between students and their teachers, or among teachers and administrators. Their research on these questions usually helps answer questions asked by those with other sociological perspectives as well. For example, observation of classroom interactions might reveal that without knowing it, teachers are following what is sometimes called a "hidden curriculum" that communicates different expectations for girls and boys, with boys expected to do better at math and science and girls expected to do better at analyzing characters and emotions, typical gender-stereotypical roles (Lynch, 1990).

In their research on global educational issues, interactionist sociologists ask questions about how schools work to reach as many of a nation's children as possible, how well students actually learn in those schools, and how the schools function with regard to other major social institutions. Are the schools secular or religious institutions, or both? How free are educators to decide on what is to be taught? In more formal terms, how differentiated are the schools from the society's other social institutions? This

This photo of Tibetan refugee children in a classroom in northern India illustrates the similarity of classroom organization in many parts of the world.

© George Holton/Photo Researchers, Inc.

GLOBAL PERSPECTIVES ON EDUCATION

PERSPECTIVE	TYPICAL ISSUES RAISED	
	DEVELOPED REGIONS	**DEVELOPING REGIONS**
Functionalism	How can schools be better organized to carry out their mission?	Are schools devoted to elite or mass education?
		How independent are the schools from other social institutions, such as mosques and political parties?
Conflict Theory	Do schools promote equal opportunity and mobility, or do they reproduce the status quo of inequality?	Whose children actually get to go to school?
		Do schools allow freedom of thought and critical thinking?
	Do they foster free inquiry or stifle it?	
Interactionism	How does learning take place in classroom interactions?	Questions are essentially the same, based on observation of classroom interactions, but perhaps with more emphasis on how traditional cultures are dealt with in school and classroom interaction.
	What else is being communicated and taught in addition to the lessons?	
	How do peer interactions work to assist or impede learning?	

question is the familiar one of separation of church and school, or of political party and school. Even in relatively secular nations such as the United States, where separation of church and school is the law, there are continual battles over issues like prayer in school and the teaching of "creationism" or "intelligent design" (the idea that God set in motion the mechanisms of evolution). In less secular societies, such as many Islamic nations, religious institutions are entirely responsible for running the schools, in which case little value may be placed on scientific objectivity or freedom of inquiry.

THE CONFLICT PERSPECTIVE: MOBILITY VERSUS REPRO-DUCTION   Conflict theorists view education in modern societies as serving to justify the status quo of class inequality. They ask whether the education produces genuine upward mobility for new generations or simply reproduces the existing class structure by giving students from less advantaged backgrounds mediocre education and schools (Arrow, Bowles, & Durlauf, 2000; Bowles & Gintis, 2000; Castells et al., 1998). Their emphasis on the reproduction of inequality through education challenges the more popular view that education is the main route to social mobility and that it can offset inequalities in family background (Bell, 1973, 1999). When sociologists analyze the impact of educational institutions on

society, they generally conclude that the benefits of education are unequally distributed and tend to reproduce the existing stratification system (Aronowitz & Giroux, 1985; Fullan, 1993).

As noted earlier, sociologists with a conflict perspective on social research often ask whether schools are actually involved in creating equal opportunities for social and group advancement or whether they are in fact working to justify and reproduce existing patterns of inequality. Are they preparing all students, regardless of class, race, ethnicity, or gender, to rise in the social-class hierarchy, for example, or are they preparing students to accept their positions in society, especially when those positions are less advantaged?

The different perspectives generate many specific questions and diverse research projects. This is especially true when one takes a global perspective because educational issues vary widely across different regions of the world. The Study Chart above summarizes the researchable questions these basic sociological perspectives raise in developing and developed regions. Note that the question of who actually goes to school is a critical one. In most urban industrial societies, over 95 percent of all children attend school, but home schooling is becoming more popular, and differential rates of school leaving (dropping out) mean that questions about who goes to school at different

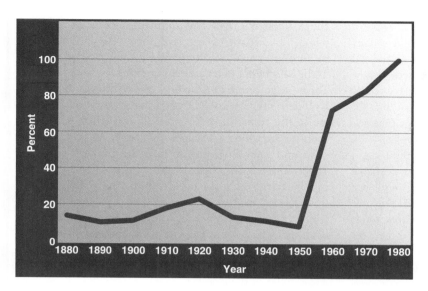

Figure 18.1   Percentage of Nations Developing Systems of Mass Education, by Decade

Source: Adapted from Meyer, Ramirez, & Soysal, 1992.

levels of education are just as relevant in the developed nations as they are in the developing regions of the world.

Who Goes to School?

The idea that all children should be educated is a product of the American and French Revolutions of the late eighteenth century. In the European monarchies, the suggestion that the children of peasants and workers should be educated would have been considered laughable. In those societies, children went to work with adults at an early age, and adolescence was not recognized as a distinct stage of development. Formal schooling, which was generally reserved for the children of the elite, typically lasted 3 or 4 years, after which the young person entered a profession.

Even after the creation of republics in France and the United States and the beginning of a movement for universal education, the development of a comprehensive system of schools took many generations. In the early history of the United States, the children of slaves, Native Americans, the poor, and many immigrant groups, as well as almost all female children, were excluded from educational institutions. The norm of segregated education for racial minorities persisted into the twentieth century and was not overturned until 1954 in the Supreme Court's famous ruling in *Brown* v. *Board of Education of Topeka*. Even after that decision, it took years of civil rights activism to ensure that African Americans could attend public schools with whites. Thus, although the idea of universal education in a democracy arose early, it took many generations of conflict and struggle to transform it into a strong social norm (Cremin, 1980; Krueger, 1998).

The idea of mass education based on the model created in the United States and other Western nations has spread throughout the world. Mass education differs from elite education, which is designed to prepare a small number of privileged individuals (generally sons of upper-class families) to run the institutions of society (e.g., the military, the clergy, the law). Mass education focuses instead on the socialization of all young people for membership in the society. It is seen as a way for young people to become citizens of a modern nation-state. Mass education establishes an increasingly standardized curriculum and tries to link mastery of that curriculum with personal and national development (Benavot et al., 1991; Meyer, Ramirez, & Soysal, 1992).

Figure 18.1 indicates that by 1980 all the nations of the world had adopted the basic model of a mass educational system (although many had not extended educational opportunities to the majority of young citizens). Note the sharp upsurge in the 1950s. This was the decade when large numbers of colonial nations in Africa and Asia became independent. Commitment to a mass educational system became a hallmark of modernity for these and other new nations. It was also a time when agencies like the World Bank, UNESCO (United Nations Educational, Social, and Cultural Organization), and the U.S. Agency for International Development began to actively encourage and provide financial support for mass educational institutions.

PROBLEMS OF SCHOOLING IN THE DEVELOPING WORLD In a recently released study, *The State of the World's Children 1999,* the United Nations Children's Fund (UNICEF) warns that "hundreds of millions of children throughout the world are denied the right to quality basic education, and are therefore growing up ill-equipped to make decent lives for themselves." According to the research documents on which the report is based, nearly 1 billion people—one-sixth of humanity—are classified as functionally illiterate, and two-thirds of these adults are female. (For more on the consequences of this situation, see the Global Social Change box on pages 525–527.)

The report says that children who grow up without basic education find it harder not only to sustain themselves and their families but also to make their way as adults in society with a spirit of tolerance and understanding. Girls who are excluded from school and remain illiterate are even more subject to the dictates of patriarchal figures than those who have received some education and can voice their opposition, at least among themselves. At present, at least 90 million children worldwide are denied any schooling at even the first-grade level, and 232 million have no access at all to secondary education. The UNICEF researchers calculated that in order to provide basic education for all children worldwide, governments would need to spend only an additional $7 billion per year over the next 10 years, which is less than one-tenth of the world's annual military spending.

Turning their attention to educational issues in the developed nations, the UNICEF researchers' findings echo those of critical sociologists. They found that academic underachievement, especially in math and science, is a problem in industrialized as well as developing nations, and that violence is a major problem in schools around the world. The gap between educational haves and have-nots is widening, the research showed, partly as a result of the influence of new learning technologies that are unequally distributed. Most important, the study signaled the long-term negative effects of ignorance and illiteracy caused by the educational exclusion of so many children in the world's poor nations (United Nations, 2001).

In the more affluent industrial nations, extremely high proportions of students who complete secondary school go on to universities and colleges or some kind of professional or occupational training. The demand for greater access to higher education was pioneered in the United States and Canada. An extension of mass education in the United States was the expansion of public institutions of postsecondary education (and the parallel expansion of private colleges and universities, often with federal aid and research funding). This expansion was fueled by the post–World War II baby boom and the massive increase in the college-age population in the 1960s. During those years, there was a parallel boom in employment for elementary school teachers and then for high school teachers and college professors. But after the boom came the bust: The birthrate fell sharply beginning in the late 1950s, and by the mid-1970s college enrollments also began to de-

cline. These changes had dramatic effects on primary schools, but at the college level they were partially offset by an unprecedented countertrend: the immense increase in the number of older students seeking higher education. Today large numbers of adults are returning to college. Unlike the typical student of earlier years, adult students are in the labor force, are married and living with their spouses, are going to school part-time, and are seeking skills and knowledge to enhance their careers (Mulkey, 1993; Torres & Mitchell, 1998).

The return of so many adults to educational institutions has led many social scientists to describe a future in which education will be a lifelong process in which people of all ages will move in and out of educational institutions. Nevertheless, the most rapidly growing area of education is preschool programs, an important trend that is discussed later in the chapter.

Schools and Adolescent Society

A key feature of education is the fact that schools structure the lives of children and adolescents. This is particularly true at the high school level. A famous study of the effect of schools on adolescents and youth, *The Adolescent Society,* was published by James Coleman in 1961. Its main point was that schools help create a social world for adolescents that is separate from adult society. According to Coleman, this is an almost inevitable result of the growing complexity of industrial societies, in which, as we saw earlier, functions that were formerly performed by the family are increasingly shifted to other institutions, especially educational institutions. Yet schools cannot provide the same kind of support and individual attention that the family can. As a result, according to Coleman, the student is pushed into associations primarily with others of the same age. These small groups of age-mates come to "constitute a small society, one that has most of its important interaction within itself, and maintains only a few threads of connection with the outside adult society" (1961, p. 3).

Coleman's research was not unique. Other social scientists have analyzed what has come to be known as the "youth culture" in terms of changes in the structure of American society. Briefly, what has happened is that the rising level of expectations regarding educational attainment has placed more and more demands on the student. This pressure often is not matched with a clear means of meeting the new demands. This mismatch between ends and means can lead to the emergence of deviant individuals and groups, as we saw in our discussion of Merton's typology of deviance in Chapter 7. The

GLOBAL SOCIAL CHANGE

Poverty and Illiteracy

There is a strong correlation between illiteracy and poverty throughout the world (see the map on pages 526–527). The poor nations of the Sahel, such as Mali, Chad, Niger, Ethiopia, and the Sudan, suffer from some of the highest rates of illiteracy in the world. High rates of illiteracy are also evident in much of South Asia, especially on the Indian subcontinent. On the other hand, the correlation is not absolute: Illiteracy rates are quite low in poor nations such as Mexico and Cuba, where the ideology of social development places strong emphasis on educating the mass of citizens to the fullest extent possible.

Sociological theories of modernization stress the need for populations to become literate so that their members will be better-informed voters, more highly skilled workers, more careful parents, and generally better able to realize their human potential. Reductions in the level of ignorance yield improvements in every aspect of a nation's social and civic life.

This line of argument is clearly supported by the correlation between poverty and illiteracy in India (see the accompanying chart). Overall, the chart shows that as illiteracy decreases, the amount of money a household is able to spend each month increases. The chart also shows that illiteracy and the poverty associated with it are much more prevalent among women than among men, with rural women showing the highest rates of illiteracy and poverty (about 90 percent illiterate in the high-poverty category). That men are far more likely than women to become literate in India is a reflection of the immense gap in prestige between the sexes in that society; men are considered far more worthy of education than women.

Research on the effects of literacy on vital measures of social change such as reduced fertility clearly shows the importance of educating women. Data from research conducted in Thailand and other Southeast Asian nations suggest that until women gain access to

at least minimal educational opportunities, fertility rates in those nations will remain high. This research confirms the hypothesis that "demographic change is unlikely if the movement towards mass schooling is confined largely to males" (London, 1992, p. 306).

These relationships among gender, illiteracy, and social indicators like poverty and fertility offer a warning that investments in literacy alone are necessary but not sufficient to accelerate social change in a population. Investments in literacy must be accompanied by strategies to reach the most impoverished and discriminated against segments of the population (such as rural women in many societies). Such strategies, in turn, are difficult to develop in a society in which the powerful may fear their effects. In nations where poor rural women are offered more education, for example, the women often begin to demand greater equality. It takes farsighted leadership to actively promote such strategies.

Another consequence of increasing literacy and education in poor societies is that some of the "best and brightest" are attracted by opportunities in richer societies. This phenomenon is known as the "brain drain" and is a significant problem for developing nations (Alam, 1988; Cortes, 1980). Relatively well-educated people, often with professional training, are an important source of migration from Third World nations to the wealthier nations of North America and Western Europe. Indeed, immigration policies in North America actively

encourage immigration by well-trained individuals and establish quotas that discourage less educated persons from seeking entry.

In order to address the problems created by the brain drain phenomenon, the poorer nations have developed policies requiring that people trained at public expense (e.g., through scholarships and training programs) must serve in their own nation until it has recouped its investment in their education. Such policies are not popular with educated people in those nations, especially if they are aware of more attractive opportunities outside their own society. But if the full benefits of literacy and education are to be applied to national development, such policies are necessary.

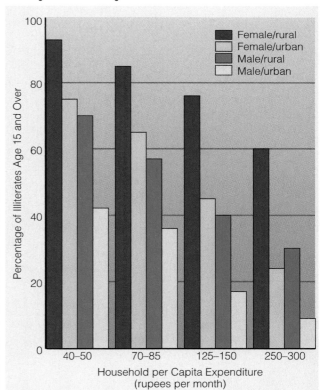

Poverty and Illiteracy in India

Source: Data from third quinquennial survey on employment and unemployment, Ministry of Planning, New Delhi, India.

continued

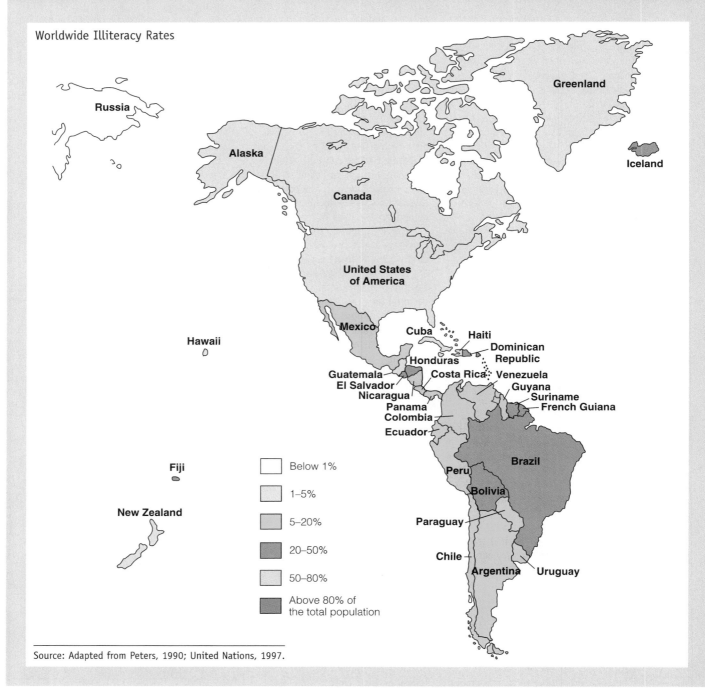

Worldwide Illiteracy Rates

Russia

Greenland

Alaska

Iceland

Canada

United States
of America

Hawaii

Mexico   Cuba   Haiti

Dominican
Republic

Honduras

Guatemala   Costa Rica   Venezuela
El Salvador   Guyana
Nicaragua   Suriname
Panama   French Guiana
Colombia

Fiji   Ecuador

Brazil

New Zealand   Peru

Bolivia

Paraguay

Chile

Argentina   Uruguay

	Below 1%
	1–5%
	5–20%
	20–50%
	50–80%
	Above 80% of the total population

Source: Adapted from Peters, 1990; United Nations, 1997.

resulting frustration often leads teenage peer groups to become extremely ambivalent and even cynical about adult expectations. They develop fierce loyalty and conformity to the peer group, strictly observing group norms and not tolerating any deviance from those

norms, which themselves may deviate from those of their teachers and parents.

The risk for society in the development of isolated adolescent cultures is that teenagers will fail to learn how they can become involved in shaping their own society.

1 Czech Republic
2 Slovakia
3 Austria
4 Hungary
5 Estonia
6 Latvia
7 Bosnia and Herzegovina
8 Yugoslavia

9 Macedonia
10 Bulgaria
11 Lithuania
12 Moldova
13 Belarus
14 Syria
15 Jordan
16 Israel

Great cultural gaps between youth and their parents are often a signal that the older generation has not offered young people enough opportunities to work with adults for constructive social change (Gilligan, cited in Norman, 1997; Moscos, 1988).

Education and Citizenship

Another important aspect of education in the United States is the relationship between education and citizenship. Throughout its history, this nation has emphasized public education as a means of transmitting democratic values, creating equality of opportunity, and preparing new generations of citizens to function in society. In addition, the schools have been expected to help shape society itself. During the 1950s, for example, efforts to combat racial segregation focused on the schools. Later, when the Soviet Union launched the first orbiting satellite, American schools and colleges came under intense pressure and were offered many incentives to improve their science and mathematics programs so that the nation would not fall behind the Soviet Union in scientific and technological capabilities.

Education is often viewed as a tool for solving social problems, especially social inequality. The schools, it is thought, can transform young people from vastly different backgrounds into competent, upwardly mobile adults. Yet these goals seem almost impossible to attain (Cahill, 1992). In recent years, in fact, public education has been at the center of numerous controversies arising from the gap between the ideal and the reality. Part of the problem is that different groups in society have different expectations. Some believe that students need better preparation for careers in a technologically advanced society, others that children should be taught basic job-related skills, still others that education should not only prepare children to compete in society but also help them maintain their cultural identity (and, in the case of Hispanic children, their language). On the other hand, policymakers concerned with education emphasize the need to increase the level of student achievement and to involve parents in their children's education (Wilson, 1993).

Some reformers and critics have called attention to the need to link formal schooling with programs designed to address social problems. Sociologist Charles Moscos, for example, is a leader in the movement to create a system of voluntary national service. National service, as Moscos defines it, would entail "the full-time undertaking of public duties by young people—whether as citizen soldiers or civilian servers—who are paid subsistence wages" and serve for at least a year (1988, p. 1). In return for this period of service, the volunteers would receive assistance in paying for college or other educational expenses.

Advocates of national service and school-to-work programs believe that education does not have to be confined to formal schooling. In devising strategies to provide opportunities for young people to serve their society, they emphasize the educational value of citizenship experiences gained outside the classroom. Americorps and Teach for America are examples of such programs, but they are minuscule compared to the need. Although, as noted earlier, President Bush voiced his support for these programs in his 2002 State of the Union Address, he has so far done little to dissuade his party's leaders from their efforts to cut back on nonmilitary federal programs. Moreover, massive shortfalls in state and local budgets due to federal tax cuts are making it difficult to fund mainstream educational institutions, to say nothing of expanding innovative ones like Teach for America.

ATTAINMENT, ACHIEVEMENT, AND EQUALITY

Although some educational reformers focus on the need to expand learning opportunities through nonschool service experiences, most scholars and administrators seek improvements in educational institutions themselves. Their efforts often focus on *educational attainment,* or the number of years of schooling that students receive, and *educational achievement,* or the amount of learning that actually takes place. Both aspects of education are closely linked to economic inequality and social mobility (see Chapter 12).

Educational Attainment

In any discussion of education as a major social institution, the concept of **educational attainment** (number of years of school completed) holds a central place. Educational attainment is correlated with income, occupation, prestige, attitudes and opinions, and much else. It is essential, therefore, for social scientists to understand the impact of recent trends in school enrollment on the educational attainment of the population as a whole and of various subgroups of the population.

Table 18.1 shows the median number of years of school completed by the population as a whole in the decades since 1940. Table 18.2 presents data on educational attainment by race, ethnicity, and sex. Both tables apply to the population age 25 and older. It is immediately clear that the average American today has much more education than the average American of the early 1940s. It is also clear that whites are more likely to complete high school than blacks or Hispanics and are considerably more likely to attend college. The data indicate the increasingly high value placed on education, especially college education. People older than age 75, who were born in the early decades of the twentieth century, have, on the average, considerably lower levels of educational attainment than their children and grandchildren (Farley, 1996; *Statistical Abstract,* 2002).

CHAPTER 18   Education   529

TABLE 18.1

Educational Attainment of U.S. Population, 1940–2000

Year	Median Years of School Completed
2000	12.9
1990	12.9
1980	12.5
1970	12.2
1960	10.6
1950	9.3
1940	8.6

Source: Data from U.S. Census Bureau, 2002.

Barriers to Educational Attainment

TRACKING AND INEQUALITY   The rise of mass education gave the middle and lower classes greater opportunities for upward social mobility through educational attainment. As early as the 1920s, however, many schools began to use "tracking" systems in which higher-achieving students were placed in accelerated classes while others were shunted into vocational and other types of less challenging classes. Today tracking remains a major problem in public schools. Parents of "gifted" children seek educational challenges for their sons and daughters and do not want them to be held

back by slower learners. However, tracking systems can make average students feel less valued, and there is a danger that gifted but alienated students will be labeled as nonachievers.

Figure 18.2 is based on a national study of more than 14,000 eighth-grade students in public schools. It shows clearly that white and Asian students are far more likely than black and Hispanic students to be tracked into high-ability groups. (Ability grouping is synonymous with tracking.) Some social scientists argue that these differences are a result of ability differences among racial and class groups; others assert that they are a consequence of race and class bias (Wolfe, 1998). Because there are far more Hispanic and black students in the lower socioeconomic classes, there is little question that social factors outweigh biological ones in explaining these results. In any case, tracking separates children and is increasingly viewed as leading to educational inequalities. A current trend in educational practice, therefore, is to institute detracking programs and to provide highly gifted students with additional challenges through cooperative education (in which they have opportunities to teach others) and through after-school programs (Betts, 1998; Mansnerus, 1992).

Tracking most often begins in junior high school or middle school, where students do not stay in a single classroom but move from one subject to another. It persists into high school, where it is often made explicit in tracks such as the common, academic, general, and vocational-commercial curricula of many secondary-school systems. Teachers and administrators often support tracking systems because they believe that students learn more effectively and develop

TABLE 18.2

Educational Attainment, by Race, Ethnicity, and Sex: 1947–2000

	Percent High School Graduate						Percent College Graduate					
	White		Black		Hispanic		White		Black		Hispanic	
Year	M	F	M	F	M	F	M	F	M	F	M	F
2000	88%	88%	77%	78%	56%	56%	31%	25%	14%	17%	11%	11%
1997	83	83	74	76	55	55	27	22	13	14	11	10
1991	80	80	67	67	51	51	25	19	11	12	10	9
1987	77	77	63	64	52	50	25	17	11	10	10	8
1980	71	70	51	51	46	44	22	14	8	8	10	6
1970	57	58	32	35	NA	NA	15	9	5	4	NA	NA
1962	47	50	23	26	NA	NA	12	7	4	4	NA	NA
1947	33	37	13	15	NA	NA	7	5	2	3	NA	NA

NA = Data not available.

Source: U.S. Census Bureau, 1988, 1992; Statistical Abstract, 2001.

Figure 18.2   Ability Grouping ("Tracking") in U.S. Public Schools

Source: Adapted from Mansnerus, 1992.

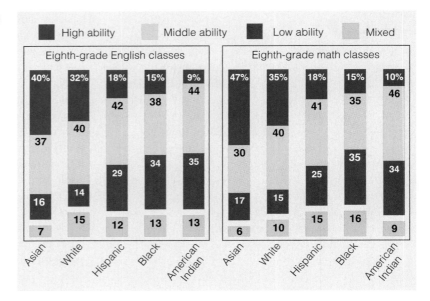

greater self-esteem when they are grouped with academically equivalent students. These claims may be legitimate, but most of the available research indicates that students are intensely aware of tracking when it exists and that it does not contribute to the academic confidence of those in lower tracks.

Research on the lasting effects of tracking gives strong support to the critical "reproduction" theories of schooling. Students in lower tracks tend to end up in lower-paid and lower-prestige occupations once they finish their schooling, as we see clearly in Table 18.3. In this longitudinal study, which compared student experience with tracking with careers later in life, the researchers found that almost 41 percent of those in the academic track were in professional, technical, or managerial careers later

in life, as opposed to less than 20 percent of those in vocational-commercial tracks. Tracking does not automatically translate into reproduction of the class system, but these data indicate that it contributes to maintaining the status quo of class inequality.

DROPPING OUT   The educational attainment of various subgroups of the population is virtually identical up to the age of 13 (Farley, 1996). The picture begins to change in the early secondary school years, however. Until recently, the dropout rate for black and Hispanic students in high school was almost twice the rate for white students. In 1970, for instance, 10.8 percent of white students dropped out without finishing high school, while among black students the proportion was 22.2 percent. By 1999,

TABLE 18.3

Cross-Tabulation of Track Placement by Occupation of Respondent

Occupation	Academic		General		Vocational-Commercial	
	N	Percent	N	Percent	N	Percent
Service	48	10.0	137	20.5	41	19.1
Operator-laborer	70	14.6	165	24.7	39	18.1
Precision production and craft	24	5.00	65	9.7	29	13.5
Administrative-sales	141	29.5	147	22.0	64	29.8
Professional technical-managerial	195	40.8	153	22.9	42	19.5

Note: Data used in this table are from the 1991 National Longitudinal Survey of Youth, a nationally representative sample of 12,686 men and women first interviewed in 1979, when they were between ages 14 and 22. Slightly more than 1,900 cases were randomly selected and analyzed.

Source: Broussard & Joseph, 1998.

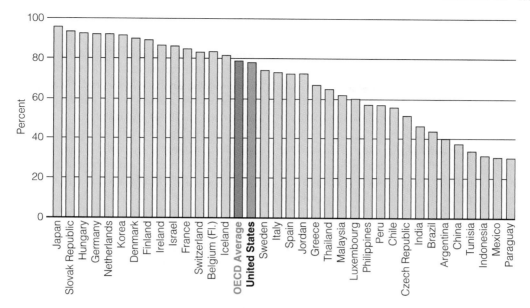

Figure 18.3 International Secondary-School Completion Rates

Source: Organization for Economic Cooperation and Development, 1999.

the situation had improved remarkably as a result of strenuous efforts by students, parents, and teachers across the United States. In that year, 7.3 percent of white students and 12.6 percent of black students dropped out (*Statistical Abstract,* 2002).

International comparisons show that with a national secondary school completion rate just below 80 percent, the United States ranks well below other nations in Europe and Asia with which it is often compared, such as Japan, Germany, and France. In the early twentieth century, the United States led the world in the rate at which its teenagers completed high school, but as Figure 18.3 demonstrates, it has slipped to the middle of the rankings (Peterson, 2003). Such comparisons lead some political and educational leaders to argue that greater school accountability, particularly through the use of standardized testing of all students annually, is required to make the United States more competitive. As we turn to issues of educational achievement, however, we will see that equating school success with test scores can lead to additional and unanticipated problems.

The main reason for dropping out of school is poor academic performance, but there are other reasons as well. Students often drop out because of the demands of work and family roles; many are married, or unmarried and pregnant, and/or working at regular jobs. Whatever the reason, the effects of dropping out can be serious.

Dropouts have less chance of joining the labor force than high school graduates; whatever jobs they find tend to be low-paying ones. Since the 1970s, the income advantage from completing college has increased for all individuals, regardless of gender or minority status. But black–white differentials are found at each level of attainment. White college graduates, for example, earn at least 20 percent more than black college graduates of the same age (National Center for Educational Statistics, 1995).

HIGH-STAKES TESTING AND DROPOUT RATES There is now conclusive social-scientific evidence that states that base their funding of school districts on how well schools do on standardized tests actually increase, rather than decrease, high school dropout rates. This is an unintended consequence of such "high-stakes testing." Mandated by the Bush administration's "No Child Left Behind" education bill of 2001, the move to increase school accountability through increased use of uniform tests, and then rating schools on how well their students do on these tests, has been a growing trend since the early 1980s. Unfortunately, new research shows that while such tests do result in small gains in student performance, it also encourages school systems to engage in "creative" measurement of school achievement.

In 2003, Texas audited 16 middle schools and high schools and found that of 5,500 teenagers who had left school in the 2000–2001 school year, about 3,000, or 55 percent, should have been reported as dropouts. The research showed that the rankings of 14 of the 16 schools should be lowered and that Houston's school system should be ranked unacceptable. Houston as a whole reported a 1.5 percent annual dropout rate, although education experts estimate that the true percentage of students who quit before graduation is nearer 40 percent. The city is appealing the recommendation and contends that it may be guilty of shoddy record-keeping, but not of fraud (Schemo, 2003).

But Houston is far from alone in using statistical sleight-of-hand to inflate graduation rates (and deflate dropout rates). Many other school districts whose funding is now based on national test results have also been found to be taking steps to make their graduation rates appear better than they are.

The congressionally mandated 1999 National Academy of Sciences report *High Stakes: Testing for Tracking, Promotion and Graduation* cites five other studies that draw similar conclusions (Orfield & Wald, 2001).

DEGREE INFLATION   The trend toward increasingly higher levels of educational attainment has had an unexpected effect known as "degree inflation" (Pedersen, 1997). Employers have always paid attention to the educational credentials of potential employees, but today they require much more education than in the past. For example, early in the twentieth century a person could get a teaching job with just a high school diploma; now a bachelor's or master's degree is usually required. The same is true of social work. And secretaries, who formerly could get by without a high school diploma, now are often required to have at least some college education or, in some cases, a college degree.

Degree inflation is discouraging to some students and prevents them from continuing their education. It also adds to the expense of education (both directly and indirectly in terms of lost income) and hence prevents less advantaged students from undertaking advanced studies. Degree inflation also increases the amount of time that must be devoted to formal education. It therefore raises questions about the meaning of educational achievement—that is, the value of the time spent attaining educational credentials.

Educational Achievement

International differences in levels of educational attainment are viewed as a sign that public education is not meeting the expectations of society in terms of the quantity of education provided to citizens. There is also controversy over the quality of education, or educational achievement as reflected in scores on standardized tests like the Scholastic Aptitude Test (SAT). **Educational achievement** refers to how much the student actually learns, measured by mastery of reading, writing, and mathematical skills. It is widely believed that the average level of educational achievement has declined drastically in recent decades. In a historic 1983 report titled *A Nation at Risk*, the National Commission on Excellence in Education pointed to the decline in the average test scores of high school students since the mid-1960s and stated that the schools have failed to maintain high educational standards. In recent years, standardized scores in math have risen somewhat, but verbal scores (reading and vocabulary) have not (Jencks & Phillips, 1999). Many observers attribute the decline in test scores to a variety of social conditions such as too much television viewing and changing values related to family life.

Critics of excessive reliance on standardized tests might agree with prominent educational reformer Ted Sizer, who points out that "none of the major tests used in American elementary and secondary education correlates well with long-term success or failure. SAT scores, for example, suggest likely grades in the freshman year at college; they do not predict much thereafter" (1995, p. 58). For better or worse, however, the SAT and other standardized tests continue to be used as primary measures of individual and school performance.

FUNCTIONAL INCOMPETENCY   Another problem related to educational achievement is the high rate of "functional incompetency" among Americans. Many people are unable to read, write, keep a family budget, and the like. Although more and more people are obtaining a college education, many others are being left behind—particularly members of the lower social classes, people for whom English is a second language, and people with learning disabilities. As increasing amounts of education are required for better jobs, this cleavage between educational haves and have-nots becomes an increasingly dangerous trend. And recent research shows that because people with less education have more stressful lives, with longer periods of unemployment and other risks to their health, mortality rates for people ages 25–64 are much higher for those with less education. In other words, people with less than 12 years of education are at greater risk of dying than are those with 12 or more years of education (Battle, 2003).

INTERNATIONAL COMPARISONS   Recent research on school achievement offers even more disturbing evidence of deficiencies in the educational achievement of U.S. students, beginning at an early age. Tests of achievement by thousands of schoolchildren in comparable U.S. and Asian cities—Minneapolis, Chicago, Sendai (Japan), Beijing (China), and Taipei (Taiwan)—found that the mathematics scores of American first-graders were lower than those of Asian first-graders. In some American schools, first-graders' scores were

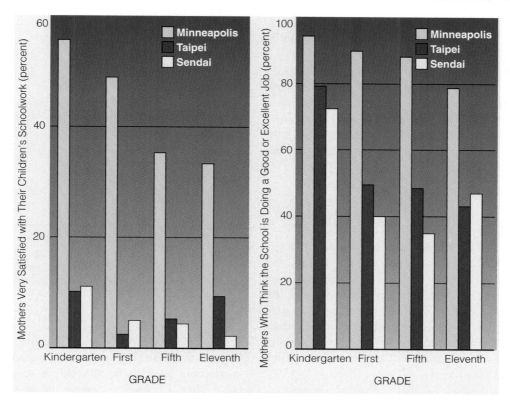

Figure 18.4 Parents' Satisfaction with Academic Performance of Students and Schools in Selected U.S. and Asian Cities

similar to those of Asian students; by the fifth grade, however, all the American students had fallen far behind. In computation, for example, only 2.2 percent of children in Beijing scored as low as the mean score for U.S. fifth-graders. On a test consisting of word problems, only 10 percent of fifth-graders in Beijing scored as low as the average U.S. student. Gaps also appeared in reading skills, although vast differences in written languages make it somewhat difficult to compare achievement in those skills (H. W. Stevenson, 1992a, 1998).

Americans are likely to suggest that these differences occur because citizens of Asian nations value education more than Americans do and that in Asian schools children are placed under great stress, learn by rote and drill, and spend long hours in school. The researchers found that only the first of these explanations is correct. It is true that Asian parents generally value education more than American parents do, but it is not true that Asian schoolchildren experience more stress, do more rote learning, and spend more time at their desks. In fact, the opposite is true: Asian children experience less stress and anxiety than American children, enjoy school more, and have far

more opportunities for recreation and breaks from classroom work despite their longer school day. The frequency of recreation breaks appears to help them pay more attention to their classroom work than is typical of children in U.S. schools.

Close observation of teaching methods revealed that Asian teachers tend to use work that the students do at their desks (seatwork) as an opportunity to pay attention to individual students. Teachers in U.S. schools are less likely to circulate through the class and comment on individual students' efforts.

Finally, Figure 18.4 shows important differences in the way parents perceive schooling in Asia and the United States. Mothers in the United States tend to be far more positive than Asian mothers about their children's schoolwork at all grade levels. They are also more likely to believe that the school is doing an excellent job in educating their children. American parents tend to believe far more in the effects of innate ability and less in the value of effort in school than Asian parents do. This difference is especially important because it seems to lead U.S. parents to more readily accept their children's performance in school and to demand less of them. Parents' belief in innate ability also appears to make them far less critical of the schools than they might otherwise be (H. W. Stevenson, 1998).

This research has many practical implications for social change in the schools. It is apparent, for example, that simply lengthening the school day in the United States would not have the desired results. Indeed, it might well have negative results without far greater provision for time when children can play and socialize with their peers as they do in Asian schools.

Education and Social Mobility

Studies by educational sociologists have consistently found a high correlation between social class and educational attainment and achievement. As we see in Table 18.4, over the past 20 years there has been a marked erosion of the income of non–college graduates.[1] Only college graduates have experienced significant increases in earnings. This fact indicates that social stratification in the United States is increasing, rather than declining as a result of greater equality of opportunity.

Changes in the nature of work and global competition at all skill levels place ever-greater pressure on educational institutions to produce better results. Nevertheless, there is evidence that the promise of equal education for all remains far from being fulfilled. Educational institutions have been subjected to considerable criticism by observers who believe that they hinder, rather than enhance, social mobility (Fullan, 1993).

As noted earlier, critical sociologists often argue that the schools actually reproduce existing patterns of stratification and inequality rather than promote social mobility. The point here is that working-class and poor children do not automatically inherit their lower-class position through the failure of education to reach them or through their own failure to accept the value of education. The influence of specific family and school environments has been demonstrated numerous times in empirical research on how inequality is reinforced by school experiences, especially in schools in low-income neighborhoods (MacLeod, 1995; Torres & Mitchell, 1998).

INEQUALITY IN THE CLASSROOM   Two contemporary studies of the school experiences of students from lower social classes offer strong support for "reproduction theory," the idea that the educational experiences of children of a given social class serve to keep them in that class once their schooling is completed.

---

[1]The table also reveals a significant gender gap in earnings. Inequalities of gender are discussed in Chapter 14.

TABLE 18.4

Average Earnings, by Level of Education, 1979 and 1998

	1979	1998
Without a High School Education		
Males	$27,690	$23,958
Females	18,302	16,482
High School Graduates		
Males	34,978	31,477
Females	23,041	22,780
College Graduates		
Males	55,068	56,524
Females	29,919	39,786

Note: Table reflects average annual earnings in 1998 dollars.

Sources: National Center for Education Statistics; Bureau of Labor Statistics; Current Population Survey, U.S. Census Bureau.

Paul Willis's research in an industrial community in England draws on the experience of a group of boys from low-income homes who thought of themselves as "the lads." They delighted in making fun of higher achievers in their school, whom they called "the earholes." In many different ways, however, the lads indicated that they believed their teachers were pushing them into low-prestige futures. Willis interpreted the hostility and alienation of these students as a way of resisting the social forces they encountered in school and in their communities that were channeling them into working-class careers (Willis, 1983).

In a study that confirms some aspects of Willis's research and challenges others, Jay MacLeod (1995) spent a great deal of time observing and interacting with two groups of students from working-class or poor backgrounds in an American high school in a poor community. MacLeod's white subjects, who called themselves the "Hallway Hangers," were very much like "the lads." In school they were angry and alienated. They believed that there was no point in raising their educational aspirations above those of their parents and older siblings. Their school experiences did nothing to change their resigned outlook. In contrast, a black peer group, "the Brothers," had taken on the higher aspirations of an African-American version of the American dream of hard work and eventual success. Although objectively they were not doing much better in school than the Hallway Hangers, in MacLeod's view their greater optimism and resolve calls into question the apparent inevitability of social-class reproduction in the public schools. While MacLeod does not deny the existence of educational forces that tend to reproduce inequalities from one generation to another, he believes that there is always the possibility of "agency"—

that is, determined efforts by individuals and groups to challenge the status quo of inequality, even if this challenge often produces very mixed results (MacLeod, 1995).

These studies are based on close observation of students in inner-city communities in England and the United States. They document the processes whereby class inequalities are reinforced in school as children from working-class and poor backgrounds are shown in subtle and not-so-subtle ways that they need not have high expectations for their educational future. If these lower expectations are not countered at home in the family environment, and if the students are not exceptionally gifted in school, the resulting cycle of school failure and lowered expectations for mobility through education is difficult to break.

In a classic study of how this cycle is established, Ray C. Rist (1973) found that "the system of public education in the United States is specifically designed to aid in the perpetuation of the social and economic inequalities found within the society" (p. 2), despite the widespread belief that education increases social mobility. He reached the following conclusion:

> Schooling has basically served to instill the values of an expanding industrial society and to fit the aspirations and motivations of individuals to the labor market at approximately the same level as that of their parents. Thus it is that some children find themselves slotted toward becoming workers and others toward becoming the managers of those workers. (1973, p. 2)

More recent studies of the reproduction of inequality in schools and classrooms often point to problems stemming from cultural differences among students and teachers. This new emphasis is a reflection of the growing impact of immigration and cultural diversity in schools throughout urban industrial nations (Castells et al., 1998). One of the primary issues in studies of culture and education is bilingualism, as shown, for example, in recent empirical research on language and culture among Latino students.

LANGUAGE AND INEQUALITY A study by Lourdes Diaz Soto (1997) traces how the recent retreat from bilingual education has affected children from homes in which Spanish is the primary language. Although they were always controversial, programs that offered instruction in the student's native language as well as in English are being cut back in U.S. schools, largely in response to demands for "English-only" instruction and what is often known as "total immersion" in a single-language environment. Diaz Soto gathered data from participant observation and interviews of teachers, students, and parents in a small industrial city in Pennsylvania where a bilingual pro-

gram had been replaced with an English-only curriculum. Her research documents the frustration and disappointment felt by Spanish-speaking students and their parents as opportunities to enhance the students' ability to speak, read, and write Spanish are withheld. Most painful is the message that only English is permitted in the schools. Diaz Soto's research shows that while this message may be motivated by the desire to have all students master one language (English), it has the negative effect of communicating to Latino students and their parents that their culture is devalued and that their voices will be silenced.

The Spanish-speaking parents argued that there was a need for earlier opportunities for students to learn a second language in elementary school so that children whose home language was not English could see that their language and culture were valued and would be taught in school. Diaz Soto, like many other educational researchers, notes the waste of human resources as children's abilities in languages other than English are lost. She points out that elsewhere in the world "second- and multiple-language learning is common: Danish schools' educational system includes compulsory second-language learning at age eleven; Swedish schools initiate second-language learning in the lower grades; France is initiating language learning for children under five; three-year-olds in northern parts of Germany are experimenting with second-language learning" (1997, p. 94). But in the United States, despite the growing emphasis on global relations and global social change, language education is extremely weak and "bilingual education continues to be suspect." Unfortunately, students who feel that their language and culture are devalued in school, be they Hispanic, Native American, Asian American, or others, often withdraw from participation and fail to develop their full potential.

Important as language and other cultural issues may be in explaining school achievement, economic class may be even more significant. It remains true that students from poor families are likely to attend schools with far fewer resources, less favorable student–teacher ratios, and more staff turnover than the schools attended by middle- and upper-class students (Torres & Mitchell, 1998). These class differences are also striking at the level of higher education.

INEQUALITY IN HIGHER EDUCATION Inequality in higher education is primarily a matter of access—that is, ability to pay. Ability to pay is unequally distributed among various groups in society, and as a result students from poor, working-class, and lower-middle-class families, as well as members of racial minority groups, are most likely to rely on public colleges and universities. Social-scientific evidence indicates that such inequalities are alleviated by federal aid to students from families with low or moderate income. It is likely that without Pell grants, work-study funds, and student loan programs, the proportion of students from such families would be far lower than it currently is. Even with such aid, the proportion of low-income students in colleges and universities is lower than that of students from high-income families (Fuller & Elmore, 1996).

Sandra Baum (1987) examined the educational careers of 2,000 students who were high school seniors in 1980. She found that college attendance rates were higher for students from high-income families than for students from low-income families (60 percent versus 46 percent). However, she found that achievement in school seemed to account for an even larger difference: Students from low-income families who scored high on achievement tests had far higher rates of college attendance than low-scoring students from affluent homes. Thus achievement in the primary school grades seems to be at least as important as family income in explaining a student's success in higher education—but remember that in the lower grades students from more affluent homes tend to achieve more than students from less advantaged homes.

Baum and other researchers have also found that low-income students tend to be concentrated in 2-year colleges and that students in such colleges are much more likely to drop out before completing a degree than students who enter 4-year colleges. On the basis of findings such as these, most educational researchers agree that without college assistance for needy students, differences in educational attainment and achievement would be much greater. And since public institutions of higher education remain the primary route to college degrees for low-income students, increased support for such institutions also tends to diminish inequality in access to higher education (Torres & Mitchell, 1998).

Education for Equality

The question of whether and in what ways education leads to social mobility remains open. Some social scientists view education as an investment like any other: The amount invested is reflected in the future payoff. This is known as *human capital theory*. In this view, differences in payoffs (jobs and social position) are justified by differences in investment (hard work in school and investment in a college education). However, critics of the educational system point out that the resources required to make such "investments" are not equally available to all members of society.

The question of whether the society as a whole, or only its more affluent members, will invest in its "human capital" through such means as preschool programs and student loans is a major public policy issue. This is especially true as technological advances coupled with degree inflation increase the demand for educated people (Castells et al., 1998; Reich, 1992). Empirical evidence of the effectiveness

of such investments may be seen in the results of numerous evaluations of Head Start and other early-education and prekindergarten educational programs (Kagan & Neuman, 1998). One of these evaluations, conducted by the High/Scope Educational Research Foundation and completed in the early 1980s, thoroughly demonstrated the lasting positive effects of a high-quality preschool program.

The subject of the study was a preschool program at the Perry Elementary School, located in a low-income black neighborhood of Ypsilanti, Michigan, a small industrial city on the outskirts of Detroit. The researchers randomly selected 123 children—3-year-old boys and girls—and assigned them either to the preschool group or to another group that would not go to the preschool program. The latter children, like most children at that time, would not be enrolled in school for another 2 years.

About twice a year for the next 20 years, the researchers traced the experiences of the experimental (preschool) and control (no-preschool) groups. The data in Table 18.5 show that the preschool experience produced important differences between the two groups. Members of the preschool group achieved more in school, found better jobs, had fewer arrests, and had fewer illegitimate children; in short, they experienced more success and fewer problems than members of the control group. These findings confirm what other, less well-known studies had shown. For example, pioneering studies by Benjamin Bloom (1976) and by Piaget and Inhelder (1969) had indicated that as much as 50 percent of variance in intellectual development takes place before the age of 4.

The most significant contribution of studies like the High/Scope research is their documentation of the actual improvements that a good preschool program can produce in disadvantaged children. The High/Scope study was also able to translate its findings into dollar figures. One year in the Perry program cost about $1,350 per child. The researchers showed that the "total social benefit" from the program (measured by higher tax revenues, lower welfare payments, and lower crime costs) was equivalent to $6,866 per person.

This research became a classic in the social-scientific study of education because it demonstrated the undeniable benefits of preschool education to society (Kagan & Neuman, 1998). It also appeared during a period when funding for public preschool programs was in danger of being drastically reduced. The findings of the High/Scope study gave congressional advocates of preschool education the evidence they needed to justify continued federal funding. In many instances, however, social scientists know what needs to be done to improve educational achievement and increase equality of educational opportunity but are frustrated by the resistance to change that is inherent in large-scale bureaucratic systems such as the public school systems of many states and municipalities.

TABLE 18.5

Major Findings at Age 19 in the Perry Preschool Study

Category	Number Responding*	Preschool Group	No-Preschool Group
Employed	121	59%	32%
High school graduation (or its equivalent)	121	67%	49%
College or vocational training	121	38%	21%
Ever detained or arrested	121	31%	51%
Females only: teen pregnancies, per 100**	49	64	117
Functional competence (APL Survey: possible score 40)	109	24.6	21.8
Percent of years in special education	112	16%	28%

*Total N = 123.

**Includes all pregnancies.

Source: Data from Berrueta-Clement et al., 1984.

THE STRUCTURE OF EDUCATIONAL INSTITUTIONS

A significant barrier to educational reform is the bureaucratic nature of school systems. We noted earlier that sociologists view the school as a specialized structure with a special socializing function and that it is also a good example of a bureaucratic organization. As any student knows, there is a clearly defined status hierarchy in most schools. At the top of the hierarchy in primary and secondary schools is the principal, followed by the assistant principal and/or administrative assistants, the counselors, the teachers, and the students. Although the principal holds the highest position in the system, his or her influence on students usually is indirect. The teacher, on the other hand, is in daily command of the classroom and therefore has the greatest impact on the students. In this section, we discuss several aspects of the structure of educational institutions and attempts to change those institutions.

Schools as Bureaucracies

As the size and complexity of the American educational system have increased, so has the tendency of educational institutions to become bureaucratized (Torres & Mitchell, 1998). The one-room schoolhouse is a thing of the past; today's schools have large administrative staffs and numerous specialists such as guidance counselors and special education teachers. Teachers themselves specialize in particular subject areas or grade levels. Schools are also characterized by a hierarchy of authority. The number of levels in the hierarchy varies, depending on the nature of the school sys-

tem. In large cities, for example, there may be as many as seven levels between the superintendent and school personnel, making it difficult for the superintendent to control the way policies are carried out. Similarly, in any given school, it may be difficult for the principal to determine what actually happens in the classroom.

The Sociological Observer

Distance learning, which involves an individual taking a college course completely online via a computer, means that classes can be taught to students who do not have access to a physical school or classroom. What are some of the advantages of this type of education? What are some things that the students may be missing? (See page 547 for further insights into the sociological content of this photo.)

AP/Wide World Photos

School bureaucracies are often criticized for being "top heavy" with administrators who do not teach and whose regulations seem to stifle creativity at the classroom level. What accounts, then, for the prominence of these complex administrations and their influence on the conduct of schooling? In attempting to answer this question, we need to consider several aspects of what makes a successful school system in a city, town, or rural area.

First, in addition to everything else they are, schools are a collection of buildings, sports fields, laboratories, and real estate. They require capital funds for building and maintenance, planning for new facilities, budgeting and accounting for fiscal oversight, and much more. As Figure 18.5 shows, in some parts of the nation overly high percentages of students are going to schools that are old and need to be refurbished or replaced. The average age of schools in the United States is 42 years. Teachers, students, and parents want to know that buildings are safe and designed to facilitate learning, but they do not have the time or ability to take care of these needs themselves. School administrators must work with political leaders and parents' groups to get the physical work of the district done, and they often labor under extremely difficult conditions of budgetary constraint and ideological conflict.

A second social force that tends to expand educational bureaucracies is their need to respond to so many different public needs and values. Children with learning disabilities need special programs; sports teams demand budgets and leagues; federal and state authorities demand compliance with new requirements for testing, record keeping, school security, student health standards, and much more. Every demand on a school system that administrators are expected to fulfill adds to their workload and produces a need for more administrative personnel. Some school administrations become large because political leaders want to place their allies in jobs (this is known as *patronage*) or because of *cronyism* within the administration (appointing people to jobs as a favor), but much of the growth of school administrations is caused by demands that citizens and their representatives place on the school system.

THE CLASSROOM   In most modern school systems, the primary school student is in the charge of one teacher, who instructs in almost all academic subjects. But as the student advances through the educational structure, the primary school model (which evolved from the one-room school with a single teacher) is replaced by a "departmental" structure in which the student is taught by several different teachers, each specializing in a particular subject. The latter structure is derived largely from that of the nineteenth-century English boarding school. But these two basic structures are frequently modified by alternative approaches

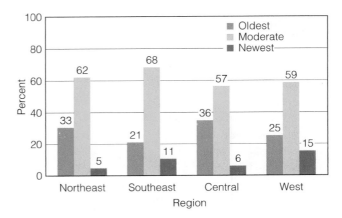

Figure 18.5   Percentage Distribution of Public Schools According to School Condition, by Region

Note: Estimates are aggregates of data collected in 1994, 1995, and 1996. Percentages may not add up to 100 as a result of rounding.

Source: U.S. Department of Education, 1999.

such as the "open" primary school classroom, in which students are grouped according to their level of achievement in certain basic skills and work in these skill groups at their own pace. The various groups in the open classroom are given small group or individual instruction by one or more teachers rather than being expected to progress at the same pace in every subject.

Open classrooms have not been found to produce consistent improvements in student performance, but they have improved the school attendance rates of students from working-class and minority backgrounds. Students in open classrooms tend to express greater satisfaction with school and more commitment to classwork. The less stratified authority structure of the open classroom and the greater amount of cooperation that occurs in such settings may help students enjoy school more and, in the long run, cause them to have a more positive attitude toward learning.

THE TEACHER'S ROLE   Given the undeniable importance of classroom experience, sociologists have done a considerable amount of research on what goes on in the classroom. They often start from the premise that, along with the influence of peers, students' experiences in the classroom are of central importance to their later development. It is rare, however, that social scientists have the opportunity to trace the influence of teachers over students' lifetimes. A classic exception to this limitation is a study (Pedersen & Faucher, 1978) that examined the impact of a single first-grade teacher on her students' subsequent adult status. As they examined the IQ scores of pupils in the school's first-grade classes, the researchers found a clear association between changes in a pupil's family background, first-grade teacher, and self-concept. Further examination of the school's records revealed a startling fact: The IQs of pupils in one particular teacher's first-grade class were significantly more likely to increase in subsequent years than those of pupils in first-grade classes taught by other teachers. And pupils who had been members of that class were more than twice as likely to achieve high status as adults as pupils who had been members of other first-grade classes (see Table 18.6).

What was so special about Miss A, as the outstanding teacher was labeled? First, she was still remembered by her students when they were interviewed 25 years after they had been in her class. More than three-quarters of those students rated her as very good or excellent as a teacher. "It did not matter what background or abilities the beginning pupil had; there was no way that the pupil was not going to read by the end of grade one." Miss A left her pupils with a "profound impression of the importance of schooling, and how one should stick to it" and "gave extra hours to the children who were slow learners." In nonacademic matters, too, Miss A was unusual:

> When children forgot their lunches, she would give them some of her own, and she invariably stayed after hours to help children. Not only did her pupils remember her, but she apparently could remember each former pupil by name even after an interval of 20 years. She adjusted to new math and reading methods, but her success was summarized by a former colleague this way: "How did she teach? With a lot of love!" (Pedersen & Faucher, 1978, pp. 19–20)

In summing up their findings, Pedersen and Faucher stated that their data "suggest that an effective first-grade teacher can influence social mobility" (p. 29). The surprising results of this study have important implications. Good teachers clearly can make a big difference in children's lives, a fact that gives increased urgency to the need to improve the quality of primary school teaching. The reforms carried out by educational leaders suggest that when good teaching is combined with high levels of parental involvement, the results can be even more dramatic.

Because the role of the teacher is to change the learner in some way, the teacher–student relationship is an important part of education. Sociologists have pointed out that this relationship is asymmetrical or unbalanced, with the teacher being in a position of authority and the student having little choice but to passively absorb the information provided by the teacher. In other words, in conventional classrooms there is little opportunity for the student to become actively involved in the learning process. On the other hand, students often develop strategies for undercutting the teacher's authority: mentally withdrawing, inter-

TABLE 18.6

Adult Status, by First-Grade Teacher

Adult Status	First-Grade Teacher Miss A	Miss B	Miss C	Others
High	64%	31%	10%	39%
Medium	36	38	45	22
Low	0	31	45	39
Total	100%	100%	100%	100%
(N)	(14)	(16)	(11)	(18)
Mean adult status	7.0	4.8	4.3	4.6

(N) = Number of students who could be located and interviewed 25 years later.

Note: "Adult status" was determined form interviews that included questions on occupational status and work history, highest grade completed, rent paid and number of rooms, and related indicators of social position.

Source: Eigil Pedersen and Terese Annette Faucher, "A New Perspective on the Effects of First-Grade Teachers on Children's Subsequent Adult Status," *Harvard Educational Review,* 1978, 48:1, 1–31. Copyright © 1978 by the President and Fellows of Harvard College. All rights reserved.

rupting, and the like (Darling-Hammond, 1997; Rose, 1995). Much current research assumes that students and teachers influence each other instead of assuming that the influence is always in a single direction.

SCHOOL PEER GROUPS AND VIOLENCE   The shootings at Columbine High School in Colorado and in other seemingly safe suburban schools in Oregon, Arkansas, Michigan, and Kentucky, along with the outbreaks of gang violence in many urban schools in the late 1990s, were generally seen as symptoms of widespread school violence and student alienation. These tragic episodes received sensational television coverage and scared millions of parents, but they are not representative of the actual data on school violence. As Figure 18.6 shows, rates of school violence have remained relatively stable over the past few decades. The most common form of crime that high school students experience is theft (about 40 percent). Rates of vandalism and threats with or without a weapon actually decreased during the 1990s (U.S. Department of Education, 1999).

Public reactions and social policies often are determined not by facts but by perceptions of social conditions. The perception that schools were becoming unsafe, even in communities assumed to be immune from severe peer violence, resulted in much new legislation intended to make schools safer. Perhaps a more positive outcome, however, is that educators, parents, and students have become more

Figure 18.6 Percentage of High School Seniors Who Reported Being Victimized at School During the Previous 12 Months, 1976–1997 (by type of victimization)

Source: Hazler, 2000.

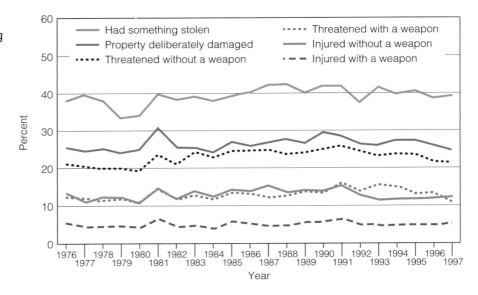

aware of the causes of school violence. Much more emphasis has been placed on the need to understand school peer groups (and identifiable cliques) and their interactions. Teachers are being taught how to recognize bullying, how to protect the rights and safety of gay and lesbian students, and how to communicate better with students about their feelings and experiences (Hazler, 2000). Much remains to be done to create school environments that are free of violence and where students can speak to adults about their problems with peers without feeling that they are "snitches." As the diversity of racial and ethnic groups in the schools continues to increase, the challenge of combating school violence will become more difficult. But the statistics show progress, even if perceptions cause some parents to seek alternatives to their local public school or, in some cases, withdraw their children from school.

Changing the System

The bureaucratic organization of school systems makes them highly resistant to change. The basic classroom unit has remained essentially unchanged since the days of the one-room school, as has the structure in which one teacher is in charge of a roomful of students. But despite the difficulties, there are endless demands for school reform and changes in the way students and teachers are evaluated. A full treatment of controversies over educational policy is offered in most courses on the sociology of education. Here we discuss three current controversies that have a direct bearing on whether schools can deliver on their promise of equality of opportunity. They concern class size, school choice, and desegregation.

COMPREHENSIVE SCHOOL REFORM *Raise the standards. Create a level playing field. End social promotion. Use vouchers for school choice.* These are only a few of the most popular slogans people use in debates over education. There is no end to the controversies over what should and should not be accomplished in the nation's schools and colleges. Most of these calls for school reform rely on one major reform, such as testing at every grade level to ensure accountability and to qualify schools for supplemental funding, a centerpiece of the Bush administration's education policy. Most of the reforms also seek to address the needs of schools that are experiencing high levels of failure and poor performance. These schools also tend to be those receiving disproportionately lower shares of public support per student.

Because measures such as universal achievement testing do not address the overall needs of failing schools, some school reformers have developed approaches to comprehensive school reform, which affects all the groups who have a stake (sometimes called stakeholders) in the quality of learning in schools. Among the most prominent of these approaches is the one developed by the pioneering educator and Yale psychiatrist James Comer. His school reform model has inspired many others that are being used to develop new schools and revamp old school systems. We therefore can consider the Comer model as a case study of current efforts at comprehensive school reform.

School districts in Prince George's County (Maryland), Chicago, Miami, New Haven (Connecticut), Dallas, and many other areas are undertaking major efforts at educational reform. Nowhere are their goals quite as ambitious as those of the Prince George's County school district. The Comer-inspired reform efforts involve schoolchildren in collaborative planning with their parents, teachers, and principals. "What I've tried to do here," Comer explains, "is to shape the system, the school, so that it becomes the advocate and support for the kid, and a believer in the kid in the same way that my parents were" (quoted in Schorr, 1988, p. 232).

Comer's research and experience convinced him that children from neighborhoods that are undergoing severe strain—because of poverty, racism, unemployment, violence, drug addiction, and related social problems—enter school with major deficits. They are often "underdeveloped in their social, emotional, linguistic, and cognitive growth." As a result, they often withdraw, act up, and do not learn. Of course, not all such students have these problems. Those who do, however, are labeled "slow learners" or "behavior problems" and consequently fall even further behind their classmates. Comer's solution appears simple on the surface: Change the "climate of demoralized schools by paying much more attention to child development and to basic management of the school" (quoted in Schorr, 1988, p. 233).

Of course, the process of changing school climates and management is much more difficult than this simple formula suggests. The Comer model of institutional change calls for the formation of a School Planning and Management Team in each school; the team is directed by the principal and has from 12 to 14 members, including teachers, aides, and parents. A second team is made up of helping professionals—the school psychologist, social workers, special education teachers, and counselors; it acts as an advisory group. The purpose of the teams is to ally the parents with the school so that, in Comer's words, "you reduce the dissonance between home and school and you give the kid a long-term supporter for education at home" (quoted in Schorr, 1988, p. 233; see also Comer, 1997; O'Neil, 1997).

Inspired by the research of Comer and others, large cities such as Chicago and New York are instituting more opportunities for parents to get involved in school issues and are seeking to reduce the size of schools so that teachers, students, and administrators feel that they are part of a "learning community" in which they all know one another and are concerned with one another's well-being—conditions that may not be possible in larger schools where bureaucratic rules and regulations often seem to take precedence over personal relations (Comer, 1997; Meier, 1995).

In many school districts, however, the pace of reform is slowed by bitter disagreements about how to fund the schools in an era of reduced public spending. There are also controversies over issues such as sex education, tolerance for homosexual students, distribution of condoms to prevent AIDS and teenage pregnancy, bilingual education,

and school prayer. These debates can divide communities and prevent structural changes like the move toward smaller schools and more local responsibility for educational decisions (McFadden, 1998; Rose, 1995).

CLASS SIZE Although the basic organization of the classroom has not changed much over time, the ratio of students to teachers varies widely. Higher-quality education is associated with lower student–teacher ratios—that is, fewer students per teacher. The more students there are in the classroom, the more difficult it is for the teacher to spend time with individual students. One of the reasons parents who can afford to do so often send their children to private schools is so their children will receive more attention and direct instruction from their teachers.

In public schools, classrooms in lower-income communities tend to have the highest student–teacher ratios. Classrooms in suburban schools in affluent communities have among the lowest student–teacher ratios in public education. This is one reason that so many families seek to move to those communities (Ballantine, 1997). Extensive studies in Tennessee and in various urban school districts provide quantitative support for the hypothesis that student performance is indirectly correlated with class size: The lower the number of students per teacher, the higher average school performance will be in terms of grades and performance on standardized tests (Gursky, 1998).

SCHOOL CHOICE One of the most controversial issues confronting educational institutions today is that of school choice. In fact, "school choice" involves several types of choices. As educational sociologist Carol H. Weiss notes:

> Choice plans include magnet schools: public schools with special emphases and/or facilities that draw students from across a district, such as technology schools or music and art schools. Choice plans include charter schools, authorized by a number of state legislatures to be free of most local school district regulations; students apply for admission. (quoted in Fuller & Elmore, 1996, p. vii)

Among conservative school reformers, school choice often means plans to allow students to choose private schools as well as public ones by giving parents vouchers to pay for tuition and leaving them free to decide where and how they will use the vouchers. These "free-market" school choice plans have been popular among conservatives since the 1950s, when they were first developed by the economist Milton Friedman.

At this writing, a great deal of research is being conducted to evaluate one or another of the school choice initiatives. Note, however, that the range of choice is so wide that no single study can demonstrate the overall effect of school choice on all the desirable outcomes of education (e.g., knowledge, mobility, equality, morality, citizenship). And there are so many actual school choice behaviors—including moving to better school districts, home schooling of children, vouchers or education grants (such as the Pell grants in higher education), and the choice among parochial, private, and public schools—that researchers are hard pressed to respond to the challenges presented by these changes in educational institutions (Fuller & Ellmore, 1996). But most liberal critics of school choice plans are afraid that while greater choice is attractive to parents in poor school districts as well as to those in more affluent ones, the overall consequence of increasing choices among different types of schools will be to increase the segregation of students by class and race. And as such segregation increases, so will rates of failure in schools that have been abandoned by better students and more aware parents (Torres & Mitchell, 1998). Indeed, from this critical perspective, increasing racial segregation in public and private education can already be viewed as an outcome of school choice.

THE HOME-SCHOOLING MOVEMENT   Between 1.2 and 1.5 million children are now being taught at home. Since approximately 44 million children are in public schools at all levels and another 10 million are enrolled in private schools, the 3 percent being schooled at home represent a small minority. On the other hand, this number has grown rapidly in the past decade. Its advocates come from all social classes and backgrounds, but a disproportionate 96 percent of home-schooled children are white, and most are Protestant (McDowell & Ray, 2000).

Most home-schooling families are motivated by the desire to teach their children more moral precepts and religious values than they would be taught in public or private schools. They usually want to keep their children away from negative peer influences, materialistic values, and the possibility of violence and intimidation. Parents who wish to educate their children outside the public schools have traditionally sought private schools, often parochial schools that combine secular and religious curricula not available in the secular public schools. Some critics of home schooling question whether children learn well outside schools, but the limited number of studies that have addressed this question indicate that home-schooled students score on the average significantly higher than children in public schools on standardized tests (Ray, 2000).

Critics of home schooling in Europe—where it is also becoming an increasingly popular alternative to public education—note that it is part of a general trend in many

societies to value private rights over public rights and private goods over public ones. We can think of education as something that the individual gains, which eventually makes the individual more competitive in the job market or a more moral person—that is, a person with more private goods to share with selected others as he or she sees fit. But we can also think of education as serving the common good of a vibrant society to which children and parents all contribute through learning; in this view, education is a public rather than a private good. By rejecting the schools, home schoolers are withdrawing the resources of their children and families from the community and thus denying this common good (Lubienski, 2000).

Home-schooling families argue that they and their children should have the right to contribute to the common good in their congregations and peer groups. They should not be obliged to send their children to a school if they so choose. Courts have tended to rule that as long as parents can demonstrate to educators in their communities that they are not depriving their children of the right to high-quality education, they can school them at home. Similar rulings exist in the United Kingdom and other European nations, with the exception of Germany, where judges have tended to rule against home schooling largely on the ground that all children need to contribute to the learning community of the public schools.

The future of home schooling may have lasting implications for the strength of public schooling in democratic societies. If the rate of its growth remains at about 7 percent per year (it is higher in some states, such as South Carolina), there will be about 3 million home-schooled children by 2010. But this growth rate will depend largely on what happens in the schools as well.

THE RETREAT FROM SCHOOL DESEGREGATION   Perhaps the most significant change in educational institutions in the late twentieth century was desegregation. Efforts to desegregate public schools began in 1954 with the Supreme Court's ruling in *Brown* v. *Board of Education of Topeka*, when the Court held that segregation had a negative effect on black students even if their school facilities were "separate but equal" to those of white students. In the first few years after this landmark decision, most of the states in which schools had been legally segregated instituted desegregation programs. However, in some states, particularly in the deep South, desegregation orders were resisted, and by 1967 only 26 percent of the nation's school districts were desegregated (Orfield & Eaton, 1996).

Further progress toward desegregated schools was made after the passage of the Civil Rights Act of 1964 and the Elementary and Secondary Education Act of 1965; by 1973, de jure (legally sanctioned) segregation had been almost entirely eliminated. However, de facto (in-practice) segregation remained common in many parts of the nation. This pattern was created by two factors: (1) school districts' traditional policy of requiring students to attend schools in their own neighborhoods, and (2) "white flight," the tendency of whites to move to the suburbs in order to take advantage of suburban housing opportunities and, in some cases, to avoid sending their children to central city schools with large percentages of black students. On the basis of an extensive study of the impact of desegregation programs, Coleman (1976) concluded that "policies of school desegregation which focus wholly on within-district segregation . . . are increasing, rather than reducing or reversing, the tendency for our large metropolitan areas to consist of black central cities and white suburbs" (p. 12).

Coleman's findings had a significant influence on the policy debates that took place throughout the 1970s and 1980s over what could be done to increase racial equality in public education, especially the issue of whether school-children should be bused across city lines. Educational policymakers are now seeking ways of promoting racial integration, not just by means of busing plans but also through changes in school curriculums and instructional methods.

When education critic Jonathan Kozol visited public schools in central cities and suburban communities, he was shocked by the stark evidence of continuing racial and class segregation he found:

> What startled me most was the remarkable degree of racial segregation that persisted almost everywhere. . . . Moreover, in most cities, influential people that I met showed little inclination to address this matter and were sometimes even puzzled when I brought it up. Many people seemed to view the segregation issue as "a past injustice" that had been sufficiently addressed. . . . I was given the distinct impression that my inquiries about this matter were not welcome. (1995, pp. 2–3)

The children Kozol interviewed understood quite well the way class and racial segregation affected their own educational opportunities. Samantha, an eighth-grader in the impoverished schools of East St. Louis, Illinois, described to Kozol the great differences in resources between the schools she attended and those in the nearby white suburbs—lack of adequate textbooks, no computers, fewer after-school programs, and the like. Her mother had tried to get her into one of the better schools but had been told that she had to stay "in her jurisdiction." "Is it a matter of race?" Kozol asked Samantha. He notes that in answering him the girl chose her words slowly and with great care: "Well, the two things, race and money, go so close together what's the dif-

ference? I live here, they live there, and they don't want me in their school" (pp. 30–31).

Clearly, the process of racial integration still has a long way to go. Although school choice plans may increase racial segregation in schools, residential segregation has a much greater impact on school segregation. As sociologist John Yinger points out, "segregation in housing obviously leads to segregation in schools" (1995, p. 142). In his view, the failure to ensure freedom of residential choice for African Americans and other people of color remains a major obstacle to equality of education through desegregation.

Samantha's comment in the interview just quoted is a reminder of the central place schools occupy in American communities. The schools can bring different groups together in the pursuit of common goals, or they can separate children and families according to class, race, or religion. The schools, especially public schools, community colleges, state colleges, and state universities, are explicitly designed to build the capabilities of communities and entire cities or states while developing competent citizens. The same can be said about specific aspects of school programs, such as school and college sports, to which we now turn for a glimpse at recent research and trends.

CRITICAL SOCIOLOGY AND SOCIAL CHANGE

Gender and School Sports

In schools throughout the world, excellent athletes are in great demand. Whether it is the ability to run fast, throw hard, knock others down, jump, skate, shoot, or dribble, athletes who make the team, and especially those who excel at their sports, win higher prestige than those who don't make the team. In many schools, the athletes of whichever sport is locally most competitive are also those who become known as leaders in other areas of school life and are most sought after by the popular girls. In fact, going with a successful athlete is one of the ways in which girls become popular in school. This is an old story, one that reflects the values of adults in societies in which men's sports become a way of achieving unprecedented success and sports spectatorship is a major form of leisure activity.

Today women in most urban industrial nations are no longer relegated to the role of spectator or cheerleader but participate fully in school sports. Historic legislation passed in 1972, largely as the result of persistent lobbying by feminists and their allies and known as Title IX, decreed that

THEN AND NOW   Pigskin Mania

Football emerged in more or less its present form in the 1890s as a popular sport among wealthy young men at elite eastern universities like Yale and Harvard. In North America, football has become not just a sport but a generator of enormous revenues and a cultural form that many people almost feel they could not live without. The growth in popularity of the sport was intimately associated with the powerful influence of the mass media, which can broadcast games to ever-larger audiences.

But the growth of media institutions, in turn, depends on the revenues made possible by the huge audiences attracted to major games. Thus there is a symbiotic relationship between television and the educational institutions that can afford to support football teams (Kriegel, 1993; Lawton, 1984). More than 50 million fans attend one or more football games in a given year, and no one attending a college or university in the United States needs to be told that football games are central events in the life of many campuses.

In fact, for many men and an increasing number of women, football has come to resemble a civil religion. There are fans whose lives become subordinated to the rituals of preparation for the Saturday game. Legendary coaches like Alabama's Bear Bryant or Penn State's Joe Paterno assume a status that is well below that of a god but far above that of an ordinary mortal (C. R. Wilson, 1987). The rivalries that emerge between regional powerhouse teams and are played out each year become material for local legends. Many will admit to having prayed for a successful third-down conversion.

The metaphors inherent in football—success, hard work, strength, speed, organization, strategy—all make the sport a study in cultural ritual that mirrors the values of the larger society in which it has flourished (Brokaw, 1994). These cultural qualities of the game also make it extremely popular to television viewers and enable broadcasters to make large payments to the universities; these, in turn, help support other, less profitable sports. The popularity of football also enhances the university's prestige and its ability to compete for students and faculty.

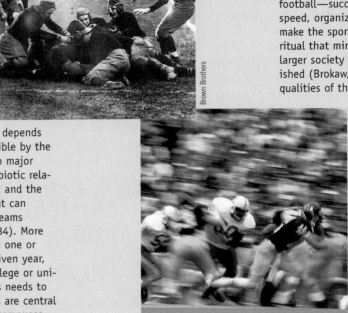

Brown Brothers

© Mark Lewis

"no person in the United States shall, on the basis of sex, be excluded from participation in, denied the benefits of, or be subjected to discrimination under any education program or activity receiving federal financial assistance." Students now take for granted the fact that women participate in school sports and compete in intercollegiate leagues in as many sports as men do, though with some differences (e.g., football is still a male sport; field hockey is still largely a female sport; lacrosse, once thought to be an exclusively male sport, is played by women at very high levels of competition but in separate female leagues).

The changes resulting from the implementation of Title IX in schools and colleges are far-ranging. Sociological research shows, for example, that the rise of school sports for girls and young women has caused dramatic changes in the relative prestige of different peer groups in American high schools. In a fascinating research report titled *Football, Fast Cars, and Cheerleading: Adolescent Gender Norms, 1978–1989*, J. Suitor and R. Reavis (1995) describe the results of a study in which they interviewed hundreds of high school graduates from different classes to find out what activities brought prestige to high school kids when they were in school. They found that far more female students gained prestige from sports and fewer said that prestige came to cheerleaders. For boys, sports remained a source of high prestige, but having a car conveyed less prestige over time as more young women began driving cars as well, primarily in suburbs and nonmetropolitan communities.

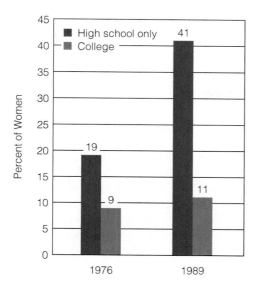

Figure 18.7 Percentage of Women Who Played High School and College Sports, 1976 and 1989

Source: Sjulmana & Bowen, 2001.

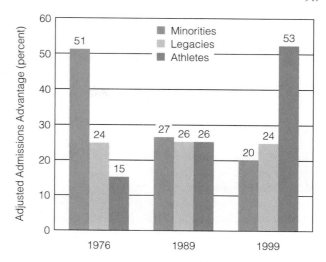

Figure 18.8 Adjusted Admissions Advantage at a Representative Nonscholarship School, Controlling for Differences in SAT Scores (females only)

Source: Sjulmana & Bowen, 2001.

In colleges and universities, the effects of Title IX have been even more dramatic. In the most thorough available research on the impact of athletics on higher education, James L. Sjulmana and William G. Bowen, in their book *The Game of Life: College Sports and Educational Values* (2001), note that an unintended consequence of gender equality in college sports has been to vastly increase the economic and social costs of campus athletics. Students and alumni not only want teams, they want winning teams. As a result, recruitment of men and women athletes becomes increasingly intense. In fact, the research shows that in 4-year schools where students are not given athletic scholarships—primarily non-NCAA Division I universities and colleges—athletic recruitment has become as important as grades and SAT scores for admission. Figure 18.7 charts the stunning rise in female participation in school sports between 1976 and 1989. The percentage of women in college sports was still low, but the rise in girls' sports in secondary schools created a huge demand for women's sports opportunities in higher education in the 1990s, with the result that most institutions of higher education were out of compliance with the law. Indeed, they are still attempting to meet the demand for gender equality in sports, a demand that has been consistently supported by the courts.

The researchers also found that while the SAT scores of college athletes have improved because of pressure from educators, they remain significantly lower than the average for all applicants. This has increased the demand for student-athletes, especially in the nonscholarship schools. The flood of athletes of both sexes into higher education has also contributed to the decline in majors in the physical and natural sciences, where more demanding curricula are difficult to master given the demands of intercollegiate sports competition. Moreover, as we see in Figure 18.8, the demand for scholar-athletes has resulted in a significant decrease in the admission of nonathlete minority students. This figure shows that when one holds SAT scores constant (by comparing applicants at each SAT level), the probability that an athlete will be admitted to a nonscholarship school is more than twice as high as the probability that a minority applicant, or someone whose parent went to the school (a "legacy"), will be admitted. This represents a major change in recruitment since 1976 and is a clear indication of how emphasis on winning in college sports distorts the values of higher education and educational equality. Of course, the effects are far more marked in the NCAA Division I schools, and the gap in school performance between athletes in the major sports and other students is widening all the time. Finally, note that although the data in Figure 18.8 are for women applicants, the data for males in nonscholarship institutions are almost identical.

VISUAL SOCIOLOGY

THE TOUGHEST JOB YOU'LL EVER LOVE

In late 2001 and early 2002, the terrorist attacks on the United States and the sinking U.S. economy created a wave of interest in teaching among Americans from all social backgrounds. This was extremely good news to U.S. educators, who face a potential shortage of teachers as retirements among older teachers thin the teaching ranks. There are now about 2.8 million teachers, but in the next 10 years another 2.4 million will need to be recruited. When the economy is doing well, it is far more difficult to recruit teachers, but now the states are finding it relatively easy to find new recruits. In time, as the economy heats up again, it will be more difficult to recruit new teachers, but programs like Teach for America will be there to fill the gaps, especially by recruiting recent college graduates.

The recruiting slogan for teachers, "The Best Job You'll Ever Love," is a reminder that, in addition to job security and a refuge from the harsh world of business, teaching offers opportunities for personal growth and a sense of having helped others that is more difficult to find in other professions. An ad in the New York City subways says, "No one goes back 10 years later to thank a middle manager" and "Your spreadsheets won't ever grow up to be doctors and lawyers" (Goodnough, 2002). These testimonials by Teach for America teachers do not ensure that they will stay in teaching or become professional educators, but they certainly show that young Americans are still able to find outlets and true challenges for their idealism.

A group of TFA teacher trainees.

Courtesy of Allison Serafin

The Sociological Observer

(See photo on page 537.)

Distance learning allows for increased educational attainment for students who are not able to take traditional college courses due to their schedule, work, and family obligations. Students are able to learn more at their own pace. However, distance learning removes interaction and socialization between students as well as the relationship between the individual student and teacher. Also, it requires actual online computer access, which is not available to all people equally.

Participants in Teach for America use their leadership skills to help students fulfill their potential.

Forth Worth Star-Telegram/Joyce Marshall

Courtesy of Orin Gutlerner

TFA teacher Orin Gutlerner with his fifth- and sixth-grade students at Clark Street Elementary School in Henderson, North Carolina.

SUMMARY

Education for a Changing World

- *Education* is the process by which a society transmits knowledge, values, norms, and ideologies and in so doing prepares young people for adult roles and adults for new roles. It is accomplished by specific institutions outside the family, especially schools and colleges.

- Schools are often cited as examples of bureaucratic organizations because they tend to be characterized by a clearly defined authority system and set of rules.

- A more interactionist viewpoint sees the school as a distinctive set of interactions and patterns of socialization.

- Conflict theorists view schools as institutions whose purpose is to maintain social-class divisions and reproduce the society's existing stratification system.

- Hundreds of millions of children throughout the world are denied the right to quality basic education.

- In the United States, the post–World War II baby boom caused a bulge in elementary school enrollments beginning in 1952 and an expansion of the college-age population in the 1960s. These trends were reversed in the 1960s and 1970s, but at the same time more and more adults have sought additional education.

- A key feature of education is the fact that schools structure the lives of children and adolescents. They help create a social world for adolescents that is separate from adult society.

- Another important aspect of education in the United States is the relationship between education and citizenship. Education is also viewed as a tool for solving social problems, especially social inequality.

Attainment, Achievement, and Equality

- *Educational attainment* refers to the number of years of school a person has completed. It is correlated with income, occupation, prestige, and attitudes and opinions.

- The average American today has much more education than the average American of the early 1940s.

- Research on the effects of tracking has found that students in lower tracks tend to end up in lower-paid and lower-prestige occupations once they finish their schooling.

- Social-scientific research has shown that states that base their funding of school districts on how well schools do on standardized tests actually increase, rather than decrease, high school dropout rates.

- One effect of higher levels of educational attainment is "degree inflation," in which employers require more education of potential employees.

- *Educational achievement* refers to how much the student actually learns, measured by mastery of reading, writing, and mathematical skills. The steady decline in mean SAT scores in the 1970s and 1980s was viewed as a sign that average levels of educational achievement have declined.

- Cross-cultural research has shown that these deficiencies are apparent from an early age. American parents are more likely than Asian parents to be satisfied with their children's schoolwork and to believe that the schools are doing a good job; they therefore are less likely to be critical of the schools or to demand more of their children.

- Educational institutions have been criticized by observers who believe that they hinder, rather than enhance, social mobility. Higher levels of educational attainment provide the credentials required for better jobs, and students who are able to obtain those credentials usually come from the middle and upper classes.

- A factor that has been shown to affect students' school careers is teacher expectations regarding students, which are affected by the teacher's knowledge of the student's family background.

- Inequality in higher education is primarily a matter of access—that is, ability to pay.

The Structure of Educational Institutions

- The American educational system is highly bureaucratized, a fact that acts as a major barrier to educational change.

- Among the factors that tend to expand educational bureaucracies are the need to maintain buildings and other real estate and the need to respond to many different public needs and values.

- Recent outbreaks of violence in schools have led to greater emphasis on efforts to understand school peer groups, recognize bullying, protect the rights of gay students, and communicate better with students about their feelings and experiences.

- Most calls for school reform rely on single reforms such as testing at every grade level. Proposals for comprehensive school reform seek to address a wide array of issues.

- The number of children schooled at home has grown rapidly in the past decade. Home-schooling families are motivated to teach their children more moral precepts and more religious values than would be the case in public or private schools.

- When educational bureaucracies have been forced to change, as in the case of school desegregation, they have often proved to be very adaptable.

GLOSSARY

education: The process by which a society transmits knowledge, values, norms, and ideologies and in so doing prepares young people for adult roles and adults for new roles. (p. 520)

educational attainment: The number of years of school an individual has completed. (p. 528)

educational achievement: How much the student actually learns, measured by mastery of reading, writing, and mathematical skills. (p. 532)

INTERNET RESOURCES

Virtual Society: The Wadsworth Sociology Resource Center
(http://sociology.wadsworth.com)
At Virtual Society you can access a wide range of enrichment material to aid your study of sociology. From the main page, click on the Student Resources link and find your course and this textbook. Next, select the chapter you are presently studying from the pull-down menu. Among the useful options for each self-study chapter are online links and exercises, flashcards, practical study tips, and practice quizzes for each chapter.

MC MicroCase Online
From the Virtual Society home page, click on MicroCase Online to access book-specific MicroCase exercises that allow you to further explore sociological issues and principles presented in the text.

InfoTrac College Edition
Another unique option available to you at the Student Resources section at Virtual Society is InfoTrac College Edition, an online library with access to hundreds of scholarly and popular periodicals. Below are suggested search terms for this chapter, but this resource also allows you to fit your study of sociology to your own interests by searching custom keywords.

Educational attainment
Communications media
Bureaucracy
School choice

The Carnegie Foundation
(www.carnegie.org)
A major sponsor of strategic research on education and educational policy in the United States. A good place to start searching for research studies.

U.S. Department of Education
(www.ed.gov)
Provides information about federal education programs and initiatives, with links to other major education sites.

United Nations Educational, Scientific, and Cultural Organization (UNESCO)
(www.unesco.org)
The UN's major education agency. Sponsors conferences and research programs on issues of global education, literacy, community development, professional development, and much more.

National Center on Educational Statistics
(http://nces.ed.gov/pubsearch)
Offers a wealth of data on school performance, especially in the United States.

Economic Institutions

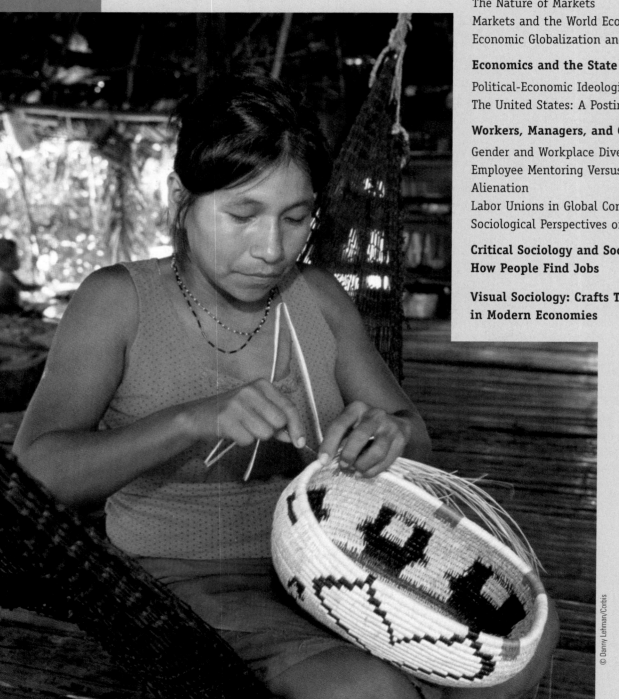

© Danny Lehman/Corbis

E. L. Winthrop, an American businessman from a major city north of the Rio Grande, was on a vacation trip to Mexico. While there he traveled to a remote and rather quaint village somewhere in the province of Oaxaca. As he wandered through the dusty streets of that little pueblo, which had neither electricity nor running water, he came upon an Indian man squatting on the earthen-floored porch of his palm hut. The Indian was weaving baskets, but these were not ordinary baskets. Winthrop had never seen such colors and such fine detail as the Indian was weaving into the little containers, using only natural fibers and dyes from the nearby jungle. Winthrop immediately decided that he must buy one no matter what the price.

When Winthrop learned that the man was selling his wares for only 50 centavos, perhaps a tenth of what he had expected to pay, Winthrop could not help thinking that here was a fine opportunity to start a thriving business. The baskets would make ideal containers for gift candy; he could sell them at home for three or four times the price. And even counting shipping costs and other expenses, both Winthrop and the Indian would surely make out very well.

"I've got big business for you, my friend," he announced to the surprised basket weaver. "Do you think you can make me one thousand of those little baskets?"

Winthrop explained that the Indian could enlist the help of his family and kin in the project, and at the prices he could pay they all stood to gain tremendously.

That might be true enough, the man admitted, but who then would look after the corn and beans and goats? Yes, he could see that he and his kin would have plenty of money to buy these things as well as many other items that they did not yet possess, but, he explained, "Of the corn that others may or may not grow, I cannot be sure to feast upon."

Not easily discouraged, Winthrop proceeded to show the basket weaver how wealthy he and his entire village could become even if they continued to sell the baskets for only 50 centavos. The Indian seemed interested, which spurred Winthrop on to more detailed descriptions of the basket assembly line they could begin together in the dusty little town. But after it was all explained, the Indian was still unmoved. The thousands of pesos that could be earned in this way were more than he could reckon with, since he had always used the few pesos from his basket selling only to supplement the modest needs of his family. There was another reason, too:

Besides, señor, there's still another thing which perhaps you don't know. You see, my good lordy and caballero, I've to make these canastitas my own way and with my song in them and with bits of my soul woven into them. If I were to make them in great numbers there would no longer be my soul in each, or my songs. Each would look like the other with no difference whatever and such a thing would slowly eat up my heart. Each has to be another song which I hear in the morning when the sun rises and when the birds begin to chirp and the butterflies come and sit down on my baskets so that I may see a new beauty, because, you see, the butterflies like my baskets and the pretty colors on them, that's why they come and sit down, and I can make my canastitas after them. And now, señor jefecito, if you will kindly excuse me, I have wasted much time already, although it was a pleasure and a great honor to hear the talk of such a distinguished caballero like you. But I'm afraid I've to attend to my work now, for day after tomorrow is market day in town and I got to take my baskets there. Thank you, señor, for your visit. Adios. (Traven, 1966, p. 72)

FOCUS QUESTIONS:

• How do markets work, and why do they play such a powerful role in shaping the growth of societies?

• What are the basic approaches that different nations employ to try to balance economic growth with social justice?

• What are some of the major issues in the job market and the workplace?

SOCIOLOGY AND ECONOMICS

This simple story captures the essence of what Max Weber meant when he observed that as societies grow in size, complexity, and rationality, there is less enchantment in human life. The Indian could never imagine himself as a captain of industry, the manager of a workforce of Indians who would buy their corn in a store with a portion of their wages. But neither could Winthrop appreciate the full meaning of the Indian's refusal and the metaphor of his song. The basket weaver feared that mass production would rob his baskets of their poetry and their maker of his soul. The businessman was used to dealing with markets and with the logic of profit and loss. He believed that he would be creating a "win-win" situation. He would profit, and he would be helping the Indian earn a better living for himself and his family. After all, the Indian was engaged in selling his baskets in the market. We will see in the Visual Sociology section at the end of this chapter that in the modern world there is a constant struggle to come out ahead in markets yet at the same time to maintain one's sense of creativity—one's soul. Nor is this the only dilemma forced upon us by modern economic institutions.

In this chapter, we turn to an analysis of the major economic institutions of modern industrial societies. As we do so, we should keep in mind examples from nonindustrial societies like that of the basket weaver in order to appreciate the enormous impact of economic and social change in the past two centuries. Such examples will also show that there is not just one path toward economic modernization, nor only one blueprint for how the economic institutions of a modern society should work.

In any society, economic institutions specialize in the production of goods and services. How we survive in modern societies depends on whether we have jobs and income, on the nature of markets, on the public policies that involve governments in economic affairs, on worker–management relations, and so on. Thus it is little wonder that sociologists have dedicated much research to these questions. But if that is true, what distinguishes sociology from economics? In our review of the sociology of economic institutions, we begin by distinguishing between these two social-scientific fields.

The Nobel Prize–winning economist Paul Samuelson (1998) defines *economics* as the study of how people and social groups choose to employ scarce resources to produce various commodities and distribute them for consumption among various persons and groups in society. Sociologists are also concerned with how individuals and societies make choices involving scarce resources such as time, talent, and money. But sociologists do not assume that scarcity or supply and demand are the only reasons for making such choices (Elster, 1997). Sociologists are deeply concerned with showing how the norms of different cultures affect economic choices. For example, we cannot assume that people with equal amounts of money or talent are free to choose the same values or activities. We often find that women who might have chosen to pursue careers in business management have been channeled into such occupations as teaching or social work. Until recently, American culture defined the latter occupations as appropriate for women, whereas managerial roles were viewed as appropriate for men. Women therefore did not have the same choices open to them even when they had equal amounts of scarce resources like talent.

It would not be accurate to stress only the differences between sociology and economics, however. Increasingly, some sociologists (and economists) use the central theory of economics to study all situations in which people choose to allocate scarce resources to satisfy competing ends (Coleman, 1986; Hechter & Kanazawa, 1996). By "central theory" we mean the central proposition of economics: *People will attempt to maximize their pleasure or profit in any situation and will also try to minimize their loss or pain.* Applying this idea to nonbusiness situations, another Nobel Prize–winning economist and sociologist, Gary S. Becker, has conducted research on racial discrimination, marriage, and household choices. In this research, he applies an economic "rational-choice" approach to the study of the behavior of people in groups and organizations that do not produce goods or services. Becker points out that even the choice of a mate or the decision to have a child can be looked upon as an economic decision because people who make these decisions intuitively calculate the "price" of their actions in terms of opportunities gained or lost (Becker, 1997). Having a child means giving up other scarce resources, such as free time or income that could be used in other ways. And we saw in Chapter 16 how intuitive calculations enter into the choice of a marriage partner.

Following the lead of rational-choice theorists like Becker, sociologist Michael Hechter (1987) has studied the larger social consequences of the individual propensity to maximize pleasure and avoid pain. He concludes, among other things, that the larger the number of individuals in an organization, the more the organization will be required to invest in inspectors, managers, security personnel, and the like in order to control its members' propensity to "do their own thing." The same point was made over a century ago by Karl Marx: "All combined labour on a large scale requires . . . a directing authority. . . . A single violin player is his own conductor, an orchestra requires a separate one" (1962/1867, pp. 330–331).

Although it is tempting to apply principles of rational choice or exchange theory to noneconomic institutions like the family and the church, in this chapter we focus specifically on behavior in economic institutions such as businesses and markets and on the social implications of changes in these institutions. We will see that sociologists are continually comparing the ways in which such institutions are organized in different societies. The comparative study of how these differences relate to other features of a society's culture and social structure are very much a part of the sociological perspective on economic institutions.

Sociologists who study economic institutions are also interested in how markets for goods and services change as people learn to use new technologies and to divide up their labor in increasingly specialized ways (Drucker, 1992). They also look at how competition for profits may lead to illegal activities and cause governments to try to regulate economic institutions. In addition, sociologists attempt to show how the labor market is organized and how professions develop. Thus markets and the division of labor, the interactions between government and economic institutions, and the nature of jobs and professions are the major subjects of sociological research on economic institutions (Wallerstein, 1999). In the rest of this chapter, we discuss each of these subjects in turn.

GLOBAL MARKETS AND THE DIVISION OF LABOR

A hallmark of an industrial society is the production of commodities and services to be exchanged in markets. In London, Hong Kong, New York, and other major cities throughout the world, there are markets for gold, national currencies, stocks and bonds, and commodities ranging from pork bellies to concentrated frozen orange juice. However, not all societies have economies dominated by industry and markets. Subsistence economies, in which people live in small villages like that of the Mexican basket weaver, do not have highly developed markets. In such economies, people seek to produce enough food and other materials to enable them to meet their own needs, raise their children, and maintain their cultural traditions. The basic unit of production is the family, rather than the business firm as is the case in a capitalist economy. But there are few, if any, purely subsistence economies in the world today. Most subsistence economies must engage in some trade in international markets to obtain goods such as medicine or tools. These markets are dominated by the larger firms and entrepreneurs of the global capitalist economy, as we saw in the case of the basket weaver and Mr. Winthrop.

Socialist economies like Cuba or China also buy and sell products in international markets. Within their societies, however, they usually try to limit the influence of markets.

Prices for essential goods, especially foodstuffs, are not entirely subject to the laws of supply and demand; often they are prevented by law from rising too high or falling too low. Many types of goods and services, including firms themselves, cannot be sold to private buyers because they are said to belong to all the people of the society. We will return to the conceptual differences among these types of economies later in the chapter. For now, remember that few contemporary societies conform to one or another of the basic economic types. Most nations encompass capitalist markets, subsistence economies, and elements of socialism as well. Nevertheless, the market is an increasingly dominant economic institution throughout the world.

The Nature of Markets

Markets are economic institutions that regulate exchange behavior. In a market, different values or prices are established for particular goods and services, values that vary according to changing levels of supply and demand and are usually expressed in terms of a common measure of exchange, or currency. A market is not the same thing as a marketplace. As an economic institution, a market governs exchanges of particular goods and services throughout a society. This is what we mean when we speak of the "housing market," for example. A marketplace, on the other hand, is an actual location where buyers and sellers make exchanges. Buyers and sellers of jewelry, for instance, like to be able to gather in a single place to examine the goods to be exchanged. The same is true for many other goods, such as clothing and automobiles.

Market transactions are governed by agreements or contracts in which a seller agrees to supply a particular item and a buyer agrees to pay for it. Exchanges based on contracts are a significant factor in the development of modern societies. As the social theorist Talcott Parsons pointed out, the use of contracts makes impersonal relations possible. Contracts neutralize the relevance of the other roles of the participants, such as kinship and other personal relationships, that govern exchanges in nonmarket situations. In contractual relations, for example, the fact that people are friends or kin does not, in principle, change the terms of their agreement and the need to repay debts (Parsons, 1991).

Among hunting-and-gathering peoples and in relatively isolated agrarian societies before the twentieth century, markets in the modern sense of the term did not exist. Think of the Mexican Indian basket weaver who could not imagine buying corn and other foods. He was used to growing foodstuffs himself and exchanging them with members of his extended family. The idea of buying them with currency was foreign to him. In social-scientific terms, a society cannot be said to have a fully developed market economy if many of the commodities it produces are not exchanged for a common currency at prices determined by supply and demand.

The spread of markets into nonmarket societies has been accelerated by political conquest and colonialism as well as by the desire among tribal and peasant peoples to obtain the goods produced by industrial societies. To illustrate this point and to show what happens as a smaller-scale society becomes integrated into world markets, consider the case of the Tiv.

MARKETS IN A SUBSISTENCE ECONOMY   In precolonial times, the Tiv, a small West African tribal society living in what is now Nigeria, were a good example of a *subsistence economy,* one in which producers try to meet the needs of their immediate and extended families and do not produce goods or services for export beyond the family, village, or tribe. Among the Tiv, the land was divided up into garden plots on which each family grew its own food. When the harvest was completed, the remaining vegetation was slashed and burned. The ashes served to fertilize the soil, but sometimes a plot was allowed to lie fallow for a few seasons. This meant that there was always a lot of discussion about which plots were to be used by which families in any given season. Never was a garden plot bought or sold—the idea that land could be bought and sold was not part of Tiv culture. The land belonged to the tribe as a whole. Individual families were granted the right to use the land, but there was no such thing as private property in the form of land that could be bought and sold.

Nor were the products of the land thought to be the property of the grower. Food was distributed according to need, and a person who accepted food was expected to return the gift at some future time. Only a few goods, mainly items of dress worn on ceremonial occasions, were traded for currency—in this case, short brass bars. The Tiv also accepted brass bars from foreign traders in exchange for carvings or woven cloths. But they would have laughed at the idea of trading the bars for food. They would have shared their food with strangers without any expectation of payment.

The conquest of Tivland by the British in the early twentieth century brought immense changes to this non-market society. The British colonial administrators were shocked when they observed Tiv weddings, in which it appeared to them that young women were being traded for ceremonial goods. In reality, these exchanges were not market transactions; the items that were given in exchange for a bride were a symbol of respect for the bride's family.

The British also noted that the Tiv seemed always to be at war, either with neighboring tribes or among themselves. To them this was a further sign that they needed to "civilize" the Tiv; in fact, however, the warfare was an outcome of the colonial system of taxation. Each tribal chief was required to pay a certain sum, either in British currency or in a commodity such as pigs. Because the Tiv had no currency and had to struggle to produce the required commodities, they were forced to cultivate more land. Their conflicts with neighboring clans or tribes were caused by the need to acquire more land. Thus the wars that the British observed were an almost immediate result of their own policies.

In this idealized depiction of British colonial rule in Africa, white administrators confer in the foreground while happy natives work in the background. In reality, the "blessings" of colonialism were extremely mixed. As we see in the case of the Tiv, the experience of becoming part of the world market system made it difficult to maintain a small-scale society and culture.

Tobacco Plantation in NYASALAND

The Granger Collection, New York

When the British succeeded in ending the warfare that had broken out among the Tiv, the only remaining source of cash to pay the taxes was wage labor on the colonial plantations. The Tiv therefore sent their sons and daughters to work for the British, and on their own land they began to grow crops that they could sell. Before long, they were part of the British market economy, selling their crops and labor for cash with which they could buy manufactured goods. Eventually, like thousands of other tribal societies, they were engulfed by the larger market system of the more powerful European nations (Bohannon & Bohannon, 1953, 1962).

Markets and the World Economic System

In the late fifteenth and early sixteenth centuries, according to sociologist Immanuel Wallerstein (1999), a "European world-economy" came into existence. The new economy was a kind of social system that the world had not known before. It was based on economic relationships, not on political empires; in fact, it encompassed empires, city-states, and the emerging nation-states.

Great empires had been a feature of the world scene for at least 5,000 years before the dawn of the modern era. But the empires of China, India, Africa, the Mediterranean, and the Middle East were primarily political rather than economic systems. Wallerstein argues that because the great empires dominated vast areas inhabited by peoples who lacked military and political power, they were able to establish a flow of economic resources from the outlying regions to the imperial centers. The means used were taxation, tribute (payments for protection by the imperial army), and trade policies in which the outlying societies were forced to produce certain goods for the imperial merchants.

But this system—exemplified most clearly in the case of the Roman empire—required a huge military and civil bureaucracy, which absorbed much of the imperial profit. Local rebellions and wars continually increased the expense of maintaining imperial rule. Political empires thus can be viewed as a primitive means of economic domination. "It is the social achievement of the modern world," Wallerstein (1974) comments, "to have invented the technology that makes it possible to increase the flow of the surplus from the lower strata to the upper strata, from the periphery to the center, from the majority to the minority" (p. 16) without the need for military conquest.

What technologies made the new world system possible? They were not limited to tools of trade, such as the compass or the oceangoing sailing vessel, or to tools of domination like the Gatling machine gun. They also in-

cluded organizational techniques for bringing land, labor, and local currencies into the larger market economy: ways of enclosing and dividing up land in order to charge rent for its use; financial and accounting systems that led to the creation of new economic institutions like banks; and many others. We discuss the role of science and technology in social change more thoroughly in Chapter 21, but it is important to note here that the term *technology* refers not only to tools but also to the procedures and forms of social organization that increase human productive capacity (Faulkner, 1997; Polanyi, 1944).

Although the European colonial powers (and the United States) often used political and military force to bring isolated societies into their markets, in the twentieth century they allowed their former colonies to gain independence yet still maintained economic control over them. This occurred because the economies of the colonial societies had become dependent on the technologies and markets controlled by the Western powers. Today former colonies are struggling to develop independent economic systems, but their ability to compete effectively in world markets is limited by the increasing power of **multinational corporations,** or *multinationals,* economic enterprises that have headquarters in one country and conduct business activities in one or more other countries (Barnet, 1994).

Multinationals are not a new phenomenon. Trading firms like the Hudson's Bay Company and the Dutch East India Company were chartered by major colonial powers and granted monopolies over the right to trade with native populations for furs, spices, metals, gems, and other valued commodities. Thus exploitation of the resources of colonial territories has been directed by multinational corporations for over two centuries. Modern multinationals do not generally have monopolies granted by the state, yet these powerful firms, based primarily in the United States, Europe, and Japan, are transforming the world economy by "exporting" manufacturing jobs from nations in which workers earn high wages to nations in which they earn far less. This process, which is particularly evident in the shoe, garment, electronics, textile, and automobile industries, has accelerated the growth of industrial working classes in the former colonies while greatly reducing the number of industrial jobs in the developed nations.

Changes in worldwide production patterns challenge Wallerstein's thesis that there is a world economic order dominated by the former colonial powers. In particular, industrial nations like the United States and Japan are increasingly losing manufacturing jobs while newly industrializing nations like Brazil and Indonesia are gaining them. But as the Global Social Change box on page 556 shows, the economic survival of millions of rural workers continues to be heavily influenced by changing markets in the highly developed nations.

GLOBAL SOCIAL CHANGE

Addictive Substances and World Markets

In 1983, when sociologist Edmundo Morales returned to his birthplace in northern Peru to conduct research on land reform, he found that the peasants of the Andes villages had become dependent on the worldwide traffic in cocaine. Their efforts to gain cooperative ownership of the land they farmed had faded. Instead, most of the able-bodied men in the villages were busy packing for the long trip down the eastern face of the Andes. Most of them would work for months in coca-processing laboratories hidden in the jungle. Some would earn cash income by selling food, especially pork and beef, to the managers of the cocaine factories. The demand for cocaine in the United States and other societies had changed their lives.

Morales was dismayed to see so much urgently needed food being shipped from the impoverished highlands to the jungles. He felt that the enormous growth of the cocaine market had led his people down a false path. They were gaining cash income, perhaps, but in the bargain they were becoming increasingly addicted to cocaine and were neglecting the need for more basic economic progress in their own villages (Morales, 1986, 1989).

Morales was able to use his knowledge of the culture and his training as a sociologist to identify the connections between the plight of the Andean peasants and the world market for addictive substances. He knew that cocaine was simply another in a long line of substances for which huge markets had emerged in the richer nations, with

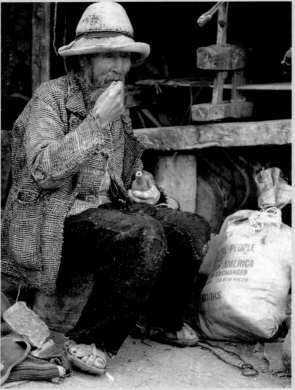

Edmundo Morales took this photo of a Peruvian highlander dipping into his sack of coca leaves. Andean Indians have traditionally chewed coca leaves to increase energy and reduce hunger. In the small bottle he carries is a form of lime paste, which he mixes with the leaves in his mouth to strengthen the effects, a process similar to what cocaine manufacturers do on a far larger scale with the leaves they buy from Indian cultivators.

drastic results for the less developed world. Foremost among those substances was sugar. In the thirteenth century, sugar was a luxury available only to royalty. But as its use as a source of energy and as a basis for alcoholic beverages—especially rum—became more widespread, the demand for sugar production became one of the main causes of European expansion into the tropical regions of the world. Moreover, sugar production required that huge amounts of land

be devoted to growing sugarcane, and many cane cutters were needed to harvest the crop.

Thus along with the expansion of sugar production went slavery, first in parts of North Africa and the Azores and later in the Caribbean islands and Latin America (Bennett, 1954; Mintz, 1985). And sugar was only the beginning. The cultivation of wheat, tea, and coffee; the extraction of iron, tin, gold, silver, and copper; and the widespread cutting of primeval forests were all spurred by the emergence of mass markets in the developed nations of the West. Andean coca for cocaine and Indochinese poppies for heroin were latecomers in a series of crops that had changed the earth and all its peoples (Capra, 2000).

Some scholars argue that economic development in the world's commercial capitals actually produced *underdevelopment*—dependency and poverty and overpopulation—in huge parts of Africa, Asia, and Latin America. But Morales questions the notion of "development of underdevelopment." He believes that despite their tendency to become addicted to cocaine, the villagers of northern Peru are becoming more sophisticated in their market dealings and their understanding of politics. When they turn their attention once again to land reform, as eventually they must, their experiences in recent years will have made them less culturally isolated and more politically effective.

Economic Globalization and Deregulation

Economic globalization can be broadly defined as a worldwide shrinkage of economic distances (costs of doing business) between nations. It includes two closely related processes: the globalization of production and trade, and the globalization of flows of finance (funds) and capital (tools, equipment, and services). These aspects of globalization have been greatly facilitated in recent decades by three important changes:

1. *Innovations and advances in transportation* (e.g., jet travel and air freight) *and communications* (computers and the Internet), which allow extremely rapid exchanges of people, funds, and capital between regional markets.

2. *Global economic liberalization*—especially the reduction of national tariffs that may create barriers to the free flow of trade and investment funds—are encouraged through global trade institutions, particularly the General Agreement on Tariffs and Trade (GATT) and the World Trade Organization (WTO) in the case of world trade in goods and services, and the International Monetary Fund (IMF) in the case of global finance and capital flows.

3. *Use of market incentives* that encourage people to rely on supply and demand rather than government-enforced quotas, regulations, or treaties to regulate economic behavior—to speed up the development of production and trade everywhere in the world (Rajan, 2001).

According to its advocates, especially in the business sector, the modern market economy encourages constant change and innovation. Some of that change, however, involves risk to jobs and incomes. If one region produces steel at a higher cost than another region, for example, a market free of protective tariffs will make the lower-cost steel more competitive and create plant closings and layoffs in the region where labor costs (wages and benefits) are higher. Advocates of worldwide free trade and rapid globalization believe that nations that lose out in market competition will find ways of adapting and changing their economies so that workers in uncompetitive industries will eventually find work in more dynamic sectors of the economy.

Globalization's opponents, including many trade union members, environmentalists, and critics of unregulated market forces, argue for "fair trade" rather than free trade. By that they mean trade that does not eliminate protections against exploitation and environmental pollution in the rush to deregulate all markets. For example, if steelworkers in the United States are able to form unions and bargain for higher wages and decent benefits, should they be vulnerable to competition from companies in nations where workers are forbidden or systematically discouraged from joining unions and are severely exploited and paid extremely low wages? Fair trade would insist that certain standards, such as bans on child labor, the right to form unions, and regulations on pollution, be applied to all trade treaties and that nations or regions that do not have such regulations be barred from markets in nations that do have these protections (Wayne, 2001).

GLOBALIZATION AND THIRD WORLD AGRICULTURE   Subsidies for the agricultural products of rich farming nations, especially the United States and Europe, present some of the most pressing problems of globalization and economic development. While Western leaders sing the praises of "free trade" and claim that global supply and demand, not political considerations, should determine the international flow of goods and services, their actions go against their ideologies. This is particularly true in the case of politically motivated subsidies for domestic agriculture. Growers of corn, cotton, sugar, tobacco, and many other crops in the United States and other affluent nations are routinely granted subsidies, often in the form of guaranteed minimum prices, that encourage more production than would otherwise be economically feasible. The surpluses that these subsidies generate, in turn, flood the world market with agricultural products that squeeze out the farm products of poor nations and add to the suffering of impoverished rural people throughout the world.

Cotton, for example, can be produced quite cheaply and in large quantities in the vast semidesert regions of Africa, where the average person lives on less than a dollar a day. But American cotton farmers have a good deal of political influence over southern and southwestern congressional representatives and use this influence to win guaranteed crop prices and other subsidies that encourage them to produce bumper crops that they would not be able to sell easily without the subsidies. In 2001, U.S. cotton farmers received $3.9 billion in subsidies from the federal government. As U.S. cotton floods the world market, prices paid to other farmers decrease, but the American farmers are guaranteed their price due to the subsidies. This is having a dire effect on cotton-producing countries in Africa, such as Mali, where a third of the population are dependent on cotton for their income. In the 2002–2003 growing season, Malian cotton farmers received just 18 cents per kilogram for their cotton whereas U.S. farmers received 80 cents per kilogram. The result is that Mali loses revenues, its population sinks

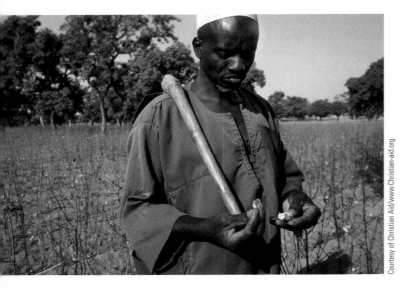

Courtesy of Christian Aid/www.christian-aid.org

Cotton farmers like Bakary Diarra face crisis due to unfair competition and trade rules that work against their interests.

further into poverty, and Third World leaders become increasingly cynical about the benefits of free trade that is not in fact free.

GLOBALIZATION AND CULTURE   Globalization and free trade may also threaten the values of people in nations where cultural products like music, movies, fast food, and fashions seem to promote deviance from strict religious and gender norms. Thus orthodox religious leaders in many nations continually protest against free markets that bring American or European movies that question religious authority, or fashions that reveal women's bodies, or music and foods that depart from local traditions and norms. (See the Popular Culture and Social Change box on page 559.)

ECONOMICS AND THE STATE

The earliest social scientists were deeply interested in understanding the full importance of modern economic institutions. In fact, since the eighteenth century, almost all attempts to understand large-scale social change have dealt with the question of how economic institutions operate. But the age-old effort to understand economic institutions has not been merely an academic exercise. The fate of societies throughout the world has been and continues to be strongly influenced by theories about how economic institutions operate, or fail to do so, in nation-states with different types of political institutions. The major economic ideologies thus are also political ideologies, and economics is often called *political economics* (Heilbroner, 1995). In this section, we review three economic ideologies—mercantilism, capitalism, and socialism—and some variations of them. (See the Study Chart on page 560.)

Political-Economic Ideologies

MERCANTILISM   The economic philosophy known as **mercantilism**, which was prevalent in the sixteenth and seventeenth centuries, held that a nation's wealth could be measured by the amount of gold or other precious metals possessed by the royal court. The best economic system, therefore, was one that increased the nation's exports and thereby increased the court's holdings of gold.

The mercantilist theory had important consequences for economic institutions. For example, the guilds, or associations of tradespeople, that had arisen in medieval times were protected by the monarch, to whom they paid tribute. The guilds controlled their members and determined what they produced. In this way, they were able to produce goods cheaply, and those goods were better able to compete in world markets, thereby increasing exports and bringing in more wealth for the court. But the workers were not free to seek the best jobs and wages available. Rather, the guilds required them to work at assigned tasks for assigned wages, and the guildmasters fixed the price of work (wages), entry into jobs, and all working conditions. Land in mercantilist systems was not subject to market norms either. As in feudalism, land was thought of not as a commodity that can be bought and sold—that is, a commodity subject to the market forces of supply and demand—but as a hereditary right derived from feudal grants.

LAISSEZ-FAIRE CAPITALISM   The ideology of **laissez-faire capitalism** attacked the mercantilist view that the wealth of nations could be measured in gold and that the state should dominate trade and production in order to amass more wealth. The laissez-faire economists believed that a society's real wealth could be measured only by its capacity to produce goods and services—that is, by its resources of land, labor, and machinery. And those resources, including land itself, could best be regulated by free trade in world markets (Halevy, 1955; Smith, 1965/1776).

The ideology of laissez-faire capitalism also sought to free workers from the restrictions that had been imposed by the feudal system and maintained under mercantilism. Thus it is no coincidence that the first statement of modern economic principles, Adam Smith's *The Wealth of Nations,* was published in 1776. Revolution was in the air—not only political revolution but the Industrial Revolution as well.

POPULAR CULTURE & SOCIAL CHANGE   Hating and Loving It

While the Taliban were seeking to eliminate all Western cultural influences from Afghanistan—by banning popular music and women's fashions other than veil and full body covering, and closing all movie houses—Afghan women were secretly going to Western-style beauty parlors, often at severe risk to their safety. Even Osama Bin Laden, seen on video condemning the United States and its "decadent culture," was noted to be wearing what looked very much like a Timex Ironman Triathlon wristwatch (Rothstein, 2002). What explains this love–hate relationship with Western, and especially American, popular culture and its products?

Fundamentalists often hate aspects of capitalism and free markets that permit all kinds of goods and services to be bought and sold even if they violate religious norms. Critical intellectuals often hate the products of popular

culture—the music, fast food, violent movies, and much more—because they seem to drive more traditional or more refined cultural products out of the market. Fast-food stores and mass-produced clothing may drive local and regional cuisines and fashions out of

existence or make them seem antiquated to impressionable young people in developing societies.

On the other hand, these popular cultural forms allow people new freedoms—to eat in public, to sing and dance and create new ways of

One effect of globalization is to make the popular cultures of other nations more familiar and to allow them to influence our own.

expressing feelings publicly, and much more. When they are identified as outside influences, they may appear threatening, but eventually, as we see in Japan, India, China, and much of Latin America, creative individuals in these nations and regions are fully capable of developing their own contributions to a global popular culture. An example is the rise of world music, which combines regional and popular musical styles in many exciting forms.

And some of the most revolutionary ideas came from the pens of people like Adam Smith, Jeremy Bentham, and John Stuart Mill, who understood the potential for social change contained in the new capitalist institutions of private property and free markets.

Private property (as opposed to communal ownership) is not merely the possession of objects, but rather, a set of rights and obligations that specify what their owner can and cannot do with them. The laissez-faire economists believed that the owners of property should be free to do almost any-

thing they liked with their property in order to gain profit. Indeed, the quest for profit would provide the best incentive to produce new and cheaper products, and therefore required free markets in which producers could compete to provide better products at lower prices.

These economic institutions are familiar to us today, but the founders of laissez-faire capitalism had to struggle to win acceptance for them. No wonder they thought of themselves as radicals. In fact, their economic and political beliefs were so opposed to the rule of monarchs and to feudal institutions

STUDY CHART

POLITICAL-ECONOMIC IDEOLOGIES

IDEOLOGY	DESCRIPTION	EXAMPLE
Mercantilism	An economic philosophy based on the belief that the wealth of a nation can be measured by its holdings of gold or other precious metals and that the state should control trade.	European nations under feudalism
Laissez-Faire Capitalism	An economic philosophy based on the belief that the wealth of a nation can be measured by its capacity to produce goods and services and that these can be maximized by free trade.	England at the time of the Industrial revolution
Socialism	An economic philosophy based on the concept of public ownership of property and sharing of profits, together with the belief that economic decisions should be controlled by the workers.	The Soviet Union before 1989; China and Cuba today
Democratic Socialism	An economic philosophy based on the belief that private property may exist at the same time that large corporations are owned by the state and run for the benefit of all citizens.	Holland and the Scandinavian nations
Welfare Capitalism	An economic philosophy in which markets determine what goods will be produced and how, but the government regulates economic competition.	The United States

like guilds that they could readily be seen as revolutionary. They believed that the state should leave economic institutions alone (which is what *laissez-faire* means). In their view, there is a natural economic order, a system of private property and competitive enterprise that functions best when individuals are free to pursue their own interests through free trade and unregulated production.

Smith opens *The Wealth of Nations* by describing how wealth and prosperity are created through a self-regulating system of markets in which participants enter into contracts to buy and sell without outside influences or constraints. This classical model of capitalism and free markets hinges on three primary characteristics:

1. *Freedom:* the right to produce and exchange products, labor, and capital.
2. *Self-interest:* the right to pursue one's own business and appeal to the self-interest of others.
3. *Competition:* the right to compete in the production and exchange of goods and services.

Smith's observations of markets convinced him that these three characteristics would produce a "natural harmony" among workers who contribute their labor power, landlords who rent land and other property, and capitalists who buy and build the machines and equipment and

develop new enterprises to produce goods and services. When free to buy and sell their products or services in unfettered markets, the self-interest of millions of individuals creates an orderly and wealthy society without the need for central direction from the state (government). As Smith wrote:

> It is not from the benevolence of the butcher, the brewer, or the baker, that we expect our dinner, but from their regard to their own interest. We address ourselves, not to their humanity, but to their self-love. . . . Every individual . . . [who] . . . employs capital . . . and . . . labours . . . neither intends to promote the public interest, nor knows how much he is promoting it. . . . He is . . . led by an invisible hand to promote an end which was no part of his intention. . . . By pursuing his own interest he frequently promotes that of the society.

This doctrine of enlightened self-interest, often called "the invisible hand," is the central idea of laissez-faire or classical economics. As we will see, it is an idea that is continually invoked by those who wish to make markets the primary institution regulating economic and other transactions within and across the world's nations (Skousen, 2001).

SOCIALISM As an economic and political philosophy, **socialism** began as an attack on the concepts of private property and personal profit. These aspects of capitalism, socialists believed, should be replaced by public ownership of property and sharing of profits. As we have noted in earlier chapters, this attack on capitalism was motivated largely by horror at the atrocious living conditions caused by the Industrial Revolution. The early socialists thought of economics as the "dismal science" because it seemed to excuse a system in which a few people were made rich at the expense of the masses of workers. They detested the laissez-faire economists' defense of low wages and wondered how workers could benefit from the Industrial Revolution instead of becoming "wage slaves." They proposed the creation of smaller-scale, more self-sufficient communities that would produce modern goods but would do so within a cooperative framework.

Karl Marx viewed these ideas as utopian dreams. He taught that the socialist state must be controlled by the working class, led by their own trade unions and political parties, which would do away with markets, wage labor, land rent, and private ownership of the means of production. These aspects of capitalism would be replaced by socialist economic institutions in which the workers themselves would determine what should be produced and how it should be distributed.

Marx never completed his blueprint of how an actual socialist society might function. That chore was left to the political and intellectual leaders of the communist revolutions—Lenin, Leon Trotsky, Rosa Luxemburg—and, finally, to authoritarian leaders like Joseph Stalin, Mao Ze-dong, and Fidel Castro. They believed that all markets and all private industry must be eliminated and replaced by state-controlled economic planning, collective farms, and worker control over industrial decision making. Unless capitalist economic institutions were completely rooted out, they believed, small-scale production and market dealings would create a new bourgeois class.

In the socialist system as it evolved under the communist regimes of the Soviet Union and China, centralized planning agencies and the single legal party, the Communists, would have the authority to set goals and organize the activities of the worker collectives, or soviets. Party members and state planners would also devise wage plans that would balance the need to reward skilled workers against the need to prevent the huge income inequalities found in capitalist societies. In Soviet-style societies, markets were not permitted to regulate demand and supply; this vital economic function was supposedly performed by government agencies. Societies that are managed in this fashion are said to have *command economies*. The state commands economic institutions to supply a specific amount (a quota) of each product and to sell it at a particular price. (Note that not all command economies are dominated by communist parties. Germany under the Nazis and Italy under the fascists were also command economies.)

With the collapse of the Soviet political empire, the economies of Russia and the other nations of the former Soviet Union (as well as its satellites in Eastern Europe) are attempting to make a transition to capitalist economic institutions. It has become evident that command economies provided these nations with overdeveloped industrial infrastructures and limited capability to compete in world markets for goods and services. Indeed, it has been said that the command economic system of the former Soviet Union gave it "the most impressive nineteenth century industrial infrastructure in the world, 75 years too late" (Ryan, 1992, p. 22).

The Soviet system was notorious for the inefficiency of its economic planning and industrial production. Under the command system, factory managers must continually hoard supplies, or raid supplies destined for similar factories in other regions, in order to meet their production quotas. Or they must trade favors with other factory managers to obtain supplies, a system that creates a hidden level of exchange based on bribes and favoritism. And because there

These children worked in a Rhode Island textile mill in the 1890s. Children were preferred as workers in this industry because it was believed that their nimble fingers helped maintain the pace of production.

are no free markets, goods that are desired by the public often are not available simply because the planners have not ordered them. In fact, in the Soviet-style economies there were always clandestine markets that operated outside the control of the authorities and supplied goods and services to those with the means to pay for them. These underground markets thereby increased inequality in those societies and generated greater public disillusionment with command economies and one-party communist rule.

The massive social upheavals of 1989 and 1990 brought an end to the communist command economic system, but they also initiated a period of great economic and social uncertainty in the former Soviet-dominated nations. At present, efforts to privatize their economies and use market forces to regulate the supply of goods and services, including labor, have begun to produce economic growth in some of those nations. Rapid changes have also produced new forms of insecurity and corruption that have caused many people there to wish for the relative stability and security of the communist past (Ash, 1999; Woo, 1994). These problems are made even worse by the collapse of the political system in some nations of the former Soviet empire, which has enabled organized criminal gangs known as the *mafiya* (not related to the Mafia) to flourish. Without the rule of law established by a legitimate system of government, it is extremely difficult to modernize an economy and prevent severe abuses of power through violence and terror. (The role of legitimacy is discussed further in Chapter 20.) In recent elections in Russia, Slovakia, and the former East Germany, many people voted for former Communist party officials who wish to slow down the conversion to a capitalist economy (Tagliabue, 1998).

DEMOCRATIC SOCIALISM   A far less radical version of socialism than that attempted in the Soviet bloc is known as **democratic socialism.** This economic philosophy is practiced in the Scandinavian nations, especially Sweden, Denmark, and Norway, as well as in Holland and to a lesser extent in Germany, France, and Italy. It holds that the institution of private property must continue to exist because people want it to, and that competitive markets are needed because they are efficient ways of regulating production and distribution. But large corporations should be owned by the nation or, if they are in private hands, required to be run for the benefit of all citizens, not just for the benefit of their stockholders. In addition, economic decisions should be made democratically.

Democratic socialists look to societies such as Sweden and Holland for examples of their economic philosophy in practice (Harrington, 1973). In Sweden, for instance, workers can invest their pension benefits in their firm and thereby gain a controlling interest in it. This process is intended to result in socialist ownership of major economic organizations.

In the United States, there is a long history of conflicted relations between workers and owners of capital. Cooperative systems in which authority and even ownership are shared are developing, but more slowly than in the social democracies of Europe. Social scientists who study the U.S. economy note that in recent years there has been a reaction among owners of capital against the principles of democratic socialism, especially those that stress cooperation between labor and management and the right of workers to organize unions and engage in collective bargaining (Freeman, 2000). Employers have also shown diminished commitment to welfare capitalism, the political-economic model that until recently has had a great deal of influence in the noncommunist modern economies (Harrison, 1994).

WELFARE CAPITALISM   Emerging to some extent as a response to the challenge posed by the Russian Revolution (which called attention to many of the excesses of uncontrolled or laissez-faire capitalism), **welfare capitalism** represented a new way of looking at relationships between governmental and economic institutions. Welfare capitalism affirms the role of markets in determining what goods and services will be produced and how, and it also affirms the role of government in regulating economic competition (e.g., by attempting to prevent the control of markets by one or a few firms).

Welfare capitalism also stresses the role that governments have always played in building the roads, bridges, canals, ports, and other facilities that make trade and industry possible. Expanding on this role, the theory of welfare capitalism asserts that the state should also invest in the society's human resources—that is, in the education of new generations and the provision of a minimum level of health care. Welfare capitalism also guarantees the right of workers to form unions in order to reach collective agreements with the owners and managers of firms regarding wages and working conditions. It creates social-welfare institutions like Social Security and unemployment insurance. And in order to stimulate production and build confidence in times of economic depression, welfare capitalism asserts that governments must borrow funds to finance large-scale public works projects like the construction of the American interstate highway system during the 1950s.

The theory of welfare capitalism is associated with the writings of John Maynard Keynes, Joan Robinson, John Kenneth Galbraith, and James Tobin, all of whom contributed to the revision of laissez-faire economic theory. Welfare capitalism dominated American economic policy from World War II until the 1970s, when a succession of economic crises—inflation, energy shortages, and unemployment—turned the thoughts of many Americans once again toward laissez-faire capitalism. Today, how-

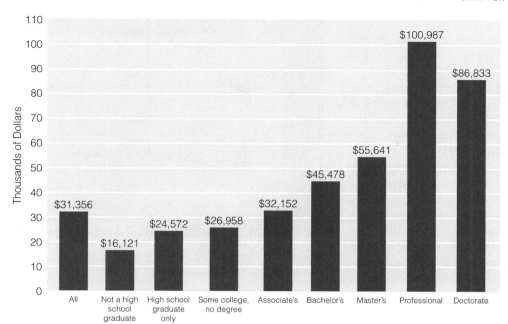

Figure 19.1 Mean Earnings, by Highest Degree Earned

Source: U.S. Census Bureau, 2000.

ever, the increasingly evident gap between the haves and the have-nots in U.S. society has created renewed interest in enhancing the institutions of the welfare state—unemployment insurance, health insurance, low-income housing, public education, and others. At the same time, fear of governmental control over people's lives, and its costs in the form of higher taxes, has generated a revolt against the "welfare state" in many segments of the population in the United States and other industrial nations. This trend has resulted in conservative electoral victories and unprecedented reductions in social spending. What is not clear is whether the public's desire for relative security from economic stress will outweigh the desire for lower taxes and reductions in the scope of government bureaucracies.

The United States: A Postindustrial Society?

Although many people in the United States see the failure of socialism in the Soviet bloc as a victory for capitalism, sociologists and poll takers have called attention to a growing sense of unease about the U.S. economy. As demographer Valerie Kincade Oppenheimer observes: "Since about 1970, the average real earnings position of young men has deteriorated considerably. This has been true not only for high school dropouts but also for high school and college graduates" (1994, p. 331). (Figure 19.1 shows the value of continuing one's education through college and beyond.) The declining incomes of U.S. workers over the past quar-

ter century have contributed to the growth in dual-earner households.

The disparity between the incomes of people with professional and technologically sophisticated jobs and those of people with less intellectually demanding jobs is likely to increase as economic growth centers on computers, telecommunications, and biological technologies. Jobs that require lower levels of education and training may be more onerous, but the number of people who can perform them is relatively large. The basic economic laws of supply and demand therefore drive up the wages of highly educated workers while those of less-educated workers are driven downward.

In an influential study, *The Coming of Post Industrial Society,* sociologist Daniel Bell (1973, 1999) reviewed changes in American economic institutions indicating that we are undergoing a transition from an industrial to a postindustrial society. A postindustrial society "emphasizes the centrality of theoretical knowledge as the axis around which new technology, economic growth, and the stratification of society will be organized" (p. 116). As societies undergo the transition to postindustrial economic institutions, an "intellectual technology" based on information arises alongside machine technology. Industrial production does not disappear, but it becomes less important. New industries devoted to providing knowledge and information become the primary sources of economic growth (Block, 1990; Sabel, 1995).

Changes in the distribution of jobs in the goods-producing and service-producing sectors of the American economy clearly show the growing importance of services, especially those employing professional and technical workers. For Bell, this change is inevitable. Industries decline, but new ones appear. A century ago, for example, over 70 percent of Americans were employed in agriculture and related occupations. Now this figure is below 3 percent. Similar transformations are taking place in manufacturing today, and they can be made less painful if the society is willing to invest in education and the retraining of workers in declining industries like mining, steel production, or manufacturing for military purposes (Harrison, 1994).

Other social scientists view these changes less optimistically. Some note that declines in industrial production have pushed thousands of skilled workers into lower-paying jobs in the service sector (e.g., in the fast-food industry or as janitors or security guards), which helps explain the decline in average wages (Aronowitz, 1996; Fallows, 1996). Others are concerned that the gains made by blacks and women in access to better-paying industrial jobs since World War II are being erased. William Julius Wilson (1998), for example, has observed that access to control over the means of production is increasingly based on educational criteria and thus threatens to solidify the subordinate position of the black lower class.

European sociologists have criticized the theory of postindustrial society on even broader grounds, saying that it tends to promote belief in the inevitability of an increasingly impoverished working class with even more reason to demand a more equal distribution of wealth (Touraine, 1998). In the United States, the theory of postindustrial society has been criticized on the ground that even though manufacturing accounts for a declining share of the labor force, the society still depends on manufactured goods of all kinds. Critics argue that the United States cannot relinquish its manufacturing base simply because a theory says it is outmoded (Wilson, 1998).

A CHANGING SOCIAL CONTRACT?   Conversion from a wartime to a peacetime economy, together with the massive changes brought about by economic globalization, technological advances, and the growth of service industries, is increasing the pressure on employers to keep their costs down in order to be competitive. This focus on cost savings results, as we have seen, in declining real wages and widening economic inequalities. In the social democracies of Europe, especially Scandinavia, the impact of these changes is eased by social-welfare policies. In the United States, the welfare state and its "safety net" of economic and social policies (e.g., Medicare, the minimum wage, unemployment insurance) are considered important by those who need to be protected from the harshest consequences of sudden economic change. Others, however, attack the policies as wasteful and costly government intervention in the economy.

The 1994 congressional elections brought in a conservative leadership committed to a "contract with America"

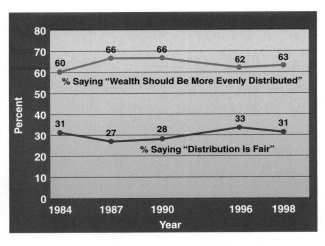

Figure 19.2   Opinions on the Distribution of Money and Wealth in the United States

Do you feel that the distribution of money and wealth in this country today is fair, or do you feel that the money and wealth in this country should be more evenly distributed among a larger percentage of the people?

Source: © 1983–1989. The Gallup Organization, Princeton, NJ. Reprinted with permission.

that promised to balance the federal budget, reduce the size of government, and cut taxes. These and related measures are consistent with laissez-faire principles that argue against government intervention in the economy and insist that individual choices about how to spend income and wealth should be protected to the extent possible. But these issues are controversial. As can be seen in Figure 19.2, a large percentage of Americans believe that wealth should be more evenly distributed. Responses to other questions on the survey indicate that Americans also believe that government has the primary responsibility to address the issue. Note that these proportions change somewhat over time.

During the relatively affluent 1990s, before the recession of 2001–2002, fewer people believed that the distribution of wealth was unfair, but even before the recession, in 1998, the trend was moving toward the belief that wealth should be more evenly distributed. Over the past decade or more, there has been a consistent majority in favor of some kind of income redistribution. Despite these trends, it appears that the conservative attack on the welfare state has persuaded large numbers of Americans to oppose taxation for the purpose of reducing inequality. It remains to be seen how stable this trend will be as the gap between rich and poor widens.

In his analysis of postindustrial society, Daniel Bell (1973, 1999) assumed that the "social contract" in the United States and other advanced nations would be maintained. In return for hard work, saving, and efforts to improve their skills, citizens could expect modest increases in their living standards, adequate health care, protection from crime, decent public education for their children, and protection of their rights. However, the Reagan administration of the 1980s and the conservative Congress of the 1990s challenged the assumption that government would provide these benefits if they were not provided by the economy itself. This alteration in the basic social contract that has guided social policy for the past half century will have far-reaching consequences (Blau, 1993; Davey, 1995).

WORKERS, MANAGERS, AND CORPORATIONS

During the 1990s, the United States enjoyed its longest period of sustained economic growth in the twentieth century. Unemployment dropped to lows not seen since the post–World War II boom years. Worker productivity increased steadily. In the financial markets, there were record increases in the prices of securities and mutual funds, and since a large proportion of U.S. employees have their pension funds in these securities, there was a widespread sense of well-being during most of the decade. This positive outlook was not shared by workers in the lower ranks of labor, who continued to experience erosion of their spending ability. However, in relation to the major European and Asian economies, where economic crisis and chronic unemployment were serious problems, the U.S. economy assumed a position of almost undisputed dominance.

In the midst of this overall prosperity, sociologists noted that there remain unresolved social problems. Feminist sociologists pointed to the persistence of discrimination against women in the workplace. Others warned of worker alienation, while still others focused on the increasing power and dominance of corporations over the lives of individuals (Chang, 2003; Odaka, 1998; Touraine, 1998).

Gender and Workplace Diversity

One of the most outstanding results of affirmative action efforts over the past generation has been the entry of women into jobs and professions that were formerly closed to them. Although affirmative action to correct racial discrimination and inequality has drawn fire from critics of quotas and admissions policies in education, conflicts arising in the workplace have also been fierce on occasion. In 1998, for example, Texaco Inc. agreed to settle a gender discrimination claim by a group of its female employees.

The women were working at all levels of the company but were paid less than their male counterparts for the same work. Though not admitting its guilt, Texaco agreed to pay $3.1 million in back pay to the 186 women in the lawsuit brought on their behalf by the U.S. Department of Labor. This settlement sent a clear signal to other major domestic and global corporations that the push for gender equality in workplaces continues (Stevenson, 1999). In fact, in the same year, the Supreme Court ruled against the Virginia Military Institute's exclusion of women and in so doing made it clear that affirmative action to achieve gender equality is justified on economic grounds (Skaggs, 1998).

Feminist sociologists note that as important as these victories may be, they should not convey a sense of uniform progress toward greater gender equality and tolerance of diversity in the workplace (Bradley, 1998; Epstein, 1995). Major corporations like Texaco often adopt far more conciliatory positions on these issues than do smaller corporations, which are less likely to be in the public spotlight. For example, the Walt Disney Company recognized the growing diversity of its labor force by conceding the right of cohabiting adults, no matter what their gender, to receive the same health and other employee benefits as heterosexual married couples. But for every company like Disney there are scores of others in which the forms of inequality that produce differences in pay for women and members of minority groups persist.

Globalization of the activities of major corporations has an immense impact on gender relations outside the United States. On the Mexican border, for example, there are hundreds of so-called *maquilladora* industries. These factories do production work of all kinds, often on a contract basis, for larger corporations. Women and men employed in these factories often experience conditions and hours of work that would be illegal in the United States. But in Mexico workers are often thankful to have the work and feel that they must endure the hardships. As *maquilladora* workers begin to protest and seek to join labor unions, they find themselves enmeshed in class conflict and labor struggles that may be entirely new to them. The experiences of earning their own wages and, especially, taking on leadership roles at work often motivate female workers to challenge traditional male-dominated family and community relations as well. Thus experiences in the workplace produce a movement for more egalitarian gender relations in other institutions. Nor is this trend limited to Mexico. Sociologists who study economic globalization and gender relations are finding many instances of these changes throughout the world (Cowie, 1998; Nelson, 1998).

Increases in the demand for part-time workers, the trend toward contracting for services by freelance workers (who may be highly skilled professionals), decreases in the willingness of employers to pay health care benefits, and efforts to prevent employees from joining labor unions are only a few of the major trends in the economies of industrialized nations that are causing workplace conflict and employee alienation. As we see next, alienation is not a new problem, but it takes on new aspects as the nature of work and economic institutions changes.

Employee Mentoring Versus Worker Alienation

Many sociologists use the concept of alienation to explain the gap between workers and managers. Karl Marx first applied the term *alienation* to the situation of workers under early capitalism. The worker in a factory performed only a fraction of the work that went into a product and therefore could feel little sense of ownership of the final product. And because the worker typically could not control the work process very much, he or she came to feel like a mere cog in a giant machine, a feeling that produced a sense of not being able to control one's own actions on the job (Fromm, 1961; Marx, 1961/1844). Today the term *alienation* is often used to describe the feeling of being powerless to control one's own destiny (Burawoy, 1996; Freeman, 2000). At work, people may feel alienated because their labor is divided up into activities that are meaningless to them. For example, in a classic study of autoworkers, oil workers, and others in different factory settings, Robert Blauner (1964) found that workers who perform highly repetitive tasks on an assembly line are more alienated than workers in groups whose tasks involve teamwork.

In a study of organizational techniques that have been used successfully in Japan, Ezra Vogel (1979) pointed out that Japanese firms tend to avoid worker alienation by strengthening the role of the small group:

> The essential building block of a company is not a man with a particular role assignment and his secretary and assistants. The essential building block of the organization is the section. . . . The lowly section, within its sphere, does not await executive orders but takes the initiative. . . . For this system to work effectively leading section personnel need to know and to identify with company purposes to a higher degree than persons in an American firm. They achieve this through long experience and years of discussion with others at all levels.
> (pp. 143–145)

The irony of this finding and others like it is that even before World War II American and European industrial

sociologists had demonstrated the benefits of team approaches to work (McCord, 1991). The famous studies by Elton Mayo, discussed in Chapter 2, were designed to find out how workers at any level of an organization could be made to feel less alienation and a greater sense of ownership of their jobs. This research demonstrated the importance of primary-group relationships at work. But the function of the manager is to motivate employees to work more efficiently and at higher levels, a goal that is not easily achieved (Hickins, 1998).

Large companies are often extremely concerned about worker alienation. Because they invest heavily in personnel training, losing employees to other businesses or having their productivity decrease because of feelings of discontent can result in lower profits. Employee mentoring programs are a popular approach to preventing alienation. Mentoring usually matches an experienced employee with a newcomer; it is also used to groom employees for advancement in the organization.

In essence, a mentor is a personal teacher and helper. The experienced employee shows the newcomer how to do the work more effectively, how to avoid "burnout" (the sense that one has no more energy to devote to the job), how to deal with the quirks and foibles of certain supervisors, and much more. The mentoring approach is widely used in business, education, health care, and government—and, of course, some programs are more effective than others.

Sociologists or people with sociological training are often asked to evaluate mentoring programs. For example, in one large metropolitan hospital, evaluators studied more than 600 professional, administrative, and clerical employees who were involved in a mentoring program. They found a strong negative correlation between time spent in mentoring and measures of employee alienation. This means that the more mentoring an individual received, the less alienation he or she felt. The evaluation also suggested ways to measure the effectiveness of mentoring aside from merely looking at whether the employee had a mentor or how much time the mentor and the employee spent together. Overall, organizations that institute mentoring programs and attempt to improve them through ongoing monitoring and evaluation are extremely pleased with the results (Koberg, Chapell, & Ringer, 1997).

Mentoring is especially important for professional workers, whose success often depends on social skills, and those in service occupations that require a great deal of interpersonal skill. But throughout the world, for workers in manufacturing and service occupations, especially in the middle and lower ranks, any improvements in wages, benefits, and working conditions are most influenced by whether or not they are represented by labor unions.

TABLE 19.1

U.S. Union Wage and Benefit Premium, 2001

| | Hourly Pay | | | Total |
	Wages	Insurance	Pension	Compensation
All workers				
Union	$21.40	$2.48	$1.52	$27.80
Nonunion	16.67%	1.14%	0.51%	19.98%
Union premium				
Dollars	$4.73	$1.34	$1.01	$7.82
Percent	28.4%	117.5%	198.0%	39.1%
Blue collar				
Union	$21.10	$2.66	$1.70	$28.07
Nonunion	13.72%	1.12%	0.37%	16.93%
Union premium				
Dollars	$7.38	$1.54	$1.33	$11.14
Percent	53.8%	137.5%	359.5%	65.8%

Source: Mishel, Bernstein, & Boushey, 2003.

Labor Unions in Global Context

Labor unions promote and defend the interests of workers in the private and public sectors of the economy. They negotiate with owners and managers on behalf of the workers for pay and benefits. In the United States, there are approximately 16.3 million union members out of 121 million workers in the labor force. The highest proportion of union members are in police and other protective services, and the lowest in farming, but unions represent workers in thousands of job settings and are especially important in construction, manufacturing, hospitals, county and state governments, retail trades, airlines, and many other major sectors of the economy (*Statistical Abstract*, 2003).

COLLECTIVE BARGAINING The union–management negotiating process occurs only after management has agreed to sign a union contract and to engage in *collective bargaining* with the union on issues of pay, benefits, and job conditions. These contracts and the negotiations they lead to are by far the most important reform of laissez-faire capitalism in the past two centuries. Under laissez-faire capitalism, workers can only bargain as individuals with their employer. The owner or manager reserves the right to set wages, establish working conditions, and decide on whether to pay benefits or not. A highly valued worker might get more pay and benefits than others, but most will be told, if they ask for improvements in their situation, to accept the status quo or quit. The employees as individuals do not have any real power to influence these decisions except by finding another job. But if they are represented by a union that has a collective bargaining contract with the employer, this contract will allow union leadership to bargain with the boss for improvements in wages and working conditions. Union contracts also provide for some measure of justice and due process at work by establishing a grievance process whereby workers who feel that they have been unfairly disciplined or subjected to unsafe conditions can appeal to the union to represent them in a grievance against the company or agency. Nonunion workplaces sometimes have a grievance system put in place by company owners, but these systems invariably give almost all the decision-making power to management (Freeman & Rogers, 2002).

WHAT UNIONS ACHIEVE FOR THEIR MEMBERS Workers represented by labor unions earn more pay and receive better insurance and pension benefits than workers in nonunion jobs. These facts are clearly demonstrated in Table 19.1. The wage premium, or gain, for union membership is 28.4 percent, and almost 40 percent if one considers all elements of hourly compensation (including insurance and pensions). The U.S. Department of Labor recently reported that a typical union job pays $640 a week compared to $478 a week for nonunion workers. This difference means an extra $8,400 a year for a union member.

Labor unions also bargain for vacations, holidays, sick pay, family leave, and hours of employment, including overtime pay. Improvements like overtime pay, pay for working on holidays, compensation for injuries suffered on the job, and many more improvements in the conditions of employees can be credited to the efforts of the labor movement and dedicated workers over many years of struggle with the owners of capital and with high-level managers in the public sector. In 2003, for example, the Bush administration issued new regulations, through the U.S. Department of Labor, that defined many thousands of workers as part of management or as contingent workers (not full-time employees), and therefore not subject to the regulations that require overtime pay after 8 hours of work in a day or 40 hours in a week. It claimed this would lead to improvements in the wages of many part-time workers and give parents more flexibility to spend more time with their children. But unions and their members are fighting this directive as an attack on the incomes of their members and all workers in the U.S. economy (Swindell, Allen, & Graham-Silverman, 2003).

WHAT UNIONS ACHIEVE FOR SOCIETY AS A WHOLE   Sociologists and historians credit the labor movement (along with its allies in Congress) for spearheading many of the most significant reforms of American capitalism, including the 40-hour workweek, social security, health and welfare plans, job safety, generous pensions, and a host of other benefits that many Americans now take for granted and many others still only dream about (Bronfenbrenner, 2003). With some exceptions, unions have been in the front ranks of other social movements that have brought forth positive changes for minorities, women, the elderly, gays and lesbians, and many others. In the case of the civil rights movement, for example, internationally respected union leaders like A. Philip Randolph, president of the Brotherhood of Sleeping Car Porters, were instrumental in bringing about many of the key rallies and events leading up to the great 1963 March on Washington at which Dr. Martin Luther King, Jr. gave his "I Have a Dream" speech.

UNIONS AND "FREE RIDERS"   Unions play a significant role in improving wages and working conditions and reducing inequality even for employees who are not union members and, often without knowing it, are "free riding" on the efforts of union members. Because of the efforts of unionized workers in many industries, employers seek to pay something close to the "prevailing wage" in their region and industry. These wages are often set by union workers, who may have to make sacrifices, and even go on strike, to win gains in wages and benefits from their employers. Although nonunion workers in these regions and industries rarely get the same raises and improved benefits, those they do get are often the result of "free riding" on the efforts of unionized workers (Wallerstein & Moene, 2003).

DECLINES IN U.S. UNIONS   Despite all their positive achievements, unions in the United States have been losing membership and strength since they reached their peak numbers in the 1950s. In 2002, about 13.2 percent

of U.S. workers were union members, although the percentage varies widely from the major industrial states of the Midwest, where union densities (the proportion of workers in unions) are over 20 percent, to those of the South, where union densities are generally lower than 9 percent. But union densities have been declining in other Western nations as well, as shown in Table 19.2.

The table also shows, however, that with the exception of France, the United States has the lowest union density among the nations listed. The Scandinavian nations, where social inequalities are lower than anywhere else on earth, show the highest union densities, and unions in these nations have played a major role in decreasing inequality. But if unions are so good for workers, why is their strength declining?

DEINDUSTRIALIZATION AND GLOBALIZATION OF LABOR   Much of the reduction in union density in the United States and other Western nations is due to deindustrialization and the transformation of the economy from one dominated by manufacturing to one in which services predominate, although industrial production remains in a highly automated form. Manufacturing plants in major industries like steel, mining, textiles, and garment manufacturing have been moved to places where it is much more difficult, even impossible, for workers to form unions (Scruggs & Lange, 2002). Automation has also eliminated hundreds of thousands of union jobs in the United States and Europe. Automation increases the productivity of the remaining workers, and as such it is of great value to every nation's economy, but it is always an open question whether the new jobs created in the economy will be as high-paying and secure as those that are lost to globalization and automation.

ANTI-UNIONISM   What about those jobs that cannot be "exported" to low-wage nations and regions? Are they more likely to be unionized because the owners of capital cannot send them away? The answer is no, in large part because of the strenuous efforts of employers and their allies among conservative political leaders to oppose union representation. Compared to those in Europe, where there is greater acceptance of labor unions and collective bargaining, employers in the United States are extremely anti-union. Although major unionized employers like the auto companies have long recognized their workers' rights to bargain collectively—through the United Auto Workers and other unions—many U.S. employers, including major ones like General Electric, IBM, and Wal-Mart, have never willingly accepted unions and actively engage in efforts to prevent their workers from joining unions. In smaller nonunion companies, owners often feel that unionization of their workers deprives them of their right to run their businesses

TABLE 19.2

Union Density Trends, Selected Countries, 1960–1994

Country	1960	1974	1980	1990	1994	Change
Sweden	70.7%	71.9%	78.3%	82.4%	88.6%	16.7%
Denmark	59.6	63.8	77.5	74.5	79.5	15.7
Austria	57.8	51.7	50.8	45.2	39.4	−12.3
Norway	51.6	51.1	54.1	53.1	52.6	1.5
Australia	47.9	47.5	46.4	42.6	35.0	−12.5
Belgium	40.7	49.9	56.6	56.7	58.8	8.9
United Kingdom	44.3	50.4	52.8	40.9	33.8	−16.6
Netherlands	39.4	35.1	32.6	22.3	22.3	−12.8
Switzerland	37.0	29.2	30.6	26.3	23.3	−5.9
Germany	34.2	32.9	33.6	29.9	27.4	−5.5
Finland	31.9	63.4	70.0	72.5	78.9	15.5
Japan	31.0	33.2	29.9	24.5	23.2	−10.0
United States	28.0	24.2	20.5	14.6	13.9	−10.3
Canada	27.5	31.3	33.2	31.2	30.8	−0.5
Italy	22.4	42.7	44.4	33.6	33.2	−9.5
France	19.2	21.0	17.1	9.2	8.8	−12.2%

Note: Union density figures represent the proportion of workers who are in unions among all workers, so that union membership can be growing, as it is slowly in the United States, but the labor force can be growing at a faster rate, which results in lowering union density figures.

Source: Ebbinghaus & Visser, 2000.

the way they wish and forces them into labor agreements that drive up the cost of making their products or delivering their services. When faced with union efforts to organize their workers, the majority threaten to move their production facilities (where feasible) to lower-wage regions of the world rather than agree to pay union wages and benefits. In situations where the owners cannot globalize their production by moving it to low-wage regions, unions are somewhat more successful in winning contracts, but in the United States many employers simply threaten to move to anti-union regions of the country (Bronfenbrenner, 2000).

FALSE CONSCIOUSNESS Another important reason non-union workers seem complacent about their lack of bargaining power at work, their lack of adequate health care benefits, and their overall passivity is that they often identify with their bosses because they want approval, rather than with other workers in the same situation who are seeking union representation. And workers in low-wage jobs, where there is a great deal of turnover of personnel, are typically reluctant to confront their supervisors with demands for better treatment, pay, or benefits. They know that if they begin inquiring about their rights or their need to have a union, they may be fired. While these responses are understandable under the circumstances of their employment, they are also a form of *false consciousness;* that is, as workers they are aware of their lower status and inequality, but they don't think there is much they can effectively do about it.

To make matters worse, nonunion workers tend to believe that they have rights at work that they actually do not have. In a survey of what American workers think about how much voice they should have and what rights they have in their workplaces, economist Richard Freeman and sociologist Joel Rogers found that "employees vastly exaggerate their workplace rights" (Freeman & Rogers, 2002, p. 118). Here is a list of questions they asked about this issue. How would you answer each of them?

Is it legal or illegal for your employer to:
Fire you for no reason?
Move you to a lower-paying job because you wanted to form a union?
Refuse to let you take time off from work to take care of your sick baby?
Fire you for refusing to do hazardous work?
Permanently replace you if you went on strike?
Avoid hiring minorities for "good business reasons"?

Percentage of Employees Who Believe Legal Acts are Illegal

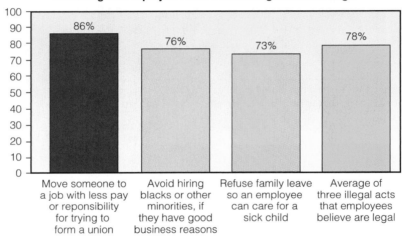

Percentage of Employees Who Believe Illegal Acts are Legal

Figure 19.3   Employee Beliefs About the Legality of Selected Actions by Employers

Source: Freeman & Rogers, 2002.

Figure 19.3 indicates that an average of 74 percent of American workers believed that three or more acts that are actually legal are against the law. Eighty-three percent believed, wrongly, that it is illegal to fire a worker for no reason; 83 percent thought it is illegal to fire a worker for refusing hazardous work. In fact, these acts are perfectly legal and are fundamental principles of laissez-faire capitalism. Extremely high proportions of workers also believe, wrongly, that illegal acts by employers, such as firing or moving someone to a lower-paying job for trying to form a union, avoiding hiring minorities for "good business reasons," or refusing family leave for a sick child (all of which are illegal according to U.S. labor laws) are legal (Freeman & Rogers, 2002).

CAN THE LABOR MOVEMENT REJUVENATE ITSELF?   Anti-unionism, globalization and deindustrialization, and worker misunderstandings and false consciousness are some of the main reasons for the decline in union strength in the United States, but it is also true that as a social movement, labor is confronted with a negative climate due to the prevalence of far more conservative thinking in U.S. society today than in the early twentieth century. The Bush administration is opposed to doing anything that will help unions organize new members. But this is not a new situation, for many other administrations have been unsympathetic to organized labor; moreover, the movement's original victories were won in an extremely anti-union social environment during the first decades of the twentieth century. The prospects for a rejuvenated labor movement, therefore, will depend on aggressive and creative leadership in the unions (Bronfenbrenner, 2003).

One currently popular strategy is for unions to open up their membership and the benefits they can supply to workers in nonunion workplaces. This "open source" unionism can bring lower medical costs, better insurance plans, and many more benefits, short of actual union contracts, which still need to be won in local representation elections. But such a strategy can eventually convince more and more workers to take on the responsibilities of helping to organize actual union membership drives in their workplaces. Successful modern labor unions like the Service Employees International Union (SEIU) are currently using such strategies to take on major anti-union employers like Wal-Mart.

Sociological Perspectives on the Workplace

Industrial sociology is concerned with the social organization of work and the types of interactions that occur in the workplace. Like sociologists in other fields, industrial sociologists use the functionalist, conflict, and interactionist perspectives in their research. The results of that research have been used to support various approaches to labor–management relations.

HUMAN RELATIONS IN INDUSTRY: A FUNCTIONALIST PERSPECTIVE The *human relations* perspective on management is associated with the research of Elton Mayo and his colleagues at Western Electric's Hawthorne plant and in aircraft and metal production plants. Their goal was to use experimental methods and observation of workers and managers on the job in an attempt to understand how the factory's formal organization and goals are affected by patterns of informal organization within the workplace. This was in sharp contrast with earlier approaches to labor–management relations, especially the *scientific management* approach developed early in the twentieth century by Frederick W. Taylor.

Scientific management (or Taylorism, as it is often called) was one of the earliest attempts to apply objective standards to management practices. After rising through the ranks from laborer to chief engineer in a large steel company, Taylor turned his attention to the study of worker productivity. He noticed that workers tend to adhere to informal norms that require them to limit their output. For example, he found that the rate of production

The Sociological Observer

These members of the Service Employees International Union in the Sacramento metropolitan region are picketing outside a Wal-Mart as part of their effort to sign up new union members and gain public sympathy for their efforts to unionize Wal-Mart "associates." The Wal-Mart store, seen in the background, is typical of the "big box" shopping center retail outlets that now dominate the metropolitan landscape. Wal-Mart is the nation's single largest employer and the world's leading retailer. It is an extremely powerful company and one that prides itself on its "union-free" environment.

So why are these picketers laughing? Don't they know the odds are stacked against their success? What can you say about them from closer observation of the photos? (See page 577 for further insights into the sociological content of this photo.)

Dick Wood

in a machine shop was only about one-third of what might normally be expected. Taylor decided to use the authority of management to speed up the workers.

He fired stubborn men, hired "green hands" who did not know the norms of the experienced workers, and experimented with ways of breaking down the labor of each worker into its components. Every job, he claimed, could be scientifically studied to determine how it could be performed most efficiently. Such "time and motion studies," combined with piecework payment systems that induced workers to produce more because they were paid for each unit produced above a set number, became the hallmarks of scientific management (Miller & Form, 1964). Taylor's principles were quickly incorporated into the managerial practices of American businesses, but they were often resisted by workers and their unions (Braverman, 1974).

Mayo's experiments were intended to determine what conditions would foster the highest rates of worker productivity. His observations convinced him that increased productivity could be obtained by emphasizing teamwork among workers and managers, rather than through pay incentives or changes in such variables as lighting, temperature, and rest periods (Bendix, 1974). We saw in Chapter 2 that Mayo's research showed that it was the attention given to the workers that mattered, not the various experimental conditions. But Mayo drew another, more important conclusion from the Hawthorne experiments:

> The major experimental change was introduced when those in charge sought to hold the situation humanly steady . . . by getting the cooperation of the workers. What actually happened was that six individuals became a team and the team gave itself wholeheartedly and spontaneously to cooperating in the experiment. (Mayo, 1945, pp. 72–73)

Although Mayo's research focused on the interactions between workers and managers, the human relations approach that grew out of that research can be said to represent the functionalist perspective on the workplace because it stresses the function of managerial efforts in increasing worker productivity. The functionalist perspective is also illustrated by William F. Whyte's classic study of the restaurant industry. In a small restaurant, the organization's structure is simple: "There is little division of labor. The owner and employees serve together as cooks, countermen, and dishwashers." But when the restaurant expands, various supervisory and production occupations are added to its role structure. According to Whyte, this magnifies old problems and creates new ones:

> In a large and busy restaurant a waitress may take orders from fifty to one hundred customers a day (and perhaps several times at each meal) in addition to the orders (much less frequent) she receives from her supervisor. When we add to this the problem of adjusting to service pantry workers, bartenders, and perhaps checkers, we can readily see the possibilities of emotional tension—and, in our study, we did see a number of girls break down and cry under the strain. (1949, p. 304)

Whyte discovered that tension and stress could be reduced, and customers served more happily, if the restaurant was organized so that lower-status employees were not required to give orders directly to higher-status ones. For example, waiters and waitresses should not give orders directly to cooks but should place their orders with a pantry worker or use a system of written orders. By changing the organization of statuses and roles in the restaurant (and, thus, the way they functioned as a social system), it would be possible to increase work satisfaction and output.

CONFLICT AT WORK The human relations approach just discussed seeks to improve cooperation between workers and managers in order to achieve the organization's goals. Industrial sociologists who take a conflict perspective believe that this approach automatically condones the goals of managers and fails to consider more basic causes of worker–management conflict such as class conflict (Touraine, 1998). This results in continual fine-tuning of organizational structures rather than in more thorough reforms.

In an influential study of a midwestern metal products factory, Michael Burawoy (1980) found that even after changes were made on the basis of the human relations approach, the workers continued to limit their output. The workers called this "making out" and saw it as a way of maximizing two conflicting values: their pay and their enjoyment of social relations at work. But instead of wondering why the workers refused to produce more, Burawoy asked why they worked as hard as they did. He concluded that the workers were actually playing into the hands of the managers and owners because neither they nor the unions ever questioned management's authority to control basic production decisions. The norms of the shop-floor culture, of which "making out" is an example, caused the workers to feel that they were resisting the managers' control. As a result, they did not feel a need to engage in more direct challenges to the capitalist system itself (Burawoy, 1996).

A fundamental problem for conflict sociologists is that class conflict must be shown to exist; it cannot be assumed to exist simply because Marxian theory defines workers and business owners as opposing classes. In fact, there is considerable evidence that despite their misfortunes, workers do not view their interests as automatically opposed to those of owners and managers. As workers and supervisory personnel lost their jobs in the severe recession of the early 1990s, they often expressed discontent with the nation's leadership and with company managers. Generally, however, the anguish of the unemployed tends to be turned inward, taking the form of depression rather than militant class consciousness. Class consciousness may be popularized in the lyrics of a Bruce Springsteen song— "They're closing down the textile mill/across the railroad track/Foreman says these jobs are going boys/and they ain't coming back/to your hometown"—but it has not produced much overt class conflict or new social movements (Bensman & Lynch, 1987).

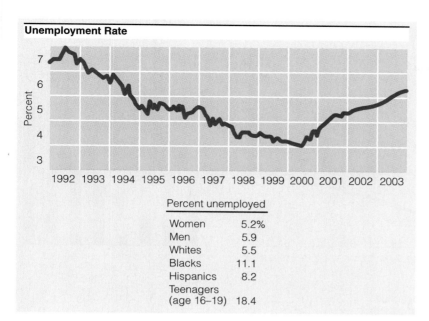

Figure 19.4 Conditions in the U.S. Labor Market, 2003

Unemployment Rate

Percent unemployed

Women	5.2%
Men	5.9
Whites	5.5
Blacks	11.1
Hispanics	8.2
Teenagers (age 16–19)	18.4

In addition to class conflict between workers and management, there are problems of inequality in the workplace. As mentioned earlier, during the decade of the 1990s the U.S. economy experienced unprecedented growth and low inflation, just about the best possible conditions for businesses and workers (Nasar, 1999). Jobs were being created in record numbers. Civilian employment stood at 133.1 million, up from 108.4 million in 1992. And all this was occurring despite severe economic crises in Asia and parts of Latin America. This powerful surge in the U.S. economy vastly aided the absorption of immigrants into the labor force without increasing intergroup tensions caused by competition for scarce jobs. Unemployment began to increase during the recession of 2001–2002, which was accelerated by the decline in the stock market following the bursting of the "dot-com bubble." As we see in Figure 19.4, the unemployment rate began increasing in 2000 but did not come close to the high rates reached during the severe recession of 1992. On the other hand, the unemployment rate among black workers remained twice that of whites. And the unemployment rate among teenagers, usually a far higher figure, remained over 18 percent in 2003.

These employment figures present a picture of a nation with relatively high rates of employment but with underlying problems of employment inequity (e.g., black–white differences in unemployment) that often become far worse when the economy enters a downward phase of the business cycle. Another trend that worries both economists and sociologists is the rise in rates of consumer debt and bankruptcies in the United States, as shown in Figure 19.5. About two-thirds of domestic production in the United

States is purchased by U.S. consumers, a fact that helps explain the intense pressure on those consumers to go to the mall or order merchandise from mail-order catalogs. But credit card and other forms of consumer debt, which fuel the economy in good times, can become a major problem if the economy weakens and bankruptcies rise. This is especially true for people employed in part-time service work or in manufacturing, where workers are most vulnerable to plant closings and layoffs.

PROFESSIONS: AN INTERACTIONIST PERSPECTIVE Factory workers and other low-status employees are not the only subjects of research by sociologists who study work and employment. Because they are a growing segment of modern economic institutions, professionals have also been studied extensively. A **profession** is an occupation with a body of recognized knowledge and a developed intellectual technique. Its knowledge is transmitted by a formal educational process, and entry into the profession is regulated by testing procedures. A code of professional ethics governs each profession and regulates relations with colleagues, clients, and the public. Most professions are licensed by the state (Cant & Sharma, 1998; Montagna, 1977). This definition could be applied to a variety of occupations. For example, doctors and attorneys have long been considered professionals, but what about nurses and stockbrokers? Sociologists have addressed this question in their research on the "professionalization" of occupations—that is, on the way different occupations attempt to achieve the status of professions.

According to Everett C. Hughes (1959), a profession is a set of role relations between "experts" and "clients," in

Figure 19.5 Consumer Debt and Personal Bankruptcies, 1991–2002

Source: Federal Reserve Board, Administrative Office of U.S. Courts.

*Excludes home mortgages.
**Includes overdraft protection.

which the professional is an expert who offers knowledge and judgments to clients. The professional often must assume the burden of the client's "guilty knowledge": The lawyer must keep secret the client's transgressions, and the physician must hide any knowledge of the sexual behavior or drug use of famous and not-so-famous patients. Professions thus "rest on some bargain about receiving, guarding, and giving out communications" (Hughes, 1959, p. 449; see also Abbott, 1993).

Interactionist sociologists pay special attention to the role relations that develop in various professions. They are particularly interested in the processes of *professional socialization*—learning the profession's formal and informal norms. For example, in a well-known study of professional socialization in medical schools, Howard Becker and his colleagues (1961) found that in the later years of their training, medical students' attention is devoted more and more to learning the informal norms of medical practice. The formal science they learn in class is supplemented by the practical knowledge of the working doctor, and the student's skill at interacting with higher-status colleagues becomes extremely important to achieving the status of a professional physician. In a highly acclaimed study on the same subject, Charles Bosk (1979) showed that resident surgeons in a teaching hospital are forgiven if they make mistakes that the older surgeons believe to be "normal" aspects of the learning process, but not when their mistakes are repeated or are thought to be caused by carelessness. The point of these and similar studies is that role performance is learned through interaction. Role expectations vary from one profession to another, as do the ways

in which these expectations are experienced by members of the profession (Abbott, 1988).

Our discussion of professions can serve as a reminder of a basic characteristic of economic institutions, one that we noted early in the chapter: Economic institutions are concerned with allocating scarce resources to satisfy competing ends. Thus, just as the guilds of feudal societies controlled access to skilled trades in medieval times, professional associations like the American Medical Association attempt to control access to the professions. Efforts by nation-states to regulate markets and trade, and efforts by managers to increase the productivity of workers, are all concerned with achieving the most advantageous use of scarce resources. This fundamental fact is at the heart of the sociological study of economic institutions.

CRITICAL SOCIOLOGY AND SOCIAL CHANGE

How People Find Jobs

How do people find their jobs? Do they rely on the want ads? Family contacts? College placement services? From a strictly economic viewpoint, the question is answered by relying on market mechanisms. Employers seek workers at given wages for particular kinds of work. Potential employees seek employers who need their skills and will pay the highest rate for their services. The supply and de-

TABLE 19.3

Level of Income of Respondent in Present Job, by Job-Finding Method Used

| Income | Method Used | | | | |
	Formal Means	Personal Contacts	Direct Application	Other	Total
Less than $10,000	28.0%	22.7%	50.0%	5.3%	27.6%
$10,000–14,999	42.0%	31.8%	30.8%	26.3%	33.1%
$15,000–24,999	24.0%	31.2%	15.4%	52.6%	28.4%
$25,000 or more	6.0%	14.3%	3.8%	15.8%	10.9%
N	50	154	52	19	275

Source: Adapted from Granovetter, 1995. *Getting A Job,* 2nd edition. Copyright 1995 University of Chicago Press. Used with permission of the University of Chicago Press.

mand for particular services will explain changes in the prevailing wages for those services. But how do people actually learn about available jobs, and how do they obtain them once they know about them? Market models of job-seeking behavior often assume that there is a perfect flow of information. In fact, however, sociological research uncovers some surprising gaps in the flow of information and reveals that both employers and employees actually behave in ways that are not the most rational from an economic viewpoint.

Mark Granovetter (1974, 1995), one of the nation's foremost economic sociologists, is largely responsible for discovering what is now known as "the strength of weak ties." This discovery turns out to be a key to explaining how a large proportion of people actually go about finding their jobs. By "weak ties," Granovetter refers to people who are part of our social networks even if we are not always aware that they are. They are acquaintances or friends of acquaintances. It turns out that these weak ties, as opposed to stronger ties of kinship, can be essential in the success of job searches. Here is how Granovetter formulated his research problem and collected the data for his pioneering research.

While a graduate student in sociology at Harvard, Granovetter developed an interest in chains of contact and flows of information through them. His mentor, the economic sociologist Harrison White (1970), had made some important discoveries about how information in markets flows through chains of acquaintance, and Granovetter wanted to extend this research to labor market and job-seeking behavior. He decided to interview a sample of prospective employees in order to determine whether they also relied on chains of acquaintance within social networks to help them find jobs. To reduce the possible variance among different occupa-

tions, and because he could not afford to interview more than about 280 respondents, Granovetter decided to limit his sample to professional, technical, and managerial workers. He conducted the interviews in the Boston suburb of Newton, obtaining the names of eligible male respondents through a commercial directory service that lists residence, occupation, and related information for each entry. (In subsequent research, he broadened his study to include women.) In collecting the data, he combined in-person interviews with career histories and basic demographic information—age, education, race or ethnicity, place of birth, and so on.

The first surprises in Granovetter's research came as he looked at the data about which job-finding methods worked for which types of job seekers. Examples of these findings from his original survey are presented in Tables 19.2 and 19.3. In no case do formal job search methods—that is, the use of impersonal intermediaries (newspaper ad, placement service, employment agency, professional association, and the like)—account for the majority of job placements. Direct application, in which the applicant shows up at the employer's office without an appointment, and personal contacts through social networks are more important than formal searches, especially at the middle levels of the salary scale. Table 19.3 shows that 154 of 275 respondents (56 percent) found their jobs through personal contacts, clearly the most effective of the three methods of job seeking. Table 19.4 on page 578 shows that personal contacts are particularly important when the position being filled is newly created. Indeed, the lengthy interviews Granovetter conducted with his respondents revealed a pattern in which a personal contact mentioned a job that another contact in a certain company had mentioned as just being created—thus providing the job seeker with "insider information" in seeking the position.

Text continues on page 578.

VISUAL SOCIOLOGY

CRAFTS TRADITIONS IN MODERN ECONOMIES

As these photos show, crafts traditions are flourishing. The Indian basket maker whom we met at the beginning of the chapter is not alone. In fact, in industrial nations like England and the United States, many people are engrossed in using their creative powers to make traditional and modern craft objects of all kinds. Millions of people throughout the industrial world are facing the same problem as the Indian basket weaver: how to market their goods while maintaining their pride in their skills and their love of the process.

Contrary to the dire predictions of many social critics and early sociologists, such as Karl Marx and Max Weber, who lived more than a century ago during the earlier phases of capitalism, the enchantment people find in creating arts and crafts has not withered in the face of mass production and mass marketing. On the contrary, the easy availability of mass-produced goods seems to have made people even more eager to buy unique objects made by people who are

carrying out enduring cultural traditions. And global forms of marketing like the World Wide Web are proving to be extremely powerful institutions for disseminating information about craftspeople and their products.

Although craftspeople will always face an uphill struggle to make a living from their work, particularly in traditional societies, we see proof that the struggle can pay off. Early in the era of industrial capitalism, William Morris, a

© Michael Newman/PhotoEdit

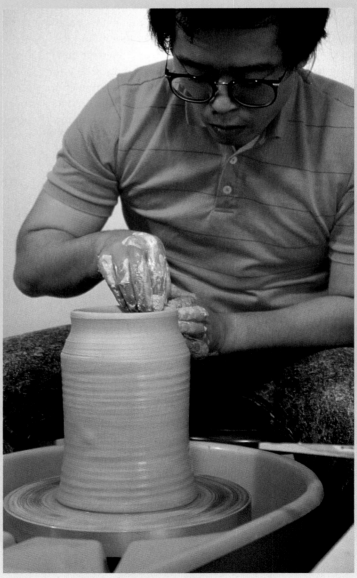

© Gary A. Conner/PhotoEdit

man with keen sociological insights and a passion for arts and crafts, started what became known as the Arts and Crafts movement. Morris, a contemporary of Marx, was deeply concerned that industrial expansion and urbanization would wipe out craft traditions throughout the world. If he were alive today, he would still be concerned about the loss of traditional skills and techniques for producing baskets and other objects of everyday life, but he would be extremely gratified to see the burgeoning activity in this area of life—which we can observe by simply browsing the Web.

The Sociological Observer
(See photo on page 571.)

When people join picket lines and try to present their case to other workers and to the public, they often encounter responses that make them laugh. Those who support them shout encouraging words that make the pickets joke back and all laugh together. Those who shout negative taunts may also make pickets laugh because they know they are having some effect, making people think. The worst responses for people on a picket line are apathy and indifference.

These people are proud union members, which one can tell from the buttons on their clothing and the signs they are carrying. They are wearing jeans and casual clothing of the kind that Wal-Mart workers often wear when they are not in the red smocks that mark them as "associates." For this and similar union organizing drives to be successful, it is extremely important that many women be involved, because the majority of retail workers are women.

Courtesy of Susan Dueckman

William Morris.

Brown Brothers

© Billy E. Barnes/PhotoEdit

TABLE 19.4

Origin of Job, by Job-Finding Method of Respondent

	Method Used				
Origin of Job	Formal Means	Personal Contacts	Direct Application	Other	Total
Direct replacement	47.1%	40.5%	58.0%	38.9%	44.9%
Added on	31.4%	15.7%	18.0%	27.8%	19.9%
Newly created	21.6%	43.8%	24.0%	33.3%	35.3%
N	51	153	50	18	272

Note: Percentages may not add up to 100 because of rounding.

Source: Adapted from Granovetter, 1995.

Many readers may think that these findings are not actually surprising. Don't we often hear it said that "it's not what you know, but who you know" that explains how people succeed in getting jobs? Indeed, this is a time-honored cliché—but Granovetter explored its meaning more fully. After all, "who you know" should include family members and close kin. Yet family and close kin contacts and referrals accounted for a minority of the personal referrals that paid off in terms of obtaining a job. Far more important were links between friends and acquaintances. The following three cases from Granovetter's original study illustrate how weak ties actually work:

> George C. was working as a technician for an electrical firm, with a salary of about $8,000 and little apparent chance for advancement. While courting his future wife, he met her downstairs neighbor, the manager of a candy shop, a concession leased from a national chain. After they were married, Mr. C. continued to see him when visiting his mother-in-law. The neighbor finally talked him into entering a trainee program for the chain, and arranged an interview for him. Within three years, Mr. C. was earning nearly $30,000 in this business.

> Herman D. was the owner of a fruit and vegetable store, which he sold (at age 45) because of ill health. He took a vacation; meanwhile his brother, a business executive, attended a meeting where a colleague mentioned that he was looking for someone to do inventory management. Mr. D. had done similar work before buying his store, and his brother therefore suggested him. He was hired several days later.

> Gerald F. was a salesman for a wholesale liquor distributor. A friend who was a doctor asked him if he would be interested in managing a nursing home, and if so, to put together a resume. One of the references Mr. F. used for the resume was his wife's cousin, owner of a fashionable antique shop. When the nursing home job didn't come through, the wife's cousin, now aware that Mr. F. was considering changing jobs, offered him a job as business manager of his shop, which he accepted. (Granovetter, 1974, p. 49)

These are not the family ties that one often associates with "who you know." In fact, another surprising finding of Granovetter's research is that on the average it takes about two or more contacts in the chain of network associations to get the job applicant to appear as a likely candidate for the prospective employer, so it is not the direct contact but the contact through network chains that makes the difference in the successful job search.

One implication of this research is that people who are on the margins of society because of their race, gender, or social class are less likely to have the network resources to draw upon when looking for a job. Granovetter used this finding to argue in favor of affirmative action in hiring. African Americans and other groups that have experienced systematic exclusion from particular types of jobs and careers have plenty of personal contacts and social networks, Granovetter explains. But because they are underrepresented in the existing structures of employment, these contacts do not produce chains of referral into these careers. Once a core of formerly excluded people are included, largely through intentional efforts like affirmative action, the normal network system of weak ties will work for them as it does for others.

SUMMARY

Sociology and Economics

- *Economics* is the study of how individuals and societies choose to employ scarce resources to produce various commodities and distribute them among various groups in the society.

- Sociologists are also concerned with how individuals and societies make such choices, but much of their research focuses on how cultural norms affect those choices.

- The main subjects of sociological research in this area are markets and the division of labor, the interactions between government and economic institutions, and the nature of jobs and professions.

Global Markets and the Division of Labor

- A hallmark of an industrial society is the production of commodities and services to be exchanged in markets. A *market* is an economic institution that regulates exchange behavior.

- In a market, different values are established for particular goods and services; those values are usually expressed in terms of a common measure of exchange, or currency. Market transactions are governed by agreements, or contracts, in which a seller agrees to supply a particular item and a buyer agrees to pay for it.

- The spread of markets throughout the world began in the late fifteenth century as a result of the development of new *technologies* that facilitated trade.

- Today world markets are dominated by *multinational corporations,* economic enterprises that have headquarters in one country and conduct business activities in one or more other countries.

- An important modern trend is economic globalization, a worldwide shrinkage of economic distances between nations.

Economics and the State

- The fate of societies throughout the world has been strongly influenced by the economic ideologies of mercantilism, capitalism, and socialism.

- *Mercantilism* held that the wealth of a nation could be measured by its holdings of gold, so the best economic system was one that increased the nation's exports and thereby increased its holdings of gold.

- *Laissez-faire capitalism,* on the other hand, argued that a society's wealth could be measured only by its capacity to produce goods and services—that is, its resources of land, labor, and machinery. The major institutions of capitalism are private property and free markets.

- *Socialism* arose out of the belief that private property and personal profit should be replaced by public ownership of property and sharing of profits. According to Marx, the socialist state would be controlled by the workers, who would determine what should be produced and how it should be distributed.

- Soviet-style socialist societies were characterized until recently by command economies, in which the state commands economic institutions to supply a specific amount of each product and to sell it at a particular price.

- *Democratic socialism* holds that private property must continue to exist but that large corporations should be owned by the nation or, if they are in private hands, required to be run for the benefit of all citizens.

- In *welfare capitalism,* markets determine what goods and services will be produced and how, but the government regulates economic competition. Welfare capitalism also asserts that the state should invest in the society's human resources through policies promoting education, health care, and social welfare.

- In the United States, the transition from an economy based on the production of goods to one based on the provision of services has resulted in the displacement of thousands of skilled workers into lower-paying jobs in the service sector. These trends appear to signal a change in the basic social contract in which individuals who work hard can expect increases in their living standards.

Workers, Managers, and Corporations

- Many sociologists use the concept of *alienation* to explain this gap. This term refers to the feeling of being powerless to control one's own destiny. At work, people may feel alienated because their labor is divided up into activities that are meaningless to them.

- Mentoring programs have been found to raise employee morale and prevent burnout.

- Labor unions promote and defend the interests of workers in the private and public sectors of the economy. Workers represented by labor unions earn more pay and receive better insurance and pension benefits than workers in nonunion jobs.

- Unions in the United States have been losing membership and strength since they reached their peak numbers in the 1950s. Much of the reduction in union density is due to deindustrialization and the transformation of the economy from one dominated by manufacturing to one in which services predominate. Other factors are anti-union attitudes among employers and "false consciousness" (identification with the employer's interests) among workers.

Sociological Perspectives on the Workplace

- The scientific management approach to labor–management relations attempted to increase productivity by determining how each job could be performed most efficiently and by using piecework payment systems to induce workers to produce more.

- Efforts to determine what conditions would result in the highest rates of worker productivity led to the recognition that cooperation between workers and managers is an important ingredient in worker satisfaction and output. A result of this recognition was the human relations approach to management, which seeks to improve cooperation between workers and managers.

- Conflict theorists believe that the human relations approach fails to consider the basic causes of worker–management conflict. They study how social class and status both at work and outside the workplace influence relations between workers and managers.

- Interactionist theorists have devoted considerable study to professionalization, or the way in which occupations attempt to gain the status of *professions,* and to the processes of professional socialization (i.e., learning the formal and informal norms of the profession).

GLOSSARY

market: An economic institution that regulates exchange behavior through the establishment of different values for particular goods and services. (p. 553)

technology: Tools, procedures, and forms of social organization that increase human productive capacity. (p. 555)

multinational corporation: An economic enterprise that has headquarters in one country and conducts business activities in one or more other countries. (p. 555)

mercantilism: An economic philosophy based on the belief that the wealth of a nation can be measured by its holdings of gold or other precious metals and that the state should control trade. (p. 558)

laissez-faire capitalism: An economic philosophy based on the belief that the wealth of a nation can be measured by its capacity to produce goods and services (i.e., its resources of land, labor, and machinery) and that these can be maximized by free trade. (p. 558)

socialism: An economic philosophy based on the concept of public ownership of property and sharing of profits, together with the belief that economic decisions should be controlled by the workers. (p. 561)

democratic socialism: An economic philosophy based on the belief that private property may exist at the same time that large corporations are owned by the state and run for the benefit of all citizens. (p. 562)

welfare capitalism: An economic philosophy in which markets determine what goods will be produced and how, but the government regulates economic competition. (p. 562)

alienation: The feeling of being powerless to control one's own destiny; a worker's feeling of powerlessness caused by inability to control the work process. (p. 566)

profession: An occupation with a body of knowledge and a developed intellectual technique that are transmitted by a formal educational process and testing procedures. (p. 573)

INTERNET RESOURCES

Virtual Society: The Wadsworth Sociology Resource Center
(http://sociology.wadsworth.com)
At Virtual Society you can access a wide range of enrichment material to aid your study of sociology. From the main page, click on the Student Resources link and find your course and this textbook. Next, select the chapter you are presently studying from the pull-down menu. Among the useful options for each self-study chapter are online links and exercises, flashcards, practical study tips, and practice quizzes for each chapter.

MC   MicroCase Online
From the Virtual Society home page, click on MicroCase Online to access book-specific MicroCase exercises that allow you to further explore sociological issues and principles presented in the text.

InfoTrac College Edition

Another unique option available to you at the Student Resources section at Virtual Society is InfoTrac College Edition, an online library with access to hundreds of scholarly and popular periodicals. Below are suggested search terms for this chapter, but this resource also allows you to fit your study of sociology to your own interests by searching custom keywords.

Markets

Technology

Welfare capitalism

Socialism

The World Bank
(www.worldbank.org) and the
Organization for Economic Cooperation and Development (OECD)
(www.oecd.org)
Two sources of extensive data on social indicators such as health and education in different nations and regions.

African Studies Department at the University of Pennsylvania
(www.sas.upenn.edu/African_Studies/AS.html)
A valuable site for those interested in the economics and politics of a rapidly changing continent.

Politics and Political Institutions

We are living through one of the most momentous political experiments in the history of world politics. American-led occupation forces and their Iraqi supporters are attempting to build the institutions of a democratic nation so that constitutional democracy, the rule of law, and protection of minorities will replace cruel repression, tribalism, and rampant corruption.

From a sociological standpoint, this is a political experiment because there were only very limited democratic institutions in Iraq before it was invaded by forces of the United States and Great Britain. After World War II, there were successful efforts by the Allies to help Japan and Germany rebuild their economies and create democratic political institutions. Iraq, however, had been ruled for generations by kings and dictators, and before that had been a British colony. In fact, like so many nations in the Middle East and Africa that were created by the colonial powers after World War I, the modern nation of Iraq is a legacy of the colonial period of world domination by the great powers of Europe. Another aspect of the nation-building work in Iraq that makes it such a momentous experiment is that Western-style democratic institutions have proven difficult to export to Islamic nations.

The deposed ruler of Iraq, Saddam Hussein, was a notorious and brutal dictator and killer who used mass assassination and genocidal warfare against his own people to maintain himself, his sons, and their corrupt political party in power. Hussein ruled as a despot for almost a quarter of a century, waged war on Iran (with American backing), and lined his pockets and those of his family and friends while his once oil-rich nation collapsed into poverty and despair.

Through its invasion and occupation of Iraq, the Bush administration is seen by most world leaders as responsible for the outcome of this experiment in nation building. Ironically, President Bush was extremely wary of committing the United States to costly and risky "nation building" efforts in the Third World. But the War on Terror he began after the terrorist attacks of September 11, 2001, has led to major commitments of U.S. military and civilian personnel in Iraq, Afghanistan, and elsewhere in the world, but especially in the Middle East. In consequence, Americans and their allies are working day and night to help build democratic institutions based on a constitution that the people feel is legitimate. But this experiment in building democracy during a military occupation is full of risks to all parties. The creation of stable democratic political institutions in Iraq will have to occur despite the tensions and mistrust that exist between Iraqis and their occupiers, and among the many religious, ethnic, and regional factions of Iraqis themselves. Enemies of the United States and Great Britain who oppose the occupation have been doing everything possible to thwart these efforts. At this writing, the Bush administration, which earlier decided not to wait for United Nations sanction for the invasion, is belatedly seeking more help from the international community.

As the world watches, the stakes of this political experiment increase. Social scientists and experts on democracy note that it is not easy to manufacture the conditions for liberal democracy. No quick fix replaces the hard work of building trust in laws, establishing checks and balances, and encouraging civil debate. Recent attempts to impose democracy in countries such as Cambodia, Bosnia, and Angola have failed dismally (Carnegie Endowment for International Peace, 2003; Zakaria, 2003). More critical voices claim that the United States and Britain have selfish eyes fixed on Iraq's oil wealth and simply want to get American troops out of Iraq. But once a major effort at building democracy is under way, as it is in Iraq, much depends on the hard, slow work of getting groups and leaders together to create the specific institutions of rule that will make the experiment work for Iraq's people. That will be the true test of whether the political experiment is a success or a failure.

FOCUS QUESTIONS:

• How do different types of political institutions establish their legitimacy?

• What are the main characteristics of different types of political regimes in the world today?

• What aspects of societies seem to facilitate the development of democracy and the rule of law?

THE NATURE OF POLITICS AND POLITICAL INSTITUTIONS

"Politics," Max Weber liked to tell his students, "is the slow boring of hard boards." By this he meant that political change is almost never achieved easily. Creating new political institutions or changing old ones, even just changing the leadership of existing institutions, usually requires years of effort. There will be endless meetings, ideological debates, fundraising, negotiations, and campaigning. At times, however, especially during times of revolutionary social change, the pace of political change is fast and furious.

We are living through a period of severe crisis and dramatic change in world politics. It is not at all clear that the democratic nation-state, the rule of law, and guarantees of the rights of minorities can be established in many parts of the world (Kaplan, 2001). In the view of many political sociologists, the twentieth century ended with the world in a state of political unrest and nationalistic conflict much like that at the end of the nineteenth century (Abu-Lugod, 1996). This uncertainty in world and national politics makes the comparative study of political institutions a major growth area in sociology.

Well before the invasion of Iraq in 2003, the fall of the Berlin Wall in 1989 symbolized the beginning of a new era in world politics. The cold war between the former Soviet Union and the Western capitalist democracies had dominated the politics of many parts of the world for more than 40 years. Although many nations, including the United States, still feel the effects of the arms race that accompanied the competition between the superpowers, with the end of the cold war has come an end to the nuclear "balance of terror" and to the suppression of political expression within the former Soviet empire. Nationality groups in the former Soviet republics are asserting their desire for independence or, at least, for protection of their rights within a multiethnic state.

The decline of authoritarian communist parties means that there is often no central authority to restrain populations who yearn to form their own independent nation or who covet the lands of their neighbors. The situation is not encouraging. The political upheavals in the former Yugoslavia, Africa, the Middle East, and India and Pakistan; the struggle to transform South Africa into a truly democratic state; and the rise of militias and other violently antigovernment hate groups in the United States—all these changes and others promise to make the comparative study of politics a central area of social-scientific research for years to come.

We can gain much insight into what the nationality groups in Eastern Europe, the black majority in South Africa, and others who are trying to effect political change are experiencing by looking more carefully at politics and political institutions and the place they occupy in national life. This section of the chapter reviews some of the essential concepts of politics, with special emphasis on power, authority, and legitimacy.

The second section explores the evolving nature of the nation-state, and the third section describes the political institutions that are typical of modern nations and compares the political regimes of states and territories throughout the world. The fourth section explores the major theories that have been proposed to explain why political institutions operate as they do and how they change or resist change. In the final section, we look at the role of the military in the political life of contemporary nations.

Politics, Power, and Authority

In any society, Harold Lasswell (1936) argued, politics determines "who gets what, when, and how." Different societies develop their own political institutions, but everywhere the basis of politics is competition for power. **Power** is the ability to control the behavior of others, even against their will. To be powerful is to be able to have your way even when others resist (Mills, 1959). The criminal's power may come through a gun and the threat of injury, but many people wield power over others without any threat of violence, merely through the agreement of the governed. We call such power *authority.* **Authority** is institutionalized power—power whose exercise is governed by the norms and statuses of organizations. Those norms and statuses specify who can have authority, how much authority is attached to different statuses, and the conditions under which that authority can be exercised.

Political institutions are sets of norms and statuses that specialize in the exercise of power and authority. The complex set of political institutions—judicial, executive, and legislative—that operate throughout a society forms the **state** (see Figure 20.1). This chapter will concentrate primarily on these explicitly political institutions, but keep in mind that in modern societies many institutions that are active in politics are not part of the state. Labor unions, for example, are economic institutions because they represent their members in bargaining with business owners and managers, but they play an active role in politics when they support particular political candidates or when they lobby for government-funded benefits for workers and their families.

When we look at the way in which conflicts over scarce resources such as wealth, power, and prestige occur, we are

Institutional Sector	Major Institutions	Examples of Key Organizations
The State	Executive	The President and his advisers The Cabinet
	Legislative	The U.S. Senate The U.S. House of Representatives
	Judicial	The U.S. Supreme Court Federal courts State courts
	Military	The armed forces The National Guard
	National security	The FBI The CIA Local police forces
Civil Politics	Political parties	The Democratic party The Republican party
	Interest groups	National Organization for Women National Rifle Association

Figure 20.1 Political and Military Institutions of the United States

looking at politics. From this perspective, there can be a politics of the family, in which its members vie for attention, respect, use of the family car, money, and other resources. There can be a politics of the school, in which teachers compete for benefits such as smaller class size or better students. And the politics of government at all levels of society determines how the society's resources are allocated among various groups or classes. This view of politics, which looks at competition for power and at conflict over the use of power in a variety of settings, was reflected in the works of Karl Marx and Max Weber, two pioneering sociologists who devoted much of their work to the analysis of politics and change in political institutions. According to Marx, the way power is distributed in a society's institutions is a feature of its system of stratification. People and groups that have power in economic institutions are most likely to have power in political institutions as well. However, much research in political sociology is devoted to the analysis of competition for power in political parties and electoral campaigns (Lipset, 1998). A central problem of political sociology is whether the electoral process can sustain people's belief in legitimate authority in a society despite inequalities in power and wealth (Kloby, 1997).

Legitimacy and Authority

A basic dilemma that every political institution must solve is how to exercise legitimate authority—that is, how to govern with the consent and goodwill of the governed. "You can't sit on bayonets," goes an old political expression. This is a way of saying that although a state can exercise its power through the use of police force or coercion, in the long run the use of force will not be sufficient to gov-

ern a society. When the Soviet Union abandoned the use of force to control its satellite states in Eastern Europe, the governments of those nations (Poland, Czechoslovakia, East Germany, Romania) were soon toppled by popular revolts. The communist parties in those nations had governed for too long without the consent of the governed—that is, without legitimacy.

But why do people consent to be governed without the use of force? For political sociologists since Weber's time, the answer to this question begins with the concept of legitimacy. As defined by political sociologist Seymour Martin Lipset (1981), **legitimacy** is the capacity of a society "to engender and maintain the belief that the existing political institutions are the most appropriate for the society" (p. 64). In other words, legitimacy results from citizens' belief in the norms that specify how power is to be exercised in their society. Even if they disagree with some aspects of their political institutions or dislike their current leaders, they still hold to an underlying belief in their political system.

TRADITIONAL, CHARISMATIC, AND LEGAL AUTHORITY Weber (1947) recognized that shared beliefs about legitimate authority may differ widely in different groups or societies. These differences result in three basic types of authority—traditional, charismatic, and legal—that have important effects on the way societies cope with social change. (See the Study Chart on page 586.)

1. *Traditional authority.* In tribal and feudal societies, Weber observed, **traditional authority** prevails. The rulers usually attain authority through heredity, by succeeding to power within a ruling family or clan. Traditional authority is legitimated by the people's idea of the sacred, and traditional leaders are thought

WEBER'S THREE TYPES OF AUTHORITY

TYPE	DEFINITION	EXAMPLE
Traditional Authority	Authority that is hereditary and is legitimated by traditional values, particularly people's idea of the sacred.	Tribal chiefs; absolute monarchs
Charismatic Authority	Authority that comes to an individual through a personal calling, often claimed to be inspired by supernatural powers, and is legitimated by people's belief that the leader does indeed have God-given powers.	Joan of Arc; Mahatma Gandhi
Legal Authority	Authority that is legitimated by people's belief in the supremacy of the law; obedience is owed not to a person but to a set of impersonal principles.	Presidents; prime ministers

to derive their authority from God. The absolute monarchs of Europe, for example, were believed to rule by "divine right." Traditional leaders usually embrace all the traditional values of the people they rule. This gives immense scope to their authority but makes it difficult for them and their systems of government to adapt to social changes that challenge those values. Thus the absolute monarchs of Europe had difficulty adapting their methods of governing to the growing power of new social classes like the proletariat and the bourgeoisie. The traditional chiefs of African societies today find it difficult to retain their authority as people in those societies gain more education and wealth and abandon their traditional village and agrarian way of life.

2. *Charismatic authority.* **Charismatic authority,** Weber's second type, finds its legitimation in people's belief that their leader has God-given powers to lead them in new directions. A charismatic leader, such as Jesus or Joan of Arc, comes to power not through hereditary succession but through a personal calling, often claimed to be inspired by supernatural powers. The charismatic leader usually develops a new social movement that challenges older traditions. Charismatic leaders may appear in all areas of life, "as prophets in religion, demagogues in politics, and heroes in battle. Charismatic authority generally functions as a revolutionary force, rejecting the traditional values and rebelling against the established order" (Blau & Scott, 1962, pp. 30–31).

Charismatic authority tends to bring about important social changes but is usually unstable because it depends on the influence of a single leader. Moreover, as noted in Chapter 8, charisma tends to become institutionalized as the charismatic leader's followers attempt to build the values and norms of their movement into an organization with a structure of statuses and roles and its own traditions. This process occurred in the early history of Christianity as the disciples built organizations that embodied the spirit and teaching of Christ.

3. *Legal authority.* Weber's third type of authority, **legal authority,** is legitimated by people's belief in the supremacy of the law. This type of authority "assumes the existence of a formally established body of social norms designed to organize conduct for the rational pursuit of specified goals. In such a system obedience is owed not to a person—whether a traditional chief or a charismatic leader—but to a set of impersonal principles" (Blau & Scott, 1962, p. 31). The constitutions of governments establish legal forms of authority. All formal organizations, not only modern nation-states but also factories, schools, military regiments, and so on, have legal forms of authority.

Ideally, legal forms of authority adhere to the principle of "government of laws, not of individuals." We may be loyal to a leader, but that leader, in turn, must adhere to the laws or regulations that establish the rights and obligations of the leader's office. In practice, individual leaders often abuse their office by using their authority for private gain, as we have seen in cases of government corruption ranging from Watergate to the Enron scandal. But legal systems and the rule of law cannot maintain their legitimacy for long if official wrongdoing is not punished (Breiner, 1996).

Of Weber's three basic types, legal systems of authority are the most adaptable to social change. In legal systems, when the governed and their leaders face a crisis, they can modify the laws to adapt to new conditions. Such modifications do not always occur easily or without political conflict, however, especially when momentous changes are under way.

POLITICAL CULTURE   Because the stability of political institutions depends so directly on the beliefs of citizens, we can readily see that political institutions are supported by cultural norms, values, and symbols like the Statue of Liberty. These are commonly referred to as the society's *political culture.* When we look at other societies, it is clear that their political cultures differ significantly from ours. Americans justify a political system based on competitive elections by invoking the values of citizen participation in politics and equality of political opportunity. Chinese Communist party leaders justify their single-party political system by downplaying the value of citizen participation in politics and asserting the need for firm leaders and a centralized state that will hold the society together and reduce inequalities. Because there is widespread skepticism about the ability of most people to participate in the political process, political sociologists believe that it will be difficult to promote democracy and the rule of law in many parts of the world (McCrone, 1996; Moore, 1968).

NATIONALISM   Perhaps the strongest and most dangerous political force in the world today is nationalism. **Nationalism** is the belief of a people that they have the right and the duty to constitute themselves as a nation-state (Hechter, 2000). Religion, language, and a history of immigration or oppression are among the shared experiences that can cause a people to feel that they ought to have their own state. The situation of the French-speaking population of Quebec is a good example. Their language and their history of discrimination in English-dominated workplaces set the Quebecois

The Lincoln Memorial is a shrine not only to a great President but also to the essential values of American political culture. It evokes feelings of reverence for the ideas of national unity and the rule of law.

apart from English-speaking Canadians. In 1995, the people of Quebec narrowly defeated a separatist referendum, but it is still possible that nationalist sentiments in Quebec may result in the formation of a new nation on the North American continent.

In the case of Quebec, where political institutions and the rule of law are well established, such a change would not necessarily be traumatic. But elsewhere in the world the rise of ethnic hostility and nationalism threaten to produce chaos. As former secretary of state Warren Christopher noted in a statement before the House Foreign Relations Committee, "If we don't find some way that the different ethnic groups can live together in a country, how many countries will we have? We'll have 5,000 countries rather than the one hundred plus we have now" (quoted in Blinder & Crossette, 1993, p. A1). Although the numbers may be exaggerated, few political sociologists doubt that new nations will be created as a consequence of nationalist conflicts in coming years.

CRISES OF LEGITIMACY   Societies occasionally undergo political upheavals like those that are occurring at this writing in Nigeria, Zimbabwe, the former Yugoslavia, the former Soviet Union, and Colombia. When these periods of unrest and instability involve enough of the citizens to such a degree that they challenge the legitimacy of the nation's political institutions, sociologists call the situation a *crisis of legitimacy.* For example, the Declaration of Independence was written during a crisis in which the American colonists challenged the legitimacy of British rule. In modern South Africa, where the black majority now rules with the cooperation and participation of the white minority, it still remains to be seen whether political legitimacy can be maintained in the face of extremes of wealth and poverty (Kloby, 1997).

In sum, as we scan the globe today, it is evident that the world's political ecology includes many states that are extremely stable and many others in which political instability threatens to develop into a crisis of legitimacy.

THE NATION-STATE IN CRISIS

The most important political territory in world affairs is the **nation-state,** the largest territory within which a society's political institutions can operate without having to face challenges to their sovereignty. Throughout the world, however, we see nation-states in crisis. In Africa, there has been persistent civil strife in many nations, particularly Somalia, Sierra Leone, Liberia, Angola, and Nigeria. In India, the world's most populous democracy, strife between Hindus and Muslims continues to threaten peace and political stability. In Indonesia, economic crisis and rampant corruption led to the fall of the Suharto regime. The nations of Central America are threatened by dictatorship and civil strife. At this writing, the stability of Afghanistan's national government and its ability to effect a peaceful leadership transition is very much in question. Nor is the United States immune from terrorism directed against the legitimacy of the nation—as we saw in the case of the Oklahoma City bombing and in the threats of terrorism by armed militia groups that challenge the state's legitimacy, detest the United Nations and other agencies of world government, and claim that the U.S. federal government's protection of abortion clinics or the rights of homosexuals and other minorities justifies armed resistance (Horowitz, 1999).

Fortunately, one can also point to improvements in the stability of some nations that have faced severe threats to their existence and to social peace within their borders. Northern Ireland, Chile, and Mali are examples of nations that have experienced marked improvements in national legitimacy in the recent past. On balance, however, the world has begun a new millennium facing serious challenges to the stability and viability of many of its nations.

We noted in Chapter 4 that nation-states claim a legitimate monopoly over the use of force within their borders. By this we mean that within a nation-state's borders, only organizations designated by the state (i.e., the government) may use force. But if the citizens believe that their government is legitimate, why is force necessary at all? The answer is that even when citizens believe their government to be legitimate, force (or, more often, the threat of force) may be needed to maintain order and ensure compliance with the law. For example, citizens may agree in principle that some of their income should be taken by the state through taxes to cover its expenses, but some individuals or groups (such as the Freemen in the United States) may attempt to avoid paying taxes.

In many parts of the world, bribery and corruption among public officials are commonplace. When elites do not observe the rule of law, it is difficult to convince less powerful and less wealthy citizens to do so. Conflicts arising from this issue take the form of scandals such as the Enron bankruptcy or the collusion between politicians and corrupt businesspeople in Russia. The point is that those charged with enforcing the laws should be beyond reproach. Otherwise the legitimacy of government and the laws is diminished in the minds of citizens—and in their behavior.

People who believe that the state uses its power in an illegitimate manner are not allowed to form private armies to resist the state. They may challenge the legitimacy of a particular law in the courts, where rational arguments and interpretations of law replace violent conflict. Neverthe-

less, all the institutions of the state, including the courts, are ultimately based on the state's monopoly over the use of force (Breiner, 1996). In societies in which the state is weak or in which its legitimacy is denied by particular groups, as in Afghanistan, it is common to find bandits, guerrilla armies, or terrorist groups.

Citizenship and the Rule of Law

The term *citizenship* refers to the status of membership in a nation-state. Like all statuses, citizenship is associated with a specific set of rights and obligations (Transaction, 1997). As political sociologist Reinhard Bendix put it: "A core element of nation-building is the codification of the rights and duties of all adults who are classified as citizens" (1969, p. 89). In other words, the roles of citizens in the society's political life must be made clear to all.

In feudal societies, most of the members of the society did not participate in political life. The needs of various groups in the population were represented, if at all, by the edicts of powerful landholders, generals, and clergymen. In modern nation-states, as a result of major social movements, this form of representation has been replaced by a form based on citizen participation, in which representatives elected by the citizens are entitled to vote on important public issues. But as societies adopted the principle of citizen participation, conflicts arose over the question of who would be included among a society's citizens. This is illustrated by the violent struggle over citizenship and political participation for blacks in South Africa, led by Nelson Mandela and the African National Congress, that finally resulted in a new constitution and majority rule.

RIGHTS OF CITIZENSHIP   The rights of citizenship include much more than the right to vote. T. H. Marshall (1964) defined those rights as follows:

- *Civil rights* such as "liberty of person, freedom of speech, thought and faith, the right to own property and to conclude valid contracts, and the right to justice."
- *Political rights* such as the right to vote and the right of access to public office.
- *Social rights* ranging from "the right to a modicum of economic welfare and security to the right to share fully in the social heritage and to live the life of a civilized being according to the standards prevailing in the society" (pp. 71–72).

This list does not necessarily imply that these rights actually exist in a given society or that they are shared

These new citizens at a swearing-in ceremony have had to demonstrate knowledge of basic English and awareness of the rights and responsibilities of U.S. citizens.

equally by all of the society's citizens. In the United States, for example, before 1920 women were considered citizens but were denied the right to vote. No society in which these rights are denied to citizens can be said to have established the rule of law within its boundaries.

PARTICIPATION IN LOCAL POLITICS   The question of who is entitled to full participation in politics is a key issue at the local level as well as at the national level. At the national level, participation is vital to a group's position in society, as can be seen in the struggles by women and blacks to win the right to vote. But in the cities and towns and communities in which daily life is lived, the same guarantee of full participation plays a role in social mobility.

W. E. B. Du Bois's *The Philadelphia Negro,* which we discussed in Chapter 1, includes this poignant petition by black community leaders to the city's mayor:

> We are here to state to your excellency that the colored citizens of Philadelphia are penetrated with feelings of inexpressible grief at the manner in which they have thus far been overlooked and ignored by the Republican party in this city. . . . We are therefore here, sir, to earnestly beseech of you as a faithful Republican and our worthy chief executive, to use your potent influence as well as the good offices of your municipal government, if not inconsistent with the public weal, to procure for the colored people of this city a share at least, of the public work and the recognition which they now ask for and feel to be justly due to them. (1967/1899, p. 374)

At the turn of the twentieth century, Philadelphia, like most American cities, was dominated by leaders who were among the town's richest and most powerful citizens. Immigrant workers and the poor were effectively excluded from political participation. The Great Depression drastically altered this pattern. Fearing that the misery created by the Depression would lead to unrest among the lower classes that could result in social disorder and even revolution, upper- and middle-class Americans began to look more favorably on the call for the creation of new social-welfare institutions. Such institutions would ease the plight of the poor and the unemployed without fundamentally changing capitalist economic institutions. At the same time, the poor and the working class began to exercise the right to vote in increasing numbers.

In the 150 years since the Civil War, the extension of full rights of citizenship and political participation has helped the United States avoid crises of legitimacy and civil strife. As we will see in the next section, however, by no means do all nations experience the same political developments, nor are they necessarily striving to extend the rights of participation in democratic political institutions to all citizens. Nor have all nations been as fortunate as the United States and others that have managed to solve their political crises without civil strife.

POLITICAL INSTITUTIONS: A GLOBAL VIEW

The central problem of contemporary politics, according to Seymour Martin Lipset, is this: "How can a society incorporate continuous conflict among its members and social groups and yet maintain social cohesion and legitimacy of state authority?" (1979, p. 108). This question has taken on particular urgency since World War II, when the colonial empires of Europe crumbled in the face of nationalistic movements and hundreds of new nations were created. In comparing the political institutions of the world's nations, it is helpful to begin by outlining the nature of the political institutions one expects to find in any modern state and noting the problems associated with their development.

Characteristics of Modern Political Systems

A RATIONAL ADMINISTRATION   Modern nations are governed by elected and appointed officials whose authority is defined by laws. To the extent possible, they are expected to use their authority for the good of all citizens rather than for their own benefit or for that of particular groups. They are forbidden to use their authority in illegitimate ways—that is, in ways that violate the rights of the citizens.

Modern political institutions usually specify some form of separation of powers. The authors of the U.S. Constitution, for example, were careful to create a system of checks and balances among the nation's legislative, executive, and judicial institutions so that abuses of authority by one could be remedied by the others. Thus when agents of the Nixon campaign organization were caught breaking into the Democratic party headquarters during the 1972 presidential election campaign and the President and some of his advisers were found to have covered up their role in this and other illegal activities, the impeachment proceedings initiated by the legislative and judicial branches of the government led to the President's resignation.

In many other nations, abuses of state authority are far more common. The power of rulers is unchecked by other political institutions, and although citizens may question the legitimacy of their rule, they are powerless to prevent the rulers' use of coercion in violation of their rights. Such states are often ruled by **demagogues,** or leaders who use personal charisma and political symbols to manipulate public opinion. Demagogues appeal to the fears of citizens and essentially trick them into giving up their rights of political participation. Hitler's ability to sway the suffering German masses made him the outstanding example of demagoguery in the twentieth century.

A PARTY SYSTEM   Organizations of people who join together in order to gain legitimate control of state authority—that is, of the government—are **political parties.** Parties may be based on ideologies, or they may simply represent competing groups with the same basic values. Many American political sociologists assert that nations must make certain that other political parties are able to compete with the ruling party (Janowitz, 1968; Lipset, 1995). Failure to protect the existence of an opposition party or parties leads to **oligarchy**—rule by a few people who seek to stay in office indefinitely rather than for limited terms of office.

Parties that seek legitimate power and accept the rule of other legitimate parties form a "loyal opposition" that monitors the actions of the ruling party, prevents official corruption, and sustains the hopes of people whose needs are not adequately met by the ruling party. Revolutionary political parties, it should be noted, do not view the state as legitimate. They therefore do not agree to seek authority through legitimate procedures like elections. For this reason they tend to be banned by most governments. On the other hand, many modern nations, including the United States, have banned or repressed nonrevolutionary communist parties, largely because of their opposition to private property and their sympathy for the communist-dominated regime of the former Soviet Union.

INSTITUTIONS FOR MAINTAINING ORDER   We have seen that states control the use of force within their borders. They also seek to protect their territories against attacks by other states. For these purposes, most states maintain police forces and armies. But sometimes the state's leaders have difficulty controlling these institutions, and military factions often seize power in what is called a *coup d'état* (or simply *coup*).

A coup usually results in the establishment of an oligarchy in which the state is ruled by a small elite that includes powerful members of the military. The *junta* is a special type of oligarchy in which military generals rule, usually with the consent of the most powerful members of the nation's nonmilitary elite. Their rule is commonly opposed by members of the intellectual professions, especially journalists, professors, writers, and artists. The dissent expressed by these individuals often leads to censorship and further repression of nonmilitary political institutions. Juntas have appeared in all parts of the world, especially where military institutions are strong and institutions that stand for democracy and the rule of law are weaker, as is the case in many developing nations.

Regimes that accept no limits to their power and seek to exert their rule at all levels of society, including the neighborhood and the family, are known as **totalitarian regimes;** Nazi Germany and the Soviet Union under Stalin are examples. Such regimes cannot exercise total power without the cooperation of the military. It would be incorrect, however, to attribute the existence of oligarchies and totalitarian regimes to the power of the military alone. On many occasions, military leaders have led coups that deposed the state's existing rulers and then turned over state power to nonmilitary institutions.

Nevertheless, in modern societies military institutions have become extremely powerful. Even before the end of World War II, Harold Lasswell (1941) warned that nations might be moving toward a system of "garrison states—a world in which the specialists in violence are the most powerful group in society" (p. 457). This theme was echoed by Dwight D. Eisenhower, one of the nation's celebrated soldier-Presidents. As he was leaving office, Eisenhower warned that the worldwide arms buildup, together with the increasing sophistication of modern weapons, was producing an "industrial-military complex." By this he meant that the military and suppliers of military equipment were gaining undue influence over other institutions of the state. (We discuss military institutions more fully in the final section of the chapter.)

SECULAR GOVERNMENTAL INSTITUTIONS   It is extremely difficult for minorities in a nation-state, be they religious minorities, ethnic or racial groups, or others, to feel that their rights are protected and honored if the institutions of government are dominated by members of the majority group. This is the case in Israel, where the Arab minority feels that, because Israel is a Jewish state, the institutions of government are biased against them. It is even more true in other nations of the Middle East, such as Saudi Arabia, Jordan, and Iran. These governments may be theocracies like Saudi Arabia, where religious leaders dominate the courts and the agencies of government, or democracies like Iran, where separation of church and state has made some progress in recent years but clerics still dominate many of the vital institutions of government and the press. As the world witnessed in the case of the Taliban regime in Afghanistan before 2002, a state ruled by religious tyrants can ensure law and order among its people, but lacking legitimacy among minority groups and the educated, it has great difficulty promoting economic and social development.

Abdullahi An-Na'im, a professor at Emory University in Atlanta and a political exile from the repressive regime in the African nation of Sudan, is an expert on political reform in the Islamic world. "It takes time," he observes, "and certain conditions of stability and prosperity, for societies to relax their defenses and actively allow civic engagement. It took the Americans 200 years, including a horrendous civil war and a long civil rights movement, and still you have far to go" (2002, p. 20). He also points out that every Muslim country

in the world today was either colonized by Western powers or controlled by Western powers the way Iran and Saudi Arabia were, and that "Colonialism was not in the business of promoting democratic values or institutions." The long struggle for separation of church and state and democratization of Muslim societies will never be imposed by Western power, he observes; it will have to come from democratic political movements in the Islamic world itself. There are already many precedents to draw on, despite the more visible influence of antidemocratic fundamentalists. This can also be said of many other nations in Asia, Africa, and Latin America: Democratic reforms will depend on the efforts of leaders within those regions as well (Reardon, 2002).

Democratic Political Systems

In contrast to oligarchies and totalitarian regimes, democratic societies offer all of their citizens the right to participate in public decision making. Broadly defined, **democracy** means rule by the nation's citizens (the Greek *demos*, from which the word *democracy* is derived, means "people"). In practice, democratic political institutions can take many different forms as long as the following conditions are met:

1. The political culture legitimizes the democratic system and its institutions.
2. One set of political leaders holds office.
3. One or more sets of leaders who do not hold office act as a legitimate opposition (Lipset, 1995, 2000).

The two most familiar forms of democratic political rule are the British and American systems. In the British *parliamentary* system, elections are held in which the party that wins a majority of seats in the legislature "forms a government," meaning that the leader of the party becomes the head of the government and appoints other party members to major offices. Once formed, the government generally serves for a specified length of time. If no party gains a majority of the legislative seats, a coalition may be formed in which smaller parties with only a few seats can bargain for positions in the government. Such a system encourages the formation of smaller parties.

In the American *representative* system, political parties attempt to win elections at the local, state, and national levels of government. In this system, the President is elected directly, and the party whose candidate is elected President need not have a majority of the seats in the legislature. Success therefore depends on the election of candidates to national office. In the United States, two political parties, the Republicans and the Democrats, have developed the resources and support necessary to achieve this goal.

Abdullahi An-Na'im on the Emory University campus. He sees a need for internal discourse "that has to be done by Muslims."

REPRESENTATIVE VERSUS DIRECT DEMOCRACY: CALIFORNIA DREAMIN'   Efforts to create direct democratic institutions, whereby everyone in the electorate votes to decide on an issue, periodically arise in representative democracies. Many Americans become impatient with representative democracy and its legislative deliberations and wish for more immediate solutions to high taxes, open immigration, or whatever problems are most troubling to them. California's 2003 gubernatorial recall election, in which movie star Arnold Schwarzenegger was much in the political spotlight, is a highly instructive case in the problems of direct democracy as applied to a large and complex society. California is larger than many nations of the world and boasts the world's fifth most important economy (Kolbert, 2003).

Twenty-five years ago, Californians voted on Proposition 13, an anti–property tax measure that was placed on the statewide ballot after voters signed enough petitions to qualify it as a referendum issue. The measure passed, and voters seemed so pleased with their experience in direct democracy that an average of 64 initiatives have been filed in California each year since then. The latest of these was a recall of the state's elected governor, Gray Davis, whom many voters blame for the state's multibillion-dollar deficit. But the referendum before that one, Proposition 49, initiated about $500 million a year of new expenditures but provided no new revenues for them, thus helping to drive up the state deficit. That referendum was financed in part by Arnold Schwarzenegger. Sociologist Mark Baldassare, research director of the Public Policy Institute of California, finds that many of the problems of

California's economy can be traced directly to changes in the way revenues are collected that resulted from Proposition 13. The state's education ratings, for example, once the pride of the nation, have declined sharply, and there is a growing crisis in housing and basic infrastructure, also largely due to the inability of local governments to fund needed rehabilitation projects. So while it may feel good to reject an unpopular governor or pass one's favorite piece of legislation immediately, the state has suffered from its rush to pass referendums. Direct democracy works well in small communities where town hall meetings and local citizen involvement are longstanding traditions, but as we see in the case of California, it is far from the best way to ensure political stability and legitimacy in a large polity (Baldassare, 2003).

SMALL PARTIES IN REPRESENTATIVE SYSTEMS   A disadvantage of representative democratic systems like that of the United States is that smaller parties, which have no hope of electing candidates to national office or even to offices in most statewide elections, are effectively barred from sharing power with the larger parties, as they often do in parliamentary systems. Even when they do win a few seats in a state legislature or in Congress, they are not asked to form coalitions that would place their leaders in high cabinet positions. But small parties do exist in American politics, and they often exert an extremely important influence on the outcomes of elections.

The Reform party created by Ross Perot and the Green party headed in the 2000 presidential election by Ralph Nader are examples of smaller parties that have garnered enough votes on the national level to alter the outcomes of presidential elections. Votes for Perot in 1992, many taken

Ross Perot of the Reform party and Ralph Nader of the Green party have both had an enormous impact on presidential elections, even though their parties did not win.

away from the Republican column, helped defeat George Bush; similarly, votes for Nader in 2000, most of which ordinarily would have gone to Al Gore, helped elect George W. Bush. In close elections, smaller parties can play a decisive role in the outcome of national elections. Ironically, however, their impact is often to swing hotly contested elections toward the candidate who is least in favor of their ideas. Does this mean that smaller parties have no positive effects? On the contrary, the existence of smaller parties, which represent specific sets of issues such as greater concern for the environment and consumer affairs, or reform of government, often push the major parties to adopt platforms that incorporate their demands. They also tend to enlist people in active political life who would otherwise be uninvolved or apathetic. So while the third parties or smaller, narrow-issue parties in a representative system like that of the United States normally do not share power after elections, they can have an enormous impact on the course of political history (Cohen, 2000).

ONE-PARTY SYSTEMS   Suppose that a nation has only one political party. Does this mean that it is undemocratic? Not in principle. A one-party state or region can be democratic as long as the citizens are free to form other parties, as long as the party's leaders can be replaced through democratic processes, and as long as the leaders do not violate the rights of citizens. But how likely are these conditions to be met if there are no opposing parties? The evidence suggests that the odds are against democracy in one-party states and regions, as we see in communist one-party states and many noncommunist one-party dictatorships (McCrone, 1996).

A Typology of Regimes

Social scientists use analyses of political institutions to develop typologies of political regimes. One such typology, which is widely used, was developed by J. Denis and Ian Derbyshire (1996). They classify national regimes into these categories:

1. *Liberal democracies.* These regimes are marked by multiparty elections, competitive parties, separation of powers, and guarantees of the rights of minorities and individuals. Examples are the United States, Canada, Great Britain, France, Brazil, and Japan.

2. *Emergent democracies.* These have constitutions that specify all or most of the institutions and processes of liberal democracies but are marked by problems in fully establishing democratic processes caused by one-party dominance, insurgencies, corruption, and so forth. They are often viewed as "liberal democracies on trial." Examples are Chile, Ivory Coast, Mali, Haiti, Morocco, Tunisia, and the Philippines.

The Sociological Observer

The boy on the throne is Faisal II, who became king of Iraq at the age of 4, when his father, King Ghazi, himself the son of Iraq's King Faisal I, was killed in a suspicious auto accident. The boy king ruled with the help of an adult regent until he himself was assassinated at the age of 18.

Although your answer will of course be highly subjective, what do you think Faisal seems to be feeling in this photo? In your opinion, what does this striking photo reveal about some of the weaknesses of hereditary rule? (See page 607 for further insights into the sociological content of this photo.)

Sotheby's Picture Library, London

3. *Communist regimes.* These are run by a "revolutionary dictatorship" and a single communist party that in principle is serving the interests of the working class. There are very limited guarantees of individual or minority rights. Political command over economic institutions is widespread but subject to market experimentation. China, North Korea, and Cuba are examples of existing communist regimes.

TABLE 20.1

World Political Regimes, 1989 and 1995

| | Number of States by Regime Type | | | | | | | |
Year	Lib-Dem	Em-Dem	Communist	Nat-Soc	Auth-Nat	Military	Islam-Nat	Absolutist
1989	50	33	16	21	16	16	0	12
1995	73	72	5	8	13	7	2	12
Change	+23	+39	−11	−13	−3	−9	+2	—

Key

Lib-Dem	Liberal Democratic	Auth-Nat	Authoritarian Nationalist
Em-Dem	Emergent Democratic	Islam-Nat	Islamic Nationalist
Nat-Soc	Nationalistic Socialist		

Source: Denis & Derbyshire, 1996.

4. *Nationalistic socialist regimes.* These are similar to communist regimes, with a single socialist party; however, they are more inclined to promote the interests of one national group over others and to allow private commerce. There is little or no protection of individual or minority rights. Examples are Iraq, Libya, Tanzania, and Syria.

5. *Authoritarian nationalist regimes.* The extreme nationalism of these regimes leads to intolerance and the exclusion of other races and creeds, often in the most brutal or genocidal fashion as in Nazi Germany or contemporary Zimbabwe.

6. *Military regimes.* These are ruled by a military elite or junta, usually with extremely limited protection of citizens' rights and no free elections. Current examples are Sierra Leone, Sudan, and Myanmar, although many emergent democracies and some liberal democracies are plagued by problems of civilian control over the military.

7. *Islamic nationalist regimes.* These are ruled by nationalistic political regimes devoted to fundamentalist Islam. Afghanistan under the Taliban and Iran are examples of this type of regime.

8. *Absolutist regimes.* These are usually ruled by an absolute monarch who passes power to successors through a hereditary line. Constitutional forms of government, popular assemblies, judiciary rules that counter the executive power, and political parties are banned. Sultanates, emirates, and traditional monarchies such as Jordan, Saudi Arabia, and Swaziland are examples of this type of regime.

Most of the world's people live in liberal or emergent democracies, although China, the world's most populous nation with more than 1 billion people, is ruled by a communist regime. Table 20.1 shows that there has been a trend toward more democratic regimes over the last few years, but this trend cannot be viewed as an inevitable progression. There are far too many obstacles to true democracy, even in the most stable democratic regimes, to allow us to take the future of democracy for granted. Indeed, we will see in the next section that persistent problems of poverty and inequalities in the distribution of power are among the most serious obstacles to the emergence of democratic institutions.

PERSPECTIVES ON POLITICAL INSTITUTIONS

Our description of democratic political institutions leaves open the question we posed earlier: How can a society accommodate competition or conflict among its members and social groups and yet maintain social cohesion and legitimacy of state authority (Lipset, 1998)? One answer is that a society can resolve conflicts through democratic processes. But this leads us to ask what conditions allow democratic institutions to form and, once formed, what ensures that they actually function to reduce the inequalities that engender conflict. The broadest test of democratic institutions is not whether they are embodied in formal organizations like legislatures and courts but whether they are able to address the problems of inequality and injustice in a society.

There are at least three schools of sociological thought regarding these questions. The first, derived from the functionalist perspective, asserts that democratic political institutions can develop and operate only when certain "structural prerequisites," such as a large middle class, exist in a society. The second school of thought, often referred to as the **power elite model**, is based on the conflict perspective. It is highly critical of the functionalist view, supporting its criticism with evidence of the ways in which so-called democratic political institutions actually operate to favor the affluent. A third position, known as the **pluralist model**, asserts that the existence of ruling elites does not mean that a society is undemocratic, as long as there are divisions within the elite and new groups are able to seek power and bargain for policies that favor their interests.

Structural Prerequisites of Democracy and the Rule of Law

Seymour Martin Lipset (1981, 1994) argues that democratic political institutions are relatively rare because if they are to exist and function well, the society must have attained a high level of economic and cultural development. To prove his theory, Lipset surveyed data on elections, civil rights, freedom of the press, and party systems in 48 nation-states, and subsequently in many other countries (Lipset, 1994). He found that the presence of these institutions was correlated with a nation's level of economic development, its degree of urbanization, the literacy of its citizens, and the degree to which its culture values equality and tolerates dissent. The Sociological Methods box on page 596 presents Lipset's findings in more detail.

In this cross-cultural research and in his research on democracy in the United States, Lipset attempted to show that the growth of a large middle class is essential to democracy. The middle-class population tends to be highly literate and, hence, able to make decisions about complex political and social issues. Moreover, middle-class citizens believe that they have a stake in their society and its political institutions. Accordingly, they often support policies that would reduce the class and status cleavages—the distinctions between the haves and the have-nots—that produce social conflict.

Sociologists who study voting behavior tend to support Lipset's thesis that the stability of democratic institutions rests on structural features that diminish conflict in a society. But their research has revealed something less than complete stability. Morris Janowitz (1978) made this observation, which is even more true today:

> Since 1952, there has been an increase in the magnitude of shifts in voting patterns from one national election to the next. . . . Increasingly important segments of the electorate are prepared to change their preference for president and also to engage in ticket splitting [voting for candidates of different parties]. (p. 102)

These shifts in voting behavior may represent new alignments of voters that could lead to major changes in the nation's public policies. The important point, however, is that these realignments, while they influence which parties and political leaders gain or lose power, do not affect the process of democratic competition itself.

The Power Elite Model

However important elections are to the functioning of democratic institutions, there are strong arguments against the idea that they significantly affect the way a society is governed. Some social scientists find, for example, that political decisions are controlled by an elite of rich and powerful individuals (Zweigenhaft & Domhoff, 1998). This "power elite" tolerates the formal organizations and procedures of democracy (elections, legislatures, courts, etc.) because it essentially owns them and can make sure that they act in its interests no matter what the outcome of elections may be. C. Wright Mills, the chief proponent of this point of view, has described the power elite as follows:

> The power elite is composed of men whose positions enable them to transcend the ordinary environments of ordinary men and women. They are in positions to make decisions having major consequences. . . . They are in command of the major hierarchies and organizations of modern society. They rule the big corporations. They run the machinery of the state. . . . They direct the military establishment. They occupy the strategic command posts of the social structure. . . . The power elite are not solitary rulers. . . . Immediately below the elite are the professional politicians of the middle levels of power, in the Congress and in the pressure groups, as well as among the new and old upper classes of town and city and regions. Mingling with them in curious ways . . . are those professional celebrities who live by being continually displayed. (1956, p. 4)

When it was first published, Mills's *The Power Elite* created a stir among sociologists. Mills challenged the assumption that societies that have democratic political institutions are in fact democratic. He asserted instead that party politics and elections are little more than rituals. Power is exercised by a ruling elite of immensely powerful military, business, and political leaders that can put its members into positions of authority whenever it wishes to do so. Mills's claim was significant for another reason as well: Although Mills appreciated Marx's views on the role of class conflict in social change, he did not believe that

SOCIOLOGICAL METHODS   Diagramming Social Change

The accompanying chart is an example of how a diagram can effectively communicate ideas about the directions and influences of social change. This diagram presents the social structures from which democratic political institutions arise (listed on the left) and some possible further consequences of the emergence of those political institutions (on the right).

The arrows in the diagram indicate either conditions that contribute to democracy or possible consequences of the emergence of democratic institutions. As in most social-scientific analysis, the author, political scientist Seymour Martin

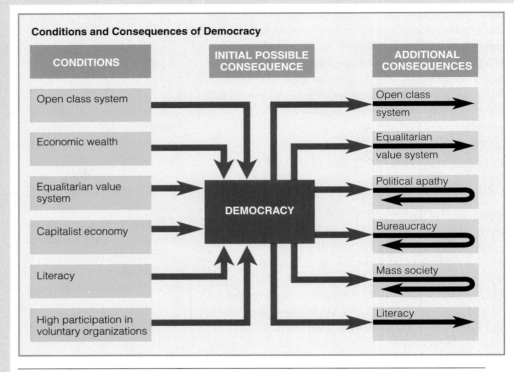

Conditions and Consequences of Democracy

CONDITIONS — INITIAL POSSIBLE CONSEQUENCE — ADDITIONAL CONSEQUENCES

Open class system, Economic wealth, Equalitarian value system, Capitalist economy, Literacy, High participation in voluntary organizations → DEMOCRACY → Open class system, Equalitarian value system, Political apathy, Bureaucracy, Mass society, Literacy

Source: From *Political Man: The Social Bases of Politics,* by Seymour Martin Lipset (Baltimore: Johns Hopkins University Press, 1981, expanded and updated edition). Reprinted by permission of the author.

Lipset, is careful not to make direct assertions about causality. He does not state, for example, that an open class system (measured by upward and downward social mobility) inevitably leads to the emergence of democratic regimes. Instead, social mobility and the other aspects of social structure listed on the left are "necessary but not sufficient" preconditions for the emergence of democracy. That is, they must exist to some degree in a society, but they are not sufficient to "cause" democracy. For that to happen, other conditions must also be present, such as the leadership of people who can sacrifice their desire for personal power in the interest of creating democratic political institutions. George Washington, for example, is revered as a pioneer of democracy, because when he had the chance to become a monarch, he chose to relinquish personal power and lead the newly independent colonies toward the creation of a constitutional monarchy.

Note that the arrows on the right side of the diagram suggest that democratic rule is associated with the emergence of social phenomena that run counter to democracy. Bureaucracy, for example, is a common consequence of democratic regimes. Laws passed by democratic processes tend to spawn administrations designed to deliver services, provide protection, enforce regulations, and much more. These bureaucracies, in turn, may stifle democracy by replacing the will of the majority with rules, regulations, and procedures. Note, however, that these excesses can be corrected by the actions of democratic institutions (e.g., further legislation). The arrows merely indicate that democratic rule has certain counterdemocratic consequences.

In an expansion of the comparative research on which this diagram is based, Lipset makes the following comment:

Not long ago, the overwhelming majority of the members of the United Nations had authoritarian

systems. As of the end of 1993, over half, 107 out of 186 countries, have competitive elections and various guarantees of political and individual rights—that is, more than twice the number two decades earlier in 1970. (1994, p. 1)

But Lipset, a veteran of many decades of close observation of democratic rule in nations throughout the world, is cautious about predicting a trend toward the emergence of democratic regimes. Too many nations, like Nigeria and Russia, have turned toward more authoritarian rule after promising attempts to develop democratic political institutions. Above all, Lipset warns:

[If nations] can take the high road to economic development they can keep their political houses in order. The opposite is true as well. Governments that defy the elementary laws of supply and demand will fail to develop and will not institutionalize genuinely democratic systems. (1994, p. 1) the working class could win power without joining forces with the middle class. He therefore attempted to demonstrate the existence of a ruling elite to an educated public, which would then, he hoped, be able to see through the rituals of political life and make changes through legitimate means.

Other sociologists have questioned the power elite thesis on methodological grounds. For example, Talcott Parsons (1960) noted that the power elite was supposed to act behind the scenes rather than publicly. Therefore its actions could not be observed, and the power elite thesis could not be either proved or disproved. The power elite thesis therefore was not scientifically sound, according to Parsons.

Numerous adherents of the power elite thesis have attempted to show that a ruling elite does indeed exist and that its activities can be observed. One of the best known of these researchers is Floyd Hunter (1953), whose classic studies of Atlanta's "community power structure" attempted to show that no more than 40 powerful men were considered to have the ability to make decisions on important issues facing the city and its people. Most of these men were conservative, cost-conscious business leaders. The Hunter study stimulated many attempts to find similar power structures in other cities and in the nation as a whole (Domhoff, 1983; Zweigenhaft & Domhoff, 1998). But although the term *power structure* has found its way into the language of politics, these studies have been strongly criticized for basing their conclusions on what people say about who has power rather than on observations of what people with power actually do (Oppenheimer, 1999). On the other hand, recent corporate scandals—especially the Enron case—lend support to Mills's original power elite thesis because of the cozy relationships that exist between many energy and media corporate leaders and core members of the Bush administration (see the Global Social Change box on page 598).

The Pluralist Model

The power elite thesis has not gone unchallenged in the research literature. In another famous study of politics—this one in New Haven, Connecticut—Robert Dahl (1961) found that different individuals played key roles in different types of decisions. No single group was responsible for all of the decisions that might affect the city's future. No power elite ruled the city, Dahl argued. Instead, several elites interacted in various ways on decisions that affected them. In situations in which the interests of numerous groups were involved, a plurality of decision makers engaged in a process of coalition building and bargaining.

The pluralist model calls attention to the activities of interest groups at all levels of society (Reidy, 2001). **Interest groups** are not political parties; they are specialized organizations that attempt to influence elected and appointed officials on specific issues. These attempts range from **lobbying**—the process whereby interest groups seek to persuade legislators to vote in their favor on particular bills—to making contributions to parties and candidates who will support their goals. Trade unions seeking legislation that would limit imports, organizations for the handicapped seeking regulations that would give them access to public buildings, and ethnic groups seeking to influence U.S. policy toward their country of origin are among the many kinds of interest groups that are active in the United States today (Oberschall, 1996).

In recent decades, as the number of organized interest groups has grown, so has the complexity of the bargaining that takes place between them and the officials they want to influence. Social scientists who study politics from the pluralist perspective frequently wonder whether the activities of these groups threaten the ability of elected officials to govern effectively. For example, a study of a federal economic development project in Oakland, California, found that the personnel in the agency responsible for such projects had to learn to deal with supporting and opposing interest group leaders and elected officials throughout the life of the project. It took 6 years of constant negotiation on many unanticipated issues—affirmative action in employment, environmental concerns, design specifications—before a firm could win a contract to build an airplane hangar (Pressman & Wildavsky, 1984).

Politics and Social Interaction

From the interactionist perspective, political institutions, like all others, are "socially constructed" in the course of human interaction. They do not simply come into being as structures of norms, statuses, and roles and then continue to function without change. Instead, they are continually being shaped and reshaped through interaction. This view closely parallels the popular notion that democratic political institutions must be continually challenged if they are to live up to their ideals. Otherwise they will become oligarchies that rule for the benefit of small cliques rather than for the mass of citizens (Oberschall, 1996).

The question of how social interaction affects a society's political institutions was a central concern of the leading philosophers of ancient Greece. In his *Politics,* for example, Aristotle "held that humans were made for life in society just as bees were made for life in the hive" (Bernard, 1973, p. 30). Because humans are "political animals," Aristotle believed, their constant discussions of political issues and their ability to form coalitions allow them to arrive at a consensus regarding what a good society is and how it should be

GLOBAL SOCIAL CHANGE   The Power Grid

Scrutiny and criticism come with being the Earth's sole superpower. World attention and, often, harsh criticism of problems with democracy and the rule of law in the United States are to be expected. If the United States is to successfully promote democracy elsewhere in the world, it must practice it at home. This article in the London *Financial Times*, published as the Enron bankruptcy scandal was beginning to unfold, shows how closely American politics is watched abroad:

Enron was, politically speaking, the best connected company in America. It donated millions to both main political parties but was closer to Republicans, especially Mr Bush, who, when he was governor of Texas, referred to Mr Lay [Enron's Chief Executive Officer] as "Kenny Boy." Half a dozen senior officials in the administra-

tion either worked directly for the company or held substantial amounts of equity in it.

Last week it emerged that Vice-President Dick Cheney spoke to Indian government officials in June in an effort to help Enron recoup large debts on an investment in an Indian power plant. The White House said he had not been asked to speak to India by Enron.

There have not been, though, any specific allegations that anyone acted improperly, still less evidence of wrongdoing. But corporate contributions are the life-blood of the American political system, and companies do not give money unless they think they are getting something in return. Enron clearly benefited from a number of policy initiatives, although its defenders claim the policies would have been implemented anyway and the com-

pany did not always succeed in winning changes.

The risk for Mr Bush—indeed, for all politicians who received donations from the company—is the sheer scale of the investigations now under way. No company can withstand the current level of scrutiny without yielding up embarrassing information, and the record of such investigations suggests they acquire a momentum of their own that can result in unpredictable consequences. (Barker et al., 2002)

The Enron bankruptcy, the largest in U.S. history, and the scandals it revealed have indeed sent shock waves rippling throughout the American economy and its political system. The U.S. Attorney General, John Ashcroft, had to recuse himself from the investigation because he had earlier accepted Enron campaign funds for his unsuccessful Senate campaign. The Attorney General's entire staff of U.S. attorneys in Houston had to recuse themselves because of conflicts of interest. As chair of the President's energy policy committee, Vice President Cheney met with Enron and other corporate energy executives more than six times, but he agreed to meet with representatives of environmental groups only once, when the energy task force's report was essentially ready for public release. To many Americans of all political parties, these facts were a sad reminder of the problem of undue influence of powerful actors on American politics and social policy.

The Enron Corporation and its accounting firm, Arthur Andersen, were among the largest contributors to the President's campaign in 2000. No major party or leader, however, was free of criticism; the tainted funds were spread widely in both houses of Congress and among members of both major political parties.

M. Wuerker

governed. Unfortunately, he concluded, existing political systems were flawed. The divisions and gaps in interaction created by wealth prevented consensus and created conflict. Moreover, people in occupations like farming did not have enough time to examine all the sides of an issue and work toward agreement with their fellow citizens. In a good society, therefore, all the citizens must be free to devote their full attention to political affairs. (In practice, Greek democracy required an economy based on the labor of slaves.)

Nearly 2,000 years later, the Italian political adviser Niccolò Machiavelli (1469–1527) again took up the relationship between human interaction and political institutions. Machiavelli believed that political institutions had to be based on the recognition that all human beings are capable of evil as well as good. In his *Discourses,* he made this observation:

> All those who have written upon civil institutions demonstrate . . . that whosoever desires to found a state and give it laws, must start by assuming that all men are bad and ever ready to display their vicious nature, whenever they may find an occasion for it. (1950/1513, vol. 1, p. 3)

Some people, he admitted, are merciful, faithful, humane, and sincere, but even though there are virtuous people in every society, political leaders must anticipate the worst possible behavior. In his most famous work, *The Prince,* Machiavelli suggested that the wise ruler or prince would be a master of astuteness—the ability to "read" the intentions of allies and opponents in the tiniest of gestures and reactions—and would also have mastered the skills of diplomacy. He used the following comparison to make this point:

> A prince . . . must imitate the fox and the lion,
> for the lion cannot protect himself from the traps,
> and the fox cannot defend himself from wolves.
> One must therefore be a fox to recognize traps,
> and a lion to frighten wolves. Those that wish
> to be only lions do not understand this. (1950/1513, vol. 1, p. 66)

In the five centuries since they were originally formulated, these ideas have had a powerful influence on political thinkers. The authors of the U.S. Constitution, for example, attempted to avoid situations in which "foxes" or "lions" could take advantage of the weaknesses of others. They anticipated the more self-serving aspects of political interaction rather than simply assuming that a new society would bring about cooperation among citizens: "If men were angels, no government would be necessary" (*The Federalist,* No. 51). This is why, as noted earlier in the chapter, they planned a government in which each of the major branches would be able to check any abuse of power by the other branches.

POLITICAL INTERACTION IN THE "DEMOCRATIC EXPERIMENT" In the 1830s, Alexis de Tocqueville, a young French aristocrat, visited the world's first experiment in national democracy. Although the United States was by no means a true democracy, since it condoned slavery, indentured servants, and war against Native Americans, European social thinkers took a keen interest in the model of citizen rule through democratic institutions that was being established in the new nation. Tocqueville was stunned by the "tumult" of American political interactions, which "must be seen in order to be understood." In America, he wrote, political activity was in evidence everywhere:

> A confused clamor is heard on every side; and a thousand simultaneous voices demand the immediate satisfaction of their social wants. Everything is in motion around you; here, the people of one quarter of a town are met to decide upon the building of a church; there, the election of a representative is going on; a little further, the delegates of a district are traveling in a hurry to the town in order to consult upon some local improvements; or, in another place, the labourers of a village quit their plows to deliberate upon the project of a road or a public school. (1980/1835, p. 78)

Tocqueville expressed surprise at the fact that although they were denied the vote, in the United States "even the women frequently attend public meetings, and listen to political harangues as recreation after their household labours" (p. 79). In fact, the culture of America was so suffused with political issues that he believed Americans could not converse except to discuss issues. The typical American, he observed, "speaks to you as if he were addressing a meeting" (p. 79).

Tocqueville was concerned that democratic societies might encourage the rise of demagogues who could manipulate the masses, but his observations persuaded him that the immense number of competing groups in the American political system would prevent this from happening. And while he worried about the possibility of political conflict tearing the young nation apart, he became convinced that Americans' love of liberty and belief in the legitimacy of their political institutions would carry them through any crisis that might arise.

THE MEDIA AND POLITICAL COMMUNICATION Television has brought about vast changes in the politics of democratic societies. The televised debate between Vice President Richard Nixon and John F. Kennedy in 1960 marked the first time an entire nation could watch candidates for the nation's highest office as they presented themselves and their views to a mass audience. Most viewers believed that Kennedy came across as the more attractive candidate, and he subsequently won the election. From then on, all election campaigns in the United States, except those for the smaller local offices, increasingly relied on the media to reach voters with political messages. Campaigns had always made extensive use of newspapers and other print media, but after 1960 television and radio became by far the dominant media of political communication.

Table 20.2 demonstrates the overwhelming importance of television viewing as compared to other forms of media consumption in the United States. To understand the influence of the major networks (i.e., ABC, CBS, NBC, Fox, and TBS), one needs only to see that the average adult in the United States spends 865 hours per year watching network broadcasts. Radio is also an extremely important medium, but these comparative figures suggest that newspapers command a relatively insignificant proportion of media attention. In fact, however, individuals who influence other people's opinions of events and political leaders tend to spend far more time reading newspapers and magazines than the average citizen does. Sociologists refer to such individuals, who are well informed and like to reach independent judgments about current events, as *opinion leaders*. Although they may be a minority in any community, their views can help sway the opinions and votes of others. In consequence, political campaigns attempt to get their positions and candidates covered in the print media, but as the actual election approaches, they spend millions of dollars on television advertising designed to reach the mass of voters, many of whom are undecided until just before election day.

Today television dominates most major political campaigns, and its influence has stimulated the movement for campaign finance reform. Candidates who can afford to buy television advertising have advantages that other candidates simply cannot match. Thus, in recent elections in the United States, billionaires like Ross Perot, Michael Bloomberg, John Corzine, Steven Forbes, and many others have relied on personal funds to buy enough television advertising to make their names household words among voters who might never have heard of them before the campaign. For nonbillionaires, the greatest amount of campaign time is now spent not meeting crowds of voters but meeting crowds of rich donors. As we have seen in the case of Enron, this imbalance of influence in American politics has stimulated a powerful campaign finance reform movement.

In many European nations, political candidates and parties receive free television time and there are structured debates that present candidates and issues to voters. Candidates cannot simply purchase as much media advertising as they can afford. The United States probably will not

adopt a similar system in the near future, but sociological research and polling data show that most U.S. voters want significant reforms in the current system of campaign finance (Duffy et al., 2002; Goidel, Gross, & Shields, 1999).

For those out of power, political communication and the ability to gain the attention of the mass media are major concerns. Sociologist Todd Gitlin (1993) reminds us how important this aspect of politics was to the student radicals who challenged U.S. policies in Vietnam in the 1960s and 1970s. They were only one among many social movements of that period that discovered the great power of television in a society with mass publics (see Chapter 8). Through skillful use of television coverage of staged confrontations, sit-ins, and demonstrations, it was possible for a relatively small group of activists to mobilize larger numbers of supporters. The labor movement had used similar tactics in earlier decades, but by the 1960s it had become easier to communicate to mass audiences and sway public opinion—at least in a society in which the press, including the television news, is relatively free from governmental interference.

In a world in which the techniques of communication are increasingly sophisticated, it becomes ever more important to analyze political communications and to read between the lines of political rhetoric. Political jargon often masks deeds that leaders would rather not admit to.

TABLE 20.2

Average Media Consumption, United States, 2002 (persons 18 and over)

	Hours per Person
Total	3,560
Television	1,655
Broadcast TV	865
Network stations	804
Independent stations	61
Cable and satellite	789
Basic cable and satellite	653
Premium cable and satellite	137
Radio	985
Recorded music	247
Daily newspapers	148
Consumer magazines	104
Consumer books	88
Home video	67
Video games	90
Box office	12
Consumer Internet	164

Note: These figures are projected from partial data.

Source: *Statistical Abstract*, 2002.

THEN AND NOW

Television Reshapes the Campaign Trail

In 1948, Harry Truman campaigned across the United States, making speeches from a special car at the back of a train. This was one of the last "whistle stop" campaigns in American presidential politics. The older style of campaign, in which the candidate attempted to meet as many voters as possible, was accompanied by a great deal of "back room" politics—the candidate met with local political leaders, who bargained for favors in return for bringing out their supporters on election day. These dealings, of course, were not visible to the people who gathered at the "whistle stops."

Today the power of television brings the candidate and the campaign message into the homes of millions of voters, diminishing the importance of town-by-town campaigning. But television demands camera skills that many politicians do not necessarily possess. Television has also vastly increased the importance of fundraising to pay the high costs of television advertising. The influence of local political party leaders has declined, but "back room" politics and the influence of wealthy and powerful contributors have yet to disappear.

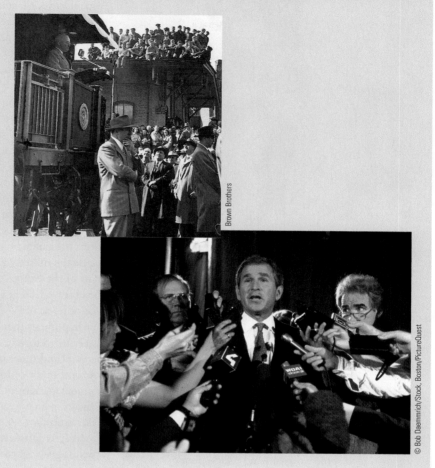

Brown Brothers

© Bob Daemmrich/Stock, Boston/PictureQuest

George Orwell, a master of political commentary, made this point in his essay "Politics and the English Language":

> Political speech and writing are largely the defense of the indefensible. . . . Defenseless villages are bombarded from the air, the inhabitants driven out into the countryside, the cattle machine-gunned, the huts set on fire with incendiary bullets: this is called *pacification.* Millions of peasants are robbed of their farms and sent trudging along the roads with no more than they can carry: this is called *transfer of population* or *rectification of frontiers.* People are imprisoned for years without trial, or shot in the back of the neck or sent to die of scurvy in Arctic lumber camps: this is called *elimination of unreliable elements.* Such phraseology is needed if one wants to name things without calling up mental pictures of them. (1950, p. 136)

If Orwell sounds highly pessimistic about the conduct of politics, remember that he was writing in a time of even greater political cruelty and chaos than our own. In his lifetime, he had seen nations with the most advanced constitutions commit the most brutal acts of war and repression. The point of his essay is that to be politically objective, to seek the true meanings of political acts and the consequences of political beliefs, we must "start at the verbal end":

> The great enemy of clear language is insincerity. When there is a gap between one's real and one's declared aims, one turns as it were instinctively to long words and exhausted idioms, like a cuttlefish squirting out ink. . . . If you simplify your English . . . when you make a stupid remark its stupidity will be obvious, even to yourself. Political language . . . is designed to make lies sound truthful and murder

George Orwell, the author of *Animal Farm* and *1984*, addressed the abuse of language for political purposes in his essay "Politics and the English Language."

respectable, and to give an appearance of solidity to pure wind. One cannot change this all in a moment, but one can at least change one's own habits, and from time to time one can even, if one jeers loudly enough, send some worn-out and useless phrase . . . into the dustbin where it belongs. (p. 140)

MILITARY INSTITUTIONS

The problem of civilian control of the military remains the most important issue in many of the world's nation-states. At this writing, for example, Nigeria, the largest emergent democratic regime in Africa, is experiencing a difficult transition from military absolutism to constitutional democracy. After years of harsh military dictatorship, extreme political and economic corruption, and suppression of the media, universities, and the courts by a military "strongman," two major parties are competing peacefully for electoral support. The press is thriving again, and exiled intellectuals and artists are returning (DARE, 1999). Nigeria, however, is not an isolated example of the problem of social control over the military. Throughout the world, the problem of how to maintain

the allegiance of the military often looms as the largest threat to democracy and to the legitimacy of governments. These situations raise a major question in political sociology: How can states control their military institutions? Answers are to be found in knowledge about the nature of the modern military as a social institution as well as in the political culture of different nations.

A key question about military institutions in all societies, and especially in democracies, is how the military can be made to submit to the guidance of civilian political institutions. A democratic society cannot remain democratic for long if the military usurps the authority granted to it by the civilian institutions of the nation-state. This is a common occurrence—taking the form of coups led by military "strongmen"—in nations in which the military is not adequately controlled by other institutions.

The problem of civilian control of the military was recognized by Tocqueville, who noted that in aristocratic nations the military could be controlled by the government because the military leaders were aristocrats and therefore were part of the court. "The officer is noble, the soldier is a serf," he observed. "The one is naturally called upon to command, the other to obey" (1980/1835, p. 128). Tocqueville formed the hypothesis that greater equality would make a nation less likely to go to war, since its citizens would have more to lose in wars and more power to prevent them. Yet he also feared the ambitions of military leaders in democratic nations. "In democratic armies," he wrote, "all the soldiers may become officers, which . . . immeasurably extends the bounds of military ambition" (p. 129).

Morris Janowitz (1960), a highly innovative political sociologist, responded to Tocqueville's concerns in his analysis of the history of military institutions in democratic nations. He argued that the military has often played a crucial role in establishing and protecting democratic institutions. In the Greek city-states and the Roman republic, as well as the democracies that emerged from the revolutions of the late eighteenth century, citizens were obligated to serve in the armed forces. The military institution could function only through the enlistment of "citizen soldiers." Because the citizen soldier was committed to democratic institutions and was serving because such service was a requirement of citizenship, the military would be unlikely to take over the functions of democratic political institutions. Soldiers would presumably place the values of their society above the demands of the military.

When Janowitz reviewed the impact of new methods of warfare on the military, he concluded that because of the increasing sophistication of military technology, the military in many modern nations had become staffed by "professional soldiers" for whom service in the armed forces is a career. In addition, the shift to a volunteer military, rather than one that depends on citizen soldiers, may threaten the control of the military by civilian institutions (Janowitz, 1960).

The Economic Role of the Military

Even in the United States, where the threat of a coup is not considered great, the military has so much influence on the economy that social control of the military becomes difficult. The function of the armed forces is, of course, the defense of the nation-state; in the United States, however, the military also serves an important economic function as a producer of jobs and revenue. The economies of states like Alaska, Connecticut, Maryland, California, and Virginia became highly dependent on the wealth gained from defense contracts during the decades of the cold war and the arms race. In addition, the private companies that vie for military contracts became a major source of employment, often providing some of the most highly paid and secure jobs in their regions. Throughout the United States, the influence of the military "pork barrel"—federal spending on defense contracts and the resulting employment—often makes it difficult for legislators to support cuts in military budgets and programs.

The growth of military production in different parts of the United States also adds to the potential for armed conflict elsewhere in the world. Faced with declining domestic sales, U.S. arms makers seek to supply advanced weapons to buyers in other nations. Indeed, weapons account for a significant portion of U.S. exports; the United States is the world's leading exporter of conventional weapons (Boese, 1998).

Military Socialization

Social control of the military is partially explained by the professional socialization of military personnel. This point was vividly illustrated by Tom Wolfe in *The Right Stuff* (1980). "There were many pilots in their thirties," Wolfe wrote, "who to the consternation of their wives, children, mothers, fathers, and employers, volunteered to go active in the reserves and fly in combat in the Korean War." This was in vivid contrast to the attitude of the foot soldiers in that war, whose morale during some periods of the prolonged conflict "was so bad it actually reached the point where officers were prodding men forward with gun barrels and bayonets" (p. 32).

This contrast between the "fighter jocks," socialized to want to prove they had "the right stuff" and thus win pro-

motion to higher ranks, and the far more cautious draftees and recruits on the ground, raises a series of questions: What motivates a person to face death in war? Is it desire for glory and advancement? Is it fear of punishment? Is it the pressure of collective action? From an interactionist perspective, this contrast results from the ways in which people are socialized in military institutions, coupled with their definitions of the situation. The fighter jocks define the situation as one in which they must act as they do—it is the job for which they have volunteered. The draftees do not define the situation in the same way; they are more interested in their own survival and in adhering to group norms like "Never volunteer."

In his classic study of socialization in a military academy, Sanford Dornbusch (1955) showed that traditional military socialization processes are designed to develop a high level of motivation and commitment to the institution. Those processes include the following:

- *Suppression of previous statuses.* Through haircuts, uniforms, and the like, the recruit is deprived of visible clues to his or her previous social status.
- *Learning of new norms and rules.* At the official level, the recruit is taught obedience to the rules of the military; through informal socialization, he or she is taught the culture of the military institution.
- *Development of solidarity.* Both informal socialization and harsh discipline build solidarity and lasting friendships among recruits; they learn to depend on one another.
- *The bureaucratic spirit.* The recruit is taught unquestioning acceptance of tradition and custom; orders are taken and given from morning to night.

The controversy that greeted President Bill Clinton's order that the military cease discriminating against homosexuals is an indication of the sensitivity that surrounds issues of military socialization. Gay men and women have been serving in the armed forces for decades but have had to deny their sexual preferences in military examinations and screening procedures. Objections to openly admitting homosexuals into the military centered on the possibility that gay sexuality would be a divisive influence and a detriment to fighting morale. Gay activists in and outside the military answered that there is no reason why the norms of military conduct would not apply to openly gay soldiers just as they always have to gay and nongay military personnel.

Despite his personal opposition to the President's order, General Colin L. Powell, then chairman of the Joint Chiefs of Staff, stated that "we know that there will be changes and . . . you and the Commander in Chief [the President] can always count on us for faithful support and execution of your decisions" (quoted in Schmitt, 1993, p. A1). General Powell was referring not only to the issue of acceptance of homosexuals in the military but also to the issue of cuts in military budgets. His statement indicates the control the constitutional rule of law provides over the powerful institution of the military.

Social Change and Military Institutions

Like all major social institutions, the military has undergone many changes, some of which can be seen in the transformation of American military institutions in the past two centuries. In the era of the citizen soldier, people expected to be called into service only in emergency situations and to be trained by a small cadre of professional officers. Today, in contrast, the permanent armed forces have more than 1.5 million uniformed members, and the annual military budget amounts to $348 billion (*Statistical Abstract,* 2002). In response to the war on terrorism and the projected need for more—and more sophisticated—military hardware and training, the Bush administration requested an increase of 14 percent in the defense budget, to $379 billion in 2003, with further increases projected for subsequent years. The world's only superpower now spends more on defense than all of its allies combined.

Today the requirements of highly technological forms of warfare and the need to maintain a complex set of military organizations throughout the world have changed our concept of a military career. The military as a modern social institution requires professionally trained officers who commit themselves to spending much of their working lives in the military. Thus, as the military has evolved, so has its need to recruit and train career officers in specialized military academies.

Over time, the institutions that train professional soldiers have had to adapt to certain changes. For example, as the larger society has accepted the demand for gender equality and women have gained access to occupations that were previously reserved for men, the military has had to redefine its historical perception that women soldiers are better equipped for desk duty than for service in combat. Although to date few women have fought in ground warfare, women in the military are now being trained for combat roles. The idea of women engaging in ground combat remains controversial among military traditionalists—primarily males—but the increasing automation of air and ground combat makes it more reasonable for women to assume the same military roles as men (West, 1998), as some are doing in Iraq at this writing. Yet the massive military buildup for the war against

terrorism will have important consequences for other institutions for many years to come. Education, Social Security, health care, and many other social-welfare activities of the federal and state governments will be under greater stress because of shifts in spending toward defense and domestic security (Thompson, 2002).

CRITICAL SOCIOLOGY AND SOCIAL CHANGE

Is the United States Becoming a Nation of Solitary Bowlers?

In "Bowling Alone," a famous and controversial article, political scientist Robert Putnam (1995) presented evidence that Americans have become far less a "nation of joiners" than they were when Tocqueville visited the United States. In fact, they are becoming less inclined to join social groups, to become informed about current events, to trust other Americans, and perhaps more important, to vote in elections. Just after the terrorist attacks of September 11, 2001, Putnam and colleagues were able to conduct another poll to determine whether, as a result of the attack and its aftermath, Americans were more likely to volunteer and to join social groups. The results were mixed, with small increases in voluntarism and community activity but no clear indications that the increases would continue (Sander & Putnam, 2002).

Putnam's phrase "bowling alone" is a metaphor or catch phrase for a range of phenomena that point to growing social isolation and what he and other social scientists term a "decline in social capital." *Social capital* refers to all forms of engagement in civic life in communities, congregations, political parties, and voluntary associations. This engagement can be thought of as "capital" because it supplies the much-needed energy and individual activity that make civic life possible. As we saw earlier in the chapter, the legitimacy of democratic political institutions depends on citizen participation. If voters are alienated from political institutions and do not believe that government acts in their interests, the consequences can be devastating. Political alienation results in apathy and the feeling that no political action matters (Putnam, 1995). It results in resentment of government and a weakening of the rule of law. Catastrophic violence like the Oklahoma City bombing may be a symptom of a growing crisis of political legitimacy. As Putnam points out:

> Consider the well-known decline in turnout in national elections over the last three decades.
> From a relative high point in the early 1960s,

Figure 20.2 Group Membership, by Newspaper Readership and Education

Source: Data from NORC.

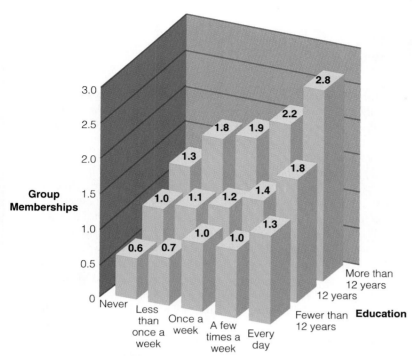

voter turnout had by 1990 declined by nearly a quarter; tens of millions of Americans had forsaken their parents' habitual readiness to engage in the simplest act of citizenship. Broadly similar trends also characterize participation in state and local elections.

It is not just the voting booth that has been increasingly deserted by Americans. A series of identical questions posed by the Roper Organization to national samples ten times each year over the last two decades reveals that since 1973 the number of Americans who report that "in the past year" they have "attended a public meeting on town or school affairs" has fallen by more than a third (from 22 percent in 1973 to 13 percent in 1993). Similar (or even greater) relative declines are evident in responses to questions about attending a political rally or speech, serving on a committee of some local organization, and working for a political party. By almost every measure, Americans' direct engagement in politics and government has fallen steadily and sharply over the last generation, despite the fact that average levels of education—the best individual-level predictor of political participation—have risen sharply throughout this period. Every year over the last decade or two, millions more have withdrawn from the affairs of their communities. (1995, p. 4)

Putnam and others who study changing patterns of civic engagement trace these declines to major generational shifts over the course of the twentieth century. The generations born earlier in the century fought the world wars and experienced devastating economic depression and the rebuilding of the economy through concerted corporate and civic action. The boom in participation in higher education after World War II, spurred by the GI Bill and growing demand for a skilled labor force, also contributed enormously to a sense of civic involvement, which translated into participation in groups of all kinds. Now these generations are being replaced by people born after the mid-1940s, the baby boomers and those in the so-called Generation X, who account for about 60 percent of the nation's adult population (Putnam, 1996). These cohorts appear far less interested in civic engagement than their parents and grandparents were, but the causes of this change are not well established.

Putnam attributes much of the change to the influence of television, the most powerful of the new media that became available in the second half of the twentieth century. He admits that available data do not fully prove this hypothesis, but he maintains that they are extremely suggestive. Two pieces of evidence for this claim are revealed in Figures 20.2 and 20.3, which relate group membership to education and media consumption. Group membership is measured in terms of the number of groups people say they belong to (including church congregations, labor unions,

Text continues on page 608.

VISUAL SOCIOLOGY

BUILDING DEMOCRACY IN OCCUPIED NATIONS

"You can't sit on bayonets," said Max Weber, meaning that it is one thing to conquer a nation or society and quite another to institute a government that its people believe is legitimate. In the nineteenth century, the colonial powers, including the United States, found it easy to conquer people all over the less industrialized and militarized world, but ruling the colonized peoples in ways they believed to be fair and representative of their own wishes proved almost impossible for any length of time. The photo of an American soldier on a tank delivering food in Somalia is a graphic

reminder that even humanitarian missions like the American-led, U.N.-sanctioned mission to restore order in Somalia and feed its starving people can end in disaster when there is no legitimate national government to maintain order (Dobbins et al., 2003).

The photo of the chief of the U.S.-led occupation of Iraq, Ambassador Paul Bremer, is also a reminder of how difficult it has proven to be to bring stability and democratic political institutions to Iraq. This photo was taken just after the terrorist bombing of the United Nations headquarters in Baghdad, which led to added controversy over whether the occupying coalition (primarily the United States and Great Britain) had "enough boots on the ground" to offer security to Iraqis who were cooperating

with the goals of the occupation. Chief among those Iraqis are the members of the provisional Government Council, many of whom were formerly living as exiles in the United States and England and are viewed by many Iraqis who lived through the Saddam years as interlopers and agents of the U.S. occupiers.

When the British ended their rule in Iraq in 1921, they created the new nation's first king, Faisal. But aside from his friendships with the British, Faisal, whose parents came from Mecca in what is now Saudi Arabia, had never lived in Iraq and was a Sunni Muslim in a land dominated by the Shia Muslims who make up about 60 percent of the population. After years of political unrest, Britain decided to reassert its control over Iraq and its valuable oil fields after World War II. This occurred during the reign of one of Iraq's least effective monarchs, the unfortunate Faisal II (depicted in the Sociological Observer box on page 593).

Unfortunately, the key lesson of Iraq's history, as well as that of so many former colonial regions, is that people prefer bad rule of their own kind to good rule by somebody whom they see as foreign. And the occupying nation's growing desire to extricate itself from its costly responsibilities in the conquered nation often results in a rush to create a government and hold

AP/Wide World Photos

© Stephanie Sinclair/Corbis

elections. In this regard, the Democracy and Rule of Law Project at the Carnegie Endowment for International Peace notes that rushing elections reinforces the divisions that already exist in a society. As a nation rapidly "decompresses," tribal and religious loyalties fill the vacuum. Citizens attach themselves to what is familiar—often the most belligerent separatists. If elections were held today in Iraq, the report warns, radical Shiite clerics and Kurdish separatists would be elected.

During the buildup to invasion of Iraq in 2003, Muslims—including these women shown carrying antiwar signs in London—joined in some of the largest antiwar protests the world had ever seen. Ironically, however, if efforts to build democratic institutions in occupied Iraq fail, or if Iraqis use their new democratic rights to elect a highly conservative Shia Muslim national leadership, the rights to speak freely and to voice their protests are highly unlikely to be extended to the women of Iraq.

The Sociological Observer
(See photo on page 593.)

The boy king sits uneasily on the throne, as any boy king would. He hardly fills half the space on the throne and seems quite wistful, as if he wishes he could be a regular little boy out playing with his friends. Of course, there isn't a spot on his white sandals and short pants suit, and

perhaps there is just the slightest trace of fear in his glance, or is that reading something into the photo that isn't there? Whatever our interpretations, the photo is a vivid reminder of a major weakness of hereditary forms of rule: Succession to the throne becomes political crisis when there is no clear and competent choice to replace the dead king or queen.

AP/Wide World Photos

Dmitri Kessel/Getty Images

Peter Marshall/Alamy

مَجلِس الحُكْم

Figure 20.3 Group Membership, by Television Viewing and Education

Source: Data from NORC.

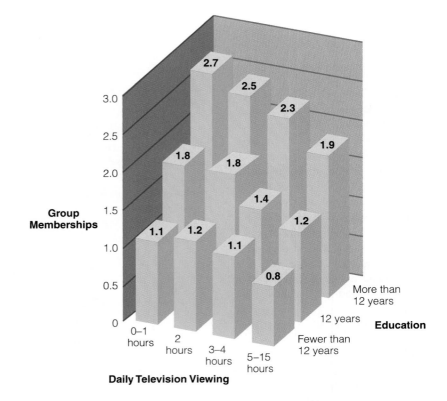

sports teams, and so on). Adding the education variable helps control for the effects of years of schooling on media consumption. The two graphs deal with newspaper readership and hours of television viewing. They offer a striking visual comparison of the effects of different media on civic engagement at each level of education. Clearly, the effects of the two media diverge. At each level of education, the more people read newspapers, the more group membership they report. But the more television they watch, the less group affiliation they report. These effects do not change with age; in fact, younger people are more likely to watch television rather than read newspapers and less likely to report membership in social groups than people in older generations. Note also that group membership and political participation are highly correlated—in other words, the same effects are found for voting.

These trends are disturbing. No social scientist can predict whether they will continue or how and why they might improve. Putnam himself believes that more Americans will be "bowling alone" in the future. He offers this comment:

> The most whimsical yet discomfiting bit of evidence
> of social disengagement in contemporary America
> that I have discovered is this: more Americans are

bowling today than ever before, but bowling in organized leagues has plummeted in the last decade or so. Between 1980 and 1993 the total number of bowlers in America increased by 10 percent, while league bowling decreased by 40 percent. (Lest this be thought a wholly trivial example, I should note that nearly 80 million Americans went bowling at least once during 1993, nearly a third more than voted in the 1994 congressional elections and roughly the same number as claim to attend church regularly. Even after the 1980s' plunge in league bowling, nearly 3 percent of American adults regularly bowl in leagues.)

The rise of solo bowling threatens the livelihood of bowling-lane proprietors because those who bowl as members of leagues consume three times as much beer and pizza as solo bowlers, and the money in bowling is in the beer and pizza, not the balls and shoes. The broader social significance, however, lies in the social interaction and even occasionally civic conversations over beer and pizza that solo bowlers forgo. Whether or not bowling beats balloting in the eyes of most Americans, bowling teams illustrate yet another vanishing form of social capital. (1995, p. 10)

SUMMARY

The Nature of Politics and Political Institutions

- Politics determines "who gets what, when, and how." The basis of politics is competition for *power,* or the ability to control the behavior of others, even against their will.

- *Authority* is institutionalized power, or power whose exercise is governed by the norms and statuses of organizations.

- Sets of norms and statuses that specialize in the exercise of power and authority are *political institutions,* and the set of political institutions that operate in a particular society forms the *state.*

- Although a state can exercise its power through the use of force, in the long run the use of force will not be enough to govern a society. When people consent to be governed without the use of force, the state is said to be legitimate.

- *Legitimacy* is a society's ability to engender and maintain the belief that the existing political institutions are the most appropriate for that society. Legitimacy is the basis of a society's political culture—the cultural norms, values, and symbols that support and justify its political institutions.

- According to Max Weber, the political cultures of different societies give rise to three different types of authority: *traditional, charismatic,* and *legal.*

- Perhaps the strongest and most dangerous political force in the world today is *nationalism,* the belief of a people that they have the right and the duty to constitute themselves as a nation-state.

The Nation-State in Crisis

- The most important political territory in world affairs is the *nation-state,* the largest territory within which a society's political institutions can operate without having to face challenges to their sovereignty.

- Throughout the world, there are nation-states in crisis. Even when citizens believe that their government is legitimate, force may be needed to maintain order and ensure compliance with the law.

- *Citizenship* is the status of membership in a nation-state.

- The rights of citizenship include civil rights (e.g., freedom of speech, thought, and faith), political rights (e.g., the right to vote), and social rights (e.g., the right to a certain level of economic welfare and security).

- The question of who is entitled to full participation in politics is a key issue at the local level as well as at the national level.

Political Institutions: A Global View

- Modern nations are governed by elected and appointed officials whose authority is defined by laws. In order to prevent abuses of authority, modern political institutions usually specify some form of separation of powers in which abuses by one institution can be remedied by others.

- *Political parties* are organizations of people who join together in order to gain legitimate control of state authority. Parties that accept the rule of other legitimate parties form a "loyal opposition" that monitors the actions of the ruling party and prevents the emergence of *oligarchy,* or rule by a few people who stay in office indefinitely. Regimes that accept no limits to their power and seek to exert their rule at all levels of society are known as *totalitarian regimes.*

- It is extremely difficult for minorities in a nation-state to feel that their rights are protected and honored if the institutions of government are dominated by members of the majority group.

- *Democracy* means rule by the nation's citizens: Citizens have the right to participate in public decision making, and those who govern do so with the explicit consent of the governed.

- In the British parliamentary system, elections are held in which the party that wins a majority of the seats in the legislature "forms a government": The leader of the party becomes the head of government and appoints other party members to major offices.

- In the American representative system, the party whose candidate is elected President need not have a majority of seats in the legislature.

- Although third parties in a representative system normally do not share power after elections, they can have an enormous impact on the course of political history.

- National regimes can be classified into several categories: liberal democracies, emergent democracies, communist regimes, nationalistic socialist regimes, authoritarian nationalist regimes, military regimes, Islamic nationalist regimes, and absolutist regimes. Most of the world's people live in liberal or emergent democracies.

Perspectives on Political Institutions

- Functionalist theorists assert that certain "structural prerequisites" must exist in a society for democratic political institutions to develop and operate. Among these are high levels of economic development, urbanization, and literacy, as well as a culture that tolerates dissent.

- The *power elite model* holds that the presence of democratic institutions does not mean that a society is democratic; political decisions are actually controlled by an elite of rich and powerful individuals.
- This view is challenged by the *pluralist model,* which holds that political decisions are influenced by a variety of *interest groups* through a process of coalition building and bargaining.
- Many political thinkers have been concerned with the relationship between social interaction and political institutions. Among the most influential was Machiavelli, who argued that political institutions must be based on the recognition that human beings are capable of evil as well as good. This recognition played a major part in the planning of the government of the United States, in which each branch of the government is able to check abuses of power by the other branches.
- Today television dominates most major political campaigns, and its influence has stimulated the movement for campaign finance reform.
- In modern nation-states, political communication is a major concern for those out of power as well as those in power. Analyzing political communications and reading between the lines of political rhetoric are important, particularly in societies characterized by mass publics and sophisticated communication techniques.

Military Institutions

- A major question in political sociology is how states can control their military institutions. A society cannot remain democratic for long if the military usurps the authority granted to it by civilian institutions.
- One factor that contributes to this problem is the fact that the military is staffed by professional soldiers for whom service in the armed forces is a career.
- Another factor is the immense influence of the military on the economy. On the other hand, military socialization instills norms and values that may contribute to social control of the military.

GLOSSARY

power: The ability to control the behavior of others, even against their will. (p. 584)

authority: Power whose exercise is governed by the norms and statuses of organizations. (p. 584)

political institution: A set of norms and statuses pertaining to the exercise of power and authority. (p. 584)

state: The set of political institutions operating in a particular society. (p. 584)

legitimacy: The ability of a society to engender and maintain the belief that the existing political institutions are the most appropriate for that society. (p. 585)

traditional authority: Authority that is hereditary and is legitimated by traditional values, particularly people's idea of the sacred. (p. 585)

charismatic authority: Authority that comes to an individual through a personal calling, often claimed to be inspired by supernatural powers, and is legitimated by people's belief that the leader does indeed have God-given powers. (p. 586)

legal authority: Authority that is legitimated by people's belief in the supremacy of the law; obedience is owed not to a person but to a set of impersonal principles. (p. 586)

nationalism: The belief of a people that they have the right and the duty to constitute themselves as a nation-state. (p. 587)

nation-state: The largest territory within which a society's political institutions can operate without having to face challenges to their sovereignty. (p. 587)

citizenship: The status of membership in a nation-state. (p. 588)

demagogue: A leader who uses personal charisma and political symbols to manipulate public opinion. (p. 590)

political party: An organization of people who join together to gain legitimate control of state authority. (p. 590)

oligarchy: Rule by a few people who stay in office indefinitely rather than for limited terms. (p. 590)

totalitarian regime: A regime that accepts no limits to its power and seeks to exert its rule at all levels of society. (p. 590)

democracy: A political system in which all citizens have the right to participate in public decision making. (p. 591)

power elite model: A theory stating that political decisions are controlled by an elite of rich and powerful individuals even in societies with democratic political institutions. (p. 595)

pluralist model: A theory stating that no single group controls political decisions; instead, a plurality of interest groups influence those decisions through a process of coalition building and bargaining. (p. 595)

interest group: An organization that attempts to influence elected and appointed officials regarding a specific issue or set of issues. (p. 597)

lobbying: The process whereby interest groups seek to persuade legislators to vote in their favor on particular bills. (p. 597)

INTERNET RESOURCES

 Virtual Society: The Wadsworth Sociology Resource Center
(http://sociology.wadsworth.com)
At Virtual Society you can access a wide range of enrichment material to aid your study of sociology. From the main page, click on the Student Resources link and find your course and this textbook. Next, select the chapter you are presently studying from the pull-down menu. Among the useful options for each self-study chapter are online links and exercises, flashcards, practical study tips, and practice quizzes for each chapter.

MC MicroCase Online
From the Virtual Society home page, click on MicroCase Online to access book-specific MicroCase exercises that allow you to further explore sociological issues and principles presented in the text.

InfoTrac College Edition
Another unique option available to you at the Student Resources section at Virtual Society is InfoTrac College Edition, an online library with access to hundreds of scholarly and popular periodicals. Below are suggested search terms for this chapter, but this resource also allows you to fit your study of sociology to your own interests by searching custom keywords.
Legitimacy
Citizenship
Nation-state
Interest groups

The New York Times
(www.nytimes.com)
An unparalleled source for political events and trends in the world. To receive the full range of available materials, you will have to register at this address.

Stanford University, Hoover Institution on War, Revolution, and Peace
(www-hoover.stanford.edu)
Analyzes social, political, and economic change in the world.

The White House
(www.whitehouse.gov)
A comprehensive site that features an Interactive Citizens' Handbook providing information about the U.S. federal government. The site also offers a list of commonly requested federal services and ways to communicate with the President and Vice President via electronic mail.

United States Federal Judiciary
(www.uscourts.gov)
The function of the courts' official Web site is to provide a clearinghouse for information from and about the judicial branch of the U.S. government. The site offers guidelines for understanding the federal court system and publishes press releases about recent decisions.

Technology, Environment, and Health

© Ilkka Uimonen for Newsweek/Magnum

Children hunting for berries or edible plants are a common sight throughout the world, but there is something ominous about this photo that the chain-link fence topped with barbed wire only hints at. In fact, the fence bars these children from entering a tract of contaminated land near Anniston, Alabama. Cancer-causing pollutants have poisoned the ground and made the eating of any local vegetables or berries quite hazardous. The pollutants, polybichlorinated phenols (PCBs), are used in many industrial applications but are also among the most carcinogenic agents known. Their presence in the Anniston vicinity makes it extremely hazardous to eat the plants that grow within and around the fence, which was erected by a subsidiary of the Monsanto Chemical Corporation when it was revealed that the company had been dumping the pollutants into the ground and local waterways for decades. "I was exposed to PCBs from the time I was born into the world right up until today," says a longtime resident of a neighborhood next to the old Monsanto plant. "It's scary. It's like a death sentence" (Grunwald, 2002, p. A17).

Anniston's official Web site advertises it as a peaceful and lovely southern town with some of the region's best restaurants and plentiful outdoor recreational opportunities, including bicycling, fishing, camping, and golfing. But the town is now fighting to overcome a far more threatening reputation as a toxic city. The pollution caused by the Monsanto Corporation, which many residents of the poorer neighborhoods near the dump sites believe has caused themselves and their kin to contract cancer and other life-threatening illnesses, is only one of its grave problems. More recently the U.S. Army, which has a large incinerator near Anniston, began burning highly toxic nerve gas, which residents fear will add to their health risks. During the summer of 2003, the Defense Department announced that it would burn hundreds of obsolete rockets containing nerve gas and other highly toxic pollutants. Although the department takes great care not to release these lethal gases into the local environment, many of Anniston's residents are extremely nervous and also concerned that their property has lost much of its value.

Sociologist Kai Erikson has conducted research in many communities like Anniston. Some of the people he has spoken to face nuclear contamination because they live near nuclear waste dumps or former bomb sites; other sites, like those in the Anniston area, are toxic because of industrial pollution due largely to illegal or ignorant disposal of toxic chemicals. In Erikson's view, the threat of contamination that troubles the people who live in these high-risk environments is "a new species of trouble." Although they are continually told that pollutants or nuclear wastes are contained and will not cause them any harm, the residents of such communities fear the presence of dangerous, cancer-producing materials in the area. "We live in a precarious world," Erikson writes, "and those people who must make their way through it without the capacity to forget those perils from time to time are doomed to a good deal of anxiety" (1998, p. 154).

Another of the communities that Erikson has studied is located near the new federal underground storage facility for radioactive waste in Yucca Mountain, New Mexico. Like residents of the Alabama town, many residents of Yucca Mountain lobbied hard to have the facility built in their region and were glad to take jobs in it. In Yucca Mountain, what once was a semidesert region of ranchers and miners will experience the growth spurt associated with industrialization. The daily arrival of huge transports of potentially deadly wastes will become a part of everyday life. All this would be less troubling if there was consensus among scientists that the disposal facility is safe.

FOCUS QUESTIONS:

• What do we mean by technological dualism, and how does it affect our lives?

• What are the key norms of science, and how are they continually being challenged by new developments in society?

• How do cultural lags create problems for societies as they experience new technologies?

Many people who worry about the risks posed by nuclear dump sites or army incinerators or industrial plants that produce hazardous wastes will cite Murphy's Law, which says that anything that can go wrong will eventually go wrong. Scientists explain this "law" in terms of probabilities of bad events occurring and by pointing out all the turbulence that exists in nature, which is often unpredictable and makes all forms of regularity and stability suspect (Matthews, 1997). None of this uncertainty makes people in the region sleep any easier. Nor does it help people who live on the coasts and fear the ultimate effects of global warming, or who live near nuclear plants and fear earthquakes, or who live near any of a hundred types of chemical or other manufacturing facilities that produce hazardous wastes. An extremely problematic aspect of our technologically sophisticated consumer society is found in the waste and pollution problems it produces. At best, scientists can tell us that our chances of not being poisoned by it are extremely small—but never zero.

Some of the most important changes that technologies are creating involve greater risk and hazards, as we see in the example of Anniston or Yucca Mountain, or, conversely, major improvements in our ability to fight illness and disease. Thus, in the second half of the chapter, we will focus primarily on issues of health and medicine, where new technologies offer great promise of better health, while other technologies of information (especially television and computers) and transportation (especially the automobile) are leading people to be more sedentary and bringing about new changes and challenges, such as runaway medical costs and nutritional conditions like obesity.

THE NATURE OF SCIENCE AND TECHNOLOGY

Our optimism about science and technology is frustrated not just by problems of nuclear waste disposal but by many other consequences of technological change. Depletion of the ozone layer in the atmosphere, air and water pollution, controversies over access to AIDS drugs, global warming, unemployment caused by technological change—these and many other problems result from our dependence on modern technologies and the scientific research that develops them. But if technologies are a source of negative change and global problems, they are also the basis of much of our material well-being. For better and, too often, for worse, science and technology are among the most powerful forces for social change in our world. In this chapter, we explore the ways in which science and technologies are developed and controlled and how they can be used to meet the challenges of our future existence on Earth.

Science Versus Technology

Science is a major institutional sector of modern societies: A hallmark of the modern social order is the conduct of scientific research in universities and other research organizations. And as we saw in Chapter 19, the control of information, especially scientific and technical information, is a source of prestige and power in postindustrial societies. The study of science and technology is therefore an increasingly important sociological specialty.

Science is, essentially, knowledge. (The Latin word *scientia*, from which *science* is derived, means "knowledge.") But science is a particular kind of knowledge: Knowledge that has been obtained through the scientific method (see Chapter 2)—that is, as a result of the process of developing and testing hypotheses. Even so, science encompasses an extremely diverse array of subjects—"from subatomic reactions to mental processes; from mathematical laws of thermodynamics to the economics of race relations; from the births and deaths of stars to the migration of birds; from the study of ultramicroscopic viruses to that of extragalactic nebulas; from the rise and dissolution of cultures and crystals to the rise and dissolution of atoms and universes" (*Encyclopaedia Britannica*, 1967, vol. 20, p. 7). These diverse topics are grouped together under the label "Science" because they all involve systematic and repeated observations.

Science is customarily divided into "pure" and "applied" branches. *Pure science* is scientific investigation that is devoted exclusively to the pursuit of knowledge for its own sake, with no immediate concern for using that knowledge to solve practical problems. For example, for more than 30 years Barbara McClintock did genetics research on corn plants, which had no immediate application to agricultural technology but eventually was recognized as having applications in molecular biology. *Applied science,* in contrast, is the application of known scientific principles to a practical problem; the outcome in many cases is new technologies. And those technologies can have a tremendous impact on the quality of human life.

We saw in Chapter 3 that **technology** is an aspect of culture. It can be defined as the use of tools and knowledge to manipulate the physical environment in order to achieve desired practical goals. Although modern technologies are often based on scientific discoveries, technology is much older than science; it has its roots in the tool-making and fire-building skills of the earliest human groups. People have always needed to find better ways of doing things or ways of making their lives more comfortable. Technological innovations have met those needs for thousands of years. In fact, technological change proceeded without the benefit of scientific knowledge for the bulk of human history. Science as we know it today is a relatively recent development. Although its origins may be traced to the mathematicians and philosophers of the ancient world, its emergence as a separate sphere of knowledge, with its own norms and values, dates from the late sixteenth century. From that time on, science tested and experimented on nature and progressed far beyond what nature spontaneously had ever revealed (Hess, 1997).

Accelerated by the discoveries of modern science, technology rapidly expanded the human capacity to live in and exploit different habitats. Indeed, in the past two centuries it has changed the face of the earth (Merton, 1996). Airports, skyscrapers, housing developments, oil refineries, superhighways, the Panama Canal, and the rocket launching pad at Cape Canaveral are all products of technology that have transformed the surroundings in which human beings live and work. This interrelationship between science and technology is responsible for the breathtaking speed of technological change in the twentieth century.

The benefits of technological change are not always distributed equally. Quite often, in fact, technologies allow people in wealthier nations to produce substances that formerly could be obtained only from poorer nations. For example, sugar beets grown in Europe and the United States are replacing the sugarcane produced in tropical nations as a source of sugar. At the same time, new technologies designed to increase crop yields—the fertilizers and pesticides that created the so-called green revolution in parts of Asia—appear to be adding excessive amounts of pollution to the environment, thereby creating huge costs for future generations. These problems of technology and industrial side effects have led many social scientists and environmental activists to call for **sustainable development**, or development that does not damage the environment or create new environmental burdens (World Commission on Environment and Development, cited in Keyfitz, 1991). Sustainable development leads to economic and social growth without compromising the ability of future generations to meet their needs.

The concept of sustainability can also be applied to many other issues involving new technologies. In health care, for example, technological breakthroughs in drug therapies for HIV or new imaging techniques like MRIs

and CAT scans promise to aid millions of people in their battles against deadly diseases, but the added cost of these measures creates unsustainable conditions for many societies' health care systems. In consequence, as an especially revealing example of how technological change can shape the values and institutions of a society, we will examine the evolution and social impact of medical technology. First, however, we need to explore some of the key relationships between science and technology and some of the sociological aspects of technological change.

The Norms of Science

We saw in Chapter 3 that every social institution develops norms that specify how its special functions are to be carried out. This is readily illustrated by the institutions of science. The function of those institutions is to extend knowledge by means of a specific set of procedures (i.e., the scientific method). The norms of science are derived from that function (Merton, 1996). (See the Study Chart on page 616.)

UNIVERSALISM One of the basic norms of scientific institutions is *universalism,* which holds that the truth of scientific knowledge must be determined by the impersonal criteria of the scientific method, not by criteria related to race, nationality, religion, social class, or political ideology. This would seem to be self-evident until one remembers that international rivalries have been part of the history of science since the Renaissance.

Consider the case of the Russian geneticist Trofim D. Lysenko, who, on the basis of some extremely unscientific research on plant genetics during the Stalinist era, claimed that acquired characteristics of plants could be inherited by the next generation (Rossianov, 1993). This claim seemed to offer hope for improvement of the Soviet Union's faltering agricultural production. It also fit well with Soviet ideology, which held that better human beings could be created through adherence to the ideals of the revolution. To Stalin and his advisers, science seemed to have proved the value of the Soviet culture and social system. Lysenko was granted a virtual dictatorship over biological research in the Soviet Union, and hundreds of geneticists lost their jobs (Sakharov, 1990). Lysenko was deposed during the Khrushchev era, but the damage done to Soviet agriculture and biological research in the name of ideology lasted many years longer.

COMMON OWNERSHIP Another norm of science is *common ownership of scientific findings.* Those findings are a result of collaboration and hence are not the property of any individual, although in some cases they may bear the name

THE NORMS OF SCIENCE

SCIENTIFIC NORM	THE NORM IN PRACTICE	VIOLATIONS OF THE NORM
Universalism	Proof of scientific knowledge must be based on impersonal and strict scientific method	Political influence; desire for national glory (e.g., the case of Russian geneticist Lysenko)
Common ownership and publication	Scientific findings are available to all through open publications	Private companies or agencies may conduct "proprietary research," intending to use results for business and profit (e.g., much contemporary genetic research)
Disinterestedness	Research is not done for personal motives or gain but to share results with scientific community freely	Desire for personal glory or gain may lead to abuses such as falsification of data or unsubstantiated claims (e.g., the case of "cold fusion")

of the person who first published them, as in "Darwin's theory of evolution" or "Einstein's theory of relativity." One outcome of this norm is frequent conflicts over scientific priority—that is, over who was the first to discover or publish a particular item of scientific knowledge. Thus there may be disagreements over who discovered the differential calculus—Newton or Leibniz—but there are no limitations on the use of that calculus. A further consequence of the norm of common ownership is the norm of *publication*—the requirement of full and open communication of scientific findings in journals that are accessible to all. Secrecy is out of place in science.

However, because scientific research is so often conducted in the interests of national defense or under the sponsorship of private firms that hope to profit from applications of the findings, the norms of common ownership and publication are often suspended. Such situations have led to innumerable conflicts in scientific circles. An outstanding example is the race to publish the complete map and inventory of the human genome—all the sequences of human DNA that constitute our genes. In 2001, two rival groups raced to be the first to complete the research, one in the private sector, the Celera Genomics Corporation, led by J. Craig Venter, and the other a government-funded laboratory headed by Francis Collins. An argument raged over whether the private corporation was trying to establish patents on human genetic sequences, a violation of the norm of openness. The public laboratory had, or claimed to have, no such business interest. Eventually the competing teams compromised and issued a joint publication of the map, but the controversy and legal battles over issuing patents for genetic material continue.

Another lesson from the human genome project is that modern genetic research and its applications cannot be funded by conventional academic science alone. Government-supported and private-sector research, acting in collaboration, will be needed to integrate the work of

computer scientists, mathematicians, and biologists who engage in huge scientific enterprises. These collaborations will make the norm of common ownership ever more difficult to apply (Butcher, 2001; Young, 2001).

DISINTERESTEDNESS   A further norm of scientific institutions is *disinterestedness.* The scientist does not allow the desire for personal gain to influence the reporting and evaluation of results; fraud and irresponsible claims are outlawed. In fact, more than most other activities, scientific research is subject to the scrutiny of others. This characteristic is part of the nature of that research, which involves the search for results that can be verified; in other words, science is, in a sense, self-policing. The norm of disinterestedness does not imply that scientists cannot hope to profit from their findings, and there are many instances in which scientists have held lucrative patents for their discoveries. But it does imply that related norms of scientific research, such as unbiased observation and thoroughness in reporting findings, must take precedence over any selfish motives.

Sociologists are concerned that the pressure on scientists to make discoveries that will earn large sums of money will damage the credibility of scientific institutions. The trend toward partnerships between private corporations and scientific institutions may also put pressure on scientists to violate scientific norms. The Monsanto Chemical Corporation, for example, gave $23.5 million to Washington University for biological research, and a West German pharmaceutical company invested $40 million in research at Harvard Medical School. Dorothy Nelkin (1996), one of the nation's leading experts on scientific policy, warns that when businesses form alliances with universities to conduct research in such areas as biological technologies, the scientists involved must keep their findings secret until patents have been applied for. Nelkin concludes that such secrecy violates the norm that science should be shared.

Similarly, when chemists at universities in Utah and Great Britain announced in 1989 that their collaboration had achieved "cold fusion," the production of energy through the fusion of hydrogen atoms at low temperatures (a reaction that scientists believe requires extremely high temperatures), it appeared that a new era of low-cost energy might be on the horizon. But other scientists were highly skeptical. The so-called discoveries had not been published in scientific journals before their announcement to the press—a violation of the norm of publication. The cold fusion apparatus was also kept secret for a time so that the scientists and their universities could apply for patents and enlist the support of major corporations for further research. These actions made scientists suspicious. Before too long the results were found to be incorrect, an outcome perhaps of too much hope for profit and not enough careful measurement (Frazier, 1998).

The norms just described are well-established aspects of modern science, which is increasingly differentiated from other institutions, particularly religion and the state. But science was not always viewed as a legitimate institution or a respectable occupation. In fact, early in its history, science was often regarded as a dangerous activity with the potential to threaten the existing social order (Rhodes, 1999). This can be seen clearly in the repression of Galileo by the Inquisition.

The first person to use a telescope to study the skies was Galileo Galilei, an Italian mathematician who lived from 1564 to 1642. His observations convinced him that the earth revolved around the sun. Up to that time it had been taken for granted that the earth was the center of the universe, and this belief was strongly entrenched in the doctrines of the Catholic church. Galileo's views were so radical that he was tried by the Inquisition, ordered to deny what he knew to be the truth, and forced to spend the last 8 years of his life under house arrest.

Galileo's fate illustrates a principle we have mentioned at numerous points in this book: As societies become more complex, the process termed *differentiation* removes various functions from existing institutions and creates new institutions to perform them. Galileo was tried by the Inquisition because in his time science had not yet become differentiated from philosophy and religion. A scientist must on no account discover anything that contradicted the doctrines of the church.

Today scientists are studying subatomic particles called quarks. They have proposed that dinosaurs had feathers rather than scales, and they have suggested that the universe began with a big bang and that stars eventually become black holes. They have discovered the process by which the continents were formed and the structure of human genes. In none of these cases have the findings been challenged by "the authorities," religious or otherwise. Rather, they have been judged by the standards of scientific investigation, one of the functions of the institution we call science.

But the process of differentiation is never complete. In recent years, the ancient tension between science and religion has taken a new turn: The scientific theory of evolution has been challenged by fundamentalist religious groups because it contradicts statements made in the Bible. These groups have put pressure on publishers to delete discussions of evolution from school and college textbooks, or at least to mention "creation science" as well as evolution. Although their efforts have had only limited success, they have not been ignored.

TECHNOLOGY IN MODERN SOCIETIES

We noted earlier that a significant aspect of modern science is its contribution to the rapid pace of technological change. The technologies produced by scientific research are applied to all aspects of human life and hence are a major force in shaping and changing other institutions in addition to scientific institutions themselves. An example is the impact of technological change on the institutions of mass communication. The advent of radio and then television dramatically changed the ways in which social and cultural values are transmitted to various

New York Public Library Picture Collection/New York Public Library, Astor, Lenox & Tilden Foundations

The astronomer Galileo Galilei was brought before the Inquisition in 1632, charged with the heresy of asserting that the earth moves around the sun.

groups in society. Now it is possible for people in regions of the world that lack up-to-date telephone systems to "leapfrog" over technological problems by purchasing cellular phones, which do not require a vast telecommunications infrastructure. We will note other examples of the impact of technology in the following pages, but first it is necessary to enlarge our understanding of what is meant by the term *technology*.

Dimensions of Technology

In Chapter 19, we pointed out that technology encompasses more than tools and skills, that ways of organizing work are also part of technology. Technology has three dimensions, which may be summarized as follows:

1. Technological tools, instruments, machines, gadgets, which are used in accomplishing a variety of tasks. These material objects are best referred to as *apparatus,* the physical devices of technical performance.

2. The body of technical skills, procedures, routines— all *activities* or behaviors that employ a purposive, step-by-step, rational method of doing things

3. The *organizational networks* associated with activities and apparatus (Winner, 1977, pp. 11–12)

The last of these dimensions may be clarified by an example. Organizational networks are sets of statuses and roles. All technologies establish or modify such networks. Thus the automobile owner is part of a network that includes dealers, mechanics, parts suppliers, insurers, licensing agents, and junkyard owners. Our great-great-grandparents were probably part of a network of horse dealers, harness makers, buggy suppliers, and blacksmiths, a network that has been largely eliminated by the advent of motorized vehicles.

Technological change can occur in any or all of the dimensions just listed. The most far-reaching changes involve all three, especially the third. For example, the Industrial Revolution completely changed the organization of economic institutions and also had significant effects on other institutions, such as the family. Likewise, the internal combustion engine, which made possible the development of the automobile, has completely transformed the ecology of North America (Flink, 1988). Since 1969, the total number of vehicles in the United States has grown six times faster than the total population (Wald, 1997). On the other hand, some technological changes are limited to modifications in the apparatus or technical skills needed for a particular task (the surgical stapler is an example) and do not affect large numbers of people or have major social impacts.

Not only do technological changes affect various groups and institutions within a society, and sometimes transform a society, but technology itself is affected by the social conditions prevailing at any given time. The acceptance of a particular technological innovation may depend on prior changes in other aspects of a society. Thus television might not have had as great an impact if it had been invented in the nineteenth century, when working people had far less leisure time than they do today. Other innovations have failed to gain acceptance because the institutional frameworks were not established that would permit their widespread acceptance. A good example of this problem is the current crisis in the music industry, in which the free sharing of music files downloaded over the Internet has caused a drastic decline in the sales of CDs and has resulted in lawsuits and threats of major cutbacks in recordings of new music. Here the problem is that the record companies and the major Internet service providers failed to develop a system for marketing and distributing music and films over the Internet that consumers would pay for. In the meantime, innovative companies like Napster saw that the new Internet-based technologies would allow them to provide a service by linking music file sharers with those who wanted to download music. The music companies were able to show that this was a violation of existing copyright laws, but they have not been able to prevent new groups or individuals from sharing music files. Eventually there will be more and more legal ways of downloading music files for a reasonable fee, but the music companies' desire to maintain their immensely profitable hold over CD sales prevented them from adapting to the new technologies before suffering huge losses in revenue. At the same time, many new, less well-known music groups are happy to post their music on the Web as a way of becoming known to a larger public without having to sign a contract with a record label (Rubell, 2003).

Technological Dualism

It should be noted that the effects of new technologies are not always positive. The phrase *technological dualism* is sometimes used to refer to the fact that technological changes often have both positive and negative effects. The introduction of diesel locomotives, for example, greatly increased the efficiency of railroad operations, but it also led to the decline and eventual abandonment of railroad towns whose economies were based on the servicing of steam locomotives (Cottrell, 1951). Another example is the automation of industrial production. Automation has greatly improved manufacturing processes in many industries. It has increased the safety of certain production tasks and led to improved product quality in many cases. But it has also replaced thousands of manual workers with machines, and significant numbers of those workers find themselves unemployed and lacking the skills required by

GLOBAL SOCIAL CHANGE

Worker Responses to High Technology

The rapid growth of employment (interrupted briefly by the 2001–2002 recession) in industrial regions like California's "Silicon Valley," Route 128 outside Boston, and the "Silicon Prairie" in the Dallas–Fort Worth area, as well as in hundreds of industrial parks throughout the United States, is viewed as one of the benefits of investment in high-technology industries. The term *high technology* is associated with computers, advanced electronics, genetic engineering, and other frontiers of technological change, but it is rarely well defined. And without a clear definition of this term, it is almost impossible to assess its impact on society.

As the term is used by academics, policymakers, and journalists, *high technology* refers to at least one of the following features of technology:

- An extensive degree of technological sophistication embodied in a product
- A rapid rate of employment growth associated with an innovative product
- A large research and development effort associated with production (Markson & Bloch, 1985)

One implication of this definition is that it includes job-creating processes like research and development as well as technologies like computers, which also have created new growth in employment. Yet the employment-producing features of high technology can be problematic. Many high technologies, such as robotics and computer-aided design, are intended to reduce employment by substituting the work of machines guided by computers for human production of all kinds. Early machine technologies tended to replace human labor power, but high technology tends to reduce the need for human brain power. Employment in occupations like drafting and industrial drawing in engineering and architecture, for example, is threatened by the accelerating use of computer design and graphics programs (Shaiken & Lopez, 1997).

During the Industrial Revolution in England, workers sometimes rioted and wrecked the machinery that was replacing their labor. Such violence against machines was termed *Luddism* after an English stocking maker, Ned Ludd, who smashed his employer's knitting frame

with a sledgehammer and thereby touched off the famous Luddite riots of 1811 and 1812 (Hobsbawm, 1975; Rudé, 1964). Outbursts of collective behavior directed against automation have been relatively rare, however. Instead, workers have generally accepted their fate and looked for other sources of employment. Nevertheless, the effects of high technology are so threatening to so many workers that unions have taken some initiatives designed to alleviate those effects.

An example occurred at Britain's Lucas Aerospace, a maker of landing gear and electronic equipment, in the mid-1970s. Automation had reduced the Lucas workforce from 18,000 to 13,000. At that point, the employees and their union leaders conducted an ambitious study that showed that highly skilled workers were losing their jobs at the same time that many of the society's needs remained unmet. The study suggested hundreds of ways in which the company could employ its skilled workforce to meet these needs and still earn profits. Although the plan was rejected, it has served as a model for other worker strategies.

---

the high-tech occupations of postindustrial society (see the Global Social Change box above).

Some observers go so far as to say that technology is a danger to the modern world. They believe that it has become an autonomous force, that it is out of control. This is a recurrent theme in movies and science fiction—HAL, the computer that takes over the ship in *2001: A Space Odyssey,* is a good example. But it is also claimed that technology is increasingly independent from human control in the real world. Events like the toxic gas leak that killed more than 2,000 people in Bhopal, India, in 1984; the disaster at the Chernobyl nuclear power plant in the Soviet Union in 1986; the historic power blackout in much of the United States in August 2003; the problem of global warming caused by excessive emissions of gases from cars and other users of fossil fuels (oil and coal); and fear of the spread of nuclear arms to terrorist organizations seem to indicate that human beings cannot control the technologies they have created.

The Bhopal facility produced a pesticide that made possible larger harvests of much-needed grain; machines that use gasoline have become, for better or worse, vital to the economies of entire regions of the world. The result of our dependence on the benefits of complex technologies is an increasingly complex set of organizations and procedures for putting those technologies to work. This requires more human effort and skill, and the chances of error and breakdown are greater. The point is not that technology is out of control but that often a lag exists between the introduction of new technologies and the development of adequate controls over the application of those technologies (Winner, 1996).

One of the main issues that concerns social scientists in this regard is why such lags occur. Consider the problem known as wind shear. Numerous major plane crashes have been caused by sudden downdrafts associated with severe thunderstorms on the approaches to airport runways. These downdrafts literally slam large aircraft to the ground.

This spectacular display of nature's power is a reminder of the precarious existence of humans on the earth. Thunderstorms, tornadoes, and hurricanes destroy billions of dollars worth of property and disrupt untold numbers of lives every year.

Industry and government officials have known about the wind shear problem since at least 1975, when an Eastern Airlines jet crashed at New York's Kennedy Airport under such conditions. But not until a similar crash occurred in New Orleans in 1984 were airports ordered to install instruments that could predict such conditions.

Why the delay? Some sociologists have argued that the pressure on corporations to show a profit causes them to neglect spending on safety measures. Others, taking a more functionalist view, tend to explain such lags in terms of the time required for organizations to recognize the causes of the problem and develop new statuses and roles to cope with them (Perrow, 1984, 1996).

Technology and Social Change

Among catalysts of social change, technological innovation ranks extremely high, along with major social forces such as population growth, war, epidemics, and rising expectations for better lives. Technological change can also rapidly effect large-scale social change, often well within an individual life span. One need only think of the impact of television. This powerful communications medium, introduced in the United States on a mass basis in the 1950s, has significantly altered the way people receive information about their society and the world, how they behave as consumers, how they engage in politics, and how they use their leisure time.

In Chapter 10, we discussed William Fielding Ogburn's theory of **cultural lag,** the classic sociological treatment of how societies adjust to technological change and the problems that can result. One example of cultural lag can be seen in the case of cable and satellite television. The actual technological change occurred rapidly, with the result that many new broadcasting channels became available. But the social development of new material for those channels requires further investment, creativity, and organization. Thus a lag exists between the immediate effects of technological change and the social adjustments necessary to make effective use of the new technology.

POWER AND CULTURAL LAG   A problem with the cultural lag theory is that it often fails to account for the effects of social power. For example, AIDS activists and public health officials would like to see condoms advertised on television. They argue that people who are already suffer-

Here is a vivid example of the risks and unintended effects of technology. This bizarre accident, which occurred in France early in the twentieth century, proved to some skeptics that humans could not control the power of their technology. As technology advances, the risks generally increase in proportion to the benefits.

TABLE 21.1

Long Booms and Associated Industries

Dates	Industry	
1790–1815	Cotton	Mechanization of spinning
1848–1873	Textiles	Mechanization of spinning and weaving
	Engineering	Production by machine of textile machinery, steam engines, and locomotives
1896–1921	Engineering	Batch production; semiautomatic machinery; marine engineering; automobiles
	Electrical	
	Chemical	Rise of science-based industries
	Steel	Bulk production
1945–1974	Automobiles	
	Mechanical and electrical consumer durables	Assembly-line mass production
	Petrochemicals	Continuous-flow process production
Present	Computers	Information and telecommunications technologies

Source: Adapted from CSE Microelectronics Group, 1980. Reprinted with permission from CSE Books, London.

ing from AIDS, as well as people who might be exposed to AIDS and other sexually transmitted diseases, need as much information as possible about safe sex. Condom companies want to advertise on television, as is common in other nations, especially in Europe. However, television stations generally do not accept condom ads because they are worried about the reaction of powerful religious organizations or political leaders who oppose public discussion of sex and birth control. The power to block advertising of condoms on television is an example of a cultural lag that will not necessarily be overcome, because it stems from a deep and unresolved cultural conflict in American society. Other cultural lags resulting from technological change may be more amenable to intentional efforts to address them, as can be seen in the case of air pollution.

TECHNOLOGY ASSESSMENT The lags described by Ogburn can be at least partially reduced by the process of **technology assessment,** or efforts to anticipate the consequences of particular technologies for individuals and for society as a whole. For instance, the massive plan to reduce air pollution in the Los Angeles basin requires careful assessment. According to the National Environmental Policy Act and related state laws, any major action by a public agency that affects the environment must be assessed for its impact on the environment and on the citizens involved. Laws that require technology assessment—especially those that require corporations to abide by the findings of such assessments—tend to increase the power of citizens in communities affected by technological change. They are therefore a source both

of conflict and of movements for social reform. In the Los Angeles case, a few small, inadequately funded environmental organizations have succeeded in forcing the California Environmental Policy Administration to fund the plan to reduce air pollution (Browne & Keil, 2000; Kahn, 2000).

CYCLES OF TECHNOLOGICAL CHANGE Theories that view technological innovations as a source of social change must also recognize that technological changes do not occur at an even pace. Some analysts, such as economist N. D. Kondratieff, believe that technological innovation follows a cyclical pattern. They have shown that the growth of particular industries produces a "long boom," a period of economic expansion and prosperity that lasts about 25 years and is followed by a period of decline and depression of about the same duration or slightly longer (Schilling, 1991). This pattern is illustrated in Table 21.1, which shows the cycles of industrial development in Britain since the late 1700s.

Despite the crash of the high-flying dot-com stocks in 2000 and 2001, it is still possible that the new technologies of computers and automation will begin another long boom or wave of economic growth, as many people in advanced industrial societies hope. But it is clear that in the late 1970s the previous long boom, stimulated in part by the availability of cheap energy, was over. Some sociologists and economists believe that a new long boom is occurring based on computers, telecommunications, and biotechnologies, and perhaps on new breakthroughs in energy technologies, such as electric automobiles (Korotz, 1998).

The Quest for Energy

Throughout human history, a central aspect of technological change has been the quest for new sources of energy to meet the needs of growing populations. That quest has resulted in a succession of energy technologies, each more sophisticated than the last. Animal power gave way to steam-driven machinery, which in turn was replaced by the internal combustion engine. Reliance on oil and its derivatives, especially gasoline, encouraged the growth of powerful energy corporations, which often lobby government agencies for assistance in developing new technologies like nuclear energy. And today the technologically advanced nations are attempting to control the fusion reaction, in which hydrogen atoms are fused into helium, thereby producing an enormous release of energy. The implications of this energy technology, if it can be achieved, are staggering. Fusion promises to create a major revolution in human existence. It could make possible the colonization and exploration of space, the rapid development of the less developed nations, the elimination of energy technologies based on oil and coal (which pollute the environment), and much else. But the effort to develop fusion power also signals a fundamental crisis in modern life: the dwindling supply of finite energy resources.

The problem of oil depletion is only the most recent in a series of energy crises that began with the depletion of the supply of game animals by hunting in Paleolithic times. The shortage of meat created conditions that spurred the development of agriculture. Later, in the waning years of the Roman empire, a shortage of labor power to grind flour encouraged the use of water power. The Industrial Revolution had its origins in the depletion of the supply of wood during the Renaissance. Coal was plentiful, and experiments with its use as an energy source led to the development of new techniques for producing energy—and new machinery and processes for manufacturing goods. Today, as supplies of oil and coal diminish, the search for new energy sources continues (Brown, 2001).

It would seem from what we have said so far that the quest for energy is a positive force that results in new, sometimes revolutionary technologies that greatly improve the quality of human life. Many people believe that societies can meet their growing energy needs by continually investing in more sophisticated technologies. This approach has led to the development of huge nuclear power plants to replace oil-fueled generators, and it is widely hoped that investment in fusion, an even more complex technology, will eliminate the dangers posed by nuclear power.

"HARD" VERSUS "SOFT" ENERGY PATHS This view is subject to considerable criticism, however. Amory Lovins (1977, 1998), for example, distinguishes between "hard" and "soft" energy paths. The former "relies on rapid expansion of centralized high technologies to increase supplies of energy, especially in the form of electricity." The latter "combines a prompt and serious commitment to efficient use of energy [and] rapid development of renewable energy sources" (p. 25). Present and proposed energy policies favor the hard path, which involves intensive use of available coal, oil, and natural gas plus heavy investment in nuclear power. These are *capital-intensive* technologies because they rely heavily on sophisticated equipment (capital) rather than labor power.

Soft energy technologies depend on renewable sources like sun and wind and tend to be *labor-intensive* in that larger numbers of people are needed to produce a given amount of energy (Grose, 2001). They are more diverse than hard energy technologies and are more directly matched to energy needs. (Solar energy, for example, can be used to heat water without first being converted into electricity.) But the major difference between the two paths, according to Lovins, is that whereas the soft path depends on "pluralistic consumer choice in deploying a myriad of small devices and refinements, the hard path depends on difficult, large-scale projects [e.g., nuclear power plants and fusion reactors] requiring a major social commitment under centralized management" (1977, p. 54). Such projects are characterized by a "remote and . . . uncontrollable technology run by a faraway, bureaucratized, technical elite who have probably never heard of you" (p. 55).

Whether or not one accepts Lovins's thesis, the use of nuclear power to generate electricity remains a major social and political issue (Perrow, 1996). Underlying the conflict over the safety of nuclear power plants is the issue of control. In the ancient world, those who controlled the irrigation systems were the ruling elite; in the United States, the "robber barons" of the late nineteenth century often gained both wealth and political influence from their control of oil and coal supplies. Thus much of the opposition to nuclear power plants stems from the recognition that control over energy supplies is a key source of economic and political power.

IMPACTS OF TECHNOLOGY

Technological Systems

The propensity of people in highly industrialized societies to seek technological solutions to problems like pollution or hazardous waste disposal is often referred to as the "technological fix." The belief that new technologies can solve existing environmental and other problems can itself have adverse consequences. This is especially true in relation to technologies like nuclear energy, which require complex social systems to operate them. As Charles Perrow (1984) has written, "Human-made catastrophes appear to have increased with industrialization as we built devices that could crash, sink, burn, or explode" (p. 11). Perrow also points out that the increasing complexity of modern technology has led to a new kind of catastrophe: the failure of whole systems (i.e., activities and organizational networks as well as apparatus)—for example, the Three Mile Island accident or the *Challenger* and *Columbia* disasters.

The enormous risks associated with complex technologies have led many observers to call for a more thorough assessment of the potential impact of new technologies before they are put into operation. According to Perrow, it is important to study technological systems in their entirety rather than focusing on individual components of those systems. For example, in the case of Three Mile Island, the accident was not a simple matter of a faulty valve but the consequence of a combination of factors—an overworked maintenance staff, equipment failures, ineffective safety precautions, inadequate training, and the unwillingness of scientists and bureaucrats to admit that they might be mistaken. Similar conditions led to the explosions of the *Challenger* and *Columbia* space shuttles in 1986 and 2003. Once again we are reminded that technology consists not only of apparatus that can malfunction but also of knowledge and skills that may be deficient and of organizational networks that occasionally break down.

Environmental Stress

New technologies often cause new forms of pollution and environmental stress. *Pollution* may be defined as the addition to the environment of agents that are potentially damaging to the welfare of humans or other organisms (Ehrlich & Ehrlich, 1997). *Environmental stress* is a more general term that refers to the effects of society on the natural environment. Pollution is the most common form of environmental stress, but it is not the only one.

One example of environmental stress resulting from technology is the surprising finding that winter fish kills in Wisconsin lakes were caused by snowmobiles. Heavy snowmobile use on a lake compacts the snow, thereby reducing the amount of sunlight filtering through the ice and thus interfering with photosynthesis by aquatic plants. As the plant life dies, its decomposition further reduces the amount of oxygen in the water. The fish then die of asphyxiation.

The fish–plant–oxygen relationship is a natural ecological system. The snowmobile is a technological innovation whose potential uses are highly varied. The production, marketing, and use of snowmobiles are elements of a social system. This social system is responsible for the environmental stress resulting from snowmobile use. The land available for snowmobiling is increasingly scarce in an urban society like the United States. Frozen lakes near urban centers thus seem

ideal for this purpose, but snowmobiles cause environmental stress in the form of fish kills and thereby create the need for new social controls over the uses of this technology.

The need for such controls often does not become apparent until a great deal of damage has been done. Nor is it ever entirely clear that new social controls or new technologies can solve the problem at hand. For example, as described at the beginning of this chapter, in a recent study of comparative environmental risks, sociologist Kai T. Erikson (1994b) examined the vast area of Nevada where the U.S. government carried out its nuclear bomb testing and where it now plans to bury large quantities of high-level nuclear wastes. These wastes can remain extremely dangerous for thousands of years. Erikson points out that scientists can assess the geological risks of storing nuclear waste deep underground but have much less experience in assessing the social risks. As seen in the Visual Sociology feature at the end of the chapter, symbols for danger that are familiar to us could easily be as indecipherable to our descendants in 10,000 years as the writing on many ancient tombs is to us today.

Class and Racial Inequalities in Technological Impacts

Studies of the impact and social control of technologies are an active frontier of sociological research. The Environmental Sociology section of the American Sociological Association routinely publishes research reports that assess the polluting and environmentally stressful impacts of technology. Many such studies have shown that the people who bear the heaviest burden of pollution are most often those who are least able to escape its effects. The poor, minorities, and workers and their families in industrial regions are exposed to higher levels of air, water, and solid-waste pollution than are more affluent people (Erikson, 1994a). This finding is not surprising. People whose livelihoods depend on polluting industries generally learn to tolerate and even ignore the pollution associated with those industries. In fact, when environmental activists protest against the polluting effects of mines and smelters, they often find that their most vocal opponents are those who are most negatively affected by the pollution. In the past 30 years, however, there has been a significant change in attitudes, especially on the part of trade union leaders in polluting industries; such leaders are more likely to press for pollution controls than they were in the past.

The place of technology in modern societies is a subject of continuing controversy. Key issues include not only pollution and other impacts of technology but also the need to control the development and uses of technological innovations so that they benefit all sectors of society. The complex interactions between technology and other aspects of the social order can be seen in the case of technology and health.

THEN AND NOW

The Impact of Major Disasters

In 1993, more than 500 hundred miles of the Mississippi and Ohio rivers reached flood levels after weeks of drenching rains. The floods were the worst in decades, and certainly the worst in the contemporary era, in which modern systems of levees and dikes have been constructed in the great river valley. Billions of dollars worth of property was destroyed. Thousands of people lost their homes. Many more thousands were forced to dig out their homes, which had been polluted by oil-soaked mud. For months a five-state area in the Midwest was a federal disaster area. Even now the rebuilding continues, and fierce controversies rage about how much of the built environment in the flood plain can be restored and how much should be declared ineligible for flood insurance, which would preclude rebuilding. So thousands of families in the agricultural heartland of the United States continue to face agonizing uncertainties and severe economic, social, and psychological hardships caused by the flooding. And yet in the national media, this story is considered old, and one almost

never reads about it outside the region. Other disasters have crowded it out.

In the summer of 1998, the worst hurricane ever to hit Central America devastated much of coastal Honduras, Nicaragua, El Salvador, and parts of Guatemala. The storm, known as Hurricane Mitch, struck a region of extreme poverty. Many thousands of people lost their lives. Almost 300,000 were made homeless. The storm unleashed a desperate new wave of migration to the U.S. border that continues at this writing (Zarembo, 1999). Within these impoverished nations, demographers estimate that

the number of homeless, orphaned street children has also grown dramatically since the hurricane, and in Nicaragua and Honduras the number continues to increase by several thousand a year (Collymore, 2002). It will take years to rebuild the economies of Honduras and Nicaragua.

For years people will suffer the consequences of a storm that commanded the world's attention for a few weeks and resulted in news articles for

a few months. The point here is that public attention is short but the consequences of natural disasters are long, and much of the poverty that one witnesses in the United States and elsewhere in the world is brought on by disruptions in people's efforts to build their local economies. Technologies of weather prediction, flood control, and water containment cannot keep up with population growth and the many attractions of living near rivers and coasts.

HEALTH AND TECHNOLOGICAL CHANGE

Throughout most of human history, limitations on food production, together with lack of medical knowledge, have placed limits on the size of populations. Dreadful diseases like the bubonic plague have actually reduced populations. In England, the plague, known as the Black Death, was responsible for a drastic drop in the population in 1348 and for the lack of population growth in the seventeenth century (see Figure 21.1). In 1625 alone,

35,417 residents of London died of the plague. Smallpox and dysentery have had similar, though less dramatic, effects (Davis, 1992; Wrigley, 1969).

Until relatively recently, physicians were powerless either to check the progress of disease or to prolong life. In fact, they often did more harm than good—that is, their remedies were more harmful than the illnesses they were intended to cure. As Lewis Thomas (1979) has stated:

Bleeding, purging, cupping, the administration of infusions of every known plant, solutions of every known metal, every conceivable diet including total fasting, most of these based on the weirdest

Figure 21.1 Long-Term Population Trends in England and Wales, 1000–1800

Source: Reprinted with permission from *Wrigley's Population and History,* 1969. Copyright © McGraw-Hill Book Company.

imaginings about the cause of the disease, concocted out of nothing but thin air—this was the heritage of medicine up until a little over a century ago. (p. 133)

Thomas's point is that before the nineteenth century, when scientists finally began to understand the nature of disease, physicians based their treatments on folklore and superstition. In fact, with few exceptions, the practice of healing, like many other aspects of science, was closely linked to religion. In ancient Greece, people who suffered from chronic illnesses and physical impairments would journey to the temple of Asclepius, the god of healing, in search of a cure. In medieval times, pilgrims flocked to the cathedral at Lourdes in France (as many still do today) in the belief that they would thereby be cured of blindness, paralysis, or leprosy. Not until Louis Pasteur, Robert Koch, and other researchers developed the germ theory of disease did medicine become fully differentiated from religion. Their discoveries, together with progress in internal medicine, pathology, the use of anesthesia, and surgical techniques, led to the twentieth-century concept of medicine as a scientific discipline (Cockerham, 2001).

During the nineteenth century, scientific research resulted in the discovery of the causes of many diseases, but at first this progress led physicians to do less for their patients rather than more: They began to allow the body's natural healing processes to work and ceased to engage in damaging procedures like bloodletting. At the same time, they made major strides toward improving public health practices. They learned about hygiene, sterilization, and other basic principles of public health, especially the need to separate drinking water from waste water. These innovations, which occurred before the development of more sophisticated drugs and medical technologies, contributed to a demographic revolution that is still under way in

some parts of the world. Suddenly rates of infant mortality decreased dramatically, births began to outnumber deaths, and life expectancy increased. As we saw in Chapter 9, this change resulted not from the highly sophisticated techniques of modern medicine but largely from the application of simple sanitation techniques and sterilization procedures (Rosner, 1995). In fact, these simple technologies have had such a marked effect on infant survival that the rate of infant mortality in a society is often used as a quick measure of its social and economic development (see Figure 21.2).

In sum, as medical science progressed toward greater understanding of the nature of disease and its prevention, new public health and maternal care practices contributed to rapid population growth. In the second half of the nineteenth century, such discoveries as antiseptics and anesthesia made possible other life-prolonging medical treatments. In analyzing the effects of these technologies, sociologists ask how people in different social classes gain access to them and how they can be more equitably distributed among the members of a society. The ways in which medical technologies have been institutionalized in hospitals and the medical profession are a central focus of sociological research on these questions.

The Hospital: From Poorhouse to Healing Institution

In the twentieth century, the nature of medicine changed dramatically as scientific investigation expanded our knowledge of the causes and cures of disease. That knowledge led to the development of a vast array of technologies for the prevention and cure of many known illnesses, as well as the long-term care of terminally ill patients. Because

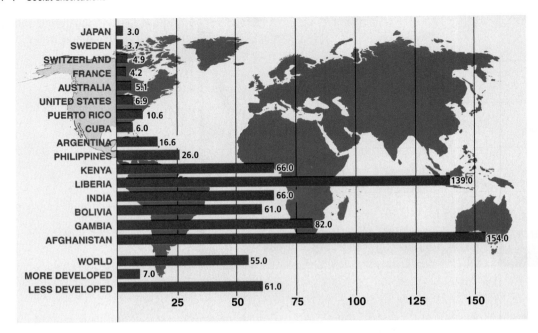

Figure 21.2   Infant Mortality Rates for Selected Countries

Note: The infant mortality rate is the number of deaths of infants younger than 1 year of age per 1,000 live births in a given year.

Source: Data from Population Reference Bureau, 2003.

the more complex of these technologies are applied in a hospital setting, it is worthwhile to consider the development of the hospital as the major social institution for the delivery of health care.

Historically, hospitals evolved through several stages, beginning as religious centers and eventually developing into centers of medical technology (Cockerham, 2001). The first hospitals were associated with the rise of Christianity; they were community centers for the care of the sick and the poor, providing not only limited medical care but also food, shelter, and prayer. During the Renaissance, hospitals were removed from the jurisdic-

tion of the church and became public facilities. Because they offered food and shelter to the poor regardless of their health, they soon became crowded with invalids, the aged, orphans, and the mentally ill. The third phase in the development of hospitals began in the seventeenth century, when physicians gained influence over the care of patients in hospitals. Gradually the nonmedical tasks of hospitals disappeared, and the hospital took on its present role as an institution for medical care and research.

This painting by Jan Beerblock (1739–1806) depicts the sick wards in Sint-Janshospital in Bruges, Belgium, a bleak forerunner of modern hospital organization.

Saint-Janshospitaal, Bruges

The modern hospital began to emerge at the end of the nineteenth century as a result of the development of the science of medicine. Especially important were advances in bacteriology and increased knowledge of human physiology, along with the use of ether as an anesthetic. Because the new medical technologies were more complex and often more expensive than earlier forms of treatment, they were centralized in hospitals so that many physicians could use them. Physicians also began to refer patients of all social classes to hospitals, and those patients paid for the services provided to them there. In the United States, the number of hospitals grew rapidly in the twentieth century—from a few hundred at the turn of the century to more than 6,500 in the 1990s.

Today hospitals play an important role in the control of medical practice and access to medical care. For example, doctors who want to practice in a particular hospital must be accepted by the hospital's medical board. Patients who want high-quality care in private hospitals must be able to pay the fees charged by those hospitals or have the necessary insurance coverage. And hospitals have a monopoly on advanced medical technologies, a fact that has had a major impact on the American health care system.

Medicine and Technological Change

Today the technologies available for the diagnosis and treatment of serious illnesses are often described as "miracles of modern medicine." The magnetic resonance imaging (MRI) scanner, for example, allows hospital technicians to observe a patient's internal organs without the use of X-rays; renal dialysis is used to prevent patients from dying of kidney failure; open-heart surgery is practically a routine operation, with the patient kept alive during the process by an external heart-lung machine; other surgical procedures involve the use of laser beams and fiber optics to perform delicate operations. All of these technologies require the use of extremely expensive equipment and highly trained personnel.

The development of increasingly sophisticated and costly medical technologies, together with the practice of requiring patients (or their insurance companies) to pay for hospital services, has led to a crisis in American medical care. The high cost of medical care has become a major public issue, as has the fact that some groups in the population are unable to obtain adequate care. (Over 43 percent of Americans have inadequate medical insurance, or none at all.) Some critics claim that the American health care system is suffering from *hypertrophy*, by which they mean that it has expanded to a size and complexity at which it has become dysfunctional. In their view, excessive emphasis on technological progress has created a situation in which the needs of the patient are subordinated to those of the providers of health care.

According to Paul Starr (1982, 1995), the problems of the American health care system stem from the way in which medical institutions evolved. As medical knowledge increased and technological advances were made, physicians developed narrow specialties and hospitals invested in specialized equipment. The physicians referred their patients to the hospitals for sophisticated medical testing and treatment. At the same time, the institution of health insurance emerged in response to demands for a more equitable distribution of health care. Insurance companies or the government began to pay for the services provided by hospitals. Physicians and hospitals became highly interdependent, so much so that they began to "assert their long-run collective interests over their short-run individual interests" (Starr, 1982, p. 230). Their collective interests involve continued investment in complex technologies, with the result that medical care is becoming more and more expensive. The high cost of medical care makes it more difficult for the poor, the elderly, and other groups to afford high-quality care and heroic life-preserving measures. In the opening years of the twenty-first century, efforts to make health care less costly while preserving the insurance systems that provide medical coverage for the majority of Americans are proving to be one of the most controversial and rancorous issues in U.S. political life.

MEDICAL SOCIOLOGY Starr's 1982 study of the evolution of health care institutions had a major impact on the health care reform movement of the 1990s. It is an excellent example of *medical sociology*. This relatively new field of study has emerged in response to the development of medicine as a major institution of modern societies. Many sociologists are employed by health care institutions, and some medical schools have established faculty positions for sociologists. When they work in medical research, sociologists often conduct studies that add to our knowledge of epidemiology, especially social epidemiology.

SOCIAL EPIDEMIOLOGY Social epidemiology is a new and important subfield of epidemiology that draws heavily on research in medical sociology. *Epidemiology* is the study of how diseases originate and spread in human populations and how societies can develop better public health systems to attack the causes of illness. Epidemiologists trace the outbreaks of new diseases like Ebola or severe acute respiratory syndrome (SARS), and they also track the spread and decline of epidemics like AIDS, malaria, and many others. Epidemiologists are trained in biology and some aspects of medicine, and they are particularly well trained in biostatistics.

The Sociological Observer

These schoolchildren in Hong Kong are wearing masks to protect them against severe acute respiratory syndrome (SARS). This contagious respiratory virus killed hundreds of people, caused more than 3,400 confirmed or suspected cases of the disease in more than 30 countries, and generated worldwide panic. How does the response to this disease represent an interaction between technology and medicine? How can technology have a negative impact on an outbreak of a contagious disease such as SARS? (See page 632 for further insights into the sociological content of this photo.)

Peter Parks/AFP/Getty Images

Social epidemiology looks for the fundamental causes of health problems in basic social and cultural conditions that are often the precursors of health problems. The policies they advocate, based on their research, often address social issues like poverty, racism, gender bias, and the stresses working people encounter on their jobs (Burris, 2002).

AIDS AND SOCIAL EPIDEMIOLOGY   In the United States, the Centers for Disease Control and Prevention (CDC), with headquarters in Atlanta, Georgia, is a pioneer in social epidemiology and the use of medical-sociological research. The CDC is the lead federal agency for protecting the health and safety of Americans both at home and abroad. It is expected to provide credible information to enhance health decisions and to promote health through strong partnerships with community groups of all kinds. For example, it is the CDC that is responsible for developing programs to detect and combat possible terrorist use of bioweapons. And since the emergence of AIDS in the 1980s, the CDC has taken a major leadership role in tracking the course of the AIDS epidemic in the United States and elsewhere in the world.

Since the start of the AIDS epidemic, the CDC has been the leading agency helping to prevent the spread of HIV (the virus that causes AIDS) as well as providing surveillance. "As of December 2000, 774,467 AIDS cases have been reported in the U.S., including 640,022 cases reported among men and 124,441 among women. By race/ethnicity, 330,160 AIDS cases have been reported among whites, 292,522 among blacks, and 141,694 among [Latinos]." Currently, according to the CDC, African Americans are most at risk for contracting the virus. Figure 21.3 shows that African Americans accounted for 50 percent of reported HIV infections in 2001; however, African Americans make up only 12.3 percent of the U.S. population. Whites accounted for 29 percent of reported HIV infections and Latinos accounted for 19 percent of HIV infections in 2001.

Figure 21.4 shows reported HIV infections by gender and race in 2001. The chart that addresses HIV infection among men shows that 43 percent of those infected were African American, 35 percent were white, and 20 percent were Latinos.

In general, men who have sex with men, or MSMs, represent the largest proportion of reported new HIV infections at 42 percent, followed by heterosexual men at 32 percent. In fact, men make up the largest proportion of new infections at 70 percent of new HIV infections.

The CDC suggests that heterosexual contact followed by injection drug use is the leading cause of HIV infection among African-American women. It cautions people not to think of race and ethnicity as risk factors in themselves, because they are not, but people from certain racial and ethnic groups have to endure many challenges that are associated with the risk of HIV infection, such as poverty, denial and discrimination, partners at risk, substance abuse, and a connection to sexually transmitted diseases. Currently, and due in part to the research conducted by the CDC, people are living longer with HIV/AIDS than they have in the past.

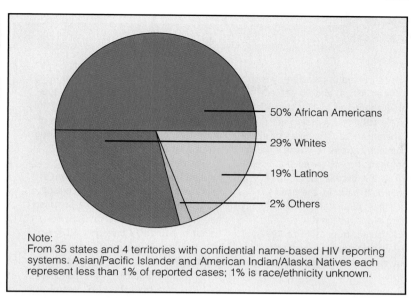

Figure 21.3 Reported HIV Infections by Race, 2001 (N = 35,575)

Source: Centers for Disease Control.

The CDC employs a number of strategies to prevent the spread of HIV and AIDS; such strategies "include monitoring the epidemic to target prevention and care activities, researching the effectiveness of prevention methods, funding local prevention efforts for high-risk communities, and fostering linkages with care and treatment programs." The CDC also provides counseling, testing, community outreach services, and even treatment and prevention for other sexually transmitted diseases. It also encourages creative approaches to communicating with the public about sexual behavior and HIV/AIDS. The creative use of soap operas by AIDS activist Miguel Sabido, described in the Popular Culture and Social Change box on page 630, is an example of highly innovative forms of public education about the disease in Mexico. Conflicts over public discussion of sexuality in the United States make such television programming far more difficult to find in the media.

THE SOCIAL EPIDEMIOLOGY OF OBESITY Another serious threat to public health in the United States and other affluent nations is obesity. A certain amount of body fat is essential to good health—for stored energy, heat insulation, shock absorption, and other functions. Women as a rule have more body fat than men, but men with more than 25 percent and women with more than 30 percent body fat are obese, according to most public health

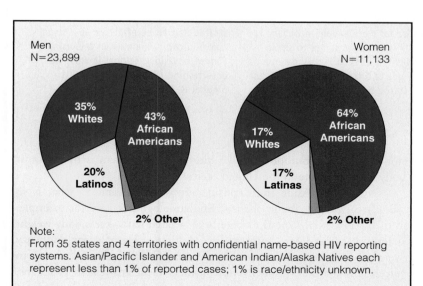

Figure 21.4 Reported HIV Infections by Gender and Race, 2001

Source: Centers for Disease Control.

POPULAR CULTURE & SOCIAL CHANGE   Radio Soaps and the Fight Against AIDS

Miguel Sabido is not a media star. Few people in the United States, outside the world of professional media, know his name. But this Mexican social activist, television executive, and soap opera writer/producer is one of the world's most important influences in the global battle against the exploitation of women and the spread of AIDS. Sabido's social-content soap operas, which he began producing in Mexico in 1977, have become so popular that his approach to using popular culture to teach about sensitive and critical issues is considered one of the most important tools in the fight against AIDS.

Sabido's work, based in part on the highly influential social-learning theories of Stanford University social psychologist Alfred Bandura, uses the media and a culture's forms of folk entertainment to motivate family planning, AIDS prevention, and respect for women. His approach has been used in India, many parts of Africa, and Latin America. Here is a glimpse at the Sabido method in action in the African nation of Tanzania (Ryerson, 2002).

The problem of HIV/AIDS in sub-Saharan Africa, particularly in eastern and southern African countries such as Tanzania, Uganda, Botswana, and South Africa, represents a social catastrophe of historic proportions. Sub-Saharan Africa has the highest rate of infection among adults and children in the world. At least 70 percent of the

total HIV-infected population lives in sub-Saharan Africa, and 90 percent of children infected by HIV through mother-to-child transmission are in sub-Saharan Africa. The need for effective communications to young African women about how to avoid the disease is critical, but because southern Africa is highly paternalistic, the need to educate men about safe sex and family planning is just as great.

In Tanzania, from 1993 to 1997, Radio Tanzania's radio broadcasts of a serial melodrama (radio soap opera)

Miguel Sabido.

Courtesy Population Media Center, www.populationmedia.org

based on the Sabido model became wildly successful among men and women. Sabido and his followers use radio more often than television because far more people in high-poverty areas have access to small, portable radios even if they cannot easily get to a television. A main character in the popular Tanzanian soap

opera was a truck driver who had many girlfriends along his route. In the program, he contracts AIDS, and all of his women friends are put in situations of grave risk, a common occurrence along Africa's vital trucking routes.

The broadcasts were so entertaining and humorous, and yet filled with important content, that 82 percent of the listeners surveyed said the programs had caused them to change their behavior to avoid HIV infection. Most said that they were beginning to use condoms and limiting the number of their sexual partners. Independent data from the AIDS Control Programme of the government of Tanzania found a 153 percent increase in condom distribution in the broadcast areas during the first year of the soap opera. Condom distribution in a temporary control area that did not receive the broadcasts increased only 16 percent in the same period.

Sabido argues that the mass audiences commercial communication can create are absolutely essential for social change. To effectively address enormous human problems like AIDS, abuse of women, and poverty, one needs to reach mass audiences and hold their attention as important social learning takes place. Sabido's work demonstrates that to be effective as a social communicator, commercial television cannot have low ratings: It must be entertaining (Panford et al., 2001; Singhal & Rogers, 1999).

experts. Measuring how much fat one carries is not a simple matter, however, because of other aspects of body mass such as height and bone density.

By calculating a person's body mass index (BMI) to control for height, and studying the distribution of BMI in different populations, epidemiologists can determine the proportions of a population that are overweight or obese. By these measures, approximately 25 percent of Americans are obese, and rates of obesity are rising rapidly

in Europe as well, although the problem is by far most acute in the United States.

Aside from considerations of appearance, what is so bad about obesity? Epidemiologists know, for example, that Type II diabetes is associated with excess body weight and the consumption of high levels of sugar and fatty foods. Cardiovascular disease is also closely related to obesity. When one considers all health-related problems, obesity costs an estimated $96 billion a year in excess

Race, Income, and Obesity

A study done by the Centers for Disease Control and Prevention shows that obesity rates in the United States have a direct correlation to race, ethnicity, and income level.

Figure 21.5 Race, Income, and Obesity

Source: Barboza, 2000.

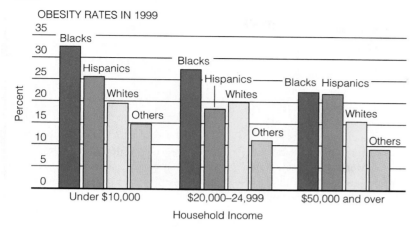

OBESITY RATES IN 1999

health care costs, making it second only to smoking as a public health problem. And it is also a social problem in that it is closely related to other aspects of inequality and to the way high-fat foods are marketed in the U.S. food industry (Stephen, 2003).

Social epidemiologists have shown that the increases we are seeing in obesity are fundamentally related to inequalities of class and race. Poor people, who are also more likely to be members of minority groups, are less likely to have access to healthy diets and more likely to have fast-food stores in their neighborhoods, where sugars and fatty foods become a staple of the family diet. People in low-income urban communities or more isolated rural areas have far fewer choices in available foods. "They don't have big supermarkets in their areas," notes sociologist William Julius Wilson, an expert on the lifestyles of the poor, and people on low incomes eat large amounts of more inexpensive but delicious starchy-fat foods like fried potatoes and macaroni with cheese, which are extremely high in calories. As Figure 21.5 shows, people whose household income is under $10,000 are especially prone to obesity, an effect that minority status only increases (Barboza, 2000).

In addition to low income, the number of hours parents spend at work—the hours that children spend watching television and sitting around eating during the day—is highly correlated with children's body fat. And these practices are more common in neighborhoods where parents are afraid to let their children go outside for exercise. Cuts in school budgets for athletics and physical education and more emphasis on cramming for high-stakes standardized tests are other afflictions of the poor that are implicated in the obesity epidemic.

So are the practices of the fast-food industry, which markets its high-fat and high-sugar content foods to children and adults with particular success in communities of the working poor, where harried parents have less time to prepare more nutritious dinners and less knowledge about the dangers of high-fat diets. In response to criticism and to lawsuits by obese consumers, the major fast-food chains have begun to offer more vegetables and salads, and less fat-saturated foods (Carpenter & Bartley, 1994; Gale, 2003).

CRITICAL SOCIOLOGY AND SOCIAL CHANGE

Patients' Rights and Medical Practice

In recent years, medical sociologists have faced a new and serious challenge: helping society cope with the ethical issues that arise as it becomes increasingly possible to prolong human life by artificial means. Procedures such as heart transplants are extremely expensive and cannot possibly be made available to all patients who need them. Are they to be limited to those who can pay for them? If not, how should the patients who will benefit from such procedures be chosen? Medical sociologists are often asked to conduct research that will affect decisions of this nature—a form of technology assessment.

An issue that has arisen as a result of advances in medical technology—as well as the sensational actions of "assisted suicide" advocate Dr. Jack Kevorkian—is what exactly constitutes death. Should a person whose brain has stopped functioning be considered dead even if other life functions

Text continues on page 634.

VISUAL SOCIOLOGY

12001 AD: ARE YOU LISTENING? CAN YOU UNDERSTAND?

As sociologist Kai Erikson learned in his study of new forms of risk and danger, the disposal of dangerous radioactive wastes poses a staggering variety of technical and social dilemmas. From a sociological standpoint, however, few are as challenging as that of how to communicate with people in a future civilization that might have nothing in common with our own.

Radioactive waste products remain dangerous for thousands of years. Even if these wastes are buried in caverns deep below the desert, it will be necessary to post warnings in case, for whatever reason, people penetrate the barriers and come near the dangerous materials. Conventional symbols or signs, such as "DANGER, RADIOACTIVE WASTES—DO NOT ENTER," might suffice if we could assume that the intruders read English. But can we make that assumption?

Archaeologists can often interpret the purpose of ancient monuments like the Sphinx, although they may not be entirely sure of their interpretations. For example, they cannot always decipher hieroglyphics like those shown here, found in ancient Assyria. How to communicate in a universal fashion with people who do not know our language and culture is the subject of a recent study by the Sandia National Laboratories. The photos and diagrams shown here illustrate some of the possible warnings that could be posted near the materials buried at Yucca Mountain, Nevada, the most likely site for the deposition of nuclear wastes in the United States.

The Sandia researchers doubt that the well-known symbol

for radiation will stand the test of time. They believe that if we are to communicate with people from a future civilization, we must find more universal symbols. For example, some ancient monuments used masks that might evoke dread, like those pictured here from Medinet el Fayyum, Egypt. Perhaps warnings using such universal symbols of fright would work. Another proposed solution involves using dangerous shapes such as the "landscape of thorns" to warn away the curious without relying on language. Still another noncultural, nonlinguistic means of communication is the "black hole" design that evokes fear.

The Sociological Observer

(See photo on page 628.)

The outbreak of SARS raised many questions about how to deal with outbreaks of new, highly contagious diseases. Technology was used to attempt to identify and isolate individuals carrying the virus, as well as to find a medical cure for those

© C.J. Pickerell

D:2   D:3

F:2

F:3

H:2

H:3

© Joel Simon/Getty Images

who were infected. Surgical masks were used to control the spread of the virus, and communication technology was used to inform the public about the dangers of the disease. However, high-speed communication technology can also raise the level of concern about a disease to the level of panic, which can interfere with careful, deliberate medical research. Further, because humans can now travel so freely around the world, so can diseases like SARS.

© concept by Michael Brill, illustration by Safdar Abidi

Metropolitan Museum of Art, New York/Carnarvon Collection, Edward S. Harkness Gift, 1926.

© concept by Michael Brill, illustration by Safdar Abidi

can be maintained by artificial means? Do patients have a "right to die"—that is, to request that life-sustaining equipment be disconnected if the brain has ceased to function? These are extremely difficult questions, and health care institutions, whose function is to strive to maintain life whatever the cost, are ill equipped to deal with them. Critics charge that medical technologies simply prolong the dying process, but courts and legislatures have been reluctant to accept the notion of a right to die—a good example of what Ogburn meant by the phrase *cultural lag.*

The courts have recognized, however, that patients do have the right to decide what medical treatment they will receive and when to terminate treatment. This has resulted in the development of what are called "living wills," in which a patient signs a statement expressing the wish not to be resuscitated in the event of incurable medical conditions in which only artificial life support systems would maintain life. Patients often wish not to cause themselves or their families needless suffering when death is the inevitable outcome. "Heroic" medical interventions such as CPR or other efforts to prevent death may interfere with what is, after all, the natural outcome of a severe illness. In consequence, the living will and instructions not to resuscitate are becoming more common in hospitals in the United States and elsewhere in the world.

Aside from the ethical questions that may arise in situations in which doctors and family members must decide how inevitable death may be and how soon it may occur, several important sociological issues emerge as well. These are well illustrated in a recent national study sponsored by the Robert Wood Johnson Foundation, which examined doctors' actual behavior in situations in which patients have signed living wills.

Under the leadership of William Knaus of the University of Virginia, investigators followed doctors and nurses in five major teaching hospitals as they treated 4,301 desperately ill patients. Among their findings:

- While a third of the patients had asked not to be revived with cardiopulmonary resuscitation, half the time "Do Not Resuscitate" was never written on their charts.

- Nearly 40 percent of patients spent at least 10 days in intensive care, kept alive only by breathing machines.

- Half the patients able to communicate in their last 3 days of life reported that they were in severe pain (Jaroff, 1995).

Joanne Lynn of George Washington University, a codirector of the study, observed that "We don't decide to let patients die in peace until almost the last moment. This is hard on patients, their families, and the health professionals who care for them." The investigators were convinced that poor communication is the primary cause of disregard of the patient's wishes and instructions. They designed a follow-up study of another 4,800 dying patients to test this hypothesis. Half the patients were treated in conventional fashion. The other half were assisted by a specially trained nurse who "consulted with patients and their families, forced them to confront the realities of dying, and kept doctors informed about their patients' conditions and wishes." The investigators were stunned to find that the nurses' intervention had no significant effect on the outcome. "The tools that experts thought would work didn't," Lynn comments. "Physicians are taught to save lives, that death is failure," she says. "Patients and families have come to expect miracles in every case. No one wants to give up too soon."

Even if doctors, nurses, and often the patients' families are unwilling to end heroic efforts to prolong life, sociologists observe forces within medical institutions that are putting pressure on doctors to honor patients' right to die in peace (Prough, 2001). About 30 percent of all Medicare payments go to patients in their last year of life. This suggests that medical insurance companies and health maintenance organizations will increasingly place pressure on doctors to question what they see as a moral obligation to use life-saving technologies even when there is no chance of success. "We have to recognize," Lynn concludes, "that there are alternatives to ending life hooked up to high-tech machines" (quoted in Jaroff, 1995, p. 76).

SUMMARY
The Nature of Science and Technology

- A hallmark of the modern social order is the conduct of scientific research in universities and other research organizations.

- *Science* is knowledge obtained as a result of the process of developing and testing hypotheses.

- Pure science is scientific investigation devoted to the pursuit of knowledge for its own sake. Applied science is the application of known scientific principles to a practical problem.

- *Technology* involves the use of tools and knowledge to manipulate the physical environment to achieve desired practical goals.

- Technology is much older than science, but the discoveries of modern science are creating new technologies at a rapid rate and have greatly expanded the human capacity to live in and exploit different habitats.

- Negative effects of technological change have led to calls for *sustainable development,* or development that does not damage the environment or create new environmental burdens.

- One of the most basic norms of scientific institutions is *universalism,* which holds that the truth of scientific knowledge must be determined by the impersonal criteria of the scientific method.

- Another norm of science is the *common ownership* of scientific findings (although such findings sometimes bear the name of the person who first published them).

- A third norm of scientific institutions is *disinterestedness,* meaning that scientists do not allow the desire for personal gain to influence the reporting and evaluation of results.

- The technologies produced by scientific research are a major force in shaping and changing other institutions.

Technology in Modern Societies

- The basic dimensions of technology are physical devices or apparatus, the activities associated with their use, and the organizational networks within which those activities are carried out.

- The fact that technological changes often have both positive and negative effects is sometimes referred to as *technological dualism.*

- Sociologists recognize that social institutions are often slow to adapt to changing technologies. This recognition forms the basis of the theory known as *cultural lag.*

- The time required for social institutions to adapt to technological change can be reduced by the process of *technology assessment,* or efforts to anticipate the consequences of particular technologies for individuals and for society as a whole.

Impacts of Technology

- The increasing complexity of modern technology has led to a new kind of catastrophe: the failure of whole systems.

- The enormous risks associated with complex technologies have led many observers to call for a more thorough assessment of the potential impact of new technologies before they are put into operation. This is especially important from the standpoint of protection of the environment.

Health and Technological Change

- The complex interactions between technology and other aspects of the social order are illustrated by the case of medical technology.

- Until relatively recently, physicians were powerless either to check the progress of disease or to prolong life. Scientific research led to the discovery of the causes of many diseases during the nineteenth century, but in the twentieth century a vast array of technologies were developed both for the prevention and cure of illnesses and for the long-term care of terminally ill patients.

- The technologies used in the diagnosis and treatment of serious illnesses require extremely expensive equipment and highly trained personnel. This has caused health care to become very expensive, and as a result some groups in the population are unable to obtain adequate care.

- Some critics claim that extreme emphasis on technological progress has created a situation in which the needs of the patient are subordinated to those of the providers of health care.

- Social epidemiology looks for the fundamental causes of health problems in basic social and cultural conditions that are often the precursors of health problems. The policies they advocate often address social issues like poverty, racism, gender bias, and job stress.

- The Centers for Disease Control and Prevention is a pioneer in the use of epidemiological studies to track the AIDS epidemic, increasing rates of obesity, and other serious health conditions.

GLOSSARY

science: Knowledge obtained as a result of the process of developing and testing hypotheses. (p. 614)

technology: The use of tools and knowledge to manipulate the physical environment in order to achieve desired practical goals. (p. 614)

sustainable development: Development that does not damage the environment or create new environmental burdens. (p. 615)

cultural lag: The time required for social institutions to adapt to a major technological change. (p. 620)

technology assessment: Efforts to anticipate the consequences of particular technologies for individuals and for society as a whole. (p. 621)

INTERNET RESOURCES

Virtual Society: The Wadsworth Sociology Resource Center
(http://sociology.wadsworth.com)

At Virtual Society you can access a wide range of enrichment material to aid your study of sociology. From the main page, click on the Student Resources link and find your course and this textbook. Next, select the chapter you are presently studying from the pull-down menu. Among the useful options for each self-study chapter are online links and exercises, flashcards, practical study tips, and practice quizzes for each chapter.

MC MicroCase Online

From the Virtual Society home page, click on MicroCase Online to access book-specific MicroCase exercises that allow you to further explore sociological issues and principles presented in the text.

InfoTrac College Edition

Another unique option available to you at the Student Resources section at Virtual Society is InfoTrac College Edition, an online library with access to hundreds of scholarly and popular periodicals. Below are suggested search terms for this chapter, but this resource also allows you to fit your study of sociology to your own interests by searching custom keywords.

Sustainable development

Medicine

Energy

Cultural lag

National Institutes of Health
(www.nih.gov)

Health information, press releases about scientific discoveries, and a link to scientific resources are all found at this site. The site also has links to major support services, including CancerNet, AIDS information, and clinical alerts.

UNAIDS: The Joint United Nations Programme on HIV/AIDS
(www.unaids.org)

A good place to begin searching for health resources on a global basis. The AIDS page provides many links to other health resources.

Women's Health Interactive
(www.womens-health.com)

Offers interactive sessions on a wide variety of critical health issues affecting women throughout the world.

Appendix

CAREERS IN SOCIOLOGY

What could be more stimulating than to spend a lifetime learning and teaching about human society? But can one really make a living as a sociologist? And what use is a sociology major if one does not go on to do graduate work in sociology?

In attempting to answer these questions, it is helpful to distinguish between careers in sociology itself and applications of sociology in other fields. It may also help to know that throughout the world many government and business leaders are sociologists.

In North America, most sociologists with graduate degrees teach and conduct research in colleges and universities. This has been true since the early decades of the twentieth century, but there is a growing trend toward the application of sociology in many fields outside academia. More than 25 percent of sociologists now work for nonacademic employers (American Sociological Association, 2003; Lyson & Squires, 1993). But sociological training does not have to lead to a sociological career. It can be valuable preparation for careers in a wide variety of other professions, including law, business, education, architecture, medicine, social work, politics, and public administration. Whatever the specific occupation, the emphasis will be on understanding human behavior and relationships in different kinds of social settings.

For most careers in sociology, a graduate degree is necessary—a Ph.D. in the case of academic sociology, and an M.A. or Ph.D. for most jobs in applied fields. However, a B.A. in sociology can often be of value in occupations outside of sociology. At any educational level, a sociologist is likely to specialize in a particular area, such as the family, education, health, environmental issues, sex roles, the military, or law enforcement.

The majority of sociologists earn more than $50,000 a year. As in many professions, men tend to earn more than women. The American Sociological Association continues to promote equality of opportunity for women and minorities; a survey of sociologists found that about 70 percent of the women thought their opportunities for promotion and advancement were either very good or pretty good (Lyson & Squires, 1993). The association has also established a minority scholarship program and continually seeks to improve the representation of minority groups in sociology.

Academic Careers

Colleges and universities may place differing amounts of emphasis on teaching and on conducting research. At major universities, professors of sociology are expected to devote a significant portion of their time to original research and writing for publication, while at smaller colleges there is more emphasis on teaching. This is not to say that sociologists in smaller institutions do not do research, just that more importance is attached to their teaching.

A professor of sociology at a large university must have a Ph.D. He or she may teach four or five courses a year, including advanced seminars for graduate students. But research and writing are likely to play a greater role in his or her career development. Research projects may be financed by grants from federal or other research agencies, and graduate students may be hired as research assistants using funds from the grant. The professor then can use the project as a means of teaching at the graduate level, while concentrating on publishing scholarly articles and, sometimes, books. The latter are an important element in the university's decision regarding tenure, or guaranteed employment, which is generally made during the individual's fifth or sixth year on the faculty.

A sociology instructor in a community college may have an M.A., although many of these institutions now require a Ph.D. He or she typically does a great deal of teaching—perhaps five courses a semester. Although this teaching load becomes less demanding as courses are repeated, the instructor must continually seek out up-to-date materials and be alert to innovations in teaching techniques. In addition to preparing for courses, he or she is expected to serve on academic and research committees, meet with individual students, and keep abreast of new developments in sociology and related fields.

Another important consideration is that sociologists at colleges and universities not only teach sociology to graduate and undergraduate sociology majors, but also teach students in other disciplines such as law, education, medicine, social work, and nursing. Almost eight out of ten practicing sociologists are teaching in universities, colleges, and high schools.

Careers in Applied Sociology

Opportunities for sociologists in government, business, and not-for-profit organizations are extremely varied and can be categorized in a number of ways. One approach (Rossi & Whyte, 1983) is to divide applied sociology into three main branches: applied social research, social engineering, and clinical sociology. Applied social research is similar in many ways to the basic research conducted at universities, except that it is conducted in order to obtain empirically based knowledge of applied issues. It may take the form of descriptive studies such as victimization surveys, analytical research such as studies of voter preferences, or evaluation research—that is, systematic attempts to estimate the potential effects of a proposed social program or a new approach to management in a business firm. Social engineering goes a step further and attempts to use sociological knowledge to design social policies or institutions with a specific purpose. An example is the federally funded preschool program known as Head Start. Clinical sociology refers to the use of sociological knowledge in providing assistance to individuals and organizations. A clinical sociologist might, for example, work with a large corporation to find ways of improving employee morale.

To get an idea of the variety of job opportunities in applied sociology, consider the following examples (American Sociological Association, 2003):

RESEARCH DIRECTOR IN A HEALTH CENTER Sociologists employed by state-supported health science centers teach future physicians, nurses, and other health care professionals about the sociological aspects of health care. Among other things, they provide data about the population groups served by the center and the distribution of disease and health care needs in those groups.

STAFF RESEARCHER IN A FEDERAL AGENCY Many sociologists are employed in various positions by federal agencies. An example is a staff member of a program that administers grants to researchers at universities throughout the country. This involves discussing research plans with applicants and monitoring grants that have been awarded.

MEMBER OF THE PLANNING STAFF IN A STATE DEPARTMENT OF TRANSPORTATION Opportunities for sociologists in state agencies are also varied. An example is performing long-range forecasting for the transportation department, which entails projecting population shifts in major urban and suburban areas. The sociologist must keep informed about relevant research and prepare frequent reports and analyses based on recent studies.

STAFF ADMINISTRATOR IN A PUBLIC ASSISTANCE AGENCY In local government, a sociologist might serve as program coordinator for a city social-service department. This job would include processing reports and legal forms as well as direct contact with clients of the agency—particularly individuals who are poor, disabled, aged, or members of minority groups. In addition, it would involve helping clients solve personal problems by referring them to other public and private agencies that provide assistance of various kinds.

STAFF MEMBER OF A RESEARCH INSTITUTE A sociologist employed by a private research institute might help carry out studies of specific problems at the request of government agencies, businesses, or political organizations. This could involve developing new research projects (including writing grant proposals) as well as supervising existing ones.

Careers in Other Fields

People with sociological training often work in other occupations that use their training, even if they are not specifically referred to as sociologists. For example, a personnel manager in a small manufacturing firm would be considered a business executive rather than a sociologist. But training in industrial sociology and social psychology can be immensely valuable in carrying out the responsibilities of a personnel manager—for instance, in setting strategies and programs for hiring, training, supervising, and promoting employees. Many businesses and other organizations have come to recognize that sociological training is worthwhile for administrators and executives.

Kenneth Donow, a senior adviser to the Public Service Satellite Consortium in Washington, D.C., is an example of a sociologist who has made a successful transition from an academic career to a career in business. Although his training was geared toward a university position, Donow's interest in communications and information policy steered him toward the business world. He was hired by a consulting firm to analyze the worldwide semiconductor industry. It soon became clear to him that business analysis involves the study of formal organizations and social networks, something for which sociologists are ideally suited. He was able to convince other business clients to incorporate sociological approaches into their operations and notes that today "sociological practice has become fully integrated into the largest U.S. corporations" (1990, p. 6). Donow believes that people with sociological training will be increasingly sought by American businesses during the next few decades.

There are many other areas in which sociological training is viewed as appropriate preparation for employment. A publication of the American Sociological Association (2003) lists the following positions among those that can be obtained with an undergraduate degree in sociology: interviewer, research assistant, recreation worker, group worker, teacher (if certified), administrative assistant, probation and parole worker, career counselor, community planner, editorial assistant, social worker (not certified), and statistical assistant. A graduate degree can also be useful outside of sociology. For example, if you seek a career in a particular industry or field—such as transportation—participating in original research in that field as part of a graduate degree program can provide a means of entering the field with the help of individuals who notice and respect your work.

Employment Prospects

The directors of the American Sociological Association believe that "the future appears bright for sociology. The [present] century may be the most exciting and critical period in the field's history." The Association anticipates a surge in the hiring of younger sociologists as professors, research personnel, and administrators with sociological backgrounds who are part of the baby boom generation retire from the workforce. Moreover, "internationalization of both higher education and the profession of sociology will also lead to new opportunities inside academia and in applied settings" (American Sociological Association, 1995, p. 22).

In the 1980s, a study of the specific types of jobs held by recipients of M.A. and Ph.D. degrees in sociology found that close to half the M.A.s and one-third of the Ph.D.s were employed by government agencies. About one-third of the Ph.D.s were employed by not-for-profit organizations, as were about one-fourth of the M.A.s. About a fifth of each group were employed in the private sector (Huber, 1984). These patterns hold true today as well, but with some significant changes. More sociologists are working in the private sector—especially in advertising, telecommunications, computers and software development, and personnel—and somewhat fewer are working in the public sector.

Not-for-profit foundations and companies continue to look to people with sociological training. In this era of corporate downsizing and reductions in funding for public institutions, people with diverse training in sociological methods and theories often find that they have the flexibility required in today's employment market. The American Sociological Association notes that "solid training in sociology at the undergraduate or graduate levels forms a foundation for flexible career development. The better your training and the more skills you have acquired, the better you will be able to take advantage of new opportunities" (1995, p. 22).

Preparing for a Career in Sociology

A bachelor's degree in sociology provides excellent preparation for either graduate study or employment. However, few employers look specifically for sociology B.A.s in preference to other liberal arts degrees. To enhance the value of a B.A. in sociology relative to degrees in other fields, it is advisable to emphasize courses in research methods and statistics.

A graduate degree is necessary to become a practicing sociologist. It is required for any career in academic sociology and for most careers in applied sociology. An M.A. or M.S. is sufficient for teaching in high schools or 2-year colleges, or for employment in public agencies and private firms. A Ph.D. is usually necessary for teaching and research in universities and for high-level positions in research institutes, private industry, and government agencies.

The Ph.D. generally requires 4 or 5 years of study, often including the completion of an M.A. In many graduate schools, work is available as part of the learning experience; the graduate student may be employed as a teaching assistant (TA) or research assistant (RA). A TA typically grades exams, meets with students who need extra help, and leads discussion sections. As noted earlier, RAs are generally hired by faculty members who have received grants for specific research projects.

Most graduate degree programs begin with courses on basic theoretical issues, research methods, and statistics. After a year of such courses, the student may take an examination and perhaps be awarded the master's degree. Subsequently the emphasis shifts from course work to actual research. In this phase, the student is exposed to a wide variety of research methods, including computer skills, in-depth interviewing, participant observation, and use of census materials, questionnaires, and surveys. This is followed by a set of Ph.D. examinations, which may be written or oral, and then by the writing of a dissertation. The dissertation must be an original piece of scholarship. Usually it entails submitting a formal proposal to a committee of faculty advisers, who also preside over the student's oral defense of the dissertation when it is completed.

More than 130 universities in the United States offer a Ph.D. in sociology, and most of them also offer an M.A. or M.S. More than 150 other schools offer only an M.A.

Some graduate programs in sociology are designed specifically to prepare students for nonacademic careers in business or government. They may, for example, substitute internships in agency offices for the traditional TA or RA experience.

Applicants to graduate sociology programs do not have to have an undergraduate major in sociology, but the requirements of graduate departments differ considerably in such areas as foreign language skills and statistics courses. Many departments require applicants to take the Graduate Record Examination (GRE) and have scores available by the beginning of the calendar year. This is particularly important for financial aid decisions. Letters of recommendation can greatly influence the decisions of graduate admissions committees.

The reputation of the institution from which an individual receives a graduate degree can have a significant effect on career opportunities. In addition, graduate departments differ in the quality of their programs in various specialties, such as criminology, demography, the study of the family, and so on. The prospective degree candidate should pay careful attention to the department's reputation in specific areas as well as the reputation of the college or university itself. And, of course, it is a good idea to apply to several graduate programs.

To aid students in choosing a graduate program in sociology, the American Sociological Association issues an annual publication titled *Guide to Graduate Departments of Sociology*. This guide contains information about more than 200 degree programs in the United States and Canada— including degrees awarded, names and specialties of faculty members, special programs, tuition and fees, availability of fellowships and assistantships, deadlines for applications, and how to obtain further information and application forms. The guide is available in college libraries or can be ordered from the American Sociological Association, 1722 N Street N.W., Washington, D.C. 20036.

References

American Sociological Association (1995). *Careers in sociology*. Washington, DC: American Sociological Association.

American Sociological Association (2003). www.asanet.org/research/reportcard.htm.

Donow, K. R. (1990, April). On the transition from the academy to a career in business. *Footnotes* (American Sociological Association), p. 6.

Huber, B. J. (1984). *Career possibilities for sociology graduates*. Washington, DC: American Sociological Association.

Lyson, T. A., & Squires, G. D. (1993, February). The "lost generation" of sociologists. *Footnotes* (American Sociological Association), pp. 4–5.

Rossi, P. H., & Whyte, W. F. (1983). The applied side of sociology. In H. E. Freeman, R. R. Dynes, P. H. Rossi, and W. F. Whyte (Eds.), *Applied sociology*. San Francisco: Jossey-Bass.

Glossary

accommodation: The process by which a smaller, less powerful society is able to preserve the major features of its culture even after prolonged contact with a larger, stronger culture.

acculturation: The process by which the members of a civilization incorporate norms and values from other cultures into their own.

achieved status: A position or rank that is earned through the efforts of the individual.

age cohort: A set of people of about the same age who are passing through the life course together.

age grade: A set of statuses and roles based on age.

ageism: An ideology that justifies prejudice and discrimination based on age.

agencies of socialization: The groups of people, along with the interactions that occur within those groups, that influence a person's social development.

agents of socialization: Individuals who socialize others.

alienation: The feeling of being powerless to control one's own destiny; a worker's feeling of powerlessness caused by inability to control the work process.

animism: A form of religion in which all forms of life and all aspects of the earth are inhabited by gods or supernatural powers.

anomie: A state of normlessness.

anticipatory socialization: Socialization that prepares an individual for a role that he or she is likely to assume later in life.

ascribed status: A position or rank that is assigned to an individual at birth and cannot be changed.

assimilation: The process by which culturally distinct groups in a larger civilization adopt the norms, values, and language of the host civilization and are able to gain equal statuses in its groups and institutions; a pattern of intergroup relations in which a minority group is absorbed into the majority population and eventually disappears as a distinct group.

authority: Power that is considered legitimate both by those who exercise it and by those who are affected by it; power whose exercise is governed by the norms and statuses of organizations.

behaviorism: A theory stating that all behavior is learned and that this learning occurs through the process known as conditioning.

bisexuality: Sexual orientation toward either sex.

bureaucracy: A formal organization characterized by a clearly defined hierarchy with a commitment to rules, efficiency, and impersonality.

capitalism: A system for organizing the production of goods and services that is based on markets, private property, and the business firm or company.

caste: A social stratum into which people are born and in which they remain for life.

charisma: A special quality or "gift" that motivates people to follow a particular leader.

charismatic authority: Authority that comes to an individual through a personal calling, often claimed to be inspired by supernatural powers, and is legitimated by people's belief that the leader does indeed have God-given powers.

church: A religious organization that has strong ties to the larger society.

citizenship: The status of membership in a nation-state.

class: A social stratum that is defined primarily by economic criteria such as occupation, income, and wealth.

class consciousness: A group's shared subjective awareness of its objective situation as a class.

civil religion: A collection of beliefs and rituals that exist outside religious institutions.

civil society: The sphere of nongovernmental, nonbusiness social activity carried out by voluntary associations, congregations, and the like.

civilization: A cultural complex formed by the identical major cultural features of several societies.

closed question: A question that requires the respondent to choose among a predetermined set of answers.

closed society: A society in which social mobility does not exist.

closed stratification system: A stratification system in which there are rigid boundaries between social strata.

cohort: All persons born in a specified time span.

collective behavior: Nonroutine behavior that is engaged in by large numbers of people responding to a common stimulus.

community: A set of primary and secondary groups in which the individual carries out important life functions.

conditioning: The shaping of behavior through reward and punishment.

confidentiality: The promise that the information provided to a researcher by a respondent will not appear in any way that can be traced to that respondent.

control group: In an experiment, the subjects who do not experience a change in the independent variable.

controlled experiment: An experimental situation in which the researcher manipulates an independent variable in order to observe and measure changes in a dependent variable.

conflict perspective: A sociological perspective that emphasizes the role of conflict and power in society.

core state: A technologically advanced nation that has a dominant position in the world economy.

correlation: A specific relationship between two variables.

counterculture: A subculture that challenges the accepted norms and values of the larger society and establishes an alternative lifestyle.

crime: An act, or omission of an act, that is prohibited by law.

crowd: A large number of people who are gathered together in close proximity to one another.

crude birthrate: The number of births occurring during a year in a given population, divided by the midyear population.

crude death rate: The number of deaths occurring during a year in a given population, divided by the midyear population.

cult: A new religion.

cultural evolution: The process by which successful cultural adaptations are passed down from one generation to the next.

cultural lag: The time required for social institutions to adapt to a major technological change.

cultural relativity: The recognition that all cultures develop their own ways of dealing with the specific demands of their environments.

culture: All the modes of thought, behavior, and production that are handed down from one generation to the next by means of communicative interaction rather than by genetic transmission.

de facto segregation: Segregation created and maintained by unwritten norms.

de jure segregation: Segregation created by formal legal sanctions that prohibit certain groups from interacting with others or place limits on such interactions.

deference: The respect and esteem shown to an individual.

demagogue: A leader who uses personal charisma and political symbols to manipulate public opinion.

demeanor: The ways in which individuals present themselves to others through body language, dress, speech, and manners.

democracy: A political system in which all citizens have the right to participate in public decision making.

democratic socialism: An economic philosophy based on the belief that private property may exist at the same time that large corporations are owned by the state and run for the benefit of all citizens.

demographic transition: A set of major changes in birth and death rates that has occurred most completely in urban industrial nations in the past 200 years.

denomination: A religious organization that is on good terms with the institution from which it developed but must compete with other denominations for members.

dependent variable: The variable that a hypothesis seeks to explain.

developing nation: A nation that is undergoing a set of transformations whose effect is to increase the productivity of its people, their health, their literacy, and their ability to participate in political decision making.

deviance: Behavior that violates the norms of a particular society.

differential association: A theory that explains deviance as a learned behavior determined by the extent of a person's association with individuals who engage in such behavior.

differentiation: The processes whereby sets of social activities performed by one social institution are divided among different institutions.

discrimination: Behavior that treats people unfairly on the basis of their group membership.

diversity: A term used to refer to the heterogeneous nature of a society made up of numerous different racial, ethnic, religious, and other population groups.

double standard: The belief that women must adhere to a different and more restrictive moral code than that applied to men.

downward mobility: Movement by an individual or group to a lower social stratum.

dramaturgical approach: An approach to research on interaction in groups that is based on the recognition that much social interaction depends on the desire to impress those who may be watching.

education: The process by which a society transmits knowledge, values, norms, and ideologies and in so doing prepares young people for adult roles and adults for new roles.

educational achievement: How much the student actually learns, measured by mastery of reading, writing, and mathematical skills.

educational attainment: The number of years of school an individual has completed.

ego: According to Freud, the part of the human personality that is the individual's conception of himself or herself in relation to others.

endogamy: A norm specifying that a person brought up in a particular culture may marry within the cultural group.

endogenous force: Pressure for social change that builds within a society.

equality of opportunity: Equal opportunity to achieve desired levels of material well-being and prestige.

equality of result: Equality in the actual outcomes of people's attempts to improve their material well-being and prestige.

ethnic group: A population that has a sense of group identity based on shared ancestry and distinctive cultural patterns.

ethnic (or racial) nationalism: The belief that one's own ethnic group constitutes a distinct people whose culture is and should be separate from that of the larger society.

ethnic stratification: The ranking of ethnic groups in a social hierarchy on the basis of each group's similarity to the dominant group.

ethnocentrism: The tendency to judge other cultures as inferior to one's own.

ethnomethodology: The study of the underlying rules of behavior that guide group interaction.

exogamy: A norm specifying that a person brought up in a particular culture may marry outside the cultural group.

exogenous force: Pressure for social change that is exerted from outside a society.

experimental group: In an experiment, the subjects who are exposed to a change in the independent variable.

expulsion: The forcible removal of one population from a territory claimed by another population.

extended family: An individual's nuclear family plus the nuclear families of his or her blood relatives.

family: A group of people related by blood, marriage, or adoption.

family of orientation: The nuclear family in which a person is born and raised.

family of procreation: The nuclear family a person forms through marriage or cohabitation.

feral child: A child reared outside human society.

field experiment: An experimental situation in which the researcher observes and studies subjects in their natural setting.

folkways: Weakly sanctioned norms.

formal organization: A group that has an explicit, often written, set of norms, statuses, and roles that specify each member's relationships to the others and the conditions under which those relationships hold.

frequency distribution: A classification of data that describes how many observations fall within each category of a variable.

functionalism: A sociological perspective that focuses on the ways in which a complex pattern of social structures and arrangements contributes to social order.

gemeinschaft: A term used to refer to the close, personal relationships of small groups and communities.

gender: The culturally defined ways of acting as a male or a female that become part of an individual's personal sense of self.

gender role: A set of behaviors considered appropriate for an individual of a particular gender.

gender socialization: The ways in which we learn our gender identity and develop according to cultural norms of masculinity and femininity.

generalized other: A person's internalized conception of the expectations and attitudes held by society.

genocide: State-sponsored mass killing explicitly designed to completely exterminate a population deemed to be racially or ethnically different and threatening to the dominant population.

gerontology: The study of aging and older people.

gesellschaft: A term used to refer to the well-organized but impersonal relationships among the members of modern societies.

ghetto: A section of a city that is segregated either racially or culturally.

group: Any collection of people who interact on the basis of shared expectations regarding one another's behavior.

Hawthorne effect: The unintended effect that results from the attention given to subjects in an experimental situation.

hegemony: Undue power or influence.

hermaphrodite: A person whose primary sexual organs have features of both male and female organs, making it difficult to categorize the individual as male or female.

heterosexuality: Sexual orientation toward the opposite sex.

homogamy: The tendency to marry a person who is similar to oneself in social background.

homosexuality: Sexual orientation toward the same sex.

horticultural society: A society whose primary means of subsistence is raising crops, which it plants and cultivates, often developing an extensive system for watering the crops.

human ecology: A sociological perspective that emphasizes the relationships among social order, social disorganization, and the distribution of populations in space and time.

hypothesis: A statement that specifies a relationship between two or more variables that can be tested through empirical observation.

id: According to Freud, the part of the human personality from which all innate drives arise.

ideas: Ways of thinking that organize human consciousness.

identification: The social process whereby an individual chooses role models and attempts to imitate their behavior.

ideologies: Systems of values and norms that the members of a society are expected to believe in and act on without question.

impression management: The strategies one uses to "set a stage" for one's own purposes.

in-group: A social group to which an individual has a feeling of allegiance; usually, but not always, a primary group.

independent variable: A variable that the researcher believes causes a change in another variable (i.e., the dependent variable).

informal organization: A group whose norms and statuses are generally agreed upon but are not set down in writing.

informed consent: The right of respondents to be informed of the purpose for which the information they supply will be used and to judge the degree of personal risk involved in answering questions, even when an assurance of confidentiality has been given.

institution: A more or less stable structure of statuses and roles devoted to meeting the basic needs of people in a society.

institutional discrimination: The systematic exclusion of people from equal participation in a particular institution because of their group membership.

interactionism: A sociological perspective that views social order and social change as resulting from all the repeated interactions among individuals and groups.

interest group: An organization that attempts to influence elected and appointed officials regarding a specific issue or set of issues.

intergenerational mobility: A change in the social class of family members from one generation to the next.

internal colonialism: A theory of racial and ethnic inequality that suggests that some minorities are essentially colonial peoples within the larger society.

intragenerational mobility: A change in the social class of an individual within his or her own lifetime.

Jim Crow: The system of formal and informal segregation that existed in the United States from the late 1860s to the early 1970s.

kinship: The role relations among people who consider themselves to be related by blood, marriage, or adoption.

labeling: A theory that explains deviance as a societal reaction that brands or labels people who engage in certain behaviors as deviant.

laissez-faire capitalism: An economic philosophy based on the belief that the wealth of a nation can be measured by its capacity to produce goods and services (i.e., its resources of land, labor, and machinery) and that these can be maximized by free trade.

laws: Norms that are written by specialists, collected in codes or manuals of behavior, and interpreted and applied by other specialists.

legal authority: Authority that is legitimated by people's belief in the supremacy of the law; obedience is owed not to a person but to a set of impersonal principles.

legitimacy: The ability of a society to engender and maintain the belief that the existing political institutions are the most appropriate for that society.

life chances: The opportunities an individual will have or be denied throughout life as a result of his or her social-class position.

life course: A pathway along an age-differentiated, socially created sequence of transitions.

life expectancy: The average number of years a member of a given population can expect to live.

lifetime negative experiences: Experiences that cause long-term stress, such as the death of a child or spouse.

linguistic-relativity hypothesis: The belief that language determines the possibilities for thought and action in any given culture.

lobbying: The process whereby interest groups seek to persuade legislators to vote in their favor on particular bills.

macro-level sociology: An approach to the study of society that focuses on the major structures and institutions of society.

market: An economic institution that regulates exchange behavior through the establishment of different values for particular goods and services.

mass: A large number of people who are all oriented toward a set of shared symbols or social objects.

mass public: A large population of potential spectators or participants who engage in collective behavior.

master status: A status that takes precedence over all of an individual's other statuses.

material culture: Patterns of possessing and using the products of culture.

megalopolis: A complex of cities distributed along a major axis of traffic and communication, with a total population exceeding 25 million.

mercantilism: An economic philosophy based on the belief that the wealth of a nation can be measured by its holdings of gold or other precious metals and that the state should control trade.

metropolitan area: A central city surrounded by several smaller cities and suburbs that are closely related to it both socially and economically.

micro-level sociology: An approach to the study of society that focuses on patterns of social interaction at the individual level.

middle-level sociology: An approach to the study of society that focuses on relationships between social structures and the individual.

minority group: A population that, because of its members' physical or cultural characteristics, is singled out from others in the society for differential and unequal treatment.

modernization: A term used to describe the changes that societies and individuals experience as a result of industrialization, urbanization, and the development of nation-states.

monotheistic: A term used to describe a theistic belief system centered on belief in a single all-powerful God.

mores: Strongly sanctioned norms.

multinational corporation: An economic enterprise that has headquarters in one country and conducts business activities in one or more other countries.

nation-state: The largest territory within which a society's political institutions can operate without having to face challenges to their sovereignty.

nationalism: The belief of a people that they have the right and the duty to constitute themselves as a nation-state.

natural selection: The relative success of organisms with specific genetic mutations in reproducing new generations with the new trait.

nonterritorial community: A network of relationships formed around shared goals.

normative order: The array of norms that permit a society to achieve relatively peaceful social control.

norms: Specific rules of behavior.

nuclear family: Two or more people related by blood, marriage, or adoption who share a household.

objective class: In Marxian theory, a social class that has a visible, specific relationship to the means of production.

occupational prestige: The honor or prestige attributed to specific occupations by adults in a society.

oligarchy: Rule by a few people who stay in office indefinitely rather than for limited terms.

open question: A question that does not require the respondent to choose from a predetermined set of answers; instead, the respondent may answer in his or her own words.

open society: A society in which social mobility is possible for everyone.

open stratification system: A stratification system in which the boundaries between social strata are easily crossed.

out-group: Any social group to which an individual does not have a feeling of allegiance; may be in competition or conflict with the in-group.

paradigm: A model comprising existing theories and methods; a general way of seeing the world that dictates what kind of scientific work should be done and what kinds of theory are acceptable.

participant observation: A form of observation in which the researcher participates to some degree in the lives of the people being observed.

pastoral society: A society whose primary means of subsistence is herding animals and moving with them over a wide expanse of grazing land.

patriarchy: The dominance of men over women.

peer group: An interacting group of people of about the same age that has a significant influence on the norms and values of its members.

percent analysis: A mathematical operation that transforms an absolute number into a proportion as a part of 100.

peripheral area: A region that supplies basic resources and labor power to more advanced states.

plea bargaining: A process in which a person charged with a crime agrees to plead guilty to a lesser charge.

pluralist model: A theory stating that no single group controls political decisions; instead, a plurality of interest groups influence those decisions through a process of coalition building and bargaining.

pluralistic society: A society in which different ethnic and racial groups are able to maintain their own cultures and lifestyles while gaining equality in the institutions of the larger society.

political institution: A set of norms and statuses pertaining to the exercise of power and authority.

political party: An organization of people who join together to gain legitimate control of state authority.

political revolution: A set of changes in the political structures and leadership of a society.

polytheistic: A term used to describe a theistic belief system that includes numerous gods.

power: The ability to control the behavior of others, even against their will.

power elite model: A theory stating that political decisions are controlled by an elite of rich and powerful individuals even in societies with democratic political institutions.

prejudice: An attitude that prejudges a person on the basis of a real or imagined characteristic of a group to which that person belongs.

primary deviance: An act that results in the labeling of the offender as deviant.

primary group: A small group characterized by intimate, face-to-face associations.

privacy: The right of a respondent to define when and on what terms his or her actions may be revealed to the general public.

profane: A term used to describe phenomena that are not considered sacred.

profession: An occupation with a body of knowledge and a developed intellectual technique that are transmitted by a formal educational process and testing procedures.

projection: The psychological process whereby we attribute to other people behaviors and attitudes that we are unwilling to accept in ourselves.

psychosocial risk behaviors: Behaviors that are detrimental to health, such as smoking and heavy drinking.

public opinion: The values and attitudes held by mass publics.

race: An inbreeding population that develops distinctive physical characteristics that are hereditary.

racism: An ideology based on the belief that an observable, supposedly inherited trait is a mark of inferiority that justifies discriminatory treatment of people with that trait.

rate of reproductive change: The difference between the crude birthrate and the crude death rate for a given population.

recidivism: The probability that a person who has served a jail term will commit additional crimes and be jailed again.

reference group: A group that an individual uses as a frame of reference for self-evaluation and attitude formation.

relative deprivation: Deprivation as determined by comparison with others rather than by some objective measure.

religion: Any set of coherent answers to the dilemmas of human existence that makes the world meaningful; a system of beliefs and rituals that helps bind people together into a social group.

religiosity: The depth of a person's religious feelings.

resocialization: Intense, deliberate socialization designed to change major beliefs and behaviors.

rite of passage: A ceremony marking the transition to a new stage of a culturally defined life course.

ritual: A formal pattern of activity that expresses symbolically a set of shared meanings.

role: The way a society defines how an individual is to behave in a particular status.

role conflict: Conflict that occurs when in order to perform one role well, a person must violate the expectations associated with another role.

role expectations: A society's expectations about how a role should be performed, together with the individual's perceptions of what is required in performing that role.

role strain: Conflict that occurs when the expectations associated with a single role are contradictory.

role taking: Trying to look at social situations from the standpoint of another person from whom one seeks a response.

sacred: A term used to describe phenomena that are regarded as extraordinary, transcendent, and outside the everyday course of events.

sample: A set of respondents selected from a specific population.

sample survey: A survey administered to a selection of respondents drawn from a specific population.

sanctions: Rewards and punishments for abiding by or violating norms.

scapegoat: A convenient target for hostility.

science: Knowledge obtained as a result of the process of developing and testing hypotheses.

scientific method: The process by which theories and explanations are constructed through repeated observation and careful description.

secondary deviance: Behavior that is engaged in as a reaction to the experience of being labeled as deviant.

secondary group: A social group whose members have a shared goal or purpose but are not bound together by strong emotional ties.

sect: A religious organization that rejects the beliefs and practices of existing churches; usually formed when a group leaves the church to form a rival organization.

secularization: A process in which the dominance of religion over other institutions is reduced.

segregation: The ecological and institutional separation of races or ethnic groups.

semiperipheral area: A state or region in which industry and financial institutions are developed to some extent but that remains dependent on capital and technology provided by other states.

sex: The biological differences between males and females, including the primary sex characteristics that are present at birth (i.e., the presence of specific male or female genitalia) and the secondary sex characteristics that develop later (facial and body hair, voice quality, etc.).

sexism: An ideology that justifies prejudice and discrimination based on sex.

sexuality: The manner in which a person engages in the intimate behaviors connected with genital stimulation, orgasm, and procreation.

significant other: Any person who is important to an individual.

simple supernaturalism: A form of religion in which people may believe in a great force or spirit but do not have a well-defined concept of God or a set of rituals involving God.

slavery: The ownership of one racial, ethnic, or politically defined group by another group that has complete control over the enslaved group.

social category: A collection of individuals who are grouped together because they share a trait deemed by the observer to be socially relevant.

social change: Variations over time in the ecological ordering of populations and communities, in patterns of roles and social interactions, in the structure and functioning of institutions, and in the cultures of societies.

social conditions: The realities of the life we create together as social beings.

social control: The set of rules and understandings that control the behavior of individuals and groups in a particular culture.

social Darwinism: The notion that people who are more successful at adapting to the environment in which they find themselves are more likely to survive and to have children who will also be successful.

social group: A set of two or more individuals who share a sense of common identity and belonging and who interact on a regular basis.

social mobility: Movement by an individual or group from one social stratum to another.

social movement: Organized collective behavior aimed at changing or reforming social institutions or the social order itself.

social revolution: A complete transformation of the social order, including the institutions of government and the system of stratification.

social stratification: The process whereby the members of a society are sorted into different statuses; a society's system for ranking people hierarchically according to such attributes as wealth, power, and prestige.

social structure: The recurring patterns of behavior that people create through their interactions, their exchange of information, and their relationships.

socialism: An economic philosophy based on the concept of public ownership of property and sharing of profits, together with the belief that economic decisions should be controlled by the workers.

socialization: The processes whereby we learn to behave according to the norms of our culture.

society: A population that is organized in a cooperative manner to carry out the major functions of life.

sociobiology: The hypothesis that all human behavior is determined by genetic factors.

socioeconomic status (SES): A broad social-class ranking based on occupational status, family prestige, educational attainment, and earned income.

sociological imagination: According to C. Wright Mills, the ability to see how social conditions affect our lives.

sociology: The scientific study of human societies and human behavior in the groups that make up a society.

spatial mobility: Movement of an individual or group from one location or community to another.

state: A society's set of political structures; the set of political institutions operating in a particular society.

status: A socially defined position in a group.

status group: A category of people within a social class, defined by how much honor or prestige they receive from society in general.

status symbols: Material objects or behaviors that indicate social status or prestige.

stereotype: An inflexible image of the members of a particular group that is held without regard to whether it is true.

stigma: An attribute or quality of an individual that is deeply discrediting.

structural mobility: Movement of an individual or group from one social stratum to another, caused by the elimination of an entire class as a result of changes in the means of existence.

subculture: A group of people who hold many of the values and norms of the larger culture but also hold certain beliefs, values, or norms that set them apart from that culture.

subjective class: In Marxian theory, the way members of a given social class perceive their situation as a class.

superego: According to Freud, the part of the human personality that internalizes the moral codes of adults.

sustainable development: Development that does not damage the environment or create new environmental burdens.

technology: Tools, procedures, and forms of social organization that increase human productive capacity; the use of tools and knowledge to manipulate the physical environment in order to achieve desired practical goals.

technology assessment: Efforts to anticipate the consequences of particular technologies for individuals and for society as a whole.

territorial community: A population that functions within a particular geographic area.

theism: A belief system that conceives of a god or gods as separate from humans and from other living things on the earth.

theoretical perspective: A set of interrelated theories that offer explanations for important aspects of social behavior.

theory: A set of interrelated concepts that seeks to explain the causes of an observable phenomenon.

total institution: A setting in which people undergoing resocialization are isolated from the larger society under the control of a specialized staff.

totalitarian regime: A regime that accepts no limits to its power and seeks to exert its rule at all levels of society.

traditional authority: Authority that is hereditary and is legitimated by traditional values, particularly people's idea of the sacred.

transsexuals: People who feel strongly that the sexual organs they were born with do not conform to their deep-seated sense of what their sex should be.

triad: A group consisting of three people.

unobtrusive measures: Observational techniques that measure behavior but intrude as little as possible into actual social settings.

upward mobility: Movement by an individual or group to a higher social stratum.

urbanization: A process in which an increasing proportion of a total population becomes concentrated in urban settlements.

values: The ideas that support or justify norms.

variable: A characteristic of an individual, group, or society that can vary from one case to another.

voluntary association: A formal organization whose members pursue shared interests and arrive at decisions through some sort of democratic process.

welfare capitalism: An economic philosophy in which markets determine what goods will be produced and how, but the government regulates economic competition.

References

Abbott, A. D. (1988). *The system of professions: An essay on the division of expert labor.* Chicago: University of Chicago Press.

Abbott, A. D. (1993). The sociology of work and occupations. *Annual Review of Sociology, 19,* 187–209.

Abbott, A. D. (2001). *Chaos of disciplines.* Chicago: University of Chicago Press.

Abbott, C. (2001, May 14). PW talks with Barbara Ehrenreich. *Publishers Weekly,* p. 68.

Abu-Lugod, J. (1996, January). Personal communication.

Addams, J. (1895). *Hull House maps and papers.* New York: Crowell.

Adler, J., & McCormick, J. (1999, May 10). The truth about high school. *Newsweek,* p. 56.

Adler, M. (1997). *Drawing down the moon: Witches, druids, goddess-worshippers, and other pagans in America today.* New York: Viking.

Adorno, T. (1950). *The authoritarian personality.* New York: Harper.

Africa News Service (2000, July 24). Ethnic violence makes sovereign confab imperative—Soyinka.

Aganbegyan, A. (1989). *Perestroika 1989.* New York: Scribner.

Ahlburg, D. A., & De Vita, C. J. (1992, August). New realities of the American family. *Population Bulletin* (Population Reference Bureau).

Alam, M. (1988). *Studies on brain drain.* Monticello, IL: Vance Bibliographies.

Alan Guttmacher Institute (2001). *Teenage sexual and reproductive behavior in developed countries, 2001.*

Albom, M. (1997). *Tuesdays with Morrie.* Garden City, NY: Doubleday.

Albrecht, D. G. (1997). The changing structure of U.S. agriculture. *Rural Sociology, 62,* 474–490.

Aldous, J. (1982). From dual-earner to dual-career families and back again. In J. Aldous (Ed.), *Two paychecks: Life in dual-career families.* Newbury Park, CA: Sage.

Allen, F. L. (1931). *Only yesterday: An informal history of the 1920s.* New York: Harper.

Allen, G. (1997). Abolishing parole saves lives and property. *Corrections Today, 59,* 22.

Amato, P. R., & Sobolewski, J. M. (2001). The effects of divorce and marital discord on adult children's psychological well-being. *American Sociological Review, 66,* 900–921.

Ammerman, N. T. (1990). *Baptist battles: Social change and religious conflict in the Southern Baptist Convention.* New Brunswick, NJ: Rutgers University Press.

Ammerman, N. T. (1997). Organized religion in a voluntaristic society. *Sociology of Religion, 58,* 203–216.

Ammerman, N. T. (2000, March 15). New life for denominationalism. *Christian Century,* pp. 302–307.

Anderton, D. L. (1997). *The population of the United States* (3rd ed.). New York: Free Press.

Andrews, E. L. (2003, January 23). Economic inequality grew in 90's boom, Fed reports. *New York Times,* pp. 1, 7.

An-Na'im, A. (2002). *Islamic family law in a changing world: A global resource book.* London: Zed Books.

Annie E. Casey Foundation. Annual. *Kids count: A pocket guide on America's youth.* Washington, DC: Population Reference Bureau.

AP (Associated Press) (2002, January 3). A nation challenged: American Muslims. *New York Times,* p. A14.

Applebome, P. (1998, May 10). No room for children in a world of little adults. *New York Times,* sec. 4, pp. 1, 3.

Archibald, K. (1947). *Wartime shipyard.* Berkeley: University of California Press.

Ariès, P. (1962). *Centuries of childhood.* New York: Vintage.

Arnot, M. (2002). Making the difference to sociology of education: Reflections on family–school and gender relations. *Discourse: Studies in the Cultural Politics of Education, 23,* 347–355.

Aron, R. (1955). *The century of total war.* Boston: Beacon.

Aronowitz, S. (1996). Losing and winning in a conservative age. *Social Policy, 27,* 10–21.

Aronowitz, S. (1998). *From the ashes of the old.* Boston: Houghton Mifflin.

Aronowitz, S. (2003). *How class works.* New Haven, CT: Yale University Press.

Aronowitz, S., & DiFazio, W. (1994). *The jobless future: Sci-tech and the dogma of work.* Minneapolis: University of Minnesota Press.

Aronowitz, S., & Giroux, H. A. (1985). *Education under siege.* South Hadley, MA: Bergin and Garvey.

Arrow, K., Bowles, S., & Durlauf, S. (Eds.) (2000). *Meritocracy and economic inequality.* Princeton, NJ: Princeton University Press.

Asch, S. E. (1966). Effects of group pressure upon the modification and distortion of judgments. In H. Proshansky & B. Seidenberg (Eds.), *Basic studies in social psychology.* Fort Worth: Holt, Rinehart and Winston.

Ash, T. G. (1999, February 15). Helena's kitchen. *New Yorker,* pp. 32–39.

Ashmawi, M. S. (1998). *Against Islamic extremism: The writings of Muhammad Sa'id al-'Ashmawy.* Gainesville: University Press of Florida.

Aspaklaria, S. (1985, September 12). A divorced father, a child, and a summer visit together. *New York Times,* p. C1.

Ayala, V. (1996). *Falling through the cracks: AIDS and the urban poor.* Putnam Valley, NY: Social Change Press.

Baber, Z. (2001). Modernization theory and the cold war. *Journal of Contemporary Asia, 31,* 71.

Bacci, M. (1997). *A concise history of world population* (2nd ed.). Malden, MA: Blackwell.

Backer, B. (1982). *Death and dying: Individuals and institutions.* New York: Wiley.

Baker, P. (2003, April 5). Daring rescue of Pvt. Lynch. *Washington Post,* p. A5.

Bakke, E. W. (1933). *The unemployed man.* London: Nisbet.

Balandier, A. (1971/1890). *The delight makers.* Orlando: Harcourt Brace Jovanovich.

Balch, E. G. (1910). *Our Slavic fellow citizens.* New York: Charities Publication Committee.

Baldassare, M. (1986). *Trouble in paradise: The suburban transformation in America.* New York: Columbia University Press.

Baldassare, M. (2003, June 27). How the West is taxed. *New York Times,* p. A27.

Bales, R. F., & Slater, P. E. (1955). Role differentiation in small decision-making groups. In T. Parsons & R. F. Bales (Eds.), *Family, socialization, and interaction process.* New York: Free Press.

Ballantine, J. H. (1997). *The sociology of education: A systematic analysis* (4th ed.). Upper Saddle River, NJ: Prentice Hall.

Baller, R. D., & Richardson, K. K. (2002). Social integration, imitation, and the geographic patterning of suicide. *American Sociological Review, 67.*

Barash, D. (2002). *Peace and conflict studies.* Thousand Oaks, CA: Sage Publications.

Barboza, D. (2000, December 26). Rampant obesity, a debilitating reality for the urban poor. *New York Times,* p. F5.

Barfield, J. (2003, Summer). Single-parent families and the food safety net. *Focus* (Institute for Research on Poverty), pp. 19–23.

Barker, M. (2002, January 21). The day of reckoning. *London Financial Times,* p. 1.

Barnet, R. J. (1994, December 19). Lords of the global economy: Stateless corporations. *The Nation,* pp. 754–758.

Barrett, D. V. (1996). *Sects, "cults," and alternative religions: A world survey and sourcebook.* London: Blandford.

Bashi, V. (1991). Mentoring of at-risk students. *Focus* (University of Wisconsin, Institute for Research on Poverty), *13,* 26–32.

Bassuk, E. L. (1984, July). The homelessness problem. *Scientific American,* 40–45.

Bates, A. (1999, February 15). The siege at Waco: Deadly inferno. *Booklist,* pp. 1050–1051.

Batson, C. D., Batson, J. G., & Todd, R. M. (1995). Empathy and the collective good: Caring for one or the others in a social dilemma. *Journal of Personality and Social Psychology, 68,* 619–631.

Battaglia, L., & Zecchin, F. (1989). *Chroniques siciliennes.* Paris: Centre Nationale de la Photographie.

Battle, J. (2003, August). Unpublished manuscript.

Baum, S. (1987). *Financial aid to low-income college students: Its history and prospects* (Institute for Research on Poverty Discussion Paper No. 846-87). Madison: University of Wisconsin.

Bayer, R. (1988). *Private acts, social consequences: AIDS and the politics of public health.* New York: Free Press.

Bayer, R. (1991). The great drug policy debate. *Millbank Quarterly, 69,* 341–364.

Bearak, B. (1997, April 28). Eyes on glory. *New York Times,* p. A1.

Becker, G. S. (1997, December 29). Why every married couple should sign a contract. *Business Week,* p. 30.

Becker, H. S. (1961). *Boys in white: Student culture in medical school.* Chicago: University of Chicago Press.

Becker, H. S. (1963). *The outsiders: Studies in the sociology of deviance.* New York: Free Press.

Becker, H. S. (2002). Studying the new media. *Qualitative Sociology, 25,* 337–343.

Beebe, S. A. (1997). *Communication in small groups: Principles and practices* (5th ed.). New York: Longman.

Beer, F. A. (1981). *Peace against war: The ecology of international violence.* San Francisco: Freeman.

Bell, D. (1962). Crime as an American way of life. In D. Bell, *The end of ideology.* New York: Free Press.

Bell, D. (1973). *The coming of post industrial society: A venture in social forecasting.* New York: Basic Books.

Bell, D. (1973, 1999). *The coming of post industrial society: A venture in social forecasting.* New York: Basic Books.

Bellah, R. N. (1970). *Beyond belief.* New York: Harper.

Bellah, R. N., Madison, R., Sullivan, W. M., Swidler, A., & Tipton, S. M. (1985). *Habits of the heart: Individualism and commitment in American life.* Berkeley: University of California Press.

Belsky, J. (1988). The "effects" of infant day care reconsidered. *Early Childhood Research Quarterly, 3,* 235–272.

Belsky, J., & Steinberg, L. D. (1991). *Infancy, childhood & adolescence: Development in context.* New York: McGraw-Hill.

Bem, S. L. (1993). *The lenses of gender: Transforming the debate on sexual inequality.* New Haven, CT: Yale University Press.

Benavot, A., et al. (1991). Knowledge for the masses: World models and national curricula, 1920–1986. *American Sociological Review, 56,* 85–91.

Bendix, R. (1969). *Nation-building and citizenship.* Garden City, NY: Doubleday.

Bendix, R. (1974). *Work and authority in industry.* Berkeley: University of California Press.

Bendix, R., & Lipset, S. M. (1966). *Class, status, and power: Social stratification in comparative perspective* (2nd ed.). New York: Free Press.

Beneckson, R. E., Dunn, M., Gonzalez, A., & Marichal, C. (2000). Racial and ethnic disparities in Florida welfare reform: A study of income levels for black, Hispanic and white post-welfare recipients. www.fla-spp.com/research.

Bengston, V., & Schaie, K. W. (Eds.) (1999). *Handbook of theories of aging.* New York: Springer.

Bennett, M. K. (1954). *The world's food.* New York: Harper.

Benokraitis, N. V. (1996). *Marriages and families: Changes, choices, and constraints* (2nd ed.). Upper Saddle River, NJ: Prentice Hall.

Bensman, D., & Lynch, R. (1987). *Rusted dreams: Hard times in a steel community.* New York: McGraw-Hill.

Bentham, J. (1789). *An introduction to the principles of morals and legislation.* London: T. Payne.

Berger, A. A. (2000). *Ads, fads, and consumer culture: Advertising's impact on American character and society.* Oxford, England: Rowman & Littlefield.

Berger, B. (1961). The myth of suburbia. *Journal of Social Issues, 17,* 38–48.

Berger, E. (2002, January 23). Study finds a growing gap between managerial salaries for men and women. *New York Times,* p. A24.

Bergmann, B. R., & Hartmann, H. (1995, May 1). A program to help working parents. *The Nation,* pp. 592ff.

Berlin, I. (1998, May 14). My intellectual path. *New York Review of Books,* pp. 53–60.

Berman, P. (2003). *Terror and liberalism.* New York: Norton.

Berman, S. (1997). *Children's social consciousness and the development of social responsibility.* Albany: State University of New York Press.

Bernard, J. (1964). *Academic women.* University Park: Pennsylvania State University Press.

Bernard, J. (1973). *The sociology of community.* Glenview, IL: Scott, Foresman.

Bernard, J. (1982). *The future of marriage* (2nd ed.). New Haven, CT: Yale University Press.

Berrueta-Clement, J. R., Schweinhart, L. J., Barnett, W. S., Epstein, A. S., & Weikart, D. P. (1984). *Changed lives: The effects of the Perry preschool program on youths through age 19.* Ypsilanti, MI: High/Scope Press.

Berry, B. (1978). Latent structure of urban systems: Research methods and findings. In L. S. Bourne & J. W. Simmons (Eds.), *Systems of cities: Readings on structure, growth, and policy.* New York: Oxford University Press.

Betts, J. R. (1998, March). The two-legged stool: The neglected role of educational standards in improving America's public schools. *Federal Reserve Bank of New York Economic Policy Review,* pp. 97–117.

Bianchi, S. M., & Casper, L. M. (2000). American families. *Population Bulletin,* vol. 55, no. 4. Washington, DC: Population Reference Bureau.

Bianchi, S. M., & Spain, D. (1986). *American women in transition.* New York: Russell Sage.

Bianchi, S. M., & Spain, D. (1996). Women, work, and family in America. *Population Bulletin,* vol. 51, no. 3. Washington, DC: Population Reference Bureau.

Bierstedt, R. (1963). *The social order.* New York: McGraw-Hill.

Binstock, R. K., & George, L. K. (Eds.) (2001). *The handbook of aging and the social sciences* (5th ed.). New York: Academic Press.

Bittman, M. (1993). Australians' changing use of time, 1974–1987. *Social Indicators Research, 30,* 91–109.

Black, D. (Ed.) (1984). *Toward a general theory of social control.* Orlando: Academic Press.

Blau, J. R. (1993). *Social contracts and economic markets.* New York: Plenum.

Blau, P. (1964). *Exchange and power in social life.* New York: Wiley.

Blau, P., & Duncan, O. D. (1967). *The American occupational structure.* New York: Wiley.

Blau, P. M., & Scott, R. W. (1962). *Formal organizations: A comparative approach.* San Francisco: Chandler.

Blauner, R. (1964). *Alienation and freedom.* Chicago: University of Chicago Press.

Blauner, R. (1969). Internal colonialism and ghetto revolt. *Social Problems, 16,* 393–408.

Blauner, R. (1972). *Racial oppression in America.* New York: Harper.

Blauner, R. (Ed.) (1989). *Black lives, white lives: Three decades of race relations in the United States.* Berkeley: University of California Press.

Blinder, D., & Crossette, B. (1993, February 7). As ethnic wars multiply, U.S. strives for a policy. *New York Times,* p. A1.

Bloch, M. (1964). *Feudal society* (Vol. 1). Chicago: University of Chicago Press.

Block, F. (1990). *Post industrial possibilities: A critique of economic discourse.* Berkeley: University of California Press.

Bloom, B. S. (1976). *Human characteristics and school learning.* New York: McGraw-Hill.

Bluestone, B. (1992). *Negotiating the future: A labor perspective on American business.* New York: Basic Books.

Blumenfeld, W. J. (Ed.) (1992). *Homophobia.* Boston: Beacon.

Blumer, H. (1969a). Elementary collective groupings. In A. M. Lee (Ed.), *Principles of sociology* (3rd ed.). New York: Barnes & Noble.

Blumer, H. (1969b). *Symbolic interactionism.* Englewood Cliffs, NJ: Prentice Hall.

Blumer, H. (1978). Elementary collective behavior. In L. E. Genevie (Ed.), *Collective behavior and social movements.* Itasca, IL: Peacock.

Bobrick, B. (1997). *Angel in the whirlwind: The triumph of the American Revolution.* New York: Simon & Schuster.

Bodenhorn, H. (2002). Banking panics of the gilded age, by Almus Wicker. *Journal of Interdisciplinary History, 32,* 497–498.

Boese, W. (1998). U.S. retains top spot in latest UN conventional arms register. *Arms Control Today, 28,* 27.

Boggs, V. W., & Meyersohn, R. (1988). The profile of a Bronx salsero: Salsa's still alive! *Journal of Popular Music and Society, 11,* 7–14.

Bogue, D. J. (1969). *Principles of demography.* New York: Wiley.

Bogue, D. J. (1985). *The population of the United States: Historical trends and future projections.* New York: Free Press.

Bohannon, L., & Bohannon, P. (1953). *The Tiv of central Nigeria.* London: International African Institute.

Bohannon, L., & Bohannon, P. (1962). *Markets in Africa.* Evanston, IL: Northwestern University Press.

Bonner, R. (1994, August 25). Hutu and Tutsi mill the rice and set an example. *New York Times,* p. A1.

Bonnett, A. W. (1981). *Institutional adaptation of West Indian immigrants to America.* Lanham, MD: University Press of America.

Booth, A., & Edwards, J. N. (1985, February). Age at marriage and marital instability. *Journal of Marriage and the Family,* pp. 67–75.

Bornstein, D. (1996). *The price of a dream: The story of the Grameen Bank and the idea that is helping the poor to change their lives.* New York: Simon & Schuster.

Bose, C. E., & Rossi, P. H. (1983). Gender and jobs. *American Sociological Review, 48,* 316–330.

Boserup, E. (1965). *The conditions of agricultural growth.* London: Allen and Unwin.

Bosk, C. (1979). *Forgive and remember: Managing medical failure.* Chicago: University of Chicago Press.

Bosworth, B., & Burtless, G. (Eds.) (1998). *Aging societies: The global dimension.* Washington, DC: Brookings Institution.

Bott, E. (1977). Urban families: Conjugal roles and social networks. In S. Leinhardt (Ed.), *Social networks: A developing paradigm.* Orlando: Academic Press.

Bottomore, T. (Ed.) (1973). *Karl Marx.* Englewood Cliffs, NJ: Prentice Hall.

Bourdieu, P. (1993). *Sociology in question.* London: Sage.

Bower, B. (2002, March 16). Heads up. *Science News,* pp. 1–3.

Bowker, J. W. (1997). *World religions.* New York: DK Publishers.

Bowles, S., & Gintis, H. (1976). *Schooling in capitalist America.* New York: Basic Books.

Bowles, S., & Gintis, H. (2000). Schooling in capitalist America revisited. *Sociology of Education, 75,* 1–18.

Boxer, D. (2002). Nagging: The familial conflict arena. *Journal of Pragmatics, 34,* pp. 49–61.

Bracey, J. H., Meier, A., & Rudwick, E. (1970). *Black nationalism in America.* Indianapolis: Bobbs-Merrill.

Bradley, H. (1998). A new gender(ed) order? Researching and rethinking women's work. *Sociology, 32,* 869–874.

Braidwood, R. S. (1967). *Prehistoric man* (7th ed.). Glenview, IL: Morrow.

Braudel, F. (1976/1949). *The Mediterranean and the Mediterranean world in the age of Philip II.* New York: Harper.

Braudel, F. (1981). *The structures of everyday life: Vol. 1. Civilizations and capitalism: 15th–18th century.* New York: Harper.

Braudel, F. (1984). *The perspective of the world: Vol. 3. Civilizations and capitalism: 15th–18th century.* New York: Harper.

Braudy, L. (1997). *The frenzy of renown: Fame and its history.* New York: Oxford University Press.

Brauss, P. (1995). The baby boom at mid-decade. *American Demographics, 17,* 40–46.

Braverman, H. (1974). *Labor and monopoly capital.* New York: Monthly Review Press.

Breese, G. (1966). *Urbanization in newly developing countries.* Englewood Cliffs, NJ: Prentice Hall.

Breiner, P. (1996). *Max Weber and democratic politics.* Ithaca, NY: Cornell University Press.

Brimelow, P. (1995). *Alien nation: Common sense about America's immigration disaster.* New York: Random House.

Brody, D. (1960). *Steelworkers in America: The non-union era.* Cambridge, MA: Harvard University Press.

Brody, J. (1992, August 11). To predict divorce, ask 125 questions. *New York Times,* pp. C1, C9.

Brokaw, T. (1994, January 2). Learning lessons for life in football. *New York Times,* sec. 8, p. 11.

Bronfenbrenner, K. (2000, December). Raw power. *Multinational Monitor,* pp. 24–29.

Bronfenbrenner, K. (2003, May). Declining unionization, rising inequality. *Multinational Monitor,* pp. 21–24.

Bronfenbrenner, U., & Ceci, S. J. (1994). Nature-nurture reconceptualized in developmental perspective: A bioecological model. *Psychological Review, 101,* 568–586.

Brooke, J. (1997, April 28). Former cult member warns of continuing cult loyalties. *New York Times,* p. A16.

Brotherton, D., & Salazar-Atias, C. (2003). Amor de reina! The pushes and pulls of group membership among the Latin

Queens. In L. Kontos, D. Brotherton, & L. Barrios (Eds.), *Gangs and society: Alternative perspectives*. New York: Columbia University Press.

Broussard, C. A., & Joseph, A. L. (1998). Tracking: A form of educational neglect? *Social Work in Education, 20*, 110–120.

Brown, C. (1966). *Manchild in the Promised Land*. New York: Macmillan.

Brown, D. (1970). *Bury my heart at Wounded Knee*. New York: Washington Square Press.

Brown, K. M. (1991). *Mama Lola: A Vodou priestess in Brooklyn*. Berkeley: University of California Press.

Brown, K. M. (1992, April 15). Writing about "the other." *Chronicle of Higher Education*, p. A56.

Brown, L. R. (1995, December 10). Facing food security. *World Watch*.

Brown, L. R. (2001). *Building an economy for the earth*. New York: Norton.

Brown, L. R., Flavin, C., & French, H. F. (1997). *State of the world 1998: A Worldwatch Institute report on progress toward a sustainable society*. New York: Norton.

Browne, D. R., & Keil, R. (2000). Planning ecology: The discourse of environmental policy making in Los Angeles. *Organization and Environment, 13*, 158–205.

Browne, M. W. (1987, September 1). Relics of Carthage show brutality amid the good life. *New York Times*, pp. C1, C10.

Brundtland, G. H. (1989, September). How to secure our common future. *Scientific American*, p. 190.

Bucholtz, M. (2002). Youth and cultural practice. *Annual Review of Anthropology, 31*, 525–552.

Bullard, R. D. (2003, January-February). Environmental justice for all. *The New Crisis*.

Bulmer, M. (1986). *The Chicago school of sociology*. Chicago: University of Chicago Press.

Bumpass, L. L., & Raley, R. K. (1995). Redefining single-parent families: Cohabitation and changing family reality. *Demography, 32*, 97–110.

Bumpass, L. L., Raley, R. K., & Sweet, J. A. (1995). The changing character of stepfamilies: Implications of cohabitation and nonmarital childbearing. *Demography, 32*, 425–437.

Bumpass, L. L., & Sweet, J. A. (1989). Children's experience in single-parent families: Implications of cohabitation and marital transitions. *Family Planning Perspectives, 21*, 256–260.

Burawoy, M. (1980). *Manufacturing consent*. Chicago: University of Chicago Press.

Burawoy, M. (1996). A classic of its time. *Contemporary Sociology, 25*, 296–300.

Burdman, P. (2003, April 24). Investigating below the surface. *Black Issues in Higher Education*, pp. 30–33.

Burgess, E. W. (1925). The growth of the city: An introduction to a research project. In R. E. Park & E. W. Burgess (Eds.), *The city*. Chicago: University of Chicago Press.

Burris, S. (2002). Introduction: Merging law, human rights, and social epidemiology. *Journal of Law, Medicine, and Ethics, 30*, 498–509.

Burstein, R. (1991). Legal mobilization as a social movement tactic: The struggle for equal employment opportunity. *American Journal of Sociology, 96*, 1201–1225.

Burtless, G. (1998, Summer-Fall). Can the labor market absorb three million welfare recipients? *Focus* (Institute for Research on Poverty), pp. 1–6.

Burum, I., & Margalit, A. (2002, January 17). Occidentalism. *New York Review of Books*, pp. 4–8.

Buruma, I. (1984). *Behind the mask: On sexual demons, sacred mothers, transvestites, gangsters, drifters and other Japanese cultural heroes*. New York: Pantheon.

Bury, J. B. (1932). *The idea of progress: An inquiry into its origin and growth*. New York: Dover.

Butcher, J. (2001). Neurogenomics—a capital investment? *The Lancet, 357*, 1420.

Butler, R. (1989). Dispelling ageism: The cross-cutting intervention. *Annals of the American Academy of Political and Social Science, 503*, 138–148.

Butterfield, F. (1992b, January 13). Studies find a family link to criminality. *New York Times*, pp. A1, A16.

Butterfield, F. (1998a, August 9). Prison population growing although crime rate drops. *New York Times*, p. 18.

Byrd-Bredbenner, C., & Murray, J. (2003). A comparison of the anthropometric measurements of idealized female body images in media directed to men, women, and mixed gender audiences. *Topics in Clinical Nutrition, 18*, 117–129.

Caccamo, R. (2000). *Back to Middletown: Three generations of sociological reflections*. Stanford, CA: Stanford University Press.

Cahil, T. (2002, February 3). The one true faith: Is it tolerance? *New York Times*, sec. 4, pp. 1, 4.

Cahill, S. E. (1992). The sociology of childhood at and in an uncertain age. *Contemporary Sociology, 21*, 669–672.

Cain, L. D. (1964). Life course and social structure. In R. F. Faris (Ed.), *Handbook of modern sociology*. Chicago: Rand McNally.

Caldwell, J. (2000, March). Rethinking the African AIDS epidemic. *Population and Development Review, 26*, 117–136.

Caldwell, J., & Caldwell, P. (1988). Women's position and child mortality and morbidity in LDCs. In *Conference on women's position and demographic change in the course of development*. Liège: International Union for the Scientific Study of Population.

Califano, J. A. (1998, February 21). A punishment-only prison policy. *America*, pp. 3–4.

Cameron, W. B. (1966). *Modern social movements: A sociological outline*. New York: Random House.

Campbell, B. (1984). *Wigan Pier revisited: Poverty and politics in the eighties*. London: Virago.

Cancian, F. M. (1994). *Romantic longings: Love in America, 1830–1980*.

Cancian, M., et al. (2003, Summer). Income and program participation among early TANF recipients: The evidence from New Jersey, Washington, and Wisconsin. *Focus* (Institute for Research on Poverty), pp. 1–10.

Cant, S., & Sharma, U. (1998). Reflexivity, ethnography and the professions (complementary medicine): Watching you watching me watching you (and writing about both of us). *Sociological Review, 46*, 244–264.

Cantril, H., with Gaudet, H., & Herzog, J. (1982/1940). *The invasion from Mars*. Princeton, NJ: Princeton University Press.

Caplan, A. L. (1978). *The sociobiology debate: Readings on ethical and scientific issues*. New York: Harper.

Caplow, T. (1969). *Two against one: Coalition in triads*. Englewood Cliffs, NJ: Prentice Hall.

Caplow, T., Bahr, H. M., Chadwick, B. A., Hill, R., & Williamson, M. H. (1983). *Middletown families: Fifty years of change and continuity*. New York: Bantam.

Caplow, T., Bahr, H. M., Modell, J., & Chadwick, B. A. (1991). *Recent social trends in the United States 1960–1990*. Montreal: McGill-Queen's University Press.

Capra, F. (2000, February). The challenge of the 21st century. *Tikkun*.

Carnegie Endowment for International Peace (2003). www.ceip.org.

Carnoy, M., Castells, M., & Benner, C. (1997). Labour markets and employment practices in the age of flexibility: A case study of Silicon Valley. *International Labour Review, 136*, 27–48.

Carpenter, L., & Bartley, M. (1994). Fat, female, and poor. *Lancet, 344*, 1715–1716.

Carter, L. J. (1975). *The Florida experience*. Baltimore: Johns Hopkins University Press.

Carter, L. J., & Pigford, T. H. (1998). Getting Yucca Mountain right. *Bulletin of the Atomic Scientists, 54*, 56–62.

Casper, L. M., McLanahan, S. S., & Garfinkel, I. (1994). The gender-poverty gap: What can we learn from other countries? *American Sociological Review, 59,* 594–605.

Cassidy, J. (1995, October 16). Who killed the middle class? *New Yorker,* pp. 113–124.

Castells, M., Flecha, R., Freire, P., Giroux, H. A., Macedo, D., & Willis, P. (1998). *Critical education in the new information age.* Totowa, NJ: Rowman and Littlefield.

Cecco, J. P., & Parker, D. A. (1995). The biology of homosexuality: Sexual orientation or sexual preference? *Journal of Homosexuality, 28,* 1–27.

Chaddock, G. R. (1999, October 27). Teach for America turns 10—and thrives. *Christian Science Monitor,* p. 10.

Chadwick, B. A., & Heaton, T. B. (1999). *The statistical handbook on the American family* (2nd ed.). Phoenix: Oryx Press.

Chalk, F., & Jonassohn, K. (1990). *The history and sociology of genocide.* New Haven, CT: Yale University Press.

Chambliss, D. F. (1996). *Beyond caring: Hospitals, nurses, and the social organization of ethics.* Chicago: University of Chicago Press.

Chambliss, W. J. (1973, December). The Saints and the Roughnecks. *Society,* pp. 23–31.

Chang, T. F. H. (2003). A structural model of race, gender, class, and attitudes toward labor unions. *Social Science Journal, 40,* 189–200.

Chenault, C. (1996). *Maasai.* Unpublished manuscript, Calhoun Community College, Decatur, AL.

Cherlin, A. J. (1981). *Marriage, divorce, remarriage.* Cambridge, MA: Harvard University Press.

Cherlin, A. J. (1996). *Public and private families: An introduction.* New York: McGraw-Hill.

Chernin, K. (1981). *The obsession: Reflections on the tyranny of slenderness.* New York: Harper.

Chernow, R. (1998). *Titan: The life of J. D. Rockefeller Sr.* New York: Random House.

Chirot, D. (1986). *Social change in the modern era.* San Diego: Harcourt Brace Jovanovich.

Chirot, D. (1994a). *How societies change.* Thousand Oaks, CA: Pine Forge.

Chirot, D. (1994b). *Modern tyrants: The power and prevalence of evil in our age.* New York: Free Press.

Chodorow, N. (2002). Mother and child: Feminist psychology. *Feminism and Psychology, 12,* 11–17.

Chomsky, N. (1965). *Aspects of the theory of syntax.* Cambridge, MA: MIT Press.

Chwast, J. (1965). Value conflicts in law enforcement. *Crime and Delinquency, 2,* 151–161.

Clairborne, W. (1998, July 24). Farmers face harvest of despair. *Washington Post,* p. 4.

Clarke, L. H. (2002). Older women's perceptions of ideal body weights: The tensions between health and appearance motivations for weight loss. *Ageing and Society, 22,* 751–773.

Clausen, J. A. (1968). *Socialization and society.* Boston: Little, Brown.

Clay, G. (1980). *Close-up: How to read the American city.* Chicago: University of Chicago Press.

Clay, G. (1994). *Real places: An unconventional guide to America's landscape.* Chicago: University of Chicago Press.

Cloward, R., & Ohlin, L. (1960). *Delinquency and opportunity: A theory of delinquent gangs.* New York: Free Press.

Clydesdale, T. T. (1997). Family behaviors among early U.S. baby boomers: Exploring the effects of religion and income change, 1965–1982. *Social Forces, 76,* 605–635.

Coates, J. F. (2002, September–October). What's next? Foreseeable terrorist acts. *Futurist,* p. 23.

Cochran, M., Larner, M., Riley, D., Gunnarson, L., & Henderson, C. R., Jr. (1990). *Extending families: The social networks of parents and their children.* Cambridge, England: Cambridge University Press.

Cockerham, W. C. (2001). *Medical sociology* (8th ed.). Upper Saddle River, NJ: Prentice Hall.

Cohen, B. E., & Burt, M. R. (1990).The homeless: Chemical dependency and mental health problems. *Social Work Research and Abstracts, 26,* 8–17.

Cohen, J. E. (1998, October 8). How many people can the earth support? *New York Review of Books,* pp. 29–31.

Cohen, N. (1961). *The pursuit of the millennium.* New York: Harper.

Cohen, R. (2000, October 22). Third party time. *New York Times Magazine,* pp. 44–45.

Coleman, J. S. (1961). *The adolescent society.* New York: Free Press.

Coleman, J. S. (1964). Research chronicle: The adolescent society. In P. E. Hammond (Ed.), *Sociologists at work.* Garden City, NY: Doubleday.

Coleman, J. S. (1976). Liberty and equality in school desegregation. *School Policy, 6,* 9–13.

Coleman, J. S. (1982). *The asymmetric society.* Syracuse, NY: Syracuse University Press.

Coleman, J. S. (1986, May). Social theory, social research, and a theory of action. *American Journal of Sociology, 91,* 1309–1335.

Coleman, J. S. (1994). Social *capital,* human *capital,* and investment in youth. In A. C. Petersen & T. J. Mortimer, *Youth unemployment and society.* Cambridge, England: Cambridge University Press.

Collins, E. G. C., & Scott, P. (Eds.) (1978). Everyone who makes it has a mentor. *Harvard Business Review, 56,* 89–101.

Collymore, Y. (2002, February–March). Migrant street children on the rise in Central America. *Population Today.*

Comer, J. P. (1997). *Waiting for a miracle: Why schools can't solve our problems and how we can.* New York: Dutton.

Comte, A. (1971/1854). The positive philosophy. In M. Truzzi (Ed.), *Sociology: The classic statements.* New York: Random House.

Conger, D., Ge, X., & Elder, G. H., Jr. (1994). Economic stress, coercive family process, and developmental problems of adolescence. *Child Development, 65,* 541–561.

Conley, D. (1999). *Being black, living in the red: Race, wealth, and social policy in America.* Berkeley: University of California Press.

Conley, D. (2003, February 15). The cost of slavery. *New York Times,* p. A25.

Connell, R. W. (1995). *Masculinities.* Berkeley: University of California Press.

Constantine, N., & Huberman, B. (2000, August). European approaches to adolescent sexual health and behavior. Florence Crittendon Roundtable, San Francisco, California.

Cookson, P. W. (1997). New kid on the block? A closer look at America's private schools. *Brookings Review, 15,* 22–25.

Cookson, P. W., & Persell, C. H. (1985). *Preparing for power: America's elite boarding schools.* New York: Basic Books.

Cooley, C. H. (1909). *Social organization: A study of the large mind.* New York: Scribner.

Cooley, C. H. (1956/1902). *Human nature and the social order.* New York: Free Press.

Corsaro, W. (1997). *The sociology of childhood.* Thousand Oaks, CA: Pine Forge.

Cortes, C. E. (Ed.) (1980). *The Latin American brain drain.* New York: Arno.

Coser, L. A. (1966). *The functions of social conflict.* New York: Free Press.

Cottrell, W. F. (1951). Death by dieselization: A case study in the reaction to technological change. *American Sociological Review, 16,* 358–365.

Cowie, J. (1998). The terror of the machine: Technology, work, gender and ecology on the U.S.–Mexico border. *Labor History, 39,* 502.

Cramer, E., & Boyd, J. (1995). The tenure track and the parent track: A road guide. *Wilson Library Bulletin, 69,* 41–42.

Cranz, G. (1982). *The politics of park design: A history of urban parks in America.* Cambridge, MA: MIT Press.

Creel, M. W. (1988). *"A peculiar people": Slave religion and community-culture among the Gullahs.* New York: New York University Press.

Cremin, L. A. (1980). *American education: The national experience 1783–1876.* New York: Harper.

Cressey, D. R. (1971/1953). *Other people's money: A study in the social psychology of embezzlement.* Belmont, CA: Wadsworth.

Cronon, W. (1983). *Changes in the land: Indians, colonists, and the ecology of New England.* New York: Hill and Wang.

Crosley, N. (2002). *Making sense of social movements.* London: Open University Press.

Crowder, M. (1966). *A short history of Nigeria* (rev. ed.). New York: Praeger.

Cuber, J. F., & Haroff, P. B. (1980). Five types of marriage. In A. Skolnick & J. Skolnick (Eds.), *Family in transition.* Boston: Little, Brown.

Cumming, E., & Henry, W. (1971). *Growing old: The process of disengagement.* New York: Basic Books.

Cummings, J. (1983, November 20). Breakup of black family imperils gains of decades. *New York Times*, p. 56.

Current Population Survey (2002). Food security supplement. Washington, DC: U.S. Government Printing Office.

Curtin, P. D. (1969). *The Atlantic slave trade.* Madison: University of Wisconsin Press.

Curtiss, S. (1977). *Genie: A psycholinguistic study of a modern-day "wild child."* New York: Academic Press.

Dahir, M. (2001, July 17). Why are we gay? *Advocate*, p. 1.

Dahl, R. (1961). *Who governs?* New Haven, CT: Yale University Press.

Dahrendorf, R. (1990). *The modern social conflict: An essay on the politics of liberty.* Berkeley: University of California Press.

Dahrendorf, R. (1997). *After 1989: Morale, revolution, and civil society.* New York: St. Martin's Press.

Daniel, K. (1996). The marriage premium. In Tommasi, M., & Tommasi, K. (Eds.), *The new economics of human behavior.* Cambridge, England: Cambridge University Press.

Dankert, C. E., Mann, F. C., & Northrup, H. R. (Eds.) (1965). *Hours of work.* New York: Harper.

Danziger, S., & Gottschalk, P. (Eds.) (1993). *Uneven tides: Rising inequality in America.* New York: Russell Sage.

DARE (1999, March 8). Letter from Lagos. *The Nation*, p. 8.

Darling-Hammond, L. (1997, November). What matters most: 21st-century teaching. *Education Digest*, pp. 4–10.

Das, S., & Srinivasan, K. (1997). Duration of firms in an infant industry: The case of Indian computer hardware. *Journal of Development Economics, 53,* 157–167.

Dasgupta, P. (2000). Population and resources: An exploration of reproductive and environmental externalities. *Population and Development Review, 26,* 643–690.

Davey, J. D. (1995). *The new social contract: America's journey from welfare state to police state.* Westport, CT: Praeger.

Davidson, D. (1973). The furious passage of the black graduate student. In J. Ladner (Ed.), *The death of white sociology.* New York: Vintage.

Davies, J. C. (1962). Toward a theory of revolution. *American Sociological Review, 27,* 5–19.

Davis, K. (1939). Illegitimacy and the social structures. *American Journal of Sociology, 45,* 215–233.

Davis, K. (1947). Final note on a case of extreme isolation. *American Journal of Sociology, 52,* 432–437.

Davis, K. (1955). The origin and growth of urbanization in the world. *American Journal of Sociology, 60,* 429–437.

Davis, K. (1968). The urbanization of the human population. In S. F. Fava (Ed.), *Urbanism in world perspective: A reader.* New York: Crowell.

Davis, K. (1991). Population and resources: Fact and interpretation. In K. Davis and M. S. Bernstam (Eds.), *Resources, environment, population: Present knowledge, future options.* New York: Oxford University Press.

Davis, K., & Moore, W. E. (1945). Some principles of stratification. *American Sociological Review, 10,* 242–249.

Davis, K. C. (1995, September 3). Ethnic cleansing didn't start in Bosnia. *New York Times*, sec. 4, pp. 1, 6.

Davis, L. (1992). *Natural disasters: The black plague.* New York: Facts on File.

Davis, M. (1998). *Ecology of fear: Los Angeles and the imagination of disaster.* New York: Metropolitan Books.

Davis, N. J. (1975). *Deviance: Perspectives and issues in the field.* Dubuque, IA: Brown.

Dawson, T. L. (2002). New tools, new insights: Kohlberg's moral judgement stages revisited. *International Journal of Behavioral Development, 26,* 154–167.

Deaux, K., & Wrightsman, L. S. (1988). *Social psychology* (5th ed.). Pacific Grove, CA: Brooks/Cole.

Defina, M. P., & Wetherbee, L. (1997, October). Advocacy and law enforcement: Partners against domestic violence. *FBI Law Enforcement Bulletin*, pp. 22–26.

De Jong, G. F., & Tran, Q. G. (2001). Warm welcome, cool welcome: Mapping receptivity toward immigrants in the U.S. *Population Today, 29,* 1, 4–5.

Deierlein, K. (1994). Ideology and holistic alternatives. In W. Kornblum & C. D. Smith (Eds.), *The healing experience: Readings on the social context of health care.* Englewood Cliffs, NJ: Prentice Hall.

D'Emilio, J., & Freedman, E. B. (1988). *Intimate matters: A history of sexuality in America.* New York: Harper.

Denis, J., & Derbyshire, I. (1996). *Political systems of the world.* New York: St. Martin's Press.

Denno, D. W. (1990). *Biology and violence: From birth to adulthood.* New York: Cambridge University Press.

de Rougemont, D. (1983). *Love in the western world.* Princeton, NJ: Princeton University Press.

Deshpande, A. (2000). Recasting economic inequality. *Review of Social Economy, 58,* 381–399.

de Tocqueville, A. (1955/1856). *The old regime and the French revolution* (S. Gilbert, Trans.). Garden City, NY: Doubleday.

de Tocqueville, A. (1956/1840). *Democracy in America.* New York: Vintage.

de Tocqueville, A. (1980/1835). *On democracy, revolution, and society* (J. Stone & S. Mennell, Trans.). Chicago: University of Chicago Press.

Dewey, R. (1948). Charles Horton Cooley: Pioneer in psychosociology. In H. F. Barnes (Ed.), *An introduction to the history of sociology.* Chicago: University of Chicago Press.

De Witt, K. (1994, August 15). Wave of suburban growth is being fed by minorities. *New York Times*, pp. A1, B6.

De Zwart, F. (2000). The logic of affirmative action: Caste, class and quotas in India. *Acta Sociologica, 43,* 235.

Diaz Soto, L. (1997). *Language, culture, and power: Bilingual families and the struggle for quality education.* Albany: State University of New York Press.

Djilas, M. (1982). *The new class: An analysis of the communist system.* Orlando: Harcourt Brace Jovanovich.

Dobbins, J., McGinn, J. G., Crane, K., Jones, S. G., Lal, R., Rathmell, A., Swanger, R., & Timilsina, A. (2003). *America's role in nation-building: From Germany to Iraq.* Santa Monica, CA: RAND.

Dodgson, R. A. (1987). *The European past: Social evolution and spatial order.* London: Macmillan.

Dollard, J. (1937). *Caste and class in a southern town.* New Haven, CT: Yale University Press.

Dollard, J., Miller, N., & Doob, L. (1939). *Frustration and aggression.* New Haven, CT: Yale University Press.

Domhoff, G. W. (1983). *Who rules America now?* New York: Simon & Schuster.

Donow, K. R. (1990, April). On the transition from the academy to a career in business. *Footnotes* (American Sociological Association), p. 6.

Dornbusch, S. (1955). The military as an assimilating institution. *Social Forces, 33,* 316–321.

Dowd, M. (1985, November 17). Youth, art, hype: A different bohemia. *New York Times Magazine,* pp. 26ff.

Drake, S. C., & Cayton, H. (1970/1945). *Black metropolis: Vol. 1. A study of Negro life in a northern city* (rev. ed.). Orlando: Harcourt Brace Jovanovich.

Dreifus, C. (1998, April 14). She talks to apes, and, according to her, they talk back. *New York Times,* p. F4.

Drucker, P. F. (1992). The new society of organizations. *Harvard Business Review, 70,* 95–105.

Du Bois, W. E. B. (1967/1899). *The Philadelphia Negro: A social study.* New York: Schocken.

Dudley, W. (Ed.) (2002). *Religion in America: Opposing viewpoints.* San Diego: Greenhaven Press.

Duffy, M., Dickerson, J. F., Thomas, C. B., Tumulty, K., & Weisskopf, M. (2002, February 4). Enron spoils the party. *Time,* pp. 16–23.

Dugger, C. W. (2001, June 22). Relying on hard and soft sells, India pushes sterilization. *New York Times,* p. A1.

Duncan, G. J., & Brooks-Gunn, J. (Eds.) (1997). *Consequences of growing up poor.* New York: Russell Sage.

Duneier, M. (1992). *Slim's table: Race, respectability, and masculinity.* Chicago: University of Chicago Press.

Durkheim, E. (1964/1893). *The division of labor in society* (2nd ed.). New York: Free Press.

Durkheim, E. (1951/1897). *Suicide, a study in sociology.* New York: Free Press.

Duster, T. (2001, September 14). Buried alive: The concept of race in science. *Chronicle of Higher Education,* pp. 1–5.

Dyer, J. (1996, November-December). Ground zero. *Utne Reader,* pp. 80ff.

Dymski, G. A. (2000). Illegal-seizure and market-disadvantage approaches to restitution: A comparison of the Japanese American and African American cases. *Review of Black Political Economy, 27,* 49–80.

Ebbinghaus, B., & Visser, J. (2000). *Trade unions in Western Europe since 1945.* London: Macmillan.

Eckholm, E. (1985, June 25). Kanzi the chimp: A life in science. *New York Times,* pp. C1, C3.

Eckholm, E. (1992, October 6). Learning if infants are hurt when mothers go to work. *New York Times,* pp. A1, A21.

The Economist (2001, July 21). How do you house a quarter of a nation? El Salvador. *The Economist,* p. 31.

Edleson, J. I., & Tan, N. T. (1993). Conflict and family violence: The tale of two families. In P. G. Boss, W. J. Doherty, R. LaRossa, W. R. Schumm, & S. K. Steinmetz (Eds.), *Sourcebook of family theories and methods: A contextual approach.* New York: Plenum.

EEOC (U.S. Equal Employment Opportunity Commission) (1993). *Guidelines on discrimination because of sex.* Washington, DC: U.S. Government Printing Office.

Egan, T. (1995, September 3). Many seek security in private communities. *New York Times,* pp. A1, A22.

Eggers, D. (2003, August 2). Muting the call to service. *New York Times,* p. A15.

Ehrenreich, B. (2001). *Nickel and dimed: On (not) getting by in America.* New York: Metropolitan Books.

Ehrlich, P. R., & Ehrlich, A. H. (1990). *The population explosion.* New York: Simon & Schuster.

Ehrlich, P. R., & Ehrlich, A. H. (1997). Erlichs' fables. *Technology Review, 100,* 38–48.

Eibl-Eibesfeldt, I. (1989). *Human ethology.* Hawthorne, NY: Aldine.

Eisenberg, S. (1998). *We'll call if we need you: Experiences of women working in construction.* Ithaca, NY: Cornell University Press.

Eisley, L. (1961). *Darwin's century.* Garden City, NY: Doubleday Anchor.

Eisley, L. (1970). *The invisible pyramid.* New York: Scribner.

Elder, G. H. (1981). History and the life course. In D. Berteaux (Ed.), *Biography and society: The life history approach to the social sciences.* Newbury Park, CA: Sage.

Eldridge, C. C. (1978). *Victorian imperialism.* Atlantic Highlands, NJ: Humanities Press.

Elias, N. (1978/1939). The civilizing process. In N. Elias (Ed.), *The development of manners.* New York: Urizen.

Elkin, F., & Handel, G. (1989). *The child and society: The process of socialization* (5th ed.). New York: Random House.

Elkind, D. (1970). *Children and adolescents: Interpretative essays on Jean Piaget.* New York: Oxford University Press.

Ellul, J. (1964). *The technological society.* New York: Vintage.

Ellwood, D. (1988). *Poor support: Poverty in the American family.* New York: Basic Books.

Elshtain, J. B. (1997, May 5). Heaven can wait. *New Republic,* p. 23.

Elster, J. (1997). Accounting for tastes. *University of Chicago Law Review, 64,* 749–764.

Enloe, C. (2000). The surprised feminist. *Signs, 25,* 1023.

Epstein, C. (1995, Fall). Affirmative action. *Dissent,* pp. 463–465.

Epstein, C. F. (1985). Ideal roles and real roles. *Research in Social Stratification and Mobility, 4,* 29–51.

Epstein, C. F. (1988). *Deceptive distinctions: Sex, gender, and the social order.* New Haven, CT: Yale University Press.

Epstein, H. (2002, May 9). The hidden cause of AIDS. *New York Review of Books,* pp. 43–48.

Epstein, H. (2003, July 17). The invisible cure for AIDS. *New York Review of Books,* pp. 44–49.

Erikson, E. (1963). *Childhood and society.* New York: Norton.

Erikson, E. (Ed.) (1965). *The challenge of youth.* Garden City, NY: Doubleday Anchor.

Erikson, K. T. (1962). Notes on the sociology of deviance. *Social Problems, 9,* 307–314.

Erikson, K. T. (1966). *Wayward puritans: A study in the sociology of deviance.* New York: Wiley.

Erikson, K. T. (1976). *Everything in its path.* New York: Simon & Schuster.

Erikson, K. T. (1994a). *A new species of trouble.* New York: Norton.

Erikson, K. T. (1994b, March 6). Out of sight, out of our minds. *New York Times Magazine,* pp. 34ff.

Erikson, K. T. (1998). Trauma at Buffalo Creek. *Society, 35,* 153–162.

Etzioni, A. (2002, August 4). When it comes to ethics, business schools get an F. *Washington Post,* p. B4.

Etzkowitz, H., & Glassman, R. (1991). *The renaissance of sociological theory: Classical and contemporary.* Itaska, IL: Peacock.

Ewald, W. (1996). *I dreamed I had a girl in my pocket.* New York: Norton.

Ezorsky, G. (1991). *Affirmative action.* Ithaca, NY: Cornell University Press.

Faison, S. (1997, August 17). Chinese happily break the "one child" rule. *New York Times,* pp. 1, 10.

Fallows, D. (1985). *A mother's work.* Boston: Houghton Mifflin.

Fallows, J. (1996, May). They only look dead: Why progressives will dominate the next political era. *Washington Monthly,* pp. 48–50.

Farley, R. (1996). *The new American reality.* New York: Russell Sage.

Farley, R., & Allen, W. R. (1987). *The color line and the quality of life in America.* New York: Russell Sage.

Farnsworth, C. H. (1994, August 15). With her songs, Eskimo bares her people's pain. *New York Times,* p. A4.

Farrington, K., & Chertok, E. (1993). Social conflict theories of the family. In P. G. Boss, W. J. Doherty, R. LaRossa, W. R. Schumm, & S. K. Steinmetz (Eds.), *Sourcebook of family theories and methods: A contextual approach.* New York: Plenum.

Faulkner, R. R. (1997). Karl Polanyi meets the masters of the universe. *Contemporary Sociology, 26,* 688–692.

Fava, S. (1956). Suburbanism as a way of life. *American Sociological Review, 21,* 34–38.

Fava, S. (1985). Residential preferences in the suburban era: A new look? *Sociological Focus, 18,* 109–117.

FBI (Federal Bureau of Investigation) (2002). *Crime in the United States 2001* (Uniform Crime Reports). Washington, DC: U.S. Department of Justice.

Feachem, R. G. A., et al. (Eds.) (1993). *The health of adults in the developing world.* New York: Oxford University Press.

Feagin, J. R. (1991, November 27). Blacks still face the malevolent reality of white racism. *Chronicle of Higher Education,* p. A44.

Feagin, J. R. (2001). Social justice and sociology: Agendas for the twenty-first century. *American Sociological Review, 66,* 21–48.

Feiler, A., & Webster, A. (1999). Teacher predictions of young children's literacy success or failure. *Assessment in education: Principles, policy, and practice, 6,* 341–355.

Feldman, S. (2001). Exploring theories of patriarchy: A perspective from contemporary Bangladesh. *Signs, 26,* 1097.

Felson, M. (1998). *Crime and everyday life.* Thousand Oaks, CA: Pine Forge Press.

Fernandes, F. (1968). The weight of the past. In J. H. Franklin (Ed.), *Color and race.* Boston: Beacon.

Fine, G. A. (1987). *With the boys: Little League baseball and preadolescent culture.* Chicago: University of Chicago Press.

Finke, R., & Stark, R. (1992). *The churching of America 1776–1992.* New Brunswick, NJ: Rutgers University Press.

Fischer, C. S. (1976, 1987). *The urban experience.* Orlando: Harcourt Brace Jovanovich.

Fischer, C. S. (1982). *To dwell among friends: Personal networks in town and city.* Chicago: University of Chicago Press.

Fishman, R. (1987). *Bourgeois utopias: The rise and fall of suburbia.* New York: Basic Books.

Fiske, M., & Chiriboga, D. A. (1990). *Change and continuity in adult life.* San Francisco: Jossey-Bass.

Fitzgerald, L, Swan, S., & Magley, V. J. (1997). But was it really sexual harassment? Legal, behavioral, and psychological definitions of the workplace victimization of women. In W. O'Donohue (Ed.), *Sexual harassment: Theory, research, and therapy.* Boston: Allyn & Bacon.

Flink, J. J. (1975). *The car culture.* Cambridge, MA: MIT Press.

Flink, J. J. (1988). *The automobile age.* Cambridge, MA: MIT Press.

Flores, J. (1988, Fall). Rappin', writin', and breakin': Black and Puerto Rican street culture in New York. In *In search of New York* [Special issue]. *Dissent,* pp. 580–585.

Fontana, B. (1993). *Hegemony and power.* Minneapolis: University of Minnesota Press.

Fortunato, S. J., Jr. (2002, Summer). Corporate crime and voting rights. *Dissent,* pp. 56–61.

Foster, J. (1990). *Villains: Crime and community in the inner city.* London: Routledge.

Foster, L., Martin, J. W., Chidester, D., & Ammerman, N. T. (1998). Forum: Interpreting Waco. *Religion and American Culture, 8,* 1–30.

Foucault, M. (1973). *Madness and civilization: A history of insanity in the Age of Reason.* New York: Vintage.

Foucault, M. (1977). *Discipline and punishment.* London: Allen Lane.

Foucault, M. (1984). *The Foucault reader.* New York: Pantheon.

Frank, A. G. (1966). The development of underdevelopment. *Monthly Review, 18,* 3–17.

Frank, R. H. (1988). *Passions within reason: The strategic role of the emotions.* New York: Norton.

Frazier, E. F. (1957/1939). *The Negro family in the United States* (rev. ed.). New York: Macmillan.

Frazier, E. F. (1966). *The Negro church in America.* New York: Schocken.

Frazier, K. (1998, May-June). Cold fusion saga ends at its University of Utah birthplace. *Skeptical Inquirer,* pp. 8–9.

Freeman, J. (1973). The origins of the women's liberation movement. In J. Huber (Ed.), *Changing women in a changing society.* Chicago: University of Chicago Press.

Freeman, R. (1994). *Working under different rules.* New York: Russell Sage.

Freeman, R. B. (2000). *What workers want.* Ithaca, NY: ILR Press.

Freeman, R. B., & Rogers, J. (2002, June 24). A proposal to American labor. *Nation.*

French, H. R. (2003, July 25). Japan's neglected resource: Female workers. *New York Times,* p. A3.

Fried, M. (1963). Grieving for a lost home. In L. J. Duhl (Ed.), *The urban condition.* New York: Basic Books.

Friedan, B. (1963). *The feminine mystique.* New York: Dell.

Friedman, M. (1962). *Capitalism and freedom.* Chicago: University of Chicago Press.

Friend, T. (2000, September-October). Chimp culture. *International Wildlife,* pp. 28–35.

Fromm, E. (1961). *Marx's concept of man.* New York: Ungar.

Fullan, M. (1993). *Change forces: Probing the depths of educational reform.* New York: Falmer.

Fuller, B., & Elmore, R. F. (1996). *Who chooses? Who loses? Culture, institutions, and the unequal effects of school choice.* New York: Teachers College Press.

Furedi, F. (1997). *Population and development: A critical introduction.* New York: St. Martin's Press.

Furstenberg, F. (1976). *Unplanned parenthood: The social consequences of unplanned childbearing.* New York: Free Press.

Furstenberg, F. E. (2000). Teenagers; adolescence; adulthood. *Journal of Marriage and the Family, 62,* 896–1000.

Furstenberg, F. E., & Cherlin, A. J. (1991). *Divided families: What happens to children when parents part.* Cambridge, MA: Harvard University Press.

Fyfe, C. (1976). The dynamics of African dispersal. In M. L. Kilson & R. I. Rothberg (Eds.), *The African diaspora.* Cambridge, MA: Harvard University Press.

Gabriel, T. (1995, June 12). A new generation seems ready to give bisexuality a place in the spectrum, *New York Times,* p. A12.

Gaines, D. (1998). *Teenage wasteland* (2nd ed.). Chicago: University of Chicago Press.

Galbraith, J. K. (1995, September 19). Blame history, not the liberals. *New York Times,* p. A21.

Gale, E. A. M. (2003). Is there really an epidemic of type 2 diabetes? *Lancet, 362,* 503–504.

Gallup Organization. (1997, March). *The Gallup Poll Monthly,* pp. 8–13.

Gallup Organization. (2003). www.gallup.com/poll/releases/pr030417.asp.

Galtung, J. (1985). War. In A. Kuper & J. Kuper (Eds.), *The social science encyclopedia.* London: Routledge and Kegan Paul.

Gamson, J. (1994). *Claims to fame: Celebrity in America.* Berkeley: University of California Press.

Gamson, W. A. (1992). *Talking politics.* Cambridge, England: Cambridge University Press.

Ganong, L. H., & Coleman, M. (1999). Family obligations following divorce and remarriage. Mahwah, NJ: Erlbaum.

Gans, H. (1962, 1984). *The urban villagers.* New York: Free Press.

Gans, H. (1967, 1976). *The Levittowners: Way of life and politics in a new suburban community.* New York: Pantheon.

Gans, H. (1985). The uses of poverty: The poor pay all. In W. Feigelman (Ed.), *Sociology: Full circle* (4th ed.). Fort Worth: Holt, Rinehart and Winston.

Gans, H. (1995). *The war against the poor.* New York: Basic Books.

Garcia, A. (1996). Moral reasoning in interactional context: Strategic uses of care and justice arguments in mediation hearings. *Sociological Inquiry, 66,* 197–214.

Gardner, H. (1983). *Frames of mind: The theory of multiple intelligences.* New York: Basic Books.

Gardner, H. (2002). Performance standards. *Organizational Behavior, 15,* 88-90.

Garfinkel, H. (1991). Respecification. In G. Button (Ed.), *Ethnomethodology and the human sciences.* New York: Cambridge University Press.

Garfinkel, H. (1967). *Studies in ethnomethodology.* Englewood Cliffs, NJ: Prentice Hall.

Garfinkel, H. (2000). Studies in ethnomethodology. In W. Sharrock & M. J. Lynch (Eds.), *Harold Garfinkel,* 3rd ed. Newbury Park, CA: Sage.

Garfinkel, I., & McLanahan, S. S. (1986). *Single mothers and their children: A new American dilemma.* Washington, DC: Urban Institute.

Garmezy, N. (1993). Children in poverty: Resilience despite risk. *Psychiatry, 56,* 127–136.

Garner, R., & Tenuto, J. (1997). *Social movement theory and research: An annotated bibliographical guide.* Lanham, MD: Scarecrow Press.

Garreau, J. (1991). *Edge city: Life on the new frontier.* Garden City, NY: Doubleday Anchor.

Garrett, M. (1997). The effects of infant child care on infant-mother attachment security: Results of the NICHD Study of Early Child Care. *Child Development, 68,* 860–879.

Geertz, C. (1973). The growth of culture and the evolution of mind. In C. Geertz, *The interpretation of culture.* New York: Basic Books.

Genevie, L. E. (Ed.) (1978). *Collective behavior and social movements.* Itasca, IL: Peacock.

Geoghegan, T. (1991). *Which side are you on?* New York: Farrar Straus Giroux.

Gerbner, G. (1990). *Violence profile.* Philadelphia: Annenberg School of Communications.

Gerth, H., & Mills, C. W. (1958). *From Max Weber: Essays in sociology.* New York: Oxford University Press.

Geschwender, J. A. (1977). *Class, race and worker insurgency.* New York: Cambridge University Press.

Gibbs, J. P. (1994). *A theory about control.* Boulder, CO: Westview.

Giddens, A. (1984). *The constitution of society.* Berkeley: University of California Press.

Gilbert, J. B. (1997). *Redeeming culture: Religion in an age of science.* Chicago: University of Chicago Press.

Gilder, G. (1982). *Wealth and poverty.* New York: Basic Books.

Gilligan, C. (1982). *In a different voice: Psychological theory and women's development.* Cambridge, MA: Harvard University Press.

Gilligan, C. (1987). Adolescent development reconsidered. In C. E. Irwin, Jr. (Ed.), *New directions for child development: No. 37. Adolescent social behavior and health.* San Francisco: Jossey-Bass.

Gilligan, C., Ward, J. V., Taylor, J. M., & Bardige, B. (Eds.) (1998). *Mapping the moral domain.* Cambridge, MA: Harvard University Press.

Gist, N. P. (1968). Urbanism in India. In S. F. Fava (Ed.), *Urbanism in world perspective: A reader.* New York: Crowell.

Gitlin, T. (1993). *The sixties.* New York: Bantam.

Glausiusz, J. (1997, August). The ecology of language. *Discover,* p. 30.

Glazer, N. (1975). *Affirmative discrimination: Ethnic inequality and public policy.* New York: Basic Books.

Glazer, N., & Moynihan, D. P. (1970). *Beyond the melting pot: The Negroes, Puerto Ricans, Jews, Italians, and Irish of New York City* (2nd rev. ed.). Cambridge, MA: MIT Press.

Glick, P. C., & Parke, R., Jr. (1965). New approaches in studying the life cycle of the family. *Demography, 2,* 187–202.

Glueck, S., & Glueck, E. T. (1950). *Unraveling juvenile delinquency.* New York: Commonwealth Fund.

Goffman, E. (1958). Deference and demeanor. *American Anthropologist, 58,* 488–489.

Goffman, E. (1959). *The presentation of self in everyday life.* Garden City, NY: Doubleday.

Goffman, E. (1961). *Asylums.* Garden City, NY: Doubleday.

Goffman, E. (1963). *Stigma: Notes on the management of spoiled identity.* Englewood Cliffs, NJ: Prentice Hall.

Goffman, E. (1965). *Interaction ritual: Essays on face-to-face behavior.* Garden City, NY: Doubleday.

Goffman, E. (1972). Territories of the self. In E. Goffman (Ed.), *Relations in public.* New York: Harper.

Goffman, E. (2000). *Erving Goffman* (Sage Masters of Modern Thought). London: Sage.

Goidel, R. K., Gross, D. A., & Shields, T. G. (1999). *Money matters: Consequences of campaign finance reform in U.S. House elections.* Lanham, MD: Rowman & Littlefield.

Goldhamer, H., & Shils, E. (1939). Types of power and status. *American Journal of Sociology, 45,* 171–182.

Goleman, D. (1985, March 19). Dislike of own body found common among women. *New York Times,* pp. C1, C5.

Gonzalez-Mena, J. (1998). *The child in the family and the community.* Upper Saddle River, NJ: Merrill.

Goodall, J. (1994). Digging up the roots: Relationships with the Gombe chimpanzees. *Orion, 13,* 21–21.

Goodall, J. V. L. (1968). A preliminary report on expressive movements and communications in Gombe Stream chimpanzees. In P. Jay (Ed.), *Primates: Studies in adaptation and variability.* New York: Holt, Rinehart and Winston.

Goode, Eric (1994). *Deviant behavior* (4th ed.). Englewood Cliffs, NJ: Prentice Hall.

Goode, Erica (2001, July 17). A rainbow of differences in gays' children. *New York Times,* p. 1.

Goode, W. J. (1964). *The family.* Englewood Cliffs, NJ: Prentice Hall.

Goodman-Draper, J. (1995). *Health care's forgotten majority: Nurses and their frayed white collars.* Westport, CT: Auburn House.

Goodnough, A. (2002, February 11). More applicants answer the call for teaching jobs. *New York Times,* p. A1.

Goodstein, L. (2003, July 19). Homosexuality issue threatens to break Anglicanism in two. *New York Times,* p. A1.

Gordon, M. (1964). *Assimilation in American life.* New York: Oxford University Press.

Gorn, E. J., & Goldstein, W. (1993). *A brief history of American sports.* New York: Hill and Wang.

Goslin, D. A. (1965). *The school in contemporary society.* Glenview, IL: Scott, Foresman.

Gottmann, J. (1978). Megalopolitan systems around the world. In L. S. Bourne & J. W. Simmons (Eds.), *Systems of cities: Readings on structure, growth, and policy.* New York: Oxford University Press.

Gould, S. J. (1981). *The mismeasure of man.* New York: Norton.

Gould, S. J. (1995, February). Ghosts of bell curves past. *Natural History,* pp. 12–19.

Gould, S. J. (1996). *Full house: The spread of excellence from Plato to Darwin.* New York: Harmony Books.

Gramling, R., & Krogman, N. (1997). Communities, policy and chronic technological disasters. *Current Sociology, 45,* 41–57.

Gramsci, A. (1971). *Selections from prison notebooks.* London: Routledge and Kegan Paul.

Gramsci, A. (1992/1965). *Prison notebooks.* New York: Columbia University Press.

Gramsci, A. (1995). *Further selections from the prison notebooks.* Minneapolis: University of Minnesota Press.

Granovetter, M. (1974, 1995). *Getting a job: A study of contacts and careers.* Chicago: University of Chicago Press.

Graves, J. L., Jr. (2001). *The emperor's new clothes: Biological theories of race at the millennium.* New Brunswick, NJ: Rutgers University Press.

Gray, J. (1992). *Men are from Mars, women are from Venus.* New York: HarperCollins.

Greeley, A., Michael, R. T., & Smith, T. (1990). Americans and their sexual partners. *Society, 27,* 36–42.

Greenhouse, L. (2003, June 27). Justices, 6-3 legalize gay sexual conduct. *New York Times,* pp. 1, 19.

Greenhouse, S. (2003, July 20). Hiring for looks can get legally ugly for stores. *New York Times.*

Grodin, D., & Lindlof, T. R. (Eds.) (1996). *Constructing the self in a mediated world.* Thousand Oaks, CA: Sage.

Groesz, L. M., Levine, M. P., & Murnen, S. K. (2002). The effect of experimental presentation of thin media images on body satisfaction: A meta-analytic review. *International Journal of Eating Disorders, 31,* 1–16.

Grose, T. K. (2001, December 31). Wind turbines, solar panels and fuel cells—is alternative energy ready for prime time? *Time,* pp. 108–110.

Gross, J. (1992, March 29). Collapse of inner-city families creates America's new orphans. *New York Times,* pp. 1, 20.

Grunwald, M. (2002, January 1). In dirt, water and hogs, town got its fill of PCBs. *Washington Post,* p. A17.

Gugler, J. (Ed.) (1997). *Cities in the developing world: Issues, theory, and policy.* New York: Oxford University Press.

Gursky, D. (1998). Class size does matter. *Education Digest, 64,* 15–19.

Gusfield, J. (1966). *Symbolic crusade: Status politics and the American temperance movement.* Urbana: University of Illinois Press.

Gusfield, J. (1981). *The culture of public problems: Drinking, driving and the symbolic order.* Chicago: University of Chicago Press.

Gusfield, J. (1996). *Contested meanings: The construction of alcohol problems.* Madison: University of Wisconsin Press.

Gutman, H. (1976). *The black family in slavery.* New York: Pantheon.

Haber, L. D., & Dowd, J. E. (1994, January). *A human development agenda for disability: Statistical considerations* (Working Paper for the Statistical Division of the United Nations Secretariat). New York: United Nations.

Hacker, A. (1995, Fall). Affirmative action. *Dissent,* pp. 465–467.

Hacker, A. (1997). *Money: Who has how much and why.* New York: Simon & Schuster.

Hackett, D. G. (Ed.) (1995). *Religion and American culture: A reader.* New York: Routledge.

Hadaway, C. K., & Marler, P. L. (1998, May 6). Did you really go to church this week? Behind the poll data. *The Christian Century,* pp. 472–476.

Hagestad, G. O., & Neugarten, B. L. (1985). Age and the life course. In R. H. Binstock & E. Shanas (Eds.), *Handbook of aging and the social sciences* (2nd ed.). New York: Van Nostrand Reinhold.

Halbwachs, M. (1960). *Population and society: Introduction to social morphology.* Glencoe, IL: Free Press.

Halevy, E. (1955). *The growth of philosophic radicalism* (M. Morris, Trans.). Boston: Beacon.

Hall, J. R. (1987). *Gone from the promised land: Jonestown in American cultural history.* New Brunswick, NJ: Transaction.

Halle, D. (1984). *America's working man: Work, home and politics among blue-collar property owners.* Chicago: University of Chicago Press.

Halsey, M. (1946). *Color blind.* New York: Simon & Schuster.

Halstead, T. (2003, January). The American paradox. *Atlantic Monthly.*

Hamilton, C. V. (1969). The politics of race relations. In C. U. Daley (Ed.), *The minority report.* New York: Pantheon.

Hammond, J. (1998). *Fighting to learn: Popular education and guerilla war in El Salvador.* New Brunswick, NJ: Rutgers University Press.

Handel, G. (2001). Socialization. In L. Balter (Ed.), *Parenthood in America: An encyclopedia.* Santa Barbara, CA: ABC-CLIO.

Handlin, O. (1992). The newcomers. In P. S. Rotherberg (Ed.), *Race, class and gender in the United States.* New York: St. Martin's Press.

Hanna, S. L. (1994). *Person to person: Positive relationships don't just happen.* Englewood Cliffs, NJ: Prentice Hall.

Harbison, F. H. (1973). *Human resources as the wealth of nations.* New York: Oxford University Press.

Harden, B. (2001, August 12). 2-parent families rise after change in welfare laws. *New York Times,* p. 1.

Harding, S. (1998). Women, science, and society. *Science, 281,* 1.

Hardt, M., & Negri, A. (2001). *Empire.* Cambridge, MA: Harvard University Press.

Hare, A. P. (1992). *Groups, teams, and social interaction.* Westport, CT: Praeger.

Hare, A. P., Blumberg, H. H., Davis, M. F., & Kent, V. (1994). *Small group research: A handbook.* Norwood, NJ: Ablex.

Harlow, H. F. (1986). *From learning to love: The selected papers of H. F. Harlow.* New York: Praeger.

Harlow, H. F., & Harlow, M. K. (1962, November). Social deprivation in monkeys. *Scientific American,* pp. 137–147.

Harper, C. L. (1993). *Exploring social change* (2nd ed.). Englewood Cliffs, NJ: Prentice Hall.

Harper, D. A. (1982). *Good company.* Chicago: University of Chicago Press.

Harrington, M. (1973). *Socialism.* New York: Bantam.

Harrington, M. (1987). *The next lift: The history of a future.* New York: Holt.

Harris, M. (1980). *Culture, people, nature: An introduction to general anthropology.* New York: Harper.

Harrison, B. (1994). When government gets it right. *Technology Review, 97,* 66.

Harrison, B. B., Tilly, C., and Bluestone, B. (1986, March-April). Wage inequality takes a great U-turn. *Challenge,* pp. 26–32.

Hauser, P. M. (1957). The changing population pattern of the modern city. In P. K. Hatt & A. J. Reiss (Eds.), *Cities and society.* New York: Free Press.

Hawkins, G. (1976). *The prison: Policy and practice.* Chicago: University of Chicago Press.

Hazler, R. J. (2000). When victims turn aggressors: Factors in the development of deadly school violence. *Professional School Counseling, 4,* 105–112.

Hechter, M. (1974). *Internal colonialism.* Berkeley: University of California Press.

Hechter, M. (1987). *Principles of group solidarity.* Berkeley: University of California Press.

Hechter, M. (2000). *Containing nationalism.* New York: Oxford University Press.

Hechter, M., & Kanazawa, S. (1996, March 29). Sociological rational choice theory. In Elster, J. (Ed.), Doing our level best (rational-choice theory—a symposium). *Times Literary Supplement,* pp. 12–14.

Heilbroner, R. L. (1995). Putting economics in its place. *Social Research, 62,* 883–898.

Heitzeg, N. (1996). *Deviance: Rulemakers and rulebreakers.* Minneapolis: West.

Helmreich, W. B. (1982). *The things they say behind your back.* Garden City, NY: Doubleday.

Henry, D. O. (1989). *From foraging to agriculture.* Philadelphia: University of Pennsylvania Press.

Henslin, J., & Briggs, M. (1971). Dramaturgical desexualization: The sociology of the vaginal examination. In J. Henslin (Ed.), *Studies in the sociology of sex.* New York: Appleton-Century-Crofts.

Herek, G. M. (2002, Spring). Gender gaps in public opinion about lesbians and gay men. *Public Opinion Quarterly*, pp. 40–66.

Herlihy, D. (1995). Biology and history: The triumph of monogamy. *Journal of Interdisciplinary History, 25,* 571–583.

Herrnstein, R., & Murray, C. (1994). *The bell curve.* New York: Free Press.

Hess, D. (1997). *Science studies: An advanced introduction.* New York: New York University Press.

Hewes, G. W. (1954). A conspectus of the world's cultures in 1500 A.D. *University of Colorado Studies,* no. 4, pp. 1–22.

Hickins, M. (1998). Reconcilable differences. *Management Review, 87,* 54–59.

Higgins, T. (2003, February 14). State of emergency. *Commonweal.*

Hill, J. (1978). Apes and language. *Annual Review of Anthropology, 7,* 89–112.

Himes, C. L. (2001). *Elderly Americans.* Population Bulletin, Vol. 56, No. 4.

Hinton, W. (1966). *Fanshen: A documentary of revolution in a Chinese village.* New York: Vintage.

Hobsbawm, E. (1975). *The age of capital.* New York: Scribner.

Hochschild, A. (1989). *The second shift: Working parents and the revolution at home.* New York: Viking.

Hochschild, A. (1997). *The time bind: When work becomes home and home becomes work.* New York: Henry Holt.

Hodge, R. W., & Treiman, D. J. (1968). Class identification in the United States. *American Journal of Sociology, 73,* 535–547.

Hoecker-Drysdale, S. (1992). *Harriet Martineau: First woman sociologist.* New York: Berg Publishers.

Hoffman, L. M. (1989). *The politics of knowledge: Activist movements in medicine and planning.* Albany: State University of New York Press.

Holden, C. (1996). New populations of old people. *Science, 273,* 46–48.

Hollingshead, A. (1949). *Elmtown's youth.* New York: Wiley.

Holmes, S. A. (1998, July 1). Birth rate falls to 40-year low among unwed black women. *New York Times,* pp. A1, A16.

Holt, T. C. (1980). Afro-Americans. In *Harvard encyclopedia of American ethnic groups.* Cambridge, MA: Belknap.

Holy, L. (1985). Groups. In A. Kuper & J. Kuper (Eds.), *The social science encyclopedia.* London: Routledge and Kegan Paul.

Homans, G. (1950). *The human group.* Orlando: Harcourt Brace Jovanovich.

Homans, G. (1961). *Social behavior: Its elementary forms.* Orlando: Harcourt Brace Jovanovich.

Hopkins, T. K., & Wallerstein, I. (Eds.) (1996). *The age of transition: Trajectory of the world-system 1945–2025.* London: Zed Books.

Horgan, J. (1997, May). Seeking a better way to die. *Scientific American,* pp. 100–105.

Horowitz, M. (1979). The jurisprudence of Brown and the dilemmas of liberalism. *Harvard Civil Rights–Civil Liberties Review, 14,* 599–610.

Horowitz, R. (1985). *Honor and the American dream: Culture and identity in a Chicago neighborhood.* New Brunswick, NJ: Rutgers University Press.

Horowitz, T. (1999, March 15). Run, Rudolph, run: How the fugitive becomes a folk hero. *New Yorker,* pp. 46–52.

House, J. S., Lepkowski, J. M., Kinny, A. M., Mero, R. P., Kessler, A., & Herzog, R. (1994). The social stratification of aging and health. *Journal of Health and Social Behavior, 35,* 213–234.

Hout, M., & Greeley, A. M. (1987). The center doesn't hold: Church attendance in the United States, 1940–1984. *American Sociological Review, 52,* 325–345.

Howe, I. (1983). *1984 revisited: Totalitarianism in our century.* New York: Harper.

Huang, C. (1994). *Immigration and the underclass.* Unpublished doctoral dissertation, City University of New York Graduate School.

Hughes, E. (1945). The dilemmas and contradictions of status. *American Journal of Sociology, 50,* 353–359.

Hughes, E. (1958). *Men and their work.* New York: Free Press.

Hughes, E. (1959). The study of occupations. In R. K. Merton, L. Broom, & L. S. Cottrell, Jr. (Eds.), *Sociology today: Problems and prospects.* New York: Basic Books.

Human Rights Watch, The Sentencing Project. (1998). Felony disenfranchisement: overview. www.hrw.org/reports98/vote/usvot980.htm.

Hummin, D. (1990). *Commonplaces: Community ideology and identity in American cities.* Albany: State University of New York Press.

Humphreys, L. (1970, 1975). *Tearoom trade: Impersonal sex in public places.* Hawthorne, NY: Aldine.

Hunsberger, B. (1995). Religion and prejudice: The role of religious fundamentalism, quest, and right-wing authoritarianism. *Journal of Social Issues, 51,* 113–130.

Hunt, G., & Joe-Laidler, K. (2001). Situations of violence in the lives of girl gang members. *Health Care for Women International, 22,* 1.

Hunt, M. (1985). *Profiles of social research: The scientific study of human interactions.* New York: Russell Sage.

Hunt, M. (1999, Summer). The biological roots of religion. *Free Inquiry,* pp. 30–33.

Hunter, F. (1953). *Community power structure: A study of decision makers.* Chapel Hill: University of North Carolina Press.

Hussein, M. (1994, December). Behind the veil of fundamentalism. *UNESCO Courier,* pp. 25–28.

Iannaccone, L., Stark, R., & Finke, R. (1998). Rationality and the "religious mind." *Economic Inquiry, 36,* 373–390.

Ianni, F. A. J. (1998). New Mafia: Black, Hispanic and Italian styles. *Society, 35,* 115–129.

Iglesia, R. (1990). *Cronistas e historiadores de la conquista de Mexico.* Mexico City: Biblioteca de la Ciudad de Mexico.

Jackman, M. R., & Jackman, R. W. (1983). *Class awareness in the United States.* Berkeley: University of California Press.

Jackson, B. (1972). *In the life: Versions of the criminal experience.* New York: NAL.

Jackson, K. (1985). *The crab grass frontier: The suburbanization of the United States.* New York: Oxford University Press.

Jacobson, J. L. (1992). Improving women's reproductive health. In L. R. Brown (Ed.), *State of the world.* New York: Norton.

Jacobson, L. (2001, July 11). Looking to France. *Education Week,* www.edweek.org/ew.

Jacobson-Hardy, M. (1995). The changing landscape of labor: Workers and workplace. *Labor's Heritage, 6,* 40–57.

Jacot, M. (1999, October). The death penalty: Abolition gains ground. *UNESCO Courier,* p. 37.

Jahoda, M. (1982). *Employment and unemployment: A social-psychological analysis.* London: Cambridge University Press.

Jahoda, M., Lazarsfeld, P., & Zeisel, H. (1971). *Marienthal: A study of an unemployed community.* Hawthorne, NY: Aldine.

Janowitz, M. (1960). *The professional soldier: A social and political portrait.* New York: Free Press.

Janowitz, M. (1968). Political sociology. In D. Sills (Ed.), *The international encyclopedia of the social sciences.* New York: Free Press.

Janowitz, M. (1978). *The last half century: Societal change and politics in America.* Chicago: University of Chicago Press.

Janowitz, M., & Shils, E. A. (1948). The cohesion and disintegration of the Wehrmacht in World War II. *Public Opinion Quarterly, 12,* 280–315.

Jargowsky, P. A. (1997). *Poverty and place: Ghettos, barrios, and the American city.* New York: Russell Sage.

Jaynes, G. D., & Williams, R. M., Jr. (1989). *A common destiny: Blacks and American society.* Washington, DC: National Academy Press.

Jencks, C. (1993). *Rethinking social policy: Race, poverty and the underclass.* Cambridge, MA: Harvard University Press.

Jencks, C. (1994). *The homeless.* Cambridge, MA: Harvard University Press.

Jencks, C., & Phillips, M. (1999, January). The black-white test score gap: How to reduce it. *Current,* pp. 9–16.

Jennings, F. (1975). *The invasion of America: Indians, colonialism and the cant of conquest.* New York: Norton.

Johnson, D. K. (1988). Adolescents' solutions to dilemmas in fables: Two moral orientations—two problem solving strategies. In C. Gilligan, J. V. Ward, J. M. Taylor, & B. Bardige (Eds.), *Mapping the moral domain.* Cambridge, MA: Harvard University Press.

Johnson, J. H., Jr., & Farrell, W. C., Jr. (1995, July 7). Race still matters. *Chronicle of Higher Education,* p. A48.

Johnson, P. (1987). *A history of the Jews.* New York: Harper.

Jones, C. (2002, November 12). The AIDS memorial quilt. *Advocate,* p. 99.

Judt, T. (2003, May 1). Anti-Americans abroad. *New York Review of Books,* pp. 24–28.

Kagan, J. (2000, October). Adult personality and early experiences. *Harvard Mental Health Letter,* pp. 4–5.

Kagan, J., Pals, J. L., McCrae, R. R., Paunonen, S. V., Saarni, C., Shiner, R. L., Tellegen, A., Masten, A. S., & Whitbourne, S. K. (2001). Commentaries on "Personality development across the life course: The argument for change and continuity" and "Issues in the study of personality development." *Psychological Inquiry, 12,* 16–23.

Kagan, R. (2003). *Of paradise and power.* New York: Knopf.

Kagan, S. L., & Neuman, M. J. (1998). Lessons from three decades of transition research. *Elementary School Journal, 98,* 365–380.

Kagay, M. R., & Elder, J. (1992, August 9). Numbers are no problem for pollsters. Words are. *New York Times,* sec. 4, p. 5.

Kahl, J. A. (1965). *The American class structure.* Fort Worth: Holt, Rinehart and Winston.

Kahn, M. E. (2000). Smog reduction's impact on California county growth. *Journal of Regional Science, 40,* 565–582.

Kahneman, D., Knetsch, J., & Thaler, R. (1986). Fairness and the assumptions of economics. *Journal of Business, 59,* S285–S300.

Kaiser Family Foundation (2001). Inside-OUT: A report on the experiences of lesbians, gays and bisexuals in America and the public's view on issues and policies related to sexual orientation. www.kff.org.

Kammerman, S. B. (1995). *Starting right: How America neglects its youngest children and what we can do about it.* New York: Oxford University Press.

Kammerman, S., & Kahn, A. (1981). *Child care, family benefits, and working parents: A study in comparative policy.* New York: Columbia University Press.

Kammerman, S., & Kahn, A. J. (1993, Fall). What Europe does for single parent families. *The Public Interest,* pp. 70–86.

Kanter, R. M. (1977). *Men and women of the corporation.* New York: Basic Books.

Kanter, R. M., & Stein, B. A. (Eds.) (1980). *Life in organizations: Workplaces as people experience them.* New York: Basic Books.

Kaplan, D. E. (1998, April 13). Yakuza Inc.: U.S. investors snapping up bad loans from Japanese banks will collide with organized crime. *U.S. News & World Report,* pp. 40–41.

Kaplan, R. (2001). *The coming anarchy.* New York: Vintage.

Karnoe, P. (1997). Only in social action! *American Behavioral Scientist, 40,* 419–430.

Karras, T. (2003, March). You'll never believe what I heard! *Good Housekeeping.*

Kasarda, J. D. (1988). *Metropolis era.* Newbury Park, CA: Sage.

Kasarda, J. D. (1989). Urban industrial transition and the underclass. *Annals of the American Academy of Political and Social Science, 501,* 26–47.

Katz, E. (1957). The two step flow of communication: An up-to-date report on an hypothesis. *Public Opinion Quarterly, 21,* 61–78.

Kazemipur, A., & Rezaei, A. (2003). Religious life under theocracy: The case of Iran. *Journal for the Scientific Study of Religion, 42,* 347–361.

Keith, J. (1982). *Old people, new lives: Community creation in a retirement residence* (2nd ed.). Chicago: University of Chicago Press.

Kelley, T. (1998, February 3). Charting a course to ethical profits. *New York Times,* sec. 3, p. 1.

Kemper, T. D. (1990). *Social structure and testosterone: Explorations of the socio-bio-social chain.* New Brunswick, NJ: Rutgers University Press.

Keniston, K. (1965). Social change and youth in America. In E. H. Erikson (Ed.), *The challenge of youth.* Garden City, NY: Doubleday Anchor.

Keniston, K. (1977). *All our children.* Orlando: Harcourt Brace Jovanovich.

Kennedy, R. J. R. (1944). Single or triple melting pot? *American Journal of Sociology, 49,* 331–339.

Kessler, S. J., & McKenna, W. (1978). *Gender: An ethnomethodological approach.* Chicago: University of Chicago Press.

Keyfitz, N. (1991). Toward a theory of population-development interaction. In K. Davis & M. S. Bernstam (Eds.), *Resources, environment and population: Present knowledge and future options* (special edition of *Population and Development Review*). New York: Population Council.

Killian, L. (1952). Group membership in disaster. *American Journal of Sociology, 57,* 309–314.

Kilson, M. (1995, Fall). Affirmative action. *Dissent,* pp. 469–470.

Kim, I. (1981). *New urban immigrants: The Korean community in New York.* Princeton, NJ: Princeton University Press.

King, S. (1994, May). Diamonds are forever. *Life,* p. 26.

Kingston, P. W., Hubbard, R., Lapp, B., Schroeder, P., & Wilson, J. (2003). Why education matters. *Sociology of Education, 76,* 53–70.

Kinsey, A. C., Pomeroy, W. B., & Martin, C. E. (1948). *Sexual behavior in the human male.* Philadelphia: Saunders.

Kinsey, A. C., Pomeroy, W. B., & Martin, C. E. (1953). *Sexual behavior in the human female.* Philadelphia: Saunders.

Kitano, H. H. I. (1980). *Race relations.* Englewood Cliffs, NJ: Prentice Hall.

Klandermans, B. (1997). *The social psychology of protest.* Cambridge, MA: Blackwell.

Klass, P. (1988, October 30). Wells, Welles and the Martians. *New York Times Book Review,* pp. 1, 48–49.

Kleinberg, O. (1935). *Race differences.* New York: Harper.

Kloby, J. (1997). *Inequality, power and development: The task of political sociology.* Atlantic Highlands, NJ: Humanities Press.

Kluger, J. (2001, May 21). Can gays switch sides? *Time,* p. 62.

Koberg, C. S., Chappell, D., & Ringer, R. C. (1997). Correlates and consequences of protégé mentoring in a large hospital. *Annual Review of Sociology, 23,* 191–215.

Kohut, A. (2002). *The Pew global attitudes survey: How the world views America.* Washington, DC: Pew Foundation.

Kolbert, E. (2003, September 1). Pox populi. *New Yorker,* pp. 25–26.

Koler, S. R., & Freeman, B. J. (1994). Analysis of environmental deprivation: Cognitive and social development in Romanian orphans. *Journal of Child Psychology and Psychiatry and Allied Disciplines, 35,* 769–781.

Koretz, G. (2003, April 21). Demographic time bombs. *Business Week,* pp. 17–18.

Koretz, G. (2003, June 30). Equality? Not on death row. *Business Week,* pp. 6–7.

Kornblum, W. (1974). *Blue collar community.* Chicago: University of Chicago Press.

Kornblum, W. (1995). Times Square as a field research site. In R. P. McNamara, *Sex, scams, and street life: The sociology of New York City's Times Square.* Westport, CT: Greenwood.

Kornblum, W., & Julian, J. (2004). *Social problems* (10th ed.). Englewood Cliffs, NJ: Prentice Hall.

Kornblum, W., & Lawler, K. (1999). *Handbook of park user research.* Washington, DC: Urban Institute and Lila Wallace Readers Digest Foundation.

Kornhauser, W. (1952). The Negro union official: A study of sponsorship and control. *American Journal of Sociology, 57,* 443–452.

Korotz, G. (1998, January 12). What's moving today's economy? *Business Week,* p. 32.

Kosmin, B. (1991). *Research report: The national survey of religious identification.* New York: Center for Jewish Studies, City University of New York Graduate Center.

Kozol, J. (1995). *Amazing grace: The lives of children and the conscience of a nation.* New York: Crown.

Kremer, P. (1998, February 4). Sociologists rediscover the links between suicide and economic crisis. *Le Monde,* p. 8.

Kriegel, L. (1993). From the catbird seat: Football, baseball, and language. *Sewanee Review, 101,* 213–225.

Kroc, R. (1977). *Grinding it out: The making of McDonald's.* Chicago: Henry Regnery.

Kronus, C. L. (1977). Mobilizing voluntary associations into a social movement: The case of environmental quality. *Sociological Quarterly, 18,* 267–283.

Krueger, A. B. (1998, March). Reassessing the view that American schools are broken. *Federal Reserve Bank of New York Economic Policy Review,* pp. 29–44.

Kübler-Ross, E. (1969). *On death and dying.* New York: Macmillan.

Kunen, J. S. (1995, July 10). Teaching prisoners a lesson. *New Yorker,* pp. 34–39.

Kurtz, L. (1995). *Gods in the global village.* Thousand Oaks, CA: Pine Forge.

Kutner, B., Wilkins, C., & Yarrow, P. R. (1952). Verbal attitudes and overt behavior involving racial prejudice. *Journal of Abnormal and Social Psychology, 47,* 649–652.

Kwamena-Poh, M., Tosh, J., Waller, R., & Tidy, M. (1982). *African history in maps.* Burnt Hill, England: Longman.

Kwong, P. (1998). *Forbidden workers: Illegal Chinese workers and American labor.* New York: New Press.

Lachs, M. S., & Boyer, P. (2003, August). When rivalry won't die. *Prevention,* p. 3.

Ladner, J. (Ed.) (1973). *The death of white sociology.* New York: Vintage.

Lai, C. S. L., Fisher, S. E., Hurst, J. A., Vargha-Khadem, F., & Monaco, A. P. (2001). A forkhead-domain gene is mutated in a severe speech and language disorder. *Nature, 413,* 519–523.

Lai, H. M. (1980). The Chinese. In S. Thornstrom (Ed.), *Harvard encyclopedia of ethnic groups.* Cambridge, MA: Harvard University Press.

Lampman, J. (2001, June 14). Homosexuality remains focus of denominational controversy. *Christian Science Monitor,* p. 14.

Lampman, J. (2002, January 10). Muslims in America. *Christian Science Monitor,* p. 15.

Land, K. C. (1989). Review of *Predicting Recidivism Using Survival Models,* by Peter Schmidt and Ann Dryden Witte. *Contemporary Sociology, 18,* 245–246.

LaPiere, R. (1934). Attitudes vs. actions. *Social Forces, 13,* 230–237.

Lash, S. (1992). *Modernity and identity.* Cambridge, MA: Blackwell.

Laslett, P. (1972). Introduction. In P. Laslett & R. Wall (Eds.), *Household and family in past time.* Cambridge, England: Cambridge University Press.

Laslett, P. (1983). *The world we have lost* (3rd ed.). London: Methuen.

Lasswell, H. (1936). *Politics: Who gets what, when and how.* New York: McGraw-Hill.

Lasswell, H. D. (1941). The garrison state. *American Journal of Sociology, 46,* 455–468.

Latané, B., & Darley, J. (1970). *The unresponsive bystander: Why doesn't he help?* New York: Meredith.

Laumann, E. O., Gagnon, J. H., Michaels, R. T., & Michaels, S. (1994). *The social organization of sexuality: Sexual practices in the United States.* Chicago: University of Chicago Press.

Lawton, J. (1984). *The all American war game.* Oxford, England: Blackwell.

Lazreg, M. (1994). *The eloquence of silence: Algerian women in question.* New York: Routledge.

Leacock, E. (1978). Women's status in egalitarian society: Implications for social evolution. *Current Anthropology, 19,* 247–275.

LeBon, G. (1947/1896). *The crowd.* London: Ernest Bonn.

Lee, S. M. (1998). Asian Americans: Diverse and growing. *Population Bulletin,* p. 53.

Lehman-Haupt, R. (1999, January 24). Rooming with a guy named Mom. *New York Times,* p. 9.

LeMasters, E. E. (1975). *Blue collar aristocrats.* Madison: University of Wisconsin Press.

Lengermann, P. M., & Niebrugge-Brantley, J. (1998). *The women founders.* New York: McGraw-Hill.

Lenski, G., & Lenski, J. (1982). *Human societies* (4th ed.). New York: McGraw-Hill.

Lerman, H. (1996). *Pigeonholing women's misery.* New York: Basic Books.

Lever, J. (1976). Sex differences in the games children play. *Social Problems, 23,* 478–487.

Lever, J. (1978). Sex differences in the complexity of children's play and games. *American Sociological Review, 43,* 471–483.

Levi, P. (1989). *The drowned and the saved.* New York: Vintage International.

Levi-Strauss, C. (1995). *Saudades do Brasil: A photographic memoir.* Seattle: University of Washington Press.

Levy, S. (1997, April 7). Blaming the Web. *Newsweek,* pp. 46–47.

Lewin, T. (1989, November 14). Aging parents: Women's burden grows. *New York Times,* pp. A1, B12.

Lewis, M., & Feiring, C. (1982). Some American families at dinner. In L. M. Laosa & I. E. Sigel (Eds.), *Families as learning environments for children.* New York: Plenum.

Lewontin, R. C. (1995, April 20). The social organization of sexuality. *New York Review of Books,* pp. 24–29.

Lewontin, R. C. (2003). The truth about DNA. *New York Review of Books,* 39–42.

Lieberson, S. (1980). *A piece of the pie: Blacks and white immigrants since 1880.* Berkeley: University of California Press.

Liebow, E. (1967). *Tally's corner: A study of Negro streetcorner men.* Boston: Little, Brown.

Lin, M. (1995, November 1). Interview by Terri Gross on *Fresh Air,* National Public Radio.

Linton, R. (1936). *The study of man.* New York: Appleton.

Lippman, P. (2003, June). Bosnia and Herzegovina: A state under threat. *Washington Report on Middle East Affairs.*

Lipset, S. M. (1979). *The first new nation.* New York: Norton.

Lipset, S. M. (1981). *Political man.* Baltimore: Johns Hopkins University Press.

Lipset, S. M. (1994). The social prerequisites of democracy revisited. *American Sociological Review, 59,* 1–22.

Lipset, S. M. (1995, December). America today: Malaise and resiliency. *Current,* pp. 3–11.

Lipset, S. M. (1998). One nation after all. *Wilson Quarterly, 22,* 100–102.

Lipset, S. M. (2000). The indispensability of political parties. *Journal of Democracy, 11,* 48–55.

Livernash, R., & Rodenburg, E. (1998). Population change, resources, and the environment. *Population Bulletin,* vol. 53, no. 1.

Lofland, J. F. (1981). Collective behavior: The elementary forms. In N. Rosenberg & R. H. Turner (Eds.), *Social psychology: Sociological perspectives.* New York: Basic Books.

Lofland, L. (1998). *The public realm: Exploring the city's quintessential social territory.* Hawthorne, NY: Aldine.

Loke, M. (2002, August 6). Critic's notebook: A camera-toting Odysseus looks into the face of pain. *New York Times,* p. E2.

Lombroso, C. (1911). *Crime: Its cause and remedies.* Boston: Little, Brown.

London, B. (1992). School-enrollment rates and trends, gender, and fertility: A cross-national analysis. *Sociology of Education, 65,* 305–318.

Lorber, J. (1994). *Paradoxes of gender.* New Haven, CT: Yale University Press.

Loseke, D. R. (2003, February). "We hold these truths to be self-evident": Problems in pondering the pedophile priest problem. *Sexualities,* pp. 6–14.

Lovins, A. (1977). *Soft energy paths: Toward a durable peace.* Cambridge, MA: Ballinger.

Lovins, A. (1998, October 10). On the rebound. *New Scientist,* p. 521.

Low-Beer, D., & Stoneburner, R. (2004). Uganda and the challenge of AIDS. In A. Whitehead & N. Poku (Eds.), *The political economy of AIDS in Africa.* London: Ashgate.

Lowey, I. S. (1990). World urbanization in perspective. In K. Davis & M. S. Bernstein (Eds.), *Resources, environment, and population. Population and Development Review, 15* (Suppl.), 148–178.

Lowry, E. H. (1993). *Freedom and community: The ethics of interdependence.* Albany: State University of New York Press.

Lubienski, C. (2000). Whither the common good? A critique of home schooling. *Peabody Journal of Education, 75,* 207–232.

Luce, I. (1964). *Letters from the Peace Corps.* Washington, DC: Robert B. Luce.

Lurie, A. (1981). *The language of clothes.* New York: Random House.

Lye, K. (1995). *The complete atlas of the world.* Austin: Raintree Steck-Vaughn.

Lynch, K. (1990). *The hidden curriculum.* London: Falmer Press.

Lynd, R. S., & Lynd, H. M. (1929). *Middletown: A study in American culture.* Orlando: Harcourt Brace Jovanovich.

Lynd, R. S., & Lynd, H. M. (1937). *Middletown in transition: A study in cultural conflicts.* Orlando: Harcourt Brace Jovanovich.

Lyson, T. A., & Squires, G. D. (1993, February). The "lost generation" of sociologists. *Footnotes* (American Sociological Association), pp. 4–5.

Machiavelli, N. (1950/1513). *The prince* and *The discourses.* New York: Modern Library.

Machlis, G., & Tichnell, D. L. (1985). *State of the world's parks: An international assessment.* Boulder, CO: Westview.

Mack, P. (2001). Women and gender in early modern England. *Journal of Modern History, 73,* 379.

MacLeod, J. (1987, 1995). *Ain't no makin' it: Leveled aspirations in a low-income neighborhood.* Boulder, CO: Westview.

MacWhinney, B. (1998). Models of the emergence of language. *Annual Review of Psychology, 49,* 199–227.

Majundar, R. C. (Ed.) (1951). *The history and culture of the Indian people.* London: Allen and Unwin.

Makela, K. (1996). *Alcoholics Anonymous as a mutual-help movement: A study in eight societies.* Madison: University of Wisconsin Press.

Malinowski, B. (1927). *Sex and repression in savage society.* London: Harcourt Brace.

Malson, L. (1972). *Wolf children and the problem of human nature* (E. Fawcett, P. Aryton, & J. White, Trans.). New York: Monthly Review Press.

Malthus, T. (1927–1928/1798). *An essay on population.* New York: Dutton.

Mannheim, K. (1941). *Man and society in an age of reconstruction.* Orlando: Harcourt Brace Jovanovich.

Mansnerus, L. (1992, November 1). Should tracking be derailed? *Education Life, New York Times,* pp. 14–16.

Mark, N. (1998). Beyond individual differences: Social differentiation from first principles. *American Sociological Review, 63,* 309–330.

Marks, J. (1994, December). Black, white, other. *Natural History,* pp. 32–35.

Marks, P. M. (1998). *In a barren land: American Indian dispossession and survival.* New York: Morrow.

Markson, A. R., & Bloch, R. (1985). Defensive cities: Military spending, high technology, and human settlements. In M. Castells (Ed.), *High technology, space, and society.* Newbury Park, CA: Sage.

Marshall, T. H. (1964). *Class, citizenship and social development.* Garden City, NY: Doubleday.

Martinson, R. (1972, April 29). Planning for public safety. *New Republic,* pp. 21–23.

Marwell, G., & Ames, R. E. (1985). Experiments on the provision of public goods II: Provision points, stakes, experience, and the free-rider problem. *American Journal of Sociology, 90,* 926–937.

Marx, K. (1961/1844). *Economic and philosophical manuscripts of 1844.* Moscow: Foreign Languages Publishing House.

Marx, K. (1962/1867). *Capital: A critique of political economy.* Moscow: Foreign Languages Publishing House.

Marx, K. (1963/1869). *The eighteenth Brumaire of Louis Bonaparte.* New York: International Publishers.

Marx, K., & Engels, F. (1955). Wage labor and capital. In *Selected works in two volumes.* Moscow: Foreign Languages Publishing House.

Marx, K., & Engels, F. (1969/1848). *The communist manifesto.* New York: Penguin.

Mascie-Taylor, C. G. N. (1990). *Biosocial aspects of social class.* New York: Oxford University Press.

Massey, D. S., & Denton, N. A. (1993). *American apartheid: Segregation and the making of the underclass.* Cambridge, MA: Harvard University Press.

Massey, D. S., & Fischer, M. J. (2000). How segregation concentrates poverty. *Ethnic and Racial Studies, 23,* 670–691.

Matthews, R. A. J. (1997). The science of Murphy's law. *Scientific American, 276,* 88–92.

Mauss, M. (1966/1925). *The gift.* New York: Free Press.

Mawson, A. R. (1989). Review of *Homicide,* by Martin Daly and Margo Wilson. *Contemporary Sociology, 18,* 238–240.

Maxwell, M. (1991). *The sociobiological imagination.* Albany: State University of New York Press.

Mayfield, L. (1984). *Teenage pregnancy.* Doctoral dissertation, City University of New York.

Maynard, M. (2002). Studying age, "race" and gender: Translating a research proposal into a project. *International Journal of Social Research Methodology, 5,* 31–40.

Mayo, E. (1945). *The social problems of an industrial civilization.* Boston: Harvard University, Graduate School of Business Administration.

McAdam, D. (1988). *Freedom summer.* New York: Oxford University Press.

McAdam, D. (1992). Gender as a mediator of the activist experience: The case of Freedom Summer. *American Journal of Sociology, 97,* 1211–1240.

McAdam, D., McCarthy, J. D., & Zald, N. (1988). Social movements. In N. J. Smelser (Ed.), *The handbook of sociology.* Newbury Park, CA: Sage.

McAdam, D., McCarthy, J. D., & Zald, M. N. (Eds.) (1996). *Comparative perspectives on social movements: Political opportunities, mobilizing structures, and cultural framings.* New York: Cambridge University Press.

McAdam, D., & Snow, D. S. (1997). *Social movements: Readings on their emergence, mobilization, and dynamics.* Los Angeles: Roxbury.

McAdam, D., Tarrow, S., & Tilly, C. (2001). Dynamics of contention. Cambridge University Press.

McAndrew, M. (1985). Women's magazines in the Soviet Union. In B. Holland (Ed.), *Soviet sisterhood.* Bloomington: Indiana University Press.

McBrien, R. P. (1990, March 12). A papal attack on Vatican II. *New York Times,* p. A17.

McCord, W. (1991). *The dawn of the Pacific century: Implications for three worlds of development.* New Brunswick, NJ: Transaction.

McCrone, D. (1996). *The sociology of nationalism.* London: Routledge.

McDowell, S. A., & Ray, B. D. (2000). The home education movement in context, practice, and theory: Editors' introduction. *Peabody Journal of Education, 75,* 1–7.

McFadden, R. B. (1998). Review of *Waiting for a miracle,* by James P. Comer. *Black Issues in Higher Education, 15,* 30.

McGoldrick, M., & Carter, E. A. (1982). *The family life cycle in normal family processes.* London: Guilford.

McGuire, M. B. (1987). *Religion: The social context* (2nd ed.). Belmont, CA: Wadsworth.

McIntyre, M. (1995). Altruism, collective action, and rationality: The case of LeChambon. *Polity, 27,* 537–557.

McKendrick, N., Brewer, J., & Plump, J. H. (1982). *The birth of a consumer society.* Bloomington: Indiana University Press.

McKenzie, E. (1994). *Privatopia: Homeowner associations and the rise of residential private government.* New Haven, CT: Yale University Press.

McManus, P. A., & DiPrete, T. A. (2001). Losers and winners: The financial consequences of separation and divorce for men. *American Sociological Review, 66,* 246–268.

McNamara, R. P. (1994). *Crime displacement: The other side of prevention.* East Rockway, NY: Cummings and Hathaway.

McNamara, R. P. (1995). *Sex, scams, and street life: The sociology of New York City's Times Square.* Westport, CT: Greenwood.

McNeill, W. (1963). *The rise of the West: A history of the human community.* Chicago: University of Chicago Press.

McNeill, W. H. (1982). *The pursuit of power: Technology, armed force, and society since A.D. 1000.* Chicago: University of Chicago Press.

Mead, G. H. (1971/1934). *Mind, self and society.* Chicago: University of Chicago Press.

Mead, M. (1950). *Sex and temperament in three primitive societies.* New York: NAL Mentor.

Mead, M. (1971). Comment. In J. Tanner & B. Inhelder (Eds.), *Discussions on child development.* New York: International Universities Press.

Medalie, J. H., & Cole-Kelly, K. (2002). The clinical importance of defining family. *American Family Physician, 65, 1277.*

Meier, D. (1995). *The power of their ideas: Lessons from a small school in Harlem.* Boston: Beacon.

Melton, J. G. (1989). *The encyclopedia of American religions* (3rd ed.). Detroit: Gale Research.

Merton, R. K. (1938). Social structure and anomie. *American Sociological Review, 3,* 672–682.

Merton, R. K. (1948). Discrimination and the American creed. In R. M. MacIver (Ed.), *Discrimination and national welfare.* New York: Institute for Religious and Social Studies; dist. by Harper.

Merton, R. K. (1968). *Social theory and social structure* (3rd ed.). New York: Free Press.

Merton, R. K. (1996). *On social structure and science.* Chicago: University of Chicago Press.

Merton, R. K. (1998). Personal communication.

Merton, R. K., & Kitt, A. (1950). Contributions to the theory of reference group behavior. In R. K. Merton & P. Lazarsfeld (Eds.), *Continuities in social research.* New York: Free Press.

Meyer, D. S., & Tarrow, S. (Eds.) (1998). Contentious politics for a new century. Lanham, MD., and Oxford, England: Rowman & Littlefield.

Meyer, J. W., Ramirez, F. O., & Soysal, Y. N. (1992). World expansion of mass education, 1870–1980. *Sociology of Education, 65,* 128–149.

Meyersohn, R., & Katz, E. (2004). Notes on a natural history of fads. In Peters, J.D. and Simonson, P. (Eds.), *Mass communication and American social thought: classic texts, 1919–1968.* Oxford, U.K.: Rowman and Littlefield.

Milgram, S. (1970). The experience of living in cities. *Science, 167,* 1461–1468.

Milgram, S. (1974). *Obedience to authority: An experimental view.* New York: Harper.

Miller, A. T. (1993). African American families. In M. B. Katz (Ed.), *The "underclass" debate: View from history.* Princeton, NJ: Princeton University Press.

Miller, D. C., & Form, W. H. (1964). *Industrial sociology* (2nd ed.). New York: Harper.

Miller, N. (1989). *In search of gay America: Women and men in a time of change.* New York: Atlantic Monthly Press.

Miller, W. B. (1958). Lower class culture as a generating milieu of gang delinquency. *Journal of Social Issues, 14,* 5–19.

Millman, M. (1976). *The unkindest cut: Life in the backrooms of medicine.* New York: Morrow.

Mills, C. W. (1951). *White collar.* New York: Oxford University Press.

Mills, C. W. (1956). *The power elite.* New York: Oxford University Press.

Mills, C. W. (1959). *The sociological imagination.* New York: Oxford University Press.

Mintz, S. (1985). *Sweetness and power: The place of sugar in modern history.* New York: Viking.

Minuchin, S. (1974). *Families and family therapy.* Cambridge, MA: Harvard University Press.

Mishel, L., Bernstein, J., & Boushey, H. (2003). *State of working America 2002/2003.* Ithaca, NY: Cornell University Press.

Mitchell, J. D. (1998). Before the next doubling. *World Watch, 11,* 20–27.

Mitra, A. (1997). Diasporic Web sites: Ingroup and outgroup discourse. *Critical Studies in Mass Communication, 14,* 158–181.

Mixner, D., & Bailey, D. (2002). *Brave journeys: Profiles in gay and lesbian courage.* London: Random House International.

Modell, J., & Hareven, T. K. (1973). Urbanization and the malleable household: An examination of boarding and lodging in American families. *Journal of Marriage and the Family, 35,* 466–479.

Moen, P. (2001). The career quandary. *PRB Reports on America,* vol. 2, no. 1. Washington, DC: Population Reference Bureau.

Mollenkopf, J. (1985). *The contested city.* Princeton, NJ: Princeton University Press.

Money, J., & Tucker, P. (1975). *Sexual signatures.* Boston: Little, Brown.

Monnier, M. (1993). *Mapping it out: Expository cartography for the humanities and social sciences.* Chicago: University of Chicago Press.

Montagna, P. D. (1977). *Occupations and society.* New York: Wiley.

Moody, H. R. (1998). *Aging: Contexts and controversies* (2nd ed.). Thousand Oaks, CA: Pine Forge.

Moore, B. (1968). *The social origins of dictatorship and democracy: Lord and peasant in the making of the modern world.* Boston: Beacon.

Moore, H. E. (1958). *Tornados over Texas.* Austin: University of Texas Press.

Moore, J. W. (1991). *Going down to the barrio: Homeboys and homegirls in change.* Philadelphia: Temple University Press.

Moore, J., & Pachon, H. (1985). *Hispanics in the United States.* Englewood Cliffs, NJ: Prentice Hall.

Moore, R., & Muller, J. (2002). The growth of knowledge and the discursive gap. *British Journal of Sociology of Education, 23,* 627–637.

Morales, E. (1986). Coca and the cocaine economy and social change in the Andes of Peru. *Economic Development and Cultural Change, 35,* 143–161.

Morales, E. (1989). *Cocaine: White gold rush in Peru.* Tucson: University of Arizona Press.

Morgan, D. L. (1998). Introduction: The aging of the baby boom. *Generations, 22,* 5–10.

Morgan, R. (Ed.) (1970). *Sisterhood is powerful: An anthology of writings from the women's liberation movement.* New York: Random House.

Morris, W. F., & Foxx, J. J. (1987). *Living Maya.* New York: Abrams.

Moscos, C. A. (1988). *Call to civic service.* New York: Free Press.

Mosley, W. H., & Cowley, P. (1991, December). *The challenge of world health.* Washington, DC: Population Reference Bureau.

Moynihan, D. P. (1988, Spring). Our poorest citizens. *Focus* (Institute for Research on Poverty), p. 5.

Mulkey, L. M. (1993). *Sociology of education: Theoretical and empirical investigations.* Fort Worth: Harcourt Brace.

Murdock, G. (1949). *Social structure.* New York: Macmillan.

Murdock, G. (1983). *Outline of world cultures* (6th ed.). New Haven, CT: Human Relations Area Files.

Murray, C. (1984). *Losing ground.* New York: Basic Books.

Murray, C. (2000, June 4). Press release. New York: World Health Organization.

Murray, C. A. (1988). *In pursuit: Of happiness and good government.* New York: Simon & Schuster.

Myrdal, G. (1944). *An American dilemma.* New York: Harper.

Myrdal, J. (1965). *Report from a Chinese village.* New York: Random House.

Nagel, T. (1994, May 12). Freud's permanent revolution. *New York Review of Books,* pp. 34–39.

Naipaul, V. S. (1998). *Beyond belief: Islamic excursions among the converted peoples.* New York: Random House.

Naisbitt, J., & Aburdene, P. (1990). *Megatrends 2000.* New York: Morrow.

Napier, A. Y., & Whitaker, C. (1980). *The family crucible.* New York: Bantam.

Naples, N. (1998). *Grassroots warriors: Activist mothering, community work, and the War on Poverty.* London: Routledge.

Nasar, S. (1999, March 6). Economic growth still at fast pace as hiring surges. *New York Times,* p. 10.

National Catholic Reporter (1997, April 11). Low-intensity war against liberation theology, p. 28.

National Center for Children in Poverty (2001). http://cpmcnet.columbia.edu/dept/nccp/ycpf.html.

National Commission on America's Urban Families (1993). *Families first.* Washington, DC: U.S. Government Printing Office.

National Opinion Research Center (NORC). Annual. *General social survey, cumulative codebook.* Chicago: University of Chicago Press.

Neihardt, J. G. (1959/1932). *Black Elk speaks: Being the life story of a holy man of the Oglala Sioux.* New York: Washington Square Press.

Nelkin, D. (1996). Conjuring science. *Nature, 384,* 423.

Nelson, B. (1998, November). Motivating workers worldwide. *Workforce,* pp. 7–9.

Neurology (2002). Mental activity may delay Alzheimer's. *Neurology, 59,* 1910–1914.

Neugarten, B. L. (1996). *The meanings of age.* Chicago: University of Chicago Press.

Newcomb, T. (1958). Attitude development as a function of reference groups: The Bennington study. In E. Maccoby, T. M. Newcomb, & E. L. Hartley (Eds.), *Readings in social psychology* (3rd ed.). Fort Worth: Holt, Rinehart and Winston.

Newman, K. S. (1988). *Falling from grace.* New York: Free Press.

Niebuhr, G. (1995, October 3). With every wave of newcomers, a church more diverse. *New York Times,* p. B6.

Niebuhr, G. (2001, September 14). After the attacks: Finding fault; U.S. "secular" groups set tone for terror attacks, Falwell says. *New York Times,* p. A18.

Niebuhr, H. R. (1929). *The social sources of denominationalism.* New York: Meridian.

Ning, P. (1995). *Red in tooth and claw: Twenty-six years in communist Chinese prisons.* New York: Grove.

Nisbet, R. A. (1969). *Social change and history.* New York: Oxford University Press.

Nisbet, R. A. (1970). *The social bond.* New York: Knopf.

Norman, M. (1997, November 9). From Carol Gilligan's chair. *New York Times Magazine,* p. 50.

Nurge, D. (2003). Liberating yet limiting: The paradox of female gang membership. In L. Kontos, D. Brotherton, & L. Barrios (Eds.), *Gangs and society: Alternative perspectives.* New York: Columbia University Press.

Nussbaum, M., & Sen, A. (Eds.) (1993). *The quality of life.* New York: Oxford University Press.

Nyden, P. (1984). *Steelworkers rank and file.* New York: Praeger.

Obermeyer, C. M. (1992). Islam, women, and politics: The demography of Arab countries. *Population and Development Review, 18,* 33–60.

Oberschall, A. (1996). *Social movements.* New Brunswick, NJ: Transaction.

Odaka, K. (1998). Portraits of the Japanese workplace: Labor movements, workers, and managers. *Journal of Comparative Economics, 26,* 825–829.

Office of Technology Assessment, U.S. Congress (1986). *Technology, public policy, and the changing structure of agriculture: Vol. 2. Background papers: Part D. Rural communities.* Washington, DC.

Ofosu-Amaah, V. (1998). Declines in fertility levels evident in Africa, notes UN Population Fund. *UN Chronicle, 35,* 20–21.

Ogbu, J. U. (1994, Winter). Racial stratification and education in the United States: Why inequality persists. *Teachers College Record,* pp. 264–298.

Ogburn, W. F. (1942). Inventions, population and history. In American Council of Learned Societies, *Studies in the history of culture.* Freeport, NY: Books for Libraries Press.

Ogburn, W. F. (1957). Cultural lag as theory. *Sociology and Social Research, 41,* 167–174.

Ogburn, W. F., & Nimkoff, M. F. (1934). *The family.* Boston: Houghton Mifflin.

O'Hare, W. (1996). A new look at poverty in America. *Population Bulletin,* vol. 51, no. 2.

Oldenburg, R. (1997). *The great good place.* New York: Marlowe.

Oliver, M. L., & Shapiro, T. M. (1990). Wealth of a nation: A reassessment of asset inequality in America shows at least one third of households are asset-poor. *American Journal of Economics and Sociology, 49,* 129–150.

Oliver, M.L., & Shapiro, T.M. (1995). *Black wealth/white wealth: A new perspective on racial inequality.* New York: Routledge.

Olojede, D. (1995, June 5). Chaos lurks in Nigeria. *Newsday,* pp. A6, A22.

Olson, M. (1965). *The logic of collective action.* Cambridge, MA: Harvard University Press.

O'Neil, J. (1997). Building schools as communities: A conversation with James Comer. *Educational Leadership, 54,* 6–11.

O'Neill, B., & Balk, D. (2001). World population futures. Population Bulletin, vol. 56, no. 3.

Opie, I., & Opie, P. (1969). *Children's games in street and playground.* Oxford, England: Oxford University Press.

Oppenheimer, M. (1999, September). We made it, so what? *Monthly Review,* pp. 5–6.

Oppenheimer, V. K. (1994). Women's rising employment and the future of the family in industrial societies. *Population and Development Review, 20,* 293–342.

Orfield, G., & Eaton, S. E. (1996). *Dismantling desegregation: The quiet reversal of Brown v. Board of Education.* New York: New Press.

Orfield, G., & Wald, J. (2001, April 29). High stakes tests attached to high school graduation lead to increased drop-out rates, particularly for poor and minority students. *In Motion,* pp. 1–2.

Ornish, D. (1998). *Love and survival: The scientific basis for the healing power of intimacy.* New York: HarperCollins.

Orwell, G. (1950). *Shooting an elephant and other essays.* New York: Harcourt Brace Jovanovich.

Palmer, J. (1995, July-August). Windows of opportunity (the motion picture industry in other countries). *UNESCO Courier,* pp. 29–31.

Panford, S., Nyaney, M. O., Amoah, S. O., & Aidoo, N. G. (2001). Using folk media in HIV/AIDS prevention in rural Ghana. *American Journal of Public Health, 91,* 1559–1562.

Papernow, P. (1988). Stepparent role development: From outsider to intimate. In W. R. Beer (Ed.), *Relative strangers.* Totowa, NJ: Rowman and Littlefield.

Park, R. E. (1914). Racial assimilation in secondary groups. *Publications of the American Sociological Society, 8,* 66–72.

Park, R. E. (1967/1925). The city: Suggestions for the investigation of human behavior in the urban environment. In R. E. Park & E. W. Burgess (Eds.), *The city.* Chicago: University of Chicago Press.

Park, R. E. (1967/1926). The urban community as a spatial pattern and a moral order. In R. H. Turner (Ed.), *Robert E. Park on social control and collective behavior.* Chicago: University of Chicago Press.

Park, R. E., & Burgess, E. W. (1921). *Introduction to the science of sociology* (rev. ed.). Chicago: University of Chicago Press.

Parsons, T. (1937). *The structure of social action.* New York: McGraw-Hill.

Parsons, T. (1940). An analytic approach to the theory of social stratification. *American Journal of Sociology, 45,* 841–862.

Parsons, T. (1951). *The social system.* New York: Free Press.

Parsons, T. (1960). *Structure and process in modern societies.* New York: Free Press.

Parsons, T. (1966). *Societies: Evolutionary and comparative.* Englewood Cliffs, NJ: Prentice Hall.

Parsons, T. (1968). The problem of polarization along the axis of color. In J. H. Franklin (Ed.), *Color and race.* Boston: Beacon.

Parsons, T. (1991). The integration of economic and sociological theory. *Sociological Inquiry, 61,* 10–60.

Parsons, T., & Bales, R. F. (1955). *Family, socialization, and interaction process.* New York: Free Press.

Partin, M., & Palloni, A. (1995, Spring). Accounting for the recent increases in low birth weight among African Americans. *Focus* (Institute for Research on Poverty), pp. 33–38.

Patterson, O. (1982). *Slavery and social death.* Cambridge, MA: Harvard University Press.

Patterson, O. (1991). *Freedom: Vol. 1. Freedom in the making of Western culture.* New York: Basic Books.

Patterson, O. (1999). *Rituals of blood: Consequences of slavery in two American centuries.* Washington, DC: Civitas/Counterpoint.

Pavlov, I. (1927). *Conditioned reflexes: An investigation of the physiological activity of the cerebral cortex* (G. V. Anrep, Trans. & Ed.). London: Oxford University Press.

Pear, R. (1993, July 8). Big health gap, tied to income, is found in U.S. *New York Times,* pp. A1, B10.

Pedersen, D. (1997, March 3). When an A is average. *Newsweek,* p. 64.

Pedersen, E., & Faucher, T. A., with Eaton, W. W. (1978). A new perspective on the effects of first-grade teachers on children's subsequent adult status. *Harvard Educational Review, 48,* 1–31.

Peek, C. W., Zsembik, B. A., & Cloward, R. T. (1997). The changing caregiving networks of older adults. *Research on Aging, 19,* 333–361.

Peplau, L. A., Hill, C. T., & Rubin, Z. (1993). Sex role attitudes in dating and marriage: A 15-year follow-up of the Boston couples study. *Journal of Social Issues, 49,* 3–25.

Perin, C. (1977). *Everything in its place: Social order and land use in America.* Princeton, NJ: Princeton University Press.

Perls, T. T., & Silver, M. H. (1999). *Living to 100.* New York: Basic Books.

Perrow, C. (1984). *Normal accidents: Living with high-risk technologies.* New York: Basic Books.

Perrow, C. (1996). Prosaic organizational failure. *American Behavioral Scientist, 39,* 1040–1056.

Perutz, M. F. (1992). The fifth freedom. *New York Review of Books, 39,* 5–7.

Peters, A. (1990). *Peters atlas of the world.* New York: HarperCollins.

Peterson, P. E. (2003, July-August). Schools after twenty years. *Current,* pp. 7–9.

Pettigrew, T. F. (1980). Prejudice. In *Harvard encyclopedia of American ethnic groups.* Cambridge, MA: Belknap.

Pew Foundation (2003, March 18). America's image further erodes. Washington, DC: Pew Foundation.

Pfeiffer, E., Verwoerdt, A., & Davis, G. (1972). Sexual behavior in middle life. *American Journal of Psychiatry, 128,* 1262–1267.

Phelan, J. C., & Link, B. G. (1999). Who are "the homeless"? Reconsidering the stability and composition of the homeless population. *American Journal of Public Health, 89,* 1334–1338.

Phillips, T. (1998). The end of the rope, part three: The capital punishment revival. *Contemporary Review, 272,* 181–186.

Piaget, J., & Inhelder, B. (1969). *The psychology of the child.* New York: Basic Books.

Pifer, A., & Bronte, L. (Eds.) (1986). *Our aging society: Paradox and promise.* New York: Carnegie Corporation of New York.

Pillari, V. (1998). *Human behavior in the social environment: Families, groups, organizations, and communities.* Pacific Grove, CA: Brooks/Cole.

Pittman, J. F. (1993). Functionalism may be down, but it surely is not out. In P. G. Boss, W. J. Doherty, R. LaRossa, W. R. Schumm, & S. K. Steinmetz (Eds.), *Sourcebook of family theories and methods: A contextual approach.* New York: Plenum.

Piven, F. F. (1997). *The breaking of the American social contract.* New York: New Press.

Platt, A. M. (1977). *The child savers* (2nd ed.). Chicago: University of Chicago Press.

Ploch, D. R., & Hastings, D. W. (1995). Some church; some don't. *Journal for the Scientific Study of Religion, 34,* 507–516.

Polansky, N. A., Chalmers, M. A., Buttenweiser, E., & Williams, D. P. (1981). *Damaged parents, an anatomy of child neglect.* Chicago: University of Chicago Press.

Polanyi, K. (1944). *The great transformation.* Boston: Beacon.

Polsby, N. (1980). *Community power and political theory* (2nd ed.). New Haven, CT: Yale University Press.

Popenoe, D. (1999, September-October). The institution of marriage is weakening. *Society*, pp. 2–3.

Population Reference Bureau (1998). Parents whose children need day care often face daily crisis. *Population Today, 26,* 1–2.

Population Reference Bureau (2002). *2002 world population data sheet.* Washington, DC: U.S. Government Printing Office.

Population Reference Bureau (2001, December). *Population Bulletin #4.* Washington, DC: Government Printing Office.

Portes, A., & Rumbaut, R. G. (1996). *Immigrant America: A portrait.* Berkeley: University of California Press.

Portes, A., & Stepick, A. (1985). Unwelcome immigrants. *American Sociological Review, 50,* 493–514.

Press, J. E., & Townsley, E. (1998). Wives' and husbands' housework reporting: Gender, class, and social desirability. *Gender and Society, 12,* 188–219.

Pressman, J. L., & Wildavsky, A. (1984). *Implementation* (3rd ed.). Berkeley: University of California Press.

Pressman, S. (1998). The gender poverty gap in developed countries: Causes and cures. *Social Science Journal, 35,* 275–287.

Preston, J. (1998, March 6). Mexico's overtures to the Zapatistas bring tensions in Chiapas to a new boiling point. *New York Times,* p. A8.

Preston, S. H. (1984). Children and the elderly: Divergent paths for America's dependents. *Demography, 21,* 435–457.

Prough, D. S. (2001). Are enough explicit resuscitation directives obtained for critically ill patients? *The Lancet, 358,* 1920–1921.

Putnam, R. (1995). Bowling alone: America's declining social capital. *Journal of Democracy, 6,* 65–78.

Putnam, R. D. (1996, Winter). The strange disappearance of civic America. *American Prospect,* pp. 34–49.

Pyle, R. E. (1996). *Persistence and change in the Protestant establishment.* Westport, CT: Praeger.

Quadagno, J. S. (1979). Paradigms in evolutionary theory—Sociobiological models of natural selection. *American Sociological Review, 44,* 100–109.

Quinn, B. A. (2000). The paradox of complaining: Law, humor, and harassment in the everyday work world. *Law and Social Inquiry, 25,* 1151–1185.

Quinney, R. (1978). The ideology of law: Notes for a radical alternative to legal oppression. In C. E. Reasons & R. M. Rich (Eds.), *Sociology of law: A conflict perspective.* Toronto: Butterworths.

Quinney, R. (1980). *Class, state, and crime.* White Plains, NY: Longman.

Radelet, M. L., & Bedau, H. A. (1992). *In spite of innocence: Erroneous convictions in capital cases.* Boston: Northeastern University Press.

Rajan, R. S. (2001, April). Globalization. *ASEAN Economic Bulletin,* pp. 1–11.

Randall, V. (1998). *Political change and underdevelopment: A critical introduction to Third World politics* (2nd ed.). Durham, NC: Duke University Press.

Rathje, W. L. (1993). Less fat? Aw, baloney. Garbage Project studies indicate misreporting of fatty meat consumption. *Garbage, 5,* 22–23.

Ray, B. D. *Peabody Journal of Education, 75,* 71–106.

Reardon, C. (2002, Winter). Islam and the modern world. *Ford Foundation Report,* pp. 18–23.

Redfield, R. (1947). The folk society. *American Journal of Sociology, 52,* 293–308.

Reese, S. (1998, August). Religious spirit. *American Demographics,* p. 62.

Reich, R. B. (1992, Winter). Training a skilled work force. *Dissent,* pp. 42–46.

Reid, L. L. (1998). Devaluing women and minorities: The effects of race/ethnic and sex composition of occupations on wage levels. *Work and Occupations, 25,* 511–537.

Reid, S. T. (1993). *Criminal justice.* New York: Macmillan.

Reidy, D. A. (2001). Pluralism, liberal democracy, and compulsory education: Accommodation and assimilation. *Journal of Social Philosophy, 32,* 585–609.

Reiman, J. (2002). *The rich get richer and the poor get prison* (7th ed.). Boston: Allyn & Bacon.

Rejwan, N. (1998). *Arabs face the modern world: Religious, cultural, and political responses to the West.* Gainesville: University of Florida Press.

Renzetti, C. M. (1999). Editor's introduction. *Violence Against Women, 5,* 227–229.

Rhodes, R. (1999). *Visions of technology.* New York: Simon and Schuster.

Richards, E. (1989). *The knife and gun club: Scenes from an emergency room.* New York: Atlantic Monthly Press.

Richmond-Abbott, M. (1992). *Masculine and feminine: Gender roles over the life cycle* (2nd ed.). New York: McGraw-Hill.

Riesman, D. (1957). The suburban dislocation. *Annals of the American Academy of Political and Social Science, 314,* 123–146.

Riis, J. A. (1890). *How the other half lives: Studies among the tenements of New York.* New York: Scribner.

Riley, M. W., Foner, A., & Waring, J. (1988). The sociology of age. In N. E. Smelser (Ed.), *The handbook of sociology.* Newbury Park, CA: Sage.

Riley, M. W., Kahn, R. L., & Foner, A. (1994). *Age and structural lag.* New York: Wiley.

Riley, M. W., & Riley, J. W., Jr. (1989). The lives of older people and changing social roles. *Annals of the American Academy of Political and Social Science, 503,* 14–28.

Rist, R. C. (1973). *The urban school: A factory for failure.* Cambridge, MA: MIT Press.

Robbins, W. (1985, February 10). Despair wrenches farmers' lives as debts mount and land is lost. *New York Times,* pp. 1, 30.

Roberts, A. E., Koch, J. R., & Johnson, D. P. (2001). Religious reference groups and the persistence of normative behavior: An empirical test. *Sociological spectrum, 21,* 81–96.

Roberts, S. (1995, April 27). Women's work: What's new, what isn't. *New York Times,* p. B6.

Robertson, R. (1985). The sacred and the world system. In P. Hammond (Ed.), *The sacred in a secular age.* Berkeley: University of California Press.

Robinson, J. (1988). *The rhythm of everyday life.* Boulder, CO: Westview.

Robinson, J. P., & Godbey, G. (1997). *Time for life: The surprising ways Americans use their time.* University Park: Pennsylvania State University Press.

Robinson, P. (1994). *Freud and his critics.* Berkeley: University of California Press.

Robinson, R. (2003, February). Reparations—More than just a check. *Black Collegian,* pp. 96–98.

Rochon, T. R. (1998). *Culture moves: Ideas, activism, and changing values.* Princeton, NJ: Princeton University Press.

Rock, P. (1985). Symbolic interactionism. In A. Kuper & J. Kuper (Eds.), *The social science encyclopedia.* London: Routledge and Kegan Paul.

Rodriguez, C. E. (1992). The Puerto Rican community in the South Bronx: Contradictory views from within and without. In P. S. Rotherberg (Ed.), *Race, class and gender in the United States.* New York: St. Martin's Press.

Roer-Strier, D., & Rosenthal, M. K. (2001). Socialization in changing cultural contexts: A search for images of the "adaptive adult." *Social Work, 46,* 215–228.

Rosario, V. (2001, September-October). The "gay gene" is born. *Gay and Lesbian Review,* pp. 13–15.

Rose, M. (1995). *Possible lives: The promise of public education.* Boston: Houghton Mifflin.

Rosen, E. I. (1987). *Bitter choices: Blue-collar women in and out of work*. Chicago: University of Chicago Press.

Rosenhan, D. L. (1973). On being sane in insane places. *Science, 179,* 250–258.

Rosoff, S. M., Pontell, H. N., & Tillman, R. (2002). *Profit without honor: White-collar crime and the looting of America*. Upper Saddle River, NJ: Prentice Hall.

Rosow, I. (1965). Forms and functions of adult socialization. *Social Forces, 44,* 38–55.

Ross, H. L. (1963). *Perspectives on the social order*. New York: McGraw-Hill.

Rossi, A. (1964). Equality between the sexes: An immodest proposal. In R. J. Lifton (Ed.), *The woman in America*. Boston: Beacon.

Rossi, A. (1977). The biosocial basis of parenting. *Daedalus, 106,* 1–31.

Rossi, A. (1980). Aging and parenthood in the middle years. In P. B. Baltes & O. G. Brim, Jr. (Eds.), *Life-span development and behavior* (Vol. 3). Orlando: Academic Press.

Rossi, A. (1994). *Sexuality across the life course*. Chicago: University of Chicago Press.

Rossianov, K. D. (1993). Editing nature: Joseph Stalin and his "new" Soviet biology. *Isis, 84,* 728–745.

Roszak, T. (1969). *The making of a counterculture*. Garden City, NY: Doubleday.

Rothenberg, P. S. (Ed.) (1992). *Race, class and gender in the United States* (2nd ed.). New York: St. Martin's Press.

Rothstein, E. (2002, March 2). Damning (yet desiring) Mickey and the Big Mac. *New York Times,* p. B9.

Rubell, P. (2003, August 26). Technology law and practice. *New York Law Journal*.

Rubin, Z. (1980). The love research. In A. Skolnick & J. H. Skolnick (Eds.), *Family in transition*. Boston: Little, Brown.

Rubington, E., & Weinberg, M. S. (1999). *Deviance: The interactionist perspective* (7th ed.). Boston: Allyn & Bacon.

Rudé, G. (1964). *The crowd in history*. New York: Wiley.

Ruggles, S. (1997). The rise of divorce and separation in the United States, 1880–1990. *Demography, 34,* 455–467.

Ruskin, C. (1988). *The quilt: Stories from the NAMES Project*. New York: Pocket Books.

Ryan, A. (1992). Twenty-first century limited. *New York Review of Books, 39,* 20–24.

Rybczynski, W. (1987). *Home: A short history of an idea*. New York: Penguin.

Ryerson, W. (2002, Winter). The effectiveness of entertainment mass media in changing behavior. *Population Media Center Newsletter,* p. 1.

Rymer, R. (1992a, April 13). A silent childhood. *New Yorker,* pp. 41–53.

Rymer, R. (1992b, April 20). A silent childhood, part II. *New Yorker,* pp. 43–47.

Sabel, C. F. (1995). Bootstrapping reform: Rebuilding firms, the welfare state, and unions. *Politics & Society, 23,* 5–49.

Sadik, N. (1995). Decisions for development: Women, empowerment and reproductive health. In *The state of the world population 1995*. New York: United Nations Population Fund.

Sagarin, E. (1975). *Deviants and deviance: A study of disvalued people and behavior*. New York: Praeger.

Sahagun, L., & Stammer, L. B. (1998, February 20). Entire Promise Keepers' staff to be laid off. *Los Angeles Times* p. A1.

Sahlins, M. D. (1960, September). The origin of society. *Scientific American,* pp. 76–87.

Sahlins, M. D. (1976). *The use and abuse of biology: An anthropological critique of sociobiology*. Ann Arbor: University of Michigan Press.

Sakharov, A. D. (1990, May 14). The poisonous legacy of Trofim Lysenko. *Time,* p. 61.

Salgado, S. (1990). *An uncertain grace*. New York: Aperture.

Salgado, S. (1993). *Workers*. New York: Aperture.

Salisbury, R. F. (1962). *From stone to steel*. Parkville, Australia: Melbourne University Press.

Samuelson, P. A. (1998). How Foundations came to be ("Foundations of Economic Analysis"). *Journal of Economic Literature, 36,* 1375–1387.

Sanchez-Jankowski, M. S. (1991). *Islands in the street: Gangs and American urban society*. Berkeley: University of California Press.

Sandefur, G. D., & Tienda, M. (Eds.) (1988). *Divided opportunities: Minorities, poverty, and social policy*. New York: Plenum.

Sander, T. H., & Putnam, R. D. (2002, February 19). Walking the civic talk after September 11. *Christian Science Monitor,* p. 11.

Sanderson, W., & Scherbov, S. (1997). Doubling of world population unlikely. *Nature, 387,* 803–805.

Sapir, D. (1997, October). Women in the front line. *The UNESCO Courier,* pp. 27–29.

Sapolsky, R. (1998, April). How the other half heals: Links between health and socioeconomic status. *Discover,* pp. 46–72.

Sassen, S. (1991). *Global city*. Princeton, NJ: Princeton University Press.

Sassen, S. (1994). *Cities in a world economy*. Thousand Oaks, CA: Pine Forge.

Sassen, S. (1998). *Globalization and its discontents: Essays on the new mobility of people and money*. New York: Free Press.

Satir, V. (1972). *Peoplemaking*. Palo Alto, CA: Science and Behavior Books.

Savage-Rumbaugh, E. S., & Shanker, S. G. (1998). *Ape language and the human mind*. New York: Oxford University Press.

Sbraga, T. P., & O'Donohue, W. (2000). Sexual harassment. *Annual Review of Sex Research,* 11, 258–286.

Scanzoni, J. (1995). *Contemporary families and relationships: Reinventing responsibility*. New York: McGraw-Hill.

Scarf, M. (1995). *Intimate worlds: Life inside the family*. New York: Random House.

Schaller, G. B. (1964). *The year of the gorilla*. Chicago: University of Chicago Press.

Schemo, D. J. (2003, July 26). Education secretary defends school system he once led. *New York Times,* p. A9.

Scheper-Hughes, N., & Devine, J. (2003, February). Priestly celibacy and child sexual abuse. *Sexualities,* pp. 15–40.

Schilling, A. G. (1991, March 18). This could be the eve of a false recovery. *Forbes,* pp. 74–75.

Schmitt, E. (1993, February 6). The top soldier is torn between 2 loyalties. *New York Times,* p. A1.

Schmitt, E. (2001, April 4). Analysis of census finds segregation along with diversity. *New York Times,* p. A15.

Schooler, C., & Miller, J. (1985). Work for the household: Its nature and consequences for husbands and wives. *American Journal of Sociology, 90,* 97–124.

Schorr, L. B. (1988). *Within our reach: Breaking the cycle of disadvantage*. Garden City, NY: Doubleday.

Schubeck, T. L. (1995). Ethics and liberation theology. *Theological Studies, 56,* 107–123.

Schuman, H., & Scott, J. (1989). Generations and collective memories. *American Sociological Review, 54,* 359–381.

Schumpeter, J. A. (1950). *Capitalism, socialism, and democracy* (3rd ed.). New York: Harper.

Schur, E. M. (1984). *Labeling women deviant: Gender, stigma, and social control*. New York: Random House.

Schwartz, B. (1976). Images of suburbia: Some revisionist commentary and conclusions. In B. Schwartz (Ed.), *The changing face of the suburbs*. Chicago: University of Chicago Press.

Scott, T. G. (1998). *The United States of suburbia*. Amherst, NY: Prometheus.

Scruggs, L., & Lange, P. (2002). Where have all the members gone? Globalization, institutions, and union density. *Journal of Politics, 64,* 22–39.

Scull, A. T. (1988). Deviance and social control. In N. J. Smelser (Ed.), *The handbook of sociology*. Newbury Park, CA: Sage.

Seligson, M. A., & Passe-Smith, J. T. (1993). *Development and underdevelopment: The political economy of inequality*. Boulder, CO: Renner.

Selizer, V. (1985). *Pricing the priceless child: The changing social value of children*. New York: Free Press.

Selznick, P. (1952). *The organizational weapon: A study of Bolshevik strategy and tactics*. New York: McGraw-Hill.

Selznick, P. (1966). *TVA and the grass roots: A study in the sociology of formal organization*. New York: Harper.

Sen, A. (1992). *Inequality reexamined*. New York: Russell Sage.

Sen, A. (1993, May). The economics of life and death. *Scientific American*, pp. 40–47.

Sen, A. (1997). Maximization and the act of choice. *Econometrica, 65*, 745–779.

Sennett, R., & Cobb, J. (1972). *The hidden injuries of class*. New York: Random House.

Shaiken, H., & Lopez, S. (1997, January). Two routes to team production: Saturn and Chrysler compared. *Industrial Relations*, pp. 17–45.

Shapiro, I., & Greenstein, R. (2001). *The widening income gulf*. Washington, DC: Center on Budget and Policy Priorities.

Shaw, C. R. (1929). *Delinquency areas: A study of the geographic distribution of school truants, juvenile delinquents, and adult offenders in Chicago*. Chicago: University of Chicago Press.

Shibutani, T., & Kwan, K. M. (1965). *Ethnic stratification*. New York: Macmillan.

Shils, E. (1970). Tradition, ecology and institution in the history of sociology. *Daedalus, 99*, 760–825.

Shils, E. (1985). Sociology. In A. Kuper & J. Kuper (Eds.), *The social science encyclopedia*. London: Routledge and Kegan Paul.

Shorris, E. (1992). *Latinos: A biography of the people*. New York: Norton.

Shotland, R. L. (1985). When bystanders just stand by. *Psychology Today, 19*, 50–55.

Shuck, P. (2001, Winter). Affirmative action. *Brookings Review*, pp. 24–27.

Siegel, A. (1992, March). Felice Schwartz tries to set the record straight. *Working Woman*, p. 17.

Silberman, C. (1980). *Criminal violence, criminal justice*. New York: Random House.

Silk, L. (1989, May 12). Rich and poor: The gap widens. *New York Times*, p. D2.

Simmel, G. (1904). The sociology of conflict. *American Journal of Sociology, 9*, 490ff.

Simmons, J. L. (1985). The nature of deviant subcultures. In E. Rubington & M. S.

Weinberg (Eds.), *Deviance: The interactionist perspective*. New York: Macmillan.

Simon, J. (1996). *The ultimate resource*. Princeton, NJ: Princeton University Press.

Simpson, C. E., & Yinger, J. M. (1953). *Racial and cultural minorities: An analysis of prejudice and discrimination*. New York: Harper.

Simpson, J. H. (1983). Moral issues and status politics. In R. C. Liebman & R. Wuthnow (Eds.), *The new Christian right: Mobilization and legitimation*. Hawthorne, NY: Aldine.

Singer, M. (1999, August). The population surprise. *Atlantic Monthly*, pp. 22–24.

Singhal, A., & Rogers, E. M. (1999). Miguel Sabido and the entertainment-education strategy. In *Entertainment-education: A communication strategy for social change*. London: Erlbaum.

Siwolop, S. (1995, August 27). Have I got a business opportunity for you. *New York Times*, pp. D1, D8.

Sizer, T. (1995, January 8). What's wrong with standard tests. *Education Life, New York Times*, p. 58.

Sjoberg, G. (1968). The preindustrial city. In S. Fava (Ed.), *Urbanism in world perspective: A reader*. New York: Crowell.

Sjulmana, J. L., & Bowen, W. G. (2001). *The game of life: College sports and educational values*. Princeton, NJ: Princeton University Press.

Skaggs, J. M. (1998). Justifying gender-based affirmative action under *United States v. Virginia's* "exceedingly persuasive justification" standard. *California Law Review, 86*, 1169–1210.

Skocpol, T. (1979). *States and social revolutions*. New York: Cambridge University Press.

Skousen, M. (2001). *The making of modern economics: The lives and ideas of the great thinkers*. Armonk, NY: M. E. Sharpe.

Smelser, N. J. (1962). *Theory of collective behavior*. New York: Free Press.

Smelser, N. J. (1966). The modernization of social relations. In M. Weiner (Ed.), *Modernization*. New York: Basic Books.

Smigel, E. O. (1964). *The Wall Street lawyer: Professional organizational man*. New York: Free Press.

Smil, V. (2001). *Feeding the world*. Cambridge, MA: M.I.T. Press.

Smiley, J. (1992). *A thousand acres*. New York: Ballantine.

Smith, A. (1965/1776). *The wealth of nations*. Modern Library.

Smith, C., Denton, M. L., Faris, R., & Regnerus, M. (2002). Mapping American adolescent religious participation. *Journal for the Scientific Study of Religion, 41*, 597–612.

Smith, C. D. (1994). *The absentee American: Repatriates' perspectives on America and its place in the contemporary world*. Putnam Valley, NY: Aletheia.

Smith, C. D. (Ed.) (1996). *Strangers at home: Essays on the effects of living overseas and coming "home" to a strange land*. Putnam Valley, NY: Aletheia.

Smith, D. (1989). *Promises* (Letter from Madurai). Oberlin, OH: Oberlin Shansi Memorial Association.

Smith, D. M., & Gates, G. J. (2001, August). Gay and lesbian families in the United States: Same-sex unmarried partner households, a preliminary analysis of 2000 census data. Washington, DC: D.C. Human Rights Campaign.

Smith, R. A. (1968). Los Angeles, prototype of supercity. In S. F. Fava (Ed.), *Urbanism in world perspective: A reader*. New York: Crowell.

Snipp, C. M. (1991). *American Indians: The first of this land*. New York: Russell Sage.

Snow, D. A., & Benford, R. D. (1992). Master frames and cycles of protest. In A. D. Morris & C. M. Mueller (Eds.), *Frontiers in social movement theory*. New Haven, CT: Yale University Press.

Sorenson, A. B., Weinert, F. E., & Sherrod, L. R. (Eds.) (1986). *Human development and the life course: Multidisciplinary perspectives*. Hillsdale, NJ: Erlbaum.

Sorokin, P. (1937). *Social and cultural dynamics: Vol. 3. Fluctuation of social relationships, war, and revolution*. New York: American Book.

Sowell, T. (1972). *Black education: Myths and tragedies*. New York: McKay.

Spencer, H. (1874). *The study of sociology*. New York: Appleton.

Spengler, O. (1965/1918). *The decline of the West*. New York: Modern Library.

Spitz, R. A. (1945). Hospitalism: An inquiry into the genesis of psychiatric conditions in early childhood. In A. Freud (Ed.), *The psychoanalytic study of the child*. New York: International Universities Press.

Stacey, J., & Biblarz, T. J. (2001). (How) does the sexual orientation of parents matter? *American Sociological Review, 66*, 159–183.

Stack, C. (1974). *All our kin*. New York: Harper.

Staggenborg, S. (1998). *Gender, family, and social movements*. Thousand Oaks, CA: Pine Forge.

Starr, P. (1982). *The social transformation of American medicine*. New York: Basic Books.

Starr, P. (1995, Winter). What happened to healthcare reform? *American Prospect*, pp. 20–31.

Statistical abstract of the United States. Annual. Washington, DC: U.S. Bureau of the Census.

Steen, G. R. (1996). *DNA and destiny: Nature and nurture in human behavior*. New York: Plenum.

Stein, J. (1994, December). Space and place. *Art in America*, pp. 66–71.

Steltzer, U. (1982). *Inuit: The north in transition*. Chicago: University of Chicago Press.

Stephen, A. (2003, August 25). More junk food, ever-larger portions and more hours spent in front of the television have made the United States the fattest nation in the world. Is it too late to reverse the trend? *New Statesman*, p. 12.

Stevens, W. K. (1988, December 20). Life in the Stone Age: New findings point to complex societies. *New York Times*, pp. C1, C15.

Stevenson, H. W. (1992, December). Learning from Asian schools. *Scientific American*, pp. 70–76.

Stevenson, H. W. (1998, March). A study of three cultures: Germany, Japan, and the United States. *Phi Delta Kappan*, pp. 524–530.

Stevenson, R. W. (1992, July). U.S. judge orders $7.5 million award to whistle-blower. *New York Times*, pp. 1, 12.

Stevenson, R. W. (1999 January 6). Texaco is said to set payment over sex bias. *New York Times*, p. C1.

Steward, J. H. (1955). *The theory of culture change: The methodology of multilinear evolution*. Urbana: University of Illinois Press.

Stewart, C. T., Jr. (2002). Inequality of wealth and income in a technologically advanced society. *Journal of Social Political and Economic Studies, 27*, 495–512.

Stewart, G. R. (1968). *Names in the land*. Boston: Houghton Mifflin.

Stimson, C. (1980). Women and the American city. *Signs, 5* (Suppl.).

Stockard, J., & Johnson, M. M. (1992). *Sex and gender in society*. Englewood Cliffs, NJ: Prentice Hall.

Stolberg, C. G. (1997, November 23). Gay culture weighs sense and sexuality. *New York Times*, sec. 4, pp. 1, 6.

Stouffer, S. A., Suchman, E. A., DeVinney, L. C., Star, S. A., & Williams, R. A., Jr. (1949). *Studies in social psychology in World War II: Vol. 1. The American soldier: Adjustment during army life*. Princeton, NJ: Princeton University Press.

Strange, M. (1988). *Family farming: A new economic vision*. Lincoln: University of Nebraska Press.

Sudman, S., & Bradburn, N. (1982). *Asking questions: A practical guide to questionnaire design*. San Francisco: Jossey-Bass.

Sudnow, D. (1967). *Passing on: The social organization of dying*. Englewood Cliffs, NJ: Prentice Hall.

Suitor, J., & Reavis, R. (1995). Football, fast cars, and cheerleading: Adolescent gender norms. *Adolescence, 30*, 265–272.

Sullivan, K. (1998, November-December). Defining democracy down. *American Prospect*, pp. 91–96.

Sumner, W. G. (1940/1907). *Folkways*. Boston: Ginn.

Sumner, W. G. (1963/1911). *Social Darwinism: Selected essays*. Englewood Cliffs, NJ: Prentice Hall.

Suro, R. (1992, May 26). For women, varied reasons for single motherhood. *New York Times*, p. A12.

Sutherland, E. H. (1940). White collar criminality. *American Sociological Review, 5*, 1–12.

Suttles, G. (1967). *The social order of the slum*. Chicago: University of Chicago Press.

Suttles, G. (1972). *The social construction of communities*. Chicago: University of Chicago Press.

Sutton-Smith, B., & Rosenberg, B. G. (1961). Sixty years of historical change in the game preferences of American children. *Journal of American Folklore, 74*, 17–46.

Swedberg, R. (1994). *Explanations in economic sociology*. New York: Russell Sage.

Swift, D. C. (1998). *Religion and the American experience: A social and cultural history*. Armonk, NY: Sharpe.

Swindell, B., Allen, J., & Graham-Silverman, A. (2003, June 7). "Family friendly" bill to foster comp time flexibility gets laid off House schedule. *CQ Weekly*, p. 1.

Szelenyi, I. (1983). *Urban inequalities under state socialism*. New York: Oxford University Press.

Tabb, W. (1986). *Churches in struggle: Liberation theologies and social change*. New York: Monthly Review Press.

Taeuber, K. E., & Taeuber, A. F. (1965). *Negroes in cities*. Hawthorne, NY: Aldine.

Tagliabue, J. (1998, August 19). Communists, remodeled, keep trying in Germany. *New York Times*, p. A5.

Talbot, M. (1998, May 24). Attachment theory: The ultimate experiment. *New York Times Magazine*, pp. 24–30.

Tannen, D. (1990). *You just don't understand: Women and men in conversation*. New York: Morrow.

Tannen, D. (2001). *I only say this because I love you*. New York: Random House.

Tarde, G. (1903). *The laws of imitation*. New York: Holt.

Tarrow, S. G. (1994). *Power in movement: Social movements, collective action, and politics*. Cambridge, England: Cambridge University Press.

Tawney, R. A. (1966/1932). *Land and labor in China*. Boston: Beacon.

Taylor, J. M., Gilligan, C., & Sullivan, A. M. (1995). *Between voice and silence: Women and girls, race and relationship*. Cambridge, MA: Harvard University Press.

Teitelbaum, M., & Weiner, M. (1995). *Threatened peoples, threatened borders: World migration and U.S. policy*. New York: Norton.

Temkin, L. S. (1993). *Inequality*. New York: Oxford University Press.

Tewksbury, R., & Taylor, J. M. (1996). The consequences of eliminating Pell Grant eligibility for students in post-secondary correctional education programs. *Federal Probation, 60*, 60–63.

Thio, A. (1998). *Deviant behavior* (5th ed.). New York: Longman.

Thomas, L. (1979). *The medusa and the snail*. New York: Bantam.

Thomas, W. I. (1971/1921). *Old world traits transplanted*. Montclair, NJ: Patterson.

Thomas, W. L. (1956). *Man's role in changing the face of the earth*. Chicago: University of Chicago Press.

Thompson, L. B. (2002, February 17). Defense budget battle: Did Rumsfeld get it right? *San Diego Union-Tribune*, p. G-1.

Thompson, P. M., et al. (2001). Genetic influences on brain structure. *Nature Neuroscience, 4*, 1253–1258.

Thorne, B. (1993). *Gender play: Boys and girls in school*. New Brunswick, NJ: Rutgers University Press.

Thorne, B. (2000). A telling time for women's studies. *Signs: Journal of Women in Culture and Society, 25*, 1183–1187.

Thornton, A., & Young-DeMarco, L. (2001, November 1). Four decades of trends in attitudes toward family issues in the United States: The 1960s through the 1990s. *Journal of Marriage and Family*.

Thornton, R. (1987). *American Indian holocaust and survival: A population history since 1492*. Norman: University of Oklahoma Press.

Tienda, M., & Singer, A. (1995). Wage mobility of undocumented workers in the United States. *International Migration Review, 29*, 112–138.

Tienda, M., & Wilson, F. D. (1992). Migration and the earnings of Hispanic men. *American Sociological Review, 57*, 661–678.

Tilly, C. (1993). *European revolutions, 1492–1992*. Oxford, England: Blackwell.

Tobach, E., & Rosoff, B. (Eds.). (1994). *Challenging racism and sexism: Alternatives to genetic explanations*. New York: Feminist Press at the City University of New York.

Toffler, A. (1970). *Future shock*. New York: Bantam.

Tönnies, F. (1957/1887). *Community and society* (C. P. Loomis, Trans. & Ed.). East Lansing: Michigan State University Press.

Torres, C. A., & Mitchell, T. R. (Eds.) (1998). *Sociology of education: Emerging perspectives.* Albany: State University of New York Press.

Touraine, A. (1998). Social transformations of the twentieth century. *International Social Science Journal, 50,* 165–172.

Toynbee, A. J. (1972). *A study of history.* New York: Oxford University Press.

Transaction Publishers (1997). *Foundations of political sociology.* New Brunswick, NJ: Transaction.

Traven, B. (1966). Assembly line. In *The night visitor, and other stories.* New York: Hill and Wang.

Trent, J. W., Jr. (1995, July-August). Suffering fools. *The Sciences,* pp. 18–22.

Trillin, C. (1998, February 2). New Orleans unmasked. *New Yorker,* pp. 38–43.

Truzzi, M. (1971). *Sociology: The classic statements.* New York: McGraw-Hill.

Tuch, S. A., & Martin, J. K. (1997). *Racial attitudes in the 1990s: Continuity and change.* Westport, CT: Praeger.

Tuch, S. A., Sigelman, L., & Martin, J. K. (1997). Fifty years after Myrdal: Blacks' racial policy attitudes in the 1990s. In Tuch, S. A., & Martin, J. K., *Racial attitudes in the 1990s: Continuity and change.* Westport, CT: Praeger.

Tucker, C. (1998, November 29). Working poor deserve voice. *Denver Post,* p. G-02.

Tucker, L. M. (2001, October 20). Firefighters honor wee ones. *Largo Times.*

Turner, F. J. (1920/1893). *The frontier in American history.* Fort Worth: Holt, Rinehart and Winston.

Turner, R. H. (1974). The theme of contemporary social movements. In R. E. L. Faris (Ed.), *Handbook of modern sociology.* Chicago: Rand McNally.

Uhlenberg, P. (1980). Death and the family. *Journal of Family History, 5,* 313–320.

UNDP (United Nations Development Programme). Various years. *Human Development Report.* New York: Oxford University Press.

UNIFEM (United Nations Development Fund for Women). www.unifem.org.

United Nations (1995, March). *Adoption of the declaration and programme of action of the World Summit for Social Development.* New York: United Nations.

United Nations (1997). Map #3980, Worldwide illiteracy, www.un.org/esa/population/pubsarchive/bss/bssmapil.htm.

United Nations (2001). *UNICEF reports on global education crisis.* www.unicefusa.org.

United Nations Commission on Human Rights (1998). *Report on the situation of human rights in Iraq.* Geneva: United Nations.

United Nations Department of Public Information (2002, March). DP/2264.

U.S. Census Bureau (2000). *Census of population: 2000.* Washington, DC: U.S. Census Bureau.

U.S. Department of Commerce (2001). *An aging world.*

U.S. Department of Education (1999). *How old are America's public schools?* Washington, DC: National Center for Educational Statistics.

Van Gennep, A. (1960/1908). *The rites of passage.* Chicago: University of Chicago Press.

Vanneman, R., & Cannon, L. W. (1987). *The American perception of class.* Philadelphia: Temple University Press.

Vass, W. K. (1979). *The Bantu speaking heritage of the United States.* Los Angeles: Center for Afro-American Studies, University of California.

Ventura, S. J., et al. (2001). Births to teenagers in the United States, 1940–2000. *National Vital Statistics Reports, 49,* 10.

Verbrugge, L. M., Gruber-Baldini, A. L., & Fozard, J. L. (1996). Age differences and age changes in activities: Baltimore longitudinal study of aging. *Gerontologist, 36,* 342–350.

Vest, J. (2001, December). Fourth-generation warfare. *Atlantic Monthly,* pp. 49–50.

Vilain, E. (2000). Genetics of sexual development. *Annual Review of Sex Research, 11.*

Vilas, C. M. (1993). The hour of civil society. *NACLA Report on the Americas, 27,* 38–43.

Villarosa, L. (2002, January 1). A conversation with Joseph Graves. *New York Times,* p. F5.

Vining, D. R., Jr. (1985, April). The growth of core regions in the Third World. *Scientific American,* pp. 42–49.

Vogel, E. (1979). *Japan as number one: Lessons for America.* Cambridge, MA: Harvard University Press.

Vondra, J. (1996, April). Resolving conflicts over values. *Educational Leadership,* pp. 76–79.

Wade, N. (2001, November 5). Study finds genetic link between intelligence and size of some regions of the brain. *New York Times,* p. A15.

Wald, M. L. (1997, September 21). Number of cars is growing faster than human population. *New York Times,* p. 35.

Wallerstein, I. (1974). *The modern world system: Capitalist agriculture and the origins of the European world-economy in the sixteenth century.* Orlando: Academic Press.

Wallerstein, I. (1999). The heritage of sociology, the promise of social science. Presidential address, XIVth World Congress of Sociology, Montreal, July 26, 1998. *Current Sociology, 47,* 1–43.

Wallerstein, J., & Blakeslee, S. (1989). *Second chances: Men, women and children a decade after divorce.* New York: Ticknor & Fields.

Wallerstein, J., Lewis, J., & Blakeslee, S. (2000). *The unexpected legacy of divorce.* New York: Hyperion.

Wallerstein, M., & Moene, K. O. (2003). Does the logic of collective action explain the logic of corporatism? *Journal of Theoretical Politics, 15,* 271–297.

Walsh, E. J., & Warland, R. H. (1983). Social movement involvement in the wake of a nuclear accident: Activists and free riders in the TMI area. *American Sociological Review, 48,* 764–780.

Walton, J. (1992). *Western times and water wars: State, culture, and rebellion in California.* Berkeley: University of California Press.

Waltzer, M. (1980). Pluralism. In *Harvard encyclopedia of American ethnic groups.* Cambridge, MA: Belknap.

Warhus, M. (1997). *Another America: Native American maps and the history of our land.* New York: St. Martin's Press.

Warner, R. S. (1998). Work in progress toward a new paradigm for the sociological study of religion in the United States. *American Journal of Sociology, 98,* 1044–1093.

Warner, W. L., Meeker, M., & Calls, K. (1949). *Social class in America: A manual of procedure for the measurement of social status.* Chicago: Science Research Associates.

Watson, J. B. (1930). *Behaviorism.* New York: Norton.

Wayne, L. (2001, October 28). For trade protesters, "slower, sadder songs." *New York Times,* sec. 3, p. 1.

Weaver, M. A. (1994, September 12). A fugitive from justice. *New Yorker,* pp. 46–60.

Webb, E., Campbell, D. T., Schwarz, R. D., & Sechrest, L. (1966). *Unobtrusive measures: Nonreactive research in the social sciences.* Chicago: Rand McNally.

Weber, M. (1922). *Gesammelte aufsatze zur Religionssoziologie.* Tubingen, Germany: Mohr.

Weber, M. (1947). *The theory of social and economic organization* (A. M. Henderson & T. Parsons, Trans.). New York: Free Press.

Weber, M. (1958/1913). World religion. In H. Gerth & C. W. Mills (Trans. & Eds.), *From Max Weber: Essays in sociology.* New York: Oxford University Press.

Weber, M. (1958/1922). Economy and society. In H. Gerth & C. W. Mills (Trans. & Eds.), *From Max Weber: Essays in sociology.* New York: Oxford University Press.

Weber, M. (1962/1921). *The city.* New York: Collier.

Weber, M. (1963/1922). *The sociology of religion* (E. Fischoff, Trans.). Boston: Beacon.

Weber, M. (1968). The concept of citizenship. In S. N. Eisenstadt (Ed.), *Max Weber on charisma and institution building.* Chicago: University of Chicago Press.

Weber, M. (1974/1904). *The Protestant ethic and the spirit of capitalism* (T. Parsons, Trans.). New York: Scribner.

Weinberg, H. (1994). Marital reconciliation in the United States: Which couples are successful? *Journal of Marriage and the Family, 56,* 80–88.

Wekerle, G. (Ed.) (1980). *New space for women.* Boulder, CO: Westview.

Wellins, S. (1990). *Children's use of television in England and the United States.* Doctoral dissertation, City University of New York.

Wells, M. J. (1996). *Strawberry fields: Politics, class, and work in California agriculture.* Ithaca, NY: Cornell University Press.

West, C. (1992, February 8). Learning to talk of race. *New York Times Magazine,* pp. 24–25.

West, C. (1996). *Race matters.* New York: Vintage.

West, W. (1998, March 9). The U.S. armed forces: Ready to fight—nicely? *Insight on the News,* p. 48.

Westin, A. (1967). *Privacy and freedom.* New York: Atheneum.

Wheeler, S. R. (1998, April 10). Future showing promise: Donors revitalize religious group. *Denver Post,* pp. A1, A5.

Whitchurch, G. G., & Constantine, L. L. (1993). Systems theory. In P. G. Boss, W. J. Doherty, R. LaRossa, W. R. Schumm, & S. K. Steinmetz (Eds.), *Sourcebook of family theories and methods: A contextual approach.* New York: Plenum.

White, H. (1970). *Chains of opportunity.* Cambridge, MA: Harvard University Press.

Whiting, B. B., & Edwards, C. P. (1988). *Children of different worlds.* Cambridge, MA: Harvard University Press.

Whittle, J. (2003, May). War of the world-views. *Church and State,* pp. 8–9.

WHO (World Health Organization) (2000). WHO global database on child growth and malnutrition, 2000. www.who.int/nut/documents/nhd_mip_200.pdf.

WHO (2002). Nutrition for health and development progress report 2002. Geneva, Switzerland: United Nations.

Whorf, B. L. (1961). The relation of habitual thought and behavior to language. In J. B. Carroll (Ed.), *Language, thought, and reality: Selected writings of Benjamin Lee Whorf.* Cambridge, MA: MIT Press.

Whyte, W. F. (1943). *Street corner society.* Chicago: University of Chicago Press.

Wilford, J. N. (1997, November 18). New clues show where people made the great leap to agriculture. *New York Times,* pp. F1, F6.

Wilgoren, J. (2003, April 13). Where race matters. *The New York Times,* sec. 4A, p. 20.

Wilkinson, A. (1989, July 24). Sugarcane. *New Yorker,* pp. 56ff.

Williams, T. (1989). *The cocaine kids.* Reading, MA: Addison-Wesley.

Williams, T. (1992). *Crack house.* Reading, MA: Addison-Wesley.

Williams, T., & Kornblum, W. (1994). *The uptown kids: Struggle and hope in the projects.* New York: Putnam.

Willis, P. (1983). Cultural production and theories of reproduction. In L. Barton & S. Walker (Eds.), *Race, class and education.* London: Croom-Helm.

Willmott, P., & Young, M. (1971). *Family and class in a London suburb.* London: New American Library.

Wilson, B. L. (1993). *Mandating academic excellence: High school responses to state curriculum reform.* New York: Teachers College Press.

Wilson, C. R. (1987). The death of Bear Bryant: Myth and ritual in the modern South. *South Atlantic Quarterly, 86,* 282–295.

Wilson, E. O. (1975). *Sociobiology.* Cambridge, MA: Belknap.

Wilson, E. O. (1979). *On human nature.* New York: Bantam.

Wilson, E. O. (1998). *Consilience: The unity of knowledge.* New York: Knopf.

Wilson, J. Q. (1977). *Thinking about crime.* New York: Vintage.

Wilson, W. J. (1984). The urban underclass. In L. W. Dunbar (Ed.), *The minority report.* New York: Pantheon.

Wilson, W. J. (1987). *The truly disadvantaged: The inner city, the underclass, and public policy.* Chicago: University of Chicago Press.

Wilson, W. J. (1998). Inner-city dislocations. *Society, 35,* 270–278.

Winch, R. F. (1958). *Mate selection.* New York: Harper.

Winik, M. F. (1996, November 13). Sharing a legacy of rescue. *The Christian Century,* pp. 1112–1116.

Winner, L. (1996, February-March). Know-nothing technology policy. *Technology Review,* p. 55.

Winner, L. (1997, August-September). The neverhood of Internet commerce. *Technology Review,* p. 31.

Wirth, L. (1945). The problem of minority groups. In R. Linton (Ed.), *The science of man in the world crisis.* New York: Columbia University Press.

Wirth, L. (1968/1938). Urbanism as a way of life. In S. F. Fava (Ed.), *Urbanism in world perspective: A reader.* New York: Crowell.

Wise, D. A. (Ed.) (2001). *Themes in the economics of aging.* Chicago: University of Chicago Press.

Witt, S. D. (1997). Parental influence on children's socialization to gender roles. *Adolescence, 32,* 253–360.

Wittfogel, K. (1957). *Oriental despotism: A comparative study of total power.* New Haven, CT: Yale University Press.

Wixen, B. N. (1979). Children of the rich. In J. D. Call, J. D. Noshpitz, R. L. Cohen, & I. N. Berlin (Eds.), *Basic handbook of child psychiatry.* New York: Basic Books.

Wolf, A. (1998). *One nation after all.* New York: Viking.

Wolf, E. R. (1984a, November 4). The perspective of the world. *New York Times Book Review,* pp. 13–14.

Wolf, E. R. (1984b, November 4). Unifying the vision. *New York Times Book Review,* p. 11.

Wolf, N. (1991). *The beauty myth.* New York: Morrow.

Wolfe, A. (1998, October 25). The black-white test score gap. *New York Times Book Review,* p. 15.

Wolfe, T. (1980). *The right stuff.* New York: Bantam.

Wolfgang, M. E., & Riedel, M. (1973). Race, judicial discretion, and the death penalty. *Annals of the American Academy of Political and Social Science, 407,* 119–133.

Women's Health Weekly (2003, May 15). White women three times more likely to commit suicide than black women. P. 23.

Woo, W. T. (1994). The art of reforming centrally planned economies: Comparing China, Poland, and Russia. *Journal of Comparative Economics, 18,* 276–308.

World Bank (1997). *World development indicators.* Washington, DC: World Bank.

Wren, D. J. (1997). Adolescent females' "voice" changes can signal difficulties for teachers and administrators. *Adolescence, 32,* 463–470.

Wright, E. O. (1979). *Class structure and economic determination.* Orlando: Academic Press.

Wright, E. O. (1989). *The debate on classes.* New York: Verso.

Wright, E. O. (1997). *Class counts: Comparative studies in class analysis.* New York: Cambridge University Press.

Wright, E. O., Costello, C., Hachen, D., & Sprague, J. (1982). The American class structure. *American Sociological Review, 47,* 702–726.

Wrigley, E. A. (1969). *Population and history.* New York: McGraw-Hill.

Wrigley, J. (1995). *Other people's children.* New York: Basic Books.

Wrong, D. H. (1961). The oversocialized conception of man in modern sociology. *American Sociological Review, 24,* 772–782.

Wrong, D. H. (1999). *The oversocialized conception of man.* New Brunswick, NJ: Transaction.

Wu, H., & Wakeman, C. (1995). *Bitter winds: A memoir of my years in China's gulag.* New York: Wiley.

Wuthnow, R. (1988). Sociology of religion. In N. J. Smelser (Ed.), *The handbook of sociology.* Newbury Park, CA: Sage.

Wuthnow, R. (1994). *Sharing the journey: Support groups and America's new quest for community.* New York: Free Press.

Yahia, L. (2002). http://espn.go.com/oly/s/2002/1220/1480103.html#.

Yinger, J. (1995). *Closed doors, opportunities lost: The continuing costs of housing segregation.* New York: Russell Sage.

Young, S. N. (2001). Beyond the human genome. *Journal of Psychiatry and Neuroscience, 26,* 291–292.

Youniss, J., & Yates, M. (1997). *Community service and social responsibility in youth.* Chicago: University of Chicago Press.

Zakaria, F. (2003). *The future of freedom: Illiberal democracy at home and abroad.* New York: Norton.

Zangwell, I. (1909). *The melting pot.* New York: Macmillan.

Zarembo, A. (1999, March 15). A hurricane's orphans. *Newsweek,* p. 47.

Zeisel, H. (1982). *The limits of law enforcement.* Chicago: University of Chicago Press.

Zill, N. (1995, Spring). Back to the future: Improving child indicators by remembering their origins. *Focus* (Institute for Research on Poverty), pp. 17–24.

Zonana, H. (1997). The civil commitment of sex offenders. *Science, 278,* 1248–1249.

Zurcher, L. A., & Snow, D. A. (1981). Collective behavior and social movements. In M. Rosenberg & R. Turner (Eds.), *Social psychology: Sociological perspectives.* New York: Basic Books.

Zweigenhaft, R., & Domhoff, G. W. (1998). *Diversity in the power elite: Have women and minorities reached the top?* New Haven, CT: Yale University Press.

Photo Credits

Chapter 1. 2: © Lee Celano/Reuters/Getty Images. 6: M. Dwyer/Stock, Boston. 9: center, Bettmann/Corbis. 9: left, Culver Pictures Inc. 9: right, Culver Pictures Inc. 10: bottom right, Courtesy of Manjula Giri. 10: left, Harriet Martineau by Richard Evans, Courtesy of the National Portrait Gallery, London. 10: top right, Hulton/Archive/Getty Images. 12: © UPI/Bettmann/Corbis. 14: AP/Wide World Photos. 16: AP/Wide World Photos. 17: © Michael Newman/PhotoEdit. 18: © Bill Lai/The Image Works. 19: © Marleen Daniels/Getty Images. 20: left, © Crandall/The Image Works. 20: right, © Zbigniew Bzdak/The Image Works. 21: left, © Alain Evrard/Photo Researchers, Inc. 21: center, © Nour/Getty Images. 21: right, AP/Wide World Photos.

Chapter 2. 25: © Mary Kate Denny/PhotoEdit. 28: right, AP/Wide World Photos. 28: left, © UPI/Bettmann/Corbis. 30: top right, © Bill Ross/Corbis. 30: bottom left, © Brian Willer/NYT Pictures. 34: top right, AP/Wide World Photos. 34: top left, © Franco Zecchin. 44: both, AP/Wide World Photos. 44: center, AP/Wide World Photos.

Chapter 3. 49: © Dan Groshong/Corbis Sygma. 53: left, © Douglas Mazonowicz/Photo Researchers. 53: right, Egyptian Museum, Cairo. 54: right, © Matthew Neal McVay/Stock, Boston. 54: left, © Mitchell Gerber/Corbis. 56: © Chenault Photography Studio, Decatur, Alabama. 57: right, AP/Wide World Photos. 57: left, Coram Foundation, London/Bridgeman Art Library, London. 59: bottom, © Ron Angle/Getty Images News. 59: top, © Underwood & Underwood/Corbis. 63: © Manoj Shah/Getty Images. 65: © Richard B. Levine. 66: © Hans Georg Roth/Corbis. 67: JJFOXX/NYC. 72: personal property of Margaret Washington. 74: all, Jeffrey Jay Foxx. 75: right, Jeffrey Jay Foxx.

Chapter 4. 79: © Eugene Richards. 88: © Gerhard Hinterleitner/Getty Images. 90: top right, © John Neubauer/PhotoEdit. 90: bottom left, copyright Nicholas Sapieha/Art Resource, NY. 94: bottom, © Paul De Maria/Corbis Sygma. 94: top, © Rick Maiman/Corbis Sygma. 97: AP/Wide World Photos. 100: AP/Wide World Photos. 101: © Reuters NewMedia Inc./Corbis. 102: both, © Eugene Richards. 103: both, © Eugene Richards.

Chapter 5. 108: © Richard Hutchings/PhotoEdit. 114: S. Curtiss, Genie: A Psycholinguistic Study of a Modern Day "Wild Child" (Academic Press, 1977). Used by permission. 118: Rich Puchalsky. 123: The New York Public Library, Astor, Lenox & Tilden Foundations. 125: © Spencer Grant/PhotoEdit. 127: left, AP/Wide World Photos. 127: right, © 1995 Newsday, Inc. 128: © Preston Mack/Getty Images News. 129: © Will & Deni McIntyre/Photo Researchers, Inc. 131: Courtesy NYFD Photo Archives. 134: left, AP/Wide World Photos. 134: center, © Michael Newman/PhotoEdit. 135: left, © Eric Miller/Getty Images News. 135: center, AP/Wide World Photos. 135: right, AP/Wide World Photos. 136: Courtesy Lofton-Croteau family.

Chapter 6. 140: Steve Hart © 2002. 143: © Gregg Hadel. 146: © Ken Heyman/Woodfin Camp & Associates. 153: Courtesy of Galerie Patrice Triggano, Paris. 162: right, AP/Wide World Photos. 162: left, © Corbis. 164: all, © Ken Heyman/Woodfin Camp & Associates. 165: left, © Ken Heyman/Woodfin Camp & Associates. 165: center, © Ken Heyman/Woodfin Camp & Associates. 165: top right, © Ken Heyman/Woodfin Camp & Associates. 165: bottom right, © Michael Newman/PhotoEdit.

Chapter 7. 170: © Margaret Morton, author/photographer The Tunnel (Yale University Press, 1995). 172: Essex Institute, Salem, Massachusetts. 173: © Erich Schlegel/Dallas Morning News/Corbis. 177: American Cancer Society. 178: © Rafiqur Rahman/Reuters NewMedia Inc./Corbis. 179: top right, © REENTS/SIEMONEIT/Corbis Sygma. 179: bottom left, © Ronnie Wright/Corbis. 180: left, Stock Montage, Inc. 180: top center, © Bettmann/Corbis. 180: right, © A. Ramey/PhotoEdit. 180: bottom center, © Patrick Ward/Stock, Boston. 181: Food For The Poor, Inc. 189: © Alon Reininger/Contact/Woodfin Camp & Associates. 190: left, AP/Wide World Photos. 190: right, © The Granger Collection, New York. 196: right, © Margaret Morton author/photographer The Tunnel (Yale University Press, 1995). 197: all, © Margaret Morton author/photographer The Tunnel (Yale University Press, 1995).

Chapter 8. 201: Photo courtesy Kaiser Foundation. 204: top right, AP/Wide World Photos. 204: bottom left, © Ted Streshinsky/Corbis. 208: © Matt Herron 1987. 213: © Steven Rubin/The Image Works. 214: Hulton/Archive by Getty Images. 215: Culver Pictures Inc. 219: © Jeff Greenberg/Photo Researchers. 220: top right, Cliches des Musees Nationaux. 220: bottom left, Museo del Prado, Madrid. 222: both, © Matt Herron 1987. 223: all, © Matt Herron 1987. 225: right, © Kevin Winter/DMI. 225: left, © Philippe Ledru/Corbis Sygma.

Chapter 9. 228: © Liba Taylor/Corbis. 237: Darshana Dalvi. 238: AP/Wide World Photos. 240: © Peter Menzel/Stock, Boston. 243: left, © Bettmann/Corbis. 243: right, © Kirk Condyles. 248: top left, © Dennis Stock/Magnum. 248: bottom right, © J. B. Diederich/Contact Press Images. 248: top right, © Joe Carini/The Image Works. 255: © Kirk Condyles. 256: Wendy Ewald/Chandrakant. 257: both, Wendy Ewald/Chandrakant.

Chapter 10. 260: © Betty Press/Woodfin Camp & Associates. 265: AP/Wide World Photos. 266: © Nik Wheeler/Corbis. 268: © Bettmann/Corbis. 269: both, © Traver/Getty Images. 272: © Michael Grecco/Stock, Boston. 276: © Shepard Sherbell/Corbis Saba. 277: Musee d'Orsay, Paris/Cliche des Musees Nationaux. 286: bottom left, © Betty Press/Woodfin Camp & Associates. 286: bottom right, Independent Picture Service. 286: top right, Photograph by Eliot Elisofon, 1972, Slide no. HEBR 2, Eliot Elisofon Photographic Archives, National Museum of African Art. 287: center right, A Harrist Church in Blokosso Section of Abidjian, Cote d'Ivoire. Photograph by Eliot Elisofon, 1969, Slide no. TIVC2, Eliot Elisofon Photographic Archives, National Museum of African Art. 287: bottom left, Courtesy of United Nations/DPI. 287: top, © F. Willett.

Chapter 11. 292: © Miguel Rio Branco/ Magnum Photos, Inc. 295: Rafiqur Rhaman/ Reuters. 298: AP/Wide World Photos. 300: © PhotoEdit. 301: © Reuters NewMedia, Inc./Corbis. 303: © Bettmann/Corbis. 304: © C. Lee/New York Times. 305: © Carolyn D. Smith. 308: top left, AP/Wide World Photos. 308: bottom right, © David Kampfner/Getty Images. 316: both, © Sebastiao Salgado/Contact Press Images. 317: bottom left, © Bernard Pierre Wolff/ Magnum Photos, Inc. 317: © bottom right, Sebastiao Salgado/Contact Press Images. 317: top, © Sebastiao Salgado/Contact Press Images. 318: Lois Kleffman, Sand Gap, KY. 319: Reprinted with permission of Funcionamiento CIAZO.

Chapter 12. 322: © Jose More. 326: © Jeff Greenberg/PhotoEdit. 330: top right, Gift of Mr. & Mrs. Earle Ludgin. 1947.39. Photograph © 1999, The Art Institute of Chicago. All Rights Reserved. 330: bottom left, Philadelphia Museum of Art: Given by Wright S. Ludington. 337: right, © A. Ramey/ Woodfin Camp & Associates. 337: left, Bettmann/Corbis. 338: © Barbara Norfleet. 341: top right, © Elliot Erwitt/Magnum. 341: left, © Michael Jacobson-Hardy. 347: © Nathan Benn/Woodfin Camp & Associates. 350: both, © Michael Jacobson-Hardy. 351: all, © Michael Jacobson-Hardy. 352: left, AP/Wide World Photos. 352: top right, © Chapman/The Image Works.

Chapter 13. 355: AP/Wide World Photos. 356: top right, AP/Wide World Photos. 359: top, AP/Wide World Photos. 359: bottom, © Maggie Steber/Stock, Boston. 366: both, Dorothea Lang. 368: Reproduced from the Collections of the Library of Congress. 372: AP/Wide World Photos. 375: © Robert Brenner/PhotoEdit. 377: right, © C. Simonpietri/Corbis Sygma. 377: left, Chicago Historical Society. 383: © Fujihira/ Monkmeyer. 384: © Dan Dry/Dan Dry & Associates. 386: © Steve Skjold/PhotoEdit. 387: both, © William Johnson/Stock, Boston.

Chapter 14. 392: © Chenault Studios/ Decatur, AL. 395: © Paul Chesley/Getty Images. 396: top right, AFP Photo/Jimin Lai © AFP/Corbis. 396: bottom left, AP/Wide World Photos. 397: The Kobal Collection. 404: © Chenault Studios/Decatur, AL. 405: Bibliotheque Royale Albert I, Brussels. 407: Catherine Ursillo/Photo Researchers, Inc. 408: AP/Wide World Photos. 410: Continental Airlines. 411: Courtesy of Daniel J. Curran. 412: Stock Montage, Inc. 415: Cour-

tesy: Mary Boone Gallery, New York. 418: all, © Chenault Studios/Decatur, AL. 419: both, © Chenault Studios/Decatur, AL.

Chapter 15. 423: The Imogen Cunningham Trust. 430: © Kevin Moloney/NYT Pictures. 432: © Terry Ashe/Getty Images. 433: © Farrell Grehan/Photo Researchers, Inc. 435: AP/Wide World Photos. 436: bottom center, © Dave Sartin/Getty Images. 436: top right, © The Curtis Publishing Company. 436: top left, The Huntington Library, Art Collections, and Botanical Gardens, San Marino, California/SuperStock. 440: © Hanson Carroll/Archive Photos/Getty Images. 442: UN/DPI Photo. 444: photograph by Heather Pillar. 446: both, The Imogen Cunningham Trust. 447: all, The Imogen Cunningham Trust.

Chapter 16. 452: © Eugene Richards. 453: © Eugene Richards. 456: top right, © Paul Conklin/Monkmeyer. 456: bottom right, © Stephanie Maze/Woodfin Camp & Associates. 469: Allison Shelley/Education Week. 472: The National Gallery, London. 475: Courtesy of the Vermont Freedom to Marry Task Force from their website www. vtfreetomarry.org, photographer Jordan Silverman. 476: © Kevin Rivoli. 480: left, © 1994 Frank Fournier/Contact Press Images. 480: right, © Donna Ferrato, 1994. 481: bottom left, © Dan Habib/Impact Visuals. 481: top right, © Jeanne Strongin, 1990.

Chapter 17. 484: AP/Wide World Photos. 486: © Leo de Wys. 488: left, © David Moore, Black Star. 488: right, © Robert Goldwitz/Photo Researchers, Inc. 489: © Dr. Chaibai Mustamandy. 492: © Edmundo Morales. 493: top right, Collection of Sandra S. Jaffe/Preservation Hall. 493: bottom left, Collection of the Museum of American Folk Art, New York. Gift of Mr. and Mrs. Edwin C. Braman, 1983.14.4. 497: Courtesy of Susan Kornblum. 498: National Anthropological Archives. 499: © Bettmann/Corbis. 501: © Ross-Marino/Corbis Sygma. 502: left, © Bob Daemmrich/Stock, Boston. 502: right, © Bob Daemmrich/The Image Works. 504: © Corbis. 506: © A. Keler/Corbis Sygma. 508: © Tony Savino/The Image Works. 512: left, AP/Wide World Photos. 512: right, © Beryl Goldberg. 513: both, © Steven Rubin/The Image Works.

Chapter 18. 518: Courtesy of Jonas Chartock. 521: © George Holton/Photo Researchers, Inc. 537: AP/Wide World Photos. 544: top left, Brown Brothers. 544: bottom right,

© Mark Lewis. 546: Courtesy of Allison Serafin. 547: bottom, Courtesy of Orin Gutlerner. 547: top right, Fort Worth Star-Telegram/Joyce Marshall.

Chapter 19. 550: © Danny Lehman/Corbis. 554: The Granger Collection, New York. 556: © Edmundo Morales. 558: Courtesy of Christian Aid/www.christian-aid.org. 559: bottom left, AP/Wide World Photos. 559: top right, Aldo Mauro. 561: Library of Congress. 571: Dick Wood. 576: right, © Gary A. Conner/PhotoEdit. 576: left, © Michael Newman/PhotoEdit. 577: top left, Brown Brothers. 577: center right, Courtesy of Susan Dueckman. 577: bottom left, © Billy E. Barnes/PhotoEdit.

Chapter 20. 582: © Attar Maher/Corbis Sygma. 587: © John Feingersh. 589: © Andrew Holbrooke/Getty Images. 591: © Pete Winkle. 592: both, AP/Wide World Photos. 593: Sotheby's Picture Library, London. 598: M. Wuerker. 601: bottom, © Bob Daemmrich/Stock, Boston/PictureQuest. 601: top, Brown Brothers. 602: Hulton/ Archive by Getty Images. 606: left, AP/Wide World Photos. 606: right, © Stephanie Sinclair/Corbis. 607: left, AP/Wide World Photos. 607: top right, Dmitri Kessel/Getty Images. 607: bottom right, Peter Marshall/ Alamy.

Chapter 21. 612: © Ilkka Uimonen for Newsweek/Magnum. 617: New York Public Library Picture Collection/New York Public Library, Astor, Lenox & Tilden Foundations. 620: bottom right, © Roger Viollet/Getty Images. 620: top left, © Warren Faidley/ Weatherstock. 624: bottom, AP/Wide World Photos. 624: top right, © Jeff Christensen/ Getty Images. 626: Saint-Janshospitaal, Bruges. 628: Peter Parks/AFP/Getty Images. 630: Courtesy Population Media Center, www.populationmedia.org. 632: center, Courtesy Nuclear Regulatory Commission. 632: bottom, © C.H. Hortsjo, in I. Eibl-Eibesfeldt, Human Ethnology, reprinted by permission of Aldine de Gruyter and Eibl-Eibesfeldt. 632: top, © C.J. Pickerell. 633: bottom left, Metropolitan Museum of Art, New York/Carnarvon Collection, Edward S. Harkness Gift, 1926. 633: top, © Joel Simon/Getty Images. 633: center right, © concept by Michael Brill, illustration by Safdar Abidi. 633: bottom right, © concept by Michael Brill, illustration by Safdar Abidi.

Name Index

Subject Index

Territorial communities, 146–147, 645
Terrorism, 266
TFR. *See* Total Fertility Rate
Theism, 492, 645
Theoretical perspective, 645
Theories
    definition, 45, 645
    natural selection, 61
    predictive, 45–46
The Power Elite (Mills), 595
The Pursuit of the Millennium (Cohen), 209
The Road to Calvary, 220
The State of the World's Children (UNICEF), 523
The Urban Villagers (Gans), 250
The War of the Worlds (Wells), 218–219
Third Word, 523–524
Thoreau, Henry David, 247
Three Mile Island, 216, 623
Thurman, Paul, 80–81
Title IX, 544–545
Title VII, 412
Tocqueville, Alexis de., 162–163
Tolerance, 489–490
Tönnies, Ferdinand, 96
To Renew America (Gingrich), 213
Total Fertility Rate, 274
Total institutions, 131, 646
Totalitarian regime, 646
Traditional authority, 646
Trailer kids, 243
Transition, demographic, 642
Transsexuals, 395, 646
Triads, 146, 646
Truman, Harry, 601
Tunnel people, 196–197
Twelve-step programs, 131

U

UNESCO. *See* United Nations Educational, Social, and Cultural Organization
UNICEF. *See* United Nations Children's Fund
Unions. *See* Labor unions
United Nations Children's Fund, 523
United Nations Educational, Social, and Cultural Organization, 523
Units of Analysis, 39–40
Universalism, 615
University of Chicago, 11
Unobtrusive measures, 33–34, 646
Unreliable elements, 601
Upward mobility, 646
Urban communities. *See also* Cities
    conflicts, 252–253
    disasters in, 253–255
    early studies, 247–249

growth of, 235–236
    inequality in, 252–253
    persistence of, 249–251
    tensions, 247
Urbanization. *See also* Cities
    definition, 235, 646
    effects of, 242–245
    large-scale, 238–231
    modernity and, 275
    society, 240–242
Urban Villagers (Gans), 250
Utilitarianism, 17

V

Valence, 145
Values
    American, 73, 75
    children, 437
    cultural, 51–52
    definition, 52, 646
    deviance and, 176–177
    family, 467
    generation X, 283
    patriarchal, 66
Variables
    definition, 28, 646
    dependent, 28, 642
    independent, 28–29, 643
    interaction among, 29
    suicide, 27–29
Victimization surveys, 176
Vietnam War, 44
Violence
    family, 469–470
    racial, 377
    school, 539–549
    against women, 411
Visual sociology, 33–34
Volunteers, 37, 157, 646

W

Wal-Mart, 571
Walt Disney Company, 475–476
Warfare
    asymmetrical, 266
    cultural impact, 267–268
    ecological impact, 266–267
    forms, 266
    gender relations, 268–269
    historical view, 265
    institutional effects, 269–270
    symmetrical, 266
Watson, John B., 112–113
Wealth inequality, 325–326
The Wealth of Nations (Smith), 558–559, 560
Weber, Max, 9

Welfare capitalism, 646
Welfare reform, 348–349
Wells-Barnett, Ida B., 10
White-collar crime, 184–185
Whitneys, 296
Wilson, Edward O., 116
Wobblies. *See* Industrial Workers of the World
Women. *See also* Gender
    aging, 434
    appearance, 408–410
    educational parity, 326
    empowering, 417, 420
    fertility control, 256
    harassment, 410–411
    homophobia and, 401–402
    liberation, 411–413
    Muslim, 396, 508
    obesity and, 629–630
    objectification of, 407, 410
    patriarchy and, 65–66
    poverty and, 343
    self-image, 408–409
    spousal abuse, 469–470
    Taliban, 396
    violence against, 411
    war's impact, 268–269
    working, 414–416
Women's International League for Peace and Freedom, 269
Working poor, 342–343, 349, 352
Workplace
    conflict model, 572–573
    crafts and, 576–577
    diversity and, 565–566
    environment, 350–351
    functionalist perspective, 571–572
    gender and, 565–566
    interactionist's perspective, 573–574
    prestige, 327
    second shifts, 413–414
    unions, 567–571
    women in, 414–416
World Trade Organization, 557
Wounded Knee, 499–500
WTO. *See* World Trade Organization

Y

Yakuza, 179
Yankee City, 331–332

Z

Zapatista rebellion, 211–212
Zecchin, Franco, 33–34
Zionism, 377

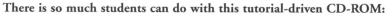